THE SCATTERED LIBRARY

Hans P. Soetaert

THE SCATTERED LIBRARY

The Various Fates of the Remnants of Magnus Hirschfeld's Institute of Sexual Science Collection in France and Czechoslovakia, 1932–1942

Bibliografische Information der Deutschen Nationalbibliothek
Die Deutsche Nationalbibliothek verzeichnet diese Publikation in der Deutschen Nationalbibliografie; detaillierte bibliografische Daten sind im Internet über http://dnb.d-nb.de abrufbar.

Bibliographic information published by the Deutsche Nationalbibliothek
The Deutsche Nationalbibliothek lists this publication in the Deutsche Nationalbibliografie; detailed bibliographic data are available on the Internet at http://dnb.d-nb.de.

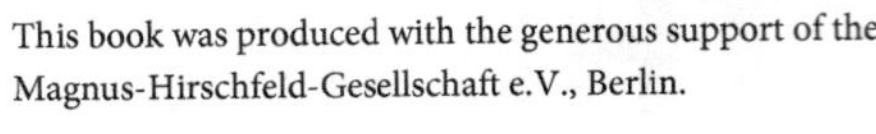

This book was produced with the generous support of the Magnus-Hirschfeld-Gesellschaft e.V., Berlin.

Dieses Buch wurde mit großzügiger Unterstützung der Magnus-Hirschfeld-Gesellschaft e.V., Berlin, hergestellt.

https://magnus-hirschfeld.de/

Cover picture: Bundesarchiv, Berlin, picture n° 183-R70391.
Book design: Typeface nv, Leuven, Belgium - www.boekopmaak.be

ISBN (Print): 978-3-8382-1895-3
ISBN (E-Book [PDF]): 978-3-8382-7895-7

Leuschnerstraße 40
30457 Hannover
info@ibidem.eu

Printed in the EU

for Harry, who was patient, with love

in memory of the people mentioned in this book, who perished in the Holocaust

in memory of Yves Feyten and Avi Haimovsky

"... [when writing the history of homosexuality,] the punishment of Sodom should not serve as the historical model".

Michel Foucault[1]

[1] "... [en écrivant l'histoire de l'homosexualité,] ce n'est pas la condamnation de Sodome qui doit servir de modèle historique" (Foucault 1982, 16).

CONTENTS

A young man in civilian clothes sorting through books looted from Hirschfeld's Institute in the student house on Oranienenburger street in Berlin. Photo dated between May 6 and 10, 1933.

1. Introduction

In June 2019, one hundred years after the German-Jewish sexologist and LGBT activist Magnus Hirschfeld (1868–1935) opened his Institute of Sexual Science (*Institut für Sexualwissenschaft*) in Berlin, the Berlin-based publisher Hentrich & Hentrich published an extensively annotated transcript and facsimile edition of a guestbook that Hirschfeld kept during the last two years of his life.[1] Hirschfeld's *Exile Guestbook 1933–1935* (*Magnus Hirschfelds Exil-Gästebuch 1933–1935*) was presented at the "Queering Memory" conference that brought together people and organizations from all over the world, working on LGBT themes in archives, libraries, museums and special collections (ALMS). The sixth ALMS conference was deliberately held in Berlin, on the occasion of the one hundredth anniversary of the opening of the Institute. The conference took place in the House of World Cultures (Haus der Kulturen der Welt), a modernist building located on the site where Hirschfeld's Institute once stood, close to the Spree river, beside the Tiergarten park.[2]

Hirschfeld started his guestbook shortly after arriving in France, in May 1933. Presumably the last contributor signed it two days before Hirschfeld's death, in the middle of May 1935.[3] The sexologist invited people he encountered in his daily life to leave an entry in this guestbook: quotes, poems, drawings, or a simple signature. "Guestbook" may not be an adequate term, since Hirschfeld also filled it with newspaper clippings of his lectures and public appearances, photos of himself and the people he met, and other memorabilia. Hirschfeld had previously named his guestbooks "memorial books" (*Erinnerungsbücher*). He kept several during his 1930–32 world trip, already filling three in the USA, during the first three months of his trip.[4] According to our present knowledge, only Hirschfeld's very last guestbook survived, and it has now come to us in the form of this wonderful facsimile and transcript edition. But what is the story behind this guestbook? How did this Hirschfeld artifact come to us and who were the people involved in the process? That is one of the main subjects of this book, which endeavors to function as an extended, contextualizing introduction to the 2019 publication of the Hirschfeld guestbook.[5]

In this book, I will also look in detail at the life of the late Magnus Hirschfeld and, even more, at the circle of people who survived him. After introducing his main ally, his life partner and coworker Karl Giese (1898–1938) in chapter 2, our story will start

[1] *Magnus Hirschfelds Exil-Gästebuch 1933–1935*, ed. Hans Bergemann, Ralf Dose, Marita Keilson-Lauritz, and Kevin Dubout (Berlin: Hentrich & Hentrich, 2019).

[2] See https://queeralmsberlin2019.de/ (accessed Nov. 12, 2020) and https://en.wikipedia.org/wiki/ALMS_Conference (accessed Nov. 14, 2020). The first ALMS conference was held in 2006 in the USA, in Minneapolis.

[3] The earliest entry (not all entries were dated) dates from November 1933. See Bergemann, Dose, Keilson-Lauritz & Dubout 2019, f. 11/55. We will see that, in all probability, people added undated entries even earlier. The last explicitly dated entry in the guestbook is from May 12, 1935. See ibid, f. 142/186.

[4] Bergemann 2019, 27 n. 1; Hirschfeld & Dose 2013, 207 n. 3. I have found strong indication that at least one other such guestbook existed, likely covering the years 1932–33. See below, chapter 15. Hirschfeld's very last guestbook, published in 2019, covered the years 1933–35.

[5] The 2019 publication of the Hirschfeld guestbook is accompanied by two excellent contributions (Dose 2019; Bergemann 2019). Two earlier texts by Marita Keilson-Lauritz, on her first dealings with the Hirschfeld guestbook, remain valuable introductions to and sources of information regarding the Hirschfeld guestbook. See Keilson-Lauritz 2004 and 2008.

in March 1932, when Hirschfeld again set foot on European soil, returning from his almost two-year world tour, one mainly spent in the US, Asia, and the Middle East. In this way, the book also picks up the thread where Rainer Herrn's excellent 2022 book on the history of Hirschfeld's Institute and the life work of Magnus Hirschfeld ended, in 1932–33.

Although Hirschfeld was hailed as a world celebrity on his tour, he was quickly reminded, on the return from his world trip, that he was much less liked in Europe. The Nazis' aversion to Hirschfeld and his ideas was already in evidence in October 1920, when Hirschfeld was physically attacked in the street and left for dead after a lecture he gave in Munich. His person and work met with the same animosity as soon as he disembarked in the port of Athens, in March 1932. Since leaving Germany to go on his world tour in November 1930, Nazi influence in his home country had only grown stronger and his friends urged him not to return to Germany after his world trip. After Athens, Hirschfeld went to Austria, before going to Switzerland, where he stayed in 1932–33, ultimately wandering to France on his birthday, May 14, 1933. Only a few days earlier, Nazi students had looted his Institute in Berlin. On May 10, in Berlin's Opernplatz, they publicly burned great portions of the Institute's vast and unique sexology collection, which consisted of books, periodicals, questionnaires, journals, manuscripts, pictures and museum artifacts acquired by Hirschfeld since he started the Institute in 1919 (see chapter 4). That Hirschfeld saw a newsreel of the Berlin auto-da-fé in a Paris cinema, leaving him understandably shattered, is well known. One year after his return to Europe, this was another serious blow, on top of his poor health, from which Hirschfeld never fully recovered.

Despite once again having to deal with an old, all-too-familiar hostility as soon as he returned from his world tour, Hirschfeld managed to find some relief in a young European country, one with which he had an excellent relationship since its founding in 1918. In Czechoslovakia, he was able to shine one more time. In September 1932, the fifth and final conference of the World League for Sexual Reform (WLSR) took place in Brno, the second-largest city of Czechoslovakia. The League was another of Hirschfeld's brainchildren, officially starting in 1928. When visiting Czechoslovakia in the months leading up to the conference, to make preparations for the event with Josef Weisskopf (1904–1977), a local doctor, Hirschfeld lectured in different parts of the country and was received with much enthusiasm (see chapter 3).

Despite the grievous blow delivered by the Nazi students in Berlin, Hirschfeld and Giese eventually, in the beginning of 1934, got back on their feet and tried to make a new start in Paris, attempting to start up a new Institute there (see chapters 5 and 7). Some of the materials that Hirschfeld had bought back from Nazi Germany in November 1933 were first sent from Berlin to Brno. In April 1934, a portion of these materials were then sent to Paris. But the Paris project did not succeed. Karl Giese, Hirschfeld's assistant and life partner, found himself entangled in a bathhouse affair, as a result of which he was expelled from France, in the autumn of 1934. This proved to be a definitive setback for the new Paris venture (see chapter 8). It is clear that the Paris police (Préfecture de Police) used the Giese case to try to contain Hirschfeld's controversial sexual reform activities in France. At the end of 1934, seeing that he was not as welcome in Paris as he had hoped, Hirschfeld moved from the French capital to Nice in the south of France, known for its mild Mediterranean winter climate. Six months later, Hirschfeld died there. It is in Nice that one can now find the grave of the sexologist who, in his time, was as famous as Einstein. On his world trip, in Chicago, he was dubbed "the Einstein of sex" and "Europe's Greatest Sex Authority".

A letter from a learned society in Agra (India), called him, referring to the author of the *Kamasutra*, "the modern-day Batsyayana (Vātsyāyana)".[6]

Concerned about his legacy, after ruminating about its precise details for years, Hirschfeld drew up his will in Nice. Principally, Hirschfeld outlined his expectation that the two men dearest to him would continue his life work. These were Karl Giese, whom Hirschfeld met in Berlin in 1914, and who had been the Head of Collections (*Archivleiter*) of the Institute of Sexual Science library until 1933; and Li Shiu Tong (1907–1993), a young Chinese man, whom Hirschfeld met on his world tour. Hirschfeld's estate was settled in Nice in 1935–36 (see chapter 9). But the posterity outlined in Hirschfeld's will was never realized.

It was also in Nice, in the months following Hirschfeld's death, that a few of the smaller remnants of the Institute's collection, along with other papers, were divided among Karl Giese, Li Shiu Tong and Hirschfeld's visiting great-nephew, Ernst Maass (1914–1975). A separate portion of the Institute materials that escaped the Berlin bonfire seems to have been inaccessible to the two principal heirs of Hirschfeld's estate, Karl Giese and Li Shiu Tong. These artifacts, most of them ethnological objects, remained in Nice and were handled by the Austrian painter Victor Bauer (1902–1959) and his circle of friends, then resident in Nice (see chapter 10).

The materials left to Li Shiu Tong were partially recovered from his estate, which came to light – thanks to a great deal of luck – shortly after his death in Vancouver, Canada, in 1993. This lot was saved from a waste container in 1993 by Adam P. W. Smith, an astute young photographer. In 2003, Smith donated these materials to the Magnus-Hirschfeld-Gesellschaft in Berlin. The cast of Hirschfeld's plaster death mask was among the objects rescued. One of Hirschfeld's personal notebooks, *Testament: Heft II*, was also part of the Li Shiu Tong lot. This notebook was not strictly a diary. It mainly contains Hirschfeld's thoughts about what he would do with his estate. In 2013, this Hirschfeld notebook was published by Ralf Dose (1950-) in Germany in an annotated facsimile edition.[7] It now constitutes a crucial primary source in Hirschfeld research.

The materials that Ernst Maass took to the USA when he emigrated there, in March 1938, were discovered in the New York home of his son, Robert Maass (1956–), in December 2009, thanks to the investigations of the University of Toronto librarian and researcher Don McLeod (1957–).[8] In 2011, these materials were donated by Robert Maass to the Magnus-Hirschfeld-Gesellschaft in Berlin. However, a larger part of the Institute's remaining materials, along with documents and personal archives belonging to Hirschfeld, ended up with Karl Giese in Brno. Once Giese had received, after a one-year delay, his small part of the Hirschfeld inheritance, he returned for the third time, at the end of May 1936, to Brno, where he settled until his death in March 1938 (see chapter 11). The Hirschfeld guestbook was in Giese's possession when he lived in Brno, together with at least around 500 and possibly as many as 900 books from the Institute library. Giese eventually lost faith, suffering partly because of a love affair with a man nine years his junior that had gone sour, but also because of his growing fear of Nazism. Germany's annexation of Austria in March 1938 made it clear that Germany would continue to expand beyond its national borders. Giese committed suicide in his Brno apartment in the same month as the *Anschluss*. Giese drew up a will in which he entrusted the Institute materials and everything else he owned to his friend Karl Fein (1894–1942), a Jewish lawyer in Brno (see chapter 12). Fein perished in the Holocaust in the beginning of May 1942, six months after being

[6] For the USA titles, see Viereck 1930, 240; Hirschfeld & Dose 2013, 98. For the Indian title, see *Tagesbote*, May 22, 1932, 8.

[7] Hirschfeld & Dose 2013.

[8] Don McLeod offers a detailed overview of his concise but effective discovery trail. See McLeod 2012.

deported from Prague to the Łódź ghetto in Poland (see chapter 13). Fein and possibly also his aunt, Elise Brecher, played a central role in the operation to buy back Institute materials in the last months of 1933 (see chapter 6).

Exactly what happened to the Hirschfeld and Institute materials that Giese guarded in Brno remains in part unclear; however, in all probability, most or even all the remaining Institute materials were thrown out in 1942, ending up in a waste paper container belonging to a scrap company. This is a painful observation, made even worse when one reflects that Giese most likely had in his possession the greater part of what remained of the Institute collection, as well as Hirschfeld's personal archives covering his years of exile. Tragically, especially after Magnus Hirschfeld's death, Giese considered himself to be their best guardian.

But not everything was lost in Brno. In 1942, along with some sexology books, the guestbook that Hirschfeld kept in France, was retrieved by an unknown person from the aforementioned container in Brno. The finder (or finders) of these artifacts handed them over to a Brno doctor, Stanislav Kaděrka (1906–1986). In the 1980s, Dr. Kaděrka asked a close family friend to sell the Hirschfeld guestbook in West Germany. In this way, in 1985, the guestbook made its way to the Deutsches Literaturarchiv in Marbach, where it is still housed. Very curiously, the Hirschfeld guestbook thus shared the same fate as *Testament: Heft II*, also saved from a dumpster in Canada.

Many people believe that the whole of the Hirschfeld Institute library was lost to the fire in the Opernlatz in Berlin in May 1933, but the truth is a little more complicated.[9] In this book, I try to gain some distance from this pervasive, almost romantic view, in which some people seem almost fascinated by the sensational and destructive Berlin bonfire, even as they are determined to wax indignant about the undoubtedly great injustice committed by the National Socialists. I rejected the idea of yet another book bearing the almost predictable title: *The Burning Library*. Yes, many things were consigned to the flames in Berlin in May 1933 by the Nazis, but that is only one part of the story; or, rather, just the beginning of the story. Nine years after the Berlin auto-da-fé, in 1942, a considerable part of Hirschfeld's library, along with other papers related to Hirschfeld, were, in all probability, deliberately disposed of in Brno. Chapters 14, 15 and 16 of this book offer some hypothetical scenarios to explain how the Hirschfeld guestbook, along with some sexology books, ended up in the Brno scrap firm's container, and also to suggest how the guestbook ended up with the aforementioned Dr. Kaděrka. We will mainly look at two plausible scenarios about what may have happened. One scenario involves a group of seven gay men from Brno, who founded the short-lived gay magazine *Kamarád* in 1932. The other scenario revolves around an aunt of Karl Fein, Elise Brecher (1869–1943), who found temporary refuge in a small makeshift Jewish hospital in Brno in 1941–43. The fraught year 1942, when the Nazis installed a terror regime in the so-called Protectorate of Bohemia and Moravia (Protektorat Böhmen und Mähren) by appointing Reinhard Heydrich as Reichsprotektor, plausibly explains why someone deemed it safer to discard the Institute materials. Holding on to such materials, which had belonged to Magnus Hirschfeld, one of Nazi Germany's archenemies, was considered too dangerous and even life-threatening in occupied Czechoslovakia. One key figure, the Czech Jaroslav Růžička (1905–1978), curiously makes an appearance in both scenarios. He was the manager (but not the owner) of the company from whose container the Hirschfeld guestbook and some sexology books were salvaged. This man, and what he did with the Institute materials, is the only truly certain factor in the diffuse and still

[9] For a recent example of the strangely persistent idea that everything was lost in May 1933, see Stefano Evangelista's claim in "Institute of Sexual Science", https://happy-in-berlin.org/institute-of-sexual-science/ (accessed Aug. 6, 2021).

unresolved matter of exactly what happened to the part of the Hirschfeld estate that Giese guarded in Brno.

This book is an attempt, then, to try to determine in as much detail as possible what happened in the years 1932–42 to the remainder of Magnus Hirschfeld's estate. The consequence is that the reader of this book will encounter a vast number of names, facts, and details. This is not an easily digestible novel or Netflix movie. Readers interested in a quicker read may want to skip the footnotes. Details are especially prodigious in chapters 14–17, containing the Czechoslovak part of our story. This profusion is closely related to the fact that exactly what happened in Czechoslovakia in 1939–42 remains partly unresolved. These final chapters should therefore be read as a sort of investigative report on the partly unsolved crime of the discarding of the Institute materials in Brno in 1942. In these chapters, the probable actors involved, as well as the possible scenarios regarding what may have happened, will be described at length. In reporting in detail on the research trails followed, my wish is to help future researchers, saving them from repeating work already done, and thus speed up the progress of Hirschfeld research. Since much of this uncertainty is intrinsically linked to the deportation and annihilation of the Jewish population – and the concomitant destruction of their personal archives and memories – I have tried to follow as many trails of Jewish survival as possible, hoping to find some answers there. My hope, in spelling out these rare trails of Jewish survival (relegated to the footnotes in most cases), is to reach some Jewish readers who may recognize names of relatives. I would like to ask any who do to contact me so that we may determine whether something new can be learned that may shed further light on our story. I also hope that this book will make a useful contribution to – and serve as an instrument for – the justified quest to find yet other possible remainders of Hirschfeld's estate.

Finally, and most of all, my ambition is that this book will bring further appreciation for and restore some dignity to (as hinted by his first name) the "great" Magnus Hirschfeld, by contributing to the detailed history of what happened to his greatly admirable life's work when confronted by the multifaceted catastrophe named National Socialism, which infested all of Europe in the 1920s and 1930s, ultimately culminating in World War II and the Holocaust.

2. Karl Giese and Magnus Hirschfeld

MEETING MAGNUS HIRSCHFELD

In the winter of 1914, Karl Giese boldly visited Magnus Hirschfeld in his doctor's office in Berlin-Charlottenburg. Giese was sixteen years old at the time and Hirschfeld forty-six. In June 1935, one month after Hirschfeld's death, Giese told a journalist in Vienna: "As a 16-year-old apprentice merchant, I sought advice from Dr. Hirschfeld regarding a family matter. I had previously only read a brochure by him, never even seeing a picture of him. So I stood in the elegant villa 'in den Zelten' on a gloomy December morning".[1] In previous research, there are already a few indications that Giese met Hirschfeld when he was very young. Most commonly, one relies on the Danish Dr. Ellen Bækgaard's statement that Karl Giese was "very young" (*blutjung*) when they met. But what age did Bækgaard have in mind when she characterized Giese as "very young"?[2] And what did Hirschfeld's housekeeper, Adelheid Schulz (1909–2008), mean when she said that Giese came to Hirschfeld "as a young boy"?[3]

It's hard to think of any reasons for Giese to be mistaken or simply lie about the date of the encounter when talking to the Austrian journalist. Hirschfeld himself, on two occasions, indirectly suggested that he had indeed met Giese, thirty years his junior, in December 1914. In a 1934 entry in *Testament: Heft II,* Hirschfeld wrote that he had been working together with Giese for twenty years. Hirschfeld had no reason to be circumspect in such an intimate personal document.[4] In a July 1934 letter to the French Ministry of the Interior, Hirschfeld stated – in somewhat faulty French –

[1] "Magnus Hirschfelds Erbe in Wien", *Der Morgen – Wiener Montagblatt*, Jun. 24, 1935, 10: "Als 16 jähriger Kaufmannslehrling suchte ich in einer Familienangelegenheit Rat bei Dr. Hirschfeld. Ich hatte vorher nur eine Broschüre von ihm gelesen, hatte nie ein Bild von ihn gesehen. So stand ich an einem trüben Dezembervormittag in der eleganten Villa 'in den Zelten'". There appears to be, at first sight at least, a small problem with Giese's claim that he went to see Hirschfeld in the elegant villa in In den Zelten. This seems to refer to the villa-like corner building with a front garden where, in 1919, the famous Institut für Sexualwissenschaft (Institute of Sexual Science) was established. The exact address was 9, 10 In den Zelten / 3 Beethovenstrasse. Hirschfeld started the Institute in July 1919, buying the building in November 1920. See Dose 2015, 11–12. However, in 1914, Hirschfeld was not yet living at this address but in another house on the same street: 19 In den Zelten. See, for example, *Berliner Adressbuch* 1914, 252; *Berliner Adressbuch* 1915, 253. The typescript "Hirschfeld in Berliner Adreß- und Telefonbüchern" gives the 19 In den Zelten address for the year 1917. See Wellcome Institute, London, fonds Charlotte Wolff, folder n° 6-8-4 I. In the fourth edition of the 1915 *Psychobiologischer Fragebogen*, the same address is given but with the addition of the Roman numeral "I", likely indicating the floor number on which Hirschfeld then lived in the building. Cf. Dose 2015, 69. This inconsistency does not necessarily undermine Giese's claim, though. Likely, Giese was simply aligning in his mind the important, romantic story of his meeting with Hirschfeld and, in his eyes, the equally significant story of the Institute. It would also explain then why Giese wrote that it was Hirschfeld who opened the door. Once the Institute was established, Hirschfeld no longer answered the door. This was done by a doorman. In the early 1930s, a woman, Mrs. Helene Helling, took on this role, see Dose 2021, 13–15.

[2] "Er [Karl Giese] war blutjung zu Magnus Hirschfeld gekommen, nachdem er einen von dessen Vorträgen über Homosexualität gehört hätte. Am Tag danach hat er Hirschfeld aufgesucht, der selbst [die Tür des Instituts] geöffnet hat. [...] Magnus Hirschfeld erzog Karl Giese und ließ ihn zum Archivleiter ausbilden und zum Sekretär des Instituts und seiner selbst" (He [Karl Giese] had come to Magnus Hirschfeld as a very young man after hearing one of his lectures on homosexuality. The day after, he went to see Hirschfeld, who himself opened [the door of the Institute]. [...] Magnus Hirschfeld educated Karl Giese and had him trained as the Head of Collections and as his own and the Institute's secretary) (Bækgaard 1985, 33). In 1986, Ellen Bækgaard also told Manfred Herzer that Giese was actually fifteen when he saw Hirschfeld for the first time. See Herzer 2017, 369.

[3] Schulz 2001, 72.

[4] Hirschfeld & Dose 2013, f. 87/186, n. 494. See also Hirschfeld & Dose 2013, f. 2/16, n. 2.

that "[f]or nearly 20 years, Mr. Giese has administered as an archivist this valuable scientific material".[5] The specification "for nearly 20 years" is especially remarkable. We can see that Hirschfeld was acutely aware of the upcoming important twentieth anniversary in December 1934. And Hirschfeld was a man who was sensitive to anniversaries, most of all his own. Lastly, an unknown journalist who reported on Hirschfeld's funeral ceremony in Nice, in May 1935, also mentions Giese having been Hirschfeld's secretary for twenty years.[6]

Most likely, explaining the relative discretion of the two women who referred to Giese's being quite young when he met Hirschfeld, there must have been some kind of taboo around the matter in Hirschfeld's lifetime. In this sense, it was likely no coincidence that Giese was happy he could finally be open about this decisive moment in his life, when he spoke to a foreign journalist a month after Hirschfeld's death. It was a sort of grateful release of a love secret kept too long. But, on reflection, it was wise to be very discreet about Giese's exact age when he met Hirschfeld. Probably, Hirschfeld himself urged his closest friends and associates never to bring it up. Even though the age of consent was fourteen, as stipulated in paragraph 176 of the German criminal code (*Strafgesetzbuch*, StGb), the preceding infamous paragraph 175 forbade any sex between men, rendering the issue of the age of consent irrelevant.[7] And yet, as Laurie Marhoefer has shown, a *higher* age of consent (*Schutzalter*) for boys than for girls lay at the heart of the 1929 Criminal Code Reform Committee (*Strafgesetzausschuss*) debates around repealing the infamous paragraph 175. Boys were considered more prone to homosexual seduction than girls, one reasoned. At the same time as repealing paragraph 175, the intention was to introduce twenty-one as the age of consent in paragraph 297.[8] So, even though Giese was already sixteen years old – and not fourteen or fifteen – when he and Hirschfeld met, it certainly would have compromised Hirschfeld as a relatively respected human sexuality researcher (*Sexualforscher*) had it come to public knowledge that he had an affair with a very young working-class man. His opponents would doubtless have used the matter to attack him and accuse him of "corrupting German youth".[9]

[5] AN, site de Pierrefitte-sur-Seine, Ministère de l'intérieur, Direction générale de la sûreté nationale (fonds de Moscou), file Karl Giese, dossier n° 15843, letter from Magnus Hirschfeld to Interior Ministry (dated Jul. 12, 1934), cote 19940448/186: "Mr. Giese a depuis près de 20 ans administré comme archiviste ce précieux matériel scientifique". A time frame of twenty years was already mentioned in an earlier letter (dated Jun. 17, 1934, f. 1) sent by Hirschfeld to the French authorities, but I think that claim less poignant because the word "presque" (almost) is not used. In another, later letter sent to the French Interior Minister, Hirschfeld repeated the number of years ("depuis vingt ans") one more time; see ibid., letter (dated October 23, 1934) from Magnus Hirschfeld to Ministre de l'Intérieur.

[6] *L'Eclaireur de Nice et du Sud-Est*, May 22, 1935, 3. Yet another source shines more light on the matter. In July 1937, Giese claimed that he had worked eighteen years for Magnus Hirschfeld (see MZA, Brno, fonds B 40, Zemský úřad Brno (Landesbehörde in Brünn), kart. n° 2138, sign. 5274/38, f. 6b). If we take 1933, the year the Institute was looted, as the end of the journey, this brings us to the year 1915. So they might indeed have met in December 1914, with Giese moving into the Institute in the course of the year 1915.

[7] Kerchner 2005, 269 n. 108. Laurie Marhoefer writes that the age of consent for girls was sixteen (Marhoefer 2015, 240 n. 181). Jens Dobler provides the best discussion on the issue of the *Schutzalter* (age of consent) in relation to paragraph 175. See Dobler 2020, 55–60, 155–56, 170–75. Dobler also mentions concern about sexual abuse in a work relationship as another important factor that could have hindered free expression. See Dobler 2020, 166.

[8] Marhoefer 2015, 44–45, 76, 120–28. In 1935, the Nazis made twenty-one the age of consent, and made it clear that, in very light cases, a young man (read: an innocent seduced by an older "predatory" gay man) might escape punishment. See https://de.wikipedia.org/wiki/§_175 (accessed May 5, 2020). About this akward victimization of young men, Magnus Hirschfeld wrote: "Wenn man von einem jungen Mädchen beansprucht, daß es sich selbst, ohne gesetzliche Unterstützung, vor Verführung schützt, kann man es von einem jungen Mann wohl auch verlangen." (If you expect a young girl to protect herself from seduction without legal support, you can probably expect the same from a young man). See Hirschfeld & Beck 1927, 59.

[9] For some examples of the National Socialist discourse on the corruption of youth "promoted" by Hirschfeld, taken from the Nazi publications *Völki-*

KARL GIESE'S FAMILY

Karl (Otto Bernhard) Giese was born into a working-class family on October 18, 1898, at 17 Schulstraße, in what was then known as Berlin Norden.[10] The house where Giese was born escaped the intense World War II bombing of Berlin and still stands today [ill. 1].[11] Nowadays the building houses low-income immigrant families. During the Weimar republic, the Wedding neighborhood was known as "Roter Wedding" (Red Wedding) since almost half of its residents voted Communist. Giese's parents were no exception.[12] Karl Giese's father, Hermann Giese (1862–1904), was a helmsman (*Steuermann*) by profession.[13] His mother was Anna Noack (1860–?).[14] The couple

scher Beobachter (Oct. 31, 1928) and *Der Angriff* (Nov. 19, 1928), see Herrn 2010, 125–26, 128.

[10] Karl was delivered by the *Hebamme* (midwife) Marie Haupt in his parents' house at 9 a.m. The baby was baptized in either the Neue Nazarethkirche or the Alte Nazarethkirche. See ELAB, Berlin, Taufbuch Berlin-Wedding, Gemeinde Nazareth 1898–1899, n° 3150, folio 17, n° 1267, Carl Otto Bernhard Giese. A copy of Karl Giese's birth certificate can be found in MZA, Brno, fonds C 107, Německý úřední soud Brno (Deutsches Amtsgericht Brünn), kart. n° 256, sign. 5a V 3/41 (Karl Giese inheritance file). I saw the original birth certificate in the Standesamt of the Bezirksamt Berlin Mitte in 2012 (Bezirksamt Berlin Mitte Berlin, Archiv im Standesamt, Bestand P Rep. 920, Geburtsregister, Standesamt Berlin XIII [zurückgeführtes Erstregister], year 1898, certificate n° 3711). Since 2014, the birth certificate can be found online at Ancestry.com (under Berlin, Germany, Births, 1874–1906). The administrative division at the time was Bezirk Berlin Wedding (with Ortsteilen Berlin Wedding and Berlin Gesundbrunnen). Since 2001, this Bezirk has been part of the greater Bezirk Berlin Mitte. The birth certificate indicates that Giese's first name was officially spelled "Carl", but I will retain the usual spelling, "Karl", since this had already been current in Giese's lifetime. In October 2012, I further inquired with the Landesarchiv Berlin about any trace of Giese or his parents in the fragmentary archival fonds of Berlin residents' registration cards (Berliner Einwohnermeldekartei, EMK, 1875–1960, Bestand B Rep. 021). This search, a paid service, proved unsuccessful. See Landesarchiv Berlin's letter to the author, dated November 1, 2012.

[11] The house has several wings (*Vorderhaus, Seitenflügel, Quergebäude*, etc.) with many apartments and is located just across from the neo-Gothic, evangelical Neue Nazarethkirche located between two U-Bahn stations, Nauener Platz and Leopoldplatz. The 1893 Neue Nazarethkirche is not to be confused with the older nearby (towerless) 1835 Alte Nazarethkirche, situated on Leopoldplatz. The house number has not changed since 1898, the year Giese was born, as testified by an email (dated Mar. 27, 2013) from Bernhard Wittstock (Bezirksamt Mitte von Berlin, Stadtentwicklungsamt, Kataster und Vermessung) to the author: "Aus einer hier archivierten historischen Übersichtskarte und der Eintragung im Original des hier vorliegenden Preußischen Gebäudesteuerbuches geht hervor, dass das in Rede stehende Grundstück Schulstraße 17 diese Hausnummer auch im Jahr 1913 hatte. Daher ist davon auszugehen, dass eine Veränderung der Hausnummer nicht stattgefunden hat und diese auch in der Zeit von 1899 bis 1918 bestand" (From a historical survey map archived here and the entry in the original of the Prussian building tax book available here, it is clear that the property in question, 17 Schulstraße, also had this house number in 1913. Therefore, it can be assumed that no change of the house number took place and that it was also in existence from 1899 to 1918).

[12] Berlin Wedding and Berlin Neukölln were the two main neighborhoods involved in the so-called Communist workers' *Blutmai* (Bloody May) revolt of 1929. Ralf Dose communicated to me that the Giese family was Communist. See the comment (n. 7) added by Dose to the English translation of the letter (dated Dec. 29, 1937) sent by Karl Giese to Ernst Maass (Archiv MHG, Berlin, fonds Ernst Maass). This fact appears to correspond to what Giese wrote about his relatives in the same letter: "Meinen Geschwistern geht es sagen wir mal einigermaßen. Sie leiden allerdings alle sehr unter dem, was sie, trotzdem sie keine Juden sind, als schweres und unverdienstes Joch empfinden" (As for my siblings, let's say they are pretty ok. However, they all suffer greatly from what they feel to be a heavy and undeserved yoke, although they are not Jews). Hirschfeld's housekeeper Adelheid Schulz once complained that Antonie Mertens, one of Giese's two sisters, always tried to get her to join the Communist Party with her ideological talk. See Schulz 2001, 74.

[13] Karl (August Hermann) Giese, was born in Neuendorf (present-day Babelsberg). His death certificate is held at Landesarchiv Berlin, Sterberegister, Standesamt Berlin XIIIa (zurückgeführtes Erstregister), year 1904, certificate n° 814. It is now available online at Ancestry.com (under Berlin, Germany, Deaths, 1874–1920). His birth year was inferred from the death certificate. I thank Ralf Dose for helping me decipher the handwriting on the death certificate. Hermann Giese's profession appears on the birth certificate of his first son, Georg, as well as on his and Anna's 1885 marriage certificate.

[14] Anna Dorothea Luise Noack was born in Zossen, a small city fifty kilometers south of Berlin. Initially, I could only find her first and middle names, along with her birth name, when I consulted the ELAB Berlin Wedding Taufbücher for the births of some of her children. Armed with this information, Ralf Dose traced her exact year of birth and the Berlin Standesamt in which her birth was registered. The exact death date of Giese's mother is still unknown; however, it must be before 1938, since her name does not appear in a document naming possible

married on January 17, 1885, in Zossen and a first son, Georg, was born two and a half years later.[15] Karl Giese's father died in 1904, when Giese was five years old. In 1908, four years after the death of her first husband, Giese's mother married Karl Müller (1849–1910). But, two years later, Anna Noack was widowed again.[16]

Karl Giese was the Benjamin of the family and had five older siblings. Not counting the two children who died in infancy,[17] there were three brothers and two sisters.[18] His brothers were Georg (1887–1945),[19] Reinhold (1894–1927)[20] and Adolf (1895–1975) Giese.[21]

heirs drawn up after Karl Giese's death in 1938. See MZA, Brno, fonds C 107, Německý úřední soud Brno (Deutsches Amtsgericht Brünn), kart. n° 256, sign. 5a V 3/41. Adelheid Schulz possessed an undated picture of people from the Institute in costume for a play, show or party [ill. n° 3]. It shows Giese's mother on the far left. For Schulz's identification of Giese's mother (and many other Institute collaborators) in the photo, see Schulz 2001, 30. Based on the date of the photo, Giese's mother was still alive in 1919. So, for now, we can only surmise that she must have died between 1919 and 1938.

15 Unable to find the date of the couple's marriage in either the ELAB Berlin Wedding Trauungsbücher or in the marriage registers for Berlin Wedding (Standesamt Berlin XIII) for the years 1886 and 1887 that I consulted in the Landesarchiv Berlin, I started to think that the couple may have married in another Berlin Bezirk or even in another German city. Ralf Dose suggested to me that the couple may have married in Zossen, where Anna Noack was born. I obtained a copy of the *Eheurkunde* (marriage certificate) from the Standesamt in Zossen in July 2020. I thank Alice Gutsche (Ordnungsamt, Standesamt Zossen) for her help.

16 The first indication that Karl Giese's mother had remarried was found in a French document of 1934 in which Giese gave "Luisa Muller" [*sic*: Müller] as the name of his mother. See Archives départementales des Alpes-Maritimes, Nice, Archives administratives de 1940 à nos jours, Direction départementale de la sécurité publique des Alpes-Maritimes, Sûreté départementale, unité technique d'aide à l'enquête (caserne Auvare), file Karl Giese, file n° 104801, cote 1440W 0236, f. titled "examen de situation" (examination of the situation). Ralf Dose eventually identified the name of the man whom Anna Giese (née Noack) married on November 4, 1908: Karl Friedrich Theodor Ludwig Müller (1849–1910). See Landesarchiv Berlin, Heiratsregister, Standesamt Berlin XIIIa (zum Erstregister erklärtes Zweitregister), year 1908, certificate n° 877; available online on Ancestry.com, under Germany, Marriages, 1874–1920. For Karl Müller's death certificate, see Landesarchiv Berlin, Sterberegister, Standesamt Berlin XI (zurückgeführtes Erstregister), year 1910, certificate n° 1574; available online on Ancestry.com, under Berlin, Germany, Deaths, 1874–1920.

17 Hermann Karl Fritz Giese (Feb. 24, 1897–Mar. 31, 1897) died at the age of five weeks. See Landesarchiv Berlin, Geburtenregister, Standesamt Berlin XIII (zurückgeführtes Erstregister), year 1897, certificate n° 747; available online at Ancestry.com, under Berlin, Germany, Births, 1874–1899. For his death certificate, see Landesarchiv Berlin, Sterberegister, Standesamt Berlin XIII (zum Erstregister erklärtes Zweitregister), year 1897, certificate n° 595; available online at Ancestry.com, under Berlin, Germany, Deaths, 1874–1920. Anna Giese (Aug. 28, 1892–Apr. 25, 1893) was eight months old when she died. For her birth certificate, see Landesarchiv Berlin, Geburtsregister, Standesamt XIII (zurückgeführtes Erstregister), year 1892, certificate n° 2706; available online at Ancestry.com, under Berlin, Germany, Births, 1874–1899. For her death certificate, see Landesarchiv Berlin, Sterberegister, Standesamt XIII (zurückgeführtes Erstregister), year 1893, certificate n° 852; available online on Ancestry.com, under Berlin, Germany, Deaths, 1874–1920.

18 Giese is a common German name. Previous researchers simply did not know in which Berlin neigborhood Giese was raised or which of the many Karl Gieses born in Berlin was "the right one". The initial crucial "access key" to identifying Giese's parents and siblings was a 1938 document in the Giese inheritance file, listing four of his surviving siblings: Georg Giese, Marthe Thal (née Giese), Antonie Mertens (née Giese, widowed) and Adolf Giese. Reinhold Giese, who died in 1927, was not mentioned in this file. See MZA, Brno, fonds C 107, Německý úřední soud Brno (Deutsches Amtsgericht Brünn), kart. n° 256, 5a V 3/41, f 16b. Armed with this crucial information, I gathered information on Giese and his family from four sources: 1) research in the *Kirchenbücher* (church registers) of the Evangelisches Landeskirchliches Archiv in Berlin (ELAB) (I thank Ralf Dose for his help in preparing the genealogical research that I conducted in the ELAB in February 2012); 2) research in the Standesamt archive of the Bezirksamt Berlin Mitte in 2012; 3) the "Berlin, Germany, Births, 1874–1899" database at www.ancestry.com, first accessed Dec. 24, 2015 (the originals scanned by Ancestry.com are in the Landesarchiv Berlin); 4) additional information gathered by Ralf Dose after I shared the results of my ELAB research on Giese's family with him in 2013 and 2016.

19 For Karl Hermann Georg Giese (1887–1945), see Landesarchiv Berlin, Geburtenregister, Standesamt Berlin XII (zum Erstregister erklärtes Zweitregister), certificate n° 1635; available online at Ancestry.com, under Berlin, Germany, Births, 1874–1899. On March 29, 1913, he married Martha Hahn (1891–1965). See Landesarchiv Berlin, Heiratsregister, Standesamt Berlin XIIIa (zurückgeführtes Erstregister), year 1913,

Karl Giese's two sisters were Martha Thal (1889–1948)[22] and Antonie (Toni) Mertens (1891–1963).[23] That these two daughters were not born in Berlin Wedding but in smaller

certificate n° 228. For Martha Hahn's birth certificate, see Landesarchiv Berlin, Geburtenregister, Standesamt Berlin VIIa (Erstregister), year 1891, certificate n° 679. Both documents are available online at Ancestry.com, under Berlin, Germany, Births, 1874–1899; and under Berlin, Germany, Marriages, 1874–1920 (accessed Dec. 24, 2015). The couple had one child, Vera Sadlowski (?–?), who remains at present unidentified. I thank Ralf Dose for sharing Martha Hahn's death certificate with me (Standesamt Berlin Wedding, Sterberegister, year 1965, certificate n° 1988/1965). Georg Giese fought in Verdun during World War I.

[20] For the birth certificate of Reinhold Hermann Fritz Giese (1894–1927), see Bezirksamt Berlin Mitte, Archiv im Standesamt, Geburtsregister, Berlin XIII, year 1894, certificate n° 159; available online at Ancestry.com, under Berlin, Germany, Births, 1874–1906. Giese's parents were still living at 22 Ruheplatzstrasse when Reinhold was born, not far from the house and street to which they would later move, and where Giese was born. The Ruheplatzstrasse house number no longer exists, but it seems that most or even all of the houses on this street were rebuilt (and renumbered) after the war. Reinhold's birth certificate records the year and the city district where he died in 1927 (Standesamt Berlin-Reinickendorf, death certificate n° 351/1927). Once I supplied him with this information, Ralf Dose was able to trace the exact death date of Reinhold Giese.

[21] The original birth certificate for Adolf Karl Fritz Giese (1895–1975) is in Bezirksamt Berlin Mitte, Archiv im Standesamt, Geburtsregister, Standesamt Berlin XIII, year 1895, certificate n° 2967; available online at Ancestry.com, under Berlin, Germany, Births, 1874–1906. On February 21, 1920, Adolf Giese married Elsbeth Klara Hahn (August 9, 1897–?), a sister of Martha Hahn, who married Georg Giese. See Landesarchiv Berlin, Heiratsregister, Standesamt Berlin XIIIa (zurückgeführtes Erstregister), year 1920, certificate n° 167. For Elsbeth Hahn's birth certificate, see Landesarchiv Berlin, Geburtsregister, Standesamt Berlin Xb, year 1897, certificate n° 3305; available online at Ancestry.com, under Berlin, Germany, Births, 1874–1906.

[22] Martha Anna Therese Giese (1889–1948). See Kreisarchiv Dahme-Spreewald, Luckau, Standesamt Waltersdorf, Geburtenregister G 3 (1886-1890), sign. A-7, n° 47, no f. number, Martha Anna Therese Giese (July 1, 1889). On June 15, 1912, she married Adolf Moritz Friedrich Thal (1889–1967), an assistant train driver and bricklayer. For her husband's birth certificate, see Landesarchiv Berlin, Standesamt Reinickendorf (Erstregister), Geburtenregister, year 1889, certificate n° 324; and, for their marriage certificate, see Landesarchiv Berlin, Heiratsregister (zum Erstregister erklärtes Zweitregister), Standesamt Berlin XIIIa, year 1912, certificate n° 571. Both entries are available online at Ancestry.com, under Berlin, Germany, Births, 1874–1899 and Berlin, Germany, Marriages, 1874–1920 (accessed Dec. 24, 2015). The marriage certificate records a child named Dorothea Böttcher (née Thal, 1918–1946), who married an unidentified man on May 29, 1941 in Berlin Wedding (marriage certificate n° 1389). Adolf Thal's death certificate (Standesamt Berlin Kreuzberg, year 1967, death certificate n° 236) records a second child, Elli Blüthgen (née Thal, 1914–?), who married Willi Kurt Blüthgen (1914–?) in 1936 (divorced in 1951). The couple had a daughter named Gisela (1937–1943) who died young. In 1981, an Elli Blüthgen still figured in the Berlin phonebook. See *Amtliches Fernsprechbuch für Berlin* 1980–1981, A–K, 270.

[23] For Antonie Bertha Ida Giese (1891–1963), see Kreisarchiv Potsdam-Mittelmark, Bad Belzig, Standesamt Päwesin, Geburtenregister (1890–1900), sign. A-002, Antonie Bertha Ida Giese (Feb. 7, 1891), n° 2, f. 1b. Antonie Giese proved difficult to identify at first. The starting point was a 1938 Czech archive file describing her as a widow (married name, Mertens). On the basis of her chronological position in the list of Giese siblings summed up at Karl Giese's death, she had to have been born between 1890 and 1893. See MZA, Brno, fonds C 107, Německý úřední soud Brno (Deutsches Amtsgericht Brünn), kart. n° 256, sign. 5aV 3/41, f. 16b. Initially I had only seen her name in *Berliner Adreßbuch* 1943, I: 1924, listing her as living at 140 Koloniestrasse during World War II. In correspondence with Adelheid Schulz, Giese observed that his sister Toni was a good friend of Schulz's. In her interview with the MHG in Berlin, in response to a question about Antonie (Toni) Mertens, Adelheid Schulz said: "Ah ja. Und was ist aus der Schwester geworden ? [– Adelheid Schulz:] Toni Mertens? Ja, sie war sehr sehr kommunistisch und wollte mich überzeugen und solange sie was von Karl Giese zu berichten hatte, kam sie auch. Und ich glaube, sie ist auch noch gekommen, wie meine Tochter geboren wurde, aber sie war ja auch nicht ganz gesund, sie selbst hatte eine Ehe gehabt, von dem sie einen Sohn und eine Tochter hatte, von dem Sohn, da hat sie viel dummes Zeugs geredet, die Tochter sei ihr gestorben. Denn hat sie einen – ihren Max geheiratet – geheiratet nicht, aber dann mit dem Max ... weil der Mann ihr 2 Kinder gemacht hat – mochte sie ihn nicht mehr. Also son bißchen abnorm, und da hat sie mit dem Max, der war ein Eintänzer, ... so wie sagt man da ..." (Ah yes. And what became of the sister? [– Adelheid Schulz:] Toni Mertens? Yes, she was very much a Communist and wanted to convince me and as long as she had something to report about Karl Giese, she also came. And I think she also came when my daughter was born, but she was not completely healthy. She was married herself, and had a son and a daughter; about the son, she talked a lot of stupid stuff, the daughter had died. Then she married one – her Max – she did not marry him, but then with Max ... because the man gave her 2 children – she did not like him anymore. So it was a little bit abnormal, and then she got together with Max, who was a one-dancer, ... as they say ...). See Schulz

villages in Brandenburg is perhaps an indication that Giese's mother often joined her husband on the boat in the 1890s.[24]

Karl Giese's siblings remained working-class people, holding jobs as either a sheet-metal factory worker (*Stanzerin*), a locksmith (*Schlosser*), a bricklayer (*Maurer*) or an assistant train driver (*Hilfsmachinist*). In the year 1938, three of the Giese siblings lived in the Koloniestrasse in Berlin (present-day district Mitte), not far from the house where Karl Giese was born.[25] After World War II, several of Giese's siblings and their children continued to live in the same street. The widowed sister Antonie Mertens (née Giese) lived in 140 Koloniestrasse until her death in 1963. Georg Giese's widow, Martha Giese, lived in 77 Koloniestrasse until her death in 1965. In terms of their relatonships, Karl Giese's siblings did not really adhere to bourgeois marriage and sexual norms. His sister Antonie Mertens Giese had a son and a daughter outside of marriage, and his other sister Martha married, divorced, and remarried the same man.[26] His brother Adolf remarried as well but this was most likely due to the death of his first wife Elsbeth.[27] Georg Giese was the only one not to divorce. But maybe this

2001, 74. On the basis of Antonie Giese's death certificate, Ralf Dose was able to determine most of the relevant biographical information about her marriage to "her Max". Antonia Giese married Max Robert Theodor Mertens (1882–1936) on September 20, 1929. For the marriage certificate, see Landesarchiv Berlin, Heiratsregister, Standesamt Berlin XI, year 1929, certificate n° 1017. Max Mertens died in 1936, confirming the 1938 information that Antonia Giese was widowed. For the birth certificate of Max Mertens, see Landesarchiv, Berlin, Geburtsregister, Standesamt Berlin XI (zurückgeführtes Erstregister), year 1882, certificate n° 3732; available online at Ancestry.com, under Berlin, Germany, Births, 1874–1906. On the basis of Adelheid Schulz's claims, we presume that the couple had no children within their marriage. Max Mertens's marriage with Antonie Giese was in any case his second marriage, as recorded on his birth certificate. Max Mertens's first wife was Henriette Hedwig Schmidt (1886–?), whom he married in 1905 and divorced in 1920. See Landesarchiv, Berlin, Heiratsregister, Standesamt Berlin Xb (Erstregister), year 1905, marriage certificate n° 295; available online at Ancestry.com, under Berlin, Germany, Marriages, 1874–1920.

[24] According to a February 2016 remark by Ralf Dose, Martha Giese was born in Zeuthen and Antonie Giese in Päwesin, both located in Brandenburg.

[25] MZA, Brno, fonds C 107, Německý úřední soud Brno (Deutsches Amtsgericht Brünn), kart. n° 256, sign. 5a V 3/41, f. 16b. The street seems mostly to have escaped the intensive second World War II bombing of Berlin. There was also a chocolate and marzipan factory under the name Mertens & Jaenicke, founded in 1888, at 133–136 Koloniestrasse, but it is unknown if there is any relation to Max Mertens, the husband of Antonie Giese. See *Berliner Adreßbuch* 1943, II: 1924.

[26] Adelheid Schulz claimed that Antonie Mertens (née Giese) had a daughter and a son before she married Max Mertens. See Schulz 2001, 74. I discovered that, before Antonie Giese married Max Mertens, she had indeed a child named Antonia Giese (1911–1915) that she raised on her own as an unmarried woman of twenty ("Tochter des ledigen Arbeiterin"). The death of this daughter at age four accords with another of Adelheid Schulz's claims: "die Tochter sei ihr gestorben" (her daughter died). For the death certificate of this daughter, see Landesarchiv Berlin, Sterberegister, Standesamt XIIIa (zurückgeführtes Erstregister), year 1915, certificate n° 738; available online at Ancestry.com, under Berlin, Germany, Deaths, 1874–1920. I was not able to trace the name of her son. Whether or not she married the unknown man (or one of the men) who fathered her daughter and/or her son remains unknown, despite Adelheid Schulz's claim that she had the two children within marriage. Ralf Dose, on the other hand, reported that Antonie Mertens's death certificate stated that she had no children. Martha Giese and Adolf Thal divorced on December 10, 1946, as made clear by the note of a *Standesbeamte* (civil registry employee) dated March 14, 1950 in the marriage registry. Curiously, Adolf Thal's death certificate also shows that he remarried Martha Giese on June 23, 1947. See Landesarchiv, Berlin, Standesamt Berlin Wedding, marriage certificate n° 781/1947. Martha Giese's stomach cancer may have played a part in this.

[27] Adolf Giese's birth certificate records that he remarried in 1929 in Berlin Blankenberg. Ralf Dose looked up this marriage certificate and found that Adolf Giese married Luise Zühlke (1899–?) on October 5, 1929. According to a handwritten note on her birth certificate, this was Luise Zühlke's second marriage. For Luise Zühlke's birth certificate, see Landesarchiv, Berlin, Geburtenregister, Standesamt Berlin XI, year 1899 (zurückgeführtes Erstregister), year 1899, certificate n° 2377; available online at Ancestry.com, under Berlin, Germany, Births, 1874–1906. Ralf Dose further discovered that this second marriage produced a son, Hans-Peter Giese (1946–2004), who died in Berlin. See email (dated Aug. 8, 2013) from Ralf Dose to the author.

[28] Archiv MHG, Berlin, fonds Ernst Maass, letter (dated Dec. 29, 1937, 7) Karl Giese to Ernst Maass.

[29] In 2013, I tried my luck by sending letters to people with the last name Giese, Thal and Mertens,

was related to the fact he turned out to be, to the dismay of the rest of the family, a fascist.[28] Despite all this new genealogical information about Giese's family, not one living member of the Giese family has so far been found.[29] The last thing we know about Giese's youth is that he went to an elementary school (*Volksschule*) in Berlin Wedding.[30] In the above-mentioned 1935 interview with the Austrian journalist, Giese also stated that he was a merchant's apprentice (*Kaufmannslehrling*) before starting his life in the Institute.

ANDERS ALS DIE ANDERN

In May 1919, the so-called *Aufklärungs-Film* (educational movie) *Anders als die Andern* came out in Germany. The movie is now considered to be one of the first, if not the very first, "gay movies" ever made, allowing the crowd to stare in the dark at the rather troubled life of a fictitious, successful homosexual musician.[31] The young Karl Giese and Magnus Hirschfeld both participated in the movie as actors. Hirschfeld played himself, a sexologist sympathetic to the gay liberation cause. In four scenes at the beginning of the movie, the main character, the violinist Paul Körner, reminisces about his troubled years in a boarding school where he had been caught frolicking with a fellow student named Max, played by a sturdy-looking Karl Giese [ill. 2]. The school board decides to expel Körner for this homosexual transgression. For a very long time, Hirschfeld researchers used this movie to determine the *latest* time that the first encounter between Giese and Hirschfeld could have taken place.[32] Since we have seen that Giese met Hirschfeld in December 1914, we now know that Giese took

currently living in Berlin Mitte, but nobody replied. An online phonebook for Germany, http://www.das telefonbuch.de/, consulted Feb. 25, 2020, listed 243 people surnamed Giese in Berlin and 4,279 in the whole of Germany.

[30] The source for this information is Günter Maeder, one of his classmates. See Günter Maeder's undated text "Bruchstücke", obtained by Manfred Herzer from Maeder's widow Norma Maeder. See Maeder 1993; see also the introduction in Herzer 1997a, 16. I thank Manfred Herzer and Ralf Dose for sending me a copy of this twelve-page typescript. In this text, Maeder talks about the "Volksschule am Hümbidhain [*sic*]" where he met Giese "[a]ls ich ins schulpflichtige Alter kam [...]" (as I entered mandatory school age). See Maeder 1993, 1. Most probably by "Hümbidhain" he meant the Volkspark Humboldthain, about one kilometer away. Cf. Wellcome Library, London, archive Charlotte Wolff, correspondence with Günter Mäder (1981–1986), letter Maeder to Wolff, Dec. 12, 1984, [2], where Maeder spells it almost correctly as "Humboldhain". What school – Gemeindeschule or Grundschule – could it have been? There are two schools near the park and another one near the house where Giese was born. An email inquiry about these schools, dated March 6, 2013, sent to the Weddinger Heimatverein e.V., went unanswered. An initial and cursory review of the available archival sources in the Landesarchiv Berlin indicated to me that no archival records for these four schools seem to have survived the war. Maeder's father owned a *Möbel* (furniture) factory employing 150 workers. Maeder was himself forced by his father to learn *Handwerk* (woodworking) at one point. We will return on several occasions to Günter Maeder's contentious "Bruchstücke" testimony (Maeder 1993). I say "contentious" because Maeder suffered from multiple sclerosis in the last years of his life, and this seems to have negatively affected his memory. Quite often, Maeder is simply mistaken in his claims. He states, for example, that Giese and Hirschfeld went to Israel shortly after the May 1933 events. See Maeder 1993, 5. The catch is that Maeder is right about many things, partly right about some things, and also that he sometimes makes interesting claims that no one else does. So it is impossible to totally dismiss Maeder as a source.

[31] For more background information on the movie, see Nowak 2015, 96–140; Linge 2018; Steakley 2007.

[32] Volkmar Sigusch has even overlooked the simple fact, impossible to ignore, that Giese appeared in the movie in 1919, stating: "Das Arbeiterkind [Karl Giese] hatte sich 1920 nach einem Vortrag Hirschfelds über Homosexualität tags darauf bei dem Sexualforscher gemeldet" (In 1920, the day after a lecture by Hirschfeld on homosexuality, the working-class child [Karl Giese] contacted the sex researcher) (Sigusch 2008, 355). Ralf Dose's earlier, more cautious suggestion that Giese and Hirschfeld might have met *during* the shooting of the movie can now be set aside, despite a letter to Hirschfeld from his sister, Franziska Mann – used by Dose as an indication – written on New Year's Day 1918, stating "dass Du allein in Deinem schönen Hause wohnst" (that you live alone in your beautiful house). Hirschfeld's sister seems to have been unaware of Hirschfeld's liaison with Giese, perhaps indicating that Hirschfeld and Giese partly concealed it in the first years after their meeting. See Dose 2005a, 26–27.

part in the movie a little more than four years after this meeting. The movie was shot in March–April 1919.[33]

A MYSTERIOUS FAMILY MATTER

Giese makes a curious comment in the interview with the Austrian journalist in 1935. He says that he went to see Hirschfeld "regarding a family matter". This discretion contrasts strikingly with his blatant openness about the more scandalous fact that he met Hirschfeld when he was very young. I think it is possible that Giese visited Hirschfeld because one of his older brothers was gay. He may have even used the problem of his brother being gay as an alibi to visit Hirschfeld. That Giese had a gay brother seems quite certain, but the sources differ about which one it was. There are three sources. Firstly, there is a 1937 letter that Giese wrote to Ernst Maass, Hirschfeld's great-nephew. In all likelihood, Maass had previously asked Giese about there being a second gay brother in Giese's immediate family. In his reply, Giese only creates more confusion when he writes: "You are, however, mistaken about my brother. I have a brother who is very fond of Dr. H. [Hirschfeld] and me, but [he] has nothing to do with the movement".[34] Since later in the same letter he mentions his older brother Georg, Giese must have meant Adolf Giese.[35] But was Giese denying that this brother was gay or saying that he was gay but not a gay activist like Karl Giese and Hirschfeld? The second source on the matter is again Hirschfeld's housekeeper, Adelheid Schulz, who claimed that Georg, the oldest brother, was gay. She also said that he killed himself. To the dismay of the rest of the family, this brother was a Nazi sympathizer. That Georg Giese died near the end of World War II, in February 1945, is thus intriguing.[36] In his reply to Maass, Giese also mentions the older fascist brother, from whom he also felt estranged due the difference in their ages.[37] But he does not seem to say that it was the older brother who was gay. Or could he simply not get his gay activist head around the fact that his older brother was a Nazi and gay? A third, more indirect factor seems to indicate that there was indeed, at the very least,

[33] Steakley proposes this date based on a discussion about the desirability of a movie on the subject of homosexuality held in the Berlin Institute on February 10, 1919 (Steakley 2007, 67). The meeting is also mentioned in the *Vierteljahrsberichte des Wissenschaftlich-humanitären Komitees während der Kriegszeit*, Jg. XVIII, Heft n° 4, 171–72: "Demnächst werden die Filmaufnahmen vor sich gehen" (Soon the filming will go ahead). One scene in the film shows Paul Körner and Kurt Sivers taking a romantic walk in the park, where they are noticed by the ominous blackmailer Franz Bollek. The trees and bushes are bare and the actors are wearing thick coats, which suggests that the movie must have been shot in late March or at the latest in early April 1919.

[34] Archiv MHG, Berlin, fonds Ernst Maass, letter (dated Dec. 29, 1937, 7) from Karl Giese to Ernst Maass: "Bezüg meines Bruders sind Sie allerdings im Irrtum. Ich habe einen Bruder der Dr. H.[irschfeld] und mir sehr zugetan ist, aber nichts mit der Bewegung zu tun hat".

[35] For some time, I thought that the gay brother may have been Reinhold Giese, as I could find no marriage record for him. But Reinhold Giese died in 1927 and Giese does not use the past tense about this possibly gay brother in the 1937 letter to Maass. Nevertheless, it is still possible that it was indeed Reinhold who was gay and that, in 1937, neither of his two remaining brothers was gay.

[36] Schulz 2001, 73: "der älteste Bruder war homosexuell und hat sich das Leben genommen" (the oldest brother was homosexual and took his own life). The older brother's political convictions did not prevent him from living in the same street as his two sisters, possibly even living with one of them in 1938. See MZA, Brno, fonds C 107, Německý úřední soud Brno (Deutsches Amtsgericht Brünn), kart. n° 256, sign. 5a V 3/41, f. 16b. Georg Giese lived at 68 Koloniestrasse and Martha Giese at 78 Koloniestrasse. It is uncertain in which house Toni Giese lived since the document with the correct house number was overwritten: one can see that it was either 68 or 78, but the overwriting does not allow us to determine which one is correct. That Toni Giese was a staunch Communist makes one think that she would have lived with her sister rather than with her fascist brother.

[37] Archiv MHG, Berlin, fonds Ernst Maass, letter (dated Dec. 29, 1937, 7) from Karl Giese to Ernst Maass: "und einen anderen [Bruder], der zu unser aller Empörung [...] als einzigster in meiner ganzen Verwandtschaft umgesattelt hat" (and another [brother] who, to the indignation of us all [...] was the only one in my whole family to switch saddles).

a second gay brother. This requires returning to the movie *Anders als die Andern*. The movie ran for almost a full year in Berlin and was clearly also screened in the north Berlin working-class neighborhood where Giese came from: "Berlin has now seen the educational film 'Anders wie [*sic*] die andern', written by Richard Oswald and Dr. Magnus Hirschfeld, in all parts of the city. The lively attendance in the cinemas everywhere shows the great interest the Berlin audience took in the performance. [...] It is all the more regrettable that, at a screening of the film in the north of the city, some young people, known to me as homosexual, got carried away and disturbed the performance by continuous exclamations of 'Oh no', 'But sister', etc."[38] More importantly, in his excellent booklet on the movie, Steakley quotes a letter sent by a reader to the *Berliner Allgemeine Zeitung* in reply to a negative review of the movie in its pages.[39] In the letter, a north Berlin mother, who claimed to have two gay sons and a total of six children, testified about her experience seeing the movie, giving her social background: "I live in the north of Berlin, I really do not belong to the 'better circles', but the voices of the general public, which I have heard, differ considerably from the views stated in the newspaper. [...] I had to write this as a mother [...] that the homosexual suffers less from homosexuality than the non-understanding of others".[40] I think it is highly probable that the mother quoted here was Giese's mother, Anna. Several factors suggest this: where she lived, her socio-economic status, her activist insight and the number of her children, the same that Anna Giese had with Karl Giese's father, Hermann Giese. Another indication that Giese's mother was the likely author of this letter is the simple fact that, at the time, not many mothers would have been prepared to give such a partly public testimony: claiming not only one, but two gay sons. However, for now, the identity of Karl Giese's gay brother remains unresolved.

WAR AND CONSCRIPTION

Giese's discretion regarding a "family matter" he wanted to discuss with Hirschfeld could indicate something else. Did Giese contact Hirschfeld to get an exemption from possibly impending military conscription into the German army? The conscription age was twenty, but maybe Giese feared that, with the outbreak of war in July 1914, this might change and he could be drafted at any moment.[41] A not unwarranted fear given that, in the middle of the war, in December 1916, the draft age was indeed lowered to seventeen.[42] Hirschfeld was known as a pacifist but toned down his convictions during the war.[43] We may also mention that, in two 1934 letters to the French

[38] "Berlin hat sich nun wohl schon in allen Stadtteilen den von Richard Oswald und Dr. Magnus Hirschfeld verfassten Aufklärungsfilm 'Anders wie [*sic*] die andern' angesehen. Der rege Besuch, den die Kinos überall aufzuweisen hatten, zeigt, welches Interesse die Berliner Bevölkerung der Aufführung entgegenbrachte. [...] Um so bedauerlich ist es, dass sich bei einer Vorführung des Films im Norden der Stadt einige mir als homosexuell bekannten jungen Leute dazu hinreissen liessen, die Vorstellung durch fortwährende Zwischenrufe, wie 'Huch nein', 'Aber Schwester' usw. zu stören" (F. M. 1919, 3; qtd. in Steakley 2007, 73).

[39] The reader's letter appeared in the *Berliner Allgemeine Zeitung* and was also reprinted in the *Jahrbuch für sexuelle Zwischenstufen* 1919/1920, 48; qtd. in Steakley 2007, 74–75.

[40] Steakley 2007, 74–75: "Ich wohne im Norden Berlins, gehöre wirklich nicht zu den 'besseren Kreisen', aber die Stimmen des Publikums, die ich gehört habe, weichen doch ganz erheblich, von den in der Zeitung angegebenen ab. [...] Ich mußte als Mutter dies schreiben, [...] daß es weniger die Homosexualität ist, woran der Homosexuelle leidet, als das Nichtverstehen der Andern".

[41] See https://de.wikipedia.org/wiki/Wehrpflicht_in_Deutschland#Kaiserreich,_Weimarer_Republik_und_NS-Zeit (accessed Nov. 16, 2020).

[42] For the so-called Gesetz über den vaterländischen Hilfsdienst (Auxiliary Services Act) of December 1917, see Chickering 1998, 79–80; https://www.1000dokumente.de/index.html?c=dokument_de&dokument=0001_hil&object=abstract&st=&l=de (accessed Nov. 17, 2020).

[43] For a nuanced overview of Hirschfeld's evolving (or opportunistic) relationship to World War I and pacifism, see Herzer 2017, 252–73.

authorities in Paris, Hirschfeld stressed that Giese was a pacifist.[44] Unfortunately, virtually all the Prussian army's World War I-related archival materials, stored in the Heeresarchiv in Potsdam, were destroyed in a bombing raid in April 1945. So it is impossible to check whether Giese ever evaded the draft. Also, to my knowledge, the following question has not yet been posed in Hirschfeld research: did Hirschfeld help gay men escape conscription by supplying medical certificates stating that they were unfit for military service? In any case, Magnus Hirschfeld helped one of his friends, Hans Adalbert von Maltzahn (1894–1934), to withdraw from his military career.[45] It is well known that Hirschfeld issued medical certificates, so-called transvestite passes (*Tranvestitenschiene*), for men who felt compelled to cross-dress in public in Weimar Berlin, so they would receive more lenient treatment by the police when arrested.[46] Did Hirschfeld have other kinds of medical attestations up his sleeve that could also attract patients?

When Giese saw Hirschfeld in December 1914, the latter quickly supported the sixteen-year-old's boldness and urged the young Giese to send his mother to him: "And then – typical of Dr. Hirschfeld – my mother had to come. After all, Dr. Hirschfeld had a soft spot for mothers".[47] We do not know the details of the conversation between Hirschfeld and Giese's mother but we do now know that, by 1919, she was willing to write a letter to a newspaper critical of the reviewers' treatment of *Anders als die Andern* and even calling for social justice for gay men. Giese's mother also figures in a magnificent but undated photograph, presumably taken in the Institute, showing a costume party or, more likely, the actors of a play at rest [ill. 3].[48] This further indicates that Giese's mother was open-minded and willing to support her gay son, and that Hirschfeld welcomed both her and her son to the Institute. Ralf Dose also suggested to me that Karl's bonding with the wealthy Magnus Hirschfeld would most likely have delighted Giese's working-class family. The official conclusion of the war, declared in November 1918, also brought a general sense of renewal and of breaking with a restrictive past.[49] It is quite possible that Hirschfeld's – presumably – happy love affair with Giese may have further motivated him to start the Institut für Sexualwissenschaft in the summer of 1919.[50] It was an important moment for both men and likely also a happy one. Charlotte Wolff, Hirschfeld's first biographer, was likely right when, writing about Karl Giese and the Institute, she said that "[t]he one might not have succeeded so well without the other".[51]

THEATER

Giese had a passion for the theater and it is likely that, during his first years at the Institute, he was able to realize his aspirations. It was probably due to him that Theater

[44] AN, site de Pierrefitte-sur-Seine, Paris, Ministère de l'intérieur, Direction générale de la sûreté nationale (fonds de Moscou), file Karl Giese, dossier n° 15843, cote 19940448/186, letter (dated Oct. 23, 1934) from Magnus Hirschfeld to Ministre de l'Intérieur. In an earlier letter of the same year he even characterized Giese as a "pacifiste enthousiasmé" (enthusiastic pacifist). See ibid., letter (dated Jun. 17, 1934) from Magnus Hirschfeld to "Messieurs".

[45] Bergemann, Dose, Keilson-Lauritz & Dubout 2019, 218.

[46] For an example of a (female to male) *Tranvestitenschein*, see Taylor, Timm & Herrn 2017, 44; originally in Herrn 2008c: card Der "Tranvestitenschein". For further historical information on the *Transen-Schein*, see Dobler 2020, 29–30; Herrn 2022, 275–76. Cf. also Dobler 2022, 51.

[47] "Und dann – typisch für Dr. Hirschfeld – mußte meine Mutter kommen. Denn Dr. Hirschfeld hatte nun einmal einen Faibel für Mütter" ("Magnus Hirschfelds Erbe in Wien", *Der Morgen – Wiener Montagblatt*, Jun. 24, 1935, 10).

[48] The picture is also reproduced in Sigusch 2008, 351. Giese's old mother is the first figure on the left seated in the lower row. She was identified by Adelheid Schulz, Hirschfeld's housekeeper, who also donated the original picture to the MHG in Berlin.

[49] Steakley 2007, 32–33.

[50] For a good "initial introduction" to Magnus Hirschfeld and his Institute in the context of Weimar Germany and Berlin, see Bauer 2021, 75–93. In June 2022, Rainer Herrn published a detailed study on the history of the Institute (Herrn 2022).

[51] Wolff 1986, 185.

of Eros, Stage Society for Self-Owned Art (Theater des Eros, Bühnenvereinigung für Eigene Kunst) (1921–24), a gay theater group, used the Berlin Institute for its rehearsals. It is even possible that the group was founded in the Institute. We know that at least one play, written by Hans Wedell, was performed in the Institute, in the newly opened Ernst Haeckel-Saal.[52] Eduard Oskar Püttmann, one of the directors (*Spielleiter*) of the Theater des Eros, wrote: "In this way we hope to achieve by the means of art what the Scientific-Humanitarian Committee is striving to achieve through research: liberation, toleration, respect for our brothers".[53] We know that Giese made a big splash when he played his first role in one of the troupe's productions, in the summer of 1921.[54] In a review for the magazine *Uranus,* René Stelter lauded Giese's performance as the lieutenant in *The Lieutenant's Boy* (*Der Bursche vom Herrn Leutnant*), the farce by Hans Wedell.[55] Giese and Hirschfeld's continued interest in the theater as a means to further their militant LGBT causes can also be seen in their contact, around 1929, with the German playwright Peter Martin Lampel (1894–1965). He lived in the Institute for a while, but soon joined the fascist ranks.[56]

SECRETARY

Other than that Giese was presumably Hirschfeld's lover for some years, not much is known about the eighteen years that Giese lived and worked in the Institute.[57] It is common knowledge that in those days the "impossible" homosexual partners of upper-class citizens, like Hirschfeld, were often "coded" as secretaries, drivers,

[52] Püttmann 1922, 3. The Ernst Haeckel-Saal was located in the adjoining building, to the left of the Institute's corner building, at 9a In den Zelten. Hirschfeld bought this extra building in 1921. See Herrn 2022, 86.

[53] "Dadurch hoffen wir mit den Mitteln der Kunst zu erreichen, was das wissenschaftlich-humanitäre Komitee mit denen der Forschung durchzuseßen erstrebt: Befreiung, Duldung, Achtung unserer Brüder" (Püttmann 1921, 1). Cf. "Giese's active participation in the Theater des Eros reveals how closely it was allied with the Committee [Wissenschaftlich-humanitären Komitee, WhK] and Hirschfeld's projects" (Senelick 2008, 16). See also Borchers's chapter "Courts-Mahler auf homophil: das Theater des Eros" for more details on the troupe's other productions (Borchers 2001, 164–77). See also Beachy 2014, 233–34.

[54] The play opened on July 6, 1921, in Stadttheater Moabit. See M. H. D. 1921, 6.

[55] "In erster Linie hat aber Karl Giese, der hier zum ersten Male öffentlich aufgetreten ist, durch seine glänzende Erfassung und Darstellung der schwierigeren Leutnantsrolle bewiesen, daß, wie man aus seinen kleineren privaten Darbietungen wohl anzunehmen berechtigt war, ein starkes schauspielerisches Können in ihm schlummert. In Mimik, Eleganz der Bewegung und Anpassungsfähigkeit an die Situationen, eben in allem dem, was aus dieser Schwankrolle allein herauszuholen war, zeigte er sich gleich gelungen" (First and most important, however, is Karl Giese, giving his first public performance. His brilliant understanding and portrayal of the lieutenant, one of the more difficult parts, justifies the assumption one was able to form from his smaller private performances that a strong acting talent lay dormant in him. In his facial expressions, in the elegance of his movements and adaptation to situations, in everything, that is, that could be gotten out of this comic role, he showed himself immediately successful) (Stelter 1921, 213; see also Senelick 2008, 16 n. 41; M. H. D. 1921, 6). The play was based on *Die Infamen* (1906), a gay novel by Fritz Geron Pernauhm (the pseudonym of Guido Hermann Eckardt, 1873–1951). For advertising for the play, see *Die Freundschaft*, 1921, n° 43, 29/10-05/11, last page. The novel was reissued in 2010, see Pernauhm 2010.

[56] Norman Haire, one of Hirschfeld's sexologist colleagues, made an English translation of Lampel's successful play *Revolte im Erziehungshaus* (*Revolt in the Reformatory*), with a performance planned in England in April 1930. See the undated letter (probably Sep. or Oct. 1929) from Norman Haire to Karl Giese; and the letter (dated Feb. 13, 1930) from Norman Haire to Karl Giese, University of Sydney Library, Sydney, Norman Haire collection, 3.21, Karl Geise [*sic*: Giese], Typescripts, 1928–1934. There is no trace of any correspondence between Lampel and Hirschfeld (or Giese) in Lampel's archival fonds in the Staats- und Universitätsbibliothek Hamburg, which contains only an inscribed copy of Magnus Hirschfeld's *Sexualerziehung* (dated 1929). The inscription says: "Mit den besten Zukunftshoffnungen von Magnus Hirschfeld zu Weihnachten 29" (With best hopes for the future from Magnus Hirschfeld at Christmas [19]29). See emails (dated Aug. 22, 2012 and Aug. 23, 2012) from Mark Emanuel Amtstätter (Staats- und Universitätsbibliothek Hamburg) to the author. For Lampel's stay in the Institute, see Schulz 2001, 21. For more biographical information on Lampel, see Dobler 2016, 21.

[57] Wellcome Library, London, archive Charlotte Wolff (1897–1986), correspondence II, 1981–1986,

personal assistants or as other members of staff. And, indeed, Karl Giese was described most of the time as Hirschfeld's personal secretary, sometimes actually operating as such in the Institute.[58] He also claimed that he was the only one who could read Hirschfeld's handwriting.[59] However, Giese was not Hirschfeld's only secretary. Günter Maeder (1905–1993) was another. He started working for Hirschfeld in 1927 and stayed in the Institute until 1933. Giese, who had known Maeder from his school years in a Berlin elementary school (*Volksschule*), introduced him to the Institute.[60] Maeder was the Institute's second secretary, after Giese, which meant, according to Charlotte Wolff, that Maeder "had to take on everything which the first secretary [Giese] did not want to do".[61] It is possible to recognize Giese's distinctive curly handwriting – correcting typos – in some of the letters that Hirschfeld sent when exiled in Paris in 1934.[62]

HIRSCHFELD AND THE INSTITUTE

The opening of the Institute, in July 1919, was not the only important thing Hirschfeld realized in his life.[63] In 1897, together with two other men, he founded the Scientific-Humanitarian Committee (Wissenschaftlich-humanitäre Komitée, WhK) that sought to abrogate the infamous paragraph 175 that prohibited sex between men in Germany.[64] In 1899, the first volume of the imposing scholarly *Jahrbuch für sexuelle Zwischenstufen unter besonderer Berücksichtigung der Homosexualität* came out. It would run for twenty-three years.[65] Hirschfeld is also regarded as one of the driving forces behind the establishment of sexology (*Sexualwissenschaft*) as a distinct field of medicine.[66] In 1908, he was the editor of the *Zeitschrift für Sexualwissenschaft*.[67] However, near the end of the 1920s, many things changed at the Institute.[68] Several doctors left as the Institute started to move away from a narrow focus on scholarly *Sexualwissenschaft*, concentrating more on the sexual enlightenment of the population at large and on sexual reform in general.[69] The new publications *Die Aufklärung* and *Die Ehe* that originated in the Institute did indeed target a more general audience.

PSY/WOL/6/8/2, letter (undated, 1985?, f. 6) from Erhart Löhnberg to Charlotte Wolff.

[58] See von Praunheim's interview with Dr. Hanns G. (Von Praunheim & G. 1992) and Wellcome Library London, archive Charlotte Wolff (1897–1986), correspondence II, 1981–1986, PSY/WOL/6/8/2, letter (undated 1985?, f. 6) from Erhart Löhnberg to Charlotte Wolff. On the obvious sexual overtones in choosing a young secretary, see the letter (dated Dec. 12, 1932) from Norman Haire to Magnus Hirschfeld, University of Sydney Library, Sydney, Norman Haire collection, 3.20, Magnus Hirschfeld, Typescripts, 1923–1935.

[59] "Wir haben ihn alle nur den Vater genannt, der in den frühesten Morgenstunden zwischen 5 und 6 Uhr seine Gedanken zu Papier brachte, in einer Handschrift, die wirklich nur ich zu lesen imstande war" (We all just called him Father. He would put his thoughts down on paper in the wee hours of the morning between 5 and 6 a.m., in handwriting that only I was really capable of reading) ("Magnus Hirschfelds Erbe in Wien", *Der Morgen – Wiener Montagblatt*, Jun. 24, 1935, 10).

[60] Maeder ([1993]: 1-2). Giese and Maeder lost contact some time near the end of their school years, so around age twelve or fourteen, but met again by chance in 1926. For more biographical information on Maeder, see Dose 2021, 24–25.

[61] "Ab 1927 übernahmich [*sic*: übernahm ich] also meine Tätigkeit als 2. Sekretär am Institut für Sexualwissenschaft" (So from 1927, I took up my duties as 2nd secretary at the Institute of Sexual Science) (Maeder [1993], 2). The same document describes Giese as indeed the "1. Sekretär im Institut für Sexualwissenschaft" (1st secretary at the Institute of Sexual Science). See also Wolff 1986, 431; cf. Herzer 1997, 16.

[62] One can determine that Giese did indeed type at least some of the letters in Paris. The manual corrections were clearly done in his handwriting, using the blue-ink fountain pen he used to write most of his letters. See, for example, letter (dated Apr. 12, 1934) from Magnus Hirschfeld to Norman Haire, University of Sydney Library, Sydney, Norman Haire collection, 3.20, Magnus Hirschfeld, Typescripts, 1923–1935.

[63] Currently, the best overview of the history of the Institute is offered by Herrn 2004 and Herrn 2022.

[64] For more information on paragraph 175, see Herzer 1990.

[65] Keilson-Lauritz 2004b; Dobler 2004; Sigusch 2008, 108–9.

[66] Pretzel 2013; Beier 2013.

[67] Sigusch 2008, 110–11.

[68] Herrn 2004, 189–92.

[69] The heading "Abschied von der Sexualwissenschaft" (Farewell to Sexology) in Herrn 2004, 187–89 is telling.

That Hirschfeld changed his strategy can also be seen in his founding of the World League for Sexual Reform (Weltliga für Sexualreform, WLSR) in 1928, choosing to incorporate the goal of homosexual emancipation in a general agenda of progressive sexual reform.[70] All in all, one can see that, in the second half of the 1920s, the Institute moved further to the left of the political spectrum, probably also in direct reaction to the steadily growing influence of the Nazis and their hostility to Hirschfeld's life's work.[71] In November 1929, Max Hodann (1894–1946) and Richard Linsert (1899–1933), two collaborators at the Institute, strongly clashed with Magnus Hirschfeld. They questioned Hirschfeld's authority and credibility, which resulted in Hirschfeld being ousted as president (*Vorstand*) of the WhK, a position he had held for thirty-two years.[72] Suddenly, Hirschfeld ceased to be the "patron saint of the homosexuals" (*homosexuellen Schutzheiligen*).[73] This conflict left a deep wound in Hirschfeld's soul.

LOVE & SEX

It is generally assumed that Hirschfeld and Giese had a passionate love affair. But, in conformity with the discretion that both displayed regarding Giese's exact age when they met, this was swept under the carpet and remained unspoken. It was an open secret. Thus, it is simply an assumption that, at least initially, they had a sexual relationship. For those still in doubt about the matter, Giese once privately told people attending the 1930 Vienna WLSR conference that Hirschfeld was gay; the listener concluded that Giese and Hirschfeld were indeed a couple: "Today, at lunch, Carl [*sic*] Giese confessed that Magnus was homosexual. I said that I thought it would be better if he publicly acknowledged it. Giese said that it would harm his work. Giese is his friend, and lives with him in the Imperial [a luxury hotel in Vienna] and is completely dependent on him".[74] Further, an initial sexual and/or love relationship presumably created the two men's lifelong bond and emotional attachment. Even after Hirschfeld died in 1935, the great affection and loyalty that Giese felt for him remained. He wrote to Max Reiss, one of Hirschfeld's students, in May 1935: "You probably know that no kind word pleases me more than the one said about Papa".[75] "Papa" was Giese's pet name for Hirschfeld.

We know that Giese and Hirschfeld were not sexually monogamous between 1914, the year they met, and Hirschfeld's death in 1935. As Hirschfeld's housekeeper once put it, with some cirucumspection, Hirschfeld always found something sexually gratifying or important in his other sexual partners.[76] She also briefly mentioned one of Giese's sex partners, Erwin Hansen, apparently a married man.[77] Giese also felt deep jealousy in relation to another man whom Hirschfeld hired as a secretary, Franz Wimmer (? – ?), also resident in the Institute.[78] And finally, when Hirschfeld brought a young Chinese man named Li Shiu Tong (also known as Tao Li) home from his world tour, this provoked Giese to more bouts of jealousy (*Eifersuchtszenen*).[79] Even

[70] For more information on the WLSR, see Dose 1993; Dose 1999.
[71] Herrn 2010, 123–24.
[72] Hirschfeld & Dose 2013, f. 32/76 n. 119; Pfäfflin 1985, x–xv; Herrn 2022, 383, 392–96.
[73] This is how Hirschfeld was dubbed by a journalist in the National Socialist periodical *Der Angriff*, May 21, 1928; qtd. in Herrn 2010, 125; Herrn 2022, 454–55.
[74] Diary Paul Krische, entry dated Sep. 20, 1930: "Heute Mittag bekannte Carl [*sic*] Giese beim Essen, dass Magnus homosexuell sei. Ich meinte, dann hielte ich es besser, dass er es auch bekenne. Giese meinte, das würde seiner Arbeit schaden. Giese ist sein Freund, wohnt auch mit im Imperial [a luxury hotel in Vienna], ist ganz von ihm abhängig" (*Mitteilungen der Magnus-Hirschfeld-Gesellschaft*, 12 [Oct. 1988], 6).
[75] Archiv MHG, Berlin, fonds Max Reiss, letter (dated May 1935 but presumably May 28, 1935) from Karl Giese to Max Reiss: "Du weißt ja wahrscheinlich, das mir kein liebes Wort so erfreut, wie das, dass man über Papa sagt".
[76] Schulz 2010, 72.
[77] Baumgardt 2003, 10. For more on Erwin Hansen, see Schulz 2010, 123–24; Isherwood 1988, 34, 136.
[78] Schulz 2010, 3–4, 70, 67, 72, 118; Hirschfeld & Dose 2013, f. 8-9/28, 30, f. 19/50 and f. 25/62. For more biographical information on Wimmer, see Dose 2021, 20–21.
[79] Von Praunheim & G. 1992, 12.

though their sexual passion presumably faded over time, one cannot but perceive the lifelong attachment and, above all, the absolute loyalty between the two men.

SCHOOLING

Giese never had higher education. He never finished his so-called *Abitur* (a high school diploma obtained after a set of final exams), nor are there any indications that he got a degree later in life, as Hirschfeld hoped.[80] This certification would have allowed him to commence university studies to become a doctor. Hirschfeld likely started to worry about Giese's future means of existence after the French authorities forced Giese – as we will see later on – to leave Paris (and Hirschfeld) in October 1934. Until then, Giese had been able to live in the Institute under Hirschfeld's protective wing. Hirschfeld made a financial agreement with Ellen Bækgaard and Norman Haire to provide money for Giese to study to become a doctor. Despite this financial settlement, Giese most likely never obtained his *Abitur*.[81] Giese also seems to have been self-conscious about his (real or imagined) limited intellectual capacity. In a January 1938 letter to Ernst Maass, referring to a typical quote by Hirschfeld, Giese stated that his own native talents were indeed limited and that his working-class background had inescapably disadvantaged him in life.[82] Magnus Hirschfeld also saw Li Shiu Tong as the smarter pupil.[83] In this regard it was strange, and probably also unrealistic, that, as we will see, Hirschfeld entrusted Giese (and Li Shiu Tong) with the task of continuing his life's work. But it does clearly indicate how much Hirschfeld trusted and believed in Giese's abilities. Adelheid Schulz suggested that Hirschfeld himself was possibly also at fault for Giese's not living up to Hirschfeld's expectation that he become a doctor like him. She said that Hirschfeld did not allow Giese to take up medical studies when Giese lived and worked in the Institute (1915–1933) since this would mean not having his loyal secretary by his side.[84] All that said, Giese was far from unintelligent and must have at least been interested in sexological matters, if only simply from working with and being around Hirschfeld, and living and working in the Institute [ill. 4].

PUBLISHING RECORD

Despite his self-consciousness and modesty, Giese did write and publish some texts on sexological topics in the periodicals produced by the Institute, and in other publications.[85] Compared to the immense quantity of publications by Magnus Hirschfeld, his mentor, Giese's record is of course rather meager. As an author, Giese is best known for his two-part text on the gay Danish writer Hans Christian

[80] University of Sydney Library, Sydney, Norman Haire collection, 3.21, Karl Geise [*sic*: Giese], Typescripts, 1928–1934, letter (dated Mar. 27, 1935) from Norman Haire to Karl Giese, which contains talk of a medical degree for Karl Giese and Li Shiu Tong. See also Hirschfeld & Dose 2013, f. 91/194, where Hirschfeld clearly expressed his hope that Giese would obtain a medical degree.

[81] When Kurt Hiller asked Giese fleetingly about his "Abiturientenpläne" (Abitur plans), in a letter of April 1937, Giese ignored the question in his reply. See Archiv Kurt Hiller Gesellschaft, Neuss, letter (dated Apr. 29, 1937, 2) from Kurt Hiller to Karl Giese. In an August 1935 letter to Max Hodann, Giese claimed he had started his studies but was not sure he would be able to continue due to a lack of funds. See Arbetarrörelsens arkiv och bibliotek, Stockholm, Max Hodann samling, vol. 15, letter (dated Aug. 2, 1935, [2, 4]) from Karl Giese to Max Hodann. Copies of these letters, procured by Max Hodann's biographer, Wilfried Wolff, are held at the MHG, Berlin. I thank Ralf Dose for sending me copies of this Hodann-Giese correspondence in January 2013. As a consequence of a reorganization of the Swedish archive, the precise archival description of these letters has since changed. See email (dated Apr. 3, 2013) from an Arbetarrörelsens arkiv och bibliotek, Stockholm, collaborator to the author.

[82] Archiv MHG, Berlin, fonds Ernst Maass, letter (dated Jan. 21, 1938, 4) from Karl Giese to Ernst Maass: "auf Grund mangelnder Veranlagung (Sie wissen, 'Anlage und Lage'!)" (due to inadequate predisposition [you know, "predisposition and circumstance"!])

[83] Hirschfeld & Dose 2013, f. 57/126.

[84] Schulz 2001, 72.

Andersen, most famous for his fairy tales,[86] which appeared in *Der Eigene* at a time when relations between Hirschfeld and Adolf Brand (1874-1945) were still good.[87] In this text, Giese tried to "out" Andersen as a gay man by identifying aspects in the fairy tales that indicate a gay sensibility. Unlike his mentor and lover Hirschfeld, Giese seems to have been more interested in the psychological aspects of the homosexual experience. He always wanted to look beneath the surface and outward, odd-seeming phenomena to uncover the hidden (homo)sexual motive. There is one striking and consistent feature in almost all of Giese's texts: he nearly always mentions the name of Magnus Hirschfeld at least once. The unpublished and undated "The Sexual Causes Behind Self-Inflicted Death", in which Giese comments on a 1923 case of auto-erotic asphyxiation in England,[88] is a typical text. A young man named Francis John Ellis was found dead. At first it was thought that the boy had been strangled by a friend since they were rivals for the same woman. It seems that Giese's analysis, suggesting that Ellis died from his own actions and was therefore not murdered, was pretty much on target.[89] Giese proposed replacing the common heteronormative explanatory motto "cherchez la femme" (look for the woman) with "cherchez le sexe" (look for the sex, where "sex" is understood as sexuality or sexual activity). Against the usual heteronormative bias, Giese argued that (sexual rivalry over) a woman did not always lie in the background, explaining mysterious deaths. Sometimes it was necessary to look for a more self-centered (homo)sexual explanation. The young man had not been murdered by a male rival but died from auto-erotic asphyxiation. One could say that Giese had a predilection for gossipy journalism, somewhat enriched with sexological knowledge. It is no wonder then that the bulk of Giese's texts were written for the Institute's more popular magazines, *The Enlightenment* (*Die Aufklärung*) and,

[85] I have listed all of Giese's currently known texts in the bibliography. Very likely there are more. Perhaps significantly, no nonfiction bibliography on the topic of homosexuality that I have seen includes any of Giese's texts. See, for example, Herzer 1982; Bullough et al. 1976; Sigusch 2008. Does this omission tell us something about how Giese's texts are perceived? The single exception is Jacob Schorer's 1922 printed library catalogue, which mentions Giese's article on Hans Christian Andersen. See Schorer 1922, 42. The database of the MHG, Berlin, contains the most complete bibliography of Giese's writings that I have seen. It is missing only one text written by Giese and Richard Linsert, on an English transsexual or transvestite named Captain Barker. See Giese & Linsert 1929a. Barker was a woman who posed as a man; she was also the secretary of a London fascist organization. The incident is also (anonymously) mentioned in *Die Ehe: Monatsschrift für Ehe-Wissenschaft,-Recht u.-Kultur*, Jg. 4, n° 4, Apr. 1, 1929: 124; and in *Die Freundschaft*, Jg. 11, n° 4, 1929: 60–61.

[86] Giese 1921/1922. This text is indeed Giese's most well-known and cited text. See, for example, the chapter on Andersen in Detering 1994, 195.

[87] Herrn 2022, 260–64.

[88] Giese, n.d. The typescript is in the University of Sydney Library, Sydney, Norman Haire collection, 3.21, Karl Geise [*sic*: Giese], Typescripts, 1928–1934. Determining its exact date of composition is problematic. Since the case occurred in 1923, one would at first presume the text could be dated to that year (or at the latest to 1924), something its opening line seems to suggest: "The English Press [*sic*] is at present occupied with the highly sensational death of Francis John Ellis". However, it is probable that the text was written around 1930–31, when the mysterious case was still in the British press. It also needs to be added that this unpublished text only survived because of Giese's contact with the British sexologist Norman Haire. Giese was trying to get Haire's help in publishing it in England. But Haire, seeing the poor quality of the text, quickly informed Giese that publication would not happen any time soon. Giese subsequently wrote to Haire to say that he intended to publish the text in Germany in the periodical *Die Ehe*, but this publication never came about either. *Die Ehe*'s *Erscheinugsverlauf* (publication dates) – 1926 to 1933 – seem to further indicate a composition date of 1930–31. That *Die Ehe* never published the article was confirmed to me by Ralf Dose (personal communication, January 2012). Finally, we also know from a letter to Norman Haire that Giese's text, written in tentative English, was cleaned up a bit with the assistance of Christopher Isherwood – again supporting a 1930–31 date. Isherwood had not lodged in the Institute in 1923–24. See letter (dated Mar. 16, 1931) from Karl Giese to Norman Haire; and letter (dated Mar. 18, 1931, 1) from Norman Haire to Karl Giese; both in University of Sydney Library, Sydney, Norman Haire collection, 3.21, Karl Geise [*sic*: Giese], Typescripts, 1928–1934.

[89] For more information on the 1923 case, which gained the attention of the English criminologist Sir Bernard Spilsbury (1877–1947), see Rose, Apr. 2, 2009, [7].

between 1926 and 1933, *Marriage: A Monthly Journal of Marriage Science, Marriage Law and Marriage Culture* (*Die Ehe: Monatsschrift für Ehe-Wissenschaft, -Recht und –Kultur*).[90]

HEAD OF COLLECTIONS AT THE INSTITUTE

In the fourteen years that Giese lived and worked in the Institute, his tasks probably evolved. But he is best known as the Head of Collections (*Archivleiter*) of the Institute library, archive and the sex-related objects in the Sexualmuseum. On the letterhead of a surviving letter, it is indeed clear that Giese is called *Archivleiter* [ill. 5].[91] In July 1937, Giese said that he had been a secretary and librarian at the Institute for eighteen years, which would mean that he had taken up this function in 1915 – when the Institute was not yet in existence.[92] Most likely, at the earliest, he only became a full-fledged *Archivleiter* in 1919, the year the Institute was founded.[93] Giese also kept the Institute collection under lock and key.[94] This strictness was justified since there was considerable interest, especially from gay visitors, in the juicier parts of the Institute's collection, which was prone to theft.[95] Even after Giese left Germany, likely deeply affected by the tragic destiny of the Institute's archive and library, Giese often continued to describe himself as an archivist (*Archivar*) in official documents, and probably also when speaking with others.

Giese conducted tours and gave lectures on sexological topics to the general public visiting the Institute.[96] Karl Giese was considered intelligent and sufficiently well-read to give these tours. He was even allowed to lead tours for university professors who had taken their students to the Institute. If Giese felt that they were testing

[90] Giese 1929b; Giese 1929c; Giese 1930a; Giese 1930b; Giese 1931a; Giese 1931b; Giese 1932a; Giese 1932b.

[91] Giese used this letterhead when Hirschfeld was on his world tour in 1930–32. See the letters (dated Mar. 16, 1931; Jan. 31, 1932; Feb. 9, 1932) from Karl Giese to Norman Haire in the University of Sydney Library, Sydney, Norman Haire collection, 3.21, Karl Geise [*sic*: Giese], Typescripts, 1928–1934. See also Giese's above-mentioned undated and unpublished text "The Sexual Causes Behind Self-Inflicted Death", in which Giese states his qualification as "Keeper of the Archives of the Institute for Sexual Science". See also Giese 1929c, 139, where Giese signs himself "Archivleiter Karl Giese". In October 1932, Hirschfeld himself described Giese as *Archivar* (archivist) of the Institute. See Hirschfeld & Dose 2013, f. 68/148.

[92] MZA, Brno, fonds B 40, Zemský úřad Brno (Landesbehörde in Brünn), kart. n° 2138, sign. 5274/38, f. 6b.

[93] On the other hand, Sigusch says that Giese was responsible for the Institute's archive and library between 1924 and 1932 (Sigusch 2008, 355).

[94] Wolff quotes the author of this claim, another secretary working at the Institute, Bruno Vogel (1898–1987): "Giese was guardian of the Archive, which was properly closed up and secured" (Wolff 1986, 422).

[95] On the erotic attraction of some of the items in the library, see the interview Rosa von Praunheim conducted with a patient of the Institute, Hanns Grafe: "RvP [Rosa von Praunheim]: Und es kamen dann auch viele Schwule von ausserhalb, die die Bibliothek benutzten und an den Tees teilnahmen? Dr HG [Hanns Grafe]: Ja, die haben sich das angeguckt und konnten ja gar nicht genug haben, von den Fotos, Fotoalben mit nackten jungen Burschen und Männern, die gabs da. Es mussten auch welche aufpassen, weil da immer gestolen wurde, die Bilder mitgenommen" (RvP [Rosa von Praunheim]: And then there were also many gays from outside who used the library and joined the tea parties? Dr HG [Hanns Grafe]: Yes, they looked at it and could not get enough of the photos, the photo albums of naked young boys and men. Someone also had to watch out, because they were always stealing, taking the pictures) (Von Praunheim & G. 1992, 14). For a bare idea of the variety of the objects in Hirschfeld's Sexualmuseum, see the rather tittilating photographs in a 1932 issue of the French popular magazine *Voilà* (Scize, Oct. 22, 1932). See also Giese 1929c, 139–42.

[96] See the *Jahresbericht* (annual report), *Jahrbuch für sexuelle Zwischenstufen mit besonderer Berücksichtigung der Homosexualität* 1923, 211; Hirschfeld 1929, 130; where there is talk of "regular Saturday evening tours". See also Schulz 2001, 71; Herrn 2022, 327–28. Wolff writes that "Hirschfeld entrusted him [Giese] with lecturing to the general public on questions of sexual conflict and homosexuality" (Wolff 1986, 185). Rosa von Praunheim's interview with Hanns Grafe points in the same direction: "RvP [Rosa von Praunheim]: "Der [Giese] hat doch dann auch die Fragestunden geleitet im Institut? Dr HG [Hanns Grafe]: Genau. Und er hat auch so Führungen gemacht und Vorträge gehalten. RvP: Uber was waren die Vorträge? Dr HG: Na ja, über Homosexualität, über die Verbreitung in der Welt, von der Antike her, wie sie sich entwickelt hat. Da waren so'n paar Standardmuster" (RvP [Rosa von Praunheim]: Didn't [Giese] also lead the Q&A sessions at the Institute? Dr HG [Hanns Grafe]: Exactly. And he also gave guided tours and lectures. RvP: What were the lectures about? Dr HG: Well, about homosexuality,

him, he always knew how to handle the matter and ended with a light joke.[97] In addition to the many locals, a considerable number of foreigners, perhaps drawn by the sensational rumors about what could be seen there, found their way to the Institute and sometimes wrote about their visit.[98] An Institute tour was "one of the Berlin attractions of the Weimar period" [ill. 6].[99] It is therefore only correct that Karl Giese was listed among the Institute's twenty collaborators (*Mitarbeiter*) in Sigusch's reference work on the history of German sexology.[100]

Thanks to his pivotal position in the Institute, Karl Giese knew Hirschfeld's professional network very well and was also perfectly aware of the topics and issues at hand. That Giese likely joined Hirschfeld at all five WLSR conferences would only have deepened his intimate knowledge of Hirschfeld's personal and professional network.[101] Giese's thorough knowledge of this network is further illustrated by a letter Giese sent to Ernst Maass at the end of 1937, two years after Hirschfeld's death. In this letter, Giese listed, possibly from memory, an impressive number of American professional contacts Hirschfeld made on his world trip. Although Giese likely never met most of these people, he must have learned their names from his intense cooperation with Hirschfeld when the latter was on his world trip in the USA in 1930–31.[102]

GIESE'S EMOTIONAL INTELLIGENCE

Giese was very close with the above-mentioned Adelheid Schulz, who worked as a housekeeper in the Institute.[103] Schulz started work in the Institute in 1928, when she was nineteen years old.[104] She personally witnessed the ransacking of the Institute in May 1933 and, quite heroically, attempted to talk some sense to the Nazi students in an effort to stop their mad actions. After it was looted, she stayed in the Institute for a few months but finally left her former workplace for good on July 1, 1933.[105] It is thanks to her that so many intimate details about the Institute's daily life are known to us [ill. 7]. In 2001, representatives of the MHG in Berlin interviewed her a few times about all kinds of subjects relating to the Institute and Magnus Hirschfeld and the people around him. It was indeed a unique occasion.[106] If one reads the transcript

about its spread in the world, from Antiquity, how it developed. There were some standard patterns) (Von Praunheim & G. 1992, 13). Günter Maeder said he and Giese alternated their evening lectures (Maeder 1993, 3).

[97] Wellcome Library, London, archive Charlotte Wolff (1897–1986), correspondence II, 1981–1986, PSY/WOL/6/8/2, letter (undated 1985?, f. 6-7) from Erhart Löhnberg to Charlotte Wolff. Cf. Wolff's conclusion: "He had a great sense of humour and was brilliant at repartee" (Wolff 1986, 427).

[98] Giese 1929c, 141–42; Dose & Hern 2006, 37. A good written account by a French visitor, who also lodged in the Institute, is Royer 1930.

[99] "Eine der Berliner Attraktionen der Weimarer Zeit" (Dose 2005a, 78). Another well-known picture shows Giese lecturing in the Institute's Ernst-Haeckel-Saal as well. The picture was published in *Die Aufklarung*, Jg. 1, Heft 5, 1929, 130.

[100] Sigusch 2008, 355–56.

[101] It is not known if Giese attended the first conference in Berlin in 1921, but Giese can be clearly seen in a picture of the participants at the second WLSR conference in Copenhagen (Jul. 1–5, 1928) (Riese & Leunbach 1929, n.p.). He is also included in the list of conference participants (Riese & Leunbach 1929, 306). We know that Giese attended the third London conference (Sep. 8–14, 1929), as he later told Norman Haire that he was recovering from the conference. See University of Sydney Library, Sydney, Norman Haire collection, 3.21, Karl Geise [*sic*: Giese], Typescripts, 1928–1934, letter (dated Sep. 21, 1929) from Karl Giese to Norman Haire. Giese can be seen in a picture of the fourth conference held in Vienna (Sep. 16–23, 1930) (Sigusch 2008, 103). Finally, Giese appears in the front row of a well-known photo of the attendees at the fifth and final WLSR conference in Brno (Sep. 20–26, 1932), seated in an auditorium. See illustration n° 10 in chapter 3.

[102] Archiv MHG, Berlin, fonds Ernst Maass, letter (dated Dec. 29, 1937) from Karl Giese to Ernst Maass. It is unclear why exactly Giese informed Ernst Maass about Hirscheld's American contacts. See also Soetaert 2014, 67.

[103] Very soon after being hired, Schulz grew very close to both Giese and Hirschfeld. See Schulz 2001, 2, 14, 43. For more biographical information on Schulz, see Dose 2021, 12, 17.

[104] Schulz 2001, 2–3, 25, 44, 83.

[105] Schulz 2001, 92.

[106] Schulz 2001. On December 12, 2002, Adelheid Schulz was interviewed again, this time by Manfred

of the interview, one notices that she mentions Giese's name very often, stressing several times that her relationship with Giese was very good, and that she thought of him as a brother.[107] That Giese and Schulz both had a working-class background likely played a part in their warm connection. The correspondence between Giese and "Delchen", as Giese fondly called her, clearly shows that they had a very strong bond, one that did not diminish after Giese left Germany in 1933. He kept in written contact with Schulz.[108] Adelheid Schulz kept the letters and postcards that Giese sent her after his departure. She donated this correspondence to the MHG in Berlin some time after the MHG interviewed her.[109]

Giese also had a strong bond with his sister Toni (Antonie) Mertens. She often visited Adelheid Schulz in the Institute. Giese was clearly the connection between the two women, but they remained in contact after Giese left Germany in May 1933. They would tell each other the latest news about Giese, who was clearly aware that the two women were sharing this information. Giese often wrote to his sister Toni Mertens, who reported what Giese said in his letters on her almost weekly visits to Schulz.[110] After Giese died in 1938, Toni Mertens's visits to Schulz stopped.[111]

Giese was an avid letter writer, often noting in his letters that he had "correspondence owing" (*Briefschulden*), meaning that he had to write to this or that person and was lagging behind in answering letters.[112] In Giese's surviving letters, we encounter a man who not only mastered his mother tongue but also possessed a good amount of what we would now call emotional intelligence. Giese's letters have proved to be a crucial source for my own research. It is highly possible that more of Giese's letters are extant. I think one could do greater justice to the centrality of the figure of Karl Giese in Hirschfeld research simply by continuing to look for the doubtless many letters that Giese sent to people he knew.[113]

Baumgardt and Ralf Dose. See Baumgardt 2003.

[107] Schulz 2001, 44, 111.

[108] Schulz 2001, 33. In his letters, Giese always fondly addressed Adelheid as "Delchen". Adelheid never failed to send Giese a card on his birthday.

[109] See https://magnus-hirschfeld.de/gedenken/historisches/institut/innenansichten/ (accessed May 21, 2021).

[110] In a 1936 letter that Giese sent to Schulz, Giese referred Schulz to his sister for more details about what had happened to him. See Archiv MHG, Berlin, fonds Adelheid Schulz, letter (dated May 26, 1936, 1) from Karl Giese to Adelheid Schulz. In a postcard to Schulz, later that year, Giese referred to a long letter he sent to his sister, indicating that Schulz should talk to his sister to learn what he had said. See Archiv MHG, Berlin, fonds Adelheid Schulz, postcard (dated Oct. 20, 1936) from Karl Giese to Adelheid Schulz.

[111] Schulz 2001, 74, 103, 123.

[112] I found three indirect indications that Giese wrote – or at least intended to write – several letters. In two letters Giese complained he was behind in answering letters. See Archiv MHG, Berlin, fonds Günter Maeder, undated letter (but likely Jan. 10, 1934, n.p.) from Karl Giese to Günter Maeder: "Auch ich habe ja noch so viele 'Briefschulden'" (I also still have so much "correspondence owing"). See also Archiv MHG, Berlin, fonds Adelheid Schulz, letter (dated Aug. 6, 1933, 1) from Karl Giese to Adelheid Schulz: "denn ich habe so vielen zu schreiben" (for I have so many still to write); letter (dated May 26, 1936, 1) from Karl Giese to Adelheid Schulz: "Ich habe aber so viele Briefschulden" (I still have so much correspondence owing).

[113] Even *within* archives that house Giese's letters, they struggle to be noticed. When, in 2011, I asked the Arbetarrörelsens arkiv och bibliotek in Stockholm about the Giese letters in the Max Hodann fonds, they replied that it contained none. See their email (dated Feb. 1, 2011) to the author. Fortunately, I knew this was incorrect and I thank Ralf Dose for sending me copies of the Giese-Hodann correspondence, copies of which were given to the MHG Berlin by Hodann's biographer, Wilfried Wolff, in 1990. See letter (dated Jan. 30, 2013) from Ralf Dose to the author; and email (dated Mar. 7, 2013) from Ralf Dose to the author. Giese's name does not even appear in the inventory of the Max Hodann fonds. This omission could perhaps be explained by the fact that Giese's handwriting is not always very legible. But the real lesson is that inventory lists can be incomplete and constitute no guarantee of the contents. In the online inventory of the Hirschfeld and Giese letters in the Norman Haire fonds of the Rare Books and Special Collections department of the University of Sydney Library, Giese's name is misspelled "Geise". An attempt on my part to point out this mistake did not result in anyone rectifying the spelling in the online catalogue of the archival fonds.

[114] "Femininer Sohn und Mutter gleichzeitig photographiert" (Herrn 2008c: card Karl Giese – der Freund als "Fall"). The original photo is to be found in Hirschfeld 1926–1930, 1930: vol. IV, Bilderteil, 327, image n° 422.

CHERCHEZ LA FEMME?

There seems to be a good deal of agreement about the feminine character of Giese's actions, gestures and appearance. Giese himself was not afraid to be perceived and labeled this way. In the picture volume (*Bilderteil*) of Hirschfeld's magnum opus *Geschlechtskunde*, the following legend appears under the photo of Giese and his mother: "Feminine son and mother photographed at the same time" [ill. 8].[114] The most famous characterization of Karl Giese is, of course, Christopher Isherwood's description of Giese in one of his novels. He recalled Giese as a "sturdy peasant youth with a girl's heart".[115] Yet one should also not forget what Isherwood immediately adds, that Giese is a "dedicated earnest intelligent campaigner for sexual freedom".[116] Regarding Giese's feminine appearance, Erhart Löhnberg wrote to Charlotte Wolff, Hirschfeld's biographer: "Giese was a Berlin youth who looked like a woman or, more precisely, like a girl. This was because of his facial features, and the way he cut his hair".[117] In his memoir, Günter Maeder wrote that "Giese was an arch-fairy. It was sometimes embarrassing to walk in his company". Yet Maeder also claimed that Giese's feminine traits somewhat diminished with age.[118] In her MHG interview, Adelheid Schulz also mentioned that Giese looked like an effeminate gay man because of the way he walked: "Ah yes. You could tell from a distance because there was a real sway to his movement".[119] In a March 1935 letter, Hirschfeld wrote about Giese's "eidetic-feminine nature".[120] The niece of Adolf Brand (the publisher of *Der Eigene*, the very first gay magazine in the world) also remembered Giese as acting feminine (*tuntig*) when he and Hirschfeld visited Brand in Berlin-Wilhelmshagen. She further described Giese in diminutive terms, as still not grown up, naming him "Karlchen Giese" (little Karl Giese). Of course, this might simply be a reference to Karl Giese being still very young at the time. In addition, Dieter Berner revealed that Giese was nicknamed Karola Gisela in one of Friedrich Radszuweit's gay magazines.[121] In 1921, Giese signed one of his articles with the pseudonym Androgynos.[122]

Giese was also handy with a needle and thread, adept at embroidery and upholstery, and loved decorating.[123] He was a collector of precious stones, which he kept in a showcase (*Vitrine*). At the foot of his bed in his room in the Institute, there was a round table covered with little statuettes. And he had an unusual but impressive

[115] Isherwood 1977, 26–27. Bernd-Ulrich Hergemöller used this quote as an epigraph to his lemma on Karl Giese in his major reference work *Mann für Mann* (Hergemöller 1998, 279). Seeing the surviving fragments of *Anders als die Andern*, one is indeed reminded of Isherwood's description of Giese. In the movie, the very young Karl Giese seems to be a rather tall and robust young man. Giese's acting is indeed exaggerated and somewhat feminine in some scenes; however, it must also be stated that exaggerated dramatic gestures were part and parcel of the silent movie acting conventions of the time.

[116] Isherwood 1977, 26–27; Isherwood 1988, 33.

[117] Wellcome Library, London, archive Charlotte Wolff (1897–1986), correspondence II, 1981–1986, PSY/WOL/6/8/2, letter (undated 1985?, f. 6) from Erhart Löhnberg to Charlotte Wolff: "Giese war ein Berliner Jüngling, der so aussah wie eine Frau, genauer: wie ein Mädchen. Das lag an seinen Gesichtszügen, und an seinem Haarschnitt". Compare Wolff's treatment of the information from "Dr. L. E.": Giese looked like a girl "not in the build of his body, but in his facial expressions and hairstyle" (Wolff 1986, 427).

[118] Wellcome Library, London, archive Charlotte Wolff (1897–1986), correspondence II, 1981–1986, PSY/WOL/6/8/2, letter (dated Feb. 2, 1982, f. 2) from Günter Maeder to Charlotte Wolff: "Giese war eine Erztunte. Es war manchmal peinlich, in seiner Gesellschaft zu gehen". And: "Er hat sich aber später sehr zu seinem Gunsten gewandelt" (However, it must be noted that Giese later shed some of his feminine manner and, according to Maeder, this was very much in Giese's favor).

[119] "Ah ja. Man kannte es ja von weitem, weil er eine richtige schaukelnde Bewegung hatte" (Schulz 2001, 35, 74). All through the interview, one can see that Schulz held several other common views on homosexuality.

[120] Archiv MHG, Berlin, fonds Max Reiss, letter (dated Mar. 3, 1935, 3) from Magnus Hirschfeld to Max Reiss: "eidetisch-femininen Natur".

[121] Brand, Herzer & Berner 2000, 99.

[122] Giese 1921b.

[123] Schulz 2001, 45–46, 97, 103 and Wellcome Library, London, archive Charlotte Wolff (1897–1986), correspondence II, 1981–1986, PSY/WOL/6/8/2, letter (undated 1985?, f. 9) from Erhart Löhnberg to Charlotte Wolff.

collection of candle snuffers (*Lichtputzscheren*) that he later gave to his brother Adolf, possibly when he had to leave Berlin in 1933.[124] Giese was also fond of cats and kept a few in the Institute.[125] The pair of cats photographed for an issue of Hirschfeld's periodical *Die Ehe* may have belonged to Giese. That the male and female cats were gaily named "Miss Purzel" (Fräulein Purzel) and "Mr. Puck" (Herr Puck) seems to suggest that this was indeed the case.[126] Other than shiny precious stones, Giese also collected cat figurines.[127]

Ellen Bækgaard, a Danish acquintance of Hirschfeld's, wrote that Giese helped Hirschfeld stay attuned to the "real world" outside: "However difficult it was to get to Magnus Hirschfeld, it was easy to approach his secretary. With him it was always an 'open house', and Mrs. Heller [who supervised the entrance to the Institute; in reality, Helene Helling] always let his private friends pass. It was a 'sanctuary' for them in the middle of the city; they could come in at any time and unload and feel safe – there was no pretence there".[128] Bækgaard went so far as to conclude that Giese "was [...] the absolute go-between between Magnus Hirschfeld and the world around him".[129]

Besides the many comments about his many feminine traits, Giese was looked down upon a little as someone who, especially in his younger years, lived for fun and enjoyed socializing in his room in the Institute with friends who were also interested in having a gay old time. Schulz often repeated that Giese was an "extremely cheerful person".[130] He organized revues (*Revuen*) in the Ernst-Haeckel-Saal in the Institute and also loved dressing-up parties. He did indeed have a large circle of friends and acquaintances.[131] Some of his more well-known personal friends were the archeologist Francis Turville-Petre (1901–1942),[132] the English writer Christopher Isherwood (1904–1986), and the actor Michael Rittermann (1910–1989).

One must be cautious, of course, about the tendency to perceive and identify feminine traits in gay men.[133] This deprecatory attitude towards feminine gay men is likely one of the reasons that Giese has for so long been regarded as a less relevant or valuable source in Hirschfeld research. Giese's lack of schooling, due to his working-class background, probably only strengthened this negative sentiment. I believe this implicit depreciation of Giese to be unjustified. On the contrary, Giese should be considered an important figure and source in Hirschfeld research. He stood *closest*

[124] Schulz 2001, 100, 122.

[125] Schulz 2001, 33.

[126] *Die Ehe: Monatsschrift für Ehe-Wissenschaft, -Recht u. -Kultur*, n° 4, Apr. 1, 1927: 117. The picture was used for a (rather silly) April Fool's joke, suggesting that the Institute's *Eheberatungstelle* (marriage counseling center) brought the cat couple together. Schulz mentions two cats in the Institute, one named Grauli and a white one called Hasi (Schulz 2001, 33, 100).

[127] Schulz 2001, 46–47, 100, 102.

[128] "So schwierig wie es war, zu Magnus Hirschfeld zu kommen, so leicht war es, zu seinem Sekretär zu gelangen. Dort war immer 'offenes Haus', und Frau Heller [who supervised the entrance to the Institute; in reality, Helene Helling] ließ seine privaten Freunde immer passieren. Das war eine "Freistatt' für die mitten in der Stadt, sie konnten jederzeit hereinkommen und konnten abladen und sich in Sicherheit fühlen – es gab keine Verstellung dort" (Bækgaard 1985, 35).

[129] "[W]ar [...] das absolute Zwischenglied zwischen Magnus Hirschfeld und der Umwelt" (Bækgaard 1985, 33).

[130] "[Ä]ußerst fröhlicher Mensch" (Schulz 2001, 35–37).

[131] Wolff 1986, 186; and Wellcome Library, London, archive Charlotte Wolff (1897–1986), correspondence II, 1981-1986, PSY/WOL/6/8/2, letter (undated, 1985?, f. 6) from Erhart Löhnberg to Charlotte Wolff.

[132] Sigusch 2008, 351; Schulz 2001, 124.

[133] Whatever the situation, one must certainly condemn von Praunheim's attitude in the interview he conducted with Dr. Hanns Grafe. Von Praunheim appears to have had clear, preconceived gender-stereotypical ideas about "who the man was and who the wife" in Giese and Hirschfeld's relationship. After hearing Hanns Grafe talk all through the interview about Giese's predilection for perfumes, scarves, etc., von Praunheim summed up the clear-cut gender divide he had in his mind near the end. In conclusion, he asked Grafe to tell him "if Hirschfeld had a deep voice and if Giese was very effeminate". See von Praunheim & G. 1992, 16.

[134] "[d]er beste Kenner meiner Ziele und Werke" (Hirschfeld & Dose 2013, f. 72/156).

[135] University of Sydney Library, Sydney, Norman Haire collection, 3.20, Magnus Hirschfeld, Type-

to Hirschfeld and had a great amount of intimate knowledge about the man and his projects. At one point, Hirschfeld himself described Giese as "the best specialist of my aims and works".[134] That Giese increasingly became Hirschfeld's alter ego can be seen in the surviving correspondence between Giese and the English sexologist Norman Haire. In one of these letters, for example, Giese wrote "we", meaning him and Hirschfeld.[135] When, in his *Testament: Heft II*, Hirschfeld restlessly revolved who was best suited to continue his legacy, Giese was always the first.[136] It is certain that Hirschfeld and Giese constituted a sturdy tandem. In what follows we will look further at the lives of these two men, who were very close to each other, and who preserved a close bond to the end of their lives. As we will see, Giese's loyalty to Hirschfeld endured even after the latter's death. When Hirschfeld embarked on his world tour, in 1930–32, Hirschfeld relied on Giese as the most reliable conduit for accurate information about the Institute and its operation in his absence. Indeed, Giese's intimate knowledge of Hirschfeld's work and professional network allowed Giese to manage things in a satisfactory way for Hirschfeld when the latter was abroad [ill. 9].

HIRSCHFELD GOES ON A WORLD TOUR

Having been invited to give a lecture in the USA, Hirschfeld sailed from Bremerhaven in Germany to New York on November 15, 1930.[137] Hirschfeld would end up staying three months in the USA (with side trips to Canada and Mexico) before setting out on a year-long world tour, mainly through Asia and the Middle East, leaving the USA from San Francisco.[138] Hirschfeld's true motivations for leaving his beloved home country are a little unclear. His personal writings indicate some discontent with the Institute's petty rivalries, as well as with the difficulties of finding and keeping reliable staff, and he may have been glad to get away.[139] He was also trying to get away from the growing animosity towards him expressed in the National Socialist press.[140] In the introduction to the book that he later wrote about his world tour, he claimed that he had not planned the longer trip prior to setting off from Bremerhaven. But the success he enjoyed in the USA, and an invitation to lecture in Japan, apparently made him realize that he could extend his trip, financing it by giving lectures.[141] The 1929 stock market crash, and its presumably dramatic consequences for Hirschfeld's financial situation, may also have contributed to Hirschfeld finding it opportune to extend (and enjoy) the reach of his name and fame more globally.[142] We also need to take into account that Hirschfeld always intended to find new markets for the Titus Pearls (Titus Perlen), marketed as pills to improve one's sex life, since he already gained a considerable income from the license he co-owned.[143] Lastly, I also think that, due to the darkening political climate and the ascendancy of the fascists, Hirschfeld

scripts, 1923-1935, letter (dated Jan. 16, 1930) from Karl Giese to Norman Haire.

[136] Soetaert 2014, 14.

[137] Dose 2019, 11; Hirschfeld 1933b/2006, 23. Hirschfeld made his first trip to the USA in 1893, shortly after finishing his medical studies.

[138] Hirschfeld 1933b/2006, 39.

[139] Hirschfeld & Dose 2013, f. 47/108; Wiesner 2003, 424. For more on the many troubles in the Institute, see also Herrn 2004; Herrn 2010, 124.

[140] For an excellent overview of the worsening political climate in Germany, starting around 1927, when the fascists imposed themselves more and more, see Herrn 2010, 123–29.

[141] Hirschfeld 1933b/2006, 24.

[142] Cf. Herrn 2010, 123; and Hirschfeld & Dose 2013, f. 48/108, where Hirschfeld records what he told reporters about the purpose of his trip: "Recreation – Studies – Lectures". Hirschfeld added that, at least in theory, his lectures could now reach 250 million people – presumably referring to the population of the USA. The problem is that the USA had only around 125 million inhabitants at the time.

[143] Herrn 2022, 447. For more information on the Titus Pearls, see Hirschfeld & Dose 2013, f. 10/32 n. 28, 29; Herzer 2017, 307–10; Herrn 2022, 364–70. Ralf Dose is preparing a study on the subject under the working title "Die Testifortan-Story oder: Weimars Viagra?".

might have been looking for possible (academic) escape routes for himself and his life's work on this second trip to the USA. The anonymous introduction to the English edition of his world tour book claims that Hirschfeld left Germany in 1930 because of antisemitism and was advised to continue the tour indefinitely because, when he was in New York, "another wave of Anti-Semitism broke over Germany".[144] But there were also arguments *against* embarking on a world tour. Hirschfeld was quite aware of its risks due to his poor health and the possibility of contracting tropical diseases.[145] Prior to starting the trip, he was intensely deliberating, in *Testament: Heft II,* on who his successor should be.[146]

Hirschfeld set foot on European soil again on March 17, 1932. He arrived by ship in Piräus, the port of Athens. But Hirschfeld brought along a new partner, a young Chinese man named Li Shiu Tong (or also Tao Li) whom he met in Shanghai around May 1931 [ill. 10].[147] On the advice of his friends and the Institute staff, Hirschfeld did not return to Berlin.[148] Karl Giese, eager to see his beloved mentor again after an absence of sixteen months, traveled to Athens to welcome Hirschfeld.[149] Hirschfeld told a Vienna newspaper that he had traveled around the world for 500 days and arrived in Vienna's Ostbahnhof on April 1, 1932, with Giese and Li Shiu Tong, on the Orient Express.[150] Later, Hirschfeld told a French magazine that he had given 178 lectures on his world tour and also took – or, rather, allowed Li Shiu Tong to take – around 1,200 photos on the trip.[151] Hirschfeld would stay in Vienna until the autumn of 1932.

The difficulties from which Hirschfeld had run away reappeared as soon as he landed in Athens. He had to deal with hostile local newspapers and death threats. Hirschfeld wrote: "I had hardly set foot on European soil again on 17/III. [1932] when the old agitation began again".[152] Things were no better in Austria. On May 9, 1932, Nazis interrupted a screening of the movie *Laws of Love: From the Portfolio of a Sexologist* (*Gesetze der Liebe: Geheimnisse aus der Mappe eines Sexualforschers*) in the Schubert cinema in Graz.[153] They threw stink bombs and smeared the screen with

[144] Hirschfeld 1935c, ix.

[145] Hirschfeld & Dose 2013, f. 48-49/108, 110.

[146] Hirschfeld & Dose 2013, f. 1-37.

[147] Hirschfeld & Dose 2013, f. 57/126 n. 328. I have chosen to use the name Li Shiu Tong for Hirschfeld's Chinese pupil throughout this text, thus avoiding the Chinese spelling of his name, in accordance with how he is named in most instances in Hirschfeld research. I have also avoided the other name that is sometimes used, Tao Li. For more explanations of both of these names, see Berner 1989a; Berner 1989b. See also Panel 19, https://magnus-hirschfeld.de/ausstellungen/exil-gastebuch/exile-guestbook/ (accessed Jul. 14, 2020).

[148] Hirschfeld & Dose 2013, f. 59/130.

[149] Dose 2005a, 87; Hirschfeld & Dose 2013, f. 62/136; Schulz 2001, 115. Giese went to Greece with Francis Turville-Petre, a close friend. See University of Sydney Library, Sydney, Norman Haire collection, 3.21, Karl Geise [*sic*: Giese], Typescripts, 1928–1934, letter (dated Jan. 31, 1932, 1) from Karl Giese to Norman Haire. See also Herzer 2017, 370.

[150] See "Magnus Hirschfeld hat seine Weltreise beendet", *Neues Wiener Journal*, Apr. 2, 1932, 9. See also Hirschfeld & Dose 2013, f. 63/138. The date of Hirschfeld's arrival in Vienna corresponds to the stamp (dated Apr. 1, 1932) in Hirschfeld's passport. See Archiv MHG, Berlin, fonds Ernst Maass, Hirschfeld's Reisepass (passport) (May 19, 1928–May 18, 1933, 22). The name discernible from the semi-legible stamp ("Gr … dorf") could not be found under the sections "*Eisenbahnübergänge*" (railroad crossings) on the Wikipedia page "Österreichische Grenzübergängen in die Nachbarstaaten" (Austrian border crossings to neighboring countries), but of course this list only gives the *current* railway border crossings. See https://de.wikipedia.org/wiki/Österreichische_Grenzübergänge_in_die_Nachbarstaaten#Eisenbahnübergänge (accessed May 15, 2020). I thank Ralf Dose for sending me a copy of his working paper on the stamps in Hirschfeld's passport.

[151] *Voilà*, Jul. 1, 1933, 5.

[152] "Kaum hatte ich am 17/III. [1932] wieder europäischen Boden betreten, als die alte Hetze wieder begann" (Hirschfeld & Dose 2013, f. 62/136).

[153] See, for example, *Salzburger Chronik für Stadt und Land*, May 11, 1932, 7; *Reichspost*, May 11, 1932, 5; and (Linzer) *Tages-Post*, May 10, 1932, 12. An article from *Neuen Freien Presse* (May 10, 1932, 20) is reproduced in Hirschfeld & Dose 2013, f. 62/136. The Schubert movie theater is still located at the same address, 2 Mehlplatz.

[154] *Mein Film* 323 (1932): 22. The movie played at the Lichtbildbühne cinema in the 11th *Bezirk* (district), March 8–10, 1932.

red paint forcing the screening to stop. The movie had started showing in Vienna in March.[154] By the end of the month, one cinema announced that it would show the movie only once, adding that it would be a late-night screening and explicitly forbidden to young people.[155] Almost ten years earlier, in February 1923, a lecture in Vienna by Hirschfeld was severely disrupted by Hitler adepts. They fired shots, pulled knives, threw stink bombs and harassed the audience. Several people were injured, some seriously. Hirschfeld himself escaped the mob at the last moment.[156]

[155] The movie was screened at the Weltbild cinema on April 30, 1932; see *Mein Film* 331 (1932): 24. To the announcement of the screening of the film, one added the warning: "Strengstes Jugendverbot!" (Strictly no Young People!). The film started at 10:45 or 11:45 p.m.

[156] See "Neue Heldentaten der Wiener Hakenkreuzler: Schüsse und Stinkbomben beim Vortrag Magnus Hirschfeld", *Wiener Morgenzeitung*, Feb. 5, 1923, 1. This newspaper article was unearthed by Erwin In het Panhuis, see https://magnus-hirschfeld.de/netzwerk/veroffentlichungen-publications/ausdem-archiv-storaktion-gegen-eine-vortrag-magnus-hirschfelds-in-wien-1923/ (accessed Jul. 21, 2024).

1. The birth house of Karl Giese at 17 Schulstraße in what is now Berlin Mitte, November 2010.

2. Film still from Anders als die Andern (Different from the others) (1919), dir. Richard Oswald. Karl Giese plays the role of the young violinist Paul Körner. In this scene he is pushed to "go after the girls" at a party.

3. Undated photograph, presumably taken in the Institute, of a costume party or actors of a play at rest. Giese's old mother is the first figure on the left, seated in the lower row. Karl Giese is the sixth person and Magnus Hirschfeld the eighth person in that same row. Giese and Hirschfeld are holding hands.

4. Group photo of Institute collaborators and visiting Prussian social-democratic politicians, March 1, 1920. The young Karl Giese with bow tie (second row, fifth person from the right) stands behind a seated Magnus Hirschfeld (first row, fourth person from the right).

KARL GIESE
ARCHIVLEITER AM INSTITUT FÜR SEXUALWISSENSCHAFT / BERLIN NW 40, IN DEN ZELTEN 10
FERNSPRECHER: A 2 FLORA 4356

Locarno
Moscia Den 17. V. 33.

Lieber Dr. Haire!

Nachdem ich vorläufig hierher zurückgekehrt bin, möchte ich Ihnen gleich schreiben, dass „Papa" wünscht, dass niemand seine Briefadresse erfährt. Eine eigentliche Adresse hat er ja überhaupt noch nicht. Es bestehen insofern für ihn auch Gefahren, als die Schweiz auch nicht frei ist von Nazi-Elementen und außerdem von Deutschland aus versucht wird, ihm ein Korruptionsverfahren (auf dem Umweg über Stiftungsbehörde u. Steuer) anzuhängen und ihn nach Deutschland ausliefern zu lassen.

Mir persönlich wird auch aus Berlin mitgeteilt, dass ich besser nicht dahin käme, da man auch an die Mitarbeiter heran will. So ist auch meine Zukunft unklar, ganz abgesehen davon, dass das Institut zwar noch nicht endgültig geschlossen ist, aber doch in einem solchen Zustand der Auflösung sich befindet, dass an ein Arbeiten dort für mich und andere nicht in Frage kommt.

5. Letterhead "Karl Giese, Head of Collections at the Institute of Sexual Science" (Karl Giese Archivleiter am Institut für Sexualwissenschaft), letter dated May 17, 1933. University of Sydney Library, Sydney, Norman Haire collection.

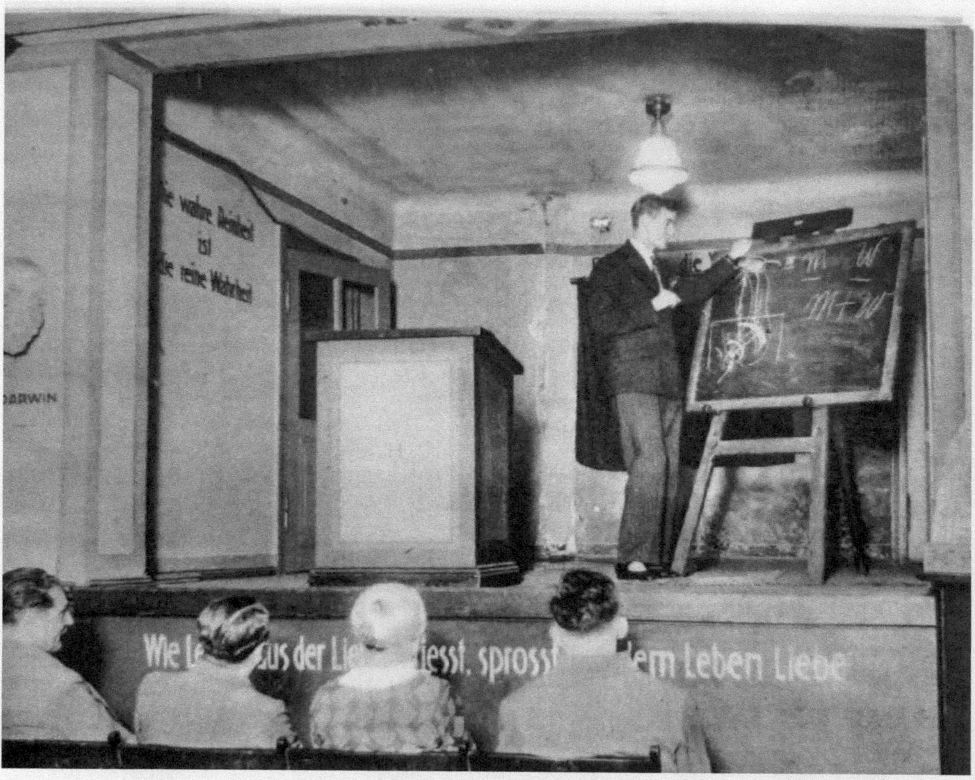

6. Karl Giese giving one of his regular Saturday evening lectures in the Institute's Ernst Haeckel room, undated photo but likely second half of the 1920s.

7. Hirschfeld's housekeeper Adelheid Schulz, undated photo but presumably 1928-1933.

8. Karl Giese with his mother Anna Müller (née Noack, 1860-?), undated photo but presumably 1920s. Subtitle: Feminine son and mother photographed at the same time (Femininer Sohn und Mutter gleichzeitig photographiert).

9. Dedicated portrait photo Karl Giese, September 28, 1931 (in Berlin).

10. Photo of the young Li Shiu Tong, undated.

3. The September 1932 World League for Sexual Reform Conference in Brno

MAGNUS HIRSCHFELD AND CZECHOSLOVAKIA

Luckily, Hirschfeld was soon able to find some relief in Czechoslovakia. Hirschfeld had a special affection for the young country led by president Tomáš Garrigue Masaryk. In many ways, the country represented for Hirschfeld a model democracy, one that embraced the many aspects of modernity much better than reactionary Germany. Hirschfeld also regularly took vacations in the spas of Karlsbad (Karlovy Vary) or Marienbad (Mariánské Lázně).[1] Starting in the 1920s, he gave lectures when he was in the country on his annual spa tour. In June 1927, for example, he gave two lectures in Marienbad.[2] The following year, he was in Marienbad again and lectured once more.[3] Indeed, Hirschfeld's lectures in Czechoslovakia were met with much less hostility than in Germany.[4] Only in the Sudetenland was there some opposition when Hirschfeld lectured.[5] Hirschfeld was also aware that the Slovak part of the country was more conservative, but he did not hesitate to spread the word in Pressburg (Bratislava) when he visited Czechoslovakia.[6] Hirschfeld clearly had ambitions in the young country. In 1921, he toured there for three weeks, lecturing in Prague, Brünn (Brno), Marienbad, Aussig (Ústí nad Labem), and Pilsen (Plzeň). Hirschfeld's lectures, larded with scientific seriousness and slides, were met with respectful enthusiasm across Czechoslovakia, as reported by the Berlin gay magazine *Die Freundschaft*, extensively quoting from a few Czechoslovak newspapers, among them the *Marienbader Zeitung*: "Through his tireless research work, Hirschfeld proved irrefutably that homosexuals are neither sick people nor degenerates, but that their sexual disposition is innate".[7] There was even talk that an Institute like the one in Berlin would start in Prague under the direction of the venerologist and dermatologist Dr. Ferdinand Pečírka (1859–1922), who taught at the Faculty of Medicine of Charles University in Prague between 1920 and 1922, and who may have been Europe's first university professor of sexology.[8] The

[1] For example, Hirschfeld is mentioned in the *Seznam Karlovarských lázeňských hostů = Karlsbader Kurliste = Visitors-list of Carlsbad = Liste des baigneurs à Carlsbad*, Jul. 4, 1907; Aug. 15, 1916; and also in the 1924 and 1928 volumes of the *Liste der angekommenen Kur- und Badegäste in der königl. Stadt Kaiser-Karlsbad*. See also Dose 2014, 64; Soetaert 2014, 38 n. 98.

[2] "Das Recht auf Liebe", *Pilsner Tagblatt*, Jun. 21, 1927, 2.

[3] "Vortrag Dr. Magnus Hirschfeld", *Pilsner Tagblatt*, May 30, 1928, 2.

[4] "Sanitätsrat Hirschfeld gibt seiner Befriedigung über den ungestörten Verlauf, den seine Vorträge in Brünn nun schon zum drittenmal [*sic*] nehmen, Ausdruck" (Sanitätsrat Hirschfeld expresses his satisfaction at the undisturbed course that his lectures in Brno are taking now for the third time) (Fein, Nov. 4, 1930, 3).

[5] In 1930, far-right forces organized against Hirschfeld in Teplitz (Teplice). See "Gegen die Kulturschänder" (Against the Abusers of Culture), *Brünner Tagespost*, Aug. 9, 1930, 3. For an excellent introduction to Hirschfeld's activities as a lecturer, see Dose 2020b. See also Herzer 1989.

[6] Fein, Nov. 4, 1930, 3.

[7] According to the article, Hirschfeld's tour in Czechoslovakia ran May 1–22, 1921. See Ploto 1921, 6: "Hirschfeld hat durch seine unermüdliche Forscherarbeit unumstößlich bewiesen, daß die Homosexuellen weder Kranke noch Entartete sind, sondern daß ihre Sexualveranlagung angeboren ist".

[8] Ploto 1921, 6; Bondy, Oct. 15, 1921, 677. In the same article, Hugo Bondy also wrote that a Prague Institute could be started at "any moment". Bondy was very interested in the supposed biological causes of homosexuality. See Bondy, Jul. 30, 1921, 468; Bondy 1921, 21–23. See also email (dated May 4, 2020) from Marek Suk (Archiv Univerzity Karlovy, Praha) to the author; Seidl et al. 2012, 286 n. 189; Jepsen 1998, 118. Pečírka's name was one of three university professors on a list that would, in Hirschfeld's opinion, help the gay cause in Czechoslovakia: Ferdinand Pečírka, Arthur Biedl

planned initiative was already announced by Pečírka at the first WLSR conference in Berlin in 1921.[9] Pečírka's death, in January 1922, meant that the Prague Institute of Sexual Science, which had received full approval from the board of the Faculty of Medicine, ultimately did not come about [ill. 1]. It was Josef Hynie (1900–1989) who, in 1935, would take up the chair of sexology at Charles University, a position he held for several decades, and Hynie is now considered the father of Czechoslovak sexology.[10] Not coincidentally, Hynie went to Berlin in 1929 and 1931 to study with Hirschfeld.[11]

The influence of Hynie, the sexologist Antonín Trýb (1884–1960) from Brno, and ultimately even Kurt Freund (1914–1996), helps explain how homosexuality was decriminalized in Czechoslovakia as early as 1961.[12] It is clear that Hirschfeld's visits to Czechoslovakia in 1921 and 1922 played a role in the formation of the Czechoslovak homosexual emancipation movement, mainly led by the lawyer František Čeřovský (1881–1962) and the doctor Hugo Bondy (1897–1939). As early as October 1921, Bondy reported on Hirschfeld's Berlin Institute in the Czechoslovak medical periodical *Journal of Czech Physicians (Časopis lékařů českých),*[13] ultimately visiting the Institute in October 1926.[14] In 1928, Bondy also attended the WLSR conference in Copenhagen, where he gave a lecture on the reform of the Czechoslovak criminal code, writing an extensive article on the gathering afterwards.[15] In May 1921, Hirschfeld also gave a talk to the Purkyněs Society for the Study of the Soul and the Nervous System (Purkyněs Gesellschaft für Studium der Seele und des Nervensystems; Purkyňova společnost pro studium duše a nervstva), one that would play a somewhat curious role in the history of the homosexual emancipation movement in Czechoslovakia.[16]

On May 3, 1921, on the same tour in Czechoslovakia, Hirschfeld also lectured on the topic of Sexual Enlightenment (or Education) (*Sexuelle Aufklärung*) in Brno, probably the very first time that he spoke in this city. He held his lecture in the local bulwark of German culture, the German House (Deutsches Haus, Německy dům).[17] Hirschfeld must also have been in Prague in 1924, since that is when he inscribed a reprint of his three-volume *Sexualpathologie* to someone there.[18] In an informative

and Antonín Trýb. Four other doctors were also added to this list: Otto Lampl, Hugo Bondy, Josef Weisskopf and Josef Hynie. See Hirschfeld 1933a, 1. During the 1930 Vienna WLSR conference, Arthur Biedl, Otto Lampl and Josef Weisskopf were elected as the Czechoslovak WLSR representatives. See Weisskopf, Mar. 5, 1931, 140.

[9] See "Československo na mezinárodním sjezdu pro sexuální reformu v Berlíně", *Československá republika*, Sep. 21, 1921, 2; Pečírka 1922, 7–8; E. H., Sep. 25, 1921.

[10] Jepsen 1998, 119.

[11] Jepsen 1998, 120. For Hynie's two trips to the Berlin Institute, see Schindler 1999; Schindler 2000.

[12] Seidl et al. 2012, 121–25, 202–4, 286–99; Jepsen 1998; Lišková 2018, 232; Schindler 2013. Antonín Trýb is mentioned in the Brno phonebook as a member of the *Vorstand* (Board) of the "Klinik für Haut- u.[nd] Geschlechtskrankheiten" (clinic for dermatology) at 53/58 Bäckergasse (Pekařská) (*Adressbuch von Brünn* 1934, 34), the address of the still existing St. Anne's University Hospital. For more information on Trýb, see http://encyklopedie.brna.cz/home-mmb/?acc=profil_osobnosti&load=404 (accessed Dec. 13, 2014). In a *Voilà* issue covering the 1932 WLSR conference, Trýb is wrongly identified as Dr. Fischl (whose name is also misspelled "Fischel"). See Scize, Oct. 1, 1932, 5.

[13] Bondy, Oct. 15, 1921, 677.

[14] Interestingly, in the same article, Bondy also mentions that there was another institute of sexual science in Germany, led by the dermatologist Max Jessner (1887–1978) at the University of Königsberg. For Bondy's 1926 visit, see *Mitteilungen des Wissenschaftlich-Humanitären Komitees* 3 (1926): 18.

[15] Bondy, Sep. 21, 1928, 1350–51.

[16] See Seidl 2012, 123–27; "Purkyňova společnost. Zpráva o schůzi Purkyňovy společnosti, konané dne 18. prosince 1920", *Časopis lékařů českých* 6 (Feb. 5, 1921): 72–75. More generally, it can be said that talk of reforming the Czechoslovak penal code was clearly influenced by what was happening in Germany regarding homosexuality. See Kubista, Oct. 7, 1922, 1-2. Despite his censorious attitude, Kubista seems to have been very well-informed about the matter. See also the reactions by Hugo Bondy and František Čeřovský to Kubista's article (Bondy, Oct. 13, 1922, 4; Čeřovský, Oct. 24, 1922, 5–6).

[17] See the announcement in *Tagesbote*, May 1, 1921, 5. It would be interesting to determine if this was also the first and last time he lectured in this right-wing venue. When Hirschfeld visited Brno in later years, he usually gave his lectures in the left-wing DOPZ-building.

[18] The second edition of the three volumes of *Sexualpathologie*, originally published in 1917–20, bore the following inscription: "Mit besten Zukunft(?)-wünschen vom Verfasser DR. HIRSCHFELD Prag.

book on homosexuality, published by František Jelínek in 1924, Hirschfeld's principal activist motive appeared on the very first page: "per scientiam ad iustitiam!" (through science to justice!).[19] Despite its title, *Homosexuality in the Light of Science* (*Homosexualita ve světle vědy*), Hugo Bondy condemned the book for being partisan and unscientific, which shows that, even among the first Czechoslovak activists, there was disagreement about how to pursue progress in the area of sexual justice.[20] But all this nevertheless shows that Hirschfeld and his ideas had an immense, unignorable influence in Czechoslovakia as early as the 1920s [ill. 2].[21]

JOSEF WEISSKOPF PREPARES THE FIFTH WLSR CONGRESS

In 1932, Hirschfeld added another chapter to the story of his love for Czechoslovakia. During his world trip, Hirschfeld had already declared his intention to go to Karlsbad (Karlovy Vary) to recover from his journey in *Testament: Heft II*.[22] Hirschfeld was also looking for a suitable place to convene the fifth WLSR congress. Initially, the plan was to hold the conference in Moscow and the sixth congress, the following year, in Paris. But both cities dropped out.[23] Starting with the second WLSR conference in Copenhagen, in 1928, the decision was taken to organize a conference every year; however, because of Hirschfeld's world trip, one was not held in 1931. In discussing matters with the young Brno doctor Josef Weisskopf (1904–1977), on April 24, 1932, presumably in Vienna, the latter jokingly suggested hosting the conference in Brno.[24] A week later, after Hirschfeld discussed the matter with Haire and Leunbach, this lighthearted suggestion was accepted, and Weisskopf was left with only five months to organize the conference planned for September 1932.[25]

Josef Weisskopf was a young Jewish doctor who graduated from Brno's Masaryk University in 1929.[26] In 1932, he was an assistant at the university's Institute for Social Medicine (Ústav pro sociální lékařství, Institut für Sozialmedizin).[27] Weisskopf was married to Božena Jordan (1906–1996) and the couple had two children, Vera (1926–

7.I.24" (With best wishes for the future from the author DR. HIRSCHFELD Prague. 7.I.24). In 2020, a German rare book dealer had it for sale.

[19] Jelínek 1924, 3.

[20] Bondy, Jun. 28, 1924, 999. See also Seidl 2005, 62.

[21] For a succinct overview of the advances of gay activism in Czechoslovakia (and, since 1993, the Czech Republic), see Schindler 2013. Schindler's article contains some errors. He states, for example, that Josef Weisskopf died in Auschwitz-Birkenau (he emigrated to the USA) and that the Brno WLSR conference was the fourth WLSR conference (it was the fifth). For an extensive overview of the history of the LGBT movement in Czechia, see Seidl et al. 2012.

[22] Hirschfeld & Dose 2013, f. 60/132 and f. 63/138.

[23] See Weisskopf, Mar. 5, 1931, 140; Kinsey Institute Library & Special Collections, Bloomington (Indiana), Hirschfeld scrapbook, call n° X7910463, letter (dated Aug. 1, 1932) from WLSR to WLSR members, written by Magnus Hirschfeld and the secretary of the WLSR, Wilhelm Kaufmann.

[24] Weisskopf 1933, 26 (for the Apr. 24, 1932 date). In a letter to Hirschfeld, Norman Haire mentioned that he received a postcard (sent from Vienna ?) signed by Hirschfeld, Li Shiu Tong, Josef Weisskopf, Sidonie Fürst (1891–1973) and Ludwig Chiavacci (1896–1970) on May 11, 1932. Fürst and Chiavacci had organized the 1930 Vienna WLSR congress. See Hirschfeld & Dose 2013, f. 47/108 n. 309; University of Sydney Library, Sydney, Norman Haire collection, 3.20, Magnus Hirschfeld, Typescripts, 1923–1935, letter (dated May 11,1932, 1) from Norman Haire to Magnus Hirschfeld. The conference took place later than Hirschfeld initially intended. Judging from his *Testament: Heft II*, he wanted the conference to take place before August 1932. See Hirschfeld & Dose 2013, f. 60/132.

[25] Weisskopf 1933, 26. See also Schindler 2001, 31; but no source is given in the latter (the text was published in a Masaryk University magazine with no notes added). Weisskopf became the *Generalsekretär* (general secretary) of the conference. See the official program (WLSR 1932 Brno conference, [2]).

[26] See the Brno Masaryk University "Recover an Alumnus" database, https://is.muni.cz/absolventi/oziveni?fakulta=1422;lang=en (accessed May 18, 2020).

[27] MZA, Brno, fonds B 40, Zemský úřad v Brně, presidiální registratura, kart. n° 175, sign. 553/32, protokol (dated Dec. 15, 1932); Schindler 2001, 31; *Adreßbuch von Groß-Brünn* 1932, 74; *Zdravotnická ročenka československá* 1931, 197. The address given there, 73 Dra Bedřicha Macků (Dr-Bedřich-Macků-Gasse), is the conference hall's old address. The corner building's current address is 53 Údolní (formerly Talgasse) and 33 Úvoz (formerly Hohlweg). See chapter 12, p. 406, n. 76 on the changed house numbering for this street.

1988) and Rudolf (1931–1998). The family lived in the northern Brno suburb of Královo Pole (Königsfeld).[28] Hirschfeld and Weisskopf held each other in high esteem; Hirschfeld even considered Weisskopf the perfect successor to lead the Institute in Berlin.[29] It is possible that Hirschfeld first learned of Weisskopf when the latter contributed to Hirschfeld's two-volume *Sittengeschichte des Weltkrieges,* published in 1930.[30] In an April 1931 letter, Weisskopf expressed the hope that Hirschfeld would quickly return to Brno to lecture there once more, which indicates that they must have met before when Hirschfeld lectured in Brno.[31] Weisskopf had also been a participant in three discussion panels at the 1930 WLSR conference in Vienna, writing a laudatory article in the Czech medical journal *Medical practitioner* (*Praktický lékař*) about the Vienna conference and Hirschfeld's WLSR project.[32] Weisskopf was known as an eloquent lecturer and also gave radio talks on topics related to sexology [ill. 3].[33] In organizing the conference, Weisskopf was assisted by a preparatory committee (*vorbereitendes Kongreßkomitee*) which included several Brno representatives: Dr. Siegfried Fischl; the lawyer Karl Fein; Jan Amos Kajš; Josef Weisskopf's wife, Božena Weisskopfová; Dr. Vladimír Zapletal; Dr. Karel Hora; and the instructor, Lothar Spielmann.[34] We will return to these people later.

In May 1932, Hirschfeld traveled from Vienna to Czechoslovakia, planning to stay in the country for several months. His final goal was the spa city of Karlsbad (Karlovy Vary), in the west of the country, but he first stopped in Bratislava (Pressburg), Brno and Prague.[35] In Bratislava, Hirschfeld met and was joined by the gay militant Imrich Matyáš (1896–1974). Matyáš was a great admirer of Hirschfeld and his cause. Later that year, Matyáš attended the Brno WLSR conference.[36] Matyáš also accompanied Hirschfeld on his trip through Czechoslovakia until the latter's arrival in Karlsbad

[28] Weisskopf lived at 15 Serbische Gasse (Srbská). He and his family lived on the first floor of the house, as confirmed to me by a grandson of Josef Weisskopf, Tom N. See his email (dated Oct. 18, 2012) to the author. Weisskopf had moved from his former address, 2 Tyršgasse (Tyršova), to Serbische Gasse (Srbská) around 1934–35. See MZA, Brno, fonds B 40, Zemský úřad v Brně, presidiální registratura, kart. n° 175, sign. 553/32, protokol (dated Dec. 15, 1931); *Adreßbuch von Groß-Brünn* 1934, 599; *Nezávislá politika*, May 18, 1935, 5.

[29] Hirschfeld & Dose 2013, f. 65/142, f. 67/146. Hirschfeld already bragged about Weisskopf and named him his *Mitarbeiter* (coworker) in an interview he gave to Karl Fein in November 1930. See Fein, Nov. 4, 1930, 4.

[30] Hirschfeld, Gaspar et al. 1930.

[31] Kinsey Institute Library & Special Collections, Bloomington (Indiana), Hirschfeld scrapbook, call n° X7910463, letter (dated Apr. 9, 1931) from Josef Weisskopf to Magnus Hirschfeld. Since Hirschfeld was then on his world tour, Weisskopf must have meant some time before November 1930, the month that Hirschfeld left.

[32] Steiner 1931, 112–14, 374–75, 475–76; Weisskopf, Mar. 5, 1931, 139–40. For Weisskopf's attendance at the 1930 WLSR Vienna conference, see also *Tagesbote*, Sep. 20, 1930, 3.

[33] See the review of Weisskopf's book *Láska a manželství* (1931) in *Pokrokový obzor*, Apr. 18, 1931, 7. The book collects Weisskopf's radio talks. See Schindler 2013, 136 n. 27. For the announcement of a radio talk titled "*Krise manželství?*" (The Crisis of Marriage?), see *Lidové noviny*, Nov. 12, 1930, 3.

[34] J.[an] A.[mos] Kajš was only mentioned in the announcement leaflet and preliminary program for the Brno WLSR conference. His name disappears from the list of Brno conference preparatory committee members in the third and final conference brochure. The names of Hora and Spielmann *only* appear in this final brochure.

[35] That Hirschfeld first went to Bratislava (Pressburg), and not Brno, can be deduced from his passport. One or two partly legible stamps show the border railway station of Marchegg (between Vienna and Bratislava/Pressburg) instead of the expected Břeclav border railway station (between Vienna and Brno). The only problem is that one of the Marchegg border station stamps is dated May 28, 1932. It remains oddly difficult to accord the only partly legible stamps in Hirschfeld's passport with his exact itinerary. See Archiv MHG, Berlin, fonds Ernst Maass, Hirschfeld's passport (Reisepass) (May 19, 1928– May 18, 1933, 12).

[36] Imrich Matyáš published several articles on Hirschfeld in *Hlas*, as well as its successor, *Nový hlas*. See Matyáš, May 15, 1931, 4–5; Matyáš, Jul. 1, 1932, 3–6; and Matyáš, 1933, 72. See also the online exhibition "Imrich Matyáš – prvý slovenský aktivista za zrovnoprávnenie LGBTI ľudí" (Imrich Matyáš – The First Slovak Activist for the Equality of LGBTI People), http://www.matyas.sk/ (accessed Jan. 12, 2018). Its ninth chapter is especially interesting (Nacisti a 2. svetová vojna rozmetali všetky snahy o liberalizáciu európskej spoločnosti v oblasti ľudskej sexuality a intímnych vzťahov). I thank Tomáš Adamec for the reference to this online exhibition. See also Seidl et al. 2012.

(Karlovy Vary), at the end of May.[37] During this trip, Hirschfeld made two visits to Brno to oversee the preparations for the fifth WLSR conference, the first on May 20, 1932, with Matyáš.[38] When in Brno, Hirschfeld must have helped Josef Weisskopf with the first preparations for the conference since, soon afterwards, an article appeared in the Brno newspaper *Tagesbote*, announcing the September 1932 conference.[39] In the evening of his arrival day, in the DOPZ building, Hirschfeld lectured on the marriage problem. The lecture was well attended.[40] Two years earlier, shortly after the Vienna WLSR 1930 conference, in the same building, Hirschfeld had given a lecture on "The Sufferings and Aberrations of Love" (*Leiden und Irrwege der Liebe*).[41] After the May 20, 1932 lecture in the DOPZ building, Hirschfeld met with a group of gay men from Brno who intended to publish a new gay magazine called *Kamarád*. Its first (and also last) issue came out a week later. We will return to these individuals since this group of men plays a key part at the end of our story.

Hirschfeld also went to Prague where he met with the Slovak Minister of Education Ivan Dérer (1884–1973) to talk about the planned conference in Brno.[42] While in Prague, Hirschfeld spoke in the Urania lecture hall on May 30, 1932.[43] At the beginning of May, the gay magazine *Nový hlas* wrote that they had learned about Hirschfeld's trip that month to Czechoslovakia. They announced that Hirschfeld would give a lecture on May 30, 1932, in the Batex building (3 Revoluční), then known as the latest Prague gay hotspot. The magazine appeared very excited by the prospect and called upon gay men to show their support by attending the lecture. However, it is likely that this gathering for the gay in-crowd did not take place. Hirschfeld delivered his lecture in Urania only.[44]

[37] Matyáš noted that the trip with Hirschfeld ran from May 20, 1932, until May 31, 1932, and that he was with Hirschfeld in Bratislava (Pressburg), Brno and Prague (Matyáš, Jul. 1, 1932, 3).

[38] It is difficult to understand why a May 20, 1932 stamp from the Břeclav railway border station in Hirschfeld's passport says "Ausreise" (departure). See Archiv MHG, Berlin, fonds Ernst Maass, Hirschfeld's passport (Reisepass) (May 19, 1928–May 18, 1933, 22).

[39] See the article "Kongreß für Sexualreform in Brünn" (Sexual Reform Congress in Brno), *Tagesbote*, Jun. 10, 1932, 4. The conference was also briefly announced in several other newspapers. See, for example, *Lidové noviny*, Jun. 10, 1932, 5; *Národní osvobození*, Jun. 10, 1932, 2; *Prager Presse*, Jun. 10, 1932, 6; *Moravská orlice*, Jun. 18, 1932, 4.

[40] See "Vortrag Magnus Hirschfeld" (Magnus Hirschfeld Lecture), *Tagesbote*, May 22, 1932, 8–9; *Morgenpost*, May 21, 1932, 2. Curiously, the *Neues Wiener Journal* noted that both Hirschfeld and Richard Oswald, the director of the film *Anders als die Andern*, were then at the Hotel Imperial in Vienna (*Neues Wiener Journal*, May 22, 1932, 21). Did they go to Brno together?

[41] See "Zwei vollwertige Abende sind zu erwarten!" (Two Packed Evenings Are to Be Expected!), *Tagesbote*, Oct. 24, 1930, 5. The lecture was held on October 24, 1930. Previously, the lecture was announced under the title "Zwei hochinteressante Kultur-Vorträge" (Two Highly Interesting Cultural Lectures), *Tagesbote*, Oct. 5, 1930, 7. Hirschfeld also lectured twice in Brno, on February 10 and 11, 1930. See the announcement accompanied by a picture of Hirschfeld (*Tagesbote*, Feb. 8, 1930, 5) and the further announcement "Dr.-Magnus-Hirschfeld-Vorträge" (Dr. Magnus Hirschfeld Lectures) (*Tagesbote*, Feb. 9, 1930, 8). The tickets for the first lecture were too expensive (and had failed to sell well?). A second lecture was held with lower-cost tickets the next day. The topic of the lectures was "Anziehungsgesetze der Liebe" (Laws of attraction of love). See *Tagesbote*, Oct. 29, 1930, 5. For a critical review of the first lecture, see *Tagesbote*, Feb. 11, 1930, 2. Hirschfeld also lectured in Prague and Bratislava (Pressburg) in the same month, before heading to Karlsbad (Karlovy Vary) for a spa sojourn. See "Prof. Dr. Magnus Hirschfeld in Preßburg", *Neues Pressburger Tagblatt*, May 31, 1932, 3–4. This article mentions that Li Shiu Tong and an unidentified Graz colleague were with him. The topic of the Bratislava (Pressburg) lecture was "Geschlechts- und Liebesleben der Völker" (Sex and the Love Life of Nations).

[42] *Expres*, Jun. 8, 1932, 2.

[43] Announcement in *Prager Presse*, May 27, 1932, 5. Hirschfeld had previously lectured for the Urania association in 1924. See Adam 2013, 295. Urania was a left-wing German-language cultural bastion in Prague (and a rival of the right-wing Deutsches Haus). It began in 1917 and had its own magazine, *Urania: Monatsschrift für moderne Bildungspflege* (Urania: A Monthly Journal for Modern Educational Maintenance). The new, modernist lecture hall, which opened in 1933, was located at 1205/4 Klimentská (Klemensgasse). See *Von deutscher Kultur in der Tschechoslowakischen Republik: Festschrift zur Eröffnung des neuen Urania-Hauses*, Oct. 31, 1933; Adam 2013, 293–98.

[44] *Nový hlas*, Jg. 1, n° 2, May 1, 1932, 17. The Batex building was located at 1003/3 Revoluční třída (Re-

Hirschfeld undertook his 1932 Czechoslovak tour during a key moment for Czechoslovak third sexers. The month before, the Czechoslovak League for Sexual Reform (Československá liga pro sexuální reformu, ČLSR) had been established, in large part a gay initiative. The main goal of the association, as explained in paragraph 2 of their statutes, was to promote the idea that any judgment on sexual life had to be based on scientific insights, one of Hirschfeld's main refrains.[45] Earlier that same year, another gay association was formed, concentrating more on the social needs of gay men, the Friendship, Educational and Social Association (Osvětové a společenskě sdružení Přátelství, shortened as Přátelství). They convened in the Batex building in Prague.[46] Their first act, in February 1932, was to throw a costume ball with prizes. As Hirschfeld noted in an interview with *Nový hlas,* he was well aware that gay movements were active in three cities in Czechoslovakia: Prague, Brno (Brünn), and Bratislava (Pressburg).[47] Hirschfeld seems to have concluded the first part of his tour with another lecture in Liberec (Reichenberg) on May 29, 1932, this time on the topic of the war against veneral disease.[48] After this hustle and bustle, Hirschfeld took some rest, spending the whole month of June in Karlsbad (Karlovy Vary),[49] where he very probably met his good friend, Dr. Leopold Hönig (1887–1956), to whom, a few years later, Hirschfeld would bequeath a sum in his will.[50] In Karlsbad (Karlovy Vary) Hirschfeld also saw the Communist Hungarian doctor Béla Neufeld (1894–1962) who, like Hönig, had his practice in Karlsbad.[51] Hirschfeld managed to convince Neufeld to deliver a talk at the upcoming September conference.[52] Hirschfeld extended his spa tour to July, with a three-week stay in Marienbad (Mariánské Lázně), fifty kilometers south of Karlsbad.[53]

In the last week of July 1932, Hirschfeld returned to Brno to provide further assistance and oversee Weisskopf's preparatory work for the WLSR conference. Hirschfeld's interview with the local Brno academic Lothar Spielmann gives a good overview of the state of the conference planning, how intensively Hirschfeld cooperated with Weisskopf, and also, quite interestingly, the people who initially agreed to take part but eventually did not attend. It also shows how well read Hirschfeld was. After first giving it some thought, at the very beginning of the inter-

volutionsstraße), very close to the Urania lecture hall. The Hirschfeld lecture was also reported in *Expres*, Jun. 8, 1932, 2. The *Expres* writer says that Hirschfeld was interviewed in the editorial office of *Nový hlas*. The complete interview was published a month later (*Nový hlas*, Jg. 1, n° 3, Jul. 1, 1932, 1–2). The author of the anonymous article in *Polední list* says that he attended Hirschfeld's lecture on Monday, May 30, 1932, but then went to the Batex building later that night to socialize with friends (*Polední list*, Jun. 2, 1932, 5).

45 The Ministry of the Interior's approval (decree 20267-1932) of the association was announced in *Nový hlas*, Jg. 1, n° 1, May 1, 1932, 21. The fourteen paragraphs of their statutes had been previously published in *Nový hlas*, Jg. 2, n° 1, Jan. 1, 1932, 11–15. The statutes are also reproduced in Seidl 2012, 502–7.

46 On the Batex club, see Seidl 2012, 191–98; Seidl 2014a, 31–33; Seidl 2014b, 44–49.

47 *Expres*, Jun. 8, 1932, 2.

48 *Morgenpost*, May 21, 1932, 2.

49 Imrich Matyáš wrote that, in the beginning of July 1932, Hirschfeld was recovering from his world trip in Karlsbad (*Nový hlas*, Jul. 1, 1932, 6). *Der Wiener Tag* claimed that Hirschfeld went to Karlsbad on May 28, 1932, after a two-month stay in Vienna (*Der Wiener Tag*, May 29, 1932, 7). This was factually incorrect since, as we have seen, Hirschfeld left for Bratislava (Pressburg) and Brno earlier in May.

50 In 1931, Hönig lived in Karlsbad at 18 Kreuzstrasse, in a house called "Goldener Schwan" (the Golden Swan). See *Čechoslovakische Kurorte* 1931, 4. However, in 1934, he lived at 62 Alte Wiese, in a house called "Savoyen" (Savoy). See *Kurorte, Heilanstalten Sommerfrischen in der Č.S.R* 1934, section Ärzteverzeichnis, 19. The Alte Wiese house was also given as Hönig's address in ADAM, Nice, Archives notariales, minutes notariales étude Pierre Demnard, Dec. 12,1935, n° 1390, cote 03E 148/026.

51 Neufeld lived (or at least had his practice) in a house called "Weiser Hase" (the Wise Hare) on Alte Wiese in Karlsbad. See *Čechoslovakische Kurorte* 1931, 36. Neufeld was deported from Romania to Buchenwald in 1944, but survived the war.

52 Szegedi 2014, 289. Both men clearly already knew each other since Neufeld had contributed to Hirschfeld's *Sittengeschichte des Weltkrieges*, even though Hirschfeld's name alone appeared on the cover. See Hirschfeld, Gaspar & et al. 1930; Szegedi 2014, 288–89.

53 Hirschfeld & Dose 2013, f. 64/140.

view, Hirschfeld revealed that he knew about Spielmann's academic work. He also convinced Spielmann on the spot to join the conference organizing committee and to give a lecture at the conference.[54] When Hirschfeld arrived in Brno, on July 25, a reporter noticed Li Shiu Tong at his side. It is possible that Li Shiu Tong joined Hirschfeld for the whole May-to-July trip; however, since this was the only occasion that a journalist observed the exotic young man in Hirschfeld's company, it is also possible that Hirschfeld's Chinese pupil only caught up with his mentor at the end of July [ill. 4].[55] This would accord with the assumption that it was in the summer of 1932 that Li Shiu Tong went to Berlin to see Hirschfeld's Institute with his own eyes (and without Hirschfeld). In any case, a picture in the Hirschfeld guestbook, showing Li Shiu Tong and Giese in the Institute's sunny front garden, attests to that visit [ill. 5].[56] The September WLSR conference was announced on Brno radio on Friday, July 29, 1932.[57] On August 1, 1932, a letter was sent from the WLSR secretarial office in Berlin confirming that the conference would take place the following month in Brno, on September 20–26.[58] On his return to Vienna, Hirschfeld stopped once again in the Slovak part of the country. He gave some lectures in Trenčín (Trencin) and Piešťany (Pystian).[59] Presumably, Hirschfeld met Matyáš again, likely to ensure that everything decided in Brno was also aligned with the Slovak part of the country. After his extended stay in Czechoslovakia, Hirschfeld went to Switzerland where he spent the month of August with Jakob Keller, an acquaintance, in Zürich.[60] At the end of August, he spent a few days on the Salzburger Festspiele, a (still) famous music festival, and also spent some time in the Salzkammergut region, east of Salzburg.[61] It is not known whether Hirschfeld returned to Vienna for a few days' stay before heading back to Brno, on September 16, 1932, to attend the fifth WLSR conference.

HUGO ILTIS

In August and September 1932, several Czechoslovak newspapers included short announcements of the conference.[62] Josef Weisskopf, the local conference organizer, had also briefly spoken about the conference on a Brno radio broadcast in July 1932.[63] Although the conference did not start until September 20, Hirschfeld arrived early in Brno, on Friday, September 16.[64] The day after his arrival, Hirschfeld gave a well-attended Saturday evening lecture in the art deco styled DOPZ venue, the main

54 Spielmann, Jul. 28, 1932, 4–5.

55 See "Profesor Magnus Hirschfeld v Brně" (Professor Magnus Hirschfeld in Brno), *Lidové noviny*, Jul. 25, 1932, 3; "Prof. Magnus Hirschfeld in Brünn", *Prager Presse*, Jul. 26, 1932, 5; and the short notice in *Československý denník*, Jul. 26, 1932, 2. The second Brno visit seems to accord with Hirschfeld's brief note in *Testament: Heft II*: "Vor- und nachher [Karlsbad/Karlovy Vary, Marienbad/Mariánské Lázně and other spa cities] Kongressvorbereitungen in Brünn" (Before and after [Karlsbad, Marienbad and other spa cities] congress preparations in Brno) (Hirschfeld & Dose 2013, f. 64/140).

56 Bergemann, Dose, Keilson-Lauritz & Dubout 2019, f. 69/113.

57 Spielmann, Jul. 28, 1932, 5. The announcement was broadcast from 6:45 p.m. until 7:00 p.m.

58 Kinsey Institute Library & Special Collections, Bloomington (Indiana), Hirschfeld scrapbook, call n° X7910463, letter (dated Aug. 1, 1932) from WLSR to WLSR members, written by Magnus Hirschfeld and the secretary of the WLSR, Wilhelm Kaufmann.

59 Hirschfeld & Dose 2013, f. 64/140; and the exit stamp in Hirschfeld's passport, Archiv MHG, Berlin, fonds Ernst Maass, Hirschfeld's passport (Reisepass) (May 19, 1928–May 18, 1933, 15), Marchegg railway border station, stamp (dated Jul. 29, 1932).

60 Hirschfeld wrote that he stayed there from August 4 to September 4, 1932 (Hirschfeld & Dose 2013, f. 64/140 n. 385; and Dose 2019, 20 n. 66).

61 Hirschfeld & Dose 2013, f. 64/140. For the Salzburger Festspiele's month-long program for the year 1932 (Jul. 30, 1932–Aug. 31, 1932), see https://archive.salzburgerfestspiele.at/geschichte/1932 (accessed May 18, 2020).

62 See, for example, *Národní listy*, Aug. 23, 1932, 3; *Volksfreund*, Aug. 13, 1932, 3; *Deutsche Post*, Sep. 18, 1932, 6; *Prager Presse*, Sep. 18, 1932, 6.

63 See the Brno radio announcement for the (fifteen-minute) talk, *Národní listy*, Jul. 18, 1932, 3. Schindler states that Weisskopf had a regular radio program (Schindler 2001, 31).

64 Archiv MHG, Berlin, fonds Ernst Maass, Hirschfeld's passport (Reisepass) (May 19, 1928 – May 18, 1933, 6), Břeclav railway border station stamp (between Vienna and Brno).

meeting place of Brno social democrats.[65] Hirschfeld was also invited by Hugo Iltis (1882–1952) of the Brno adult education center (Volkshochschule) to deliver a talk. He was asked to speak about WLSR's ten goals and to say something about the topics of the lectures that would be given at the conference. Hirschfeld was once again met with "warm acclaim" (*warmen Beifall*), and even, as another journalist wrote, "rapturous acclaim" (*stürmischen Beifall*) by the crowd in attendance.[66] Presumably a substantial number of gay men attended this lecture.[67] Hugo Iltis, who organized the evening, was, like Weisskopf, a Brno local whom Hirschfeld knew well. Hugh Iltis (1925–2016), the son of Hugo Iltis, recalled that there was a lot of talk about Magnus Hirschfeld in his parents' house.[68]

Hugo Iltis was born in Brno and worked as a biology teacher in the Deutsches Staatsgymnasium and the Deutsche Technische Hochschule.[69] He is best known for his biographical work on the Augustinian monk Gregor Mendel. Mendel undertook his pioneering scientific experiments on heredity in the garden of his monastery

[65] DOPZ is an acronym for Družstvo obchodních a průmyslových zaměstnanců (Haus des Einheitsverbands der Privatangestellten, Cooperative Association of Trade and Industry Employees). The building is still located at the same address, 3 Moravské náměstí (in the 1930s the street was called Lažanského náměstí, Lažanský-Platz). The Scala cinema, which exists to this day, is located inside the building. On the second floor, there was a café called Kavárna (Kaffeehaus, Café) Biber. Peter Demetz thinks that Café Biber was located on the third floor of the building. See email (dated Jan. 13, 2012) from Peter Demetz to the author. Inside the building there is a memorial plaque commemorating German and Austrian exiles, Oskar Maria Graf and Thomas Theodor Heine among them, who found temporary refuge in Brno in the late 1930s. Dora Müller was one of the people who advanced the idea of the plaque. "Ihr Vater Theodor Schuster hatte im DOPZ-Gebäude eine Anwaltskanzlei und nahm als führender Sozialdemokrat seine Tochter zu den Gesprächen ins Café Biber mit. So hat sie alle kennen gelernt und hält sie lebhaft in Ehren. Auf diese Weise ist Dora Müller das lebendige Gedächtnis der Stadt an diese Zeit geworden, und ihre 'Ausstellung Drehscheibe Brünn' ist seit 1997 dauernd unterwegs" (Her father, Theodor Schuster, had a law office in the DOPZ building and, as a leading social democrat, took his daughter to Café Biber for talks. That's how she got to know everyone and grew to hold them in lively esteem. In this way, Dora Müller has become the city's living memory of that period, and her 'Turntable Brno' exhibition has been on permanent tour since 1997), http://www.literaturblatt.de/heftarchiv/heftarchiv-2004/42004-inhaltsverzeichnis-der-gedruckten-ausgabe-42004/parnass-und-pegasus-in-der-provinz.html (accessed Mar. 30, 2013). Though the building still stands today, its art deco façade vanished as the result of considerable war damage. Afterwards it was given a more "classical" façade. It seems that, in its time, the art deco façade was considered "ugly", or at least as making too great a contrast with the other, more "classical" buildings on the square. I have seen quite a few contemporary postcards of the Lažanský square and they all seem to make an effort *not* to include the art deco building in their scenic portrayal of the square.

[66] *Tagesbote*, Sep. 19, 1932, Abendblatt, 2; *Volksfreund*, Sep. 21, 1932, 6. Afterwards, the adult education center magazine, *Licht ins Volk!*, wrote: "Als Neuerung bewährten sich die Samstagabendvorträge der Volkshochschule. Als erster in der Reihe sprach am 17. September im großen Dopzsaal [*sic*] der anläßlich des Sexuologenkongresses in Brünn anwesende Dr. Magnus Hirschfeld über 'Sexualreform und ihre großen Probleme'" (The Saturday evening lectures at the adult education center proved to be an innovation. As the first in the series, on September 17 in the large DOPZ venue, Dr. Magnus Hirschfeld, who was in Brno on the occasion of the sexologist congress, spoke about 'Sexual Reform and Its Principal Problems'). See *Licht ins Volk!*, Jg. 5, Heft n° 2, Jänner [*sic*], 1933, 22.

[67] Like Magnus Hirschfeld, the Viennese Sophie Lazarsfeld, another conference attendee, gave a lecture on Saturday, September 16, 1932. She often went to Brno to give lectures. They were always a success and often sold out. See *Tagesbote*, Sep. 20, 1932, 6. It is possible that the gay crowd mostly went to see Hirschfeld and the straight crowd to listen to Lazarsfeld that day. On the last day of the conference, Monday, September 26, 1932, Lazarsfeld gave another lecture, this time for the adult education center, on her latest book *Wie die Frau den Mann erlebt* (*How Woman Experiences Man*). See *Tagesbote*, Sep. 24, 1932, 6; *Volksfreund*, Sep. 28, 1932, 6.

[68] Email (dated Jan. 20, 2012) from Hugh Iltis to the author. Hugh Iltis was thirteen years old when he fled Czechoslovakia with his family in the first months of 1939.

[69] The two schools were located right across from each other on the Komenského náměstí square (Comeniusplatz), much better known under its former name, Elisabethplatz. Both schools were important symbols of German culture in pre-war Brno. They ceased to exist at the end of World War II. For a history of the Deutsche Technische Hochschule, see Šišma 2009.

[70] Iltis 1924. Jaroslav Kříženecký (1896–1964) did the most to carry on Mendel's legacy in Brno after

in Brno.[70] Iltis was also the driving force behind the Brno adult education center (*Volkshochschule*) that opened shortly after World War I, in 1920 [ill. 6].[71] The school served as a symbol for the German-speaking, progressive leftists in Brno, who endeavored to educate and enlighten the working class by offering a wide curriculum of very affordable evening courses.[72] Their publication, which also served as a course program, was called *Enlighten the People!* (*Licht ins Volk!*). Just one year before the conference, in September 1931, the adult education center had moved to long-awaited newly built premises.[73] The magnificent modernist building further underlined their firm belief in progress and their effort to get away from a restrictive past and its old ideas. In 1934, with the Czechoslovak president approving the use of his name, the school was renamed the Masaryk Volkshochschule.[74] The progressive political left of the country strongly linked its fate to their president, Tomáš Garrigue Masaryk. In 1935, an issue of *Licht ins Volk!* declared: "As long as Masaryk lives, we feel safe. His life is a protective shield for all who struggle for freedom and peace" [ill. 7].[75]

Along with the DOPZ building, the adult education center was an important left-wing bulwark in Brno. Many adult education center lectures were held in the DOPZ building, sometimes drawing audiences of over 1,000 people. Erika Mann's cabaret performance, *The Pepper Mill* (*Die Pfeffermühle*), was always performed there on its 1935 and 1937 tours, easily selling out its 3,000 seats.[76] Despite the St. Thomas Church lying between them, preventing one from seeing the two buildings together, the DOPZ building was a sort of ideological counterpart to the nearby, right-wing German-nationalist (*Völkisch*) German House (Deutsches Haus). The latter was the German-speaking community's most important building in pre-World War II Brno.[77] Several sexology courses were given at the adult education center.[78] After the Brno WLSR

World War II, establishing the still extant Mendel department in the Moravské zemské muzeum Brno (Moravian Museum), now called the Mendelianum. See http://www.mzm.cz/en/mendelianum/ (accessed May 12, 2020).

[71] See the anonymous text "Dr. Hugo Iltis, Leiter der Masaryk-Volkshochschule, 1921–1938", *Licht ins Volk!*, Jg. 11, Heft n° 1, 1938-1939, 1-3. A good introduction to Iltis' life can also be found at https://www.wikiwand.com/en/Hugo_Iltis (accessed Dec. 3, 2020). For more on the theoretical background of Iltis' educational idealism about the working classes, see Iltis 1929.

[72] *Licht ins Volk!*, [1928?], 2.

[73] The outstanding modernist building, designed by the architect Heinrich Blum (1894–1942), was located at 2a Leoš-Janáček-Platz (náměstí Leoše Janáčka). See https://www.bam.brno.cz/en/architect/7-heinrich-blum (accessed May 11, 2020). For a picture of the front and back of the building, and also for floor plans of three (of the seven) floors of the building, see Pelčák, Sapák & Wahla 2000a, 45. Today, the building is part of Masaryk University. On April 4, 1942, Heinrich Blum and his wife Gertruda Nasch (1905–1942?) were deported from Brno on transport "Ah" to Terezín, and then transferred, on April 27, 1942, on transport "Aq" to Izbica.

[74] *Licht ins Volk!*, Jg. 7, Heft n° 1, 1934, 1.

[75] *Licht ins Volk!*, Jg. 7, Heft n° 3, 1935, 1, "Fünfundachtzig Jahre [Eighty-five Years (Masaryk's age and birthday)]": "Solange Masaryk lebt, fühlen wir uns geborgen. Sein Leben ist ein Schutz für alle, die um Freiheit und Frieden kämpfen". Even after Masaryk's death in 1937, and following Hitler's annexation of Austria, they continued to appeal to him as they faced the impending German threat: "Wir bekennen uns zu den Idealen Masaryks" (We are committed to Masaryk's ideals). See *Licht ins Volk!*, Jg. 10, Heft n° 2, 1938, 1.

[76] Bečvová 2007.

[77] The 1891 Deutsches Haus was built as a German-language pendant to the Czech Besední dům (Meeting House), built in 1873 on Komenského náměstí. The latter building now houses the Brno Philharmonic. The Deutsches Haus was heavily bombed during World War II and its ruins were removed shortly after the war. Today, star-like paths lead to the park's empty center, where the Deutsches House once stood. It is a resonant emptiness in Brno's history, reminding one of the fierce pre-war cultural conflict between Germans and Czechs, culminating in the social and cultural removal of all things German shortly after the war. That the square on which the building once stood is so significant in Brno's history is proved by its several renamings: Adolf-Hitler-Platz, a few days after the invasion of Brno, in March 1939; and náměstí Rudé armády (Red Army Square), starting in 1946.

[78] For the course that Josef Gajdeczka gave on "Kultur- und Sittengeschichte des Weibes von den Anfängen menschlicher Gesittung über die heutigen Naturvölker bis in unsere gegenwart in Europa und Amerika" (The Cultural and Moral History of Women from the Beginnings of Human Culture through Today's Indigenous Peoples and to our Present in Europe and America), see *Licht ins Volk!*, Jg. 3, n° 1,

conference, Josef Weisskopf lectured at Iltis' school on a few occasions.[79] Hirschfeld must have known about Iltis' interest in left-wing views of the theoretical debates on the race issue. Iltis lectured and authored several publications on the way the Nazis tried to rationalize their pernicious racist ideology by resorting to a particular form of social Darwinism. It would be interesting to determine whether, and how, Iltis and Hirschfeld's writings on the issue influenced each other.[80] The fact that both Iltis' famous Mendel biography and Hirschfeld's *Racism* were both translated (the first in 1932 and the second, posthumously, in 1938) by the British couple Eden and Cedar Paul is likely in itself significant.[81]

CONFERENCE PRE-OPENING

On Tuesday September 20, 1932, the WLSR conference held an evening pre-opening with an informal gathering in the marble room (*Marmorsaal, mramorový sál*) in the basement (*souterrain*) of the Provincial House (Landeshaus, Zemský dům) [ill. 8] [ill. 9].[82] Busy conference days were planned. The official program listed seventy to eighty speakers on seven topics, from twenty countries, over five days.[83] This meant

Herbst, 1930, 17, 21–22. Hirschfeld's *Geschlechtskunde* was on that course's reading list. Dr. E. Bloch's course on "Sexualethik und Sexualreform" (Sexual Ethics and Sexual Reform), on the other hand, opted to put Max Hodann's book *Geschlecht und Liebe* (*Sex and Love*) on its reading list (see *Licht ins Volk!*, Jg. 4, [n° 1], Sep. 1931, 29–30). There is no extant catalogue of the adult education center's library holdings but it is possible that the library had both Hirschfeld's five-volume *Geschlechtskunde* and Hodann's book on its shelves. The long-serving school librarian was Karl Dwořaček. The library was located in the basement of the new building, had a reading room, and its collection numbered around 4,000 books in 1934. See *Licht ins Volk!*, Jg. 7, Heft n° 1, 1934, 6, 8. It is not known what happened to the adult education center library once the Nazis took control in Brno in 1939.

[79] On March 25, 1933, Weisskopf lectured on "Geburtenregelung oder Gebärzwang?" (Birth Control or Compulsory Childbearing?). See *Licht ins Volk!*, Jg. 5, Heft n° 2 , Jan., 1933, 19–22. In February 1937, at the invitation of the Hospodářské strany pokrokové (HSP) (Economic Progressive Party), Weisskopf lectured on the topic of marital sex in the adult education center. See *Nezávislá politika*, Mar. 13, 1937, 5.

[80] In the very first issue of *Licht ins Volk!* ([Jg. 1, Heft 1, 1928–1929], 24) we see that Iltis gave a course on "Die Rassenfrage" (The Race Question) as early as the first semester of the 1928–29 school year. Of course, this does not exclude the possibility that he had worked on the theme earlier. Iltis published two pamphlets on this topic: *Volkstümliche Rassenkunde* (Iltis 1930) and *Der Mythus von Blut und Rasse* (Iltis 1936). In the single-page reading guide in *Volkstümliche Rassenkunde*, Iltis positively mentions the second volume of Hirschfeld's *Gechlechtskunde* (see Iltis 1930, 4). Excerpts of Iltis' texts on racism have appeared in English (see Iltis 2017).

[81] Hirschfeld 1938. According to Hugh Iltis, the "Pauls' translation of the Mendel biography is not very good!" See email (dated Jan. 20, 2012) from Hugh Iltis to the author. See also Frischknecht 2009, 33–34 n. 56.

[82] The Zemský dům III, also known as the Nový zemský dům (neues Landhaus), and also simply as Zemský dům (Landhaus), was (and is) located at 1 Kounicova (Kaunitzgasse). See *Adresář Republiky Československé pro průmysl, živnosti, obchod a zemědělství* 1935, 3489. The owner of the café, Jan Brychta, is identified in *Adreßbuch von Groß-Brünn* 1932, 556. For the marble room, see https://www.bam.brno.cz/en/object/c277-national-house-iii (accessed May 13, 2020); and the conversation with the historian Lenka Kudělková on http://smisenezbozi.blogspot.com/2015/06/ (accessed Mar. 26, 2021). There are two other buildings in Brno with the same name: Zemský dům II (confusingly also known as Nový zemský dům, Neues Landhaus) located at 3–5 Žerotínovo náměstí (Zierotinplatz) and Zemský dům I, located at 8 Joštova (Jodokstrasse).

[83] Dose shows that it was important for the WLSR that an ever-increasing number of countries attend its conferences (Dose 1993, 25). On the idea that efforts at both local and national sexual reform would be strengthened by a call for international coordination, see, for example, Haire & Spielmann, Sep. 30, 1932, 5. In an interview he gave after the Brno conference, Hirschfeld also stressed the growing number of countries attending every WLSR conference. See Hirschfeld, Sep. 29, 1932, 4. Hirschfeld spoke of thirty different countries represented at the Brno conference. See ibid. However, Weisskopf says that there were a total of twenty countries (Weisskopf 1933, 28). I also counted twenty countries; however, judging from the final conference progam, only seventeen were represented among the speakers and moderators. In an article written two weeks before the start of the conference, Weisskopf listed the seventeen countries then represented: England, France, Belgium, Austria, Germany, Poland, the Netherlands, Denmark, Finland, Sweden, Yugoslavia, Spain, Estonia, Switzerland, the USA, India, and China. See Weisskopf, Sep. 10, 1932, 3. Weisskopf later added Hungary, Russia and, of course, Czechoslovakia itself, bringing the total to exactly twenty countries (Weisskopf 1933, 26).

[84] *Prager Presse*, Sep. 28, 1932, 4. In an article writ-

that, on average, fifteen people lectured during the morning and afternoon sessions every day.[84] Speakers were allowed to speak for fifteen minutes. In comparison, the 1930 Vienna conference had almost eighty speakers, but spread over eight days.[85] A few Brno newspapers reported almost daily on the conference, but only mentioned some of the lectures in their reports.[86] So, it is not possible to determine whether everyone mentioned in the official conference program actually spoke or attended. Some pictures of the conference have survived or were published in newspapers. There were two main conference photographers. One was a local photographer named Eugen Faden (1892–1941?).[87] Faden was most likely hired by the local conference organizers and probably took the best-known pictures of the conference, in the anatomy auditorium of Masaryk University [ill. 10].[88] The other photographer was Dr. Rudolf Elkan (1895–1983) from Hamburg, who took more candid pictures. Elkan was also one of the lecturers at the conference.[89] In addition, Norman Haire used his own film camera to record extensively.[90] The conference participants received a medallion that could be worn like a lapel pin [ill. 11].[91] Once alerted to this, it is possible to discern the medallion in the conference photos [ill. 12]. Around seven or even eight conference lecturers were invited to deliver a group presentation that

ten two weeks before the conference, Weisskopf said that there were seventy-six speakers announced, with other speakers still coming. See Weisskopf, Sep. 10, 1932, 3. In a report written the year after the conference, Weisskopf stated that eighty-five lectures were given. See Weisskopf 1933, 26. According to the program brochure, seventy-eight speakers were announced. Panýrek claimed that the number of lectures actually given was seventy-five, since some speakers did not manage to reach Brno (Panýrek 1932, 629). Weisskopf freely admitted that some of the lectures were of rather poor quality, and expressed the hope that this could be avoided by obliging speakers next time to send a conference résumé in advance (Weisskopf 1933, 29). Approximately thirty people canceled their attendance at the last minute, leaving the conference organizers with a financial deficit. See Weisskopf 1933, 26.

[85] See Steiner 1930; and the official 1930 WLSR Vienna (Wien) conference program.

[86] The local newspaper *Tagesbote* reported on the conference in its morning and afternoon editions. I mainly checked three local German-language newspapers: *Tagesbote*, *Volksfreund* (the best in terms of the quality of reporting), and *Prager Presse*. The latter included only one article on the conference and that after it was over: "*Brünner Sexuologentagung beendet*" (Brno Sexology Conference ended) (*Prager Presse*, Sep. 28, 1932, 4). National Czech newspapers also reported on the conference – *Večer*, *Národní listy*, *Venkov*, and others – but their reports were all very brief. For a Communist appreciation of the conference, see Kroha, Nov. 2, 1932, 8. The Communist newspaper *Dělnická rovnost* reported on the conference on five different days: September 21, 24, 25, and 27; and November 2. *Lidové noviny* reported on the conference on September 21, 22 and 24. The most important primary source for determining who actually lectured is Panýrek 1932. The two main Czech-language secondary sources on the Brno conference are Schindler 2001; and Seidl et al. 2012, 214–22.

[87] The photographer's name, Faden, was added to two of the conference pictures in an issue of the popular French magazine *Voilà*. See Scize, Oct. 1, 1932, 5. Eugen Faden had taken over the business of his father, Michael Faden (1865–1936). In 1932, his photography studio was located at 13 Pragerstrasse (Pražská). Eugen Faden, his wife Tilda (1895-1941?) and son Kurt Otto (1930-1941?) were deported on the very first Jewish transport "F" from Brno to Minsk on November 16, 1941. All three perished in the Holocaust.

[88] One picture can be dated exactly to Sunday, September 25, 1932, because the blackboard in the background states that Norman Haire's film on the Gräfenberg ring was showing that day. See *Volksfreund*, Sep. 27, 1932, 4 (which mentions the discussion of the contraceptive device); *Tagesbote*, Abendblatt, Sep. 27, 1932, 4. In 1930, Haire informed Hirschfeld that he was busy researching this ring's effect on patients. See University of Sydney Library, Sydney, Norman Haire collection, 3.20, Magnus Hirschfeld, Typescripts, 1923-1935, letter (dated Feb. 22, 1930, 2) from Norman Haire to Magnus Hirschfeld.

[89] His fifteen photographs of the conference are deposited in London in the Wellcome collection (formerly Wellcome Institute), London, fonds Family Planning Association, folder World League for Sexual Reform conference including letters from Dr. E. Elkan [donor], sign. SA/FPA/A23/1. Elkan wrongly gives 1929 as the year of the pictures. The remark that some photos were taken near Mendel's tomb is in error. The conference attendees visited the Mendel monument, not his tomb. Mendel is buried, along with some other monks from his monastery, in the central cemetery in Brno.

[90] Schütz, Oct. 2, 1932, 3. It is not known if these film reels have survived.

[91] The medallion measures 8.7 cm x 3.5 cm.

was broadcast on the radio [ill. 13].[92] Flags on the main hotels in Brno displayed the conference logo.[93]

FIRST CONFERENCE DAY AND TWO VISITS

At 9:30 a.m., Wednesday, September 21, 1932, the conference opened in the steep auditorium (*Hörsaale*) of Masaryk University's Faculty of Medicine anatomy institute, located at 73 Údolní (Talgasse) [ill. 14].[94] Josef Weisskopf, the main organizer, spoke in Czech and German. He informed the audience that Masaryk, the president of Czechoslovakia, had sent a telegram congratulating the organizers and attendees.[95] This news fired up the conference crowd and the decision was made to send Masaryk a telegram of greeting in return. Hirschfeld addressed the conference, saying he was happy to see everyone gathered in the city of Mendel, and named three scholars, important to sexology, who had died since the last congress in Vienna: the Swiss psychiatrist August(e) Forel (1848–1931), the Austrian sociologist and philosopher Rudolf Goldscheid (1870–1931), and the German rejuvenation doctor Peter Schmidt (1892?–1930).[96] He also invoked Masaryk's motto "*veritas vincit*" (truth prevails), certainly annoying Dr. Duchoslav Panýrek (1867–1940), a conference participant and observer, with his extravagant adulation of Masaryk.[97] Norman Haire, the second of the three WLSR presidents, then addressed the conference, stating that the main enemy of sexual reform was the Catholic Church.[98] After him, Leunbach, the third

[92] See Patzaková et al. 1935, 533–34, where the conference is erroneously dated July 1932; cf. Schindler 2001, 31.

[93] Schütz, Oct. 2, 1932, 3.

[94] See the entry for the Institut für normale Anatomie in *Adreßbuch von Groß-Brünn* 1927, 67. The house numbers have changed and its current address is 53/244 Údolní. The auditorium is currently aula U5 on the Masaryk University campus. See https://www.muni.cz/en/map/complex-23 (accessed Mar. 6, 2021). For pictures of the auditorium (and the blackboard), hardly changed since 1932, see https://www.vutbr.cz/www_base/zav_prace_soubor_verejne.php?file_id=146116, p. 11 and https://www.vutbr.cz/vut/aktuality-f19528/favu-zahajila-plny-provoz-na-nove-adrese-udolni-53-d136700 (both accessed Mar. 6, 2021). The front-row seats have since been removed, and the aisle down the middle has disappeared as well.

[95] The telegram was dated September 6, 1932. Karl Giese had this telegram in his possession in 1937 when he was living in Brno. He quoted the whole of the telegram sent by Masaryk in a document that was redacted for the Czechoslovak authorities. See MZA, Brno, fonds B 40, Zemský úřad Brno (Landesbehörde in Brünn), kart. n° 2138, sign. 5274/38, f. 7. The text in which this telegram is quoted can be found in the addenda (n° 9), p. 740.

[96] *Volksfreund*, Sep. 22, 1932, 4. See also "Mezinárodní kongres Světové ligy pro sexuální reformu v Brně", *Československá republika*, Sep. 22, 1932, 4. Peter Schmidt is mentioned in the *Jahrbuch für sexuelle Zwischenstufen*, vol. 21, 1921, 178. Hirschfeld mentioned his death in a letter (dated Oct. 22, 1930) to Georg Sylvester Viereck, reproduced in Hirschfeld & Dose 2013, 202–3. A photograph of Peter Schmidt can be found in Hirschfeld 1926–1930, 1930, vol. IV, Bilderteil, 880. For his work on rejuvenation, see Schmidt 1928.

[97] *Neues Wiener Journal*, Sep. 28, 1932, 9. The annoyed observer was Duchoslav Panýrek (Panýrek 1932, 630). Hirschfeld also expressed his admiration for Masaryk in a letter sent to *Prager Presse* in 1934: "Da ich ein grosser Bewunderer der C.S.R. vom ersten Tage ihrer Begründung bis heute bin und ein aufrichtiger Verehrer Ihrer beide hervorragenden Staatsmänner MASARYK u. BENEČ [*sic*: Beneš]" (Since I am a great admirer of the C.S.R., from the first day of its foundation until today, and a sincere admirer of your two outstanding statesmen MASARYK and BENEČ [*sic*: Beneš]). See PNP, Praha, fonds Arne Laurin (real name Arnošt Lustig), folder Magnus Hirschfeld, letter (dated Apr. 3, 1934) from Magnus Hirschfeld to *Prager Presse*.

[98] Panýrek 1932, 628. Josef Weiskopff was also involved in fierce controversies with the Catholic Church. See *Pokrokový obzor*, Jul. 2, 1932, 3; and Weisskopf, Sep. 10, 1932, 3. Weisskopf's (and also Iltis') virulent opposition to the Catholic Church, criticizing the *Bevormundung* (patronizing attitude) of religious people, was acutely (and quickly) noted by the Benedictine monks in the Rajhrad cloister, located just outside of Brno. See the anonymous article "Pohlavní poučování" (Sexual Instruction) in *Hlídka: měsíčník vědecký se zvláštním zřetelem k apologetice a filosofii* 49, n° 9 (Sep. 1932): 316.

[99] *Volksfreund*, Sep. 22, 1932, 4. For a list of the instances supporting the conference, see Weisskopf 1933, 27–28.

[100] For Jan Bělehrádek, see Linhartová 2003. Joseph Weisskopf mentioned him and Antonín Trýb as the two individuals put forward by the Masaryk University Faculty of Medicine as conference attendees: "Masarykova universita je již nyní zastoupena dvěma vý značnými členy profesorského sboru

WLSR president, addressed the crowd in Esperanto. Following these speakers, no fewer than eight people gave welcoming speeches and addresses.[99] The first real conference talk was given by the biology professor Jan Bělehrádek (1896–1980), an important Brno university figure.[100] He spoke on the first conference topic, Eugenics and Sexuality (*Eugenik und Sexualität*), distinguishing four phases of mankind: in the first stage humans did not realize offspring were linked to sexual intercourse, but, in the last stage, humans consciously planned procreation.[101]

After the morning session, the congress crowd went to the Mendelplatz (Mendlovo náměstí) to leave a wreath at the Mendel monument. Gregor Johann Mendel (1822–1884) was a monk, and later abbot, at the Augustinian monastery in Brno, who experimented with peas (and bees) in the monastery garden and discovered the rules of heredity that ultimately paved the way for the discovery of DNA in the twentieth century. To this day, the Brno tourist office hails him as one of the world-famous celebrities to have lived and worked in the city. Hugo Iltis, Mendel's biographer, guided the tour to Mendelplatz and the adjoining Augustinian cloister, speaking in German. Three other people spoke at the monument: Jan Bělehrádek spoke in Czech, Norman Haire in English, and Bertie Albrecht, the delegate of the WLSR's French branch, in French. The plurality of languages again showed the international character of the conference.[102] Judging from the pictures taken on the occasion, Hirscheld was not present at this memorial tour [ill. 15]. The marble monument, a statue of Mendel, was inaugurated in October 1910 at the instigation of Hugo Iltis; at the same time, the Klosterplatz (Klášterní náměstí) was renamed Mendelplatz (Mendlovo náměstí). In 1950, under the Communist regime, the monument, sculpted by the Austrian artist Theodor Charlemont (1859–1938), was moved to the Augustinian monastery. The fact that Mendel was a German-speaker, and a religious figure, was likely the main reason for removing the statue from its more central location after forty years. In 1964, the statue was moved again, this time to a more central place in the front garden of the monastery, where it still stands today [ill. 16].[103]

Initially, it was planned for the conference to take place in the German adult education center, led by Iltis.[104] It is probable that, given Czech-German cultural competition, the predominance of Czech-speakers on the conference organizing commitee, and the desire to win the benevolence of the dominant Czech-speaking authorities, it was decided that it would be better not to hold the conference in a German-language bastion. Of course, German had always been the main language of the nascent discipline of sexology, and this was noticeable at the conference. But it annoyed one Czech conference observer, who noted that this undermined the equality between the Czech and German languages in Czechoslovakia. (The same

lékařské fakulty a to profesorem Venerologie drem Ant.[onín] Trýbem a profesorem biologie drem Janem Bělehrádkem vedle jiných do centů a asistentů" (Masaryk University is now represented by two distinguished members of the professorial staff of the Faculty of Medicine, namely professor of venereology Dr. Ant.[onín] Trýb and professor of biology Dr. Jan Bělehrádek, in addition to other professors and assistants). See Weisskopf, Sep. 10, 1932, 3.

[101] Bertie Albrecht wrote that Bělehrádek gave his lecture in French. See Albrecht 1932, 1. The title of his talk is indeed spelled out in French in the official conference program: "Sexualité et mesures eugéniques" (Sexuality and Eugenic Measures). Albrecht also wrote that Bělehrádek had put Mendel's manuscripts in order after his death. In 1934, Bělehrádek published the book *Dědičnost a eugenika* (*Heredity and Eugenics*). See also Engels & Glick 2008, 266.

[102] *Volksfreund*, Sep. 22, 1932, 6.

[103] *Gemeinde-Verwaltung und Gemeindestatistik der Landeshauptstadt Brünn* 1910, 292–93; Giannini, Nov. 30, 1999 (online document). Giannini gives three reasons for the removal of the statue: 1. Mendel was a German-speaker; 2. Lysenkoism; 3. the enlargement and renovation of Mendelplatz. The last reason seems incorrect because this enlargement did not happen until the mid-1960s.

[104] Initial Brno conference brochure 1932, [4]. The building is located at 2a Janáčkovo náměstí and is now part of Masaryk University.

author also complained that most lecturers were Jewish.)[105] However, Josef Weisskopf took care to give a Czech summary of every lecture given in German, and vice versa.[106]

After lunch, the crowd went to see the newly built modernist municipal swimming pool in the Brno suburb of Zábrdovice (Městské lázně v Zábrdovicích, Städtisches Bad in Obrowitz), designed by the Brno architect Bohuslav Fuchs (1895–1972). This grand bathing and swimming compound had only been finished the year before. It was considered a fine example of modern hygiene for the masses, above all as bathing, and interior plumbing, was still not common.[107] Hirschfeld loved the pool. When engaged in preparations for the conference with Weisskopf, in the summer of 1932, he scouted the swimming pool. He then told Brno's Lothar Spielmann, who interviewed Hirschfeld: "I had a look at the Obrowitz swimming pool yesterday and I am very excited about it. It is one of the most beautiful and modern pools in the world. I find that it incorporates everything that should be united in a modern swimming pool. It makes a perfect impression. The congress will officially visit the bathing facility" [ill. 17].[108]

The conference's afternoon session started with a lecture by Hugo Iltis on sexuality and Mendelism. That this lecture had initially been intended for the morning proves that the earlier introductory speeches had run longer than planned.[109] Some of the following afternoon lectures were on the same topic of Eugenics and Sexuality.[110] After the conclusion of the first day, the conference attendees could visit the so-

105 The author also suggested that one third of the lectures should have been in Czech, one third in German, and one third in French. He had no sympathy at all for the idea of Esperanto as a fourth conference language. ibid., 597-98, 1932, 599, 628. For the antisemitic stance, ibid., 597-98.

106 Ibid., 628.

107 See https://www.bam.brno.cz/en/object/c344-public-spa-in-zabrdovice (accessed May 11, 2020); Pelčák & Šlapeta 2015, 286–87.

108 Spielmann, Jul. 28, 1932, 4: "Ich habe mir gestern das Obrowitzer Bad angesehen und bin ganz begeistert davon. Es ist eines der schönsten und modernsten Bäder der Welt. Ich finde dort alles berücksichtigt, was in einem modernen Bad vereinigt sein soll. Es macht einen vollendeten Eindruck. Der Kongreß wird offiziell das Bad besuchen".

109 *Tagesbote*, Morgenblatt, Sep. 22, 1932, 6; *Volksfreund*, Sep. 21, 1932, 4.

110 The conference announcement brochure (1932, 4) claimed that there were four new topics (out of the seven covered in the conference): *Eugenik und Sexualität, Weltanschauung und Sexualität, Völkerkunde und Sexualität* and *Intersexualitätsforschung*. The other three topics were: *Sexualerziehung, Sexualpathologie*, and *Populationsprobleme – Ehe- und Sexualberatung*. In the final brochure, these seven topics appeared unchanged. Three brochures were issued for the conference: a preliminary brochure, announcing the conference; a second provisional program; and a third and final offical conference brochure. Most of the speakers listed in the provisional program were included in the final brochure. Only six of the lecturers previously announced failed to appear in the third conference brochure: section II: Univ. Doz. Dr. Jaroslav Křížencký, Brünn: "Pübertät und Geschlechtsreife"; section VI: Dr. Hugo Bondy, Prag: "Sexualpathologie"; section VII: Dr. Gruschka, Aussig a. E.: "Die unfruchtbaren Tage der Frau"; Dr. Max Popper, Prag: "Sozialversicherung und Sexualberatung"; Mrs. Edith How-Martyn, London: "Birth Control"; Dr. Abraham Stone, New York: "Genital Spasms as a Cause of Sexual Disharmonies". For a newspaper article listing all the initially planned speakers, see *Volksfreund*, Aug. 27, 1932, 5–6. Cf. the list in "Sexuologen-Tagung in Brünn", *Prager Presse*, Sep. 18, 1932, 6.

111 Program brochure WLSR 1932 conference, [4]. See also *Licht ins Volk!*, Jg. 6, Heft n° 1, 1933, 15: "Der Sexuologenkongreß veranstaltete auch eine Exkursion in das im Hause der Volkshochschule untergebrachte Gregor Mendel-Museum der Deutschen Gesellschaft für Wissenschaft und Kunst" (The sexologists' congress also organized an excursion to the Gregor Mendel museum of the German Society for Science and Art, housed in the adult education center building). See also the anonymous article (most likely written by Hugo Iltis), "Die Brünner Volkshochschule im Schuljahr 1932/33", *Licht ins Volk!*, Jg. 6, Heft n° 1, 1933, 15. There is an article on Iltis' Mendel museum in *Licht ins Volk!*, Jg. 5, Heft n° 1, Sept. 1932, 19–24.

112 See the final conference brochure, Gesellschaftlicher Teil. The periodical of the main theater in Brno reported that the opera had been requested by the WLSR conference organizers. See *Divadelní list Národního divadla v Brně*, Sep. 10, 1932, 47. It is difficult to determine what happened to the other activities planned in the Gesellschaftlicher Teil of the conference program, 10. Generally, the press did not report on the conference's leasure activities after the initial outing to the Mendel monument and the visit to the swimming complex. The program tells us that on Thursday, September 22, 1932, a sightseeing bus tour of the city was planned at eight in the morning (or perhaps the evening). On

called Gregor Mendel Museum, a somewhat permanent exhibit on Mendel's life, located in a room of Hugo Iltis' adult education center.[111] That evening, the conference participants were offered the option of attending the opera *The Bartered Bride* (*Die verkaufte Braut*) by the Czech composer Bedřich Smetana (1824–1884) in the city theater on Krapfengasse (Kobližná) [ill. 18].[112]

SECOND CONFERENCE DAY

On the second day, Thursday September 22, the morning topic was Sexual Education (*Sexualerziehung*). Twelve lecturers were listed as speaking about masturbation, or "ipsation" as it was called at the conference. According to Weisskopf, Hirschfeld invented "ipsation" out of a desire to be rid of the old biblical term "onanism".[113] In theory, this should have occupied the morning session from 9 a.m. until 12 p.m.[114] For the afternoon session, on the topic of World Philosophy [*sic*] and Sexuality (*Weltanschauung und Sexualität*), no fewer than thirteen speakers were announced.[115] Hirschfeld's new lover, Li Shiu Tong, lectured on "Chinese Philosophy in [*sic*: and] Sexual Morality" (*Chinesische Weltanschauung und Sexualität*) and Wilhelm Reich spoke in his usual jargon on "The Tasks of the Sexual-Political Mass Movement" (*Die Aufgaben der sexualpolitischen Massenbewegung*).[116]

In the evening, at 8 p.m., another public event was held, once again in the DOPZ venue, under the title "Why Sexual Reform?" (*Warum Sexualreform?, Proč sexuální*

Friday, September 23, 1932, there were other plans: a visit to the casemates on Špilberk castle, and a visit to the Brno exhibition grounds (*Výstaviště, Ausstellungsgelände*) in the Schreibwald (Pisárky) city district, which included a stop at the temporary Anthropos exhibition held there. See *Volksfreund*, Jan. 21, 1932, 6; *Lidové noviny*, Aug. 30, 1932, 11; May 25, 1930, 7. On Saturday, September 24, 1932, a visit to the Austerlitz (Slavkov) battlefield memorial was also proposed, pending agreement from the conference attendees; Schindler claims they did go (Schindler 2001, 31). Although this was announced as a possibility in the *Gesellschaftlicher Teil* of the official conference brochure, Saturday was still a regular conference day with a morning and an afternoon session. On Sunday, a screening of Fritz Lang's 1931 movie *Mörder unter uns!* (*Murderer Among Us*, better known in English and German by its later title *M*) was planned in the Kapitol cinema. On Monday, September 26, 1932, a visit to the Macocha Gorge (near Blansko), also known as the Macocha Abyss, was anticipated. See https://en.wikipedia.org/wiki/Macocha_Gorge (accessed May 11, 2020). Panýrek provided the most information on the outings but even he did not mention all the excursions. See Panýrek 1932, 630. The only other indication of this extracurricular program is a mention on the blackboard in one of the conference pictures, saying that the visit to the Macocha Gorge took place as planned in the conference brochure, on Monday, September 26, 1932. For the picture, see Scize, Oct. 1, 1932, 5. Initially, the outing to the Macocha Gorge was planned for Sunday, September 25, 1932, since there were no lectures that day. See the WLSR 1932 conference announcement brochure, 5.

113 Weisskopf 1933, 30.

114 WLSR 1932 conference program, [4]. *Tagesbote* only mentioned seven of the twelve lectures announced (*Tagesbote*, Abendblatt, Sep. 22, 1932, 2).

115 We here adopt the erroneous translations made by the conference organizers in the conference brochure. *Weltanschauung* (worldview) is not the same as world philosophy.

116 WLSR 1932 conference program, [5]. *Tagesbote* only mentioned seven speakers (*Tagesbote*, Morgenblatt, Sep. 23, 1932, 6). Li Shiu Tong's talk, "Chinese Philosophy and Sexual Morality", was judged to be one of the high points of the conference by several people. See "Sexueele hervorming. Het vijfde congres van den 'Wereldbond voor sexueele hervorming' te Brünn in Tsjecho-Slowakije", *Algemeen Handelsblad* (Amsterdam) (morning edition), Sep. 17, 1932, 9; and Lewandowski, Oct. 11, 1932, 13: "Onder de lezingen over het thema Wereldbeschouwing en Sexualiteit mag in het bizonder [*sic*] genoemd worden een lezing van Li-Schiu-Tong uit Hongkong over de rol der sexualiteit in China" (Of the lectures on the topic of Worldview and Sexuality particular mention may be made of the one by Li Shiu Tong from Hong Kong on the role of sexuality in China). Scize wrote that Li Shiu Tong's lecture on polygamy in the Far East was "brève et substantielle" (short and substantial) (Scize, Oct. 1, 1932, 6). A Czech woman, on the other hand, criticized the contribution of Hirschfeld's Chinese pupil because his English was very bad: "Poté nastoupil na řečnickou tribunu pan Li-Sching Tong z Hongkongu, aby promluvil anglicky na téma 'Čínský světový názor v pohlavní otázce'. Proslov byl velmi stručný. Prohlásil, že v jeho vlasti není našich sexuálně mravních problémů, neboť tam trvá zákonitá polygamie. Jeho angličině rozuměli velmi málo i ti, kdo angličinu ovládají dokonale" (Then Mr. Li-Sching Tong [*sic*] from Hong Kong took the podium to speak in English on the topic of 'Chinese world opinion on the sex question'. The speech was very brief. He stated that there are no sexual moral problems in his homeland because there is legal polygamy. His

reforma?).[117] Weisskopf and Hirschfeld opened the public lecture and stressed that the ultimate goal of sexual reform was not theory but the well-being and improvement of people's sexual and love lives. Weisskopf had raised this same point in a text written two weeks before the conference: "Since all people's interests intersect in sexual life, the congress is open not only to the purely scientific and medical community, but also to the general public".[118] Weisskopf quoted Hirschfeld himself in this text: "'Science is not here science for itself, but for the people' are the words of League President Dr Hirschfeld".[119] No fewer than fourteen speakers followed Weisskopf and Hirschfeld's introduction in the DOPZ venue, all conference lecturers, among them Li Shiu Tong. One journalist reported: "It was a spirited evening, with several surprising highlights. The very enthusiastic audience often interrupted the speakers with storms of applause".[120] Another newspaper noticed the enthusiasm but thought the crowd in attendance was not that large.[121] Whatever the case, Hirschfeld must have enjoyed this Czech enthusiasm immensely.

THIRD CONFERENCE DAY

On the third day, Friday, September 23, the morning session addressed the topic of Sexual Ethnology (*Sexualethnologie*). This topic was likely suggested by Hirschfeld's world tour and, indeed, Hirschfeld himself began the session with a long talk accompanied by slides from his trip.[122] Bertie Albrecht and Jean Dalsace then reported on the sexual reform situation in France and Herbert Lewandowski (1896–1996) and Coenraad van Emde-Boas (1904–1981) on the situation in the Netherlands.[123] In the afternoon, the general board (*Generalsammlung*) of the WLSR convened. This meeting was not open to the public.[124] A decision was reached, for example, that doctors specializing in sexual counseling (*sexualberatende Ärzte*) would form a separate section within the WLSR.[125]

FOURTH CONFERENCE DAY

Because Hirschfeld suffered an attack of malaria on Friday evening, the morning and afternoon sessions on the following, fourth day, Saturday, September 24, were switched.[126] The session on Sexual Pathology (*Sexualpathologie*) took place in the morning. Intersexuality Research (*Intersexualitätsforschung*), "Dr. Magnus Hirschfeld's area of expertise" (*das Spezialgebiet von Dr. Magnus Hirschfeld*), was held in the afternoon.[127] This wreaked a lot of havoc with the conference program.[128] For example, an afternoon speaker, the Prague psychiatrist Vladimír Vondráček (1895–1978), was allowed to speak in the morning on homosexual tendencies after alcohol

English was very difficult to understand even for those with perfect mastery of English).

[117] See the WLSR 1932 conference program, [5], where the event was announced as a "*grösse öffentliche Volksversammlung*" (large public assembly). The poster for the event mentioned eighteen speakers in total. Some of the speakers were not mentioned on the poster.

[118] Weisskopf, Sep. 10, 1932, 3: "Poněvadž [*sic*: pokud] se v sexuálním životě stýkají zájmy všech lidí, jest kongres přístupný ne jenom ryze vědeckému a lékařskému obecenstvu, nýbrž [*sic*: ba dolconce] i široké veřejnosti".

[119] Weisskopf, Sep. 10, 1932, 3: "'Věda tu není pro vědu samotnou, ale pro lidi,' to jsou slova presidenta Ligy dra Hirschfelda".

[120] *Tagesbote*, Morgenblatt, Sep. 23, 1932, 6: "Es war ein buntbewegter Abend, mit mehreren überraschenden Höhepunkten. Das sehr begeisterde Publikum unterbrach die Redner oft mit Stürmen von Beifallskundgebungen".

[121] *Volksfreund*, Sep. 25, 1932, 5.

[122] *Tagesbote*, Abendblatt, Sep. 23, 1932, 2. Of the seven announced speakers, five were named in the newspaper. One of the speakers mentioned, the Dutch doctor van Emde-Boas, was not announced in the offical WLSR 1932 conference program, [6].

[123] See Lewandowski & van Dranen 1933, 224–26. Lewandowski and van Dranen refer to the Brno conference and the lecture given by their Dutch colleague Coenraad van Emde-Boas on the topic of sexual consultancy in the Netherlands.

[124] WLSR 1932 conference program, [6].

[125] *Der Wiener Tag*, Sep. 27, 1932, 4. A very partial account of the board meeting was published in the sole issue of *Sexus, Vierteljahreszeitschrift für die ge-*

use. The lesbian Berlin doctor Johanna Elberskirchen (1864–1943) also delivered a talk. She may have arrived late at the conference, since her talk on "Sexual Periodicity and Eugenics" (*Sexuale Periodizität und Eugenik*) should have been given on the first day.[129] In addition, the female Vienna doctor Sidonie Fürst (1891–1973) was allowed to give her talk on ejaculatio praecox in the morning, despite the fact that she was not even mentioned in the official conference brochure.[130] Dr. Rudolf Elkan made a lasting impression when, during his lecture, which he accompanied with slides, he reasoned that the female orgasm did not exist and that women were in general frigid beings.[131] Hirschfeld, suffering from fever in the morning, did not arrive at the conference until the afternoon. He was met with applause and flowers. Weisskopf announced that the chancellery of President Masaryk replied to their telegram, which provoked more applause. Li Shiu Tong and Norman Haire presided over the Intersexuality Research session.[132] Felix Abraham, one of Hirschfeld's collaborators at the Institute in Berlin, spoke about three transsexual operations, and Karl Giese spoke of "intersex psychological projections" (*intersexuelle Psychoprojektionen*).[133] At the end of the session, two typical letters from people seeking counseling (*Ratsuchenden*) were read to the audience.

Extensive announcements for and reports on the conference appeared in some issues of the Czechoslovak gay magazine *Nový hlas*. It took special interest, of course, in the session on intersexuality.[134] Hirschfeld claimed that it was the first time that the topic was addressed at a WLSR conference and several newspapers simply repeated that claim.[135] After checking the four published WLSR conference proceedings (in Berlin, London, Copenhagen, Vienna), I can say that this is correct, if also somewhat surprising. Did Hirschfeld indeed assess that Czechoslovakia was the one country able to handle the topic of intersexuality, even having its own session in a WLSR

samte Sexualwissenschaft und Sexualreform 1933, 62–63.

[126] *Volksfreund*, Sep. 25, 1932, 5; *Volksfreund*, Sep. 27, 1932, 4. In *Testament: Heft II*, Hirschfeld speaks of "Schwere Malariaanfälle, hohes Fieber, Herzattacken in Brno (mitten beim Kongress)" (Severe malaria attacks, high fever, heart attacks in Brno [in the middle of the congress]) (Hirschfeld & Dose 2013, f. 65/142). See also Schütz, Oct. 2, 1932, 3.

[127] As put by *Prager Presse*, Sep. 28, 1932, 4. It was likely no coincidence that the *Intersexualität* topic was scheduled for Saturday. I think this was an intentional decision meant to allow a possibly interested gay and lay crowd to attend. The conference was open to anyone with an interest in sexology, not just medical professionals. See the WLSR 1932 Brno conference announcement brochure, point V. However, one may wonder if many lay men and women actually attended. Admission was 100 Czech crowns. See Humbert 1932, 1.

[128] Cf. Seidl 2012, 220, who thinks that the offical program was followed.

[129] It is also possible that time constraints meant she was not able to give her talk on the first day of the conference. Leidinger, Elberskirchen's biographer, claims that Elberskirchen did not attend the Brno conference (Leidinger 2008, 120).

[130] *Tagesbote*, Sep. 25, 1932, 6.

[131] *Volksfreund*, Sep. 25, 1932, 5. The journalist mentioned only two of the nine speakers announced. Dr. Julka Chlapcová-Gforgjovičová called this speech by Elkan, along with another speech he gave in the DOPZ building, anti-feminist (Chlapcová-Gforgjovičová 1932, 193–94; see also Weisskopf 1933, 31). Elkan was not mentioned in either of the two sessions that day but was listed as giving yet another talk on the last day of the conference, "Demonstration des Geburtenregelungsphantomes" (Demonstration of the Birth Control Phantom).

[132] *Tagesbote*, Morgenblatt, Sep. 25, 1932, 6; WLSR 1932 conference program, [6–7]. I may have missed an article in *Volksfreund* covering this session ... or the newspaper made a conscious decision not to report on the Intersexuality session.

[133] *Tagesbote*, Morgenblatt, Sep. 25, 1932, 6. This is what the journalist made of Giese's talk: "Es handelt sich um Ausdrucksformen des Seelenlebens, denen ein geschlechtsspezifischer Charakter meistens abgesprochen wird, die aber für die Persönlichkeit charakteristisch sind" (It is about expressions of the psychic life whose gendered character is usually denied, but which are characteristic of the personality nonetheless).

[134] See the article "Kongres Ligy pro sexuální reformu v Brně" in *Nový hlas*, Aug. 1932, 1. Intersexuality is the only conference topic printed in bold in the text. For a report on the conference, with extra attention on the LGBT theme, see "5. Kongres Ligy pro sexuální reformu", *Nový hlas*, Jg. 1, n°s 7-8, Nov. 1, 1932, 11–14. Panýrek may have referred to Karl Fein as one of the few lawyers at the conference (Panýrek 1932, 598).

[135] Hirschfeld 1933a, 1; Hirschfeld, Sep. 29, 1932, 4.

conference? Josef Weisskopf delivered only a brief report on this session in his conference report: "Hirschfeld and his students rightly championed the importance of predisposition and circumstances in the general discussion on homosexuality and intersexuality, as well as the liberation of affected persons from harsh outmoded laws".[136]

FIFTH AND FINAL CONFERENCE DAY

Twenty speakers were listed for the fifth and final day, Sunday, September 26, and no difference was made between a morning and an afternoon session. The seventh and last topic was Population Problems: Birth Control and Marriage Advice (*Populationsprobleme: Ehe- und Sexualberatung*). On this occasion as well, some lectures were delivered by people not mentioned in the official conference brochure. Magnus Hirschfeld had the last word. He thanked the Czechoslovak republic, the city of Brno and the Brno university for their hospitality and said that now, for sexual reform also, the "truth marches on".[137] The Brno conference was the very last time that Hirschfeld was able to shine as the scientific and activist personality that he always wanted to be. Three years earlier, in November 1929, after three decades of relentless activism, he suffered his demise as the president of the WhK in Germany. In Czechoslovakia, on the other hand, he was celebrated as a scientific authority and as thé guiding light of its burgeoning LGBT movement. It is important to perceive that Hirschfeld must have been very aware that he could live and thrive in Czechoslovakia (and on his world trip) in a way he could not in his native country.[138] But then, of course, a prophet is not without honor except in his own country.

According to Bertie Albrecht, after the conference, there was an agreement that the following year's WLSR conference would take place in Amsterdam. However, this was not to be because the WLSR's Dutch section eventually refused the offer in June 1933, despite Hirschfeld having travelled to Amsterdam from Paris.[139] The Brno conference proceedings, which would number eight hundred pages, were never published.[140] The exact reasons for this are not known, but most likely it was due to an insufficiency in the conference finances. Nothing allows one to infer that Weisskopf's relationship with Hirschfeld or Giese had in any way soured after the Brno conference. In 1934, Weisskopf positively reviewed the German-language edition of Hirschfeld's

136 Weisskopf 1933, 31: "Hirschfeld und seine Schüler verfochten mit Recht die Bedeutung von Anlage und Lage beim Homosexualitäts- und Intersexualitätsproblem überhaupt sowie die Befreiung des Betroffenen aus den harten veralteten Gesetzen".

137 *Tagesbote*, Abendblatt, Sep. 27, 1932, 4: "Auch im Bezug auf die Fragen der Sexualreform gilt der Satz, daß die Wahrheit auf dem Marsch ist" (The phrase that truth is on the march also applies with respect to issues of sexual reform).

138 A few days after the conference, in an interview Hirschfeld gave to *Prager Presse*, he immediately began by stressing how very friendly and hospitable Czechoslovakia was. See Hirschfeld, Sep. 29, 1932, 4. The interview was conducted on Tuesday, September 28, 1932. Cf. Herrn 2022, 384.

139 Warmerdam & Brandhorst 1995, 37; University of Sydney Library, Sydney, Norman Haire collection, 3.20, Magnus Hirschfeld, Typescripts, 1923–1935, letter (dated Jun. 6, 1933, f. 1) from Magnus Hirschfeld to Norman Haire. Hirschfeld was in Amsterdam June 11–17, 1933. An article in the *Neues Wiener Journal*, a Vienna newspaper, mentioned the cities of Chicago and Stockholm, in addition to Amsterdam, as possible locations for the next conference. See *Neues Wiener Journal*, Sep. 28, 1932, 9; see also Schütz, Oct. 2, 1932, 4. In a letter to Norman Haire, Hirschfeld said that Bernard Premsela (1889–1944) had written that he feared possible reactions from fascist factions in the Netherlands. See University of Sydney Library, Sydney, Norman Haire collection, 3.20, Magnus Hirschfeld, Typescripts, 1923–1935, letter (dated Nov. 16, 1933, f. 1) from Magnus Hirschfeld to Norman Haire. On his return trip, Hirschfeld stopped in Antwerp on June 18, 1933, where he met Inga Junghanns (1886–1962), a divorced Danish translator and member of the WLSR international committee, known for her work on and contact with the poet Rainer Maria Rilke. See, for example, Rilke & Junghanns 1959. See https://da.wikipedia.org/wiki/Inga_Junghanns (accessed Jun. 5, 2020). I thank Ralf Dose for providing further information on Junghanns. See his email (dated Jun. 5, 2020) to the author.

140 Albrecht 1932, 1; WLSR 1932 conference program, [9], where the publication of the proceedings of the conference are announced under the

world trip book. In addition, some details in Weisskopf's book review suggest that some of his information must have come from Hirschfeld himself, indicating that they were still in contact.[141]

MOVIE SCREENINGS

Although not announced in any of the three known conference brochures, on Sunday night, the movie *Laws of Love* (*Gesetze der Liebe*) was played in the Sokol Stadion cinema [ill. 19].[142] "On the occasion of the fifth International Congress of the World League for Sexual Reform, *Progressive Horizon* [*Pokrokový obzor*] will screen a cultural and health film depicting the tragedy of the homosexual, *Laws of Nature* [the Czech title for *Gesetze der Liebe*], a six-part documentary made with the collaboration of Ma.[gister?] Magnus Hirschfeld in Berlin".[143] *Progressive Horizon* (*Pokrokový obzor*) was the bi-weekly of the Progressive Party (*Pokrokové strany*) in Brno, in which Josef Weisskopf also published. The magazine published one of the best in-depth accounts of the conference.[144]

Gesetze der Liebe came out in Germany in 1927. The better known movie *Different from the Others* (*Anders als die Andern*), which came out in 1919, was ultimately banned in Germany and *Gesetze der Liebe* was, in a way, Hirschfeld's attempt to get past the censor and present the substance of *Anders als die Andern* to the public.[145] Hirschfeld cleverly incorporated a concise version of the latter film into *Gesetze der Liebe*, thus "neutralizing" its danger within a more general presentation of sexuality. It is unclear if *Anders als die Andern* (*Jiný než ostatní*, in Czech) was widely screened in Czechoslovakia. It was shown in the Sudeten German city of Teplitz (Teplice) in 1919.[146] Hirschfeld strongly believed in the didactic capacity of the film medium. A film department was set up in the Institute in the very year that it was founded.[147] A short interview that Hirschfeld gave to a Czech movie periodical in 1926 indicates that he did not yet accept the fact that *Anders als die Andern* had been banned.[148] The following year, *Gesetze der Liebe* appeared.

Gesetze der Liebe consists of five parts. Its fourth part presents the phenomenon of intermediary types (*Zwischenstufen*) in fauna, flora, and humans. The fifth part contains a reworked and abridged version of *Anders als die Andern* under the title *Innocently Outlawed! Tragedy of a Homosexual* (*Schuldlos geächtet! Tragödie eines Homosexuellen*). However, the fifth part was almost completely cut by the German censor.[149] Along with the movie, a sixty-four-page pamphlet, also titled *Gesetze der Liebe*, was published.[150] Two thirds of this publication was devoted to the theme of homosexuality, further revealing that situating the homosexual theme within the

title "Kongreßbericht" (Congress Report). See also Weisskopf 1933, 29, 32.

[141] Weisskopf, Feb. 20, 1934, 113–14.

[142] The cinema was located at 20–22 Kounicova (Kaunitzgasse) in Brno. The modernist building had just been built in 1928–29. See Vrabelová, Svobodová & Šlapeta 2016, 181.

[143] See https://cinematicbrno.phil.muni.cz/index.php/cs/node/38004 (accessed Feb. 18, 2023): "Při příležitosti V. Mezinárodního kongresu Světové Ligy pro sexuální reformu promítne Pokrokový obzor kulturně-zdravotní film, líčící tragedii homosexuála: Zákony přírody. Dokument doby o 6 dílech za spolupráce Ma.[gister?] Magn.[us] Hischfelda v Berlíně". See also *Pokrokový obzor*, Sept. 24, 1932, 7.

[144] Roubičkova, Oct. 1, 1932.

[145] For more information on *Gesetze der Liebe* and the difficulties it had reaching an audience in Germany, see Steakley 2007.

[146] Seidl 2012, 112. The movie is not mentioned in the https://cinematicbrno.phil.muni.cz/database (accessed Feb. 18, 2023).

[147] See the notices in the Czech movie magazine *Filmschau*, Nov. 1, 1919, 13; Jan 1, 1920, 141–42.

[148] Hirschfeld, Jul. 20, 1926, 9.

[149] Nowak 2015, 126–28. The five parts were: I. *Vom Suchen und Finden der Geschlechter*; II. *Ans Licht der Welt*; III. *Mutterliebe*; IV. *Vom Zwischengeschlecht*; V. *Schuldlos geächtet!* (I. Of Seeking and Finding the Sexes; II. Into the Light of the World, III; Motherly Love; IV. Of the Intermediate Sex; V. Innocently Outlawed!). See Hirschfeld & Beck 1927. Isherwood also wrote that *Gesetze der Liebe* was mainly a reworking of *Anders als die Andern* (Isherwood 1988, 42).

[150] Hirschfeld & Beck 1927.

broader perspective of sexuality was mostly a ruse. The pamphlet contains thirty-two photos, ten of which are stills from *Anders als die Andern*.

As with *Anders als die Andern*, only an incomplete version of *Gesetze der Liebe* survives, making it hard to determine the extent of the gay part.[151] *Gesetze der Liebe* was released in Czechoslovakia as *Laws of Nature, Sex Drive* (*Zákony přírody, pohlavní pud*) and was screened for the first time in Brno in August 1929, in the Edison, Universum, and Jas cinemas.[152] It is unknown if, at this screening, the fifth part was censored. It is likely that Hirschfeld would not have agreed to show a censored version at the WLSR conference, in September 1932. But it would be interesting to determine if a full or censored version of the movie was screened in Brno, in order to get a clearer picture of how tolerant the Czechoslovakia that Hirschfeld so admired was.

A movie by the Dutch sexologist Theodoor Van de Velde, *Marriage* (*Manželství, Die Ehe*), was screened at the conference as well.[153] This was not a Czechoslovak premiere as the movie had been shown in 1929.[154] The complaint by several conference participants about the Catholic Church's interference in sexual matters is explained by the fact that Van de Velde's famous 1926 book, *Het volkomen huwelijk* (in German, *Die vollkommene Ehe*; in English, *Ideal Marriage*), was placed on the Vatican's Index in 1931,[155] the only sexological work ever to receive that honor. Probably because of the Church's action, the book became an international bestseller. Van de Velde's classic was translated into Czech in 1930 as *Dokonalé manželství*, and was reprinted several times.[156] Lastly, the movie *Life in a Drop of Water* (*Život v kapce vody*), a cultural film directed by Dr. Mack, was also shown.

SOME POST-CONFERENCE EVENTS

On Tuesday, September 27, Hirschfeld, together with Leunbach, Haire and Elkan, went to Prague to give a presentation as the "Participants of the 5th Congress of the World League for Sexual Reform on a Scientific Basis", as the event announcement put it.[157] Hirschfeld's passport shows that he left his beloved Czechoslovakia that evening. Returning via Brno, on his way back to Vienna, he passed through the border station in Břeclav (Lundenburg).[158] Upon his arrival in Vienna, he was hospitalized in Dr. Fürth's sanatorium.

The momentum from the conference gave rise to another initiative in Brno. Only a few days after its conclusion, a new association, the Association of German Social Democratic Doctors (Verein deutscher sozialdemokratische Ärzte), was created. Probably, this was simply the Brno chapter (*Ortsgruppe*) of the association, as the organization itself had been founded in February 1930, in Prague, under

[151] The original parts (four reels) of *Gesetze der Liebe* were only very recently discovered in the Bundesarchiv by Stefan Drößler of the Filmmuseum München and will be brought out soon on DVD. See Würmann, Sep. 24, 2021.

[152] See https://www.phil.muni.cz/filmovebrno/?id=22&lang=1&abc=1929 (accessed Jan 9, 2020). As far as I could judge from the available, digitized archival sources, the movie was shown in Brno in 1929, 1932 and 1934.

[153] See the announcement in *Pokrokový obzor*, Sep. 3, 1932, 7.

[154] See, for example, *Večer*, Dec. 5, 1929, 1.

[155] For the Vatican Index Librorum Prohibitorum (Index of Forbidden Books), see https://en.wikipedia.org/wiki/Index_Librorum_Prohibitorum (accessed May 22, 2020). The news also reached Czechoslovakia. See, for example, *Večer*, Apr. 13, 1931, 4.

[156] Van de Velde 1930.

[157] An otherwise unidentified Professor D. Gamper, president of "Freie Mutterschaft für Deutschland" (Free Motherhood for Germany), and Dr. Hugo Hecht (1883–1970) from Prague also lectured. The lecture took place in the Plodinová burza (Crops Exchange Building) at 31 Havlíčkovo náměstí (now 866/30 Senovážné náměstí) in Prague. Tickets cost 3, 5 and 10 Czech crowns. Students and workers paid only 1 Czech crown. See *Rudé právo*, Sep. 25, 1932, 8; Sep 27, 1932, 6. For a more detailed account of the gathering, see "Schůze pro sexuálni reformu" (A Meeting for Sexual Reform), *Rudé právo*, Sep. 30, 1932, 2.

[158] Supposing that the Břeclav (Lundenburg) border railway station stamp (dated Sep. 27, 1932) in Hirschfeld's passport is indeed correct, he likely

the leadership of Arnold Holitscher (1859–1942).[159] Leunbach gave the opening speech, stressing the need for the association. According to one journalist, Magnus Hirschfeld, Norman Haire and Dr. Rubinraut from Warschau were supposed to have been there as well. Hirschfeld was represented by Dr. Josef Güdemann (1897–1972) from Vienna, who conveyed Hirschfeld's warmest regards.[160] As in Brno, the reason given for Hirschfeld's absence was a malaria attack.[161]

The Brno conference may have also given rise to another initiative. In March 1933, the Czech-language Union of Czechoslovak Social Democratic Doctors (Svaz československých sociálnědemokratických lékařů), started producing their own social medicine periodical, the *Social Health Journal* (*Sociálne zdravotní revue*). Starting with its fourth issue, in June 1933, the journal addressed the topic of sexology with explicit reference to Magnus Hirschfeld, whose work had been destroyed in Berlin the previous month, and also to the Brno conference.[162] Antonín Trýb and Josef Hynie wrote the two texts for that issue.[163] Sexology remained one of the main subjects treated in the magazine. In the March 1934 issue, František Čeřovský and Hugo Bondy, two old allies, addressed the topic of homosexuality, supported by a text from Dr. Max Popper (1873–1965), the editor of the magazine.[164] Popper had regularly published texts in Czech gay magazines and would continue to do so until 1938, when the sole issue of *Hlas přírody* came out. In 1935, Josef Hynie would take up again the project of creating a chair in sexology at Prague's Charles University (Univerzita Karlova, Karls-Universität), a project that, as we saw earlier, Ferdinand Pečírka had already broached with Hirschfeld in the early 1920s.

IDEA OF PROGRESS

The Brno conference adhered, of course, to the WLSR's ten principles, which were printed in all three brochures for the Brno conference: the economic, legal and sexual equality of women and men; the liberation of marriage (and divorce) from church and state tyranny; the promotion of birth control; eugenic birth selection; protection for the unmarried mother and her illegitimate child; intersex variations; the prevention of prostitution and veneral diseases; sexual abnormalities should be rationally viewed as pathological, not as criminal or sinful phenomena; consensual sexual acts between adults are a private matter, not crimes; sexual education and enlightenment should be systematic. All in all, there was the sense of wanting to leave behind a "medieval" past of inadequate or even bad and harmful information about sexuality.[165] In a text written for a Czech audience shortly before the conference, Weisskopf wrote: "The program makes it clear what the World League is about.

took the night train. See Archiv MHG, Berlin, fonds Ernst Maass, Hirschfeld's passport (Reisepass) (May 19, 1928–May 18, 1933, 6).

[159] See the chapter "Tschechoslowakei", https://de.wikipedia. org/wiki/Verein_sozialistischer _%C3%84rzte (accessed Nov. 25, 2021).

[160] Josef Güdemann worked at the Sanatorium Fürth in Vienna, where Hirschfeld was going in September 1932. See Sauer 2017, 26. Güdemann emigrated to the USA, arriving on December 15, 1938. He died in New York in 1972. See Ancestry. com, New York, State and Federal Naturalization Records, 1794–1943; the U.S. Social Security Death Index, 1935–2014. Josef Güdemann's wife was the Lithuanian-born Basia Terespolski (1905–2010). The couple were married on October 26, 1930 in Vienna and had one daughter, Frances (1934–1994). Dr. Güdemann (spelled Gudemann or Guedemann in the USA) was the son of Moritz Güdemann (1835–1918), a rabbi and scholar in Vienna. Hirschfeld mentions Güdemann's name in *Testament: Heft II* (Hirschfeld & Dose 2013, f. 65/142). Dr. Josef Güdemann also spoke at the Brno WLSR conference. His talk was part of the *Populationsprobleme* (Population Problems) section, on the Aschheim-Zondek(sche) Reaktion, a pregnancy test also known as the mouse or rabbit test. See *Der Wiener Tag*, Sep. 27, 1932, 4. Cf. Hirschfeld & Dose 2013, f. 66/144.

[161] *Volksfreund*, Oct. 1, 1932, 5.

[162] M. P., Jun. 10, 1933, 75.

[163] Trýb, Jun. 10, 1933, 76; Hynie, Jun. 10, 1933, 76–80.

[164] Čeřovský, Mar. 25, 1934, 55–59; Bondy, Mar. 25, 1934, 59–60; Popper, Mar. 25, 1934, 60.

[165] Cf. Herrn 2022, 392.

The League brings together eminent figures from around the world, periodically convening congresses for its members as well as all those who wish to cooperate earnestly and sincerely in the liberation of mankind from the bonds of medieval superstition and error".[166] This idea of moral progress, and the dawning of a new, more enlightened time for sexual matters, with the conference members as the moral vanguard, also suffused the title that Pierre Scize, the French journalist and WLSR committee member, gave to one of the articles he wrote on the conference for the French magazine *Voilà*: "Estates General of the New Times" (*États généraux des temps nouveaux*).[167]

Within the WLSR, differences were growing about how to bring about this desired renewal and modernization of sexual morality. As in the political domain, there was a growing divergence between the reformist social democrats and the more radical and revolutionary Communists. The latter were represented by Max Hodann, Wilhelm Reich, and Béla Neufeld. All three, perceived as belonging to the extreme left, spoke at the conference.[168] As was only to be expected, the Czech Communist newspaper *Dělnická rovnost* interviewed Max Hodann during the conference.[169] We have already seen that the main organizer of the conference, Josef Weisskopf, helped create the Association of German Social Democratic Doctors immediately after the Brno conference.[170] But Weisskopf was also a member of another association (*Verein*), the Brno local branch of the Proletarian Freethinkers of the ČSR, (Proletarische Freidenker in der ČSR, Ortsgruppe Brünn), made up of atheist, anti-clerical and anti-capitalist social democrats.[171] The local Brno branch was created in 1921.[172] On the first day of the Brno WLSR conference, Dr. Siegfried Fischl, representing both the Proletarian Freethinkers and also the Association of German Social Democratic Doctors, was one of the eight people who greeted the audience and opened the conference.[173] Weisskopf himself, despite being a social democrat (or at least perceived as one), seems to have been influenced by the ideals of the New Society as propagated in the Communist Soviet Union. On the occasion of the fifteenth anniversary of the Bolshevik revolution, in October 1932, Weisskopf stated that "socialism should prevail as soon as possible in the whole world". He also declared that "[o]ne of the most important gifts that the Russian Revolution has brought to humanity, conditions allowing, is the real equality of women. Woman was freed from the cruel yoke of

166 Weisskopf, Sep. 10, 1932, 3: "Z programu jest zrejmo, oc Svetové lize jde. Liga sdružuje význacné osobnosti ce lého sveta a svolává cas od casu kongresy svých príslušníku a všech zájemcu, kterí chtejí vážne a uprímne spolupracovali na díle osvobození lidstva z pout stredovekých pover a bludu". See also Weisskopf 1933, 29.

167 Scize, Oct. 1, 1932, 5. The series of three articles (Scize Oct. 1, 1932; Oct. 15, 1932; Oct. 22, 1932) appearing in the French magazine *Voilà* was presented under the title "*Aux assises des temps nouveaux*" (At the Assembly of the New Times). In 1933, the texts were reprinted in *Sexus, Vierteljahreszeitschrift für die gesamte Sexualwissenschaft und Sexualreform*. See Scize 1933.

168 Panýrek 1932, 629, 630.

169 See "Max Hodan [*sic*: Hodann] a sexuální reformě" (Max Hodan[n] and Sexual Reform), *Dělnická rovnost*, Sep. 27, 1932, 3.

170 That this was a left-wing, Marxist-inspired association of social democrats can be seen from Arnold Holitscher's welcome article published in the very first March 1933 issue of *Sociálne zdravotní revue*. See Holitscher, Oct. 10, 1933, 5–6.

171 The association issued a periodical called *Freidenkerbibliothek* (1924–30). In Germany, there was also the Proletarische Freidenker (Proletarian Freethinkers), centralized since 1911 in the Zentralstelle proletarischer Freidenker (Central Office of Proletarian Freethinkers). In 1931, it became the Verband proletarischer Freidenker Deutschlands (German Association of Proletarian Freethinkers). See Schröder 2018, 45, 50.

172 *Volksfreund*, Nov. 21, 1931, 5. The Brno police observed a reunion, on December 3, 1931, in the DOPZ building, where Weisskopf lectured on the maternal fate of women. Weisskopf was later interrogated by the police and an attempt was made to prosecute him for this lecture. See MZA, Brno, fonds B 40, Zemský úřad v Brně, presidiální registratura, kart. n° 175, sign. 553/32.

173 *Volksfreund*, Sep. 22, 1932, 4; *Adreßbuch von Groß-Brünn* 1934, 66.

174 Weisskopf, Oct. 28, 1932, 1: "Proto je jedním z nejvýznamnějších darů, který ruská revoluce lidstvu přinesla, že uskutečnila pokud to poměry dovoluji skutečnou rovnoprávnost ženy. Žena byla

forced motherhood and does not have to give birth today against her will".[174] Like so many left-wing intellectuals, Weisskopf visited the Soviet Union in 1936 and, judging by the title of the lectures he gave about his visit, was enamored by the Communist societal project.[175]

PREPARATORY COMMITTEE

Of course, the conference was mainly supported and attended by left-wing people, and this meant that the conference was denounced by the press organs of the extreme right. The *Sudetendeutsche Volkszeitung*, for example, proclaimed: "On the Congress of the World League for Sexual Reform. A systematic attempt to demoralize the people. Why are all the leading members of the World League Marxist Jews? – a small selection".[176] The writer of the article was remarkably well-informed about the conference organizers, even referring to the title of Iltis' adult education center publication, *Licht ins Volk*!: "The liberal and Marxist press, of course, glorifies everything that this congress does! And the fact that the DOPZ hall, where the lectures are being given, is full to bursting [...] is the best proof of the skillful orchestration of these 'light-unto-the-people-bearers'".[177] The 1930 Vienna WLSR conference had also been heavily criticized by the extreme-right press, even in Brno.[178]

A glance at the destinies of the Brno conference's organizing committee (*vorbereitendes Kongreßkomitee*) members suffices to reveal that the WLSR's progressive ideas for a new sexual morality frontally collided with the growing conservative order of pre-war Europe. Weisskopf fled Czechoslovakia in October 1938 and emigrated to the USA.[179] His wife Božena and their two children followed him the following year.[180] Dr. Siegfried Fischl (1877–1942) owned a laboratory specializing in the examination of bodily fluids, at 20 Rennergasse (Běhounská).[181] In March 1941, Fischl divorced his

vysvobozena z krutého jha [*sic*] nuceného mateřství a nemusí dnes proti své vůli rodit".

[175] On his two lectures on his impressions of the Soviet Union, at the end of May and the beginning of June 1936, see "'Tep nového světa', dojmy z SSSP, první máj v Moskvě 1936" ('Heartbeat of the New World', Impressions of the USSR, May Day in Moscow 1936), *Nezávislá politika*, Jun. 6, 1936, 4. Heda Margolius Kovály offers another good example of someone enamored by the socio-cultural accomplishments of the Soviet Union. See Margolius Kovály, Třeštíková & Margolius 2018, 23–24.

[176] *Sudetendeutsche Volkszeitung*, Sep. 25, 1932, 1: "Zum Kongreß der Weltliga für Sexualreform. Ein planmäßiger Versuch die Völker zu entsittlichen. Warum sind sämtliche führende Mitglieder der Weltliga marxistische Juden? – eine kleine Auslese".

[177] *Sudetendeutsche Volkszeitung*, Sep. 25, 1932, 1: "Die liberale und marxistische Presse verherrlicht selbstverständlich alles, was dieser Kongreß tut! Und daß der Dopzsaal, in welchem die Vorträge stattfinden, brechvoll ist ..., ist höchstens ein Beweis für die geschäftstüchtige Regiekunst dieser 'Licht-ins Volkträger'".

[178] See, for example, "Moralbolschewismus" (Moral Bolshevism), *Brünner Tagespost*, Oct. 2, 1930, 1.

[179] According to Josef Weisskopf's American grandson Joe Weisskopf, Josef Weisskopf left his home country in 1938. See email (dated Jun. 5, 2012) from Joe Weisskopf to the author. This is confirmed by the passenger list of the S.S. *Queen Mary*, which sailed from Southampton to New York. See National Archives and Records Administration Washington USA, New York Passenger Lists 1820–1957, List or manifest of alien passengers for the United States, list n° 23 (dated Oct. 15, 1938). I thank Ralf Dose for sending me a digital copy of this passenger list. See his email (dated Mar. 16, 2013) to the author. Weisskopf flew from Prague to Evere airport in Belgium, but he had no valid visa for Belgium. However, he did have a visa for the USA and a valid ticket for a ship to the USA leaving from England. For this reason, the Belgian police authorities granted him a temporary visa, valid for two days. This allowed him to take a ship from Oostende (Belgium) to Dover (England). See the document (dated Oct. 10, 1938) issued by the Belgian Rijkswacht, Rijksarchief, Brussels, Ministerie van Justitie, Bestuur der Openbare Veiligheid, Dienst Vreemdelingenpolitie, file Josef Weisskopf, n° A316.325.

[180] Josef's wife, Božena (1906–1996), and their two children, Vera (1926–1988) and Rudolf (1931–1998), left Le Havre (France) on August 4, 1939 on board the S.S. *Britannic* and arrived in New York on August 13, 1939. See National Archives and Records Administration Washington USA, New York Passenger Lists 1820–1957, List or manifest of alien passengers for the United States, list n° 10 (dated Aug. 4, 1939). Josef Weisskopf is buried in the cemetery in Kojetín, the town where he was born. See email (dated Oct. 18 2012) from Tom N. to the author.

[181] See, for example, the advertisement for this company in *Adreßbuch von Groß-Brünn* 1934, 597.

Russian wife, Vera Krak (1879–?), whom he had married in 1916,[182] explicitly so that she would not be persecuted for being married to a Jewish man; he meant to remarry her as soon as the war was over. Because Fischl was a freemason and had been a member of a Spanish Civil War committee, and involved in other anti-fascist activities, he was sent to Auschwitz where he was killed immediately after his arrival, on February 16, 1942.[183] Dr. Karel Hora (1901–1942) worked at the Anatomical Institute in Brno, and played a vital role in hosting the conference gatherings in the anatomy auditorium of Masaryk University.[184] Hora was active in the resistance during World War II and was sentenced to death by the so-called first court martial (*1. Standgericht*) on January 13, 1942. He was not immediately executed but sent to Mauthausen where he died on May 7, 1942.[185] His wife, Olga Horová (1908–1968), survived the war. The unmarried Jewish academic Lothar Spielmann (1904–1942?) taught in a Jewish high school in Brno and lectured on pedagogical topics at Iltis' adult education center.[186] Spielmann went to Prague in April 1939. He was deported on August 3, 1942, on the Jewish transport "AAw" from Prague to Terezín. He was then transferred to Treblinka on transport "Bx" on October 22, 1942.[187] The Brno lawyer Karl Fein, about whom we will have much to say later on, moved to Prague in October 1939, and was deported from Prague to Łódź in October 1941. He died in Łódź of undernourishment and heart failure on May 2, 1942. Dr. Vladimír Zapletal (1900–1983), a married non-Jewish man, was active in the resistance group Defence of the Nation (Obrana národa) during World War II. He survived the war and worked for the public health department of the Brno Provincial

[182] The couple married in Penza (in Russian, Пéнза). See the home certificate (*domovský list*) for Siegfried Fischl in AMB, Brno, fonds B 1/39. From here on "domovský list" (Heimatschein, in German) will be mentioned as "home certificate" only.

[183] AMB, Brno, fonds Z 1, resident registration card Siegfried Fischl; and fonds B 1/39, home certificate Siegfried Fischl. He is mentioned as a new member of the Masonic order in the periodical *Die Drei Ringe: Monatsblätter für Freimaurerei und verwandte Gebiete* 5 (1926): 75. The couple had no children. Fischl's wife survived the war and, in 1947, went to court to restore her prior legal situation, namely her marriage to Fischl, most likely for financial reasons. The divorce was in fact annulled, legally entitling her to collect a pension as Fischl's widow. I thank Miroslava Kučerová (MZA, Brno) for sending me the relevant files on this case in January 2014: MZA, Brno, fonds C 11, Krajský soud civilní Brno (Kreisgericht für Zivilsachen in Brünn), III. manipulace, kart. n° 461, sign. Ck Ia 62/41, divorce Dr. Siegfried Fischl and Vera Krak; and, for the postwar annulment of the divorce, MZA, Brno, fonds C 152, Okresní soud civilní Brno (Bezirksgericht für Zivilsachen in Brünn), III. Manipulace, year 1947, kart. n° 489, sign. Ck Ia 173/47, request Vera Fischl to annul the divorce. The date of Fischl's death in Auschwitz-Birkenau is confirmed in the ITS database. After the war, Vera Fischlová lived at 19 Vlhká. See *Adresář zemského hlavního města Brna* 1948, 82.

[184] Weisskopf 1933, 27. In the same text, Weisskopf mentioned that Otomar Völker (1871–1955), Hora's superior and the head of the Anatomical Institute, was intrumental in organizing the conference. Magnus Hirschfeld drew attention to Völker's invaluable aid in an interview. See Hirschfeld, Sep. 29, 1932, 4.

[185] MZA, Brno, fonds B 340, Gestapo Brno, n° 2870, kart. n° 310, sign. 100-310-13, file Karel Hora, f. 19. All his belongings were confiscated. The reason for his conviction, as always in such court martial verdicts, was rather generic: "Vorbereitung eines hochverräterischen Unternehmens" (Preparing to commit high treason). Hora's name appears in the Mauthausen database, https://www.mauthausen-memorial.org/ (accessed Jul. 25, 2017). See also Vašek & Štěpánek 2002, 147; http://encyklopedie.brna.cz/home-mmb/?acc=profil_osobnosti&load=876 (accessed Mar. 4, 2017).

[186] See *Jahresbericht des Öffentlichen Jüdischen Privatreformrealgymnasiums in Brünn* 1932, 13; and *Adreßbuch von Groß-Brünn* 1932, 94. For examples of his lectures, see "Vortragabend der Mizo", *Nikolsburger Wochenschrift*, Oct. 23, 1931, 5; *Volksfreund*, Sep. 20, 1933, 6. The topic of one of his courses was "Die sexuelle Frage und ihre Auswirkungen im täglichen Leben" (The Sexual Question and Its Implications in Daily Life). See *Volksfreund*, Jan. 21, 1933, 6. For one of the courses he taught at the adult education center, see *Licht ins Volk!*, Jg. 8, Heft n° 2, 1935/1936, 11.

[187] For his move to Prague, see the resident registration card in AMB, Brno, fonds Z 1. His name does not figure in the www.holocaust.cz database, but can be found in Kárný et al. 1995, 861.

[188] For his resistance activity, see Kopečný 2006, 233. For more information on Zapletal, see http://encyklopedie.brna.cz/home-mmb/?acc=profil_osobnosti&load=5368 (accessed Dec. 14, 2014). His wife, Marie Blažková (1908–2003), was also a doctor. The couple had two children, Vera (1942–d.) and Vladimír (1944–d.).

office (Zemský úřad Brno) after the war.[188] Jan Kajš (1875–1955) was in charge of the typography of the WLSR Brno conference's announcement brochure, printed the second preliminary conference leaflet, and, since he was active in the Brno Esperanto Association, may have also been responsible for translations into Esperanto for the conference.[189] In 1943, he was checked by the German Kriminalpolizei for unknown reasons but survived the war.[190] Even though, strictly speaking, he was not a member of the preparatory committee, Hugo Iltis was clearly a key figure in preparing the Brno conference, and also in its operation. In May 1938, he resigned as the leader of the adult education center.[191] Iltis fled with his wife Anna (1900–1987) and their two sons Hugh (1925–2016) and Fred (1923–2008) to the USA, shortly before the Germans completed the invasion of Czechoslovakia in March 1939. Hugo Iltis and his family departed from Cherbourg in France, arriving in New York on January 20, 1939.[192] One of Iltis' sons, Hugh Iltis, a professor of botany at the University of Wisconsin-Madison, wrote to me that his father was once on the point of killing himself because of the political circumstances, but his wife stopped him.[193]

HIRSCHFELD GOES TO ZÜRICH

After his initial stay in Austria, and his trip through Czechoslovakia, Hirschfeld went to Switzerland, where he would stay for around seven and a half months, from autumn 1932 to mid-May 1933. In *Testament: Heft II*, Hirschfeld wrote that he arrived in Zürich on October 1, 1932,[194] and that he was still in Zürich in December 1932.[195] From January until the middle of May 1933, Hirschfeld and Li Shiu Tong stayed in Ascona-Moscia.[196] Very little is known about this "Swiss period", other than that Hirschfeld stayed with his Chinese lover in Zürich and Ascona.[197] Due to the cold, and a lack of adequate medical assistance, Hirschfeld found the winter months in Zürich unpleasant.[198] However, while there, as Beat Frischknecht has suggested, Hirschfeld made use of the excellent library of the museum association (*Museumgesellschaft*),

[189] Kajš was the treasurer of the Brno Esperanto Association, founded in 1901. Kajš' wife, Adéla Boroňová (1878–?), was also active in the association. See https://encyklopedie.brna.cz/home-mmb/?acc=profil_udalosti&load=332 (accessed May 12, 2020). In the 1930s, Kajš published *Cosmoglotta*, a magazine devoted to an artificial language called Occidental (later renamed Interlingue), as well as several manuals on the language. Jan Kajš is mentioned in the section "Buch- und Steindruckereien. Lithographischen Anstalten", *Adreßbuch von Groß-Brünn* 1932, 558.

[190] AMB, Brno, fonds Z 1, resident registration card Jan Kajš. Kajš also published two books by the well-known Brno philosophy professor Josef Tvrdý (1877–1942), *Filosofie náboženství* (1921) and *Vývoj filosofického myšlení evropského* (1923). Tvrdý was an important resistance figure in Brno. In addition, Kajš published the (illegal?) poetry chapbook *České martyrium* (1938–42) by Alois Vojkůvka. See Vojkůvka 1942.

[191] See "Prof. Dr. Hugo Iltis, Leiter der Masaryk-Volkshochschule, 1921–1938", *Licht ins Volk!*, Jg. 11, Heft n° 1, 1938/1939, 1–3.

[192] See Ancestry.com, New York, Passenger and Crew Lists (including Castle Garden and Ellis Island), 1820–1957.

[193] See email (dated Jan. 20, 2012) from Hugh Iltis to the author. As a US soldier, Hugh Iltis, who spoke German, assisted in the interrogation of Himmler. See the obituary (dated Dec. 30, 2016) "Hugh Iltis, UW's [University of Wisconsin-Madison's] 'battling botanist', dies at 91", written by David Tenenbaum.

[194] Hirschfeld & Dose 2013, f. 65/142; Hirschfeld & Dose 2013, f. 64/140. Both show Hirschfeld was certainly in Zürich by October 28, 1932. The *Neues Wiener Journal* reported that Hirschfeld was staying in the Hotel Imperial at the beginning of October 1932 (*Neues Wiener Journal*, Oct. 2, 1932, 21).

[195] See, for example, "Kommunistische Wühlarbeit" (Communist Spadework), *Neue Zürcher Nachrichten*, night edition, Dec. 10, 1932, 1. Hirschfeld later wrote that he spent almost four months in the wet, fog and cold of Zürich in the winter of 1932–33, but it was rather three and a half months (Hirschfeld & Dose 2013, f. 73/158).

[196] See Hirschfeld & Dose 2013, f. 70/152. Hirschfeld gives January 14, 1934, as the date of his entry into Ascona.

[197] We need to wait for the publication of Beat Frischknecht's work, "Hirschfeld und die Schweiz" (Hirschfeld and Switzerland). Some fragments were published in Frischknecht 2009.

[198] Hirschfeld & Dose 2013, f. 65/142 and f. 73/158. The *Freundschafts-Banner* briefly announced that "Dr. Magnus Hirschfeld, soll sich schwer erkrankt in Zürich aufhalten" (Dr. Magnus Hirschfeld is said to be seriously ill in Zurich) (*Freundschafts-Banner*, Oct. 29, 1932, 3).

very popular with other German exiles.[199] Hirschfeld also worked on two book projects: the book about his world trip and his *Racism* book. The latter would only be published in English in 1938, three years after Hirschfeld's death. Despite the winter cold and his precarious health, on December 12, 1932, Hirschfeld managed to lecture in Bern's Hotel National on "The Right and Wrong Paths of Love" (*Wege und Irrwege der Liebe*).[200]

The five months he spent in Ascona were likely a more pleasant experience than the winter in Zürich. The Hirschfeld guestbook contains a picture of Hirschfeld and Li Shiu Tong posing on the sunny and scenic balcony of the villa where they were staying, bordering Lago Maggiore.[201] Ascona hosted a considerable community of educated and well-to-do exiles from Germany. Since World War I, Ascona had been a haven for pacifists and social reformers, who gathered mainly in the Monte Verità neigborhood.[202] In *Testament: Heft II*, Hirschfeld noted that exiles continued to arrive in Ascona due to the deteriorating situation in Germany.[203]

GIESE AWAY TOO LONG FROM THE INSTITUTE

But where was Giese when Hirschfeld was spending his time in Austria, Switzerland and Czechoslovakia? Much less is known. We saw that Giese traveled to Greece to meet Hirschfeld when he returned from his world trip, in March 1932. But it is not known if Giese returned to Berlin before the end of 1932. A postcard, sent at the end of December 1932 from Zürich to Hirschfeld's Berlin housekeeper, Adelheid Schulz, reveals that Hirschfeld and Giese were together in Zürich.[204] It is possible that Giese and Friedrich Haupstein, the daily manager of the Institute, suddenly went to Zürich to discuss a crisis in the Berlin Institute.[205]

I think it possible that Giese returned first to Berlin at the end of May 1932, shortly before Hirschfeld left Vienna to tour Czechoslovakia for a couple of months. Presumably, Giese went from Berlin to Brno again to attend the WLSR conference in September. Giese was certainly in Brno since, as we have seen, he gave a lecture at the conference. Another postcard, sent by Giese to Adelheid Schulz on September 30, 1932, shows that Giese was with Hirschfeld in Vienna's Fürth Sanatorium, and seems to announce Giese's second return to Berlin.[206] Whatever the dates of Giese's returns to Berlin, the important thing is that, unlike Hirschfeld, Giese did eventually go to Berlin and stood guard at the Institute until the bitter end, May 1933.

[199] Frischknecht 2009, 21. The library still exists today. See http://www.museumsgesellschaft.ch/museumsgesellschaft/geschichte (accessed May 16, 2020).

[200] *Der Freidenker*, Dec. 1, 1932, 183.

[201] Bergemann, Dose, Keilson-Lauritz & Dubout 2019, f. 137/181. The name of the villa at which Hirschfeld and Li Shiu Tong stayed was Casa Werner. For a likely explanation of the name of the house, based on the probable owner of the house, Hilde Werner, see Hirschfeld & Dose 2013, f. 86/184 n. 486.

[202] See https://www.monteverita.org/en/monteverita/history (accessed May 18, 2020). In Ascona, Hirschfeld explicitly added the name of the neigborhood when writing in *Testament: Heft II*. See, for example, Hirschfeld & Dose 2013, f. 70/152.

[203] Hirschfeld & Dose 2013, f. 77/166.

[204] Hirschfeld & Dose 2013, f. 70/152 n. 411 (for a mention of this postcard to Adelheid Schulz).

[205] Hirschfeld & Dose 2013, f. 70/152.

[206] The postcard is in Archiv MHG, Berlin, fonds Adelheid Schulz. It is reproduced in Hirschfeld & Dose 2013, f. 66/144. I am not convinced that the handwritten date (November 30, 1932) added to the postcard, which Dose accepts as the date the postcard was written, is correct. It seems unlikely that a card mailed on September 30, 1932 (postal stamp on the postcard), would not arrive in the Institute until November 30, 1932. Further, the handwriting of the added date is different from Giese's. Finally, I think that November 30, 1932, cannot be the date that the card was written since Hirschfeld wrote that he went to Zürich on October 1, 1932. See Hirschfeld & Dose 2013, f. 65/142. Herzer seems more certain about Giese's multiple returns to Berlin (and their timing) in 1932 (Herzer 2017, 371).

[207] Hirschfeld & Dose 2013, f. 73/158.

[208] See Hirschfeld & Dose 2013, f. 73/158 n. 414; Hirschfeld & Dose 2013, f. 75/162.

[209] Hirschfeld & Dose 2013, f. 70/152, f. 73/158 n. 414, f. 75/162. In 1924, the Institute was legally linked to the Magnus-Hirschfeld-Stiftung, which became an *öffentliche gemeinnützige Stiftung* (public non-profit foundation). See Hirschfeld 1929, 131. For a history

As time went on, the political situation in Germany worsened. Within the Institute, power relations were shifting. There were fears that Nazi elements might try to infiltrate the Institute, or were already active inside. In mid-March 1933, Hirschfeld wondered whether a Nazi flag possibly adorned his Institute.[207] The Institute was experiencing financial problems.[208] The Magnus-Hirschfeld-Stiftung had to sack some of the staff.[209] In addition, one of Hirschfeld's long-time collaborators at the Institute, Dr. Bernhard Schapiro, planned to sue Hirschfeld for the revenue from the Titus Pearls.[210] Hirschfeld also lost confidence in another of his collaborators, Friedrich Hauptstein.[211] Furthermore, Max Hodann and Kurt Hiller, two of Hirschfeld's former sexual emancipaton colleagues, were arrested in Germany in the first months of 1933.[212] Hirschfeld, who suffered from poor health after his world trip, lived with the fear that every day could be his last. He almost constantly rewrote his will.[213] This led him to the conclusion that, in the end, the only person he could really trust and the one who should continue his life's work, was Karl Giese.[214]

All this raises the question of whether, in hindsight, embarking on a world tour in 1930 had been a good decision. That trip clearly did not solve the problems in the Institute, problems Hirschfeld seemed to have been running away from. That Giese had also been away from the Institute on and off in 1932 likely did not help matters either.[215] We have seen that Giese was the Head of Collections (*Archivleiter*) at the Institute, but had most likely delegated this task to someone else when he left the Institute, in March 1932, to meet Hirschfeld in Athens. It is possible that Giese entrusted guardianship of the library to Arthur Röser (1879–1945). However, Röser was an ambiguous figure who likely sided with the Nazis.[216] It is possible that Giese lost access to the library on one of his returns from abroad in 1932. Perhaps Röser simply refused to return the keys to the library.[217]

and detailed analysis of the Magnus-Hirschfeld-Stiftung, including its postwar fate, and the attempts by the Berlin MHG and the Berlin Bundesstiftung Magnus Hirschfeld, among others, to fulfill the goals stipulated by Hirschfeld's foundation, see Dose 2015; Dose & Herrn 2005. Dose contains some indirect references to the Gestapo's termination of the foundation in November 1933, as well as their confiscation of its property to benefit the Prussian state (Dose 2015, 75–76, 78–79, 85). See also Eichhorn, Ngo & Löbbecke 2015, sheet In den Zelten 9A/10. Further information on the subject, and reproductions of many original documents, can be found in Baumgardt 2000. Hirschfeld himself wrote about the "Beschlagnahme meines Vermögens" (confiscation of my assets). See Hirschfeld & Dose 2013, f. 79/170. Karl Giese mentioned this Nazi maneuver in a letter to Norman Haire. See University of Sydney Library, Sydney, Norman Haire collection, 3.21, Karl Geise [*sic*: Giese], Typescripts, 1928–1934, letter (dated May 17, 1933, 1) from Karl Giese to Norman Haire. The letter is reproduced in Hirschfeld & Dose 2013, 221.

210 Hirschfeld & Dose 2013, f. 70/152, f. 71/154.

211 Hirschfeld & Dose 2013, f. 75/162; Schulz 2001, 94.

212 Hirschfeld & Dose 2013, f. 73/158; University of Sydney Library, Sydney, Norman Haire collection, 3.20, Magnus Hirschfeld, Typescripts, 1923–1935, letter (dated May 13, 1933, [2]) from Magnus Hirschfeld to Norman Haire and Jonathan Leunbach. Max Hodann was arrested on February 28, 1933; Kurt Hiller was arrested three times in 1933. See Sigusch 2008, 356; Dobler 2016, 21–22.

213 For Hirschfeld rewriting and rethinking his last will, spelling out his views regarding his legacy, see Hirschfeld & Dose 2013, f. 65/142–f. 72/156.

214 Hirschfeld & Dose 2013, f. 75/162.

215 Hirschfeld & Dose 2013, f. 65/142, f. 78/168.

216 Hirschfeld & Dose 2013, f. 18/48 n. 55, 57. Maeder later wrote that Röser "uns schon immer naziverdächtig [*sic*] war" (was always perceived by us as a possible Nazi) (Maeder [1993], 5). Schulz claimed that Röser wanted to be addressed as "Direktor Röser" (Director Röser) (Schulz 2001, 59, 63, 99). See also Wolff 1986, 433–34; Dose & Herrn 2006, 42; and Dose 2021, 23–24.

217 This possibility is indirectly suggested by Maeder [1993], 5. Maeder appears to say that he had a spare library key.

1. *Professor Ferdinand Pečírka, undated photo but presumably ca. 1911.*

2. *Book cover of Homosexuality in the Light of Science (Homosexualita ve světle vědy), by František Jelínek (1924)*

3. *Dr. Josef Weisskopf, photo ca. 1932.*

4. Magnus Hirschfeld, Liu Shiu Tong, and Imrich Matyáš taking a stroll in the Aupark park (currently Janko Kráľ park) in Bratislava (Pressburg), likely August 1932.

5. Li Shiu Tong and Karl Giese posing with a dog in the front garden of the Institute, presumably summer months of 1932.

6. The facade of the Center for Adult Education (Volkshochschule) in Brno, January 15, 1938.

7. Hugo Iltis, leader of the Brno Center for Adult Education (Volkshochschule), 1927.

8. Provincial house III (Zemský dům III, Landhaus III), located in 1 Kounicova (Kaunitzgasse), postmarked July 18, 1933.

9. The marble room (Marmorsaal, mramorový sál) in the basement (souterrain) of the Provincial House III (Landeshaus III, Zemský dům III), ca. 1924-1932.

10. Picture of attendees of the fifth WLSR Brno conference, September 21-26, 1932. Only a few people can be identified. Front row, from left to right: unknown, Jonathan Leunbach, Magnus Hirschfeld, Norman Haire, Karl Giese, Josef Weisskopf, the rest unidentified. Second row, from left to right: unknown, unknown, (blurry women's face), Li Shiu Tong, Felix Abraham, unknown (man standing up), possibly Otto Schütz, the rest unidentified. Karl Fein is presumably present as well but we cannot identify him.

11. WLSR Brno conference medallion (8,7 cm x 3,5 cm).

12. Magnus Hirschfeld wearing the WLSR Brno conference medallion, September 20-26, 1932.

13. "Radio broadcast session with some WLSR conference lecturers" (Mezinárodní sexuologický kongres v Brně zasedá před mikrofonem). From left to right: Norman Haire, possibly Jan Bělehradek, unknown, Josef Weisskopf, unknown, Jonathan Leunbach, Li Shiu Tong, Hugo Iltis, September 20-26, 1932.

14. Auditorium of the Anatomy Institute of the Medical faculty of Masaryk university (the building with the Greek-style tympanum just behind the lower corner building) at 73 Údolní (Talgasse), postmarked October 3, 1929.

15. Brno WLSR 1932 conference attendees pay a visit to the Mendel monument. The man on the right with hat, cane and glasses (looking at the photographer) is Hugo Iltis. The tall man with moustache to his left is Jonathan Leunbach. On the far left one sees, from left to right, unknown (with cane), Norman Haire (with glasses), Berty Albrecht (with white shoes) and Jan Bělehrádek (with moustache), dated September 21, 1932.

16. Mendelplatz (Mendlovo náměstí) in Brno. The small white sculpture on the right is the Gregor Mendel monument. The photo was taken from the bell tower of the Basilica of the Assumption of Our Lady (Bazilika Nanebevzetí Panny Marie), linked to the Augustinian monastery (where Mendel lived and worked). Postmarked April 27, 1931.

17. Swimming pool in the Brno city district Zábrdovice/Obrowitz (Městské lázně v Zábrdovicích, Städtisches Bad in Obrowitz), postmarked May 28, 1935.

18. The Mahen city theatre in Brno, postmarked August 10, 1931.

19. The modernist Sokol Stadion cinema, postmarked September 23, 1936.

4. The May 1933 Looting of the Institute and the Berlin Book Burning

CAMPAIGN AGAINST THE UN-GERMAN SPIRIT

At the very end of January 1933, when Hitler was finally named chancellor by President Hindenburg, everything started to change quickly. Hitler set in motion his National Socialist agenda, which descended like an avalanche. The March 1933 elections – in which the NSDAP gained more than forty percent of the vote – were the last hurdle to Hitler ruling as dictator. The Reichstag fire, which was blamed on the Communists, was an omen of what lay ahead. Soon thereafter, all political opposition was outlawed and Germany became a state led by the Nazi party alone.

On Saturday, May 6, 1933, Hirschfeld's Institute was ransacked by a group of National Socialist students from the Berlin-based German College of Physical Education (Deutschen Hochschule für Leibesübungen).[1] Books, pictures, magazines, and other papers were carried out of the Institute, loaded on a truck, and driven away.[2] The looting of the Institute was not an isolated incident, but part of a broader campaign, the so-called "Action Against the Un-German Spirit" (Aktion wider den undeutschen Geist), launched in mid-April 1933, and intended mainly to "cleanse" (*Säuberung*) from German public lending libraries any books by authors unwanted by National Socialism. In cities that had colleges (*Hochschulorten*), it would be especially easy to recruit the necessary students to carry out the campaign. The entire *Aktion* had been prepared by the umbrella organization (*Dachverband*) named German Student Union (Deutsche Studentenschaft), of which the German College of Physical Education was a member.

The starting point of the broader campaign was the publication of the "Twelve theses against the un-German spirit" (12 Thesen wider den undeutschen Geist), thought out by the Main Office for Press and Propaganda (Hauptamt für Presse und Propaganda) of the German Student Union under the leadership of Hans Karl Leistritz (1909–1994).[3] On the same morning that the Institute was looted, five other shock troups (*Stoßtrupps*) of Nazi students drove twenty-two trucks around Berlin to collect anathematized books from around 700 lending libraries. Using so-called black lists (*Schwarze Listen*), unwanted authors could be identified; however, in most cases the books had already been weeded out by librarians, who had been sent the black lists beforehand. The students only had to pick up the suddenly vilified books.[4]

FIRST LOOTING IN THE MORNING OF MAY 6, 1933

Hirschfeld's Institute had to endure two intrusions on the day it was looted.[5] At 9:30 a.m., a somewhat restrained visit took place, led by a student leader named Herbert

[1] For a history of this school, see Court 2019.
[2] Herrn has written the most informative article on the Institute looting to date (Herrn 2010). The other relevant articles are Treß 2008a and 2008b; Strätz 1968 and (slightly amended) Strätz 1983; Herzer 2009a; and Herbert Wiesner's considerably dense, but pleasant and curiously well-informed article (Wiesner 2003).
[3] Treß 2008a, 80.
[4] Herrn 2010, 117–18. How 600 libraries could have been visited in a single morning by only five companies of students remains inexplicable to me. Two Belgian newspapers noted that the collection of books continued on Monday, May 8, 1933; see, for example, *Het Handelsblad*, May 8, 1933, 3. For another book collecting Nazi actor that morning, the Reichsschundkampfstelle, see Dobler 2020, 149.
[5] Herrn 2010, 137–38.

Guthjahr (1911–1944).[6] Most sources mention around a hundred students of the German College of Physical Education, dressed in white shirts and brown pants, taking part in the looting.[7] A limited number of books, magazines, publications, photographs, and other materials were removed [ill. 1]. Some artifacts were thrown out of a window onto the sidewalk. A small brass band infused some National Socialist spirit into the scene.[8] The brass band, and the groups shouting and cursing, likely explains why Karl Giese, who would later write an (anonymously published) account of the events, curiously called himself an "eye and ear witness" (*Augen- und Ohrenzeuge*) to the looting.[9]

In pictures of the morning looting, at the Institute's side entrance in 3 Beethovenstrasse, one can see the truck of the Berlin moving firm G. Pagel on which the looted materials were loaded.[10] The students stuck a photograph of Hirschfeld they had taken from the Institute on the entrance door.[11] When the operation was finished, around noon, the students formed a military-style "protective" square around the side entrance [ill. 2]. Guthjahr then gave a speech and declared the Institute closed.[12] Legally speaking, Guthjahr had no authority to make such a declaration. Officially, the Institute was closed by the Berlin police director (*Polizeipräsident*) Magnus von Levetzow on June 14, 1933.[13]

When going through the Institute's materials, the looters stuck quite closely to the black list (or lists) they had brought.[14] In his later testimony, Karl Giese noted that a book on Tutankhamun was taken from his personal library, but claimed that, apart from some other materials, only a few hundred books were taken away in the morning.[15] *The New York Times* estimated that around 500 kg of materials were removed in this looting.[16] The rowdy students also vandalized the inside of the building – for

[6] Herbert Guthjahr was the local leader of the Berlin Group No. 10 (Kreis n° X) of the German Student Union (Treß 2008a, 135 n. 88). In newspaper articles, his name was commonly spelled erroneously as Gutjahr. A Dutch newspaper mentioned that Guthjahr was a law student. See *De Courant*, Dec. 12, 1933, 1.

[7] Herrn 2010, 145. It is questionable that there were indeed around one hundred students taking part in the action. If one examines a picture, taken during the looting, one counts around fifty students. The picture is reproduced in Herrn 2010, 133. If the number of 100 students is correct, this would mean that around 50 students were inside the Institute when the photo was taken.

[8] On one picture, reproduced in Herrn 2010, 133, one can indeed see students forming a little trumpet or cupper band (*Blechmusik*) playing music in front of the Institute.

[9] The complete text of Giese's testimony can be found in Herrn 2010, 135–39. For the omnipresent music, see Herrn 2010, 135: "und immer wieder spielte die Musik" (again and again the music played).

[10] Treß 2008a, 111. Curiously, checking the Branchen-Verzeichnis under the categories Möbeltransportgeschäfte, Lagerhausbetriebe, Möbellagerung and Speditionsgeschäfte, I could not find the firm in *Berliner Adreßbuch* 1933. There was no Umzugsbetriebe section. I did find a single mention of a Mrs. Müller, who worked as a secretary for the firm in *Berliner Adreßbuch* 1933, IV, 855. *Berliner Adreßbuch* 1934, II: 364 does mention a certain G. Pagel(s?) in Schöneberg at 58 Tempelhoferweg, under the category Möbeltransportgeschäfte (businesses specializing in moving furniture).

[11] One can see the photograph of Hirschfeld stuck to the entrance door, but it is very tiny in the newspaper picture that appeared in *Berliner Volks-Zeitung*, May 6, 1933, reproduced in Herrn 2010, 153. One can see Hirschfeld's picture (along with another portrait being carried out) a little more clearly on a photo that appeared in the French magazine *Police*, May 21, 1933, 16. One can see the same picture, with added racist drawings, on a picture of the looted materials taken in the Oranienburger Straße student house. See Herrn 2010, 146, Abbildung n° 7. The same portrait was later hung on the truck that took the books to the Opernplatz on May 10, 1933 to be burned (Herrn 2010, 155; and Herrn 2008c: card Die mediale Inszenierung der Institutsplünderung). An original copy of this picture, personally signed by Hirschfeld in 1910, can be found in the Staatsbibliothek Berlin, Handschriftenabteilung. A reproduction of this can be found in Sternweiler & Hannesen 1997, 36. The picture is also used on the cover of the periodical of the Magnus-Hirschfeld-Gesellschaft in Berlin, the *Mitteilungen der Magnus-Hirschfeld-Gesellschaft*.

[12] Herrn 2010, 145, 151.

[13] Herrn 2022, 478; Dose 2015, 34–35.

[14] This was also mentioned in the main testimony of the looting, written by Giese. See Herrn 2010, 137.

[15] Herrn 2010, 137.

[16] *New York Times*, May 7, 1933, 3, qtd. in Herzer 2009, 158: "about half a ton of books, pamphlets, photographs, charts and lantern slides".

[17] *Berliner Börsen-Zeitung*, May 6, 1933, 11, qtd. in

example, by throwing ink on the carpets and playing soccer with picture frames they had taken from the walls.

The morning visit appears to have been well-planned. It was to this event that the press was invited. In newspapers across Germany and Europe, the action had been announced beforehand. It was presented as the official start of a more general campaign to "cleanse" Berlin lending libraries and remove the condemned authors.[17] All subsequent press coverage was based exclusively on this first, more restrained visit.[18] The newspapers reported that several people were looking on as the looting happened.

SECOND LOOTING IN THE AFTERNOON ON MAY 6, 1933

The second looting, which was not expected at the Institute, started at 3 p.m. While the morning action had seemed somewhat "moderate", the afternoon visit was a no-holds-barred action.[19] This looting was carried out by veterinary college students and a student leader named Fritz Witt (?–?). The veterinary students were members of a different student umbrella organization, the National Socialist Student Union of Germany (Nationalsozialistischen Studentenbund Deutschland).[20] The afternoon intrusion may have been planned somewhat ad hoc.[21] It is not known how the afternoon students went about their looting or if they also used black lists, but this seems not to have been the case. Giese's testimony claims that works by several foreign literary authors and many sexology works were taken away in the afternoon. Curiously, his testimony also notes that the afternoon students seem to have been well-versed about the famous sexology authors they were after.[22]

When, on May 10, a Dutch journalist went to see the Institute loot deposited in the student house (*Studentenheim, Studentenhaus*) at 18 Oranienburger Straße, he spoke with a certain student named Gehlhar [ill. 3]. Gehlhar was the leader of the battle committee of the banned books campaign of the Berlin-based Kreis X (group 10) of the German Student Union.[23] If we are to believe his own statement, he was the spiritual leader of the Berlin book-burning campaign: "In one of the rooms I meet Mr. Gehlar [*sic*], a young and ardent National Socialist, who is the editor of a party paper somewhere in East Prussia, and who claims to be the spiritual father of this auto-da-fé. Already as a young student, he tells me, he agitated and fought against the filth in our patriotic literature, which was poisoning our population. 'Come with me and judge for yourself'. He led me into a room crammed with books from Magnus Hirschfeld's library. We climbed [*sic*] on a table and opened some of the books lying around. 'Does this have anything to do with science?', asks my guide".[24] The young

Herzer 2009, 157: "Der Führer des Kreises 10 der Deutschen Studentenschaft, Gutjahr [*sic*], richtete an seine Kommilitonen dann eine kurze Ansprache, in der er darauf hinwies, daß die Aktion der Studenten mit einer Säuberung der Bibliothek der Magnus-Hirschfeld-Stiftung begonnen habe" (The leader of Group No. 10 of the German Student Union, Gutjahr [*sic*], then briefly addressed his fellow students, pointing out that the students' action had begun with a purge of the Magnus Hirschfeld foundation library). See also Herrn 2010, 137, 142–45 and 164 n. 73.

[18] Herrn 2010, 147, 151–52.

[19] Herrn 2010, 145.

[20] See Herrn 2010, 144 and Raith 2006 for more information on this student organisation.

[21] For the (late) record of the second looting, written by Fritz Witt himself, see Herrn 2010, 144 n. 92, 147; Treß 2008a, 113–14.

[22] Herrn 2010, 138 and Schulz 2001, 112–13.

[23] In German, this becomes *Geschäftsführer der "Kampfausschusses wider den undeutschen Geist" aus dem Kreis X, Berlin-Brandenburg der Deutsche Studentenschaft*. Gehlhar's first name is not known. See Treß 2008a, 79, 128, 134–35 n. 85. His last name is spelled in different ways: Gelhar, Gehlar, Geelhar. The correct form is likely Gehlhar. See Herrn 2010, 166 n. 98.

[24] De Courant, May 12, 1933, 1: "In een van de vertrekken maak ik kennis met den heer Gehlar [*sic*], een jong en vurig nationaal-socialist, die de redactie voert van een partijblad ergens in Oost-Pruisen, en die er zich op beroept, de geestelijke vader te zijn van dit auto-da-fe. Reeds als jong student, vertelt hij mij, heb ik geageerd en gestreden tegen het vuil in onze vaderlandsche litteratuur, dat onze bevolking vergiftigde. 'Komt U maar eens mede en oordeelt u zelf'. Hij leidde mij naar een kamer, welke volge-

man also seemed to have known many of the names associated with sexology: "'On the list of gentlemen, related to the Institute for Sexual Research, the name of our compatriot [Theodoor] v.[an] d.[e] Velde also appears', my leader [Gehlhar] declares in a somewhat calmer tone, 'and also the name of count [von] Arco, Dr. Farel [*sic*: August Forel] and Karl Kautsky". The "count [von] Arco" mentioned by Gehlhar was most likely the radio wave engineer Georg Graf von Arco (1869–1940). He was a pacifist and, like Hirschfeld, a member (and also briefly president) of the German Monist League (Deutscher Monistenbund). This seems to reveal Gehlhar's intimate knowledge of personalities and their networks.[25] Was Gehlhar the main figure behind the more destructive afternoon looting? It would appear not, at first sight, since he was a member of the German Student Union, the organization to which the more moderate morning looters belonged. But he is clearly a character – until now known by his last name only – in need of greater scrutiny.[26]

The materials were carried out in baskets and were loaded onto one or perhaps two trucks.[27] Hirschfeld's private library and personal archive were looted as well.[28] The leader of the afternoon looting afterwards noted that 750 kg of materials were taken out of the Institute's cellar.[29] Giese's testimony claimed that around 10,000 books (*Bände*) were taken out of the Institute that afternoon.[30] There are some pictures of the materials looted, randomly thrown onto two piles in the student house of the Friedrich-Wilhelms-Universität at 18 Oranienburger Straße. In one, some materials were immediately dropped in a pile on the left side of the main entrance of the student house, but one cannot tell if this pile is from the first or the second looting.[31]

propt is met boeken uit de bibliotheek van Magnus Hirschfeld. Wij klimmen [*sic*] op een tafel en slaan enkele der rond om ons liggende boeken open. „Heeft dat nog iets met wetenschap te maken?" vraagt mijn begeleider".

[25] De Courant, May 12, 1933, 1: "'Op de lijst van heeren, welke met het 'Institut für sexuelle Forschung' in relatie hebben gestaan, komt ook de naam voor van onzen landgenoot [Theodoor] v.[an] d.[e] Velde', verklaart mijn leider [Gehlhar] op eenigszins kalmer toon, 'en ook de naam van graaf [von] Arco, dr. Farel [*sic*: August Forel] en Karl Kautsky".

[26] Armed with this new information from a Dutch newspaper (Gehlhar was a writer for a local NSDAP periodical in Ostpreußen [East Prussia, now Poland]), I tried in vain to identify the man. I inquired with the Universitätsarchiv der Humboldt-Universität zu Berlin but they could not find a student with that name, born in Ostpreußen, in their indexes for the years 1928–33; see the email (dated Jan. 18, 2021) from Heather Forster (Universitätsarchiv der Humboldt-Universität zu Berlin) to the author. An inquiry was also sent on January 25, 2021 to the Carl und Liselott Diem-Archiv (Köln), since they hold the archives of the Berlin Deutsche Hochschule für Leibesübungen. I also inquired with Christian Rohrer, the main authority on the history of National Socialism in Ostpreußen. See Rohrer 2006. However, despite the very valuable research tips he generously shared with me, the name was not familiar to him, nor could it be found in his database. See the email (dated Jan. 4, 2021) from Christian Rohrer to the author. I also had a look at the NSDAP membership index cards (*NSDAP-Mitgliederkartei*) in the Bundesarchiv in Berlin-Lichterfelde, looking specifically for men born around 1910 in East Prussia. They were not few in number, which shows that the name was not uncommon in East Prussia. But I also noticed that the name could often be spelled as Gehlhaar. The next step would seem to be checking these local East Prussian NSDAP publications for this last name.

[27] Cf. Herrn 2010, 138 for Giese's testimony ("zwei grosse Lastwagen voll" [two large truckfuls]); and Herrn 2010, 144, which quotes from a July 1933 letter by Fritz Witt where only one truck (*Lastwagen*) is mentioned, lent to them by the father of a fellow student (*Kommilitonen*). A last possibility, of course, is that one truck took two trips, and returned from the student house at 18 Oranienburger Straße to pick up the second load.

[28] Compare Herrn 2010, 141, 165 n. 87.

[29] There was mention of "15 Zentnern" of materials. One Zentner is 50 kilograms. See Treß 2008a, 114; Herrn 2010, 144.

[30] Herrn 2010, 139.

[31] The picture is reproduced in Treß 2008a, 114. Cf. the picture in Herrn 2010, 146. Another picture (Treß 2008, 113) shows a pile of other materials, but it is unclear where in the building this pile was located. The building where the student house was located in 1933 still stands today; however, an extra floor has been added. From shortly after the war until 2004, the building housed the Institut für Psychologie. The building is now the property of the Humboldt-Universität zu Berlin. Before it became a university student house, the building housed a *Herrenklub* (gentlemen's club) named Ressource. See *De Courant*, May 12, 1933, 1.

[32] Günter Maeder, the notoriously unreliable witness (see p. 23, n. 30), for example, stated that Giese

Giese was most likely in the Institute when it was looted but it is unclear if he was present during both sessions.[32] Hirschfeld's housekeeper, Adelheid Schulz, said that during the looting (but which one?)[33] some or most of the Institute staff were under guard or temporarily locked in the Institute's Ernst Haeckel Hall (Ernst-Haeckel-Saal).[34] "The [others] were [in] the Ernst Haeckel Hall, that's the building next door, there – I still remember Karl Giese soon laughing himself to death, how he looked through an upper window from the door there [...]".[35] Toni Mertens, one of Giese's sisters, and her husband Max Mertens looked on from the nearby Tiergarten park and could see Adelheid Schulz sitting in Hirschfeld's work room.[36] She was the only staff member who was not locked up and the Mertens couple later praised her for her courage. Schulz also said later that she had confronted some of the students about the "utility" of their actions, especially when they vandalized some medical equipment. The valuable books that the students focused on seemed less important to her. After the looting, some pictures were taken inside the Institute, showing the dire state of some of the rooms. Adelheid Schulz kept some of these photographs and eventually gave them to the Magnus-Hirschfeld-Gesellschaft in Berlin.[37]

BERLIN BOOK BURNING ON MAY 10, 1933

Four days after the two lootings, on Wednesday, May 10, just before midnight, a considerable amount of materials taken from the Institute's collections was thrown on a bonfire in the Opernplatz (now Bebelplatz), together with many other books deemed un-German from Berlin lending libraries.[38] Trucks loaded with books along with a procession of students, accompanied by brass bands and flanked by torch bearers, made their way in the pouring rain from the student house in Oranienburger

was not in the Institute the day it was looted because he had an appointment. See Maeder [1993], 4.

33 Curiously, in the interviews that she gave, Schulz never mentioned that there had been two looting sessions.

34 On a few occasions in her testimony, Schulz stated that she was the only one left in the Institute when it was being looted (Schulz 2001, 111, 113–14; repeated by Schulz in Baumgardt 2003, 7). She also suggested that some Institute staff members remained in their rooms out of fear. Schulz 2001, 113–14: "Ich weiß nur, daß sie alle verschwunden waren, weil sie alle ein bißchen ängstlich waren. [...] Die sind in ihrem Kabuff geblieben, waren ja sowieso ein bißchen scheu, nich. Was da vorgegangen ist, ob sie da noch ne Unterredung mit den Nazis da gehabt haben, weiß ich nicht. Ich war ja nur oben in den Räumen, die erste Etage und dann auch die Arbeitsräume" (I only know that they all disappeared because they were all a bit scared. [...] They stayed in their cubbyholes, they were a bit scared, of course. What went on there, if they had another conversation with the Nazis, I don't know. I was only upstairs in the rooms, the first floor and then also the workrooms). The seeming contradiction in her testimony can perhaps be explained by the fact that the Institute was constituted of two adjacent buildings. The second main building, which was bought after 1919, was joined to the first corner building by creating passageways between the two. The Ernst-Haeckel-Saal, where at least some of the members were locked up, was located in the second building. Schulz, however, was in the older corner building, where Hirschfeld's own work room was also located. So, possibly, Schulz meant that she was alone in the main building. Schulz was ninety-two years old when she was interviewed in 2001 by members of the Magnus-Hirschfeld-Gesellschaft. Herrn correctly stresses that she suffered from "fragmentary memories" (*bruchstückhaften Erinnerungen*) (Herrn 2010, 141).

35 Schulz 2001, 112: "Die [anderen] waren, [im] Ernst-Haeckel-Saal, das ist das Nebenhaus, da – ich weiß noch, daß Karl Giese sich bald totgelacht hat, wie der da durch ein oberes Fenster von der Tür da geguckt hat".

36 Schulz 2001, 38, 52, 74, 114. Cf. Herrn 2010, 141–42.

37 Adelheid Schulz was a bit unclear on who had taken the pictures showing the state of the Institute after the looting. At first, she said "someone" took those pictures; later on, however, she clearly said that it was Giese or another member of the Institute, Wilhelm Kaufmann. See Schulz 2001, 31, 38. At least some (or all?) of these photos were taken by the Communist Georg (Orje) Heidrich. See Schulz 2001, 71. One of these pictures of the aftermath of the looting is reproduced in Herrn 2010, 143. Schulz also said that Karl Giese's brother-in-law insisted that photos documenting the ravages of the looting inside the Institute would be made. This brother-in-law was most likely Max Mertens. Compare Herrn 2008c: card Die vandalisierte Institutsbibliothek.

38 Treß 2008a, 117–25 gives the most extensive chronological account of what exactly happened that night.

Straße to the Opernplatz, passing through the famous Brandenburger gate.[39] It was raining so hard that the fire brigade had to use gasoline to start and then keep the fire going.[40] It would appear that three trucks were mainly loaded with books.[41] A seventy-year-old widow named Pagel, who procured at least one of the trucks that collected loot from the Institute on May 6, told a Dutch journalist with evident satisfaction that she had lent five trucks from Pagel, her transport company, to carry the books from the student house to the Opernplatz [ill. 4].[42]

When the procession arrived at the Opernplatz, the students threw their torches on the pyre.[43] Adelheid Schulz went to see the spectacle with her boyfriend Hans and cried.[44] Most accounts report that around 20,000 books were thrown on the fire that night.[45] The books were solemnly consigned to the flames as nine so-called fire oaths (*Feuersprüche*) were recited by students. They held the books of the authors they were cursing in their hands, further conjuring the whole enactment.[46] As concerns books on sexuality, two names were identified by the speakers. In one fire oath, the speaker acted against the "soul-crushing overestimation of sexuality", referring to books by Freud that were then thrown on the burning pile.[47] Hirschfeld's name appeared in its own fire oath (*Feuerspruch*), but it remains somewhat uncertain if it was actually spoken or not: "We do not want the demoralization of our people; therefore burn, Magnus Hirschfeld!"[48] When all the oaths had been spoken, a bust of Hirschfeld, taken from the Institute, was ostentatiously thrown on the bonfire by two physical education teachers [ill. 5].[49] Then Goebbels spoke: "The era of extreme Jewish intellectualism is now at an end", he claimed. The newsreel of his speech is well known.[50] "The celebration was concluded with choral singing."[51]

That treasure hunters, the following morning, managed to salvage some poems Hirschfeld wrote as a student in Strasbourg from the smouldering remains on the Opernplatz, indicates that Hirschfeld's private papers had also been looted from his work room and ended up on the pyre.[52] Adelheid Schulz said that all the books from the wall of Hirschfeld's working room had been taken by the looting students.[53] There

[39] See the report in *Die Jüdische Welt: Unparteiisches Weltorgan für die Gesamtinteressen des Judentums*, Jg. 1, n° 2, June 2, 1933, 8.

[40] Treß 2008a, 119.

[41] *Le Populaire*, May 12, 1933, 3. A Dutch journalist confirmed that he had seen a third, fully loaded truck leaving from the student house in the Oranienburger Strasse for the Opernplatz. See *De Courant*, May 12, 1933, 21.

[42] *De Courant*, May 12, 1933, 2. The lady also said she lived in Berlin-Neukölln which had, in her opinion, too many Communists who harrassed her until Hitler took over. Berlin Neukölln was indeed, together with Berlin Wedding, one of the two neighborhoods involved in the 1929 Blutmai revolt. In *Berliner Adreßbuch* 1933, I: 1962, I found a Maria Pagel, retired (*Pensionärin*), living in Berlin-Neukölln at 14 Ulsterstraße, but it is not certain that this is the same lady. One can indeed see "Neukölln" on the side door of the truck parked in front of the Institute during the morning looting. See the photo in Dose 2005a, 92.

[43] *Die Jüdische Welt*, Jg. 1, n° 2, June 2, 1933, 9.

[44] Baumgardt 2013, 9.

[45] See, for example, *Grazer Tagblatt*, evening edition, May 12, 1933, 1. The Dutch newspaper *De Courant* reported that the first books were thrown on the fire at 11:20 p.m. (*De Courant*, May 12, 1933, 1).

[46] Treß 2008a, 119. One can, with some difficulty, hear the young voices screaming on https://www.dhm.de/lemo/kapitel/ns-regime/etablierung-der-ns-herrschaft/buecherverbrennung.html (accessed Nov. 27, 2021). The first voice might well belong to Herbert Guthjahr.

[47] Walberer 1983, 115: "seelenzerfasernde Überschätzung des Trieblebens". Cf. Herrn 2010, 158, 168 n. 136.

[48] "Wir wollen keine Entsittlichung des Volkes, darum brenne, Magnus Hirschfeld!" *Die Jüdische Welt* (Jg. 1, n° 2, June 2, 1933, 8) claims that this was actually spoken aloud. See also Herrn 2008c: card Der Hirschfeld gewidmete Feuerspruch, which gives *Deutsche Illustrierte*, May 16, 1933, as the source for the *Feuersprüche*. Herrn's card contains another *Feuerspruch* addressed to Emil Ludwig (Cohn) that is not in the list of nine *Feuersprüche* in Walberer 1983, 115, which itself cites Wulf 1963, 45–46. A Dutch journalist also claimed that there were only nine *Feuersprüche* (*De Courant*, May 12, 1933, 1). The same article appeared in *De Telegraaf*, May 11, 1933, 1–2.

[49] Herrn 2010, 145–47.

[50] "Die Zeit des überspitzten jüdischen Intellektualismus ist zu Ende".

[51] *Die Jüdische Welt*, Jg. 1, n° 2, June 2, 1933, 9: "Mit Chorgesang wurde die Feier abgeschlossen".

[52] See Keilson-Lauritz & Dose 2009, where the five saved handwritten pages are reproduced, and also Dose & Keilson-Lauritz 2010. These few pages were saved by Hans Graeber, who gave them to the writer

are also a few indications that some of the books confiscated from Berlin lending libraries were not burned but sold as old paper. It is not known if some portion of the Institute materials shared the same fate.[54]

The book burning in Berlin was definitely not the only one to take place in Germany on May 10, 1933. Nineteen other burnings of unwanted books were staged in other German cities where colleges had welcomed the German Student Union.[55] But the Berlin book burning was certainly the one most publicized at the time, even internationally.[56] The whole event had in fact been consciously orchestrated as a media event. Because of this media character, the Berlin auto-da-fé became, from the very day it took place, one of the key symbolic events in the rise to power of National Socialism in Germany.[57] The ostentatious burning of books signaled that National Socialism would not tolerate the European ideal of free speech and expression. The May 1933 event is now often seen as a key indication of what was soon to follow. A line from the 1821 play *Almansor* by Heinrich Heine – who was himself on the Nazis' list of unwanted authors – is frequently quoted in reference to this event, becoming part of German consciousness regarding book burnings in the Nazi period: "This was only a prelude: where they burn books, they will in the end also burn people".[58] Heinrich Heine's now famous phrase referred to the burning of the Quran in Spain by Christians after the Reconquista.

Erich Kästner (1899–1974). Graeber collected manuscripts or writers' signatures and, the morning after the book burning, went to see if he could find any treasures in the ashes. The Hirschfeld pages were apparently ripped from a book or binder and gathered, equally or unequally, by treasure hunters that morning. On the very night of the fire, people fished out remnants from the smouldering ashes, which were then sold to interested parties in the days that followed. See Treß 2008a, 125; Herzer 2009a, 158.

53 Schulz 2010, 112–13.

54 A Dutch reporter wrote that many books were in fact sold as old paper and that the companies purchasing them offered trucks to carry the books that were going to be burned in the Opernplatz. See *De Gooi- en Eemlander*, May 16, 1933, 5; *De Tijd*, May 14, 1933, 1. On the other hand, as we have seen, at least five trucks were provided by the widow Pagel. The observation that parts of the loot were sold as old paper "to pay for the torches and the bands", at the rate of 1 German mark for 100 kilograms, can also be found in a *New York Times* article. See Birchall, May 11, 1933, 12. The latter seems to have been the source used in Wiesner 2003, 426–27.

55 There were eleven other book burnings on other days in May 1933 (Treß 2008b, 20–21, 25). Separately from the German Student Union, the Hitler Jugend (Hitler Youth) had also made bonfires throughout Germany around the same time (Treß 2008b: 25–26). Treß counted around ninety-four book burnings in total staged throughout Germany in 1933, but without considering who had organized them or why (Treß 2008b, 14).

56 The USHMM, Washington, has a traveling (and online) exhibition on the US reaction to the Berlin book burning, *Fighting the Fires of Hate: America and the Nazi Book Burnings*. See https://www.ushmm.org/information/exhibitions/traveling-exhibitions/retired-exhibitions/fighting-the-fires-of-hate (accessed May 14, 2021).

57 Herzer 2009a, 160–61 is right to signal that on May 1 and 2, 1933 (i.e. a few days earlier), much more important mass events were organized by the Nazis, in which, as Herzer also claims, following Walter Benjamin, the Nazis enacted another example of their "Aesthetisierung des Terrors" (aestheticization of terror). Compared to these mass events, the looting of the Institute and the book burning some days later was, Herzer claims, "unbedeutend und marginal" (insignificant and marginal). But the truth is that the Berlin book burning simply cut much deeper into subsequent historical consciousness.

58 "Dies war ein Vorspiel nur, dort, wo man Bücher verbrennt, verbrennt man auch am Ende Menschen". See, for example, Peiffer 2010, 109; Botsch 2010, 191–92; and Wiesner 2003, 422. Treß offers a fine example of this acquired, *unpronounced* part of German cultural consciousness, linking the burning of books in May 1933, the burning down of synagogues, and, later, the incineration (in the crematoria of Auschwitz-Birkenau) of Jewish people murdered in the Holocaust (Treß 2008a, 127). Another good example is the book title *Das war ein Vorspiel nur...* (This Was Only a Prelude...), which quotes just the first part of the Heine line. See Haarmann, Huder & Siebenhaar 1983. It is unclear to me who exactly started referring to Heine but it could have begun in Paris, in 1936, on the third Tag der deutschen Bücherverbrennung (Day of the German Book Burning) (dated May 10, 1936), when the Heinrich-Heine-Preis was created by the Schutzverband Deutscher Schriftsteller, the Freiheitsbibliothek and the Association Internationale des Ecrivains pour la Défense de la Culture. See "Der Heinrich-Heine-Preis. Zum Jahrestag der Bücherverbrennung", *Pariser Tageblatt*, May 10, 1936, 3, accessible online at https://portal.dnb.de/bookviewer/view/1026577888#page/3/mode/1up (accessed May 12, 2020); Schiller 2003, 44.

From the very day it took place, writers and journalists around the world often appealed, in their moral outrage at the book burnings, to humanist or Enlightenment values of free speech and expression that should be guaranteed at all times. Implying: a society that burns books can only be barbaric. One Vienna newspaper condemned the Berlin book burning event as follows: "The improbable happens; in the middle of twentieth-century Europe, in the heart of a city that until recently was considered a symbol of European progress and freedom, as in the times of the worst barbarism and darkness of spirit, works by authors, many recognized as representatives of European culture all over the world, are consigned to the flames. The act judges itself. No words of horror at what is happening can express the magnitude of the German cultural disgrace, the disgrace of the self-emasculation of a people and its self-condemnation to slavery and barbarism!"[59] The choice of the Nazis to reenact, in the twentieth century, the centuries-old ritual of burning books continues to resonate to this day. The public burning of copies of Salman Rushdie's novel *Satanic Verses*, in 1990, showed that the ritual continues to be inspirational as an act of public protest against unwanted books.[60] The epochal May 1933 book burning in Berlin is now commemorated by a beautiful and wonderful artwork by the Israeli artist Micha Ullman (1939–), installed on the Opernplatz (currently Bebelplatz) where the books were burned. The impressive Book Burning Memorial (Denkmal zur Erinnerung an die Bücherverbrennung), installed in 1995, shows a completely white underground space with empty, white book shelves.[61] An explanatory board nearby the artwork also mentions the Heine quote.

THE LOOTING OF THE INSTITUTE WAS A LAST-MINUTE DECISION

In the communication to the press, the looting of the Institute was presented as the start of the Action Against the Un-German Spirit: "At the beginning of the German Student Union's campaign to purge the public libraries, the Institute for sexual science, founded by Prof. Magnus Hirschfeld, was occupied. [...] At the same time, five student shock troops undertook to subject all Berlin public lending libraries to a purge".[62] And yet, the decision to add the looting of Hirschfeld's Institute (and the burning on a pyre of materials coming from the Institute) to the Action Against the Un-German Spirit was most likely a last-moment decision, likely suggested to the Nazi students by people higher up in the National Socialist party hierarchy. There are several indications that this was the case. As we have seen, the Action Against

[59] R. O., May 7, 1933, 3: "Das Unwahrscheinliche geschieht; mitten im Europa des 20. Jahrhunderts, im Herzen einer Stadt, die bis vor kurzem noch als ein Symbol europäischen Fortschrittes und europäischer Freiheit galt, werden wie in den Zeiten ärgster Barbarei und Finsternis des Geistes Werke von Autoren, die vielfach als Repräsentanten europäischer Kultur auf der ganzen Welt anerkannt sind, den Flammen übergeben. Die Tat richtet sich selbst. Kein Wort des Entsetzens über das, was geschieht, vermag die Größe der deutschen Kulturschande zu erfassen, die Schande der Selbstentmannung eines Volkes und seiner Selbstverurteilung zu Sklaverei und Barbarei!"

[60] On the long history of the ritual of public book burnings, see, for example, Sauder 2010.

[61] See, for example, Endlich 2010, 371–73, 376; Meschede & Ullman 1999. Some also call the artwork a *Mahnmal* (warning memorial) rather than a *Denkmal* (memorial).

[62] *Schweizerisches Freundschafts-Banner*, May 15, 1933, 4: "Zu Beginn der Aktion der deutschen Studentenschaft zur Säuberung der öffentlichen Büchereien wurde das Institut für Sexualwissenschaft besetzt, das von Prof. Magnus Hirschfeld gegründet worden war. [...] Gleichzeitig setzten sich fünf studentische Stoßtrupps in Bewegung, um sämtliche Volksleihbüchereien in Berlin einer Säuberung zu unterziehen". The Swiss gay magazine *Schweizerisches Freundschafts-Banner*, reporting on the Berlin book burning, cited an unnamed and unidentified (German-language) publication. The *Salzburger Volksblatt*, May 6, 1933, 17 clearly used the same text as a basis for its own short article. The same can be said of the Swiss *Freiburger Nachrichten*, May 8, 1933, 3; *Oberländer Tagblatt*, May 8, 1933, 1; and *Neue Zürcher Nachrichten*, May 8, 1933, 2. Referring to an article (dated May 6, 1933) that appeared earlier in the morning in the *Berliner Lokalanzeiger*, Karl Giese's later written testimony on the looting reiterated the same message that the

the Un-German Spirit was planned by the umbrella organization (*Dachverband*) of the German Student Union in the months before the May book burning. And yet, neither Hirschfeld's name nor his Institute was mentioned in the surviving archival traces of that preparatory work.[63] The name of Hirschfeld and his Institute do not show up until the press conference given the day before the actual looting of the Institute.[64]

Raiding Hirschfeld's Institute was simply not in line with the Action's initial goal of weeding out books by forbidden authors from lending libraries in Berlin and throughout Germany. Hirschfeld's Institute was clearly not a lending library, but a specialized one, and yet the Institute library was nevertheless added to the operation at the last minute,something that seriously hampered the initial logic and consistency of the operation.[65] The attempt to present both the removal of unwanted authors from lending libraries and the looting of the Institute as one consistent action resulted in outright contradictions and also subsequent rationalizations in the press releases of the German Student Union. One Vienna newspaper wrote: "The action is directed only against libraries open to the general public. [...] Libraries that serve exclusively scientific purposes will be spared from the action".[66] In a press notice released the day after the looting, an effort was made to counter this contradiction by stating that Hirschfeld's library was accessible to the general public and thus fitted the Action: "The main focus was on the large library, which was open to the public".[67]

SIFTING OF BOOKS

Another message given to the press the day after the looting of the Institute, which can also be linked to this troubling inconsistency, concerned the possible value of some of the books looted from the Hirschfeld Institute. These books were clearly perceived as different from the much more easily replaced copies looted from lending libraries. One newspaper wrote: "The books confiscated from the Institute of Sexual Science are being subjected to close examination by experts, so as not to destroy works which have a high scientific value for medical science".[68] A journalist working for the French newspaper *L'Intransigeant* – a man clearly not insensitive to

Action began with the looting of the Hirschfeld Institute. See Herrn 2010, 135.

[63] Herrn 2010, 119, 149; Treß 2008a, 70–80.

[64] Herrn 2010, 148. See, for example, the article "Der Scheiterhaufen der Literatur: Das Berliner Autodafé findet am 10. Mai statt" (The Pyre of Literature: The Berlin Auto-da-fé will take place on May 10) in the Austrian newspaper *Die Stunde*, May 7, 1933, 1: "Außerdem wird sich eine Gruppe des Instituts für Leibesübungen der Berliner Universität mit einem Propagandaauto nach dem Magnus Hirschfeld-Institut begeben, um dieses offiziell zu schließen" (In addition, a group from the Institute for Physical Education of Berlin University will go to the Magnus Hirschfeld Institute with a propaganda car in order to officially close it).

[65] Herrn 2010, 118 agrees that, in this regard, the Institute was a true exception. When writing in 1927 about the Institute library collection, Karl Giese stressed that the books were collected for "purely scientific purposes". This does not mean that the library was accessible to scientists only. The science argument was most likely part of justification maneuvers regarding the more risqué parts of the collection. See Giese 1927, 132. Rainer Herrn stresses that the library was accessible to anyone interested, and this was explicitly communicated by the library in 1926. See Herrn 2008c: card Sammlungen und Bibliothek des Instituts. That being said, it was definitely not a lending library in the strict sense. For more information on the situation of the Berlin lending libraries, see Rürup 1999, 32.

[66] *Wiener Allgemeine Zeitung*, May 7, 1933, 3: "Die Aktion richtet sich nur gegen die der breiten Oeffentlichleit zugänglichen Büchereien. [...] Büchereien, die ausschließlich wissenschaftlichen Zwecken dienen, werden von der Aktion verschont bleiben". An almost identical rendering can be found in the *Berliner Volks-Zeitung*, May 6, 1933 (qtd. in Herrn 2010, 119). The *Salzburger Volksblatt* (May 6, 1933, 17) even made it a little more explicit: "Die Aktion richtet sich selbstverständlich nur gegen die der breiten Öffentlichkeit zugänglichen Büchereien" (The Action is, of course, directed only against libraries open to the general public).

[67] *Berliner Morgenpost*, May 7, 1933; *Germania*, May 7, 1933; qtd. in Herrn 2010, 150: "Das Hauptaugenmerk richtete sich dabei auf die große Bücherei, die dem Publikum zugänglich war". Herrn adds that this maneuvering was necessary so that the campaign would remain consistent (Herrn 2010, 167 n. 110; see also 152).

[68] *Germania*, May 7, 1933, qtd. in Herzer 2001, 233: "Die beschlagnahmten Bücher des Instituts für Sexual-

the destruction of the materials from the Institute, nor to the blondness of German boys – heard the same message from the student leader Herbert Guthjahr when he went to the Studentenhaus where the loot from the Institute had been dropped off: "A few moments before the auto-da-fé, we were able to enter the students' house in the Oranienburgerstrasse, where the impure booty had been gathered. Most of the books had already been loaded onto the trucks that were to carry them to the pyre at the Opernplatz. By an unhoped-for chance, the documentation seized from the 'Sexual Institute' of Dr. Hirschfeld, of wide renown, can still be seen in a large room where it is rather complacently displayed. Mr. Herbert Guthjahr, head of the Berlin student guilds, a very blond boy in a brown uniform who does not trifle with virtue, selects some documents of special interest and of dubious morality for us from the pile. We take a quick look at them to convince ourselves of the utility of their upcoming destruction. 'This has nothing to do with science, of course', says Mr. Guthjahr. 'Besides, to be certain that no useful documents would be lost, we asked two doctors to inventory the stock'. The German revolution, as we already knew, is proceeding methodically and only taking up the traditional revolutionary rites by adding the mark of scientific rationalization proper to our time".[69] Yet why would one want to sort through books that were after all destined to be destroyed by fire, together with the other books picked up from the Berlin lending libraries? All this shows that coupling the removal of unwanted authors from lending libraries with the

wissenschaft werden noch einer genauen Sichtung durch Sachverständige unterzogen, damit nicht Werke vernichtet werden, die für die medizinische Wissenschaft einen hohen wissenschaftlichen Wert besitzen [...]" The newspaper further stated that the same was also done with pictures (*Bilder*) and slides (*Diapositiven*) from the Institute: "Das Bildarchiv des Instituts, in dem Hunderte von Diapositiven lagerten, wurde einer eingehenden Untersuchung unterzogen und alles Undeutsche vernichtet. Ein Teil der Bilder wurde sichergestellt und wird von medizinischen Sachverständigen noch einmal geprüft werden." (The Institute's picture archive, in which hundreds of slides were stored, was subjected to a thorough examination and everything un-German was destroyed. Some of the images were seized and will be re-examined one more time by medical experts.) It remains unclear to what extent the materials that were deemed scientific enough to be sifted out, were effectively safeguarded or if this claim was mainly a soothing or justificatory message destined for the outside world. A two-and-a-half-minute-long 1933 US Paramount newsreel clearly shows (in the surviving thirty-eight second segment) two men in civilian clothes, and presumably some students, in the Berlin student house rather carelessly going through books from the Institute – recognizable by the distinctive white and circle-shaped labels on the spines – and then stacking them in baskets. The cover of *Die Aufklärung*, a magazine published by the Institute in the 1930s, is plainly visible. Paramount News Issue 84 (*Germans Burn Books!*) is held by the Sherman Grinberg Film Library, Los Angeles. The lead to the newsreel was found in the database of the USHMM, Washington, see https://collections.ushmm.org/search/catalog/irn1003188 (accessed December 15, 2023). I then informed Jens Dobler of its existence whereupon he made an effort to obtain a copy in December 2023. It is, for now, the only known filmed testimony of the sifting activity in the student house.

69 M., May 12, 1933, 5: "Nous avons pu, quelques instants avant l'autodafé, pénétrer dans la Maison des Etudiants, Oranienburgerstrasse, où avait été rassemblé l'impur butin. La plus grande partie des livres était déjà chargée sur les camions qui devaient les transporter au bûcher de la place de l'Opéra. Par une chance inespérée, la documentation saisie à l''Institut sexuel' du docteur Hirschfeld, de célèbre mémoire, est encore visible et même complaisamment étalée dans une vaste salle. M. Herbert Guthjahr, chef des corporations d'étudiants de Berlin, un garçon très blond en uniforme brun et qui ne badine pas avec la vertu, nous choisit dans le tas quelques documents d'un intérêt spécial et d'une moralité douteuse. Nous y jetons rapidement un coup d'œil d'adieu afin de nous bien convaincre de l'utilité de leur destruction prochaine. "Ceci n'a évidemment rien à voir avec la science, n'est-ce pas["], nous dit M. Guthjahr. ["]D'ailleurs, pour être sûrs de ne faire disparaître aucun document utile, nous avons demandé à deux médecins d'inventorier le stock." La révolution allemande, nous le savions déjà, se poursuit avec méthode et ne reprend les rites révolutionnaires traditionnels qu'en y ajoutant la marque de la rationalisation scientifique propre à notre temps". When looking at the reporting of the Berlin book burning in foreign, non-German language newspapers from France, the Netherlands and Belgium, I noticed that their local correspondents often investigated in person while local German newspapers tended to simply copy or slightly rework official press releases. Rainer Herrn states that this can be explained by the "gleichgeschaltete Presse" (homogenized press). See Herrn 2008c: card Die Institutsplünderung als Auftakt der Bücherverbrennung.

desire of Nazi officials to administer a heavy blow to the Hirscheld enterprise was a last minute undertaking, and definitely not an easy marriage in the Action initiated by the German Student Union.

One could say that the looting of the Institute even somewhat eclipsed the initial focus of the banned books campaign on Berlin lending libraries. "The greatest blow in the course of the action will be struck against the collection of Magnus Hirschfeld", many newspapers wrote in their May 6, 1933, editions, thereby clearly copying from the same press release.[70] This seems to indicate that, at least for some National Socialists, the true and important target that day was the Institute rather than the lending libraries. Rainer Herrn and Werner Treß both remark that the looting of the 700 lending libraries in Berlin by the other four raiding troops (*Stoßtrupps*) in around twenty-two trucks received little or no mention in the press reports they consulted.[71]

NOT A WELL-OILED MACHINE

When looking back at Nazism, people often assume that the whole phenomenon, from start to finish, ran like a well-oiled machine, most things being rationally planned and executed – the crematoria in Auschwitz-Birkenau serving as the ultimate symptomatic emblem of this supposed mechanism. But, in reality, Nazi actions and plans were often a story of different Nazi factions battling it out with the end result often being a sort of potpourri compromise imposed upon the clashing factions.[72] I think that the banned books campaign was no different. This idea of essentially piecemeal tinkering might also explain why the Institute was looted twice and not just once.

Let us take another look at the seeming reluctance of Herbert Guthjahr, the student leader who orchestrated the morning looting of the Institute. It looks like he conducted the assault on the Institute in accordance with the general, more moderate policy thought out by the German Student Union to "cleanse" (*Säuberung*) the Berlin libraries in the morning, using one or several blacklists (*schwarze Listen*). We may recall here that, as one photo clearly shows, some students carried out the materials looted during the morning action in their arms, while in the afternoon looting, as we have seen, baskets (*Körben*) were used to move the more significant loot.[73] We also saw that Giese stated that the morning looters only took a few hundred books with them.[74] It is commonly assumed that the afternoon looters simply finished the work started in the morning, possibly because not everything could be taken out in one truck load. This is also how the afternoon looters justified their return: they did not have enough time in the morning to do the job properly.[75] But this lack of time

[70] *Wiener Allgemeine Zeitung*, May 7, 1933, 3: "Der größte Schlag im Verlaufe der Aktion wird gegen die Magnus-Hirschfeld-Sammlung geführt werden". Almost exactly the same phrase appears in *Der Abend* (Vienna), May 6, 1933; and *Neue Freie Presse*, May 6, 1933; qtd. in Herrn 2010, 149, 167 n. 108.

[71] Herrn 2010, 117; Treß 2008, 109.

[72] On the other hand, Dagmar Herzog seems to see the entire attack on the Institute as a concerted and consistent campaign, calling it "eine Art Kulminationspunkt" (a sort of culminating point) (Herzog 2020, 87). Instead, I would contend, the event was rather the outcome of a rather clumsy assemblage of competing Nazi factions and structures, last-minute decisions, and possibly also of an irrational and uncontrollable desire for revenge.

[73] "Ganze Arme voll Bücher, Broschüren und Bilder usw. wurden in den Lastkraftwagen geworfen" (Armfuls of books, brochures, pictures, etc. were thrown into the truck), *Deutsche Zeitung*, May 6, 1933, qtd. in Herrn 2010, 150. On the baskets, see Herrn 2010, 138.

[74] Herrn 2010, 137.

[75] This argument – that it was impossible to load everything on one truck in the morning – was repeated in an article in the *Berliner Lokal-Anzeiger*, the day after the looting. See *Berliner Lokal-Anzeiger*, May 7, 1933, qtd. in Herrn 2010, 145. Herrn also suggests that the poor result of the morning looting, as judged by Guthjahr after going to the student house where the materials were dropped off, might have been the reason for the return in the afternoon (Herrn 2010, 145). Giese's testimony about the Institute looting also notes that the afternoon looters explained resuming the action because the morning looters did not have enough time. See Herrn 2010, 138. But Giese may well have got that view from the newspapers he read in the days afterwards, as he

explanation has been discredited for the most part.[76] The morning students were at the Institute for two and a half hours. If there were indeed, as we have seen, around a hundred students involved (or even, as we argued, only half that number), then it is frankly surprising they could not finish their somewhat light assignment in the morning. They certainly had enough manpower that morning to take out more stuff ... if they had wanted to do so.

THERE WAS NO SEXOLOGY BLACKLIST

Apart from some surplus vandalism, the morning looters mainly sorted through works with the help of one or several blacklists, supposedly finishing their task in the Institute that morning. What was there left for the afternoon crew to do, then? When we look at how the afternoon looters proceeded, we seem to perceive a different agenda. From the testimony that Giese wrote afterwards, we know that the afternoon looters appeared to focus on foreign literature and also on homosexual literary figures like André Gide and Oscar Wilde. They also focused on books of sexology and, rather curiously, seem to have been very well-versed in sexology.[77] Did this knowledge of the big names in sexology have anything to do with the medical training of the veterinary students? Archival research has shown that, in the beginning of May 1933, no blacklist yet existed specifically targeting sexology publications, which means that the afternoon students had no sexology blacklist at their disposal. The librarian Wolfgang Herrmann, who had compiled the list of German literary figures to be culled, a list which the morning students used, had not prepared a list of sexological works, simply presuming, with good reason, that hardly any were held in public lending libraries. In that sense, according to the student campaign's banned books logic, there was no real reason to loot Hirschfeld's Institute in search of any banned sexology books. A blacklist targeting sexology works specifically came out later, in June 1933.[78] So, presumably, only the morning looters had blacklists that allowed them to remove German literary figures from the Institute collection. One Vienna journalist even thought, or overheard, that there had not been any blacklists at all and that the students had acted randomly: "It was pointed out that an official index of banned books had not been published, but that this was a private action of the German Student Union".[79] It is possible that this referred specifically to the afternoon looting and was simply another justification for an inconsistent campaign.

It is strange, and also interesting, that the main author on the Berlin 1933 book burning, Werner Treß, has no real difficulties with the inconsistencies inherent to the campaign as executed and presented by the Nazi students, never bringing up the many instances as constituting a problem of sorts. He does not fail, of course, to mention the looting of the Institute as part of the many events between the moment the action was planned, in March 1933, and its culmination, the Berlin book burning of May 10, 1933. Very curiously, however, Treß gives no explanation of any kind why, suddenly, raiding the Institute became part of the plan. He simply presents the looting at the Institute as follows: "The worst hit by the book roundup was the Institute of

tried to understand the strange fact that there were two sessions of looting.

[76] Herrn 2010, 144–45.

[77] Herrn 2010, 138.

[78] Treß 2008a, 109; and, especially, Herrn 2010, 129–31.

[79] *Wiener Allgemeine Zeitung*, May 7, 1933, 3: "Man führte an, daß ein offizieller Index verbotener Bücher nicht herausgegeben wurde, sondern daß es sich da um eine Privataktion der deutschen Studentenschaft handle".

[80] Treß 2008a, 110–11: "Am schlimmsten wurde von der Büchersammelaktion das Institut für Sexualwissenschaft heimgesucht".

[81] Treß 2008a, 112: "Das Bild der Verwüstung, das die Studenten hinterließen, zeigt deutlich, dass es bei der Stürmung des Instituts für Sexualwissenschaft um mehr ging als die bloße Beschlagnahme von Büchern". This also means that the basic question, asked on the back cover of Schoeps & Treß 2010, was not really answered by Treß: "Wie kam es am 6. Mai 1933 zur Erstürmung des 'Instituts für Sexualwissen-

sexology".[80] In doing so, I think, he implicitly accepts the campaign's twisted internal logic, which suggested that the books and other materials in Hirschfeld's Institute were no different than the books taken from the Berlin lending libraries. And yet, he also later concedes: "The picture of devastation left by the students clearly shows that the storming of the Institute of Sexual Science was about more than the mere confiscation of books".[81] But with this acknowledgment that "something more" was happening, Treß's interest in the evident inconsistency ends.

COMPETITION BETWEEN TWO STUDENT UMBRELLA ORGANIZATIONS

I think there is a possibility that the afternoon raid of the Institute was initially not foreseen at all. One element above all seems to point in this direction. After the morning looting, Guthjahr declared that the Institute was henceforth closed. He gave no indication that he or his troupe of physical education students (or any other student group) would return in the afternoon to finish the job.

Let us look a bit closer at the decision making and the course of action of the afternoon looting. The veterinary students who undertook the afternoon looting were members of the National Socialist German Students' League (Nationalsozialistische Deutsche Studentenbund) whereas the morning students belonged to the competing student umbrella organization, the German Student Union. As reported repeatedly in the press, the latter was the main organizer of the whole campaign.[82] Following an indication by Hans-Wolfgang Strätz (who himself borrowed the idea from Hans Schlömer), I think that the afternoon looting can be explained in large part by the rivalry between these two student organizations. The second looting was likely simply the consequence of a local petty battle in which the National Socialist German Students' League tried to jump on the bandwagon.[83] I think a last-minute, impulsive decision lay behind the afternoon looting, which had simply not been planned beforehand. It is even possible that a trivial or petty human (*kleinmenschlich*) reason alone explained the afternoon session. Several months after the events, the leader of the afternoon looting, Fritz Witt, in a brief letter reporting on the events, wrote that the veterinary students wanted to take part in the May 6 campaign only to be told, when they arrived at their college (*Hochschule*), that the Berlin lending libraries were already closed and that they had thus missed out on the action.[84] Did the students maybe oversleep on a Saturday morning or was there another reason for their being late? Was the second looting decided upon by some frustrated students who had missed out, for whatever reason, on the "fun" of the morning session?[85] Or did some

schaft' von Magnus Hirschfeld und wer waren die Verantwortlichen?" (How did the storming of Magnus Hirschfeld's Institute for Sexual Science come about on May 6, 1933, and who was responsible?).

[82] Herrn 2010, 144 also stresses that the morning and afternoon lootings were executed by students from different (and competing) student umbrella organizations.

[83] Strätz 1968, 348–50, 352–53. Strätz 1968, 349: "Es scheint daher manches dafür zu sprechen, daß die rasche Bereitwilligkeit zur Übernahme einer derart spektakulären Aktionen, wie es die Bücherverbrennung sein würde, nicht in erster Linie mit dem 'Kalkül des Demagogen' Goebbels erklärt werden kann, sondern eher auf die zwischen der Deutschen Studentenschaft (DSt) und dem Nationalsozialistischen Deutschen Studentenbund (NSDStB) bestehende Rivalität zurückzuführen ist" (There seem to be quite a few arguments, therefore, that the quick readiness to engage in such a spectacular action as the book burning cannot be explained primarily by the 'calculus of the demagogue' Goebbels, but rather by the rivalry existing between the Deutschen Studentenschaft [DSt] and the Nationalsozialistischen Deutschen Studentenbund [NSDStB]). Hans Schlömer, a collaborator of the Archiv der Universitätsbibliothek Würzburg, was the one who pointed this idea out to Strätz.

[84] Letter (dated Jul. 21, 1933) from Fritz Witt to Hauptamt für Aufklärung und Werbung der Deutschen Studentenschaft (qtd. in Herrn 2010, 144).

[85] This seems to be confirmed by another somewhat curious note by Fritz Witt when he later reported what had happened that morning: "Der N.S.D.St.B. der Tierärztlichen Hochschule versammelte sich am ersten Tag der Aktion in der Hochschule, um einige Bibliotheken der Stadt Berlin zu untersuchen" (The N.S.D.St.B. of the Veterinary College assembled at the college on the first day of the action to examine some of the libraries of the city

students of the National Socialist German Students' League – or, rather, one of their superiors – suddenly realize they needed to join the seemingly successful campaign of the German Student Union to clearly declare and claim their part in the whole campaign as well?

The students of the National Socialist German Students' League were most likely also entangled in different ways with the Nazi apparatus and this might have resulted in differing marching orders and courses of action regarding the looting of the Institute.[86] Karl Giese certainly saw a difference between the morning and the afternoon looting sessions. He wrote that the morning looters were students and that the afternoon students arrived accompanied by "several trucks with SA people".[87] On the pictures of the morning looting one can indeed see only a *few* SA Brownshirts at the side entrance door. Months after the May events had taken place, the afternoon leader, Fritz Witt, wrote that he had been given an order at the student house in Oranienburger Straße to return to the Institute.[88] One may presume that this order came from a superior within the National Socialist German Students' League hierarchy and not from someone in the German Student Union. Another element possibly further supports the idea that the morning and afternoon looters were operating separately from each other. We have already seen that the truck used in the morning looting was provided by the Pagel firm, and that this firm was owned by an elderly woman. This firm would also have provided the trucks carrying the books from the student house to the Opernplatz. But when Fritz Witt spoke about the truck his group of students used, he said it had been provided by the father of one of his fellow students.[89]

Following this hypothesis, that the afternoon visit was possibly a separate and spontaneously organized undertaking, and recognizing that the two student umbrella organizations were in competition, it becomes conceivable that the afternoon visit was perhaps seen by the National Socialist German Students' League as an occasion to display a harsher stance against Hirschfeld and what he stood for, compared to the more civilized and restrained activity of the morning looters. It is certainly possible that, with seemingly spontaneous interference and more violent intrusion of the afternoon looting, the National Socialist German Students' League sought to make a stand which they hoped would win the notice of the Nazi establishment. It is equally

of Berlin). See the letter (dated Jul. 21, 1933) from Fritz Witt to Hauptamt für Aufklärung und Werbung der Deutschen Studentenschaft (qtd. in Herrn 2010, 144). The idea that they would assist by *investigating* some libraries could only have been purely superfluous since, as we have seen, there was little left to investigate. The books had already been sorted by the librarians and just needed to be picked up.

86 Treß 2008a, 25–26 stresses the importance of the contribution of the Hitler Youth to the campaign. They arranged a similar amount of book burnings throughout Germany. An important figure, who possibly lay behind some of the decisions taken there, was Baldur von Schirach (1907–1974). In 1933 he was the head of the Hitler Youth but had also been, from 1928 until 1931, the leader of the National Socialist German Students' League.

87 Herrn 2010, 135, 137–38: "mehrere Lastautos mit SA-Leuten".

88 See the letter (dated Jul. 21, 1933) from Fritz Witt to Hauptamt für Aufklärung und Werbung der Deutschen Studentenschaft (qtd. in Herrn 2010, 144).

89 Letter (dated Jul. 21, 1933) from Fritz Witt to Hauptamt für Aufklärung und Werbung der Deutschen Studentenschaft (qtd. in Herrn 2010, 144): "Wir fuhren darauf zum Sammelpunkt im Studentenhaus und bekamen dort Befehl mit unserem Lastwagen, den uns der Vater eines Kommilitonen zur Verfügung gestellt hatte, zum Magnus-Hirschfeld-Institut zu fahren" (We then drove to the assembly point in the student house and received orders there to drive to the Magnus Hirschfeld Institute in our truck, which the father of a fellow student had provided for us). I think that this is also further proof of the already accepted idea that all of the known photographs showing the looting of the Institute were taken in the morning. As far as I know, there are no (publicly known) photos of the afternoon looting. If any existed, they would show, according to the student's claim, a truck other than the one from the Pagel firm.

90 The name of the German Student Union's Hauptamt für Presse und Propaganda was changed, at the end of April 1933, to Hauptamt für Aufklärung und Werbung. See Strätz 1968, 359 n. 54.

91 For this letter, see Herrn 2010, 144. Witt also wrote in the letter that he had sent the report so late because of a mistake (*ein Versehen*). He undersigned

conceivable that the original organizer of the Action Against the Un-German Spirit, the German Student Union, was not all that happy about this improvised second looting carried out by the competing organization. This would explain why Fritz Witt was summoned by Hans Karl Leistritz, the director of the coordinating Main Office for Education and Recruitment (Hauptamt für Aufklärung und Werbung) of the German Student Union, to explain the afternoon looting.[90] This could also explain why Fritz Witt responded very late, on July 21, to Leistritz's questioning Witt on the matter.[91] Witt's procrastination could indicate either deliberate indifference towards the competing student umbrella organization or simply avoidance of an uncomfortable subject. Witt might have been very well aware that the afternoon's wild looting had not been part of the original morning-only plan conceived by the German Student Union.[92] It is interesting also in this regard that in the speech Herbert Guthjahr, the leader of the morning looting and member of the German Student Union, gave at the auto-da-fé, he noted that the whole campaign had been jointly organized by both student umbrella organizations.[93] A statement which was factually incorrect and likely added to counter the (already rumored?) impression of a counterproductive rivalry between the two organizations. Not surprisingly, to bring any rivalries to an end, they were merged in 1936 into the Reich Student Leadership (Reichsstudentenführung).[94]

INVOLVEMENT OF THE NAZI PARTY APPARATUS

There is a whole discussion among historians about the exact involvement of Nazi party officials in the student banned books campaign. The exiled German writer Alfred Kantorowicz, who exactly one year later would create the Library of Burned Books (Deutsche Freiheitsbibliothek) in Paris,[95] was one of many who, from the French capital, quickly pointed a finger at Joseph Goebbels. Goebbels was after all the Reich Minister of Public Enlightenment and Propaganda (Reichsminister of Volksaufklärung und Propaganda) and was the only high Nazi official to attend the auto-da-fé that night, giving a speech on the Opernplatz.[96] Research has shown that the German Student Union conceived and executed the whole campaign themselves. But, when planning their action, they had contacted high-ranking party figures for both the necessary funding and moral support.[97] The exact role – if any – of Goebbels

the letter with "Führer in der Aktion 'wider den undeutschen Geist der Ti. H. [Tierärztliche Hochschule]'", which, strictly speaking, was something of a provocation since his organization was not the main organizer of the Action.

92 Herrn seems to suggest that the letter was sent by Witt to Leistritz as this was then the normal and expected course of action for the Main Office for Education and Recruitment in using information for possible press releases (Herrn 2010, 147). Herrn concedes that this letter was indeed sent terribly late. I think that, just for starters, Witt was under no obligation to answer Leistritz because he belonged to the competing student umbrella organization. Furthermore, if the hypothesis of an improvised second looting is correct, I believe that he sent the letter, and sent it so late, because he may have been summoned (repeatedly?) to account for the wild looting of the afternoon.

93 "Die deutsche Studentenschaft habe gemeinsam mit dem NSDStB [Nationalsozialistische Deutsche Studentenbund] diese Aktion gegen den undeutschen Geist aufgenommen" (The deutsche Studentenschaft, together with the NSDStB [Nationalsozialistische Deutsche Studentenbund], had undertaken this Action Against the Un-German Spirit.), *Der Angriff*, May 11, 1933 (qtd. in Herzer 2009b, 21). Cf. Rückl & Noack 2005, 122: "Zu den spektakulärsten Aktionen, die der NSDStB [Nationalsozialistische Deutsche Studentenbund] und die Deutsche Studentenschaft je an der FWU [Friedrich-Wilhelms-Universität] organisierten, gehört die ücherverbrennung am 10. Mai 1933" (Among the most spectacular actions ever organized at FWU [Friedrich-Wilhelms-Universität] by the NSDStB [Nationalsozialistische Deutsche Studentenbund] and the Deutsche Studentenschaft was the book burning on May 10, 1933). See also Rückl & Noack 2005, 121.

94 Strätz 1968, 350.

95 On Kantorowicz and the Deutsche Freiheitsbibliothek, see below, p. 204.

96 Treß 2008b, 9–10. The Reich Ministry of Public Education and Enlightenment was created in mid-March 1933, two months before the May book burning, under the leadership of Joseph Goebbels.

97 Treß 2008a, 66–80.

(or any other NSDAP party official) in the matter remains unclear to this day.[98] Several authors stress that Goebbels joined the campaign and acted only at the last minute.[99] But this does not exclude the possibility that Goebbels, even if only at the last minute, might indeed have intervened and imposed some of his own urgent ideas here and there.[100] It is possible that Goebbels came up with the idea, perhaps when he was approached to deliver a speech, to add Hirschfeld and his Institute to the campaign, and that this explains why the attack on Hirschfeld's Institute appears so late in the campaign. As early as 1928, in the National Socialist magazine *Der Angriff*, a periodical that he himself led, Goebbels called for the closure of Hirschfeld's Institute.[101] Furthermore, on the day of the looting, the closing down of the Institute was announced in that same publication.[102]

Again, Herbert Guthjahr may not have been pleased by the possible last-moment order to add the raid on the Institute to the campaign. This may also explain why he manifested some slight resistance during the morning visit by partly hiding behind the rules (i.e. cleansing lending libraries of unwanted books), as these had been spelled out by his student umbrella organization. Herrn brings up another significant fact in this connection that might help to explain Guthjahr's reluctance: starting in 1921 (or even earlier), the German College of Physical Education, to which the morning students belonged, had published their notifications (*Mitteilungen*), together with those of the Institute, in a publication called *Sexualreform*. Though *Sexualreform* ceased publication around 1926–27, attacking the Institute would still mark a serious change of course.[103]

If this interpretation of the afternoon looting as a last-minute, unplanned action is correct, then we also have to conclude that the more destructive afternoon looting did not have to take place. The book burning campaign would have been succesful with just the morning loot. That would also mean that the attack on the Institute, and especially its devastating results, as we now know them, was not undertaken by a fierce "Nazi machine", ruthlessly rolling over its victim according to a preconceived rational plan. As we have suggested, in its more devastating effects, it was possibly the product of a petty rivalry between two student umbrella organizations.

[98] Treß warns that it would be mistaken to consider Joseph Goebbels as the "silent" spindoctor of the whole operation (Treß 2008a, 48). According to Treß, Goebbels only "joined the ranks" once he saw that the book burnings would suit his propaganda purposes. Treß prefers to speak of intertwined Nazi networks in which it is hard to determine who pulled the strings and who influenced who. For the idea of an explanatory network (*Bündnispartner*), defended by Treß, see Treß 2008a, 49. On the other hand, regarding the forces behind the campaign, Manfred Herzer prefers to give more determinative weight to the (hidden) purposeful planning and coercion of burgeoning Nazi politics (Herzer 2009, 151–54). Curiously, Rürup claims that there is uncontested agreement that the students were the sole driving force behind the entire action (Rürup 1999, 30).

[99] Yet on April 2, 1933, it was already clear that Goebbels would (be asked to) hold a speech on the day of the book burning. See Treß 2008, 70. Cf. Herrn 2010, 159: "[Goebbels] kurzfristig entschloss eine Rede zu halten" ([Goebbels] decided on short notice to give a speech). Rürup 1999, 30 claims that Goebbels only agreed to speak on May 9, 1933, the day before the book burning.

[100] Treß mentions that Goebbels' influence or mediating function in the whole matter cannot be excluded (Treß 2008, 69, 70–71, 80).

[101] Herrn 2010, 159.

[102] See "Demonstrative Schließung" (Demonstrative Closure) in *Der Angriff*, May 6, 1933 (qtd. in Herrn 2010, 152); and, especially, Herrn 2010, 159.

[103] Herrn 2010, 165–66 n. 91. The full title of the publication was *Sexualreform: Beiblatt zu Geschlecht und Gesellschaft mit offiziellen Mitteilungen des Instituts für Sexualwissenschaft und der Hochschule für Leibesübungen Berlin*. Herrn writes that this publication began in 1922; however, I own a copy of the tenth volume of *Sexualreform* from 1921, which contains the same two *Mitteilungen*. It remains unclear when the collaboration between the Institute, the College, and *Sexualreform* started; however, we know that Hirschfeld's Institute was established in 1919, and this implies, of course, that *Sexualreform*, or the Institute's insertion of its *Mitteilungen* in the periodical, began shortly thereafter. The periodical *Geschlecht und Gesellschaft* ceased publication in 1926/1927, according to the online catalogue of the DNB in Leipzig, and this was also confirmed to me by Marita Keilson-Lauritz. Cf. Sigusch 2008, 103.

[104] Herrn 2010, 113. Herrn's quintessential 2010 contribution should be read in conjunction with his con-

WAS MAGNUS HIRSCHFELD USED TO COVER UP AN UNSUCCESSFUL CAMPAIGN?

Why did the Nazis suddenly decide to add an attack on Hirschfeld and his Institute to the Action Against the Un-German Spirit? Rainer Herrn, one of the main authors on the May 1933 looting of the Institute, claims that Hirschfeld and his Institute, and the whole enemy image (*Feindbild*) the Nazis created around the man in the years before, had a central role to play in the whole campaign because the latter was not going as smoothly as they had hoped.[104] Herrn writes that adding Hirschfeld was a "media-savvy" (*medienwirksames*) tactic necessary to cover up the false start of the campaign. Indeed, the first weeks of the Action Against the Un-German Spirit did not run very smoothly. The organizers of the campaign met with resistance throughout Germany when the idea to single out undesirable authors and eventually burn their books was announced.[105] This resistance began with the founding act of the campaign: the publication of the twelve Theses Against the Un-German Spirit that, especially in Berlin, met with opposition from academic circles.[106] The pamphlet reeked of anti-Jewishness in its fourth, fifth, and tenth demands, and also announced, in its sixth demand, the cleansing of the public libraries: "The un-German spirit is being eradicated from public libraries".[107] Another event planned in the campaign was an appeal to sixty writers sympathetic to Nazism to support the campaign by writing a text. Hardly any texts came in. The call to report teachers who did not sympathize with National Socialist ideology and the idea of installing pillories (*Schandpfahlen*) with banned books nailed to them also faltered in great part due to a lack of support or occasionally even simple resistance.[108] Adding the easy rallying point of Hirschfeld at the end of the campaign had to disguise all of these failures, Herrn reasons.[109]

It is indeed likely that Hirschfeld's enemy image (*Feindbild*) functioned a little like the gasoline thrown on the bonfire that May night. But we should also not forget that, from the very outset, neither Hirschfeld nor what he stood for had likely been a part of the plan concocted by the Nazi students. If indeed the Hirschfeld element had been added as purposefully as Herrn claims, then I think Hirschfeld's name would have popped up earlier in the preparation of the campaign. And we have already seen that the raid on the Institute was only announced the day before, on May 5.[110] Also, Hirschfeld's "usefulness" to the campaign does not mean that, without him, it would

tributions printed on approximately 110 cardboard cards handed out on the occasion of the exhibition *Sex brennt: Magnus Hirschfelds Institut für Sexualwissenschaft und die Bücherverbrennung* held in the Museum der Charité in Berlin from May 7 until September 14, 2008 (Herrn 2008c). Several issues concerning the Nazis' decision to add Hirschfeld and the Institute to the 1933 forbidden books campaign, which are left out of his 2010 text, are addressed in these cards and strengthen his central thesis. Possibly because a funding source fell through, it seems that a catalogue of this exhibition was not printed. See Herrn 2008a, 11–13. One can also find the texts of thirty-nine of these cards, translated into English, and slightly adapted, in Herrn, Taylor & Timm 2017, 37–79, figs. 7–45.

[105] Herrn 2010, 113–17; and, for more detail, Treß 2008a, 80–106.

[106] Herrn 2010, 114.

[107] The pamphlet is reproduced in Treß 2008a, 77: "Der undeutsche Geist wird aus öffentlichen Büchereien ausgemerzt".

[108] Herrn 2010, 114–16; and especially Strätz 1968, 351–58.

[109] Herrn writes that Hirschfeld and the Institute were a "welcome alternative" (*willkommene Alternative*) for the Action Against the Un-German Spirit, which had not met with much enthusiasm in its first weeks (Herrn 2010, 116).

[110] Herrn concedes that the last-minute (*kurzfristig*) looting of the Institute was enacted as a spectacle to enhance the media effect of the whole campaign ("*medienwirksames Spektakel*") (Herrn 2010, 149). Cf. Herrn 2008b, 19–20. Indeed, why was Hirschfeld or his Institute not mentioned even once in the announcement by Hans Karl Leistritz, leader of the German Student Union's Main Office for Education and Recruitment, when he stated that the Action had to be conducted "in ständiger Steigerung bis zum 10. Mai — mit allen Mitteln der Propaganda durchgeführt werden, wie: Rundfunk, Presse, Säulenanschlag, Flugblätter und Sonderartikeldienst der DSt-Akademischen Korrespondenz" (in constant intensification until May 10 – to be carried out using all propaganda means, such as radio, press, pillar posts, leaflets and the special article service of the DSt-Akademische Korrespondenz). See the

not have succeeded or even failed to take place. The book burning spectacle would simply have been a little less feisty, according to Nazi standards.[111] That Hirschfeld was not a necessary part of the campaign is supported by the fact that the other book burnings set up by the German Student Union in around thirty other cities with colleges (*Hochschulorten*) hardly relied on this Hirschfeld-and-Institute constellation to carry out their local auto-da-fés.[112] Again, Hirschfeld may have been useful but was not really *necessary* for the success of the campaign. Burning books on a public pyre is sensational in itself; and this is indeed how it was remembered later on, as a general campaign targeting unwanted authors and their banned books, not as a campaign that featured Hirschfeld as one of the main culprits.

As a central piece of evidence for his thesis, Herrn points out that Hirschfeld's bust (the only one of all the authors consigned to the flames) was mounted on a stick and ostentatiously thrown into the fire [ill. 6]. But I think that this act was a last moment addition that was simply not planned in the book burning scenario prepared for the Opernplatz. I think that some of the students who raided the Institute simply found his bust there and thought (or were told) it was a good idea to add that element to the ceremony on the Opernplatz. The decision to include Hirschfeld's bust in the book burning ritual might also have been made later on in the student house. Even if throwing Hirschfeld's bust on the bonfire had been sensationally planned, it received little to no attention in the German press and was moreover hardly noticeable in the known newsreels of the book burning shown in cinemas.[113]

It is indeed correct that the campaign became a little more sensational and sadistic with the symbolic attack on the archenemy Hirschfeld as the proverbial cherry on the cake. As already suggested, incorporating the Hirschfeld complex actually eclipsed the initial focus on lending libraries. It likely delighted Goebbels. But I am not sure if this view and interpretation of the role of Hirschfeld in the banned books campaign tells the whole story. I think that the Nazis may have had yet another, much less instrumental motive in wanting to add the Hirschfeld element to the Action Against the Un-German Spirit.

letter (date unknown) from Hans Leistritz (qtd. in Strätz 1968, 350).

[111] Cf. Herrn 2010, 117.

[112] Referring to Treß 2008a, Herrn says that Hirschfeld also played a role in other *Hochschulorten* where book burnings were staged (Herrn 2010, 160 n. 6). But Treß does not claim this at all. A simple search for the name of Magnus Hirschfeld in the register of the index in that same Treß publication suffices to demonstrate that Hirschfeld hardly played a role in other book burnings events held in Germany.

[113] Cf. Herrn 2010, 158, 168 n. 138. Herrn writes that Treß made him aware of a film fragment that briefly shows this part. In the German documentary that Herrn saw, two physical education students can be seen from afar and very briefly (three seconds) walking with a stick towards the fire (at 1:28–1:30 min), but, because the artificial light is coming from only one side, the Hirschfeld bust is barely visible, and it looks like they are carrying a stick with nothing on it. See Dieter Hildebrandt's 1980 documentary *Der Gelbe Stern – Ein Film über die Judenverfolgung 1933–1945*, accessible online at https://vimeo.com/171387785 (accessed Apr. 30, 2020). The same fragment, embedded in Goebbels' speech, can also be seen in the British Pathé newsreel at 0:59-1:00 min; see https://www.britishpathe.com/video/burning-the-books-germany-1933 (accessed Dec. 10, 2020). On a third, different British Movietone newsreel fragment one can see, though again with difficulty, and only if informed, the stick with Hirschfeld's bust, held by one student, and *waiting* to be thrown in the fire (at 0:37-0:40 min); see http://www.aparchive.com/metadata/NAZIS-BURN-MARXIST-BOOKS-SOUND/073a00946e194ea784a3f9579c7d36b5?query=book+burning+berlin¤t=1&orderBy=Relevance&hits=2&referrer=search&search=%2fsearch%2ffilter%3fquery%3dbook%2520burning%2520berlin%26from%3d1%26orderBy%3dRelevance%26allFilters%3dBritish%2520Movietone%253ASource%26ptype%3dIncludedProducts%26_%3d1588280718557&allFilters=British+Movietone%3aSource&productType=IncludedProducts&page=1&b=7d36b5 or https://www.youtube.com/watch?v=Iq17XfEjNfs (accessed Apr. 30, 2020).

[114] Strätz 1968, 347: "Die öffentliche Bücherverbrennung war der Höhepunkt einer Aktion, die als Gegenschlag gegen die „schamlose Greuelhetze des Judentums im Ausland motiviert war" (The public book burning was the culmination point of an action motivated as a counter-attack against the Jewish atrocity rhetoric of Jewry abroad). For more information on the motivating factor of the "jüdi-

FEAR OF REACTIONS FROM ABROAD

When announcing and preparing the campaign, the students stressed that their Action was also meant as a response to the "Jewish atrocity rhetoric" (*jüdische Greuelhetze*) coming from abroad. Indeed, several foreign countries, and especially Jewish circles abroad, had strongly reacted to the Nazis' rise to power in the first months of 1933.[114] It is far from certain that Nazi officials would *not* have taken these foreign reactions and perceptions into account. Some newspapers wrote that even the leaders of the German Student Union found it necessary to stress that no foreign books had been burned and that this false rumor was spread to incite indignation about the Action abroad.[115] In May 1933, a *New York Times* article claimed that one of Helen Keller's books, *How I Became a Socialist,* had been burned on the pyre in Berlin.[116] This prompted the student leader Herbert Guthjahr to write a letter to the rector of the Friedrich-Wilhelms-Universität, stating that was *not* the case. The theologian Paul Humburg (1878–1945) intervened on the matter with the university rector, which again shows that the book burning organized by the students was contested by several German intellectuals.[117]

Reinhard Rürup is, to my knowledge, the only author who stresses that Nazi party officials were not necessarily happy with the students' "spontaneous", somewhat uncontrolled, and maybe excessively aggressive book burning initiative and looting of the Institute.[118] A Dutch journalist in Berlin expressed a similar opinion about the Nazi students' youthful rashness. He went to visit the student house in the Oranienburger Straße on May 10 where he met Gehlhar: "Then I get to hear a discourse, so vehement, and so sharply critical, that I decide not to make any objection nor to express any doubt as to the efficacy of this modern iconoclasm. *I understand that the [Nazi] revolution is not yet complete and that many things are still upside down and will soon be put back on their feet. Perhaps this will also happen with the Berlin students whose cultural-political activity seems somewhat premature*".[119] The students may have acted freely and wildly

sche Greuelhetze" coming from abroad, Treß 2008a, 66–70.

[115] See "Lügengerüchte" (False Rumors), *Kölner Tageblatt*, May 12, 1933, qtd. in Wulf 1963, 47. This message from the German Student Union's Kreis X (Berlin-Brandenburg) also reached some foreign newspapers. See, for example, the Belgian newspaper *Het Handelsblad*, May 14, 1933, 3.

[116] Birchall, May 11, 1933, 12.

[117] A copy of the letter can be found in American Foundation for the Blind, New York, Hellen Keller Archive, kart. n° 210 (Bibliography, Biographer, Book Burning, Publishers), folder n° 3 (Book Burning, 1933), item n° 4, letter (dated May 29, 1933) from Herbert Guthjahr (Der Führer of the Studentenschaft der Friedrich-Wilhelms-Universität zu Berlin) to Rektor der Universität, accessible online at https://www.afb.org/HelenKellerArchive?a=d&d=A-HK02-B210-F03-004&e=-------en-20--1--txt--------5-----------------0-1 (accessed Nov. 27, 2021).

[118] Rürup 1999, 35–36: "Der politischen Führung war zu diesem Zeitpunkt an einem die internationale Oeffentlichkeit erregenden Spektakel wenig gelegen. Auch innenpolitisch schien es geboten, die Dynamik der so oft beschworenen "Revolution" eher zu verlangsamen als zu beschleunigen. Die entscheidenden Machtfragen waren geklärt, und nun schien es darauf anzukommen, nicht nur die "braunen Bataillone" der SA, sondern auch die revoltierenden Studenten zu disziplinieren und eindeutig in den Dienst der politischen Führung zu stellen. [...] Dieser Wechsel der Politik spiegelt sich auch darin, daß die Berichterstattung über die "Bücherverbrennung" in den deutschen Medien der Zeit – von den Zeitungen über die Rundfunkanstalten bis zur Wochenschau – eher knapp und weniger auftrumpfend war, als zu vermuten gewesen wäre" (At the time, the political leadership had little interest in a spectacle that would excite the international public. Domestically, too, it seemed advisable to slow down rather than accelerate the momentum of the oft-invoked "revolution". The decisive questions of power had been settled, and now it seemed important to discipline not only the "brown battalions" of the SA, but also the revolting students, and to place them clearly in the service of the political leadership. [...] This change of policy is also reflected in the fact that the coverage of the "book burning" in the German media of the time – from newspapers to radio stations to newsreels – was rather scanty and less showy than might have been expected).

[119] *De Courant*, May 12, 1933, 1 (emphasis added): "Dan krijg ik een betoog te hooren, dat zoo heftig is, en zoo scherp van critiek, dat ik maar besluit geen tegenwerping te maken en geen twijfel te uiten aan de doelmatigheid van deze moderne beeldenstormerij. *Ik begrijp dat de omwenteling nog niet voltooid is en dat vele dingen nog op hun kop staan, die straks wel weer op hun pooten zullen terecht komen. Wel-*

in the months preceding the book burning, but the book burning itself seems to have been tightly choreographed according to a script worked out beforehand. One Dutch journalist noticed the event was not just spontaneous.[120] The students' spontaneous initiative, at first condoned and encouraged, could only go so far.

It is certain that, sooner or later, the Hirschfeld Institute would have been closed down by the Nazis. Several left-wing bulwarks in Berlin had already been under assault by the Nazis before May 1933: the Artists' Colony (Künstlerkolonie) in Berlin-Wilmersdorf (where the playwright Peter Martin Lampel lived), the Anti-War Museum (Anti-Kriegsmusem), and the Schöneberg State School of Art (Staatliche Kunstsschule Schöneberg) had already been plundered by March 1933.[121] As with the Berlin Institute, when these institutions were assaulted, unwanted book collections were confiscated and publicly burned.

Yet I think that in the case of the Institute, it is possible that the Nazis wanted to avoid their attack being a standalone action that would then, in its very nakedness, be open to external and especially foreign criticism. Hirschfeld's world trip cemented his status as an international star. In the USA he was even dubbed the "Einstein of sex".[122] His international renown was only reinforced with the founding of the WLSR in 1928, when a worldwide network of academics (for the most part) was created, all adhering to a sexual reform ideology abhorred by the Nazis. Including the inevitable and clearly longed-for aggressive attack on Hirschfeld, and what he stood for, in the broader, more generic Action Against the Un-German Spirit, which weeded out the books of unwanted, mainly literary authors, may have neutralized it somewhat.[123] That the assault on Hirschfeld's life work was a last minute addition to the campaign could also simply indicate the late realization that the book burning campaign provided an opportune moment to attack Hirschfeld and his Institute. But we have also seen that opportunistically adding the Hirschfeld element to a campaign devoted to burning of books from lending libraries, where it did not really belong, brought several contradictions in its wake that the Nazi students tried to explain away in the press afterwards.

A SPONTANEOUS INITIATIVE BY THE YOUNG

I think that another feature of the banned books campaign can be associated to the idea that the attack on the "Hirschfeld complex" was partly neutralized by including it in the more general campaign targeting unwanted books. A review of the speeches given at the Berlin auto-da-fé reveals a common insistence that the entire campaign was conceived and executed by the younger generation and, more specifically, the

licht zal dit ook geschieden met de Berlijnsche studenten wier cultureele politieke activiteit eenigszins voorbarig lijkt". The article also shows that the students pampered foreign journalists. The journalist was given a special card that allowed him access to the Opernplatz, which was closed to the general public during the book burning event, and to which he was also driven in a car procured by the students. The same text also mentions that Prince August Wilhelm von Preußen (1887–1949) was also present and even lauded on the event. He was the fourth son of the last German emperor, a closeted gay man who turned to Nazism, but quickly fell out of favor. See Machtan 2006.

120 *De Gooi- en Eemlander*, May 16, 1933, 5.

121 Treß 2008a, 54–58; Herrn 2010, 117.

122 The catchphrase "The Einstein of Sex" was invented by George Sylvester Viereck. See Dose 2014, 90.

123 I think a thorough check should be made one day of the extent to which the "Hirschfeld/Institute element" featured in the German press coverage of the Berlin book burning compared to press coverage abroad. My first hunch and impression is that this element was more prominent in the latter. I checked several Dutch newspapers and noticed that the names of Hirschfeld and his Institute appeared in most of them. See *Nieuwe Apeldoornsche Courant*, May 11, 1933, 1; *Nieuwe Tilburgsche Courant*, May 9, 1933, 5; *De Gooi- en Eemlander*, May 16, 1933, 5; *De Tijd*, Apr. 14, 1933, 1; *Provinciale Noordbrabantsche en 's Hertogenbossche Courant*, May 6, 1933, 2.

124 *Berliner Lokal-Anzeiger*, May 7, 1933 (qtd. in Herrn 2010, 117): "Wir haben unsere ganze Aktion aus uns allein heraus begonnen".

students of the German Student Union. "We undertook the whole campaign by ourselves alone", a local newspaper quoted one of the student leaders as saying.[124] In his speech at the auto-da-fé, Herbert Guthjahr said that it was possibly German youth who first recognized the danger flowing from everything that went against the true German spirit.[125] The same theme recurs in Goebbels' auto-da-fé speech, which indirectly suggested that the book burning action was a grassroots initiative, spontaneously emanating from the students of the German Student Union.[126]

This endeavor to draw a clear causal connection to young people was already present when the Action was being prepared in the months before the book burning. Werner Treß writes: "On the one hand, there was a deliberate emphasis on the participation of young people, because this made it possible to pretend that the Action Against the Un-German Spirit was about the struggle of the young and new against the old and outdated".[127] This was an interesting move on the part of the Nazis: they wanted to spread the message that their viewpoints were not imposed top down but, on the contrary, spontaneously arose bottom up from young people. There was an appeal to the natural, spontaneous intuition of the youth, who had acted on their own and instinctively knew what was right and wrong. The whole undertaking in which, specifically, physical education students – the epitome of health – were sent in the morning to loot the Institute seems to further confirm the point that these healthy and innocent German youths were crusading against the depraved sexual conglomerate that Hirschfeld stood for.[128]

In addition, judging from the pictures taken in front of the Institute, it seems also that only male students took part in the looting campaign, even though the students of the German College of Physical Education certainly had female members also.[129] When the morning looting was over, the students stood in front of the Institute singing, among other songs, "We Will Protect German Women and Girls" (*Deutsche Frauen, deutsche Mädchen nehmen wir in unseren Schutz*).[130] The students clearly represented healthy breeding and normal (heterosexual) sex life, in contrast to the sexual lifestyles "promoted" in the Institute. The physical education students, dressed "a little like Wandervogel youths",[131] were also deliberately put forward as a sort of moral vanguard on the day of the auto-da-fé itself.[132] Hirschfeld's bust, stolen from the Institute, was thrown on the fire in a theatrical way by two physical education students.

I think that this tactic of appealing to the young is interesting as a means to justify and ideologically consolidate the existence of the still young regime, which was most likely perceived as an imposed tyranny *pur sang*, especially abroad. The students had come up with the idea to attack these unwanted authors on their own. The responsibility for the scandalous act of looting the Hirschfeld Institute thus, it was suggested, lay on the shoulders of the young students who had only followed their

[125] Herzer 2009b, 21. His use of the word "possibly" is indeed intriguing. See also Peiffer 2010, 99, 104–8.

[126] For a fragment of Goebbels' speech, see Treß 2008a, 124.

[127] Treß 2008a, 78: "Zum einen wurde bewusst auf die Beteiligung junger Menschen gesetzt, weil sich so vortäuschen ließ, es handele sich bei der *Aktion wider den undeutschen Geist* um den Kampf des Jungen und Neuen gegen das Alte und Überkommene".

[128] Werner Treß thinks that it was no accident that the physical education students were consciously put forward as the chosen "troops" to storm the Institute during the morning looting (Treß 2008a, 112). Herrn also remarks on the "innocence" of the physical education students (Herrn 2010, 151).

[129] Peiffer 2010, 108, 110.

[130] Treß 2008a, 113.

[131] Wiesner 2003, 426: "ein wenig wandervogelhaft". The Wandervogel (wandering bird) were youth groups that existed in Germany before World War II. They traveled around, advocated a return to nature, and also had a strong nationalistic inspiration.

[132] Treß 2008a, 121. If the afternoon looting of the Institute was indeed a more ad hoc affair, then it is likely that no meaning is to be found in the fact that it was undertaken by veterinary students. Or is there?

healthy instinct(s). Finally, one may wonder also if the idea that this action could only be symbolic (since it could never eradicate all unwanted books or ideas), brought up by Goebbels in his speech, and by the student leaders Guthjahr and Gehlhar, was the symptom of a longing to add a somewhat more civilized appearance to the event.[133]

NAZI ANARCHISM

The rivalry between the two student umbrella organizations – possibly causing two separate lootings – may have been a common feature of the new Nazi apparatus that was installing itself in the first half of 1933. One sees that the new inroads made by the Nazis often started off with a "wild phase", in which people spontaneously took action, with the Nazi authorities having no full control (yet) over these burgeoning events. There was always the threat of anarchy, all the more so in the very beginning. In this vein, the book burnings that took place throughout Germany *before* the ones sanctioned by the German Student Union were branded by Werner Treß as "wild burning campaigns" (*wilde Verbrennungsaktionen*).[134] Later, we will encounter another "wild phase" in the National Socialist reign, the initial "wild" Aryanizations of Jewish companies in Czechoslovakia, in March 1939. Above all in the first months of 1933, power struggles might have still been going on, or simply been more open, resulting in different, competing views of how to attack the archenemy Hirschfeld.[135]

A curious phrase in Christopher Isherwood's well-known memoir *Christopher and His Kind* is, I think, telling here. Isherwood remarks that, if the Nazis had indeed been interested in the Institute holdings, they would likely have conducted themselves more discreetly, and would not have wildly looted the Institute.[136] Isherwood concludes that the Nazis were not really interested in the Institute. I think that he was mistaken in this interpretation and that he simply failed to perceive (or misjudged) clashing and competing Nazi factions with different views of how to handle the matter. I also think that Isherwood presupposed a fully operative rational state apparatus with a unified command. We have already drawn attention to this common view of Nazism, which lives on in our own day, and which Isherwood may also have had in mind in the 1970s when he wrote his book. But the Nazi apparatus was still installing itself in the first half of 1933. I think it is more probable that some Nazi officials would have preferred to see the Institute relatively untouched, allowing them to screen in a more controlled way the holdings of the Institute behind closed doors. The prudent morning approach, in which the Institute was only superficially and, one could even say, symbolically raided, may have seemed to some Nazi factions the most desirable and optimal one.[137] That the looting of Hirschfeld's Institute was added at the last moment to the banned books campaign, perhaps even only the day before, presumably by Goebbels himself, is a possible indication that the decision was *not* necessarily shared by the new people in power. Perhaps Goebbels, or another Nazi official, overplayed his hand a bit, driven by the powerful desire to finally strike at one of the archenemies of the National Socialist movement. A short notice that appeared in *The New York Times* suggests that there was clear disagreement on the

[133] See M., Dec. 12, 1933, 5; and, of course, Goebbels' speech itself. Talking to a Dutch journalist, Gehlhar, the student leader of the German Student Union, also stressed that the action was only symbolic. See *De Courant*, Dec. 12, 1933, 1.

[134] Treß 2008b, 14.

[135] Yet strong disagreements and infighting among high-ranking Nazi officials on the policy to be followed went on until at least 1938. See, for example, the chapter "Le coup d'envoi, version allemande" in Chaponnière 2015, 93–164.

[136] Isherwood 1988, 137.

[137] In line with this logic, a different interpretation of the two Institute lootings is possible. Was the morning looting maybe more moderate to allow the unannounced afternoon looting to hit harder without any media presence? This interpretation could also help to explain the discussion or disagreement, among the morning looting students, on the exact goal of the looting. Were they following strict orders, without always succeeding in keeping themselves under the control of this imposed

student action within the National Socialist camp, and that the disapproval of the loss of valuable books was just a symptom of this disagreement: "Lest the students 'go too far,' a commission of college professors had been named to 'separate the wheat from the chaff' and preserve valuable books from the fires. This action followed upon a warning by Captain Hermann Wilhelm Goering, the Prussian Premier, against forms of 'racketeering'".[138] So, all in all, instead of there being a unified well thought-out anti-Hirschfeld campaign, with one group or Nazi leader pulling the strings, we instead see a congeries of different factions, interests and visions coming together, bringing about a hybrid and confusing conglomerate that eventually appeared as the seemingly consistent Nazi book burning on May 10, 1933, an event supposedly fully endorsed by the new National Socialist regime and in any case showcased as such in the worldwide press.

CONCLUSION

It is clear that Hirschfeld and his looted Institute were, at least in intention, an important and exemplary aspect of the Berlin book burning of May 1933. As we have seen, the campaign started off with the looting of the Institute and – to name just one other example – a photo of Hirschfeld was hung on one of the trucks carrying books to the Opernplatz.[139] Yet I have also argued that it is important to see that, most probably, one or another Nazi official not only decided at the last minute to add the attack on Hirschfeld's Institute to the book burning campaign, but also possibly tried simultaneously to partly neutralize this aggressive act by subsuming it under the larger and more generic action where the books of unwanted authors were removed and destroyed by innocent students. In this view, Hirschfeld was just one of the many authors solemnly consigned to the fire. Showcased, certainly, but, in the end, just one of the many authors whose books (or books Hirschfeld condoned, promoted or simply collected) went up in flames. Curiously, this is also how the Berlin book burning was ultimately perceived, especially abroad, and above all in later public consciousness. Hirschfeld did indeed appear as a titillating element in the May 1933 campaign, but, at the same time, he disappeared from view soon after his proverbial fifteen minutes of dreadful fame in a mediatized Nazi event. It is indeed remarkable to observe that in later accounts of the May 1933 book burning, Hirschfeld's name is usually absent even though he was an important part of the event.[140]

It is clear that the Berlin book burning became one of the key symbolic events marking the beginning of the rise to power of Nazism in Germany. This is how it was

restraint? In Giese's testimony one can read: "Auf die Einwände eines Studenten, dass es sich um medizinisches Material handele, antwortete ein anderer, darauf käme es nicht an, es wäre ihnen nicht um die Beschlagnahme von ein paar Büchern und Bildern zu tun, sondern um die Vernichtung des Instituts" (To the objections of one student that it concerned medical materials, another replied that it did not matter, they were not concerned with the confiscation of a few books and pictures, but with the destruction of the Institute). See Herrn 2010, 137. Cf. Schulz 2001, 112–13. Schulz describes the aggressive conduct of some of the looting students as follows: "Das sind so – die wollten mal was kaputt machen" (They were like – they wanted to smash something once). But it is not known if Schulz was speaking of the first or second looting. Schulz is one of the few people who does not specifically mention two looting sessions. For the small doubt that there may *not* have been two looting sessions on May 6, 1933, see Herrn 2010, 142–44.

[138] See "20,000 Books on Berlin Pyre", *New York Times*, May 11, 1933, 12.

[139] See ill. n° 4. The photo can also be seen at https://collections.ushmm.org/search/catalog/pa1056478 (accessed Jun. 13, 2021).

[140] This curious paradox – also noticed in Herrn 2022, 457 – would benefit from more research on the matter. However, it is possibly already telling that in a 1947 booklet by Alfred Kantorowicz on the occasion of the Tag des freien Buches (Day of the Free Book), Hirschfeld does not appear in the list of the "bedeutendsten Autoren, deren Bücher in Nazideutschland verbrannt und verboten wurden" (most important authors whose books were burned and banned in Nazi Germany). See Kantorowicz 1947, 22. Kantorowicz's main text contains a brief mention of Hirschfeld's name, together with Freud

perceived, especially abroad, and very early on.[141] The very first scene one encounters when entering the permanent exhibit in the Yad Vashem Museum in Jerusalem – which impressively tries to document the Holocaust in its entirety – deals with the May 1933 book burning and is testimony to the broadly perceived significance of the event as one of the very first important Nazi campaigns. Several banned books are displayed in this first scene, but none by Hirschfeld, nor is there even a single sexology title. The book burning is presented as a kind of symbolic starting point for everything that followed. Another example of the strange omission of Hirschfeld is the 2013 initiative to reprint, on the occasion of the eightieth anniversary of the book burning, some of the "burned books". The ten books reprinted were all literary titles.[142] I would like to argue, finally, that the May 1933 book burning is nowadays perceived as a campaign in which the Nazis burned books, and more specifically, fiercely attacked literature (with a capital "L"), with literature seen as a noble and pure object, and Literature as occupying a central part in any civilization worthy of the name. In this constellation, the endlessly invoked modern admonition – expressed by Heine's words – not to burn books (any more) is *merely* the politically correct expression of a "generic perception" of the Berlin book burning event, one in which books, and what they stand for, were under attack.[143]

KAREL ČAPEK'S VIEW OF THE BERLIN BOOK BURNING

One can see that Hirschfeld's own looted library was already disappearing from view in May 1933. It could be said that the Nazis tried to fit Hirschfeld into a campaign targeting mainly literary authors. But Hirschfeld simply did not belong there; however, the miscasting was very quickly sanctioned. We have seen that the Nazi students felt obliged to issue press releases rationalizing the contradictions their hybrid book burning project engendered. That Hirschfeld's collection of sexology books did not blend very well into a self-sufficient and self-ennobling literary category can be seen in the early reaction to the Berlin book burning by the Czech literature authority Karel Čapek (1890–1938). Ten days after the Berlin book burning, in a front-page article for the Czechoslovak newspaper *Lidové noviny*, he wrote: "On the Opernplatz in Berlin they have already cleared the ashes from the pyre of burned books. The works of poets and scientists have been burned; socialism, pacifism, freedom of

(Kantorowicz 1947, 9). Yet only Freud's name shows up in the list of banned authors found in the back of the pamphlet.

[141] Especially Rürup 1999, 27–28, 36; his quoting from Thomas Mann's prophetic 1943 BBC radio speech on the Hitler regime, identified as a regime of book burning, is interesting here. There is even a spectacular 1938 book burning scene, attended by Hitler himself, in one of the blockbuster *Indiana Jones* movies, *Indiana Jones and the Last Crusade* (1989). The movie shows a much more spectacular and orchestrated event than what really happened in Berlin in May 1933. This Hollywood rendering is another prime example of the current perception of Nazism as a well-oiled machine, where everything was rationally planned, and there was a clear line of command.

[142] See the series "Bibliothek der verbotenen Bücher" published by the Axel Springer Verlag (in close collaboration with the magazine *Bild*) in 2013, see https://www.axelspringer.com/de/press einformationen/zum-80-jahrestag-der-buecher verbrennung-bild-veroeffentlicht-die-bibliothek-der-verbotenen-buecher (accessed Dec. 5, 2020): "Die ausgewählten Werke von Bertolt Brecht, Lion Feuchtwanger, Erich Kästner, Egon Erwin Kisch, Heinrich Mann, Gustav Meyrink, Erich Maria Remarque, Joseph Roth und Kurt Tucholsky und Stefan Zweig geben einen Einblick in das literarische Schaffen dieser geächteten Schriftsteller, deren Werke im Mai 1933 von den Nationalsozialisten verbrannt wurden" (The selected works of Bertolt Brecht, Lion Feuchtwanger, Erich Kästner, Egon Erwin Kisch, Heinrich Mann, Gustav Meyrink, Erich Maria Remarque, Joseph Roth, and Kurt Tucholsky and Stefan Zweig provide insight into the literary work of these ostracized writers, whose works were burned by the Nazis in May 1933).

[143] Cf. Herrn 2010, 159–60.

[144] Čapek, May 21, 1933, 1: "Na Opernplatze v Berlíně už odklidili popel z hranice spálených knih. Dohořela díla básníku a vědců ; socialismus, pacifismus, svoboda myšlení byly vrženy do ohně, jako by tím je bylo možno sprovodit se světa. Ale nebyly to jen tyto knihy. Do plamene, který by mohl být výstražnou hranicí, bylo naházeno také ledajaké

thought have been thrown into the fire, as if by doing so they could be driven out of the world. But it was not only these books. They also threw into the flames, and this should have been a cautionary boundary, all the rubbish in which the German press notoriously abounded. The proverbial *Nacktkultur* [nudism movement] and the equally proverbial pseudo-science masquerading as *Sexualwissenschaft* [sexual science] were also burned, along with other paper filth. The fire on the Opernplatz was polluted by this filthy fuel; a gross violence to culture and spiritual freedom was done by mixing it with that impure parasitism of freedom, art and culture in one lurking mass. There is no pity for all that burned on the Berlin border. It was also a piece of primitive national 'disinfection'".[144] In wanting to differentiate between noble literature and the smut of sexology that polluted the fire on the Opernplatz, Čapek implicitly predicted how the Berlin book burnings would be remembered in the eight decades that followed: as exclusively a brutal Nazi attack on literature with a capital "L". Čapek's piece did not escape the notice of Joseph Weisskopf, the conference organizer of the WLSR Brno conference. Weisskopf passionately defended his friend Hirschfeld in stating that books, *all books,* were worthy of unconditional protection in a civilization. Weisskopf retorted: "Even the worst books, in my opinion, should not be burned, but preserved in the archives as the memory of a certain human age, because they express its thinking".[145] Weisskopf tried to preserve Hirschfeld as one of the pool of authors victimized by the Nazis, but Čapek's reaction was a forewarning that Hirschfeld's sexology books would, very quickly, cease to be part of the public perception of the Berlin auto-da-fé. The first to initiate this post-event logic were the Nazis, who had added Hirschfeld to their banned books campaign, knowing very well he never fitted into the picture.

Almost two years later, in April 1935, Hirschfeld would meet Karel Čapek in Nice (France) at a banquet organized by the Permanent Committee on Arts and Letters of the League of Nations (Comité Permanent des Lettres et des Arts of the Société des Nations). The League of Nations was the forebear of the United Nations (UN). On the banquet invitation card, held at the Centre Universitaire Méditerranéen (C.U.M.) in Nice, Hirschfeld collected ten autographs of other personalities attending and later pasted the collection of international literary greats into his guestbook.[146] Čapek was one of these. It is not known if Hirschfeld and Čapek discussed Čapek's May 1933 text. Also, here in Nice, Hirschfeld may have been again the odd man out among the more decent "men of letters".

Rainer Herrn thinks that this desire to eclipse Hirschfeld from the public perception of the Berlin book burning likely derives from post-war German homophobia.[147] I am not sure that this is the only or even a truly determinative factor at play. It could well be that the almost spontaneous or automatic exclusion of Hirschfeld's books – and of the Institute's collection of sexology books – from the category of Literature simply followed, and in our own societies continues to follow, an *internal, self-sufficient logic* of what Literature is, one with certain ambitions to purity and allergic or sensitive to contamination. Not just any book is worthy of such privileged status. Like a transplanted organ, one could say, Hirschfeld's books were

svinstvo, kterým notoricky oplýval německý tisk. Byla tu pálena také pověstná Nacktkultur [nudism movement] a neméně pověstná pseudověda, která se vydávala za Sexualwissenschaft [sexual science], vedle jiného papírového neřádu. Oheň na Opernplatze byl znečištěn tímto mrzkým palivem; stalo se hrubé násilí na kultuře a svobodě duchovní tím, že byly smíšeny s oním nečistým parasitismem svobody, umění a kultury v jediném čadícím houfu. Není škoda všeho, co na tč [*sic*] berlínské hranici [*sic*] shořelo. Byl to také kus primitivní národní "desinfekce"."

145 Weisskopf, May 27, 1933, 2: "Ani ty nejhorší knihy by se podle mého mínení nesmely pálit, ale uschovat do archivu na památku toho kterého lidského veku, nebot odpovídají jeho myšlení."

146 Bergemann, Dose, Keilson-Lauritz, & Dubout 2019, f. 131/175.

147 Herrn 2010, 160.

rejected by the sacred body of Literature. This logic, when one thinks of it, could not have been anticipated or planned by the Nazis, despite their having forcefully added Hirschfeld to the generic banned books campaign targeting literary greats, in which, as they quickly realized, Hirschfeld and his sexology books simply did not blend very well. Hirschfeld's and the Institute's books were driven out of the public perception of the May 1933 auto-da-fé, almost at the very moment that they were forcibly added to the staged event.

When, in May 2016, Dr. Heike Bernhardt generously donated a stamped edition of Freud's *Three Essays on the Theory of Sexuality* (*Drei Abhandlungen zur Sexualtheorie*) from the Institute's collection to the Magnus-Hirschfeld-Gesellschaft in Berlin, she said that she had written first to the artist Micha Ullman, telling him she had a book that belonged on the empty shelves of his Berlin artwork.[148] That the Israeli artist never answered her letter is possibly symptomatic and revelatory of the now almost insurmountable chasm between the current, mainly moral and symbolic perception of the May 1933 Berlin book burning – perfectly captured by Ullman's extremely poignant and almost angelic artwork with its empty book shelves – and the still ongoing discovery of what *exactly* happened in May 1933.

THE QUESTIONNAIRES (FRAGEBOGEN) ON THE SEX LIVES OF INSTITUTE PATIENTS

In the whole history of the looting of the Institute, in May 1933, the uncertain fate of the so-called psycho-biological questionnaires (*psychobiologischer Fragebogen*) is a recurrent theme. These were questionnaires that patients who visited the Institute were asked to complete. The questions regarded details of patients' sex life and also their psychological and sociological background. According to a French journalist, every patient at the Institute was asked to fill out this questionnaire.[149] No fewer than thirteen pages covering 137 questions were printed in a pamphlet, containing on the right-hand side, and at the end, several blank pages for the answers [ill. 7].[150]

The questionnaire was not anonymous. It started by asking the patient's full name, day of birth, with whom they lived, and the organizations to which they belonged before proceeding to questions about the patient's emotional and sex life.[151] The introductory text of the questionnaire stated: "You can rely on the strictest discretion".[152] Magnus Hirschfeld considered the questionnaires filled out by the patients to be the Institute's main research material because they supplied the empirical basis for his theories on "sexual intermediaries" (*sexuele Zwischenstufen*).[153] That patients left very intimate details about their sex life in these questionnaires, which were kept in the Institute, must have been of real concern to Hirschfeld, especially after the looting of the Institute.

There is an indication that an undetermined number of these questionnaires escaped the looting. Karl Giese, above all, would have played a central role in the rescue of these questionnaires. Hirschfeld wrote somewhat evasively about the rescue of these questionnaires in one of his French books, *L'âme et l'amour*, written and published during his later exile in France: "It was with great difficulty, that my collaborator, Mr. Karl Giese, *to protect professional confidentiality*, succeeded in saving this unique documentation from the destruction it was threatened with".[154] It must have reassured some former Institute patients to read that. One finds this same concern about the fate of the questionnaires in Giese's testimony (*Zeitzeugenbericht*)

[148] See Bernhardt 2016, 24, 26 and https://magnus-hirschfeld.de/bibliothek-und-archiv/sammlungs-schwerpunkte/neuzugang-sigmund-freud/ (accessed Dec. 8, 2020).

[149] Beucler, Apr. 9, 1932, 6.

[150] I consulted the 1915 fourth edition of the *Fragebogen*.

[151] Two pages from (a version of) the *Fragebogen* can be found in Sigusch 2008, 352–53.

[152] Sigusch 2008, 352: "Auf strengste Verschwiegenheid dürfen Sie sich verlassen".

[153] Hirschfeld 1929, 129–30; Hirschfeld 1935a, 10.

[154] Hirschfeld 1935a, 10 (emphasis added): "C'est avec beaucoup de peine, que mon collaborateur

reporting on the May 1933 looting of the Institute. According to this testimony, some of the Institute inhabitants present during the looting managed to convince the students not to take these questionnaires with them. "They also wanted to haul away the completed questionnaires (several thousand) and only the explicit indication that they were medical records persuaded the students to refrain from doing so".[155] This may have been true during the morning looting but, as we have seen, it is likely that the afternoon looters took some or even all the presumably remaining questionnaires from the Institute's cellar. We will see later that at least some of these questionnaires (together with other Institute materials) were bought back by Hirschfeld from Nazi Germany in 1933, which confirms, minimally, that at least some questionnaires were left behind in the Institute. Hirschfeld certainly had an interest in making the world believe that these questionnaires were in safe hands and had not fallen prey to the Nazis. But we need to ask, nevertheless, if the claim by Hirschfeld and Giese that the questionnaires were taken to safety, was true in whole or in part.

How many questionnaires were housed in the Institute is unclear. After the war, Ludwig Levy-Lenz (1889–1966), an Institute doctor, claimed that there were around 40,000.[156] I have not seen another source giving a higher number than that. If one counted just one patient a day for the approximately thirteen years that the Institute existed, then one arrives at around 4,745 questionnaires (365 x 13). If one counted ten patients a day, the number is closer to the one Levy-Lenz reported. It might be interesting also to look at the number of gay patients Hirschfeld claimed to have treated by June 1932: 35,000 or even 36,000.[157] In *L'âme et l'amour*, Hirschfeld had himself written that "more than 10,000" of these questionnaires had been filled out in his Institute and that they had all been saved.[158] Very curiously, the English translation of this text mentions that there were questionnaires only "furnished by over one thousand men and women" in the Institute and that they had all been safeguarded by Giese.[159] This low number is quite curious. One would presume that the introduction to the English translation was written after the French original (which had a different introduction) was written or even published. Did Hirschfeld change his mind maybe? Maybe he decided to tell the plain truth and only mentioned the number of questionnaires that had been effectively preserved or bought back from Nazi Germany at the end of 1933?

It is certain that attempts to smuggle some materials out of the Institute on the day of the looting and possibly also in the days after were made. Adelheid Schulz suggested that several people had helped to smuggle out materials. Since the campaign to weed out the Berlin libraries was announced in a Berlin newspaper, on the day of the looting, there were attempts, very early in the morning, to smuggle out "valuable personal books and manuscripts" from the Institute, despite the fact that SA people had already started guarding the Institute at 8:30 a.m., one hour before the looting

M. Karl Giese a réussi, *pour défendre le secret professionnel*, à sauver cette documentation unique de la destruction dont elle était menacée". For the English translation, see Hirschfeld 1935b, xiv.

155 Herrn 2010, 138: "Man wollte auch die ausgefüllten Fragebögen fortschleppen (mehrere tausend) und nur der ausdrückliche Hinweis, dass es sich um Krankengeschichten handle, liess die Studenten davon Abstand nehmen". For further considerations of the rescue of the questionnaires, see also Herrn 2010, 138–40.

156 Levy-Lenz 1954, 404. He named these questionnaires *Selbstbeichten* (self-confessions).

157 For the 36,000 patients, see *Expres*, Jun. 8, 1932, 2. Hirschfeld talks about 35,000 patients in *Nový hlas*, Jg. 1, nos. 7–8, Nov. 11, 1932, 12.

158 Hirschfeld 1935a, 10: "plus de 10.000". Cf. Lamprecht, Nov. 15, 1935, 173. Lamprecht reproduces the number of 10,000 questionnaires, but it seems that he may have copied this directly from *L'Âme et l'amour*, since immediately afterwards he mentions, just as in Hirschfeld's book, that the patients had to answer 130 questions in the questionnaires. George Viereck speaks of 8,000 questionnaires in his 1930 text on Hirschfeld, and this makes the 10,000 questionnaires in 1933 realistic. See Viereck 1930, 247.

159 Hirschfeld 1935b, xiii–xiv. The number of one thousand was not written out in arabic numerals, so there was certainly no mistake of a zero being left out.

actually started. Other sources say there was already a guard during the night.[160] Yet this attempt to get things out, undertaken by an unidentified young man, apparently failed.[161] One newspaper wrote that it concerned "writings that were allegedly of a private character".[162] Does this indicate that it was the questionnaires? There may also have been attempts to smuggle things out between the morning and the afternoon looting sessions, when it was still unknown that there would be a second session. The Institute was still guarded then, presumably by SA people. Hirschfeld's housekeeper Adelheid Schulz mentioned that a daring Communist named Georg (Orje) Heidrich, and his girlfriend Mia, did manage to smuggle out many things, without being noticed, on the day of the looting or in the days or weeks afterwards.[163]

There is a small indication that a part of these questionnaires may have been taken away by the Nazi students in the afternoon looting. During the latter, the students headed to the Institute's cellar where they found some "not insignificant material".[164] Interestingly, Charlotte Wolff writes that Maeder had once told her that the questionnaires were kept in the cellar.[165] There is also a sentence in the anonymous introduction (presumably by Norman Haire) to the English translation (and UK edition) of Hirschfeld's world tour book, *Women East and West: Impressions of a Sex Expert*: "On May 6th, 1933, the Nazis broke into his beloved Institute in Berlin, sacked the place, tore up drawings, pictures and photographs, piled more than half of the library *and the case records* into lorries, and publicly burnt them in one great funeral pyre in the Opera Square".[166] Norman Haire knew Hirschfeld quite well and they talked a lot. This introduction was likely written and published, unsigned, after Hirschfeld's death. Did Haire or another anonymous writer describe how things *really* happened?[167]

We do know with certainty, as we will see later, that at least some of these questionnaires did indeed end up in France. But it could well be that these questionnaires formed a part of the Institute lots that Hirschfeld bought back from Nazi Germany in November 1933. So there is real possibility that Karl Giese never managed to rescue any of these questionnaires. It is perfectly possible that Hirschfeld's claim that Giese had saved these questionnaires was just soothing reassurance meant for the patients who had filled them out and who read in their newspapers that the Institute had been looted. So, we definitely need to be wary about Hirschfeld and Giese's claim that 10,000 of these questionnaires were rescued. This means that we also need to be critical of Giese's claim, contained in his testimony of the looting, that someone from the Institute convinced the afternoon looters not to take the questionnaires. This claim also entails that some, or even all the questionnaires, were in the Institute at the time of the May 6 looting. After that, it would hardly have

[160] Herrn 2010, 135: "kostbare Privatbücher und Manuskripte". According to Giese's *Zeitzeugenbericht* (testimony), the raids on Berlin public libraries had been announced in the *Berliner Lokalanzeiger*, May 6, 1933. See Herrn 2013, 135. On the (lack of) success of these rescue attempts, see Herrn 2010, 164 n. 69. On guards being posted that night, see Herrn 2013, 135. For the guard, or guards, being there at 8:30 a.m., see *Germania*, May 7, 1933 (qtd. in Herrn 2010, 164 n. 69).

[161] Herrn 2010, 135. More newspapers reported on this attempt, and even others which involved not one young man but several people. See Herrn 2010, 164 n. 69.

[162] *Germania*, May 7, 1933 (qtd. in Herrn 2010, 164 n. 69): "Schriften, die angeblich privaten Charakter trugen".

[163] Schulz 2001, 39, 71. Maeder possibly suggests how this smuggling might have worked. He claims that he was locked in the Institute and his mother-in-law had to bring him food unnoticed. The Institute was situated on a street corner and the guard was apparently able to see only one side of the L-shaped building at a time. The food was passed through a *Parterrefenster* (low-rise window) (Maeder [1993], 5). But Maeder remains an unreliable source. We also know that Adelheid Schulz remained in the Institute for another seven weeks and likely also continued to do the cooking there.

[164] Letter (dated Jul. 21, 1933) from Fritz Witt to Hauptamt für Aufklärung und Werbung der Deutschen Studentenschaft (qtd. in Herrn 2010, 144: "nicht unbedeutendes Material").

[165] Wolff 1986, 433.

been possible to get things out as the Institute was guarded. And lastly: how would Giese have managed to carry out thousands of completed questionnaires by himself? And do so maybe at the last minute? Or had he safeguarded some questionnaires before the lootings of May 6?

We also need to look at the timing of the message claiming that a great part (or even all) of the questionnaires had been saved. It is possible that Hirschfeld became aware that many former patients were inquiring about the fate of the questionnaires after May 1933 and felt that he needed to publicly address this concern. When he wrote the text in which he brought up the matter of the questionnaires, the buy-back operation had already been concluded. So it cannot be excluded that the only questionnaires that were saved were the ones bought back from Nazi Germany in the same year 1933. Hirschfeld may have deemed it necessary to twice say that he and Giese had had enough foresight to safeguard the questionnaires before the Institute was plundered, even though, in reality, they may not have done so. All in all, nothing much is really certain here. Questions regarding the number of questionnaires in the Institute and how many, if any, were "saved" by Giese, or anyone else, have no definitive answer. We also do not know how many of these questionnaires were bought back from Nazi Germany at the end of 1933.

NAZI INTEREST IN THE INSTITUTE QUESTIONNAIRES

In relation to this question of the exact fate of the questionnaires, there is a rumor that, in their attack on the Institute, the Nazis were mainly (or even exclusively) after them all along. If true, this would possibly throw more light on the afternoon looting, during which, as we have seen, a part of the questionnaire collection was removed. There is the real possibility that they expressly returned in the afternoon to (also?) find these questionnaires; and that, maybe, their lack explains why the National Socialist German Students' League, or rather their superiors, considered that the morning visit, led by Guthjahr, had simply missed its target, obliging them to pay a second visit in the afternoon. In his famous 1976 memoir, *Christopher and His Kind*, Christopher Isherwood writes that the looters that came back in the afternoon clearly knew what they were looking for.[168]

The presumed strong interest in these questionnaires on the part of some Nazi faction(s) is connected to the possibly (politically) compromising information they contained. It was rumored at the time that the Nazis were especially concerned about their possibly containing intimate details of the sex life of some National Socialists and especially those in the gay circle around the SA leader, Ernst Röhm. Isherwood mentions this same rumor.[169] Günter Maeder claims that, three years before the Institute was looted, an SA man who had had an affair with Röhm visited the Institute for treatment.[170] In 1937, Raymond-Raoul Lambert (1894–1943), a good French acquaintance of Magnus Hirschfeld, wrote that Hirschfeld had known too much about the matter: "Informed about the secret life and vices of certain leaders of the ruling party, it is infinitely probable that he [Hirschfeld] would have been

[166] Hirschfeld 1935c, xi (emphasis added).

[167] I think that Norman Haire might have written the introduction because Haire was also instrumental in getting Hirschfeld's world trip book translated into English. Haire wrote the introduction to *Sex in Human Relationships* (Hirschfeld 1935b), the English translation of Hirschfeld's *L'Âme et l'amour*. Hirschfeld did not live to see any of these English translations. See also University of Sydney Library, Sydney, Norman Haire collection, 3.20, Magnus Hirschfeld, Typescripts, 1923–1935, letter dated (Mar. 7, 1935) from Norman Haire to Magnus Hirschfeld.

[168] Isherwood 1988, 136–37.

[169] Isherwood 1988, 136–37. It is also mentioned in Wiesner 2003.

[170] Wellcome Library, London, archive Charlotte Wolff (1897–1986), correspondence II, 1981–1986, PSY/WOL/6/8/2, letter (undated, presumably January or February 1982) from Günter Maeder to Charlotte Wolff.

excluded from speaking and writing without delay".[171] Indeed, there seem to have existed real tensions around these questionnaires, the possibly politically useful sexual secrets they might contain and their fate. Hirschfeld's Chinese lover, Li Shiu Tong, wrote down in one of his personal notes (in broken English), sometime after the war: "Dr. Hirschfeld had two assistents who [were] under the pressure of the Nazi [*sic*] to get the records of the sexual behaviour of foreign patients. The assistants had already burned the records. Under continuous pressure they committed suicide".[172] If this note is reliable, it would suggest two things: that at least some of the questionnaires were indeed "saved" from the Nazis (but then deliberately burned or destroyed by Hirschfeld's two collaborators) and that the Nazis were interested in these questionnaires since they might contain information on the sex lives of foreign patients who had visited the Institute. Thus, the Nazis' possible interest in the questionnaires need not be linked to the sex lives of their own number. Rainer Herrn thinks that this idea – or myth – of the Nazis' strong interest dated from the 1950s, when the former Institute collaborator, Dr. Ludwig Levy-Lenz, wrote his memoirs. He also concedes that the idea is not entirely "implausible", but then immediately adds that it directly contradicts Giese's claim in his testimony that the questionnaires were untouched by the rampaging Nazi students and were taken into safe custody.[173] Herrn, in other words, assumes that Giese and Hirschfeld simply spoke the truth when they claimed that 10,000 questionnaires were saved from the clutches of the Nazis.

But the somewhat sensational rumor regarding the Nazis' particular interest in these Institute's questionnaires goes even further in suggesting that they might also have contained information about Hitler's supposed gayness. In a letter sent to Charlotte Wolff, Maeder brought up this idea that Hitler himself was gay and that there were materials in the Institute that "proved" this. But he also immediately added after reporting this claim or rumor he had heard that it was possibly just gay gossip ("Tuntengeschwätz?").[174] That at least the rumor about compromising materials about Hitler's possible homosexual preferences already existed in 1937 is also revealed by some surviving correspondence between Karl Giese and Kurt Hiller of that year. In

[171] Lambert, Jun. 18, 1937, 629: "Au courant de la vie secrète et des vices de certains chefs du parti au pouvoir, il est infiniment probable qu'il [Hirschfeld] eût été mis sans délai hors d'état de parler et d'écrire". Lambert is one of the main figures linking Hirschfeld to Jewish France. I thank Kevin Dubout (see his email dated Oct. 2, 2013 to the author) for pointing out this man to me. Dubout found a text by Lambert, written after Hirschfeld's death, that shows that Lambert had a very intimate knowledge of Hirschfeld. Lambert even knew that Hirschfeld kept a diary and even read it, presumably after Hirschfeld's death. See Lambert, Jun. 18, 1937, 630. It is possible that the wreath for Hirschfeld's funeral, paid for by the Ligue internationale contre l'antisémitisme (International League Against Anti-Semitism), came from one of the organizations in which Lambert was active, or through his mediation. The photo of the wreath and ribbon is in Archiv MHG, Berlin, fonds Ernst Maass. Lambert himself also kept a diary, but only the years 1940–43 have been published. See Lambert 1984. When I started looking for the other volumes of his diary, I read that they were lost, despite having been donated to a French archive. A very sad and simply incomprehensible fact. I have read the excellent introduction to the English translation (*Diary of a Witness, 1940–1943*), but there is no mention of Lambert's having been active in the Ligue internationale contre l'antisémitisme, only in several other Jewish organizations. He was the president of the Comité d'assistance aux réfugiés (CAR: Committee for Assistance to Refugees) and later of the Union générale des israélites de France (General Union of French Israelites). Lambert was clearly also a great admirer of German culture.

[172] Hirschfeld & Dose 2013, 22 n. 24. As we will see later, Giese committed suicide in 1938. Dose thinks that the second assistant alluded to here might have been Felix Abraham (1901–1937), who committed suicide in Italy a year before Giese.

[173] Herrn 2010, 139 n. 81, 82; repeated in Herrn 2022, 472–73. The information to which Herrn refers can be found in Levy-Lenz 1954, 404. Dagmar Herzog seems to agree fully with Herrn on this point (Herzog 2020, 88).

[174] Wellcome Library, London, archive Charlotte Wolff (1897–1986), correspondence II, 1981–1986, PSY/WOL/6/8/2, letter (undated but presumably January or February 1982) from Günter Maeder to Charlotte Wolff. This idea that the Nazis were intent on getting

these letters, Hiller asked Giese to make public the Institute documents about Hitler's presumed gayness, rumors of whose existence Hiller clearly must have heard.[175]

Whatever the exact truth behind these rumors, I think one can minimally state that it is indeed easily imaginable that the National Socialists were interested in these questionnaires since they simply wanted to gather as much sensitive information as possible on the people that had visited the Institute, whether their own, or other German or foreign patients. The questionnaires were simply one element in a larger operation to gather as much "intelligence" as possible on people and enemies, an interest that would only increase in the years that followed.[176] That the Nazi police apparatus was interested in any data on people, linked in any way to the Institute, is shown by Giese's testimony, which records that the afternoon looters also took with them the WLSR's address list (*Kartothek*).[177] We will later see that lists of people to be immediately arrested were prepared before the invasion and annexation of Czechoslovakia by the Germans in March 1939, by the police apparatus that would become the Reich Security Main Office (Reichssicherheitshauptamt, RSHA) in Berlin. And lastly, the Nazis' likely interest in the questionnaires might have simply been provoked by rumors about all that they contained. Their desire to get hold of them need not be based on facts. They might have reasoned that the best way to overcome rumors was to thoroughly investigate the matter. Trying to get hold of the materials in the Institute was thus the next logical step.[178]

IMPENDING DANGER AND "GOODBYE TO BERLIN"

We must dare to ask the question whether Giese and Hirschfeld demonstrated enough foresight and caution or not. Shortly after the looting, the English sexologist Norman Haire, Hirschfeld's good colleague, wrote to him: "But you must have expected the raid for some time before it actually occurred. Were you not able to remove to safety the most valuable books, papers, etc, and to destroy anything which you did not

hold of these questionnaires also explained, again according to Maeder, why, before the Institute was looted, the SA had made impromptu visits to the Institute. See Maeder [1993], 4. Maeder's claiming "that Hitler was the biggest monkey of them all" was also picked up by Wolff 1986, 438. Levy-Lenz also mentions Hitler's supposed homosexuality and also the story of a former lover of Röhm, who had been a patient in the Institute three years before it was looted. See Levy-Lenz 1954, 401–4. It is possible that Maeder's later claims were exclusively based on Levy-Lenz's book. It is one of Lothar Machtan's central claims that Hitler did all he could to prevent information on his supposed homosexual preference from coming out (Machtan 2001). But neither Machtan nor any other author has ever found clear proof that Hitler may have been a gay man. At the same time, there is, to this day, no real means, technique or instrument that would prove that a dead or even living person was gay or not. For the time being, the debate concludes with disagreement between those who believe and those who do not.

175 Later, I will return to the discussion between Giese and Hiller on this topic (see pp. 423–424).

176 Levy-Lenz seems to have been of the same opinion: the Institute was closed because it had sensitive information about NSDAP members but *also* because it had "dokumentarisches Material" (documentary material), in the form of questionnaires, on the sex life of, in his opinion, around 40,000 people (Levy-Lenz 1954, 404). Harry Benjamin repeated this in 1966: "The Institute's confidential files were said to have contained too many data on prominent Nazis, former patients of Hirschfeld, to allow the constant threat of discovery to persist". See Benjamin 1966, 12. In the National Library in Prague, for example, I saw a biographical dictionary of Czechoslovak celebrities with a Gestapo rubber stamp. This indicates that the Germans simply gathered information on notable people from many different sources.

177 Herrn 2010, 140. In a letter written to Norman Haire and Jonathan Leunbach, Hirschfeld also mentioned that the WLSR address list (*Kartothek*) had been stolen. See University of Sydney Library, Sydney, Norman Haire collection, 3.20, Magnus Hirschfeld, Typescripts, 1923–1935, letter (dated May 13, 1933, [1]) from Magnus Hirschfeld to Norman Haire and Jonathan Leunbach.

178 Dagmar Herzog writes, on the contrary, that the Nazis' possible interest in the Institute patients' questionnaires was not the true issue ("der springende Punkt ist ein anderer"). In her view, the sacking of the Institute was rather about the installment of a totalitarian state that ruthlessly imposed itself on Hirschfeld's legacy and on defenseless, fragile views of sexual morality. See Herzog 2020, 88–89.

wish to fall into the hand [*sic*: hands] of the Nazis?"[179] Certainly both Hirschfeld and Giese perceived the threat of the Nazis's rise to power and their intention to attack Hirschfeld's life work as a real possibility. We have seen that, as early as 1928, Joseph Goebbels had called for the closure of Hirschfeld's Institute in his magazine *Der Angriff*.[180] Hirschfeld also saw that the old feud against his person started again as soon as he arrived in Greece on his return from his world trip.[181] At that moment, he was reminded of a warning question in a letter he had received with disbelief two years earlier but that he now took seriously: "When will Reich president Hitler close your institute?" Hirschfeld also feared again for his life when he returned to Europe, not for the first time in his life.[182] Also, since Hitler had become Chancellor of the Reich (Reichskanzler), in January 1933, the Institute had to endure several, presumably probing visits by the Criminal Police (Kriminalpolizei), the Auxiliary Police (Hilfspolizei) and even SA people.[183] It is not known whether, or to what extent, these preliminary visits were linked to the looting of the Institute in May 1933. It seems as if they were mostly interested in getting a physical hold of Hirschfeld himself in those preliminary visits.[184]

It is probable that Giese had also seen danger heading his way and had taken precautions in the months before the dramatic events. In mid-December 1932, when he was still in Germany, he applied for a new passport.[185] As we will see later, it is certain that at least some Institute artifacts, among them a painting of a bearded lady and a carved wooden door from Melanesia, must have been taken to safety

179 University of Sydney Library, Sydney, Norman Haire collection, 3.20, Magnus Hirschfeld, Typescripts, 1923–1935, letter (dated May 19, 1935, f. 1) from Norman Haire to Magnus Hirschfeld.

180 Herrn 2010, 159.

181 Hirschfeld & Dose 2013, f. 62/136.

182 Hirschfeld & Dose 2013, f. 63/138: "Wann wird Reichspräsident Hitler Euer Institut schliessen?" Herrn gives an excellent overview of the many (mainly press) bashings of Hirschfeld over the years by the German extreme right, which intensified starting in 1927 (Herrn 2010, 119–29). Hirschfeld was physically attacked after a lecture in Munich in October 1920 and was left for dead in the street. Some rejoiced, a bit too quickly, that he had been killed. See Herrn 2010, 121–22; In het Panhuis, Oct. 2, 2020, Oct. 3, 2020, Oct. 4, 2020; and the contributions of Dose and In het Panhuis in Knoll 2020.

183 Geheimes Staatsarchiv Preußischer Kulturbesitz, Berlin-Dahlem, letter (dated Mar. 29, 1933) written by Arthur Röser, Fritz (Friedrich) Hauptstein and Ewald Lausch (three Institute collaborators) to Magnus Hirschfeld (then in Ascona) and an accompanying letter written by the same three collaborators (dated Mar. 29, 1933) adressed to Reichsminister Hermann Goering. A copy can be found in Schwules Museum, Berlin, Sammlung zum Institut für Sexualwissenschaft und Magnus Hirschfeld, "Von den Mitarbeitern des Instituts", letter (dated Mar. 29, 1933). One of these letters was reproduced in facsimile in Wolff but, strangely, only the less informative accompanying letter sent to Goering was reproduced in her book, not the copy of the letter sent to Hirschfeld in Switzerland mentioning the impromptu visits that must have taken place before March 29, 1933, the date the letter was written (Wolff 1986, 378). In the working papers of Charlotte Wolff (Wellcome Institute, London) there are copies of both the letter to Goering and the one to Hirschfeld. See also Herzer 2001, 230–31. The three letter writers deemed it relevant to distinguish between acceptable, lawful visits (presumably with a search warrant) by the Kriminalpolizei and Hilfspolizei and the much less acceptable visit from the "illegal" SA people. Apparently, one could rely on the local police to ward off the latter visit. For an interesting analysis of the letter, see Wiesner 2003, 424; see also Herrn 2022, 453–54.

184 At least this is what Giese tried to convey regarding these visits in his testimony of the looting. See Herrn 2010, 138. In a very fierce dispute with Manfred Herzer, one of Hirschfeld's first biographers, Günter Maeder, adamantly insisted that there had been looting visits to the Institute before the two on May 6, 1933. Maeder even claimed that the main looting visit occurred on January 31, 1933, the day after Hitler was named chancellor. See Herzer 1997a, 16; Maeder [1993], 4; Wellcome Library, London, archive Charlotte Wolff (1897–1986), correspondence II, 1981–1986, PSY/WOL/6/8/2, copy of letter (dated Apr. 25, 1983, f. 1) from Günter Maeder to the Magnus Hirschfeld-Gesellschaft (where he typed on a letter sent to Herzer). Maeder's insistence that the main sacking of the Institute took place on January 31, 1933 is – as Herzer 1997a already remarked – indeed quite astonishing. Maeder even added a handwritten note next to the underlined (!) date of January 31, 1933 in his text (written near the end of his life): "(versch.[iedene] Zeitungen meldeten es anders)" (various newspapers reported otherwise) (Maeder [1993], 4). This *idée fixe* required the consistent adjustment of many other later dates in his text, chronologically synchronizing them with his initial date of January 31, 1933; as a result, these are also

beforehand, presumably by Giese and possibly by other people who assisted him. Isherwood was adamant that he had later heard that the most important documents and books in the Institute had been taken to safety before disaster struck.[186] Hanns Grafe also claimed that Hirschfeld had arranged the removal of Institute books and other belongings before 1933.[187] Lastly, Hirschfeld himself reiterated afterwards that Giese had played a primary role in saving Institute materials. He even risked his life to do so, Hirschfeld claimed: "From the threat of destruction, and at the risk of his own life, he [Giese] saved a part of our archives (manuscripts etc.), the greater part of which was delivered to the flames by the fanatical supporters of the present regime in Berlin".[188] Giese's heroic feat was also confirmed by a source in Switzerland: "The other heir [of Hirschfeld's estate] is the Berlin-born 38-year-old secretary Karl Giese, to whose energetic intervention is due that part of Hirschfeld's material that was rescued from the Berlin Institute before the student detachment of the Berlin SA destroyed the premises".[189]

One or two days after the looting of the Institute, Giese left Berlin.[190] He judged that it was no longer safe for him to stay in Germany. Giese had lived and worked at the Institute for almost fourteen years. Just like Hirschfeld, he would never return

mistaken. For example, he claims he was locked in the Institute, immediately after the plundering, which he dates to February 1933. Maeder also writes that a first scouting visit of "ein Kommando von S.-Leuten" (a squad of S[A] people) took place in the evening of January 30, 1933, thus the day before – at least according to Maeder's schedule – the ransacking of the Institute. See Maeder [1993], 4–5. Interestingly, Maeder manages to sound partly convincing since he specifically mentions the name of (Herbert) Guthjahr, the man who was in charge of the morning looting on May 6, 1933. We must add that, on another occasion, Maeder gave yet another date (March 1933) for the ransacking of the Institute. See Hirschfeld & Dose 2013, 158 n. 416; Wolff 1986, 433. So, probably, Maeder was simply confused about several dates but was probably right that the May 1933 looting was not the first time Nazis set foot in the building, as also indicated by the Röser/Lausch/Hauptstein letter. The letter writers give the time of the first Nazi visits as the first weeks of February ("in den Wochen seit der nationalen Erhebung" [in the weeks since the national rising]). The fierce quarrel between Maeder and Herzer on this matter could also be explained by another mix-up in Maeder's mind: a scouting visit is not the same as a looting raid.

185 The new passport was valid for five years (until December 16, 1937) and was issued in Berlin on December 16, 1932. It was issued by the Polizei-Präsidium Berlin, Polizei-Revier 28. See Politisches Archiv des Auswärtigen Amts, Berlin, Akten des früheren Deutschen Konsulats in Brünn, Bündel 42, Passangelegenheiten, Einzelfälle gebündelt, Buchstabe G, 1935–1939, file Karl Giese. As we have already seen, a few days after receiving his new passport, Giese left for Zürich to talk to Hirschfeld about a crisis in the Institute and then returned to Berlin, possibly some time in January 1933. Is it possible that his choice to secure a new passport before leaving Germany might have been made out of fear that he would not be able to return to Germany? One can find some copies of a few pages from this passport in ADAM, Nice, Direction départementale de la sécurité publique des Alpes-Maritimes, Sûreté départementale: unité technique d'aide à l'enquête (caserne Auvare), file Giese Karl Otto Bernhard, cote 1440W 0236. I thank Kevin Dubout (Berlin) for sending me a digital copy of this file in February 2012. In 1935, Giese lost this passport when he was in Vienna.

186 Isherwood 1988, 137.

187 Von Praunheim & G. 1992, 11.

188 AN, site de Pierrefitte-sur-Seine, Ministère de l'intérieur, Direction générale de la sûreté nationale (fonds de Moscou), file on Karl Giese, dossier n° 15843, cote 19940448/186, letter (dated Jul. 12, 1934, f. 1) from Magnus Hirschfeld to unknown man within the Interior Ministry: "Il [Giese] a sauvé en exposant sa vie, de la destruction qui menaçait également cette partie de nos archives (manuscrits etc.) dont la majeure partie a été livrée aux flammes par les partisans fanatiques du régime actuel à Berlin". It needs to be noted that Hirschfeld made this claim in mid-1934. That means that Hirschfeld could have been referring to the buy-back operation that took place at the end of 1933, and to which we will return in chapter 6.

189 See the text "Magnus Hirschfelds Testament" in *Der Freidenker*, Jg. 18, n° 18, Sep. 15, 1935, 143: "Der andere Erbe [of Hirschfeld's estate] ist der in Berlin geborene 38-jährige Sekretär Karl Giese, dessen tatkräftigem Eingreifen es zu verdanken ist, dass ein Teil des Hirschfeldschen Materials aus dem Berliner Institut gerettet wurde, ehe das Studentenkommando der Berliner S. A. die Räume zerstörte".

190 In a 1937 document, Giese stated explicitly that he left Germany the day after the Institute had been looted by the Nazis, so on May 7, 1933; see MZA, Brno, fonds B 40, Zemský úřad Brno (Landesbehörde in Brünn), kart. n° 2138, sign. 5274/38, f. 6b. See n° 9 in the addenda, p. 739. In a 1935 interview he said that he left two days after the looting: "Durch einen Zufall konnte ich zwei Tage nach der Sperre des Instituts ausreisen" (By a coincidence, I was able to leave

to Germany. Giese was an avid collector of precious stones and gave Adelheid Schulz a stone from his collection shortly before he left Berlin. The sadness on Giese's face when he gave her the stone was immense, Schulz remembered.[191] On February 9, 2016, at the initiative of the Magnus-Hirschfeld-Gesellschaft, a stumbling stone (*Stolperstein*) was laid for Karl Giese where the Institute once stood.[192] The text on the *Stolperstein* reads: "Here lived / Karl Giese / Born 1898 / Fled in 1933 / France / Czechoslovakia / Fled to his death / 16/03/1938 / Brno [ill. 8]."[193]

two days after the institute was closed). See "Magnus Hirschfelds Erbe in Wien", *Der Morgen – Wiener Montagblatt*, Jun. 26, 1935, 10. It is interesting that Giese used the expression "Durch einen Zufall" (by a coincidence) a second time a few years later, when he was expelled from France and wanted to hide how he got back in to attend Hirschfeld's funeral in Nice. The Institute housekeeper, Adelheid Schulz, pretty much confirms the lack of clarity about the exact day Giese left Berlin: "Nachdem die Aktion [the plundering of the Institute] [beendet] war, ist er [Karl Giese] gleich am nächsten oder übernächstigen Tag gefahren" (After the Action [the plundering of the Institute] [was finished], he [Karl Giese] left the very next day or the day after). See Baumgardt 2003, 11. For a slightly earlier but similar account of the same facts by Adelheid Schulz, see Schulz 2001, 102. Cf. Wolff 1986, 377. Wolff claims Giese probably left on May 7, 1933.

191 Schulz 2001, 46.

192 Nowadays the modernist building of the Haus der Kulturen der Welt occupies the space where the Institute once stood. The address of the Haus der Kulturen der Welt is 10 John-Foster-Dulles-Allee, Berlin; see https://www.hkw.de/de/index.php (accessed Jul. 17, 2020). The *Stolperstein* can be found on the sidewalk in front of the main entrance door on the Tiergarten park side on the ground floor. I thank Raimund Wolfert for having invited me to deliver a short speech on the occasion of the placing of the *Stolperstein*. During the small ceremony, I presented the latest findings from my research on Giese. Raimund Wolfert (as representative of the Magnus-Hirschfeld-Gesellschaft) and Dr. Katinka Bhagwati (as representative of the Haus der Kulturen der Welt) also addressed the small group of people who attended the ceremony. See https://magnus-hirschfeld.de/forschungsstelle/veranstaltungen-und-einladungen/stolperstein-fur-karl-giese/ (accessed Jul. 17, 2020). Two notices (both dated Feb. 9, 2016) about the event can be found on the Facebook pages of the Bundesstiftung Magnus Hirschfeld and the Gesprächskreis Homosexualität der Ev. Advent-Zachäus-Kirchengemeinde. See also the mention of the event in the Chronik section of the Mitteilungen der Magnus-Hirschfeld-Gesellschaft, n° 54, June 2016, 3.

193 See https://www.stolpersteine-berlin.de/biografie/7552 (accessed Jul. 17, 2020); https://magnus-hirschfeld.de/forschungsstelle/veranstaltungen-und-einladungen/stolperstein-fur-karl-giese/ (accessed Dec. 6, 2020): "Hier wohnte / Karl Giese / Jg. 1898 / Flucht 1933 / Frankreich / Tschechoslowakei / Flucht in den Tod / 16/03/1938 / Brno". See also Soetaert & Wolfert n.d.

1. The looting of the Institute, morning session. May 6, 1933.

A Berlin, chez le Dr Magnus Hirschfelds, écrivain connu, on a fait une saisie de ses livres, considérés comme anti-allemands. Le Dr Hirschfelds traite des mœurs allemandes du point de vue sexuel. Des étudiants « nazis » assuraient le service d'ordre. (K.)

2. Another photo of the looting of the Institute in the morning. A well-known portrait of Magnus Hirschfeld is visible on the left, by a side entrance door to the Institute (3 Beethovenstrasse). To the right, a different framed portrait (of a woman?) is being carried out. A photographer is standing on the roof of the truck. May 6, 1933.

3. Student house (Studentenheim or Studentenhaus) of the Friedrich-Wilhelms-Universität in 18 Oranienburger Strasse. 1930s.

4. A truck full of Institute materials arriving at the Opernplatz in Berlin. In the back, between the two uniformed men, one can see a panel taken from the Institute's so-called "Wall of Sexual Intermediaries" (Zwischenstufenwand). A photo portrait of Hirschfeld, made at the Brno 1932 conference (see also chapter 3, ill. n° 12) is visible a little left of center. May 10, 1933.

5. A bronze bust of Hirschfeld, originally housed in the Institute's entry hall, is carried atop a wooden pole on the Opernplatz in Berlin. May 10, 1933.

6. The bronze bust was designed in 1926 by the German sculptor Kurt Harald Isenstein (1898–1980). It was given to Hirschfeld in 1928, on the occasion of his sixtieth birthday. In 1984, a new bronze cast of the bust was made by the Magnus-Hirschfeld-Gesellschaft on the occasion of their seminal exhibition, Berlin Eldorado: History, Culture and Daily Life of Homosexual Women and Men in Berlin 1850–1950 (Berlin Eldorado: Geschichte, Kultur und Alltag homosexueller Frauen und Männer in Berlin 1850–1950). The bust can now be found in the Schwules Museum library in Berlin.

Psychobiologischer
Fragebogen

herausgegeben
und mit namhaften Seelenforschern ausgearbeitet
von

Dr. Magnus Hirschfeld,
Berlin, In den Zelten 19

IV. Auflage.

BERLIN 1915

7. Cover page of the "psychobiologischer Fragebogen" questionnaire (4th edition, 1915).

8. At the instigation of the Magnus-Hirschfeld-Gesellschaft, a stumbling stone (Stolperstein) for Karl Giese was placed on the sidewalk near the entrance of the Haus der Kulturen der Welt, 10 John-Foster-Dulles-Allee, Berlin, on February 9, 2016.

5. Magnus Hirschfeld Lands in Paris and Karl Giese Tests the Waters in Brno

KARL GIESE GOES TO SWITZERLAND

Fleeing from Berlin, Karl Giese quickly joined Magnus Hirschfeld and Li Shiu Tong in Ascona-Moscia in Switzerland.[1] On May 13, 1933, in a letter to Normain Haire and Jonathan Leunbach of the WLSR, Hirschfeld wrote: "Last week our Institute was dissolved by the government, most of our library and many things were taken away by force or destroyed. Most of the books, including a lot of foreign material, were dragged away and thrown on the pyre and burned. Even my bronze bust, which I received exactly 5 years ago (for my 60th birthday) was thrown into the fire. Karl Giese, who personally witnessed the events at the Institute, has joined me in Switzerland, partly to inform me, partly because he himself is in danger. We will draw up an exact protocol of the events".[2] Indeed, Giese and Hirschfeld drew up a witness account (*Zeitzeugenbericht*) on the looting of the Berlin Institute, which we have quoted many times already.[3] Yet the question of whether Karl Giese was truly

[1] Hirschfeld stayed in Switzerland from autumn 1932 until mid-May 1933, first in Zürich and later in Villa Werner in Ascona-Moscia, idyllically bordering Lago Maggiore. A photo pasted into Hirschfeld's guestbook shows Hirschfeld and Li Shiu Tong posing on the balcony of Villa Werner, to which Hirschfeld added a handwritten note stating they were there for Easter 1933. Easter Sunday 1933 fell on April 16, 1933. That Hirschfeld and Li Shiu Tong were in Ascona, and that Giese went there when he fled from Berlin, can be inferred from an entry in Hirschfeld's *Testament: Heft II*, noting that the three left Ascona by car on May 11, 1933. See Hirschfeld & Dose 2013, f. 79/170. There is also a letter (dated May 13, 1933) written by Hirschfeld to Norman Haire, sent from Hotel Central in Zürich. See University of Sydney Library, Sydney, Norman Haire collection, 3.20, Magnus Hirschfeld, Typescripts, 1923–1935. Following Wolff, Herrn claims that Hirschfeld was in Ascona when Giese arrived in Switzerland (Herrn 2010, 134). A Swiss gay magazine also stated that Hirschfeld was in Ascona (*Freundschafts-Banner*, May 15, 1933, 4); cf. Dose 2019, 11. On the other hand, it is difficult to determine when exactly Hirschfeld moved from Zürich to Ascona. Dose writes that, at the end of 1932, Hirschfeld lived in Zürich. See Dose 2005a, 88; for the statement that Hirschfeld was in Zürich since October 1, 1932, see Hirschfeld & Dose 2013, f. 65/142. See also Hirschfeld & Dose 2013, f. 70/152, f. 73/158, f. 77/166, f. 79/170. Frischknecht has shown that Hirschfeld had good reasons to stay in Zürich: he had the excellent library of the Zürcher Museumsgesellschaft at his disposal and Zürich was also the home of the "Verleger des Exils" (exiles' publisher), Emil Oprecht (1895–1952), who intended to publish Hirschfeld's book *Der Racismus* (Frischknecht 2009, 21–23 and passim).

[2] University of Sydney Library, Sydney, Norman Haire collection, 3.20, Magnus Hirschfeld, Typescripts, 1923–1935, letter (dated May 13, 1933, [1]) from Magnus Hirschfeld to Norman Haire and Jonathan Leunbach: "In der letzten Woche wurde unser Institut von der Regierung aufgelöst, der grösste Teil unserer Bibliothek und viele Sachen mit Gewalt fortgenommen oder zerstört. Die meisten Bücher, darunter auch viel ausländisches Material wurden fortgeschleppt und auf den Scheiterhaufen geworfen und verbrannt. Auch meine Bronzebüste, die ich genau vor 5 Jahren (zu meinem 60. Geburtstag erhielt) wurde ins Feuer geworfen. Karl Giese, der den Vorgängen im Institut persönlich beiwohnte, hat sich zu mir in die Schweiz begeben, teils um mich zu informieren, teils weil ihm selber Gefahr droht. Wir werden ein genaues Protokoll der Vorgänge abfassen". The letter is reproduced in Hirschfeld & Dose 2013, 219. On Hirschfeld's bust, and its being thrown on the bonfire, see Herrn 2010, 145. The bronze bust was sculpted in 1926 by the German sculptor Kurt Harald Isenstein (1898–1980). Hirschfeld obtained it in 1928 on the occasion of his sixtieth birthday. A new bronze cast of the bust was made by the Magnus-Hirschfeld-Gesellschaft in 1984 on the occasion of their Berlin Eldorado: Geschichte, Kultur und Alltag homosexueller Frauen und Männer in Berlin 1850–1950 exhibition. Fittingly, nowadays one can find the bust in the library of the Schwules Museum in Berlin. See chapter 4, ill. n° 6.

[3] The *Zeitzeugenbericht* was initially published under the title "Vandalen. Die Plünderung des Instituts für Sexualwissenschaft in Berlin" (Vandals: The Looting of the Institute for Sexual Science in Berlin) in the Basel-based exile periodical *Unsere Zeit: Monatsschrift für Politik, Literatur, Wirtschaft, Sozialpolitik und Arbeiterbewegung*, Jg. 6, Heft n° 10,

the author of the anonymously published testimony, published in 1933, continues to be a minor point of debate.[4] The testimony itself is the primary source of this slight doubt, since the text states in its very first sentence that the witness and writer of the text was *not* a member of the Institute.[5] But this seeming contradiction may safely and quickly be explained away. In order to prevent any possible retaliation, it was wiser to say that the person decrying the looting was not related to the Institute.[6] So most likely, Giese was indeed the author, or at least the main source in providing the testimony of the event.[7] That Hirschfeld also had a hand in the text seems highly probable.[8]

MAGNUS HIRSCHFELD GOES TO PARIS

On May 14, 1933, on Hirschfeld's birthday, and just a week after Giese had arrived from Berlin, Hirschfeld left Switzerland with his Chinese lover Li Shiu Tong and went to Paris by car. One would think that Li Shiu Tong bought the car in Switzerland since it only starts showing up in pictures then.[9] But, as a French intelligence officer noted

1933, 40–42. In the same year, the text was also published in the widely distributed "Braunbuch über Reichstagsbrand und Hitler-Terror" (Brown Book on the Reichstag [German parliament] Fire and Hitler Terror). The very first edition of the "Braunbuch" was published in Basel by Universum-Bücherei. See Braunbuch 1933. A French-language edition was published in October 1933 by Editions du Carrefour. See Comité international d'aide aux victimes du fascisme hitlérien 1933. The eyewitness account in the "Braunbuch" is slightly shorter than the one published in *Unsere Zeit*, since it leaves out the last part of the text. Generally speaking, the passages that put Communism in a bad light were left out of the book version. One can compare the version published in *Unsere Zeit* (reproduced in Herrn 2010, 135–39) with the "Braunbuch" version (published in Sigusch 2008, 366–70). When quoting from this important source, I have made use of the more complete version published in Herrn. See also Sigusch 2008, 365; Herrn 2010, 130–32.

[4] Rainer Herrn has shown convincingly that many elements do indeed seem to point to Giese as the author of the *Zeitzeugenbericht*. See Herrn 2010, 130–40, 142 n. 70, 76, 78. I would like to add one small element to Herrn's case. Herrn shows that Willi Münzenberg (1889–1940) was the publisher of both the periodical *Unsere Zeit* and the "Braunbuch" in which the testimony appeared. Münzenberg and his wife Babette Groß had at one point been inhabitants of the Institute. See Schulz 2011, 5; Herrn 2010, 131–32; Dose & Herrn 2006, 38. But Münzenberg is best known as the founder of the *Arbeiter-Illustrierte-Zeitung* (1921–1938). In 1929, Giese had published, together with Richard Linsert, a text in *A-I-Z*. See Giese & Linsert 1929a. And finally, let us also remember here that Giese came from a family with Communist convictions.

[5] Qtd. in Herrn 2010, 135: "Ein zuverlässiger Augen- und Ohrenzeuge, der, ohne selbst dem Institut anzugehören, die Vorgänge genau verfolgen konnte, hat [...] folgendes Protokoll aufgenommen" (A reliable eye and ear witness, who, without himself belonging to the Institute, was able to follow the events closely, drew up [...] the following account).

[6] Herrn 2010, 134–35.

[7] Rainer Herrn believes that the details given about the bonfire of May 10, 1933, in the last passage of the *Zeitzeugenbericht*, were likely taken from newspaper articles and are for him further evidence that Giese was the author of the text. By the time of the Berlin bonfire, Giese was indeed already abroad. See Herrn 2010, 165 n. 78. Herrn also writes that Recha Tobias (1857–1942), Hirschfeld's sister who also lived in the Institute, was possibly another source for the testimony (Herrn 2010, 132, 134).

[8] Giese, for example, used the word "Protokoll" for his testimony. See Herrn 2010, 135. On May 13, 1933, in a letter to Norman Haire and Jonathan Leunbach, Hirschfeld wrote: "Wir werden ein genaues Protokoll der Vorgänge abfassen" (We will draw up an accurate record [*Protokoll*] of the events); see University of Sydney Library, Sydney, Norman Haire collection, 3.20, Magnus Hirschfeld, Typescripts, 1923–1935, letter (dated May 13, 1933, [1]) from Magnus Hirschfeld to Norman Haire and Jonathan Leunbach. The particular details about the founding of the Institute, and the mention of the Magnus Hirschfeld foundation behind the Institute, seem to suggest that Hirschfeld also helped in composing this text. See Herrn 2010, 135 n. 67, 68. There is also a small chance that Günter Maeder, another of Hirschfeld's secretaries, was a source for the *Zeitzeugenbericht*. Maeder claimed that he left for Zürich (when Giese was already there?) shortly after the dramatic events in Berlin (Maeder [1993], 1, 5–6). But Maeder fitted his version of the story into his own time logic of the chronology of events. According to this logic, Maeder left Germany in March (!) 1933 to see Hirschfeld in Zürich. In the same text, he also claimed that he later visited Hirschfeld in Paris, and even that Giese was not present in the Institute on the day of the plundering. Herrn only mentions Maeder once in his article and quickly dismisses Maeder's claims that he was the only witness in the house and that he was physically abused. On the contrary, as Schulz stressed several times, there was no use of (excessive) violence against the Institute staff during the looting. See Schulz 2001, 111–13.

[9] Herzer 2017, 374.

in a report, the car had been registered in Germany.[10] This would mean that Li Shiu Tong had bought the car when he was in Germany, presumably when he visited the Institute in Berlin, sometime in the summer of 1932. Had the young Chinese also bought the car with a view to transporting materials out of Germany?

Hirschfeld headed to France since he had heard from friends that not even Switzerland was safe for him anymore.[11] He had obtained a new German passport at the end of February 1933 in Zürich.[12] This is interesting because Hirschfeld's old passport, which he acquired in May 1928, was valid until May 1933.[13] This likely means that Hirschfeld foresaw – and correctly judged – that things would only get worse in Germany and that the German authorities might not want to extend his passport – which would leave him stuck in whatever country he was in then. We saw that Giese had also renewed his passport in December 1932. In Paris, Hirschfeld saw the newsreel on the Berlin book burning in a cinema, "in the deepest soul-wrenching emotional shock".[14] Giese had also written to Adelheid Schulz that, when he saw Hirschfeld in Switzerland, the latter was "very sick and very despairing" because of the Institute looting and the subsequent book burning.[15]

After saying goodbye to Hirschfeld and Li Shiu Tong in Zürich, Giese returned to Casa Werner in Ascona-Moscia, where Hirschfeld and Li Shiu Tong had stayed in the preceding months. Giese would remain in this idyllic place for a little more than two months.[16] Towards the end of July 1933, Giese went to Zürich, where an unknown person had invited him.[17]

[10] AN, site de Pierrefitte-sur-Seine, Ministère de l'intérieur, Direction générale de la sûreté nationale (fonds de Moscou), file on Dr. [Pierre] Vacher [Vachet], conférencier a/s de guérisons miraculeuses, anonymous note (dated Jan. 1, 1934), cote 19940482/2. Presumably the same car with German license plate (IT – 6167) can be seen in a picture in the Hirschfeld guestbook. See Bergemann, Dose, Keilson-Lauritz & Dubout 2019, f. 78-79/122-123. Max Reiss wrote to his parents that it was an Opel. See Broers 2016b, letter of Jul. 19, 1934.

[11] University of Sydney Library, Sydney, Norman Haire collection, 3.20, Magnus Hirschfeld, Typescripts, 1923–1935, letter (dated May 13, 1933, [1–2]) from Magnus Hirschfeld to Norman Haire and Jonathan Leunbach.

[12] AN, site de Pierrefitte-sur-Seine, Paris, Ministère de l'intérieur, Direction de la Sûreté Générale, Service central des cartes d'identité d'étrangers, file Magnus Hirschfeld, file n° 210400, cote 19940506/151, anonymous report (dated Dec. 1934). Presumably, Hirschfeld obtained his new passport at the German consulate in Zürich. The date of issue was February 27, 1933 and the passport number was 266. Cf. Hirschfeld & Dose 2013, 170 n. 434, which notes that requesting an extension of his passport in the Zürich consulate would have been futile and possibly even life-threatening. We also need to take into account that this was February 1933, and not yet May 1933, as this explains how Hirschfeld *succeeded* in obtaining a new passport in Zürich.

[13] Hirschfeld's older passport can be found in the Ernst Maass fonds in the Archiv MHG, Berlin. See Dose 2019, 11 n. 3. For other (and different) considerations regarding Hirschfeld's passport and any (available or missing) visas, see Dose 2019, 11–12.

[14] Hirschfeld & Dose 2013, f. 79/170: "unter tiefster seelischer Erschütterung". See also Humbert 1947, 200: "nous entendîmes le savant sexologue [Hirschfeld] nous conter, avec une tristesse que nous partagions, comment il avait eu la douleur d'assister, au cinéma, à l'holocauste de ce qui avait été toute sa vie" (we heard the erudite sexologist [Hirschfeld] tell us, with a sadness that we shared, how he had had the pain of witnessing, in the cinema, the holocaust of what had been his whole life). This conversation must have taken place in May or June 1933, at the home of the French writer Victor Margueritte. It is clear that the word "holocaust" was not used by Hirschfeld but specifically chosen by Jeanne Humbert in her memoir of her husband, published two years after the war.

[15] Archiv MHG, Berlin, fonds Adelheid Schulz, letter (dated May 25, 1933, [1]) from Karl Giese to Adelheid Schulz: "sehr krank und sehr verzweifelt".

[16] University of Sydney Library, Sydney, Norman Haire collection, 3.20, Magnus Hirschfeld, Typescripts, 1923–1935, letter (dated May 13, 1933, [2]) from Magnus Hirschfeld to Norman Haire and Jonathan Leunbach, and ibidem, letter (dated May 17, 1933, [2]) from Karl Giese to Norman Haire. The latter is reproduced in Hirschfeld & Dose 2013, 221. In a letter (dated Jul. 24, 1933) that Karl Giese sent from Ascona to Adelheid Schulz, he wrote that he would be leaving in a week's time. See Archiv MHG, Berlin, fonds Adelheid Schulz. I thank Ralf Dose for sharing copies of this correspondence that Hirschfeld's housekeeper, Adelheid Schulz, received from Karl Giese and that she kept all her life. This correspondence, together with other documents related to the Institute, was donated to the MHG in Berlin after her death.

[17] Letter (dated Aug. 6, 1933) from Karl Giese to Adelheid Schulz in Archiv MHG, Berlin, fonds Adelheid Schulz. On the timing of Giese's stay in Ascona

One month after Hirschfeld's arrival in Paris, the local newspaper *Paris-Soir* went to interview the German scholar. This is what they wrote:

> On a study trip through Europe, professor Magnus Hirschfeld is currently our guest. He has received us kindly, with good grace, without pomp. Among the scientists whose scientific work is under attack by the Nazis, Professor Hirschfeld occupies a special place. It was he who, along with Havelock Ellis in England and Auguste Forel in Switzerland, founded the World League for Sexual Reform. This well-known sexologist founded a unique institution in Berlin, the Institute of Sexual Science. Eminent doctors studied the most bizarre cases of sexology there; and, without a doubt, Professor Hirschfeld is the man best informed about different peoples' way of loving each other. On the night [*sic*] of May 6–7, a hundred Nazis broke into the Institute, and looted and ransacked everything. The 14,000 unparalleled documents they found there were piled up and made into a gigantic auto-da-fé. The conflagration of the bust of the scientist crowned this feat. – Professor Hirschfeld was not in Germany at the time, Dr. Mayer Zachart, the physician accompanying Professor Hirschfeld, told me. Fortunately, because I think that he would not have been able to bear such an act. His health is very poor and he is looking for tranquility. [...]
>
> Professor Hirschfeld entered. He is a stocky man, the face marked by a strong moustache, with rebellious hair, like Einstein, the eyes hidden behind golden glasses. His approach is cordial, and immediately the conversation starts, in German.
>
> – Do you plan to stay long in France? What are your plans?
>
> I don't know myself. I will, if my health allows it, collaborate with French scientists, and then complete a book *Weltreise eines Sexualforschers* (The Journey of a Sexologist Around the World).
>
> – What were your impressions when you heard about the act that destroyed your work?
>
> To tell the truth, I had long felt the danger. Ten years ago, in Munich, Nazis attacked me in the street. I escaped with a fractured skull.
>
> – Do you intend, Professor, to found an institution somewhere similar to the one in Berlin?
>
> That is almost impossible. Think of it! I have spent my whole life establishing my Institute and now I have nothing left but the memory of it. Here I am without a homeland; perhaps I will stay in France; I like the spiritual and artistic atmosphere of Paris, this city where, from Lamarck to Charcot and Calmette, then from Voltaire to Zola and Gide, so many persevering and courageous scientists have been able to work and teach freely. I am very grateful to my French colleagues who have welcomed me so kindly.
>
> – Would it be indiscreet, Professor, to ask you what your opinion is of current events in your country?
>
> My God, no. My countrymen are blinded. I do not abhor those who expelled me from my homeland, who burned my books and my effigy, I pity them. One day, certainly, the truth will triumph. I can only quote the words of a Being whose appearance was the best refutation of the false theories of the Nazis: "Lord, forgive them, for they know not what they do".[18]

and Zürich, see also Hirschfeld & Dose 2013, 170 n. 435, 174 n. 453.

[18] Godefroy 1933, 3: "Poursuivant un voyage d'études en Europe, le professeur Magnus Hirschfeld est actuellement notre hôte. Il a bien voulu nous recevoir, avec une bonne grâce, sans apparat. Parmi les savants dont les travaux scientifiques sont en butte aux attaques des nazis, le professeur Hirschfeld occupe une place de choix. C'est lui qui, avec Haverlok [*sic*: Havelock] Ellis, en Angleterre, Auguste Forel en Suisse, fonda la "Ligue mondiale de réforme sexuelle". Ce sexologue bien connu avait fondé, à Berlin, un établissement unique en son genre: l'Institut de Sciences Sexuelles. D'éminents docteurs y étudiaient les cas les plus bizarres de la sexologie; et sans doute le professeur Hirschfeld est-il l'homme le mieux renseigné sur la façon de s'aimer chez les différents peuples. Dans la nuit [*sic*] du 6 au 7 mai,

The doctor present mentioned by the journalist was Dr. Manfred Mayer-Zachart (1895–1942) who had arrived in Paris in April 1933.[19] One can find an undated entry for Mayer-Zachart in Hirschfeld's guestbook, but the fact that he was present at the interview makes it likely that he inscribed the guestbook around this time.[20] If correct, this would also mean that Hirschfeld started his guestbook as soon as he arrived in Paris.[21] The Mayer-Zachart entry, a quote supposedly from Oscar Wilde, gains a certain meaning when related to Hirschfeld's still being traumatized by the looting of his Institute, in June 1933: "Paris is the only city where you can live when you're unhappy" (*Paris ist die einzige Stadt, in der man leben kann, wenn man unglücklich ist*). And Hirschfeld was indeed very depressed and unhappy, as he clearly also wrote in a letter to Norman Haire, dated June 6.[22]

THE BERLIN BOOK BURNING IN VU MAGAZINE

The Berlin book burning was also discussed in the Paris press. One popular magazine stood out above all. Exactly one week after the events, in its May 17, 1933, issue, the French weekly photo magazine *Vu* published a black and white photo of the May 10 Opernplatz auto-da-fé. Beneath the photo, an announcement declared that, in the next issue, an "auto-da-fé contest" (*concours de l'autodafé*) would kick off. The magazine asked its readers almost gleefully: "which books would you burn?" (*quels livres brûleriez-vous?*).[23] The cover of the next issue showed a gloomy photo montage of a bonfire of books overlooked by three Klu Klux Klan-like figures in black gowns and caps pointing at a man with a naked torso shoveling books into a burning pile [ill. 1].[24]

une centaine de nazis pénétrèrent dans l'Institut, pillèrent, saccagèrent tout. Les 14.000 documents incomparables qui s'y trouvaient furent entassés et servirent de gigantesque autodafé. L'incinération du buste du savant couronna cet exploit. – Le professeur Hirschfeld n'était pas alors en Allemagne, me dit le docteur Mayer Zachart, médecin qui accompagne le professeur Magnus [*sic*]. Heureusement, car je pense qu'il n'aurait pas pu supporter un tel acte. Sa santé est d'ailleurs fort atteinte et ce qu'il recherche, c'est le calme. [...] Le professeur Hirschfeld entrait. C'est un homme trapu, le visage barré d'une forte moustache, les cheveux rebelles, à la Einstein, les yeux cachés derrière des lunettes d'or. L'abord est cordial, et, tout de suite, la conversation s'engage, en allemand. – Comptez-vous séjourner longtemps en France ? Quelles sont vos projets? Je les ignore moi-même. Je vais, si ma santé le permet, collaborer avec des savants français, puis achever un livre *Weltreise eines Sexualforschers* (Voyage d'un chercheur de sexologie autour du monde).– Quelle fut votre impression à l'annonce de l'acte qui ruinait votre œuvre? A vrai dire, j'avais depuis longtemps senti le danger. Il y a dix ans déjà, à Munich, des nazis m'ont attaqué dans la rue. Je m'en suis tiré avec une fracture du crâne. – Avez-vous l'intention, Monsieur le professeur, de fonder quelque part un établissement analogue à celui de Berlin? C'est une chose presque impossible. Pensez donc! J'ai passé toute ma vie à établir mon Institut et il ne m'en reste plus rien qu'un souvenir. Me voilà sans patrie; peut-être resterai-je en France; j'aime bien l'atmosphère spirituelle et artistique de Paris, cette ville où, depuis Lamarck jusqu" [*sic*: jusqu'à] Charcot et Calmette, depuis Voltaire jusqu'à Zola et Gide, tant de savants persévérants et courageux ont pu travailler et enseigner librement. J'ai beaucoup de reconnaissance pour mes confrères français qui m'ont si affablement accueilli. – Serait-il indiscret, Monsieur le professeur, de vous demander quelle est votre opinion sur les événements actuels de votre pays? Mon Dieu, non. Mes compatriotes sont aveuglés. Je n'abhorre pas ceux qui m'ont expulsé de ma patrie, qui ont brûlé mes livres et mon effigie, je les plains. Un jour, certainement, la vérité triomphera. Je ne puis que citer les paroles d'un Etre dont l'apparition fut la meilleurs [*sic*: meilleure] réfutation des théories fausses des nazis: "Seigneur, pardonnez-leur, car ils ne savent pas ce qu'ils font". Contrary to what Hirschfeld claimed here, the almost fatal Munich attack on his life took place in 1920, so thirteen and not ten years before.

[19] Bergemann, Dose, Keilson-Lauritz & Dubout 2019, 218–19.

[20] Ibid., f. 15/59.

[21] The very first, effectively dated entry in the Hirschfeld guestbook appears quite late, November 28, 1933. See Bergemann 2019, 27. I also think there is a possibility that the message from Mayer-Zachart's wife, Käte (1906–1999) (dated Apr. 6, 1934), written just under her husband's (and, thus, on the same page), was added later and that her husband's message was indeed written in June 1933.

[22] University of Sydney Library, Sydney, Norman Haire collection, 3.20, Magnus Hirschfeld, Typescripts, 1923–1935, letter (dated Jun. 6, 1933, f. 1) from Magnus Hirschfeld to Norman Haire.

[23] *Vu*, année 6, n° 270, May 17, 1933, [761-762].

[24] *Vu*, année 6, n° 271, May 24, 1933, cover page.

The main title was "AU FEU!" (INTO THE FIRE!): on the lower part of the page, the question asked in the previous issue was repeated: "which books would you burn?"

Inside, one could find the following statement: "The Hitlerites amused themselves the other night by burning the books that did not agree with their doctrine or their mood in public squares. A symbolic gesture, and, for once, innocent: this game, at least, did not harm anyone. [...] If this story amuses you, we could reenact it here. And from the unintentionally comical auto-da-fé on the other side of the Rhine, make an amusing contest here! Who do you want to burn? We invite the readers of *VU* to imitate – only once – the followers of Adolf. [...] Make a list of ten authors of all times and all places, the complete works or a particular work by whom you would like to see disappear in the flames. [...] And now, executioners, to your torches".[25] They added that simply disliking an author was reason enough to put his or her name on one's list of books to be burned. People could win a total of 5,000 French francs in prizes and had to send in their list by July 15, together with a cut-out coupon from the magazine. Whoever chose the largest number of names from the list of authors most disliked would be one of the winners of the contest. In the next issue, the competition was announced again, and they added that there would be a bonfire where literary figures and lawyers would attack or defend the nominees on the "winner's list". The first prize was a sum of 1,000 French francs ... in books. The whole event would also be broadcast on the radio.[26]

Such repeated and consistent lightheartedness could hardly have amused Hirschfeld. Did he intervene here with the editors of the magazine? A special issue of the same magazine on the topic of sexology, which came out in June 1932, makes this seem likely. In the same year, two of the authors in the issue, Édouard Toulouse and Jean Dalsace, started the Association d'Etudes Sexologiques (AES), which was, at least at first, very closely associated to the WLSR.[27] Hirschfeld may have also stayed with Dr. Dalsace for a while when he arrived in Paris in May 1933, as we will see in a moment.

In *Vu*, two issues later, another anonymous text appeared that reported on the authors and books banned in Germany. This serious and objective text, which very accurately described what was happening in Germany, also seemed to condemn the events. This time, the introduction called the event of the banned (and burned) books in Germany a "hecatomb" (*hécatombe*). The text was anonymous, yet by someone thoroughly familiar with the banned authors mentioned in the text. Did Hirschfeld have a hand in this text or even write it himself? It contrasted starkly with the frivolity of the *"concours"* announced in the previous issues. Hirschfeld was mentioned in this text: "Dr. Magnus Hirschfeld, the famous Berlin sexologist whose Institute was occupied and destroyed and whose effigy was burned. He was accused of writing a

25 *Vu*, année 6, n° 271, May 24, 1933, [774]: "Les hitlériens se sont divertis, l'autre soir, à brûler sur les places publiques les livres qui ne convenaient pas à leur doctrine, ou à leur humeur. Geste symbolique, et, pour une fois, innocent: ce jeu, du moins n'a fait de mal à personne. [...] Si cette histoire vous amuse, nous pourrions la recommencer. Et de l'autodafé involontairement comique d'outre-Rhin, faire ici un concours amusant! Qui voulez-vous brûler? Nous convions donc les lecteurs de VU à imiter – une fois n'est pas coutume – les disciples d'Adolf. [...] Dressez une liste de dix auteurs de tous les temps et de tous les pays, dont vous voudrez voir disparaître dans les flammes les oeuvres complètes ou tel ouvrage particulier. [...] Et maintenant, bourreaux, à vos torches".

26 *Vu*, année 6, n° 272, May 31, 1933, 808. I have consulted the digital radio archive of the INA but, for these pre-war years, there are hardly any recordings of the T.S.F. (*télégraphe sans fil*), as the radio was then called in France. They did have a partial recording of the book burning event in Berlin itself and more specifically of Goebbels' speech. I have also scanned some radio magazines for the period May–July 1933 (*Mon programme TSF*) but did not see any mention of a radio program on the book burning competition that was broadcast.

27 *Vu*, année 5, n° 224, Jun. 29, 1932, on the theme of "Sexologie: problème vital" (Sexology: a vital problem).

28 See the article "A l'index en Allemagne", *Vu*, année 6, n° 274, Jun. 14, 1933, 900: "[L]e docteur

book on 'morals during war' and of having undertaken a campaign against the police persecution of pederasty".[28]

A photo of the original German list of the now banned authors was added to the text. Apparently, someone passed a copy of the list of banned authors and books to the French magazine. On one of the pages of the partly photographed lists, one can clearly see Hirschfeld's name next to other famous names in early sexology: (Sigmund) Freud, (Hans) Ostwald, (Theodoor) Van de Velde, (Leo) Schidrowitz, etc. The magazine bragged they were able to obtain a copy of this list of banned books, despite Goebbels forbidding the public circulation of the list. Did Hirschfeld procure it for them?

Hirschfeld's possible intervention might also explain how Hirschfeld was introduced to the editors of the magazine since, in September 1933, he started to write for *Vu*. He began with a commentary on the Violette Nozière case, a woman who tried to kill both of her parents and ended up killing her father. In the text, a very prudent Hirschfeld claimed that hidden "sexual factors" sometimes played a role in these crimes. As Giese had done in his already mentioned unpublished text, Hirschfeld advised that one should not simply "Cherchez la femme" (look for the woman behind it) but, more broadly, "Cherchez le mobile sexuel" (look for the sexual motive).[29] Later that year, Hirschfeld wrote another one-page article for a voluminous special women's issue and a Christmas special of the same magazine. His article considered theories that stressed the basic matriarchal nature of all societies. He wrote that only in Nazi Germany was this preponderant idea now contested again.[30] It is unclear what became of the competition, whose winners would have been known in the summer of 1933; however, judging from the lack of any other traces of the contest in the magazine, it seems that the project was aborted.

The Berlin looting and auto-da-fé was also featured in another French magazine, though with more compassion. In the summer of 1933, when Hirschfeld was in Paris, the French journalist Roger Salardenne (1902–1968) wrote a series of ten articles titled "Berlin, Babylone moderne" on the Berlin underworld for the French popular periodical *Police magazine* [ill. 2].[31] Salardenne seems to have been an open-minded straight man, who made frequent tours of the Berlin nightlife with his friend Rudolf Schweitzer. He wrote three very well-informed articles about the LGBT scene in Berlin at the time.[32] Sometimes attracted to a handsome female person, he wrote that, in Berlin gay locales, you could never be really certain of the true sex of the person in front of you (i.e. tell if the person was male or female).[33]

In the August 27, 1933 issue, he wrote about the Institute which, he claimed, he had visited a few days before it was raided. At the Institute, he and Schweitzer had spoken with Dr. Felix Abraham, one of the three Institute doctors at the time. They discussed the book Abraham had published, together with Erich Wullfen (1862–1936), on the 1930–31 murder of the Berlin watchmaker Fritz Ulbrich who had photographed 1,500 women in various states of undress. The photographer and watchmaker had

Magnus Hirschfeld, le célèbre sexologue berlinois dont l'institut fut occupé et détruit et dont l'effigie fut brûlée. On lui reproche d'avoir écrit un livre sur « les mœurs pendant la guerre » et d'avoir entrepris une campagne contre la persécution policière de la pédérastie". The book on 'morals during war' referred to is Hirschfeld's *Sittengeschichte des Weltkrieges*, see Hirschfeld, Gaspar et al. 1930a.

29 Hirschfeld, Sep. 6, 1933.

30 Hirschfeld, Dec. 9, 1933.

31 The series started with issue n° 136 (Jul. 2, 1933) and ended with issue n° 145 (Sep. 3, 1933). In 1930, Salardenne had already published a book on the sexual underworld of some of Europe's capitals. In the specific case of Berlin, a separate chapter on male prostitution was added. See Salardenne 1930; and, for the German translation, Salardenne 1931. Salardenne must have been in Berlin in the first months of 1933. He also wrote two books on the German and one book on the French nudism movement.

32 *Police magazine*, Aug. 13, 1933, 11, part VII; *Police*, Aug. 20, 1933, part VIII; *Police*, Aug. 27, 1933, part IX.

33 *Police magazine*, Aug. 13, 1933, 11.

been murdered by Lisa Neumann, one of his models, her boyfriend and another accomplice.[34] Salardenne claimed that Ulbrich's photo collection, amounting to 7,000 photos, later came into the possession of the Institute, but here he possibly confused the Berlin Institute with the Wiener Institut für Sexualforschung (Vienna Institute for Sexual Research).[35] In the first part of the article, the French journalist lamented the destruction of the Institute: "It is not without emotion that I write these lines, thinking that, a few days before this new crime of the National Socialists, I had the opportunity to visit the Institute and to admire its remarkable museum. I still cannot believe in its annihilation. What! Is there nothing left of the magnificent collection so intelligently assembled by Dr. Magnus Hirschfeld and his eminent collaborators? It seems impossible. And yet, alas!"[36]

Hirschfeld seems to have recovered, though slowly, from the trauma caused by the May 1933 events.[37] On July 4, one month after the interview in *Paris Soir*, Hirschfeld delivered a lecture in Club du Faubourg (1918–1939), a popular debate club in the Salle Wagram, Paris XVII.[38] The debate club was led by Léo Poldès (1891–1970), a Jewish ex-Communist and pacifist.[39] Poldès also left a trace – if only his typical signature – in Hirschfeld's guestbook, presumably around the date of Hirschfeld's lecture in the debate club.[40] Here, we have another indication that the guestbook was being inscribed almost as soon as Hirschfeld arrived in Paris.

But despite his seeming depressed passivity, Hirschfeld also tried to earn a living in Paris from his writings. As he wrote in a later letter, he was offered two publishing contracts when he arrived in France. But it seems to me that he was the one who approached publishers to find a way to live from his writings (*"possibilités d'existence littéraire"*).[41] The first proposal came from Grasset, and included the publication of books and, together with the French doctor Pierre Vachet, the setting up of an Institute in Paris, similar to the one destroyed in Berlin. Pierre Vachet had already published several sexology books with Grasset in previous years. Hirschfeld declined this offer, choosing instead the offer from another Paris publisher, Gallimard, possibly simply because they offered him more money and better prospects.

[34] Wullfen & Abraham 1931. On the murder case, see Gordon 2000, 240–42; Herrn 2022, 437–44.

[35] *Police magazine*, Aug. 27, 1933, 7. At least two sources claim that the photographs were in the possession of the Wiener Institut für Sexualforschung, founded in 1928 by Leo Schidrowitz (1894–1956). See https://www.klinebooks.com/pages/books/45216/erich-wulffen-felix-abraham/fritz-ulbrichs-lebender-marmor (accessed Feb. 22, 2022); https://www.arthistoricum.net/werkansicht/dlf/73117/15 (accessed Feb. 22, 2022). That Wullfen and Abraham's 1931 book on Fritz Ulbrich was published by the Vienna Verlag für Kulturforschung, also led by Schidrowitz and located at the same address as the Wiener Institut für Sexualforschung, is a further argument for this view. See https://www.geschichtewiki.wien.gv.at/Leo_Schidrowitz (accessed Feb. 22, 2022). On Schidrowitz, see Marschik 2016, 106–11; Bach 2016, 267–74.

[36] *Police magazine*, Aug. 27, 1933, 6: "Ce n'est pas sans émotion que j'écris ces lignes, en songeant que, quelques jours avant ce nouveau crime des nationaux-socialistes, j'avais eu l'occasion de visiter l'établissement et d'admirer son remarquable musée. Je ne puis croire encore à son anéantissement. Quoi! ne rest-t-il donc rien de la magnifique collection si intelligemment réunie par le Dr Magnus Hirschfeld et ses éminents collaborateurs ? Il semble que ce soit impossible. Et pourtant, hélas!"

[37] This is also how Rainer Herrn summarized the life work of Hirschfeld: "Vom Traum zum Trauma" (from dream to trauma). See Herrn 2004.

[38] *Bec et ongles*, July 2, 1933, 8. Hirshfeld's speech was also reported in the October 1933 issue of the club's periodical, *Le Faubourg*.

[39] The real name of Léo Poldès was Léopold Sessler (also Szesler). He and his brother escaped to Brazil in 1940 and returned to Europe after the war.

[40] Bergemann, Dose, Keilson-Lauritz & Dubout 2019, f. 4/48. That the signature appears on one of the first pages of the guestbook is likely a further indication that it was added before November 1933, the date of the earliest dated entry in the guestbook. Poldès' signature was one of the around fifty names (out of 260 personal entries in total) the editors of the Hirschfeld guestbook were not able to identify. Poldès' name has now been added in a publication listing further discoveries, corrections, etc., to the 2019 edition of Hirschfeld's guestbook. See Bergemann, Dose & Keilson-Lauritz 2021, 4, 11–12.

[41] Bibliothèque histoire de la médecine, Paris, fonds Dalsace-Vellay, folder Ligue Mondiale pour la

BOOK CONTRACTS WITH GALLIMARD

Presumably sometime in July 1933, a contract was drafted in Paris with Gallimard, even today one of France's major publishing houses. The contract stipulated that Hirschfeld would write three books; in addition, he would also publish excerpts from his books in, and contribute to, three popular, abundantly illustrated weeklies owned by Gallimard: *Voilà*, *Détective* and the women's magazine *Marianne*.[42] That the contract did indeed include cooperation with Gallimard's magazines can be inferred from an April 1934 letter in which Hirschfeld says: "I had to collaborate with these magazines". In the same letter, he also wrote that he had to "review several scientific works" for other, more serious periodicals in Gallimard's portfolio, like *La Nouvelle Revue française* (NRF), but I have no knowledge of any such reviewing activity by Hirschfeld for the NRF.[43]

According to the contract, the titles of the books Hirschfeld would write in French were *Psychologie sexuelle*, *Sociologie sexuelle*, and *Pathologie sexuelle*.[44] Each book would number 300,000 letters or characters and include thirty photos. In terms of author's rights, Hirschfeld obtained 10 percent on the first 10,000 copies sold, 12 percent on the next 20,000, and 15 percent thereafter. Hirschfeld received an advance of 10,000 French francs on signing the contract.[45] Gallimard would eventually publish three books by Hirschfeld, though with different titles and no photos. The books were also published quite late. The first one, *L'Âme et l'amour: psychologie sexologique*, only came out around the time of Hirschfeld's death, in April–May 1935. There exists a copy of the book, signed by Hirschfeld, dated April 25, 1935, which shows that Hirschfeld saw the copies of his new book.[46] Two days earlier, together with a copy of his latest book, Hirschfeld also sent a letter to the couple Eugène and Jeanne Humbert.[47] A publicity paper sitting in my copy of *L'Âme et l'amour* is dated April 1935 and, other than mentioning Hirschfeld's publishing career, announces the two other volumes that now bore the titles *Le Corps et l'amour* (The Body and Love) and *La Société et l'amour* (Society and Love).[48] The English translation and UK edition of the first French book in the series of three, *L'Âme et l'amour*, came out in the same year under the title *Sex*

Réforme Sexuelle, letter (dated Apr. 6, 1934, f. 2) from Magnus Hirschfeld to Berty Albrecht.

[42] Starting in 2010, I made several attempts (through different media) to obtain a copy of this contract (and possible other agreements) between Hirschfeld and Gallimard but did not obtain even a single answer from the person then responsible for the Gallimard company archives. It needs to be noted that, of course, Gallimard's archives remain the property of the publishing house itself and can thus be considered private. Also, some of the archives were lost. In 1940, one of several trucks carrying Gallimard archives away from Paris, caught fire. See Grenier & Lemoine 2011, 91. Manfred Herzer had more luck and once told me he had been able to obtain a copy of Hirschfeld's Gallimard contract. He shared the first page of this contract with me, for which I wish to thank him. The full date stamp on the contract is illegible but one can make out the year 1933. On August 11, 1933, Hirschfeld mentioned the existence of this contract in *Testament: Heft II* (Hirschfeld & Dose 2013, f. 80/172). For the three popular magazines owned by Gallimard, see Thérenty 2019. *Détective*, for example, started separately in 1928 but was soon bought by Gallimard, bringing the publisher a lot of revenue (Willemin 2009, 82).

[43] Bibliothèque histoire de la médecine, Paris, fonds Dalsace-Vellay, folder Ligue Mondiale pour la Réforme Sexuelle, letter (dated Apr. 6, 1934, f. 2) from Magnus Hirschfeld to Berty Albrecht: "Je devais collaborer à ces revues"; and "rédiger plusieurs ouvrages scientifiques".

[44] This preliminary description of the three books can also be found in Hirschfeld's *Testament: Heft II*. See Hirschfeld & Dose 2013, f. 80/172: "sexuelle Psychologie (bereits im Entwurf fertig) dann Sex.[uelle] Pathologie u. Soziologie" (sexual psychology [already finished in draft], then sexual pathology and sociology).

[45] See the contract between Hirschfeld and Gallimard dated 1933, partial copy, private archive Manfred Herzer.

[46] Hirschfeld & Dose 2013, 190 n. 498.

[47] The letter (dated Apr. 23, 1935) from Magnus Hirschfeld sent to the Humbert couple is published in *La Grande Réforme* 5, n° 50 (June 1935): 3. Hirschfeld's sudden death, the month before, is also announced there.

[48] My copy of *L'Âme et l'amour* also contains a small printed card stating: "De la part de l'Auteur, absent de Paris" (from the author, absent from Paris). The online catalogue of the Bibliothèque nationale

in Human Relationships.[49] Only one of the other two books in the series would be published: *Le corps et l'amour* came out in 1937, two years after Hirschfeld's death. Later on, we will return to the possible reason for this seeming delay.

In 1938, *Le tour du monde d'un sexologue* was also published by Gallimard. It is important to note that this French translation of Hirschfeld's world trip book was part of another, separate contract that Hirschfeld must have agreed with Gallimard.[50] The third book of the initial "La Science et l'Amour" series of three books, *La société et l'amour,* was under contract but, given Hirschfeld's death in May 1935, most likely never written. Lastly, it is also likely that Hirschfeld planned to publish the French translation of his *Der Racismus* book as well (with Gallimard?) since Raymond-Raoul Lambert claimed that Hirschfeld was reading "the proofs" (*les épreuves*) of the French translation of the book in the weeks before his death.[51] Hirschfeld also mentions a French translation of *Der Racismus* in a letter of October 1933 addressed to Georg Sylvester Viereck.[52]

FRENCH POPULAR MAGAZINES

The collaboration with Gallimard's three popular magazines has some prehistory. Already in 1932, *Voilà* had shown interest in Hirschfeld's cause. In April 1932, the magazine published an article – which Hirschfeld appreciated greatly – by André Beucler on the Berlin Institute.[53] It is possible, and even likely, that Beucler helped in facilitating Hirschfeld's publishing contract with Gallimard since Beucler knew Gaston Gallimard very well.[54] In October of the same year, the magazine also reported, in three issues, on the Brno WLSR conference under the title "At the Assembly of the New Times" (*Aux assises des temps nouveaux*). The journalist who wrote the reports was the Frenchman Pierre Scize (1894–1956), a member of the French section of the WLSR.[55]

in Paris has added the date of May 17, 1935, to its description of the book, but it is unclear what this date refers to: registration at the *dépôt legal* (legal deposit) or some other event.

[49] Hirschfeld 1935b. Norman Haire facilitated the book's publication and wrote the introduction. See University of Sydney Library, Sydney, Norman Haire collection, 3.20, Magnus Hirschfeld, Typescripts, 1923–1935, letter (dated Mar. 15, 1935, f. 2) from Norman Haire to Magnus Hirschfeld. Haire also assisted Hirschfeld in getting his world trip book published in English. When Lane declined to publish the English translation of *L'Âme et l'amour,* Haire looked for another publisher. See University of Sydney Library, Sydney, Norman Haire collection, 3.20, Magnus Hirschfeld, Typescripts, 1923–1935, letter (dated Feb. 12, 1934, f. 2) from Norman Haire to Magnus Hirschfeld. The book was brought out by another London publisher, William Heinemann, in 1935 (Hirschfeld 1935c). Haire also intended to help Hirschfeld get another of his "French books" published, *Éducation sexuelle* (Hirschfeld & Bohm 1934) in March 1935. However, two months later, Hirschfeld was dead. We will return to Hirschfeld's other two French books published with Montaigne later. University of Sydney Library, Sydney, Norman Haire collection, 3.20, Magnus Hirschfeld, Typescripts, 1923–1935, letter (dated Mar. 7, 1935, f. 1) from Norman Haire to Magnus Hirschfeld.

[50] As early as November 1933, Hirschfeld knew that a French version of his world trip book would be published, possibly indicating that a contract with Gallimard for this book was already signed. For his announcement of this, see University of Sydney Library, Sydney, Norman Haire collection, 3.20, Magnus Hirschfeld, Typescripts, 1923–1935, letter (dated Nov. 16, 1933, [f. 2]) from Magnus Hirschfeld to Norman Haire. In February 1934, Hirschfeld's Czechoslovak colleague, Josef Weisskopf, was aware that there would be English and French translations of the world trip book. See Weisskopf, Feb. 20, 1934, 114. As early as May 1932, Hirschfeld started work on a world trip book, and had a working title in mind: "Asien, wie ich es sah, Sexual-ethnologische Streifzüge" (Asia As I Saw It, Sexual-Ethnic Ramblings). See *Neues Pressburger Tagblatt,* May 31, 1932, 4. The German-language version of the book was published in Switzerland in 1933. See Hirschfeld 1933b/2006.

[51] Lambert 1937, 630.

[52] This letter (dated Oct. 30, 1933) is reproduced in Hirschfeld & Dose 2013, 223.

[53] *Voilà,* n° 55, Apr. 9, 1932. Hirschfeld expressed his appreciation of that article in *Voilà,* n° 119, Jul. 1, 1933, 5.

[54] See the chapter on Gaston Gallimard in Beucler 1980, 91–105.

[55] *Voilà,* n° 80, Oct. 1, 1932; n° 82, Oct. 15, 1932; and n° 83, Oct. 22, 1932.

[56] It is necessary to add that all *Voilà* issues always had two different covers, front and back.

[57] *Voilà,* n° 119, Jul. 1, 1933, 5: "Un jeune Chinois, mince et élégant, s'approche de nous".

[58] Hirschfeld & Dose 2013, 138 n. 374.

Hirschfeld was also interviewed and centrally featured in an issue of *Voilà* dated July 1, 1933. This likely indicates that the contract with Gallimard had probably already been drafted sometime in June. This July issue of *Voilà* must have been quite the sensation in Paris since a photo of Hirschfeld and his pupil Li Shiu Tong was featured on the cover of the issue [ill. 3].[56] In the interview with Hirschfeld, the young Chinese Li Shiu Tong was very quickly introduced as Hirschfeld's *compagnon de route*: "A young Chinese man, slim and elegant, is coming towards us".[57] The journalist also noted that the young Chinese sexologist had studied medicine in Vienna, but the truth was that Li Shiu Tong had only taken some courses at the medicine faculty in Vienna in the winter of 1932–33.[58] But it is remarkable that Hirschfeld did not conceal the young man, or seem afraid that this might be perceived as (what today would be called) a coming out.[59] Another photo of Hirschfeld, taken when interviewed by *Voilà*, shows a man who had endured a severe setback: his head seems to sink into his shoulders [ill. 4].[60]

The July 1933 *Voilà* interview was only the first article in a series titled "Love and Science" (*L'amour et la science*), consisting of five articles in five consecutive issues. The last issue appeared at the end of July 1933, clearly hoping to attract a summer readership. In the first article of the series, Hirschfeld quickly turned to his favorite subject, intermediate types. In subsequent issues, Hirschfeld spoke about what he had seen on his world trip in Japan, China, India, and Egypt; and ending, in the fifth and last issue of the series, with the topics of the possible determination of the sex of an unconceived baby, forced and voluntary sterilization, the sexual education of children and the topic of premarital sex.[61] That would not be the end of Hirschfeld's liaison with *Voilà*. In December 1933, "driven by the success of the first series", as the publisher noted, another series of three articles was launched under the title "Science and Sexuality" (*Science et sexualité*).[62] The first issue appeared on December 30, 1933, in which Hirschfeld spoke about the topic of crime and sexuality, only to quickly turn to cross-dressing and what we now call transsexuals. In the second issue he spoke exclusively about sexual fetishism. The last issue addressed the sexual education of children. "Save the young from sexual fear", he concluded.[63]

These many *Voilà* articles are a rather underestimated and unknown source in Hirschfeld research. In one of the texts, for example, Hirschfeld claimed that 1,200 pictures were taken (mostly by Li Shiu Tong) on his world tour; however, since these were sent to the Institute, most were likely lost.[64] The articles also include some very rare pictures of the interior of the Berlin Institute and its collections. Three years after Hirschfeld died, in 1938, excerpts from Hirschfeld's book *Le tour du monde d'un sexologue* were published in two *Voilà* issues.[65] As for the other two Gallimard magazines, I found only one article by Hirschfeld in *Détective*, in the beginning of 1934, and, as far as I could see, no text by Hirschfeld was ever published in the women's magazine *Marianne*.[66]

[59] One of the young doctors trained by Hirschfeld in the summer of 1934, the Dutch gay man Max Reiss, was deeply inspired by this issue (and its cover?), as his last partner Jean Bart Broers noted. See Broers 2016a, 31.

[60] *Voilà*, n° 119, Jul. 1, 1933, 5.

[61] For the "L'amour et la science" series, see issues 119–23 of *Voilà*, all published in July 1933: Hirschfeld, Jul. 1, 1933, 5–6; Hirschfeld, Jul. 8, 1933, 10–11; Hirschfeld, Jul. 15, 1933, 12–13; Hirschfeld, Jul. 22, 1933, 5–6; Hirschfeld, Jul. 29, 1933, 10–11.

[62] For the second "Science et sexualité" series, see *Voilà* n° 145, Dec. 30, 1933, 10–11; n° 146, Jan. 6, 1934, 12–13; and n° 148, Jan. 20, 1934, 14–15. That the third and final part of the series was published in n° 148 (and not n° 147) was possibly due to Hirschfeld staying in Nice in January 1934.

[63] *Voilà*, n° 145, Dec. 30, 1933, 11: "Epargnez à la jeunesse la peur sexuelle".

[64] *Voilà*, n° 119, Jul. 1, 1933, 5.

[65] *Voilà*, n° 364, Mar. 11, 1938, 8–9; n° 365, Mar. 18, 1938, 11–12.

[66] For the *Détective* article, see Hirschfeld, Mar. 1, 1934. In an effort to find possible contributions to *Marianne*, I checked the digitized *Marianne* collection in the Gallica database of the French Biblio-

PARIS HOTELS AND A NEW APARTMENT

We also know, from the very first July 1933 *Voilà* issue, that Hirschfeld was staying in a hotel when he was interviewed and posed with his lover Li Shiu Tong for the magnificent cover photo.[67] On June 4, Hirschfeld was still staying in the Victoria Palace Hôtel but, on June 6, he sent a letter to Norman Haire from the Hôtel Palais d'Orsay, located at 7–9 Quai d'Orsay.[68] In the Gallimard book contract, it also said that Hirschfeld was staying in the Hôtel Palais d'Orsay. Not taking into account trips away from the hotel, he was still staying there in the first three weeks of August 1933.[69] So it is likely that he was interviewed by the *Voilà* journalist in the Hôtel Palais d'Orsay.

After his arrival in Paris, in mid-May 1933, Hirschfeld also possibly briefly stayed with Dr. Jean Dalsace, a member of the French section of the WLSR. Dalsace lived in his newly built, ultra-modern Glass House (*Maison de Verre*) at 31 Rue Saint-Guillaume, Paris VII. It is also possible that Hirschfeld only used Dalsace's address for his mail, as a precaution.[70] In October 1933, a *Voilà* journalist sensationally claimed he had seen a document stating that undercover Nazis in Paris had put a price (2,000 German marks) on the heads of Hirschfeld and other German left-wingers exiled in Paris.[71] Hirschfeld might have feared he was not safe in Paris either.[72]

In mid-August, Hirschfeld still had no fixed address, but, by August 24, he was renting a fifth-floor apartment at 24 Avenue Charles Floquet, Paris VII,[73] on the

thèque Nationale. I only found a small advertisement for Hirschfeld's book *L'Âme et l'amour* in one issue (*Marianne*, Jul. 17, 1935, 4) and an announcement of Hirschfeld's death in another (*Marianne*, May 29, 1935, 12).

[67] *Voilà*, n° 119, Jul. 1, 1933, 1, 5.

[68] See Dose 2019, 11. On June 4, 1933, Magnus Hirschfeld wrote a letter to Agnes Mann from the same Victoria Palace Hotel. See Archiv MHG, Berlin, fonds Ernst Maass, letter (dated Jun. 4, 1933) from Magnus Hirschfeld to Agnes Mann. The Victoria Palace Hotel was (and still is) located at 6 Rue Blaise Desgoffe, Paris VI. The hotel Palais d'Orsay was located right next to the Quai d'Orsay train station; the latter was changed into an art museum in 1986. For the letterhead of the Hôtel Palais d'Orsay, see University of Sydney Library, Sydney, Norman Haire collection, 3.20, Magnus Hirschfeld, Typescripts, 1923–1935, letter (dated Jun. 6, 1933, f. 1) from Magnus Hirschfeld to Norman Haire. Cf. the intelligence report on Hirschfeld (dated Jul. 20, 1933) in AN, site de Pierrefitte-sur-Seine, Ministère de l'intérieur, Direction générale de la sûreté nationale (fonds de Moscou), file on Dr. [Pierre] Vacher [Vachet], conférencier a/s de guérisons miraculeuses, "a/s du docteur HIRSCHFELD, Magnus", cote 19940482/2, which claims that Hirschfeld arrived in Paris on May 18, 1933 and took residence in the Hôtel du Palais d'Orsay. I think that the person or persons who wrote the report made a mistake and overlooked Hirschfeld's initial stay in the Victoria Palace Hotel.

[69] University of Sydney Library, Sydney, Norman Haire collection, 3.20, Magnus Hirschfeld, Typescripts, 1923–1935, letter (dated Aug. 28, 1933, f. 1) from Norman Haire to Magnus Hirschfeld.

[70] Hirschfeld & Dose 2013, 170 n. 439; University of Sydney Library, Sydney, Norman Haire collection, 3.20, Magnus Hirschfeld, Typescripts, 1923–1935, letter (dated May 13, 1933, f. 2) from Magnus Hirschfeld to Norman Haire; Archiv MHG, Berlin, fonds Ernst Maass, letter (dated Jun. 4, 1933) from Magnus Hirschfeld to Agnes Mann, where it says "31 rue St. Guillaume chez Dr. Dalsace" (31 rue St. Guillaume at Dr. Dalsace's). For the *Maison de Verre*, see https://en.wikipedia.org/wiki/Maison_de_Verre (accessed May 29, 2020).

[71] See Car, Oct. 28, 1933, 9. Car claimed that he saw (in the home of a Bavarian man named Schmutz) the list of those with a price on their heads. A commando from Kaiserlautern would take care of the assassinations. Willi Münzenberg's head was worth 7,000 German marks. The news item (or rumor) was picked up in the article "Nazi Feme in Paris: Kopfpreise auf Emigranten", *Gegen-Angriff*, Nov. 5, 1933, 1. I owe this reference to Manfred Herzer; see email (dated Dec. 31, 2014) from Manfred Herzer to the author. Car's article also appeared in the Saar/Sarre newspaper, *Die Chronik*, Nov. 5, 1933. See Brenner 2001, 151 n. 34. For the article that picked up the rumor, see *Grazer Tagblatt*, Nov. 4, 1933, 3.

[72] In a letter, sent from Switzerland around mid-May 1933, Karl Giese had asked Norman Haire to keep Hirschfeld's Paris address secret. See University of Sydney Library, Sydney, Norman Haire collection, 3.20, Magnus Hirschfeld, Typescripts, 1923–1935, letter (dated May 19, 1933, f. 1) from Norman Haire to Karl Giese (!).

[73] See Hirschfeld's Vichy entry (dated Aug. 11, 1933) in *Testament: Heft II* (Hirschfeld & Dose 2013, f. 79/170), where he writes that he had no fixed address yet. See also University of Sydney Library, Sydney, Norman Haire collection, 3.20, Magnus Hirschfeld, Typescripts, 1923–1935, letter (dated Aug. 24, 1933, [1]) from Magnus Hirschfeld to Norman Haire. Ralf Dose is mistaken in thinking that the first indication of Hirschfeld's new Avenue Charles Floquet address appears in the letter Hirschfeld sent to Norman Haire on September 15, 1933. See Dose 2019, 12.

northeast side of the building, located above the main entrance door.[74] He paid 2,300 French francs per month in rent.[75] But Hirschfeld must have been well aware that the high rent he payed for this luxury apartment served a good cause. To this day, on the corner of the facade of the building, a medallion carved in stone is visible, bearing the legend "Civil Society The Future of the Proletariat" (*Société civile L'avenir du proletariat*), and also giving the year of the building as 1910. In 1893, a real estate association (*société civile immobilière*) was started to assist workers with pensions and insurance in case of grave sickness. By 1905, the money saved by 115,000 workers was invested in upper-class rental buildings.[76] In Paris alone, in 1994, the association owned around thirty buildings before the association was disbanded and sold.[77] The posh apartment would remain Hirschfeld's permanent address until he left Paris, in November 1934 [ill. 5].[78]

The apartment's view of the nearby Eiffel Tower must have been simply magnificent. There is a picture of the Eiffel Tower pasted into the Hirschfeld guestbook, which is likely not a photo of the national monument taken by Hirschfeld's entourage, but rather a regular postcard of the famous landmark. Presumably, this postcard was specifically chosen because it was a very close match to Hirschfeld's actual – and, as already stated, simply magnificent – view of the Eiffel Tower from one of his (north-facing) apartment balconies. Above the picture, Hirschfeld added the handwritten note: "Our wonderful view" (*Unser wundervoller Blick*). I think that the publisher of the Hirschfeld guestbook made an excellent choice in selecting this postcard as the cover image of the 2019 edition of the guestbook [ill. 6].[79] In *Testament: Heft II*, Hirschfeld also wrote about the wonderful environment he could see from his new apartment, mentioning not only the Eiffel Tower but also the view of the nearby Champ de Mars park.[80]

As reported by Bertie Albrecht after the Brno 1932 WLSR conference, they had agreed that the next WLSR conference would take place in Amsterdam in 1933. This never happened because the Dutch section of the WLSR eventually refused the date of June 1933, despite Hirschfeld having traveled to Amsterdam from Paris to discuss the matter.[81] When in Amsterdam, Hirschfeld also cashed his shares from an earlier

[74] The northeast corner of the building is also the side with the building's main entrance door. This can be inferred from the fact that, in the morning, Hirschfeld could see from his bed (in the northeast) the sails of the Moulin Rouge. See Hirschfeld & Dose 2013, f. 83/178. For the apartment being on the fifth floor, see Dose 2019, 12 n. 14. In the background of a balcony picture showing Hirschfeld and Dr. Zammert (Bergemann, Dose, Keilson-Lauritz & Dubout 2019, f. 73/117), on the right, one can see the top of the eighty-four-meter-high clock tower of the Basilique du Sacré-Coeur in Montmartre. Hirschfeld mentions this view as well: "mit dem Montmartre als Hintergrund" (with Montmartre as background) (Hirschfeld & Dose 2013, f. 83/178).

[75] AN, site de Pierrefitte-sur-Seine, Ministère de l'intérieur, Direction de la Sûreté Générale, Service central des cartes d'identité d'étrangers, file Magnus Hirschfeld, file number 210400, A.S. de l'Allemand Hirschfeld, [1], cote 19940506/151.

[76] See *L'Humanité*, Mar. 17, 1905. The association issued a magazine titled *Prolétaire prévoyant* (Far-Sighted Proletarian).

[77] See https://www.liberation.fr/futurs/1995/11/28/la-famille-catteau-se-paye-l-avenir-du-proletariat-ce-systeme-de-prevoyance-atypique-etait-tres-conv_148702 (accessed May 28, 2020).

[78] Hirschfeld wrote afterwards that he had spent a year and a half in this Paris apartment, but in reality it was only one year and three months. See Hirschfeld & Dose 2013, f. 83/178.

[79] Bergemann, Dose, Keilson-Lauritz & Dubout 2019, f. 42/86.

[80] Hirschfeld & Dose 2013, f. 83/178.

[81] Warmerdam & Brandhorst [1995], 37; University of Sydney Library, Sydney, Norman Haire collection, 3.20, Magnus Hirschfeld, Typescripts, 1923–1935, letter (dated Jun. 6, 1933, f. 1) from Magnus Hirschfeld to Norman Haire. Hirschfeld was in Amsterdam June 11–17. In a Vienna newspaper, the cities of Chicago and Stockholm were mentioned (in addition to Amsterdam) as two other cities where the new conference could take place. See *Neues Wiener Journal*, September 28, 1932, 9. In a letter sent to Norman Haire, Hirschfeld wrote that Bernard Premsela (1889–1944) had written that he feared the possible reaction by fascist factions in the Netherlands. See University of Sydney Library, Sydney, Norman Haire collection, 3.20, Magnus Hirschfeld, Typescripts, 1923–1935, letter (dated Nov. 16, 1933, f. 1) from Magnus Hirschfeld to Norman Haire.

investment in the local, well-known (and still existing) Bijenkorf department store.[82] In August, Hirschfeld also went to the French spa town of Vichy.[83]

In August–September 1933, Hirschfeld was preoccupied by a book titled *Hitler's Wonderland,* published in London, which put Hirschfeld's former Institute in a bad light.[84] Norman Haire sent Hirschfeld the book, whereupon Hirschfeld started an intense correspondence with Norman Haire, trying to determine how best to deal with the matter.[85] In September, Hirschfeld gave a lecture on "The Race Problem: From Gobineau to the Present" (*Das Rassenproblem: von Gobineau bis heute*) in the Deutscher Klub in Paris.[86] Around the beginning of October 1933, Hirschfeld went to see Norman Haire in London.[87] The publishing contract with Gallimard and the payout on his Amsterdam investment must have given Hirschfeld the idea he could live comfortably for a while. The presence of Li Shiu Tong likely played a further role in Hirschfeld's slow recovery from the May 1933 trauma. The young man would leave for a trip to China in mid-November 1933.[88]

KARL GIESE GOES TO BRNO (BRÜNN) IN CZECHOSLOVAKIA

Meanwhile, in Ascona in Switzerland, Karl Giese awaited the aftereffects of the May 1933 events. Presumably, Giese and Hirschfeld corresponded continuously about what to do next in this period. But after two to three months of retreat and reflection, Giese made a decision. Like Hirschfeld, he considered that Switzerland had become unsafe.[89] The idea of starting a bureau of the WLSR in Copenhagen, with Giese as its secretary, had been floated for a while but this did not come about.[90] On July 24, Giese was still in Ascona but left for Zürich shortly after.[91]

On August 5, 1933, Giese arrived in Brno (also known as Brünn, in German) in Czechoslovakia, to this day the second-largest city in the country after the capital Prague.[92] Starting in 1933, many left-wing German exiles had sought refuge from the Nazi regime in Brno. Brno was attractive to these refugees because they could speak German there and because it was cheap to live. Also, Czechoslovakia was not as *Völkisch*-oriented as Austria. Czechoslovakia may have been a bilingual country (not counting Slovak as a third, separate language) where German-speakers and Czech-speakers had equal rights, but there was always a cultural war going on between Czech- and German-speaking citizens. In the 1920s, when the largely

[82] Hirschfeld & Dose 2013, f. 4/20 n. 5.

[83] Entry (dated Aug. 11, 1933) in Hirschfeld's *Testament: Heft II* (Hirschfeld & Dose 2013, f. 79/170).

[84] Fry 1934.

[85] See the correspondence between Hirschfeld and Haire of August–September 1934, University of Sydney Library, Sydney, Norman Haire collection, 3.20, Magnus Hirschfeld, Typescripts, 1923–1935.

[86] The lecture was held on September 9, 1933. See Frischknecht 2009, 34. The address of the venue was Université du Parthénon, 64 Rue du Rocher, Paris VIII. See *Das neue Tagebuch*, Jg. 1, n° 11, Sep. 9, 1933, 266. This last announcement was found by Marita Keilson-Lauritz. See Frischknecht 2009, 34. An overview of the (currently known) lectures that Hirschfeld gave while he was in Paris can be found in the addenda (n° 16).

[87] University of Sydney Library, Sydney, Norman Haire collection, 3.20, Magnus Hirschfeld, Typescripts, 1923–1935, letter (dated Sep. 19, 1933, f. 1) from Norman Haire to Magnus Hirschfeld.

[88] Dose 2019, 12.

[89] Archiv MHG, Berlin, fonds Adelheid Schulz, letter (dated Jul. 24, 1933) from Karl Giese to Adelheid Schulz.

[90] University of Sydney Library, Sydney, Norman Haire collection, 3.21, Karl Geise [*sic*: Giese], Typescripts, 1928–1934, letter (dated May 17 1933, [1]) from Karl Giese to Norman Haire. The letter is reproduced in Hirschfeld & Dose 2013, 221; see also ibidem, letter (dated May 19, 1933, f. 1) from Norman Haire to Karl Giese.

[91] Archiv MHG, Berlin, fonds Adelheid Schulz, letter (dated Jul. 24, 1933) from Karl Giese to Adelheid Schulz. Giese also wrote that someone had invited him to Zürich and that, when he was in Zürich, he often met Inga Junghanns, a Danish woman. See Archiv MHG, Berlin, fonds Adelheid Schulz, letter (dated Aug. 6, 1933, 1) from Karl Giese to Adelheid Schulz.

[92] Archiv MHG, Berlin, fonds Adelheid Schulz, letter (dated Aug. 6, 1933) from Karl Giese to Adelheid Schulz. Giese wrote that he had found a room in Brno on the day of his arrival, that is, the day before he sent the letter to Schulz.

Czech-speaking suburbs of Brno were added to the inner city, Czech-speakers were becoming the politically dominant group. The language battles found expression in many aspects of day-to-day life. Just to name two examples: there existed in Brno so-called Czech and German "promenades" where, according to one's mother tongue, mainly young people would take walks in their spare time. The German promenade ran from the clock on the main square, Freiheitsplatz (Náměstí svobody), to the end of Rennergasse (Běhounská), the street of Karl Fein's youth, Hirschfeld's lawyer friend in Brno. The Czech promenade started from the same clock but followed Česká street (Tschechische Gasse) until Joštova (Jodokstrasse). Walking on the right promenade was essential. Magnus Hirschfeld mentioned the two Brno promenades in his *Geschlechtskunde* as places for flirtation.[93] The already mentioned open-air and modernist swimming pool, designed by Bohuslav Fuchs, visited by the attendees of the 1932 WLSR Brno conference, was the swimming pool of the Czech-speaking crowd, while the older swimming pool located on Mendelplatz (Mendlovo náměstí) was for the German-speaking swimmers.[94]

Giese would stay five months in Brno. It would be the first of several sojourns in the city in the five years that followed. Contrary to the claim of one source, Giese's mother most likely did not join him.[95] When Giese arrived in Brno for his first prolonged stay there, he rented a furnished room from a woman named Hedi Tschauner (née Sieglová, 1908–?) in 46 Lesnická street (Forstgasse) in Brno.[96] He presumably believed the people from whom he rented were nice but they would later turn out to be convinced fascists. In 1939, the Roman Catholic couple registered for status as German nationals (Deutsche Volkszugehörigkeit).[97] Hedi Tschauner's husband, Emil Tschauner (1904–?), an architect and engineer, would also act as a certified appraiser (*gerichtlich beeideter Sachverständiger*) when confiscated Jewish furnishings had to be valued during the war years.[98]

[93] Hirschfeld 1928, 175. For another mention of the promenades, also called "A-B", see, for example, Nosková 2016, 156.

[94] See the interview of Marie Hlaváčková (1926–) in Nosková & Čermáková 2013, 404–5.

[95] It seems unlikely to me that Giese would have taken his old mother to Czechoslovakia, as Hanns Grafe claimed in an interview with von Praunheim. See von Praunheim & Grafe 1991, 14. Her name, Anna Müller (she married twice), was not found in the resident registration cards present in the AMB, Brno, fonds Z 1, where I checked under the last names Noack (her maiden name), Giese (first marriage) and Müller (second marriage). Her name could not be found in the NA, Praha, either. For a while, I thought that Hanns Grafe might have confused Giese with Kurt Hiller; however, Manfred Herzer wrote to me that Hiller's mother, Ella Hiller (1863–1936), died in 1936, referring to Hiller 1969, 318. Herzer also added that Grafe simply did not know Hiller. See email (dated Dec. 4, 2016) from Manfred Herzer to the author. For now, the matter remains unresolved, not least because the exact death date of Giese's mother is still not known.

[96] The house number 46 can be seen on Giese's resident registration card in the AMB, Brno, fonds Z 1, and in AN, site de Pierrefitte-sur-Seine, Paris, Ministère de l'intérieur, Direction de la Sûreté Générale, Service central des cartes d'identité d'étrangers, file Karl Giese, file number 198379, cote 19940506/68, letter (dated Jan. 26, 1934) from Karl Giese to the Préfet [du département des Alpes-Maritimes]. In the latter, Giese gave this as his last address before he entered France, in the beginning of 1934, which means that he stayed at this Lesnická (Forstgasse) address until he left Brno at the end of December 1933. Giese was thus mistaken when he mentioned the house number 6 in a letter (dated Aug. 6, 1933) he sent to Adelheid Schulz. See Archiv MHG, Berlin, fonds Adelheid Schulz. By 1942, the Tschauner couple lived at 23 Babičkova (Babičkagasse). See *Adresář Protektorátu Čechy a Morava pro průmysl, živnosti, obchod a zemědělství = Adressbuch des Protektorates Böhmen und Mähren für Industrie, Gewerbe, Handel und Landwirtschaft* 1939, II: 1419.

[97] See the petition in Emil Tschauner's home certificate for the candidacy and approval of Deutsche Volkszugehörigkeit status for him and his wife (AMB, Brno, fonds B 1/39). For the ambiguous notion of Deutsche Volkszugehörigkeit, which is difficult to translate into English, and which later reappeared as a notion in need of exact definition in the legal context of post-war damage compensation, see Nachum 2013, 53–58.

[98] MZA, Brno, fonds G 427, Německá správa zabaveného majetku Brno, Movitosti, vyúčtování pro t. zv. Vermögensamt, hesla Sch, St, T, U, kart. n° 16, letter (dated Nov. 13, 1940) from Emil Tschauner to Gestapo (Referat I C 3) in Brno, f. 150. The appraisal done by Tschauner was for the furnishings belonging to Baruch Ticho, a Jewish man who lived at 31 Lehmstätte (V hlinkách).

A "gentleman" (*Herr*) Giese knew from the 1932 WLSR Brno conference helped him to find the room.[99] Most likely, this gentleman was Karl Fein who, as we shall see, lived quite near Giese's new place in Lesnická street. In a letter he sent to Adelheid Schulz, shortly after he had arrived in Brno, Giese wrote that he and Fein found the room by wandering about in Brno but there is also a slight chance that Fein knew about the room being for rent, close to his own apartment, through his family.[100] The local Brno pharmacist Willy Bermann was married to Fein's niece Anna Brecher, the daughter of his aunt Elise Brecher. The sister of Willy Bermann, Marie Ernestine Bermann, was married to Otto Weiss who was, like his father Leopold, an authorized officer (*Prokurist*) of the cement and lime company Maloměřické cementárny a vápenky, founded in 1906 by Leo Czech and Max Kohn. This company was at the time one of the biggest and most important companies in Brno. Karl Fein was clearly acquainted with Leo Czech since he served as Czech's lawyer in a case in which an unnamed female friend of Czech's sued the social democratic newspaper *Rovnost* for libel.[101] Since 1926, Leo Tschauner, Emil Tschauner's brother, worked as a manager in this same cement and lime company. Leo Tschauner – and also, briefly, his brother Emil – were later actively involved in the Aryanization of the company.[102] Emil Tschauner showed up in full SS uniform when he visited the company premises during the war.[103] By January 1943, he was active in the Wehrmacht.[104]

COOPERATION WITH JOSEF WEISSKOPF

Most likely, Giese headed to Brno to inquire with Dr. Josef Weisskopf if the latter would be interested in starting up the Institute in Brno again.[105] Giese wrote to Adelheid Schulz, Hirschfeld's former housekeeper, then looking for a new employer,

[99] Archiv MHG, Berlin, fonds Adelheid Schulz, letter (dated Aug. 6, 1933) from Karl Giese to Adelheid Schulz. It is possible that that Giese did not mention Fein's name (on two occasions) in the letter out of caution, yet he does mention other last names in the letter.

[100] Archiv MHG, Berlin, fonds Adelheid Schulz, letter (dated Aug. 6, 1933) from Karl Giese to Adelheid Schulz.

[101] See "Doležal auf eine Stunde wieder Kommunistischer Chefredakteur" (Doležal in one hour again Communist editor-in-chief), *Volksfreund*, Aug. 20, 1926, 6.

[102] ABS, Praha, SÚMV, fonds n° 305, Ústředna Státní bezpečnosti, sign. 305-501-4, f. 19, 25-26. See also NA, Praha, fonds n° 375, Arizační spisy, kart. n° 186, sign. 1073, cement company Leo Czech & Co. (Brno).

[103] ABS, Praha, SÚMV, fonds n° 305, Ústředna Státní bezpečnosti, sign. n° 305-501-4, f. 26. Leo Tschauner was married to Walburga Marie Linger (1907–?). The couple had one son named Erik (1930–1988).

[104] *Volksdeutsche Zeitung*, Feb. 2, 1943, 10: "dzt. [derzeit] Wehrmacht" (currently under arms in the German army). In 1979, Hedi and Emil Tschauner were celebrating their 50 years of marriage in a city in Germany, where they then lived, see *Brünner Heimatbote*, 1979, n° 3, 58. The couple married in Brno on March 23, 1929. When Giese stayed with them in the second half of 1933, the couple had two very young children, a son born in 1930 and a daughter born in 1932. A third child would follow in 1938 and a fourth in 1943. See *Volksdeutsche Zeitung*, Feb. 2, 1943, 10.

[105] Archiv MHG, Berlin, fonds Adelheid Schulz, letter (dated Aug. 6, 1933) from Karl Giese to Adelheid Schulz. Günter Maeder is the only source known to me to explicitly claim that Giese went to Brno to start a new Institute. See Maeder [1993], 1, 5–6. But Maeder, an always problematical source, also claimed that he had joined Giese when the latter went to Brno: "Dort machten wir auch ein Institut auf, welches sich aber, aus den vorgenannten Gründen [the destruction of most of the Institute materials] niemals mit Berlin vergleichen konnte" (There we also opened an Institute, which, however, for the aforementioned reasons [the destruction of most of the Institute materials] could never compare with Berlin) (Maeder [1993], 6). I have not found another source to confirm that Maeder also went to Brno in the second half of 1933. I looked mainly for resident registration cards for Maeder in the AMB, Brno, fonds Z 1, but did not find any. Just for starters, Giese simply made no mention of arriving in Brno with Maeder in the letter to Adelheid Schulz. Erhart Löhnberg as well seems to conclude, though not with absolute certainty, that Maeder never went to Brno with Giese, since, as Löhnberg puts it, Maeder had nothing to flee from. See Wellcome Library, London, archive Charlotte Wolff (1897–1986), correspondence II, 1981–1986, PSY/WOL/6/8/2, letter (dated Mar. 8, 1985, f. 1) from Erhart Löhnberg to Charlotte Wolff. As indicated by Manfred Herzer, Maeder may have tried, after the war, to downplay his wartime involvement with Nazism and possibly embellished and invented his role in the post-May 1933 scenarios involving Giese and Hirschfeld. See also, in this regard, Maeder's opportunistic (?) involvement with

that he was going to have lunch with Weisskopf shortly after he arrived in Brno.[106] But Weisskopf did not bite. Bizarrely, Giese would make the argument that he had gone to Brno to work with Josef Weisskopf, or with the intention of doing so, several times in the five years that followed. In 1937, for example, Giese mentioned a future collaboration with Weisskopf when he tried to avoid an evacuation order from the Moravian provincial authority. In a letter Giese sent to the Czechoslovak authorities, he wrote that Hirschfeld had always esteemed Brno as the best place to continue his scientific project after his death.[107] But very early on, he must have known that this idea of working together with Josef Weisskopf had no real ground. In an August 1935 letter to Max Hodann, Giese indicated that Weisskopf "has more or less withdrawn from the movement, though for practical, not theoretical reasons".[108] In a letter from April 1937, sent to Kurt Hiller, Giese made a parallel comment about Weisskopf: "Similar [to Karl Fein's case] is the situation with Dr. Weisskopf, who is supposed to be my collaborator, and whom I almost never get to see. He has, by the way, occasionally taken some initiatives, though related to more general sexual reform questions, and has always encountered great difficulties. I know also that he has already made himself very unloved for it. And who can afford to do that?"[109] Weisskopf's ability and willingness to cooperate with Giese and Hirschfeld in his home town of Brno is a not unimportant element in our story. Had Weisskopf agreed and managed to help out his hero Magnus Hirschfeld, surely many things would have turned out differently in the years that followed. But what were these obstacles that Weisskopf had to deal with in Brno?

JOSEPH WEISSKOPF'S PUBLISHING ACTIVITIES

Despite an active support of the Czechoslovak government and Masaryk University in Brno for the 1932 Brno conference and the propagation of its sexological ideas, some other elements in Czechoslovakia had less sympathetic ideas on the matter. Josef Weisskopf was active as a writer of sexology books. He began writing in Czech a few years after graduating. In April 1931, his first book, *Love and Marriage* (*Láska a manželství*) was published in Brno, and he immediately sent a copy to Hirschfeld. On the half title page of the book there appears a catchy quote from Magnus Hirschfeld: "Life without love is misery" (*Život bez lásky je živoření*).[110] In a letter Weisskopf enclosed

a presumed secretary of Hermann Göring, a certain and still mysterious Noël Meyer-Haukohl (1906–1940), a man of English descent who, also according to Maeder, played a role in getting Kurt Hiller out of prison in 1933. Meyer-Haukohl's name is consistently misspelled as Meyer-Hawkohl in Wolff 1986.

[106] Archiv MHG, Berlin, fonds Adelheid Schulz, letter (dated Aug. 6, 1933, 1) from Karl Giese to Adelheid Schulz.

[107] MZA, Brno, fonds B 40, Zemský úřad Brno (Landesbehörde in Brünn), kart. n° 2138, sign. 5274/38, f. 6b-7. Seidl thinks that Giese's 1937 claim of cooperating with Weisskopf was a serious argument in mid-1937, not seeing that Giese was using it – along with several other, equally groundless arguments – in an ad hoc manner and instrumentally to avoid being evicted from Brno. We will return again to this eviction attempt later on.

[108] Arbetarrörelsens arkiv och bibliotek, Stockholm, Max Hodann samling, vol. 15, letter (dated Aug. 2, 1935, [4]) from Karl Giese to Max Hodann: "der sich mehr oder weniger, allerdings aus praktischen[,] nicht aus theoretischen Gründen von der Bewegung zurückgezogen hat". The precise archival description of these letters, present in the Max Hodann samling (fonds), is no longer correct due to an internal reorganization in the archive. See Soetaert 2014, 26 n. 52.

[109] Archiv Kurt Hiller Gesellschaft, Neuss, letter (dated Apr. 27, 1937, 2) from Karl Giese to Kurt Hiller: "Aehnlich [wie bei Karl Fein] steht es auch mit Dr. Weisskopf, der ja eigentlich mein Mitarbeiter sein sollte, und den ich fast nie zu sehen bekomme. Der hat übrigens in verschiedenen, allerdings mehr allgemein sexualreformatorischen Fragen gelegentlich et[w]as unternommen und ist aber auch immer wieder auf grosse Schwierigkeiten gestossen. Ich weiss, auch, dass er sich schon sehr ungeliebt damit gemacht hat. Und wer will sich das leisten?" I thank Harald Lützenkirchen (Kurt Hiller Gesellschaft) for sending me, in October 2015, copies of the correspondence between Kurt Hiller and Karl Giese.

[110] Weisskopf 1931. See also the advertisement for the book in the newspaper *Lidové noviny*, April 5, 1931, 3.

in the book, Weisskopf expressed his deep admiration for Hirschfeld, saying also that he considered himself to be Hirschfeld's scholar (*Schüler*).[111] Another pamphlet in Czech would follow, "Sexual Issues in the Education of Adolescents" (*Pohlavní otázky ve výchově dorostu*).[112] Weisskopf's publishing activity seems to have ended, at least at first sight, in 1931–32. However, it is possible that Weisskopf also pseudonymously published some sexology books in German. Unlike his Czech-language books, these were not sold over the counter but privately through mail order companies, meant only for "serious" readers of the age of majority, and not available in public libraries.

These books were not publicly sold because they ran the risk of being considered pornographic (and could thus be seized) under a Czechoslovak law dating to the Austro-Hungarian criminal code.[113] Two books above all contain several clues that indicate that Weisskopf was the writer or at least that Weisskopf was closely connected to their real writer(s). In the year 1932, *Love Paradise: The Secret of Love without Consequences* (*Liebesparadies: Geheimnis der Liebe ohne Folgen*) was pseudonymously published by a certain Dr. M. S. Miller [ill. 7]. In the forceful introduction, titled "More Light!" (*Mehr Licht!*), a strong plea was made for the emancipatory virtues of sexology. At the head of the text, one finds a Hirschfeld quote and other Hirschfeld quotes form the epigraphs of several chapters in the book. Furthermore, Hirschfeld is quoted or paraphrased very often and approvingly in the book. Lastly, several of the book's approximately two hundred illustrations were taken from Hirschfeld's magnum opus, *Geschlechtskunde*.[114] At the end of the four-page-long introduction, the author and publisher (*Verfasser und Verleger*) gives the first day of the opening of the 1932 Brno WLSR conference, September 20, 1932, as the date of his text, and explicitly refers to the first day of the conference in the introduction, strongly indicating that the book was on sale at the Brno conference.[115] The book also contains a special section on the life and accomplishments of Magnus Hirschfeld, and also includes a reference to the possibility of sexological counseling free of charge with Dr. Josef Weisskopf who, according to the same text, "belongs to the youngest generation of sexologists"; and who, in his published works, was "faithful to the example and slogan of his great teacher and master Magnus Hirschfeld". This section also includes a photo of Hirschfeld and one of Weisskopf.[116]

[111] The letter Weisskopf added to the book he sent to the Institute in Berlin (from which Hirschfeld was absent since he was then on his world tour) has curiously survived in the Kinsey Institute Library & Special Collections, Bloomington (Indiana), Hirschfeld scrapbook, call n° X7910463, letter (dated Apr. 9, 1931) from Josef Weisskopf to Magnus Hirschfeld.

[112] Weisskopf 1932a. I left aside a poetry chapbook *Krvácející rány* (Bleeding Wounds) that he published in 1938 (Weisskopf 1938), and also a 1932 small pamphlet on school reform (Weisskopf 1932b). Neither treats sexological matters.

[113] See paragraph 516 on Erregung öffentlichen Aergernisses, Verletzung der Sittlichkeit usw. (public offence, violation of morality, etc.) of the penal law book (Strafgesetzbuch, Trestní zákoník). For paragraph 516 in the Trestní zákoník of 1852, see https://www.epravo.cz/vyhledavani-aspi/?Id=17&Section=1&IdPara=1&ParaC=2, (accessed May 29, 2020). The central term in Czech is "urážka mravopočestnosti" (insult to morality). For the German-language version of paragraph 516 of the Austrian Strafgesetzbuch, see http://www.graupner.at/images/documents/Vortrag-Porno-2001-1.pdf, 2: "(w)er durch bildliche Darstellungen oder durch unzüchtige Handlungen die Sittlichkeit oder Schamhaftigkeit gröblich und auf eine öffentliches Ärgernis erregende Art verletzt(e)" (who, by pictorial representation or by lewd acts, grossly, and in a manner likely to cause public offense, offends morality or decency). For more information on the historic evolution of Czech laws on pornography, see the third chapter in Svoboda 2014, 61–84. The production and distrubution of pornography was legalized in Czechia in 1993.

[114] Miller 1932a.

[115] The introductory text ends with: "Am 20. September 1932, dem Tage der Eröffnung des Kongresses der Weltliga für Sexualreform" (On September 20, 1932, the day of the opening of the congress of the World League for Sexual Reform). See Miller 1932a, 8.

[116] Miller 1932a, 281: „gehört der jüngsten Generation der Sexuologen an". And: "treu der Losung und dem Beispiel seines großen Lehrers und Meisters Hirschfeld". The four-page-long section is titled "Sanitätsrat dr. Magnus Hirschfeld" (Miller 1932a, 278–81). The photo of Josef Weisskopf is reproduced here, see chapter 3, ill. n° 3.

This 1932 book seems to be an extended and totally reworked edition of a book of the same title that came out in 1930, by the pseudonymous author H. Elis.[117] The 1930 edition was also a privately printed book (*Privatverlag*) and, like the 1932 book, was published by Kulturverlag in Brno. In this 1930 edition, let it be clear, the name of Magnus Hirschfeld is only briefly mentioned in the chapter on sexual perversions (*sexuelle Perversionen*) and the name of Josef Weisskopf is not mentioned at all.[118] The title page of the 1930 edition of *Liebesparadies* says that it is the fifth edition, whereas the 1932 edition states that it was the seventh, reworked and greatly expanded edition of the book.[119] While the 1930 fifth edition of *Liebesparadies* was 187 pages long, the 1932 seventh edition extended to 319 pages. I think it is probable that Josef Weisskopf was the author of this 1932 edition. Possibly, he reworked and considerably extended the text of the 1930 edition, which may not have been his own text.

But there was another privately printed title, also published by the Kulturverlag Brünn, that came out in 1932 as well, the two-volume *Hochschule der Liebeskunst* by another pseudonymous author, Dr. Baldwin Strongworth. The two volumes were published in the first months of 1932 and treated all aspects of sexuality with, in the second volume especially, a very strong cultural-historical focus. When one looks a bit closer at the 600 pages of this work, one can see that a quote of Hirschfeld adorns the introduction, written in November 1931.[120] On the last pages of the second volume, Josef Weisskopf advertised sexological consultations by confidential correspondence, giving the publisher's address. Weisskopf also added that he was a member of the WLSR and that Hirschfeld was its president. In order to obtain a written answer from Weisskopf on a question, one had only to fill out a sheet added to the second and supplementary volume of the book (*Ergänzungsband*). It was also necessary to preorder the supplementary volume and prepay before February 1932. The free sexological mail consultation with Dr. Weisskopf was used, in other words, as an incentive to buy the second volume of the work.[121] A subscriber to the second volume of *Hochschule der Liebeskunst* needed to confirm with a signature that he or she was aware that the volume was a private printing (*Privatdruck*), that it was of the highest scientific level, did not violate morality, and was for one's own personal use and could not be given to others, especially not to youngsters.[122] This shows again that publishing a sexology book, or being an author of such a book, was a tricky matter in pre-World War II Czechoslovakia.

Going further back in time, we discover even more shady sexology books published by the Kulturverlag. In 1929, a book came out with the title *Liberated Marriage: Regeneration: (the secret of love without consequences)* (*Osvobozené manželství: regenera: (tajemství lásky bez následků)*). The subtitle should sound familiar by now. Judging from the printed copy numbers that I have seen, sales went well.[123] According to the

[117] Elis 1930. Besides sharing the main title, one of the two subtitles of the 1930 edition of *Liebesparadies* is also the same as the (only) subtitle of the 1932 edition: *Geheimnis der Liebe ohne Folgen*. A few chapters and themes in the 1930 *Liebesparadies* return in the extended 1932 edition. The unusual (and unscientific) sections on astrology and sexuality, above all, seem to indicate that the two editions of the book were indeed by the same author.

[118] Elis 1930, 126–27.

[119] See the title page of Miller 1932a: "siebente gänzlich umgearbeitete, stark vermehrte Auflage" (seventh, entirely revised, greatly expanded edition). In the MZK, Brno, I also saw a 1930 third edition copy, numbered 1817, indicating good sales. In *Hochschule der Liebeskunst* one reads that the next (and seventh) edition of the book (*Liebesparadies*) was meant to be titled *Das neue Paradies der Liebe* (*The New Paradise of Love*). See Strongworth 1932, 227.

[120] Strongworth 1932, 5–8.

[121] Strongworth 1932, [101]. At the back of the *Ergänzungsband* one finds indeed a form that can be torn out and sent to Kulturverlag at 21 Josefsgasse (Josefská) in Brno. See also the publicity sheet in MZA, Brno, fonds C 12, Krajský soud trestní Brno, III. manipulace, kart. n° 593, sign. Tk VII 2161/33, obžaloba (Anklage) n° 1154/33, court file Karl Večeřa.

[122] Strongworth 1932, [101].

[123] A copy of this title that I saw in the MZK, Brno, was numbered 6656. This book was also published

title page, this book was written by Karel Vespera and Jan Svoboda.[124] The printer of the book was Kajš & Fellman [*sic*] from Kralovo Polé.[125] Jan Kajš was also the printer and lay-out man of (at least) two of the three WLSR 1932 conference brochures. He would also print Weisskopf's very last chapbook of poems, published in 1938.[126]

Still more sexology books were printed after 1932. In 1937, another pseudonymous author named "docteur S. Neumann" wrote the book *Eternal Honeymoon* (*Ewige Flitterwochen*).[127] The – non-fictive – publisher was a Paris company, Editions et librairie "La Culture", but the book was printed in Brno by the printing company [Josef] Štursa, Kraut a spol.[128] From an advertisement for his company, we also know that this book was sold by Karel Večeřa.[129] But we do not know if he was involved in any way with the production of this book. The author was well read in sexology authors and Hirschfeld was quoted several times. Here again, we may wonder if Docteur Neumann was in reality Josef Weisskopf.[130] The Neuman book came out in French under the title *Lune de miel en permanence* (*Permanent Honeymoon*), also in 1937 and from the same Paris publisher.[131]

in German in 1930 as *Regenera: die Wiedergeburt der Ehe: das grosse Geheimnis der Liebe ohne Folgen*. I also saw copies of the fourth and fifth editions, also from 1930. The printer in this case was a Jewish man, Karl Prochaska, from Teschen (currently Český Těšín). See http://www.boehmischeverlagsgeschichte.at/boehmische-verlage-1919-1945/karl-prochaska-verlag/ (accessed May 22, 2020).

124 Vespera & Svoboda 1929. The publisher is given as Regenera, Karel Večeřa [*sic*] at 16 Na pískách (Sandstätte) in Brno. *Adreßbuch von Groß-Brünn* 1930, 461 lists a salesman with this surname at this address, one of five people with this last name in Brno. One of the latter was actually a theology professor (1880–1957) and the online library catalogue of the MZK, Brno, has – possibly erroneously – attributed the book to this theology professor. The choice of Svoboda ("freedom" in Czech) for the second, likely pseudonymous author's name may have been deliberate.

125 The printer's address was 16 Palackého (Palackýgasse). I found an advertisement for Kajš & Fellman in the section "Buch- und Steindruckereien. Lithographische Anstalten" (Book and lithographic printing houses. Lithographic establishments) in *Adreßbuch von Groß-Brünn* 1930, 542.

126 Weisskopf 1938.

127 Neumann 1937. The title page of the German-language edition names "*docteur* S. Neumann" as the author, seeming to indicate a desire for potential customers to believe that the book was written by a French doctor. Was this an attempt to appeal to the public cliché that the French were love specialists?

128 The printer was located at 41 Kopečná (Berggasse). See *Adreßbuch von Groß-Brünn* 1934, 577; *Adressbuch der Landeshauptstadt Brünn* 1942, 18. Interestingly, Josef Weisskopf's first book, the 1931 *Láska a manželství*, was printed there as well. One also finds at the same Parisian address given for the publisher (29 Rue de Trévise, Paris IX) another publishing house around the turn of the century. See *Journal général de l'imprimerie et de la librairie* 1892, 92. They published the journal *Psyché, revue mensuelle d'art et de littérature*, but also *L'Initiation, revue philosophique indépendante des Hautes Etudes. Hypnotisme, Théosophie, Kabbale, Franc-Maçonerie, Sciences Occultes*. See Laurant 1992, 244. The cover of the French edition of the book gives the company's registration number in the *Registre du commerce* as 684.288. See Neumann 1937b. In October 1937, a twenty-eight-year-old Polish man named Walter Rosiki, who owned a publishing house in Paris ("Besitzer eines Bücherverlags in Paris"), was on trial in Colmar for having distributed the book in France. See *Gebweiler neueste Nachrichten*, Oct. 9, 1935, 5. I sent an email to the Archives départementales du Bas-Rhin (regarding the public prosecutor [parquet] in Strasbourg) and the Archives départementales du Haut-Rhin (regarding the court in Colmar) on November 28 and 29, 2020 respectively. Unfortunately, all of the year 1937 of the Tribunal correctionnel de Colmar in the Archives départementales du Haut-Rhin is missing. See email (dated Dec. 1, 2020) from Olivier Holder (Archives départementales du Haut-Rhin, Colmar) to the author.

129 MZA, Brno, fonds C 12, Krajský soud trestní Brno, kart. n° 968, sign. Hp I 81/38, court file Karel Večeřa, publicity sheet. In the back of the book, one also finds an advertisement for Van de Velde's classic *Die Vollkommene Ehe*, also published and printed by the same publisher and printer in Paris and in Brno.

130 Hirschfeld is mentioned on pages 21, 23, 31, 72, 75, 147, 160, 163–64. The chapter on sexual life in Mussolini's Italy is in any case peculiar (Neumann 1937, 146–61).

131 Neumann 1937, 171. The Czech and French editions were certainly produced in tandem, since the French edition states that the book was printed in Czechoslovakia. I have also seen that the Czech and French language editions both have the same green boards with an embossed motif on the spine. I must add that, judging from the different front covers I have seen, there were several French editions of the book published in the same year and that at least one edition was also printed by the Imprimerie Spéciale des Editions La Culture (29 Rue de Trévise) in Paris. I was not able to obtain a copy of the book offered on sale online that contained, at least according to the sales description, a *carte de visite* (business card) inscribed by the author. Since I knew

In order to promote even more sales, the publisher Karel Večeřa marketed his products by mixing up book titles, subtitles and inventing still more pseudonymous authors. I also found a book, published in 1932 by Kulturverlag in Vienna (!), written by M. S. Miller, and titled *Eternal Honeymoon: The Secret of Love without Consequences* (*Ewige Flitterwochen: Geheimnis der Liebe ohne Folgen*).[132] Apart from the main title and the place of publication, the book is – even in terms of its layout and cover – exactly the same as the 1932 edition of *Liebesparadies*.[133] A publicity sheet from Večeřa's mail order company says of this book: "Let there be light! – in all dark, hitherto unsolved questions of sexual life! – in the newest work of the appointed sexologist, member of the World League for Sexual Reform, Berlin, Dr. M. S. Miller [...] the most delicate problems are treated without prudishness [ill. 8]!"[134] The publicity text also suggested that Dr. Miller had written other books on the same topic. So, here as well, several elements seem to point to Weisskopf.

THE PUBLISHER KAREL VEČEŘA

A few things are known about the Czech publisher of all these books, Karel Večeřa (1887–?), who was born in Napajedla (Napajedl) in the region of Zlín. After escaping from prison in Trieste (Italy), he arrived in mid-January 1912 in Amsterdam where he stayed for five weeks. There he was listed as a commercial traveler (*handelsreiziger*, in Dutch), and as an anarchist living in Vienna.[135] In Roosendaal, also in the Netherlands, he was later arrested by the police on a train and taken to the prison of Breda where he stayed for several months.[136] In June 1913, after a robbery in Amsterdam, and also being identified as a saccharine smuggler, he was extradited to Austria.[137] A resident registration card shows that he arrived in Brno in April 1930.[138]

Večeřa would have started up his thriving mail order business around 1929.[139] Besides the sexology books that he published himself, he also sold other erotic books, both fiction and non-fiction titles.[140] He also sold series of pornographic

where to find a sample of Weisskopf's handwriting and signature, I would have been able to recognize his handwriting. The book was on offer online at https://www.le-livre.fr/ (owner Adrian Rodriguez, Sablons, France) in November 2020. I bought the book but when it arrived, the business card (carte de visite) mentioned in the online description was apparently missing. This unique document might have held the answer to our question of whether Weisskopf was our pseudonymous author or not.

132 Miller 1932b.

133 Just like Miller 1932a, Miller 1932b mentions that it is the "7. gänzlich umgearbeitete, stark vermehrte Auflage" (7th entirely revised, greatly expanded edition) and that the book is 319 pages long. Presumably in an attempt to avoid prosecution, the book was issued in Vienna instead of Brno.

134 MZA, Brno, fonds C 12, Krajský soud trestní Brno, kart. n° 968, sign. Hp I 81/38, court file Karel Večeřa, publicity sheet: "Es werde Licht! – in allen dunklen bisher ungelösten Fragen des Sexuallebens! – in dem neuesten Werke des berufenen Sexuologen, Mitglied der Weltliga für Sexualreform, Berlin, Dr. M. S. Miller [...] werden die heikelsten Probleme ohne Prüderie [...] behandelt!"

135 Stadsarchief, Amsterdam, Gemeente Amsterdam, Vreemdelingenregister, archiefnummer 5225, inventarisnummer 930, n° 19, Jan .15, 1912, Karl Vecera.

136 Brabants Historisch Informatie Centrum, Gemeente Breda, 1912–1913, Inschrijvingsregister gedetineerden, exclusief voorlopig aangehoudenen, archiefnummer 55, Gevangenissen in Breda, inventarisnummer 289, n° 295, Karl Vecera, f. 95 and *Provinciale Overijsselsche en Zwolsche courant*, Feb. 25, 1913, 1.

137 *Prager Tagblatt*, Jun. 18, 1913, 4. He arrived in Purkersdorf near Vienna.

138 See his resident registration card in AMB, Brno, fonds Z 1. In October 1939, he returned to his birth town of Napajedla but, after that, I lose track of him.

139 See "1500 kg pornografie před brněnskou porotou" (1500 kg of pornography in front of Brno jury), *Polední list*, May 6, 1938, 4.

140 Typical, recurring erotic fiction titles were for example *Memoiren einer Sängerin* (*Memoirs of a Female Singer*), probably a *Raubdruck* (pirate copy) of a nineteenth-century book of letters, whose first part was supposedly written by Wilhelmine Schröder-Devrient (1804–1860). Two other titles were *Tolle Nächte Eines Frauenarztes* (*Amazing Nights of a Gynecologist*) and *City der Wollust* (*City of Lust*) written by a James Grunert. A publicity sheet for *Tolle Nächte Eines Frauenarztes* as well as a series of pornographic photos on sale by Večeřa's company can be found at https://aukro.cz/tolle-nachte-eines-frauenarztes-der-glutvollste-privatdruck-cca-1935-6966424399 (accessed Nov. 26, 2020).

photographs.[141] Večeřa's mail order business traded internationally. The company had postal checking accounts in Berlin, Krakow, Prague, Vienna, Zagreb and Zürich. In a 1937 court file, one actually finds some confiscated samples of correspondence from foreign clients.[142]

Večeřa was not the only entrepreneur with an undoubtedly thriving mail order business dealing in risqué erotic or pornographic goods. In Mährisch-Ostrau (Moravská Ostrava) there was also the Willy Saalfeld Versandbuchhandlung (mail order bookstore).[143] In Germany, such mail order companies also existed – for example, the Buchversandhaus Eros in Berlin-Halensee that openly advertised.[144] When Večeřa was on trial, in 1937, the fifty-four-year-old man, "of prophetic appearance with a beard and glasses", said he did not feel guilty since he considered the books he sold to be scientific works, cryptically adding he felt supported by a "medical certificate" he had obtained.[145]

It cannot be fully proven that Weisskopf was the real author of even one of the books described above. But it is clear that, at the very least, he used these books to introduce – or confirm – himself as a local sexology authority. It is also clear that the author of *Liebesparadies*, M. S. Miller, or Josef Weisskopf, used the momentum of the 1932 WLSR conference in Brno to publish and sell these books. Two days after the conference ended, Weisskopf placed a small advertisement in the local newspaper *Lidové noviny*: "Josef Weisskopf, MD. Brno-Král.[ovo] Pole, offers sexual counseling and treatment on a regular basis".[146]

If M. S. Miller was indeed Josef Weisskopf, then Hirschfeld may have been charmed by Weisskopf's publishing activity – combining the spirit of philanthropy and business. This might also explain why Hirschfeld thought the young man his ideal successor. Possibly, Weisskopf's use of Hirschfeld's name and fame in these books (and using illustrations from Hirschfeld's *Geschlechtskunde*) meant paying Hirschfeld a certain price (or a percentage of the sales). I also saw a September 1932 letter, sent by the Večeřa mail order business to a man (with a Dr. title), working for the tourism office of the Slovak city of Košice, containing talk of Eroton Pills (Eroton-Pillen) ordered by this man. The letter says that these pills were made under the supervision of Dr. Weisskopf, who made them in cooperation with a pharmacy in Brno.[147] This is the clearest proof that I have found that Weisskopf was intimately

[141] MZA, Brno, fonds C 12, Krajský soud trestní Brno, III. manipulace, kart. n° 968, sign. Hp I 81/38, f. 114, mimeographed publicity sheet (titled "Verzeichnis").

[142] MZA, Brno, fonds C 12, Krajský soud trestní Brno, kart. n° 968, sign. Hp I 81/38. Sales conducted through middle men in Vienna went on until at least 1935. In that year, *Liebesparadies* and *Hochschule der Liebeskunst* were confiscated in Vienna. See MZA, Brno, fonds C 12, Krajský soud trestní Brno, kart. n° 967, sign. Tk 1750/37, court file Karel Večeřa.

[143] See the series of seven bibliographical publications offered for sale by the antiquarian book dealer Fokas Holthuis in Den Haag (the Netherlands) (item 27) at https://fokas.nl/sexuality/ (accessed Nov. 27, 2020).

[144] See, for example, the advertisement in *Jugend: Münchner illustrierte Wochenschrift für Kunst und Leben*, n° 38, Sep. 15, 1931, 607.

[145] See"Nemravnost na tuny: statisícový sklad pornografické literatury zabaven v Brno" (Obscenity by the ton: hundreds of thousands' worth of pornographic literature seized in Brno), *Lidové noviny*, Sep. 30, 1937, 4: "Konečně pan spisovatel Večeřa sc necítí vinen, poněvadž prý jsou to vesměs vědecké spisy. Opatřil si na to i osvědčení odborného lékaře" (Finally, the writer Večeřa does not feel guilty, because he says they are mostly scientific writings. He has even obtained a certificate from a medical doctor). See also "Za slovo omluvy rána důtkami" (For a word of apology, a blow of reprimand), *Moravská orlice*, Oct. 3, 1937, 5.

[146] *Lidové noviny*, Sep. 28, 1932, 8: "MUDr. Josef Weisskopf. Brno-Král.[ovo] Pole, ordinuje a udílí sexuální porady opét pravidelně".

[147] MZA, Brno, fonds C 12, Krajský soud trestní Brno, III. manipulace, kart. n° 593, sign. Tk VII 2161/33, obžaloba (Anklage) 1154/33, court file Karl Večeřa, f. 13. I have seen Josef Weisskopf's signature and must conclude that the handwriting of this letter is not by Josef Weisskopf. The court file deals with a copyright infringement (*Urheberrecht*) regarding the artist Martin E. Philipp from Teplitz-Schönau (Teplice). Two of his drawings had been used in the book *Hochschule der Liebeskunst* without his permission.

involved with the business exploits of Karel Večeřa. The Eroton pills were mentioned a few times in passing in Dr. Strongworth's *Hochschule der Liebeskunst*; and, as we have suggested, Dr. Strongworth may well have been Josef Weisskopf.[148] Presumably, quite a few buyers of the Dr. Strongworth book asked the Večeřa mail order company - from which, after all, they had ordered the book - where they could obtain these potency pills. Or was there a separate advertising leaflet for these pills inserted into the mail order book when it was sent out? Of course, this raises the question of whether Weisskopf was distributing (and also producing) Hirschfeld's Titus Pearls under another name in Brno, and to what extent this was done in cooperation with Hirschfeld. All in all, we perceive here a Josef Weisskopf who either preferred or perhaps felt forced to pursue his sexology topics and related business practices in a semi-clandestine way.

The 1932 WLSR Brno conference may also have drawn too much attention to the topic of sexology. We have seen that one risqué mail order book published by Karel Večeřa, *Liebesparadies*, made explicit reference to the conference, Hirschfeld, and Weisskopf. It is possibly also significant that two books published by Karel Večeřa, *Liberated Marriage* (*Osvobozené manželství*) and *Love Paradise* (*Liebesparadies, Ráj lásky*), were taken to a Brno court in the beginning of November 1932, one month after the Brno conference. Večeřa received only a mild sentence from the Regional criminal court in Brno (Krajský soud trestní Brno).[149] It was in 1937 that Večeřa was most heavily prosecuted by the Brno justice system, when a considerable part of his sales stock was confiscated because it was deemed pornographic.[150]

It was also in October 1937 that the Brno police inquired with the Medical Chamber for the Moravian-Silesian region (Lekářská komora pro zemi Moravskoslezskou, Ärztekammer für das Land Mähren-Schlesien) about the scientific value of *Hochschule der Liebeskunst*.[151] The book was indeed closely examined a few days later by Dr. Adolf Kofranyi (1847–?), a member of this professional board.[152] Kofranyi had issues with the publicity Josef Weisskopf included in the last pages of the book.[153]

[148] Strongworth 1932, 160–61, 184. In this sense, it was incorrect to say that these pills were actively *advertised* in the Strongworth book, as claimed in a report, ordered in 1937 by the Brno police with the Lekářská komora pro zemi Moravskoslezskou (Ärztekammer für das Land Mähren-Schlesien, Doctor's Chamber for the Moravian-Silesian region). See fonds C 12, Krajský soud trestní Brno, III. manipulace, kart. n° 2980, sign. Tl I 4/38, report (dated Oct. 30, 1937) Brno police, not foliated.

[149] *Lidové noviny*, Nov. 3, 1932, 8. The newspaper article claims he was convicted on the basis of paragraph 24 of the *zákona o tisku* (press act). As early as 1930, Večeřa was convicted for his book *Osvobozené manželství: regenera: (tajemství lásky bez následků)* by the Krajský soud trestní Brno (Brno Criminal District Court). See the mention of the court file Tl I 6/30in MZA, Brno, fonds C 12, Krajský soud trestní Brno, III. Manipulace, kart. n° 631, sign. Tk VII 3507/33, indictment 573/34, f. 7; and, for the book itself, Vespera & Svoboda 1929.

[150] MZA, Brno, fonds C 12, Krajský soud trestní Brno, kart. n° 967, sign. Tk 1750/37, court file Karel Večeřa. See also the two newspaper articles in *Neues Tagblatt für Schlesien und Nordmähren*, Sep. 30, 1937, 3; and *Neues Tagblatt für Schlesien und Nordmähren*, Oct. 8, 1937, 3. In the first, there is mention of 1,500 kilograms of pornographic publications confiscated; in the second article, this becomes, erroneously, 150,000 kilograms. Cf. "1500 kg pornografie před brněnskou porotou" (1,500 kg of pornography before the Brno jury), *Polední list*, May 6, 1938, 4.

[151] Letter (dated Oct. 4, 1937) from Brno police to the Státnímu zastupitelství v Brně, MZA, Brno, fonds C 12, Krajský soud trestní Brno, kart. n° 967, sign. Tk 1750/37, court file Karel Večeřa, f. n° unknown.

[152] *Adreßbuch von Groß-Brünn* 1934, 37.

[153] See MZA, Brno, fonds G 107, Lekářská komora Brno, kart. n° 2, board meeting (dated Oct. 9, 1937), mention n° 10: "Schválen referát Dr. Kofranyiho o publikaci, zaslané komoře k vyjádření policejním ředitelstvím v Brně a usneseno v souvislosti s touto publikací předati Cestné radě závadný inserát Dr. J.[osef] W.[eisskopf] v B.[rně]" (Dr. Kofranyi's report on the publication, sent to the Chamber for comment by the Police Directorate in Brno, is approved and the decision was made to forward the objectionable insertion of Dr. J.[osef] W.[eisskopf] in B.[rno] in connection with this publication to the Honorary Council). I thank Michaela Růžičková (MZA, Brno) for sending me the relevant fragment. See her email (dated Jun. 10, 2020) to the author. The Weisskopf advertisement in the book is also mentioned in a hearing protocol in MZA, Brno, fonds C 12, Krajský soud trestní Brno, kart. n° 967, sign. Tk 1750/37, court file Karel Večeřa, folio 123b. But it also notes that Weisskopf's project was not successful (because the books were confiscated?).

That Weisskopf clearly had continuing issues with the provincial Medical Chamber (*Ärztekammer*) can also be gathered from a letter Giese wrote to Max Hodann in August 1935: "He [Weisskopf] has faced a conviction from the local medical court of honor because he has a sign on his house that says 'specialist in sexual ailments'".[154] The books published by Večeřa never disappeared from the radar. In February 1938, Strongworth's *Hochschule der Liebeskunst* was confiscated again in Brno for being pornographic.[155] But then so was Hirschfeld's *Sittengeschichte des Weltkrieges* in Liberec (Reichenberg), in August 1938. That pressure was mounting in the German-speaking Sudetenland at the time seems to have informed the public prosecutor's move in Liberec (Reichenberg).[156]

CONCLUSION

This history on the involvement of Josef Weisskopf with Karel Večeřa's mail order business is important because I think that it helps illustrate and explain why Karl Giese said, on several occasions, that it was impossible for Weisskopf to be actively and openly involved in starting a new Institute in Brno, or to enter into other types of possible cooperation with Giese and Hirschfeld.

Did the many prosecutions that the publisher Karel Večeřa had to deal with raise a red flag where Weisskopf was concerned? That is a real possibility. But this would leave it unexplained why Weisskopf openly published, in Czech, two pamphlets on sexological topics in 1931 and 1932. One can clearly see that his publishing activity in Czech simply stopped after those years.[157] That Weisskopf also had issues with his superiors at the university is attested by a letter he sent to Hirschfeld in April 1931. He wrote that his direct superior, and even the whole medical faculty, were not happy with Weisskopf's views on sexual reform and his blatant attacks on the policies of the Catholic church concerning sexual morality.[158]

But there is another crucial element. Almost all of the persecuted books published by Karel Večeřa were written in German. Did Weisskopf continue his own sexual reform battles in German only? Since sales from the mail order business went well, I think it possible that Weisskopf wanted to protect this likely not inconsiderable income by remaining a pseudonymous author. Also, one should not forget that German was, at the time, after the collapse of the Austro-Hungarian empire, what English is nowadays on the global level: an important cross-border language. Austro-Hungarian political structures may have collapsed after World War I, but German as the lingua franca did not disappear overnight in the newly independent

[154] Arbetarrörelsens arkiv och bibliotek, Stockholm, Max Hodann samling, vol. 15, letter (dated Aug. 2, 1935, [4]) from Karl Giese to Max Hodann: "Er [Weisskopf] hat hier eine Verurteilung vom hiesigen ärztlichen Ehrengericht sich zugezogen, da er ein Schild am Hause hat mit der Aufschriften "Facharzt für Sexualleiden".

[155] *Neues Tagblatt für Schlesien und Nordmähren*, Feb. 9, 1938, 4. The first name of the pseudonymous author is misspelled "Baldurin" in the newspaper article. See also MZA, Brno, fonds C 12, Krajský soud trestní Brno, III. manipulace, kart. n° 2980, sign. Tl I 4/38.

[156] *Neues Tagblatt für Schlesien und Nordmähren* (Sep. 2, 1938, 4): "Das Amtsblatt der Tschechoslowakischen Republik vom 31. August veröffentlicht auf 12 Seiten insgesamt 60 Beschlagnahmeerkenntnisse, nach Paragraph 516 des Strafgesetzbuches (Erregung öffentlichen Aergernisses, Verletzung der Sittlichkeit usw.)" (The Official Bulletin of the Czechoslovak Republic of August 31 publishes on 12 pages a total of 60 seizure notices, under Section 516 of the Criminal code [excitation of public arousal, violation of morality, etc.). For the confiscation of Hirschfeld's *Sittengeschichte des Weltkrieges*, invoking paragraphs 516 and 493 of the Trestní zákoník (penal code), see the original in *Úřední list Republiky Československé = Amtsblatt der Čechoslovakischen Republik*, n° 200, Aug. 31, 1938, 6209.

[157] Weisskopf 1938.

[158] Kinsey Institute Library & Special Collections, Bloomington (Indiana), Hirschfeld scrapbook, call n° X7910463, letter (dated Apr. 9, 1931) from Josef Weisskopf to Magnus Hirschfeld. Weisskopf's superior was Professor Dr. Josef Roček (1887–1946) who, in 1923, published a book on tuberculosis, gonorrhea, and syphilis. See Roček 1923.

countries. Večeřa had German-speaking clients spread over all parts of the fallen Austro-Hungarian empire and in other German-speaking countries. The market was therefore huge and a mail order company trading in risqué literature likely very profitable.

Weisskopf may have feared coming into further conflict with his doctor colleagues. Most likely, he chose to be very discreet about either writing these books in German or at least being closely associated with their production, above all as they always ran the risk of being considered pornographic by the law and, more subjectively, by his fellow doctors. Just as Hirschfeld profited from the considerable income of his writings when he was in France, Weisskopf was likely able to generate a sizeable revenue from his sexology books, distributed in a semi-clandestine way in Czechoslovakia and throughout Europe. He likely also profited from subsidiary lucrative practices, indirectly linked to these publications, like the more or less legal trade in potency enhancing pills, and maybe also simply by gaining more patients seeking sexological counseling in his home town of Brno. But, most of all, all this illustrates and explains why Josef Weisskopf could never live up to Hirschfeld's and Giese's expectations of starting all over in Brno with a new Institute, or even of minimally and publicly cooperating with them. Karl Giese's continued reference to a possible cooperation with Weisskopf, as we will show, went on until 1937. It was simply delusional.

1. "Into the fire! Which books would you burn?" (Au feu! quels livres brûleriez-vous?) Photo collage cover of the French pictorial magazine weekly Vu. May 24, 1933.

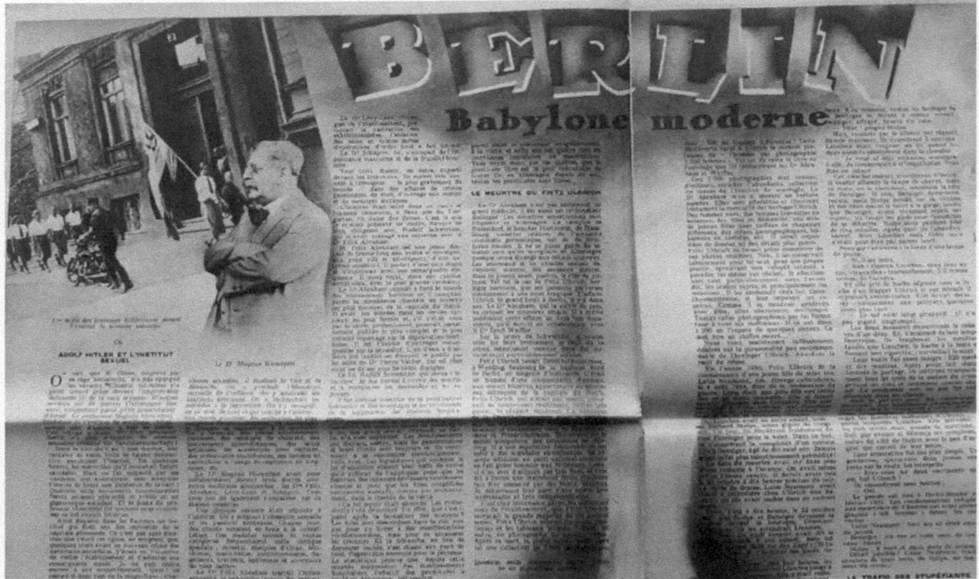

BERLIN

Babylone moderne

ADOLF HITLER ET L'INSTITUT SEXUEL

2. Photo collage of marching students arriving at the Institute on May 6, 1933, with a superimposed Magnus Hirschfeld seeming to look on. The collage appeared in the French periodical Police, part of a series on Berlin's seedy night life entitled "Berlin, Modern Babylon" (Berlin, Babylone moderne). August 1933.

3. Picture of Magnus Hirschfeld and Li Shiu Tong on the cover of the French magazine Voilà, probably taken in the Hôtel Palais d'Orsay where they stayed from June to August 1933. June 1933.

4. Picture of a mentally broken Magnus Hirschfeld, probably taken in the Hôtel Palais d'Orsay in Paris, where he stayed from June to August 1933. June 1933.

5. The apartment building at 24 Avenue Charles Floquet, Paris VII. In 1933–34, Hirschfeld lived in one of the top floors. August 2012.

6. Cover of the book Magnus Hirschfeld's Exile Guestbook 1933-1935 (Magnus Hirschfelds Exil-Gästebuch 1933-1935), published in 2019 by Hentrich & Hentrich in Leipzig.

7. Book cover Love Paradise: The Secret of Love without Consequences (Liebesparadies: Geheimnis der Liebe ohne Folgen), pseudonymously published by M. S. Miller in 1932.

8. Advertising leaflet for the publisher Kulturverlag Brünn, Karel Večeřa's mail order company, ca. 1932–33. "Let there be light! – in all the dark, still unsolved questions of sexual life! – in the newest work of the appointed sexologist, member of the World League for Sexual Reform, Berlin, Dr. M. S. Miller [...] the most delicate problems are treated without prudishness!" (Es werde Licht! – in allen dunklen bisher ungelösten Fragen des Sexuallebens! – in dem neuesten Werke des berufenen Sexuologen, Mitglied der Weltliga für Sexualreform, Berlin, Dr. M. S. Miller [. . .] werden die heikelsten Probleme ohne Prüderie [. . .] behandelt!)

6. Karl Fein and the Operation to Buy Back Institute Materials

THE LOOTED MATERIALS WERE SORTED

Not all looted materials from Hirschfeld's Institute in Berlin were burned in the Opernplatz in Berlin in May 1933. The books and materials that were looted were sorted in a professional way and thus "saved", in the days between the two looting sessions and the book burning itself, so between May 6, 1933, and May 10, 1933.[1] This sorting was mentioned in the inconsistent story the Nazis sent through press releases to the newspapers: "The books confiscated from the Institute of Sexual Science are being subjected to a meticulous examination by experts, so as not to destroy works which have a high scientific value for medical science", one Berlin newspaper reported.[2] The same newspaper further stated that the same was also done with the Institute's photos (*Bilder*) and slides (*Diapositiven*): "The Institute's picture archive, which contained hundreds of slides, was subjected to a thorough examination and everything un-German was destroyed. Some of the pictures were seized and will be examined again by medical experts".[3] Even *Der Angriff*, Goebbels' rag, declared: "We have also learned that several doctors from different faculties are busy reviewing the works handed in, to prevent important scientific works, which perhaps are unique in the world, fall victim to destruction".[4] This sorting operation is likely another indication that adding the looting of the Institute to the students' banned books campaign was a last moment decision, and one not very well thought out. It is also likely that the National Socialists met with some resistance from academic circles on this point. They may have been confronted with objections from scholarly people who pointed out that, unlike the mass-produced books from the lending libraries, some of the books and other artifacts held in the Institute were irreplaceable, as indeed was the case.

To this day, though more and more rarely, books adorned with the Institute's typical stamps continue to surface at antiquarian booksellers [ill. 1].[5] The Magnus-Hirschfeld-Gesellschaft in Berlin owns fifty-nine books and other publications bearing the Institute's stamps.[6] This is a further indication that the Institute's collection did

[1] See Dose & Herrn 2006, 45; Herzer 2001, 234; Herzer 2009a, 158; Herrn 2010, 165 n. 77.

[2] *Germania*, May 7, 1933 (qtd. in Herzer 2001, 233): "Die beschlagnahmten Bücher des Instituts für Sexualwissenschaft werden noch einer genauen Sichtung durch Sachverständige unterzogen, damit nicht Werke vernichtet werden, die für die medizinische Wissenschaft einen hohen wissenschaftlichen Wert besitzen".

[3] *Germania*, May 7, 1933 (qtd. in Herzer 2001, 233): "Das Bildarchiv des Instituts, in dem Hunderte von Diapositiven lagerten, wurde einer eingehenden Untersuchung unterzogen und alles Undeutsche vernichtet. Ein Teil der Bilder wurde sichergestellt und wird von medizinischen Sachverständigen noch einmal geprüft werden".

[4] *Der Angriff*, May 10, 1933, 3 (qtd. in Herzer 2009a, 158): "Wie wir noch ergänzend hierzu erfahren, sind mehrere Doktoren verschiedener Fakultäten mit der Durchsicht der abgegebenen Werke beschäftigt, um auf jeden Fall zu vermeiden, daß wichtige wissenschaftliche Werke, die vielleicht nur einmal in der Welt existieren, der Vernichtung zum Opfer fallen".

[5] For examples of the typical stamps in the Institute's library books, see Dose & Herrn 2006, 43. The stamps can also be seen online at: https://provenienz.gbv.de/Institut_für_Sexualwissenschaft_(Berlin) (accessed Jun. 8, 2020); and https://lootedculturalassets.de/index.php/Detail/Entity/Show/entity_id/1071 (accessed Dec. 9, 2020).

[6] Aktives Museum Faschismus und Widerstand in Berlin & Gedenk- und Bildungsstätte Haus der Wannsee-Konferenz 2018, 21; and Dose 2020a, 25. In 2006, Ralf Dose and Rainer Herrn, two collaborators of the Magnus-Hirschfeld-Gesellschaft, wrote that around twenty-five books had been identified as

not end up on the Berlin bonfire in its entirety, despite some authors continuing to claim, or simply assume, that the *whole* collection was looted and burned on the Opernplatz.[7] When writing the history of homosexuality, we have to be wary not to fall into the trap of using "the punishment of Sodom" as a historical model, as Michel Foucault once poignantly put it.[8] It is known that at least one book taken from the Institute found its way to the library of the Reich Ministry of Public Enlightenment and Propaganda (Reichsministerium für Volksaufklärung und Propaganda) headed by Joseph Goebbels.[9] In December 1934, the department of the Berlin police dealing with lewd books and images sent twenty-eight books confiscated from the Institute to the Prussian State Library in Berlin (Staatsbibliothek zu Berlin, Unter den Linden).[10]

coming from the Institute's collection (Dose & Herrn 2006, 49–51). By 2016, the MHG Berlin owned thirty-two of the Institute's books. See "Alter Institutsbestand" by Raimund Wolfert (dated May 12, 2016) in Archiv MHG, Berlin. In December 2020, another book bearing Institute stamps was discovered in the collection of the Universitätsbibliothek Greifswald and was promptly donated to the MHG Berlin, bringing their total to fifty-nine publications from the original Institute collection. See Mitteilungen der Magnus-Hirschfeld-Gesellschaft, n° 67, July 2021, 5. This demonstrates that more copies are gradually surfacing and are actively acquired by or donated to the MHG. For examples of books acquired by the MHG, see https://magnus-hirschfeld.de/bibliothek-und-archiv/sammlungsschwerpunkte/gesucht-und-gefunden/ (accessed Jul. 3, 2020). The Rosa Archiv in Leipzig (run by Jürgen Zehnle) claims to have a volume of the *Jahrbuch für sexuelle Zwischenstufen* with a WhK stamp, most likely indicating that the volume comes from the Institute collection. See https://www.jfsz.de/die-neu-edition/index.php (accessed Dec. 3, 2020). In his testimony of the May 1933 lootings, Giese claimed that all copies of the Institute's *Jahrbuch für sexuelle Zwischenstufen* had been looted. See Herrn 2010, 138.

7 In the spring of 2019, the antiquarian book seller Elysium Books (Norwich, Vermont, USA) offered for sale (asking $300) a 1922 book by Ernst Blass, *Das Wesen der neuen Tanzkunst*, which bore the usual Institute library rubber stamps. However, quite contradictorily, the seller added: "Hirschfeld's library and publications were all burned in 1933 by the Nazis and are quite rare". See Elysium Books catalogue, spring, 2019, n° 12. For an example of the persistent idea that Hirschfeld's collection was completely destroyed, see Bock 2003, 133: "Die über zehntausend Bände umfassende einzigartige Bibliothek Hirschfelds wurde vier Tage später auf dem Berliner Opernplatz vollständig verbrannt" (Hirschfeld's unique library of over ten thousand volumes was completely burned four days later on Berlin's Opernplatz).

8 Foucault 1982, 16: "ce n'est pas la condamnation de Sodome qui doit servir de modèle historique" (the punishment of Sodom should not serve as the historical model). It must be added Foucault was here referring specifically to writing the history of Greek homosexuality in Antiquity, but I think that he would have agreed that this admonition was valid, more generally, when writing the history of homosexuality across the ages. A recent text by Dagmar Herzog seems to provide an example of this "will to victimhood", at all costs, making things look even worse than they were. Addressing the more restrained morning looting of the Institute, she writes: "Diesen und ähnlichen Aufrufen folgend zerschlugen am 6. Mai 1933 dem Nationalsozialismus nahestehende Studenten die Vitrinen, verwüsteteten die 10.000 Bände in der Bibliothek und zertrampelten die 35.000 Fotos im Bestand" (Following these and similar calls, on May 6, 1933, students close to Nazism smashed the display cases, vandalized the 10,000 volumes in the library and trampled the 35,000 photographs in the collection). Her account of the afternoon looters seems to indicate that she read (and liberally rewrote) Giese's testimony, even claiming that (all?) the afternoon looters wore SA uniforms. But Giese never wrote that all of the library was removed (let alone "destroyed") during the morning looting, or that the entire photo collection had been trampled. See Herzog 2020, 88.

9 Dose & Herrn 2006, 49. It was a book by Arthur Kronfeld (1886–1941), a doctor who worked at the Institute, and bore a typical Institute stamp, showing its provenance.

10 Letter (dated Dec. 21, 1934) Polizeipräsident in Berlin (Abteilung IV, Deutsche Zentralpolizeistelle zur Bekämpfung unzüchtiger Bilder, Schriften und Inzerate) to Erwerbsabteilung Preußischen Staatsbibliothek, Berlin. This letter, in the archives of the Staatsbibliothek zu Berlin, was displayed in a mini-exhibition to mark the commemorative event (*Gedenkveranstaltung*) "90 Jahre Zerstörung des Instituts für Sexualwissenschaft" (90th anniversary of the destruction of the Institute of Sexual Science), on May 10, 2023, in the Staatsbibliothek zu Berlin (Unter den Linden), Berlin. One of these books was likely *Vita homosexualis: gesammelte Schriften*, compiled in 1902 by the Munich gay activist August Fleischmann (1859–1931). See Fleischmann (1902) and http://magnus-hirschfeld.de/bibliothek-und-archiv/sammlungsschwerpunkte/gesucht-und-gefunden/ (accessed Nov. 15, 2020). Sixteen mentions of books from the Institute located in still other German libraries (including the 8 pamphlets compiled in the above-mentioned book by Fleischmann) can be found in the database http://www.lostart.de/ by entering "Institut für Sexualwissenschaft". In October 2022, Jens Dobler of the MHG, Berlin, started a research project titled "Die Plünderung des Instituts für Sexualwissenschaft in der NS-Zeit" (The looting of the Institute of Sexual Science in the Nazi era), whose goal is to produce

It seems to indicate that at least some of the books must have found a new home in Berlin or German libraries then. Günter Maeder further claimed he had seen objects from the Institute in the Ethnological Museum (Etnologisches Museum) in Berlin.[11] Lastly, in 1935, one Swiss observer claimed that, in the weeks after the bonfire, books coming from the Institute were on offer "on the book carts around the Berlin University".[12]

WHAT WAS THE SIZE OF THE INSTITUTE COLLECTION?

As in the case of the questionnaires, the exact extent of the Institute collection, and how many of its materials – even approximately – were destroyed or saved is a question that will likely always remain unresolved.[13] In an "Autobiographical Sketch", Magnus Hirschfeld himself wrote that the Institute collection numbered approximately 20,000 volumes, 12.000 of which were removed in the lootings on May 6, 1933.[14] In his testimonial of the looting, Karl Giese mentioned that "more than 10,000" books (*Bände*) weren removed from the Institute.[15] In June 1933, Hirschfeld spoke of 14,000 books but it is unclear if he was referring to the Institute's total book collection or the estimated number of books taken away by the looters.[16] How many of these looted books were actually burned on the Opernplatz is yet another question, equally unresolved.

THE PRINTED CATALOGUE OF THE DUTCH SCIENTIFIC HUMANITARIAN COMMITTEE (NWHK)

Following the example of Germany, in 1912, the Netherlands opened a branch of the Scientific-Humanitarian Committee (Wissenschaftlich-humanitäres Komitee, WhK), the Dutch Scientific-Humanitarian Committee (Nederlandsch Wetenschappelijk Humanitair Komitee, NWHK). Its principal figure was the Dutch lawyer Jacob Schorer

a catalogue of as many of the Institute's former holdings as possible, based on surviving archival and other sources. All identified items would then be uploaded to the lostart.de database in order to improve their chances of being eventually traced by museums and libraries worldwide. The MHG, Berlin, would then plead for the restitution of any objects that would surface in this way. See Mitteilungen der Magnus-Hirschfeld-Gesellschaft, n°s 69–70, December 2022, 4.

11 Maeder [1993]: 6–7.

12 Lamprecht, Nov. 15, 1935, 173: "auf den Bücherwagen um die Berliner Universität"

13 Dose & Herrn 2006, 39.

14 Hirschfeld 1936, 319. In a June 1933 letter that Hirschfeld wrote to Agnes Mann, he also speaks of 12.000 (burned?) volumes. See Archiv MHG, Berlin, fonds Ernst Maass, letter (dated Jun. 4, 1933, [3]) from Magnus Hirschfeld to Agnes Mann. Cf. Lamprecht, Nov. 15, 1935, 173 (where the collection is said to number 20,000 books). In a French local newspaper article, written shortly after Hirschfeld's death, in May 1935, the figure of 20,000 volumes surfaced again. See van Cleeff, May 16, 1935, 2. Deriving their information indirectly from a 1929 text, most likely written by Karl Giese on the occassion of the Institute's tenth anniversary, Dose and Herrn estimate that there was room for around 10,000 titles in the Institute library rooms (Dose & Herrn 2005, 20; Dose & Herrn 2006, 42). A 1925 Berlin doctors' magazine noted that, at that point, the library numbered 4,000 volumes (*Bände*). See Herrn 2022, 206. See the (anonymous) text, almost certainly by Giese, "6. Juli 1919 – 6. Juli 1929", Kinsey Institute Library & Special Collections, Bloomington (Indiana), Hirschfeld scrapbook, call n° X7910463. In the text, Giese advanced three proposals to enlarge the Institute library. When Royer visited the Institute, around 1930, he wrote that there were eight walls filled with books, which indicates that the library was spread over two rooms (Royer 1930, 31). This also corresponds with option B in Giese's text – two ground floor rooms in the 9a In den Zelten building – and is indeed where the library was eventually moved. In Giese's 1929 text, he also suggested that the library had been operating for four years. Dose and Herrn suggest this might rather refer to the fusing of the WhK library with the one in the Institute, around 1924–25, and that the Institute library only started operating as a separate entity in 1924 (Dose & Herrn 2006, 42; Dose & Herrn 2005, 20). For more of an overview and for more details about the Institute collection, along with its size and also the changing premises inside the Institute where the collection was housed over the years, see Dose & Herrn 2006, 41–43. How the books were counted presents another problem in determining the size of the collection. For example, was a one-year periodical volume counted as one book? Was a periodical's multiyear run counted as single (book) title, if at all?

15 Herrn 2013, 139.

16 *Voilà*, Jul. 1, 1933, 5. Roger Salardenne, a French journalist, also gave this as the number of documents burned (*Police magazine*, Aug. 27, 1933, 6).

(1866–1957) from Den Haag, then known as 's-Gravenhage. The Dutch committee assembled a library of scholarly books and novels on the theme of homosexuality, though much more modest than the one in Berlin. But, unlike Berlin, the Dutch published a catalogue of the collection in the year 1922 to which, starting in 1926, around four supplements were added [ill. 2].[17] In the end, the collection numbered around 1,900 titles. But here, too, the collection was quickly attacked by the Nazis. In May 1940, the Germans invaded the Netherlands, and, in the very same month, the book collection was confiscated. It was sent in its entirety to Berlin and was never found again.[18] However, the printed catalogue at least allowed the determination of what had been lost. Soon after the war ended, Jaap van Leeuwen (1892–1978), another important Dutch LGBT activist, tried to reconstitute the lost library with the help of Schorer's printed catalogue and its supplements.[19] Around the year 2000, the contents of the original library were, as much as was possible, physically and digitally reassembled by the IHLIA in Amsterdam, which currently houses one of the biggest LGBT collections in the world.[20]

Presumably, the Berlin Institute had a card catalogue of the library holdings; if so, we may assume that this was also taken away by the looting students. That said, one fifteen-page printed WhK catalogue from around 1905 listed around 300 titles; however, it is not known if, later, other, presumably more extensive editions of this catalogue were printed or not.[21]

A FIRST BUY-BACK POSSIBILITY

Around the time Karl Giese arrived in Brno, in the beginning of August 1933, an opportunity arose to buy back some of the Institute materials that had not been consumed in the bonfire on the Berlin Opernplatz of May 10. This is another, conclusive argument for the thesis that the Nazi students did not loot and burn everything, and that the attack and thorough destruction of the Institute and its contents was likely never part of the true plans related to the Institute. As a consequence, the Berlin bonfire appears above all as a spectacle staged to convey a certain National Socialist message. If one thinks the matter through, burning the rare, expensive, and often specialized books in Hirschfeld's collection was, from a strictly economic perspective, not the wisest course.

The National Socialists also devised a way to make money out of the materials that had not ended up on the pyre. By imposing a fictive tax obligation on the official owner of the materials, the Magnus Hirschfeld Foundation (Magnus-Hirschfeld-Stiftung), the Ministry of Finance had a "valid" argument for auctioning off the

[17] Schorer 1922.

[18] On the life of Jacob Schorer and the fate of the library, see van der Meer 2007, 327–58. On the attempts to locate the Schorer library, see Snijders & Baxmann 1998; Dobler & Baxmann 1999, 87–95.

[19] See https://www.ihlia.nl/collectie/van-leeuwen-bibliotheek/ (accessed Jun. 9, 2020). A catalogue of the library constituted by van Leeuwen was made in 1983 by Martien Sleutjes (Sleutjes 1983).

[20] See https://www.ihlia.nl/collectie/schorerbibliotheek/ (accessed Jun. 9, 2020).

[21] The first page of the catalogue stated that, if needed, additions to the catalogue would follow. See *Katalog der Bibliothek des Wissenschaftlich-Humanitären Komités*, Charlottenburg, Berlinerstrasse 104 (1905, cover page). The book collection of the Wissenschaftlich-humanitären Komitee (sometimes also spelled as Komité, as in their just mentioned catalogue) merged later on with the book collection of the Institute, see Dose & Herrn (2006: 41-42).

[22] The procedure was laid out in a letter (dated Jun. 14, 1933) from the Berlin police director (*Polizeipräsident*) Magnus von Levetzow to the Prussian Minister of the Interior (copy in the Archiv MHG, Berlin; mentioned in Herrn 2010, 152–54, 167 n. 125). The letter is transcribed in Dose 2015, 34–36. Herzer mentions this document being unearthed by early collaborators of the Magnus-Hirschfeld-Gesellschaft in the former DDR Staatsarchiv Merseburg, Akten des preußischen Innenministeriums, Signatur Rep.76-Vc Sekt. 1, Tit. 8, n° 23 and Rep. 76-VIIIB, n° 2076. See Herzer 2009a, 159 n. 6. See also Dose & Herrn 2006, 38, 45; Herzer 2001, 233–34; Herrn 2022, 451–52.

[23] Adelheid Schulz also had to deal with Vieck when she asked him – in vain – if she would still receive

Institute materials.[22] In *Testament: Heft II*, Hirschfeld mentioned that, in the summer of 1933, he received an offer to buy back Institute materials from the Nazi lawyer Dr. Kurt Vieck (1891–?). At that time, Vieck was the new chairman (*Vorstand*) of the Magnus-Hirschfeld-Stiftung. He proposed that Hirschfeld buy back materials worth 4,000 German marks; otherwise, the materials would be disposed of.[23] Margarete Dost (1879–1956), a good friend of Hirschfeld's, negotiated the deal. It is not known if this offer was ever accepted by Hirschfeld.[24]

THE NOVEMBER 1934 BERLIN AUCTIONING OF INSTITUTE MATERIALS

It is uncertain if this last offer was in any way related to the auction of Institute materials that took place in mid-November 1934. The auction appears to have been announced principally in Austrian newspapers on the day it took place.[25] That this auction was mainly (and possibly exclusively) announced in Austria is not coincidental.[26] On April 28, 1933, an article appeared in the Vienna newspaper *Der Abend* saying that leather-bound volumes of literary classics from Germany were on offer for bargain prices. The title of the article was clear enough: "The German spirit is being sold off: better to sell it below cost than to have it condemned or burned at the stake" [ill. 3].[27] This means that the effect of the Action Against the Un-German Spirit and the threat of the fire pit were already felt even before the book burnings of May 1933: bookstores, laymen and possibly even libraries were selling their valuable books by unwanted authors in Austria.[28] The Nazis must have been aware of this Austrian discount book selling trend and jumped on the bandwagon in November 1933 by publishing the notice of the auction in Austria exclusively.[29]

The anonymously written newspaper article announcing the new trend of selling cut-price books in Austria at the end of April 1933 had another striking feature. In 1929, Magnus Hirschfeld and Hanns Heinz Ewers (1871–1943), both gay men, had published and introduced together a three-volume series called *Love in the Orient (Liebe im Orient)*, which comprised *Das Kamasutram des Vatsyayana*, *Anangaranga: Die Bühne des Liebesgottes*, and *Der Duftende Garten des Scheik Nefzaui*.[30] The writer of

her pay after the Institute was looted (Schulz 2001, 91–92). As we have seen, Schulz stayed in the Institute until July 1933.

[24] Hirschfeld & Dose 2013, f. 80/172 n. 442. The entry is dated Aug. 11, 1933. See also Dose & Herrn 2006, 45.

[25] Dose & Herrn 2006, 45.

[26] For the announcement of the auction in the *Neues Wiener Journal*, Nov. 15, 1933, see Herzer 2001, 233. See also Dose & Herrn 2006, 45; Hirschfeld & Dose 2013, 174, n. 446.

[27] *Der Abend*, Apr. 28, 1933, 3: "Deutscher Geist wird verramscht: Lieber unter dem Selbstkostenpreis verkaufen, als an den Schandpfahl schlagen oder auf dem Scheiterhaufen verbrennen lassen."

[28] *Der Abend*, Apr. 28, 1933, 3: "So werden denn die teuersten Werke der in Nazi-Deutschland verfehmten Autoren zu lächerlich niedrigen Preisen in Oesterreich ausgeboten, und niemals hätte der Bücherfreund in Wien bessere Gelegenheit als heute, für ein paar Schillinge die kostbarsten Bücher der Weltliteratur zu erwerben" (Thus, the most expensive works by authors who were discredited in Nazi Germany are offered for sale in Austria at ridiculously low prices, and the book lover in Vienna never had a better opportunity than today to acquire the most precious books of world literature for a few shillings).

[29] It was Ralf Dose and Rainer Herrn who claimed that the Berlin auction was only announced abroad but the basis for this claim is unclear. I checked the index of the *Börsenblatt für den deutschen Buchhandel* for the year 1933 and 1934 – by looking for mentions of "Versteigerungen" (auctions) – and did not find any sign of this November auction. I also checked the November and December 1933 and January 1934 issues of the weekly *Anzeiger für den Buch-, Kunst und Musikalienhandel*, issued by Perles in Vienna. Lastly, I also checked several German and Austrian bibliophile magazines (*Jahrbuch deutscher Bibliophilen und Literaturfreunde*, *Zeitschrift für Bücherfreunde*, *Philobiblon*, etc.) for the same period with the same negative results.

[30] Leiter & Thal 1929. The author described the three volumes as follows: "Gemeinsam haben die beiden 'Kamasutra' (Liebe im Orient), 'Die Liebesriten und Liebessitten in Indien' und die 'Arabische Liebeskunst' (Der duftende Garten des Scheik Nefzani) herausgegeben und einbegleitet" (Together, the two have edited and introduced 'Kamasutra' [Love in the Orient], 'Love Rites and Customs in India' and 'The Arabian Art of Love' [The fragrant garden of Sheik Nefzani]), *Der Abend*, Apr. 28, 1933, 3. Strictly speaking, Hirschfeld and Ewers were not the editors but only wrote three introductions each.

the newspaper article scornfully linked Hirschfeld and Ewers' uneasy marriage to the new political constellation in Germany. The allusion was clearly to the fact that Hanns Heinz Ewers was now siding with the Nazis, a decision that had consequences for his income as one of the collaborators of the 1929 books: "Hanns Heinz Ewers is known to be one of the heroes of the German revival. He holds honorary offices and hangs on to the coat-tails of his chancellor in search of success. But he has a tainted past, since in love matters he joined ranks with Magnus Hirschfeld, one of the most hated writers and scientists in the new Germany. [...] The extensive volumes [of the three-volume series], with hundreds of illustrations, are now on sale in Vienna for four to five shillings rather than thirty-three shillings. Being a bedfellow of the ostracized sex researcher is costing the minstrel of the reconverted German Empire dearly. For not only is his coat of arms marked with dark stains that cannot easily be wiped away, he is also losing the royalties that selling the works at their original price would have earned him!"[31] One of the subtitles in the newspaper article clearly referred to Hirschfeld and Ewers' shared sexual orientation : "Bed chums Magnus Hirschfeld – Hanns Heinz Ewers" (*Bettgenossenschaft Magnus Hirschfeld – Hanns Heinz Ewers*).

This is how the Berlin auction of the remaining Institute materials was announced in the Austrian newspaper *12 Uhr Blatt* on November 15, 1933:

> Magnus Hirschfeld's estate under the hammer
>
> Berlin, 14 November [1933]
>
> The tax office is arranging large auctions of the property of the notorious sex researcher Doctor Magnus Hirschfeld, containing, among other things, a library of 3,000 volumes, as well as apparatuses, instruments, furniture, etc., coming under the hammer.
>
> The reason for the auctions is Hirschfeld's failure to meet his tax obligations.
>
> Magnus Hirschfeld currently lives in Paris.[32]

This auction took place in the Institute building on November 14, 1933. Magnus Hirschfeld mentioned the auction (*Versteigerung*) in *Testament: Heft II*: "Today – November 14 – it has been three years since I left Berlin never to see it again – today

[31] *Der Abend*, Apr. 28, 1933, 3: "Hanns Heinz Ewers gehört bekanntlich zu den Heroen des deutschen Aufbruchs. Er bekleidet Ehrenämter und hängt sich Erfolg haschend an die Rockschössel Seines Kanzlers. Aber er hat eine befleckte Vergangenheit, denn er hat sich in der Liebe mit Magnus Hirschfeld gefunden und dieser wieder gehört zu den meistgehaßten Schriftstellern und Wissenschaftlern im neuen Deutschland. [...] Die umfangreichen, mit Hunderten von Illustrationen versehenen Bände [of the 3 volumed series] werden jetzt in Wien um vier bis fünf Schilling statt um 33 Schilling ausgeboten. Die Bettgenossenschaft mit dem verfemten Sexualforscher kommt dem Minnesänger des umgeschalteten Deutschen Reiches teuer zu stehen. Denn nicht nur trägt sein Schild dunkle Flecken, die sich nicht leicht wegputzen lassen, sondern er verliert auch die Tantiemen, die ihm der Verkauf der Werke zu Originalpreisen eingetragen hätte!" A Dutch journalist, writing for the Catholic newspaper *De Tijd*, believed that Ewers' "pornographic works" should have been thrown on the Berlin pyre as well, and that Ewers, who quickly penned a biography of Horst Wessel shortly after the Nazis rose to power, was simply an opportunist. See *De Tijd*, May 14, 1933, 1. On Ewers, see https://en.wikipedia.org/wiki/Hanns_Heinz_Ewers#Nazi_involvement (accessed May 15, 2020); Hergemöller 2010 307–9. From 1899 to 1920, Ewers had written for the gay literary magazine *Der Eigene*, edited by Adolf Brand. For Ewers' contributions to Der Eigene, see Keilson-Lauritz 1997, 399–400.

[32] *12 Uhr Blatt* (the midday edition of *Die Neue Zeitung*), Jg. 27, Folge 53, Nov. 15, 1933, 2: "Der Besitz Magnus Hirschfelds unter dem Hammer / Berlin, 14 November [1933] / Aus dem Besitz des berüchtigten Sexualforschers Doctor Magnus Hirschfeld lässt das Finanzamt grosse Versteigerungen durchführen, bei denen unter anderem eine 3000 Bände umfassende Bibliothek, ferner Apparate, Instrumente, Möbel usw. unter den Hammer kommen. / Der Anlass der Versteigerungen ist die Nichterfüllung der Steuerverpflichtungen Hirschfelds. / Magnus

the auction of my remaining books, materials and furniture begins in my former home – the last act (for the moment) of a tragedy of fate, which comprises a terrible mental martyrdom".[33]

The Hirschfeld biographer Manfred Herzer has dug up an article from a Berlin newspaper that is even more precise on the matter. It says that two auctions took place: one on Tuesday November 14, 1933, in the Institute, and the second on Thursday, November 16, 1933, in an auxiliary building of the State Loan Office (Staatliche Leihamt) at 74 Elsässer Straße (currently Torstraße).[34] That the auction took place at two different locations is perhaps not very surprising. It is possible that they did not want to move the materials left behind in the Institute after the morning and afternoon lootings of May 6. In that case, the materials auctioned off at the Staatliche Leihamt were the remainder of the loot that the students had taken to the Friedrich-Wilhelms-Universität student house at 18 Oranienburger Straße, and which had been sorted between May 6 and May 10. As we have seen, some of the books sorted out likely also went to libraries in Berlin or elsewhere in German. However, it is of course also possible that the libraries received books that did not sell at the auctions. There is also a chance that Margarete Dost, who, as we have also seen, was involved in negotiating the Nazi lawyer Kurt Vieck's August 1933 offer, went to see Hirschfeld in Paris on November 18, 1933, two days after the second auction. Hirschfeld inscribed the date November 18, 1933, in the copy of his world trip book that he possibly gave her as a gift, perhaps at that moment. Did she go to Paris expressly to report on the auction and the buy-back operation?[35] Of course, Hirschfeld might also simply have sent her the inscribed copy, out of gratitude for her possible help and for reporting about the auctions. Whatever the case, the proximity of the date of her inscribed copy and the dates of the two auctions in Berlin is striking.[36]

THE INSTITUTE AFTER THE RAID

The Institute was literally locked down in mid-June 1933.[37] Presumably from the day the Institute was ransacked, on May 6, 1933, it was continuously guarded by the National Socialists. Several sources mention that anyone going in or out of the building was thoroughly searched. Adelheid Schulz, who continued to live in the building after the lootings, claimed that she left the building for good in July 1933.[38] Presumably, the signs reading "Institut für Sexualwissenschaft", on the facades of

Hirschfeld lebt zur Zeit in Paris". See also *Neues Wiener Journal*, Nov. 15, 1933, 4. For the text of the latter notice, see Herrn 2008c: card Verkauf und Rückkauf der Bibliotheks- und Sammlungsbestände des Instituts. See also *Kreuz-Zeitung*, Nov. 15, 1933, reported in Herzer 2017, 375.

[33] Hirschfeld & Dose 2013, f. 81/174: "Heute – am 14. November – sind es drei Jahre, seit ich Berlin verliess u.[nd] nicht wiedersah – heute beginnt in meinem einstigen Hause die Versteigerung meiner übriggebliebenen Bücher, Materialien u.[nd] Möbel – der letzte Akt (vorläufig) einer Schicksalstragödie, die ein furchtbares seelisches Martyrium in sich schliesst".

[34] For the house number of the auxiliary building, see *Berliner Adreßbuch* 1933, III: 26. The second auxiliary building (which still stands) was located at 98 Linienstraße. See *Berliner Adreßbuch* 1933, III: 26; https://de.wikipedia.org/wiki/Königliches_Leihamt (accessed May 27, 2020). Curiously, the Linienstraße venue was closer to the student house than the one on Elsässer Straße/Torstraße. No 1933 volume of *Jahresbericht des Leihamts der Reichshauptstadt* seems to have survived in any library anywhere.

[35] Dost inscribed Hirschfeld's guestbook twice. One inscription is dated Jun. 21, 1934–Jul. 4, 1934. See Bergemann, Dose, Keilson-Lauritz & Dubout 2019, f. 39/83. In an undated inscription (perhaps linked to a possible Paris visit in November 1933) she makes a reference to Christmas (Weihnachten). See Bergemann, Dose, Keilson-Lauritz & Dubout 2019, f. 16/60. Did Hirschfeld view the successful buy-back operation as a sort of Christmas present?

[36] Hirschfeld & Dose 2013, 172 n. 443. Dost's inscribed copy was sold in 2008 by a Dutch antiquarian bookseller. I thank Jens Dobler for sending me (on February 9, 2023) a picture of Hirschfeld's inscription (*Widmung*) to Margarete Dost.

[37] Herrn 2010, 152–53; Maeder [1993], 5–6.

[38] For the letter of recommendation that Hirschfeld wrote for Schulz, saying that she stayed in the Institute until the end of July 1933, see Schulz 2001, 25.

the building at 9a In den Zelten and on the corner building at 10 In den Zelten / 3 Ecke Beethovenstrasse were removed in that very year [ill. 4].

The financing of the Institute and its operation always greatly relied on the rental income provided by rooms in the Institute's two buildings. Christopher Isherwood was one of the more famous guests to rent a room in the Institute. But sometime after May 1933, all lodgers were kicked out.[39] The building was then rented out to several National Socialist organizations and groups, among them the Association of National Socialist Legal Professionals (Bund Nationalsozialistischer Deutscher Juristen, BNSDJ), which would become, in 1936, the National Socialist Association of Legal Professionals (Nationalsozialistische Rechtswahrerbund, NSRB).[40] The Union of German Anti-Communist Associations (Gesamtverband Deutscher antikommunistischer Vereinigungen e. V.), better known as the Anti-Comintern (Antikomintern), started in October 1933, also took up residence in the Institute. When, in September 1935, the fascist Dutch priest, Anselmus Vriens, head of the Dutch Catholic Press Office (Nederlandsch Katholiek Correspondentie Bureau, RKCB) went to visit the offices of the Anti-Comintern in Berlin, he was taken by Alfred Gielen (1909–?) to the cellar of the Institute, to be shown, as he wrote, an exhibit of Bolshevik horrors and also "horrendous" photos from the "pigsty" of Hirschfeld's former Institute. Employing old biblical rhetoric about the destroyed city of Sodom, Vriens did not even want to speak of the photos.[41] The newspaper article had an interesting subtitle: "Magnus Hirschfeld's Sexual Reform Project: Disguised Communist Propaganda" (*Magnus Hirschfelds Sexualreform: een Verkapte Communistische Propaganda*).

It is interesting to observe (a possible future line of research) that the Institute's political orientation to the left, in the five years before its closure, may have been a further factor that determined the Nazis' growing intolerance of Hirschfeld and his Institute. The two main representatives of the left-wing faction in the Institute were the Institute collaborators Richard Linsert and Max Hodann. As we have seen, both were behind the November 1929 putsch against Hirschfeld as WhK chairman. Linsert died in February 1933 of the flu. Hodann was arrested by the Gestapo, at the end of the same month. Kurt Hiller, who also had more radical ideas than Hirschfeld, was arrested by the Gestapo and imprisoned for the first time in April 1933. As early as 1929, in *The Bulletin of the Scientific-Humanitarian Committee* (*Mitteilungen des Wissenschaftlich-Humanitären Komitees*), Linsert did not shrink from invoking the persistent left-wing theme that linked fascism and homosexuality. Only a little later, in 1931, the same periodical also critically reported on the case of SA leader Ernst

[39] Herzer 2009a, 160; Herrn 2010, 123.

[40] Wiesner 2003, 427. In *Testament: Heft II*, Hirschfeld also writes about the "Juristenbund" that took control of the Institute (Hirschfeld & Dose, 2013, f. 81/174). Eichhorn, Ngo and Löbbecke mention two other organizations: the Gestapo and Akademie der bildenden Künste (Academy of Fine Arts) (Eichhorn, Ngo & Löbbecke 2016, sheet In den Zelten 9A/10).

[41] *Het nieuws van den dag voor Nederlandsch-Indië*, Oct. 11, 1935, 18. The Anti-Comintern kept an office in the Institute until 1937. See https://de.wikipedia.org/wiki/Gesamtverband_Deutscher_antikommunistischer_Vereinigungen (accessed May 1, 2020). Starting in 1938, the Staats-medizinische Akademie (State Medical Academy) and Gesundheitsamt des Landkreises Niederbarnim (Niederbarnim District Health Office) were also housed in the building. See Eichhorn, Ngo & Löbbecke 2016, sheet In den Zelten 9A/10. For Vriens, see Orlow 2009, 51. Alfred Gielen (1909–?) was an assistant of Dr. Karl (Eberhard) Taubert (1904–1976), who held a key position in Goebbels' Ministry of Propaganda. See the CIA document of Apr. 23, 1947 sent to Dr. Hans Fritzsche (1900–1953), another Goebbels collaborator, at https://www.cia.gov/readingroom/document/519697e8993294098d50c4a5 (accessed Jun. 16, 2021). See also Waddington (2007). After the war, Taubert was recruited by the secret services of the Bundesrepublik Deutschland (West Germany) and several others, where he continued his fierce battle against Soviet Communism. See, for example, van Dongen, Roulin & Scott-Smith 2014; Ludwig 2003.

[42] *Mitteilungen des Wissenschaftlich-Humanitären Komitees*, 1929, 161; *Mitteilungen des Wissenschaftlich-Humanitären Komitees*, 1931, 315–16.

[43] The centers for sexual counseling were dubbed "kulturbolschewistischen Bestrebungen dienenden Organisationen für Geburtenregelung und Sexual-

Röhm.[42] One week after the Berlin book burning, other sexual counseling centers (*Sexualberatungsstellen*) were closed down, and, in their case as well, anti-Bolshevik rhetoric was used by the Nazis to justify their actions.[43]

In 1934, the sexologist Herbert Lewandowski (then living and working in the Netherlands) stopped by the building of the old Institute one last time. A plaque on the wall showed him that the Nazis had deemed it fitting to house an anti-Jewish agency in Hirschfeld's former Institute, the Institute for the Study of Jewry (Institut zur Erforschung des Judentums).[44] The full name was likely the Institute for the Study of Jewry and Bolshevism (Institut zur Erforschung des Judentums und Bolschewismus).[45] In 1943, the Institute building was badly damaged by heavy bombing. The remnants were torn down in 1950.[46]

We know from two sources that Karl Fein, the "gentleman" (*Herr*) Giese knew from the 1932 WLSR Brno conference, played a pivotal role in buying back parts of the Institute collection. In *Testament: Heft II*, Magnus Hirschfeld wrote: "The reconstruction of the Institute [in Paris] had two preconditions, firstly the re-acquisition of the materials that had been saved with the greatest difficulty from the destruction and burning of the Berlin Institute. Finally, at great expense, 2,200 kilos of books, manuscripts, documents, questionnaires, pictures and objects were brought to Paris via Prague (Dr. Fein)".[47] In an August 1935 letter sent to Max Hodann, Giese also mentioned the crucial role played by the Brno lawyer: "our lawyer friend here [Karl Fein] [...] who also repurchased the items in Berlin at the time".[48] In an intriguing diary fragment, unearthed by Ralf Dose and Rainer Herrn, we read that the Institute lot "was bought back by H.[irschfeld]'s lawyer for the immense sum of 35-40,000 [German] M[arks] on the condition that it was taken out of the country".[49] Supposing that an old book could easily weigh one kilo, we can see that the total weight of the 3,000 books announced as being auctioned off in Berlin does not correspond to 2,200 kg of the bought-back lot mentioned by Hirschfeld in *Testament: Heft II*. But it was a public auction and it was quite possible that some lots simply went to other interested buyers. This may offer one more explanation of how, to this day, though rarely, books adorned with the usual Institute library stamp continue to be offered by antiquarian booksellers.

hygiene" (organizations for birth control and sexual hygiene serving cultural Bolshevik aspirations) by The Prussian Interior Ministry (von Soden 1988, 148).

[44] See the letter (dated Dec. 13, 1984) from Herbert Lewandowski to Ilse Kokula, *Mitteilungen der Magnus-Hirschfeld-Gesellschaft* 5 (March 1985): 28.

[45] Als spelled "Institut zum Studium von Judentums und Bolschewismus" and "Institut zum Studium von Bolschewismus und Judentum". One source claims that this organization was the same as the Anti-Comintern. See Bohrmann & Toepser-Ziegert 1998, 200. In 1938 this Institute issued the booklet "Die Wanderung und Verbreitung der Juden in der Welt" (The Migration and Spread of the Jews in the World). In this regard, it is striking that the post-war Leo Baeck Institute, founded in 1947, was initially called the Institut zur Erforschung des Judentums in Deutschland seit der Aufklärung (Institute for the Study of Judaism in Germany since the Enlightenment). See also Eichhorn, Ngo & Löbbecke 2016, sheet In den Zelten 9A/10.

[46] Eichhorn, Ngo & Löbbecke 2016, sheet In den Zelten 9A/10.

[47] Hirschfeld & Dose 2013, f. 87/186: "Der Wiederaufbau des Instituts [in Paris] gründete sich auf zwei Vorbedingungen, erstens die Wiedererlangung der aus der Zerstörung und Verbrennung des Berliner Instituts mit grösster Mühe geretteten Materialien. Es gelang schliesslich mit vielen Kosten über Prag (Dr. Fein) 2200 Kilo Bücher, Manuskripte, Dokumente, Fragebogen, Bilder, Gegenstände nach Paris zu bekommen".

[48] Arbetarrörelsens arkiv och bibliotek, Stockholm, Max Hodann samling, vol. 15, letter (dated Aug. 2, 1935, [2]) from Karl Giese to Max Hodann: "unserem hiesigen befreundeten Anwalt [Karl Fein] [...] der auch seinerzeit den Rückkauf der Sachen in Berlin durchgeführt hat".

[49] One can read this in the "sex diary" entry (dated Feb. 14, 1936) of the German artist Henri Nouveau (Heinz Neumeier, 1901–1959), qtd. in Dose & Herrn 2006, 48: "[...] welches [...] durch Hs [*sic*: Hirschfeld's] Anwalt der Behörde für die horrende Summe von 35-40000 M [Deutschmark] abgekauft werden konnte unter der Bedingung, daß es ausser Landes geschafft würde."

WHO WAS KARL FEIN?

But what was the exact role of Karl Fein in all of this? Did Karl Fein go in person to Berlin to look over or even settle things? We know hardly anything about the matter. There is a slight indication that Karl Fein went to Berlin in December 1933.[50] Yet one element in Fein's life history may possibly help us to further explain who or what may have facilitated the transactions in Berlin. But let us first take a closer look at who Karl Fein was.

Karl Fein was born in Brno on March 9, 1894.[51] He was the third and youngest child in a family of three children, including his siblings Gustav (1889–1943?) and

[50] I tried to determine whether Fein went to Berlin in November 1933 by consulting the Brno police registers that documented the issuance of passports, but could not find any conclusive evidence. A 1938 police register notes that a passport was issued (or extended) for Karl Fein *for five years*, from December 8, 1938 to December 6, 1943. This may indicate that, in December 1933, Fein either renewed his passport or obtained a new one. This would mean he went to Berlin *after* the November 1933 auctions. See MZA, Brno, fonds B 26, Policenjní ředitelství Brno, book n° 79, Protokol vydaných a obnovených pasů 1938 (Protokol der ausgegebenen Reisepässe aus dem Jahre 1938), entry n° 13.304, Karl Fein. However, Fein's name does not appear in any other available 1933 passport issuance register. See MZA, Brno, fond B 26, Policenjní ředitelství Brno, Protokol vydaných a obnovených pasů, book n° 791, year 1933. In this register, I checked part of the approximately 10,000 passport registrations for 1933, from May 6 (the day of the looting of the Institute) to December 31. It is possible that Karl Fein's name appears in another (lost) 1933 register. See email (dated Jan. 17, 2014) from Miroslava Kučerová (MZA, Brno) to the author.

[51] NA, Praha, Jewish registers (Židovské matriky, Judische Matriken). See http://www.badatelna.eu/fond/1073/reprodukce/?zaznamId=163&reproId=137711 (accessed Dec. 12, 2018). In these Jewish registers, we see Fein's first name spelled as "Carl". In later documents, his first name was consistently spelled as "Karl". As we will see later, in the last years of his life, Karl Fein made the conscious chose to spell his first name the Czech way, as "Karel", probably sensing that ideas of what it meant to be German(-speaking), developed in Germany and the Sudetenland, were moving in the wrong direction. At first, I chose to use the Czech spelling of his name, but later decided to restore the original German form. I have stuck to this decision, spelling his name as "Karl Fein (the younger)" throughout. The Brno citizen and young student Alice (Licy) Rosenberg (née Kulka, 1921–2017) offers another case of changing the spelling of one's first name. She transferred from a German to a Czech school because of the changes she and her parents perceived. See Visual History Archive (USC Shoah Foundation), interview number 12303, interview (dated Feb. 21, 1996) Alice Rosenberg. My genealogical research on Karl Fein's family is based on the following sources: the archives of the AMB, Brno; visits to the Jewish cemetery in Brno and Boskovice; the database of the Jewish cemetery in Brno; the microfilmed Jewish registers (Židovské matriky, Judische Matriken) in the NA, Praha, fonds n° 167 (not yet consultable online when I started my research); Státní okresní archiv Blansko, fonds Židovská obec Boskovice (books n° 1, 2, 5 and 6); CEGESOMA, Brussel/Bruxelles, Rijksarchief/Archives de l'Etat, Brussel/Bruxelles, Felix archief, Antwerpen; the quintessential reference work Kárný et al. 1995; and the websites www.holocaust.cz, Ancestry.com and Geni.com.

[52] In a document of the Verein der Industriebeamten Brünn (Brno Association of Industrial Employees), of which Albert Fein was an active *Ausschuss-Mitglied* (board member), Fein is decribed as "Manipulant" (manual laborer). See MZA, fonds B 26, Policejní reditelství Brno, Verein der Industriebeamten Brünn, kart. n° 2578, sign. 59452, f. 61. For an example of the decisions taken in the annual meeting of the association, including mention of Albert Fein as a board member, see "Der Verein der Industriebeamten in Brünn", *Brünner Morgenpost* (*Beilage zur Brünner Zeitung*), Mar. 16, 18974, 3. The article says that Leopold Weiss was the *Vorstand* (president) of the organization. There is a family connection between Karl Fein and one of Leopold Weiss' children. The company Aron und Jakob Löw-Beer's Söhne was started in Boskovice around 1820, when Moses Löw-Beer (1794–1851) became the co-owner of a distillery. With the capital from this business, a wool spinning factory was started in nearby Svitávka. Löw-Beer's descendants later moved the company to Brno and considerably expanded it. The company was also active in the sugar and distilling industry and owned several plants in other parts of the Austro-Hungarian empire. See http://www.low-beerovy-vily.cz/podnikatelska-cinnost-low-beeru-/firma-aron-und-jakob-low-beer-s-sohne/#! (accessed Nov. 11, 2015). For the commercial activities of the well-known and very wealthy Löw-Beer clan in Brno, see also Smutný 2012, 258–63; Černá et al. 2017. Albert Fein was also a member of the Verein Deutsches Haus ("German House" Association). See "Die Hauptversammlung des Vereines 'Deutsches Haus'", *Tagesbote*, Jul. 8, 1897, 1.

[53] MZA, Brno, fonds C 152, Okresní soud civilní Brno (Bezirksgericht für Zivilsachen in Brünn), inheritance file Albert Fein, kart. n° 1817, sign. IV 1581/96, f. 5. See also "Verzeichnis der Verstorbenen vom 20. bis 27. Juli 1896", *Brünner Zeitung*, n° 176, Jul. 31, 1896, 4. It gives the cause of death as "Herzfehler" (heart failure).

Margarethe (1891–1942?). His father, Albert Fein (1854–1896), was a worker in the wool spinning company Aron und Jakob Löw-Beer's Söhne.[52] Karl Fein most likely had no memories of his father since his father died of a heart attack in the summer of 1896, when the boy was only two years old.[53] One can find Albert Fein's modest grave monument in Brno's Jewish cemetery [ill. 5].[54] Karl Fein's mother, Helene Brecher (1856?–1943), was originally from Prostějov (Prossnitz).[55] She married Karl Fein's father in May 1882.[56] Looking at the settlement of Albert Fein's estate, one sees that the sum of assets and liabilities left almost nothing, indicating that Karl Fein's parents lived in relative poverty.[57]

The paternal grandparents of Karl Fein were Simon Fein (1815–1896) and Lotti Schändl (1819–?) who married in the small village of Boskovice (then also known by the German name Boskowitz) on September 23, 1850.[58] Boskovice is situated 40 kilometers north of Brno. Karl Fein's ancestors were forced to live in the Jewish ghetto there until the mid-nineteenth century. Starting in 1848, with the abolition of the two hundred-year-old *Familianten* law which fixed the maximum number of Jewish families, Jewish emancipation in Moravian and Bohemian lands commenced. In the decades that followed, Jewish people would move out of their ancestral villages and towns to start up businesses elsewhere.[59] Simon Fein was one of the three grain traders (*Getreidehändler*) in Boskowitz (Boskovice).[60] The couple Simon and Lotti Fein had six children, three sons and three daughters, who all lived in house no. 58 in the Jewish ghetto in Boskowitz (Boskovice).[61] Albert Fein, Karl's father, was one of the three sons of Simon and Lotti Fein.

[54] Albert Fein is buried in section 36, row 1, grave 27. I thank the late Avi Haimovsky for helping me to decipher the barely legible Hebrew on the stele.

[55] Despite several efforts, it proved impossible to determine Helene's exact birth year with certainty. I found different birth years on several different official documents: 1855, 1856, 1858, 1860, etc. Missing birth registers for the city of Prossnitz (Prostějov) in the Jewish registers (Židovské matriky, Judische Matriken) for these years are the main cause of this lack of clarity. See NA, Praha, fonds n° 167. Giving wrong birth years was not uncommon at the time. If we presume that Karl Fein knew exactly how old his mother was, then she should have been born in 1856 (July 16). At the end of 1938 or the beginning of 1939, Karl Fein wrote in a document about his "82-year-old mother". See MZA, Brno, fonds C 107, Německý úřední soud Brno (Deutsches Amtsgericht Brünn), kart. n° 256, sign. 5a V 3/41, f. 26b. In August 1940, Karl Fein's brother Gustav also claimed that his mother was born on July 16, 1856. See Hessisches Hauptstaatsarchiv, Wiesbaden, Bestand 519/3, Akten der Devisenstellen Frankfurt und Kassel, Devisenstelle Frankfurt, 1940–1942, JS 10429, Erich Messing (Dec. 25, 1895), letter (dated Aug. 21, 1940) from Gustav Fein to Devisenstelle Saarbrücken, n.p. Fein's father was born in 1854; statistically, it was very common for wives to be one or a few years younger than their husbands.

[56] The marriage date can be found in MZA, Brno, C 152, Okresní soud civilní Brno (Bezirksgericht für Zivilsachen in Brünn), kart. n° 1817, sign. IV 1581/96, inheritance file Albert Fein, f. 5.

[57] MZA, Brno, fond C 152, Okresní soud civilní Brno (Bezirksgericht für Zivilsachen in Brünn), kart. n° 1817, sign. IV 1581/96, inheritance file Albert Fein.

[58] MZA, Brno, C 152, Okresní soud civilní Brno (Bezirksgericht für Zivilsachen in Brünn), kart. n° 1817, sign. IV 1581/96, inheritance file Albert Fein, f. 7.

[59] See http://www.yivoencyclopedia.org/article.aspx/Familiants_Laws (accessed Mar. 24, 2016).

[60] Simon Fein worked together with one of the other grain traders from Boskovice, Emiel Berisch (?–1904). See *Handelsadressbuch und Gewerbeadressbuch der Markgrafschaft Mähren und des Herzogthumes Schlesien* 1887, 47. In an 1890 publication, it says that Emiel Berisch and Fein rented a brewery (*Dampfbrauerei*) and a malt factory (*Malzfabrik*) in Černahora (Černá Hora). See *Neuester Schematismus der Herrschaften, Güter und Zuckerfabriken in Mähren und Schlesien sowie der auf den Gütern bestehenden Brauereien, Brennereien und sonstigen Industrien, deren Besitzer, Pächter und der dabei angestellten Beamten* 1890, 29. By 1896, they were renting similar plants in Kritschen (Podolí). See ibid., 96. The Leopold Berisch company file in the MZA, Brno, contains no information about the cooperation between Simon Fein and Emiel Berisch. See MZA, Brno, fonds C 11, Krajský soud civilní Brno, firemní agenda, Leopold Berisch, Sodawassererzeugung, Boskowitz (Boskovice), kart. n° 762, sign. Jd VII 169.

[61] This, according to an 1870 Boskovice census record that Ariel Levy-Löwy saw. See email (dated Jul. 30, 2016) from Ariel Levy-Löwy to the author. For more information on the history of the Boskowitz (Boskovice) Jewish community, see Bránský 1995; Bránský 1999.

TWO UNCLES

The other two sons of Simon and Lotti Fein (and thus Karl Fein's paternal uncles) were Moriz Fein (1858–1913) and Adolf Fein (1845–1911). Like their father, they were active in the brewing industry.[62] Possibly, they were also working for the First Brno Joint-Stock Brewery and Malt Factory (Erste Brünner Aktienbrauerei und Malzfabrik) (later the Starobrno Brewery, which still exists), founded in 1888, and located in the street where Albert Fein and his family were living [ill. 6].[63] Adolf Fein was also one of Karl Fein's godfathers.[64]

Karl Fein seems to have had a special bond with one of the three sons of Adolf Fein, Max Fein (1872–1932), twelve years his elder. The two cousins met when they spent a

[62] In an archival record, Moriz Fein is described as a *Malzfabriksverwalter* (malt factory manager). See email (dated Oct. 28, 2011) from Thomas Maisel (Archiv der Universität Wien) to the author. See also *Adressbuch von Brünn* 1897, 122, where both brothers are described as *Getreidehändler* (grain traders). Adolf Fein was not Simon Fein's son but the child of Lotti Fein and her first husband, a man named Brüll. Also, Adolf Fein was not born as Adolf Brüll but as Aron Brüll. Simon Fein adopted the child and changed his first name from Aron to Adolf. A handwritten note in the Boskovice birth register (1832–1848), probably explaining the complicated familial situation, proved illegible. See http://www.badatelna.eu/fond/1073/reprodukce/?zaznamId=136&reproId=1407252 (accessed Dec. 12, 2018). I found two men in Boskovice named Brüll who died in 1846: Moses Brüll, who died on March 7, 1846 at the age of 68, and Moses Löbl Brüll, who died at the age of 26 on October 22, 1846. The fact that he was born around 1820 makes him a good candidate for Lotti's first husband, since she was born in 1819. See the Boskovice death register (1832–1848) at http://www.badatelna.eu/fond/1073/reprodukce/?zaznamId=140&reproId=1407352 (accessed Dec. 12, 2018).

[63] See *Wohnungs-Adressbuch von Brünn und der Vororte Königsfeld, Hussowitz und Kumrowitz für 1896* 1896, 34, where Albert Fein's address is given as 3 Schreibwaldstrasse (Hlinky). A fair number of the buildings near this address were part of the factory; however, the address itself was the property of a Jewish woman named Antonie Hatschek (1848–1914). The Hatscheks also lived in the house. *Adressbuch von Brünn* 1892, 365; and the database of the Jewish cemetery in Brno at https://cemeteries.jewishbrno.eu/cemetery/search/newcemetery/1 (accessed Jul. 23, 2024). In Albert Fein's inheritance file (dated summer of 1896), a different house number is given: 37 Schreibwaldstrasse (Hlinky). This house was owned by Rosalie and Marie Hollefeld. See *Adressbuch von Brünn* 1895, 417; and MZA, Brno, fonds C 152, Okresní soud civilní Brno (Bezirksgericht für Zivilsachen in Brünn), inheritance file Albert Fein, kart. n° 1817, sign. IV 1581/96. In a newspaper announcing Albert Fein's death, this same house number 37 is also given. See "Verzeichnis der Verstorbenen vom 20. bis 27. Juli 1896", *Brünner Zeitung*, Jul. 31, 1896, 4. Karl Fein's two former family homes no longer exist. See http://encyklopedie.brna.cz/home-mmb/?acc=profil_domu&load=369 (accessed Dec, 18, 2020).

[64] The other godfather was a Brno doctor named Emil Wassertrilling (1869–1917), originally from Boskovice. I was not able to determine how or if he was related to the Fein family. He is buried in the Brno Jewish cemetery in parcel 22B, row 2, grave 8. For mention of Karl Fein's two godfathers in the Jewish registers (Židovské matriky, Judische Matriken) in the NA, Praha, fonds n° 167, see http://www.badatelna.eu/fond/1073/reprodukce/?zaznamId=163&reproId=137711 (accessed Dec. 12, 2018). Adolf Fein had at least six children with his wife Hermine (1847-1931), three sons and three daughters. One son was Oskar Fein (1882–1944?), who became a court stenographer and a journalist associated with the newspaper *Neue Freie Presse*. He was also one of the more than five hundred people who lectured in Terezín, see Makarova, Makarov & Kuperman (2004, 94-95 and 451). Arthur Fein (1884-1944) was another son. He moved to Budapest in the 1920s where he married and was killed in a 1944 bombing raid. The fate of Adolf Fein's last son, Rudolf (1924–?), is unknown. Margit Koch, Arthur Fein's wife, died in 1944, a month later then her husband. See email (dated Sep. 10, 2013) from Beatrix Baros (Budapest city archives) to the author. Finally, Adolf Fein also had three daughters, Martha Fein (1878–?), Helene Fein (1874-?), and Irma Brammer (née Fein, 1883–1944). We will return to Irma Brammer later on.

[65] Max Fein, who emigrated to Belgium in 1899, is buried in the Jewish cemetery in Boskovice. It is certain that Karl Fein met his elder cousin Max Fein in Boskovice during the 1914-1918 war. Karl Fein moved to Boskovice in 1914. Max Fein arrived there in 1916, together with his son Alfred (1903–1942?). In 1919, Karl and Max Fein left their ancestral village again. See Státní okresní archiv Blansko, fonds Židovská obec Boskovice, book n° 6, 1906–1920. So it must have been in 1916–18 that Karl Fein decided to model his typical signature on that of Max Fein's. (It seems unlikely that it would have been the other way round, since Max Fein was then thirty-four years old and Karl Fein twenty-two.) I have followed the trail of Max Fein's relatives in Belgium and in the United States, as well as that of the Boskovice Lamm family into which Max Fein married. Many members of this Lamm family also emigrated to Belgium. A second Fein family member, Helene Fein (1874–?), a daughter of Adolf Fein, married a Belgian Lamm as well. Lucienne Fischel (née Fein, 1914–1996) was the only child of Max Fein to survive the Holocaust, having emigrated to South America before the start of World War II. Eliane M. (née Fischel, 1937–) and

few years in their ancestral village of Boskowitz (Boskovice) during World War I. It is at this time that Karl Fein must have modeled his lifelong, deeply characteristic signature on the signature of his older cousin Max Fein.[65] Like Karl Fein's father, Moriz and Adolf Fein are buried in Brno's Jewish cemetery. As already mentioned, Simon and Lotti Fein also had three daughters, but hardly anything is known about the two eldest: Rosi (1848–1921?), Marie (1850–?) and Emilie Löwy (1852–1908).[66]

After the death of her husband Albert, Karl Fein's widowed mother and her three children first lived at 5 Giskra-Strasse (later to become Kaunitzgasse or Kounicova) in Brno. Around the year 1900, the family of four then moved in with Helene Fein's mother, the widowed Amalie Brecher (1818–1905) at 19 Rennergasse (Běhounská) in Brno. It is unclear if this was done in order to relieve the Fein family financially or to help the elderly woman Amalie Brecher with her daily chores (or both).[67] In November 1905, Karl Fein's maternal grandmother died.[68]

KARL FEIN'S EDUCATION AND CAREER AS A LAWYER

The young Karl Fein attended the Deutsches Staatsgymnasium in the Elisabethplatz (Komenského náměstí) in Brno [ill. 7]. He ended his eight-year-long classical study in the summer of 1912, passing his matriculation exam (*Reifeprüfung*) with distinction, one of the seven pupils out of the thirty-four tested to do so. Together with the Deutsche Technische Hochschule, located right across, the school was one of the German cultural monuments of pre-war Brno.[69] It is clear that the German-speaking Jewish and non-Jewish elite of the city wanted to send their children to this school. In the winter of 1912, the young student headed to Vienna where he studied law at the university until 1916. Even then, he seems to have been busy with gender and race issues, as a letter he wrote to the Czech feminist Božena Viková-Kunětická (1862–

Susana D. (née Fischel, 1946–) are Lucienne Fischel two daughters. One family member related to the Lamm family, who was initially willing to help me out, ultimately forbade me – in a rather unpleasant way – to continue communicating with her. She also claimed that the granddaughter of Max Fein, Eliane M., simply did not want to talk to me. I also found a public Boskovice Lamm family tree on the Ancestry.com website, posted by Roberto Altschul. I asked him twice (through the same Ancestry.com website) to contact me, the last time on Jan. 5, 2014. I received no reply. I also sent an email (dated Mar. 24, 2016) through Geni.com to Claudia Heller, who had added information on Eliane M. and her two children on the Geni.com website in 2015. She forwarded my email to some family members but it resulted in no responses. I also sent a message (dated Apr. 2, 2016) through the Geni.com platform to Sandra D., a daughter of Susi D. She kindly responded the next day and forwarded my message to her mother and her aunt. No further reply was received. It became very clear to me that this branch of the Fein family preferred not to talk to me.

66 I had been aware early on that at least one sister existed but only found, in July 2016, an online life tree for Simon and Lotti Fein, posted by Ariel Levy-Löwy (1947–) on the website Geni.com on April 23, 2016. Ariel Levy-Löwy is related to Emilie Löwy (née Fein, 1852–1908), the third and youngest daughter of Simon and Lotti Fein. Emilie Löwy married Jakob Löwy (1841–1907) and the couple had three children, the engineer Oskar Löwy (1880–1941 or 1942?), Wilma Raubiczek (née Löwy, 1883–1942) and Elsa Polacek or Polack (née Löwy, 1888–1942?). The three children of Oskar Löwy and Olga Bass (1887–1941 or 1942 ?) survived the war. Ariel-Löwy Levy (1947–) is the son of one of these children, Ernst Löwy (1912-1948). The latter was killed in the Israeli war of independence.

67 See *Adressbuch von Brünn* 1897, 121; 1901, 134. For the digitized census information about the Fein and Brecher families for the year 1900 in the Brno census database, see http://digiarchiv.brno.cz/ (accessed Dec. 13, 2014). Amalie Brecher is buried in the Jewish cemetery in Brno in section 15, row 4, grave 1. She was born on December 12, 1818. See NA, Praha, fonds n° 167, Jewish registers (Židovské matriky, Judische Matriken), inv. n° 137, Brno, Z, 1884–1922, reproduction n° 103, f. 201, n° 2546. The 19 Rennergasse (Běhounská) address where she lived at the time of her death is also confirmed there.

68 *Tagesbote*, Nov. 18, 1905, 6, death notice.

69 See the "Verzeichnis der Approbierten" list in the *Jahresbericht des Staatsgymnasiums mit deutscher Unterrichtssprache in Brünn für das Schuljahr* 1912–1913, 34–35. The school building was built by the architect couple August Sicard von Sicardsburg and Eduard van der Nüll – reputed by some to be gay – who also built the Vienna State Opera. See Zatloukal 2006, 46–47; Schock 2007, 36–37. The building now houses the Janáčkova akademie múzických umění v Brně (Janáček Academy of Music and the Performing Arts in Brno). The Hochschule across the street is currently part of the Faculty of Medicine of Brno's Masaryk University.

1934) attests.[70] Fein did not obtain his law degree until 1919 and this delay can most likely be explained by circumstances arising from World War I (*kriegsbedingt*).[71]

Fein was admitted to the bar in 1923.[72] It is a bit unclear what Karl Fein did professionally between 1919 and 1923 but it is possible that, in 1922-1923, he interned at the practice of the non-Jewish lawyer Franz Nawratil, who, as we shall see, will play a crucial role in our story.[73] After his internship, in October 1923, Fein joined the law practice of Friedrich August Herrmann (1859–1923).[74] But this lawyer died only a month later. By 1924, Fein was working in the law office of Artur Feldmann senior.[75] The Jewish Feldmann family from Brno played an important role in the career of Karl Fein. Artur Feldmann Sr. (1877–1941) was a successful lawyer in Brno. Several lawyers worked for his practice.[76] Yet, in 1925, Fein had a law office of his own in the

[70] PNP, Praha, fonds Božena Viková-Kunětická, letter (dated Jun. 14, 1912) from Karl Fein to Božena Viková-Kunětická. I found it impossible to read Fein's handwriting. Presumably, the letter was critical of Viková-Kunětická's work. It remains possible that the letter was in fact written by the elder Karl Fein, one year older than his cousin, the younger Karl Fein, who, as we will see, also studied in Vienna. On Viková-Kunětická, see Malečková 2016, 51–52, 54–55.

[71] Email (dated Oct. 28, 2011) from Thomas Maisel (Archiv der Universität Wien) to the author.

[72] *Seznam advokátů dle stavu koncem roku 1928* 1929, 16; *Seznam advokátů dle stavu koncem roku 1935* 1936, 14.

[73] The extant sources do not allow to determine with certainty that Fein did his apprenticeship with Nawratil, yet this seems likely. The volumes for the years 1922–1925 of the *Seznam advokátů* series (which ran from 1921 to 1939) are missing in the collections of the MZK, Brno, the Klementinum, Praha, or any other library I checked on www.worldcat.org. A strange coincidence though may help explain their acquaintance and even Fein's internship of Fein in Nawratil's law office. From November 11, 1930, until November 1, 1932, Fein's home address was 1 Schlossergasse (Zámečnická), in the same building where Franz Nawratil had his practice from 1923 until his death in 1942. See *Adreßbuch von Groß-Brünn* 1923, 443; 1925, 477; 1927, 461; 1930, 495; 1932, 517; 1934, 535; and *Adressbuch der Landeshauptstadt Brünn 1942* 1943, 1. Since it was a corner building, the alternative address, 18 Freiheitsplatz (náměstí Svobody), was sometimes also given. It is also interesting that Nawratil was admitted to the bar in 1922 and Fein in 1923 See *Seznam advokátů dle stavu koncem roku 1928* 1929, 16. Lastly, Nawratil was, like Fein, a former pupil of the Deutsches Staatsgymnasium in Brno.

[74] "Mitteilungen aus dem Leserkreise", *Tagesbote*, Oct. 16, 1923, 4. It is unclear if Fein took over the office or associated with Herrmann in some other way. It says: "daß er seine Advokaturskanzlei im Anschluß an die Kanzlei des Herrn Dr. Friedr. Aug. Herrmann, Brünn, […] eröffnet hat" (that he has opened his law office in connection with the law office of Dr. Friedr. Aug. Herrmann, Brünn). For more info on Friedrich August Herrmann, see https://encyklopedie.brna.cz/home-mmb/?acc=profil_osobnosti&load=20622 (accessed Mar. 2, 2020). Herrmann is buried in the Jewish cemetery in Brno in parcel 25C, row 1, grave 7. Herrmann's wife was Hermine Schüller (1873–1939).

[75] See *Politický kalendář občanský a adresář zemí koruny České na rok 1924* 1924, 361. Karl Fein's name appears at the same address as the law office of Artur Feldmann Sr., 19 Krapfengasse (Kobližná).

[76] Letter (dated Apr. 25, 2016) from Uri Peled-Feldmann, the grandson of Artur Feldmann Sr., to the author: "Mein Großvater gründete sehr bald seine eigene Kanzlei, eine sehr große Kanzlei mit vielen Rechtsanwälten" (My grandfather started his own law firm very early on, a very large firm with many lawyers). See also Caruso 2015, 35.

[77] *Politický kalendář občanský a adresář zemí koruny České na rok 1925* 1925, 367; and the same guide for the following years. See also the *Advokaten* (lawyers) section in *Adressbuch von Gross-Brünn* 1925, 172, 477; *Seznam advokátů dle stavu koncem roku 1928*, 1929, 16, 33. This also used to be the address of the law office of Friedrich August Herrmann with whom Fein had associated himself in 1923. See "Mitteilungen aus dem Leserkreise", *Tagesbote*, Oct. 16, 1923, 4.

[78] For one year alone, Karl Fein and "Feldmann Ad" appear as the only two lawyers in the small town of Pohrlitz (Pohořelice). See *Politický kalendář občanský a adresář zemí koruny České na rok 1931* 1931, 386. I thank Uri Peled for confirming to me that this was Adolf Feldmann (?–1938), the brother of Artur Feldmann Sr. (1877–1941). See email (dated Jul. 21, 2016) from Uri Peled-Feldmann to the author. A short notice published in *Morgenpost* said that Karl Fein was transferring from Brno to Pohrlitz (*Morgenpost*, Nov. 6, 1928). So it looks probable that Karl Fein and Adolf Feldmann were only temporarily working together in Pohrlitz. Different people seem to have joined Adolf Feldmann in Pohrlitz over the years: Bedřich Greger, Karl Fein, Karel Högn, Egon Kreutzer, and Bedřich Adler. In 1938, as many as three names show up next to the name of Adolf Feldmann. Had he grown his law office in Pohrlitz as the years progressed? See *Politický kalendář občanský a adresář zemí koruny České na rok 1938* 1938, 268. When Adolf Feldmann died, in 1938, his law office was taken over by Egon Kreutzer. See *Nikolsburger Kreisblatt*, May 9, 1939, 8.

[79] *Politický kalendář občanský a adresář zemí koruny České na rok 1932* 1932, 392–93.

[80] It is possible that the good relations between the Fein and the Feldmann families had something

main shopping street of Brno, at 25–27 Masarykstrasse (Masarykova).[77] Starting in November 1928, Fein then worked for a few years in the law office of Artur Feldmann Sr.'s brother, Adolf Feldmann, in Pohrlitz (Pohořelice).[78] But Fein returned to Brno in 1932 where he would practice his profession on his own until 1939.[79] Artur Feldmann Sr.'s son, Otto Feldmann (1904–1956), was also a lawyer. Possibly, there was a familial relationship between the Fein and the Feldmann family.[80] This tie, or simply their good relations, likely also explains why, in 1936, Karl Fein moved to 35 Glacis (Koliště), exactly one day after Otto Feldmann and his wife moved to that address. Did Fein live with the Feldmann couple?[81] We will return to the Feldmann family a few more times later.

Karl Fein would also use 35 Glacis (Koliště) as both his home and work address. Fein's living and working at the same address, possibly even staying with a couple, may indicate that he was not thriving professionally. However, that Fein was living in a large newly built modernist building, located on one of the poshest streets in Brno, speaks against this impression. On the resident registration card recording Fein's move, one can see that the office of the engineer Artur Eisler (1887–1944) signed as the building's property manager (*Hausverwalter*).[82] Artur Eisler was, together with his brother Moriz Eisler (1888–1972), the owner of one of the most important construction companies in pre-war Brno. The Eisler brothers' company built the world-famous Tugendhat villa designed by the architect Mies van der Rohe.[83] Artur and Moriz were only two of the five Eisler brothers. Another, more famous Eisler brother, Otto Eisler (1893–1968), was one of Brno's foremost modernist architects. He designed the building where Fein and the Feldmann couple took up residence in 1936.[84] The Eisler company not only built this new building, but also managed the rental of its apartments. The owners of the building, the Jewish couple Richard (1875–1967) and Jenny (1882–1961) Stein, lived in Vienna [ill. 8].[85] I think that Karl Fein might have

to do with Karl Fein's paternal grandmother since Lotti Fein's first husband was a Brüll. Valerie Feldmann (née Brüll, 1909–1986) was married to Karel Feldmann (1909–1989), another of Artur Feldmann Sr.'s sons. (Karel Feldmann was thus the brother of Otto Feldmann.) Valerie Feldmann's father was Max Brüll (1883–1941?) who was married to Elsa Brüll (née Stránská, 1891–1941?). Valerie Feldmann's parents both perished in the Holocaust. However, judging from an online family tree for the Brüll branch, there was no relation to Karl Fein's grandmother. See https://www.geni.com/family-tree/index/6000000121834954907 (accessed Apr. 20, 2021).

[81] The virtual convergence of the moving dates seems to suggest that the bachelor Fein moved in with the couple, or that there was at least some kind of connection. See the resident registration cards for Otto Feldmann (dated Oct. 2, 1936) and Karl Fein (dated Oct. 3, 1936) in the AMB, Brno, fonds Z 1. Otto Feldmann's wife was the Berlin jurist Hanna Schmoller (1909–?). See http://encyklopedie.brna.cz/home-mmb/?acc=profil_osobnosti&load=12677 (accessed Apr. 30, 2016). Uri Peled-Feldmann found no trace in his family archives of a familial relationship or an acquaintance between Karl Fein and the Feldmann family. See letter (dated Apr. 25, 2016) from Uri Peled-Feldmann to the author.

[82] The resident registration cards for Otto Feldmann and Karl Fein in AMB, Brno, fonds Z 1, bear the same stamp of Artur Eisler and also the same illegible *Hausverwalter* (property manager) signature. The Feldmann couple moved out in July 1938, but Fein stayed at this address until mid-October 1938. I thank Uri Arthur Peled-Feldmann for sending me a copy of Otto Feldmann's resident registration card in April 2016. For Artur Eisler, see http://encyklopedie.brna.cz/home-mmb/?acc=profil_osobnosti&load=3192 (accessed Jan. 29, 2015); Kudělková 2007.

[83] See http://www.tugendhat.eu/en/brno-construction-office.html?timeline=1 (accessed Jan. 10, 2015).

[84] The building is registered as C 104 in the Brno Architecture Manual (BAM) database. See https://www.bam.brno.cz/en/object/c104-apartment-building (accessed Jan. 30, 2021). It is important to note that today the building's house number is 29/645; in 1936, it was 35/645. See also Vrabelová, Svobodová & Šlapeta 2016, 268; Pelčák & Šlapeta 2015, 290–91.

[85] The couple emigrated to the USA in March 1939, sailing from Southampton to New York. See the National Archives, Philadelphia (Pennsylvania), Declarations of Intention for Citizenship, Jan. 19, 1842–Oct. 29, 1959, Records of District Courts of the United States, 1685-2009, U.S. District Court for the Southern District of New York, Roll 561, Declarations of Intention for Citizenship, 1842-1959 (No 438701-439600), declaration of intention n° 438781, Richard Stein (born 1875); available online at Ancestry.com, U.S., State and Federal Naturalization Records, 1794-1943 (accessed Feb. 1, 2021). The Stein couple had two daughters, who emigrated to the USA

known Otto Eisler since the latter was also part of the Jewish upper classes and a gay man.[86] Such knowledge may have played a role in Fein moving to a building that had just been finished by the Eisler brothers.

I first took notice of Otto Eisler when I read about one of his designs, the House for Two Bachelors (Haus für zwei Junggesellen), constructed for him and his brother in 1930–31.[87] My hunch that Otto Eisler might have been a gay man (at least before the war) was confirmed later in my research. I found a diary fragment by the American architect Philip Johnson (1906–2005), a gay man himself, that stated this clearly. Johnson mentioned Otto Eisler's sexual preference in his account of an impromptu visit to Otto Eisler in Brno in the summer of 1939. From the same source we also learn that Otto Eisler was tortured by the Gestapo in the Spielberg (Špilberk) castle, shortly before Johnson's visit, and, as a consequence, was physically almost unable to speak with Johnson.[88] Two of Otto Eisler's brothers were imprisoned for six weeks.[89] Otto Eisler managed to flee to Norway with his brother Hugo and his family in the second half of 1939.[90] In Oslo, Otto Eisler was imprisoned in the Bredtveit concentration camp for political prisoners.[91] When he tried to flee to Sweden, in 1943, he was shot and wounded "only a few yards from the border", and was deported to Auschwitz in February 1943.[92] Of the five Eisler brothers, only Otto and Moriz would survive the Holocaust. After the war they would both marry.[93] We will encounter Otto Eisler a few more times in our story.

soon after: Mary Hoffman (née Stein, 1905–2005) and Hetty Bloch (née Stein, 1913–1993). Behind the already impressive Koliště building's street-facing wing, there is another, even larger wing that cannot be seen from the street. During the German occupation, the apartment building was entrusted to a *Treuhänder* (trustee) and sold under duress. See MZA, Brno, fonds B 392, Vystěhovalecký fond, úřadovna Brno, kart. n° 14, inv. n° 302, building 35 Glacis (currently 29 Koliště).

86 Karl Fein's later intern, the lawyer Robert Herrmann, was in any case related to Otto Eisler's later wife, Truda Herrmann (1902–1982). Robert Herrmann was also asked to assist with settling Otto Eisler's inheritance in Czechoslovakia after his death in 1968. See Library and Archives Canada/Bibliothèque et archives Canada, Ottawa, manuscript division, fonds Stephen S. Barber, MG 31, H 113, Personal records and correspondence, vol. 12, file n° 1, letter (dated May 1, 1971, 1) from Robert Herrmann to Stephen Barber. I thank John Panofsky for pointing out the existence of the two men's correspondence to me. See also "Karl Fein and the Brno building industry" in the addenda (n° 3) for some more elements that might further shed light on our claim that Karl Fein knew Otto Eisler.

87 The address of this Brno house is 10 Neumangasse (Neumannova). The following phrase caused my gaydar to tingle: "Der geöffnete Teil der Dachterrasse mit einer Dusche wurde für vielseitige sportliche Betätigungen genutzt" (The open section of the roof terrace with a shower was used for varied sporting activities). This entry about the house and its owners' activities has since curiously disappeared. See http://slavnestavby.cz/ (accessed Jan. 11, 2015). See also http://www.bam.brno.cz/de/objekt/c058-haus-fur-zwei-junggesellen?filter=code (accessed Jan. 11, 2015). For some photos and architectural plans of the house, see Pelčák, Škrabal & Wahla 1998, 30–33; Pelčák, Sapák & Wahla 2000a, 49.

88 Schulze 1994, 136–37. Basing themselves on Schulze, Voight and Bresan repeat the claim (Voight & Bresan 2022, 268–71). For another reference to Eisler suffering physical ailments after being released from the Špilberk (Spielberg) castle prison, see Malt & Juříčková 2016, 80.

89 Wladika 2009, 7; http://encyklopedie.brna.cz/home-mmb/?acc=profil_osobnosti&load=3188 (accessed Jan. 10, 2015).

90 Wladika 2009, 7. Otto Eisler tried first to find refuge in Sweden, in February 1940, but his request for a residence permit was not granted. See his application card in the Passport office section of the archival fund Statens utlänningskommission (Immigrant Services Bureau); see email (dated Jul. 1, 2015, with reference number 2015/06246) from Åke Norström (Riksarkivet, Stockholm) to the author. Hugo Eisler died of cancer in 1944 and his wife later moved to Uppsala. For this information from the *flyktingakt* (refugee file), see email (dated Jul. 1, 2015) from Paul Epäilys (Region- och stadsarkivet i Göteborg) to the author.

91 AJJDC, New York, 1941–1967, Stockholm Collection, Olika Organisation P-S 1941–1949, document ID 944740, letter (dated Jan. 12, 1943) [the inventory of the AJJDC records the date of the letter incorrectly as Jan. 21, 1943] from Otto Schütz to Mr. [Marcus] Levin. I thank Andrés Sorin for his help in translating this letter from Norwegian to French and Daniël Christiaens for his mediation in this matter. See also https://en.wikipedia.org/wiki/Bredtveit_Prison (accessed Nov. 11, 2015).

92 See https://en.wikipedia.org/wiki/Otto_Eisler (accessed Sep. 5, 2015).

93 I tried to determine if Otto Eisler left any personal papers, letters, or even a diary behind where I might have found some information on Karl Fein's

KAREL RŮŽIČKA, THE LAWYER

Karl Fein possibly worked with the lawyer Karel Růžička (1895–1942) in the 1930s when both Fein and Růžička were renting their law offices at 6 Masarykgasse (Masarykova).[94] The building was and still is centrally located in the main shopping street leading from the main train station to the main Brno square, the Freiheitsplatz (náměstí Svobody).[95] The building then belonged the city of Brno, which explains why the building had a central pedestrian passage way leading from Masarykgasse (Masarykova) to the bell tower of the former city hall (*Rathaus, radnice*).[96]

Like Karl Fein, Karel Růžička was on the left of the political spectrum. During the war, he joined the Czechoslovak resistance movement, Defense of the Nation (Obrana národa). Růžička was arrested and found guilty of high treason (*Hochverrat*) by a summary court martial (*Standgericht*) on January 10, 1942.[97] Like so many other political opponents of the Nazis, Růžička was sent to the Mauthausen concentration camp where he was killed on July 12, 1942.[98]

KARL FEIN'S PERSONAL LIFE

Not much is known about Karl Fein's personal life because there are hardly any archival traces of his life. As we will see in chapter 13, his personal archives and his estate were, along with his life, wiped out mercilessly in the Holocaust. Here and

life. Attempts to contact the current Eisler family through their lawyer in Prague received no reply whatsoever. I thank Michael Wladika of the Leopold Museum in Vienna for his help in mediating. See email (dated Dec. 16, 2011) to the author. In 2011, the Eisler family successfully challenged the ownership of two artworks then held by the Leopold Museum in Vienna. See http://www.leopoldmuseum.org/de/presse/meldungen/10 (accessed Jan. 10, 2015); and Wladika 2009. The paintings had belonged to Otto Eisler and were confiscated by the Gestapo. The fact that Otto's homosexuality is virtually unknown in Brno indicates that this is a sensitive issue, something confirmed to me by Petr Pelčák, a Brno architecture expert. See his email (dated Dec. 19, 2011) to the author: "I'm perhaps the only one in this city [Brno] who knows it [i.e. that Eisler was gay]". Anne Newman, in the USA, who works on the architect and the history of her Jewish family in Brno, told me that many people she spoke to knew Eisler was gay, and that only Eisler's close relatives consistently denied this fact. See conversation (dated Jun. 15, 2018) between Anne Newman and the author in Paris.

[94] See *Adreßbuch von Groß-Brünn* 1932, [517]; *Seznam telefonních ústředen, hovoren a účastníků pro zemi Moravskoslezskou* 1938, 128. In the year 1931, Fein is listed at 6 Masarykova and Karel Růžička at 4 Starobrněnska, see *Politicky kalendař občansky a adresař zemi koruny Česke na rok 1932* 1932, 392. Is this an indication that Růžička followed Fein to the Masarykova address? Although both lawyers had their offices in the same large building, it is unclear if they ever worked together in any way or even shared the same office space. I noticed that the law practices of Fein and Růžička had different phone numbers. See *Seznam advokátů dle stavu koncem roku 1935* 1936, 27, 31.

[95] The building was designed by the Jewish architect Maximilian Johann Monter (1865–1942) who was deported from Vienna to Terezín on June 20, 1942, where he died. His Terezín death certificate states that he was a Roman Catholic. See http://www.holocaust.cz/databaze-dokumentu/dokument/85309-monter-maximilian-johann-oznameni-oo-umrti-ghetto-Terezín/ (accessed Aug. 18, 2016). His wife Irma (1878–1944?) was deported from Terezín to Auschwitz-Birkenau on transport "Dz" on May 15, 1944.

[96] There are no archival records in the AMB, Brno, on the rent that the two lawyers would have paid to the city of Brno starting in 1932. See email (dated Feb. 13, 2015) from Jana Dosoudilová (AMB, Brno) to the author. It is unclear if, in pre-war Brno, there were many law offices employing several lawyers, such as are so common nowadays. Judging by the addresses of Brno lawyers from that period, this seems to have been a rarity. See also chapter 6, p. 168, n. 76.

[97] MZA, Brno, fonds B 340, Gestapo Brno (1939–1945), kart. n° 147, n° 8489, sign. 100-147-7, file Karel Růžička.

[98] A post-war inheritance file contains Karel Růžička's official death certificate issued in Mauthausen. See MZA, Brno, fonds C 152, Okresní soud civilní Brno (Bezirksgericht für Zivilsachen in Brünn), Pozůstalost po Dru. Karlu Růžičkovi zemřelém Jul. 12, 1942 (inheritance file Karel Růžička d. Jul. 12, 1942), sign. D XVIII 53/50, Todfallsaufnahme Karel Růžička (dated Jul. 15, 1942). Because Karel Růžička seems an important figure, possibly linked to Karl Fein, I tried my utmost to contact the living relatives of Karel Růžička's wife Marie Vavrouch (1885–?). With difficulty, I managed to locate a son of Marie, born after the war, but this did not result in my being able to see the archives he claimed to have kept on his mother and Karel Růžička at his home. One can find in the addenda (n° 4) further information on Karel Růžička's life and my search for his surviving personal archives.

there, I have found some traces of his professional life as a lawyer in the local press.[99] In 1935, for example, he was hired by the Moravian Society for the Prevention of Cruelty to Animals (Tierschutzverein) in connection with financial embezzlement by one of its board members.[100] In March 1934, for the Jewish Women's Organization (Jüdische Frauenorganisation), Fein gave a lecture on legal forays into everyday life (*Juristische Streifzüge durch den Alltag*) in the Café Esplanade, a well-known Jewish community hangout in Brno.[101]

Karl Fein was surely also a homosexual man. Late one night, in March 1929, he got into a quarrel with a policeman in the public park in front of the Prague Main Railway Station (Praha hlavní nádraží). According to the policeman, Fein had lingered too long in the public lavatory. Most likely, Fein was cottaging in the public lavatory. Fein refused to leave the premises when ordered to do so by the police man. There followed some pushing and raised voices and Fein insulted the police officer, calling him "you dog" (*du Hund*). The juridical case that ensued over the following months shows that Fein at first refused to pay the fine of 100 Czech crowns for abusing the police officer, but yielded in the end. This incident seems to illustrate that Fein had no wish to let the Czechoslovak state easily intrude into what he may have considered his private (sexual) life.[102]

Karl Fein was described as "a very temperamental man" by a reporter of the Czechoslovak gay magazine *Nový hlas,* who was struck by the heated discussion on paragraph 129b of the Czechoslovak penal code (prohibiting sex between men), held between conference sessions at the 1932 WLSR Brno conference.[103] One of Hirschfeld's activist comrades, the Frenchman Eugen Wilhelm (aka Numa Praetorius, 1866–1951), wrote about Karl Fein in his diary, noting that he was "a rather peculiar man[,] lacking in order[,] in his very bohemian way of life".[104] According to Giese's tongue-in-cheek remark about Fein's private life, made in a letter to Kurt Hiller, Fein seems to have had a busy professional life and also an active sex and/or love life, implying that the latter left little time for gay activism.[105] As we will see later, during the last years of his life in Prague, Fein possibly had a lover or boyfriend or was at least involved with young working-class men, willing to spend time – probably in exchange for payment – with a middle-class gay man.

It is important to point out that Karl Fein was open about his sexual preference. That, uncommonly for the time, Fein was an openly gay man is indicated by his taking part in organizing the 1932 WLSR Brno conference, his association with Hirschfeld, and, as we will see, by writing under his own name for Czechoslovak gay magazines. His immediate family knew about his sexual preference. It is not known

[99] See, for example, "Advokaten vor dem Richtertisch", *Morgenpost*, Nov. 29, 1935, 3; and an untitled piece on Matthias Kuditz, one of Fein's clients, *Tagesbote*, Jul. 25, 1933, 3.

[100] See "Mährischer Tierschutzverein", *Morgenpost*, Aug. 8, 1935, 3. See also *Morgenpost*, Aug. 18, 1935, 3. A letter that Karl Fein wrote as legal representative of the association can be found in MZA, Brno, fonds B 26, Mährischer Tierschutzverein mit dem Sitz in Brünn, kart. n° 3154, sign. 1703/746, f. 188.

[101] *Tagesbote*, Mar. 21, 1934, 6. The owner of the Café Esplanade was Jewish, Alois Strompf (1871–1942?). He was deported on January 28, 1942, from Brno to Terezín on transport "U" and further deported from Terezín to Warsaw on transport "An" on April 25, 1942.

[102] For a brief mention of the importance and size of the gay life *outside* bars and venues in Prague, see Seidl 2012, 191. The park in front of the Prague railway station is to this day a cruising area for gay men but the public lavatory is gone. See NA, Praha, Policejní ředitelství Praha II, všeobecná spisovna 1931-1940, kart. n° 5661, sign. F 271-1, Fein Karel JUDr 1893 (!). The elder Karl Fein, born in 1893, was Karl Fein's one year older nephew, see further. Even in the filing of police files, both were mixed up with each other. The birth date given in the police file mentioning the park incident makes clear that it was the one year younger Karl Fein, born in 1894, who was cruising in the toilets of the Prague park in the middle of the night.

[103] *Nový hlas*, Jg. 1, n°s 7-8, Nov. 1, 1932, 13. The discussion most likely took place on Saturday Sep. 24, 1932, in the afternoon.

[104] Diary of Eugen Wilhelm, carnet 39, entry (dated Jul. 25, 1936–Sep. 26, 1936 and Oct. 3, 1936): "un homme assez singulier[,] sans ordre[,] dans sa manière de vivre très bohème". I thank Kevin

when exactly Karl Fein sought contact with Magnus Hirschfeld, but it might have been at the fourth WLSR conference in Vienna, in September 1930. Ten days after the conference, Karl Fein interviewed Hirschfeld for the local Brno newspaper *Tagesbote*, when Hirschfeld stopped in Brno to give a lecture.[106]

KARL FEIN, THE COUSIN

In terms of career, Karl Fein clearly seems to have followed in the footsteps of his very slightly elder cousin, Karl Fein (1893–1932), the son of Albert Fein's brother, Moriz Fein. This cousin, like the Karl Fein whom we have followed thus far, went to the State Grammar School (*Staatsgymnasium*) in Brno and then to Vienna, where he also studied at the university and finished his studies with a PhD in law.[107] Yet, this cousin seems to have had more success in life than Karl Fein. The cousin was a specialist in fiscal law. In 1920, he made German translations of a few books by the Czechoslovak economist Karel Engliš (1880–1961); in company with Bohumil Novotný (1882–?), published on matters related to tax; served as an editor on the *Steuer- und Bilanzrevue*; and also wrote for the newspaper *Prager Presse*.[108] Later, he worked for a period as an expert in the legislative department of the Czechoslovak Ministry of Finance and ended up working as a banker for the prestigious Petschek Bank in Prague, near the Main Railway Station.[109] Last but not least, this cousin was also a freemason.[110] He also traveled around Europe quite a lot, as his surviving passport testifies.

In the sources I consulted, there is occasional mention of an incurable disease, and that it was for his health that Fein traveled so extensively. However, the extant sources do not allow to determine with certainty what his exact affliction was. His military file tells us that he was hospitalized with malaria during his military service in 1917.[111] A Vienna newspaper reported that the affliction was a neurological ailment (*Nervenleiden*).[112] Another source speaks on the contrary about a kidney affliction.[113] Whatever it may have been, the disease had depressed the man's morale for years. In September 1932, after a few weeks in a Viennese sanatorium, and after visiting relatives in Vienna, he committed suicide in the house of an acquaintance living in

Dubout for kindly sending me this text fragment on March 11, 2018.

[105] Archiv Kurt Hiller Gesellschaft, Neuss, letter (dated Apr. 27, 1937, 2) from Karl Giese to Kurt Hiller.

[106] Fein, Nov. 4, 1930. We may also wonder if, in 1923, Karl Fein was the author of an article (undersigned by "n."), titled "Liebe unter Männern" (Love among Men), in the same newspaper, defending love between men and agitating against its unjust persecution. See n. Jun. 9, 1923.

[107] Email (dated Oct. 28, 2011) from Thomas Maisel (Archiv der Universität Wien) to the author. The similarity of the two cousins' lives is sometimes astounding. They behave almost like twin brothers. During World War I, both were sent to relatives in the relative safety of the ancestral town of Boskowitz (Boskovice). See the information, copied by hand, on the resident registration cards in Státní okresní archiv Blansko, fonds Židovská obec Boskovice, book n° 6, 1906-1920.

[108] See Engliš 1920; and, for example, Novotný & Fein 1921.

[109] Karel Engliš later became the Minister of Finance and procured him the job. Fein was one of the few German-speakers working there. See Schütz, Oct. 14, 1932, 4. The bank building would later become the Prague Gestapo headquarters, where many people were tortured. A plaque commemorates this part of the building's history. For a contemporary photo of the building, see Padevět 2016, 149. For more information on Karel Engliš, see Jančík & Kubů 2006, 129–45.

[110] See the (seemingly?) cryptic *Nachruf* (obituary) for Karl Fein (the elder cousin) in an issue of the masonic magazine *Die drei Ringe: Monatsblätter für Freimaurerei und verwandte Gebiete*, Jg. 8, n° 11, 1932, 227. The best comprehensive text on this Karl Fein's life is "Dr. Karl Fein gestorben" (Dr. Karl Fein deceased), *Prager Presse*, Oct. 5, 1932, 6.

[111] One newspaper article cryptically said: "Dr. Fein, jenž byl mezi svými známými velmi oblíben, trpěl již dlouhou dobu utkvělou představou, že je dědičně zatížen a nevyléčitelně nemocen" (Dr. Fein, who was popular among his acquaintances, long believed that he had an incurable genetical disease). See "Sebevražda pražského advokáta ve Vídni" (Suicide of Prague lawyer in Vienna), *Lidové noviny*, Oct. 4, 1932, 1. A photocopy of the elder Karl Fein's military file was kindly sent to me by the Vojenský ústředni archiv in Prague in January 2012. I was also told that there was no military file for the younger Karl Fein.

[112] See "Aus Fürcht vor geistiger Umnachtung in den Tod", *Neues Wiener Journal*, Oct. 4, 1932, 9.

[113] Schütz mentions a kidney affliction (*Nierenleiden*) (Schütz, Oct. 14, 1932).

Wien-Döbling, on October 3, 1932, shooting himself in the head.[114] Karl Fein's cousin committed suicide exactly one week after the 1932 WLSR Brno conference that Karl Fein helped organize. It makes one wonder, of course, if the unmarried elder cousin may have been a gay man as well. Or did having the same name as his younger cousin – a pretty much out homosexual – sometimes mean that he was regarded as a homosexual against his will? The ashes of the elder cousin were added to the family plot in the Jewish cemetery in Brno.[115] Their having identical names, of course, created confusion, especially in official records.[116] For now, their homonymy and the great similarity of both their lives remains somewhat coincidental, but it is important to clear up any possible confusion between the two men.

MARIANNA BECKOVÁ

The elder Karl Fein also had a sister, Gertrude Fein (1890–1944), who, in 1913, married Richard Kahn (1883–1935). In the summer of 2013, I went to Prague to interview Marianna Becková (née Kahnová, 1920–), the last surviving daughter of Richard and Gertrude Kahn.[117] Marianna Becková claimed not to know who the younger Karl Fein was. She did remember her uncle, the banker and financial specialist Karl Fein, her mother's brother who visited them once in a while. That Mrs. Becková did not know the younger Karl Fein can possibly be explained by the fact that her maternal grandmother, Kamilla Feinová (née Biachová, 1862–1934), divorced Moriz Fein, and this possibly resulted in an estrangement from or even rift with the Fein family.[118] During the interview it became clear that Marianna's emotional ties were to the Biach family.[119]

Marianna Becková also had a sister named Anna Ascherová (1914–2007). In chapter 16, we will briefly encounter Anna's husband, Albert Ascher, and, more importantly, his brother, the lawyer Siegfried Ascher. Marianna and Anna and their mother Gertruda were imprisoned in Terezín during the war.[120] After the interview,

[114] Email (dated Jun. 18, 2012) from Wolf-Erich Eckstein (Abteilung Matriken Israelitische Kultusgemeinde Wien/Vienna Jewish Records Office, Wien) to the author; *Kleine Volks-Zeitung*, Oct. 4, 1932, 9.

[115] The father, mother, and sister of the elder Karl Fein are buried in the same family grave, parcel 27A, row 1, grave 15. The grave is to be found just to the left of one of the most famous graves in the Brno Jewish cemetery, the family plot of the actor Hugo Haas (1901–1968), the composer Pavel Haas (1899–1944), and other Haas family members. The ashes of the elder Karl Fein (he was cremated in Vienna) were first burried *next* to the grave of his parents and later transferred to the family plot. See the record for the elder Karl Fein in the Jewish cemetery Brno database, https://cemeteries.jewishbrno.eu/ (accessed Dec. 18, 2020). See also email (dated Jun. 18, 2012) from Wolf-Erich Eckstein (Abteilung Matriken Israelitische Kultusgemeinde Wien/Vienna Jewish Records Office, Wien) to the author.

[116] In the police files in NA, Praha, for example, some papers relating to the two Karl Feins are mixed up in both of their files. When the younger Karl Fein was in Nice, in 1935, in relation to the Hirschfeld bequest, he lost his passport. He applied for a new passport with the Czechoslovak consulate in Marseille. The process did not go as smoothly as expected. The Czechoslovak authorities were confused about a Karl Fein asking for a new passport when a Karl Fein had died two years previously. This explains why Fein stayed five weeks in France, even though the initial plan was to stay there only one week. See letter (dated Sep. 24, 1935, [1]) from Karl Giese to Max Hodann, Arbetarrörelsens arkiv och bibliotek, Stockholm, Max Hodann samling, vol. 15. See also chapter 9, p. 278 and n. 137.

[117] I thank the Beck family for their hospitality when I visited them in Prague, and Katka Linhardtová for her assistance with the translations that day.

[118] The MZA, Brno, was not able, due to missing or incomplete archive indexes, to look up the exact divorce date of the couple, which must lie between 1899, the year the couple married, and 1913, the year of Moriz Fein's death. See email (dated Apr. 14, 2015) from Jana Fasorová (MZA, Brno) to the author.

[119] For an overview of the Biach family tree, see http://www.geni.com/family-tree/index/6000000020775457470 (accessed Jul. 28, 2015).

[120] I discovered the trail to Marianna Becková when I noticed that someone must have added the name of her mother, Gertrude Kahnová, to the Moriz Fein family plot grave stone – in the Brno Jewish cemetery – *after* the war. Marianna's mother died in Terezín. Gertrude Kahnová's name did not appear in the database of the Brno cemetery, which meant that her body was not buried there. The added inscription thus signaled that at least one family member had survived the war and had added the mother's name to the grave stone. A search message placed at my initiative in the *Časopis Terezínská*

Marianna Becková also informed me of family archival materials, linked to their Holocaust fate, that she had donated to the Jewish Museum in Prague (Židovské muzeum v Praze). One 1942 postcard found in that archival fonds plays a key role in one of the final chapters of this book.

THE L. & A. BRECHER BOOKSTORE

Because of the premature death of Karl Fein's father, at the age of forty-two, the brother of Karl Fein's mother, Alois Brecher (1853–1912), became the guardian (*Vormund*) of the young Karl and the two other children, Gustav and Margarete.[121] When Alois Brecher died, in 1912, another uncle, Siegfried Kohn (1865–1931), took over the guardianship of the three children [ill. 9].[122]

Alois Brecher was the owner of one of the approximately seven German-language bookstores in Brno. Readers in Brno could find their books in either German language or Czech bookstores. The L. & A. Brecher bookstore was very centrally located at 11 Freiheitsplatz (Náměstí svobody) in Brno and thus on the city's "German promenade". Alois Brecher's father, Ignaz Brecher (1815?–1880), who started the bookstore in 1866, was a brother of one of the main intellectual figures of the Moravian Jewish Enlightenment (Haskalah), Dr. Gideon Brecher (1797–1873). A detailed history of the L. & A. Brecher bookshop is presented in the addenda.[123]

In a memoir, the writer Fritz Beer (1911–2006), who was born and raised in Brno, briefly mentioned the Brecher bookstore when he recorded his impressions of the city's German-language bookstore landscape: "Bookseller Brecher on Freiheitsplatz, the aristocrat of his guild, had an ever-changing selection of modern novels in the displays, which saved me embarrassing conversations with the shop assistants". In Beer's code, "modern" often indicated books with erotic passages. And he added: "I believe the bookstore was [...] also the first to allow people, to some extent, to take books off the shelves and leaf through them". This was indeed exceptional since, as Beer writes, "[a]t that time, books were sold over the counter like medicine. You could not wander along the shelves, leaf through the books, get the flavour of a few pages. [...] Since I rarely knew what I was looking for, the shop assistants quickly grew impatient and sometimes snooty".[124]

After Alois Brecher died, in November 1912, his widow, Elise Brecher (née Löw, 1869–1943), inherited and took over the running of the Brno bookstore [ill. 11].[125] Alois

iniciativa (Terezín Initiative Newsletter) (issue 64, May 2013, 18) brought me in contact with Marianna Becková.

121 *K. k. Staatsgymnasium mit deutscher Unterrichtssprache in Brünn*, Hauptkataloge 1911–1912, Skoly 5418, n° 46, where the name of Alois Brecher as *Vormund* is mentioned in Karl Fein's entry (no. 9). See also MZA, Brno, fonds C 152, Okresní soud civilní Brno (Bezirksgericht für Zivilsachen in Brünn), inheritance file Albert Fein, kart. n° 1817, sign. IV 1581/96.

122 Siegfried Kohn (1865–1931) was the second husband of the sister of Karl Fein's mother, Josefina Brecher (1860–1942?). MZA, Brno, fonds C 152, Okresní soud civilní Brno (Bezirksgericht für Zivilsachen in Brünn), kart. n° 1817, sign. IV 1581/96, inheritance file Albert Fein, f. 36. Alois Brecher is buried in the Brno Jewish cemetery, in parcel 14, row 3, grave 1. His grave stone erroneously gives 1854 as his year of birth.

123 See n° 1 in the addenda.

124 Beer 1992, 78: "Buchhändler Brecher auf dem Freiheitsplatz, der Aristokrat seiner Innung, hatte eine ständig wechselnde Auswahl moderner Romane in den Auslagen, was mir peinliche Gespräche mit den Verkäufern ersparte"; "Ich glaube, er war [...] auch der erste, der im beschränkten Maße zuließ, daß man Bücher aus den Regalen nahm und durchblätterte"; "Bücher wurden damals in allen Läden wie Arzneimittel über den Ladentisch verkauft. Man konnte nicht zwischen den Regalen wandern, in den Büchern stöbern, den Geschmack von ein paar Seiten kosten. [...] Da ich nur selten wußte, was ich suchte, wurden die Verkäufer schnell ungeduldig und manchmal hochnäsig". For the section on Brno's German-language bookstore and library landscape, see Beer 1992, 76–81.

125 Elise Brecher's father was Max Löw (1842–1911) and her mother was Hermine Gomperz (1846 or 1847–1922). Elise Brecher's father may have been known as Max Löw, but his birth name was Emanuel Löw. Emanuel Löw left the Jewish faith in 1900 and changed his name to Friedrich Max Lehnstett.

and Elise Brecher had four children: Anna Bermann (née Brecher, 1893–1944), Ida Brecher (1895–1904),[126] Fritz Brecher (1901–1942), and Heinrich Brecher (1904–1955). Fritz, the oldest son, Fritz took over the bookstore from his mother in January 1938.[127] When the Germans annexed the so called Rest-Tschechoslowakei (also Rest-Tschechei, the rest of Czechoslovakia), in 1939, the Brecher bookstore was forcibly taken over by two of its employees, Ludmilla Schaal (1900–?) and Josef Cižek (1901–?). Soon afterwards, the store was Aryanized and was renamed Ostland Buchhandlung. It ceased operation, presumably in 1944, when Ludmilla Schaal sensed that the Germans were going to lose the war and fled, most likely to Germany.

See Staudacher 2009, 373, 706; and the remark in the birth register for Emanuel Löw in NA, Praha, Jewish registers (Židovské matriky, Judische Matriken), Rychnov nad Kněžnou (Reichenau an der Knieschna), inv. n° 1843, N, 1840-1876, reproduction n° 9, birth registration n° 20, Emanuel Löw, born on Aug. 13, 1842, accessible online at http://www.badatelna.eu/fond/1073/reprodukce/?zaznamId=2425&reproId=57290 (accessed Jan. 31, 2017). However, the Jüdische Kultusgemeinde (JKG) in Vienna was not able to locate the marriage date of Max and Hermine Löw in the Jewish registers (Židovske matriky, Judische Matriken). See email (dated Jan. 30, 2017) from Sabine Koller (Archiv der Israelitischen Kultusgemeinde, Wien) to the author. Perhaps this is related to Max Löw/Lehnstett's leaving of the Jewish religion and his name change. All three of the Löw/Lehnstett daughters were born in Vienna. The couple divorced in the same year that Löw's left his faith. Friedrich Max Lehnstett died in Vienna in 1911 and received a Protestant burial in Vienna. Hermine Löw/Lehnstett (née Gomperz) is buried in the Jewish cemetery in Brno in parcel 1A, row 3, grave 6, together with her mother Julia Gomperz (née Pollatschek, 1822–1884) and one of Elise Brecher's two sisters, the *Malerin* (painter) Dorette Löw (1873–1933). Hermine Löw's father, Jacob Moriz Gomperz (1811–1876) is buried in the grave next to it, in parcel 1A, row 3, grave 5. Elise Brecher's other sister was Marianne Löw (1876–1942?). She married Professor and Doctor Emil Waelsch (1863–1927), who taught at the Deutsche Technische Hochschule in Brno. He is buried in the Brno Jewish cemetery in parcel 26B, row 2, grave 3. After his death, the Emil-Waelsch-Fonds, which would procure study stipends, was started. Two days after its announcement, Elise Brecher, Dorette Löw, and Elise Brecher's daughter, Anna Bermann, and her husband Willy (and his father David Bermann) donated money. See *Tagesbote*, Jul 7, 1927, 3; Jul. 9, 1927, 7. Marianne Waelsch was deported on transport "Ae" on March 27, 1942, from Brno to Terezín and transported further from Terezín to Izbica on transport "Aq" on April 27, 1942. Her son, Heinrich Benedict Waelsch (1905–March 1966), emigrated to the USA in January 1939. See Ancestry.com database, Passenger and Crew Lists of Vessels Arriving at New York, New York, 1897–1957. Microfilm Publication T715 (1897–1957), roll 6275, 952–53. The original is in the National Archives, Washington D.C., Records of the Immigration and Naturalization Service. In the USA, Heinrich B. Waelsch became a specialist in neurochemistry. In December 1942, he married Salome Gluecksohn (1907–2007), who herself had a renowned academic career. On two occasions, October 23, 2019 and February 10, 2020, I sent a letter to Naomi Waelsch Kerest (1944–) in the USA, one of the couple's two children. I received an answer (dated Feb. 16, 2020) that she regretted that she did not know anything about her family's past. The couple's other child, Peter Waelsch (1947–d.), is deceased. Emil and Marianne Waelsch's other two children were Karla Waelsch (1903–?) and Hans Herbert Waelsch (1909–1978). The fate of Karla is unknown. Hans Herbert was a doctor and cancer specialist, who lived and practiced in Germany after the war. See Grundmann, Sep. 21, 1979. We know only that Elise Brecher's paternal grandfather was a certain Josef Löw (?–?) who was married to Dorothea Löw (née Mansfeld, ?–?). So, it was not possible to determine if Elise Brecher might have been related to another important figure of the Moravian Haskalah, Rabbi Leopold Löw (1811–1875). For more information on Leopold Löw, see Brocke, Carlebach & Wilke 2014, 618–19. For Leopold Löw and his relationships with the other Haskalah epigones, see Miller 2011, 92–93. What is certain is that Elise Brecher's maternal great-grandfather was Rabbi Jehuda Lion (Lyon) Loeb Gomperz (1782–1849). The mother of Max Löw's three daughters, Hermine Gomperz, was one of the seven daughters of Jacob Moriz Gomperz (1811–1876). The latter was a well-known Brno businessman. See Smutný 2004, 12; Smutný 2012, 131. In chapter 16, pp. 642-43, we will encounter again the name of the art collector Heinrich Gomperz (1843(?)-1894), who was one of the three sons of Jacob Moriz Gomperz (out of eleven children in total). For more information on the notable Jewish Gomperz family, of German origin, see https://de.wikipedia.org/wiki/Gomperz_%28Familie%29#Wien (accessed Feb. 1, 2017).

126 Ida Brecher died in childhood. For the record of her birth, see NA, Praha, fonds Matriky židovských náboženských obcí v českých krajích, Brno, N 1880–1895, f. 272, n° 2436, Ida Brecher (Mar. 31, 1895). The child died in Vienna of heart failure due to hypothyroidism and is buried in the Wiener Zentralfriedhof, section T1, group 49, row 6, grave 4. She was in a sanatorium for mentally disabled children, the Heilpädagogische Anstalt Wien-Grinzing, founded by Dr. Theodor Heller. I owe most of the information on this child to Andreas Franck, see his email (dated Feb. 10, 2021) to the author.

ELISE BRECHER

Even though nothing is certain or provable here, it seems to me at least plausible that, because the bookstore belonged to his aunt and uncle, and because his uncle was his guardian, Karl Fein may have had a certain affinity for books. It's even possible that Karl Fein was also formed intellectually and politically by his left-wing aunt and uncle. His aunt, Elise Brecher, in particular seems not to have been a conservative woman. When, in 1900, an upper-class women's organization called the (German) Women's Association ([Deutscher] Frauenbund), working for the education and equal treatment of women, started up in Brno, she was one of its three founders (*Gründer*) and also one of its leading figures, a position she held until at least 1914.[128]

In the texts and book reviews she wrote for the Vienna-based periodical *New Women's Life* (*Neues Frauenleben*) (1902–1918), Elise Brecher reveals herself to be an intelligent woman. This periodical did not shy from reporting on the new ideas and theories of sexual reform. Marianne Tuma von Waldkampf reported on the first International Congress for Maternity Protection and Sexual Reform (Internationaler Kongress für Mutterschutz und Sexualreform) in Dresden in 1911, where Magnus Hirschfeld was a prominent speaker.[129] Elise Brecher was also active in the local Brno group of the Association of Abstinent Women (Bund Abstinenter Frauen).[130] The L. & A. Brecher bookstore advertised in almost every issue of *Licht ins Volk!*, the periodical of the German Adult Education Center (Deutsche Volkshochschule) led by Hugo Iltis, one of the central figures, as we have seen, organizing the 1932 WLSR Brno conference.[131] In 1921, Iltis also wrote a pamphlet on the malaria mosquito in Moravia, published by the Brecher bookstore.[132]

A LINK BETWEEN THE BOOKSTORE AND THE BUY-BACK OPERATION?

I think there is a real possibility that Karl Fein may have relied on his aunt's booksellers' network for help with the buy-back operation to retrieve Institute materials from Nazi Germany. After all, would the Nazis have been willing to knowingly, and publicly, sell the Institute materials to Hirschfeld directly? Elise Brecher's booksellers' network might have provided a good screen for the operation to return the Institute materials to Hirschfeld.

Giese's 1935 statement that the buy-back operation was carried out through middlemen (*Mittelmänner*), in the plural, seems to minimally support this viewpoint.[133] One Slovak newspaper wrote that, besides Karl Fein, Josef Weisskopf also played a

[127] *Adressbuch des deutschen Buchhandels* 1938, 68; and NA, Praha, fonds Arizačni spisy, kart. n° 191, sign. 1119, file L. & A. Brecher, Brno.

[128] *Frauenleben*, Jg. 12, n° 3, Mar. 1, 1900, 8 (*Zuschriften*). For the announcement of the founding of the association, see *Neues Wiener Journal*, Jg. 8, n° 2252, Jan. 31, 1900, 3. Elise Brecher is mentioned on p. [2] as the *1. vorsitzende-Stellvertreterin* (first vice president) in *XV. Jahres-Bericht des Vereines 'Frauenbund', Brünn für das Jahr 1914*, [2]. See also http://www.fraueninbewegung.onb.ac.at/Pages/OrganisationenDetail.aspx?p_iOrganisationID=12359751 (accessed Jul. 16, 2016). For a review of a book on Otto Weininger's mysogynistic theory, as well as a text by Elise Brecher on voting rights for women, see Brecher 1904; Brecher 1911. More articles by her can be found at http://www.onb.ac.at/ariadne/vfb/02guinfl.htm (accessed Jul. 16, 2016). Karl Fein's mother Helene was also a regular member of the Frauenbund, paying the annual fee of two Czech crowns. See *XV. Jahres-Bericht des Vereines 'Frauenbund', Brünn für das Jahr 1914*, [13].

[129] Tuma von Waldkampf 1911.

[130] *Tagesbote*, Nov. 16, 1910, 3.

[131] Hugh Iltis, one of the sons of Hugo Iltis, was not aware of any special tie between his father and the Brecher family or bookstore. He only remembered buying a Christmas present in the Brecher bookstore as a child. See email (dated Jan. 20, 2012) from Hugh Iltis to the author.

[132] Iltis 1921.

[133] See "Magnus Hirschfelds Erbe in Wien", *Der Morgen – Wiener Montagblatt*, Jun. 24, 1935, 10: "Karl Giese erzählt von der Arbeit, die ihm bevorsteht. [...] Das Sammeln jener Gegenstände des Instituts, die durch Mittelsmänner auf der Versteigerung erstanden wurden" (Karl Giese speaks of the work that lies ahead. [...] Collecting the Institute items that were purchased through middlemen at the auction).

role in the buy-back operation.[134] We also saw that a first deal (it is unknown if it went through or not) was negotiated through a friend of Hirschfeld, Margarete Dost, who had no (family) relation to Hirschfeld. Not being related to Hirschfeld may have helped the negotiations with the Nazi lawyer Vieck in Berlin.

It is not clear whether the National Socialists in Berlin tried to ascertain, in one way or another, who purchased the Institute lots auctioned in November 1933. But Karl Fein's name may have presented a possible obstacle, since the Germans might have known him as one of the organizers of the 1932 WLSR conference. It was in any case almost impossible for them to know that Karl Fein – who might also have been known to them as a Hirschfeld follower – was in any way linked to the L. & A. Brecher bookstore in Brno. Relying on Elise Brecher, the sister-in-law of Fein's mother, would have provided good cover. But, possibly, the auctioned Institute lots were not directly purchased by the L. & A. Brecher bookstore either.

The L. & A. Brecher bookstore may have seemed simply a small, local bookstore but it occasionally served as a publisher, though rarely.[135] They also traded internationally, as their published sales catalogues testify [ill. 10]. One can easily find evidence of the Brecher bookstore being linked to the buying and selling of expensive manuscripts.[136] Most booksellers were then represented abroad by so-called commission agents (*Kommissionäre* or *Kommissionsgeschäfte*). These companies were part of the so-called intermediate book trade (*Zwischenbuchhandel*). Commission agents would buy and sell for the bookstore that they represented.[137] The L. & A. Brecher bookstore worked with three foreign commission agents, in Leipzig, Vienna, and London.[138]

In 1933, the Leipzig Kommissionsgeschäft Curt Fernau was headed by Curt Fernau (1895–1962), the son of the founder of the company, another Curt Fernau. The company had been acquired by the firm of Koehler & Volckmar in 1931. By that time, Koehler & Volckmar AG already controlled 80 percent of the German intermediate book trade.[139] Fernau continued to work at his company but under the umbrella of Koehler & Volckmar. Yet Curt Fernau would prove to be one of the principal figures in Koehler & Volckmar's tumultuous company history, marked by a never-resolved power struggle between different factions of the firm's founding families (*Gründerfamilien*). Fernau was a specialist in Koehler & Volckmar's foreign section (*Ausland-Abteilung*), specifically responsible for relations with Austrian booksellers.[140] The Brecher bookstore was also represented in Vienna by the Kommissionsgeschäft Lechner & Sohn. A further possible British representative, the London firm J. & E. Bumpus, seems far-fetched.[141]

To be clear, I have found no archival or other sources that indicate that these commission agents played any part in our story. However, I think there is a real

[134] See "Institut für sexualwissenschaftliche Forschung in Paris", *Neues Pressburger Tagblatt*, Apr. 28, 1934, 5.

[135] The DNB, Leipzig, has eight titles published by the bookstore in their collection. See, for example, Soffé 1922; Lamm 1934. Among the books not in their holdings are Baculus 1912 and Kreisler 1912. OCLC mentions at least five additional titles.

[136] See, for example, http://www.handschriftencensus.de/20659 (accessed, Dec. 17, 2014). The Franciscan manuscript, known as Stimulus amoris ("St. a."), is another example. A fifteenth-century Bohemian copy was sold to the National Library in Prague by the Brecher bookstore between 1934 and 1938. See Eisermann 2001, 172. See also the 1938 protocol of a Fritz Brecher hearing, in which he mentioned that he was trading with Paris. See MZA, Brno, fonds C 12, Krajský soud trestní v Brně, kart. n° 2381, sign. Tk XI 1852/38, f. 62.

[137] See the definition of *Kommissionsgeschäft* (commission company) at http://www.boersenverein.de/de/portal/glossar/174393?glossar=K&wort=220797 (accessed Dec. 17, 2014).

[138] In the addenda (n° 2), one can find more information on the three foreign *Kommissionäre* (commissionaries) representing the L. & A. Brecher bookstore abroad.

[139] Keiderling 2008, 22.

[140] Keiderling 2008, 244.

[141] The approximate time periods that these *Kommissionsgeschäfte* represented the Brecher bookstore are taken from the yearly records in the annual *Adressbuch des deutschen Buchhandels*.

[142] I think it could prove useful for future research-

possibility that the Institute materials were bought back with help from either the Kommissionsgeschäft Curt Fernau in Leipzig or the Kommissionsgeschäft Lechner & Sohn in Vienna. Some skilled book professionals were possibly required to assess the value of the books and other Institute lots auctioned by the Nazis. Furthermore, these companies had the know-how to transport these materials from Berlin to Czechoslovakia or Austria and also knew how to deal with the necessary export requirements. Nearby Vienna was always a logical partner for the German-speaking residents of Brno, and we have already seen that a great many books were dumped in Vienna at bargain prices as soon as the 1933 Action Against the Un-German Spirit started. What seems to speak against this hypothesis of a Vienna representative's possible involvement with the Brno bookstore is Hirschfeld's statement, in *Testament: Heft II*, that the materials bought back came through Prague. This last element would rather plead for a possible involvement of the Leipzig Kommissionär Curt Fernau rather than the Vienna firm Lechner & Sohn.[142]

Again, that Giese spoke in 1935 of several middlemen (*Mittelsmänner*) helping out with the buy-back operation minimally suggests that Karl Fein was not acting on his own. Moreover, it might have been simply a smart move to send several parties to the Berlin November 1933 auctions. These parties may have agreed beforehand to divide the cake (so as not to arouse any suspicion?), for example, by not bidding against each other in the auctions. If Karl Fein's aunt's bookseller network was indeed involved in the buy-back operation, then it is possible that the National Socialists were duped into believing that they were selling the lots of the remaining Institute materials to so-called *Kommissionsgeschäfte*, or "regular" book traders, associated with "disinterested" commercial interests, which certainly had no visible ties to the archenemy Magnus Hirschfeld.

When the buy-back operation took place, in mid-November 1933, Giese was still in Brno. Most likely, he was closely involved with Fein's dealings and made continuous reports to Hirschfeld on how things were going. At the end of December 1933, one and a half months after the Berlin auctions, Giese left Brno again, which likely means that the materials bought back had already arrived safely in the city. In any case, the materials were not immediately sent to Paris. Only a part of these materials, most likely sorted beforehand by Giese in Brno, was sent to Paris once Giese had arrived safely there, in the beginning of April 1934. We will return to this moment later on, when we shall look at the Brno expedition company that most likely handled this shipment.

OTTO SCHÜTZ, THE LAWYER

Trying to find more sources that could possibly shed light on this still largely obscure buy-back operation, I looked at another interesting Brno figure. In 1931–36, Fein had an intern named Otto Schütz (1892–1970) in his law office.[143] We have seen that Karl Fein may have gone to Berlin in December 1933. If he did, then Schütz would have handled affairs while Fein was away. Like Karl Fein, Otto Schütz was Jewish and left-wing. Schütz was the president of the Brno branch of the League for Human Rights (Liga für Menschenrechte, Liga pro lidská práva) and, in 1938, also started

ers to further investigate Curt Fernau in order to determine if he was indeed in any way involved with (or simply facilitated) the November 1933 auctions of Institute materials. Researchers could seek out surviving relatives who may have kept Curt Fernau's personal archives. In any case, a scan of Koehler & Volckmar's archival fonds, held in the Sächsisches Staatsarchiv Leipzig (Bestand Koehler & Volckmar Leipzig, 1877–1953), revealed no detailed traces of the administration of the company's commercial activities.

143 *Seznam advokátů dle stavu koncem roku 1931* (1932, 46), *Seznam advokátů dle stavu koncem roku 1932* (1933, 46) *Seznam advokátů dle stavu koncem roku 1933* (1934, 46), *Seznam advokátů dle stavu koncem roku 1934* (1935, 46), *Seznam advokátů dle stavu*

a committee to assist German exiles arriving in Brno, most of whom were Jewish, the Central Office for the Assistance of Refugees in Brno (Zentralhilfsstelle für Flüchtlinge in Brünn, Pomocné ústředí pro uprchlíky v Brně).[144] Schütz was also in contact with Kurt Hiller.[145] The Czech-speaking branch of the League was also concerned about the fate of gay men, as an article published in the very first year of their national publication *Lidská práva* attests.[146] Schütz also attended the 1932 WLSR Brno conference, reporting on it afterwards in the local newspaper *Tagesbote*.[147]

When the Germans invaded Czechoslovakia, in March 1939, Schütz managed to flee in time, despite being on a list of those to be immediately arrested. The engineer Bohumil Přikryl (1893–1965), the 1933–38 president of the Prague branch of the Czechoslovak League for Human Rights (Československá liga pro lidská práva), had already been arrested.[148] The Prague police banned the League for Human Rights as early as November 1938.[149] Schütz ended up in Scandinavia, working tirelessly during the war years for the well-being of the Jewish refugees from Brno. It is mainly in relation to this heroic work that some archival traces have remained. Schütz emigrated to the USA in the beginning of the 1950s. There are some indications that Schütz might have been a gay man; if so, it might be another reason for his possible intimate familiarity with Karl Fein, Karl Giese, and all matters related to Hirschfeld and the Institute.[150]

Since Schütz survived the Holocaust, I followed the trail of his living relatives; however, no archival files documenting what happened in the 1930s seem to have survived. A relative living in New York, whom I managed to track down, wrote to me that Schütz sent his archival files, testifying to his anti-Nazi activities, to the United States, but the boat transporting them sank. One can find more details on the admirable life of the still largely unknown Otto Schütz in the addenda.[151]

In line with her own strong interest in the women's movement, her professional activity as a bookseller, and her identity as a Jewish woman, Elise Brecher might have been aware of, and even concerned about Hirschfeld's own story, above all because his Institute was looted and a considerable part of its collection thrown into the

koncem roku 1935 (1936, 47), *Seznam advokátů dle stavu koncem roku 1936* (1937, 47). It is unclear why Schütz was an intern for such a long time – five years – in Fein's law office.

[144] Starting as early as 1933, and clearly linked to Hitler's rise to power in Germany, the Liga für Menschenrechte (League for Human Rights) also looked after émigrés. See Bloch & Tugendhat 1937, 4; Schütz, Sep. 15, 1934; Soetaert 2024.

[145] Archiv Kurt Hiller Gesellschaft, Neuss, letter (dated Apr. 29, 1937, 2) from Kurt Hiller to Karl Giese.

[146] Solařik 1930–31, 77–79. No such interest in the LGBT cause is to be found in *Aufruf* (1930–34) and its successor, *Europäische Hefte* (1934–35), the magazines of the German-speaking membership of the Czechoslovak Liga für Menschenrechte (League for Human Rights). On the other hand, they published the texts by Hirschfeld and Klaus Mann on the murder of Ernst Röhm. See Hirschfeld, Jul. 15, 1934; Mann 1934.

[147] Schütz, Oct. 2, 1932, 3–4.

[148] Bohumil Přikryl ended up in the Buchenwald concentration camp but survived the war. The PNP, Praha, holds the literary part of Přikryl's archives (archival fonds n° 1378). According to its online inventory, this archival fond contains no letters by Otto Schütz. See http://www.badatelna.eu/fond/5161/uvod/ (accessed Dec. 27, 2015). One transcribed letter by Schütz (dated Jun. 4, 1945), sent to an unidentified Czechoslovak minister, can be found in the PNP, Praha, fond Zdeněk Kalista (1900–1982), archival fond n° 726. See email (dated Jan. 11, 2016) from Naděžda Macurová (Památník národního písemnictví, Praha) to the author. Some of the archives of Bohumil Přikryl's stepson, Vladimír Přikryl-Čech (1914–1992), in the Národní filmový archiv, Praha, also contain some information about his stepfather's resistance activities. However, they contain no correspondence between Otto Schütz and Bohumil Přikryl. See email (dated Jan. 14, 2016) from Marcela Týfová (Národní filmový archiv, Praha) to the author. For genealogical information on Bohumil Přikryl, see http://www.geni.com/people/Bohumil-P%C5%99ikryl/6000000010145521296 (accessed Jan. 11, 2016).

[149] *Tagesbote*, Nov. 10, 1938, 4. The very short newspaper notice ends with: "Die Liga war eine stark links orientierte Organisation" (The League was very much a left-wing organization).

[150] See also Soetaert (2024).

[151] See n° 5 in the addenda.

flames. She might indeed have used her professional network, or simply given advice to Karl Fein when he assisted Giese and Hirschfeld with the auction of the Institute materials in Berlin. As we will suggest later on, Elise Brecher possibly played a decisive role during the war years in the subsequent fate of the Institute materials bought back from Nazi Germany and ultimately sent to Brno. Lastly, it also cannot be excluded that Hirschfeld visited Elise Brecher‘s bookstore on the Freiheitsplatz (Náměstí svobody) during his wanderings through the streets of Brno with Karl Fein on one of the three visits he made to Brno in 1932.

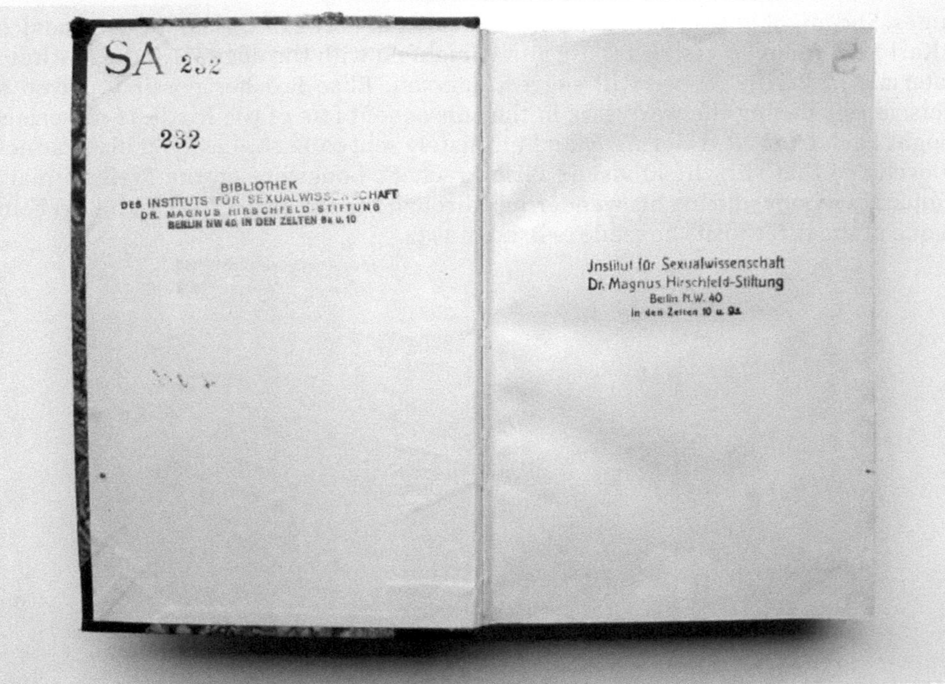

1. A 1907 sexology book with two different Institute library stamps in its front pages. "SA" (Sexualarchiv?) is likely a catalogue reference to the part of the collection under which it was filed.

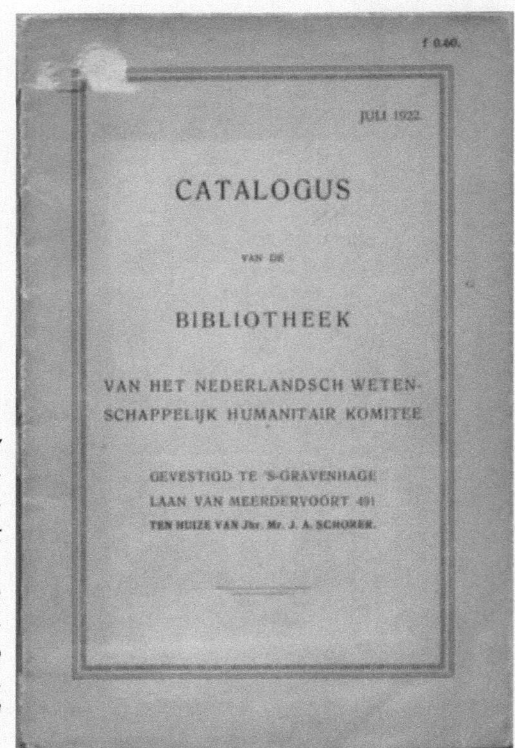
f 0.60.

JULI 1922.

CATALOGUS

VAN DE

BIBLIOTHEEK

VAN HET NEDERLANDSCH WETEN-SCHAPPELIJK HUMANITAIR KOMITEE

GEVESTIGD TE 'S-GRAVENHAGE
LAAN VAN MEERDERVOORT 491
TEN HUIZE VAN Jhr. Mr. J. A. SCHORER.

2. Cover page of a catalogue of the library of the Dutch Scientific-Humanitarian Committee (NWHK), established in 's Gravenhage (The Hague), 491 Laan van Meerdervoort [address], at the home of Squire Mr. J. A. Schorer (Catalogus van de bibliotheek van het Nederlandsch Wetenschappelijk Humanitair Komitee [NWHK], gevestigd te 's Gravenhage [The Hague] Laan van Meerdervoort 491 ten huize van Jhr. [Jonkheer] Mr. J. A. Schorer). July 1922.

Der Abend 28. April 1933 Seite 3

Deutscher Geist wird verramscht

Lieber unter dem Selbstkostenpreis verkaufen, als an den Schandpfahl schlagen oder auf dem Scheiterhaufen verbrennen lassen. — Beitgenossenschaft Magnus Hirschfeld-Hanns Heinz Ewers

Die bedeutendsten Bücher der besten deutschen Dichter, Wissenschaftler, Philosophen sind auf den „braunen Index“ gesetzt worden. Demnächst sollen sie an den Schandpfahl geschlagen oder in loderndem Feuer verbrannt werden. Die deutschen Buchhändler sind natürlich „gleichgeschaltet“ und sollte einer von ihnen noch immer etwas von den Brüdern Mann, von Wassermann oder Schnitzler, von Lenin, Marx oder Kautsky halten, so würde er doch niemals wagen, daß bestehende Verbot zu übertreten und diese „Asphaltliteratur“ in seinem Laden feilzubieten.

Aber schließlich läßt sich von der Begeisterung für den aufgebrochenen neuen deutschen Geist allein nicht gut leben und so muß man trachten, dem Scheiterhaufen und damit der völligen Vernichtung des Geschäfts zu entgehen.

So werden denn die teuersten Werke der in Nazideutschland verfehmten Autoren zu lächerlich niedrigen Preisen in Oesterreich ausgeboten, und niemals hätte der Bücherfreund in Wien bessere Gelegenheit als heute, für ein paar Schillinge die kostbarsten Bücher der Weltliteratur zu erwerben.

Demnächst kommen die schönen Fischer-Ausgaben in Halblederbänden (Artur Schnitzler, Jakob Wassermann) zum Preise von S 4,80 auf den Markt. Jetzt schon kann man die Werke Heinrich und Thomas Manns, Ernst Tollers, Stefan und Arnold Zweigs um einen Bruchteil des festgesetzten Ladenpreises erstehen. Das prachtvolle Werk „Sergeant Grischa“, eines der meistgelesenen Bücher der letzten Jahre, wird um S 4,73 statt S 13,20, Ernst Gläsers „Jahrgang 1902“, ein Gegenstück zu Remarques „Im Westen nichts Neues“, um S 2,10 verkauft.

Die Liste ließe sich ins Unendliche fortsetzen, denn was vor der Umwandlung des deutschen Geistes in spießerischen Ungeist Klang und Namen hatte, ist ja ausgemerzt und ausgerottet und darf dem nationalen Bürger nicht mehr unter die Augen kommen.

Hanns Heinz Ewers gehört bekanntlich zu den Heroen des deutschen Aufbruchs. Er bekleidet Ehrenämter und hängt sich Erfolg haschend an die Rockschössel seines Kanzlers. Aber er hat eine befleckte Vergangenheit, denn er hat sich in der Liebe mit Magnus Hirschfeld gefunden und dieser wieder gehört zu den meistgehaßten Schriftstellern und Wissenschaftlern im neuen Deutschland. Gemeinsam haben die beiden „Kamasutra“ (Liebe im Orient), „Die Liebesriten und Liebessitten in Indien“ und die „Arabische Liebeskunst“ (Der duftende Garten des Scheik Nefzani) herausgegeben und einbegleitet.

Hanns Heinz Ewers und Magnus Hirschfeld wurden gegeneinander ausgewogen und Hirschfeld als zu schwer, das heißt als zu große Belastung für den großen deutschen Dichter Ewers befunden.

Folge: Die umfangreichen, mit Hunderten von Illustrationen versehenen Bände werden jetzt in Wien um vier bis fünf Schilling statt um 33 Schilling ausgeboten. Die Bettgenossenschaft mit dem verfemten Sexualforscher kommt dem Minnesänger des umgeschalteten Deutschen Reiches teuer zu stehen.

Denn nicht nur trägt sein Schild dunkle Flecken, die sich nicht leicht wegputzen lassen, sondern er verliert auch die Tantiemen, die ihm der Verkauf der Werke zu Originalpreisen eingetragen hätte!

3. April 28, 1933 Austrian newspaper article, “The German spirit is being sold off: better to sell it below cost than put it in the pillory or let it be burned at the stake. Bedfellows Magnus Hirschfeld – Hanns Heinz Ewers”. (Deutscher Geist wird verramscht: Lieber unter dem Selbstkostenpreis verkaufen, als an den Schandpfahl schlagen oder auf dem Scheiterhaufen verbrennen lassen. Bettgenossenschaft Magnus Hirschfeld – Hanns Heinz Ewers).

4. Drawing of the two Institute buildings with the name "Institut für Sexualwissenschaft" appearing on the two façades at 9a In den Zelten and on the corner building at 10 In den Zelten / 3 Ecke Beethovenstrasse. Presumably, these inscriptions were hastily removed in 1933. The drawing is undated, but likely made between 1929 and 1933.

5. Photo of Albert Fein's grave monument (on the left) in the Jewish cemetery in Brno. February 2013.

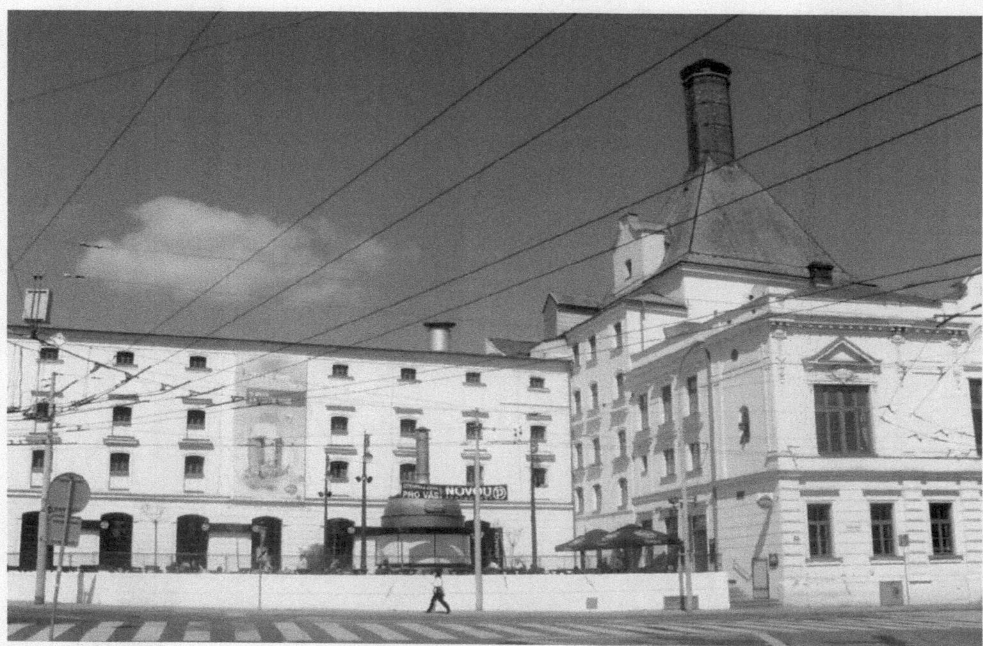

6. The Starobrno Brewery. February 2014.

7. Postcard of what before World War I was known as Elisabethplatz (currently Komenského náměstí). On the right, there is the Deutsches Staatsgymnasium (the German-language, state-run grammar school) where Karl Fein the younger and Karl Fein the elder both went to school, aged 12–18. Hand-dated September 13, 1909.

8. Apartment building (designed by Otto Eisler) to which Karl Fein moved in 1936, and where Karl Fein lived and worked. Its address has changed from 35 Koliště (Glacis) to 29 Koliště. Ca. *1936–40. By Courtesy of Museum of the City of Brno.*

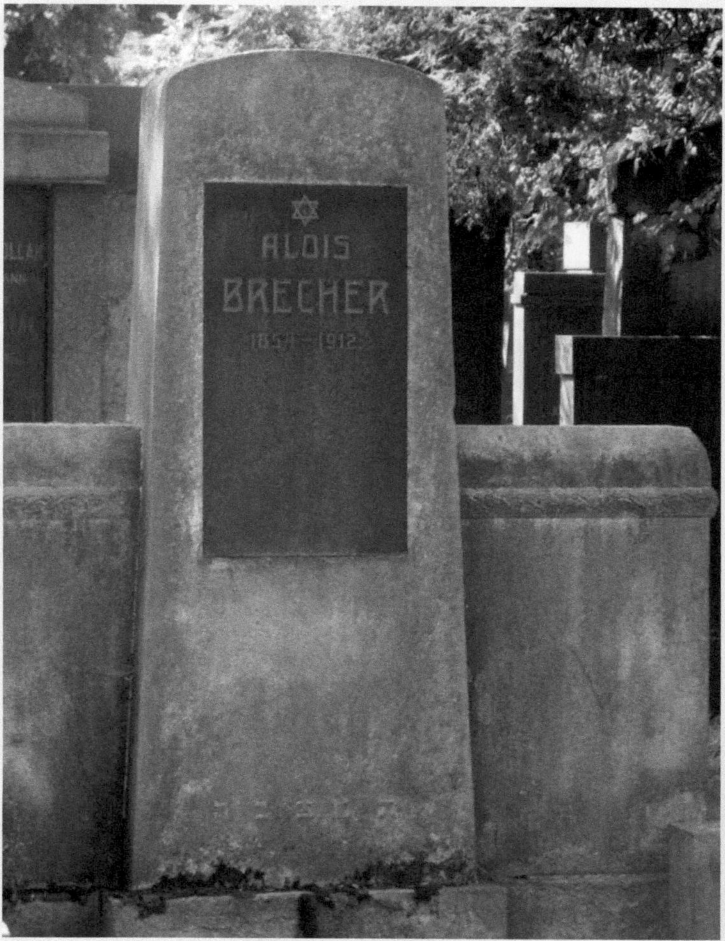

9. Grave of Alois Brecher in the Jewish cemetery in Brno. April 2012.

10. Advertisement for the L. & A. Brecher bookstore in an issue of Licht ins Volk!, the periodical of the German Adult Education Center (Deutsche Volkshochschule), led by Hugo Iltis. 1931.

11. Elise Brecher (or a bookstore employee) standing in the doorway of the L. & A. Brecher bookstore on the Freiheitsplatz (náměstí Svobody) in Brno. On the right hand side of the photo, one sees the House of the Four Mamlases (Dům u Čtyř mamlasů). 1918.

COLLECTION D'ÉTUDES SEXOLOGIQUES

Dr MAGNUS HIRSCHFELD

LE SEXE INCONNU

ÉDITIONS MONTAIGNE

7. Attempts at a New Beginning in France and Czechoslovakia[1]

KARL GIESE JOINS MAGNUS HIRSCHFELD IN FRANCE

As soon as the buy-back operation was brought to a successful completion, at the end of December 1933, Giese left Czechoslovakia again, intending to join Hirschfeld in Paris. On December 22, 1933, Giese obtained a transit visa from the French consulate in Prague, which allowed him to stay in France for one month. On December 29, 1933, Giese entered France from Italy, at the border city of Breil-sur-Roya near Nice.[2] In Nice, he was received by Magnus Hirschfeld who went there from Paris shortly after Christmas 1933.[3] The two stayed together in Nice for almost two months. Hirschfeld was likely glad to escape the harsh Paris winter.[4] They both stayed at the Hôtel de la Méditerranée et de la Côte d'Azur at 25 Promenade des Anglais.[5] Before taking rooms there, they might have both stayed in the Hotel Westminster for a while [ill. 1].[6]

Giese's months-long stay in Nice was mainly a consequence of his unresolved legal situation, as Giese had only obtained a one-month authorization to stay in

[1] Considerable parts of this chapter were based upon Soetaert 2015.

[2] ADAM, Nice, Archives administratives de 1940 à nos jours, Direction départementale de la sécurité publique des Alpes-Maritimes, Sûreté départementale, unité technique d'aide à l'enquête (caserne Auvare), file Karl Giese, file number 104801, cote 1440W 0236; and AN, site de Pierrefitte-sur-Seine, Ministère de l'intérieur, Direction de la Sûreté Générale, Service central des cartes d'identité d'étrangers, file Karl Giese, file number 198379, cote 19940506/68. For more information on Breil-sur-Roya as a border city, see Dereymez 2008, 172, 256. See also Hirschfeld & Dose 2013, f. 86/184.

[3] AN, site de Pierrefitte-sur-Seine, Ministère de l'intérieur, Direction générale de la sûreté nationale (fonds de Moscou), file on Dr. [Pierre] Vacher [Vachet], conférencier a/s de guérisons miraculeuses, anonymous note (dated Jan. 1, 1934), cote 19940482/2. See also Hirschfeld & Dose 2013, f. 85/182.

[4] Herzer writes that Maeder returned from Paris to Germany in January 1934 at the latest, and also believes that Maeder spoke the truth when he said he had joined Hirschfeld in Paris in 1933 (Herzer 1997a, 17). Giese and Hirschfeld wrote a letter (dated Jan. 10, 1934) to Maeder from Nice. The letters written by Hirschfeld and Giese were given to Manfred Herzer by Maeder's widow Norma Maeder. Giese inserted his own letter with Hirschfeld's in the same envelope; however, only the last (unnumbered) page of Giese's undated (probably Jan. 10, 1934) letter has survived. Copies of these two letters are now in Archiv MHG, Berlin. I thank Ralf Dose for sending me copies of these letters and Manfred Herzer for mediating.

[5] We can deduce their stay in this hotel from an entry from Hirschfeld's *Testament: Heft II*. See Hirschfeld & Dose 2013, f. 90/192: "Nun wohne ich hier wieder (mit Tao [Li Shiu Tong]) in demselben Zimmer mit dem gleichen in seiner unendlichen Meeresschönheit nie nachlassenden Ausblick, wie einen Winter zuvor mit K. G. [Karl Giese]" (Now I am living here again [with Tao (Li Shiu Tong)] in the same room and with the same view, which never diminishes the sea's infinite beauty, as last winter with K. G. [Karl Giese]). See also the police report (dated Feb. 2, 1934) and Giese's request (dated Jan. 26, 1934) to extend his stay in France, addressed to the Préfet des Alpes-Maritimes, AN, site de Pierrefitte-sur-Seine, Ministère de l'intérieur, Service central des cartes d'identité d'étrangers, Direction de la Sûreté Générale, Service central des cartes d'identité d'étrangers, file Karl Giese, file n° 198379, cote 19940506/68. Hirschfeld also wrote three letters (on the Hôtel de la Méditerranée's letterhead) to Ernst Maass on February 11, 16, and 21, 1934. See Archiv MHG, Berlin, fonds Ernst Maass. The building of the Hôtel de la Méditerranée et de la Côte d'Azur was demolished before World War II. The site is currently occupied by the Jean-Jacques Mecatti apartment building, completed in 1939, and designed by the Armenian architect Kevork Arsenian (1898–1980). See http://www.emporis.com/application/?nav=building&lng=5&id=1151646) (accessed Jun. 27, 2020). A sign on the facade gives the current name of the building: Les Immeubles de la Méditerranée.

[6] AN, site de Pierrefitte-sur-Seine, Paris, Ministère de l'intérieur, Direction générale de la sûreté nationale (fonds de Moscou), file on Dr. [Pierre] Vacher [Vachet], conférencier a/s de guérisons miraculeuses, cote 19940482/2, anonymous typed note (dated Jan. 1, 1934).

France.[7] At the end of January 1934, Giese sent the Préfet des Alpes-Maritimes a letter asking to extend his stay in France for six months. Giese cited reasons of health and added a medical certificate written by a good friend of Hirschfeld's, Dr. Leo Klauber (1890–1935), then residing at Nice, in support of his request.[8] Meanwhile, Giese and Hirschfeld worked on the final version of the text that was to become Hirschfeld's book *Racism*, not published in English until 1938.[9] In a letter, Giese said that it was the first time in years that he and Hirschfeld had had time to talk about many things.[10]

In February 1934, Giese obtained a permit to stay (*permis de séjour*) in France for six months. The permit was valid until July 29, 1934, a condition being that Giese not take paid employment. Giese was considered a political refugee (*réfugié politique*), and the permit stated that he had come to France "due to a change of regime" (*pour cause de changement de régime*).[11] Hirschfeld stayed in Nice until the end of February and then left for Trieste (in Italy) to pick up Li Shiu Tong, who was returning from China by ship.[12] Giese eventually moved out of the hotel as well and rented a furnished room in Madame Camille Buisson's pension at 4 Rue Halévy.[13]

[7] Archiv MHG, Berlin, fonds Günter Maeder, undated letter (but likely dated Jan 10, 1934) from Karl Giese to Günter Maeder: "das ist noch ein 'ungelegtes Ei'" (that egg has not been laid yet).

[8] Klauber certified that Giese "est atteint d'une pharyngite et d'une bronchite chroniques et qu'il a besoin d'un séjour d'à peu près 6 mois en France méridionale pour suivre une cure d'air et de repos" (is suffering from chronic pharyngitis and bronchitis and needs to stay in southern France for about six months to take a cure of fresh air and rest). AN, site de Pierrefitte-sur-Seine, Ministère de l'intérieur, Service central des cartes d'identité d'étrangers, Direction de la Sûreté Générale, Service central des cartes d'identité d'étrangers, file Karl Giese, file n° 198379, cote 19940506/68, certificat médical (dated Jan. 26, 1934) Léon [*sic*] Klauber. The papers in this archival fonds indicate that Klauber worked as an internal medicine specialist in the Nice University Hospital. Klauber attended Hirschfeld's funeral in May 1935, and also appears in a picture in the Hirschfeld guestbook. See Bergemann, Dose, Keilson-Lauritz & Dubout 2019, f. 102/146. See also McLeod & Soetaert 2010, 30 n. 49. For more information on Klauber, see Hirschfeld & Dose 2013, f. 86/184 n. 474.

[9] See Hirschfeld & Dose 2013, f. 86/184. For more information on the publishing history of the book and the book's English translators, the couple Maurice Eden Paul (1865–1944) and Cedar Paul (1880–1972), see Hirschfeld & Dose 2013, f. 86/184 n. 482. The dustcover of the book mentions that Hirschfeld handed the German typescript to Eden and Cedar Paul in 1934, four years before the translation was published. Large sections of the text were already published serially in the Czechoslovak periodical *Wahrheit* in 1934–35 under the title "Phantom Rasse: Ein Hirngespinst als Weltgefahr" (Race Delusion: A Mind Phantasy as Global Threat). See Frischknecht 2009, 32; Herrn 2003. Manfred Herzer wrote to me that the text is mainly a reworking of quotes from the third volume of Hirschfeld's *Geschlechtskunde*. See his email (dated Sep. 6, 2014) to the author.

[10] Archiv MHG, Berlin, fonds Günter Maeder, copy of letter (probably Jan. 10, 1934, last unnumbered page) from Karl Giese to Günter Maeder.

[11] The permit was granted to him "par décision ministérielle" (by ministerial decision) on February 11, 1934, but Giese was only informed of this decision on February 28, 1934. See ADAM, Archives administratives de 1940 à nos jours, Direction départementale de la sécurité publique des Alpes-Maritimes, Sûreté départementale: unité technique d'aide à l'enquête (caserne Auvare), file on Karl Giese, cote 1440W 0236. In the document, the date is erroneously given as February 28, 1924. The date of the extension (February 11, 1934) agrees with the letter (stamped Feb. 15, 1934) acknowledging the extension sent by the Ministre de l'intérieur, addressed to the Préfet des Alpes-Maritimes. See AN, site de Pierrefitte-sur-Seine, Ministère de l'intérieur, Direction de la Sûreté Générale, Service central des cartes d'identité d'étrangers, file Karl Giese, file number 198379, cote 9940506/68.

[12] Hirschfeld & Dose 2013, f. 86/184 n. 484. A postcard (dated Mar. 8, 1934) sent by Hirschfeld to Ernst Maass informs us that Hirschfeld was in Venice with Li Shiu Tong by March 8, 1934. See Archiv MHG, Berlin, fonds Ernst Maass.

[13] *Annuaire des Alpes-Maritimes* 1934, 387. The Rue Halévy is a side street off the Promenade des Anglais, then bordering the Hôtel Ruhl. Camille Hiatt (née Buisson, 1877–1964) was married to the American Walter Saunders Hiatt (1878–1956). She went bankrupt in April of 1934. See ADAM, Nice, Archives administratives de 1800 à 1940, Tribunal de commerce de Nice, année 1934, dossier Buisson Camille épouse Hiatt Walter, hôtelière à Nice (liquidation), cote 06U 04/0933. When, in January 1936, one of the beneficiaries of the Hirschfeld estate, Leopold Hönig (1887–1956), was in Nice to collect his portion of the inheritance, he stayed at this address. That means that, by then, the pension must have been taken over by someone else. Was this pension-hotel popular with gay men? See also Soetaert 2014, 38–39 n. 100.

STARTING ALL OVER AGAIN IN PARIS

Around the end of March 1934, Giese joined Magnus Hirschfeld and Li Shiu Tong, who had returned from their trip to Italy and Switzerland, in Paris. It is still a bit unclear why Giese stayed in Nice for another month after receiving the six-month permit to stay in France. Because Hirschfeld and Li Shiu Tong had still not returned to their Paris flat? That seems likely.[14] The three lived in the posh top-floor apartment at 24 avenue Charles Floquet, where Hirschfeld had stayed in the last four months of 1933.[15] We do not know how well Giese and Hirschfeld's new lover Li Shiu Tong got along in this new ménage à trois.[16] Several other people were also living with Hirschfeld and helped him as either household staff or secretaries.[17] Hirschfeld stayed at this address from the end of March until November 1934.[18]

In Paris, Giese and Hirschfeld hoped to resume the life they enjoyed in the Institute in Berlin. For example, Giese helped Hirschfeld by typing his correspondence. Giese's characteristic handwriting can be clearly seen in the corrections to typos in some of the letters sent by Hirschfeld.[19] In an April 8, 1934 letter to Norman Haire, Hirschfeld confirmed Giese's arrival in Paris and its importance: "As you can see from the attachment, we have finally come to the point where we can lay the foundations for an Institute of Sexual Science on a smaller scale in Paris. 'We' means first of all Karl Giese, who has now moved here, not only to examine the rescued materials but also to maintain continuity between the past and the future".[20] Later, when Hirschfeld

[14] Hirschfeld & Dose 2013, f. 86/184. For the date of Giese's arrival in Paris, see the letter (dated Jul. 19 or 29, 1934) from police headquarters to the French Minister of the Interior: "GIESE a logé du 26 mars au 14 avril 1934" (GIESE stayed from 26 March to 14 April 1934), AN, site de Pierrefitte-sur-Seine, Ministère de l'intérieur, Direction générale de la sûreté nationale (fonds de Moscou), file on Karl Giese, dossier n° 15843, cote 19940448/186. Indirectly, Hirschfeld confirms this in a letter sent to the French authorities. See AN, site de Pierrefitte-sur-Seine, Ministère de l'intérieur, Direction générale de la sûreté nationale (fonds de Moscou), file on Karl Giese, dossier n° 15843, cote 19940448/186, letter (dated Jul. 17, 1934) from Magnus Hirschfeld to Interior Ministry. The date can also be inferred from a letter (dated Jun. 17, 1934, 1) from Magnus Hirschfeld to "Messieurs", which says that Giese clashed with the police (see chapter 8) on April 14, 1934, "deux semaines après son arrivé à Paris" (two weeks after his arrival in Paris). See AN, site de Pierrefitte-sur-Seine, Ministère de l'intérieur, Direction générale de la sûreté nationale (fonds de Moscou), file on Karl Giese, dossier n° 15843, cote 19940448/186.

[15] That Giese actually lived in the apartment at 24 avenue Charles Floquet after arriving in Paris can be seen in Archives départementales du Val-de-Marne, Créteil, établissement pénitentiaire de Fresnes, registre d'écrou, cote 2Y5 277, JO22, mention of Karl Giese in the section "Allemagne".

[16] For reports of "*Eifersuchtsszenen*" (scenes of jealousy) between Giese and Li Shiu Tong, see von Praunheim's interview with Hanns G. (Hanns G. 1991, 12). For an indication of a more peaceful cohabitation, see, for example, the short letter (dated Aug. 3, 1934) from Norman Haire to Hirschfeld, ending with "Kind regards to Carl Giese and Tao-Li". Giese himself had no problem mentioning Li Shiu Tong's name in letters. He ended a letter (dated Aug. 11, 1934, [3]) to Norman Haire with: "Mit den besten grüssen von Dr. Hirschfeld, Tao Li und mir bin ich Ihr Karl Giese [signature]" (With best regards from Dr. Hirschfeld, Tao Li and myself, I am your Karl Giese [signature]). Another letter (dated Sep. 16, 1934), sent to Norman Haire, is personally signed by all three members of the likely "uneasy trio": Hirschfeld, Giese, and – a rarity – Li Shiu Tong (signing himself "Tao-Li"). All letters are in University of Sydney Library, Sydney, Norman Haire collection, 3.21, Karl Geise [*sic*: Giese], Typescripts, 1928–1934. A picture in the Hirschfeld guestbook also shows Giese and Li Shiu Tong, relaxed and smiling, in the front garden of the Institute. See illustration n° 5 in chapter 3. Presumably, the photo was taken in the summer of 1932. For further discussion of the possible timing of this (undated) picture, see also chapter 3, p. 53, and chapter 10, p. 330. Erhart Löhnberg heard it from Günter Maeder that Li Shiu Tong had indeed been sent by Hirschfeld to Berlin to see the Institute in 1932. See Wellcome Library, London, archive Charlotte Wolff (1897–1986), correspondence II, 1981–1986, PSY/WOL/6/8/2, letter (dated Apr. 18, 1984, 2–3) from Erhart Löhnberg to Charlotte Wollf. See also Herzer 2017, 412.

[17] See Hirschfeld & Dose 2013, f. 85/182 n. 468. The two couples – Heinz Cohn (1903–1994) and Lore Cohn (née Marcus, 1904–1974), and Karl Nohr (1905–1975) and Genia Nohr (née Goldberg, 1905–1985) – were the staff. For more biographical details about these people, see Bergemann, Dose, Keilson-Lauritz & Dubout 2019, 209, 220.

[18] Hirschfeld & Dose 2013, f. 86/184.

[19] The letters are in University of Sydney Library, Sydney, Norman Haire collection, 3.20, Magnus Hirschfeld, Typescripts, 1923–1935.

[20] University of Sydney Library, Sydney, Norman Haire collection, 3.20, Magnus Hirschfeld, Typescripts, 1923–1935, letter (dated Apr. 8, 1934, [1])

looked back at his Paris period, he linked the success of the endeavor to the fulfillment of two conditions: saving and buying back the Institute materials (and bringing them to Paris), and, secondly, the presence of Karl Giese as the only one able to order and assess these materials.[21]

Whereas, in the second half of 1933, Hirschfeld appeared a bit numb from the heavy blow of the May 1933 Berlin events, in the first half of 1934 he began to make actual plans to start a new Institute in Paris. As we have seen, as soon as Giese arrived in Paris, the decision was taken to send part of the (bought back) Institute materials from Brno to Paris. Hirschfeld and Giese clearly waited to request the materials until they were certain where exactly in Paris Giese would land after his five-month stay in Brno. Once the request was sent to Brno, Hirschfeld started to execute a plan thought out in the first months of 1934. The success of the buy-back operation – and the knowledge that the Institute materials were on their way to Paris – was the real impetus for Hirschfeld to start all over again.

While in Nice, in the first two months of 1934, Hirschfeld worked out an agreement to set up a medical practice with Leo Klauber. As we have just seen, Klauber provided a sick note for Giese. In *Testament: Heft II,* Hirschfeld himself mentioned meeting Klauber in Nice.[22] Klauber was born in Forbach (in the Alsace region of France) and, like Hirschfeld, studied medicine in Strasbourg, which was then German and spelled "Straßburg".[23] Klauber had a medical practice in Berlin and served as the doctor of the Russian embassy until 1928, the year of his expulsion from the German Communist Party (KPD).[24] He was a council member of the Association of Socialist Doctors (Verein sozialistischer Ärzte). He was also active against the German paragraph on abortion, and, in 1926, contributed a chapter on abortion to the book *Sexual-Katastrophen: Bilder aus dem modernen Geschlechts- und Eheleben*.[25] That he was indeed progressive and on the left is further attested by the fact that, in the 1920s, he worked with the newspaper *Tribune du peuple* published in Metz.[26] He also promoted working-class Esperanto as a member of the Sennacieca Asocio Tutmonda (SAT) organization.[27] Before his arrest in Berlin, in March 1933, Klauber tried to join the French army as a reserve doctor.[28]

A six-page-long, handwritten, detailed draft of the agreement between Klauber and Hirschfeld, titled "draft for an 'Institut sexologique Hirschfeld'" (*Entwurf für ein "Institut sexologique Hirschfeld"*) can be found in the cahier (*Heft*) "Remarks on Ascona" (*Bemerkungen über Ascona*).[29] The title itself indicates that Hirschfeld was counting again on his name brand as a way to attract patients to his new project and medical practice. Indeed, in the first article of the agreement, Hirschfeld wrote

from Magnus Hirschfeld to Norman Haire: "Wie Sie aus der Anlage ersehen, sind wir nun endlich soweit, das wir das Fundament zu einem Institut für Sexualwissenschaft im verkleinerten Masstabe in Paris legen konten. 'Wir' bedeutet erstens Karl Giese, der nun auch nach hier übergesiedelt ist, nicht nur für die Sichtung der geretteten Materialien sondern auch für die Aufrechterhaltung der Continuität der Vergangenheit zur Zukunft". Cf. Hirschfeld & Dose 2013, f. 83/178, where Hirschfeld wrote: "mit Karl [Giese] [...] als Brücke zur Vergangenheit u.[nd] in die Zukunft" (with Karl Giese [...] as bridge between past and future).

[21] Hirschfeld & Dose 2013, f. 87/186, entry dated December 9, 1934.

[22] Hirschfeld & Dose 2013, f. 86/184.

[23] See, for example, *Amtliches Verzeichnis des Personals und der Studenten Kaiser Wilhelms-Universität Strassburg* (Sommer-Halbjahr 1909, 46).

[24] Bergemann, Dose, Keilson-Lauritz, Dubout 2019, 215.

[25] AN, site de Pierrefitte-sur-Seine, Paris, Ministère de l'intérieur, Direction générale de la sûreté nationale (fonds de Moscou), file Léon [Leo] Klauber, sign. 19940457/125 ; Levy-Lenz 1926.

[26] AN, site de Pierrefitte-sur-Seine, Paris, Ministère de l'intérieur, Direction générale de la sûreté nationale (fonds de Moscou), file Léon [Leo] Klauber, sign. 19940457/125, letter (dated Mar. 16, 1933, 2) contrôleur général to unknown.

[27] His membership fee payments for the SAT from 1923 until 1929 can be found in *Jarlibro* 1923, 86 (first payment), and *Jarlibro* 1929, 76 (last payment). During all that time, Klauber lived at 222 Kaiserallee in Berlin-Wilmersdorf. For details on the Esperanto SAT, started in 1921, see https://nl.wikipedia.org/wiki/Sennacieca_Asocio_Tutmonda (accessed Jun. 1, 2020).

he would function as a "figurehead" (*Aushängeschild*) for the new venture.[30] The slimmed-down Paris version of the Institute was in the first place a regular medical office specializing in sexual troubles like impotence and sexual intermediate types. In the draft, Hirschfeld also referred to the laboratoires Dupraz, responsible for the promotion and distribution of the Titus Pearls (Perles Titus) in France. The many advertisements for these potency pills in French newspapers were another, indirect way to draw new patients.[31] The people holding the French license for the Titus Pearls would also fund Hirschfeld's new Paris undertaking with a monthly payment of 1,000 French francs.[32] In addition to its medical practice, the Paris project would also include a scientific and educational department that would build on the Institute materials bought back from Berlin, materials that would be managed by Karl Giese. Moreover, the primary and principal goal of the new Paris Institute was first of all scientific investigation and education: "The Institute is to be primarily a center of scientific research and education with a special archive and library, whose collection consists of the salvaged remains of the dissolved Institute in Berlin".[33] The new practice would be located somewhere near the Arc de Triomphe (place Etoile) and would count six to eight rooms, some of which would serve as private rooms for Dr. Klauber and his wife Erna Klauber. Hirschfeld and Klauber each had one consulting room. Another room would house the WLSR archive and its secretarial activities.[34] In addition to a number of financial and practical agreements, there was also an agreement to begin on April 1, 1934, and the project being tried for one year.[35] However, for reasons that are not clear, the project arranged with Klauber did not go ahead. Ralf Dose thinks that this could be explained by Hirschfeld and Klauber not having permission to practice in France, but, as we have already seen, Klauber was a practicing doctor in Nice, since he wrote a sick note for Giese in January 1934.[36] Another reason offered is the fact that Klauber was imprisoned and tortured in Germany in 1933. Possibly, he never fully recovered from this traumatic experience.[37] Klauber died in Nice in September 1935, five months after Hirschfeld. He attended Hirschfeld's funeral in May 1935.[38]

Hirschfeld did find another partner to help execute his Paris plans, Edmond Zammert (1861–1937), a French doctor Hirschfeld knew through his brother, Immanuel Hirschfeld, who had studied medicine with Zammert in Strasbourg.[39] After not

[28] AN, site de Pierrefitte-sur-Seine, Paris, Ministère de l'intérieur, Direction générale de la sûreté nationale (fonds de Moscou), file Léon [Léo] Klauber, sign. 19940457/125.

[29] For a facsimile of the five-page-long agreement, as well as a transcription, see Dose 2015, 49–55.

[30] For Article 1 of the agreement, see Dose 2015, 52.

[31] For Article 2 of the agreement, see Dose 2015, 52.

[32] For Article 5 of the agreement, see Dose 2015, 53.

[33] Letter (dated Apr. 7, 1934) signed by Edmond Zammert and Magnus Hirschfeld in *La grande réforme*, année n° 4, n° 38, June 1934, 2: "L'Institut doit être en premier lieu un foyer d'investigation et d'instruction scientifiques avec des archives et une bibliothèque spéciale, dont le fonds est formé des restes qui purent être sauvés de l'Institut supprimé à Berlin".

[34] For Articles 3–4 of the agreement, see Dose 2015, 52–53. Hirschfeld does not refer to the WLSR but mentions the "sexualwissenschaftliches Centralbüro" (Central Sexological Office).

[35] For Articles 5–10 of the agreement, see Dose 2015, 53–55.

[36] See Hirschfeld & Dose 2013, 184, n. 474. I think that two parts of the agreement indicate that Klauber was indeed allowed to practice in France. Article 1 says that Hirschfeld was a German and Klauber a French specialist (Dose 2015, 52). Article 4 (Dose 2015, 53) also says that Klauber "bereits das französische Bürgerrecht besitzt" (already has French citizenship). Does the word "bereits" (already) signify that Hirschfeld was trying to become (or thinking of becoming) a French citizen? In Bergemann, Dose, Keilson-Lauritz & Dubout 2019, 215, on the other hand, the authors clearly realize that only Hirschfeld had a problem.

[37] Bergemann, Dose, Keilson-Lauritz & Dubout 2019, 215.

[38] McLeod & Soetaert 2010, 28.

[39] Hirschfeld & Dose 2013, f. 86/184, University of Sydney Library, Sydney, Norman Haire collection, 3.20, Magnus Hirschfeld, Typescripts, 1923–1935, letter (dated Apr. 8, 1934, 1) from Magnus Hirschfeld to Norman Haire; *Amtliches Verzeichnis des Personals und der Studenten Kaiser Wilhelms-Universität Strassburg* (Sommer-Halbjahr 1883, 23, 40). A file folder exists for Edmond Zammert in the Parisian fonds de Moscou but it is empty. See AN, site de Pierrefitte-sur-Seine, Paris, Ministère de l'intérieur, Direction générale de la sûreté nationale (fonds

seeing each other for forty years, Hirschfeld and Zammert met again in Paris.[40] It was agreed with Zammert that the new medical practice would be housed in the avenue Charles Floquet apartment. A photo of Hirschfeld and Zammert posing on one of its balconies appears in Hirschfeld's guestbook.[41]

To make everything look neat, three batches of blank letter paper were printed with the appropriate letterheads. The first batch had the following letterhead (in French): "INSTITUTE OF SEXOLOGICAL SCIENCES for the scientific investigation of normal and abnormal instincts and of the psychobiological constitution" [ill. 2].[42] Hirschfeld also commissioned a batch to be printed with a personal letterhead bearing his new Paris address: "Dr Magnus Hirschfeld – Founder of the Berlin Institute of Sexology".[43] The third batch of letter paper was destined for the WLSR, now also based in Paris: "Central Headquarters, at the Sexological Institute, transferred from Berlin to Paris", whose "general secretary" Karl Giese now was.[44] Hirschfeld's solitary decision to move the WLSR central office from Berlin to Paris caused quite a row with Norman Haire and Jonathan Leunbach, the two other WLSR presidents. They objected that they had not been consulted at all about the decision to move the seat from Berlin to Paris.[45] The new practice with Zammert, as Hirschfeld later wrote, was never a great success and the undertaking only covered the costs.[46]

MONTAIGNE BOOK CONTRACT

Besides the publishing contract with Gallimard, Hirschfeld also negotiated with another Paris-based French publisher, Éditions Montaigne, at 13 Quai de Conti, Paris VI. Hirschfeld may have been moved to contact this publisher because a former Institute colleague, Max Hodann, published a book, *Love and Sexuality* (*Amour et sexualité*), with Montaigne in April 1933, in the series "Collection d'études sexologiques".[47] Hirschfeld would eventually publish two books in the same series: *Sexual Education* (*Education sexuelle*), in September 1934,[48] and *The Unknown Sex* (*Le sexe inconnu*), published in the summer of 1935, a few months after Hirschfeld's

de Moscou), file Edmond Zammert, sign. 19940508/2058. See also Bergemann, Dose, Keilson-Lauritz & Dubout 2019, 227.

[40] Dose 2019, 17. See also the entry (dated Sep. 17, 1934) for Zammert in the Hirschfeld guestbook (Bergemann, Dose, Keilson-Lauritz & Dubout 2019, f. 63/107). By then, Zammert, who was already in his early seventies, had given up his medical practice in Creutzwald (German Kreuzwald). See *Journal officiel de la République française*, Oct. 3, 1941, 4260. Creutzwald lies next to the border with Germany, close to Forbach (where the Klauber family lived), and was French territory before the war.

[41] Bergemann, Dose, Keilson-Lauritz & Dubout 2019, f. 73/117.

[42] University of Sydney Library, Sydney, Norman Haire collection, 3.20, Magnus Hirschfeld, Typescripts, 1923–1935, letter dated (Apr. 11 [12], 1934, 2) from Magnus Hirschfeld to Norman Haire: "INSTITUT DES SCIENCES SEXOLOGIQUES pour la recherche scientifique des instincts normaux et anormaux et de la constitution psychobiologique".

[43] University of Sydney Library, Sydney, Norman Haire collection, 3.20, Magnus Hirschfeld, Typescripts, 1923–1935, letter dated (Sep. 15, 1933) from Magnus Hirschfeld to Norman Haire: "Dr Magnus Hirschfeld – Fondateur de l'Institut de Sexologie de Berlin".

[44] University of Sydney Library, Sydney, Norman Haire collection, 3.21, Karl Geise [*sic*: Giese], Typescripts, 1928–1934, letter (dated Aug. 11, 1934) from Karl Giese to Norman Haire: "Siège Central: à l'Institut Sexologique transféré de Berlin à Paris" and "Secrétaire Général".

[45] University of Sydney Library, Sydney, Norman Haire collection, 3.20, Magnus Hirschfeld, Typescripts, 1923–1935, letter (dated Apr. 10, 1934, 1) from Norman Haire to Magnus Hirschfeld, where Haire protested against this *fait accompli*. In a nine-page-long letter (dated Apr. 12, 1934) Hirschfeld made an extensive reply.

[46] Hirschfeld & Dose 2013, f. 86/184.

[47] Hodann 1933. The book was a French translation of the successful *Geschlecht und Liebe in biologischer und gesellschaftlicher Beziehung*, reprinted in 1932 with the Berlin publisher Universitas. For Hodann's publishing contract with Montaigne, see IMEC Abbaye d'Ardenne, Saint-Germain-la-Blanche-Herbe, fonds Aubier-Montaigne, P 3.3., Droits dérivés, contract Hodann-Montaigne, dated Sep. 8, 1932, sign. BO4 DO1 C.

[48] Hirschfeld & Bohm 1934a. The book was published on August 29, 1934 (see Hirschfeld & Bohm 1934a, 271) and was translated from German into French by René Scherdlin (1883–?). A small advertisement for the book appeared in *Marianne*, Nov.

death.[49] The "unknown sex" of the title refers to Hirschfeld's notion of the third sex, the category of those with a mixed, intermediate sex or gender, one which was, in Hirschfeld's view, still largely unknown (*inconnu*) to the general public [ill. 3].

But quite soon, Hirschfeld found himself in conflict with Montaigne. The point at issue was *Education sexuelle,* which was not a new text by Hirschfeld, but a French translation of *Sexualerziehung* (1930), which Hirschfeld co-authored with Ewald Bohm, and which was published by Universitas in Berlin.[50] Montaigne had apparently come to an agreement with Universitas. However, Bohm had either not been consulted on the matter, or changed his mind afterwards, in any case deciding that his portion of the royalties was insufficient. Through his lawyer, Bohm demanded 1,500 French francs from Montaigne. This sum was more than twice the 600 French francs paid each to Hirschfeld and Universitas. In a letter to Fernand Aubier (1876–1961), the owner of Éditions Montaigne, Hirschfeld wrote that he was not involved in the matter, and that it was something that needed to be resolved by the two publishers.[51] It's not clear what the – financial – end result was, but it looks like the French publisher lost a considerable sum of money, if only because it had to pay their lawyer Gil Baer to handle the affair.

To avoid further difficulties, Montaigne demanded an explicit declaration in the contract for Hirschfeld's second book, *Le sexe inconnu,* that Hirschfeld was the sole author.[52] But the relationship between Hirschfeld and Aubier was permanently strained due to the issues with Hirschfeld's first Montaigne book. However, Hirschfeld was already thinking of a French translation of a third title, *Sexualität und Kriminalität*.[53] He also had ideas for a new, original book on the prostitution problem or the rejuvenation problem (*das Verjüngungsproblem*).[54]

The publisher's negative feelings about Hirschfeld also curiously came out in a handwritten suggestion for a blurb for *Le sexe inconnu,* whose anonymous writer proposed that, despite Hirschfeld's claim, the phenomenon of the "unknown sex"

21, 1934, 4; and in *Les Nouvelles littéraires*, Nov. 24, 1934, 2.

[49] Hirschfeld 1935e. The record for the book in the online catalogue of the Bibliothèque nationale in Paris gives the date as May 23, 1936. It is unclear whether this date refers to the book's issuance, publication, or *dépôt legal* (legal deposit) at the Bibliothèque nationale. Initially, this made me think that the book was published in 1936. A book review (doubling as a eulogy of Hirschfeld's life's work), in the French periodical *La grande réforme*, indicated, on the contrary, that the book was published in the summer of 1935. See C. B. C. 1935. The book was translated from German into French by a certain W. R. Fürst (?–?). Given the May 1935 correspondence between Éditions Montaigne and Hirschfeld about the *Korrekturbogen* (printer's proofs) being delayed due to a postal strike, and the publisher not knowing Hirschfeld's correct address in Nice, it is possible that – considering that Hirschfeld died on May 14, 1935 – it was Karl Giese, and not Hirschfeld, who made the last adjustments to the book, presumably when he was in Vienna in 1935. See IMEC Abbaye d'Ardenne, Saint-Germain-la-Blanche-Herbe, fonds Aubier-Montaigne, P 7.1., Service éditorial, letter exchange (dated May 3, 1935; May 7, 1935; May 9, 1935) between Magnus Hirschfeld and Éditions Montaigne, cote 658ABM/16/18. In September 2007, Gerard Koskovich kindly showed me his copy of this book, inscribed by Karl Giese. The inscription is written in blue fountain-pen ink on the recto free end page: "von einem Schüler des Verfassers / zur Erinnerung an eine / gemeinsame Arbeitszeit in / Paris- / Karl Giese / Wien. 20 Okt. 35" (from a student of the author / in memory of a / cooperation in / Paris- / Karl Giese / Vienna. Oct., 20 [19]35).

[50] Hirschfeld & Bohm 1930.

[51] IMEC Abbaye d'Ardenne, Saint-Germain-la-Blanche-Herbe, fonds Aubier-Montaigne, P 7.1., Service éditorial, letter (dated Jan. 9, 1934) from Magnus Hirschfeld to Éditions Montaigne, cote 658ABM/16/18.

[52] IMEC Abbaye d'Ardenne, Saint-Germain-la-Blanche-Herbe, fonds Aubier-Montaigne, P 3.1., Service juridique, contract *Le sexe inconnu* (date illegible: April 1934?) for 4,500 copies.

[53] Letter (dated Sep. 22, 1934) from Magnus Hirschfeld to Éditions Montaigne; letter (dated Sep. 25, 1934) from Éditions Montaigne to Magnus Hirschfeld; both in IMEC Abbaye d'Ardenne, Saint-Germain-la-Blanche-Herbe, fonds Aubier-Montaigne, P 7.1., Service éditorial, cote 658ABM/16/18. Hirschfeld's *Sexualität und Kriminalität* appeared in Germany in 1924 (Hirschfeld 1924).

[54] IMEC Abbaye d'Ardenne, Saint-Germain-la-Blanche-Herbe, fonds Aubier-Montaigne, P 7.1., Service éditorial, cote 658ABM/16/18, letter (dated Sep. 22, 1934) from Magnus Hirschfeld to Éditions Montaigne.

should maybe rather be judged "the all-too-well-known sex" (*le sexe trop connu*).[55] The publisher's homophobic backlash continued after Hirschfeld's death, inserting the following simultaneously hot and cold publisher's notice (*note des éditeurs*) in the first pages of *Le sexe inconnu*: "We thought that, in a collection of sexological studies, homosexuality could not be silenced. So we did not fail to welcome the scholarly study proposed by Dr. Magnus Hirschfeld. It certainly did not escape us that this study could have been conducted with greater scientific rigor in the field of observation and controlled facts. In other words, we would have preferred greater reserve in the philosophical and social appreciation of these facts. But the reader will be able to make his own judgment of the author's too openly displayed complacency regarding the supporters of sexual inversion. The morality of homosexuals does not fall within the scope of this collection. Whatever the sentiment that emerges from such a study, one is obliged to agree that, until now, homosexuality has never been treated with a surer or more definitive mastery".[56] The cooperation with Montaigne came to an end in April 1936, almost a year after Hirschfeld's death.[57]

MORE CONFLICTS: MADAME BERTY ALBRECHT AND THE MAGAZINE LE PROBLÈME SEXUEL

But the conflict with Montaigne was not the only problem Hirschfeld had to deal with during his stay in Paris in 1934. He also clashed with Berty (also spelled Bertie) Albrecht (1893–1943), a member of the French section of the WLSR. Albrecht is most known (and honored) in France for her resistance activities during World War II.[58] Albrecht met Hirschfeld through Norman Haire in 1930, when she was still living in London, and quickly became a big admirer of Hirschfeld.[59] Madame Albrecht, as she was usually called, attended the Vienna WLSR conference in 1930 and was also, as we have seen, one of the speakers at the WLSR Brno conference in September 1932.[60] At the Brno conference, it was also decided that Albrecht would be responsible for the articles published in French in the issues of *Sexus*, the new WLSR magazine.[61]

Energized by the Brno conference, Albrecht returned to France, reported on the conference in the newspaper *La grande réforme*, and decided to start a quarterly magazine called *The Sexual Problem* (*Le problème sexuel*), a total of six issues of which would come out between 1933 and 1935.[62] The programmatic subtitle of the magazine was "morality, eugenics, hygiene, legislation" (*morale, eugénique, hygiène, législation*). The first issue of *Le problème sexuel* came out in November 1933 [ill. 4]. The periodical was in reality issued by the Association d'Etudes Sexologiques (AES), started in 1932.

55 IMEC Abbaye d'Ardenne, Saint-Germain-la-Blanche-Herbe, fonds Aubier-Montaigne, P 8.1. Service de fabrication, feuille manuscrite *Le sexe inconnu*, sign. SO6 B13 D20.

56 Hirschfeld 1935e, [7]): "Nous avons pensé que, dans une collection d'études sexologiques, l'homosexualité ne pouvait être passé sous silence. Aussi nous n'avons pas manqué de faire bon accueil à l'étude savant que nous en proposait le Dr Magnus Hirschfeld. Il ne nous a pas échappé, assurément, que cette étude aurait pu se cantonner avec plus de rigueur scientifique dans le domaine de l'observation et des faits contrôlés. C'est dire que nous aurions préféré plus de réserve dans l'appréciation philosophique et sociale de ces faits. Mais le lecteur saura opposer lui-même son propre jugement aux complaisances que l'auteur manifeste trop ouvertement pour les partisans de l'inversion sexuelle. La moralité des homosexuels n'entre pas dans le cadre de cette collection. Quel que soit le sentiment qui se dégage d'une pareille étude, on sera bien obligé pourtant de convenir que l'homosexualité n'avait jamais été exposée, jusqu'à ce jour, avec une plus sûre et plus définitive maîtrise".

57 IMEC Abbaye d'Ardenne, Saint-Germain-la-Blanche-Herbe, fonds Aubier-Montaigne, P 7.1., Service éditorial, cote 658ABM/16/18, letter (dated May 30, 1939) from Éditions Montaigne to Karl Fein.

58 Missika 2005, 141–284. Albrecht committed suicide in May 1943 while in Fresnes Prison (Missika 2005, 284). See also Dose 2019, 18 n. 46.

59 Dose 2019, 18; Missika 2005, 62.

60 Missika 2005, 76–78, 81.

61 See the 1933 cover of *Sexus, Internationale Vierteljahreszeitschrift für die gesamte Sexualwissenschaft und Sexualreform*. This would be the first and last issue of the magazine. For an earlier, April 1931 attempt to launch *Sexus*, then subtitled *Internationale Monatsschrift für Sexualwissenschaft und Sexualreform*, see Herzer 2017, 316.

62 Albrecht 1932. Jean Dalsace, who also lectured in Brno, gave a talk on the Brno conference in Paris.

The AES editorial board largely overlapped with the local chapter of the French section of the WLSR. In May or June 1933, Hirschfeld was still friendly with Albrecht when he was invited to visit – along with Pierre Vachet, the sexual reform couple Eugène and Jeanne Humbert, and others – the home of the French writer Victor Margueritte (1866–1942).[63]

In the first half of 1934, Hirschfeld and Albrecht entered into conflict over an issue related to *Le problème sexuel*.[64] What happened? On December 1, 1933, Hirschfeld told (or perhaps promised) Albrecht that he would give her, free of charge, an article on the topic of compulsory sterilization (*stérilisation obligatoire*) in Germany for the second issue of *Le problème sexuel*, whose first issue appeared in November 1933. The article was a comment on the Law for the Prevention of Hereditarily Diseased Offspring (Gesetz zur Verhütung erbkranken Nachwuchses) that came into effect in Germany in April 1934 and legalized forced sterilization (*Zwangssterilisation*) by so-called Hereditary Health Courts (Erbgesundheitsgerichte).[65] Eugenics was a common topic in the medical sexological establishment before World War II, and Hirschfeld felt it necessary to spell out his stance on the view of eugenics being implemented in Nazi Germany. In the article, Hirschfeld wrote that he was in favor of marital counseling (*Eheberatung*), in which "science, education, and one's own judgment" (*Wissenschaft, Bildung und eigene Erkenntnis*) were the core values, and opposed that to the "coercion, violence" (*Zwang, Gewalt*) of the German Hereditary Health Courts.[66] Initially, as one of the ten people on its editorial board (*comité de redaction*), Hirschfeld was closely involved with starting up the AES's new magazine.[67]

The second issue of the magazine, which came out in April 1934, included four articles on the topic of eugenics and sterilization, but not Hirschfeld's article.[68] Hirschfeld's name was also removed from the issue's masthead.[69] Moreover, Hirschfeld's article on forced sterilization in Germany had actually appeared a little earlier, in the March issue of the popular magazine *Détective*, under the title "Sterilized People" (*Stérilisés*),[70] for which Hirschfeld received the considerable sum of 1,000 French francs. The *Détective* article was a reworked French version of an earlier article that appeared under the title "The Hereditary Health Court: Reflections on the German Sterilization Law" (*Das Erbgericht: Betrachtungen zum deutschen Sterilisationsgesetz*) in the February 1934 issue of Klaus Mann's exile magazine *Die Sammlung*, published in Amsterdam by Querido.[71] According to Norman Haire, Hirschfeld had already

See *Le Matin*, Nov. 23, 1932, 2. Hélène Gosset, a French journalist, who went to Brno for the WLSR conference, reported on it in several articles in *L'Oeuvre* (between September 24, 1932 and October 10, 1932).

[63] Humbert 1947, 200.

[64] Missika does not mention this conflict (Missika 2005, 62). It is also unclear if Albrecht was exclusively or principally the instigator of the quarrel. According to the AES letterhead, Albrecht was the "secrétaire pour l'extérieur" (secretary for external relations). See Bibliothèque histoire de la médecine, Paris, fonds Dalsace-Vellay, letter (dated Nov. 20, 1934) from J. M. Lahy to Jean Dalsace. In *Testament: Heft II*, Hirschfeld wrote of Albrecht that she was "eine äusserst intrigante ehrgeizige Person" (an extremely scheming, ambitious person) who gave him many problems (Hirschfeld & Dose 2013, f. 86/184).

[65] See https://de.wikipedia.org/wiki/Gesetz_zur_Verhütung_erbkranken_Nachwuchses (accessed May 7, 2020).

[66] Hirschfeld 1934c, 319. In 1935, Hirschfeld would briefly repeat the point in an issue of *Détective*, where he said that the question of sterilization was a purely scientific matter, adding: "Il ne peut pas se résoudre, comme en Allemagne, par un recours à la coercition, à la justice arbitraire ou à la violence. Il ne peut pas se résoudre, non plus, sans un examen approfondi des conséquences qu'il peut entraîner" (It cannot be resolved, as in Germany, by resorting to coercion, arbitrary justice, or violence. Nor can it be resolved without careful consideration of the consequences it may entail) (*Détective*, Apr. 11, 1935, 2). Cf. Herrn 2003.

[67] *Le problème sexuel* 1 (November 1933).

[68] See, for example, Maier 1934.

[69] *Le problème sexuel* 2 (February 1934).

[70] Hirschfeld, Mar. 1, 1934. Steakley missed this *Détective* article (Steakley 2021, 145–49).

[71] Hirschfeld 1934c. The same article also appeared (in German) under the title "Das Erbgericht" in the *Pariser Tageblatt* in February 1934. See Hirschfeld, Feb. 6, 1934, 4.

given the article to Albrecht (who kept it for several months) but then published it in *Détective*, without letting Albrecht know.[72] This incident initiated the conflict between Hirschfeld and the French section of the WLSR, specifically with Bertie Albrecht.[73]

Apparently, the editorial board of *Le problème sexuel* convened without Hirschfeld to address the matter and decided to oust Hirschfeld. In an April 5, 1934, letter to Hirschfeld, Albrecht informed him of the editorial board's decision.[74] But, clearly, Madame Albrecht must have complained about Hirschfeld's other questionable activities in the same letter. These included Hirschfeld's writing for popular magazines and his commercial involvement with the Titus Pearls. On the whole, in the six issues of the French sexual reform periodical, there is a strong and even scientifically strict Anglo-Saxon orientation perceptible, likely related to Norman Haire, who lived and worked in London, and had provided Albrecht with her sexological initiation when she lived in London.[75] The implicit reproach to Hirschfeld was that he had chosen popular magazines over science. The Titus Pearls advertisements were also considered very inappropriate as some of the ads for the potency pills included Hirschfeld's picture. Advertisements for the Titus Pearls could be found in many French newspapers and magazines, even after Hirschfeld's death, in May 1935 [ill. 5].[76] Norman Haire had to explain to Hirschfeld that a doctor publicizing a medical product with his own image was simply not the "done thing" in England and France.[77] But Hirschfeld retorted that this was a decision made by the people distributing the Titus Pearls in France, not his own, and that this "strictly juridical matter" was in the hands of lawyers he had hired. In his letter, Haire also mentioned that there was talk of a Titus Pearls ad in a pharmacy window near the Paris Gare d'Austerlitz train station, which included Hirschfeld's name. The letters forming his name were supposed to be two feet high. Hirschfeld wrote to Haire that he had investigated that rumor and found nothing.[78]

THE GAY REPROACH

From the letters exchanged between Hirschfeld and Norman Haire during this period, we can also gather that yet another incident was added to the list of the many reproaches against Hirschfeld. Withdrawing Hirschfeld's article on forced sterilization in Germany had been no more than the proverbial drop in the ocean. In the winter 1933 issue of *Voilà*, which centrally featured Hirschfeld, there was a photo

[72] University of Sydney Library, Sydney, Norman Haire collection, 3.20, Magnus Hirschfeld, Typescripts, 1923–1935, letter (dated Apr. 13, 1934, 1) from Norman Haire to Magnus Hirschfeld.

[73] See University of Sydney Library, Sydney, Norman Haire collection, 3.20, Magnus Hirschfeld, Typescripts, 1923–1935, letter (dated Apr. 12, 1934, [f. 5]) from Magnus Hirschfeld to Norman Haire. I think that this incident was truly the *starting point* of the clash between Hirschfeld and the French section of the WLSR (and/or Albrecht) and also think it is the explanatory "missing link" in the contributions of Wolff 1986, 394; Dose 2019, 17–19; and Herzer 2017 323, regarding the conflict between Hirschfeld and Albrecht.

[74] It is only from Hirschfeld's reply letter that we can deduce what Albrecht said in her letter. A copy of the letter Albrecht sent to Hirschfeld may have survived in a lot, sold in 2014 for 3,000 Euros, by an antiquarian bookseller in Paris. The lot contained the correspondence of the periodical *Le problème sexuel* and part of Berty Albrecht's archive. It is not known who bought the lot or if the archival fonds is now publicly accessible or not. Lot 187 numbered around 300 folios and was on offer with Les librairies associés (owned by Alban Caussé and Jacques Desse) in Paris.

[75] See also Dose 1993, 24.

[76] Simply by looking at the magazine *Voilà*, for example, one can see an advertisement in issue 123 (Jul. 29, 1933, 15). That was the last issue of a series on Hirschfeld titled "L'Amour et la science" (Love and Science). An advertisment also appeared in issue 148 (Jan. 20, 1934, 15), the last issue of a second series of articles focusing on Hirschfeld, this time titled "Science et sexualité" (Science and Sexuality). But neither advertisement included a picture of Hirschfeld.

[77] University of Sydney Library, Sydney, Norman Haire collection, 3.20, Magnus Hirschfeld, Typescripts, 1923–1935, letter (dated Apr. 13, 1934, 1–2) from Norman Haire to Magnus Hirschfeld.

[78] University of Sydney Library, Sydney, Norman Haire collection, 3.20, Magnus Hirschfeld, Typescripts, 1923–1935, letter (dated Apr. 12, 1934, [6–7]) from Magnus Hirschfeld to Norman Haire; and letter (dated Apr. 10, 1934, 2) from Norman Haire to Magnus Hirschfeld.

of a male transvestite (in women's clothes) reading a copy of the far-right French newspaper *L'Action française*.[79] The latter immediately took notice of the photo and raised havoc in its next issue.[80] Next to the *Voilà* photo of the cross-dressing man, one can see the name "Hirschfeld", suggesting that the picture came from Hirschfeld's sexology photo collection. Hirschfeld wrote to Haire that the picture was not his and that he was not responsible for the mistaken attribution by the French journalist.[81] But we simply do not know if Hirschfeld spoke the truth. On the whole, it must be said that the article in *Voilà* focused mainly on the topic of homosexuality and cross-dressing, and that the outrage over the picture was likely again only a proverbial drop.

Another very intriguing picture in the same issue – which, apparently, did come from Hirschfeld's collection (since his name appears next to it) – shows three people, and is accompanied by the following text: "A villa in Provence where Professor Hirschfeld's sick patients are treated" (*Une villa de Provence où sont soignés des malades du professeur Hirschfeld*). The scene in the picture seems relaxed and lighthearted, and includes a man holding up a shield saying "be good to abnormal people" (*soyez bon pour les anormaux*). The location of this peculiar house is unknown. It may have been in Toulon since Hirschfeld stopped there when he moved to Nice, in December 1934.[82] I think it possible that this is, strictly speaking, the very first (photographed) public display of a gay activist banner (*pancarte*) [ill. 6].[83]

Outspoken or not, it seems probable that the French section of the WLSR also thought Hirschfeld too focused on gay issues. This can be inferred from a passage in a letter Hirschfeld sent to Haire, stating that he neither could nor would abide by the French section's wish to focus mainly on birth control.[84] Referring specifically to this issue, Norman Haire warned Hirschfeld not to go to France (after Switzerland) in

[79] *Voilà*, Dec. 30, 1933, 11. This issue was part of the second series of articles focusing on Hirschfeld and his teachings, titled "Science et sexualité".

[80] Hirschfeld described the havoc as "unliebsamen Folgen" (unpleasant consequences). See University of Sydney Library, Sydney, Norman Haire collection, 3.20, Magnus Hirschfeld, Typescripts, 1923–1935, letter (dated Apr. 12, 1934, [5]) from Magnus Hirschfeld to Norman Haire. The French newspaper wrote: "Dans le dernier numéro de l'illustré Voilà, le docteur juif chassé d'Allemagne Magnus Hirschfeld, transplantant chez nous son musée de cochonneries pseudo-scientifiques, publie une photographie représentant un hybride innomable, homme déguisé en femme, lisant un numéro de *L'Action française*! [...] C'est ainsi que cette tourbe immonde reconnaît POLICIEREMENT [*sic*] notre popularité! Mais quel est donc le voyou qui dirige *Voilà*?" (In the last issue of the illustrated magazine *Voilà*, the Jewish doctor chased out of Germany, Magnus Hirschfeld, transplanting his museum of pseudo-scientific junk to our country, published a photograph representing an unspeakable hybrid, a man disguised as a woman, reading an issue of *L'Action française*! [...] This is how this filthy mob recognizes POLICELY [*sic*: using police methods] our popularity! But who is the thug who runs *Voilà*?") (*L'Action française*, Jan. 1, 1934, 1)

[81] The two series of Hirschfeld articles in *Voilà*, published in the summer and winter of 1933, which seem to be articles written by Hirschfeld, were in reality redactions of long interviews with Hirschfeld, in which the journalist was likely responsible for the transcription and editing. Possibly, the journalist decided unilaterally on the pictures to be added. University of Sydney Library, Sydney, Norman Haire collection, 3.20, Magnus Hirschfeld, Typescripts, 1923–1935, letter (dated Apr. 12, 1934, [5]) from Magnus Hirschfeld to Norman Haire; and letter (dated Oct. 10, 1934, 2) from Norman Haire to Magnus Hirschfeld. Haire also wrote that there had been a physical fight between a transvestite (the one in the picture?) and a journalist (the *Voilà* journalist?), some time after the publication of photo. It is unclear what another incident, also mentioned by Haire, and also involving Hirschfeld, this time in the newspaper *Le Figaro*, was about. Wolff seems to confuse the *Voilà* and the *Figaro* incidents (Wolff 1986, 394).

[82] Hirschfeld & Dose 2013, f. 89/190.

[83] *Voilà*, Dec. 30, 1933, 10.

[84] University of Sydney Library, Sydney, Norman Haire collection, 3.20, Magnus Hirschfeld, Typescripts, 1923–1935, letter (dated Apr. 12, 1934, [9]) from Magnus Hirschfeld to Norman Haire: "Birth Control in allen Ehren, aber schliesslich ist sie doch nur ein Teilgebiet der so ungemein positiven Aufgaben, die wir zu erfüllen haben und bei deren Lösung ich meine beiden Copräsidenten solange ich lebe stets an meiner Seite zu finden hoffe" (Birth control, for all its importance, is in the end only one part of the immensely positive tasks we have to accomplish and in whose accomplishment I hope always to find my two co-presidents by my side for as long as I live).

1932: "People tend to identify your name with the subject of homosexuality and do not hesitate to say that you are a homosexual yourself. Perhaps this is especially marked in France because they always like to find things to ridicule and abuse in Germany".[85] It is indeed probable that the members of the French section of the WLSR, either in part or whole, had a problem with the topic of homosexuality, or rather the automatic and inevitable association of Hirschfeld with homosexuality. One perceives an implicit homophobia in the French section's rewriting of the ten goals of the WLSR. They produced only eight demands. Points 6 and 8 of the ten official statutes of the WLSR were as follows:

> 6. Correct assessment of intersexual variations, especially also of homosexual men and women (*Richtige Beurteilung der intersexuellen Variationen, insbesondere auch der homosexuellen Männer und Frauen*).
>
> 8. The view of sexual drive disorders not as, hitherto, crimes, sins, or vices, but as more or less pathological phenomena (*Die Auffassung sexueller Triebstörungen nicht wie bisher als Verbrechen, Sünde, oder Laster, sondern als mehr oder weniger krankhafte Erscheinungen*).

The French section combined these two goals into one recommendation and removed any explicit reference to homosexuality:

> 6. Impartial judgment of the anomalies of the sexual instinct, scientifically considered as more or less pathological phenomena (*Jugement impartial des anomalies de l'instinct sexuel, considérés scientifiquement comme des phénomènes plus au moins pathologiques*).[86]

Let us also recall here the July 1933 *Voilà* cover, which showed Hirschfeld and Li Shiu Tong as clearly affectionate, and must have certainly raised eyebrows in Paris for its boldness. This might have been yet another ingredient added to the bubbling pot of Hirschfeld's publicly perceived gayness.[87]

Hirschfeld responded to the attack by Berty Albrecht (or the French section of the WLSR?) with a vehement four-page letter, likely written on the same day that Albrecht's letter arrived, April 6, 1934.[88] First of all, he wrote, he was very offended by the entire matter and considered it an affront that he had been removed from the editorial board of *Le problème sexuel* without a hearing. He asked the board to reconvene so he could present his side. That the clash started because Hirschfeld's text appeared in *Détective*, and not in *Le problème sexuel*, is certain; but it remains unclear why *exactly* it failed to appear in the second issue of the AES periodical [ill. 7]. One reason, suggested by Hirschfeld, seems to have been bad communication. Hirschfeld was in Nice with Giese, and then in Venice with Li Shiu Tong, in the first months of 1934. Possibly, he missed some of Albrecht's letters. Or, perhaps, Hirschfeld was simply hiding behind false explanations. On the other hand, Charlotte Wolff thinks that Albrecht simply failed to respond to Hirschfeld when he sent his text to her, and that this was the start of the quarrel.[89]

[85] University of Sydney Library, Sydney, Norman Haire collection, 3.20, Magnus Hirschfeld, Typescripts, 1923–1935, letter (dated Dec. 12, 1932, 2) from Norman Haire to Magnus Hirschfeld.

[86] Bibliothèque histoire de la médecine, Paris, fonds Dalsace-Vellay, folder Ligue mondiale pour la réforme sexuelle, undated and anonymous "Statuts moraux de la Ligue mondiale pour la réforme sexuelle sur une base scientifique". If one compares the official list of ten WLSR demands with the eight on the French list, one sees that the same basic causes are really all there. In addition to demand 8, demand 9 is also missing from the French version, but the latter could indeed be subsumed under demand 6 since it seems to hint vaguely at tolerance for all kinds of consensual sex. Cf. Dose 2019, 18–19 n. 56, 57. Dose seems to base his judgment on the nine (!) programmatic demands published in the first November 1933 issue of *Le problème sexuel*, from which the gay element seems indeed almost completely absent as well. For a general remark on the "non-synergy" of the WLSR's ten demands in its national sections, see also Dose 1993, 26.

[87] *Voilà*, Jul. 1, 1933.

[88] Bibliothèque histoire de la médecine, Paris, fonds Dalsace-Vellay, folder Ligue mondiale pour la réforme sexuelle, letter (dated Apr. 6, 1934, 1–4) from Magnus Hirschfeld to Berty Albrecht.

[89] Wolff 1986, 394.

Probably, Hirschfeld was first and foremost motivated by the considerable payment offered by *Détective*. Hirschfeld mentioned this financial reason in his letter to Albrecht, immediately adding that he needed new sources of income because his life's work had been attacked by Hitler. Also, *Détective* was a magazine owned by Gallimard and the deal he struck with that publisher included both books and magazine publications. In much the same vein, he defended his commercial activities with the Titus Pearls.[90] In his long letter, Hirschfeld wrote that two "possibilities to live from his literary output" (*possibilités d'existence littéraire*) were offered to him when he arrived in France. One was with the publisher Grasset and involved the publication of books, as well as restarting the Institute with the French Dr. Pierre Vachet. But Hirschfeld plainly stated in the letter that he had refused any collaboration with Vachet.[91] The second offer was the one from Gallimard, an offer that, as we have seen, he accepted.

A meeting between Hirschfeld and the editorial board of *Le problème sexuel* to settle matters never took place. When Hirschfeld died, in May 1935, a very brief, one-sentence notice was added to the sixth (June 1935) issue of *Le problème sexuel*, promising a biographical article on Hirschfeld in the next issue.[92] But this sixth issue also turned out to be the very last since the French magazine was not profitable.[93]

Things only got worse. At the end of April 1934, the French section of the WLSR decided to leave the WLSR altogether. The members of the French section had been elected at the September 1932 WLSR Brno conference: Victor Basch (1863–1944), Justin Sicard de Plauzoles (1872–1968), Jean Dalsace (1893–1970), and Pierre Scize (whose real name was Michel-Joseph Piot, 1894–1956).[94] Norman Haire wrote to Hirschfeld that the French section was also upset with Hirschfeld because he had not consulted with them when he decided to establish the WLSR office in Paris.[95] Haire, as one of the three WLSR presidents, took their side. The French section's dramatic next step coincided with Hirschfeld's opening a medical practice with Zammert in Paris, in the beginning of April 1934. The reply Hirschfeld wrote to the French section of the WLSR, following their second lashing out, has also survived. On its basis, we can infer that the earlier reproaches were repeated. Once again, Hirschfeld did not want to apologize for his commercial activities. He ended his letter with a nasty parting kick, saying that the French section's departure would be no great loss to the WLSR as they had hardly ever paid their dues to the Berlin central office since they joined.[96] Norman Haire judged that Hirschfeld simply lacked tact in the whole matter.[97] A "good conversation", in May 1934, between Hirschfeld and Victor Basch,

[90] Bibliothèque histoire de la médecine, Paris, fonds Dalsace-Vellay, folder Ligue mondiale pour la réforme sexuelle, letter (dated Apr. 6, 1934, 1–4) from Magnus Hirschfeld to Berty Albrecht.

[91] It is possible that Hirschfeld was sensible here, in the first months of 1934, of the influence of the Stavisky affair in French politics, in which Vachet had been involved. We will return to this affair later on.

[92] *Le problème sexuel* 6 (June 1935): 32.

[93] Missika 2005, 101–3, 106.

[94] *La grande réforme*, November 1932, 1.

[95] University of Sydney Library, Sydney, Norman Haire collection, 3.20, Magnus Hirschfeld, Typescripts, 1923–1935, letter (dated Apr. 10, 1934, 1–2) from Norman Haire to Magnus Hirschfeld. One can also infer this reproach indirectly from a letter (dated Apr. 26, 1934, 4) Magnus Hirschfeld wrote to the French section of the WLSR. See Bibliothèque histoire de la médecine, Paris, fonds Dalsace-Vellay, folder Ligue mondiale pour la réforme sexuelle. Cf. Dose 2019, 17.

[96] Bibliothèque histoire de la médecine, Paris, fonds Dalsace-Vellay, folder Ligue mondiale pour la réforme sexuelle, letter (dated Apr. 26, 1934, 5–6) from Magnus Hirschfeld to Comité français de la Ligue mondiale pour la réforme sexuelle sur une base scientifique.

[97] See Bibliothèque histoire de la médecine, Paris, fonds Dalsace-Vellay, letter (dated Apr. 19, 1934, 2) from Norman Haire to Jean Dalsace. After Hirschfeld's death, Haire would repeat his judgment of Hirschfeld more publicly: "Like the rest of us, he had his imperfections. He was not always tactful; he did not always stop to think how his actions might be interpreted by persons of ill-will; he could be very selfish and exigent in small matters". See Norman Haire's introduction to Hirschfeld's *Sex in Human Relationships* (Hirschfeld 1935b, vii–viii). Li Shiu Tong came across Haire's introduction when he was

the president of the French section of the WLSR, did not help to resolve the conflict.[98]

THE GERMAN FREEDOM LIBRARY (DEUTSCHE FREIHEITSBIBLIOTHEK)

In Paris, Hirschfeld was again reminded of the Berlin book burning. On May 10, 1934, exactly one year afterwards, he attended the opening of the German Freedom Library (Deutsche Freiheitsbibliothek), also called the Library of Burned Books (Bibliothek des verbrannten Buches), located in a painter's atelier at 65 Boulevard Arago, Paris XIII (apartment n° 17).[99] The library collected the books of banned authors whose works ended up on the pyre in Germany. Hirschfeld and other German intellectuals spoke in addition to the principal figure behind the Paris-based library, Alfred Kantorowicz (1899–1979). An article in the newspaper *Paris-Midi* included a photo showing Hirschfeld addressing the attending crowd.[100] A clipping of the newspaper article was pasted into the Hirschfeld guestbook, which also includes a real photo of Hirschfeld giving his speech.[101] Shortly afterwards, attempts were made to rescind Hirschfeld's German citizenship (*Ausbürgerung*) but this was never concluded.[102] It is fair to say that, in general, Hirschfeld did not constantly – or even very aggressively – speak against the Nazi regime while in exile. As we will see later, he wrote only a few texts on the Röhm affair. In the beginning of October 1933, he briefly commented on the Dutch Communist Marinus van der Lubbe (1909–1934), the presumed Reichstag arsonist, when he was on trial in Leipzig.[103]

COOPERATION WITH THE CZECHOSLOVAK GAY PERIODICAL NEW VOICE (NOVÝ HLAS)

During his five-month stay in Czechoslovakia and Brno, from August to December 1933, Karl Giese raised the question of starting a new Institute with Josef Weisskopf, but, as we have seen, Weisskopf had his own local battles and demons to deal with. We have also seen that, during Giese's time in Brno, especially in November and December 1934, he oversaw the buy-back operation led by the lawyer Karl Fein. But, during these five months in Czechoslovakia, Giese must have also been in contact with the people around the Czechoslovak gay magazine *New Voice: A Periodical for Sexual Reform* (*Nový hlas: list pro sexuální reform*). *Nový hlas* started in 1932 as the monthly successor to the biweekly *Voice of the Sexual Minority* (*Hlas sexuální menšiny*) whose first issue appeared in April 1931.[104] The first issue of *Nový hlas* came out in May 1932, one month after the founding of the Czechoslovakian League for Sexual Reform on a Scientific Basis (Ceskoslovenská liga pro sexuální reformu na sexuálně vědeckěm podkladě) [ill. 8].[105] That Giese was in contact with the people behind *Nový Hlas* in

in London, around December 1935, and it upset him. See Archiv MHG, Berlin, fonds Max Reiss, letter (Oct. 10, 1935, 3) from Karl Giese to Max Reiss. See also Dose 2019, 19 n. 59. Dose quotes a postcard (dated Apr. 28, 1934) that Max Hodann sent to Fritz and Paulette Brupbacher in which he wrote about the Paris clash: "Magnus hat sich hier wieder unmöglich aufgeführt" (Magnus has behaved impossibly here once again).

98 University of Sydney Library, Sydney, Norman Haire collection, 3.20, Magnus Hirschfeld, Typescripts, 1923–1935, letter (dated May 15, 1934, 1–2); and letter (dated Jun. 12, 1934, 1) from Magnus Hirschfeld to Norman Haire.

99 *Le Populaire*, May 11, 1934, 2; *L'Œuvre*, May 21, 1934, 5. See also Gruner 2006, chapter 7; and, specifically on the Freiheitsbibliothek, 301–4.

100 *Paris-Midi*, May 12, 1934, 1. More detailed information on the opening and other aspects of the Freiheitsbibliothek can be found in Dose 2019, 21–23.

101 Bergemann, Dose, Keilson-Lauritz & Dubout 2019, f. 45/89 and f. 41/85.

102 Magnus Hirschfeld's name does not figure in Hepp 1985. See, above all, Dose 2019, 22 n. 81. Cf. Herrn 2008c: card Literatentreffen anlässlich der Eröffnung der Pariser Freiheitsbibliothek.

103 See "Magnus Hirschfeld über van der Lübbe [*sic*]", *Wiener Allgemeine Zeitung*, Oct. 5, 1933, 4; https://de.wikipedia.org/wiki/Marinus_van_der_Lubbe (accessed Dec. 23, 2020).

104 Following a common practice, *Hlas sexuální menšiny* will hereafter be abbreviated as *Hlas*.

105 For a more extensive overview of the history of these two Czechoslovak gay magazines, see Jepsen 1998; Seidl 2007a; Lishaugen 2007. Huebner mentions the gay magazines briefly, quoting from them throughout her dissertation (Huebner 2008, 178–81). For the situation of these gay magazines in the general framework of other Czechoslovak sex reform publications, see Huebner 2010.

the second half of 1933 does not exclude that they may have met earlier already. As we have seen, starting as early as 1920, Magnus Hirschfeld had been closely involved with Czechoslovak efforts to abolish paragraph 129b, the Czechoslovak counterpart to the much better known German paragraph 175, punishing sex between men.[106] The Czechoslovakian League for Sexual Reform on a Scientific Basis intended to function as the national chapter of the WLSR, though in reality it only worked on gay issues.[107] Most likely, Hirschfeld's earlier activities and encounters in Czechoslovakia brought Giese into contact with at least some of the people involved in these Czechoslovak sexual reform initiatives, and that prior to his first five-month stay in Czechoslovakia.

Magnus Hirschfeld was a real hero for the editors of these pioneering Czechoslovak gay magazines. The second, May 15, 1931, issue of *Hlas* already contained an article on Magnus Hirschfeld. In March 1932, there was even a bus trip planned to Berlin and Hirschfeld's Institute.[108] But it was especially in *Hlas*'s successor, *Nový hlas*, that Hirschfeld's great prominence was simply remarkable: his name appeared in almost every issue at least once. There were interviews with the sexologist and also several articles written by Hirschfeld himself. A version of the psycho-biological questionnaires (*psychobiologische Fragebogen*; in Czech, *Psychobiologický dotazníck*) appeared in the February 1932 issue, and *Nový Hlas* both announced and extensively covered the Brno WLSR conference.[109] Hirschfeld's sixty-fifth birthday and his Paris exile were considered newsworthy items as well.[110]

It was agreed with the editor-in-chief of the magazine, the jurist Vladimír Vávra (whose real name was Vladimír Kolátor, 1903–1986), that Giese would publish regularly with the Czechoslovak gay magazine. Vávra and Giese even intended to make the German-language supplement of the magazine a regular section, so that *Nový hlas* would appeal to people living outside Czechoslovakia.[111] Starting in April 1934, an attempt was made to establish a German-language supplement (*deutsche Beilage*) of only a few pages. Five German-language supplements in total would appear in *Nový hlas* between April and October 1934.[112] This was the second attempt to start a German-language supplement in a Czechoslovak gay magazine.

Giese's first and, as we will see, also last text for the magazine was titled "The Gay Murders" (*Vraždění homosexuelních, Die Homosexuellenmorde*). It appeared in Czech in the January 1934 issue of *Nový hlas*.[113] In this short text, Giese wrote about the gay Parisian theater director Oscar Dufrenne (1875–1933), who was murdered on September 25, 1933. Dufrenne was found dead late in the evening in his office in Paris's Palace Theater, which he owned and managed. The Palace Theater at 8 Rue du Faubourg Montmartre, Paris IX, was and still is a well-known venue.[114] While it

[106] Jepsen 1998, 117–24.

[107] Jepsen 1998, 122.

[108] This planned trip must not be confused with either of the two trips made to the Institute, in 1929 and 1931, by the Czechoslovak doctor Josef Hynie (1900–1989), considered the founder of Czechoslovak sexology. See Schindler 1999; Schindler 2000.

[109] *Nový hlas* 4, Aug. 1932; *Nový hlas* 7–8, Nov. 1932.

[110] *Nový hlas* 5, May 1934, German-language supplement, 8.

[111] Seidl 2007a, 138.

[112] The supplements appeared in *Nový hlas* 4, Apr. 1934, 1–4; *Nový hlas* 5, May 1934, 5–8; *Nový hlas* 6, Jun. 1934, 9–12; *Nový hlas* 7–8, Jul.–Aug. 1934, 13–16; and, finally, skipping the ninth issue, *Nový hlas* 10, Oct. 1934, 17–19. Due to some questionable – but then commonplace – choices made by the bookbinder of the 1934 *Nový hlas* volume in the Klementinum, the Czech national library in Prague, it was not easy to determine the issues in which the five supplements appeared. The bookbinder bound together all the German supplements – with their own pagination, distinct from that of the Czech part of the magazine – at the end of the volume.

[113] Giese 1934. The Czech translation of Giese's German text was done by Vladimír Vávra.

[114] Between 1978 and 1983, the Palace Theater was renowned as a party venue. It was headed by another gay man and Parisian nightlife trendsetter, Fabrice Emaer (1935–1983). He turned the club into a very hot ticket for gay nightlife, with international appeal, as he tried to emulate the atmosphere of New York's Studio 54. Many gay icons like Roland Barthes, Andy Warhol, the young and still largely unknown Madonna, Grace Jones – to name a few – frequented the club and added to its cult status. See Garcia 1999.

operated as a revue theater most days, the Palace Theater was being used as a cinema the evening of Dufrenne's murder. Its walkway (*promenoir*), an underlit area with standing room only, was well-known among Parisian gays as a cruising place, which Dufrenne frequented as well. Dufrenne's half-naked dead body was found rolled up in a carpet. His skull had been fractured by repeated blows from a pool cue. The son of a wallpaper hanger from Lille, a city in the north of France, Dufrenne was a self-made man in the world of revue theater. Starting out as an impresario, he ended up owning the Palace Theater and also managed several other Parisian theater venues, including the Casino de Paris where he invited Josephine Baker and Mistinguett, among others, to perform. He was also an elected left-wing city councilor for the Radicaux-Socialistes in the Paris city council (*conseil municipal*).

The murder caused quite a stir, not only because Dufrenne was a well-known public figure in Paris, but also because the public was confronted with the saucy details of the murder and the homosexual lifestyle of certain people. The murder case was in and out of the press until the end of 1935, when the details came up again at the murder trial. Although the case was never really solved, it is likely that Dufrenne was murdered during some kind of sexual tryst. From the start, many unresolved questions surrounded the case. Despite some quite precise clues, the murderer was not caught in the first few days after the murder. Dufrenne's staff informed the police, though only the following day, that a sailor, or at least a man wearing a sailor's costume, had been seen around the Palace Theatre in the days before the murder and on the evening of the murder itself. Because this was not immediately taken into account by the investigating police, the press and the public started to wonder if there was some sort of concerted effort to shield the murderer. After all, the list of sailors on leave in Paris, fitting the witnesses' description of the suspect, could not have been endless. Maybe, so the rumors went, they were not very eager to find the murderer because they did not want to expose a whole sexual network involving other highly-placed Parisian names [ill. 9]? Because of the mystery surrounding the case, and also because many people in the Parisian underworld suddenly claimed that they had information, another wild story began circulating in Paris. It was rumored that Dufrenne had fellated the sailor, possibly his murderer. One person who spoke to the police claimed that Dufrenne had severely bitten the man's penis and that this may have been why Dufrenne was beaten to death.[115]

A year later, in 1935, Paul Laborie (alias "Paulo les belles dents", Paulo with the beautiful teeth), a sailor with a long criminal record, characterized as a "pédéraste professionnel" (meaning a male prostitute), who had sought refuge in Barcelona, was extradited to France, where he was tried for the murder. But the accused was acquitted for lack of evidence. Finally, there were also rumors that the murder may have had a political aspect since it preceded the Stavisky affair by a few months. Serge Alexandre Stavisky (1886–1934) was a professional crook involved with several unsavory matters associated with several French politicians. Shortly after the scandal broke, Stavisky presumably committed suicide. That Dufrenne knew Stavisky personally, and sold him a theater, was reason enough to link the two cases. The Stavisky affair plunged French politics into a deep crisis, forcing the French government to resign in the beginning of 1934.[116]

[115] See Tamagne 2006, 133–34; Tamagne 2017. To date, Tamagne has published the most extensive texts on the murder case, even though her main subject is the view of the event (and homosexuality in general) in French news media. Most of the factual information related to the case that I present here is taken from her work. I have also consulted two popular press titles on the murder case: *Voilà* and *Détective*. Bringuier, a journalist with *Détective*, wrote discreetly about the rumor of a wounded penis (Bringuier 1934, 7).

[116] Tamagne 2007, 141–42.

Giese's text for *Nový hlas*, which appeared in the January 1934 issue, was likely written when he was still in Czechoslovakia. Giese was certainly in Czechoslovakia when Dufrenne was murdered, in September 1933, and it is also certain that the spectacular news of the French gay sex scandal made headlines in Czechoslovakia. For example, it was front page news in an issue of the newspaper *Lidové noviny* in the beginning of October.[117] Giese's first sentence seems to indicate that news of the Parisian affair had indeed reached Czechoslovakia, both immediately and afterwards: "Once again the world press was full of reports of the murder of a homosexual man".[118] It is also quite conceivable, of course, that Magnus Hirschfeld, who was in Paris, informed Giese about the many rumors circulating in the French capital about the case.

In his text, Giese stated that, from its beginning, the case was bathed in mystery but that he quickly sensed what was *really* going on. As was typical of many of Giese's writings, he was interested in the hidden (homo)sexual side of things, as explaining unresolved social phenomena. "Of course, I don't like to think it a coincidence that, from the very first newspaper report, before its connections were publicly known, I suspected that this murder might have a homosexual background".[119] Giese believed that he had a good "gaydar", an ability to look beneath the presumed heterosexual appearance of things. But despite the many mysteries surrounding the case, it cannot be said that its gay aspects only became visible over time, as Giese claimed. After all, Dufrenne was known to be gay and, from the start, it was quite clear that Dufrenne had picked up a man in a sailor costume from the cinema's promenoir with sexual intent. That some men prostituted themselves dressed up as sailors, in order to attract more customers, was also mentioned in the press. It must be said, however, that the *Lidové noviny* article teemed with double entendres and innuendo in a way that would be unthinkable nowadays.[120] That Dufrenne was gay was hinted at in a very oblique way by saying that Dufrenne had a "very Parisian" (*très Parisienne*) personality, unlike, as the article noted, the French writer Paul Valéry, who was certainly *not* "très Parisienne". Yet most of the known elements of the case – Dufrenne inviting a sailor with a big nose and gold teeth to his office – were mentioned in the Czech article as well. So it is possible that, when writing his piece, Giese was thinking of actual evasiveness in the (at least Czech-language) press, but falsely concluded that the gay aspects had been wholly omitted.

In his analysis of the murder case, Giese tried to determine the common characteristics of similar affairs he encountered when working in Hirschfeld's Berlin Institute. In many homosexual murder cases, a suspect was often not from the victim's social environment. Often neighbors had information on the "unusual" people suddenly seen in the company of the victim, shortly before the murder. In his *Nový hlas* text, Giese also brought up the case of Hans Friedmann (1887–1923), a Berlin banker, with a sexual predilection for athletic men, who was murdered by one of

[117] See "Vrazi privilegovaní", *Lidové noviny*, Oct. 3, 1933, 1–2. The newspaper continues to exist to this day in Czechia. The article appeared on October 3, but was dated September 30, 1933, five days after the murder. The possible objection that Giese could not read Czech can be countered by the fact that one of his best gay friends in Brno, Karl Fein and, to a much lesser extent, also Willi Bondi, were at least bilingual. I did not systematically study the handling of the affair by the Czechoslovak press. When checking some Belgian newspapers (1933–38) I saw that the sensational murder case was front page news in Belgium as well.

[118] Giese 1934, 9: "Wieder mal war die Weltpresse voll von Berichten über die Ermordung eines homosexuellen Mannes".

[119] Giese 1934, 9: "Ich mag es natürlich nicht für einen Zufall halten, dass ich schon beim ersten Zeitungsbericht, bevor diese Zusammenhänge bekannt waren, den Verdacht hatte, dieser Mord könnte eine homosexuelle Grundlage haben".

[120] Tamagne explains that the French press had to be partly evasive about certain "obscene" facts since the 1881 Loi sur la liberté de la presse (Law on Freedom of the Press) still allowed the prosecution of "l'outrage aux bonnes moeurs" (outrage to public morals). See Tamagne 2006, 132–33.

these athletic men and an accomplice.[121] It was Friedmann's collection of "homemade" photos of athletic young men from Berlin that led to his murderers. Giese also mentioned another gay murder (mystery) in Berlin-Tegel, presumably in the winter of 1932–33. Soon after the murder of another gay man, the people at a gay party in the street In den Zelten, where the Institute was also located, were suddenly all suspects. Giese also brought up the infamous gay murder of the German art historian Johann Joachim Winckelmann (1717-1768), mentioning two literary treatments of the murder. He concluded his text by repeating what these murderers of gay men had in common: "the milieus of the murderer and the murdered person show a great disparity. [...] Often the murdered person hardly knows his murderer".[122] In these ways, Giese continued, these gay murders were quite similar to the murders of prostitutes. Gays and prostitutes, Giese claimed, knew that, if they were to fall victim, there was a good chance that their murderers might never be found. That is the price they have to pay as social outsiders. Interestingly, this accorded surprisingly well with the conclusion of the October 1933 *Lidové noviny* newspaper article mentioned above, which called the murderers of gay men "privileged murderers" (*vrazi privilegovaní*) since they were seldom found and thus escaped punishment for their crimes.

On April 19 and 20, 1934, the movie *Gesetze der Liebe,* renamed *Laws of Nature* (*Zákony přírody, pohlavní pud*) in Czechoslovakia, was screened one more time at the Elektra cinema in Opava in Czechoslovakia. Did Giese have a hand in this, before or after his return to Paris?[123]

MAGNUS HIRSCHFELD'S FURTHER AMBITIONS FOR CZECHOSLOVAKIA

We saw that, starting in April 1934, *Nový hlas* added a German-language supplement to the Czech-language magazine. That this happened around the time of Giese's arrival and starting the new Institute in Paris was most likely no coincidence. It was part of the "new beginning" Hirschfeld and Giese imagined for themselves from their new pied-à-terre in Paris. That they saw Czechoslovakia as a promising new hunting ground is indicated by a surviving letter, in which Hirschfeld offered to write articles, for a fee, in the Prague-based newspaper *Prager Presse,* focusing on one of his specialties: "Eugenics, heredity, racial issues, the sterilization problem, sexology, population politics, psychological problems, etc.".[124]

Magnus Hirschfeld wrote a forceful opening piece in the very first German-language supplement of the April 1934 *Nový hlas* issue, under the title "The State of Affairs of the (Gay) Movement in the Spiritual Liberation Struggle of Homosexuals" (*Stand der Bewegung im geistigen Befreiungskampf der Homosexuellen*).[125] The byline made it clear that Hirschfeld indeed wrote the text in Paris, his new exile home.

[121] On Hans Friedmann, see Hergemöller 2010, 355. Hergemöller says that Friedmann was a "Börsenmakler" (stockbroker).

[122] Giese 1934, 10: "dass die Milieus des Mörders und des Ermordeten einen großen Unterschied aufweisen. [...] Oft kennt der Ermordete seinen Mörder kaum".

[123] See the announcement for the movie screening in *Neues Tagblatt für Schlesien und Nordmähren*, Apr. 19, 1934, 7, where the movie also has the subtitle "Aus der Mappe des berühmten Sexualforschers Prof. Dr. Magnus Hirschfeld" (From the portfolio of the famous sex researcher Dr. Magnus Hirschfeld). In Germany, the movie's subtitle was the rather more generic and less provocative "Aus der Mappe eines Sexualforschers" (From the portfolio of a sex researcher). For some information on the Elektra cinema in Opava, see https://opavsky.denik.cz/zpravy_region/kino-elektra08092013.html (accessed Jan. 23, 2021).

[124] PNP, Praha, fonds Arne Laurin (real name Arnošt Lustig), folder Magnus Hirschfeld, letter (dated Apr. 3, 1934, 1–2) from Magnus Hirschfeld to Prager Presse: "Eugenik, Vererbung, Rassenfragen, Sterilisationsproblem, Sexualwissenschaft, Bevölkerungspoli[tik: *sic*], psychische Probleme, etc." See also ibid., letter (dated Sep. 26, 1934) from Magnus Hirschfeld to Prager Presse. In Paris, Hirschfeld was receiving the Prague-based newspaper free of charge. When copies were sent to one of his old hotel addresses, he asked them to send copies to his new and permanent address in the avenue Charles Floquet.

[125] Hirschfeld 1934b, 1–3.

In this short but important text, Hirschfeld clearly alluded to the Nazi takeover in Germany, the looting of the Berlin Institute, and his forced exile in France. As already noted, Hirschfeld was devastated by the Nazis' destructive and devastatingly successful attack on his life's work; however, with the passage of time, he became more resilient. In the same text, he wrote: "Even if books on sexology, and especially on the homosexual question, are burned and banned, even if they are pulped and destined for the flames, we stick to the word of the Bible: 'A remnant will be saved'. Yes, a remnant will be saved, a seed from which new life will blossom again".[126] Hirschfeld also wrote that the written word would eventually triumph over arms, making it clear that it was thanks to his words and actions, over several decades, that it was possible for some, now in power in Germany, to be openly homosexual. Of course, the allusion was clearly to gay cliques within the SA, with Ernst Röhm as their emblematic representative: "If today, in Germany, indeed in the world, no one, or hardly anyone, finds anything wrong with the fact that persons in high executive positions are generally regarded as homosexuals, these gentlemen owe this tolerance essentially to the men they now disown and chase away, partly simply because they do not fit into their racial scheme".[127] In the same text, Hirschfeld also quoted extensively from a letter sent to him by someone in Germany, who was close to the NSDAP before their rise to power in 1933.[128] The letter writer observed how hard it must be for Röhm to save face as a homosexual in Nazi Germany. The writer also mourned the destruction of Hirschfeld's life's work and the general prohibition on "all sexological works".[129] The same writer even asked Hirschfeld if he could perhaps intervene.

There was also mention of the compromising letters that Ernst Röhm (1887–1934) had written to Karl-Günther Heimsoth (1899–1934) around 1928, and which were published in facsimile in Germany by Helmut Klotz (1894–1943) in 1932.[130] These letters were also published (in a Czech translation) in issues 3 (March 1934) and 4 (April 1934) of *Nový hlas*.[131] Hirschfeld's opening text appeared in the issue that contained the second and final part of the Röhm-Heimsoth correspondence. Did Hirschfeld or Giese have a hand in all of this? It seems likely. Hirschfeld clearly meant to attack the National Socialists by pointing out their untenable position: seemingly supporting their open and not-so-open gay members, while at the same time being utterly intolerant of Hirschfeld and his life's work for the emancipation of (homo)sexuality. It is important to realize that, in this text, we see a rather unusual Hirschfeld at work, taking on the role of a fierce gay militant. In his Berlin years, Hirschfeld had always been somewhat discreet about his sexual orientation, conducted himself

[126] Hirschfeld 1934b, 3: "Mag man auch die Bücher über die Sexualwissenschaft und insbesondere auch über die homosexuelle Frage verbrennen und verbieten, mag man sie auch als Makulatur einstampfen und sie in Hetzschrifen umwandeln, wir halten uns an das Wort der Bibel: 'Ein Rest wird bleiben!' Ja ein Rest wird bleiben, ein Keim, aus dem wieder neues Leben erblüht". The Bible passage comes from the Old Testament Book of Isaiah. Isaiah was referring to the Jewish people and their persecution. Hirschfeld could not then have imagined that the Holocaust would ensue and this Bible passage would assume a completely new meaning. Hirschfeld likely got the idea to refer to this Biblical author from Heinz Cohn (1903–1994), who wrote the passage from Isaiah in the Hirschfeld guestbook on December 24, 1933. See Bergemann, Dose, Keilson-Lauritz & Dubout 2019, f. 15/59. See also Keilson-Lauritz 2004, 86; Keilson-Lauritz 2008, 36; Herzer 2017, 395.

[127] Hirschfeld 1934b, 1: "Wenn heute in Deutschland, ja in der Welt niemand oder kaum jemand etwas dabei findet, dass Personen in hohen leitenden Stellungen allgemein als homosexuell gelten, so haben die Herren diese Toleranz im wesentlichen den Männern zu verdanken, die sie jetzt, zum Teil nur deshalb, weil sie nicht in ihr Rassenschema passen, verleugen und verjagen". It remains of course an open question if Hirschfeld implicitly referred here to Adolf Hitler as well.

[128] Hirschfeld 1934b, 1.

[129] Hirschfeld 1934b, 2: "alle sexualwissenschaftlichen Werke".

[130] For more information on this correspondence, see Zinn 1997, 46.

[131] *Nový hlas* 3, Mar. 1934, 33–35; *Nový hlas* 4, Apr. 1934, 49–50.

diplomatically, and always took refuge behind scientific respectability. In the German-language supplement of a Czech gay magazine, on the contrary, he took a clear and powerful gay activist stand.[132] Was this a man who, thinking that his life might soon end, realized that he had little left to lose? The same man who, a year earlier, was no longer afraid of posing with his new young lover Li Shiu Tong for the cover of the July 1933 issue of *Voilà*?

In 2015, in the estate (*Nachlass*) of Hans Blüher, held in the Staatsbibliothek zu Berlin, Manfred Herzer found a text written by Marcel Herckmans (1893–1978), most likely the account of a conversation Herckmans had with Hirschfeld in 1934, presumably in Paris. Though it is likely colored by Herckmans' own views and convictions, one still perceives a more gay-activist Hirschfeld, one who thinks gay men should organize in "fraternal lodges" (*philadelphische Logen*), similar to Masonic lodges. The sacking of the Institute, Röhm's liquidation, and the fact that the National Socialists persecuted people of Jewish descent, despite many – like Hirschfeld himself – being thoroughly assimilated, seem to explain Hirschfeld's new stance.[133]

But other things were also at play in the cooperation between Hirschfeld and *Nový hlas*. It was only understandable that Hirschfeld felt like launching a counterattack against the National Socialists from abroad. Both parties – the pair of Hirschfeld and Giese, the editors of *Nový hlas* – must have known that pursuing the battle from abroad, by means of a German-language supplement in a Czechoslovak gay magazine, was only a small gay activist act of resistance against the Third Reich, a regime that, as soon as the National Socialists came to power in 1933, had totally wiped out the German gay movement, the country's gay night life and its bars, and all gay publications.[134] Apparently, Hirschfeld hoped that the German-language supplement would join the many other exile publications critical of National Socialist Germany. Hirschfeld wrote rather dramatically in his opening piece: "The very fact that after the destruction of our work in our German homeland, in neighboring Czechoslovakia, where we often and gladly spent time, personalities have come together who want to work, and have already worked in the same spirit, is proof of the indestructibility of this cultural task, which is as important as it is necessary: the liberation of unhappy people from undeserved stigma".[135] The gay colleagues in Czechoslovakia, or so he hoped at least, would take up the (homo)sexual reform torch lit by Hirschfeld. And maybe, like an Olympic flame, that inspiring light would one day shine as far as Germany: "The flame that went out in the land of Goethe, Kant and Nietzsche will shine in new splendor in the land of Huss, Commenius [*sic*] and Masaryk and will one day cast its rays back to where the light started. Thank you, Czechoslovak comrades and torchbearers!"[136] Harald Hartvig Jepsen has pointed out, in his splendid text on the early Czechoslovak homosexual emancipation movement, that the Czecho-Slovak Socialist Republic (ČSSR), several decades later, would indeed "reflect back"

[132] I discussed this picture of a more radical gay activist with Manfred Herzer, who disputed it, referring to Magnus Hirschfeld's articles from 1922–23 in the Berlin gay magazine *Die Freundschaft*. Herzer later collected these articles in Hirschfeld 1986.

[133] For the "Zitaten aus den letzten Aussprachen mit Dr. Magnus Hirschfeld", see Herzer 2015, 135–37.

[134] Dobler 2003, 179–81.

[135] Hirschfeld 1934c, 3: "Gerade die Tatsache, dass sich nach der Zerstörung unserer Arbeit in unserer deutschen Heimat, in der benachbarten Tschechoslowakei, in der wir so oft und gern weilten, Persönlichkeiten zusammenfanden, die ihrerseits im gleichen Sinne wie wir arbeiten wollen und schon gearbeitet haben, ist ein Beweis für die Unzerstörbarkeit dieser ebenso wichtigen wie nötigen Kulturaufgabe: Der Befreiung unglücklicher Menschen von unverdienter Schmach".

[136] Hirschfeld 1934c, 3: "Die Flamme, die im Lande Goethes, Kants und Nietzsches erlosch, wird im Lande eines Huss, Commenius [*sic*] und Masaryk in neuem Glanze aufleuchten und ihre Strahlen einst wieder dorthin zurückwerfen, wovon das Licht seinen Ausgang nahm. Dank Euch, tschechoslowakische Kameraden und Fackelträger!"

[137] Jepsen 1998, 126. Jepsen also quotes Hirschfeld's Fackelträger passus in his article (Jepsen 1998, 123–24) but, curiously, does not include Hirschfeld's

this light to Germany and close the circle again. The 1961 Czechoslovak initiative to no longer punish homosexual acts between adults over the age of eighteen would inspire the German Democratic Republic (Deutsche Demokratische Republik, DDR) to abolish the infamous war survivor, paragraph 175, in 1968.[137] It was only in 1994 that paragraph 175 would disappear completely in a reunified Germany.

Hirschfeld and the editors of *Nový hlas* probably also tried to use the German-language supplement to reach German gay men who fled to trilingual Czechoslovakia after the Nazi takeover in Germany. At the time, Czechoslovakia indeed still stood as a German-language democracy where, starting in 1933, many German democrats and left-wingers fled. Karl Giese was one of them and Kurt Hiller, Hirschfeld's fellow gay activist, was another. The latter's arrival in Prague, in October 1934, was mentioned in an issue of *Nový hlas*.[138]

The *Nový hlas* people were aligned with Hirschfeld (and Giese) in wanting to create such a German-language supplement. Their ambitions were indeed great. *Nový hlas* would take the lead in a global gay activist battle: "Today these [gay] periodicals have been discontinued [in Germany], some who are interested in the homosexual movement, for whatever reason, are staying abroad. [...] We have contacted German cultural workers with the aim that *Nový hlas*, as the only homosexual magazine in the world, take the first step towards becoming a world journal".[139] In the third *Nový hlas* German-language supplement of June 1934, another *Nový hlas* collaborator repeated this global gay activist ambition. Due to the new political situation in Germany and the disappearance of the gay press there, *Nový hlas* had become de facto "the only magazine in the whole world [...] which strives for and advocates the abolition of the old-fashioned provisions of the penal law against homosexuality in various states".[140]

PICKING AN OLD IDEOLOGICAL BATTLE WITH KARL MEIER IN SWITZERLAND

This claim that *Nový hlas* was at that moment the only periodical in the world working on gay emancipation was clearly incorrect. In 1934, the Swiss periodical *Schweizerisches Freundschafts-Banner* was already in its second year of publication. Changing titles a few times, it would last until 1971; especially after the war, it was best known under the title *Der Kreis – Le Cercle*.[141] But it is utterly striking that their principal figure, Karl Meier (1897–1974), better known as Rolf, began his involvement with the magazine in the month after Hirschfeld's opening piece appeared in *Nový hlas* [ill. 10].

Karl Meier wrote his first piece, "Call to All!" (*Appell an Alle!*), under the pen name Rudolf Rheiner in the *Schweizerisches Freundschafts-Banner* issue of May 15, 1934.[142] It

important text, "Stand der Bewegung im geistigen Befreiungskampf der Homosexuellen" (Hirschfeld 1934c) in his bibliography.

138 *Nový hlas* 12, Dec. 1934, last page. The date of Hiller's arrival in Prague (October 15, 1934) is mentioned in NA, Praha, fonds Policejní ředitelství Praha II, evidence obyvatelstva sheet, Kurt Hiller 1885.

139 V. [Vladimír Vávra] 1934a, 4: "Heute sind diese [schwule] Zeitschriften [in Deutschland] eingestellt, mancher von denen, die an der homosexuellen Bewegung aus welchem Grunde immer interessiert sind, weilen in der Fremde. [...] Wir haben mit deutschen kulturellen Arbeitern in den Bestreben Fühlung genommen, dass der Nový hlas als einzige homosexuelle Zeitschrift auf der Welt den ersten Schritt dazu tue, ein Weltblatt zu werden".

140 Holm 1934, 11: "die einzige Zeitschrift auf der ganzen Welt [...] welche die Abschaffung der veralteten Bestimmungen des Strafgesetzes gegen die Homosexualität in den verschiedenen Staaten anstrebt und verficht".

141 In 1937, *Schweizerisches Freundschafts-Banner* (1932–36) would be followed up by *Menschenrecht: Blätter zur Aufklärung gegen Ächtung und Vorurteil* (1937–42) to become, in 1943, *Der Kreis: eine Monatsschrift = Le Cercle: revue mensuelle* (1943–67). Finally, the gay magazine was renamed *Club 68* (1968–71) before it came to a final end in 1971. For more information on *Schweizerisches Freundschafts-Banner*, see Herzer 1997b.

142 Rheiner, May 15, 1934. Karl Meier's birth name was in reality Carl Rudolf Rheiner. Shortly after his birth, he was abandoned by his unmarried mother, Elisabeth Rheiner, and the boy was later adopted by the Meier family, hence his official last name. See Kennedy 1999, 36. I thank Jens Dobler for his assistance in obtaining a copy of this text.

is remarkable that, in relation to one of the important gay cultural divides, which continue to exist in our own day, Karl Meier clearly announced his adherence to the *eros* school by using the word "homoerotic" to describe gay men. He sided, in other words, with the masculinist and sexually sublimating viewpoints of Adolf Brand and his German periodical *Der Eigene*. Which almost automatically meant that he was opposed to the *sexus* (as in "sexuality") school around the sexologist Hirschfeld.[143] Was this old feud within the German gay movement, the conflict between the cultural and the sexual strands of gay matters, now being continued on foreign territory? That could very well be.

Rolf had worked and lived in Germany since 1924 and was often in Berlin. He returned to his native Switzerland in 1932. It was Adolf Brand, already realizing that Germany would soon no longer be safe for gay people, who urged Karl Meier to return to Switzerland.[144] Very curiously, Adolf Brand also used the image of a torch in a letter he sent (in 1932) to Karl Meier: "You, Swiss, have the duty to carry back the torch, lit by your compatriot [Heinrich] Hössli, so that it may – with luck – survive there, to be re-lit again later in a brighter and better Germany".[145] Heinrich Hössli (1784–1864) was an important precursor Swiss LGBT activist.[146] The emblem of *Der Kreis*, a stylized illuminated oil lamp, originated in Brand's mandate [ill. 11]. Although the similarity of the reflecting light imagery used by Brand in 1932 and Hirschfeld in 1934 is striking, it is likely coincidental. Nevertheless, that both used the metaphor of a torch, and spoke of its light being cast back to Germany one day, does not exclude the possibility that one might have copied it from the other. It is possible, for example, that Adolf Brand saw Hirschfeld's April 1934 text in *Nový hlas* and then appealed to Karl Meier to launch an alternative in Switzerland. That the influence ran the other way, with Brand instigating Hirschfeld, is less plausible.

Adolf Brand was very aware of the existence of *Nový hlas*. He even thought, erroneously, that it stood for "New Greece" (*Neues Hellas*). Quite aware that all gay publications in Germany would have to cease publication very soon, in a two-page issue of the magazine *Extrapost des Eigenen*, he wrote, some time in 1933, that the Czechoslovak gay magazine was now "the only homoerotic magazine in the world" (*das einzige homoerotische Blatt der Welt*).[147] This clearly resonates with the previously mentioned ideas the *Nový hlas* people had about their publication in 1934.

But there are other, more synchronic events, in April–May 1934, which look much less coincidental. It is certain that the editorial board of *Nový hlas* was in contact with the people behind *Schweizerisches Freundschafts-Banner* (or just Karl Meier?) since both magazines swapped texts. A piece written by Vladimír Vávra on *Simplicus*

[143] The pioneering and standard reference work on Brand and *Der Eigene*, and the circle around it, remains Keilson-Lauritz 1997. On Meier's involvement in the 1920s with *Der Eigene*, see Keilson-Lauritz 1997, 137–38.

[144] See the paragraph "Karl Meier und Adolf Brand", in chapter 2, titled "Weg zur Selbstbestimmung", at www.schwulengeschichte.ch (accessed Jul. 31, 2020). Cf. Salathé 1997, 8, where Rolf firmly denies the idea that he was a disciple of Adolf Brand; Keilson-Lauritz 1997, 141–42.

[145] "Du, Schweizer, die Pflicht hast, die Fackel, von deinem Landsmann [Heinrich] Hössli entzündet, wieder zurückzutragen, damit sie – mit Glück – dort überlebe, um später einmal wieder in einem helleren und besseren Deutschland neu entzündet zu werden". Karl Meier framed and hung Brand's letter to him on the wall of his bedroom, where it was seen by several people. See https://schwulengeschichte.ch/epochen/2-weg-zur-selbstbestimmung/nachfolger-der-pioniere/adolf-brand/karl-meier-und-adolf-brand/ (accessed Dec. 27, 2020).

[146] See https://schwulengeschichte.ch/epochen/2-weg-zur-selbstbestimmung/vorkaempfer-und-opfer/heinrich-hoessli/?sword_list%5B0%5D=heinrich&sword_list%5B1%5D=federer&sword_list%5B2%5D=heinrich&cHash=f4358f1e9051560bb0a98199da69ee5a&L=0 (accessed Jun. 17, 2021); Thalmann 2014.

[147] Qtd. in Keilson-Lauritz 1997, 140.

[148] See "Die Zeitschrift Simplicus", *Schweizerisches Freundschafts-Banner*, Jg. 2, n° 18 (Sep. 15, 1934), 3. For the original source in *Nový hlas*, see V. V. 1934b. No author is given in the *Schweizerisches Freundschafts-Banner* issue, but we know from the *Nový hlas* issue that the text was written by Vlad-

(the Prague-based exile successor of the German satirical weekly *Simplicissimus*), in the second German-language supplement of the May 1934 *Nový hlas* issue, was also published in a September 1934 issue of *Schweizerisches Freundschafts-Banner*, though anonymously.[148] Because the two magazines swapped texts, it is very likely that Karl Meier (aka Rudolf Rheiner) knew about Hirschfeld's April 1934 *Nový hlas* text "The State of Affairs of the (Gay) Movement in the Spiritual Liberation Struggle of Homosexuals". The striking resemblance or resonance between Karl Meier's text "Call to All!" and Hirschfeld's text is a further clue that Meier was taking a stand against Hirschfeld. While in Hirschfeld's text the homosexuals were described as "unhappy people "(*unglücklicher Menschen*), in Rheiner's text they are called "discouraged people of our kind" (*mutlosen Menschen unserer Art*). The title of Hirschfeld's piece speaks of the "spiritual liberation struggle of homosexuals", which might have also inspired Rheiner, who says: "But one thing is important for every human being, for every homoerotic [person] in particular: *only the spiritually struggling person* shapes life! [emphasis in original]" Immediately afterwards, Rudolf Rheiner (or Karl Meier) referred to the disastrous situation of the gay subculture in Germany, eliminated "with the stroke of a pen".[149]

But more was to come. In the next, June 1, 1934, issue of the Swiss gay magazine, Karl Meier, now writing under the pen name Gaston Dubois, in a text titled "The False Image" (*Das falsche Bild*) condemned "[t]he platitudinous term 'homosexuality'" as opposed to "the pure image of a *life-felt experience* [emphasis in original]".[150] An indication of the importance Karl Meier attached to these two texts – "Call to All!" and "The False Image" – is that both were reprinted in a 1957 issue of the then trilingual *Der Kreis – Le Cercle – The Circle*, celebrating the twenty-fifth anniversary of the organization and the periodical.[151] Meier's second text was highly critical of Hirschfeld's gay worldview but also opened with a mysterious sentence: "The past weeks' internal events make it necessary to make a statement". Immediately afterwards, Meier explained his view on the ideological difference – eros or sexus? The reference of the first sentence is not known. But, possibly, the ideological divide caused a serious dispute within the editorial board of the *Schweizerisches Freundschafts-Banner*.[152] Bearing all this in mind, and knowing Karl Meier's strong ideological bond with Adolf Brand, I think that one may wonder whether the now current story of how Karl Meier got involved with the *Schweizerisches Freundschafts-Banner*, and the timing of his involvement, tells the whole truth: "At the end of April 1934, he [Karl Meier]

imír Vávra. The *Nový hlas* text was based on the longer Czech text that appeared in the same April issue of Nový hlas (62–63). Interestingly, the words "von Homosexuellen" – words Karl Meier would have despised – *disappear* from a sentence (and make it nonsensical) in the *Schweizerisches Freundschafts-Banner* version: "Mit dieser Art des Kampfes sollte endlich einmal Schluss gemacht werden, insbesondere wenn man sich bei dieser tschechisch-deutschen, angeblich emigrantischen Zeitschrift dessen bewusst würde, welcher Prozentsatz [von Homosexuellen] gerade in den Reihen der Emigranten vorhanden ist" (This kind of struggle would finally be discontinued, especially if this Czech-German, supposedly émigré magazine, was made aware of the precise percentage [of homosexuals] in the ranks of émigrés). The text is also quoted in Zinn 1997, 124. Zinn also noticed "dass der anonyme Autor mit vielen deutschen Emigranten zumindest in Kontakt stand, wenn er nicht selbst sogar Emigrant war" (that the anonymous author was at least in contact with many German émigrés, if he wasn't an émigré himself). I thank Alexander Zinn for his friendly help in obtaining a copy of this short text from the *Schweizerisches Freundschafts-Banner*.

149 Rheiner, May 15, 1934, 1: "Eines aber ist für jeden Menschen wichtig, für jeden Homoeroten besonders: *Nur der geistig Kämpfende* gestaltet das Leben!" [emphasis in original]; and: "mit einem Federstrich".

150 Dubois, Jun 1, 1934, 1: "[d]ie platte Bezeichnung "Homosexualität"; and: "das reine Bild eines *Lebensgefühls* [emphasis in original]".

151 *Der Kreis – Le Cercle – The Circle* 9, Sep. 1957, 6–8.

152 "Die internen Ereignisse der letzten Wochen machen eine Feststellung notwendig". One may also wonder whether Hirschfeld had possibly tried to contact Karl Meier (or vice versa) on the matter after Meier's first article. Had it become clear, through the encounter, that the ideological gulf between the two was too deep?

noticed the *Schweizerische Freundschafts-Banner* at a kiosk [in Zürich], bought it and immediately planned to get in touch with the publisher. At the beginning of May, he visited the club's premises for the first time and met Anna Vock [1885–1962] there".[153] Is it not rather strange that Karl Meier was able to have such a strong impact on the editorial board of the Swiss magazine so soon after joining it?

Despite its clear opposition to Hirschfeld's line of thought, one cannot say that Hirschfeld's name was taboo in the Swiss magazine. When Hirschfeld moved to Paris and tried to rebuild his Institute there, this was announced in the magazine.[154] And when the world-famous sexologist died, in 1935, an article marking this event appeared on the first page of the Swiss periodical.[155] And yet, to top things off, Meier's text "Das falsche Bild" also appeared, though without the just-mentioned unclear first sentence, in the fifth and last German-language supplement of *Nový hlas* in October 1934. In this case, Karl Meier used his other pseudonym, Rudolf Rheiner.[156] It is not unreasonable to think that the Hirschfeld/Giese cooperation with *Nový hlas* came to a sudden end because of the inclusion of this ostentatiously anti-Hirschfeld text in *Nový hlas*.

Whatever the precise antagonistic interactions between Hirschfeld's opening text, in the German supplement of *Nový hlas*, and Meier's two founding texts in the Swiss magazine, it was not *Nový hlas*, as the people behind it had announced and hoped, but the *Schweizerisches Freundschafts-Banner*, and later on its successor *Der Kreis – Le Cercle*, that would ultimately become, for a while, the one and only gay magazine in the world, carrying the torch of Hirschfeld, or Adolf Brand or Heinrich Hössli. *Der Kreis* was indeed likely the only gay publication in the world to hold aloft the gay activist torch through World War II.[157] It was particularly after the war that *Der Kreis – Le Cercle* would gain wider international circulation and could indeed aspire to fulfill the global ambitions that *Nový hlas* and Hirschfeld had only dreamt of in the 1930s. Other postwar gay magazines would clearly take their inspiration from *Der Kreis – Le Cercle* and continue its legacy, the homophile *Arcadie* in France and *One Magazine* in the USA being the principal two.[158] So it is interesting to suggest that, despite their clear ideological differences, Karl Meier (Rolf) might himself have been another Hirschfeld torchbearer – maybe not positively inspired by Hirschfeld, but rather spurred on by him. In other words, the Czechoslovak case shows, once again, the extent to which Hirschfeld was indeed *the* main inspirational source for the burgeoning European gay movement before World War II, and why he has been dubbed, I think rightly, the (grand)father of the modern LGBT movement.[159]

[153] Qtd. in the paragraph "Karl Meier", in chapter 2, "Weg zur Selbstbestimmung", at www.schwulengeschichte.ch (accessed Jul. 31, 2020): "Ende April 1934 bemerkte er [Karl Meier] an einem Kiosk [in Zürich] das Schweizerische Freundschafts-Banner, erwarb es und plante sofort, mit der Herausgeberin in Kontakt zu treten. Anfang Mai besuchte er erstmals das Vereinslokal und traf mit Anna Vock [1885–1962] zusammen". Anna Vock, better known as Mammina, was one of the precursor lesbian Swiss activists active in the lesbian association Amicitia (Zürich). Vock also wrote for the *Schweizerisches Freundschafts-Banner*.

[154] See "Ein Sexualinstitut", *Schweizerisches Freundschafts-Banner*, Jg. 2, Sep. 15, 1934, n° 18, 3.

[155] V., Jun. 1, 1935. In 1945, on the occasion of the tenth anniversary of Hirschfeld's death, a text by Kurt Hiller, which first appeared shortly after Hirschfeld's death in 1935, was reprinted in *Der Kreis – Le Cercle*. See Hiller 1945. Meier wrote a short introduction to Hiller's text. While laudatory of Hirschfeld's important contribution to the gay emancipation cause, Meier was also quite critical of Hirschfeld, saying that Hirschfeld had a great many shortcomings, often sensed by those who collaborated with him ("Trotz mancher "Schwächen", die gerade auch in "Mitarbeiternähe" manchmal fühlbar wurden"). See Hiller 1945, 2.

[156] Rheiner 1934. Meier published the original text in the *Schweizerisches Freundschafts-Banner* under his pen name Gaston Dubois. See Dubois, Jun. 1, 1934.

[157] Cf. Herzer 1997b, 134; Keilson-Lauritz 1997, 139–42.

[158] For a more extensive description of the postwar international influence of *Der Kreis*, see Steinle 1999, 12–16.

[159] Referring to Magnus Hirschfeld, Ralf Dose writes of "the origins of the gay liberation movement"

The editors of *Nový hlas* likely also had other, more self-centered reasons for wanting to work with Hirschfeld and Giese in 1934. Since Czechoslovak subscribers on their own could not keep the magazine afloat, the editors hoped to gain an additional base of German readers to help preserve the magazine.[160] But this never happened. The German-language supplement endeavor never produced the hoped-for new batch of German-speaking subscribers. Besides the lack of new German-speaking readers and subscribers, there were simply not enough contributors, writing in German, prepared to carry Hirschfeld's activist torch. That the German-language supplement experiment fell apart after a few months was visible in the magazine itself. From the third, June 1934 German-language supplement on, the supplement simply provided German translations of the Czech-language articles in the same issue, or from previous issues. That Giese and Hirschfeld did indeed have a strong hand in the idea for a German-language supplement can perhaps also be deduced from the fact that Giese's (and later Hirschfeld's) departure from Paris, in the second half of 1934, virtually coincided with the date of the last German-language supplement in *Nový hlas*, in October 1934. A few months later, in December 1934, the very last issue of *Nový hlas* would come out.

All in all, we can say that Giese's projected contributions to *Nový hlas*, most likely planned while he was still in Czechoslovakia in the second half of 1933, simply fell apart at the start. The editors of *Nový hlas* wrote that this was because Giese was sick. In the fifth and last German-language supplement of October 1934, it said: "Karl Giese, Dr. M. Hirschfeld's secretary, has fallen ill and was therefore unable to write his promised contribution 'Castrated Biographies'".[161] This was probably true, but the whole truth was a little more complicated than that. Only two weeks after Giese arrived in Paris, the new start that Hirschfeld and Giese had envisioned would come to an abrupt halt.

(Dose 2014), while Robert Beachy, more generally, characterizes gay Berlin as the birthplace of modern homosexual identity (Beachy 2014). The case of the German born LGBT-precursor Henry Gerber (1892-1972, real name Josef H. Dittmar) and his pioneering organization Society for Human Rights (SHR) and short-lived magazine *Friendship and Freedom* shows that Hirschfeld's influence also reached Chicago in the 1920s, see Elledge 2023, 27, 42.

160 Holm 1934.

161 *Nový hlas* 10, Oct. 1934, 19: "Der Sekretär Dr. M. Hirschfelds Karl Giese ist erkrankt und konnte daher seinen zugesagten Beitrag 'Kastrierte Biographien' nicht verfassen".

1. The Promenade des Anglais in Nice (France). On the right, the art deco-style Palais de la Méditerranée, designed by the architect Charles Dalmas (1). In early 1934, Magnus Hirschfeld and Karl Giese stayed in the Hotel Westminster (3), 27 Promenade des Anglais, and in the Hôtel de la Méditerranée et de la Côte d'Azur (2) at 25 Promenade des Anglais. The latter was demolished before World War II. On the far left, the well-known Negresco hotel (4). Undated postcard, but presumably 1930s.

INSTITUT DES SCIENCES SEXOLOGIQUES

pour la recherche scientifique des instincts normaux et anormaux et de la constitution psychobiologique

24, AVENUE CHARLES FLOQUET, PARIS (VIIe)
(CHAMP DE MARS)

TÉLÉPHONE : SUFFREN 64-76 ET 64-77

DR MAGNUS HIRSCHFELD
FONDATEUR DE L'INSTITUT DE SEXOLOGIE DE BERLIN
DIRECTEUR DE L'INSTITUT DE SEXOLOGIE A PARIS
PRÉSIDENT DE LA LIGUE MONDIALE
POUR LA
RÉFORME SEXUELLE SUR UNE BASE SCIENTIFIQUE

PARIS, LE 11. April 19

II

keiner Bewegung ausbleibt und dass an diesen inneren Hader,diesen Angriffen unter- und gegeneinander viel mehr gute Bewegungen gescheitert sind,wie an den Argumenten sachlicher Gegner.Ich habe es aus diesem Grunde stets für taktvoller gehalten,meinen Freunden möglichst den Aerger zu ersparen,der aus der Wiedergabe dieser ewigen Vorwürfe hervorgeht.Meist handelt es sich tat-

2. Letterhead of the Paris Institute: "INSTITUTE OF SEXOLOGICAL SCIENCES for the scientific investigation of normal and abnormal instincts and of the psychobiological constitution" (INSTITUT DES SCIENCES SEXOLOGIQUES pour la recherche scientifique des instincts normaux et anormaux et de la constitution psychobiologique). April 1934. University of Sydney Library, Sydney, Norman Haire collection.

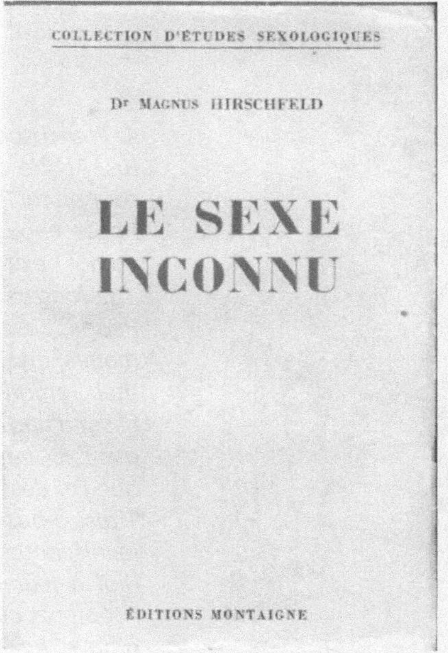

3. Cover of Magnus Hirschfeld's book Le sexe inconnu (The Unknown [Third] Sex), published in 1935.

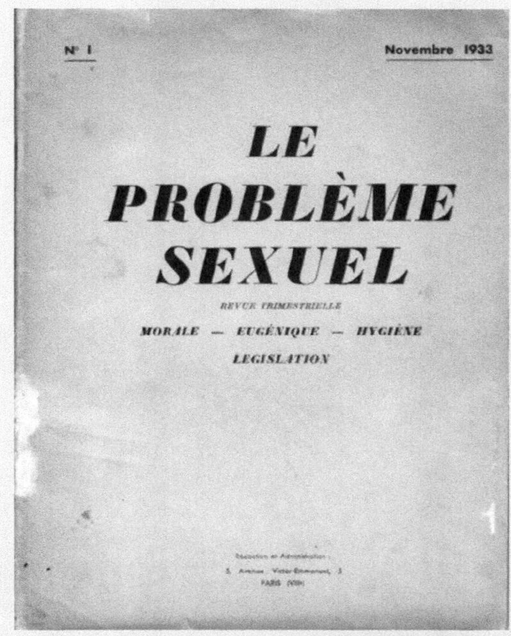

4. Cover page of the first issue of Le problème sexuel, revue trimestrielle, morale, eugénique, hygiène, legislation (The Sexual Problem: A Quarterly Review: Morality, Eugenics, Hygiene, Legislation). November 1933.

5. French advertisement for Perles Titus: At the court of King Pausole (A la cour du roi Pausole), ca. 1934–35: "Me … I have enough with one, and you, Sire, do not hesitate to have 365 wives? – No … as long as I have 'TITUS PEARLS'. Titus Pearls, based on rejuvenating sex hormones, owe their worldwide success to their remarkable action" (Moi … j'en ai assez d'une et vous n'hésitez pas, Sire, à avoir 365 femmes? … Non … du moment que j'ai des "PERLES TITUS". Les Perles Titus, à base d'hormones sexuelles rajeunissantes, doivent leur succès mondial à leur remarquable activité). Les Aventures du roi Pausole was originally a novel by Pierre Louÿs, first published in 1900, whose fictionalized king had 366 women at his disposal in his harem. In 1930, the book was turned into an operetta in Paris. In 1933, a movie came out under the same title.

6. "A villa in Provence where Professor Hirschfeld's sick patients are treated" (Une villa de Provence où sont soignés des malades du professeur Hirschfeld). A man in the picture is holding up a shield saying "be good to abnormal people" (soyez bon pour les anormaux).

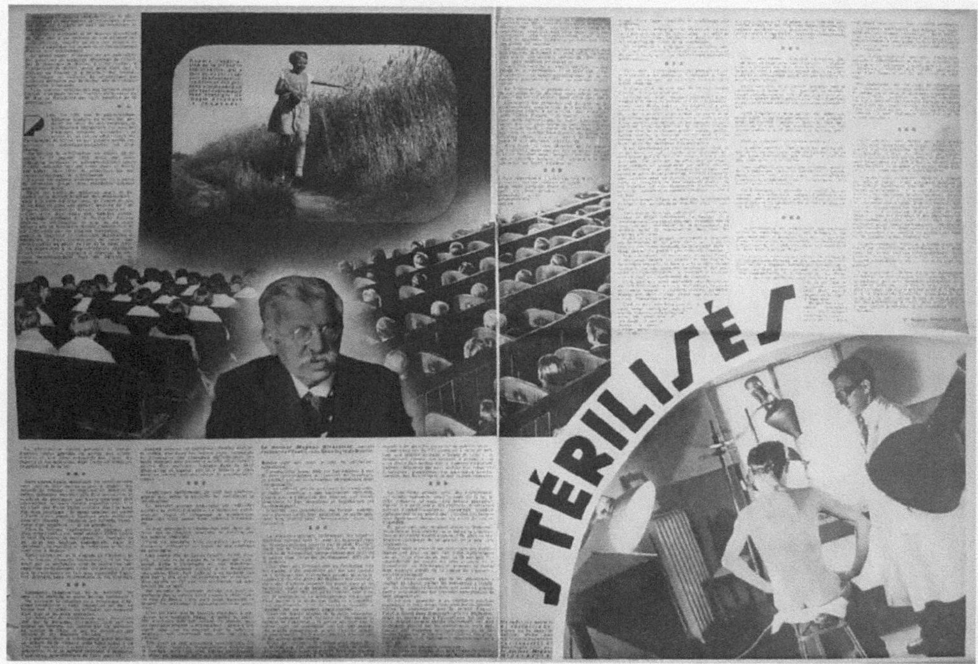

7. *Magnus Hirschfeld's text "Sterilized People" (Stérilisés), which appeared in the popular French magazine Détective on March 1, 1934.*

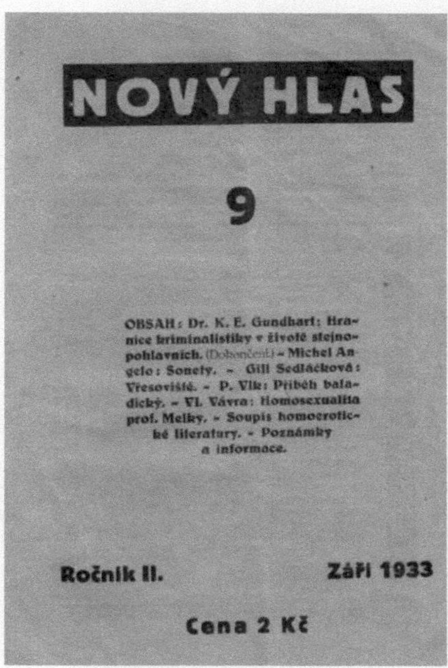

NOVÝ HLAS

9

OBSAH: Dr. K. E. Gundhart: Hranice kriminalistiky v životě stejnopohlavních. (Dokončení.) – Michel Angelo: Sonety. – Gill Sedláčková: Vřesoviště. – P. Vlk: Příběh baladický. – Vl. Vávra: Homosexualita prof. Melky. – Soupis homoerotické literatury. – Poznámky a informace.

Ročník II. Září 1933

Cena 2 Kč

8. *Cover page of the September 1933 issue of the Czechoslovak gay periodical Nový hlas (New Voice).*

SEPTEMBRE 33

LA PATIENCE

L'affaire Dufrenne est une affaire remarquable dans ce sens qu'elle est un cas type où la police est terriblement gênée.

Un personnage important de la cité, à peu près célèbre, riche, qui tient par cent liens à tous les gens en place et au gouvernement, est assassiné dans des conditions qui jettent dans le plus cruel embarras ses proches et ses amis, tous ceux enfin qui ont le souci de faire respecter sa mémoire.

Parmi tant de vertus, le prodigieux animateur de spectacles, le conseiller municipal honnête et avisé, le mécène de tant d'œuvres de bienfaisance avait une tare, un vice, une faiblesse, la paille de cette poutre de métal. Probablement écœuré d'avoir, dans sa vie, regardé professionnellement trop de jambes nues, vu trop de peau féminine à bon marché, scruté trop de cœurs frelatés, il avait accordé un nouveau crédit sentimental aux jeunes gens. Ses familiers, ses employés mêmes connaissaient ses manies et comment, souvent, le soir, il faisait le tour du promenoir de son cinéma, le Palace, pour y découvrir l'éphèbe louche avec lequel il passerait le reste de la soirée.

Un soir de septembre, il arrive comme d'habitude, erre un peu derrière les spectateurs debout, fait un signe à un marin qui, d'ailleurs, l'attendait, et monte avec lui dans son bureau. A minuit, son administrateur le trouve mort, assommé et étouffé par le tapis dans lequel l'assassin l'avait roulé.

Il a presque fallu un an de patientes recherches, depuis le meurtre de Dufrenne, pour que la police, éliminant plus de cent pistes, ne retienne plus que celle de Paul Laborie, réfugié dans le Barrio-Chino.

Paul BRINGUIER.

SEPTEMBRE 34

9. *"September 33–September 34: Patience" (Septembre 33-septembre 34: la patience). Article about the murder of Oscar Dufrenne, appearing in an issue of the magazine Détective. The "patience" in the title alludes to the fact that, a year after the murder, the presumed murderer of Dufrenne, a man disguised as a sailor, had still not been put on trial.*

10. Karl Meier (alias Rolf) in Biel/Bienne (Switzerland). 1938.

Der Kreis EINE MONATSSCHRIFT
Le Cercle REVUE MENSUELLE

Redaktion: Postfach Fraumünster 547 Zürich 22
Rédaction: Case postale Fraumünster 547 Zürich 22
Postcheckkonto: / Compte de chèques postaux
Lesezirkel »Der Kreis«, Zürich VIII 25753

XX. Jahrgang/Année Oktober/Octobre 1952 Nr. 10

11. Cover of the monthly Swiss gay magazine The Circle (Der Kreis/Le Cercle), issue of October 1952 (year 20, issue 10). The magazine was founded in 1932 as Das Freundschaftsbanner (The Friendship Banner) and renamed Der Kreis/Le Cercle in 1943.

BAINS-VOLTAIRE

8. Karl Giese's Paris Bathhouse Affair[1]

PUBLIC INDECENCY IN THE PARISIAN BATHHOUSE, BAINS VOLTAIRE

In May 1948, in the Swiss gay magazine *Der Kreis – Le Cercle*, Kurt Hiller briefly mentioned that Karl Giese had got entangled in a "bathhouse affair" (*Badeanstalts-Affäre*) when he was in France and was expelled as a consequence. "About two years after Hirschfeld died, Karl Giese committed suicide (in Vienna or Brno, the cities where he had alternately stayed, after France expelled him for a bathhouse affair)".[2] More correctly, and as we will see later, Giese committed suicide in Brno in March 1938; Hirschfeld died in May 1935, almost three years earlier. After Giese joined Hirschfeld in Paris, Hirschfeld's *Testament: Heft II* records several times that Giese had problems, without explicitly stating their exact nature.[3] Based on the extant archival sources, mainly found in the Archives de Paris and the Archives nationales in Paris, a clearer picture can be given of the bathhouse incident and its consequences for the fate of Karl Giese and also Magnus Hirschfeld.

On Saturday, April 14 (or possibly Sunday, April 15), 1934, Karl Giese visited a bathhouse named Bains Voltaire, located at 93 Rue de la Roquette, Paris XI.[4] The bathhouse was known to cater to gay men on certain days of the week.[5] The entrance to the bathhouse was located in the inner courtyard of the building housing the address. Today the building is made up of private residences, but one can still see a mosaic with the name of the bathhouse above the main entrance, as well as the artistic motifs – also laid out in mosaic tiles – on the façade next to the entrance [ill. 1].[6]

[1] This chapter is a revised version of Soetaert 2019.

[2] Hiller 1948, 353: "Karl Giese, beging etwa zwei Jahre nach Hirschfeld's Heimgang Selbstmord (in Wien oder in Brünn, den Städten, in denen er sich abwechselnd aufhielt, nachdem Frankreich ihn wegen einer Badeanstalts-Affäre ausgewiesen hatte)".

[3] See Hirschfeld & Dose 2013, f. 83/178: "ein unglückliches Verhängnis" (an unfortunate fate); ibid., f. 84/180: "um einer nichtssagenden Bagatelle" (because of a meaningless trifle); and some references to Giese's expulsion in ibid., f. 87/186: "kurz nach K's. Unverhoffter Abreise" (shortly after K's unexpected departure); ibid., f. 88/188: "ein jähes Ende durch seine Ausweisung ('Expulsion')" (an abrupt end due to his expulsion).

[4] There is some confusion in the available archival sources regarding the exact date of Giese's sexual transgression; however, most sources give the date as April 14, 1934. The court file containing Giese's *jugement* (conviction) mentions April 14, 1934 as the date of the offense. See Archives de Paris, Archives judiciaires, Tribunal correctionnel de la Seine, jugements, 19 au 20 avril 1934, n° 1692, Tribunal de première instance, 10ième chambre, audience publique du jeudi 19/04/1934, cote D1U6 2864. I also found this same April 14 date in the appeal dated June 8, 1934. See Archives de Paris, Archives judiciaires, Cour d'appel de Paris, arrêts correctionnels, 1-15 juin 1934, Jun. 8, 1934, arrêt n° 36.2316, cote D3U9 577. In a letter (dated Jul. 12, 1934) addressed to an unknown man in the French Interior Ministry, Magnus Hirschfeld also mentioned the date of April 14. In another letter (dated Jun. 17, 1934) to Paris police headquarters (?), Hirschfeld anticipated Giese's release from prison three months later, on July 14, 1934. For these two letters, see AN, site de Pierrefitte-sur-Seine, Ministère de l'intérieur, Direction générale de la sûreté nationale (fonds de Moscou), file on Karl Giese, dossier n° 15843, cote 19940448/186. For the sources that say it was Sunday, April 15, 1934, see p. 224, n. 7.

[5] A notice for the bathhouse specifies "Mardi et jeudi pour dames" (Tuesdays and Thursdays for women) in the Parisian *Annuaire et almanach du commerce et de l'industrie* 1934, 1949.

[6] Recent photos of the entrance of the bathhouse (showing the mosaic of the name "Bains-Voltaire") as well as some mosaics inside have been added to two blogs: https://monnouveauparis.wordpress.com/category/passe/, blog entry (dated Dec. 10, 2014) with the following comment: "Quelle ne fut pas ma surprise de découvrir que cet endroit fut un des lieux de consommation homosexuelle gratuits durant la guerre 1940. Que les très nombreuses vespasiennes de Paris vont tourner « à plein » et que les soldats allemands ne seront pas les derniers à les fréquenter" (What a surprise it was for me to discover that this spot was one of the places for free homosexual trysts during the 1940 war, that the many public urinals in Paris ran 'at capacity' and that the German soldiers were not the last ones to make use of them.) See also http://nalouisintheair.blogspot.

Giese had sex in this bathhouse with an unknown man and was arrested by the Paris police for public indecency (*outrage public à la pudeur*) that day, or the next.[7] For this sexual misdemeanor, Giese was given the minimum sentence of three months' imprisonment (the maximum sentence was two years). Starting on April 16, 1934, Giese was imprisoned in Paris's La Santé prison where he would remain two months.[8] On Thursday, April 19, 1934, Giese was actually found guilty of his "crime" by the Criminal Court of the Seine (Tribunal correctionnel de la Seine) in Paris. He also had to pay a fine of 105.15 French francs (the maximum fine was 200 French francs). The French judgment stated: "in the bathhouse [...], a public place[,] Giese committed an act of public indecency by engaging in lewd acts and, in particular, by having his penis sucked by an unknown person".[9] The court added that the minimum sentence of three months was a result of – unspecified – "mitigating circumstances" (*circonstances atténuantes*). Two months later, on June 14, 1934, Giese was transferred to Fresnes prison [ill. 2].[10]

be/2015/03/when-saints-go-machine-dans-mes.html, blog entry (dated Mar. 10, 2015) (both accessed Mar. 12, 2016). In order to discover more about the bathhouse owner, I checked the following index card register: Archives de Paris, Archives judiciaires, Tribunal de commerce de la Seine puis Paris, Registre du Commerce, fichier des enseignes [signposts] 1920–1954, fichier général 1920–1954, boîte "Bains-Bol", cote D34U3 2761. On an index card (dated Feb. 17, 1932), the owner is listed as Pierre Richard Robin (the third being the family name). The bathhouse had previous owners. The oldest index card on the Bains Voltaire dates to December 16, 1922.

7 Only the Parisian police headquarters administration consistently stated that Giese was arrested on Sunday, April 15, 1934; most other sources, as we have seen, give April 14, 1934, as the date of the misdeed and also as the likely date of the arrest in the bathhouse. In a letter (dated Jul. 19 or 29, 1934), the Paris police headquarters wrote: "Le 15 avril 1934, l'Allemand Karl-Otto GIESE fut surpris dans l'établissement de bains" (On April 15, 1934, the German Karl-Otto GIESE was caught in the bathhouse); and: "A Paris depuis le 29 décembre 1933 [this was in reality the date of Giese's arrival in Nice], GIESE a logé du 26 mars au 14 avril 1934, *veille de son arrestation*, avenue Charles-Floquet 24" (emphasis added) (In Paris since December 29, 1933 [this was in reality the date of Giese's arrival in Nice], from March 26 to April 14, 1934, *the day before his arrest*, GIESE stayed at 24 avenue Charles-Floquet) (emphasis added). See AN, site de Pierrefitte-sur-Seine, Ministère de l'intérieur, Direction générale de la sûreté nationale (fonds de Moscou), file on Karl Giese, dossier n° 15843, cote 19940448/186. I noticed that a substantial amount of information on Giese and Hirschfeld in other Paris police archival documents was factually incorrect. The *registre d'écrou* (prison register) in Fresnes says that Giese was indeed released on July 15, 1934, and this could be further evidence that he was arrested and imprisoned on April 15, 1934. See Archives départementales du Val-de-Marne, Créteil, archives judiciaires et notariales, Prisons, Etablissement de Fresnes, Prison des hommes: registres d'écrou (1898–1940), n° 98, 1934, 29 mai-7 juillet, section Allemagne, entry Karl Giese (dated Jun. 14, 1934), 7022, cote 2Y5 277. I thank Éric Jingeaux (Archives départementales du Val-de-Marne, Créteil) for sending me a digital scan of the relevant pages from the prison register in April 2013. A possible explanation for the confusion regarding the exact date of Giese's "crime" lies in the sequence of events. The misdeed may indeed have taken place on April 14, with Giese possibly only arrested the next day. However, as we will see in a moment, this would appear to contradict the usual procedure, in which bathhouse visitors were observed and arrested on the same day.

8 Archives de Paris, fonds des établissements pénitentiaires, prison de la Santé, registres d'écrou, registre n° 272, entry Karl Giese (dated Apr. 16, 1934), f. 550, cote D2Y14 268.

9 Archives de Paris, archives judiciaires, Tribunal correctionnel de la Seine, jugements, 19 au 20 avril 1934, n° 1692, Tribunal de première instance, 10ième chambre, audience publique du jeudi 19/04/1934, cote D1U6 2864: "dans l'établissement de bains [...], lieu public[,] Giese a commis un outrage public à la pudeur en se livrant à des actes obscènes et notamment en se faisant succer la verge par un inconnu".

10 Archives départementales du Val-de-Marne, Créteil, archives judiciaires et notariales, Prisons, Etablissement de Fresnes, Prison des hommes: registres d'écrou (1898–1940), n° 98, 1934, 29 mai-7 juillet, section Allemagne, entry Karl Giese (dated Jun. 14, 1934), n° 7022, cote 2Y5 277. This document contains two black-ink fingerprints of Giese, likely taken at his arrival (or departure ?) from Fresnes prison. For some additional information on both prisons, see also Hirschfeld & Dose 2013, f. 84/180 n. 457. In Hirschfeld's Ministry of the Interior file there is a small handwritten note referring to a certain Paul de Rémusat, with the cryptic addition "secrétaire géneral du comité Français", who paid a visit (or telephoned) on June 15, 1934. I was not able to determine exactly who this was, nor the purpose for the visit, nor the identity of the "comité Français". However, since Giese had been transferred the day before from La Santé to Fresnes, it is possible that the visit was related to this transfer. For more information on the French Rémusat family, possibly involved in this case, see http://fr.wikipedia.org/wiki/Famille_R%C3%A9musat (accessed Jun. 24, 2021). The note is in AN, site de Pierrefitte-sur-Seine, Ministère de l'intérieur, Direction de la Sûreté Géné-

An attempt to appeal the verdict at the Parisian Appeals Court (Cour d'Appel), on June 8, 1934, failed.[11] Giese was released from Fresnes on July 15, 1934.[12] This means that he served his whole prison sentence of three months. These are the summary facts of Giese's Parisian bathhouse affair. Yet this bathhouse affair did not turn out to be a mere "trifle" (*bagatelle*), as Hirschfeld dubbed it in *Testament: Heft II*.[13]

CURIOUS PARADOX

That Karl Giese was convicted in a country known for its relative leniency regarding homosexuality is rather paradoxical. According to Adelheid Schulz, Hirschfeld's housekeeper in the Berlin Institute, Giese had been imprisoned once in Germany for (forbidden) homosexual conduct and so must have fallen foul of the infamous German paragraph 175 of the German Criminal Code (Strafgesetzbuch, StGB).[14] But homosexuality as such was not prosecuted in France since Napoleon – or rather his justice minister, Cambacérès – decriminalized it.

However, the French Criminal Code contains three principal sexual offences under which gay men were (and can still be) prosecuted.[15] Article 331, "indecent assault" (*attentats à la pudeur*), relates to the violent or nonviolent sexual assault of minors. Article 334, "incitement of minors to debauchery" (*excitation des mineurs à la débauche*) mainly targets pimps luring minors into male prostitution. The most "effective", however, in terms of the number of convictions, is Article 330, "public indecency" (*outrage public à la pudeur*). This article is mainly focused on (gay) sex in public places, a centuries-old gay predilection. The question of whether (gay) sex in a bathhouse is public or not (and the relationship between gay sex, the law and privacy in general) is of course a judicial discussion with a long history in many countries, and which continues to linger. Although the Bains Voltaire was a private business, in 1934 it was considered a public place and the Paris police "ascertained" (*a constaté*) that a "public indecency" was committed. Indeed, the text of the judgment describes the bathhouse explicitly as a "public place" (*lieu public*).[16]

rale, Service central des cartes d'identité d'étrangers, file Magnus Hirschfeld, file n° 210400, cote 19940506/151.

[11] Archives de Paris, Paris, archives judiciaires, Cour d'appel de Paris, arrêts correctionnels, 1–15 juin 1934, Jun. 8, 1934, arrêt n° 36.2316, cote D3U9 577. Giese's lawyer was a woman or man named Massot (at 66 Boulevard St-Michel in Paris). In *Testament: Heft II*, Hirschfeld also indirectly gave the trial day at the Appeals Court: "Am Verhandlungstage von K. G. wurde er [Hans-Adalbert von Maltzahn (1894–1934), a good friend of Hirschfeld] begraben" (On the day of K. G.'s trial, he [Hans-Adalbert von Maltzahn (1894–1934), a good friend of Hirschfeld] was buried) (Hirschfeld & Dose, 2013, f. 85/182, n. 469–70). Von Maltzahn died on June 4, 1934 and was buried two days later. Most likely, Hirschfeld got the days confused, since several archival sources confirm June 8, 1934 as the date of the court session at the Appeals Court. We need to add – as likely explaining the mistake – that Hirschfeld wrote this at the beginning of December 1934, six months after the events took place. See Hirschfeld & Dose 2013, f. 82/176; see also Hirschfeld, Jun. 10–11, 1934. For more biographical information on von Maltzahn, see Seuss 2022.

[12] Archives départementales du Val-de-Marne, Créteil, archives judiciaires et notariales, Prisons, Etablissement de Fresnes, Prison des hommes: registres d'écrou (1898–1940), n° 98, 1934, 29 mai-7 juillet, section Allemagne, entry (dated Jun. 14, 1934) Karl Giese, n° 7022, cote 2Y5 277.

[13] Hirschfeld & Dose 2013, f. 84/180: "einer nichtssagenden Bagatelle" (a meaningless trifle).

[14] Adelheid Schulz seems to have been well-informed on the matter, since she also remembered that Giese had been imprisoned for homosexual conduct a second time when abroad, although she could not remember if this was in France or in Czechoslovakia (Schulz 2001, 74, 94). On the other hand, in a letter (dated Jul. 12, 1934) to an unknown man in the French Interior Ministry, Magnus Hirschfeld stated that Giese had never before been convicted. See AN, site de Pierrefitte-sur-Seine, Ministère de l'intérieur, Direction générale de la sûreté nationale (fonds de Moscou), file on Karl Giese, dossier n° 15843, cote 19940448/186.

[15] For more detailed information on French law and the issue of homosexuality, see Jackson 2009, 27–28; and especially Peniston 2004, 13–22.

[16] Archives de Paris, Paris, archives judiciaires, Tribunal correctionnel de la Seine, jugements, 19 au 20 avril 1934, n° 1692, Tribunal de première instance, 10ième chambre, audience publique du jeudi 19/04/1934, cote D1U6 2864.

These difficult (and clearly debatable) entanglements between state authorities exercising their authority (by defining a crime and punishing it), and the private intimacies of daily life, are visible in how Giese was arrested in the bathhouse. It needs to be said, firstly, that Giese was likely a victim of a roundup (or "*rafle*" as it is still called in French) of the kind quite commonly organized by the vice squad (*brigade mondaine*), a department of the Paris police located at 36 quai des Orfèvres, Paris I.[17] This police department handled illicit sex, prostitutes and pimps (*proxénétisme*), drugs and gambling. It was established in 1901 and then known as Police des moeurs. After World War I, it was renamed Brigade mondaine.[18] In the years 1910–40, this police department was clearly aware there were certain bathhouses (dubbed "vaps", short for "bains à vapeur" or steam baths) in Paris where gay men gathered.

It seems now that, initially, the Paris police did not have a real procedural solution for arresting people committing a sexual transgression in a bathhouse. A 1909 police report on the Bains Voltaire makes it clear that police officers stripping naked and mingling with the guests was not an option: "In order to carry out surveillance in the reported baths, it is necessary for the inspectors to act like ordinary customers, that is to say, to move about in the establishment entirely naked, as is the custom. I don't think I can ask them to make an arrest in flagrante delicto this way. On the other hand, if they wait until the individuals observed are dressed, they leave themselves open to the reproach of not having caught them in the act. Under these conditions, I think it is better not to intervene".[19]

But, after World War I, these reservations were set aside and a procedure to observe and arrest people in a bathhouse was apparently worked out. In a memoir about his work for the Brigade mondaine in the 1930s, Louis Métra described a roundup in a gay bathhouse.[20] He stated clearly that the members of the brigade, moving around in the bathhouse, were as naked as the guests so as to be able to observe what was going on. "Our intrusion into this aquatic fairyland went unnoticed because we took care to stagger our arrivals. Completely unclothed, our staff mingled with the bathers".[21] The goal was to observe so as to be able to make concrete accusations. "We had been given instructions to establish certain facts, note down the details from memory, so as to identify the perpetrators in relation to a procedure to be drawn up later. When at the hour H, the commissioner [Adolphe] Caron burst into the establishment, there was a great deal of panic among all these depraved people. To restore order, we had to employ fierce energy. Without my baton-wielding colleague, I believe that many of these naked men would have fled into the street, undressed as they were. Finally, all

[17] Girardet, Aug., 24, 1933, 12–13. The address of 36 quai des Orfèvres, the police department, is iconic in France. Two movies took their titles from the (in) famous address, one from 1947, *Quai des Orfèvres* (dir. Henri-Georges Clouzot), and the other from 2004, *36, quai des Orfèvres* (dir. Olivier Marchal).

[18] Willemin 2009, 51, 55. Today, the department is known as the Brigade des stupéfiants et du proxénétisme.

[19] Archives de la Préfecture de Police de Paris, Paris, report (dated Sep. 1, 1909) of the Brigade Mobile, dossier Bains Voltaire, 163.457 M. R., cote JC 96: "Pour exercer une surveillance dans les bains signalés, il est nécessaire que les inspecteurs s'y rendent ainsi que des clients ordinaires, c'est-à-dire qu'ils circulent dans l'établissement entièrement nus, comme c'est la coutume. Je ne crois pas pouvoir leur demander d'opérer, dans ce costume, une arrestation en flagrant délit. D'autre part, s'ils attendent que les individus observés par eux soient rhabillés[,] ils s'exposent au reproche de ne pas les avoir pris sur le fait. Dans ces conditions, j'estime qu'il est préférable de ne pas intervenir".

[20] Louis Métra, or rather his ghost writer René Delpêche, does not give a specific date for this roundup but, judging from Métra's career, it must have taken place somewhere between 1930 and 1935 (Delpêche 1955, 232–36; 10). The raid caused a sensation in the press. It's not at all certain that this was, as Métra/Delpêche claims, the very first such raid conducted by the brigade in a gay bathhouse in the French capital.

[21] Delpêche 1955, 233: "Notre intrusion dans cette fééerie [*sic*: féerie] des eaux était passée inaperçue car nous avions pris soin d'échelonner nos arrivées. Complètement dénudé, notre effectif se mêlait aux baigneurs". The bathhouse mentioned was located in the quartier des Ternes, Paris VII.

was restored to order and we returned at midnight to the quai des Orfèvres with more than seventy bathers".[22]

The inspectors' practice of going naked into the bathhouses persisted. When, in 1933, René Girardet, a journalist for the popular magazine *Détective*, wanted to write a series of six articles about the different activities of the *brigade mondaine*, the brigade proposed that he join them and have a look at a gay bathhouse. "Concerning this point, it was enough to know that there were steam baths in the capital where, naked as Adam, abnormal people indulged all of their physical fantasies".[23] The journalist quickly declined the invitation when he heard what went on in such places: "I was given in this regard a number of details that were so sickening that I would not even dare to write them in Latin. I no longer had the slightest desire to go and see for myself. Fortunately, you do not have to commit a crime to report on convicts, nor do you have to be guillotined to report on a capital execution, otherwise the profession of journalism would become, let's admit it, impossible".[24] A "live" and, in all probability, naked visit to a gay bathhouse was clearly a bridge too far for the journalist. Having vented his homophobic revulsion by linking the acts taking place there to capital offences – and thereby implicitly confirming his own (sexual) normality – the journalist added he would confine himself to a few raids on "more regular" gay and lesbian bars.[25] In these place, it would be easier to catch a few "samples" (*échantillons*) in the company of the vice squad, as if the "pederasts" were exotic insects to be pinned to a board.[26] But the mention of "samples" implicitly indicated that the police would never completely eradicate vice, and that their work was, after all, only a drop of water on a hot plate. It also seems that these roundups were conducted, at least in 1933, with a relatively small number of police – Girardet's article mentions eight – and without making much noise or causing much disruption in the neighborhood. The time of large-scale raids in which whole streets were closed off was no more.[27]

In the Archives de la Préfecture de Police in Paris, there is an April 1935 police report describing in detail exactly what went on in the different rooms of the Bains Voltaire:

[22] Delpêche 1955, 235: "La consigne qu'on nous avait donnée était de nous attacher à constater des faits certains, d'en noter le détail de mémoire, pour pouvoir à coup sûr reconnaître leurs auteurs en vue de la procédure à dresser ultérieurement. Lorsqu'à l'heure H, le commissaire [Adolphe] Caron fit irruption dans l'établissement, ce fut un bel affolement chez tous ces dépravés. Pour rétablir l'ordre, il nous fallut déployer une énergie farouche. Sans mon collègue au baton [*sic*, bâton], je crois bien que bon nombre de ces hommes nus se seraient enfuis dans la rue, ainsi dévêtus. Enfin, tout rentra dans l'ordre et c'est avec plus de soixante-dix baigneurs que nous sommes revenus à minuit quai des Orfèvres".

[23] Girardet, Aug. 24, 1933, 13: "Il m'a suffit sur ce point de savoir qu'il existait dans la capitale des bains de vapeurs où, dans la tenue d'Adam, des anormaux se livraient à toutes leurs fantaisies physiques".

[24] Girardet, Aug. 24, 1933, 13: "On m'a donné à cet égard un certain nombre de détails tellement écoeurants que je n'oserais même pas les écrire en latin, et que je n'ai plus eu la moindre envie d'aller me rendre compte d'aussi près. On n'est heureusement pas obligé de commettre un crime pour faire un reportage sur les forçats, ni d'être guillotiné pour raconter une exécution capitale, sinon le métier de journaliste deviendrait impossible, avouez-le".

[25] Girardet, Aug. 31, 1933, 12: "J'ai préféré borner ma curiosité à visiter quelques boîtes où la brigade mondaine sait pouvoir trouver, quand elle y opère une descente, les éléments des délits poursuivis par la loi" (I preferred to limit my curiosity to visiting a few clubs where the vice squad knows it can find, when it raids them, the elements of the offences prosecuted by the law).

[26] Girardet, Aug. 24, 1933, 12: "les invertis dont on va rafler quelques échantillons" (the inverts of which we are going to round up a few samples).

[27] Girardet, Aug. 31, 1933, 13: "Depuis des années, il n'y a plus de rafles à grand déploiement de forces policières. [...] On a modernisé, heureusement, cette méthode. Au lieu du grand coup de filet, on pêche comme à la ligne, peut-on dire, pièce par pièce. Un commissaire, quelques inspecteurs. Pas de cris. Pas de discussions. Mais une ruelle voisine abrite une camionnette qui s'emplit progressivement" (For years now, there have been no more raids using a large-scale deployment of police forces. [...] Fortunately, this method has been modernized. Instead of a big net, we fish by line, so to speak, piece by piece. A commissioner, a few inspectors. No shouting. No discussions. But a nearby alley contains a van that is gradually filling up).

> Witness, the bath located at n° 93, rue de la Roquette, which includes a sweat room, a shower room and a steam room.
>
> The excessive heat that reigns in the first room does not allow the customers to stay long. They gather in the shower room to wait for the steam room to open.
> It is then a rush into this room, in the middle of which one finds benches where the amateurs strike the most lascivious poses.
> As soon as the dimly lit room is filled with steam, unheard-of scenes of debauchery are committed: acts of sodomy, masturbation, sucking, obscene touching ... And for half an hour, willing actors and spectators, entangled, live in an unbreathable atmosphere, but satisfy their vices without restraint.
>
> When the half hour is over, the bathing boy, who never intervenes in the session, carefully closes the door, after having ushered out the customers, who then spill into the shower room or go to the bar that is part of the establishment.[28]

According to the verdict of the Criminal Court of the Seine, Giese had "committed public indecency by engaging in obscene acts and in particular by having his penis sucked by an unknown person".[29] So, Giese's being fellated by an unidentified man in the Bains Voltaire must have been observed by a naked vice squad policeman, whose testimony must have served as the basis for Giese's arrest. However, it remains unclear how exactly the arrest took place and if Giese was in fact taken in a police car to the Quai des Orfèvres on the day of his misdemeanor or if, given the already mentioned confusion in the sources regarding the exact date of Giese's "offense", he was arrested the next day.[30]

The sexual crime Giese committed was considered so serious by the French authorities that he was expelled from the country on the orders of the Minister of the Interior in the autumn of 1934. French law allowed the expulsion of any foreigner who committed a crime. The ministerial decision, called an *arrêté*, was issued on August 28, 1934; however, Giese and Hirschfeld were only informed of the decision

[28] Archives de la Préfecture de police, Paris, Rapports divers concernant les Pédérastes, report on "Bains Voltaire", report (dated Apr. 1, 1935), sign. BA 1690, f. 1: "Témoin, le bain sis au N° 93 de la rue de la Roquette, qui comprend une salle de sudation, une salle de douches et une salle de vapeur. La chaleur excessive qui règne dans la première pièce ne permet pas un séjour prolongé aux clients. Ils se rassemblent dans la salle de douches en attendant que s'ouvre la chambre de vapeur. C'est alors une ruée dans ce local, au milieu duquel s'élèvent des gradins où les amateurs prennent les poseslesles [*sic*, poses les] plus lascives. Dès que la salle, peu éclairée, est remplie de vapeur, des scènes inouies de débauche se consomment: actes de sodomie, masturbation, succion, attouchements obscènes ... Et pendant une demi-heure, acteurs et spectateurs complaisants, enchevêtrés, vivent dans une atmosphère irrespirable, mais satisfont leurs vices sans aucune retenue. La demi-heure écoulée, le garçon de bain, qui n'intervient jamais pendant la séance, ferme soigneusement la porte, après avoir fait sortir les clients qui se répandent dans la salle de douches ou se rendent dans le débit dépendant de l'établissement". A collaborator at the Archives de la Préfecture de Police told me that there may possibly be other police files on other bathhouse raids from the 1930s but claimed these documents were not yet inventorized. I am not sure how reliable this remark is.

[29] Archives de Paris, Paris, Archives judiciaires, Tribunal correctionnel de la Seine, jugements, 19 au 20 avril 1934, n° 1692, Tribunal de première instance, 10ième chambre, audience publique du jeudi 19/04/1934, cote D1U6 2864: "commis un outrage public à la pudeur en se livrant à des actes obscènes et notamment en se faisant sucer la verge par un inconnu".

[30] Cf. Girardet, Aug. 31, 1933, 12: "Jusque dans les bars spéciaux et les hôtels, la 'Secrète' [brigade mondaine] pourchasse les invertis qui, cueillis par les cars de la police, sont amenés à la P. J. [Police Judiciaire] où l'on consulte les sommiers pour savoir s'ils ont déjà commis des délits" (Even into the special bars and hotels, the 'Secrète' [vice squad] chases the inverts who, picked up by police buses, are taken to the P. J. [Judicial Police] where they consult the records to see if they have already committed crimes).

[31] One finds Giese's name in an official list of people expelled published on a monthly basis by the French Interior Ministry: "245. GIÉSÉ [*sic*] *(Karl)*, né à Berlin (Allemagne), le 18-10-1898, fils de Hermann et de Noac [*sic*] Léonie. Signalement: taille 1 m. 74 c.[entimètres], cheveux châtain moyen, sourcils arqués, barbe châtain foncé, yeux azuré clair, front vertical, grand [*sic*: word missing], nez rectiligne, bouche grande, visage allongé. Expulsé par arrêté ministériel du 28-8-1934. Notifié" (245. GIÉSÉ [*sic*] [Karl], born in Berlin [Germany], on 18-10-1898, son

– at least officially – on October 22, 1934.[31] The date of the notification is also indirectly confirmed by a letter that Hirschfeld wrote to the Minister of the Interior on the following day, October 23, 1934, obviously trying to reverse the fatal decision.[32]

ATTEMPTS TO STOP GIESE'S PENDING EXPULSION

Magnus Hirschfeld tried everything he could to prevent Giese from being expelled.[33] He wrote at least three rather moving letters to the French authorities that have survived in the Archives nationales in Paris.[34] These letters allow us to reconstruct a bit more precisely what exactly happened in the summer of 1934. But they also raise new issues and, more importantly, further questions about the exact role of the French authorities in the Giese bathhouse affair and about the effect of this affair on Hirschfeld and his stay in France.

On June 17, 1934, Hirschfeld wrote a first, typed and rather dramatic letter (on WLSR letterhead), addressed to "*Messieurs*" (Gentlemen, in the plural), where he asked them "to refrain from expelling Giese".[35] This indicates that Hirschfeld was already aware early on that expulsion would be the logical outcome of Giese's offense after his release from prison. In this letter, Hirschfeld resorted to all kinds of offers and justifications to persuade his addressees: he would later donate a large part of his collection to the Bibliothèque Nationale; he gave his assurance that Giese would never again do anything of the kind; he stressed that, in the 1920s, the French embassy in Berlin had recommended a visit to the Berlin Institute to many people; he asked if Giese could be expelled from Paris only, etc.[36]

Although we know that Giese was eventually expelled, things did not at first look so bleak. Sometime in June 1934, Hirschfeld was in contact with someone inside the French Ministry of the Interior who told Hirschfeld that there was a good chance that Giese would not be expelled. We can infer this from a letter of July 12, 1934, sent by Hirschfeld to this person.[37] In the letter, Hirschfeld expressed his gratitude for

of Hermann and Noac [*sic*] Léonie. Description: height 1 m. 74 c.[entimeters], medium brown hair, arched eyebrows, dark brown beard, light azure eyes, vertical forehead, large [*sic*: word missing], straight nose, large mouth, elongated face. Expelled by ministerial order of 28-8-1934. Notified). See AN, site de Pierrefitte-sur-Seine, Ministère de l'intérieur, direction de la Sûreté générale (2ième Bureau), Etat signalétique des étrangers expulsés de France, nouvelle série, n° 727, novembre 1934, n° 245, p. 21, cote F/7/14657. Giese's Nice police file also contains a card bearing the name "Giésé Charles [*sic*]", mentioning his expulsion with the numbers "727-245", clearly corresponding to the numbers given in the above description. See ADAM, Nice, Archives administratives de 1940 à nos jours, Direction départementale de la sécurité publique des Alpes-Maritimes, Sûreté départementale, unité technique d'aide à l'enquête (caserne Auvare), file Karl Giese, file n° 104801, cote 1440W 0236.

32 The date is also confirmed on the front page of the folder of Giese's Interior Ministry file, which says "notifié 22-10-1934 Paris" (notified 22-10-1934 Paris). Finally, inside the same file there is a delivery confirmation for the *arrêté d'expulsion* (expulsion decision) (dated Nov. 6, 1934) from the Prefect of Police to the Sûreté Générale. See AN, site de Pierrefitte-sur-Seine, Ministère de l'intérieur, Direction générale de la sûreté nationale (fonds de Moscou), file Karl Giese, dossier n° 15843, cote 19940448/186.

33 Hirschfeld also mentioned his efforts in this regard in *Testament: Heft II*: "der Unmöglichkeit [...], einen Widerruf von Karls Ausweisung trotz aller Mühen zu erreichen" (the impossibility [...] to obtain a revocation of Karl's expulsion, despite all efforts) (Hirschfeld & Dose 2013, f. 84-85/180-181).

34 AN, site de Pierrefitte-sur-Seine, Ministère de l'intérieur, Direction générale de la sûreté nationale (fonds de Moscou), file on Karl Giese, dossier n° 15843, cote 19940448/186.

35 AN, site de Pierrefitte-sur-Seine, Ministère de l'intérieur, Direction générale de la sûreté nationale (fonds de Moscou), file on Karl Giese, dossier n° 15843, letter (dated Jan. 17, 1934) from Magnus Hirschfeld to police headquarters (?), cote 19940448/186: "de vous abstenir de l'expulsion de Giese".

36 Ibid.: "Recommandé par l'ambassade de France, pendant les années de 19 19 [*sic*] jusqu'à l'année 19 32 [*sic*] presque toutes les personnalités prominentes qui étaient en passage à Berlin rendaient visite à l'archive dirigé par GIESE" (On the recommendation of the French embassy, from 1919 to 1932, almost all prominent personalities who were in Berlin visited the archive directed by Giese).

37 Ibid. In the same letter, Hirschfeld also thanked the collaborator from the Ministry of the Interior for his letter of June 20, 1934. There is no copy of this letter in the archival file.

him (or her) wanting to help Hirschfeld and Giese, and underlined once again the importance of Giese to continue his work and re-establish his sexological collection in France. The letter clearly shows Hirschfeld trying to win good will from the French authorities by focusing on the cultural asset of his (surviving) sexological collection. We can also see Hirschfeld repeating his already mentioned intention to donate his remaining sexology collection to the French state at some point, and that Hirschfeld was also working out plans for a new sexological collection in cooperation with the French government: "We could still acquire the Vienna Sexological Encyclopedia we mentioned during our last visit".[38] Sometime before writing this letter, Hirschfeld had clearly visited the unidentified person working inside the Ministry of the Interior. During the visit, the latter asked Hirschfeld to send another reminder of Giese's case on July 16, 1934, the day after Giese's release from prison. In the same letter, Hirschfeld also announced he would make so bold as to visit the office of the collaborator in the Ministry of the Interior in person on that day. Hirschfeld expressed the hope that, when he would stop by again, he would obtain the final confirmation that Giese would not be expelled. It is not known if Hirschfeld actually made this visit but, one way or the other, Hirschfeld must have been told – by this same person? – that the decision about Giese's fate really lay in the hands of the Paris police headquarters.

It is possible that Hirschfeld's presumed second visit was what provoked the Ministry of the Interior to send a letter to the Prefect of Police (Préfet de Police) on July 21, 1934, that is, almost a week after Giese's release. But it was also common practice for the Ministry of the Interior to order a file from the police headquarters on a person they planned to expel.[39] The letter asked the Prefect of Police to send "as soon as possible" all the information they had on Giese and his behavior. On July 29, 1934, the Prefect of Police sent a letter in reply and added a small file on Giese. In this letter, the Prefect of Police – or rather his administration – recommended expelling Giese.[40] So it looks like the Paris Prefect of Police decided Giese's fate even though, according to the law, the police headquarters operated under the Ministry of the Interior. In his study of the police's control of immigrants in interwar Paris, Clifford Rosenberg concludes that it was the Paris police headquarters that functioned as the steadier authority, when compared to the "Third Republic's notorious ministerial instability".[41] The official ministerial decision (*arrêté*), which confirmed Giese's ex-

[38] Ibid.: "Nous pouvions encore aquérir [*sic*: acquérir] l'Encyclopédie sexologique de Vienne dont nous avons parlé durant notre dernière visite".

[39] Rosenberg 2006, 88.

[40] AN, site de Pierrefitte-sur-Seine, Ministère de l'intérieur, Direction générale de la sûreté nationale (fonds de Moscou), file on Karl Giese, dossier n° 15843, letter (dated Jul. 19 or 29, 1934) from Prefect of Police to the Minister of the Interior, cote 19940448/186. The illegible date of the Prefect of Police's letter has some consequences. Likely, the date is July 29, 1934 since the ministry's letter asking for extra information on Giese's case was mailed on July 21, 1934. But if the date on the police headquarters letter is July 19, 1934, then the Prefect of Police's decision to write was simply motivated by Giese's prison release four days earlier, on July 15, 1934. If so, then it was *not* prompted by the letter sent by the Ministry of the Interior on July 21, 1934. If so, this would be further evidence that the Prefect of Police – and not the Minister of the Interior – was indeed the first and primary decision maker in this case. In the Fresnes *livre d'écrou* (prison register), one reads in addition that Giese's "dossier d'expulsion" (expulsion file) was sent on June 15, 1934 – one month before Giese's release – to the Prefect of Police. See Archives départementales du Val-de-Marne, Créteil, archives judiciaires et notariales, Prisons, Etablissement de Fresnes, Prison des hommes: registres d'écrou (1898–1940), n° 98, 1934, 29 mai–7 juillet, section Allemagne, entry Karl Giese dated Jun. 14, 1934, 7022, cote 2Y5 277. Another document, also filled out in Fresnes Prison on June 15, 1934, further indicates that Giese's expulsion was inevitable. See AN, site de Pierrefitte-sur-Seine, Ministère de l'intérieur, Direction générale de la sûreté nationale (fonds de Moscou), file on Karl Giese, dossier n° 15843, cote 19940448/186, Prisons de Fresnes, étrangers détenus passibles d'expulsion, notice individuelle Karl Giésé [*sic*].

[41] The February 6, 1934, riots in Paris, in the wake of the Stavisky affair, were also inspired by the firing of the right-wing Prefect of Police (Préfet de Police), Jean Chiappe (1878–1940). An all-new government of national unity, led by Gaston Doumergue, which was to last only nine months, also brought, in February 1934, a new left-wing Minister of the Interior, Albert Sarraut (1872–1962). A month before Giese

pulsion, mentioned that the Minister of the Interior had made the decision "on the proposal of the Prefect of Police" (*sur la proposition du Préfet de Police*). In the Prefect of Police's July 1934 cover letter, the events in the bathhouse were raised as the main and "obvious" reason why Giese had to be expelled: "Karl-Otto Giese was caught in the bathing facility of 93 rue Roquette, as he *incited* the obscene practices of another bather. [...] Since this foreigner has proved to be clearly immoral, I have the honor, on the occasion of his conviction, to propose his expulsion" (emphasis added).[42]

Florence Tamagne has shown that a generally anti-vice, and specifically anti-homosexual, policy was implemented by Jean Chiappe, the Prefect of Police, in the years before Giese's misstep. She has also shown that the murder of the French theater director Oscar Dufrenne (1875–1933) – on which Giese, as we have seen, had written – and the extensive publicity of Dufrenne's homosexual life in the press, afterwards, only exacerbated this hostile, homophobic atmosphere.[43] Chiappe's successor, Roger Langeron, continued this policy and decided Giese's fate accordingly [ill. 3].

Hirschfeld's third and final letter to the French authorities, dated October 23, 1934, trying to prevent Giese's expulsion, was written the day after he and Giese were officially informed that Giese had to leave the country. This time, the letter was directly addressed to "the Minister of the Interior" (*Monsieur le Ministre de l'Intérieur*), Albert Sarraut. Even though Hirschfeld indicated some understanding of the authorities' strict stance towards "foreigners who have committed a crime" (*les étrangers ayant commis un délit*), he again pleaded for an exception to be made in the case of Giese. On the handwritten, one-page-long letter, another person – likely someone in the Ministry of the Interior – added in blue fountain ink: "Classified as undesirable" (*Classé indésirable*). Although Rosenberg's study of interwar French immigrant policy makes it clear that, in general, the different police units and the French authorities were *not all* xenophobic right-wingers, it also makes it clear, nevertheless, that police headquarters had a real admiration for Nazi Germany.[44] Another unfriendly added handwritten comment to the same letter says: "If he can't go to Germany, let him go somewhere else! [ill. 4]"[45] Hirschfeld's repeated appeal that Giese was a victim of the German National Socialist authorities, and that it was impossible for him to return to Germany, must have fallen on deaf ears.

THE ROLE OF ANDRÉ GIDE

In despair, Hirschfeld also appealed to the French literary figure and cultural authority André Gide (1869–1951), hoping that the latter could somehow intervene to stop the expulsion of Giese. In a letter, dated September 24, 1934, held in the Fondation Catherine Gide in Paris, Hirschfeld tried to settle an appointment with André Gide.[46] In this letter, Hirschfeld does not mention Giese but instead the

got in trouble, a new Prefect of Police, Roger Langeron (1882–1966), was appointed. Albert Sarraut would not last longer than the Doumergue government but Langeron would keep his post for seven years ... and, in that time, tried to take seriously the authority of twelve different Ministers of the Interior. In 1940, Langeron was replaced by the pro-German Jean Chiappe. See Rosenberg 2006, 87; and http://www.sfhp.fr/index.php?post/2009/05/17/Notice-biographique-Roger-LANGERON (accessed May 17, 2016).

42 AN, site de Pierrefitte-sur-Seine, Ministère de l'intérieur, Direction générale de la sûreté nationale (fonds de Moscou), file on Karl Giese, dossier n° 15843, cote 19940448/186, letter (dated Jul. 19 or 29, 1934) from the Prefect of Police to the Ministry of the Interior: "Karl-Otto GIESE fut surpris dans l'établissement de bains de la rue Roquette 93, alors qu'il *provoquait* les pratiques obscènes d'un autre baigneur. [...] Puisque cet étranger a fait preuve d'une immoralité évidente, j'ai l'honneur, à l'occasion de sa condamnation, de vous proposer son expulsion" (emphasis added).

43 Tamagne 2017, 181–94, 237–38.

44 Rosenberg 2006, 81 n. 9.

45 "S'il ne peut aller en Allemagne[,] qu'il se rende ailleurs!" I thank Kevin Dubout for assisting me in correctly reading the handwriting. See email (dated Jul. 23, 2019) from Kevin Dubout to the author.

46 Fondation Catherine Gide, Paris, letter (dated Sep 24, 1934) from Magnus Hirschfeld to André Gide, cote gamma 598(1). The letter is reproduced in Foucart 1986, 42–43.

problems in Russia regarding the changed attitude towards homosexuality there, as reported to Hirschfeld by his Russian friends.[47] Because of Gide's initial sympathy for Communist ideas and the Soviet Union, and of course because of Gide's own homosexuality, Hirschfeld deemed it useful to go and talk to the French writer.[48] In the letter, Hirschfeld recalled that Gide visited the Institute in Berlin and perhaps remembered meeting Giese then.[49]

Hirschfeld likely visited Gide on October 13, 1934, since that is the date of Gide's signature in Hirschfeld's guestbook.[50] If Giese, Hirschfeld and Li Shiu Tong indeed visited Gide, we may presume that Hirschfeld also brought up Giese's case and likely inquired if Gide, a national cultural authority, would intervene for Giese.[51] Hirschfeld probably used the Russians' report as a good excuse to meet Gide. Yet the sought-for contact with the French cultural monument André Gide did not produce the desired effect in Giese's case.[52]

[47] The Bolsheviks had quickly decriminalized homosexuality when they came to power in 1917. Starting in 1934, however, the Soviet Union began the process of recriminalizing homosexuality under the pretext that it was antisocial. Initially, a few gay intellectuals and artists were arrested, incarcerated, and even banned. In March 1934, a new law was passed making the punishment of homosexuality three to eight years in prison. Wilhelm Reich reported on this new development in the chapter "Die Wiedereinführung des Homosexalitätsparagraphen" (The Reintroduction of the Paragraph on Homosexuality) in his 1936 book *Die Sexualität im Kulturkampf* (*The Sexual Revolution*) (Reich 1936, 187–90). Presumably, some gay Russians affected had informed Hirschfeld in Paris about the new terror regime. Reich wrote: "Anlässlich der Massenverhaftungen entstand eine Panikstimmung unter den Homosexuellen in der Sowjetunion" (As a result of mass arrests, there was panic among homosexuals in the Soviet Union) (Reich 1936, 190). After all, as Wilhelm Reich also pointed out, the Russians had initially decriminalized homosexuality by referring specifically to Hirschfeld's work and ideas. "Die sowjetistische Sexualgesetzgebung hatte den alten zaristischen Homosexualitäts-Paragraphen, [...] einfach gestrichen. Die offizielle grosse Sowjet-Enzyklopädie, die unter der Kontrolle der Regierung erschien, stützte sich in ihrer Darstellung der Sexualität hauptsächlich auf Magnus Hirschfeld und teilweise auch auf Freud" (Soviet sexual legislation, by a stroke of the pen, had abolished the old Tsarist law on homosexuality. [...] In its presentation of sexuality, the official Soviet encyclopedia drew mainly from Magnus Hirschfeld and partly from Freud) (Reich 1936, 187). See also Epstein 1935.

[48] That would change after Gide's visit to the Soviet Union, in 1936, and the publication of *Retour de l'U.R.S.S.* (*Return from the USSR*), the following year, which was very critical of the Bolshevik project and immediately rejected by the French Communist Party.

[49] Gide knew Berlin well and visited the city often. He also visited the Institute more than once. A first source is a letter by the French writer Jean Paulhan: "Berlin est agréable et surprennant: l'on y marche entouré de respect (je ne m'étais jamais senti respecté). Gide nous a emmenés au musée sexuel du Dr Magnus Hirschfeld" (Berlin is pleasant and surprising: one walks around surrounded by respect (I had never felt respected). Gide took us to the sex museum of Dr. Magnus Hirschfeld). See letter (dated Jun. 11, 1930) from Jean Paulhan to Valery Larbaud, in Paulhan et al. 1986, 186, n° 148. Christopher Isherwood also mentioned one of Gide's Institute visits and noted that it was Hirschfeld himself who gave the tour (Isherwood 1988, 24–25). In a 1932 letter to André Gide, the French writer and Nobel Prize winner Roger Martin du Gard (1881–1958) mentioned that Gide had visited the Institute in Berlin. Gide's diary specifies that it was in the year 1928 (see Emeis 2007, 236).

[50] Bergemann, Dose, Keilson-Lauritz & Dubout 2019, f. 78/122. I thank Marita Keilson-Lauritz for pointing this out to me. See also Keilson-Lauritz 2008, 44.

[51] Hirschfeld presumably visited Gide in the company of Giese and Li Shiu Tong. It is certain in any case that Li Shiu Tong visited Gide once by himself (see Keilson-Lauritz 2008, 44 n. 50).

[52] That Hirschfeld contacted Gide before the official announcement of Giese's expulsion (on Oct. 22, 1934) shows that Hirschfeld must have known from the start that an expulsion was the logical outcome for a foreigner who had committed a sexual crime. In other words, Hirschfeld did not want to wait for the official expulsion order since then it would be too late to do anything. Marita Keilson-Lauritz pointed out to me that Gide did intervene, with the desired positive outcome, for the German writer Werner Vordtriede (1915–1985). See Vordtriede 2002; and the correspondence between him and Robert Hichens in the Literaturarchiv in Marbach. Later on, Hirschfeld appealed to Gide about another matter. In *Testament: Heft II*, Hirschfeld wrote that he had asked Gide to assist with his delayed book publications with Gallimard. See Hirschfeld & Dose 2013, f. 89/190.

[53] See AN, site de Pierrefitte-sur-Seine, Ministère de l'intérieur, Direction générale de la sûreté nationale (fonds de Moscou), file on Karl Giese, dossier n° 15843, cote 19940448/186, letter (dated Oct. 23, 1934) from Magnus Hirschfeld to the French Minister of Justice, written the day after he had received Giese's expulsion notice: "[o]n n'a accordé à Mr. Giese qu'un délai de 4 jours pour quitter le territoire

GIESE LEAVES PARIS

The inevitable literally arrived on Hirschfeld and Giese's doorstep when, on October 22, 1934, they received the notice that Giese had to leave the country within four days. This expulsion order still came as a surprise to Hirschfeld, since he wrote in a final letter to the French Minister of the Interior that it was curious that Giese's residence permit (*permis de séjour*) had been extended until November 20, 1934. Apparently, the news of the extension of the residence permit was delivered to Hirschfeld's apartment on the same day as the expulsion notice.[53] Regarding this indeed remarkable twist I have found no further clues in the extant archives. But it does raise the question: was this coincidence an absurd accident or cynically planned by the French authorities?

In the Hirschfeld guestbook, in 1934, "M. H." (Magnus Hirschfeld) wrote a little riddle about the seemingly ineluctable paradisal character of Paris: "A riddle: If you make seven letters out of five / It still remains what it is / Answer: Paris Par – ad – is". However, underneath, Karl Giese wrote: "But one from which you can also be expelled!"[54] There are also two pictures in the Hirschfeld guestbook of Giese's farewell on the sidewalk in front of the Paris apartment. The quote under one of the two pictures reads: "Departure of K. G. on 2[?].10.34" (*Abreise von K. G. am 2[?].10.34*).[55] It appears that Li Shiu Tong was preparing to drive since he is holding the car keys and two pieces of Giese's luggage are stored in the back of the car. Did he take Giese to one of the Paris train stations or did he even drive Giese out of the country [ill. 5]? Li Shiu Tong was not averse to going long distances by car. When Hirschfeld arrived in France, in mid-May 1933, coming from Switzerland, it was in the car of the young Chinese.[56] Giese left Paris a week after his thirty-sixth birthday. It was in any case

français" (Mr. Giese was only given four days to leave French territory).

54 Bergemann, Dose, Keilson-Lauritz & Dubout 2019, f. 29/73: "Ein Rätsel: Machst du aus fünf Buchstaben sieben / So ist demnoch, was es ist, geblieben / Lösung: Paris Par – ad – is". And: "Aber eins aus dem man auch vertrieben werden kann!" Hirschfeld's entry (dated Jul. 7, 1934) and Giese's entry (dated Aug. 11, 1934). The theme of Paris as a paradise resonated later in the Hirschfeld guestbook. On February 18, 1935, in Grenoble, Arno Sachs (1906–1989) wrote an almost exact quote from the German writer (and Rousseau admirer) Jean Paul (1763–1825) in the guestbook: "Erinnerung ist ein Paradies, aus dem man nicht vertrieben werden kann!" (Memory is a paradise from which you cannot be expelled!). See Bergemann, Dose, Keilson-Lauritz & Dubout 2019, f. 111/155. This seems to indicate that people other than Giese also sometimes leafed through the guestbook for inspiration before making their own addition, sometimes in dialogue with what was there already. I follow here the pagination of the Hirschfeld guestbook proposed in Bergemann, Dose, Keilson-Lauritz & Dubout 2019. They did not follow the pagination initiated by Marita Keilson-Lauritz in her two pioneering articles on the Hirschfeld guestbook (Keilson-Lauritz 2004; Keilson-Lauritz 2008). One has now to subtract one from the page references given in Keilson-Lauritz, to correspond to the page numbering of the 2019 edition of the guestbook. See Bergemann 2019, 27 n. 2.

55 See Bergemann, Dose, Keilson-Lauritz & Dubout 2019, f. 78/122 and f. 79/123. It is interesting to see that the photographer, the young Dutch Dr. Max Reiss (in whose estate the negatives of these pictures were recently discovered), made two versions of the farewell scene. In one picture, Li Shiu Tong is part of the troupe of six people in the picture; but, in the other, Li Shiu Tong is curiously left out of the frame. It is likely that the photographer was making an implicit statement about the difficulty of joining Hirschfeld's two partners, Giese and Li Shiu Tong. Besides Hirschfeld, Giese and Li Shiu Tong, the other three people are unknown but it is possible that Genia Nohr (1905–1985) is one of the women (see Bergemann, Dose & Keilson-Lauritz 2021, 5). There are varying opinions on Giese's exact departure date because of the unclear second handwritten date number in the handwriting: is it October 21, 22, 26 or 27? For more on the dispute about the "exact departure date", see Keilson-Lauritz 2008, 44 n. 53; and Hirschfeld & Dose 2013, f. 84/180 n. 458. Given that Hirschfeld received the expulsion notice on October 22, 1934, and that Giese had four days to leave the country, I think that the date range can now be limited to October 25, 26 or even 27 (and most likely not earlier than Oct. 24, 1934). We may also presume that Giese stayed in France for all or most of the four days before he had to leave, departing on one of the last days or even the very last day of his reprieve. It is further unclear if the four-day period started on the day the message was officially issued (Oct. 21, 1934) or on the day it was received (Oct. 22, 1934) by Giese and Hirschfeld, presumably with an inscribed letter.

56 AN, site de Pierrefitte-sur-Seine, Ministère de l'intérieur, Direction générale de la sûreté nationale (fonds de Moscou), file on Dr. [Pierre] Vacher [Vachet], conférencier a/s de guérisons miraculeu-

the last time Giese and "Papa", as Giese used to call Hirschfeld, would see each other alive [ill. 6]. Six months later, in May 1935, Hirschfeld would die in Nice without either Giese or Li Shiu Tong near him.

AFTEREFFECTS

One should not underestimate the influence of these unfortunate events. First of all, it is noticeable that Hirschfeld and Giese did their very best to be very discreet about Giese being imprisoned. Two weeks after his release, in the beginning of August 1934, Karl Giese wrote a letter to the British sexologist Norman Haire. Normally, in his communications with Haire, Giese was quite open about his personal life, but in this case showed himself suddenly quite evasive. He wrote: "I was away from Paris for a long time due to private matters and also, among other things, because I was quite sick".[57] Rather understandably, Giese preferred to hide his having been locked away for three months. Giese must have also suffered from the – according to Hirschfeld – "horrible conditions" (*furchtbaren Umständen*) in prison, possibly even getting sick.[58] In the pictures of the farewell scene in the Hirschfeld guestbook, just mentioned, Giese looks quite emaciated in the face, even a few months after his release from prison.[59] Giese's transfer from the Santé prison to Fresnes could indicate his having been sick in the Santé prison or its indeed being a horrific place to be locked up in. Fresnes was certainly a more "tolerable" prison.[60]

An only recently surfaced source, on the other hand, suggests that Giese only fell sick shortly *after* his release. On July 20, 1934, five days after Giese gained his freedom, Hirschfeld left for Vichy with Li Shiu Tong. But on the day Hirschfeld wanted to leave, Giese fell sick and had a high fever.[61] Hirschfeld entrusted the care of Giese to the young Dutch Dr. Max Reiss (1909–2000), whom Hirschfeld was tutoring in Paris in

ses, "a/s du docteur HIRSCHFELD, Magnus" (dated Jul. 20, 1933), cote 19940482/2.

57 University of Sydney Library, Sydney, Norman Haire collection, 3.21, Karl Geise [*sic*: Giese], Typescripts, 1928–1934, letter (dated Aug. 11, 1934, [1]) from Karl Giese to Norman Haire: "Ich war jetzt längere Zeit in privaten Angelegenheiten von Paris fort und u. a. [unter anderen] auch ziemlich krank". In the same letter, Giese indicated that his *permis de séjour* (residence permit) was another problem that needed to be resolved: "Selbstverständlich gibt es Schwierigkeiten auch hier genug – beispielswiese ist es nicht ganz geklärt ob ich eine längere Aufenthaltsbewilligung bekomme oder nicht – aber wir versuchen doch unser möglichsten. Und wenn es auch nicht gelingt, mit den französischen Kreisen in Kontakt zu kommen, so sind doch die internationalen Beziehungen sehr aktiv wirksam. Das gibt doch immer wieder eine gewisse Hoffnung" (Of course, there are enough difficulties here as well – for example, it is not quite clear whether I will get a longer residence permit or not – but we are trying our best. And even if we don't succeed in getting in touch with the French circles, the international relations are working very actively. That always gives some hope) (ibid., [3]).

58 This is at least how Hirschfeld described Giese's prison conditions in his *Testament: Heft II*. See Hirschfeld & Dose 2013, f. 84/180.

59 It is possible that Hirschfeld was referring to the fact that Giese never fully recovered from his three months in prison in a final letter he sent to the French authorities in October 1934: "Me référant aux communications antérieures se trouvant dans le dossier de Mr. Giese[,] j'ajoute qu'il est *souffrant* et a toujours besoin de mes soins" (With reference to previous communications that you can find in Mr. Giese's file, I add that he is *suffering* and still needs my care). See AN, site de Pierrefitte-sur-Seine, Ministère de l'intérieur, Direction générale de la sûreté nationale (fonds de Moscou), file on Karl Giese, dossier n° 15843, cote 19940448/186, letter (dated Oct. 23, 1934) from Magnus Hirschfeld to Ministre de l'Intérieur (emphasis in original).

60 Hirschfeld's (own?) wish to get Giese transferred to another prison may have been inspired by the book *Sous la cagoule: à Fresnes, prison modèle*, by Jeanne Humbert (1890–1986), a French sexual reform activist whom Hirschfeld also knew. The book had just come out in February 1934 (Humbert 1934). Compared to the Santé prison, Fresnes was a more recent and modern prison. Fresnes had single prison cells and also housed sick prisoners from other prisons in the Seine department. In 1907 a lawyer dubbed it "prison Eden". See https://criminocorpus.org/fr/expositions/prisons/histoire-des-prisons-de-paris/breve-histoire/ (accessed Jun. 19, 2020); see also Chaponnière 2015, 74.

61 Broers 2016b, entry dated Jul. 20, 1934.

62 Max Reiss introduced himself to Hirschfeld around the middle of November 1933 and arrived in Paris in mid-June 1934, when Giese was in prison.

the summer of 1934, and who also lived for some time in the avenue Charles Floquet apartment.[62] Hirschfeld even supposed that Max Reiss would be a good candidate to be his successor [ill. 7].[63] In another letter, sent six days later, Hirschfeld asked Reiss if Giese had already left his sick bed.[64] But Giese was still ailing.[65] Hirschfeld returned from Vichy on August 6, a week earlier than planned, but this was probably due to Hirschfeld's own health not being very good.[66]

We have already mentioned Giese's "paradise lost" entry, made in the Hirschfeld guestbook on August 11, 1934. On the same day, Giese wrote the above-described evasive letter to Norman Haire. In all likelihood, this was one of the first days that Giese was back on his feet and catching up on things. In *Testament: Heft II*, Hirschfeld wrote that, from the middle of August until the middle of October, he and Giese worked together intensively on all kind of projects, most likely preparations for Hirschfeld's publications.[67] Since Giese had been released from prison on July 15, 1934, this means that it took almost a month before Giese recovered. All in all, Giese's stay in "paradisal Paris" was short. He was already arrested two weeks after his arrival. Not counting his prison term and his one-month convalescence, Giese would spend another nine weeks in Paris in the late summer and autumn of 1934.

But Giese's sudden "disappearance" from the Paris scene helps to explain several events. It explains, first of all, why Giese and Hirschfeld's cooperation with the gay Czechoslovak periodical *Nový hlas* failed almost from the start and did not end well. As we have seen, in October 1934, the editors of *Nový hlas* wrote, in the fifth and last German-language supplement, that Giese was not able to deliver his second promised text due to illness.[68] We know now that Giese being sick was only part of the truth. At the beginning of April 1934, two weeks after the German-language supplement project was launched in *Nový hlas*, Giese was imprisoned for three months. Possibly, this caused some frustration in the *Nový hlas* editorial board – as it meant a lack of German-language texts – and their frustration possibly played a role in the already mentioned ideological mid-1934 clash between Karl Meier and Hirschfeld. We saw that the inclusion of Meier's text "The False Image" (Das falsche Bild), in what was to be the very last German-language supplement, in the October 1934 issue of *Nový hlas*, was possibly the reason that Giese and Hirschfeld ceased all cooperation with the Czechoslovak gay magazine. But we need to recognize that Meier's text was included in the magazine simply due to the lack of German-language texts, texts that Giese presumably had promised when planning the whole project in the second half of 1933, when still in Czechoslovakia. It is possible that, as a retaliatory gesture, the editorial board of *Nový hlas* knowingly published Meier's anti-Hirschfeld text, but it is also possible that, as suggested already, Meier simply took advantage of the space left open by Giese and Hirschfeld.

The different parties' irritations can perhaps be observed in another hiccup between the Swiss and Czechoslovak gay magazines. Karl Fein, Giese's and Hirschfeld's Brno ally, had published two short articles on the topic of homosexual legislation in the German-language supplement of *Nový hlas* in May and June 1934. This was quite courageous of Fein since both articles were written shortly after Hirschfeld's forceful

See Archiv MHG, Berlin, fonds Max Reiss, letters (dated Nov. 16, 1933; Jun. 9, 1934; and Jun. 12, 1934) from Magnus Hirschfeld to Max Reiss. Reiss returned to Holland in the beginning of 1935, after visiting Hirschfeld in Nice at the end of 1934. See Broers 2016b, letter Aug. 21, 1934; and Broers 2016a, 31.

[63] Archiv MHG, Berlin, fonds Max Reiss, letter (dated Mar. 30, 1935, 3) from Magnus Hirschfeld to Max Reiss.

[64] Archiv MHG, Berlin, letter (dated Jul. 26, 1934, 4) from Magnus Hirschfeld to Max Reiss. On Hirschfeld's stay in Vichy, see also Dose 2019, 19–20.

[65] Broers 2016b, entry dated Jul. 26, 1934.

[66] Hirschfeld & Dose 2013, f. 88/188; and Broers 2016b, entry dated Aug. 8, 1934. Two days later, on August 8, 1934, in another letter to his parents, Reiss wrote that Giese *had been* sick (past perfect tense).

[67] Hirschfeld & Dose 2013, f. 88/188.

[68] *Nový hlas*, October 1934, 19.

opening text "The State of Affairs of the (Gay) Movement in the Spiritual Struggle of Homosexuals for Liberation" that had appeared in the very first German-language supplement in April 1934.[69] Probably because of these two texts, Fein was catapulted into becoming one of the important gay activists in Czechoslovakia at the time.[70] In a two-part article, titled "Homosexuals and the Law" (*Die Homosexuellen und das Gesetz*), Fein wrote about the legal situation of Czechoslovak gay men. He tried to get the message across that a Czechoslovak gay man, whom he characterized as "an often playful character" (*einem oft spielerischen Wesen*), should be more informed about his legal rights. Too often, he wrote, a gay man arrested for homosexual conduct – sometimes for the first time in his life – is startled and nervous and confesses things during his interrogation that he should not.[71] He further pointed out that Czechoslovak officials' recent harsher treatment of blackmailers did not mean that gay men simply got away with their still illegal homosexual behavior. The article makes it clear that Fein certainly had gay clients in his law practice who ran afoul of paragraph 219b, and this experience with gay clients informed the article.

The first part of Fein's two-part text also appeared in the October 1934 issue of the *Schweizerisches Freundschafts-Banner*.[72] That is, in the same month that Meier's text "The False Image" appeared in the last German-language supplement of *Nový hlas*.[73] This was possibly another intentional move by Karl Meier (or the editorial board of *Schweizerisches Freundschafts-Banner*) to further annoy Hirschfeld and Giese. Or had the magazines simply decided to swap some articles? A swap would maybe explain the odd situation of a Swiss magazine running an article on the legal situation of gay men in Czechoslovakia, and also the editorial note at the beginning of the article stating that it specifically concerned "Czech relations and conditions" (*tschechische Verhältnisse*). That this possible swap did not go unnoticed by Giese and Hirschfeld can perhaps be inferred from the fact that the second part of Fein's article did not appear in the *Schweizerisches Freundschafts-Banner*.[74] It is possible that Giese and Hirschfeld intervened and let their Brno friend Karl Fein know they were unhappy about Fein's cooperation with the *Schweizerisches Freundschafts-Banner*. But had Fein been informed beforehand about the two magazines' decision to swap articles? Maybe it was only afterwards that Fein intervened and let *Nový hlas* know he did not agree (or no longer agreed) with their decision to publish the first part of his text in the *Schweizerisches Freundschafts-Banner* and forbade them to publish the second part. Whether or not this haggling over Fein's text was yet another episode in the whole clash between Giese, Hirschfeld and Meier, involving *Nový hlas* and *Schweizerisches Freundschafts-Banner*, remains for now undetermined. If so, it was in any case the very last episode in the whole cat fight since all cross-border text deliveries and exchanges between the different parties came to a complete stop thereafter.

[69] Fein 1934a; Fein 1934b.

[70] It is unclear if Karl Fein asked Giese and/or Hirschfeld to write for *Nový hlas* or if it was the other way around. The dramatic plundering of the Berlin Institute and the book burning may have radicalized both Giese and Fein.

[71] See also, in this regard, Sulzenbacher's excellent text on gay Vienna in 1938 (Sulzenbacher 1999, 155–56). He refers to the widespread ignorance about homosexuality and the law among Viennese gay men.

[72] Fein, Oct. 1, 1934.

[73] Rheiner 1934.

[74] On the other hand, it must also be noted that no indication was given that the second part of Fein's text would be published in a later issue of *Schweizerisches Freundschafts-Banner*. The customary "Fortsetzung folgt" (to be continued) was not added at the end of Fein's article.

[75] AN, site de Pierrefitte-sur-Seine, Ministère de l'intérieur, Direction générale de la sûreté nationale (fonds de Moscou), file on Karl Giese, dossier n° 15843, cote 19940448/186, letter (dated Jun. 17, 1934, 1) from Magnus Hirschfeld to Gentlemen (Messieurs): "Après de longs débats et avec beaucoup de frais il était encore possible, au mois d'avril de cette année [1934], à transporter ces matériaux non remplaçables en partie à Paris, où il [*sic*: ils] sont encore en dépot à cause de l'arrestation de GIESE [*sic*]".

INSTITUTE MATERIALS STUCK IN PARIS DUE TO GIESE'S IMPRISONMENT

Giese's three-month imprisonment sheds light on another matter. In a letter Hirschfeld sent to the French authorities, in June 1934, he wrote the following about the Institute materials: "After long debates, and at much expense, it was still possible, in April of this year [1934], to transport part of these irreplaceable materials to Paris, where they are still in storage because of Giese's arrest".[75] And in another letter, also addressed to the French authorities, Hirschfeld wrote: "this precious scientific material, which has been lying unclaimed for several months at the Central customs office in Paris".[76] It appears that it had been decided that Giese and not Hirschfeld would receive the materials sent from Brno to Paris, likely out of caution. This further indicates that the materials were only sent after Giese had actually arrived in Paris, around the beginning of April. It was only once the materials had safely arrived, and the buy-back operation was successfully completed, that Giese and Hirschfeld were open in the media about who had played a central role in the operation. A Slovak newspaper article, published at the end of April 1934, mentioned that Karl Fein and Josef Weisskopf, both from Brno, had played key roles in the buy-back operation.[77] But by the time the materials arrived in Paris, Giese was already in prison. However, it is possible that the materials had in fact arrived shortly before Giese started his sentence, but were not picked up immediately. This would also explain the timing of Hirschfeld's letter to Norman Haire of April 12, 1934: "that, after all, I succeeded with Giese, and after very onerous labors, to save the materials which form the foundation of a restitution".[78] Had the materials arrived in Paris on or around April 12, the date of the letter? As we have seen, Giese was arrested on April 14 or 15 and released from prison three months later, on July 15.

In a letter to Max Reiss, sent from the spa town of Vichy on July 26, 1934, Hirschfeld inquired if Reiss and Giese had already started to put the materials in order. This means that the materials must have been picked up at the Central customs office (*douane centrale*) sometime in the second half of July.[79] But we have also seen that Giese got sick in the weeks after his release, only recovering in August. In a letter sent out to his parents on August 21, Max Reiss, the Dutch doctor and Hirschfeld's pupil who was in Paris in the summer of 1934, reported that he and Giese were going over twenty wooden boxes (*kisten*, in Dutch) filled with bought-back materials in a house in the Boulevard Haussmann, Paris IX, at the end of August.[80]

[76] AN, site de Pierrefitte-sur-Seine, Ministère de l'intérieur, Direction générale de la sûreté nationale (fonds de Moscou), file on Karl Giese, dossier n° 15843, cote 19940448/186, letter (dated Jul. 12, 1934, 1) from Magnus Hirschfeld to an unknown man in the Ministry of the Interior: "ce précieux matériel scientifique qui se trouve déjà depuis quelques mois sans être réclamé [?] à la Douane centrale de Paris". "Réclamé" (claimed) could also be "déclaré" (declared). I thank Pol Timmerman for his assistance in the attempt to decipher this unclear handwritten word. See email (dated Jun. 8, 2020) from Pol Timmerman to the author. The Paris customs office's strictly administrative archives have in large part not been preserved. See email (dated Jun. 8, 2020) from Sandrine Faure (Musée national des douanes, Bordeaux) to the author; and email (dated Jun. 17, 2020) from Audrey Ceselli (Archives de Paris) to the author.

[77] See "Institut für sexualwissenschaftliche Forschung in Paris", *Neues Pressburger Tagblatt*, Apr. 28, 1934, 5. This text also shows that Hirschfeld's companions were able to think that not all had been lost in May 1933: "Seine [Hirschfeld's] Bibliothek wurde teils verbrannt, teils beschlagnahmt" (His [Hirschfeld's] library was partly burned, partly confiscated).

[78] University of Sydney Library, Sydney, Norman Haire collection, 3.20, Magnus Hirschfeld, Typescripts, 1923–1935, letter (dated Apr. 12, 1934) from Magnus Hirschfeld to Norman Haire: "dass es mir mit GIESE [*sic*] nach sehr schweren Mühen doch noch gelungen ist, die Materialien zu retten, die das Fundament zu einer solchen Restitution bilden".

[79] Archiv MHG, Berlin, fonds Max Reiss, letter (dated Jul. 26, 1934) from Magnus Hirschfeld to Max Reiss. Cf. a letter Hirschfeld wrote to the French authorities: "matériaux que nous avons reçus que tout récemment" (materials we received only recently). See AN, site de Pierrefitte-sur-Seine, Ministère de l'intérieur, Direction générale de la sûreté nationale (fonds de Moscou), file Karl Giese, dossier n° 15843, cote 19940448/186, letter (dated Oct. 23, 1934) from Magnus Hirschfeld to the Ministre de l'Intérieur.

[80] Broers 2016b, letter Aug. 21, 1934.

Just as it was decided to send the materials from Brno only once Giese had arrived in Paris, it was possibly also decided, dictated by the same caution, not to take the materials to the apartment in the avenue Charles Floquet. Reiss wrote that only a part of the materials, twenty crates, had arrived in Paris.[81] Interestingly, Hirschfeld spoke of thirty boxes of materials bought back from Germany in the draft cooperation agreement he made with Leo Klauber.[82] This seems again to show that a part was indeed still in Brno. We will suggest later that the latter was probably mostly made up of books. Reiss' expressions in the letter to his parents, I think, indicate that some or most of the boxes may have contained questionnaires (*Fragebogen*) of Institute patients.[83]

Hirschfeld stressed several times in the three letters he sent to the French authorities that he needed Giese's assistance to sort through these materials. This might have been an ad hoc reason meant to convince the French authorities not to expel Giese, but it was also, at least in part, close to the truth: as the former Institute archivist, Giese knew these materials best. Soon after Giese's expulsion from France, Hirschfeld left for Nice and wrote, in his diary-like *Testament: Heft II*, that he had to put the bought-back materials in storage. The name of the storage company (*garde-meuble, Möbellager*) he used was Garde-meuble Bedel & Co. in Paris.[84] When Hirschfeld finalized his last will and testament, in January 1934, he mentioned, in article 5, that a part of the collection was still stored with this Parisian company [ill. 8].[85] Most likely, in the following months, he transferred the materials stored in Paris to Nice, but we will return again to this issue later on.

[81] Broers 2016b, letter Aug. 21, 1934: "Er is in twintig kisten een deel van het archief in Parijs aangekomen" (Part of the archive arrived in Paris in twenty crates).

[82] Dose 2015, 52.

[83] Broers 2016b, letter Aug. 21, 1934: "Het materiaal is van enorm veel gewicht, het ressorteert alles onder ambtsgeheim en is onder groote offers in Duitsland opgekocht en naar hier gezonden. Ik ben niet erg politiek maar als men ziet, hoe was omgesprongen met dat deel van het menschelijk bestaan, dat de meeste waarde heeft en het meest persoonlijk is" (The materials are of enormous importance, everything is subject to official secrecy and was bought in Germany at great sacrifice and sent here. I am not very political but if one sees how that part of human existence which has the most value and is the most personal was handled).

[84] Hirschfeld & Dose 2013, f. 87/186. The same storage company is later mentioned one more time (see Hirschfeld & Dose 2013, f. 90-91/193-194). That only Giese was able to collect the materials from the Paris customs office in August 1934 shines another light on the idea, put forward by Ralf Dose, that the July 19, 1933, rental of a storage room by Franz Herzfelder, later the executor of Hirschfeld's will, could be linked to Hirschfeld's Parisian storage plans. See Hirschfeld & Dose 2013, 186 n. 495. See also Dose & Herrn 2006, 47. My attempt to build on the initial work, started by Ralf Dose, assisted by Susanne Andrukowicz, on the archives of the Bedel company failed. The current company, Groupe Bedel, let me know in 2014 that the company had, after relocating several times, destroyed the older company archives. See email (dated Oct. 8, 2014) from Anita Federici (Groupe Bedel, Neuilly-sur-Marne) to the author. On the other hand, Rainer Herrn claims that the relevant Bedel company *Findbuch* (register) was lost in a fire (see Herrn 2008c: card Vom Finder des Koffers, Adam Smith, ins Netz gestelltes Foto).

[85] See the transcription of the text of Hirschfeld's last will in Hirschfeld & Dose 2013, 224; or Baumgardt 1984, 10. Hirschfeld mentions the address 18 Rue St. Augustin, Paris II. I have visited this Paris address. It was clear, from to the size of the current shop at this location, that only the administrative office of the Bedel company could have been located there. The mention of "Bureau central" for this address (in the *Annuaire et almanach du commerce et de l'industrie* 1935, 3187) further confirms this. All of the Bedel company's actual warehouses (called *entrepôts*) were located in other parts of Paris. One address of a Bedel warehouse – 194 Rue Championnet, Paris XVIII – is mentioned in Hirschfeld & Dose 2013, 186 n. 495. In an advertisement in *Revue illustrée* (Jan. 10, 1912, unpaginated advertisement page) one finds three more addresses for the Bedel company storage premises: 67 Avenue Victor-Hugo, 308 Rue Lecourbe (Vaugirard) and 14 Rue de la Voûte (Reuilly). The locations in the Rue Lecourbe and the Avenue Victo-Hugo were the closest to Hirscheld's Avenue Charles Floquet apartment. Hirschfeld's mentioning only the address of the representation office – and not of the actual warehouse – suggests discretion and prudence.

[86] See for example an anonymous – and very subjective and judgmental – Ministry of the Interior report on Hirschfeld, which speaks of "les préoccupations commerciales de ce personnage" (the business concerns of this character). See AN, site de Pier-

AFTEREFFECTS ON MAGNUS HIRSCHFELD

Even in the privacy of his *Testament: Heft II*, Hirschfeld was very discreet about the Giese bathhouse affair. This makes it a bit improbable that the social circle around Hirschfeld knew about the stigma of Giese's imprisonment. But we may presume that, if the news got out, Hirschfeld would have lost public credit in Paris as a result. As we have seen, in his conflict with Bertie Albrecht and the editorial board of *Le problème sexuel*, Hirschfeld was already under scrutiny by colleagues within the French medical profession for activities deemed too commercial. The oft-advertised Perles Titus (Titus Pearls), the French counterpart of the Titus Perlen sold in Germany, as well as Hirschfeld's eager cooperation with the popular magazines *Voilà* and *Détéctive*, were all considered unworthy of a serious scientist.[86] It is possible that in France, as in antisemitic Germany, some had the opinion that Jewish doctors "always mixed medicine with business and still boasted they were great saviors of men".[87] An anonymous July 1933 Ministry of the Interior report on Hirschfeld stated the following: "Professor HIRSCHFELD is considered by French medical personalities as a 'para-scientist', and he is held in only very relative esteem".[88]

A more public aversion to Hirschfeld, who had found refuge in France, could be noticed in some French newspapers as well. The animosity varied between light mockery to outright right-wing hate speech in *L'Action française*. *Paris-Midi*, for example, wrote: "He has finally found a publisher and has just published, under the candid title 'L'Ami et l'Amour', a series of reflections which will win him the support of all the scientific minds of the 'Petite Chaumière'. In the evening, you can see Dr. Magnus Hirschfeld prowling the Champs-Elysées. He goes under the big trees, meditating and dreaming. Then, at the terrace of a café where the beer is from Munich and the sausages from Frankfurt, you will find him sniffing with his big nose the perfumes of the absent fatherland" [ill. 9].[89] There are several elements of mockery here: Hirschfeld's book *L'Âme et l'amour* (lit. the soul and love) is changed to *L'Ami et l'amour* (the friend and love), a clear reference to his homosexuality. In the 1920s, the "Petite Chaumière" was a transvestite cabaret in Montmartre.[90] In addition to Hirschfeld, as a stereotypical German, going after beer and sausage, the mention of his big nose refers to his Jewishness. The truly curious aspect of this article is that, at the end of April 1935, Hirschfeld had already been away from Paris for almost half a year.

At the end of November 1934, Hirschfeld left Paris, in all probability once again fleeing the winter cold.[91] Sometime in the beginning of 1935, he decided to settle definitively in Nice. In a March 1935 letter to Norman Haire, Hirschfeld tried to sum up, in hindsight, the reasons why he had left Paris for Nice: "Paris is a charming

refitte-sur-Seine, Ministère de l'intérieur, Direction générale de la sûreté nationale (fonds de Moscou), file on Dr. [Pierre] Vacher [Vachet], conférencier a/s de guérisons miraculeuses, cote 19940482/2, anonymous text dated Jul. 5, 1933, [2].

[87] Kater 1989, 204.

[88] AN, site de Pierrefitte-sur-Seine, Ministère de l'intérieur, Direction générale de la sûreté nationale (fonds de Moscou), file on Dr. [Pierre] Vacher [Vachet], conférencier a/s de guérisons miraculeuses, « a/s du docteur HIRSCHFELD, Magnus » (dated Jul. 20, 1933), cote 19940482/2: "Le professeur HIRSCHFELD est considéré par des personnalités médicales françaises comme un 'para[-] scientifique', et l'on n'a pour lui qu'une estime très relative".

[89] See "Herr Doktor aux Champs-Elysées", *Paris-Midi*, Apr. 28, 1935, 2: "Enfin, il a trouvé un éditeur et vient de publier sous le titre candide « L'Ami et l'Amour » une suite de réflexions qui lui vaudront les suffrages de tous les esprits scientifiques de la « Petite Chaumière ». Vous pourrez voir rôder, le soir, aux Champs-Elysées, le docteur Magnus Hirschfeld. Il va sous les grands arbres, méditant et rêveur, puis à la terrasse de ce café ou [*sic*, où] la bière est de Munich et les saucisses de Francfort, vous le retrouverez humant de son large nez les parfums de la patrie absente".

[90] Pénet 2006, 117.

[91] AN, site de Pierrefitte-sur-Seine, Ministère de l'intérieur, Direction de la Sûreté Générale, Service central des cartes d'identité d'étrangers, file Magnus Hirschfeld, file n° 210400, cote 19940506/151, letter (dated Jul. 20, 1935) from Paris Police headquarters to the Minister of the Interior. According to this letter, Hirschfeld left Paris on November 27, 1934.

city, but I did not like the climate there, and the life there was too strenuous for me, in addition to the very unpleasant entanglements of the movement, where, instead of unity, people plotted against each other, and finally the difficulties with K-G. [*sic*: Karl Giese] – in short: Paris was spoiled for me".[92] Although Hirschfeld mentioned the problems with Giese as the very last reason for leaving Paris, he may have rather meant "last but not least". But is this all there is to say about Hirschfeld's seemingly voluntary exile from the hustle and bustle of Paris to cosy and provincial Nice? It would seem not.

GIESE AS HIRSCHFELD'S ACHILLES' HEEL

On June 8, 1934, the very day of the failed attempt to appeal Giese's conviction for public indecency (*outrage public à la pudeur*) at the Appeals Court, Hirschfeld was warned by the Paris police headquarters about his activities in the sexological sphere being too loud and boisterous. An internal report of the Ministry of the Interior about Hirschfeld's Parisian activities (dated December 1934) states: "His lectures as well as his publications on sexual questions have been judged of a realism likely to shock public opinion, and he was *invited*, on June 8 of this year [1934], to cease all activity in this field. Hirschfeld appears to have complied with these instructions, and we have not observed him publishing any new articles since then; his last known lecture took place on June 7, 1934, at the venue (*salle*) l'Akadémia Raymond Duncan, 31 rue de Seine" (emphasis added).[93] In another, earlier police report of June 1934, the same meeting was described as follows: "Summoned on June 8 to the 4th Section of the Renseignements Généraux, this foreigner was *invited* to cease publication of articles, in some newspapers, on sexual questions, full of a realism shocking to public opinion, as well as his public lectures on the subject. Mr. Hirschfeld Magnus [*sic*] expressed regret that his activity, which he declares to be purely scientific, could have provoked this kind of reaction and *implicitly* committed to put an end to it" (emphasis added).[94] Hirschfeld himself mentioned the caution in *Testament: Heft II*: "On the same day [June 8, 1934, the day of the attempt to appeal Giese's conviction], I received a warning from the Préfecture [de Police] that, as a guest of France, I should keep extremely quiet".[95]

[92] University of Sydney Library, Sydney, Norman Haire collection, 3.20, Magnus Hirschfeld, Typescripts, 1923–1935, letter (dated Mar. 15, 1935, [1]) from Magnus Hirschfeld to Norman Haire: "Paris ist eine charmante Stadt, aber das Klima bekam mir nicht, auch war mir das Leben dort zu anstrengend, dazu die höchst unerfreulichen Verhältnisse in der Bewegung, in der statt Einigkeit, Einer gegen den Anderen intrigierte und schliess-[lich] die Schwierigkeiten mit K-G. [*sic*: Karl Giese] – kurz : Paris war mir verleidet".

[93] AN, site de Pierrefitte-sur-Seine, Ministère de l'intérieur, Direction de la Sûreté Générale, Service central des cartes d'identité d'étrangers, file Magnus Hirschfeld, file number 210400, A.S. de l'Allemand Hirschfeld, Décembre 1934, [2], cote 19940506/151: "Ses conférences, ainsi que ses publications sur les questions sexuelles ayant été jugées d'un réalisme de nature à choquer l'opinion publique, il a été *invité* le 8 Juin [1934] dernier à cesser toute activité dans ce domaine. Hirschfeld parait [*sic*: paraît] s'être conformé à ces instructions, et on n'apprend pas qu'il ait, depuis cette époque, fait publier de nouveaux articles; sa dernière conférence connue a eu lieu le 7 Juin 1934, salle de l'Akadémia, Raymond Duncan, 31 rue de Seine" (emphasis added). The date of the lecture (titled "Die sexualwissenschaft") is likely incorrect. According to the *Pariser Tageblatt*, this lecture took place on Wednesday Jun. 6, 1934. See "Magnus Hirschfeld spricht", *Pariser Tageblatt*, Jun. 6, 1934, 3. The announcement also says that the lecture was given in French.

[94] AN, site de Pierrefitte-sur-Seine, Ministère de l'intérieur, Direction générale de la sûreté nationale (fonds de Moscou), file on Dr. [Pierre] Vacher, conférencier a/s de guérisons miraculeuses, anonymous two-page-long report (dated Jun. 14, 1934), cote 19940482/2: "Convoqué le 8 Juin courant à la 4ème Section des Renseignements Généraux, cet étranger a été *invité* à cesser la publication, dans certains journaux, d'articles, [*sic*] sur les questions sexuelles, empreints d'un réalisme de nature à choquer l'opinion publique, ainsi que ses conférences publiques sur le même sujet. M. Hirschfeld Magnus [*sic*] a exprimé des regrets que son activité, qu'il déclare être purement scientifique, ait pu provoquer des réactions et il s'est engagé, *implicitement*, à y mettre un terme" (emphasis added).

[95] Hirschfeld & Dose 2013, f. 85/182: "Am gleichen Tage [June 8, 1934, the day of the attempt to appeal

That Hirschfeld received a warning from the Paris police headquarters on the day of the appeal clearly shows that the French authorities waited for final confirmation of Giese's conviction. Giese's three-month sentence acted as a clear symbolic warning to Hirschfeld, indicating who was in charge. It was a way of indirectly telling Hirschfeld: "behave or you'll be next". The French authorities did not have to actually expel a person they considered a nuisance. It was enough simply to reassess an always temporary residence permit.[96]

"French politicians and bureaucrats could not stand to see foreigners abuse their hospitality", Rosenberg writes; and, on this topic, Albert Sarraut, the Minister of the Interior, had similar ideas to the Prefect of Police.[97] Hirschfeld was well aware of this line of thinking in the French authorities. In one of Hirschfeld's three letters to the French authorities regarding Giese's expulsion, he explicitly referred to this preoccupation: "I believe I can affirm that [Giese] [...] will henceforth make himself doubly deserving of the hospitality that France has so generously shown him".[98]

Hirschfeld had at first felt welcome when he arrived in France, in 1933, but this was only his subjective perception of the situation. In *Testament: Heft II*, Hirschfeld wrote that the initially hospitable climate changed into its opposite shortly after his arrival in France. Hirschfeld claimed that Giese was now simply one of hundreds, possibly even thousands of Germans being expelled from France. Although Hirschfeld recognized the importance of the Stavisky affair, and the ensuing February 1934 riots, it's far from certain that the affair alone could explain the changed attitude towards immigrants that he perceived.[99] In his book on refugees in pre-war Paris, Clifford Rosenberg shows that the increased mistrust (*méfiance*) of foreigners began before the affair and that the harsher attitude to which they were subject started later.[100]

And yet, Hirschfeld might still have had a point about the Stavisky affair playing a role in Giese's expulsion. Ralf Dose has pointed out that the French sexologist Pierre Vachet (1892–1990?) was entangled in the Stavisky affair. He was one of the witnesses at Stavisky's wedding and had provided Stavisky with false sick notes. This was another reason why the French authorities also considered Vachet a suspect personality.[101] In a 1934 letter to Norman Haire, Hirschfeld claimed that he declined offers from Vachet to work with him shortly after his arrival in France, but an index card for Magnus Hirschfeld in the National Security Central Index (*Fichier central de la Sûreté nationale*) explicitly links Vachet and Hirschfeld.[102] A handwritten reference on one of the index cards for Magnus Hirschfeld in this Central Index states: "See file Vacher [*sic*: Vachet], Pierre (doctor). Report 20.7.33".[103] And in Pierre Vachet's Ministry of the Interior file there are, curiously, two important reports on Hirschfeld's activities and

Giese's conviction] musste ich auf der Präfektur [de Police] eine Warnung entgegennehmen, mich als Gast Frankreichs äusserst ruhig zu verhalten".

96 Rosenberg 2006, 93: "The police resorted to administrative forced return [*refoulement*] and refusal of residence [*refus de séjour*] much more often than formal expulsion".

97 Rosenberg 2006, 91.

98 AN, site de Pierrefitte-sur-Seine, Ministère de l'intérieur, Direction générale de la sûreté nationale (fonds de Moscou), file on Karl Giese, dossier n° 15843, letter (dated Jul. 12, 1934, [2]) from Magnus Hirschfeld to an unknown man in the French Interior Ministry, cote 19940448/186: "je crois pouvoir affirmer que [Giese] [...] se rendra dorénavant doublement digne de l'hospitalité que la France lui a si généreusement accordée".

99 Hirschfeld & Dose 2013, f. 84/180.

100 Rosenberg 2006, 100–101.

101 Hirschfeld & Dose 2013, f. 84/180 n. 462. But that was most likely only an *additional* reason. Vachet's activities as a sexologist and a harsh left-wing critic of religious folk beliefs was already reason enough for the French authorities to keep an eye on him. See AN, site de Pierrefitte-sur-Seine, Ministère de l'intérieur, Direction générale de la sûreté nationale (fonds de Moscou), file on Dr. [Pierre] Vacher, conférencier a/s de guérisons miraculeuses, anonymous report (dated Jul. 20, 1933), cote 19940482/2.

102 University of Sydney Library, Sydney, Norman Haire collection, 3.20, Magnus Hirschfeld, Typescripts, 1923–1935, letter (dated Apr. 11, 1934, 3, III) from Magnus Hirschfeld to Norman Haire.

103 AN, site de Pierrefitte-sur-Seine, Ministère de l'intérieur, Direction générale de la sûreté nationale (fonds de Moscou), fichier central de la Sûreté natio-

life in France that should, at the very least, have been included in the ministry's file on Magnus Hirschfeld as well. In one of these reports, it says: "In Paris, *his* [Hirschfeld's] *relations* with Dr. Pierre Vachet and also with a large number of German political refugees *are being tracked*" (emphasis added).[104]

Also, the French authorities may have been aware of (and possibly also quite annoyed by) the book *Perversions sexuelles*, published in 1931 in France, written by one of Hirschfeld's Berlin Institute colleagues, Dr. Felix Abraham (1901–1937). The latter based the book on Hirschfeld's sexological expertise. The title page declares: "Sexual perversions – from the teaching of Dr. Magnus Hirschfeld, official court expert, director of the institute of sexual science – by his first assistant, Dr. Felix Abraham – translated and adapted by Dr. Pierre Vachet, professor at the school of psychology in Paris".[105] Besides translating and adapting the text for a French readership, the book also contained a short introduction by Pierre Vachet [ill. 10]. Vachet pleaded for birth control, and this was the complete opposite of what the French government wanted. After World War I, the French authorities deemed it important to encourage the birth rate, so it comes as no surprise that contraceptive "propaganda" was banned in 1920.[106] Gay men, considered to be non-reproductive, were of course the very antithesis of this procreative ideal.

The French authorities were also clearly aware of Hirschfeld's homosexuality. One page of an incomplete July 1933 report on Hirschfeld reveals that at least one collaborator at the Ministry of the Interior clearly suffered from paranoid homophobia: "He [Magnus Hirschfeld] is, in reality, neither Jew nor Aryan. He serves a religion which is not new, which no one thinks of proscribing (for they are too many) and to which it is absolutely useless to raise altars". The word "they" was underscored three times when typed.[107] So it cannot be excluded that the French authorities' clear link between Hirschfeld and the contested Pierre Vachet played an additional negative part in the treatment of Giese's (and Hirschfeld's) case.

nale, fiches Magnus Hirschfeld, cote 19940508/1153: "V.[oir] dos.[sier] Vacher [*sic*: Vachet], Pierre (docteur). Rap.[port] 20.7.33".

[104] AN, site de Pierrefitte-sur-Seine, Ministère de l'intérieur, Direction générale de la sûreté nationale (fonds de Moscou), file on Dr. [Pierre] Vacher, conférencier a/s de guérisons miraculeuses, anonymous report (dated Jul. 20, 1933), cote 19940482/2: "À Paris, il [Hirschfeld] est en *relations suivies* avec le Dr. Pierre Vachet et avec un grand nombre de réfugies [*sic*: réfugiés] politiques allemands" (emphasis added). One may also wonder if Hirschfeld joined Vachet on a day when the latter took the elevator up the Eiffel Tower to give his radio talk, "Causeries médicales" (Medical Chats) on national radio. Maybe Hirschfeld spoke as well? Hirschfeld's Paris apartment was located right next to the Eiffel Tower. For a mention of Vachet's radio talks, see Ministère de l'intérieur, Direction générale de la sûreté nationale (fonds de Moscou), file Dr. [Pierre] Vacher [Vachet], conférencier a/s de guérisons miraculeuses, cote 19940482/2, anonymous report on Pierre Vachet (dated July 1932).

[105] Abraham & Hirschfeld 1931, title page: "Perversions sexuelles – d'après l'enseignement du docteur Magnus Hirschfeld[,] expert officiel des tribunaux[,] directeur de l'institut de la science sexuelle – par son premier assistant, le docteur Félix Abraham – traduit et adapté par le docteur Pierre Vachet[,] professeur à l'école de psychologie à Paris". For Felix Abraham, see, for example, https://magnus-hirschfeld.de/gedenken/erinnern/hirschfeld-familie-und-freunde/gedenktafel-felix-abraham/ (accessed Aug. 16, 2018); Dose 2016.

[106] See Tamagne 2017, 22. Tamagne speaks of the "obsession démographique française" (French demographic obsession). Cf. Friedjung, Sep. 29, 1932, 5: "Paris sollte nun den [WLSR] Kongreß vorbereiten [after Moscow dropped out]; aber die damalige französische Regierung Tardieu hatte seine Freude daran; insbesondere dürfe über Geburtenregelung nicht gesprochen werden. Ausländer, die dies dennoch wagen sollten, würde man an die Grenze abschieben" (Paris was now to prepare the [WLSR] Congress [after Moscow dropped out]; but the French Tardieu government then took pleasure in it; in particular, birth control was not to be discussed. Foreigners who nevertheless ventured to do so would be deported to the border).

[107] See Ministère de l'intérieur, Direction générale de la sûreté nationale (fonds de Moscou), file Dr. [Pierre] Vacher [Vachet], conférencier a/s de guérisons miraculeuses, anonymous report (dated Jul. 5, 1933), 2, cote 19940482/2: "Il [Magnus Hirschfeld] n'est, à vrai dire, ni juif, ni aryen. Il sert une religion qui n'est pas nouvelle, que nul ne songe à proscrire (car ils sont trop) et à laquelle il est absolument inutile d'élever des autels".

[108] AN, site de Pierrefitte-sur-Seine, Ministère de l'intérieur, Direction de la Sûreté Générale, Service

Hirschfeld was also linked to some Communist figures, also in exile in Paris. The pre-war French authorities (along with those of many other European countries) felt a general repugnance for Bolshevik sympathies and Communists. A General Inquiries (Renseignements Généraux, RG) handwritten note, for example, recorded that Hirschfeld was a friend of the Marxist politician and intellectual Rudolf Hilferding (1877–1941).[108] Another index card for Magnus Hirschfeld refers to the "[Willi] Münzenberg affair" (*affaire Munzenberg* [sic: *Münzenberg*]), the German Communist who published the infamous *Brown Book of the Reichstag Fire and Hitler Terror* (*Braunbuch über Reichstagsbrand und Hitlerterror*) and had lived in the Berlin Institute for a few years.[109] On another loose note sitting in a report on Hirschfeld, it was noted that he was part of a "proscribed group of communist, anti-French and anti-English [*sic*] intellectuals" (*groupement d'intellectuels proscrits communiste, anti français & anti anglais* [sic]).[110] But the same note also stated that Hirschfeld was a social democrat ...[111]

Magnus Hirschfeld clearly misjudged that he would be able simply to continue – or even restart – his sexological life's work in France. It is clear that, with regards to Giese, he undertook a cultural argument in his first letters to the French authorities: he needed Giese in order to continue his life's work and, therefore, Giese should not be expelled. But as we have seen, at least some of the French authorities did not have a high opinion of Hirschfeld's work and simply thought that Hirschfeld caused too much social upheaval.

HIRSCHFELD GOES ON

However, curiously, Hirschfeld did not take the June 8, 1934, warning too seriously since, on July 20, 1934, he published a piece titled "Male Bonding Groups" (*Männerbunde*) in the *Pariser Tageblatt*, signed with his full name. This text presented the events of the Night of the Long Knives in which the gay SA leader Ernst Röhm, along with other gay and non-gay undesirables in the National Socialist flock, were executed

central des cartes d'identité d'étrangers, file Magnus Hirschfeld, file n° 210400, cote 19940506/151, handwritten note in pencil (dated May [?] 23, 1935). Hilferding was one of the Jewish people featured, along with Hirschfeld, in Hans Diebow's *Der ewige Jude* (*The Eternal Jew*). See Diebow 1938.

[109] AN, site de Pierrefitte-sur-Seine, Ministère de l'intérieur, Direction générale de la sûreté nationale (fonds de Moscou), fichier central de la Sûreté nationale, fiches Magnus Hirschfeld, cote 19940508/1153. I was not able to locate the file in the fonds de Moscou in the Archives nationales on the Communist publisher Willi Münzenberg (1889–1940), who worked in Paris (Editions du Carrefour). Münzenberg was the publisher of the so-called *Braunbuch*, which denounced Nazi politics, and which also contained Giese's testimony about the sacking of the Hirschfeld Institute in Berlin.

[110] AN, site de Pierrefitte-sur-Seine, Ministère de l'intérieur, Direction de la Sûreté Générale, Service central des cartes d'identité d'étrangers, file Magnus Hirschfeld, file number 210400, handwritten note (dated Oct. 15[?], 1934), cote 19940506/151.

[111] Another file on Hirschfeld states that he also had relations with Gerald Hamilton (1890–1970), a British subject, who was indeed a spy. See AN, site de Pierrefitte-sur-Seine, Ministère de l'intérieur, Direction générale de la sûreté nationale (fonds de Moscou), file on Dr. [Pierre] Vacher [Vachet], conférencier a/s de guérisons miraculeuses, "a/s du docteur HIRSCHFELD, Magnus", intelligence report (dated Jul. 20, 1933) on Hirschfeld, cote 19940482/2, [2]. It also says that Hamilton was the secretary of the British branch of the (Communist) League against Imperialism and Colonial Oppression (1927–1936). Hamilton knew Willi Münzenberg and also Christopher Isherwood, who fictionalized him as Arthur Norris in his 1935 novel *Mr. Norris Changes Trains*. For a biography of Hamilton, see Cullen 2014. Another loose note contains the names (and respective file numbers) of Hirschfeld and the translator and antiquarian bookseller Susi Eisenberg-Bach (1909–1997). It is not clear if the latter scrap is just the jotting of a clerk who needed to look up files or if the names of Hirschfeld and Eisenberg were linked here in any way. See AN, site de Pierrefitte-sur-Seine, Paris, Ministère de l'intérieur, Direction de la Sûreté Générale, Service central des cartes d'identité d'étrangers, file Magnus Hirschfeld, file n° 210400, cote 19940506/151. Eisenberg lived at 47 Rue Claude Bernard in Paris. She managed to flee to Brazil during the war. See Kosch & Hagestedt 2000, 44. She does not mention meeting Hirschfeld when she was in Paris in any of her published memoirs. See Eisenberg-Bach 1986; Bach 1991.

in a few days.[112] Two weeks earlier, a text on the same subject, titled "Putting It to the Test: Roehm and Race Theory" (*Die Probe aufs Exempel: Roehm und die Rassentheorie*), appeared in the same newspaper, but only signed with the initials "H. M.".[113] Hirschfeld researchers argue whether or not the latter text is by Magnus Hirschfeld's hand.[114] That Hirschfeld received a warning may explain why he would have used his initials. Yet it does not explain, of course, why Hirschfeld used his full name in the July 20 *Pariser Tageblatt* article. Was it due to a misunderstanding or was Hirschfeld already dipping his toe in the water in July 1934? He might have also reasoned that a political article had nothing to do with sexology, and that the French authorities would appreciate an article critical of Nazi Germany. Possibly significantly, Giese had been released from prison five days earlier.

The warning given to Hirschfeld can also be linked to another article whose authorship by Hirschfeld is debated. In the very first 1935 issue of the *Pariser Tageblatt*, another article on the situation of homosexuals in the Third Reich was published. This time the article was signed by a certain "Expertus".[115] Karl Giese stated in a 1938 letter that Hirschfeld was the author of this text.[116] In this case we can see that Hirschfeld was using a pseudonym to get around the warning. But what is most important to see here is that Hirschfeld simply could not keep silent. The link between homosexuality and the new people in power in the country of his birth was a very painful issue for him. He had been, after all, the main apostle of the gay cause in pre-war Germany.

Hirschfeld's articles for the French popular magazine *Voilà* came to a halt in May 1934, when a last article by him on the erotic aspects of dancing appeared.[117] As far as I am able to determine, Hirschfeld's last article in *Détective* appeared in March 1934.[118] Only two other articles by Hirschfeld, both titled "Rivierabrief", appeared in the *Pariser Tageblatt*, in March and April 1935.[119] The first text concerned the traditional February Carnival in Nice, and the fact that the people flocking to Nice were part of an aristocracy of the spirit (*Geistesaristokratie*) rather than an aristocracy of birth (*Geburtsaristokratie*), noting that Nietzsche had also sought refuge in Nice, in the winter of 1885–86.[120] The text also stressed that, even though his writings were appropriated by the Nazis, Nietzsche refused to attend the marriage of his sister Elisabeth to an antisemite. In the second text, Hirschfeld reported on the opening

[112] Hirschfeld, Jul. 20, 1934. This text was (for the most part) an abridged version of one that appeared five days earlier in *Der Aufruf*, the periodical of the German-speaking branch of the Czechoslovak Liga für Menschenrechte. See Hirschfeld, Jul. 15, 1934, 512–15.

[113] H. M., Jul. 5, 1934.

[114] I have contributed to this attribution debate in Soetaert 2015, 15–16. The best indication I discovered that this text might be by Hirschfeld – though, to be clear, it is not actual proof – is that "H. M." quotes a small phrase from Nietzsche's *Also sprach Zarathustra*: "Nicht nur fort sollst du dich pflanzen, sondern hinauf!" (You should propagate yourself not only onward but upward!). In a slightly earlier text on forced sterilization in Germany, published in Klaus Mann's exile periodical *Die Sammlung*, Hirschfeld uses the same quote, though in another context. See Hirschfeld 1934c, 319. Andreas Seeck has shown that Hirschfeld often used this quote. See Seeck 2003, 193. Texts by Hirschfeld and others on the subject of the homosexual Nazi as a stereotype have been extensively analyzed by Alexander Zinn. See Zinn 1997. But it is remarkable that "Die Probe aufs Exempel", which appeared very shortly after the Röhm purge, is absent from Zinn's analysis. I also inquired into whether the book review of Bodo Uhse's *Sölder und Soldat*, also signed "H. M.", could have been by Hirschfeld. See H. M., Apr. 28, 1935; Soetaert 2015, 28–29 n. 25.

[115] Hirschfeld = Expertus, Jan. 1, 1935.

[116] Archiv MHG, Berlin, fonds Ernst Maass, letter (dated Dec. 29, 1937, [6]) from Karl Giese to Ernst Maass. I do not believe there is any reason to doubt Giese's claim, even though he is confusing two texts by Hirschfeld: "Männerbünde: Sexualpsychologischer Beitrag zur Roehm-Katastrophe" (Hirschfeld, Jul. 20, 1934) and "Die 'Ausrottung' der Homosexuellen im Dritten Reich" (Hirschfeld = Expertus, Jan. 1, 1935). In the same letter, Giese mistakes the title of the former article, naming it "Männerhelden". Cf. Hirschfeld & Dose 2013, 186 n. 496; Steakley 2021, 151.

[117] Hirschfeld, May 5, 1934.

[118] Hirschfeld, Mar. 1, 1934. The last article that Hirschfeld published in the French magazine *Vu* appeared in December 1933. See Hirschfeld, Dec. 9, 1933.

[119] Hirschfeld, Mar. 3, 1935, 4; Hirschfeld, Apr. 14, 1935, 4.

of a new (or rather renovated) building of the Centre Universitaire Méditerranéen (C.U.M) in Nice, a local cultural institute that still exists.[121] These two, very untypical Hirschfeld texts are quite lighthearted and almost leisurely. Only the former is explicitly hostile to Nazi Germany. With the exception of the casual mention of "giant women, bearded ladies, female impersonators" (*Riesenweibern, Bartdamen, Damenimitatoren*) in a long list of characters seen in the Nice Carnival, there is no hint of anything sexological in either text [ill. 11].[122] So here we can see the influence of the publishing ban but also that Hirschfeld nevertheless wanted to publish, even on something trivial. We need to point out another article by Hirschfeld published in October 1934 in the Paris-based medical journal *Archives de neurologie*; however, I think that the French authorities were only concerned about (or even aware of) Hirschfeld's more noticeable publishing activities, like his articles in newspapers and popular magazines like *Voilà*.[123]

When we look at the books published by Hirschfeld we see a similar trend. Two of his books were indeed published in France during his exile. *L'Âme et l'amour: psychologie sexologique,* published with Gallimard, appeared in 1935. Hirschfeld saw the first copies near the end of his life, in the last week of April 1935.[124] But, as early as August 1934, Karl Giese wrote to Norman Haire that the printer's proofs (*Umbruchkorrekturen*) were already there and that the book would be published soon.[125] This means it would take almost another year for the book actually to come out. Hirschfeld's other French book, *Education sexuelle,* published with Montaigne, appeared in 1934, possibly before he received the warning.[126] But it is striking, especially in the light of what we now know, that three books were published only after Hirschfeld's death. *Le corps et l'amour* was published in 1937 and *Le tour du monde d'un sexologue* in 1938, both with Gallimard. Excerpts from the latter were published in *Voilà* in 1938. The third book, *Le sexe inconnu,* published by Montaigne, came out in the summer of 1935. So it is possible that Hirschfeld asked the publishers to postpone these publications. On the other hand, Hirschfeld's 1934 appeal to André Gide, apparently to accelerate the publication of *L'Âme et l'amour,* seems to contradict this.[127]

When Hirschfeld was summoned to the Paris police headquarters, they also let him know they found advertising for the Titus Pearls disturbing. Hirschfeld replied that he had no power over the publicity initiatives of the pharmacist Dupraz, who held the French license to distribute the Hirschfeld "sex pills".[128] It is possible that

[120] Hirschfeld brought this up because he had heard an apparently excellent lecture, presumably in the C.U.M., titled "Frédéric Nietzsche à Nice" (Friedrich Nietzsche in Nice). See Hirschfeld, Mar. 3, 1935, 4. The lecture may have been given by Jean-Edouard Spenlé (1873–1951), who published an article on the topic in *Mercure de France* in October 1935. See Spenlé, Oct. 15, 1935. However, the fact that Spenlé was pro-Nazi argues against this identification.

[121] For more general information on the history of the C.U.M., see Arnal 1998.

[122] Presumably, this could also explain *how* Hirschfeld signed the French translation of one of his texts, "Männerbünde", originally appearing in the *Pariser Tageblatt* in July 1934. See Hirschfeld, Jul. 20, 1934. The translation was published in the French anarchist publication *L'en dehors*. See Hirschfeld 1935f. It was signed "d'après le Docteur MAGNUS HIRSCHFELD" (after Dr. MAGNUS HIRSCHFELD). This formulation gave Hirschfeld at least some cover.

[123] See Hirschfeld 1934e. Hirschfeld published another article (on sexual impotence) in this medical journal. See Hirschfeld 1934d. But this article was published in May–June 1934. Hirschfeld only received the French authorities' warning in June 1934.

[124] Hirschfeld & Dose 2013, f. 89/190 n. 498.

[125] University of Sydney Library, Sydney, Norman Haire collection, 3.21, Karl Geise [*sic*: Giese], Typescripts, 1928-1934, letter (dated Aug. 11, 1934) from Karl Giese to Norman Haire.

[126] Cf. Hirschfeld & Dose 2013, f. 89/190 n. 501.

[127] Hirschfeld & Dose 2013, f. 89/190. Why the publication of this book was delayed remains a mystery. Was it because the publisher procrastinated or because Hirschfeld asked the publisher to wait? The exact nature of Gide's expected involvement is also unclear. Was he expected to intervene with the publisher or with the French authorities?

[128] AN, site de Pierrefitte-sur-Seine, Ministère de l'intérieur, Direction de la Sûreté Générale, Service central des cartes d'identité d'étrangers, file Magnus Hirschfeld, file n° 210400, A.S. de l'Allemand Hirschfeld, Décembre 1934, [2], cote 19940506/151.

Hirschfeld resorted to a similar argument about some of his books, saying that these were already in the pipeline with the publisher and that he was bound to contracts struck earlier on. All in all, we can conclude that the warning that Hirschfeld received at the Paris police headquarters did have a certain paralyzing effect on Hirschfeld's publishing activities in France, but not in any clear-cut way. It certainly did not sit well with Hirschfeld, who "burst out" a few times in writing anyway.

MAGNUS HIRSCHFELD'S PARIS LECTURES

When we look at the lectures that Hirschfeld gave in Paris, we can only conclude that, in this case especially, he did not take seriously the French authorities' warning. Or did Hirschfeld, in his defense, also rely on the fact that agreements were worked out before June 1934? According to announcements in the *Pariser Tageblatt*, Hirschfeld gave a lecture in October and another in November 1934, long after the June warning.[129] And Hirschfeld's last lecture in Paris was certainly not the least. The November 1934 lecture was organized by the Philosophical and Scientific Study Group for the Examination of New Trends (Groupe d'études philosophiques et scientifiques pour l'examen des tendances nouvelles) led by the psychoanalyst René Allendy (1889–1942). This organization, founded in 1922, aimed to bring together scientific, artistic and philosophical innovators to give lectures.[130] Hirschfeld was in the company of other celebrities invited by the Group, like Marinetti, Le Corbusier, Artaud, Poulenc, Eisenstein, etc. It is possible that the French rejuvenation doctor, Serge Voronoff (1866–1951), played a role in Hirschfeld lecturing there [ill. 12]. Voronoff had already lectured for the Group in 1924, in the second year of its existence. He also became a member of the patron's committee (*comité de patronage*) in the same year.[131] Hirschfeld likely knew Voronoff quite well. Voronoff can be placed alongside Eugen Steinach (1861–1944). Whatever their competition, Voronoff and Steinach set up all kinds of experiments in search of the ultimate source of "rejuvenation", a theme that bewildered Hirschfeld.[132] Allendy also published on the issue of modern sexuality and its "perversions".[133] For Hirschfeld, Allendy's Group lecture was *the* high point of

[129] On October 31, 1934, the lecture "Was eint und trennt das Menschengeschlecht?" (What Unites and Divides the Human Race?) was delivered to the Association des émigrés Israélites d'Allemagne en France. See *Pariser Tageblatt*, Oct. 27, 1934, 319, 3; and *Pariser Tageblatt*, Oct. 28, 1934, 320, 5. On November 22, 1934, the lecture "La situation actuelle de la pathologie sexuelle" (The Current Situation of Sexual Pathology) was delivered at the Sorbonne in Paris for the Groupe d'Etudes philosophiques et scientifiques pour l'examen des tendances nouvelles (Philosophical and Scientific Study Group for the Examination of New Trends). See *Pariser Tageblatt*, Nov. 21, 1934, 344, 3. A copy of the announcement of that lecture is pasted into the Hirschfeld guestbook (Bergemann, Dose, Keilson-Lauritz & Dubout 2019, f. 93/137). The newspaper clipping pasted below it is from the *Pariser Tageblatt*, Nov. 21, 1934, 344, 3.

[130] See *Bulletin du groupe d'études philsosophiques et scientifiques pour l'examen des idées nouvelles* 1 (1923). A few years later, the organization (and bulletin) was renamed Groupe d'études philosophiques et scientifiques pour l'examen des tendances nouvelles. Even though the organization lasted until 1939, the holdings of the bulletin in the Bibliothèque nationale in Paris only covers the years 1923–31. The IMEC, Saint-Germain-la-Blanche-Herbe, has the archives of René Allendy and his wife, the artist Yvonne Allendy, but the archival fonds does not contain the text of Hirschfeld's lecture. See email (dated Jan. 29, 2016) from Marjorie Delabarre (IMEC, Saint-Germain-la-Blanche-Herbe) to the author. It does contain the announcement card for Hirschfeld's lecture, which is also in the Hirschfeld guestbook. See Bergemann, Dose, Keilson-Lauritz & Dubout 2019, f. 93/137.

[131] Voronoff lectured on April 19, 1924, on "Les greffes animales et humaines" (animal and human transplants). See *Bulletin du groupe d'études philosophiques et scientifiques pour l'examen des idées nouvelles* 2 (1924): 6, 16. For more on Voronoff, see, for example, Grau 2009, 732–35.

[132] See Mildenberger 2009, 663–65; Grau 2009; Herrn 2022. For an account of a Voronoff-like operation conducted in Berlin by Ludwig Levy-Lenz (1889–1966), an Institute collaborator, in which parts of a monkey's testicles were transplanted to a human patient, see Lehnerdt, Feb. 1, 1928.

[133] See, for example, his long texts in the 1937 and 1938 special issues of *Le Crapouillot* (Allendy 1937; Allendy 1938).

his stay in France, or so he esteemed it when looking back on his Paris period, in the beginning of December 1934.[134]

The French authorities presumed that the lecture he gave on June 6 or 7, 1934, was Hirschfeld's last. It is strange that the French authorities did not notice that Hirschfeld gave two more lectures in Paris, after the warning, in the second half of 1934. Or was it possible that these two lectures were the last provocation that made the French authorities banish Hirschfeld from Paris? There are no clear traces to suggest this scenario in the French archives on Hirschfeld I consulted, but I think it possible that Hirschfeld did not leave Paris for Nice just for the winter. Because of these two lectures, the French authorities may have informed Hirschfeld that they would not prolong his residence permit. It is possible that Hirschfeld then proposed a compromise, and suggested that leaving the capital for Nice would be an acceptable alternative. When Giese's expulsion was still pending, Hirschfeld suggested something similar when he tried to convince the French authorities not to expel Giese from French soil: "If there is a possibility that the expulsion would be only from Paris, GIESE would be very happy because he would in that case be able to work on the restoration of scientific materials in some small location, for example in the south of France".[135]

Indeed, five elements seem to hint at this possibility that Hirschfeld was banished from Paris to Nice by the French authorities. Firstly, the date of his lecture at the Sorbonne, on November 22, 1934, is curiously close to his departure from Paris at the end of November. Hirschfeld left Paris on November 27, 1934.[136] Secondly, in December 1934, Hirschfeld noted in *Testament: Heft II* that his residence permit was being extended only on a monthly basis.[137] That means something must have changed (to Hirschfeld's disadvantage) since, when he arrived in France in 1933, the Prefect in Vichy granted him a residence permit (*Aufenthaltsbewilligung*) valid until the end of 1935.[138]

The third element remains unresolved but seems possibly relevant as well. Hirschfeld's Fonds de Moscou file contains an unfortunately undated letter from the Ministry of the Interior to the Paris Prefect of Police: "I have the honor of informing you that I am granting this foreigner a reprieve of *three months*, on the condition that he has no dealings with medicine in France or with anything related to Sexology" (emphasis in original).[139] Judging from other handwritten scraps of paper included

[134] Hirschfeld & Dose 2013, f. 89/190. The entry is dated December 9, 1934. For a claim that this lecture prompted Hirschfeld's lifelong enemy, Dr. Albert Moll, to send a letter denouncing him to the dean of the Sorbonne Faculty of Medicine, see Hirschfeld & Dose 2013, 190 n. 503. However, this is not possible since Hirschfeld gave his lecture in November 1934 and Moll's letter was sent in January 1934. Cf. Dose 2019, 22–23. Dose also thinks Moll's letter may have played a part in Hirschfeld's conflict with the French section of the WLSR. He speaks of an "auffällige Koinzidenz" (striking coincidence). See also Herrn 2022, 480.

[135] AN, site de Pierrefitte-sur-Seine, Ministère de l'intérieur, Direction générale de la sûreté nationale (fonds de Moscou), file on Karl Giese, dossier n° 15843, letter (dated Jun. 17, 1934) from Magnus Hirschfeld (to Paris police headquarters?), cote 19940448/186: "Si il [*sic*: S'il] y a une possibilité que l'expulsion sera seulement pour Paris, GIESE serait très heureux parcequ'il [*sic*: parce qu'il] serait capable en ce cas de travailler à la restauration des matériaux scientifiques à un petit endroit quelconque, par exemple au sud [*sic*: Sud] de la France".

[136] AN, site de Pierrefitte-sur-Seine, Ministère de l'intérieur, Direction de la Sûreté Générale, Service central des cartes d'identité d'étrangers, file Magnus Hirschfeld, file n° 210400, cote 19940506/151.

[137] Hirschfeld & Dose 2013, f. 85/182: "Auch ich bekam immer nur von einem Monat zum anderen Aufenthaltsbewilligung" (I am also only getting residence permits from one month to the next).

[138] Cf. Hirschfeld & Dose 2013, f. 85/182 n. 465; Hirschfeld & Dose 2013, f. 79/170–72 n. 437 and n. 440.

[139] AN, site de Pierrefitte-sur-Seine, Ministère de l'intérieur, Direction de la Sûreté Générale, Service central des cartes d'identité d'étrangers, file Magnus Hirschfeld, file number 210400, undated letter (but likely Jan. 1935 or later) from Directeur 8ième Bureau (Cartes d'identité) to the Prefect of Police, cote 19940506/151: "j'ai l'honneur de vous informer que j'accorde à cet étranger un sursis de *trois mois*, sous réserve qu'il ne s'occupe pas de médicine en

in the file, apparently used to prepare the case, this letter can be dated to the second half of May 1935, after Hirschfeld's death. The letter remained undated possibly because it was never sent due to Hirschfeld dying in mid-May 1935. (We will see later on that the news that Hirschfeld died in Nice reached Paris only very slowly and in a distorted way.) I think it is possible that police headquarters also noticed that Hirschfeld published *L'Âme et l'amour* with Gallimard, in April–May 1935, and thus breached his agreement with the French authorities again. The Prefecture may have conferred with the Ministry of the Interior on the matter and the latter then redacted the letter giving Hirschfeld a reprieve (*sursis*) of three months. For now, the matter of what exactly happened with regards to Hirschfeld's residence permit coming under scrutiny again in the first half of 1935 needs to remain unresolved. To be completely clear, Magnus Hirschfeld was never officially expelled from France since, unlike Giese, he had not committed a crime.[140]

The fourth element indicating that Hirschfeld might have been banished from Paris is the already mentioned text published under the pseudonym Expertus on January 1, 1935, as well as the harmless "Rivierabrief" on the C.U.M. that he published under his own name in mid-April 1935. Setting aside his books, we could say that, in this case, Hirschfeld strictly respected the French authorities' wish that he either not publish on sexological topics or only published pseudonymously and on different subjects.

The fifth factor are the lectures that seem to have come to a definitive halt once Hirschfeld was in Nice. More than a decade ago, when doing research with my Canadian friend Don McLeod in Nice on Hirschfeld's stay in the city, I remember being quite surprised at not finding any trace of Hirschfeld having given a lecture in the C.U.M. archives.[141] The venue and its underlying ideas about providing easily accessible education for a lay public – similar to those of the Collège de France in Paris – must have delighted Hirschfeld. Even to this day, anyone interested can listen to lectures on specialized topics given by invited specialists. On top of that, the C.U.M. was located right next to Hirschfeld's residence, the Gloria Mansions I building on the Promenade des Anglais. It is likely that Hirschfeld did not lecture there as a consequence of a possibly final warning from the French authorities. But that he could not do so must certainly have been hard on him. As Ralf Dose very poignantly and justly wrote of Hirschfeld: "Lecture halls filled to capacity were his element".[142] The "harmless" text on the C.U.M. that he did publish is maybe testimony to this frustration.

Hirschfeld's stay in France was, like any other foreigner's, always conditional and limited in time, and dependent on "good behavior". The warning given to Hirschfeld at the Prefecture in Paris was serious and one may presume that the French authorities kept an eye on his activities. This scrutiny seems to have extended to Hirschfeld's stay in Nice in the first half of 1935. Internal documents dating to February 1935

France et de ce qui trait à la Sexologie" (emphasis in original).

140 I checked whether Magnus Hirschfeld's name appeared in the 1933–36 alphabetical registers of the "Etats signalétiques des étrangers expulsés de France" (Lists of Foreigners Deported from France), AN, site de Pierrefitte-sur-Seine, Paris, Ministère de l'intérieur, Fichier central de police judiciaire (1899–1938), Etats signalétiques des étrangers expulsés de France, années 1931–1938, cote 19980182/3. It was not there.

141 Archives Municipales, Nice, fonds C.U.M, année 1934–1935, pp. 3–10, cote 168 W80 and Liste des conférenciers et titres, A à L, cote 168 W125.

142 Dose 2020b, 23: "Bis auf den letzten Platz gefüllte Vortragssäle waren sein Element".

143 AN, site de Pierrefitte-sur-Seine, Ministère de l'intérieur, Direction de la Sûreté Générale, Service central des cartes d'identité d'étrangers, file Magnus Hirschfeld, file n° 210400, internal note (dated Feb. 21, 1935) from Ministry of the Interior (publications obscènes) to Service central des cartes d'identité des étrangers, cote 19940506/151.

repeated that Hirschfeld could stay in France as long as he did not engage with sexological matters.[143] But it is also noticeable that Paris's surveillance of Hirschfeld was simply less efficient in Nice. All in all, judging from the rather sloppy Ministry of the Interior archive file on Hirschfeld, these surveillance activities were neither very well coordinated nor consistent.[144] In Hirschfeld's file, for example, some notes and letters reveal that there was confusion in Paris even about the exact date and place of Hirschfeld's death in May 1935.[145]

THE ROLE OF THE FRENCH AUTHORITIES

There is one more aspect we still need to consider regarding the coincidence of the attempted appeal of Giese's conviction in the Appeals Court and the clear warning Hirschfeld received. Was Giese's "usefulness" for the French authorities as a warning to Hirschfeld the outcome of a random roundup at a gay bathhouse or had this roundup been planned from the start knowing that Giese would visit the bathhouse that day?

Foreign men were more vulnerable targets in these bathhouses than French nationals. The latter, who had similar homosexual interests, were generally left alone.[146] One French author claims that "surveillance is initiated by the vice squad as soon as a foreign person visits France".[147] It is certain that Hirschfeld was sometimes shadowed in Paris. We can deduce this from a report on Hirschfeld in the Fonds de Moscou. The police were well aware that, by June 1934, Hirschfeld had returned to Paris from Nice, and that he had taken residence again in his "furnished apartment" (*appartement meublé*) at the avenue Charles Floquet.[148] When his departure for Nice was noted, in the beginning of 1934, the informer added: "His return will be reported" (*Son retour sera signalé*).[149] We may presume that Giese was also followed sometimes. It is clear in any case that the vice squad kept an eye on the private life of notable individuals, foreigners and nationals. In his memoir, Louis Métra wrote about Albert Priolet (1882–1942),[150] one of the chief inspectors of the vice squad: "Under his direction, the 'Mondaine' was at the height of its power. Day after day, he noted the secrets of our Excellencies, the foibles of our masters of the moment, the underbelly of high society life, harassed drug addicts and their dream merchants. He supplied information to the Prefect of Police, Mr. Chiappe, who was considered the best-informed man in the world. Today, all these secrets lie dormant in the archives, in the drawers of the directors; formidable forgotten papers, *which are only brought out*

[144] AN, site de Pierrefitte-sur-Seine, Ministère de l'intérieur, Direction de la Sûreté Générale, Service central des cartes d'identité d'étrangers, file Magnus Hirschfeld, file n° 210400, cote 19940506/151 and, from the same archival file, the internal handwritten note in pencil (presumably dated February 1935) of the Ministry of the Interior with a reply from a certain Mr. Nativel: "il y aurait lieu également de s'assurer de l'activité d'Hirschfeld à Nice où il irait comme hivernant" (it would also be necessary to ascertain Hirschfeld's activities in Nice, where he will be spending the winter).

[145] AN, site de Pierrefitte-sur-Seine, Ministère de l'intérieur, Direction de la Sûreté Générale, Service central des cartes d'identité d'étrangers, file Magnus Hirschfeld, file n° 210400, letter (dated Jun. 8, 1935) from the Ministry of the Interior to the Préfet des Alpes-Maritimes, cote 19940506/151.

[146] Buot 2013, 192, 194–95. See also Archives de la Préfecture de Police de Paris, loose undated note, dossier Bains Voltaire, 163.457 M. R., cote JC 96. Willemin claims that the majority of bathhouse visitors were mostly left in peace but, in exchange, owners had to inform the vice squad about their patrons (Willemin 2009, 91).

[147] Willemin 2009, 87: "Une surveillance est établie de fait par la Mondaine [brigade mondaine], dès qu'une personnalité étrangère se rend en visite en France".

[148] AN, site de Pierrefitte-sur-Seine, Ministère de l'intérieur, Direction générale de la sûreté nationale (fonds de Moscou), file on Dr. [Pierre] Vacher [Vachet], conférencier a/s de guérisons miraculeuses, cote 19940482/2, anonymous two-page text (dated Jun. 14, 1934).

[149] Ibid., anonymous note (dated Jan. 1, 1934).

[150] See http://www.sfhp.fr/index.php?post /2015/01/21/Notice-biographique-Albert-Priolet (accessed May 17, 2016).

in case of absolute necessity, a real 'high society' directory of drugs and vice whose most sensational details are kept behind an impregnable iron door" (emphasis added).[151]

Did the bathhouse roundup take place *because* the police knew that Giese was there? Did Giese act as Hirschfeld's Achilles' heel? Unfortunately, the police file on Karl Giese in the Paris police headquarters archive that could have told us what exactly happened was discarded after the war.[152] Possibly, it would have enabled us to learn more about the vice squad's planned or random raid on the Bains Voltaire in April 1934.

It also seems that Hirschfeld himself had some suspicions, seeming to make a slight allusion to the possibility of a set-up in a July 1934 letter written to the French authorities: "[Giese] embarked on this extremely distressing affair only out of ignorance, *seduced by another person who was not even identified*" (emphasis added).[153] Why indeed was the man who fellated Giese not identified or prosecuted? Because they were only after Giese? Because the other man was just a regular local? Here, Hirschfeld seems to blame the other person for having provoked Giese into this behavior while Paris police headquarters always claimed, as we have seen, that it was Giese who lured the other man into sexual activity. The least that we can say is that Giese alone being punished offended Hirschfeld's sense of justice. But it also remains possible that Hirschfeld thought that police headquarters may have had their own reasons for only bringing Giese to trial.

It is possible that Giese was simply caught in the vice squad's net, and that someone in the Paris police department realized that they could exploit Giese's "crime" to police Hirschfeld. The statistics gathered by the French historian Romain Jaouen show that, for the period 1918–39, the highest number of vice squad roundups occurred in 1934. In that year they conducted at least twenty-one. This could simply mean that Giese had the bad luck of being caught at the worst possible time.[154] It also remains possible that some more malicious intent was at work in the Paris police headquarters and its vice squad. Was the other man in the bathhouse maybe an *agent provocateur*? It

[151] Delpêche 1955, 14: "Sous sa direction, la 'Mondaine' a connu l'apogée de sa puissance. Il notait jour après jour, les secrets de nos Excellences, les travers de nos maîtres du moment, les dessous de la vie mondaine, harcelait les drogués et leurs marchands de rêve. Il armait de renseignements le Préfet de Police, M. Chiappe, qui passait pour l'homme le plus documenté du monde. Aujourd'hui, tous ces secrets dorment dans les archives, dans les tiroirs des principaux ; redoutables papiers oubliés, *et qu'on ne ressort qu'en cas d'absolue nécessité* [emphasis added], véritable bottin « mondain » de la drogue et du vice dont les plus sensationnelles manifestations sont conservées derrière une porte de fer inviolable". Cf. Willemin 2010, 51. Delpêche noted that, even before World War I, the precursor of the Brigade mondaine had a similar function: "Quelque chose d'analogue, mais trop sommaire, existait déjà sous forme d'archives spéciales des garnis, où les inspecteurs avaient accumulé dossiers et photos sur l'activité secrète des personnalités parisiennes" (Something analogous, but much more basic, already existed in the form of special supplementary archives, in which investigators gathered files and photos on the secret activities of Parisian persons" (Delpêche 1955, 12). The files on notables thus established were called "les blancs" (the whites) and these were kept in a coffer named "Les étoiles" (the stars) on the second floor of the Quai des Orfèvres building. See Willemin 2009, 51, 85. But it seems unlikely that these files could fit in a single coffer.

[152] A microfilm in the archives of the Paris police headquarters indicates that, at some point, a file on Giese existed "en vue de l'obtention d'un permis de séjour en France" (in order to obtain a residence permit in France). The microfilm further says: "Numéro du dossier: CC1485020 (dossier détruit). / Date d'ouverture du dossier: 31 août 1934. / [...] / Fin de validité du document: dossier d'expulsion (n° 52640 du 6 juin 1957)" (File number: CC1485020 [file destroyed]. / Date file opened: 31 August 1934 / [...] / End of validity of document: expulsion file [no. 52640 of 6 June 1957]). See email (dated Dec. 30, 2010) from Richard Wagner (Archives Préfecture de Police, Paris) to the author. When I sent another email asking for further explanation, I received no reply.

[153] AN, site de Pierrefitte-sur-Seine, Ministère de l'intérieur, Direction générale de la sûreté nationale (fonds de Moscou), file on Karl Giese, dossier n° 15843, typed letter (dated Jul. 17, 1934) from Magnus Hirschfeld to Paris police headquarters (?), [2], cote 19940448/186: "en cette affaire extrêmement pénible il [Giese] s'est lancé seulement par l'ignorance, *séduit par une autre personne, pas même identifiée*" (emphasis added).

is known that, in the eighteenth century, the Paris police did not hesitate to use so-called "mouches", handsome men arrested and released to act as agents provocateurs, eliciting illegal conduct in order to arrest those seduced afterwards.[155] But were such practices still in use in the 1930s? In a letter to Hirschfeld, Norman Haire wrote that the use of agents provocateurs for persecuting queer activities was very common in England in the 1930s.[156] In Nazi-occupied Vienna of the 1940s, they did not hesitate to use agents provocateurs in bathhouses to catch gay men in flagrante delicto.[157] The 2021 Netflix movie *Madame Claude* clearly suggests that French state security remained interested in the private sexual dealings of French dignitaries and other notable people until at least the 1970s and also did not hesitate to stage "information gathering" sexual encounters, compromising notables so as to blackmail them if necessary. When the closeted Hungarian European parliament member József Szájer, an active member of the anti-homophobic Fidesz party, was caught in the act at a Brussels gay sex party during Covid lockdown, in November 2020 (when all private gatherings of more than two people were forbidden), the Hungarian press deduced that Szájer had been ambushed by local police tipped off by "secret services". The arrest took place shortly after Poland and Hungary blocked plans for large-scale EU funding for the pandemic, short-circuiting the entire EU apparatus.[158] But does this indicate that Giese was also purposefully ambushed in 1934? Nothing much can be said with any real certainty. In these matters, one can only grapple with the difficult and unresolved choice (due to missing archival sources on the workings of state secret services) of not being paranoid and not being naive.

One may conclude, at the very least, that Giese's misstep was effectively used by the French authorities as a means to influence and caution against Hirschfeld's sexual reform activities in France. The clear coincidence of the dismissal of the appeal against Giese's sentence for public indecency and Hirschfeld's summons to Paris police headquarters (Préfecture de Police), both on June 8, 1934, seems to strongly confirm the conclusion that Paris police headquarters acted and operated forcefully and semi-independently in the French state apparatus to proactively control notable foreigners.[159] Hirschfeld was, as we have seen, "invited" to give up the things that had fired his passion all his life. The threat behind the friendly invitation for Hirschfeld to rein himself in was the heavy shadow of Giese's confirmed three-month prison sentence and the ensuing expulsion later that year. It was made clear to Hirschfeld that he could *not* continue his life's work in France, as he had hoped.

[154] Jaouen 2018, 115. The author stresses that, because the sources are incomplete, these numbers are no more than indicative; however, in a twenty-year period, the highest observed number of operations took place in 1934.

[155] Rey 1989, 130–32.

[156] University of Sydney Library, Sydney, Norman Haire collection, 3.20, Magnus Hirschfeld, Typescripts, 1923–1935, letter (dated Jan. 27, 1933, 2) from Norman Haire to Magnus Hirschfeld.

[157] Pettinger 2021, 81–94 ("Agent Provocateur im Dampfbad").

[158] GVV, Dec. 3, 2020, 4.

[159] See also Jaouen 2018, 47–53.

1. Entrance of the former bathhouse Bains Voltaire. March 2015.

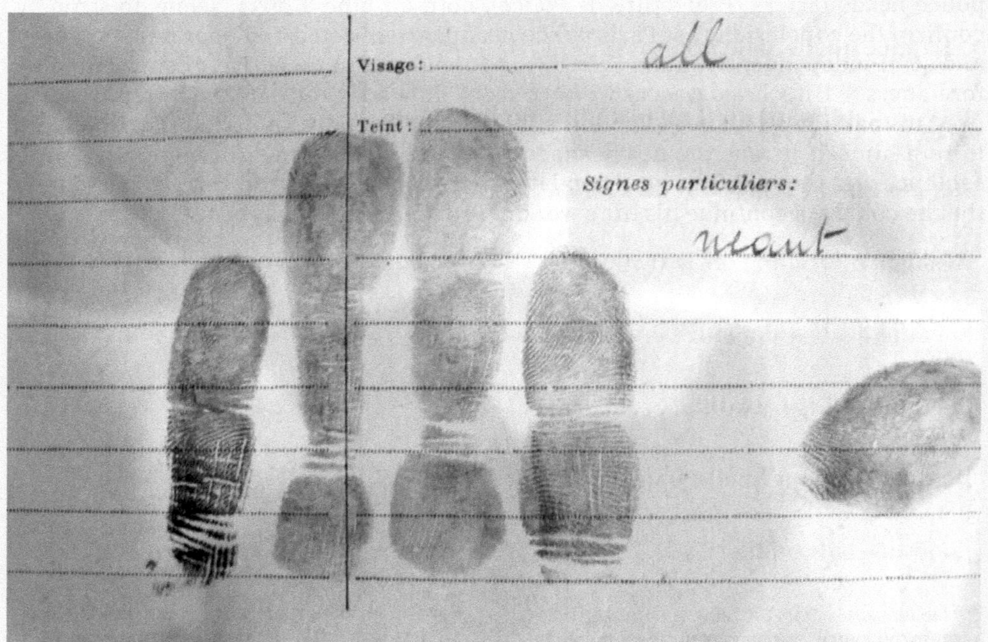
Visage: all

Teint:

Signes particuliers:

neant

2. Karl Giese's left hand fingerprints, on a document assembled in Fresnes Prison. June 15, 1934.

3. Roger Langeron, the Parisian Prefect of Police. 1934.

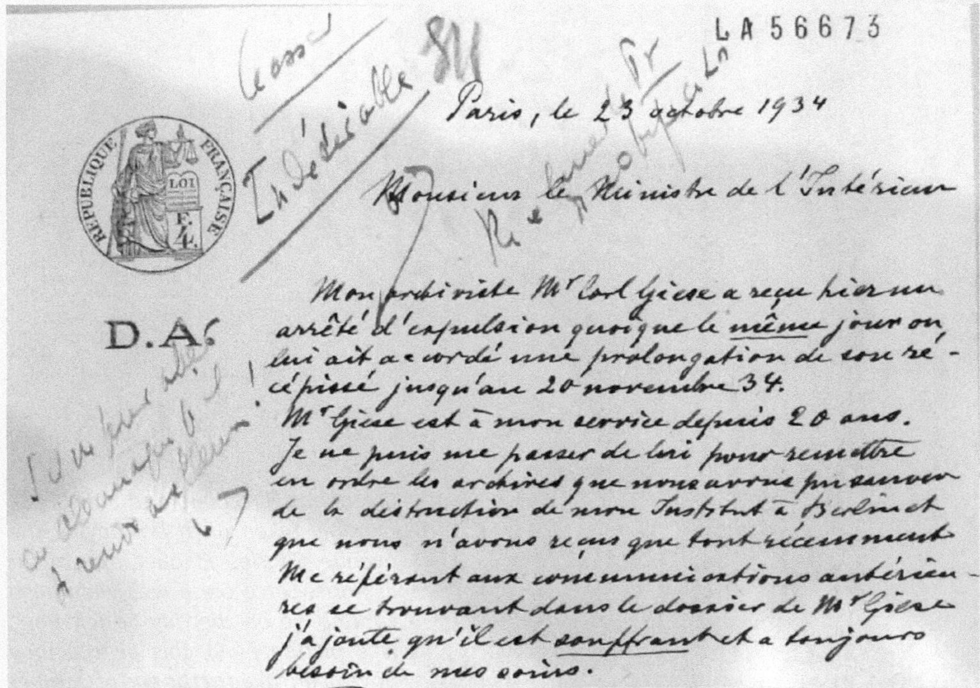

LA 56673

Classé Indésirable

RÉPUBLIQUE FRANÇAISE

LOI

D.A.

Paris, le 23 octobre 1934

Monsieur le Ministre de l'Intérieur

Mon archiviste Mr Carl Giese a reçu hier un arrêté d'expulsion quoique le même jour on lui ait accordé une prolongation de son récépissé jusqu'au 20 novembre 34.
Mr Giese est à mon service depuis 20 ans.
Je ne puis me passer de lui pour remettre en ordre les archives que nous avons pu sauver de la destruction de mon Institut à Berlin et que nous n'avons reçus que tout récemment.
Me référant aux communications antérieures se trouvant dans le dossier de Mr Giese j'ajoute qu'il est souffrant et a toujours besoin de mes soins.

4. Magnus Hirschfeld's certified handwritten letter of October 1934, asking the French Minister of the Interior not to expel Karl Giese. Someone has added in blue fountain-pen ink handwriting: "classified as undesirable" (Classé indésirable). The letter was written the day after Giese received his notice of expulsion.

5. Shortly after his thirty-sixth birthday, Karl Giese had to leave both Paris and France. A last picture was taken on the sidewalk in front of the avenue Charles Floquet apartment before Li Shiu Tong escorted Giese to a Paris train station or to the French border. Ca. October 25–27, 1934.

6. Magnus Hirschfeld and Karl Giese, possibly taken on a balcony of the avenue Charles Floquet apartment in Paris. Since Giese was wearing a spotted tie on the day he left Paris (see picture n° 5), this picture may have been taken at the end of October 1934, on the day Giese had to leave Paris. If so, then this is one of the very last pictures showing Magnus Hirschfeld and Karl Giese together.

7. From left to right, Karl Giese, Magnus Hirschfeld and Max Reiss posing for a (blurry) picture on the Champ de Mars park in August 1934. The park is adjacent to the avenue Charles Floquet apartment where Hirschfeld was living. Giese had been released from prison the month before.

8. Envelope of the Garde-meuble Bedel storage company in Paris, showing its main office address on the Rue Saint-Augustin. Postmarked June 2, 1930.

9. "Sir Doctor on the Champs-Elysées" (Herr Doktor aux Champs-Elysées). Caricature of Magnus Hirschfeld drinking beer and eating sausage in the newspaper Paris-Midi. April 1935.

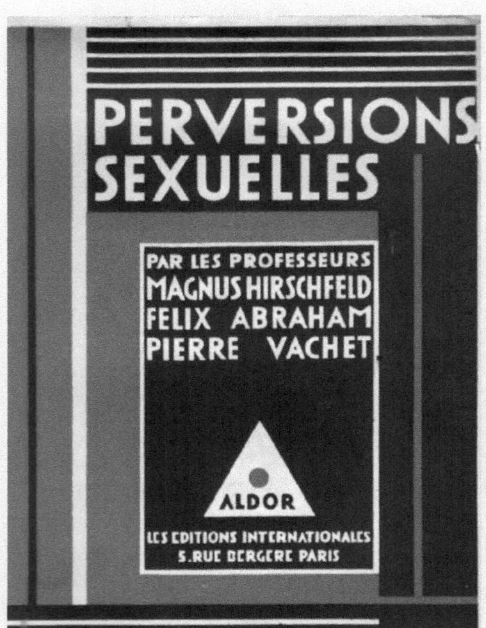

10. Front cover of Perversions sexuelles – d'après l'enseignement du docteur Magnus Hirschfeld (Sexual Perversions: Inspired by the Teachings of Doctor Magnus Hirschfeld), published in France in 1931, written by one of Hirschfeld's Berlin Institute colleagues, Felix Abraham.

11. Costumed participants in the Nice Carnival, held every February, pass in front of Café Monnot on Massena square (Place Massena), one of the main meeting points for German exiles in the city. Presumably 1930s.

12. Dr. Serge Voronoff, the French rejuvenation specialist. Before 1909 (?).

9. The Handling and Settlement of Magnus Hirschfeld's Estate in Nice

GIESE'S SECOND STAY IN BRNO, FOLLOWED BY THE MOVE TO VIENNA

After his eight-month sojourn in Paris (three months of which he spent in prison) and his subsequent expulsion from France, Giese headed back to Brno, where he arrived on November 2, 1934, staying a little less than three months, until January 23, 1935.[1] We do not know why he went there again. Did he inquire with Josef Weisskopf, as in 1933, if there was a possibility to start up an Institute there? In Brno, Giese took a room with a Jewish couple on the second floor at 5 Hutterteich (Hutterův rybník), very close to where two of his Brno friends, Karl Fein and Willi Bondi, lived.[2] (We will return to Willi Bondi later on.) Nothing else is known about Giese's second three-month stay in Brno.

At the end of January 1935, for unknown reasons, Giese moved to Vienna.[3] It's possible that he inquired again if there were any opportunities to start up the Institute in Vienna. From a letter he later wrote to Max Hodann, in August 1935, we learn that, in the preceding months, Giese had spoken to several Austrian people who had been, or still were, close to the WLSR, and this at least indicates that he was in close contact with many of them.[4] Giese would stay in the Austrian capital for approximately a year and a half. He lived at 27 Mariahilferstrasse (Wien 6), where he rented a room in the apartment of the Jewish doctor Zalman Schneyer (1875–1942?) and his wife Sofie (1880–1942?) [ill. 1].[5] Giese had been in Vienna before when he attended the 1930 WLSR conference.[6] He also stayed there for a while with Hirschfeld after the latter returned

[1] AMB, Brno, fonds Z 1, resident registration cards Karl Giese.

[2] The owners or renters of the apartment were Ferdinand Beamt (1867–1943?) and Ida Beamt (1876–1943?), who had moved there only the month before. See their resident registration cards in the AMB, Brno, fonds Z 1. The couple and their unmarried daughter Gertruda Beamtová (1902–1942?), who was living with them since October 1938, were deported from Brno to Terezín on transport "Ad", on March 23, 1942. The couple was transported further to Auschwitz-Birkenau on transport "Dr" on December 15, 1943. Their daughter Gertruda was put on transport "Al" on April 23, 1942, deporting her from Terezín to Lublin.

[3] On January 30, 1935, Giese was officially registered as living in Vienna, exactly one week after he left Brno, on January 23, 1935, see his resident registration cards in AMB, Brno, fonds Z 1. See also email (dated Dec. 10, 2010) from Wiener Stadt- und Landesarchiv to the author, who looked in the archival fonds, Bundespolizeidirektion Wien, Historische Meldeunterlagen.

[4] See Arbetarrörelsens arkiv och bibliotek, Stockholm, Max Hodann samling, vol. 15, letter (dated Aug. 2, 1935, [3-4]) from Karl Giese to Max Hodann. After Hirschfeld's death, in May 1935, some people from his Viennese network affectionately offered their condolences to Giese (ibid., [4]).

[5] The apartment was located on the third floor of the building, as attested by the Roman numeral III on an envelope of a letter (dated Oct. 20, 1935) sent by Karl Giese to Max Reiss. See Archiv MHG, Berlin, fonds Max Reiss. Giese also mentioned this address and noted "bei Dr Schneyer" (at Dr. Schneyer's) at the top of a letter (dated Sep. 24, 1935, [1]) that he sent to Max Hodann. See Arbetarrörelsens arkiv och bibliotek, Stockholm, Max Hodann samling, vol. 15. Both Zalman and Sofie Schneyer were of Romanian origin and perished in the Holocaust. They were deported from Vienna to Izbica on June 5, 1942. The building in which they lived was designed in 1908 by the architects Franz Kupka and Gustav Orglmeister and stands to this day. See Kulturgüterkataster Wien: http://www.wien.gv.at/kulturportal/public/grafik.aspx?FeatureByID=010597&featureClass=inventarisiertegebaeude&ThemePage=1 (accessed Aug. 16, 2012).

[6] For Giese's resident registration card (dated Sep. 11–14, 1930), see the email (dated Dec. 10, 2010) from Wiener Stadt- und Landesarchiv to the author: "Als Addresse wird Wien 1., Ebendorferstraße 8/1/8 und als Beruf Privatsekretär angegeben". The information comes from Wiener Stadt- und Landesarchiv, fonds Bundespolizeidirektion Wien, Historische Meldeunterlagen.

from his world tour, in March 1932.[7] In order to find a place to stay, Giese most likely relied on Hirschfeld's network, which was of course very familiar with Hirschfeld's secretary. The fact that Zalman Schneyer was a doctor and was included in a list of "Friends of Magnus Hirschfeld", assembled by Ernst Maass, strongly points in this direction.[8]

The building where Giese lived lay in the heart of what was then a gay (and red-light) neighborhood. Only two blocks away, one could find Hubertus Keller, the renowned gay restaurant.[9] Likely due to the proximity of the Stifts-barracks (Stiftskaserne), there was also a gay cruising area (*Strich*) in the neighborhood. Could Giese observe the activity going on there from the room he was likely renting?[10] For the rest, we have no real idea what Giese did in Vienna. What is clear is that he did not start his medical studies in Vienna, although he intended to finally work on completing his high school diploma (*Abitur*, also called *Matura* in Austria), as he told an Austrian journalist in June 1935, shortly after he arrived in Vienna from France.[11] Giese had

[7] "Magnus Hirschfelds Erbe in Wien", *Der Morgen – Wiener Montagblatt*, Jun. 24, 1935, 10; Herrn 2004, 193.

[8] The list titled "Freunde von Magnus Hirschfeld" is in Archiv MHG, Berlin, fonds Ernst Maass. Because of the handwriting, Robert Maass also thinks this list was assembled by his father, see email (dated Jul. 17, 2020) from Robert Maass to the author. This list has an intriguing characteristic. It is written on similar letter paper as that used by Giese to write his last will in Brno, in March 1938. The letter paper has the same crenelated border and yellowish appearance. This leads one to think that Giese possibly gave Maass the sheet of paper with the names of the seven Giese deemed to be "good friends" of Magnus Hirschfeld: Karl Fein, Ellen Bækgaard, Norman Haire, Jonathan Leunbach, Edmond Zammert, Leopold Hönig, and the lawyer and notary Johannes Werthauer (1866–1938). Other names were added later (given the difference in ink and different handwriting) by Ernst Maass. Since Giese's address at Dr. Schneyer's is also mentioned down the list, this could indicate that the list was started in Nice in the month after Hirschfeld's death. The handwritten testament of Karl Giese is in MZA, Brno, fonds C 152, Okresní soud civilní Brno (Bezirksgericht für Zivilsachen Brünn), rubber stamp (dated Mar. 23, 1938), ad DV 206/38/2, sign. s.l. 69/38.

[9] The St. Hubertus Keller restaurant (owned by a Josef Dörner) was located at 49 Mariahilferstrasse (Wien VI). This was likely not the gay restaurant that Hirschfeld described in his 1901 article on gay Vienna: "Ostersamstag Abend geleitete mich Baron X in ein, wohl nur sehr wenigen Normalsexuellen Wiens bekanntes urnisches Restaurant. Vier mittelgrosse Zimmer waren von Homosexuellen so überfüllt, das wir kaum Sitzplätze fanden" (On Easter Saturday evening, Baron X took me to a Viennese restaurant known only to very few sexually-normal people. Four medium-sized rooms were so crowded with homosexuals that we could hardly find seats). See Hirschfeld 1901, 788. Hannes Suzelbacher informed me that Hubertus Keller became a hangout for gay men in the 1920s; see email (dated Feb. 25, 2011) from Hannes Suzelbacher to the author. This seems to be confirmed by Brunner 2016, 125. See also Brunner & Sulzenbacher 2016, 261.

[10] Hannes Sulzenbacher spoke of this *Strich* during a conversation in Vienna on March 12, 2012.

[11] "Magnus Hirschfelds Erbe in Wien", in *Der Morgen – Wiener Montagblatt*, Jun. 24, 1935, 10. "Magnus Hirschfelds Testament", published in the Brno newspaper *Tagesbote* (Jun. 21, 1935, 5), contains the following: "Interessant ist es übrigens, daß Giese sich zur Zeit in Wien befindet, um sich dort aus das Abitur vorzubereiten. Der an sich sehr gebildete Sekretär ist Autodidakt und will jetzt systematisch gewisse Fachlücken ausfüllen, um als Testamentsvollstrecker einwandfrei fungieren zu können" (It is interesting to note, by the way, that Giese is currently in Vienna to prepare for the Abitur there. The secretary, who is well-educated, is self-taught and now wants to systematically fill in certain gaps in his expertise in order to be able to function flawlessly as executor of the will). See also Arbetarrörelsens arkiv och bibliotek, Stockholm, Max Hodann samling, vol. 15, letter (dated Aug. 2, 1935, [1-2]) from Karl Giese to Max Hodann. In the same letter, Giese wrote that he was too "nervös" (nervous) to work on his "Schularbeiten" (school work) (ibid., [4]). There are no traces to indicate that Karl Giese studied at the university medical faculty in Vienna any time between 1934 and 1936. See email (dated Mar. 10, 2011) from Martin G. Enne (Archiv der Universität Wien) to the author: "Auch als außerordentlicher Hörer ist er nicht verzeichnet. Soweit ich weiß, gab es damals auch keine andere Möglichkeit, in Wien Humanmedizin zu studieren" (He is also not listed as an external student. As far as I know, there was no other way to study human medicine in Vienna at the time). And yet, in a letter Magnus Hirschfeld sent to Max Reiss, in March 1935, he wrote that Giese (then in Vienna) was working hard and Hirschfeld hoped he would succeed. See Archiv MHG, Berlin, fonds Max Reiss, letter (dated Mar. 30, 1935, 3) from Magnus Hirschfeld to Max Reiss. In his own and later letter to Max Reiss, Giese said that he had to abandon his studies due to a lack of money but would resume them as soon as he received the money from the inheritance. See Archiv MHG, Berlin, fonds Max Reiss, letter (dated Oct. 20, 1935, 2) from Karl Giese to Max Reiss.

learned his lesson in Paris and managed to stay out of sexual trouble in Vienna.[12] This did not prevent him from having an idyllic affair with a visiting Viennese man who lived in Japan.[13]

GIESE'S FINANCIAL FUTURE

Shortly after Giese was forced to leave Paris, Hirschfeld started to worry about Giese's future means of existence. Giese had always been able to live under Hirschfeld's protective wing. The Paris debacle must have made it clear that Giese, who had been with Hirschfeld for at least fifteen years in the Berlin Institute, was no longer going to be by his side. We saw that Giese met Hirschfeld when he was sixteen and this likely meant that he exchanged his parents' home for one at Hirschfeld's Institute. Giese always self-evidently found food and shelter there, even when Hirschfeld was on his world tour.[14] Simply adding his precarious health to the equation was enough for Hirschfeld to realize that something needed to be done. In the months after Giese had left Paris, Hirschfeld managed to work out an agreement with Norman Haire. Haire would pay £50 annually to support Giese.[15] Hirschfeld also contacted another friend of his, the Danish doctor Ellen Bækgaard with the same request for financial support. She also agreed to contribute but it is clear that both she and Haire were uncomfortable with the request to support Giese financially.[16] Haire stressed that he neither would nor could contribute more since he was already helping out others financially and had bought a country house in need of renovation. He asked Hirschfeld to suggest the names of other possible contributors so that Bækgaard could contact them.[17] Hirschfeld himself contributed £40 per year.[18] Although it is nowhere explicitly stated, the allowance system set up to finance Giese's medical studies was likely also a way to ensure that Giese would not suddenly have access to large sums of money. Possibly, Hirschfeld knew that Giese would not be able to handle large amounts of money responsibly. Hirschfeld clearly hoped that Giese would gain a medical degree and carry on Hirschfeld's legacy and earn his own living.[19] But this never happened.

[12] Email (dated Dec. 10, 2010) from Wiener Stadt- und Landesarchiv to the author: "In der Datenbank zu den Strafakten des Landesgerichts Wien scheint der Name Karl Giese nicht auf" (Karl Giese's name does not appear in the database of the criminal files of the Vienna Regional Court).

[13] Archiv MHG, Berlin, fonds Max Reiss, letter (dated Oct. 20, 1935, 4) from Karl Giese to Max Reiss.

[14] When Giese stayed in Brno the first time, in the second half of 1933, it was clearly the first time in his life he had to live on his own and take care of himself. Suddenly, he realized he needed to pay attention and not spend too much money even on simple things like water. In a postcard sent from Brno to Adelheid Schulz, he wrote: "Das Zimmer ist ja wunderschön [...], aber vorläufig ist es mir schrecklich zu denken, dass ich mit jedem Tropfen Wasser an die Rechnung denken muss und was so alles beim möbiliert wohnen herauskomt" (The room is wonderful [...], but for the time being, it's horrible to think that I have to think of the bill with every drop of water, and of what comes with living furnished). See Archiv MHG, Berlin, fonds Adelheid Schulz, postcard (dated Aug. 6, 1933) from Karl Giese to Adelheid Schulz. While brooding over the stipulations for his will, Hirschfeld considered it obvious that Giese would continue to enjoy "freier Kost u.[nd] Logis" (free board and lodging) (Hirschfeld & Dose 2013, f. 68/148).

[15] University of Sydney Library, Sydney, Norman Haire collection, 3.20, Magnus Hirschfeld, Typescripts, 1923–1935, letter (dated Jan. 12, 1935) from Norman Haire to Magnus Hirschfeld. See also Wolff 1986, 408; Hirschfeld & Dose 2013, f. 91/194 n. 509 (where Hirschfeld confirmed this settlement).

[16] In May 1934, Hirschfeld also asked Norman Haire to keep an eye on a member of his own family, his nephew Walter Mann (1880–1942). Later, in 1935, Mann actually appealed to Haire for financial help. See University of Sydney Library, Sydney, Norman Haire collection, 3.20, Magnus Hirschfeld, Typescripts, 1923–1935, letter (dated May 15, 1934) from Magnus Hirschfeld to Norman Haire; and letter (dated Jan. 12, 1935) from Norman Haire to Magnus Hirschfeld. For more information on Walter Mann, see Wolfert Oct. 28, 2020.

[17] University of Sydney Library, Sydney, Norman Haire collection, 3.20, Magnus Hirschfeld, Typescripts, 1923–1935, letter (dated Dec. 22, 1934, 1) from Norman Haire to Magnus Hirschfeld.

[18] Wolff 1986, 408; Hirschfeld & Dose 2013, f. 91/194 n. 509.

[19] University of Sydney Library, Sydney, Norman Haire collection, 3.21, Karl Geise [*sic*: Giese], Type-

MAGNUS HIRSCHFELD SETTLES DOWN IN NICE

In December 1934, when Hirschfeld was already in Nice, he and his Chinese pupil and lover Li Shiu Tong were toying with the idea of moving to the United States. The young man especially wanted to go to the USA and study there. Later, from 1940 until 1944, Li Shiu Tong would actually study at Harvard.[20] The young Chinese was even prepared to finance the whole undertaking.[21] In June 1934, Hirschfeld also proposed to work together with Dr. Harry Benjamin in the USA for half a year, starting in September 1934.[22] But Hirschfeld also had his doubts: he found the hustle and bustle of New York too much for him, and also felt his health inadequate to handle the new project. Had Hirschfeld gone to the USA, many things might have turned out differently. But Nice won out and Hirschfeld would spend the last six months of his life there. The relaxed atmosphere and the year-round mild climate, which he had experienced the year before, must have made it more attractive.[23] As already suggested, it is not completely certain that Hirschfeld left Paris voluntarily on November 27, 1934, five days after his successful lecture at the Sorbonne.[24] Hirschfeld, Edmond Zammert and Max Reiss drove south in Li Shiu Tong's car, stopping over in Marseille and Toulon.[25] By December 9, Hirschfeld was staying in the Hôtel de la Méditerranée et de la Côte d'Azur at 25 Promenade des Anglais.[26] He remembered staying in the same hotel the previous winter with Giese.[27]

Hirschfeld must have soon realized that he would stay longer in Nice since, on February 1, 1934, he signed a one-year lease for a luxurious apartment with a magnificent sea view, also located on the famous Promenade des Anglais.[28] The six-storey building housing Hirschfeld's apartment, Gloria Mansions I, was built in 1924 by the French architect Charles Dalmas (1865–1938).[29] Further to the north, lying just behind the building, were the two neighboring apartment buildings, Gloria Mansions II and Gloria Mansions III.[30]

scripts, 1928–1934, letter (dated Mar. 27, 1935) from Norman Haire to Karl Giese (where there is talk of Karl Giese and Li Shiu Tong getting a medical degree).

[20] Hirschfeld & Dose 2013, 194 n. 511.

[21] Hirschfeld & Dose 2013, f. 91/194.

[22] Letter (dated Apr. 29, 1934) from Magnus Hirschfeld to Harry Benjamin, http://www.sexarchive.info/GESUND/ARCHIV/WLSR.HTM (accessed Jun. 28, 2020): "America is our hope, our future, Europe is very sick, nearly dead. I would like to come to America and stay there from September [19]34 to the spring [19]35, perhaps longer, when I can work there, publish books in English, give courses and lectures etc. etc."

[23] Hirschfeld & Dose 2013, f. 83/178 (for Hirschfeld complaining about the Paris winter weather).

[24] AN, site de Pierrefitte-sur-Seine, Ministère de l'intérieur, Direction de la Sûreté Générale, Service central des cartes d'identité d'étrangers, file Magnus Hirschfeld, file n° 210400, cote 19940506/151.

[25] Hirschfeld & Dose 2013, f. 89/190; f. 90/192.

[26] Hirschfeld & Dose 2013, f. 82/176. An entry in a transcribed fragment of Hirschfeld's diary was dated December 1, 1934, and was written in Nice. See MHG, Berlin, fonds Ernst Maass, manuscript (dated May 16–17, 1935) Ernst Maass (consisting of fragments copied from Hirschfeld's – presumably – last diary, entry 43, page 1).

[27] Hirschfeld & Dose 2013, f. 90/192.

[28] The *Dépôt d'envoi* of the Magnus Hirschfeld inheritance procedure clearly stated that Hirschfeld started renting the apartment on February 1, 1935. See ADAM, Nice, Archives notariales, minutes notariales étude Pierre Demnard, Sep. 28, 1935, n° 976, cote 03E 148/019. The same document also explains that it was a rental agreement signed by two private parties, Hirschfeld and the owner of the building, Joachim Nahapiet, registered on February 8, 1935. I have not found any mention of the registration of this private contract. I checked ADAM, Nice, Archives administratives de 1800 à 1940, Enregistrement, Bureau de Nice, 2e bureau des successions, Actes sous seing privé, Jan. 16, 1935-May 15, 1935, vol. 126, cote 03Q 08234. In *Testament: Heft II*, Hirschfeld mentioned the one-year lease: the date of the entry is February 8, 1935. See Hirschfeld & Dose 2013, f. 92/196. The one-year term is also mentioned in a letter to Norman Haire, University of Sydney Library, Sydney, Norman Haire collection, 3.20, Magnus Hirschfeld, Typescripts, 1923–1935, letter (dated Mar. 15, 1935, [1]) from Magnus Hirschfeld to Norman Haire: "Jahreswohnung" (one-year rental).

[29] For further information on the history of the building, see Steve 1989, 103–9. Charles Dalmas also built the Palais de la Méditerranée (1927) at 15 Promenade des Anglais, whose art deco façade alone survived until a few years ago. A new building has now been built behind the façade.

[30] Gloria Mansions II is a quite small, three-storey building located at 123 Rue de France. Gloria Mansions III, at 125–29 Rue de France, was completed in

The Gloria Mansions I building was divided into two main wings: West wing A and East wing B. Each wing had its own staircase. There were four apartments, two per wing, on each floor. Every apartment in the building had three south-facing windows with a sea view. There was also a certain status hierarchy in the set-up of the apartments: the south or sea-facing rooms were meant for owners and tenants, whereas the north-facing rooms and the kitchens were for the serving staff. There were even two separate servants' staircases (one per wing) on the north (servants') side, leading to a patio shared by Gloria Mansions I, II and III. In the Rue de France, between Gloria Mansions II and III, there was (and still is) a narrow entrance (with a decorative art deco iron gate) leading to this patio with access to the three rear entrances of Gloria Mansions I.

If one looks at the building from the sea side, Hirschfeld's former apartment was located on the far left (and thus west) side of the building, marked as "wing A" inside. The fifth floor is under the recessed penthouse apartments of the sixth and top floor [ill. 3].[31] Approaching from the sea (or south) side, Hirschfeld's former apartment could be reached by entering the building through the front middle entrance, then turning left, into wing A, after passing the posh transversal hallway. Two elevators have now been installed, but in Hirschfeld's time there were only the two main stairways.[32] Hirschfeld's apartment had an entry hall, two bedrooms in the front (the south or sea side), each with a window, a two part living room (with one south-facing window), a bathroom and, on the north side of the apartment, a kitchen and two servants' bedrooms.[33] At the time, the building also had a large front garden with all kinds of rocks and greenery. Unfortunately, one of the building's later owners decided to build another apartment block after World War II, Gloria Mansions IV, on the site of this front garden, completely blocking the sea view of the residents of Gloria Mansions I.[34] This is important to know, since both buildings have the same address, 63 Promenade des Anglais, and people who want to see where Hirschfeld lived risk thinking it the one closer to the sea, but this is Gloria Mansions IV … built in 1952 [ill. 2].[35] But in 1935, there was an unimpeded view from Hirschfeld's fifth-floor

1934. It is an art deco style building with Egyptian motifs. For more details on the three apartment blocks, see McLeod & Soetaert 2010, 16–19.

[31] Hirschfeld's floor is mentioned in van Cleeff, May 16, 1935, 2. A later appraisal of the apartment's contents allowed the certain determination that Hirschfeld indeed resided in the left (west) side of the building (and also specifically mentions the apartment being on the fifth floor), further mentioning "une pièce éclairée par une fenêtre ovale à l'ouest" (a room illuminated by an oval window to the west). See ADAM, Nice, Archives notariales, minutes notariales étude Pierre Demnard, May 24, 1935, n° 569, cote 03E 148/011. None of the other three apartments on the floor had such a west-facing window. In January 2010, during a visit to some of the Gloria Mansions I apartments, I saw such an oval window in the dining room of a top-floor apartment (on the sixth floor), but the one in Hirschfeld's fifth-floor apartment must have been replaced at some point by a rectangular stained-glass window.

[32] In January 2010, I visited three apartments in Gloria Mansions I, also seeing the one where Hirschfeld stayed between February and May 1935. I want to thank Mrs. Madeleine Duarte, the building concierge, for making this possible. Hirschfeld's old apartment, which was being renovated, had been fully stripped in the months before. Almost all of the inner walls had been removed. The only original piece I found was the marble chimney piece that one can see in the background of a picture taken in Gloria Mansions I, when Hirschfeld was still living there. See Bergemann, Dose, Keilson-Lauritz & Dubout 2019, f. 151/195, top picture. The unrenovated top-floor apartment, directly above Hirschfeld's, gave me a better idea of what Hirschfeld's apartment must have looked like at the time. But since these penthouse apartments are receded, they are smaller, and thus not isomorphic to the ones on the fifth floor.

[33] This accords with Hirschfeld writing that the apartment had five rooms (four bedrooms and one living room, not counting the kitchen or bathroom). See letter (dated Mar. 30, 1935, 2) from Magnus Hirschfeld to Max Reiss, Archiv MHG, Berlin, fonds Max Reiss.

[34] Very few buildings along the long Promenade des Anglais still have a front garden. A proud exception is the Furtado-Heine complex, lying directly to the east of Gloria Mansions I, at 61 Promenade des Anglais. On this Furtado-Heine building, see Gayraud 2005, 118.

[35] McLeod & Soetaert 2010, 19. On the window above the entrance to Gloria Mansions IV one can

apartment. This doubtlessly magnificent sea view was important to Hirschfeld for two reasons. When at the Berlin Institute, his study looked out to the neighboring Tiergarten park, and the sea view in Nice also reminded him of Kolberg (currently Kołobrzeg, Poland), the town of his birth, on the Baltic Sea. One journalist, who must have visited Hirschfeld in his apartment, wrote: "In his studio, whose wide windows open onto the blue expanse, he continued to work. The Mediterranean reminded him of the Baltic. Without the sea, he said, he could do nothing good. It was a great inspiration for him".[36] The French journalist also noticed a melancholic mood in Hirschfeld: "Dr. Magnus Hirschfeld was a great admirer of Napoleon, and many engravings of him adorn his studio. Under one, depicting the emperor on St. Helena, he traced in his own hand this thought: 'Far from his homeland, but so near all the same, he looks out to the sea and thinks of his ideal. This is the fate of men in exile'".[37]

Looking at Glora Mansions I from the sea, one can see on the left the adjacent Centre Universitaire Méditerranéen (C.U.M.) at 65 Promenade des Anglais.[38] This educational institution was and is still located in the old Villa Guiglia, a former hotel school refurbished in the beginning of the 1930s by the architect Roger Seassal (1885–1967).[39] As stated in the previous chapter, this is the institution where Hirschfeld never lectured. At the time, the French poet, essayist, and philosopher Paul Valéry (1871–1945) was the administrator of the C.U.M. It is not known how well Valéry and Hirschfeld knew each other, but it is likely that they met, since Hirschfeld attended the official opening of the newly refurbished C.U.M. Promenade des Anglais building in the beginning of April 1935 [ill. 3].[40]

STROLLING ON THE PROMENADE DES ANGLAIS

The French journalist also wrote the following: "Dr. Magnus Hirschfeld lived in retirement in Nice. However, he had good friends there. And, on the Promenade des Anglais, where he often walked, numerous émigrés recognized and greeted him. He loved our city very much and greatly appreciated the climate".[41] Hirschfeld simply felt better in Nice, for the first time in a long time. In a letter to Norman Haire, he wrote: "I already feel much calmer and more refreshed here on the sunny Côte d'Azur than I have in the 4 ½ years that separate me from my homeland".[42] Besides its year-round mild climate, Nice was (and remains to this day) attractive because it is a walkable city. The rich and famous could be seen and see each other strolling along the Promenade

indeed see the roman numeral IV. Dr. Dieter Berner confused this seafront building with Gloria Mansions I in a 1993 series of articles on Magnus Hirschfeld for the German magazine *Gay News*. Berner also mistook the art deco style building of the Palais de la Méditerranée as being the Hôtel de la Méditerranée et de la Côte d'Azur where Hirschfeld also stayed (Berner 1993, 10).

[36] Van Cleeff, May 16, 1935, 2: "Dans son studio, dont les larges baies s'ouvrent sur l'immensité bleue, il continuait à travailler. La Méditerranée lui rappelait la Baltique. Sans la mer, disait-il, il ne pouvait rien faire de bon. C'était pour lui une grande inspiratrice".

[37] Van Cleeff, May 16, 1935, 2: "Le docteur Magnus Hirschfeld était un grand admirateur de Napoléon, dont de nombreuses gravures ornent son studio. Sous l'une d'elles, représentant l'empereur à Sainte-Hélène, il a tracé de sa main cette pensée: 'Loin de sa patrie, mais si proche quand même, il regarde la mer et pense à son idéal. C'est le sort des hommes en exil'".

[38] The building of the C.U.M. bordered Rue Henri-Khron (now renamed Rue Paul Valéry).

[39] See the mention "école hotelière" at https://recherche.archives.nicecotedazur.org/viewer/viewer/VDN_0085/FRAC006088_002T0682_401_06.jpg (accessed Aug. 12, 2021).

[40] The program of the Cinquième session du comité permanent des Lettres et des Arts, Société des Nations, Nice du 1er au 3 Avril 1935, inscribed by Valéry and many other celebrity attendees, is pasted into Hirschfeld's guestbook. See Bergemann, Dose, Keilson-Lauritz & Dubout 2019, f. 130–131/174–175.

[41] Van Cleeff, May 16, 1935, 2: "Le docteur Magnus Hirschfeld vivait retiré à Nice. Il y avait pourtant de bons amis. Et, sur la promenade des Anglais, où il passait souvent, de nombreux émigrés le reconnaissaient et le saluaient. Il aimait beaucoup notre ville, dont il appréciait énormément le climat".

[42] University of Sydney Library, Sydney, Norman Haire collection, 3.20, Magnus Hirschfeld, Typescripts, 1923–1935, letter (dated Mar. 15, 1935, [1]) from Magnus Hirschfeld to Norman Haire: " ich fühle

des Anglais.[43] Indeed, several photos of Hirschfeld strolling with friends there can be found in the Hirschfeld guestbook.[44] A picture from the guestbook, showing the small scale and cozy, village-like character of the place has Hirschfeld posing with an otherwise unidentified Dr. Waldenburg. In the background, one can see part of the east wing of Gloria Mansions I, with the front garden and fence on the street side that still existed at the time. In contrast to today, there was much less traffic on the Promenade des Anglais, further contributing to the atmosphere of a relaxed seaside resort where one could meet friends along the strand. Carrying a small parcel, Dr. Waldenburg appears to be returning from a shop and has stopped, along the way, for a little chat with Hirschfeld, whom he seems to have met by chance in front of his seaside home [ill. 4].[45] Hirschfeld must have been happy to wander around in Nice and socialize in the cafés on the Place de Masséna and the Rue de France. He was likely also a customer of the Scotch Tea House, a restaurant that still exists and whose interior has remained in large part unchanged.[46]

Many other German exiles also found refuge in Nice. Two lived in the same building as Hirschfeld: Theodor Wolff (1868–1943), from 1906 until 1933 the editor-in-chief of the *Berliner Tageblatt* newspaper, and the writer Alfred Neumann (1895–1952).[47] Among Hirschfeld's good friends in Nice was the couple Frédéric (Fritz) Gordon and Sophie Gordon (née Boehm), who owned the Pension Floréal at 51 Boulevard Carnot.[48] Most likely, Hirschfeld and Giese knew Sophie Gordon because she had been married to Dr. Ludwig Levy-Lenz, an important Institute collaborator.[49] A picture in the Hirschfeld guestbook shows Hirschfeld visiting the Gordons.[50]

mich hier an der sonnigen Côte d'Azur schon viel ruhiger and frischer, als seit dem Zeitabschnitt, 4 ½ Jahre, der mich von der Heimat trennt".

43 In 1935, greater Nice had a population of around 220,000. See *Annuaire des Alpes-Maritimes* 1935, 47.

44 Bergemann, Dose, Keilson-Lauritz & Dubout 2019, f. 102/146, f. 105/149, f. 123/167, f. 133/177.

45 The picture is also in Bergemann, Dose, Keilson-Lauritz & Dubout 2019, f. 149/193, top photo.

46 The restaurant's previous address was 4 Jardin du Roi Albert. The current address is 4 Avenue de Suède. The restaurant is mentioned several times in Robert Hichens's novel *That Which Is Hidden*. See, for example, Hichens 1939, 13. The novel's main character, Ko Ling, is based on Li Shiu Tong and the narrative gives some clues about the life Hirschfeld (Dr. R. Ellendorf in the novel) led with his Chinese pupil in Nice.

47 McLeod & Soetaert 2010, 21. In the Gloria Mansions IV garden, by the eastern path leading to Gloria Mansions I, there is a historical marker stating that Wolff lived there in 1933. See also Isnard & Isnard 1989, 242.

48 Hirschfeld mentioned them among the few good friends he knew in Nice in Hirschfeld & Dose 2013, f. 90/192 n. 508. That they were good friends is also indicated by the fact that Max Reiss stayed with the couple when he was in Nice around December 1933–January 1934. Personal communication between Jean Bart Broers and Marita Keilson-Lauritz, see email (dated Oct. 9, 2021) from Marita Keilson-Lauritz to the author. Fritz (Frédéric) Gordon (1888–?) was born in Germany. In 1924, he married the Belgian Sophie Boehm (1891–1979), who worked as a stage artist between 1910 and 1924. Fritz Gordon had been a banker in Berlin and the couple fled Germany in 1933 because he was Jewish. They had a son named Armand, born on October 31, 1931 (or 1930) in Berlin. The Gordon couple ran the Floréal pension until May 1936, when they moved to Paris. All three survived the war and returned to Nice, where they applied for French citizenship. In 1948, they moved one more time from Nice to Paris. ADAM, Archives administratives de 1940 à nos jours, Direction départementale de la sécurité publique des Alpes-Maritimes, Sûreté départementale: unité technique d'aide à l'enquête (caserne Auvare), file Gordon Frédéric & Boehm Sophie, cote 1440W 212. In the 1936 Nice *recensement* (census), Frédéric Gordon, his wife Sophie, and their son Armand are indeed mentioned as living at 50–52 Boulevard Carnot. See ADAM, Fonds de la préfecture, Recensement, année 1936, 2ème canton, tome 1, p. 507, cote 06M 0169. The house numbers are given as 50–54 in *Annuaires des Alpes-Maritimes* 1935, 319. See also the *notoriété après le décès* procedure in the handling and settlement of the Hirschfeld inheritance, of which Sophie Gordon was one of the four witnesses: ADAM, Nice, Archives notariales, minutes notariales étude Pierre Demnard, May 20, 1935, n° 553, cote 03E 148/011. See also Soetaert 2014, 23 n. 40. Cf. Bergemann, Dose, Keilson-Lauritz & Dubout 2019, f. 101/145 n. 293, rectified by Bergemann, Dose & Keilson-Lauritz 2021, 3, 6, 9–10.

49 Bergemann, Dose & Keilson-Lauritz 2021, 10.

50 Bergemann, Dose, Keilson-Lauritz & Dubout 2019, f. 101/145. The photo is dated January 28, 1935, and shows Sophie Gordon on a deck chair, most likely in the Pension Floréal garden. The boy in the picture is the couple's four-year-old son, Armand. The original house was demolished and replaced with a modern apartment building that is also called

OUTINGS WITH THE SECRETARY ROBERT KIRCHBERGER

Hirschfeld occasionally took little trips away from Nice. Some destinations are documented in his guestbook: Cannes, Juan-les-Pins, and also nearby Monte Carlo, where he went a few times. He also visited the artist's colony at Haut-de-Cagnes, a small village in the hills above Nice.[51] The outing took place on March 31, 1935, and the picture of the visit also shows a young man who reappears in later pictures in the guestbook.[52] Since Giese was no longer there to do the secretarial work, Hirschfeld hired the young German-Jewish Robert Kirchberger (1904–1981) in Nice.[53] Kirchberger was born into a wealthy Jewish family in the German spa town of Bad Ems and moved to France in November 1933, after shortly being imprisoned after the Nazi takeover in Germany. His brother, André Kirchberger (1899–1942), was certainly gay and it is possible that Hirschfeld got to know Robert through an acquaintance with his brother's. Bad Ems was yet another spa town Hirschfeld may have visited and where he may have sought contact with local gay men. André Kirchberger was murdered in Mauthausen in 1942, but Robert Kirchberger joined the Légion étrangère (Foreign Legion, Fremdenlegion) during the war and died in Paris in 1981 [ill. 5].[54]

On March 29, 1935, Hirschfeld's Chinese lover and pupil left Nice in his car to continue his medical studies in Zürich. The goodbye was clearly emotionally difficult for both men.[55] The two had been in each other's company for a full year. It was the last time that they would see each other alive. Other than his new secretary Robert Kirchberger, and a cook, also living in the Gloria Mansions I apartment, Hirschfeld was now on his own again.[56] Hirschfeld felt invigorated by his new secretary and was motivated to start anew. Hirschfeld hoped that he would be able to cooperate with Kirchberger for a long time.[57] Several people noted that Hirschfeld thought of starting an Institute in Nice. In the introduction to *Women East and West*, Norman Haire wrote (anonymously): "Here [in Nice] he again began to collect, with an indomitable spirit, for a new and greater Institute".[58] The couple Eden Paul (1865–1944) and Cedar Paul (1880–1972), who translated Hirschfeld's *Der Racismus* into English, also reported Hirschfeld's intense wish to start anew in Nice in the first months of 1934: "He seemed to us tolerably content and was full of plans for the future when we last saw

Le Floréal (with house numbers 50–54). The adjoining hotel, Villa Léonie (house number 48), probably gives an idea of what the guesthouse might have looked like. Giese commented on the picture (and identified the people), which strongly suggests that he also knew the couple. Presumably then, Hirschfeld and Giese visited the couple in January–February 1934, when they were together in Nice. It is impossible that Giese was present on the visit on January 28, 1935, since he had been expelled from the country. It's amusing that Giese also referred to the shadow of the photographer, Frédéric Gordon. But he may have made a mistake since he named Sophie "Diane" – or was this maybe her artist's name? I looked up Sophie Gordon's birth certificate in the civil registry of the city archive of Bruges (Belgium), but the name Diane does not show there. Her three first names were Sophie Marie Josephine. See https://www.archiefbankbrugge.be/Archiefbank, Akten burgerlijke stand, Sint-Kruis, year 1891 (accessed Jan. 7, 2020).

[51] For more details, see McLeod & Soetaert 2010, 21–22 and Gaudet 2001.

[52] Bergemann, Dose, Keilson-Lauritz & Dubout 2019, f. 128/172. The young man is sitting on a reed chair in the middle picture on the page.

[53] See also the letter (dated Mar. 30, 1935) from Magnus Hirschfeld to Max Reiss, Archiv MHG, Berlin, fonds Max Reiss. On May 1, 1935, Kirchberger also wrote something in the Hirschfeld guestbook. See Bergemann, Dose, Keilson-Lauritz & Dubout 2019, f. 144/188.

[54] Kirchberger remained unidentified for the longest time. For more details on his life and that of his family, see Soetaert 2018.

[55] Archiv MHG, Berlin, fonds Max Reiss, letter (dated Mar. 30, 1935, 2) from Magnus Hirschfeld to Max Reiss.

[56] For Kirchberger and a cook living in the apartment, see letter (dated Apr. 24, 1935) from Magnus Hirschfeld to Li Shiu Tong, Archiv MHG, Berlin, fonds Li Shiu Tong; also qtd. in McLeod & Soetaert 2010, 23; Dose 2003a, 17.

[57] Letter (dated Mar. 30, 1935, 2) from Magnus Hirschfeld to Max Reiss, Archiv MHG, Berlin, fonds Max Reiss.

[58] Hirschfeld 1935c, xi.

[59] Hirschfeld 1938a, 27–28. Likely, part of their introduction was based on information Karl Giese gave them. In *Testament: Heft II*, Hirschfeld also mentioned that he had met William J. Robinson and

him. He and [Dr.] W.[illiam] J. Robinson [1867–1936] drove up to our cottage in the hills above Grasse. Over the huge fire of spluttering olive wood logs he outlined his hopes of reviving the Institute in the hospitable and beautiful town which was his adoptive home, both pleasure city and important commercial and maritime centre. By the time we were able to visit him in Nice, his plans were further matured. As we walked up and down the Promenade des Anglais in the brilliant February [1934] sunshine, with the mimosas aglow beneath a background of towering snowfields and the sapphire sea sparkling and dancing in a delicate southerly breeze, the *Rex* glided out of Villefranche Roads on her voyage to the west. Dr. Robinson, at sight of this majestic liner, exclaimed: 'But why here? Why not rebuild your Institute in New York? We're a go-ahead people, and we'll give you the welcome and the generous help you need.' Hirschfeld protested he would never be able to stand the rigours of such a climate, and it were better to do things on a less imposing scale than that suggested by his friend – anyway at the start. Also, being as he said with a roguish smile 'a good European,' he felt that such an enterprise must be mothered on European soil".[59] Christopher Isherwood also wrote that Hirschfeld intended to start a new institute in Nice.[60]

MAGNUS HIRSCHFELD DIES ON HIS SIXTY-SEVENTH BIRTHDAY

In the beginning of May 1935, a young man named Ernst Maass (1914–1975), a distant relative of Hirschfeld's who worked for a publishing company in Milan, visited Hirschfeld in Nice intending to celebrate Hirschfeld's upcoming birthday in his company [ill. 6].[61] In the Hirschfeld guestbook there is a picture of Hirschfeld sitting behind his desk on the morning of his birthday, May 14, 1935, around 10 a.m. He is flanked by Maass and Kirchberger, going over the birthday wishes in his mail.[62] Around noon, the trio went for lunch, and on their return, the seemingly happy "two colorful youths" (*zwei bunte Jünglinge*), who supported the slightly swaying Hirschfeld, were noticed by the German writer Hermann Kesten (1900–1996), sitting and writing at the no longer existing Café de France (64 Rue de France).[63] Hirschfeld apparently retraced his steps to tell the writer how much he admired him.[64] Back from their lunch, it was in the front garden of Gloria Mansions I that Hirschfeld had a stroke and died on the day of his sixty-seventh birthday.[65] Exactly two years earlier, on his sixty-

the Paul couple in Nice in the first months of 1934 (Hirschfeld & Dose 2013, f. 86/184).

[60] Isherwood 1988, 137.

[61] For more detailed biographical information on Ernst Maass, a great-nephew of Hirschfeld, see McLeod & Soetaert 2010, 22 n. 25; Soetaert 2014, 41; Bergemann, Dose, Keilson-Lauritz & Dubout 2019, 218.

[62] See the handwritten addition to the photo added by Karl Giese in the Hirschfeld guestbook: "Beim Lesen der Geburtstagspost mit E.[rnst] Maas [*sic*, Maass] u.[nd] R.[obert] Kirchberger am 14. V. 35 10. Uhr vorm.[ittags]" (While reading the birthday mail with E.[rnst] Maas [*sic*, Maass] and R.[obert] Kirchberger on 14 V. 35, at 10 o'clock in the morning). See Bergemann, Dose, Keilson-Lauritz & Dubout 2019, f. 151/195, top photo.

[63] It was a seven minutes' walk from the former Café de France to Gloria Mansions I. In 2010, the art deco style café was in ruins. It was later demolished to make room for a new, inverted-circle building which now has a "bio" grocery store on the lower floor.

[64] Qtd. in McLeod & Soetaert 2010, 24. See also Wolff 1986, 412–13; Dose 2019, 23–24. There is, however, some doubt about the veracity of Kesten's story of meeting Hirschfeld (or meeting him specifically on the day he died) since the punchline of his story – that so many German literature celebrities had died – is based on incorrect facts. First of all, since Kesten refers to Carnival confetti being strewn around, the story takes place in the month of February. Hirschfeld died in May 1935. Secondly, as was recently pointed out by Jakob Michelsen, three personalities whom Kesten reported being dead were still living in May 1935. On the other hand, several details of Kesten's meeting Hirschfeld reported in this story seem to indicate that he did indeed meet Magnus Hirschfeld when the latter returned from lunch, possibly on the day of his death. See Bergemann, Dose, Keilson-Lauritz 2021, 3.

[65] Archiv MHG, Berlin, fonds Max Reiss, letter (undated but presumably May 27 or 28, 1935, 1) from Karl Giese to Max Reiss; Schulz 2001, 43. See also Bergemann, Dose, Keilson-Lauritz & Dubout 2019, 195 n. 429. Cf. "Magnus Hirschfelds Erbe in Wien",

fifth birthday, Hirschfeld entered France from Switzerland. His death certificate says he died at 1:30 p.m.[66] Having to climb the stairs to his fifth-floor apartment – at least once a day – was probably not beneficial for a man of Hirschfeld's age and physical condition.[67] Giese wrote afterwards that it gave him peace that Hirschfeld's last moments were happy ones.[68] "In the name of those that stayed behind", Ernst Maass made the funeral arrangements. His name is printed on the formal funeral card that was sent out to friends and family. A copy of the funeral card is glued in the Hirschfeld guestbook.[69] The card says that the funeral would take place in the Jewish section of the Nice Château cemetery on Tuesday, May 21, at 10 a.m.[70] Brief burial ceremony notices also appeared in the local newspapers *L'Eclaireur de Nice et du Sud-Est* and *Le Petit Niçois*.[71] Of course, Hirschfeld's death was reported in many newspapers all over Europe.

Suffering from diabetes and hypertension, Hirschfeld's health was already unstable before embarking on his world trip, and the tropical climate of Asia had only made it worse. Hirschfeld never fully recovered from the malaria that he contracted in September 1931 in Agra, the Indian city best known for its Taj Mahal.[72] In April 1934, Hirschfeld wrote to his Chinese pupil that he had momentarily feared for his life one night, when he suffered from very high blood pressure, fainted, and laid unconscious for hours.[73] That Hirschfeld was well aware that the end could be near is also suggested by the fact that he prepared the final version of his last will in Nice.

HIRSCHFELD'S LAST WILL

Hirschfeld constantly changed his mind about who was best suited to continue his intellectual legacy. He was already preoccupied by the issue at the end of the 1920s. On his world trip, sensing that his health was quite precarious, he wrote down his thoughts on the matter. The main document in which Hirschfeld spelled out his ideas

Der Morgen – Wiener Montagblatt, Jun. 24, 1935, 10, where angina pectoris is given as the cause of death. On the other hand, Kurt Hiller claimed that Hirschfeld wanted to visit a sick friend but dropped dead in the front garden of Gloria Mansions I when *leaving* his home. See Hiller 1945, 5. Hermann Kesten's mentioned, somewhat dubious story (see p. 267, n. 64) claims that Hirschfeld had a heart attack in the *Hausgang* (entrance hall) of Gloria Mansions I.

[66] The text of the death certificate is transcribed in McLeod & Soetaert 2010, 24. The death certificate is reproduced in Hirschfeld & Cardon 1908/2001, 208. The Hirschfeld guestbook contains a picture of Hirschfeld on his deathbed in Gloria Mansions I. Giese's handwritten note underneath states that it was taken on May 14, 1935 at 12 p.m. (noon). See Bergemann, Dose, Keilson-Lauritz & Dubout 2019, f. 152/196. This was not the correct time, since the death certificate states that Hirschfeld died at 1:30 p.m.

[67] If it is indeed true that Hirschfeld collapsed in the front garden of the building, it must indeed have been a difficult operation to carry his dead body to the fifth floor up the slippery white marble stairs. The photo of Hirschfeld on his deathbed shows him on clearly crumpled sheets and with a pillow in a similar state, and this seems to suggest that his body was indeed carried up to the fifth floor before it was removed by the undertaker. See Hirschfeld & Dose 2013, f. 93/199. Since a whole week passed before Hirschfeld was cremated, his body would have been kept in a cooling cell at the funeral home in Nice belonging to Roblot, a company to which we shall return later.

[68] Archiv MHG, Berlin, fonds Max Reiss, letter (dated May 1935 but presumably May 27 or 28, 1935, 3) from Karl Giese to Max Reiss.

[69] Bergemann, Dose, Keilson-Lauritz & Dubout 2019, f. 154/198: „Im Namen der Hinterbliebenen". The two other currently known copies of the funeral card are in the Archiv MHG, Berlin, fonds Max Reiss, and in the IMEC, Saint-Germain la Blanche Herbe, fonds Aubier-Montaigne.

[70] To avoid confusion with the larger Château cemetery, the handwritten adjective "jüd.[ischen]" (Jewish) was added to the funeral card. The cemetery is located high up on the Coline du Château, just east of the Old Nice city center.

[71] *L'Eclaireur de Nice et du Sud-Est*, May 19, 1935, 3, 8; May 20, 1935, 3; May 21, 1935, 3; *Le Petit Niçois*, May 19, 1935, 8.

[72] See "Magnus Hirschfeld hat seine Weltreise beendet", *Neues Wiener Journal*, Apr. 2, 1932, 9; Hirschfeld 2003, 37.

[73] Archiv MHG, Berlin, fonds Ernst Maass, letter (dated Apr. 24, 1935) from Magnus Hirschfeld to Li Shiu Tong; also qtd. in McLeod & Soetaert 2010, 23; Dose 2003a, 17.

[74] Hirschfeld & Dose 2013, 13.

is *Testament: Heft II*, started in Kolberg (Kołobrzeg), the town of his birth, on August 1, 1929.[74] This primary document – which came from the partially discarded estate of Hirschfeld's pupil, Li Shiu Tong – was saved from the dumpster by Adam P. W. Smith in Canada.[75] This handwritten document was meant as a sort of manual to explain and contextualize Hirschfeld's true intentions for his intellectual posterity.[76] Initially Hirschfeld thought that the Institute's senior administrator (*Verwaltungsleiter*), Friedrich Hauptstein, Karl Giese and, later on, Bernhard Schapiro, were most suited to lead the WLSR and the Institute in Berlin. With the passage of time, and with the growing Nazi influence in the Institute, he realized that, finally, the only person he could really trust was his loyal life partner, the Institute's archivist, Karl Giese.[77] Although it may well have been true that Giese was indeed very devoted and loyal to Hirschfeld until the end of his own life, in March 1938, whether Giese was up to this demanding task was another matter. It was during Hirschfeld's world trip, in October 1931, that Hirschfeld also clearly decided to add Li Shiu Tong (1907–1993) as his second principal trustee and administrator (*Verwalter*).[78]

When Hirschfeld was at the Hôtel de la Méditerranée et de la Côte d'Azur in Nice, he drafted a handwritten last will. He wrote it in German and dated it January 10, 1935 [ill. 7].[79] Hirschfeld reformulated and rewrote his testamentary dispositions so often that the standard legal disposition of a will came in handy: article 1 revoked all previous testamentary proposals and formulations. Summarizing Hirschfeld's wishes, as formulated in his last will (*Testament*), the main determination was that his two pupils, Karl Giese and Li Shiu Tong, were the two equal principal beneficiaries ("alleinige Erben zu gleichen Teilen", article 4).[80] In the French legal terminology they were designated as the two *légataires universels* (universal legatees). This stipulation mainly referred to monetary funds that would be available after Hirschfeld's death. Hirschfeld explicitly added the express condition ("mit der ausdrücklichen Auflage") that Karl Giese and Li Shiu Tong were to use the inheritance only to continue the intellectual legacy ("geistige Erbe") of Hirschfeld's life's work in sexology (article 2). That this was truly crucial for Hirschfeld is attested by the repetition of this explicit condition in three more articles of his last will (articles 4, 5, and 6). Hence the funds

[75] Hirschfeld & Dose 2013, f. 1/14. Its predecessor, *Heft I*, a *blauen Heft* (booklet with blue cover), is lost. But the existence of this volume indicates that Hirschfeld already started thinking about his legacy some time before 1929.

[76] Hirschfeld & Dose 2013, f. 29/70: "*Mischung von Chronik, Richtlinien u.[nd] Testament*" (*Mixture of chronicle, guidelines and last will*) (emphasis in original).

[77] See Hirschfeld & Dose 2013, f. 2/16, esp. n. 3, on Hauptstein; f. 54/120; and f. 67/146. On Hauptstein's subsequent fall from grace and Giese alone remaining as the trustworthy candidate, see Hirschfeld & Dose 2013, f. 75/162, f. 78/168. On Schapiro's candidacy, see Hirschfeld & Dose 2013, f. 24/60, f. 34/80, and f. 67/146; for his own subsequent fall from grace, see Hirschfeld & Dose 2013, f. 70/152-71/154. See also Arbetarrörelsens arkiv och bibliotek, Stockholm, Max Hodann samling, vol. 15, letter (dated Sep. 24, 1935, 1) from Karl Giese to Max Hodann. In this letter, Giese mentions the conflict between Hirschfeld/Giese and Schapiro and Hauptstein – and a lawyer named Marcus Birnbaum (1890–1941) – in the months before the Nazi raid of the Institute. I could not determine if Marcus Birnbaum was related to Dora Birnbaum, see also further, chapter 10, p. 313.

[78] Hirschfeld & Dose 2013, f. 57/126. Right after his world tour, Hirschfeld still had the idea of adding Li Shiu Tong. See Hirschfeld & Dose 2013, f. 63/138. In his later testamentary ponderings, Li Shiu Tong disappeared – though only temporarily – from view. For example, at one point, Giese is mentioned as the "alleinigen Vollstrecker meines letzten Willens" (sole executor of my last will) (Hirschfeld & Dose 2013, f. 78/168).

[79] Hirschfeld's original handwritten testament can be found in Demnard's notarial minutes. See ADAM, Nice, Archives notariales, minutes notariales étude Pierre Demnard, May 22, 1935, n° 563, cote 03E 148/011. The full text of Hirschfeld's testament was first published in Baumgardt 1984, 7–12. A transcript of the last will, based on the original hand written version (and an English translation), can be found in the addenda (n° 17). The text can also be found on the MHG Berlin website, http://www.hirschfeld.in-berlin.de/frame.html?http://www.hirschfeld.in-berlin.de/testament.html (accessed Jun. 28, 2020) and is also reproduced in Hirschfeld & Dose 2013, 224–25, Anhang.

[80] The French translation of this is "comme seuls héritiers pour parts égales".

that would become available to the two principal inheritors could only be used for projects furthering the sexological cause that Hirschfeld started in his lifetime.

Hirschfeld also stipulated the items and sources of income bequeathed to Giese and Li Shiu Tong. In article 5, Hirschfeld specified that Giese would obtain all the objects saved from the disastrous looting of the Berlin Institute in May 1933. In addition, he was entitled to all the income from Hirschfeld's German and foreign language books, and from the medical licenses for Testifortan and Titus Pearls.[81] Li Shiu Tong, Hirschfeld's last partner, would have the disposition of all the couple's papers, books, and pictures when Hirschfeld passed.[82] Li was also entitled to the "Aktien und shares" (article 5) in his and Hirschfeld's names in a Paris safe. Likely Hirschfeld meant "shares and bonds" (*Aktien und Obligationen*) since *Aktien* and shares are one and the same.

The last main monetary dispensation in Hirschfeld's last will was spelled out in article 7. It stated that five of Hirschfeld's family members (Jenny Hauck, Wally Rosa Hirschfeld, Walter Mann, Franz Richard Mann, Ernst Maass) and three of Hirschfeld's friends and acquaintances (Leopold Hönig, Margarete Dost, Franz Wimmer) were to receive specific bequests (*legs*, in French) to the extent that the funds available after Hirschfeld's death allowed.[83] In French law, these people were designated as the *légataires particuliers* (individual legatees).[84] These bequeathed sums totalled 113,000 French francs (hereafter FF). In today's value, this would amount to €86,260.[85] The will also contained instructions about the cost and location (Nice or Paris) of Hirschfeld's grave, as well as a monetary provision to refund the allowance (*Stipend*) the Danish doctor Ellen Bækgaard was paying for Giese's education. We have seen that Bækgaard and the English sexologist Norman Haire were paying £50 and Hirschfeld £40 a year.

Hirschfeld's handwritten last will (*testament olographe*, in French) was not composed or certified at a notary's office.[86] Hirschfeld's five-page-long handwritten testament is quite legible, unlike most of his handwritten documents that I have seen, which probably means that he made an effort at making his writing easier to

[81] Hirschfeld had already meant these two bequests for Giese at the end of 1932. See Hirschfeld & Dose 2013, f. 68/148.

[82] Indirectly, this is of course revelatory of how Hirschfeld judged and valued his relationship with Li Shiu Tong. He apparently took it for granted that Li Shiu Tong would be his enduring partner, at his side at the time of his death.

[83] For more biographical information on Hirschfeld's five relatives, see Soetaert 2014, 14, table 2. For further information on Franz Mann and his destiny in Czechoslovakia, see NA, Praha, fonds Policejní ředitelství Praha II – všeobecná spisovna, 1941–1950, kart. n° 6996, sign. M 746/4; Walter Mann 1880; Wolfert, Oct. 28, 2020. Mann committed suicide in Mauthausen on April 15, 1942.

[84] Hirschfeld initially thought of leaving bequests to two other people from his former Institute staff: Henrike Friedrichs and Bertha Swiderski (Zander). See Hirschfeld & Dose 2013, f. 69/150.

[85] The historical conversion rate is: 1.31 (old) FF = 1 current €. See the online converter of the Institut national de la statistique et des études économiques, a part of the French Ministère de l'Économie et des Finances, http://www.insee.fr/fr/themes/calcul-pouvoir-achat.asp (accessed Dec. 26, 2013). These FF are the "old" FF (*anciens Francs*) in use until 1959. Starting in 1960, 100 old FF would equal 1 new FF.

[86] Last wills composed and certified at a notary's office are called *testaments authentiques* in French. Demnard's notarial minutes contain no trace of Hirschfeld depositing his last will at Demnard's office. I checked Demnard's minutes from mid-November 1934 to mid-March 1935. See ADAM, Nice, Archives notariales, minutes notariales étude Pierre Demnard, cotes 03E 124/228 (Nov. 16, 1934-Nov. 30, 1934), 03E 124/229 (Dec. 1, 1934–Dec. 15, 1934), 03E 124/230 (Dec. 17, 1934–Dec. 31, 1934) and cotes 03E 148/001 until 03E 148/006 (covering the period from Jan. 1, 1935 to Mar. 15, 1935). The absence can likely be explained by the fact that the deposit of a *testament olographe* (handwritten last will) is simply not mentioned in these minutes, unlike last wills redacted at the office of a notary and certified by the latter. I have seen a few *testaments authentiques* in Demnard's minutes.

[87] The handwritten last will matches, apart from a few insignificant details, the already mentioned transcript that Manfred Baumgardt found in Germany in 1984. I thank Harry Devolder for meticulously checking this for me. Hirschfeld likely used the typed draft of his last will (dated December 1934) for his handwritten copy. He kept this typed

read.[87] In article 10 of his last will, Hirschfeld appointed Dr. Franz Herzfelder (1901–1998), a lawyer originally from Munich and then a so-called "legal counselor" (*conseil juridique*) in Nice, as the executor (*exécuteur testamentaire, Testamentsvollstrecker*) of his estate [ill. 8].[88] Indeed, in *Testament: Heft II*, Hirschfeld wrote that he had put his last will "into the hands of lawyer Herzfelder, 6 rue [*sic*: it is a boulevard] Carlone".[89] Significantly, this is the very last phrase in Hirschfeld's *Testament: Heft II*.

Once Hirschfeld sealed the envelope containing the very last version of his wishes, it seems that finally, after years of revolving the issue, he stopped thinking about his posterity. He had peace of mind at last. The envelope was dropped off at the office of the notary Pierre Demnard on February 23, 1935.[90] The envelope bore Hirschfeld's typed Gloria Mansions address. As we have seen, Hirschfeld only started living there at the beginning of February 1935. Since the final version was dated January 10, 1935, this means that Hirschfeld waited another six weeks before he (or Herzfelder) took his handwritten last will to Demnard's notary office. This possibly indicates that Hirschfeld wanted to be quite certain about his final choices.[91] Another disposition, this time regarding his funeral, was spelled out in a letter Hirschfeld sent to Karl Giese while he was still in Ascona, in April 1933. Hirschfeld wrote that he did not want a religious funeral, but wanted to be cremated, Mendelssohn and Schubert to be played, and some last farewell speeches by friends.[92]

THE FUNERAL CEREMONY

Hirschfeld's funeral ceremony took place on Tuesday, May 21, 1935, in Nice. But how could Giese, who was expelled from France in October 1934, attend the funeral of his "Papa"? Against all odds, Giese, who was in Vienna when Hirschfeld died, managed to obtain a two-weeks French visa. In a letter, he wrote that he had to travel through Brno and Prague, fly, take a train, and even take a motorcycle to arrive in Nice on Sunday May 19, 1935. Apparently, Li Shiu Tong arrived from Zürich on the same day.[93]

copy in a sealed envelope that only he could open, but which was unsealed, presumably after his death, nevertheless. This typed version can be found in Archiv MHG, Berlin, fonds Ernst Maass.

[88] The designation *conseil juridique* basically meant that a foreign lawyer's degree was not recognized in France. The term set foreign lawyers apart and restricted their professional activity considerably.

[89] Hirschfeld & Dose 2013, f. 92/196: "in die Hände von Rechtsanwalt Herzfelder, rue [*sic*: it is a boulevard] Carlone 6".

[90] A phrase typed on the sealed yellow envelope confirms that the document was indeed dropped off then: "Testament / de Monsieur le Docteur Magnus Hirschfeld demeurant à Nice, 63 Promenade des Anglais, Gloria-Mansion [*sic*] / aux bons soins de Maître Demnard, Notaire à Nice 2, Place Masséna" (Last will / of Doctor Magnus Hirschfeld living in Nice, 63 Promenade des Anglais, Gloria-Mansion [*sic*] / in the care of Maître Demnard, Notary in Nice, 2 Place Masséna). Underneath, there was a handwritten addition: "deposé le 23 Février 1935" (deposited on February 23, 1935). To this day, 2 Place Masséna in Nice houses a notary's office. Demnard's later professional address – where he likely moved some time in 1935 – was the very nearby 1 Avenue de la Victoire (currently Avenue Jean Médecin). The premises nowadays house a BNP Paribas bank office. Demnard lived at 31 Boulevard Victor Hugo. See *Annuaire des Alpes-Maritimes* 1938, 572.

[91] It is also possible that Hirschfeld did not mean that his last will "was now in the hands of Herzfelder" literally. He may simply have meant that the handling and settling of his inheritance was up to Herzfelder since he had been appointed as the *exécuteur testamentaire* (executor). This could also mean that it was Hirschfeld himself who dropped off his last will at Demnard's office. ADAM, Nice, Archives notariales, minutes notariales étude Pierre Demnard, May 22, 1935, n° 563, cote 03E 148/011. In all subsequent documents dealing with Hirschfeld's estate in the *minutes notariales*, the composition date of Hirschfeld's last will (January 10, 1935) is mentioned as the date that it was deposited at Demnard's office; in reality, as we have seen, it was only dropped off on February 23, 1935.

[92] Hirschfeld & Dose 2013, f. 78/168.

[93] *L'Eclaireur de Nice et du Sud-Est*, May 19, 1935, 3: "Les héritiers de l'illustre défunt sont attendus aujourd'hui" (The heirs of the illustrious deceased are expected to arrive today); and Archiv MHG, Berlin, fonds Max Reiss, letter (dated May – presumably 27 or 28 – 1935, 2) from Karl Giese to Max Reiss (where Giese wrote that he arrived on Sunday). In a letter (dated Aug. 2, 1935, 1) to Max Hodann, Giese wrote that he had managed to get into France "durch einen Zufall" (by a coincidence). See Arbetarrörelsens arkiv och bibliotek, Stockholm, Max Hodann samling, vol. 15.

On his arrival in Nice, Giese fell sick and had to stay in bed. Against the advice of a doctor, possibly Leopold Hönig, Giese attended Hirschfeld's funeral anyway.[94]

The ceremony was held in the tiny building of the morgue (*reposoir*) located in the Jewish section of the Château cemetery on the steep Colline du Château, in the old Nice city center [ill. 9]. The local newspaper *L'Eclaireur de Nice et du Sud-Est* reported that Giese and Li Shiu Tong stood close to the coffin, accompanied by Hirschfeld's "two cousins", likely referring to Ernst Maass and the secretary Robert Kirchberger.[95] Giese delivered a eulogy for the love of his life and called Hirschfeld a "soft fanatic" (*weicher Fanatiker*).[96] Speaking these last words by Hirschfeld's coffin was for Giese, as he later wrote in a letter, "a great satisfaction" (*eine große Genugtuung*).[97] Going against Hirschfeld's wishes for a non-religious service, the ceremony was led by the local rabbi Samuel Schumacher (1874–1941), who also praised Hirschfeld.[98] Schumacher was supported by his assistant Georges Barach (1879–1943).[99] Only three not very good snapshots of Hirschfeld's funeral, likely taken by Ernst Maass, have survived. Two mainly show Schumacher and Barach, and the third shows the large wreath inside the morgue from the Ligue Internationale contre l'Antisémitisme (LICA) bearing the text "to the great exiled scientist" (*au grand savant exilé*).[100] The reporter of a local newspaper listed thirty-eight mourners, including the pharmacist Félix-Henri Dupraz (1897–1973), the principal figure behind the commercial distribution of Perles Titus in France, Hirschfeld's local friend Sophie Gordon, the notary Pierre Demnard, and Dr. Leo Klauber.[101]

94 Archiv MHG, Berlin, fonds Max Reiss, letter (dated May 1935 – presumably 27 or 28 – 1935, 2) from Karl Giese to Max Reiss. I believe that Leopold Hönig might have been the doctor attending Giese because I think there is a chance that Hönig appears, next to Karl Giese and Li Shiu Tong, in front of the entrance of Gloria Mansions I, in a loose picture from the guestbook. See Bergemann, Dose, Keilson-Lauritz & Dubout 2019, 202, middle row, left-side picture. I have compared the picture of the man with the hat with another picture of Hönig, reproduced in Soetaert 2014, 39. It is also possible that the man with the pipe in the guestbook picture was the notary Pierre Demnard. However, I do not think that Demnard would have been willing to take Giese's arm so fondly. Also, Demnard was ten years younger than Hönig. As we will see later, an advance payment of FF500 each was made to Giese and Li Shiu Tong on the day of the funeral, and this would indicate that it was indeed Demnard who appears in the picture. This advance payment was decided upon in the *notoriété après le décès* procedure of May 20, 1935. See below.

95 *L'Eclaireur de Nice et du Sud-Est*, May 22, 1935, 3. The newspaper article is quoted in full in McLeod & Soetaert 2010, 28.

96 Arbetarrörelsens arkiv och bibliotek, Stockholm, Max Hodann samling, vol. 15, letter (dated Aug. 2, 1935, [1]) from Karl Giese to Max Hodann; Wolff 1986, 414. Giese's speech is also mentioned in M.J.S., May 31, 1935, 410; and by Erhart Löhnberg, see Wellcome Library, London, archive Charlotte Wolff (1897–1986), correspondence II, 1981–1986, PSY/WOL/6/8/2, letter (undated – first page missing – but likely 1984, 9) from Erhart Löhnberg to Charlotte Wolff. Günter Maeder claimed he had a copy of Giese's eulogy, writing to Charlotte Wolff that he had given it to publisher and LGBT activist Egmont Fassbinder (1945-2023), who possibly gave it to Manfred Herzer. See Wellcome Library London, archive Charlotte Wolff (1897–1986), correspondence II, 1981–1986, PSY/WOL/6/8/2, undated letter II, f. 2. Giese also sent a copy of this text to Max Hodann. See letter (dated Aug 2, 1935, 1) from Karl Giese to Max Hodann, Arbetarrörelsens arkiv och bibliotek, Stockholm, Max Hodann samling, vol. 15. I sent an email (dated Mar. 24, 2013) to the Arbetarrörelsens arkiv och bibliotek in Stockholm asking for a copy of this text. They informed me that the text was not present in the Max Hodann fonds.

97 Archiv MHG, Berlin, fonds Max Reiss, letter (dated May – presumably 27 or 28 – 1935, 2) from Karl Giese to Max Reiss.

98 More biographical information on Schumacher can be found in his candidacy file as a *chevalier* (knight) de la Légion d'Honneur. See ADAM, Nice, fonds Légion d'Honneur, dossiers individuelles des candidatures, file Samuel Schumacher, 1929, cote 01 M0598.

99 Schumacher died a natural death. However, Barach, who was the *chamas* (officiating minister) at the synagogue (Temple Israélite) in Nice, perished in Auschwitz-Birkenau on October 12, 1943. He was deported on convoy n° 60 (leaving on October 7, 1943 from Drancy to Auschwitz-Birkenau), on which the widow of rabbi Samuel Schumacher, Sarah Schumacher (1874–1943), was also deported.

100 The three photos are in Archiv MHG, Berlin, fonds Ernst Maass.

101 *L'Eclaireur de Nice et du Sud-Est*, May 21, 1935, 3. The anonymous journalist misspelled many of the mourners' names, possibly indicating he or she noted them down as (s)he asked around who was who. Félix-Henri Dupraz' last partner was the secretary Marie Madeleine Chaudron (1913–2020).

After the funeral, the body was transported to Marseille where it was cremated, either that day or the day after.[102] Giese went in the van carrying the coffin to Marseille.[103] The Nice firm in charge of the funeral and the transport was Pompes funèbres Roblot (2 Rue de l'Hôtel de ville).[104] Hirschfeld's ashes were laid to rest in the columbarium in the Marseille St.-Pierre cemetery for approximately one year.[105] It would take some time to get Hirschfeld's posh grave stone in the Nice Caucade cemetery ready. And money would also be needed to pay for the whole operation, money that would come from settling Hirschfeld's estate.

THE HANDLING AND SETTLEMENT OF HIRSCHFELD'S ESTATE

Magnus Hirschfeld's estate was handled by the local notary Maître Pierre Demnard (1896–1980) [ill. 10].[106] We will now look at the different legal stages of the long procedure. All in all, it took six months for the formal, required legal steps to be completed. The actual paying out of the bequests, the second main part of the Hirschfeld procedure, would only commence at the beginning of 1936. The final settlement of the procedure, with the inventory of assets and liabilities and payment of the estate tax to the tax office (*Bureau de l'Enregistrement*) in Nice, would take place in the first half of 1936.[107] In August 1936, the whole procedure was concluded, the same month that Hirschfeld's grave was finally finished and paid for. On the day of Hirschfeld's death – May 14, 1935 – the notary Pierre Demnard delivered Hirschfeld's handwritten will to the Tribunal civil de première instance in Nice,[108] which validated the document. By May 16, the German text was translated into French by a court translator.[109]

[102] *L'Eclaireur de Nice et du Sud-Est*, May 21, 1935, 3. A *registre des inhumations* (burial registry) (dated May 1935, 212) in the Marseille St-Pierre cemetery archive states that Hirschfeld was indeed cremated on May 21, 1935, the day of the burial ceremony. His coffin was identified with the label 183, upper case 5. On the other hand, in a letter to Max Reiss, Giese wrote that the cremation only took place the next day and that he was in attendance. See Archiv MHG, Berlin, fonds Max Reiss, letter (dated May– but presumably 27 or 28 – 1935, 2) from Karl Giese to Max Reiss.

[103] Archiv MHG, Berlin, fonds Max Reiss, letter (dated May – presumably 27 or 28 – 1935, 2) from Karl Giese to Max Reiss.

[104] The firm still exists under the same name and at the same address. I visited its Nice branch on February 27, 2014. I was informed that client files were destroyed after ten years, and that a register summarizing client cases was only started some time after 1950. As early as the 1930s, Roblot was a nationwide funerary services chain (with historical roots in Paris). It was eventually incorporated into the immense monopolist Pompes Funèbres Générales (P.F.G.). See Bellanger 2008, 106–7; http://www.roblot.fr/ (accessed Sep. 23, 2013).

[105] His ashes were laid to rest in case 24 of the Columbarium section of the Marseille St-Pierre cemetery. See the *registre des inhumations* (burials register) (May 1935, 212) in the Marseille St-Pierre cemetery archive. Most likely, a more extensive file on Hirschfeld's cremation is present in the administrative service archives of the Marseille cemetery, but I was only allowed to see the above-mentioned burial register (which took approximately one minute to bring up) after my request to obtain more information on Hirschfeld's cremation in Marseille received three successive negative answers from three different staff members. It was also indirectly made clear to me by the third and final staff member – who finally gave in – that she did not at all feel like digging up the extensive Hirschfeld file from the cemetery archives.

[106] The *minutes notariales* (notarial minutes) of the handling of the Hirschfeld inheritance were only released for consultation by researchers in 2013. In France, the *délai de communication* (statutory restriction) for these kinds of archives (*minutes et répertoires des notaires* [notaries' minutes and directories]) is seventy-five years. Demnard's notary minutes for 1935 and 1936 are deposited in the ADAM in Nice, Archives notariales, minutes notariales étude Pierre Demnard, cote 03E 148.

[107] ADAM, Nice, Archives administratives de 1800 à 1940, Enregistrement, Bureau de Nice, Déclarations de mutations par décès (deuxième série), volume 49, Dec. 2, 1935–Jan. 31, 1936, cote 03Q 08851; volume 50, Feb. 3, 1936–Mar. 30, 1936, cote 03Q 08852 and volume 51, Apr. 1, 1936–Jun. 10, 1936, cote 03Q 08853.

[108] ADAM, Nice, Archives administratives de 1800 à 1940, Fonds du Tribunal de première instance de Nice, Constats de testaments, Jan. 1, 1935–Dec. 31, 1938, n° 138, registered on May 22, 1935, cote 03U 01/1447. For a more detailed account of this procedure, see Soetaert 2014, 21–23.

[109] ADAM, Nice, Archives notariales, minutes notariales étude Pierre Demnard, May 22, 1935, n° 563, cote 03E 148/011. I have checked the French translation of

PARTS OF THE GLORIA MANSIONS APARTMENT SEALED

On May 17, 1935, three days after Hirschfeld's death, parts of the Gloria Mansions apartment, where Hirschfeld had lived since February, were officially sealed.[110] It is possible that this was done at Giese's request, since he was not in Nice at that time. As the Berlin Institute's former archivist, and after the lootings of May 1933, Giese must have been very sensitive of the value and fragility of the materials in the apartment. Certain formulations in Hirschfeld's last will itself might have given rise to some discussion. Article 5 stipulated that Giese was entitled to the materials saved from the Berlin bonfire and that Li Shiu Tong could keep papers and other objects from the Gloria Mansions apartment. Giese's later letters show that he and Li Shiu Tong got along well, but there may still have been some distrust at that moment. So, possibly, the request to seal off parts of the apartment was made by Giese out of caution. That Giese may not have known what Hirschfeld's last will stipulated, or had only a slight idea, may also have played a role in Giese's decision. The request to seal off the apartment may thus have been a rather nervous overreaction by someone abroad who had virtually no control over things happening in Nice in the days after Hirschfeld's death.

"NOTORIÉTÉ APRÈS LE DÉCÈS" (NOTORIETY AFTER DEATH) PROCEDURE

On May 20, 1935, six days after Hirschfeld's death, one of the initial formal procedures, "notoriety after death" (*notoriété après le décès*), was handled in Demnard's office.[111] This legal procedure specifically applied to foreigners for whom one had no birth certificate (or other valid civil registry document) at hand to prove the identity of the deceased.[112] Four witnesses who declared that they knew Hirschfeld in Nice signed the document: Hirschfeld's last secretary, Robert Kirchberger; his good friend Sophie Gordon, living in the pension Floréal; and two other unidentified witnesses.[113] The four stated that they knew where Hirschfeld had lived, when he died, that he was single and without any particular profession, that he had no ascendants or descendants, and that an inventory of his belongings had not been drawn up yet. The strange thing, and against usual practice, is that not one of the four witnesses stood to inherit. This likely indicates that Giese and Li Shiu Tong had other things on their mind than signing official papers so soon after their arrival in Nice. (They arrived in Nice the day before, on Sunday.) We have also seen that Giese fell sick immediately after his arrival, likely from the stress of reaching Nice in time. Most likely, the decision about who would participate in this legal procedure was taken at the last moment.[114]

Hirschfeld's last will and found the translation factually reliable. There are only a few minor errors: in article 5, "Dokumente, Manuskripte" (documents, manuscripts) becomes "documents manuscrits" (written documents). The interpretation of article 2 is also questionable.

110 ADAM, Archives administratives de 1800 à 1940, Justice de Paix Nice Ouest, Actes, 2ème trimestre 1935, Apr. 1, 1935–Jun. 30, 1935, apposition de scellés d'office (dated 17/05/1935), cote 04U 12/0301. There one speaks confusingly of "opposition [*sic*: apposition] et levée des scellés". That the apartment had not been sealed off completely is confirmed by a later document, detailing the situation just before the seals were broken, which says that Giese and Li Shiu Tong were both "actuellement en résidence" (currently staying) in Gloria Mansions. ADAM, Nice, Archives notariales, minutes notariales étude Pierre Demnard, May 24, 1935, n° 569, cote 03E 148/011.

111 ADAM, Nice, Archives notariales, minutes notariales étude Pierre Demnard, May 20, 1935, n° 553, cote 03E 148/011.

112 Farcy 1992, 149–50: "Acte établi par le juge de paix ou un notaire constatant les déclarations de personnes qui attestent d'un fait notoire dont il est impossible de produire la preuve écrite. Il sert principalement à rectifier ou remplacer un acte de naissance (art. 70 du Code civil), ou tout acte d'état-civil lorsque les registres se trouvent en territoire ennemi" (A document drawn up by the justice of the peace or a notary giving the declarations of persons who attest to a known fact for which it is impossible to produce written proof. It is mainly used to correct or replace a birth certificate [article 70 of the Civil Code], or any civil status certificate when the registries are in enemy territory).

113 Gaston Mauclair [?], "hôtelier demeurant à Saint Jean Cap Ferrat, Hotel de la plage" and a certain

The notoriety after death procedure also allowed heirs to receive an advance payment on their eventual inheritance. Such an advance payment of FF2,000 was indeed made on the day of Hirschfeld's funeral ceremony, on May 21, 1935. Giese and Li Shiu Tong were each given FF500 and Herzfelder received FF1,000. It is possible that Giese made an explicit request for such and advance payment, since he may have realized that his financial situation had (or certainly would) become quite precarious with Hirschfeld's death. But such an advance payment may simply have been common practice in the procedure.

INVENTORY OF THE GLORIA MANSIONS I APARTMENT

On May 24, 1935, one week after the apartment had been partially sealed, and three days after Hirschfeld's funeral, the official seals in the Gloria Mansions I apartment were broken and Robert Kirchberger was dismissed from his duties as custodian of the seals *(gardien des scellés)*.[115] The seals applied on May 17 were removed so that an official inventory could be made of the contents of the apartment.[116] The inventory was drawn up by Gaston Giauffer, a certified appraiser of the Nice arrondissement (*commissaire-priseur de l'arrondissement de Nice*).[117] No fewer than five people witnessed the appraisal: Franz Herzfelder, Karl Giese, Li Shiu Tong, Robert Kirchberger and, lastly, the notary Pierre Demnard, who made the whole procedure official.[118]

In the official inventory document, the certified appraiser Gaston Giauffer recorded room by room the furniture and any decorative items of value present in the apartment. Beside the notations of mainly antique furniture and thirty-three picture frames (with photos and reproductions) hanging on a living room wall,[119] Demnard's handwritten notes, stating the appraiser's valuations, pointed out three intriguing items:

- in the living room: "a portrait of a bearded woman with inscription dated 1622" (*une peinture portrait de femme à barbe avec inscription en date 1622*), valued at FF100

Mr. Bouloward [?], "rentier, demeurant à Nice, Boulevard Carnot N° 51". The latter was the address of the Floréal pension, so we may assume that Sophie Boehm brought Bouloward along as an ad hoc witness.

114 The notary document points in this direction. It had clearly been typed out beforehand and only the names of Robert Kirchberger and Sophie Boehm were included, the other two names remaining blank, possibly indicating that they still thought it possible that Giese and Li Shiu Tong might show up to sign the document.

115 ADAM, Archives administratives de 1800 à 1940, Justice de Paix Nice Ouest, Actes, 2ème trimestre 1935, Apr. 1, 1935–Jun. 30, 1935, délégation pour levée de scellés (dated May 24, 1935), cote 04U 12/0301.

116 ADAM, Nice, Archives notariales, minutes notariales étude Pierre Demnard, May 24, 1935, n° 569, cote 03E 148/011. A title appears above the appraisal: *Prisée du mobilier* (appraisal of the furnishings). Ensuring an inventory is one of the executor's tasks prescribed by French law: "L'exécuteur testamentaire doit: [...] 2. Faire dresser inventaire en présence ou après appel des héritiers présomptifs" (The executor must: [...] 2. Have an inventory made in the presence of or after a request by the presumptive heirs). See Taithe & Taithe 1986, 22.

117 Gaston Giauffer (1886–?) was one of the two appointed *commissaires-priseurs* (auctioneers, certified appraisers) of the Nice arrondissement and was active in this function from 1919 until 1936. See ADAM, Archives administratives de 1800 à 1940, Officiers publics et ministériels, Jan 1, 1919–Dec. 31, 1946, Office de commissaire-priseur de Nice, Gaston Giauffer (1919–1936), cote 08U 0062. Giauffer's colleague was Jean-Joseph Terris (1889–1976). After the war, Terris was an associate of the Robiony art gallery in Nice. For more information on Terris, see the article in *Nice-Matin*, Sep. 28, 1976, 3. The Hôtel des Ventes where Terris and Giauffer worked was located at 3 Rue Provana (*Annuaire des Alpes-Maritimes* 1936, 1150). Under the heading "Salle de ventes" in the same directory, it says: "Hôtel des Ventes publiques des Commissaires-Priseurs" (*Annuaire des Alpes-Maritimes* 1936, 1296).

118 ADAM, Nice, Archives notariales, minutes notariales étude Pierre Demnard, May 24, 1935, n° 569, cote 03E 148/011.

119 One of the pictures in the Hirschfeld guestbook is of the inside of the Gloria Mansions apartment and shows one of the living room walls decorated with some of these picture frames. See Bergemann, Dose, Keilson-Lauritz & Dubout 2019, f. 151/195, top picture.

- in a room in the back (north side) of the apartment:[120] "A set of various books, mostly in foreign languages" (*Un lot livres [sic] divers en majeure [?] partie en langue étrangère*), estimated at FF100
- in the same room: "Seventeen casts related to sexology" (*Dix-sept moulages ayant trait à la sexologie*), also estimated at FF100

Giauffer estimated the total value of the household effects at FF4,195. What exactly became of the furnishings is mostly unclear, but, according to article 5 of Hirschfeld's will, Li Shiu Tong was entitled to these items.

KARL GIESE LEAVES NICE AGAIN

We saw that Giese obtained a two-week visa so that he could attend Hirschfeld's funeral. He arrived in Nice on May 19, 1935. Giese was well aware that his unplanned stay in France was only temporary, giving him little leeway in protecting the Institute materials. Giese vented his frustration in a letter to Max Hodann: "Unfortunately, my stay in France has been made impossible. Not only can I no longer work together with him [Li Shiu Tong] on the reconstruction and preservation of the materials – [...] – but neither do I have the necessary opportunity to take care of these things on the spot".[121] Yet Giese did not respect the two-week term of his visa. He wrote to Max Reiss that he had to stay longer in Nice "for technical reasons".[122] But ultimately, Giese had no other choice than to leave Nice.[123] On June 6, 1935, Giese formally declared that a collaborator of the notary Pierre Demnard, Raoul Leclerc, would legally represent him and have his power of attorney.[124] The next day, the day of Giese's departure, Li

[120] Possibly, these books were found in Robert Kirchberger's bedroom. See what Hirschfeld wrote in an April 1935 letter to Li Shiu Tong, in which he reported feeling very sick one night, fearing for his life, and trying to call for help: "I called before [*sic*] Robert [Kirchberger] and the cook, but because they both sleep behind [i.e., in the north-facing bedrooms] they could not hear me". See Archiv MHG, Berlin, fonds Li Shiu Tong, letter (dated Apr. 24, 1935) from Magnus Hirschfeld to Li Shiu Tong, qtd. in Dose 2003a, 17. The letter is reproduced and transcribed in *Mitteilungen der Magnus-Hirschfeld-Gesellschaft* 37–38 (June 2007): 13–14. Given where Kirchberger slept, Giese and Li Shiu Tong likely took the two south-facing "master" bedrooms (with a view of the sea) after Hirschfeld's death, but one wonders how they decided who would sleep in Hirschfeld's former bedroom (and deathbed?).

[121] Arbetarrörelsens arkiv och bibliotek, Stockholm, Max Hodann samling, vol. 15, letter (dated Aug. 2, 1935, [1]) from Karl Giese to Max Hodann: "Unglücklicher Weise [*sic*: unglücklicherweise] ist mir doch der Aufenthalt in Frankreich unmöglich gemacht, sodass ich nicht nur nicht mehr mit ihm [Li Shiu Tong] gemeinsam am Wiederaufbau und Erhaltung der Sache arbeiten konnte – [...] – sondern mir auch jetzt nicht die so notwendige Möglichkeit gegeben ist, mich an Ort und Stelle um die Erledigung dieser Sachen zu kümmern".

[122] Archiv MHG, Berlin, fonds Max Reiss, letter (dated May 1935 but presumably May 27 or 28, 1935, 3) from Karl Giese to Max Reiss: "aus technischen Gründen".

[123] In the final settlement of the Hirschfeld inheritance file, there is mention of a telegram sent to a lawyer in Paris on June 4, 1935. I found only one charge for a telegram in the final settlement. Possibly this telegram was linked to Giese's attempt to extend his stay or even to his illegally overstepping his two-weeks limit. See "Coût télégramme à M. Ferry [*sic*: Féry] d'Esclands à Paris", ADAM, Nice, Archives notariales, minutes notariales étude Pierre Demnard, Aug. 10, 1936, n° 1039, cote 03E 148/041.

[124] See ADAM, Nice, Archives notariales, minutes notariales étude Pierre Demnard, Sep. 2, 1935, n° 886, cote 03E 148/018, which contains a copy of the affidavit (dated Jun. 6, 1935) made by one of Demnard's notary colleagues, Louis Larboullet. That another notary was required seems to indicate that the matter was urgent and needed to be settled as soon as possible. The registration of the Giese-Leclerc procuration at the Nice Court of first instance can be found in ADAM, Nice, Archives administratives de 1800 à 1940, Fonds du Tribunal de première instance de Nice, Procurations annexées aux actes de renonciations et acceptations en matière de succession et conseils de famille, Jan. 1, 1935–Dec. 31, 1935, n° 196, procuration (dated Jun. 6, 1935) from Karl Giese to Raoul Leclerc, cote 03U 01/1464. I could not trace any mention of the procuration in Larboullet's répertoire du notaire. See ADAM, Archives administratives de 1800 à 1940, Officiers publics et ministériels Nice, Répertoires des notaires, Louis Larboullet (Jan. 3, 1927–Jul 29, 1936), cote 08U 0008. I was not able to check the Larboullet minutes for the year 1935 as they were not yet deposited in 2013 in the ADAM in Nice.

[125] ADAM, Nice, Archives notariales, minutes notariales étude Pierre Demnard, May 29, 1936, n° 727, cote 03E 148/036. Cf. the letter (dated Jun. 11, 1935) that François Herzfelder wrote to Ernst Maass: "Herr Giese musste schon *vor einigen Tagen* wegfahren,

Shiu Tong lent him the sum of FF1,700, likely in cash.[125] This shows that both were getting along well, a cordiality that continued until August 1935, when Giese wrote to Max Hodann: "Otherwise, he [Li Shiu Tong] is being very nice and comradely to me".[126] Shortly after his return to Vienna, Giese must have spoken to a journalist working for the Brno newspaper *Tagesbote* since it published an article precisely and openly reporting about what the Hirschfeld estate had in store for both Giese and Li Shiu Tong. Some of the details in the article clearly show that the journalist had to have spoken to Giese in person. This possibly indicates that Giese went to Brno in June 1935. If so, he most likely went there to talk to his lawyer Karl Fein.[127]

STANDSTILL

As soon as Giese left Nice, the inheritance procedure came to a virtual standstill, which would last until the end of August 1935. This could have been a consequence of the summer recess but it is also possible that Li Shiu Tong's behavior played a part. Hirschfeld's Chinese pupil was not very keen on the rather demanding conditions of the inheritance. Technically speaking, according to the stipulations in article 4 of Hirschfeld's last will, this would not present a real problem: Giese would inherit Li's part if Li Shiu Tong turned down the inheritance he was entitled to.[128] Li Shiu Tong was likely wary of Hirschfeld's explicit condition that he and Giese should only use the money to further Hirschfeld's intellectual legacy (*geistige Erbe*). Maybe Li Shiu Tong already knew he would not be able to realize Hirschfeld's wishes. One could even say that Li Shiu Tong's life afterwards was indeed proof of this early self-knowledge.[129] Coming from a very well-to-do family, he never felt any real need to study or work for a living. In other words, Li Shiu Tong, in clear contrast to Giese, had no financial incentive to accept the bequest. In the beginning of August, in a letter to Max Hodann, Karl Giese wrote that Li Shiu Tong was indeed in doubt on the matter: "Also, whether he [Li Shiu Tong] will accept his part of the inheritance together with me is still very much in question, as he fears that this will bind him too much for his age".[130]

In the beginning of August 1935, Giese went to Brno again to discuss with Karl Fein how matters were going with the Hirschfeld inheritance.[131] Apparently, it was decided that Fein would go to Nice to try to unblock matters. Around mid-August, Fein in fact headed to Nice as Giese's legal representative.[132] At the end of the month,

weil er die Verlängerung seiner Aufenthaltserlaubnis nicht erlangen könnte" (Mr. Giese already had to leave *a few days ago* already because he could not obtain an extension of his residence permit) (emphasis added). The letter is in the Archiv MHG, Berlin, fonds Ernst Maass.

[126] Arbetarrörelsens arkiv och bibliotek, Stockholm, Max Hodann samling, vol. 15, letter (dated Aug. 2, 1935, [3]) from Karl Giese to Max Hodann: "Sonst stellt er [Li Shiu Tong] sich sehr nett und kameradschaftlich zu mir". In October 1935, Giese let Max Reiss know that, out of his love for Hirschfeld, he intended to be a good friend to Li Shiu Tong. See Archiv MHG, Berlin, fonds Max Reiss, letter (dated Oct. 20, 1935, 3–4) from Karl Giese to Max Reiss.

[127] "Magnus Hirschfelds Testament", *Tagesbote*, Jun. 21, 1935, 5.

[128] Article 4 of the will indeed specified: "Sollte einer dieser Erben [Giese or Li Shiu Tong] vor mir Sterben, oder aus einem sonstigen Grunde nicht meine Erbe werden, so wächst sein Anteil dem anderen zu" (If either of these heirs [Giese or Li Shiu Tong] should die before me, or not become my heir for any other reason, his share shall go to the other). I thank Ralf Dose for pointing this out to me.

[129] See Dose 2003 for a biography of Li Shiu Tong.

[130] Arbetarrörelsens arkiv och bibliotek, Stockholm, Max Hodann samling, vol. 15, letter (dated Aug. 2, 1935, 3) from Karl Giese to Max Hodann: "Auch ob er [Li Shiu Tong] seinen Erbteil gemeinsam mit mir annimmt, ist noch sehr fraglich, da er befürchtet sich damit für sein Alter zu sehr zu binden". Li Shiu Tong's doubt is also mentioned in Archiv MHG, Berlin, fonds Max Reiss, letter (dated May 1935 but presumably 27 or 28, 1935, 1–2 and 3) from Karl Giese to Max Reiss.

[131] Arbetarrörelsens arkiv och bibliotek, Stockholm, Max Hodann samling, vol. 15, letter (dated Aug. 2, 1935, 2) from Karl Giese to Max Hodann. At the top of this letter, there is the note: "z. Zt. [*zur Zeit*, currently] in Brünn [Brno]".

[132] In MZA, Brno, fonds C 107, Německý úřední soud Brno, kart. n° 256, sign. 5a V 3/41, there is an undated procuration (*Vollmacht*), signed by Giese, naming Fein as his legal representative. It is not certain if this procuration was the one already used in 1935.

in a letter to Ernst Maass, François Herzfelder wrote: "The opening of the bank safe and the handing over of bank accounts are still not settled. At the moment, Dr. Fein, Mr. Giese's lawyer, is here. We hope to have the matter settled in a short time".[133] Fein went to Nice to try to stir things up a bit or at least to find out what was going on. He certainly spoke to Li Shiu Tong when he was there, as Giese attested in a letter.[134] Possibly it was also one of Fein's tasks to help Li Shiu Tong to come to a final decision on whether he would accept his share of the inheritance or not. News of the going-on with the Hirschfeld estate in Nice reached Switzerland in mid-September 1935. In an article published in the magazine *Der Freidenker*, it was said that the contents of Hirschfeld's last will were now known and that, other than private stipulations, the main beneficiaries were Li Shiu Tong and Karl Giese, who, beyond granting them money on which to live, had to use the estate to continue Hirschfeld's life's work.[135]

One month after Fein's arrival in Nice, Giese complained in a letter to Max Hodann that things were still not moving as he had hoped: "Shortly after the arrival of your letter, my friend and lawyer, Dr. Karl Fein from Brno [...] went to Nice because, in our opinion, the matter was not being handled with sufficient vigor there. [...] After all, in the 5 weeks of Dr. Fein's stay there (1 week was originally planned), he could not even manage to gain the opening of the safe and the ascertainment of ownership".[136] Opening Hirschfeld's bank safe in Nice was of course the centerpiece of the inheritance. How much money would it contain? The exact amount would determine the further course of the inheritance. One does not have to accept – as Giese's letter seems to suggest – that Fein was in Nice for five weeks because the inheritance procedure was delayed. There was another reason: Fein lost his passport in Nice and, because of a misunderstanding, the Czech consulate in Marseille took rather long to issue him a new one. Fein was likely confused with his homonymous elder cousin and lawyer Karl Fein, who died in 1932. The Czech authorities were very cautious since they did not want to issue a passport to a dead man.[137]

[133] Archiv MHG, Berlin, fonds Ernst Maass, letter (dated Aug. 23, 1935) from François Herzfelder to Ernst Maass: "Öffnung der Banksafes und Aushändigung der Bankkonten sind immer noch nicht geregelt. Zur Zeit ist Herr Dr. Fein, der Anwalt Herrn Gieses hier. Wir hoffen, in kurzem die Sache in Ordnung zu bringen".

[134] Arbetarrörelsens arkiv och bibliotek, Stockholm, Max Hodann samling, vol. 15, letter (dated Sep. 24, 1935, 2) from Karl Giese to Max Hodann.

[135] See the anonymous article "Magnus Hirschfelds Testament", *Der Freidenker*, Jg. 18, n° 18, Sep. 15, 1935, 143: "Die beiden Erben erhalten das Vermächtnis mit dem ausdrücklichen Vermerk überwiesen, dass die Einnahmen daraus, soweit sie nicht ihren persönlichen Unterhalt decken müssen, ausschliesslich zur Fortführung des wissenschaftlichen Werkes Hirschfelds zu dienen haben." The author of the text was possibly Herbert Lamprecht (1889?–1969?), who wrote a text (published in two parts) on Hirschfeld's life work for the same publication, some months after Hirschfeld's death. See Lamprecht, Nov. 15, 1935; and Lamprecht, Dec. 1, 1935. However, the writer could also have been a certain R. Staiger, who reviewed Hirschfeld's *Die Weltreise eines Sexualforschers* for *Der Freidenker*. See Staiger, Jun. 15, 1934.

[136] Arbetarrörelsens arkiv och bibliotek, Stockholm, Max Hodann samling, vol. 15, letter (dated Sep. 24, 1935, 1) from Karl Giese to Max Hodann: "Kurz nach Ankunft Ihres Briefes ist mein Freund und Anwalt, Herr Dr. Karl Fein aus Brünn [...] nach Nizza gefahren, da sich herausstellte, dass nach unserer Meinung die Sache dort nicht mit dem genügenden Elan angefasst wurde. [...] Immerhin ist es auch Dr. Fein in den 5 Wochen, die er dort verbrachte, (1 Woche war ursprünglich vorgesehen) nicht einmal gelungen, die Safeeröffnung und Fesstellung [*sic*, Feststellung] des Besitzes zu erwirken". The phrase "shortly after the arrival of your letter" indicates that Fein must have headed to Brno soon after August 8, 1935, the date that Hodann sent his letter to Giese (to which Giese was replying).

[137] See the correspondence in NA, Praha, Policejní ředitelství Praha II, všeobecná spisovna, 1931–1940, kart. n° 5661, sign. F 271/9, Fein Karel JUDr 1894. See also p. 174, n. 116.

[138] Here as well, we can see that the summer recess may indeed have been a factor delaying the inheritance procedure. See the definition of "Chambre des vacations", https://fr.wiktionary.org/wiki/vacation (accessed Jul. 2, 2020).

[139] ADAM, Nice, Archives notariales, minutes notariales étude Pierre Demnard, Sep. 2, 1935, n° 886, cote 03E 148/018. The original "acceptance under benefit of inventory" court decision can be found in ADAM, Archives administratives de 1800 à 1940, Fonds du Tribunal de première instance de Nice, Acceptations et renonciations à successions (décembre 1932-

THE "ACCEPTATION BÉNÉFICIAIRE" PROCEDURE

Although it is unclear if Fein played any role, on August 28, a further step was taken in the inheritance procedure. In the vacation court (*chambre des vacations*)[138] of the Nice Court of first instance it was noted that Hirschfeld's two universal legatees (*légataires universels*), Karl Giese and Li Shiu Tong, accepted the inheritance, though "only under benefit of inventory" (*sous bénéfice d'inventaire seulement*).[139] This was – and continues to be – a common legal expression and procedure stating that inheritors are entitled, prior to accepting an inheritance, to ascertain if the amount of the inheritance (activa) is greater than the debts and costs (passiva) associated with the inheritance. Li Shiu Tong attended court in person that day. Giese was represented by the notary Raoul Leclerc. Most likely, Li Shiu Tong left Nice shortly afterwards. On that day, he signed a power of attorney (*procuration*), as Giese had done before in June, allowing another clerk in Demnard's office, François Pierrugues, to represent him in all other undertakings related to the inheritance.[140]

THE TRUE DELAYING FACTOR?

In a letter that Karl Giese wrote to Max Hodann, in September 1935, he mentioned two factors delaying the inheritance procedure. The first reason he gave for the summer standstill looks rather subjective. Giese opined that "the persons entrusted with the estate probably did not have the necessary knowledge and motivation".[141] Contrary to what Giese suggests here, one may wonder to what extent "professional ability" was indeed a real hindrance. For a very long time, Nice was a place where many well-off French citizens and foreigners decided to spend the last years of their life. It seems highly unlikely that a professional like Demnard, who dealt with inheritances on a daily basis, would not have really known what he was doing. That he may have not been zealous enough is another matter. The summer recess, as already suggested, may have been another delaying factor.

However, in the same letter to Hodann, Giese also raised another delaying factor. Most likely, this was the main cause for the delay in handling the Hirschfeld inheritance in the summer of 1935. Apparently there was a discussion about Hirschfeld's actual domicile address and whether French or rather German law would therefore apply in the inheritance. In the letter to Hodann, Giese also wrote: "In fact, it turned out that the situation prompted by the circumstance that Dr. H.[irschfeld] was not yet regarded as fully resident in France etc., weighed very heavily".[142] When Hirschfeld embarked on his world tour, in November 1930, he most likely never imagined that he would never return to Germany. We know that his life as a German exile started after his return from his world tour, and that likely also means that he never had the opportunity (or wish) to officially declare to the German authorities that he had given up his Berlin domicile. In another, earlier letter to Max Hodann, Giese wrote: "When there is a safe with unknown contents, the bank requires a document that can only be

mars 1937), n° 196, dated Aug. 28, 1935, cote 03U 01/1457.

[140] ADAM, Nice, Archives notariales, minutes notariales étude Pierre Demnard, Aug. 28, 1935, n° 878, cote 03E 148/017. This power of attorney was conferred on the already mentioned notary Louis Larboullet, see above, p. 276, n. 124. Interestingly, the document also makes it clear that Li Shiu Tong was still residing in Gloria Mansions I at this time.

[141] Arbetarrörelsens arkiv och bibliotek, Stockholm, Max Hodann samling, vol. 15, letter (dated Sep. 24 1935, 1) from Karl Giese to Max Hodann: "die mit der Nachlassenschaft betrauten Personen wohl nicht die notwendige Kenntnis und Aktivität aufbrachten". In a letter sent to Max Reiss, Giese also complained that it was taking unbelievably long to settle the inheritance. See Archiv MHG, Berlin, fonds Max Reiss, letter (dated Oct. 20, 1935, 1) from Karl Giese to Max Reiss.

[142] Arbetarrörelsens arkiv och bibliotek, Stockholm, Max Hodann samling, vol. 15, letter (dated Sep. 24, 1935, 1) from Karl Giese to Max Hodann: "Tatsächlich zeigte es sich, dass die Situation infolge des Umstandes, dass Dr. H.[irschfeld] noch nicht als ganz ansässig in Frankreich anzusehen war etc. sehr schwer wog".

[143] Arbetarrörelsens arkiv och bibliotek, Stockholm, Max Hodann samling, vol. 15, letter (dated Aug. 2,

obtained from the German embassy, from which we have tried to stay away foremost. For this reason, the settlement of the affair is already taking so long".[143] Giese does not specify the exact document the French bank demanded, but it was possibly related to the just-mentioned domicile issue. In June 1935, François Herzfelder wrote to Ernst Maass: "Now we are still waiting for the issuance of the *certificat de coutume*, without which, as we all know, the disposal of the assets held by the banks is not possible".[144] In any case, this seems to have been the missing document for which they were waiting. Generally speaking, a *certificat de coutume* explains the legislation regarding a certain matter in the country of origin, and this certificate could only be obtained through a consulate or embassy of that country.

It is possible that the authorities in the German embassy were, at least initially, not prepared to deliver this or that required document or simply not in a hurry to do so. After all, Hirschfeld was one of their showcase enemies. This was perhaps another or even the main reason that explains the summer delay.[145] This problem was most likely solved through the intervention of the Parisian Jewish lawyer Edgard Sée (1873–1943?), who was then working as a legal advisor (*conseiller juridique*) for the German embassy in Paris. Delivering *certificats de coutume* was indeed one of his specialties.[146] Interestingly, Armin Fuhrer has pointed out that, in 1935, the Nazis were clashing with some of the Paris embassy staff, who were not sufficiently loyal to the new regime in Germany.[147] However, it is in any case clear that a solution to the evident, serious delay was eventually found. It is likely that Hirschfeld, when

1935, [2]) from Karl Giese to Max Hodann: "Es wird von Seiten der Bank, bei der sich ein Safe unbekannten Inhalts befindet, ein Dokument verlangt, das eigentlich nur über die deutsche Botschaft zu erlangen ist, die wir zu umgehen al le [*sic*: alle] Ursache haben. Auf diese Weise dauert die Erledigung der Affaire [*sic*] schon so lange". Apparently, the *envoi en possession* (possession of the consignment) procedure also functioned as a sort of security that banks demanded before handing over the moneys of the deceased. See in this regard the very similar current Belgian situation (also modeled on the Napoleonic *Code civil*): "L'accomplissement des formalités d'envoi en possession est souvent exigée par les banques lorsque le montant des dépôts du défunt est important. Il est normal que, dans ce cas, les institutions financières décident de s'entourer de toutes les garanties avant de libérer les fonds" (The completion of the formalities of the envoi en possession procedure is often required by the banks when the amount of the deceased's deposits is significant. It is normal that, in this case, financial institutions decide to surround themselves with all the guarantees before releasing the funds). See http://www.notaire.be/donations-successions/prise-de-possession-et-partage-de-la-succession/envoi-en-possession-des-biens-du-defunt (accessed Nov. 22, 2013).

[144] Archiv MHG, Berlin, fonds Ernst Maass, letter (dated Jun. 11, 1935) from François Herzfelder to Ernst Maass: "Jetzt warten wir noch auf die Erledigung des certificat de coutume, ohne das ja bekanntlich die Verfügung über die bei den Banken liegende Werte nicht möglich ist". In Britain and the USA this *certificat de coutume* is known as an affidavit or legal opinion.

[145] In this regard, I inquired with the Politisches Archiv des Auswärtigen Amts in Berlin, which houses the archives of the German embassy in Paris. Gerhard Keiper (Politischen Archiv des Auswärtigen Amts, Archive of the Foreign office, Berlin) let me know that neither the register of the Registratur der Rechtsabteilung nor that of the Frankreich-Referats (Länderabteilung II) for the year 1935 contained any mention of Hirschfeld, Edgard Sée (see next note), or Herzfelder. See emails (dated May 2, 2014, and several emails from June 2014) from Gerhard Keiper (Politischen Archiv des Auswärtigen Amts, Berlin) to the author.

[146] An honorary fee for services rendered was paid to Sée in the settlement of the Hirschfeld inheritance. See the mention (dated Jan. 29, 1936) "Envoi à M. Edgard See [*sic*: Sée], Avocat s/honoraires" in ADAM, Nice, Archives notariales, minutes notariales étude Pierre Demnard, Aug. 10, 1936, n° 1039, cote 03E 148 041. The Paris 1935 annuaire mentions, besides Sée's Paris address, 20 Rue Chauchat, Paris IX: "avocat, docteur en droit des universités de Paris et de Heidelberg. Certificats de coutume, contentieux. Allemagne, Autriche, Tchéco-Slovaquie". Sée was born in Colmar and, as a resident of Alsace, was perfectly bilingual. He obtained two PhDs in law from the universities of Heidelberg and Paris and specialized in inheritance law. He became French in 1892 and married in 1901. Starting in 1933, he was involved with German exiles arriving in Paris. During the war he worked for the Jewish community but was eventually deported, aged seventy, on October 27, 1943. His granddaughter, Michèle Feldman, has published a booklet on his 1942–43 war diary. See Feldman 2012.

[147] Fuhrer 2013, 74–80.

[148] Hirschfeld & Dose 2013, f. 92/196: "Im Dezember habe ich hier ein Testament nach hiesigen Gesetzen gemacht".

preparing his last will, had discussed with Herzfelder or Demnard what French law would require of him (and his belongings) as an exiled German citizen, now residing in France. In *Testament: Heft II*, he wrote: "In December, I made a last will here in accordance with local laws".[148] Had some matters been overlooked and was Giese right that the professionals in Nice were not sufficiently capable to foresee these issues? Although Hirschfeld might have discussed several aspects of his last will with Demnard or Herzfelder, or both, we need to point out again that Hirschfeld wrote out his last will by hand and that they possibly neither saw nor were involved with the final version that Hirschfeld finally put to paper. Possibly, Hirschfeld had failed to notice some legal points that complicated his case. Or perhaps Demnard was not willing to point out certain issues because Hirschfeld was not willing to register his last will with him (*testament notarial* or *testament authentique*). Legal advice comes, of course, at a certain cost.

THE "ENVOI EN POSSESSION" PROCEDURE

At the end of September, the French courts' summer recess apparently still going on, the final legal procedure called *procédure d'envoi en possession* ("putting into possession" procedure) was initiated.[149] This was the last and decisive legal hurdle that needed to be passed in the case of non-related universal legatees and in the specific case of a handwritten last will.[150] It was the judge of the Court of first instance who issued an order as soon as several documents (among them the *acte de notoriété* and the *acte de décès*) were presented to and verified by the court. This would finally allow the universal legatees, Giese and Li Shiu Tong, to "take possession" (*prendre en possession*) of Hirschfeld's former movable belongings. Today this procedure is done by a lawyer representing his clients, but in Hirschfeld's time it was the exclusive

[149] ADAM, Nice, Archives notariales, minutes notariales étude Pierre Demnard, Sep. 28, 1935, n° 976, cote 03E 148/019. The request was addressed to the president of the vacation court of the Court of first instance.

[150] One would think that, following article 1008 of the French *Code civil*, this *envoi en possession* procedure would not have been necessary had Hirschfeld let Demnard validate his last will, thus producing a so-called *testament notarial* or *testament authentique* instead of a *testament olographe*. But, apparently, the issue of Hirschfeld possibly having belongings abroad was also addressed in this procedure. We know from article 5 in Hirschfeld's last will that Institute materials were stored in Saarbrücken, Berlin, and Wiesbaden. However, it could be argued that these materials belonged to the foundation behind the Institute and not to Hirschfeld himself. But then again, some or most of the items stored in these cities had been bought back by Hirschfeld and were therefore, in a juridical sense, his own belongings. One can also see that, as early as May 1935, this issue of Hirschfeld possibly having belongings abroad was already mentioned in the *notoriété après le décès* procedure, where the notary Pierre Demnard, under the heading "mention", added the following: "Conformément à l'article 222 du décrêt [*sic*] du vingt huit décembre mil neuf cent vingt six [Dec. 28, 1926], portant codification des textes législatifs concernant l'enregistrement, mention est faite ici que dans tous les cas où une succession ouverte en France et régie par la Loi française, comprend des biens mobiliers ou immobiliers de quelque nature que ce soit, déposés ou existant à l'étranger, les ayants-droits à cette succession, doivent pour se faire remettre les dits biens, obtenir *l'envoi en possession spécial*, prévu par l'article 218 du décrêt précité" (In accordance with article 222 of the decree of December twenty-eight nineteen hundred and twenty-six [Dec. 28, 1926], codifying the legislative texts concerning registration, mention is hereby made that in all cases where an estate opened in France and governed by French law includes movable or immovable property of any kind whatsoever, deposited or existing abroad, the beneficiaries of this estate, in order to receive the said property, must obtain the *envoi en possession spécial* [special "putting into possession" procedure], provided for by article 218 of the above-mentioned decree) (emphasis added). See ADAM, Nice, Archives notariales, minutes notariales étude Pierre Demnard, May 20, 1935, n° 553, cote 03E 148/011. The decree entitled "Décret du 28 décembre 1926 portant codification des textes législatifs concernant l'enregistrement des actes et mutations et l'application des droits d'enregistrement, d'hypothèques et de greffe" (dated Dec. 28, 1926) referred to by Demnard can be found in *Le Bulletin législatif Dalloz lois, décrets, arrêtés, circulaires, etc.*, 1926, 1103–62. Articles 218 and 222, which Demnard mentioned, can be found in ibid., 1129–30.

[151] For the *envoi en possession* procedure see Taithe & Taithe 1986, 23–24. The *avoué* was – like notaries, bailiffs and certified appraisers – an *officier*

task of a so-called *avoué* (literally, an avowed person).[151] This request to be "sent into possession" (*requête aux fins d'envoi en possession*) was prepared by the avoué René Neveu (1909–2006) who represented Li Shiu Tong, Karl Giese, and Herzfelder.[152] René Neveu addressed the request to the president of the vacation court of the Nice Court of first instance on September 26, 1935.[153]

Aside from the formal legal obligations that were duly noted there, the text of the request addressed to the court contained a few interesting passages :

a. that the Hirschfeld estate concerned "to the best knowledge of the applicants only movable goods located in France" (*à la connaissance des exposants que des biens mobiliers tous situés en France*);
b. that, if possessions of any nature were found later, even abroad, these would be treated according to the "special formalities provided by French law" (*formalités spéciales prévu par la loi Française*);[154]
c. that, since Hirschfeld was domiciled in Nice, "one cannot apply to his estate any law other than French law, the law of the de facto residence of the deceased." (*on ne peut appliquer à sa succession, d'autre loi que la loi Française, loi du domicile de fait du défunt*);[155]

ministériel (legal official). See http://fr.wikipedia.org/wiki/Officier_minist%C3%A9riel (accessed Dec. 29, 2013). This function, initially hereditary, was long contested before its definitive disappearance from the juridical scene in 2012. Douxchamps even used the term "un parasite" (a parasite) when he wrote about the (to him superfluous) function of an *avoué* (Douxchamps 1907, 458).

[152] ADAM, Nice, Archives notariales, minutes notariales étude Pierre Demnard, Sep. 28, 1935, n° 976, cote 03E 148/019. For the original court source of the *envoi en possession* procedure, see ADAM, Nice, Archives administratives de 1800 à 1940, Fonds du Tribunal de première instance de Nice, Jugements civils sur requête, Jan. 1, 1935–Dec. 31, 1935, septembre-décembre, cote 03 U 01/0530. During a visit to Berlin (on May 10, 2010), Ralf Dose showed me the original of Hirschfeld's *Testament: Heft II*. I quickly noticed a rubber stamp on the cover of the document bearing a French name and profession: "M. René Neveu, Licencié en droit, avoué; 13, Rue Honoré Sauvan (étude) Nice". Only much later did I learn that Neveu played a role in the *envoi en possession* procedure in settling the Hirschfeld estate. I think that the explanation given by Ralf Dose and Nora Pester for the stamp does not cover the whole truth. See Hirschfeld & Dose 2013, 7. They suggest it is connected with the real friendship between Neveu and Demnard, and that this was a way to protect the document in case it got lost. The stamp certainly had this protective function but I think that the stamp was rather added for strictly professional reasons. Neveu simply wanted to study the Hirschfeld inheritance case (and the relevant sources) before presenting it in court. Interestingly, an *avoué* had to hold on to the pieces and documents related to a case for five years (Douxchamps 1907, 521 and 523). If this was in fact the case, then it could mean that Hirschfeld's *Testament: Heft II* was possibly only returned to Li Shiu Tong around 1940. Because the *avoué* also had the monopoly on presenting appeals to the Court of Appeals, I have also checked the archives of the Aix Court of Appeals (Nice falls under Aix as regards appeals) for traces of the Hirschfeld inheritance. Since the *répertoires des arrêts civiles* (directories of civil judgments) were not alphabetically ordered, I checked the alphabetical indexes at the end of each volume of court judgments for the years 1935–38. I did not find any trace of a possible (appealed) dispute regarding the Hirschfeld inheritance. See Archives départementales des Bouches-du-Rhône (ADBR), Centre d'Aix, fonds de la cour d'appel et de la cour de cassation d'Aix, Cour d'appel, 1795–1954, répertoires des arrêts civils (cotes 2 U 2 704 (1920-1936) and 2 U 2 705 (1936-1949)) and the arrêts civil, 1935–1938, cote 2 U 2 675 (1935, first room) until cote 2 U 2 691 (1938, fourth additional room).

[153] There is a handwritten inscription on the reverse side of the brown cover page for the *acceptation bénéficiaire* in Demnard's *minutes notariales*. See ADAM, Nice, Archives notariales, minutes notariales étude Pierre Demnard, Sep. 2, 1935, n° 886, cote 03E 148/018. It says that a copy was sent to the *avoué* Gabriel Hancy, who lived at 55 Rue Gioffredo. See *Annuaire des Alpes-Maritimes* 1935, 1078. Was he the initial *avoué* called upon to represent Giese, Li Shiu Tong, and Herzfelder in handling the *envoi en possession* procedure?

[154] Not being a specialist in French law nor even a jurist, I was not able to determine what these "formalités spéciales" (special formalities) might have been.

[155] French legislation is in any case clear on foreigners resident in France: "Si le défunt est étranger et domicilié en France, c'est la loi française qui régira sa succession mobilière" (If the deceased is a foreigner and resident in France, French law will govern his movable estate). See Taithe & Taithe 1986, 14.

d. "that, indeed, the deceased, of German nationality, was considered by the current leaders of Germany as a political enemy, meaning that, at the end of a world trip he made at the time of the German Nazi Revolution, the deceased was not able to return to Germany, where his property and his works as a professor of sexology were destroyed and expropriated".[156]

The judge accepted the request the next day, on September 26, 1935, and issued, as expected, an order:

> "In view of the above request and the provisions of the law, we convey Mr. HERZFELDER, in his capacity as executor of the will, and the Gentlemen GIESE and LI SCHIU [*sic*] TONG, in their capacity as universal legatees, to take possession of the property comprising the estate of Dr. Magnus // HIRSCHFELD de cujus,[157] excepting the property located abroad, under reserve, as concerns Mr. GIESE and LI SCHIU TONG, of the benefit of inventory that they have reserved for themselves, so as to dispose of the goods in accordance with the will of the deceased and the law".[158]

We see here that the issue of any movable and immovable possessions belonging to Hirschfeld abroad was again addressed and also conclusively dealt with by the court.

OPENING HIRSCHFELD'S BANK SAFE IN NICE

It is clear that the slowness of the inheritance procedure only made Giese more and more restless as time went on. By October 1935, he suffered "horrible tensions" (*schrecklichen Spannungen*) as a result.[159] But on October 22, 1935, three weeks after the completion of the *envoi en possession* procedure, Hirschfeld's bank safe at the Barclays Bank in Nice (7 Promenade des Anglais) was opened at 2:30 p.m. by five official witnesses.[160] Giese must have been informed on an almost daily basis about the

[156] ADAM, Nice, Archives notariales, minutes notariales étude Pierre Demnard, Sep. 28, 1935, n° 976, cote 03E 148/019: "qu'en effet, le défunt de nationalité allemande était considéré par les dirigéants actuels de l'Allemagne comme ennemi politique en sorte que à la fin d'un voyage qu'il accomplissait à travers le monde au moment de la Revolution Nazeiste [*sic*] allemande le défunt n'a pu rentrer en Allemagne, où ses biens et ses oeuvres de professeur de Sexologie avaient été détruits et expropriés".

[157] The full expression is "de cujus successione agitur" (the person of whose inheritance we speak). See https://www.dictionnaire-juridique.com/definition/de-cujus.php and https://www.sogeni.com/de_cujus.php (accessed Jan. 9, 2021).

[158] ADAM, Nice, Archives notariales, minutes notariales étude Pierre Demnard, Sep. 28, 1935, n° 976, cote 03E 148/019: "Vu la requête qui précède et les dispositions de la loi; Envoyons Monsieur HERZFELDER en sa qualité d'exécuteur testamentaire et Messieurs GIESE et LI SCHIU [*sic*] TONG en leur qualité de légataires universels, en possession des biens composants la succession du docteur Magnus // HIRSCHFELD de cujus, à l'exception des biens situés à l'étranger, sous réserve, en ce qui concerne M. GIESE et LI SCHIU TONG du bénéfice d'inventaire qu'ils se sont réservés et ce pour disposer des biens conformément au testament du défunt et à la loi".

[159] Archiv MHG, Berlin, fonds Max Reiss, letter (dated Oct. 20, 1935, 4) from Karl Giese to Max Reiss.

[160] ADAM, Nice, Archives notariales, minutes notariales étude Pierre Demnard, Oct. 22, 1935, n° 1082, cote 03E 148/022. The title page of this document in Demnard's minutes (bearing the title "Continuation de l'Inventaire"), seems also to suggest that opening the bank safe had indeed proved to be legally more complicated to execute compared to the inventory of the furnishings of the Gloria Mansions I apartment, made a few days after Hirschfeld's burial. In the introduction of this document, Demnard also referred to the *envoi en possession* court order of Sep. 26, 1936, a prerequisite for opening the bank safe. A copy of the *envoi en possession* procedure, as recorded in the notarial minutes, was already sent by Demnard's *étude* (office) to Barclays and Chase on October 4, 1935. See Demnard's handwritten note on the reverse side of the brown cover page, ADAM, Nice, Archives notariales, minutes notariales étude Pierre Demnard, Sep. 28, 1935, n° 976, cote 03E 148/019. So, this time, it was the banks that were slow and took more than two weeks to act. Lastly, it is important to note that in the final settlement (in French, *Dépôt de compte d'administration*) of the Hirschfeld estate, the date given for the opening of the bank safe is September 22, 1935, but the correct date should be October 22, 1935. See ADAM, Nice, minutes Demnard, Aug. 10, 1936, n° 1039, cote 03E 148/041, under the heading "Continuation d'inventaire".

[161] Archiv MHG, Berlin, fonds Max Reiss, letter (dated Oct. 20, 1935, 1) from Karl Giese to Max Reiss. Giese must have obtained the information from François

goings-on in Nice since, two days earlier, he had written to Max Reiss that the opening of the safe was imminent. Giese could easily be reached by phone, presumably in the Schneyer couple's apartment in Vienna.[161] The notary Demnard was again officializing the event in his usual, rather difficult handwriting. Also present were Herzfelder and the "special auditor of the Alpes-Maritimes tax collecting department" (*contrôleur spécial de l'enregistrement des Alpes-Maritimes*), a man named Raoul Coste. Giese and Li were represented by their respective proxies.

In the safe, paper money in different, mainly European currencies (guilders, French francs, British pounds) and dollars was found. But the bulk of the cash amounts were in Swiss francs: 53,000 Swiss francs was found in the safe, amounting to around FF250,000. Some traveller's checks were also in the safe. Later on, around FF21,000 altogether, was found in accounts held in Barclays Bank in Nice (funds released on January 6, 1936) and the Chase Bank in Paris (41 Rue Cambon; funds released on May 25, 1936).[162] Hirschfeld's funds consisted mainly of cash found in the Nice bank safe and the amounts in these two bank accounts. The income side of the inheritance totalled FF341,886.61, which would amount to approximately €260,849.58 in today's money.[163]

Two days after the opening of the bank safe, on October 24, 1935, Herzfelder wrote a letter to Ernst Maass informing him about what they found in the Nice bank safe: "The Barclays Bank safe has now finally been opened on the 22nd of this month. In it, there were sums of money, mainly non-French money, with a value of about FF313,000. To this must be added the approximately FF31,000, in free accounts in Chase and Barclays Bank. That makes a total of about FF344,000 [...][164] In my opinion, it is therefore safe to expect that all the legacies stipulated in the last will, including yours, will be paid out in full".[165]

Herzfelder or through his lawyer Karl Fein. It is interesting that, on an address list assembled by Ernst Maass and titled "Freunde von Magnus Hirschfeld", there are sixteen names, but Maass noted a telephone number for only one person and that person was Karl Giese. This undated address list is in Archiv MHG, Berlin, fonds Ernst Maass. François Herzfelder also informed Ernst Maass about the imminent opening of the bank safe: "Erfreulicher Weise habe ich jetzt endlich von der Barclays bank die Zustimmung zu der Eröffnung des Safes erlangt" (Pleasingly, I have now finally obtained approval from Barclays Bank to open the safe). See Archiv MHG, Berlin, fonds Ernst Maass, letter (dated Oct. 18, 1935) from François Herzfelder to Ernst Maass.

162 In a letter to Ernst Maass, Herzfelder also pointed out that some formal obstacles still had to be overcome before Barclays Bank would actually release the funds in the safe and the bank accounts. It is not clear what these obstacles were. See Archiv MHG, Berlin, letter (dated Oct. 24, 1935, 1) from Franz Herzfelder to Ernst Maass. I sent a letter inquiring about this matter to the Chase Bank in Paris (14 Place Vendôme) on October 10, 2014, but went unanswered.

163 Assuming €1 = FF1.31. See also above, p. 270, n. 85. Three archival sources spell out the details of Hirschfeld's monetary funds, the cash found in the safe, and the amounts in the two bank accounts: 1. The difficult to decipher inventory of the contents of the safe (see ADAM, Nice, Archives notariales, minutes notariales étude Pierre Demnard, Oct. 22, 1935, n° 1082, cote 03E 148/022); 2. A document of the Bureau d'Enregistrement (see ADAM, Déclarations de mutations par décès [deuxième série], o.c., Apr. 1, 1936–Jun. 10, 1936, volume 51, n° 261, May 1, 1936, cote 03Q 08853): this document is the most detailed; 3. The final settlement (see ADAM, Nice, Archives notariales, minutes notariales étude Pierre Demnard, Aug. 10, 1936, n° 1039, cote 03E 148/041). For a more detailed overview of Hirschfeld's monetary funds, see Soetaert 2014, 37, Table 1.

164 The total amount mentioned by Herzfelder corresponds very nearly – the difference being little more than FF2,000 – to the total amount of the *recettes* (income side) of the inheritance: FF341,886.61. The slight difference can be explained by the advance payment already made on May 20, 1935, during the *notoriété après le décès* procedure. However, there is a difference of around FF10,000 as regards the amount found in the two bank accounts. Possibly, the lower total amount found in the latter was an educated guess by Herzfelder (based on what Li Shiu Tong had told him?) since the money from the Paris Chase Bank account was not released until the end of May 1936.

165 Archiv MHG, Berlin, fonds Ernst Maass, letter (dated Oct. 24, 1935, 1) from François Herzfelder to Ernst Maass: "Das Safe der Barclays Bank ist nun also endlich am 22. ds. [dieses Monats] geöffnet worden. Es fanden sich darin Geldbeträge, hauptsächlich nicht französisches Geld, im Werte von ca. 313000

Giese visited Brno again in mid-November 1935, shortly after obtaining a new passport from the German embassy in Vienna, replacing the one he had lost in September of that year.[166] There, he went to see Karl Fein again. Giese returned to Brno again at the end of December 1935. From Brno, he wrote to Max Reiss in the Netherlands that he was not doing very well, "also psychically" (*auch psychisch*).[167] Giese made two more trips from Vienna to Brno after that, in January and February 1936, most likely always in relation to the inheritance procedure that continued to unfold in France.[168] The money may have been released by the banks, but this did not mean that the amount from the estate Giese was entitled to was immediately paid out to him. He did receive a few smaller advance payments, in January and March 1936, but he would obtain the bulk of his share only in June of that year.[169]

BEQUESTS (*LEGS*)

The precaution that Hirschfeld displayed in article 7 of his last will, stipulating that the amounts of the bequests (totaling FF113,000 or €86,260 in today's money) be "diminished proportionally" (*verhältnismäßig gekurzt*) in case of insufficient funds, turned out to be superfluous. Sufficient funds for all bequests were found. The total amount of the bequests was of course deducted from the FF341,886.61 constituting the income side (*recettes*) of the Hirschfeld estate. A letter that François Herzfelder sent to Ernst Maass in October 1935 makes it clear that it was only after the opening of the safe, and at last gaining some certainty about its actual monetary contents, that Herzfelder started work on identifying and locating the eight beneficiaries (*légataires particuliers*) entitled to bequests in Hirschfeld's will. Herzfelder also asked Maass to explain his exact relation to Hirschfeld.[170]

On January 27, 1936, the five bequests intended for Ernst Maass, Jenny Hauck (née Hirschfeld), Wally Rosa (Röschen) Hirschfeld, Walter Mann and Franz Richard Mann

französischen Francs. Dazu kommen die ca. 31000 frs, die sich auf freiem Konte bei der Chase- und Barclays Bank befinden. Das macht zusammen ca. 344000 frs. [...] Es ist also m. E. [meines Erachtens] sicher damit zu rechnen, dass die sämtlichen im Testament ausgesetzten Vermächtnisse, also auch das Ihrige, voll ausbezahlt werden können".

[166] For mention of Giese losing his passport and some money (Austrian schillings), see the letter (dated Sep. 24, 1935, 1) from Karl Giese to Max Hodann: Arbetarrörelsens arkiv och bibliotek, Stockholm, Max Hodann samling, vol. 15 and Archiv MHG, Berlin, fonds Max Reiss, letter (dated Oct. 20, 1935, 4) from Karl Giese to Max Reiss. On Nov. 5, 1935, Giese was issued a new passport, valid for only one year, from the *Passabteilung* (passport office) of the Deutsche Gesandtschaft (German embassy) in Vienna (see p. 2 and p. 4 of the passport). This passport, Giese's last, survived in MZA, Brno, fonds C 107, Německý úřední soud Brno, kart. n° 256, sign. 5a V 3/41.

[167] Archiv MHG, Berlin, fonds Max Reiss, postcard (dated Dec. 28, 1935) from Karl Giese to Max Reiss.

[168] Giese's new passport bears German and Czech language rubber stamps from the border police in Břeclav (Lunenburg in German, on the border between Austria and Czechoslovakia) for November 13, 1935 (no return stamp), January 14, 1936 (day return), and February 22, 1936 (day return). On November 13, 1935, there is also a stamp of the "Bank- u.[nd] Wechslergeschäft J. Fischer Filiale Ostbahnhof" (bank and currency exchange company J. Fischer, branch Ostbahnhof) (p. 32 of the passport). The Ostbahnhof was then one of Vienna's main train stations but no longer exists. See https://www.geschichtewiki.wien.gv.at/Ostbahnhof (accessed Jul. 2, 2020).

[169] Soetaert 2014, 51, Table 7.

[170] Archiv MHG, Berlin, letter (dated Oct. 24, 1935, 1) from Franz Herzfelder to Ernst Maass. Ernst Maass was both Magnus Hirschfeld's *Großvetter* (great cousin) and *Großneffe* (great nephew). See Hirschfeld & Dose 2013, 184 n. 483. In a later letter from Herzfelder to Maass (dated Jan. 28, 1936), he asked, "[d]a die Sache pressant ist" (since the matter is urgent), and Maass was a "Spezialist für genealogische Fragen" (specialist in genealogical questions), to clarify the precise family relation of Magnus Hirschfeld to Jenny Hauck, Wally Rosa Hirschfeld, and Walter and Franz Mann. This may seem at first a bit strange since – as we will see in a moment – the five bequests had already been settled the day before, on January 27, 1936. But the letter makes it clear that the information was mostly required to determine the exact amount of the inheritance taxes. Maass made a handwritten note on this letter that he answered Herzfelder a few days later, on January 30, 1936. See Archiv MHG, Berlin, fonds Ernst Maass, letter (dated Jan. 28, 1936) from Franz Herzfelder to Ernst Maass. The matter was urgent as the longer one delayed, the higher the late

were all paid out.[171] While Maass was represented by Paul Nillus from Demnard's office,[172] the other Hirschfeld relatives agreed on taking as their legal representative a German named Waldemar Speyer (1903–?) resident in Nice.[173] In order to make this possible, procurations were composed with several local notaries in Germany, Czechoslovakia, and England in December 1935.[174] In that month, possibly to discuss and coordinate the whole operation, Herzfelder was also in contact with Günter Hauck (1901–1976), the son of Hirschfeld's sister, Jenny Hirschfeld. Of the eight beneficiaries, Jenny Hirschfeld received the highest bequeathed amount, FF30,000.[175] It is also noteworthy that Li Shiu Tong was in Nice again – arriving from London – when these first five bequests were settled. He signed the official documents for the bequests in his own name instead of using his proxy. Giese was represented by Stéphane Dantot-Auclair, one of Demnard's clerks.[176] The documents also make it clear that Li Shiu Tong was staying in the Hôtel de la Méditerrannée, no longer in Gloria Mansions I.[177]

fees payable to the tax office would be. See p. 289 and notes 192 until 194.

171 ADAM, Nice, Archives notariales, minutes notariales étude Pierre Demnard, Jan. 27, 1936, n° 109, cote 03E 148/028: legs Walter Mann, n° 105; legs Richard Mann, n° 106; legs Röschen Hirschfeld, n° 107; legs *veuve* (widow) Hauck, n° 108; legs Ernst Maass, n° 109.

172 ADAM, Nice, Archives notariales, minutes notariales étude Pierre Demnard, Jan. 27, 1936, n° 109, cote 03E 148/028. Already on May 16, 1935, Maass signed a *procuration* (power of attorney) naming Paul Nillus from Demnard's office as his legal representative in all matters related to the Hirschfeld estate. See ADAM, Nice, Archives notariales, minutes notariales étude Pierre Demnard, May 16, 1935, n° 542, cote 03E 148/011. Three weeks after Maass's bequest was settled, Maass dismissed Paul Nillus. To complicate matters further, on December 23, 1935, in Milan, Maass signed a procuration stating that Herzfelder and not Nillus would be his proxy thereafter. Because Nillus had accepted the bequest in Maass's name, in January 1936, another document had to be drawn up to rectify this awkward situation. For all this, see ADAM, Nice, Archives notariales, minutes notariales étude Pierre Demnard, Feb. 21, 1936, n° 239, cote 03E 148/030; and also a copy (or perhaps draft copy?) of an undated procuration in which Maass conferred his power of attorney on Herzfelder. See the notarized document (LL 58615) in Archiv MHG, Berlin, fonds Ernst Maass.

173 How the bequeathed sums eventually reached Germany is unclear. Waldemar Speyer was the son of Gustav Speyer (1869–1933) and Lucie Meyer (1879–1942). The Jewish couple married on February 20, 1902, in Berlin. See Landesarchiv, Berlin, Personenstandsregister, Heiratsregister, Standesamt Berlin VIIa, 1902, Erstregister, n° 179, accessible at Ancestry.com under Berlin, Germany, Marriages, 1874–1936. Waldemar Speyer, likely their only child, was born in Berlin in 1903. See Landesarchiv, Berlin, Personenstandsregister, Geburtsregister, Standesamt Berlin VIIa, 1903, Erstregister, n° 678, accessible at Ancestry.com under Berlin, Germany, Births, 1874–1906. Lucie Speyer was deported from Berlin to Riga on September 5, 1942, where she died on September 8, 1942. See https://www.bundesarchiv.de/gedenkbuch/de/ (accessed Sep. 12, 2020). The same information can be found in the Yad Vashem Central Database of Shoah Victims' Names, where it further says that she was deported on transport 19 (train Da 403) (accessed Jan. 9, 2021). Waldemar Speyer was a trainee lawyer just starting out at the bar in Berlin. He fled Germany in 1933 (or at the beginning of 1934) because of his Jewish descent and being barred from his profession. He first went to London and then moved to Paris in 1934 where he took some courses at the Sorbonne. He claimed to arrive in Paris on October 14, 1934. See COJASOR, Paris, dossier (dated 1945–46) Waldemar Speyer (born 1903). He went to Nice in October 1935 where he lived in Villa Antoinette at 37 Boulevard de Cessole. We will return to this house later. Waldemar Speyer also claimed that relatives living in New York helped him out financially: a Brooklyn cousin named Rose Barent, for one. Speyer also declared that his parents were living in the USA, but this is incorrect since his father died in Berlin in 1933. He was also listed in Nice as a student in the Centre Universitaire Méditerranéen (C.U.M.). It is unclear if his being listed as a thirty-two-year-old *célibataire* (bachelor) might indicate that he was gay. We will see later that he may have had a girlfriend named Eva.

174 Walter Mann made a procuration with a notary in Prague (Dec. 7, 1935), Franz Richard Mann with one in London (Dec. 12, 1935), Wally Rosa Hirschfeld with a notary in Hamburg (Dec. 9, 1935), and Jenny Hauck with a Berlin notary (Dec. 11, 1935). The original notarial procurations for these four bequests, most probably sent from abroad, were added to Demnard's notarial minutes. See ADAM, Nice, minutes Demnard, Jan. 27, 1936, legs Walter Mann, n° 105; legs Richard Mann, n° 106; legs Röschen Hirschfeld, n° 107; legs *veuve* (widow) Hauck, n° 108, cote 03E 148/028. Ernst Maass was represented by Paul Nillus. See ADAM, Nice, minutes Demnard, Jan. 27, 1936, legs Ernst Maass, n° 109, cote 03E 148/028.

175 Herzfelder must have met Hauck in Paris some time after December 8, 1935. See Archiv MHG, Berlin, fonds Ernst Maass, letter (dated Dec. 8, 1935) from Franz Herzfelder to Ernst Maass.

176 Stéphane Dantot-Auclair was the substitute for Raoul Leclerc. See ADAM, Nice, Archives notariales, minutes notariales étude Pierre Demnard, Oct. 31, 1935, n° 1134, cote 03E 148/022. It is unclear why Leclerc was replaced by Dantot-Auclair.

BEQUESTS FOR UNRELATED FRIENDS

Of Hirschfeld's three unrelated, personal friends, who were also entitled to bequests, the Czechoslovak Dr. Leopold Hönig stood out. Leopold Hönig was born in 1887 in Kirchenbirk (currently Kostelní Bříza) in Czechoslovakia, and travelled around the world. In *Testament: Heft II*, Hirschfeld wrote that Hönig was "a magnificent physician" (*ein prächtiger Arzt*).[178] Presumably, Hirschfeld met Hönig for the first time on one of his many therapeutic trips to the spa town Karlsbad (Karlovy Vary) [ill. 11].[179]

Not only did Hönig come in person to Nice to collect the money he was bequeathed, he also obtained his share a week before the others, on January 21, 1936.[180] Possibly he had been in contact (by letter?) with Karl Giese, since Hönig stayed for a while at the same address where Giese had stayed the last months he was in Nice, in February-March 1934.[181] Hönig arrived from Egypt, landing by ship in Marseille in December 1935.[182] The unmarried Hönig was clearly a gay man. When questioned by the police in Nice, a letter was found in one of his pockets revealing an affair with a French air force soldier called Aimé Germain.[183] In 1931, Hönig was arrested during a roundup in a notorious gay bar called "La Perle" (owned by Louis Seguin) in the Rue d'Angleterre

[177] ADAM, Nice, Archives notariales, minutes notariales étude Pierre Demnard, Jan. 27, 1936, n° 105, cote 03E 148/028: "Ont comparu: Li Shiu Tong (actuellement à Londres, Hotel Royal, Russell Square, de passage à Nice, Hôtel de la Méditerranée)" (Appeared: Li Shiu Tong [currently in London, Hotel Royal, Russell Square, briefly in Nice, Hôtel de la Méditerranée]).

[178] For further information on Hönig, see Hirschfeld & Dose 2013, f. 37/86 and n. 137.

[179] Hirschfeld visited Karlsbad (Karlovy Vary) quite often to enjoy the therapeutic baths. See, for example, the *Liste der angekommenen und abgereisten P. T. Curgäste in Carlsbad* for the years 1907 and 1916, where Hirschfeld's name is mentioned. The cosmopolitan town, attracting visitors from all over Europe, was (therefore) also attractive to gay people. See Zinn 2011.

[180] ADAM, Nice, Archives notariales, minutes notariales étude Pierre Demnard, Jan. 21, 1936, n° 69, cote 03E 148/028. For unclear reasons, Hönig had filled out a *procuration en blanc* (blank procuration) at Demnard's office in December 1935. This may indicate that Hönig initially thought he would be unable to collect the money himself. On the reverse side of the brown cover page of the notarial document there is a note written in pencil: "attendre Délivrance legs" (awaiting delivery of bequest). But Hönig himself went to Demnard's office to settle the bequest in January 1936. See ADAM, Nice, Archives notariales, minutes notariales étude Pierre Demnard, Dec. 20, 1935, n° 1390, cote 03E 148/026. Two witnesses signed the document. The first witness was the Paris-born bachelor Germain (Martin Xavier) Roth, director of the Hôtel des Trois Epis (51 Promenade des Anglais). This pension-hotel had eighteen rooms and was demolished in 1956. See ADAM, Nice, Direction départementale de la sécurité publique des Alpes-Maritimes, Sûreté départementale: unité technique d'aide à l'enquête (caserne Auvare), dossier Roth Germain, cote 1440W 0235. The second witness was Lucien Lévy (1886–1974), a married Jewish man, who lived in 1 Rue Croix de marbre. See ADAM, Nice, Direction départementale de la sécurité publique des Alpes-Maritimes, Sûreté départementale: unité technique d'aide à l'enquête (caserne Auvare), dossier Lévy Lucien, cote 1273W 0020. See also the *Annuaire des Alpes-Maritimes* 1936, 874. In a 1946 letter, Ernst Maass claimed that this man was a friend of his and later on also a client of the notary Pierre Demnard. See ADAM, Nice, Archives notariales, minutes notariales étude Pierre Demnard, May 22, 1935, n° 563, cote 03E 148/011, letter (dated Jun. 16, 1945) from Ernest [*sic*] Maass to Pierre Demnard. For unclear reasons, the final settlement names this blank power of attorney "Procuration pour prendre connaissance" (power of attorney to take cognizance). See the transaction (dated Dec. 20, 1935) at Demnard's office in ADAM, Nice, Archives notariales, minutes notariales étude Pierre Demnard, Aug. 10, 1936, n° 1039, cote 03E 148/041.

[181] ADAM, Nice, Archives notariales, minutes notariales étude Pierre Demnard, Dec. 20, 1935, n° 1390, cote 03E 148/026: "A COMPARU [devant Demnard]: Monsieur le Docteur Léopold [*sic*] Hönig, sans profession, domicilié à KARLSBAD (Tchéco-Slovaquie) Alte Wiese, actuellement en résidence à Nice[,] rue Halevy [*sic*, Halévy] numéro 4" (Appeared [before Demnard]: Mr. Dr. Léopold Hönig, of no profession, resident in KARLSBAD (Czechoslovakia) Alte Wiese, currently residing in Nice, 4 rue Halévy). In January 1936, Hönig was already staying at another address: 14 Avenue Félix Fauré (Pension Bella).

[182] ADAM, Nice, Direction départementale de la sécurité publique des Alpes-Maritimes, Sûreté départementale: unité technique d'aide à l'enquête (caserne Auvare), dossier n° 81.301, Hönig Léopold [*sic*], cote 1292W 0018.

[183] The phrase "Vraisemblablement relation de 'Pédéraste'" (Presumably a homosexual [pederast] relationship) is used for the relationship between Hönig and Germain. See ADAM, Nice, Direction départementale de la sécurité publique des Alpes-Maritimes, Sûreté départementale : unité technique d'aide à l'enquête (caserne Auvare), dossier n° 81.301, Hönig Léopold [*sic*], cote 1292W 0018.

near the main Nice train station.[184] Hönig told the police he went to Nice every year in the winter months for the past fifteen years.

Certainly, Hönig was there during the winter of 1934–35, since Hirschfeld mentioned meeting him and his rather mysterious "Circle of the Mediterranean Sea" (Kreis von der grande Bleue) in *Testament: Heft II.*[185] This group of friends may have been a gay circle, gathering on the premises of the Bains de la grande bleue, a beach house complex and annex bar located on the beach side of the Promenade des Anglais, virtually across from Gloria Mansions I [ill. 12].[186] In the 1930s, the painter Guy Pène du Bois made a painting (or even several paintings) with the title *La Grande Bleue* when he was in Nice. According to one writer who saw the painting, it depicted "this typical rich, sporty American youth ... liberated (with boyishly styled hair) and young men with athletic bodies, all in swimming costumes".[187] This likely further explains Hönig's homoerotic interest in the beach resort.

Despite Hönig picking up his share before the others, there was nevertheless a certain hierarchy – likely born out of prudence – in the timing of the payment of the bequests. In general, the unrelated legatees were the last to be paid. This was for example the case for Franz Wimmer, a former Berlin employee (and lover) of Hirschfeld, who received his bequest at the end of March 1936.[188] The bequest made to Margarete Dost (1879–1956), a good friend of Hirschfeld's, was settled a few days after Wimmer's.[189]

INHERITANCE TAXES

In an already mentioned letter to Ernst Maass, Herzfelder wrote that, depending on the degree of kinship (*Verwandtschaftsgrad*), considerable amounts of inheritance tax (*Erbschaftssteuer*) would be deducted from the sums paid out. In Ernst Maass's case, Herzfelder estimated that, most likely, approximately 31 percent in taxes would be

[184] For more information on Louis Seguin and his gay pickup bar, see ADAM, Nice, Direction départementale de la sécurité publique des Alpes-Maritimes, Sûreté départementale: unité technique d'aide à l'enquête (caserne Auvare), dossier Seguin Louis, cote 1440W 0003.

[185] Hirschfeld & Dose 2013, f. 86/184 n. 480, 481.

[186] *Annuaire des Alpes-Maritimes* 1936, 273 and 975. The owner of the beach complex was François Raybaud, who also owned a much grander beach house in Cannes. See ADAM, Archives administratives de 1800 à 1940, fonds de la préfecture des Alpes-Maritimes, 1860–1940, Jan. 1, 1919–Ded. 31, 1927, Bains de la Croisette, cote 02Q 0157. Having looked at several vintage postcards of the liminal beach house, I was able to determine that the (several decades old) wooden complex Bains de la grande bleue was located directly across from 57 Promenade des Anglais. (In an old 1920 tourist guide, the street number of "Bains de la grande bleue" is actually given as 59.) This last building also faces a side street of the Promenade des Anglais, the Rue Honoré Sauvan, where René Neveu's office was located. At the other corner of the same street, at 61 Promenade des Anglais, there is the Villa des officiers of the Fondation Furtado Heine. Gloria Mansions I, at 63 Promenade des Anglais, was and still is situated – when looked at from the sea – to the left of the Villa des officiers. The beach is now named Plage du Voilier and lies between Plage Florida and Plage Forum. Only the original stone stairwell, giving access to the beach from the promenade, remains.

[187] Rotily 2006, 27: "cette jeunesse américaine riche et sportive typique ... libérées (aux cheveux coupés à la garçonne) et de jeunes hommes aux corps d'athlète, tous en costumes de bain". I did not find what Rotily saw in Fahlman's work (Fahlman 2004, 120–21). An email that sought to discuss the matter with the American academic Betsy Fahlman (dated Feb. 11, 2014) was not answered.

[188] Wimmer was also represented by Waldemar Speyer and received payment on March 26, 1936. See ADAM, Nice, Archives notariales, minutes notariales étude Pierre Demnard, Mar. 26, 1936, n° 427, cote 03E 148/032. Here as well, a power of attorney was drawn up, this time with a Berlin notary, in March 1936, allowing Speyer to represent Wimmer in Nice.

[189] Dost received payment on March 31, 1936, and was legally represented by Herzfelder. See ADAM, Nice, Archives notariales, minutes notariales étude Pierre Demnard, Mar. 31, 1936, n° 448, cote 03E 148/032. For more information on Dost, see Hirschfeld & Dose 2013, 172 n. 443. An overview listing all the details of these eight bequests, including their varying amounts and different inheritance taxes (and the late fees subtracted from the actually bequeathed amounts) can be found in Soetaert 2014, 41, Table 2. This overview combines information from two sources: the notarial minutes officializing the different bequests (as described in n. 171 and n. 174) and the documents from the Nice tax collection office: ADAM, Déclarations de mutations

deducted. After subtraction of all costs – including Demnard's honorary fee, taxes, and the late fee – Maass was actually paid FF2,792.90. A little more than half, in other words, of the FF5,000 that Hirschfeld had left Maass in his will.[190] Since three of Hirschfeld's legatees were not related to him and the five others had mostly only distant family ties, the inheritance taxes were quite high. The lowest percentage of 19.5 percent (on the first FF10,000) was applied to Hirschfeld's younger sister Jenny Hauck (née Hirschfeld) and the highest percentage, which reached 41.75 percent (on the second FF10,000), impacted Hirschfeld's good friend Margarete Dost.[191]

Moreover, according to French law, the inheritance tax had to be paid to the Registration Office (*Bureau de l'Enregistrement*) in Nice no later than six months after Hirschfeld's death.[192] This time limit was clearly breached since, at the beginning of 1936, the financial aspect of Hirschfeld's estate was still being arranged. This entailed further specific percentages of late fees to be substracted from the sums of the bequests as well. The eight legatees by particular title (*légataires particuliers*) lost around FF1,000 in total in late fees.[193] Karl Giese and Li Shiu Tong were of course taxed as well. From the money to which they were entitled, around FF233,000, no less than 40 percent in inheritance tax, or around FF95,000, was deducted. Giese and Li Shiu Tong also lost almost FF2,000 in late fees because the inheritance taxes were paid too late.[194]

EXPENSES

There were of course a lot of different costs involved in the handling and settlement of the estate. This constitutes the "passive" expenses (*dépenses*) associated with the inheritance as opposed to the "active" income of the money Hirschfeld kept in the bank safe and in his two bank accounts. We will now take a closer look at some of these expenses.[195]

ALLOWANCE (*STIPEND*): ELLEN BÆKGAARD

During Hirschfeld's lifetime, the Danish doctor Ellen Bækgaard had agreed to pay a monthly allowance (*Stipend*) to cover the costs of Giese's study. On February 12, 1936, in a signed document, she "expressly renounced" (*renoncer expressément*) the dispositions in Hirschfeld's will related to her.[196] A passage in article 5 of Hirschfeld's last will stated that the total sum of the allowance paid by Bækgaard was to be refunded after Hirschfeld's death, with the settling of the estate.[197] Bizarrely, in

par décès (deuxième série), o.c., vols. 49–51, Dec. 2, 1935–Jun. 10, 1936, cotes 03Q 08851, 03Q 08852 and 03Q 08853.

[190] Archiv MHG, Berlin, fonds Ernst Maass, letter (dated Oct. 24, 1935, 1) from Franz Herzfelder to Ernst Maass. In reality Maass's deduction would turn out to be 36.75 percent. See Soetaert 2014, 41, Table 2. A receipt from Demnard's office (dated 1936) found in Ernst Maass's papers in New York (now in Archiv MHG, Berlin, fonds Ernst Maass) tells us exactly how much was paid out to Maass and how the amount was calculated.

[191] Soetaert 2014, 41, Table 2.

[192] Taithe & Taithe 1986, 203–4.

[193] Soetaert 2014, 41, Table 2.

[194] See ADAM, Nice, Déclarations de mutations par décès (deuxième série), o.c., succession [final fiscal settlement], vol. 51, May 1, 1936, n° 261, cote 03Q 08853. A 40 percent discount on the late fees that normally needed to be paid was granted to Giese and Li Shiu Tong. See Soetaert 2014, 43, notes a and b under Table 4.

[195] Here, I have left out the costs associated with the notary, with Herzfelder as executor of the estate, the services of two Parisian lawyers, as well as some smaller outstanding debts Hirschfeld had at the time of his death. For these expenses, see Soetaert 2014, 50–51, 52–53 (Table 8), 53 (Table 9), 54 (Table 10).

[196] ADAM, Nice, Archives notariales, minutes notariales étude Pierre Demnard, Mar. 9, 1936, n° 316, cote 03E 148/031.

[197] Baumgardt 1984, 10: "Fernerhin ist an Frau Ellen Bakgaard [*sic*: Bækgaard], Kopenhagen 4, Aaboulevard 82/I der für das Studium des Herrn K. Giese mit ihr brieflich vereinbarte Teilbetrag auszuzahlen, am besten nach Correspondenz mit ihr in einmaliger Summe" (Furthermore, the partial amount agreed to by letter with Mrs. Ellen Bakgaard [*sic*: Bækgaard], Copenhagen 4, Aaboulevard 82/I for Mr. K.

the same document, written in somewhat murky French, Bækgaard also "allowed" (*j'autorise* [!]) the people handling the estate to anticipate the funds necessary to pay for Giese's studies. This strange document gives the impression that Bækgaard did not really know exactly what Hirschfeld's last will stipulated for her. Above all, she made it clear that she was no longer prepared to cover Giese's study costs.[198] She ended the affidavit by explicitly requesting that the sum of "five British pounds and [...] twelve hundred Austrian schillings" (*cinq Livres anglaises et [...] douze cents Schillings autrichiens*) be refunded to her. In the final settlement of the estate, a total of FF4,695 was repaid to her in March 1936.[199]

What happened concerning Norman Haire's contribution to covering Giese's studies is less clear. Whether Norman Haire had also initially agreed with Hirschfeld to a (later) repayment of his part of Giese's "study loan" is unclear. Haire's name is not mentioned in Hirschfeld's handwritten last will nor does his name show up anywhere in the documents related to the handling of the inheritance. Presumably, Haire stopped making payments in the changed circumstances. From letters Haire wrote soon after Hirschfeld's death, we learn that this was his first and immediate concern: ridding himself of the allowance for Giese.[200] Hirschfeld's own financial contribution of £40 of course ceased with his death. From a June 1935 letter, we know that Giese knew that Bækgaard's financial backing had fallen away and this left him with financial problems.[201] Now that we are aware of this settlement with Ellen Bækgaard, we are better able to understand a financial agreement regarding the Hirschfeld inheritance between Giese and Li Shiu Tong.

THE AGREEMENT BETWEEN KARL GIESE AND LI SHIU TONG

At the end of May 1936, "for them to come to a final settlement of the estate of Dr. Magnus Hirschfeld", Giese and Li Shiu Tong proposed the following in a written agreement.[202] Since Ellen Bækgaard renounced "the testamentary dispositions of Doctor HIRSCHFELD concerning her regarding the study expenses of Mr. GIESE",[203] it was agreed that FF31,500 would be paid out to Giese as compensation. And this "despite Giese having given up on his studies".[204] The document further stated that "Mr. Karl Giese and Mr. Li Shiu Tong engage to use all the money they receive from Dr. Hirschfeld's estate exclusively for sexology, in the spirit of Dr. Hirschfeld's ideas, work on and efforts for sexology, in accordance with the terms of his will. Mr. Giese

Giese's studies is to be repaid to her in a lump sum, preferably after correspondence with her).

[198] She had communicated this to Giese already in the months after Hirschfeld's death (at latest around July 1935). See Arbetarrörelsens arkiv och bibliotek, Stockholm, Max Hodann samling, vol. 15, letter (dated Aug. 2, 1935, [2]) from Karl Giese to Max Hodann.

[199] ADAM, Nice, Archives notariales, minutes notariales étude Pierre Demnard, Aug. 10, 1936, n° 1039, cote 03E 148/041. Waldemar Speyer, who represented several people receiving bequests from Hirscheld, was her legal proxy. The first repayment was made on March 9, 1936. On April 17, 1936, another FF99.85 was added to this sum, possibly because Bækgaard complained that the first repayment was insufficient or incorrect.

[200] Archiv MHG, Berlin, fonds Ernst Maass, letters (dated May 18, 1935 and May 29, 1935) from Norman Haire to Ernst Maass.

[201] Arbetarrörelsens arkiv och bibliotek, Stockholm, Max Hodann samling, vol. 15, letter (dated Aug. 2, 1935, [2]) from Karl Giese to Max Hodann. In a letter to Max Reiss, Giese also mentioned that the contributions of his two patrons fell through. See Archiv MHG, Berlin, fonds Max Reiss, letter (dated Oct. 20, 1935, 1) from Karl Giese to Max Reiss. The judgment of Dr. Hanns G., voiced in an interview with von Praunheim, is rather harsh and also incorrect: "Er [Hirschfeld] hat Giese aber nicht geholfen, und Giese mußte sehen, wie er sich selber durchschlägt" (von Praunheim & G. 1992, 14).

[202] ADAM, Nice, Archives notariales, minutes notariales étude Pierre Demnard, May 29, 1936, n° 727, cote 03E 148/036 : "[p]our arriver à un règlement définitif entre eux de la succession du Docteur Magnus Hirschfeld".

[203] Ibid.: "aux dispositions testamentaires du Docteur HIRSCHFELD la concernant au sujet des frais d'études de Monsieur GIESE".

[204] Ibid.: "malgré l'abandon qu'il [Giese] fait de ses études".

[205] "Monsieur Karl Giese et Monsieur Li Shiu Tong prennent l'engagementd'utiliser [*sic*: l'engagement

particularly undertakes to use his share of the said sums, including the amount of 31,500 Francs stated above, for a sexological archive which he undertakes to found in BRNO (C.S.R.) with the help of Dr. Weisskopf, living in Brno".[205] In this same agreement between Giese and Li Shiu Tong, named according to French convention, *règlement de la succession*, it was also agreed that the sum of FF1,700 that Giese had borrowed from Li Shiu Tong on June 7, 1935, would be withheld from Giese's share and would be paid to Li Shiu Tong.[206] To make ends meet after Hirschfeld's death, Giese also had to borrow money from Leopold Fleischer from Brno, the stepbrother of Willi Bondi, a good friend of Giese. He also twice received an advance payment from the people settling the estate.[207] But there were still other costs that had to be covered in connection with the Hirschfeld estate.

LIBRAIRIE GALLIMARD

One considerable sum paid out in the final settlement is intriguing. An amount of FF4,333.35 was sent to Librairie Gallimard in Paris on May 29, 1936. One's first inclination would be to think this covered the bill of Hirschfeld's open account at the Gallimard bookstore. But this in fact indeed concerned the publisher Gallimard (then known as Librairie Gallimard).[208] Part of this sum was likely repayment of the advances that Hirschfeld received for presumably one, or even two, French books that were to be published by Gallimard. As already mentioned, Hirschfeld would have written three books for Gallimard in the series "La science et l'amour": *L'Âme et l'amour*, *Le corps et l'amour*, and *La société et l'amour*. The latter was never published, likely because Hirschfeld was never able to write it. As we have already seen, there was even the possibility that a French translation of *Der Racismus* was also under contract with Gallimard. So, most likely, this was indeed a repayment of advances Hirschfeld received on signing book contracts with Gallimard, Hirschfeld's death partially breaching the legal agreements with the French publisher.

FINISHING THE GRAVE

Hirschfeld never suffered from the human psychological trait called "false modesty". He was well aware that he was someone of importance and that his life achievements deserved credit during his lifetime and adulation in posterity. In Italy, Hirschfeld himself thought it fitting to visit the graves of gay icons and precursors like Winckel-

d'utiliser] toutes les sommes qu'ils recevront de la succession du Dr. Hirschfeld, exclusivement aux fins de la sexologie dans l'esprit des idées, travaux et efforts sur la sexologie du Dr. Hirschfeld conformément aux termes de son testament. Spécialement Monsieur Giese s'engage à employer sa part dans lesdites [*sic*, les dites] sommes y compris le montant de 31.500 frs ci-dessus énoncé, pour des archives sexologiques qu'il s'engage à fonder à BRNO (C.S.R.) avec le concours de Monsieur le Docteur WEISSKOPF demeurant à Brno". This agreement was signed by Giese in Brno on May 22, 1936 (which means that he returned to his Brno lawyer Karl Fein for the purpose), and by Li Shiu Tong in Zürich on May 27, 1936. Herzfelder also signed the paper on May 29, 1936, depositing the agreement that day at Demnard's notary office. According to the notarial minutes, Giese was at that time still living at 27 Maria Hilferstrasse [*sic*: Mariahilferstrasse] in Vienna while Li Shiu Tong was staying in the Royal Hotel on Russell Square in Londen (but "actuellement à Zürich, Studentenheim" [currently in Zürich, student house]). Interestingly, the word "étudiant" (student), which had been added to both Giese's and Li Shiu Tong's names in virtually all of the Hirschfeld estate documents, was on this occasion added only to Li Shiu Tong's name.

206 Li Shiu Tong's financial help to Giese was also mentioned in a letter Giese wrote to Max Reiss, see Archiv MHG, Berlin, fonds Max Reiss, letter (dated Oct. 20, 1935, 1) from Karl Giese to Max Reiss.

207 For the full details of these arrangements and Giese's financial situation after the completion of the inheritance procedure, see Soetaert 2014, 44, 50–51 and Table 7.

208 On one of the endpapers in my copy of the fourth edition of Hirschfeld's *L'Âme et l'amour*, it says: "achevé d'imprimer sur les presses de [...] pour la librairie Gallimard / 5, Rue Sébastien-Bottin Paris. 1935" (printed by the presses of [...] for the Gallimard bookshop / 5 Rue Sébastien-Bottin Paris. 1935). Grenier & Lemoine 2011 also confirm that the *publisher* Gallimard, which started operations in 1911, had been housed at this same Paris address since 1930.

mann, Platen, and Ulrichs.[209] Hirschfeld had also toyed with the idea of being buried next to the other personages in the Père Lachaise cemetery in Paris.[210] Today, Hirschfeld's grave in Nice's Caucade cemetery has itself become a modest, mainly LGBT pilgrimage destination. This is probably as Hirschfeld would have wished.

In his last will, Hirschfeld stipulated the sum of FF15,000 for the construction of his tomb.[211] The cost of his grave, finally settled at FF13,200, was of course included in the expenses of the estate. It is unclear how much was paid to the artist Arnold Zadikow (1884–1943) who designed the bronze bas relief plaque of Hirschfeld's profile [ill. 13] [ill. 14].[212] But on top of the cost of the grave there still had to be paid the almost FF7,000 for an eternal permit. This brought the total cost of his funerary monument (*monument funéraire*) to around FF20,000. Then there was still the added cost of the burial ceremony and the cremation, FF7,366, paid to Roblot, the funerary firm, in Nice.[213] On April 6, 1936, Hirschfeld's executor François Herzfelder already registered a two-square-meter cemetery plot in perpetuity at the Caucade cemetery.[214] It would take another three months before Hirschfeld's ashes were transferred from Marseille to Nice so that these could be interred in the funerary monument. A mason needed to construct a fortification to support the Belgian gray granite grave stone.[215]

On August 29, 1936, Hirschfeld's ashes arrived in Nice from Marseille.[216] Most likely, Li Shiu Tong was present when Hirschfeld's ashes were interred in the Caucade cemetery, if only because article 8 of Hirschfeld's will entrusted the care of his grave to him: "I place the care of my grave in the hands of my disciple Li Shiu Tong".[217] Giese knew, in May 1935, that he would probably not be able to attend this final goodbye.[218]

209 See Hirschfeld 1910/2006; McLeod & Soetaert 2010, 31 n. 53. Towards the end of his life, as recorded in *Testament: Heft II*, Hirschfeld started to see himself as one more exiled German gay personality who would die outside of his native country. See Hirschfeld & Dose 2013, f. 63/138 and n. 372.

210 G. D. May 20, 1935, 1; *Freundschafts-Banner*, Oct. 5, 1935, 1. In article 8 of his will, Hirschfeld expressed a wish to be buried either in Nice or Paris. See Baumgardt 1984, 11.

211 See article 8 of his last will in Baumgardt 1984, 11.

212 Arnold Zadikow was deported with transport "Au 1" from Prague to Terezín on May 15, 1942. He died in Terezín on March 8, 1943, after an appendix operation. His wife Hilda Löwy/Lohsing (1890–1974) and daughter Marianna (1923–) were deported from Prague on the same transport but were liberated from Terezín. After the war, they emigrated to the USA.

213 For a more detailed overview of these costs, see Soetaert 2014, 55, 58, Table 11.

214 A copy of this concession registration can be found in Archiv MHG, Berlin.

215 See letter (dated May 18, 1936) from François Herzfelder to Ernst Maass in Archiv MHG, Berlin, fonds Ernst Maass: "Die Fertigstellung des Grabmales durch den Steinmetz wird aber dann ca. 3 Monate dauern" (However, the completion of the tombstone by the stonemason will then take about 3 months).

216 Registre des inhumations (Mai 1935, 212). See also Archiv MHG, Berlin, fonds Ernst Maass, letter (undated, but presumably June–July 1936) from François Herzfelder to Ernst Maass: "Die Einweihung des Grabmales wird also voraussichtlich Anfang August stattfinden" (The inauguration of the tomb is expected to take place in the beginning of August).

217 Baumgardt 1984, 11: "Die Pflege meines Grabes lege ich in die Hände meines Schülers Li Shiu Tong".

218 Archiv MHG, Berlin, fonds Max Reiss, letter (dated May 1935 but presumably May 28, 1935, 4) from Karl Giese to Max Reiss: "Zur Uberführung der Asche nach Nice bist Du [Max Reiss] selbstverständlich verkündigt. Vielleicht kannst Du dann kommen. Ob ich dann werde hier sein können ist allerdings eine andere Frage" (For the transfer of the ashes to Nice you [Max Reiss] will, of course, be notified. Perhaps you can come then. Whether I will be able to be here then, however, is another question). See also Archiv MHG, Berlin, fonds Ernst Maass, letter (dated Jun. 1, 1935) from François Herzfelder to Ernst Maass: "Giese wird wohl kaum eine neue Einreiseerlaubnis bekommen. Er wird daher bei der Überführung der Urne und bei der für diese Gelegenheit geplanten Feier nicht anwesend sein können" (Giese is unlikely to be granted a new entry permit. He will therefore be unable to attend the bringing of the urn and the ceremony planned for the occasion).

219 It is unclear why Hirschfeld was buried in this cemetery rather than the Cimetière Israélite du Château but this was possibly due to his decision to be cremated. The Caucade cemetery has a small Jewish section but his grave is not located in it. At the entrance of the Caucade cemetery, one can obtain a "Liste des personnages célèbres inhumées au cimetière de Caucade" (List of famous people buried in the Caucade cemetery) which includes Hirschfeld. Online, one can locate Hirschfeld's grave by entering concession number 18543 on: https://sig.nicecotedazur.org/public/apps/as/lanceur.jsp?

Hirschfeld was buried at the Caucade cemetery in the west of Nice (near the current city airport) where he has an eternal concession (*concession perpétuelle*, no. 18543) on parcel (*carré*) no. 9, grave (*emplacement*) no. 210, located on the Allée des Pins inside the cemetery.[219] For a very long time, a kitschy porcelain crucifix made of colored flowers lay on Hirschfeld's grave [ill. 15]. It is not known who put it there, but it is possible that it was laid on the grave in an effort to protect the grave from possible anti-Jewish sentiment during World War II. The cross may have been laid by Ernst Maass. As soon as World War II was over, Maass wrote a letter from New York to the notary Pierre Demnard in Nice: "Do you know, by any chance, if Doctor Hirschfeld's tomb in Nice was desecrated during the German occupation or if it is still intact?"[220] So far, after eighty-nine years, the grave has remained in good condition.

When Don McLeod and I visited Nice, in October 2009, we tried to see the file on Hirschfeld's grave (permit) in the Funeral Administration (*Administration funéraire*) of the city of Nice, located at 45 Rue Gioffredo. After we introduced ourselves at the front desk, we were received, after a short wait, by a female senior civil servant who already had the file on Hirschfeld's grave on her desk. Since we had just started our research on "Hirschfeld in Nice", we could not play the guessing game the woman practiced on us that day. Apparently, we had to give her the name of the executor of the will, François Herzfelder, or the notary Pierre Demnard, before she would allow us to see the file. At the time, we did not know either of these names. But when we told her that a porcelain crucifix was laid on a Jewish grave, she immediately grabbed the phone and called the Caucade cemetery to say that the crucifix should be removed from the grave. It's a great pity that a French civil servant took things in hand so unprofessionally and unevenly. The cross could have been safeguarded as an important Hirschfeld artifact. It may have had some clues on its surface (or even hidden inside). It is also rather strange that, until 2009, no one seemed to have noticed or questioned the fact that a Catholic symbol adorned a Jewish grave.[221] We were not allowed to see the file on Hirschfeld's grave that day, but from my position, at the other end of the civil servant's desk, I could see that the file contained letters from other people who had inquired over the years about Hirschfeld's grave with the same administration.[222]

Now, on the flat grave stone, one sees only the black metal letters spelling out Hirschfeld's foremost activist life motto: "per scientiam ad justitiam" (through science to justice). In his diary, Hirschfeld considered adding instead the following: "A fighter for the rights of nature" (*Ein Kämpfer um die Rechte der Natur*) [ill. 16].[223]

usertoken=ZGVmYXVsdHVzZXI=&t=as&appname=signca_cime&appmode=public, (accessed Jun. 30, 2020). Serge Voronoff (1866–1951), the French rejuvenation doctor whom Hirschfeld visited when he was in Nice, is also buried in the Caucade cemetery. See Lehnerdt Feb. 1, 1928; Grau 2009.

220 Archiv MHG, Berlin, fonds Ernst Maass, letter (dated Jun. 16, 1945) from Ernest Maass (*sic*, Maass had changed his first name Ernst to Ernest when he emigrated to the USA) to Pierre Demnard: "Savez-vous, par hazard [*sic*: hasard], si la tombe du Docteur Hirschfeld à Nice a été désacrée pendant l'occupation allemande ou si elle est encore intacte?"

221 In the Hirschfeld guestbook there are two photos of the grave without the porcelain cross. Most likely, these photos were taken very soon after the grave was erected, in August 1936. See Bergemann, Dose, Keilson-Lauritz & Dubout 2019, f. 155/199. A detail of the lower grave stone, also without the porcelain cross, can be seen in a loose photo in the album. See Bergemann, Dose, Keilson-Lauritz & Dubout 2019, 202. On a YouTube video from December 20, 2016, there is a close-up of the grave, revealing the contours where the porcelain cross lay presumably for several decades: https://www.youtube.com/watch?v=ksDzNE_IDMg (accessed Jul. 15, 2020).

222 The story of the porcelain cross's removal is also partly given in Soetaert & McLeod 2010, 18.

223 Archiv MHG, Berlin, fonds Ernst Maass, manuscript (dated May 16–17, 1935) by Ernst Maass consisting of fragments copied from Hirschfeld's (presumably) last diary, page 6, entry n° 264, which also contains Hirschfeld's other ideas for possible epitaphs for his grave: Sapere aude, Amor omnia vincit, In magnis et voluisse sat est.

FINANCIAL END RESULT

The sum of all the costs, taxes, and debts associated with the settlement of the estate came to no less than FF311,212.05 ... while the initial worth of Hirschfeld's estate was estimated at FF341,886.61. This means that the balance, to which Giese and Li Shiu Tong were entitled in the end, turned out to be the rather meager sum of FF30,674.56. Around August 1936, each would receive half of this sum, or FF15,337.28. But, as we have already seen, an extra financial settlement had been worked out for Giese. In the end, Giese would receive around FF47,000 in total from the Hirschfeld estate. In this way, he finally obtained more cash than Li Shiu Tong. However, one cannot conclude from this that Giese benefited more since Giese and Li Shiu Tong were entitled to different things, stipulated by Hirschfeld in his last will. Li Shiu Tong got the shares and bonds in the Paris bank safe and the total worth of that part of Hirschfeld's estate is unknown.

On August 8, 1936, the final financial settlement of the estate (named *Dépôt de compte d'administration*) was gathered and these documents were added to the notarial minutes. It listed, in chronological order, all the procedural steps taken in the handling and settlement of the Hirschfeld inheritance during the fourteen months following Hirschfeld's death.[224] In this way, the long procedure came to an end.[225] In summary, in the years 1935–36, one can say that Hirschfeld's estate, worth FF341,886.61, was divided as follows. A little more than a third (35 percent) of the income side was spent on taxes (FF120,779.63). A little less than FF150,000 or approximately 44 percent (so not even half of the money available in the estate), was actually paid out to the universal legatees (*légataires universels*), Giese and Li Shiu Tong, and the eight particular legatees (*légataires particuliers*). The remaining 21 percent (or approximately FF71,500) was used to cover all other expenses, debts, and costs.[226]

[224] ADAM, Nice, Archives notariales, minutes notariales étude Pierre Demnard, Aug. 10, 1936, n° 1039, cote 03E 148/041. A photographic reproduction of this five-page document can be found in Soetaert 2014, 45–49.

[225] In June 1936, Karl Giese and Li Shiu Tong signed, in Brno and Zürich respectively, a "décharge de mandat" (discharge of mandate), releasing Demnard's employees from their duties as their proxies. These official statements were registered in Demnard's notarial minutes at the beginning of August 1936. See ADAM, Nice, Archives notariales, minutes notariales étude Pierre Demnard, Aug. 5, 1936, n° 1024, cote 03E 148/041.

[226] A summary financial overview of the inheritance is presented in Soetaert 2014, 70, Table 14.

1. The building at 27 Mariahilferstrasse in Vienna (Wien 6) where Karl Giese rented a room from the Jewish doctor Zalman Schneyer and his wife Sofie. April 2012.

2. The six-story, seaside apartment building Gloria Mansions IV, built in the 1950s. Gloria Mansions I stand behind this building and is partly visible on the right. The Centre Universitaire Méditerranéen (C.U.M.) is on the far left. January 2010.

3. Aerial photo of the Promenade des Anglais in Nice, showing 1. Centre Universitaire Méditerranéen (C.U.M.) (65 Promenade des Anglais); 2. front garden of Gloria Mansions I; 3. fifth-floor apartment where Hirschfeld lived (below the receded penthouse floor, three windows on the far left); 4. former location of the Bains de la grande bleue, a beach house complex (59 Promenade des Anglais); 5. Gloria Mansions I (63 Promenade des Anglais); 6. front garden of the Fondation Furtado Heine (61 Promenade des Anglais); 7. the art deco-style Gloria Mansions III (125–129 Rue de France); 8. Gloria Mansions II (123 Rue de France). Ca. 1953.

7
8
6

4. *"With Dr. Waldenburg on 13/V/35" (Mit Dr. Waldenburg am 13/V/35), handwritten text added by Karl Giese. In the background part of Gloria Mansions I and its fenced front garden are visible.*

5. *Magnus Hirschfeld and his Nice secretary Robert Kirchberger, standing on one of the three balconies of Hirschfeld's fifth-floor Gloria Mansions I apartment, dated May 14, 1935, Hirschfeld's birthday and also the day of his death. This may be the very last picture taken of Magnus Hirschfeld when still alive. A handwritten note on the back reads: "The last photo / on 14 May 35 / at 10 a.m." (Die letzte Aufnahme / am 14. Mai 35 / um 10 Uhr).*

6. *Ernst Maass. Ca. 1935.*

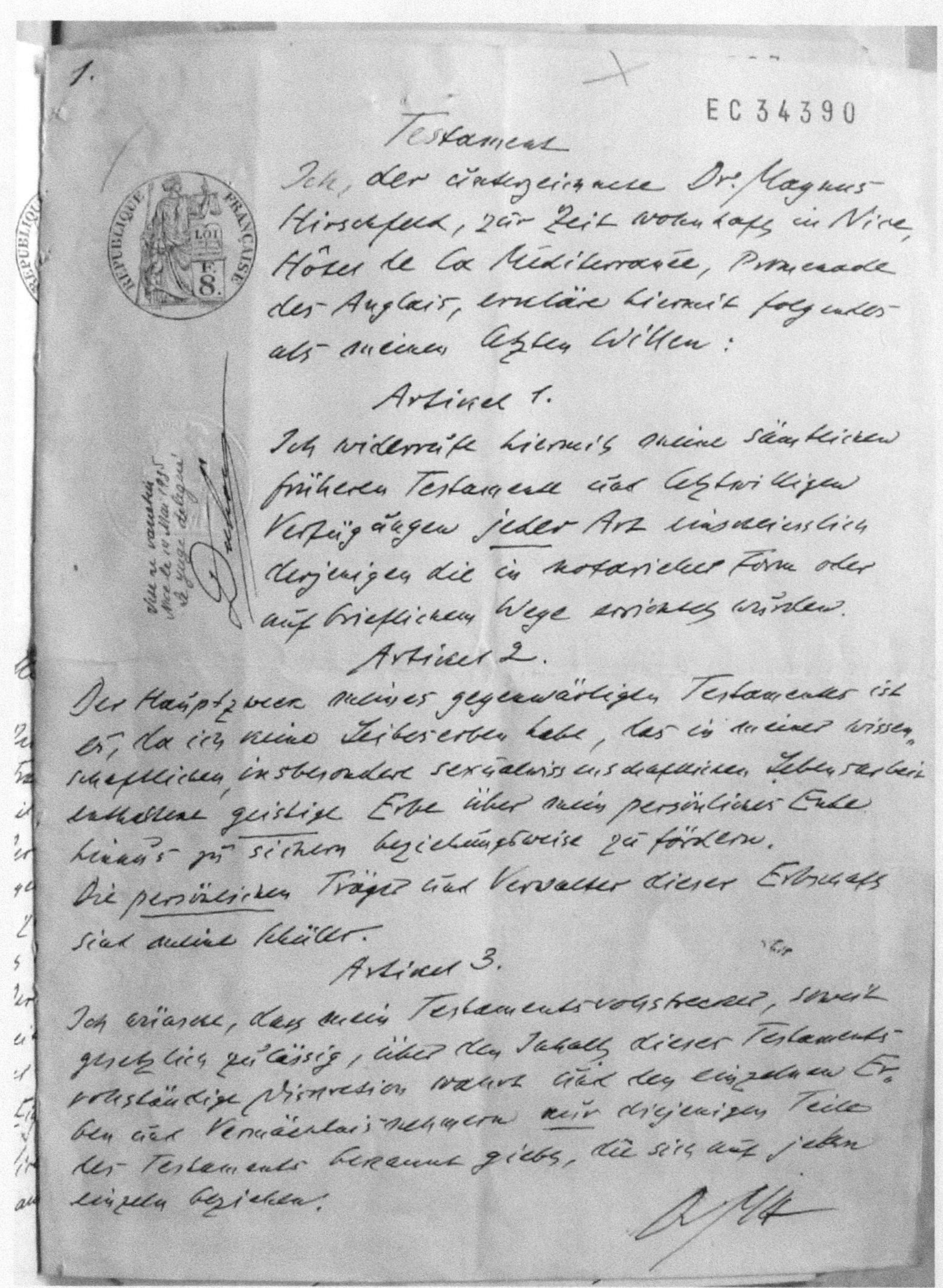

1.

EC 34390

Testament

Ich, der Unterzeichnete Dr. Magnus Hirschfeld, zur Zeit wohnhaft in Nice, Hôtel de la Méditerranée, Promenade des Anglais, erkläre hiermit folgendes als meinen letzten Willen:

Artikel 1.

Ich widerrufe hiermit meine sämtlichen früheren Testamente und letztwilligen Verfügungen jeder Art einschließlich derjenigen die in notarieller Form oder auf brieflichem Wege errichtet wurden.

Artikel 2.

Der Hauptzweck meines gegenwärtigen Testamentes ist es, da ich keine Leibeserben habe, das in meiner wissenschaftlichen, insbesondere sexualwissenschaftlichen Lebensarbeit enthaltene geistige Erbe über mein persönliches Ende hinaus zu sichern beziehungsweise zu fördern.

Die persönlichen Träger und Verwalter dieser Erbschaft sind meine Schüler.

Artikel 3.

Ich wünsche, dass mein Testamentsvollstrecker, soweit gesetzlich zulässig, über den Inhalt dieses Testaments vollständige Diskretion wahrt und den einzelnen Erben und Vermächtnisnehmern nur diejenigen Teile des Testaments bekannt giebt, die sich auf jeden einzeln beziehen.

7. The first page of Magnus Hirschfeld's handwritten last will, composed on January 10, 1935, in Nice.

8. Photobooth passport picture of François (Franz) Herzfelder. Ca. 1938.

9. Contemporary photo of the morgue (reposoir) in the Jewish section of the Château cemetery, located on the steep Colline du Château, in the old city center of Nice. October 2009.

10. The French notary Pierre Demnard. Ca. 1939.

11. Dr. Leopold Hönig, a close Czechoslovak friend of Magnus Hirschfeld. Undated, presumably 1930s.

12. The wooden complex of the Bains de la grande Bleue beach club, located at 59 Promenade des Anglais, Nice. Behind the umbrellas, the receded top floor of Gloria Mansions I is visible. To the left of Gloria Mansions I, the building that would later house the C.U.M. The beach club disappeared around World War II. Ca. 1924–34.

13. Contemporary photo of the bronze bas-relief plaque of Hirschfeld's profile, designed by Arnold Zadikow, on Hirschfeld's grave stone in the Caucade cemetery, Nice. October 2009.

14. Arnold Zadikow, the artist who designed the bronze bas-relief plaque of Hirschfeld's profile on Hirschfeld's grave in the Caucade cemetery, Nice. Ca. 1941.

15. The porcelain crucifix that adorned the grave of Magnus Hirschfeld until October 2009, when it was removed by cemetery staff. October 2009.

16. The grave of Magnus Hirschfeld. January 2010.

10. What Happened to the Institute and Hirschfeld Materials after Hirschfeld's Death in Nice?

PAINTING OF A BEARDED LADY

In a March 1935 letter to his Dutch student Max Reiss, Magnus Hirschfeld wrote that he had transferred the Institute materials in Paris to Nice.[1] In another letter to Norman Haire, two weeks earlier, he said the same: "and rented myself a flat for one year where I also stored the rest of my library and my collection".[2] So some, or even all of the Institute materials that were in a storage room of the firm Bedel & Co. in Paris were brought to Nice, shortly after Hirschfeld took residence in his Gloria Mansions I apartment, in February 1935. We have already looked at the inventory made of the contents of the apartment, shortly after Hirschfeld's death, which revealed that only a few items listed could have come from the Institute collection.[3]

One curious painting that hung on the living room wall of Hirschfeld's Nice apartment stands out. It was a painting of a bearded lady, dated 1622, valued by Gaston Giauffer, the certified appraiser (*commissaire-priseur*) of the Nice arrondissement, at FF100. This painting had belonged to the Institute collection, as it was displayed during the 1930 Vienna WLSR conference in a makeshift exhibition of Institute materials. In the list of the many items exhibited in Vienna, the painting is described as follows: "Bearded lady, 18 years old Helene Kathonia from Graz, original painting, 1622".[4] The name of the bearded lady is misspelled. It should be Helena Antonia (Galecka or also Galeckha), a woman born in 1579 in Liège (in German, Lüttich), Belgium, who suffered from hirsutism.[5] Starting to grow facial hair around the age of nine, her poor parents entrusted their child to the bishop of Liège. Through a Wittelsbach family archbishop in Cologne (Köln), the virgo barbata ended up as a curiosity at the Graz court of the Archduchess of Austria, Maria Anna of Bavaria (1551–1608), when she was eighteen years old.[6] There exist several oil paintings and illustrations of the same bearded young woman; a relatively widely distributed copperplate engraving (*Kupferstich*) by Dominic Custos is the best known. This engraving is also reproduced in Hirschfeld's *Geschlechtskunde*.[7] The two best-known oil paintings of Helena Antonia

[1] Archiv MHG, Berlin, fonds Max Reiss, letter (dated Mar. 30, 1935) from Magnus Hirschfeld to Max Reiss: "habe mir die ganzen Kisten aus Paris nachkommen lassen".

[2] University of Sydney Library, Sydney, Norman Haire collection, 3.20, Magnus Hirschfeld, Typescripts, 1923–1935, letter (dated Mar. 15, 1935, 1) from Magnus Hirschfeld to Norman Haire: "und mir eine Jahreswohnung gemietet, in der ich den Rest meiner Bibliothek und meiner Sammlung untergebracht habe".

[3] ADAM, Nice, Archives notariales, minutes notariales étude Pierre Demnard, May 24, 1935, n° 569, cote 03E 148/011.

[4] See the section "Sonderausstellung des Institutes für Sexualwissenschaft 'Dr. Magnus Hirschfeld-Stiftung' in Berlin" in the 1930 brochure IV. Kongress der Weltliga für Sexualreform auf wissenschaftlicher Grundlage, p. 9, item n° 69: "Bartdame, 18 jähr. Helene Kathonia aus Graz, Orig.-Gemälde, 1622".

[5] All Wikipedia sources (except the Polish one) give 1550 as her birth year. But Selerowicz and Babich (following Roitner 2008, 42) claim she was born in 1579, which simply makes more sense (Selerowicz 2011, 34; Babich 2019, 74). Since the portrait of Helena Antonia in Nice is dated 1622, her death date must be some time after this date. Her family name Galecka or Galeckha is only mentioned in Selerowicz 2011, 34, 35.

[6] Selerowicz 2011; Roitner 2008; Babich 2019; https://en.wikipedia.org/wiki/Helena_Antonia (accessed Jul. 10, 2020). Later, Helena Antonia was at the courts of two of Maria Anna of Bavaria's daughters, Margaret of Austria (1584–1611), queen of Spain and Austria, and Constance (1588–1631), who married Zygmund III Vasa, the king of Poland.

[7] Hirschfeld 1926–1930, 1930: vol. IV, Bilderteil, 504.

are part of the collection of the National Museum in Wrocław (Muzeum Narodowe we Wrocławiu) in Poland. This can most likely be explained by the fact that these paintings were made in Wrocław (formerly Breslau) since Helena Antonia must have been there at some point as part of the royal court. Another oil painting depicting the same bearded woman now hangs in the Velké Losiny castle in the Olomouc region in Czechia [ill. 1].[8] Still another oil painting is part of the collection of the Bayerisches Nationalmuseum in Munich.[9]

It was not possible to determine if the oil painting that Hirschfeld had in Nice was a copy of any of these or still another version. It is interesting, though, to observe that the misspelling "Helene Kathonia" in the list of exhibited items at the Vienna conference seems to correspond to the inscription on one of the two oil paintings in Wrocław. In the latter, one could indeed easily misread "An-tonia" as "Kathonia".[10] But no year appears, while in the Vienna conference description the year 1622 is clearly stated. We only find this year on the oil painting in the Velké Losiny castle. Also, the city of Graz, which is also mentioned in the Vienna description of the painting shown at the conference, is not mentioned on the Wrocław painting but it does figure in the added text for the painting in the Velké Losiny castle. Presumably, then, Hirschfeld's painting in Nice was yet another version of all the paintings just mentioned. But most likely, all or most of these paintings were originals from Wrocław or copies of these.

It is not known if the painting was part of the lot of items bought back from Nazi Germany in November 1933 or if the painting was taken out of the Institute before it was raided. In article 5 of his last will, Hirschfeld spoke about materials from the Institute stored in the cities of Paris, Saarbrücken, Berlin, and Wiesbaden. Was the painting brought to Nice from one of these places?[11] It is not known what happened to the painting of the bearded lady in Hirschfeld's Nice apartment. We only know that, according to Hirschfeld's stipulations in his will, Li Shiu Tong was entitled to it, as part of the items present in the apartment at the time of Hirschfeld's death, all of which he was entitled to.[12] What Li Shiu Tong did with all these items is not known. Pierre Demnard's notarial minutes include a bill for a moving company named Reboul & Co., dated at the end of January 1936, just before the one-year lease on the apartment expired. This bill was most likely for the furnishings that had to be packed and removed. But what happened to these furnishings afterwards, and who decided

[8] The painter is unknown. Most likely, this is a copy of an original that hung in the library of the Church of St. Mary Magdalene in Wrocław. See inventory number VL01179a in the evidenční list of the Národní památkový ústav (NPÚ); Vaňková 2009, 123–25. The painting measures 92 cm x 71.5 cm. For the Czech castle where the painting can be found, see https://www.zamek-velkelosiny.cz/en (accessed Jul. 10, 2020), and https://sumpersky.denik.cz/kultura_region/do-losin-se-vratila-vousata-dama.html (accessed Jul. 11, 2020). The painting had been in the posession of aristocratic families living in the castle for centuries: the Zierotin family and, from 1802, the Liechtenstein family. The presence of a stamp on the back of the painting ("F" for Fürst Liechtenstein) further supports this assumption. See email (dated Jul. 11, 2020) from Elena Babich to the author; and email (dated Jul. 10, 2020) from Lenka Vaňková (Národní památkový ústav, územní památková správa v Kroměříži) to the author. I also want to thank Romana Balcarová, who restored the painting in 2009, and who kindly sent me the restoration report of the painting and also gave me Lenka Vaňková's correct email address. See her email (dated Jul. 9, 2020) to the author.

[9] See https://www.bayerisches-nationalmuseum.de/veranstaltungen/helena-die-baertige-prinzessin (accessed Feb. 13, 2023).

[10] See https://pl.wikipedia.org/wiki/Helena_Antonia_z_Li%C3%A8ge (accessed Dec. 7, 2020).

[11] For article 5 in Hirschfeld's last will, see Baumgardt 1984, 10. Let us recall here that Hirschfeld deposited his last will at Demnard's Nice office on February 23, 1935; at that moment, Paris still appeared in the text of his will as one of the places where materials were stored.

[12] I have tried to locate the painting in the catalogues of public auctions held in Nice in the years 1935–36, but did not succeed. See Soetaert 2014, 56–57. Adelheid Schulz also talked about a picture of a bearded lady she saw in the Institute in one of her interviews, but it is not certain if she was talking about this particular oil painting. See Baumgardt 2003, 8.

[13] For details about the bill (dated Jan. 31, 1936) of the Nice Reboul & Co. moving company, see Soetaert 2014, 58–60. There were two other later bills from the same company to which we will return later on.

what to do with them is, as already said, not known.[13] Presumably, these furnishings were put in storage.

From the May 1935 appraisal of the apartment furnishings by Giauffer, we can infer that most of the Institute materials Hirschfeld sent from Paris to Nice were *not* present in the Gloria Mansions I apartment. Other than the painting of the bearded lady, only a few foreign-language books and seventeen wax molds of genital organs were noted by the appraiser; apart from these, no other objects seem to have come from the Institute. This most likely means that Hirschfeld rented a storage room in Nice, as he had done in Paris with Bedel & Co. For practical reasons, but likely also as a precaution. Having learnt his lesson the hard way, through the Berlin book-burning exploits of the National Socialists, it was simply wiser to store these materials away and not keep them in his publicly known living quarters.

VICTOR BAUER AND HENRI NOUVEAU

But there was another item in Nice that, with absolute certainty, had also belonged to the Institute collection, as it was part of the WLSR conference exhibition in Vienna in 1930 [ill. 2]. It was an ethnological object of considerable size, the entrance door to a Melanesian men's house. In the brochure of the Vienna WLSR conference it was described as follows: "Door of a Men's house from New Guinea, original wood carving (gift from Dr. H. Rogge, Holland)".[14] Henk C. Rogge (1876–1953), a Dutch psychiatrist who had studied with Hirschfeld in Berlin in the early 1920s, and who was also close to Jacob Anton Schorer of the Dutch section of the W.H.K., had given this door to Hirschfeld at some point.[15] In this case, too, we do not know if it was among the items bought back from Nazi Germany, in November 1933, or if it had been taken into safety before the Institute was looted. The artifact was certainly not present in the Gloria Mansions I apartment when it was appraised by Giauffer in May 1933. This is a further indication that Hirschfeld rented a storage room in Nice. We also know that the object was indeed in Nice because it showed up there after Hirschfeld's death.

[14] See under the section "Sonderausstellung des Institutes für Sexualwissenschaft ,Dr. Magnus Hirschfeld-Stiftung' in Berlin" in the 1930 brochure IV. Kongress der Weltliga für Sexualreform auf wissenschaftlicher Grundlage, p. 13, item n° 193: "Tür eines Männerhauses aus Neu-Guinea, Orig.-Holzschnitzerei (Geschenk von Dr. H. Rogge, Holland)". For more information and some picture fragments of this door, see the section "Die Tür eines Männerhauses aus Neuguinea" at https://magnus-hirschfeld.de/bibliothek-und-archiv/sammlungs-schwerpunkte/gesucht-und-gefunden/ (accessed Jul. 3, 2020). Hirschfeld already presented the door in 1914 to the Ärztlichen Gesellschaft für Sexualwissenschaft und Eugenik. See Dose & Herrn 2006, 48, n. 26. It is interesting to observe that gay men's interest in these men's houses, and the homoerotic behavior that went on inside, also fascinated another gay scientist after World War II, Gilbert Herdt. See, for example, Herdt 1993. There was also another object, a wooden phallic god statuette, also given by Henk C. Rogge to Hirschfeld, but this object does not show up either in any of the known archival sources of the 1935-36 Hirschfeld inheritance case settled in Nice. This much smaller object is also mentioned in the section "Sonderausstellung des Institutes für Sexualwissenschaft 'Dr. Magnus Hirschfeld-Stiftung' in Berlin" in the 1930 brochure IV. Kongress der Weltliga für Sexualreform auf wissenschaftlicher Grundlage, p. 12, item n° 192: "Phallusgötze aus Sumatra, Orig.-Holzschnitzerei (Geschenk von Dr. H. Rogge, Holland)". A part of this exhibition, with objects from the Institute collection in the background, can be seen in a photo taken of the WLSR 1930 Vienna conference; see https://ub.meduniwien.ac.at/blog/wp-content/uploads/2018/06/ABB-04_weblog-66_MUW-FO-IR-000670-0526_Magnus-Hirschfeld_Gruppenbild.jpg (accessed Jul. 17, 2020). Among these there is an oil (?) painting of the French transsexual and diplomat Chevalier d'Eon [see illustration n° 2].

[15] For more information on Rogge, see van der Meer 2007, 183–84, 248–49, 255–56, 259, 277, 389. For Rogge being in Berlin in 1921 and 1922, see *Jahrbuch für sexuelle Zwischenstufen* 1921 (I do not have this volume in my collection so I could not double-check the page numbers given by Dobler 2004, 309.); 1922, 99, 109. Rogge also lectured at the first WLSR congress in Berlin, in 1921, on "Die Bedeutung der Steinachschen Forschungen für die Frage der Pseudo-Homosexualität". See *Jahrbuch für sexuelle Zwischenstufen* 1922, 4, 10. Around 1933, Rogge moved to Cairo where he would stay for the rest of his life. See van Santhorst 1953, 4. In 1932, Rogge was also one of the members of the international committee of the WLSR. See the official program of the 1932 WLSR Brno conference.

The story of the entrance door revolves around the Austro-Hungarian painter Victor Bauer (1902–1959) who had been working and living in Nice since 1936 (or even earlier). Bauer was born in Vienna and lived in Nice with Irmgard Strauss (1913–1992) and some friends (to whom we will return later on). Irmgard Strauss and Victor Bauer met in 1934 in Florence.[16] Bauer was a pupil of Siegmund Freud and would have met Hirschfeld in Berlin in 1927.[17] Hirschfeld initially adhered to the psychoanalytic movement in 1910, when he joined the Psychoanalytic Society (Psychoanalytischen Gesellschaft) in Berlin.[18] Bauer visited Hirschfeld's Institute in Berlin in 1926–27.[19] He also stayed for a while in the artist's colony of Haut-de-Cagnes which, as we have seen, Hirschfeld also visited on March 31, 1935.[20] Victor Bauer was in Paris, in October 1934, but it is not known if he met Hirschfeld there since Hirschfeld left the city the following month [ill. 3].[21]

Presumably, sometime in January or February 1936, Victor Bauer obtained, bought or was entrusted with – possibly for only a limited time – some or all of the items most likely held in the storage room that Hirschfeld rented in Nice. In 2006, in a catalogue of a German antiquarian book dealer, Ralf Dose and Rainer Herrn found a biographical diary fragment by the Romanian-born artist Henri Nouveau (née Henrik Neugeboren, 1901–1959) revealing the events around the Hirschfeld estate involving both Bauer and Nouveau. In the diary text, dated February 14, 1936, two weeks after the Gloria Mansions I apartment was vacated, Nouveau described how his friend, Victor Bauer, allowed him to view, photograph, and even take a few of the items that had belonged to Hirschfeld.[22] The text fragment also mentions the "entrance door of a Melanesian men's house" (*Eingangstür eines melanesischen Männerhauses*) coming from the Institute collection and which Bauer apparently installed in the house where he lived in Nice. The title of the diary fragment, "Hirschfeld's image archive" (*Hirschfeld's Bildarchiv*), indicates that the Institute lot contained pictures and other images, either additionally or even mainly [ill. 4].

In October 1935, in a letter he sent to Max Hodann, Giese wrote about a picture of Hirschfeld, taken in the USA during Hirschfeld's world tour; a picture that he had with him in Brno and liked a lot. Giese added cryptically: "The other photos are all still in Nice, if available".[23] But we will see in a moment that the lot in Nice also contained a great many ethnological objects that escaped the Berlin flames. The lot that fell to

[16] Ehrlich, Ehrlich & Ehrlich 2015, 35. They married in 1942. Victor Bauer was also active in the resistance during World War II and was arrested and imprisoned in Italy. In June 1940, Irmgard Strauss was deported to the Gurs camp where she stayed three months. Later on, she managed to go into hiding under an assumed name. Her children interviewed her about her war experience. See http://www.campgurs.com/media/1472/ehrlicht-ir%C3%A8ne-de-nice-%C3%A0-gurs.pdf (accessed Jul. 15, 2020). This text on her Gurs camp experience was initially published in *Gurs Souvenez-vous* 142 (March 2016): 15–19; and *Gurs Souvenez-vous* 143 (June 2016): 14–19. See also ADAM, Nice, Direction départementale de la sécurité publique des Alpes-Maritimes, Sûreté départementale: unité technique d'aide à l'enquête (caserne Auvare), dossier n° 175.537, file Bauer Victor, Strauss Irmgard and Jeanne [*sic*: Jane] Rey, cote 1660W 0155 and dossier n° 104.924, file Bauer Victor, cote 1440W 0239.

[17] Richter 1977, 43, 89.

[18] Kirchhoff 2017, 53.

[19] Galerie Welz 2006, n.p.

[20] Bergemann, Dose, Keilson-Lauritz & Dubout 2019, f. 128/172.

[21] Ehrlich, Ehrlich & Ehrlich 2015, 38.

[22] The text fragment was found in the 1995 catalogue of a German antiquarian book dealer selling the original manuscript of Henri Nouveau's sex diary ("sex. Tagebuch"). See "Sexualwisssenschaft V perversiones" 1995, entry 203, n.p., the catalogue of Antiquariat Bernhard Richter; Dose & Herrn 2006, 48. The antiquarian bookseller informed Manfred Herzer that he had agreed to exercise discretion about the buyer of the sex diary. See email (dated Nov. 4, 2016) from Bernhard Richter to Manfred Herzer. I thank Manfred Herzer for sharing this information. Marita Keilson-Lauritz and Ralf Dose later managed to determine, quite admirably, that the initials "V.B." in the Nouveau diary referred to the painter Victor Bauer. See Dose 2012, 22–23.

[23] Arbetarrörelsens arkiv och bibliotek, Stockholm, Max Hodann samling, vol. 10, letter (dated Oct. 10, 1935, [3–4]) from Karl Giese to Max Hodann: "Die andere Photos sind alle noch in Nice, soweit vorhanden".

Bauer's care must indeed have been considerably large and various. In the same letter to Hodann, Giese vented his frustration at not having many of the Institute materials that he knew had survived. He wrote, resignedly: "Unfortunately, these things are all in Nice".[24] The Institute lot Bauer had at his disposal in Nice also contained (a part of?) the completed psycho-biological questionnaires (*psychobiologischer Fragebogen*) that had either been saved by Giese or bought back from Nazi Germany in November 1933. Nouveau's diary text also reveals that Bauer and several other people, including Nouveau, had to go through (i.e. read) these questionnaires to sort them. Apparently, those belonging to important people, or containing relevant content or interesting passages, were kept. Nouveau double checked the ones read by others before those deemed "irrelevant" were burned: "For days and nights on end, the many hundreds of filled out questionnaires were examined for their value; I also read many of them, after the strictest discretion was demanded. [...] A lot were burnt; I myself burnt several waste paper basketfuls of questionnaires – which VB [Victor Bauer] handed to me to weed out at the last moment any 'valuables' that might have gotten in by mistake – in the apartment's central heating".[25] The text seems to suggest that the questionnaires of important or notable people were removed and saved from the ashes. According to Nouveau, Bauer also toyed with the idea of sending the questionnaires back to the people who had filled them out, but most likely this never happened. In any case, it shows that there was a real concern about dealing correctly with these questionnaires.[26]

WILHELM REICH

In January 1936, another figure, rather more famous than Victor Bauer, showed up in Nice around the time that Hirschfeld's apartment was being cleared out. In a brief 1937 biographical introduction about Bauer, an Austrian art gallery catalogue for a 2006 exhibition of his paintings includes the statement: "He [Victor Bauer] is working with Wilhelm Reich on the estate of Magnus Hirschfeld".[27] Victor Bauer had already been in contact with the (in)famous sexologist Wilhelm Reich (1897–1957), along with other intellectuals, when he was studying medicine in Vienna in the 1920s.[28] Possibly, they got to know each other through their mutual acquaintance, Sigmund Freud. Reich had also known Magnus Hirschfeld; however, with his Sexpol movement, he clearly had different ideas on how to wage the battle for global sexual liberation.[29]

We do not know how and why Reich and Bauer met again in Nice, but it is possible that Bauer reached out to an old friend and sexologist when dealing with the Hirschfeld collection. That Reich and Bauer came together for the Hirschfeld estate is confirmed by a letter from Reich to Bauer from the end of April 1935: "I am no longer really interested in the Hirschfeld inheritance. All that remains is the memory of the loss of 1500 kr".[30] This suggests the idea that someone maybe bought, or tried to buy, the Hirschfeld materials, or at least some of them. It seems likely

[24] Arbetarrörelsens arkiv och bibliotek, Stockholm, Max Hodann samling, vol. 10, letter (dated Oct. 10, 1935, [4]) from Karl Giese to Max Hodann: "Leider sind die Sachen alle in Nizza".

[25] Dose & Herrn 2006, 48: "Tage- und nächtelang wurden die vielen 100 ausgefüllten Fragebogen auf ihren Wert hin gesichtet; auch ich las viele, nachdem strengste Diskretion von mir gefordert worden war. [...] Es wurde viel verbrannt; ich selbst habe mehrere Papierkörbe voll, welche mir VB [Victor Bauer] zwecks letzter Suche nach evtl. irrtümlich hineingeratenen "Werten" aushändigte, in der Zentralheizung der Wohnung verfeuert".

[26] "Sexualwisssenschaft V perversiones" 1995, entry 203, n.p., catalogue of Antiquariat Bernhard Richter.

[27] Galerie Welz 2006, n.p.: "Mit Wilhelm Reich bearbeitet er [Victor Bauer] den Magnus Hirschfeld Nachlass." See also the short biographical introduction on Bauer on the website of the art gallery: http://www.galerie-welz.at/de/kuenstler/kuenstler.php?id=103 (accessed Sep. 23, 2013).

[28] See also Ehrlich, Ehrlich & Ehrlich 2015, 46.

[29] See, for example, Turner 2012, 130–31.

[30] I thank Jim Strick for sharing with me this (translated) fragment of the letter (dated Apr. 30, 1936)

that the "1500 kr" is a reference to krone (crowns). Since Reich was staying in Oslo at the time, these were most likely Norwegian crowns. If this is the case, then, in April 1936, 1,500 Norwegian crowns would have been worth FF410.85.[31] This considerable amount does indeed seem to suggest a purchase scenario.

ROGER DU TEIL

There was yet another figure who may have possibly played a part here as well, though his exact role cannot, at the moment, be clarified. The pen name of this third figure was Roger du Teil (1886–1974). In 1936, he was a philosophy professor at the Centre Universitaire Méditerranéen (C.U.M.), located right next to Gloria Mansions I.[32]As a young man, du Teil was mainly a literary figure, writing under his real last name (and second middle name), Gustave Rouger.[33] In 1935, he obtained a PhD in philosophy.[34] One source indirectly tells us that Reich met du Teil around January 1936.[35] Again, we see that this was around the time that Hirschfeld's Gloria Mansions I apartment was vacated. I have found several indications that Roger du Teil, at least in his younger years, might have been a gay man.[36] Could this be an explanatory element here as well? Did anyone from this or that gay network in Nice play a decisive

from Wilhelm Reich to Victor Bauer. I also thank Kevin Hinchey (co-director of the Wilhelm Reich Infant Trust, Rangeley, Maine, USA) for his mediation in September 2013. This letter from the Reich archive was already published (translated from German to English) in 1994 (Reich 1994, 63–64), but the editor omitted the Hirschfeld and other passages. The same letter reveals that Bauer was doing German-to-French translation work for Reich. We will return to the idea that Reich lost money because of it.

[31] In April 1936, the conversion rate was NOK100 (Norwegian krone) = FF27.39. See the historical monthly exchange rates of the Norwegian National Bank (Norges Bank): http://www.norges-bank.no/Upload/HMS/historical_exchange_rates/p1_c7.htm (accessed Mar. 17, 2014). I thank Anne-Grethe Frøyland from the bank's communications section for her prompt reply. See her email (dated Mar. 17, 2014) to the author. The possibility that the "1500 kr." were Austrian crowns, the currency of the (Austro-Hungarian) country of Reich's birth, seems excluded as this would amount to FF0.60, at the 1936 exchange rate.

[32] For more, if rather succinct biographical information on du Teil, see Pascal 1979, 31–34. See also Strick 2015.

[33] For the pseudonym, see, for example, https://www.journals.uchicago.edu/doi/abs/10.1086/692705?journalCode=isis (accessed Jul. 11, 2020).

[34] Du Teil 1935. For more biographical information, see also https://gw.geneanet.org/hdelatouche?lang=en&pz=clemence+isabelle&nz=molliet&ocz=0&p=roger&n=du+teil (accessed Dec. 1, 2021).

[35] Reich 1979, 86: "Dr. Reich visited me [Roger du Teil] to tell me of his work. I translated some of his writings to make them available in France. However, *for a year* [emphasis added], I heard nothing more about his detailed research, when suddenly, on January 8 of this year (1937), he sent me a letter and a brief report with two sealed and sterilized ampoules which he asked me to examine". The German original is more precise: "Dr. Reich hatte mich selbst während einer zu diesem Zweck unternommenen Reise über seine Arbeiten informiert. Er hatte mir einige seiner Schriften zur Ubersetzung überlassen, um sie in Frankreich bekanntzumachen. Ich hatte jedoch seit einem Jahre nichts mehr von diesen eingehenden Forschungen gehört, als er mir plötzlich, am 8. Januar dieses Jahres (1937) mit einem Brief und einem kursorischen Bericht zwei versiegelte und sterilisierte Ampullen sandte, die er mich [...] zu untersuchen bat". See Reich, du Teil & Hahn 1938, 42. The renewed contact, at the beginning of 1937, is confirmed several times in the publication. But did Reich indeed contact du Teil specifically to talk about his work? That seems odd. Kevin Hinchey, co-director of the Wilhelm Reich Infant Trust, who is working on a film about Reich wrote to me that "Reich and DuTeil [*sic*] first met in early 1936 in Paris, when two of Reich's colleagues took him to see a lecture by DuTeil [*sic*]. Afterwards, the two men discussed Reich's recently completed bio-electrical experiments". See email (dated Sep. 27, 2013) from Kevin Hinchey (the Wilhelm Reich Infant Trust, Rangeley) to the author. Cf. Strick 2015, 99. Strick also claims that Reich's students took him to a lecture given by du Teil. Du Teil was also fired from his job at the C.U.M. in June 1938 because of his participation in Reich's dubious Bion experiments. See Turner 2012, 192; Strick 2015, 243–51. The C.U.M. archives of former staff members (cote 168 W 06) remain at present inaccessible to researchers.

[36] There is, for example, his pre-World War II stay in North Africa about which Pascal writes: "dans ce pays [Algeria] il attire par ses goûts et son rayonnement bien des auteurs comme: Gide, Giraudoux, Francis Carco et Colette" (in this country [Algeria] he attracts by his tastes and his influence many authors like: Gide, Giraudoux, Francis Carco and Colette). (Pascal 1979, 32). After the war, Roger du

role in all of this? Many gay men there must surely have known that the then world-famous Hirschfeld had lived and died in Nice.[37] Let us also recall here the presumably gay circle around Leopold Hönig (*Kreis von der grande Bleue*) and that Hönig was also in Nice at the end of February 1936. Did he or this circle play a role in any of this? Even Victor Bauer was viewed at one point – but likely incorrectly – as a gay man by a policeman in Nice when Bauer was there on another visit in 1934.[38]

ERNST MAASS' LIST OF NAMES

I would like now to add an element that makes the above-mentioned three names of Bauer, Reich and du Teil even more intriguing. There exists a short letter, sent in March 1938 by François Herzfelder to Ernst Maass, that mentions a Paris appointment

Teil published in the French, so-called homophile magazine *Arcadie*. See the issues of February and May 1955 and November 1956. Du Teil was married to Andrée Yvonne Namias (?–?). When I contacted du Teil's daughter, Jannik Rouger du Teil (1928–2022) in 2015, not only did she vehemently deny my implicit "allegations" of her father's homosexual inclinations, but also wrote that her father left no personal archives since he had deliberately discarded these. See email (dated Feb. 22, 2015) from Jannik Rouger du Teil to the author. In 2015, Jannik Rouger du Teil was a secretary at the literary periodical *Souffles*, with which her father had also collaborated. See http://www.revuesouffles.fr/ (accessed Jul. 11, 2020).

[37] Hirschfeld's publications were read by some gay French men at the time. The French author André du Dognon wrote: "La seule chose qui existait en grand nombre, c'était les livres médicaux. On faisait venir les livres de Hirschfeld, mais on finissait par limiter nos lectures à des cas cliniques; pour les avoir, ces livres, je me qualifiais de docteur, et je les cachais sous mon lit" (The only thing that existed in large numbers was medical books. We used to bring in Hirschfeld's books, but we ended up limiting our reading to clinical cases; to get these books, I called myself a doctor and hid them under my bed). See Barbedette & Carassou 1981, 60.

[38] Because Victor Bauer and Irmgard Strauss both spoke German, the Bauers were always watched and shadowed by Nice civilians and police alike. After receiving a 1934 letter denouncing Bauer for loitering in the Albert I Garden in Nice (known to be frequented by gay men), a policeman determined that Bauer not only ran around the streets of Nice in a sailor's costume but also spoke with a feminine voice and "avait des manières de pédé" (had the manners of a faggot). This despite Victor Bauer declaring in the same document: "ne pas se livrér [*sic*: livrer] à la pédérastie" (did not indulge in pederasty [slang for homosexuality]). It is of course far from certain that this allows us to infer that Bauer may have been gay or bisexual. Maybe he was a sexual libertine or a free spirit regarding (sexual) relationships. ADAM, Nice, Direction départementale de la sécurité publique des Alpes-Maritimes, Sûreté départementale: unité technique d'aide à l'enquête (caserne Auvare), dossier n° 104.924, file Bauer Victor, cote 1440W 0239. From another police file, we learn that Bauer and Strauss had a student named Jane (Delphine Elise) Rey (the police file speaks of Jeanne Rey), who lived with them at 219 Boulevard du Mont Boron in the years before the war, or starting around 1940. The file describes the three living together as a "faux ménage" (counterfeit household). The *maîtresse* (mistress) of the household was likely Jane Rey. ADAM, Nice, Direction départementale de la sécurité publique des Alpes-Maritimes, Sûreté départementale: unité technique d'aide à l'enquête (caserne Auvare), dossier n° 175.537, file Bauer Victor, Strauss Irmgard and Jeanne [*sic*: Jane] Rey, cote 1660W 0155. See also Ehrlich, Ehrlich & Ehrlich 2015, 76. In 2013, Lothar Neumann also told Ralf Dose that, during his marriage to Bianca Bauer, Victor Bauer carried on open extramarital affairs. "The ménage à trois with Jeanne Rey did not come as a surprise to him". See email (dated Jul. 29, 2013) from Ralf Dose to the author. Born in 1912 in Nyons (département du Drôme), Jane Rey studied at the Université d'Aix from 1933 until 1940. See ADBR, Centre d'Aix, Dossiers des étudiants, bourses, équivalences, Examen Spécial d'Entrée à l'Unive[rsité], Faculté des lettres, 1897-1990, cote 1597 W 66. In another Aix university register, I found that Irmgard Strauss and Jane Rey both studied in Aix and were indeed living at the same address in Nice in 1938–39. See ADBR, Centre d'Aix, o.c., 193–1954, 4th registre (1938–1941), cote 1597 W 184. With the help of several regional *annuaires* (phone books) in the ADBR, I was able to determine that Jane's father, Fernand Rey, was an engineer and that her parents lived in Aix before the war at 12 Traverse des Dominicaines. My attempts to find her current relatives were unsuccessful. During World War II, Rey was in Nyons, her birth town, and helped fugitives there. See Ehrlich, Ehrlich & Ehrlich 2015, 77. In 1977, in Aix-en-Provence, Jane Rey married the Jewish-born (Catholic convert) lawyer and local literary and resistance personality Eugène David-Moyse (also known as Maurice David) (1901–1985). See email (dated Sep. 4, 2020) from Marie-Elisabeth Combet (Archives départementales de la Drôme, Valence) to the author; https://fr.wikipedia.org/wiki/Maurice_David_(r%C3%A9sistant) (accessed Sp. 5, 2020). A rugby stadium in Aix-en-Provence, built in 1975, was named after him. See https://laixois.fr/mais-qui-etait-maurice-david-stade-aix/ (accessed Sep. 5, 2020). Jane Rey possibly died as Jane Donaho David in Wichita Falls, Texas, USA in February 1985.

between Herzfelder and Maass.[39] The date of the letter is itself interesting. Why did Maass contact Herzfelder at the beginning of March 1938 when the Hirschfeld inheritance had been finally settled in August 1936? Maass and his mother would leave France and Europe by ship and head to the USA one week later. What did Maass want to discuss with Herzfelder in Paris? But the letter is also intriguing for another reason. On the letter (from which a piece has been torn out), the two names we have just looked at – "Prof. Du Theil [*sic*], Centre Universitaire, Nice" and "Dr. Wilhelm Reich, Oslo" – were added in Maass' handwriting. The other five names on the paper are "Arnold Zadikoff [*sic*, Zadikow] Paris-Malakoff", "Dr. Frau Helen Baakgard [*sic*: Ellen Bækgaard] Kopenhagen", "Dr. [Josef] Weisskopf Brünn", "[Jonathan H.] Leunbach Kopenhagen", and finally "Dr. Siegfried Bernfeld [1892–1953], San Francisco, 3301 Broderick Str.[eet]".[40] Victor Bauer's name is missing but did it appear on the small torn-out piece?[41] Why did Ernst Maass assemble this list of names? And why are Reich's and du Teil's names there as well? Because they were in fact involved with the handling of Hirschfeld's remaining materials and legacy [ill. 5]?

SIEGFRIED BERNFELD

One name that shows up here for the first time can also be linked to Hirschfeld. In September 1934, the psychoanalyst Siegfried Bernfeld moved from Vienna to Menton, a city on the French Riviera. Menton is thirty kilometers east of Nice. He and his close family would leave the French Riviera and emigrate to England at the end of 1936.[42] Bernfeld had a link with the Czechoslovak Stross family. His sister, Lilly Bernfeld (1895–1986), was married to Walter Stross (1883–1946).[43] The latter was a nephew of Vilém Stross (1894–?) whose name, along with his mother's, Ewa Stross (1866–1940), shows up in the Hirschfeld guestbook. Ewa Stross signed the guestbook in Nice on March 3, 1935, calling Hirschfeld "my dear friend" (*mon cher ami*).[44] This is a bit coincidental and may seem far-fetched as an explanation for Bernfeld's appearance in Maass' list of names; however, there is another list, also assembled by Ernst

[39] Archiv MHG, Berlin, fonds Ernst Maass, letter (dated Mar. 3, 1938) from Franz Herzfelder to Ernst Maass. It is not known if Maass and Herzfelder also actually met in Paris or only exchanged information over the phone.

[40] This San Francisco address is explained by Siegfried Bernfeld having moved with his family to the USA in 1937. Before that, they were living as exiles on the French Rivièra. See http://www.hagalil.com/archiv/2010/05/16/bernfeld/ (accessed Jan. 1, 2013). Bernfeld was married to the Belgian-born Suzanne Aimée Cassirer (1896–1963). The couple raised the two children from Suzanne's earlier marriage, Peter Hans Paret (1924–) and Renate Marie Paret (1926–?). Both Siegfried and Suzanne Bernfeld were psychoanalysts and Siegfried worked with Siegmund Freud in Vienna. Likely significant as well: Arthur Kronfeld, one of the Institute doctors, was in psychoanalytic therapy with Bernfeld. See Herrn 2022, 309. I sent an email (dated Jul. 11, 2020) inquiring about this matter to Bernfeld's son, Peter Hans Paret, a distinguished retired Princeton historian. He wrote back the same day to say that he was Bernfeld's stepson but knew nothing about Hirschfeld, nor did he know of any relevant archives of his late father on the matter. No clues were found in the online inventory of the Siegfried Bernfeld archives (1910–1922) kept at YIVO, New York. But Bernfeld's personal archives are housed in several other places and these should be checked one day. See Dudek 2012, 599–600.

[41] The layout of the names noted by Maass, and the dimensions of the tear, suggest that there were one or two more names initially written on the page, but that these extra names were ripped out at one point, for one reason or another.

[42] Dudek 2012, 528, 530.

[43] Dudek 2012, 532 n. 374.

[44] Bergemann, Dose, Keilson-Lauritz & Dubout 2019, f. 115/159. Vilém Stross signed his name on March 3, 1935. See Bergemann, Dose, Keilson-Lauritz & Dubout 2019, f. 127/171. The grandparents of Walter and Vilém Stross were Noe Stross (1822–1897) and Josephine Wolf (1827–1895). Vilém Stross' father, Sigmund Stross (1854–1923), was the brother of Ludwig Stross (1851–1913), the father of Walter Stross. For more information on Vilém and his mother Ewa Stross, see NA, Praha, Policejní ředitelství Praha II, všeobecná spisovna 1941–1951, kart. n° 11154, sign. S 6776/2, Vilém Stross MUDr. 1894 and NA, Praha, Policejní ředitelství Praha II, všeobecná spisovna 1931–1940, kart. n° 11221, sign. S 6897/20, Ewa Stross. nar. 1866.

[45] The list "Freunde von Magnus Hirschfeld" is in Archiv MHG, Berlin, fonds Ernst Maass. It is also possible that Hirschfeld and Ewa Stross had already met in Paris since one of her residential registration

Maass, and titled "Friends of Magnus Hirschfeld" (*Freunde von Magnus Hirschfeld*), where the name of Ewa Stross appears with an address in Nice: Avenue Emilia, (no house number is given).[45] In the latter list one also finds the name Birnbaumova [*sic*: Birnbaumová], with the same Nice address as Ewa Stross. From the 1936 Nice census, it turns out that this was Mrs. Dora Birnbaum (née Ginsberg, 1867–?) and her daughter Marie (1898–?), and that Dora Birnbaum was the sister of Ewa Stross. The census also states that Marie was an archivist by profession.[46] So it is quite possible that it was Ewa Stross who suggested Siegfried Bernfeld as yet another expert in the matter [ill. 6]. The one thing that seems to speak a bit against Bernfeld's involvement is that he and Reich had a quarrel.[47] Marie Birnbaum being an archivist is, of course, yet another intriguing element. Was she consulted in the matter as well?

THE UNCLEAR ROLE OF THE NICE PUBLIC PROSECUTOR

Let us now return to Victor Bauer. Nouveau added in the diary fragment that Bauer was allowed to handle these Hirschfeld materials with the approval of the Nice public prosecutor (in French, *ministère public*, *procureur* or *parquet*; in German, *Staatsanwalt*) and that Bauer apparently had to return the Melanesian wood carved door (but to whom?) later. This return of ethnological objects and artifacts seems to accord with Wilhelm Reich's statement that he had paid for an item from the Institute lot, which he then had to return, losing the money he paid. The Nouveau diary fragment, if we try to interpret its insinuations, also seems to say that the sorting of the questionnaires was possibly also ordered by the Nice public prosecutor. So, it is possible that, when he studied the questionnaires, Victor Bauer was acting on a mandate. After "inspection", as we have seen, most of these Institute questionnaires were apparently burned by Bauer. Nouveau photographed some before they were turned to ashes. But there is, for now, no real explanation of why or when or how the Nice public prosecutor was involved in the matter; or why the prosecutor allowed Victor Bauer, specifically, to do these things. Unfortunately, the available archival sources that document the activity of the Nice public prosecutor in this period offer no explanation either.[48] Returning

forms (in NA, Praha) states that she moved to Paris in 1923, moving back to Prague in October 1935. See NA, Praha, Policejní ředitelství Praha II, všeobecná spisovna 1931–1940, kart. n° 11221, sign. S 6897/20, Ewa Stross. nar. 1866.

[46] ADAM, Nice, Ville de Nice, dénombrement de la population (recensement), 1936, 4ème canton, partie 1, cote 6M 173, Avenue Emilia n° 27, f. 837. This is available online at http://www.basesdocumentaires-cg06.fr/archives/ImageZoomViewerRP.php?cote=06M%200173&date=1936,%204%E8me%20canton,%20(partie%201)&c=Nice (accessed Jan. 23, 2021). Both women had Russian nationality – according to the census – but Dora Birnbaum was born in Łódź and her daughter Marie Birnbaum was born in Warsaw. Curiously, the house number given in the census is 27, whereas it is 4 in the *Annuaires des Alpes-Maritimes – Liste alphabétique des abonnés au téléphone, Antibes, Beaulieu, Beausoleil, Cagnes Sur Mer, Cannes, Grasse, Menton, Puget-Théniers, Monaco, Hyères* 1936, 13. Dora's husband was a certain Joseph Birnbaum (?–?). See https://www.geni.com/people/Joseph-Birnbaum/6000000018861882144 (accessed Jan. 24, 2021).

[47] Dudek 2012, 479–91, ch. 7.8.

[48] The Nice *parquet* has not deposited all of its archives at the ADAM in Nice and the archives of the Nice state prosecutor that the ADAM does have contain no traces related to my specific question. See email (dated Jan. 20, 2014) from staff member (ADAM, Nice) to the author. It is unclear if the undeposited archives are still with the *parquet* or have been destroyed. Because it seems that all dealings with the Nice justice system regarding the Hirschfeld inheritance began and likely also remained at the level of the Tribunal de première instance, I checked in the ADAM in Nice – over the course of several manageable sessions – the very voluminous Répertoire chronologique des actes civils of the Tribunal de première instance de Nice, which is only chronologically ordered and has no added alphabetical indexes. In several places, of course, I did find the name "Hirschfeld". In all cases the dates corresponded to important court decisions regarding the Hirschfeld inheritance procedure. I checked this register for the period from January 1935 until December 1937. A "Hirschfeld" mention with the (abbreviated) addition "constat testament" for October 25, 1935 (n° 9878) most likely refers to the case of Gustav(e) Charles (Carl) Hirschfeld, another Demnard client, who died in Nice in 1934. For his case, see ADAM, Nice, Archives notariales, minutes notariales étude Pierre Demnard, Dec. 23, 1935, n° 1397, cote 03E 148/025. The two volumes that I consulted can

to the possible role of Roger du Teil in this matter, could it be that the Nice *parquet* contacted the C.U.M., the forebear of the post-war Nice University, for some scholarly advice on what should be done with the Hirschfeld papers? Or had they called upon du Teil to gather scientists to decide what to do?[49] Lastly, it is of course also possible that Bauer simply bought the Hirschfeld lot and decided, as a medically trained professional, to be very careful with these sensitive and "private" questionnaires.

IRÈNE EHRLICH'S INTERVIEW

In July 2020, I contacted the relatives of Victor Bauer's first wife, Irmgard (Irène) Ehrlich (née Strauss, 1913–1992). Bauer married Irmgard Strauss in 1942 and divorced her in 1947.[50] Both survived the war despite their being active in the resistance. Victor Bauer was arrested in May 1943 and taken to Italy by the Italian fascists who then occupied Nice.[51] Irène Ehrlich went into hiding under a false name in the French city of Manosque along with the dentist Wolf Ehrlich (1902–1975) whom she married after the war.[52] It was in Manosque also that the couple's first child, Robert Ehrlich (1944–), was born.[53] After the war, the couple had two more children: Monique (1947–) and Jacques Ehrlich (1949–). In 1990–91, Jacques Ehrlich interviewed his mother about her life. She mentioned the dealings of Victor Bauer with the Hirschfeld estate in 1936. I quote here the relevant passage from the interview:

> There was also someone who lived here, he was the former director of the Berlin Institute of Sexology – it was the only thing that existed at that time and in this field: Institut für Sexualwissenschaft in Berlin. It was Hirschfeld. He was very, very famous. He did research all over the world, he studied tribes ... He was interested in many things: be it in the forms of sexual life in Japan, in Malaysia ... everywhere! He had two secretaries, both homosexuals. One of them, Kirchberger, was Jewish and therefore had to leave Germany. He lived on the Promenade des Anglais, next to the university centre [C.U.M.]. The other one was Chinese. They were very intelligent, very nice. Hirschfeld had just died and there was the whole Hirschfeld estate to be studied. It was a lawyer who was in charge of this, Dr Hertzberger [Herzfelder], who lived on Boulevard François Grosso. As he had very little knowledge of psychology, sexology or psychoanalysis, he asked Bauer to see what was of value, what should be kept, what should be done with all of that. So we opened all the boxes. Henri Nouveau was there too. We found some very interesting things. There were wedding scrolls by [inaudible] Naro [artist Kitagawa Utamaro (1753–1806)?], a Japanese engraver, a splendid engraving: when a young girl got married, she

be found in ADAM, Nice, Archives administratives de 1800 à 1940, Fonds du Tribunal de première instance de Nice, Répertoire chronologique des actes civils, Jan. 1, 1932–Dec. 31, 1937 [despite the official archival description, the register in fact ends on Mar. 30, 1937], cote 03U 01/0166; and also, in the same location, Mar. 30, 1937–Jan. 5, 1941, cote 03U 01/0167. An inquiry sent to the Nice Procureur de la République asking about the fate of the 1936 archives of the Nice *parquet* resulted in a letter saying no help could be offered. See letter (dated Dec. 11, 2014) from Tribunal de grande instance de Nice to the author.

49 Although it does not seem very promising, one should nevertheless maybe one day check the approximately 675 "rapports d'expertises civiles" presented to the Tribunal de première instance, in 1935 and 1936, to ascertain if the court itself relied on external expertise in the matter. Because there was no separate register for these reports, I did not check the eight relevant archival boxes of this fonds. See ADAM, Nice, Archives administratives de 1800 à 1940, Fonds du Tribunal de première instance de Nice, Rapports d'expertises civiles, 1935-1936, cotes 03U 01/1310 until 03U 01/1317. I also checked – maybe significant sums were involved? – the two registers of the Tribunal de grande instance from May 1935 until June 1938. ADAM, Archives administratives de 1940 à nos jours, Tribunal de grande instance de Nice, Dépôts de rapports d'experts : répertoire (avec indication du nom de l'expert, noms des parties, nom de l'avoué), Aug. 2, 1926–Dec. 31, 1935, cote 1334W 0341; and, in the same location, Jan. 3, 1936–Dec. 31, 1954, cote 334 W 0342. And finally, I also checked on the expertise relied upon at the level of the Justice de Paix for the year 1936. Archives administratives de 1800 à 1940, Justice de Paix, Nice Ouest, Rapports d'experts, 1936, cote 04U 12/0345. Nothing relevant was found in these two archival fonds.

50 Ehrlich, Ehrlich & Ehrlich 2015, 171.

51 Ehrlich, Ehrlich & Ehrlich 2015, 88, 92.

52 Ehrlich, Ehrlich & Ehrlich 2015, 98.

> was given wedding scrolls – it was a kind of initiation to her life as a woman. There were engraved panels that came from Malaysia ... an extraordinary artistic wealth. So we saw all that. It was distributed a little bit here and there because nobody knew its value. I don't know what happened to it. I think Henri [Goetz] has one that Bauer gave him. That was in 35–36.[54]

We can see that this interview fragment contradicts nothing of what we have just seen and it lists several names that we have looked at. What is new here is that François Herzfelder took the initiative to ask Victor Bauer what to do with the Hirschfeld materials. Irmgard Strauss also says that she met Robert Kirchberger and Li Shiu Tong, and also seems to imply that both were aware of Victor Bauer's involvement. That Robert Kirchberger was paid (a second time) with money from the Hirschfeld estate, at the end of January 1936, possibly indicates that he might also have been involved in the 1936 operations.[55] We also learn that Kirchberger may have been gay, a fact that was still somewhat uncertain.[56] Irène Ehrlich also states that many things were given away to people. One item from the Institute lot was given to the painter Henri Goetz (1909–1989), who met Victor Bauer in Paris in 1934. Bauer was Goetz's intellectual mentor.[57] Goetz was active in the resistance during the war, together with his wife, the Dutch painter Christine Boumeester (1904–1971). Henri Goetz died in Nice, in the summer of 1989, by jumping out of a window in the hospital where he was staying.[58] After Boumeester died, in 1971, Irène Ehrlich, who was a close friend of Goetz since they met in Paris in 1934, became Goetz's last partner.[59] Goetz

[53] Ehrlich, Ehrlich & Ehrlich 2015, 6. I wrote an email to Robert Ehrlich on July 15, 2020, after finding his name in Irmgard Strauss' already mentioned testimony about the Gurs camp experience.

[54] Ehrlich, Ehrlich & Ehrlich 2015, 48: "Il y avait également quelqu'un qui vivait ici, c'était l'ancien directeur de l'Institut de sexologie de Berlin – c'était la seule chose qui existait, à cette époque-là, dans ce domaine: Institut für Sexualwissenschaft in Berlin. C'était Hirschfeld. Il était très, très célèbre. Il a fait des recherches dans le monde entier, il a étudié les tribus ... Il s'est intéressé à beaucoup de choses: aussi bien aux formes de vie sexuelle au Japon, en Malaisie ... partout ! Il avait deux secrétaires, tous deux homosexuels. L'un, Kirchberger, était juif et a donc dû quitter l'Allemagne. Il habitait Promenade des Anglais, à côté du centre universitaire [C.U.M.]. L'autre était chinois. Ils étaient très intelligents, très gentils. Hirschfeld venait de mourir et il y avait toute la succession Hirschfeld à étudier. C'est un avocat qui était chargé de ça, le docteur Hertzberger [Herzfelder], qui habitait Boulevard François Grosso. Comme il avait très peu de connaissances en psychologie, en sexologie, en psychanalyse, il a demandé à Bauer de voir un peu ce qui était valable, ce qu'il fallait conserver, ce qu'il fallait faire de tout ça. On a donc ouvert toutes les caisses. Henri Nouveau était là aussi. On a trouvé des choses très intéressantes. Il y avait des rouleaux de mariage de [inaudible] Naro [artist Kitagawa Utamaro (1753–1806)?] – un graveur japonais – une splendeur de gravure: quand une jeune fille se mariait, on lui remettait des rouleaux de mariage – c'était une sorte d'initiation à sa vie de femme. Il y avait des panneaux gravés qui venaient de Malaisie ... une richesse artistique extraordinaire. On a donc vu tout ça. Ça a été distribué un peu aux uns et aux autres puisque personne n'en connaissait la valeur. Je ne sais pas ce que c'est devenu. Je crois que Henri [Goetz] en a un que Bauer lui avait cédé. C'était en 35–36". The interview, initially conducted by Jacques (Jacky) Ehrlich, was typed out by his daughter Anne Ehrlich (1970–1996) and also enriched with footnotes and extra information by Robert's Ehrlich's wife, Nicole Ehrlich (née Weber, 1943–). Later, Monique Ehrlich and Robert's daughter, Armelle Pérennès (née Ehrlich, 1973–) contributed to further documenting the interview. Most of all, the Ehrlich family wanted the interview with Irène Ehrlich (nicknamed Mayou) to be a group project by and for the future Ehrlich family. I thank the Ehrlich family for their friendliness and cooperation and for allowing me to quote from the unpublished interview here. See the email correspondence (dated 2020–21) between Nicole Ehrlich and Robert Ehrlich and the author.

[55] Soetaert 2014, 56.

[56] Cf. Soetaert 2018, 15 n. 12.

[57] Ehrlich, Ehrlich & Ehrlich 2015, 237.

[58] Ehrlich, Ehrlich & Ehrlich 2015, 240. For a schematic biographical overview of Goetz's life, see https://henrigoetz.com/wp-content/uploads/biographie.pdf (accessed Jul. 20, 2020). Some (donated) paintings by Goetz and Boumeester are on permanent exhibit in a little museum bearing their name in the citadel of Villefranche-sur-Mer, next to Nice. See https://villefranche-sur-mer.fr/goetz-boumeester/ (accessed Jul. 20, 2020).

[59] Email (dated Jul. 17, 2020) from Nicole Ehrlich to the author; Ehrlich, Ehrlich & Ehrlich 2015, 43.

and Boumeester were also good friends of Henri Nouveau, something that further illustrates the interrelations of the network.[60]

Irène Ehrlich's interview also mentions a few other things: that it was Victor Bauer who invited Wilhelm Reich to Nice, that Bauer knew Reich very well, and that Siegfried Bernfeld, who lived in nearby Menton, gave a lecture in Nice in 1935 in the Café de Lyon. Ehrlich attended this lecture, presumably with Bauer.[61] We also learn that Ehrlich and Bauer already knew Henri Nouveau, the author of the diary fragment indicating Victor Bauer's role, when they were briefly in Paris in 1934.[62] Irmgard Strauss also mentions Roger du Teil of the C.U.M., whom she also knew. She says that Reich and du Teil, the C.U.M. secretary, contacted each other in Nice and that she typed notes for Reich, who was already engaged in his controversial research on the orgon.[63]

All this confirms that the names on the list redacted by Ernst Maass in 1938 (handwritten on a letter from François Herzfelder), were indeed interrelated and linked to the handling of a significant part of the Hirschfeld estate in 1936. Presumably, the lot entrusted to Victor Bauer contained the materials that Hirschfeld had kept in a storage room in Nice. With this information, the network involved in the further handling of the Hirschfeld estate in 1936, clearly gathered around the pivotal figure of Victor Bauer, becomes almost unmanageably large because Bauer knew so many people, especially in the Parisian art world. That Paris harbored many exiled artists, in the years before World War II, only further expands the network of people Bauer may have known.[64]

Perhaps not coincidentally, a questionnaire, completed by the French anthropologist Arnold van Gennep (1873–1959), was sold in 1944 at a Parisian antiquarian bookstore. It is possible that this questionnaire came from Bauer's troupe in Nice.[65] To name just one other example of the dense network relied upon in Nice and Paris in 1936, I discovered that Victor Bauer also knew André Beucler, one of the *Voilà* journalists who visited the Institute in Berlin.[66] We have already suggested that Beucler may have

[60] Cohen 2002, 193.

[61] Ehrlich, Ehrlich & Ehrlich 2015, 47. The café exists to this day, still located at 33 Avenue Jean Médecin in Nice. Siegfried Bernfeld's stepson, Peter Paret, also confirmed to me that he and his stepfather lived in Menton. See email (dated Jul. 11, 2020) from Peter Paret to the author.

[62] Ehrlich, Ehrlich & Ehrlich 2015, 40–41.

[63] Ehrlich, Ehrlich & Ehrlich 2015, 47. For more on Wilhelm Reich in Nice, see Soetaert 2014, 62. In Ehrlich, Ehrlich & Ehrlich 2015 one reads: "Ici, le centre universitaire [C.U.M.] a été créé à cette époque-là. Je ne sais plus comment ça s'est passé, mais on avait des rapports avec le secrétaire du centre universitaire, monsieur Duteil [*sic*]. C'était un littéraire, mais il était très intéressé par la psychologie. Bauer a fait venir Wilhelm Reich chez nous, à Nice et voulait le faire connaître. Il voulait qu'il [Reich] publie quelque chose ici. Il espérait que ce monsieur Duteil pourrait être un intermédiaire pour trouver quelqu'un qui publie ses travaux" (The university centre [C.U.M.] here was created at that time. I do not remember how it happened, but we had a relationship with the secretary of the university centre, Mr. Duteil [*sic*]. He was a literary scholar, but he was very interested in psychology. Bauer invited Wilhelm Reich to visit us in Nice and wanted to make him known. He wanted him [Reich] to publish something in here. He hoped that Mr. Duteil could act as an intermediary in finding someone to publish his work) (Ehrlich, Ehrlich & Ehrlich 2015, 46).

[64] On Bauer knowing a great many people, see Ehrlich, Ehrlich & Ehrlich 2015, 41–42. For an overview of all the exiled artists in Paris before World War II, see Yagil 2015.

[65] This questionnaire has survived and was shown at the mini-exhibition held at the *Gedenkveranstaltung* (commemorative event) marking "90 Jahre Zerstörung des Instituts für Sexualwissenschaft" (The 90th anniversary of the destruction of the Institute of Sexual Science), that took place at the Staatsbibliothek zu Berlin (Unter den Linden), Berlin on May 10, 2023. However, it remains uncertain when this questionnaire was filled out. It might have been after 1933. The questionnaire was bought by a collaborator of the Staatsbibliothek zu Berlin (or a person working for them) from the Librairie Orientaliste Paul Geuthner in Paris. That Paul Geuthner (1877–1949), the original owner of the bookstore founded in 1901, was born in Germany and thus German-speaking, is intriguing for our story. See https://en.wikipedia.org/wiki/Librairie_orientaliste_Paul_Geuthner (accessed May 17, 2023). Did one of Bauer's German-speaking friends sell the questionnaire to the antiquarian bookseller? The bookseller further intrigues because he interned

facilitated Hirschfeld signing a publishing contract with Gallimard.[67] So Beucler might also have been consulted about the handling of the Hirschfeld estate and may have received some items from it.

THE TROUPE OF FRIENDS AROUND VICTOR BAUER

We have already mentioned the young man Waldemar Speyer, the German lawyer who fled Nazi Germany in 1933, and took care of the transfer of some of the monetary bequests Hirschfeld made to German relatives and friends. In August 2020, I found out that, in Nice, in 1936, Speyer lived with Victor Bauer, Irène Ehrlich, the Czechoslovak painter Rodolphe (Rudolf) Pollak (1910–1998) and Odette Jorel (1909–2008) at 37 Boulevard de Cessole, on the third floor of a villa named Villa Antoinette.[68] This finding has several consequences.

Firstly, it means that we finally know with certainty where the Institute artifacts ended up in Nice in 1936, and the house where Henri Nouveau saw the carved Melanesian men's house door.[69] Villa Antoinette is located in a cul-de-sac, at 5 Allée du souvenir, a very small side street off the Boulevard de Cessole in Nice's Mantega neigborhood [ill. 7].[70] Secondly, and more importantly, it makes it even clearer

with Koehler & Volckmar, a company we encountered when looking at Elise Brecher's bookstore (L. & A. Brecher), and also because his wife, Walburga Seidl, was Czech-born. See Messaoudi 2012, 24. The archives of the bookstore, which is still in business, are kept in the IMEC, Saint-Germain-la-Blanche-Herbe.

[66] Beucler, Apr. 9, 1932.

[67] See the chapter on Gaston Gallimard in Beucler 1980, 91–105.

[68] The ball started rolling when I read in the Ehrlich family's interview with Irène Ehrlich that Bauer lived in a villa in the Boulevard de Cessole in Nice, though she did not give the house number. See Ehrlich, Ehrlich & Ehrlich 2015, 46: "On avait décidé de s'installer à Nice. Odette Jaurel [*sic*], Polack [*sic*] et Schweier [*sic*] sont venus aussi. On a trouvé un appartement très confortable, Boulevard de Cessole, un grand appartement où nous nous sommes installés tous les cinq – Eva était restée chez Milhaud, elle n'était pas encore venue ici. C'était une petite villa. Au rez-de-chaussée habitait une vieille dame – à l'époque, elle me paraissait une vieille dame – elle avait peut-être 55 ans. Elle vivait là avec sa nièce. Cette nièce était mariée à un psychanalyste, mais elle était séparée et elle travaillait" (We decided to move to Nice. Odette Jaurel [*sic*], Polack [*sic*] and Schweier [*sic*] came too. We found a very comfortable flat on Boulevard de Cessole, a large flat where the five of us settled – Eva had stayed with Milhaud, she had not been here yet. It was a small villa. On the ground floor there was an old lady – at the time, she looked like an old lady to me – she was maybe 55. She lived there with her niece. The niece was married to a psychoanalyst, but she was divorced and working). I remembered that Speyer had also lived in the Boulevard de Cessole and it suddenly occurred to me that Speyer sounded like Schweier. I then started searching in the 1936 Nice census but was at first unable to find the owner of the villa at 37 Boulevard de Cessole. I then looked at the small dead-end street lying just behind the Boulevard de Cessole, the Allée du souvenir, and under house number 1 found the owner of Villa Antoinette, Antoinette Deroo (1875–?) and her *filleule* (goddaughter), Mariette Tramontana (1909?–?); and then, under house number 3, the troupe of five people living with Victor Bauer. There I was also able to see that Odette Jaurel was in fact Odette Jorel and Rodolphe Polack was Rodolphe Pollak. See ADAM, Nice, Ville de Nice, dénombrement de la population (recensement) 1936, 4ème canton, tome 3, cote 6M 175, f. 2501. Available online at http://www.basesdocumentaires-cg06.fr/archives/indexRP.php (accessed Aug. 14, 2020). The widow (Marie) Antoinette Deroo (née Miquel) is also listed as the owner of the Villa Antoinette under the Allée du souvenir address in *Annuaires des Alpes-Maritimes* 1936, 327, 549, 621, 755. The other names listed as living at the same address are Anna Arnaud, Alvara and Calderon.

[69] In 2014, I still believed that Victor Bauer and Irmgard Strauss (and their group of friends) were living in 1936 at 219 Boulevard du Mont Boron, the address where they lived starting around 1940. See Soetaert 2014, 59. Victor Bauer and Irmgard Strauss lived in apartment n° 20 at this address, on the third floor. See ADAM, Nice, Direction départementale de la sécurité publique des Alpes-Maritimes, Sûreté départementale: unité technique d'aide à l'enquête (caserne Auvare), dossier n° 175.537, file Bauer Victor, Strauss Irmgard and Jeanne [*sic*: Jane] Rey, cote 1660W 0155.

[70] My attempts to find the current relatives of the former owner of Villa Antoinette, Antoinette Deroo, have so far been unsuccessful. I started my search by sending a letter to Jean-Christophe Deroo in Nice on August 14 2020, asking him if he might be related to Mrs. Deroo. He replied that he was not. See his email (dated Aug. 25, 2020) to the author. I also sent a letter (on Aug. 19, 2020) to the four people named Fornari currently living in Nice. According to the 1936 census, the Fornari family lived on the second floor of the house. No one replied. I also called (on Aug.

that Victor Bauer and his troupe were very closely involved with the handling and settlement of the Hirschfeld estate, which Hirschfeld's will put in the hands of François Herzfelder. Irène Ehrlich said that Herzfelder turned to Bauer, because he was not sufficiently well-informed to deal with the Institute materials, but Herzfelder also relied, in the first half of 1936, on Waldemar Speyer to deliver Hirschfeld's monetary bequests to several people. The trust Herzfelder had in the Bauer troupe was thus considerable. This also means, at least apparently, that Victor Bauer was not contacted only after the legal settlement was finalized, in the summer of 1936, and that he and his troupe did not gain access to Institute materials in an accidental or irregular way.

We need to return once again to Henri Nouveau's diary fragment and recall that he dated the entry titled "Hirschfelds Bildarchiv" February 14, 1936. If one reads the text closely, one can see that Nouveau was taking a backward look, i.e. after all the dealings with the Hirschfeld estate were finished. He mentions, for example, that, "later on" (*später*), Victor Bauer had to return the Melanesian men's house wooden door, indicating that Bauer and his troupe were already involved earlier than February 1936, possibly even as early as the second half of 1935. This could also mean that the already mentioned cost of the moving company Reboul & Co., for a service delivered on the last day of January 1936, was indeed linked to emptying the Gloria mansions apartment *exclusively*. That was also the very last day of the annual lease Hirschfeld had signed for the Gloria Mansions I apartment. Yet it is curious, though simply possible, again following Nouveau's February 14, 1936, sex diary fragment, that the clique around Bauer dealt with some Institute materials in the two weeks after the emptying of the Gloria Mansions apartment. This could also mean that, at the end of January, the apartment was vacated and the Institute ethnological objects were moved as well. Thinking this through some more, this could mean that the artifacts Bauer and his troupe dealt with were actually stored in the Gloria Mansions I building ... and that there never was a storage room in Nice. Since these objects were not registered by Giauffer in 1935, this would also mean, if this was indeed the case, that these objects were stored in another Gloria Mansions apartment (Theodor Wolff's, for example) or in another spare storage space in the building. Another possibility, which would illuminate the curious proximity of the date of Nouveau's diary fragment and the emptying of the apartment, is that they maybe simply tried to save money by emptying out the Gloria Mansions I apartment and moving the Institute materials to Bauer's place on the same day. These last two possibilities do not seem to exclude each other. Two later bills, from May and June 1936, from the moving and storage company Reboul & Co., and a smaller bill from another moving company named Martini et Cie, of July 7, 1936, remain for now unexplained. We will return one more time in chapter 12 to these last three moving company bills and offer a plausible explanation for them.[71]

18 2020) Gilles Mordant who currently owns the third floor of the house. He told me the Allée du souvenir used to be the entrance way to one of the three Nice villas owned by Victor de Cessole (1859–1941). See https://www.victordecessole.org/dwn/Victor_de_Cessole_02.pdf (accessed Aug. 18, 2020). (In April 1937, de Cessole donated, with strict conditions, the family's rich library to the city of Nice, where it is now kept in the Bibliothèque du Chevalier Victor de Cessole, located on the third floor of the Musée Masséna.) On September 21, 2020, Gilles Mordant also kindly sent me the "reglement de copropriété" of the building in which he lives, listing the names of the building's previous owners. From that document, I learned that the building was bought in 1918 by Joseph Marie Deroo (?–1925) from the noble family of Spitalieri de Cessole. Deroo's wife, Marie Antoinette Miquel (1875–1979), inherited the property after his death. Antoinette Deroo remarried, presumably in 1978, Albert Henri Schubnel (1902–1993), who thus became the next owner of the building. In the online phonebook *Pages blanches France*, I found the name of Marie Schubnel in Nice and wrote a letter to her on September 23, 2020, but received no reply.

71 For an overview of the three bills for the Reboul & Co. moving company, see Table 13 in Soetaert 2014,

I tried, of course, to find more information about the destinies of the other people in Bauer's troupe. In her interview, Irène Ehrlich also said that Odette Jorel was very much in love with the Czechoslovak and Jewish painter Rodolphe Pollak. However, Pollak fell for her sister, Yvonne Jorel (1910–2005). This unhappy love resulted in Odette Jorel attempting suicide, but she was saved at the last moment by Victor Bauer and Irène Ehrlich. Pollak and Yvonne Jorel married in Nice in December 1936 and had a daughter, Irène Pollak (*c.* 1937–), soon after.[72] Because Pollak was Jewish, the couple separated around 1942 so as not to jeopardize Irène Pollak's life. Apparently, Rodolphe managed to escape from France and arrived in Switzerland in May 1943.[73] According to Irène Pollak, her father then went to England where he joined the armed forces and later participated in the Allied invasion of Europe, ending up in Berlin at the end of the war. He then returned to Prague to learn that his parents, the banker Ernst Pollak (1874–1942?) and Hermina Kauders (1880–1942?), had died in the Shoah.[74] Rodolphe Pollak stayed in Czechoslovakia until at least 1955 and died in Paris in 1998. Irène Pollak wrote to me that she did not know anything about her parents' time in Nice.[75] In 1940, Odette Jorel, who later became a medical doctor, married Pierre Duviard (1911–2001) in Marseille.[76]

Waldemar Speyer's further fate is only partly known. From the interview with Irène Ehrlich we also learn that Speyer, who was a lawyer, started doing photography when he was in Paris and had a German female friend (maybe a girlfriend) named Eva (whom I was not able to identify), working as a nanny in Aix-en-Provence for the French and Jewish composer Darius Milhaud (1892–1974). Apparently, this female friend of Speyer, Victor Bauer and Irène Ehrlich, helped Milhaud to translate the text for an opera project on the Renaisance artist Matthias Grünewald (1475–1528) from German to French, but the opera never saw the light of day. Later on, this Eva joined Bauer's troupe in Nice.[77] Speyer's trail continues into August 1939, when he was treated in a sanitarium in Villiers-sur-Marne.[78] Villiers-sur-Marne happened to be next to Champigny-sur-Marne, the place where Odette Jorel's father had a holiday home and where Bauer's troupe often spent time along the river Marne while they were still living in Paris.[79] Speyer survived the war but it is not clear how exactly. As

58. For some initial arguments on why these bills were there, see Soetaert 2014, 58–60.

[72] Ehrlich, Ehrlich & Ehrlich 2015, 44–46. The couple married on December 3, 1936 in Nice. The owner of the house in the Boulevard de Cessole/Allée du souvenir, Antoinette Deroo, was one of the two witnesses at the marriage. See their marriage certificate at http://genebour.fr/media/an16/160504-18.jpg (accessed Jan. 13, 2021).

[73] I found Rudolf Pollak's name in "Switzerland, Jewish Arrivals, 1938–1945" at Ancestry.com, indicating he arrived there on May 13, 1943. The evidence obyvatelstva sheet for Pollak in the NA, Praha, gives April 30, 1943, as the date he left Prague, but instead of a destination the word "revision" is added. See NA, Praha, fonds Policejní ředitelství Praha II, evidence obyvatelstva, Rudolf Pollak 1910. More biographical information on the man can also be found in NA, Praha, fonds Policejní ředitelství Praha II, všeobecná spisovna, 1941–1950, kart. n° 8890, sign. P 2760/2, Rudolf Pollak 1910.

[74] Both were deported on transport "AAe" from Prague to Terezín, on June 20, 1942, and further transferred to Treblinka on transport "Bv" on October 15, 1942. See www.holocaust.cz (accessed Jan. 12, 2021).

[75] See the messages exchanged on the https://www.geneanet.org message board (dated Jan. 12, 2021) between Irène Pollak (account holder "ipollak") and the author.

[76] The couple had one daughter, M. Duviard, born during the war. I left a message (dated Jan. 12, 2020) for her account on the https://www.geneanet.org message board, but she preferred not to answer my inquiry about her uncle Rodolphe Pollak.

[77] Ehrlich, Ehrlich & Ehrlich 2015, 45–46.

[78] For Speyer's stay in the sanitarium in Villiers-sur-Marne, just outside of Paris, see AN, site Pierrefitte-sur-Seine, Direction générale de la sûreté nationale (fonds de Moscou), Walter Speyer 1903, file n° 211878, cote 19940474/374. This sanitarium still exists, but under the name CRF Villiers, Centre de Rééducation Fonctionnelle. An email and a letter sent to them in 2020 were ignored. The Archives départementales du Val-de-Marne, Créteil, does not hold the archives of the institution. See email (dated Sep 15, 2020) from Manon Isnard (Archives départementales du Val-de-Marne, Créteil) to the author. I also sent an online message to the city administration of Villiers-sur-Marne on January 9, 2021, but there was no reply.

[79] Ehrlich, Ehrlich & Ehrlich 2015, 44.

a Jewish man, he might have been shielded by his stay in the Joffre sanitarium in Champrosay (Draveil), just thirty kilometers south of Paris, bordering the vast Forêt de Sénart. Speyer suffered from tuberculosis and also had serious kidney problems. He had no income or financial resources whatsoever and claimed he had no one he could rely on. The Comité Juif d'Action Sociale et de Reconstruction (COJASOR) helped him out financially.[80] In February–March 1946, Speyer moved from Paris to the Agra sanitarium near Lugano. There he wrote two letters to the Swiss branch of the Intergovernmental Committee on Refugees in Geneva, asking for financial support. But there the trail ends.[81]

KARL GIESE AND VICTOR BAUER DO NET SEEM TO GET ALONG

Since 2014, when I published on the handling and settlement of Hirschfeld's estate, some progress has been made in trying to determine what happened in Nice, specifically on the involvement of Victor Bauer and his troupe, but several questions and issues still remain unresolved.[82] Above all, the exact role of the Nice public prosecutor continues to be very mysterious. For starters, supposing that Hirschfeld had a storage room, how was it possible that it and its contents were kept out of the inheritance procedure? Would this not be a case of fraud, possibly requiring the intervention of the Nice public prosecutor? Did the Nice prosecutor take the matter in hand, perhaps trying to find an elegant solution for the Institute materials? It is also strange that, on the basis of the existing archival sources, Karl Giese seems not to have been aware of the Nice dealings that, as we have seen, were handled, probably as early as the second half of 1935, by the group around Victor Bauer.

When, in January 1938, Ernst Maass sent a letter to Giese in which he asked for names of people in Nice he could contact regarding the Hirschfeld inheritance, Giese could think of no one except the Gordons and François Herzfelder, who had all by then moved to Paris.[83] That Giese did not even mention Victor Bauer is simply surprising. Nevertheless, Giese might have known something about the matter. In a letter to Max Hodann in September 1935, Giese said cryptically: "As far as the material lying in Nice is concerned, I cannot give any precise information about it, as I do not know exactly myself. [...] The valuable ethnological material is still not 'available' at the

[80] COJASOR, Paris, dossier Waldemar Speyer (born 1903), index card renseignements fournis par l'assisté (dated 1945). The Joffre sanitarium was also known as hôpital Joffre-Dupuytren. Champrosay is located in the région Île-de-France, département Essonne.

[81] See ITS database, Registrierungen und Akten von Displaced Persons, Kindern und Vermissten, Unterstützungsprogramme unterschiedlicher Organisationen, IRO "Care and Maintenance" Programm, 3.2.1.4 CM, Akten aus der Schweiz, Formulare und Begleitdokumente von DP´s in der Schweiz, sowie Schriftwechsel von IRO-Dienststellen in Deutschland, Österreich und dem Nahen Osten mit dem IRO-Hauptquartier in Genf, letters (dated Mar. 8, 1946 and Mar. 20, 1946) from Waldemar Speyer to Comité intergouvernemental pour les réfugiés in Genève/Genf. A letter (dated Apr. 4, 1946) in the same archival fonds from Mr. De Sibert of the French branch of the Comité, sent to Mr. Zwerner of the Swiss branch of the comité, advised that Waldemar Speyer would contact the COJASOR in Paris. But Speyer did not do that, as his COJASOR file points out. I thank Laure Politis (Fondation Casip-Cojasor, Paris) for her help in seeing the COJASOR file on Speyer in the summer of 2021. There was no further information on Speyer in the Archivio Storico Città di Lugano. See email (dated Feb. 23, 2021) from Damiano Robbiani (Archivio Storico Città di Lugano, Castagnola) to the author. On one of the sheets in the small ITS file on Speyer, there was also mention of a file on Speyer with the Eidgenössische Fremdenpolizei (file number n° 149.519) but most of these files have been discarded. See email (dated Feb. 16, 2021) from Guido Koller (Schweizerisches Bundesarchiv, Bern) to the author. The question on a stay permit for Speyer was also checked in the Archivio di Stato del Cantone Ticino but there was no archival trace of a *permesso di soggiorno* (residency permit) for Speyer in the archival fonds of the Ufficio degli Stranieri. See emails (dated Mar. 12, 2021) from Stefano Anelli (Archivio di Stato del Cantone Ticino, Bellinzona) to the author.

[82] Soetaert 2014.

[83] Archiv MHG, Berlin, fonds Ernst Maass, letter (dated Jan. 21, 1938, 2–3) from Karl Giese to Ernst Maass.

[84] Arbetarrörelsens arkiv och bibliotek, Stockholm, Max Hodann samling, vol. 15, letter (dated Sep. 24, 1935) from Karl Giese to Max Hodann: "Was das in

moment, I would say. I cannot be more specific about it".[84] Were the ethnological materials, for example, still stuck in customs in 1935–36 (because they had been sent from abroad?) or was the French justice system involved in some other way? Maybe the latter had confiscated the ethnological art objects because they were suspicious about their origins? In another letter to Max Hodann, a month later, on the topic of Hirschfeld's pictures still in Nice, Giese wrote about "sorrowful experiences" (*traurige Erfahrungen*) trying (in vain) to obtain reproductions. Another passage in the same letter seems to refer to the same stymied situation: "The other photos are all still in Nice, if they are available".[85] It is possible that Giese was aware of Victor Bauer's dealings with the Hirschfeld estate in Nice but had, legally or otherwise, nothing to say about it.

One may also wonder if the consideration that these (ethnological?) objects had belonged to the Institute foundation, and not Hirschfeld personally, might have operated as an argument preventing Giese from legally interfering here? But we have also seen that the deliberate omission from the estate of the (possible) Nice storage room might have backfired and alerted the Nice public prosecutor (*parquet*). This may have happened, for example, unlikely as it may seem, if payment of the rent for such a storage room was stopped, at which time, or some time afterwards, the contents surfaced. Was it maybe then that the contents of the storage room were auctioned off? It is also possible that the Nice public prosecutor only intervened once the objects had been auctioned off. Maybe there were suspicions about the provenance of the (mainly) ethnological objects. This might also explain why Wilhelm Reich had to return what he bought. And, last but not least, it is important to realize that Giese was abroad and not allowed to enter France. He must have felt quite frustrated that he could not really intervene.

It is possible that Giese asked Victor Bauer to make copies of the Hirschfeld pictures in Nice but received a negative answer or even no answer at all. A mysterious and unexplained part of the Nouveau diary fragment seems to point to Giese (and also Li Shiu Tong?) being in some kind of conflict with Bauer regarding the questionnaires and their further destiny. The fragment seems to indicate that Nouveau heard from Bauer that Giese and Li Shiu Tong had pressured Bauer regarding the completed questionnaires they were reviewing. Apparently, Giese wanted questionnaires of notable people to be anonymized.[86] We have already seen that, shortly after the looting of the Institute, Hirschfeld and Giese felt it important to let the outside world and the former Institute patients know that these questionnaires had not fallen into the wrong hands. In the same place, we also mentioned that Li Shiu Tong was also aware there were pressing issues with these questionnaires.

VICTOR AND BIANCA BAUER'S ATTEMPTS TO SELL SOME OF THE INSTITUTE MATERIALS

Victor Bauer might have given away some items from the Institute lot here and there but there are strong indications that he held onto some of the materials. Bauer

Nizza liegende Material anbelangt, so kann ich keine genaue Auskunft darüber geben, da ich es selbst nicht genau weiss. [...] Das wertvolle ethnologische Material ist zur Zeit noch immer nicht 'disponibel', wie ich mal sagen möchte. Ich kann mich da nicht näher auslassen".

[85] Arbetarrörelsens arkiv och bibliotek, Stockholm, Max Hodann samling, vol. 10, letter (dated Oct. 10, 1935, [3–4]) from Karl Giese to Max Hodann: "Die andere Photos sind alle noch in Nice, soweit vorhanden".

[86] "Sexualwisssenschaft V perversiones" 1995, entry 203, n.p., catalogue of Antiquariat Bernhard Richter: "Laut VB [Victor Bauer] wurden zwecks Vermeidung der von den Erben geplanten Erpressung, wichtige Fragebogen als 'Fälle' ohne Namen (= weggeschnitten) behalten" (According to VB [Victor Bauer], in order to avoid the extortion planned by the heirs, important questionnaires were kept as 'cases' without names (= cut away)". I have discussed this strange matter with Ralf Dose and he thinks that Victor Bauer and/or Henri Nouveau may have been fabulating. See email (dated Jan. 11, 2021) from Ralf Dose to the author.

remarried in 1950, after his 1947 divorce of his first wife, Irène Strauss.[87] In 1959, the year in which Victor Bauer died, his widow and second wife, Bianca Bauer (1905–1997), offered to sell all or some of the Institute materials still in their possession to the Kinsey Institute (Bloomington, Indiana, USA).[88] The widow asked for FF200,000, approximately €3,420 in today's money. But the Kinsey Institute chose not to accept the offer.[89]

On the other hand, the Kinsey Institute collection contains the so-called "Hirschfeld scrapbook", which possibly originated from the remains of Hirschfeld's estate that Bauer had in his possession in Nice. Alfred Kinsey himself would have acquired this scrapbook himself after World War II from someone in Nice.[90] Since Kinsey died in 1956, this sale must therefore have happened some time before.[91] Kinsey was in Europe in the last months of 1955, but a report about his trip makes no mention of his buying anything in France, where he visited. There is only a mention

[87] Victor Bauer married Irmgard Strauss on May 28, 1942 and divorced her on May 6, 1947. See email (dated Jul. 17, 2020) from Nicole Ehrlich to the author, with an attached digital copy of the divorce papers. See also Richter 1977, 89; Neumann 2011, 203.

[88] This means that some of the Hirschfeld and Institute materials were likely in the Villa Coromandel (1 Avenue Gravier) in the north of Nice until 1959. Following her husband's death, Bianca Bauer then moved to Saint-Paul-de-Vence, where she died in 1997. She was also a Freud specialist. Bianca Bauer's previous married name was Seybert. She was deported from Drancy to Auschwitz-Birkenau (as Blanche Seybert) in convoy n° 70 on March 27, 1944. Her husband was likely Salvator Seybert (1900–?), a medical student in Vienna before being rejected by the university. See https://gedenkbuch.univie.ac.at/index.php?id=435&no_cache=1&L=2&person_single_id=12622&person_name=&person_geburtstag_tag=not_selected&person_geburtstag_monat=not_selected&person_geburtstag_jahr=not_selected&person_fakultaet=not_selected&person_kategorie=not_selected&person_volltextsuche=&search_person.x=1&result_page=123 (accessed Jul. 21, 2020). He was deported on the same convoy as Bianca Bauer. It is not known if he survived the war but an Austrian database of Holocaust victims claims he perished in the Shoah: https://www.doew.at/result (accessed Jul. 21, 2020). The biography of his sister, the photographer Lisette Model (1901–1983), gives a good idea of the societal position of the Vienna family. See https://www.deutsche-biographie.de/sfz63795.html#ndbcontent_sfz64682 (accessed Jul. 21, 2020). There are some postcards (from 1938–40) that mention Salva and Bianca in the Lisette Model fonds in the National Gallery of Canada.

[89] Seehttps://www.insee.fr/fr/information/2417794 (accessed Jul. 14, 2020). In response to inflation, the new French franc was introduced the following year, in 1960. To compare, the income side of the Hirschfeld inheritance, in 1936, was around FF340,000, then still worth €260,849. See Soetaert 2014, 35 and n. 84. The information on Bianca Bauer's 1959 offer comes from the Paul Gebhard correspondence at the Kinsey Institute and was communicated to MHG, Berlin, by Annette F. Timm, professor of history at the University of Calgary in Alberta (Canada). See the editor's note in Soetaert 2014, 60 n. 151.

[90] For the rumor that Alfred Kinsey bought it himself, see Pfäfflin & Herzer 1998, 2; Dose & Herrn 2006, 49; and email (dated Nov. 10, 2020) from Ralf Dose to the author. Since Victor Bauer was still alive in 1956, he might have been the one offering to sell the "Hirschfeld scrapbook" to Kinsey. I asked the Kinsey Institute if there existed any correspondence between Victor Bauer and Kinsey but there was none. I also asked them to check if the other names attached to the Nice story (Henri Nouveau, Henri Goetz, Siegfried Bernfeld, Roger du Teil, François Herzfelder, Waldemar Speyer, Rodolphe [Rudolf] Pollak, and Odette Jorel) might have corresponded with Kinsey, but they had not. See emails (dated Dec. 7, 2020 and Dec. 11, 2020) from Shawn Wilson (Kinsey Institute, Bloomington, Indiana) to the author.

[91] Dose & Herrn 2006, 49. The scrapbook, according to the Kinsey Institute's online library catalogue, was compiled by Carl Theodor Hoefft (1855–1927), a German member of the local Hamburg chapter of the Wissenschaftlich-humanitären Komitee (WhK). A part of the "Hirschfeld scrapbook" does indeed contain reports of reunions of local German chapters of the WhK. Hoefft died in 1927 but the scrapbook also includes documents of a later date, which indicates it is indeed a potpourri of materials. It is not known when it was assembled or by whom. Items from the "Hirschfeld scrapbook" in the Kinsey Institute Library archival collection are spread out over four flat boxes. See https://iucat.iu.edu/kinsey/7910463 and https://kinseyinstitute.org/collections/archival/sex-researchers-collections.php (both accessed Nov. 10, 2020). A list with an overview of the different items can be found in Pfäfflin & Herzer 1998, 20–21. See also Keilson-Lauritz & Pfäfflin 1999, 33–35; Keilson-Lauritz & Pfäfflin 2000, 2–33; and Keilson-Lauritz & Pfäfflin 2003, 1–2. A partly digitized version of the "Magnus Hirschfeld Scrapbook" can be seen at https://search.alexanderstreet.com/ (accessed Oct. 14, 2020). Another overview can be found in the online catalogue of the University of Toronto Libraries by typing "Magnus Hirschfeld Scrapbook" in the search bar: https://onesearch.library.utoronto.ca/ (accessed Oct. 18, 2020).

of his buying things in Spain.[92] We have already mentioned Arnold van Gennep's completed questionnaire, which showed up in a Parisian antiquarian bookstore in 1944. The Kinsey Institute also has a completed questionnaire in their holdings. It was filled out by a Jewish man in 1900 and forms part of the "Hirschfeld scrapbook".[93] The presence of this completed questionnaire seems to further confirm that Kinsey indeed bought what is now known as the "Hirschfeld scrapbook" in Nice, likely from Victor Bauer himself.

Around 1960, Bianca Bauer probably contacted the gay German sexologist Hans Giese (1920–1970) in another attempt to sell the remains of the Institute collection that stayed in Nice. Hans Giese was one of the foremost names in sexology in post-war Germany and one of the people who tried to revive, in his own way, Hirschfeld's legacy after the war. He and Kurt Hiller contributed, for example, to the short-lived attempt to bring back the Wissenschaftlich-humanitären Komitee (WhK).[94] A French translation of Giese's 1958 book, *Der homosexuelle Mann in der Welt* came out in 1959, the year that Victor Bauer died. This may explain why Bianca Bauer contacted Hans Giese [ill. 8].[95] Most likely, she momentarily mistook Hans Giese for Karl Giese.[96] Hans Giese went to see the widow, then living in Saint-Paul-de-Vence, but apparently no agreement was reached on a good price for the Hirschfeld and Institute materials. Or, possibly, Giese was not sufficiently impressed by the materials, like the person who checked them for the Kinsey Institute, a certain professor Carl Max Hasselmann (1897–1973) from Erlangen, who from 1954 until 1958 was the chairman of the Deutsche Gesellschaft für Sexualforschung (DGfS) ... an association founded by Hans Giese in 1950 (and which still exists today).[97]

Hans Giese developed a friendship with Bianca Bauer because he was interested in modern art and the work of her late husband. Giese tried to introduce Victor Bauer's work into the German art market, but failed. He had borrowed some paintings from the widow but, as a consequence of his sudden death, these were never returned and stayed in the Giese family. Apparently, Hans Giese also owned a painting by Henri Nouveau.[98] When visiting the widow, in the summer of 1970, Hans Giese was found dead after a fall from a cliff, a death still wrapped in mystery. Giese's boyfriend, the twenty-seven-year-old actor Klaus Hartmann, who had travelled with him to France, was at first suspected.[99]

In July 2013, Ralf Dose sought contact with a good friend of Bianca Bauer, Lothar Neumann (living in Saint-Paul-de-Vence), who in 2011 had published a book on Victor Bauer's paintings; however, Neumann claimed to have nothing from the Institute lot, except a few already known photos of Hirschfeld.[100] The German professor and

[92] Kinsey Institute, Bloomington (Indiana), Alfred C. Kinsey archival collection, Box 1, Series 1B, Folder 1, Alfred C. Kinsey's Journal of 1955 European Trip dictated by Dr. Kinsey at staff meetings. See p. 12/12/1955 and p. 12/17/55 (21) for Kinsey buying "sex books" that, in his own words, were plentiful in Barcelona (Spain). He might indeed have gone from Italy to Spain along the French Côte d'Azur and made a stop in Nice.

[93] Kinsey Institute Library & Special Collections, Bloomington (Indiana), Hirschfeld scrapbook, call n° X7910463, Fragebogen filled out on Apr. 21, 1932 by the Jewish man W. S. (or J.) (n° 100) born on Mar. 28, 1900.

[94] Wolfert 2015b; Dannecker 2009; and In het Panhuis Jun. 26, 2020.

[95] Giese 1959.

[96] Jens Dobler, who consulted the private archives of Hans Giese in the Bundesarchiv in Koblenz, confirmed to me that several people indeed thought that Hans Giese was Magnus Hirschfeld's assistant and thus confused Hans Giese with Karl Giese. See email (dated Feb. 9, 2023) from Jens Dobler to the author.

[97] See "Editor's Note", Soetaert 2014, 60 n. 151; Sigusch 2008, 415–16, 418; https://dgfs.info/ueber-die-dgfs/ (accessed Jul. 15, 2020).

[98] Neumann 2011, 207.

[99] In het Panhuis, Jun. 26, 2020; Neumann 2011, 207–8; "Natürlich idiotisch", *Der Spiegel*, June 26, 1971, 74–75, available online at: http://magazin.spiegel.de/EpubDelivery/spiegel/pdf/43144271 (accessed Jul. 15, 2020).

[100] Neumann 2011; email (dated Jun. 29, 2013) from Ralf Dose to the author.

sociologist Hubert W. Krantz (1942–2004), living in Aachen, was Bianca Bauer's main beneficiary after her death in 1997.[101] In the early 1970s, he managed to introduce Bauer's work into the German art market through Helmut Dreiseitel's gallery in Köln.[102] It is not known if Krantz also inherited any Institute materials. But Ralf Dose believes that Neumann, who nursed Bianca Bauer in her last years, would have known and told him if there were any left in her estate.[103] Dose also wrote to me that Bianca Bauer simply did not talk with Lothar Neumann about the prewar period.[104] Dose also thinks that Krantz most likely only inherited paintings from Bianca Bauer and therefore did not pursue that trace any further.[105] After I inquired, Dose wrote that he had indeed followed the trail of Hans Giese's boyfriend, as he was, of course, possibly a good witness regarding the matter. However, Klaus Hartmann was dead and the efforts by Dose and Lothar Neumann to get into contact in 2013 with Hartmann's boyfriend, a certain Horst Langeloh, failed because Langeloh did not answer them.

Likely, attempts to find the remains of Hirschfeld's Institute materials that ended up in France will not stop there. Jens Dobler told me that, in February 2023, he found further clues on what exactly happened in Nice in the private archives of Hans Giese in the Bundesarchiv in Koblenz.[106] That likely means that Bianca Bauer told Giese what she had heard from her husband Victor Bauer about the dealings in Nice regarding a part of Hirschfeld's estate. In 2023, Thomas Hirschbiegel, a Hamburg journalist, found two more completed Institute questionnaires in a flea market in Hamburg. One of them was filled out in May 1929 by a Hamburg merchant named Christian D.[107] Since Hans Giese lived in Hamburg for the last twelve years of his life, it is possible that these came from his estate and that Giese obtained them from Bauer's widow in Nice.[108] Maybe he picked one up specifically from a man living in Hamburg? The four *completed* questionnaires, now known worldwide, show that not all the questionnaires were burned in Nice by Bauer and Nouveau.

FRANÇOIS HERZFELDER'S ROLE

All these elements clearly show that something was indeed afoot with a significant batch of Institute materials in 1935–36, yet we still lack decisive elements that would further explain what exactly happened at the time. François Herzfelder, the executor of the Hirschfeld estate, would most probably have had the answer to many of these unanswered questions. Interestingly, Herzelfder asked the notary Pierre Demnard for several extracts from the Hirschfeld notary file in this period. For example, at the end of May 1936, he asked for a copy of the inventory of the furnishings of Hirschfeld's apartment.[109] He also asked for a copy of Hirschfeld's handwritten will in

[101] The biographical data on Hubert W. Krantz are very scarce. I only know of his 1975 dissertation on Walter Rathenau (see Krantz 1976), and that he received a Verdienstkreuz erster Klasse (Cross of Merit, First Class) in the year of his death. See https://www.aachener-nachrichten.de/lokales/aachen/er-kaempfte-um-arbeitsplaetze-in-aachen_aid-31998063 (accessed Jul. 15, 2020).

[102] Neumann 2011, 19; Richter 1977.

[103] Email (dated Jan. 28, 2014) from Ralf Dose to the author.

[104] Email (dated Jul. 29, 2013) from Ralf Dose to the author.

[105] Email (dated Jul. 15 2020) from Ralf Dose to the author.

[106] Communication (dated May 10, 2023) from Jens Dobler to the author. Dobler looked at this archival fonds for his research project, "Die Plünderung des Instituts für Sexualwissenschaft in der NS-Zeit" (the looting of the Institute of Sexual Science in the Nazi era). See *Mitteilungen der Magnus-Hirschfeld-Gesellschaft* 69–70 (December 2022): 4.

[107] Hirschbiegel, May 6–7, 2023, 46-47. I thank Ralf Dose for informing me of this spectacular find and sending me a digital copy of the newspaper clipping reporting on it.

[108] Hergemöller 2010, 403.

[109] See the handwritten inscription – "Extrait [copy] remis à M. Herzfelder le 29 mai 36. [signature Herzfelder]" – on the reverse side of the brown cover sheet in ADAM, Nice, Archives notariales, minutes notariales étude Pierre Demnard, May 24, 1935, n° 569, cote 03E 148/011.

[110] See the handwritten mentions of Demnard, also on the reverse side of the brown cover sheet of ADAM, Nice, Archives notariales, minutes notariales étude Pierre Demnard, May 22, 1935, n° 563, cote 03E 148/011.

February 1936.[110] And lastly, Herzfelder also incurred expenses, clearly related to the inheritance procedure, for a trip to Paris in February 1936.[111] But with what purpose? Were there still things stored in Paris? We do not know. But the visit might have been related to dealings with Victor Bauer in the first months of 1936.

Franz Herzfelder was born in Münich in 1901. His parents were Felix Herzfelder (1863–1944), a lawyer, and Emma Oberndoerffer (1873–1941).[112] After first moving to Istanbul, most of Herzfelder's close family members eventually emigrated to Israel.[113] Herzfelder was a lawyer in Munich and worked in his father's office.[114] In May 1931, Herzfelder married his non-Jewish wife Ierta Haensel (1907–?). In June 1933, shortly after the ban on Jewish lawyers pursuing their profession in Nazi Germany, he moved to Paris.[115] In August 1933, Herzfelder moved to Nice where he worked as a court translator in the Tribunal de première instance and as international legal advisor (*conseiller juridique international*) for an unknown Nice law firm.[116] He returned to Paris in November 1936. In December 1939, he joined the Foreign Legion for a short time. It was not very exceptional for a Jewish man at the time to join the Foreign Legion. Robert Kirchberger, Hirschfeld's last secretary, did the same but remained in the Foreign Legion ranks until 1944.[117] Starting in January 1941, joined by his wife, Herzfelder became an undercover farmhand in the village of Pardaillan in the département Lot-et-Garonne. He lived in hiding in this way until the end of the war.[118] After the war, Herzfelder worked as a lawyer specializing in war reparations linked to

[111] See the expenses (dated Feb. 12, 1936) in Soetaert 2014, 53, Table 9, overview of expenses and honorary fee Herzfelder. This Paris visit was apparently not the one Herzfelder mentioned to Ernst Maass. In a letter from early December 1935, Herzfelder told Maass that he was going to Paris to see Günter Hauck, a relative of Magnus Hirschfeld. See Archiv MHG, Berlin, fonds Ernst Maass, letter (dated Dec. 8, 1935) from François Herzfelder to Ernst Maass.

[112] Ralf Dose instigated the quest to identify Herzfelder more thoroughly, using information he found mainly in Ladwig-Winters & Rechtsanwaltskammer Berlin 2007, 96; and on Herzfelder's death certificate. See emails (February 2012) from Ralf Dose to the author. I thank Ralf Dose for sharing this information.

[113] See https://www.juedisches-museum-muenchen.de/fileadmin/redaktion/03_Museum/Publikationen/ Downloads/Exil_1_Broschu__re.pdf, 23–25 (accessed Jul. 13, 2020). François Herzfelder's two sisters were Magda Goldschmidt (1898–1941), who perished in the Holocaust, and Rosy (Rose) Hellmann (1895–1982). In October 2014, I had a telephone conversation with (Marianne) Miriam Schmidt (1928–2020), a daughter of Rosy Hellman. She gave me some good leads but these did not eventuate in anything; see further.

[114] Heusler & Sinn 2015, 220.

[115] AN, site de Pierrefitte-sur-Seine, Ministère de la Justice, Sous-direction des naturalisations (1976–1980), file Franz Herzfelder, dossier n° 52713X38, cote 19770898/197. Herzfelder's new Paris address (19 Rue du Dr. Heulin, Paris XVII) is mentioned in two sources: in a letter (dated Jan. 21, 1938, 2) from Karl Giese to Ernst Maass; and in a letter (dated Mar. 3, 1938, 1) from François Herzfelder to Ernst Maass. Both letters are in the Archiv MHG, Berlin, fonds Ernst Maass. Herzfelder stayed at this address until the beginning of the war.

[116] Heusler & Sinn 2015, 221–22. In the record of a court session, Herzfelder was described as "international traducteur [*sic*] juré près le [*sic*] Tribunal civil de Nice". See ADAM, Nice, Archives notariales, minutes notariales étude Pierre Demnard, Sep. 28, 1935, n° 976, cote 03E 148/019. Herzfelder's letterhead says the same: "Docteur en droit / conseil juridique international / [text added with rubber stamp:] traducteur juré près le [*sic*] tribunal civil de Nice / Allemand / Anglais / Italien". See Archiv MHG, Berlin, fonds Ernst Maass, letter (dated Jan. 28, 1936) from François Herzfelder to Ernst Maass. It is not known how Hirschfeld made Herzfelder's acquaintance in Nice, but Herzfelder's naturalization file states that he lived in Berlin with a certain Mrs. Hirschfeld (at 5 Landhausstrasse) for a few months in 1928. Was this lady related to Magnus Hirschfeld? See AN, site de Pierrefitte-sur-Seine, Ministère de la Justice, Sous-direction des naturalisations (1976–1980), file Franz Herzfelder, dossier n° 52713X38, cote 19770898/197.

[117] In 2015, the Mémorial de la Shoah in Paris mounted an exposition on the subject entitled "Les engagés volontaires juifs étrangers dans les armées françaises durant les deux guerres mondiales". See http://www.fondationshoah.org/memoire/les-juifs-etrangers-ont-defendu-la-france (accessed Apr. 27, 2018). The surviving Jewish volunteers and their relatives have their own association in France: http://www.combattantvolontairejuif.org/3.html (accessed Apr. 27, 2018). For more on Kirchberger joining the Foreign Legion, see Soetaert 2018, 15. The German painter Hans Hartung (1904–1989) also joined the Legion. See Neumann 2011, 206. Through Henri Goetz's wife, Christine Boumeester, Hartung was also part of Goetz's circle.

[118] AN, site de Pierrefitte-sur-Seine, Ministère de la Justice, Sous-direction des naturalisations (1976–1980), file Franz Herzfelder, dossier n° 52713X38, cote

Nazi Germany (*Wiedergutmachung*), focusing also on victims of the Spanish Civil War. There are, for example, several archival traces indicating Herzfelder's professional activity in the archives of the American Jewish Joint Distribution Committee (JDC).[119] Herzfelder was also the general secretary (*Generalsekretär*) of the Association pour la défense des intérêts de l'axe (ADIVA, 19 Rue de Téhéran, Paris VIII), which assisted Nazi war victims who could not afford a lawyer.[120] After a first unsuccessful attempt in 1937, Herzfelder and his wife Ierta Haensel reapplied immediately at the end of the war to be naturalized as French. They were both naturalized in October 1946. In 1966, Franz Herzfelder also officially changed his first and middle name from Franz Jakob to François Jacques.[121]

Herzfelder remained interested in the further fate of the Hirschfeld estate practically until his retirement. He seems to have kept in contact with Hirschfeld's former friends also. In a July 1937 letter to the French Minister of Justice regarding his naturalization, Herzfelder named as one of his two references Dr. Jean Dalsace who, as we have seen, knew Hirschfeld.[122] Hirschfeld's last secretary, Robert Kirchberger, also sought out Herzfelder after the war in relation to his reparations case against the German state in 1947–61.[123] That Herzfelder's interest in the fate of the Hirschfeld estate continued after the war is further testified by a letter he wrote to the publisher Montaigne in 1953, asking how much money the publisher still owed to Hirschfeld's heirs.[124] That his interest in the matter even persisted until he retired as a lawyer seems attested by a document seen by Ralf Dose: "I remember a letter from Herzfelder to the German Wiedergutmachungskammer [Reparations Chamber] or the Nachlassgericht [Probate Court] saying that he would give up his law practice and thus no longer be able to act as executor for Hirschfeld's will. That letter was dated some time in the 1960s".[125] In addition to being and remaining the executor of Hirschfeld's estate, Herzfelder seems to have preserved an interest in the whole Hirschfeld affair for more personal reasons, though it is not known what exactly triggered his interest and concern. In one rare letter, in which he seems to lapse from

19770898/197. One source claims Herzfelder (though presumably not his wife) was held in several French camps that imprisoned rounded-up Jewish people around 1940–41. See Heusler & Sinn 2015, 220.

[119] It is enough to type Herzfelder's name in the search bar of http://archives.jdc.org/ (accessed Jul. 11, 2020). Herzfelder also published on international law. See, for example, Herzfelder 1978.

[120] For more information on the ADIVA, its links with the London-based United Restitution Office (URO), and Herzfelder's involvement, see Herzfelder's own biographical text, "Une longue marche: souvenirs et réflexions", which mainly focuses on his professional activity. See Herzfelder 1976/2015, 220–29. For Herzfelder's specific involvement in Robert Kirchberger's case, see Kirchberger's Wiedergutmachungs file in Landesamt für Finanzen (Rheinland-Pfalz, Koblenz), Außenstelle Amt für Wiedergutmachung (Rheinland-Pfalz, Saarburg) (vormaliges Landesamt für Wiedergutmachung und verwaltete Vermögen Rheinland-Pfalz (Mainz), Bezirksamt für Wiedergutmachung und verwaltete Vermögen (Koblenz), Entschädigungssache Robert, André and Fanny Kirchberger, sign. 20007/20008/20009/c 10 M.

[121] Both were naturalized by décret 8670-46 (dated Oct. 8, 1946), see AN, site de Pierrefitte-sur-Seine, Ministère de la Justice, Sous-direction des naturalisations (1976–1980), file Franz Herzfelder, dossier n° 52713X38, cote 19770898/197.

[122] AN, site de Pierrefitte-sur-Seine, Ministère de la Justice, Sous-direction des naturalisations (1976–1980), file Franz Herzfelder, dossier n° 52713X38, cote 19770898/197, letter dated (Jul. 13, 1937) from François Herzfelder to the French Minister of Justice.

[123] AN, site de Pierrefitte-sur-Seine, Ministère de la Justice, Sous-direction des naturalisations (1976–1980), file Robert Kirchberger, dossier n° 39798x45, cote 19770907/122 ; and Soetaert 2018, 15–16.

[124] IMEC Abbaye d'Ardenne, Saint-Germain-la-Blanche-Herbe, Fonds Aubier-Montaigne, P 7.1., Service éditorial, letter (dated Jul. 20, 1956) from François Herzfelder to Editions Montaigne. The publisher replied that nothing was owing to Hirschfeld's estate. See, ibid., letter (dated Jul. 23, 1956) from Editions Montaigne to François Herzfelder. It remains unclear who exactly Herzfelder had in mind as entitled to royalties from Hirschfeld's books, since Karl Giese was dead by 1956 (as was his heir, Karl Fein).

[125] Email (dated Feb. 20, 2012) from Ralf Dose to the author. See also Dose 2012, 8: "The source included the information that Dr. Franz Herzfelder had closed his law office at the end of the 1960s, and therefore

his usual neutral professional attitude, he briefly mentions his dismay at hearing that the Hirschfeld materials were confiscated by the police after Karl Giese's suicide.[126]

Herzfelder's last wife was Heikki Aina Van Toym (1926–2012), with whom he had two (unidentified) children.[127] In 2016, I managed to contact Van Toym's last partner, Heinz-Gerd H. Over the telephone, he told me that Herzfelder's client files had been picked up shortly after his death in Paris in 1998 by an institute, archive or university – but he did not know its name. My numerous attempts to locate these files in an archive in France or elsewhere have so far been unsuccessful.[128] This means that, if Herzfelder's client files survived, the file on his handling of Hirschfeld's estate might be among them. Locating the Herzfelder client files – by trying to identify, find, and contact his current relatives – therefore remains an absolute priority if we want some day to discover and understand all the details of what exactly happened in Nice in 1935–36 in the circle around Victor Bauer and the exact involvement of the Nice public prosecutor.[129]

ERNST MAASS, KARL GIESE, AND LI SHIU TONG ALL TOOK SOME MATERIALS FROM NICE

Besides this somewhat frustrating tangle of loose threads whose precise interrelation must, for now, remain partly unexplained, in three instances there is much greater clarity about the fate of other Hirschfeld or Institute materials in Nice at the time of Hirschfeld's death in May 1935. Li Shiu Tong, Karl Giese, and Ernst Maass all took some of these materials with them when they left Nice. Li Shiu Tong eventually took these materials to Vancouver, Canada, Ernst Maass took his portion to New York, USA. And Karl Giese eventually watched over his part in Brno, Czechoslovakia in 1936–38.

asked the Berlin probate court to name someone else as an executor (which was never done)".

126 Archiv MHG, Berlin, fonds Ernst Maass, letter (dated Aug. 24, 1938) from François Herzfelder to Ernst Maass.

127 Van Toym, originally from Tallinn (Estland), worked as Herzfelder's secretary. Herzfelder ended up marrying her twice. See the telephone conversation (dated Oct. 22, 2014) between Miriam Schmidt and the author. Van Toym was buried in Estland. See the telephone conversation (dated Oct. 22, 2014) between Heinz-Gerd H. and the author. I am not certain if this last piece of information is correct since neither Van Toym (nor her married name Herzfelder) could be located at https://www.kalmistud.ee/ (accessed Jul. 12, 2020).

128 Telephone conversation (dated Oct. 22, 2014) between Heinz-Gerd H. and the author. I do not know if the information about the safeguarding of Herzfelder's client files is correct. I have asked the following if they hold the Herzfelder archives: the Archives Nationales in Paris, Archives de Paris, archive of the Sorbonne university, Archivo General de la Guerra Civil Española (Salamanca, Spain), Mémorial de la Shoah (Paris), and l'Alliance Israélite Universelle (Paris). All said they did not have them. Since 2014, I have written several letters (and also made several telephone calls) to Heinz-Gerd H., to further inquire about the matter, but all my later attempts at contacting him were ignored. Following valuable advice (given to me by Catherine Levy [and Adrien A.] of the Cercle de Généalogie Juive [Paris] in September 2021), I also contacted the Chambre interdépartementale des notaires de Paris. On November 8, 2021, following the latter's advice, I left a search message under "recherche de Notaire en charge d'une succession" (search for notary in charge of a succession) on the Paris notaries' website, https://paris.notaires.fr/, to identify the notary in charge of Herzfelder's succession. Unfortunately, no notary contacted me.

129 In 2012, Ralf Dose and Kevin Dubout also attempted to contact the current family, based on information on Herzfelder's death certificate. Herzfelder's last Paris address was 23 Rue Berlioz, Paris XVI. Thilla Koïta was the name of the employee who reported his death. On July 12, 2020, I left a message on the Facebook page of the homonymous "Thilla Koita", but there was no reply. On July 13, 2020, I contacted Miriam Schmidt's surviving husband, Mr. Zeev Schmidt, and asked him again for the contact information of Herzfelder's current relatives. My attempts – based on information given by his late wife over the telephone in 2014 – led to nothing. I thank Avi Haimovsky for his help in providing the correct spelling of Mr. Schmidt's email address, over the telephone. Unfortunately, Mr. Schmidt let me know that he could not help me further. See email (dated Jul. 18, 2020) from Zeev Schmidt to the author. A letter I sent to the Barreau de Paris (Paris Bar) was answered on September 21, 2020, by Agnès Wojciechowski (Ordre des avocats de Paris, Service du Patrimone), who told me they did not have the archives of Herzfelder's law office, nor did they know where they were, adding that Herzfelder was never a member of the Barreau de Paris.

ERNST MAASS TAKES MATERIALS TO NEW YORK

Ernst Maass took some documents related to Hirschfeld when he emigrated to New York in March 1938. He sailed from the French port of Le Havre on March 9, 1938, and arrived in the port of New York with his mother, Lotte Maass (1889–1971), on March 16, 1938.[130] In a July 1939 letter, Maass wrote: "A part of the papers [Hirschfeld] left was given to me, as I was a close friend of my uncle's".[131] These papers resurfaced in New York in December 2009. Some months after our October 2009 research trip to Nice, Don McLeod managed to contact one of Ernst Maass' two sons, Robert Maass (1956–), in New York.[132] Only a few months before, Robert Maass acquired from his mother the items his father had taken into safety in 1938. In 2010, after Don McLeod and Ralf Dose visited Rob Maass in New York, the latter generously offered to donate the many relevant materials safeguarded by his father to the Magnus-Hirschfeld-Gesellschaft in Berlin, where they are now part of the Ernst Maass fonds [ill. 9].[133]

It is not known with certainty when the decision was taken to entrust Ernst Maass with a part of the Hirschfeld papers, but it seems to have been in the weeks after Hirschfeld's death, when Giese, Li Shiu Tong, and Maass were still in Nice. It is also possible, yet much less probable, that Maass acquired materials from Victor Bauer in Nice. As we have seen, Maass was aware of the circle associated with Victor Bauer when he compiled a list of people involved in handling that part of Hirschfeld's estate possibly kept in a storage room in Nice.[134] Presumably, he obtained these names from François Herzfelder, and went to see Bauer in Nice, shortly before emigrating to the USA.[135] If Maass did indeed go to see Bauer, everything must have happened very quickly. Herzfelder only answered Maass' inquiry by letter, on March 3, saying that he could not meet Maass at the Café Weber in Paris on Saturday, March 5.[136] They may have only spoken over the phone, with Maass writing the names of the Bauer circle on the letter from Herzfelder. Theoretically, it would have been possible to travel to Nice and return to Paris; however, time was tight since Maass left Le Havre, as already noted, on Wednesday March 9. Which simply makes it much more likely that all the materials Maass safeguarded were only entrusted to him in Nice in the weeks after Hirschfeld's death, in May–July 1935.

What is certain in any case is that Maass was very anxious to safeguard the remaining Institute and Hirschfeld papers and materials. Possibly, his "uncle"

[130] McLeod 2012, 8. I thank Ralf Dose for sharing the document showing the departure date of the ship.

[131] Archiv MHG, Berlin, fonds Ernst Maass, letter (dated Jul. 13, 1939) from Ernst Maass to Françoise Lafitte-Cyon (1886–1974). The latter was a partner of the English sexologist Havelock Ellis. The familial relationship Maas expresses here – that Hirschfeld was his uncle – was not genealogically correct; however, in their letters, Hirschfeld and Maass sometimes addressed each other as uncle and nephew.

[132] The account of Don McLeod's major discovery, almost solely reliant on internet sources, is given in McLeod 2012; Dose 2011, 12–13; and Dose 2012. One important factor that prevented the earlier discovery of Ernst Maass was his changing his first name from Ernst to Ernest at some point in his emigration to the USA. The brother of Robert Maass is David Maass (1954–).

[133] An inventory list of Robert Maass' donation is in Dose 2011, 15-20.

[134] Archiv MHG, Berlin, fonds Ernst Maass, letter (dated Mar. 3, 1938) from Franz Herzfelder to Ernst Maass.

[135] Ernst Maass and his mother Lotte Maass first tried to settle in Palestine but did not like it there because of conflicts with the Arabs. Giese seems to have reacted to this theme, brought up in a letter Ernst Maass sent him earlier. See Archiv MHG, Berlin, fonds Ernst Maass, letter (dated Dec. 27, 1937, 4) from Karl Giese to Ernst Maass. Maass and his mother returned to Europe, France being their last stop before they emigrated to the USA.

[136] Café Weber was located at 31 Rue Royale, Paris VIII. The café had a superb view of the Eglise de la Madeleine. Li Shiu Tong liked to go there with Hirschfeld. See Broers 2016b, entry dated Jul. 19, 1934: "Tao sleepte ons in zijn Opel naar Weber in Rue Royal [*sic*] over de wondermooi verlichte boulevards. Ik woon inderdaad puik" (Tao dragged us in his Opel to Weber in Rue Royale, across the wonderfully lit boulevards. I live here poshly indeed). For German translations of Broers 2016b, see Bergemann & Keilson-Lauritz 2020.

[137] Ernst Maass ended his professional career working at the Dag Hammarskjöld Library at the United

Magnus Hirschfeld had instilled in him the consciousness of the fragility of the Hirschfeld papers, and of the remains of the Institute collection, which continued to be vulnerable to possible antisemitic attacks. His above-mentioned inquiry to François Herzfelder, after the war, asking if Hirschfeld's grave was still intact, seems to point to this kind of sensitivity.[137] Indeed, he also asked François Herzfelder that same question in a January 1938 letter, when returning from Palestine.[138] We also gather, from a reply that Giese sent Maass from Brno, in January 1938, that Maass had inquired about the location of the diaries and the guestbooks that Hirschfeld kept on his world trip. The same letter makes it clear that Maass intended to make a trip through France, concerning this matter, and asked Giese for names of people he should visit. This was when Giese failed to mention the name of Victor Bauer, and the people gathered around him, in the first months of 1936, regarding further dealings with the Hirschfeld estate.[139]

The Ernst Maass fonds also contains another list of names, also compiled by Ernst Maass, entitled "Friends of Magnus Hirschfeld" (*Freunde von Magnus Hirschfeld*).[140] Maass likely put together this list to further document the network around his "uncle". In any case, it is clear that Maass felt a real concern, in the three months before his departure for the USA, to help preserve the materials from Hirschfeld's estate or at least to determine where its dispersed remnants were located. Maass did so out of a sense of caution, clearly not knowing what lay ahead for Europe as the threat of war only increased. As soon as the war ended, Ernst Maass (by then Ernest Maass) took up the matter again briefly, and contacted, for example, the notary Pierre Demnard in Nice to ask for a copy of Hirschfeld's will.[141]

The materials found in New York in 2009 at the apartment of Ernst Maass' son, Robert Maass, were very diverse and also included Ernst Maass' personal and family archives and items specifically related to the Mann family. One of Hirschfeld's sisters, Franziska (1859–1927) took on the married name of Mann. The Mann family name was certainly one of the factors in choosing the Hirschfeld materials that Ernst Maass eventually took with him to New York. This could be a further argument that the triage (sorting) was done in the Gloria Mansions I apartment, supposedly with Giese's approval, in the weeks after Hirschfeld's death. There were certainly items in the Ernst Maass lot that could only have belonged to Hirschfeld: some correspondence, photographs, newspaper clippings, etc. There is also the slight possibility that, in the first months of 1938, Maass went to see Giese in Brno to pick up some materials. That is why I asked Robert Maass, in November 2014 and July 2020, if his father's passport(s) still existed. This could confirm whether Ernst Maass made such a trip to Brno or not. But, for now, there is no trace of this passport.[142]

Nations in New York, indicating a predilection for books and documents. See McLeod 2012, 9–10.

[138] Archiv MHG, Berlin, fonds Ernst Maass, letter (dated Jan. 25, 1938) from François Herzfelder to Ernst Maass.

[139] Archiv MHG, Berlin, fonds Ernst Maass, letter (dated Jan. 21, 1938) from Karl Giese to Ernst Maass. It was in this letter that Giese provided the contact infomation for François Herzfelder in Paris. It must be said that Maass procrastinated. He did not contact Herzfelder until the beginning of March 1938, only a few days before he emigrated to the USA.

[140] Archiv MHG, Berlin, fonds Ernst Maass, list "Freunde von Magnus Hirschfeld". Robert Maass also thinks that the handwriting belonged to his father. See email (dated Jul. 17, 2020) from Robert Maass to author.

[141] See Demnard's handwritten mention of this on the reverse side of the brown cover sheet of ADAM, Nice, Archives notariales, minutes notariales étude Pierre Demnard, May 22, 1935, n° 563, cote 03E 148/011. Most likely, a copy of the will was sent to New York in August 1945. The same archival folder contains a letter (dated Jun. 16, 1945) from Ernest [*sic*] Maass to Pierre Demnard, in which Maass asks for a copy; and also a letter (dated Jan. 19, 1946) from Ernest Maass to Pierre Demnard, in which Maass acknowledges receipt of the copy of the will and states that he paid Demnard for the service. A copy of the first letter (dated Jun. 16, 1945) can also be found in the Archiv MHG, Berlin, fonds Ernst Maass.

[142] Emails (dated Nov. 11, 2014 and Jul. 20, 2020) from Robert Maass to the author.

When he was still in Nice, toward the end of May 1935, Karl Giese wrote to Max Reiss in the Netherlands: "We are in the process now of sorting through the material".[143] This one phrase clearly shows that there was a deliberate and concerted effort to order and safeguard the materials that Hirschfeld had left behind after his death in the Gloria Mansions I apartment. Ernst Maass may have joined in these efforts; and perhaps it was decided then that he would take some materials, mainly related to the Mann family, despite Hirschfeld's stipulating in his will that everything found in the Gloria Mansions I apartment should go to Li Shiu Tong. It was also probably then that it was decided that Karl Giese would take with him to Vienna – where he was then living – some items as well. But let us first have a look at Li Shiu Tong since he was also entrusted with some materials in Nice.

THE MATERIALS TAKEN BY LI SHIU TONG

We have seen that Hirschfeld met his new lover Li Shiu Tong in China during his world trip and that the young man decided to stay close to Hirschfeld.[144] Likely at Hirschfeld's own instigation, Li Shiu Tong was sent to Berlin so he could see with his own eyes Hirschfeld's life project, about which Hirschfeld had presumably often spoken during his world tour in Asia.[145] In any case, there exists a photo of Giese and Li Shiu Tong posing together in the Institute's sunny front garden that must have been taken either in the spring or summer of 1932 or, less likely, in the spring of 1933.[146] If it was in the spring of 1933 that Li Shiu Tong went to Berlin, this would mean that Li Shiu Tong saw with his own eyes how the Nazis had taken over Berlin and Germany. In any case, he developed a lifelong fear of Nazism. Ralf Dose speaks of a "persecution motif" (*Verfolgungsmotiv*) noticeable in Li Shiu Tong's personal papers, which persisted long after World War II was over. Because he feared the Nazis were after him, Li Shiu Tong left Zürich in 1940 and went to the USA where he studied at Harvard University during the war years.[147]

It was possibly during his spring 1932 visit that Li Shiu Tong was asked to smuggle Institute materials out of Germany in his car. At least, that is what a family member of Li Shiu Tong told Ralf Dose, that Hirschfeld's pupil risked his own life smuggling out these materials in his car.[148] Interestingly, this last claim would be a further argument

[143] Archiv MHG, Berlin, fonds Max Reiss, letter (dated May 1935 but presumably May 27 or 28, 1935, 2) from Karl Giese to Max Reiss: "Jetzt sind wir dabei das Material zu ordnen".

[144] In one of his personal papers, Liu Shiu Tong wrote that, in 1931, he left St. Johns University in Shanghai to become Hirschfeld's assistant. See Hirschfeld & Dose 2013, 21.

[145] Hirschfeld's housekeeper said that it was indeed Hirschfeld who had deliberately sent the Chinese pupil to the Institute, where he would have stayed for two weeks (Schulz 2001, 34).

[146] See illustration n° 5 in chapter 3. The photo is in the Hirschfeld guestbook, see Bergemann, Dose, Keilson-Lauritz & Dubout 2019, f. 69/113. The main argument for it being spring or summer is that there are leaves on the trees. Since Hirschfeld returned from his world trip in mid-March 1932, Li Shiu Tong's Berlin trip could only have occurred in the spring or summer of 1932 or in April of 1933 (the Institute was looted on May 6, 1933; and, in March, there are usually no leaves on most deciduous trees in Europe). There is a chance that it was rather some time in May or June or mid-July 1932 and that Li Shiu Tong joined Hirschfeld in Karlsbad (Karlovy Vary) or Marienbad (Mariánské Lázně) again after his Berlin visit. Li Shiu Tong's presence next to Hirschfeld was noted in a local Brno newspaper article when Hirschfeld returned to Brno (in preparation for the 1932 WLSR conference) at the end of July 1932. See "Profesor Magnus Hirschfeld v Brně", *Lidové noviny*, July 25, 1932, 3. August 1932 is another possibility since Hirschfeld was then in Zürich for a month and wrote, in *Testament: Heft II*, that he was without "entsprechende Pflege u.[nd] Bequemlichkeit in Zurich" (appropriate care and comfort in Zurich). On the other hand, immediately after this fragment, Hirschfeld also noted, "Hauptstütze: Tao Li" (main support: Tao Li), perhaps indicating that Li Shiu Tong did *not* leave his side in the summer months of 1932 (Hirschfeld & Dose 2013, f. 65/142).

[147] Hirschfeld & Dose 2013, 194 n. 511; Dose 2003, 18. This *Verfolgungsmotiv* may also explain Karl Giese's complaint that Li Shiu Tong, in the years after Hirschfeld's death, did not want to cooperate with him. (A fact to which we will return later.) See, for example, the excerpt from a letter Karl Giese wrote to Kurt Hiller in April 1937 (Hirschfeld & Dose 2013, 18 n. 21).

for the idea that Li Shiu Tong visited Berlin in 1933 rather than 1932. Or did he return in 1933 as well? After all, in his will, Hirschfeld noted that Institute materials were also stored in Berlin.[149] Was it maybe these materials that Li Shiu Tong went to Berlin to collect at some point? Li Shiu Tong himself once wrote that he had "escaped with all Hirschfeld's works".[150] Exactly what he managed to smuggle out, when he did so, and where these materials ended up remains unknown. It is also possible, of course, that the apparently life-threatening "operation" took place in the years after Hirschfeld's death. Maybe it was, rather, some materials from the Nice apartment that Li Shiu Tong was trying to get out of Vichy France under Philippe Pétain's rule in 1940?[151] We do not know. But we do know that, at the time of Li Shiu Tong's death, in 1993, in Vancouver, he had materials that could only have come from the Institute in Berlin and/or from Hirschfeld's Nice apartment at the time of his death. We have already mentioned a few times that Hirschfeld's will bequeathed all the books, personal papers, picture frames and also furnishings in their Nice apartment to Li Shiu Tong. Hirschfeld's *Testament: Heft II*, from which we have already quoted many times, and Hirschfeld's plaster death mask, made in Nice shortly after his death, were among the materials saved from the dumpster in the Vancouver apartment complex where Li Shiu Tong lived. They were saved by the Canadian photographer Adam P. W. Smith (1964-), living in Vancouver, shortly after Li Shiu Tong's death, in 1993.[152]

Like the materials saved by Ernst Maass, these Canadian materials were also generously donated by Smith to the Magnus-Hirschfeld-Gesellschaft in Berlin in 2003 [ill. 10].[153] Hirschfeld's *Testament: Heft II* was part of Li Shiu Tong's miraculously rescued estate. The document was transcribed, annotated, indexed and published by Ralf Dose in 2013. It is now a primary source for Hirschfeld researchers.[154] Dose also determined that Li Shiu Tong's family has other personal writings by Hirschfeld in their possession, which they had *not* left in the garbage container after Li Shiu Tong's death. He suspects that the family is still holding onto four to six of Hirschfeld's world trip diaries.[155] Li Shiu Tong's family and the Magnus-Hirschfeld-Gesellschaft in Berlin have so far not been able to settle on a price for them.[156]

THE MATERIALS TAKEN BY KARL GIESE

It is certain that Giese also took some materials from Nice. In August 1935, François Herzfelder wrote to Ernst Maass: "The last diary [of Magnus Hirschfeld] is here [in Nice]. However, Mr. Giese took some of the diaries with him".[157] In an October

148 Hirschfeld & Dose 2013, f. 74/160 n. 418; Dose 2003, 14, 18, 21, 22.

149 See article 5 in Hirschfeld's will (Baumgardt 1984, 10).

150 Dose 2003, 21-22.

151 Judging from a text found in Li Shiu Tong's estate, he was in Zürich "towards the outbreak of war" and was warned at some point that foreign – presumably German – secret agents were after him, and this prompted him to leave Europe. See Hirschfeld & Dose 2013, 22. Li Shiu Tong mentioned that this happened after Robert Hichens's *That Which Is Hidden* was published. Hichens' book was published in 1939. See Hichens 1939.

152 Dose 2003, 10–11. For more on Hirschfeld's death mask, see Soetaert 2014, 54, Table 10, entry dated Jan. 27, 1936; and n. b. Apparently, Adam P. W. Smith was at first unsure about keeping the materials he found in the trash; however, on the advice of a female friend who was then studying psychology, and who told him that Hirschfeld's name rang a bell, he decided not to discard the materials. See https://www.queer.de/detail.php?article_id=21557 (accessed Dec. 6, 2020).

153 See https://magnus-hirschfeld.de/ausstellungen/hirschfeldforschung/ (accessed Jul. 14, 2020); https://makinggayhistory.com/podcast/magnus-hirschfeld/ (accessed Nov. 5, 2020). One obtains a good overview of what is in the donation of Adam P. W. Smith in Dose 2003a, 15-23.

154 Hirschfeld & Dose 2013.

155 See https://www.queer.de/detail.php?article_id=21557 (accessed Dec. 6, 2020). To that might possibly also be added other Hirschfeld guestbooks, like the one found in Brno, in which Hirschfeld mainly collected autographs of the people he met on his world trip. See Dose 2003, 18.

156 Hirschfeld & Dose 2013, 18.

157 Archiv MHG, Berlin, fonds Ernst Maass, letter (dated Aug. 23, 1935) from François Herzfelder to Ernst Maass: "Das letzte Tagebuch [of Magnus Hirschfeld] ist hier. Einige Tagebücher hat allerdings

1935 letter Giese sent to Max Hodann, written while Giese was in Vienna, he said that Hirschfeld's older diaries had not survived. Presumably this was an indirect statement that these diaries had been looted and perhaps were burned in the May 1933 Berlin bonfire.[158]

It is clear that the stipulation in article 5 of Hirschfeld's will, that Li Shiu Tong should receive the items in the Hirschfeld apartment, was not completely respected. Giese took most of the seventeen genital organ wax models that Giauffer had seen and assessed in Hirschfeld's apartment in May 1935.[159] After Giese committed suicide, in March 1938, the Brno police found eleven of these models in his apartment, confiscating nine of them.[160] But we have also mentioned that the Hirschfeld (and some of the Institute) materials in the Gloria Mansions I apartment were sorted and ordered shortly after Hirschfeld's death, and that Giese and Li Shiu Tong (and probably also Ernst Maass) agreed with each other about who would take what. We will see later that Karl Giese had several hundreds of books in his Brno flat and that these books likely came from the lot bought back from Nazi Germany in November 1933. These books, as suggested already, probably never left Brno after they had been bought back from Berlin. This likely also explains why, except for two copies, the four boxes of books found in the estate of Li Shiu Tong in 2002 did *not* bear the usual Institute library stamps.[161] This fact seems to confirm that the Institute library books did indeed remain in Brno (after arriving in November or December 1933 from Berlin) and were never sent to France. Leaving all or most of the Institute books in

Herr Giese mitgenommen". This appears to correspond with what Karl Giese wrote from Brno in January 1938 to Ernst Maass: "Die Tagebücher sind, als auf [possibly has to be "auch"] die Reiseerinn[erungs ?]bücher, die Tao in Händen hat, ebenfalls hier bei mir" (The diaries [and also?] the memorial travel books, which Tao has in his hands, are also here with me). See Archiv MHG, Berlin, fonds Ernst Maass, letter (dated Jan. 21, 1938, 3) from Karl Giese to Ernst Maass. It remains unclear how to correctly interpret Giese's grammatically incorrect sentence. It is possible that he mistakenly left out the word "nicht", which would make the statement more logical: "Die Tagebücher sind, als auf [likely has to be "auch"] die Reiseerinn[erungs ?]bücher, die Tao in Händen hat, ebenfalls [nicht] hier bei mir". But this would than contradict Herzfelder's claim that Giese took some diaries with him when he left Nice. Marita Keilson-Lauritz convinced me that, despite the bad grammar, the surviving Hirschfeld diaries (presumably with the exception of the travel diaries) were indeed with Giese in Brno, since Giese writes, immediately after that crooked sentence, that these diaries provide the reader with what any Hirschfeld biographer would need: a better idea of who Hirschfeld really was. I thank Marita Keilson-Lauritz for her assistance in reading Giese's sentence as correctly as possible. See her email (dated Jul. 14, 2020) to the author. That Giese did indeed have some of Hirschfeld's diaries in Brno is possibly also indicated by an element in the Hirschfeld guestbook. We have already shown that Giese added a comment in his own handwriting on a visit Hirschfeld made to the Gordon family in Nice in January 1935. See Bergemann, Dose, Keilson-Lauritz & Dubout 2019, f. 101/145. That Giese was able to state the exact date that the picture was taken (Jan. 28, 1935) may indicate that he held on to at least some of Hirschfeld's diaries in Brno. Or was the date he added in the guestbook noted on the back of the picture? What remains unexplained is why he added to his comment a quote from the American activist and lesbian Helen Keller (1880–1968): "Optimismus ist der Glaube, der zur Erfüllung hinführt; ohne Hoffnung können wir nichts tun" (Optimism is the faith that leads to achievement. Nothing can be done without hope and confidence). Cf. Bergemann, Dose, Keilson-Lauritz & Dubout 2019, f. 101/145 and n. 293; Bergemann, Dose & Keilson-Lauritz 2021, 6. Lastly, one may ask where Giese found this Helen Keller quote. Had Giese encountered it in his own reading and deemed it suitable to add beneath the picture? Or had he copied it from the diary, Hirschfeld maybe adding the quote on the occasion of his visit to the Gordon couple? We have already mentioned that a May 1933 *New York Times* article reported that a book by Helen Keller also ended up on the Berlin pyre. See Birchall May 11, 1933, 12. This may have been how Giese and Hirschfeld became aware of her work and may even have contacted her afterwards.

158 Arbetarrörelsens arkiv och bibliotek, Stockholm, Max Hodann samling, vol. 10, letter (dated Oct. 10, 1935, [1]) from Karl Giese to Max Hodann.

159 ADAM, Nice, Archives notariales, minutes notariales étude Pierre Demnard, May 24, 1935, n° 569, cote 03E 148/011.

160 MZA, Brno, fonds C 107, Německý úřední soud Brno (Deutsches Amtsgericht Brünn), kart. n° 256, sign. 5a V 3/41, f. 4-5.

Brno was perhaps also a good idea given that, as we have seen, the idea of starting up a new Institute, or something like it, in Brno with Dr. Josef Weisskopf, continued to occur to Giese until at least 1937. That Giese also had more personal papers belonging to Hirschfeld is indicated by a letter he wrote to Ernst Maass in January 1938: "First of all, thank you for your kind letter with inserts. I immediately added the latter to the Hirschfeld family archive".[162] But the strongest evidence that shows that Giese took Hirschfeld documents from Nice is the fact that the Hirschfeld guestbook, as we stated in the introduction to this book, was found in Brno in 1942. Giese resided in this city until his suicide, in March 1938. In 1942, the guestbook was saved from an old paper container in Brno. So, it is indeed very likely that Giese took this guestbook when he left Nice in the weeks after Hirschfeld's death.

I think that there is another very strong indication that Giese took the Hirschfeld guestbook to Brno. This can be found inside the Hirschfeld guestbook itself. We may presume that it was Giese who, on the last eight pages of the guestbook, pasted the pictures of Hirschfeld's final days in Nice before his death. These were pictures taken in the front garden of Gloria Mansions I, pictures of Hirschfeld's last trip to Monaco, a picture of Hirschfeld on his deathbed, a picture of Hirschfeld's death mask, and also the announcement card of the burial ceremony.[163] Giese added comments beneath these pictures in his own handwriting.[164] It could be objected that Giese could have added these pictures when he was still in Nice, in the weeks after Hirschfeld's funeral. Yet the very last picture of Hirschfeld's finished grave in Nice's Caucade cemetery, which terminates the Hirschfeld guestbook, thoroughly undermines this counter-argument [ill. 11].[165] We know that Hirschfeld was cremated in Marseille and that it took some time before his grave stone and plot in the Caucade cemetery was ready. This was due in part to the inheritance procedure only concluding around May 1936, which released the funds necessary to pay for Hirschfeld's expensive and posh grave. Until then, Hirschfeld's ashes were kept in the columbarium of the main city cemetery in Marseille. It was only at the end of August 1936 that the ashes were taken from Marseille to Nice. And it was only then that a picture could be taken of the finished grave in Nice. Likely Li Shiu Tong took the picture of the just finished grave and sent a copy to Giese. Giese must have received the picture in August or September 1936, when he was already in Brno. Only then, at the earliest, could the picture of Hirschfeld's grave have been added and pasted into the guestbook – by Giese, and in Brno. There is another, though less important, piece of evidence for Giese having the Hirschfeld guestbook in Brno. Again, it is related to the photos pasted into the final pages of the guestbook. An identical photo of Hirschfeld on his deathbed appears in the last pages of the Hirschfeld guestbook ánd in *Testament: Heft II*, which surfaced in

[161] Dose 2003, 14. More specifically, the two books bore a WhK rubber stamp. See above, p. 158 and n. 21, for the manner in which these WhK books may have been added to the Institute collection at some point.

[162] Archiv MHG, Berlin, fonds Ernst Maass, letter (dated Jan. 21, 1938, 1) from Karl Giese to Ernst Maass: "Ich danke Ihnen zunächst einmal für Ihren lieben Brief mit Einlagen. Letztere habe ich sofort dem Hirschfeld-Familien-Archiv einverleiht".

[163] Bergemann, Dose, Keilson-Lauritz & Dubout 2019: f. 148/192–f. 155/199.

[164] It is somewhat strange that the editors of the Hirschfeld guestbook explicitly state that they did not recognize Giese's typical handwriting in the comments added under the pictures. See Bergemann, Dose, Keilson-Lauritz & Dubout 2019, 192 n. 425; now rectified in Bergemann, Dose & Keilson-Lauritz 2021, 7. Several of Giese's letters have survived and clearly show his typical handwriting. It is true that the more careful handwriting seen on the last pages of the guestbook differs a little from Giese's usually more illegible handwriting in his letters. I think he simply made an effort to write a little more legibly in this guestbook destined for posterity. (I have made a similar comment about Hirschfeld's own more legible handwriting in his will. See Soetaert 2014, 7.) The fact that the text is written in Giese's usual blue fountain pen ink further supports the argument.

[165] Bergemann, Dose, Keilson-Lauritz & Dubout 2019, f. 155/199.

the estate of Li Shiu Tong in Canada.[166] This shows, I think, that Li Shiu Tong and Karl Giese each pasted the same picture into his unique Hirschfeld artifact.[167]

In a July 1939 letter to Françoise Lafitte-Cyon (1886–1974), the partner and secretary of the English sexologist Havelock Ellis, Ernst Maass wrote: "Many papers have been lost because they were given to Mr. Karl Giese, formerly secretary of the 'Institut für Sexualwissenschaft' in Berlin, who lived in Brno, Cechoslovakia [*sic*: Czechoslovakia], where they were taken by the German authorities". That many papers, books and documents were indeed lost because these ended up with Karl Giese in Brno is factually true, but this was not linked, as we will see in chapter 12, to their being confiscated, and certainly not by "German authorities".[168] Also, as we will see, the lot Giese held on to in Brno was most likely discarded in 1942 and – let this be made clear here and now – Giese cannot be said to be at fault that these papers were discarded later. For this reason, Maass' panicked July 1939 assessment was groundless and simply incorrect. But Maass was right in sensing, as early as July 1939, on the brink of war, that it was a mistake to entrust Karl Giese in Nice, in May–June 1935, with likely the greater part of Hirschfeld's remaining archives and materials. However, it seems that Giese considered himself, possibly when he was still in Nice, the better or more reliable guardian of the remains of Hirschfeld's estate. In July 1937, for example, he

166 For the deathbed picture in *Testament: Heft II*, see Hirschfeld & Dose 2013, f. 93/199. For the same picture pasted into the Hirschfeld guestbook, see Bergemann, Dose, Keilson-Lauritz & Dubout f. 152/196.

167 One could, I think, obtain further proof, one day, that Li Shiu Tong held on to *Testament: Heft II* and Giese to the Hirschfeld guestbook by analyzing and comparing a tiny sample of the glue they used when they pasted the same photo into their own Hirschfeld document. The glue should have a different chemical composition. I could also point out a third supporting element for the thesis that Giese held on to the Hirschfeld guestbook in Brno. Again it has to do with the pictures in the last pages of the guestbook. *Neither* of the two pictures of Hirschfeld's death mask in *Testament: Heft II* (on the same page as the photo of Hirschfeld on his deathbed) is the same as the *unique* picture of the death mask in the Hirschfeld guestbook. See Hirschfeld & Dose 2013, f. 93/199 and Bergemann, Dose, Keilson-Lauritz & Dubout, f. 153/197, respectively. This could mean that there were three different photos of the death mask. Li Shiu Tong may have taken two of them and Giese the third, or else the third picture was sent to Brno by Li Shiu Tong. On the other hand, it is much less clear that such a claim could be made for the other nine pictures that are pasted into the very end of the guestbook. See Bergemann, Dose, Keilson-Lauritz & Dubout, f. 148-151/192-195. Giese may have already added these pictures when he was still in Nice, in May–June 1935. This last possibility could explain how Giese could be so specific about the dates and times that he wrote beneath these pictures. He might have asked Robert Kirchberger, Hirschfeld's last secretary, or Ernst Maass, about these precise dates. But here also, an analysis of the glue used for this series of nine pictures might reveal *in what city* Giese pasted them into the guestbook. Since we now know that Giese could only have pasted in the picture of Hirschfeld's grave in Brno, the glue used for that could serve as a basis for comparison. The same "glue question" should be asked one day about another picture in the guestbook. In folio n° 101, there is a picture of Sophie Gordon and her son Armand on a deck chair enjoying the sun. See Bergemann, Dose, Keilson-Lauritz & Dubout, f. 101/145. Here as well, Giese added comments beneath the picture. I think that it is possible that Giese pasted this particular picture into the guestbook himself. We already indicated above (pp. 265-66 and n. 50) that the well-informed comments that Giese added could indicate that he held on to the Hirschfeld diaries in Brno. But one could object that the date that the picture of Sophie Gordon and her son was taken might simply have been written on the back, and that Giese might have added the picture and the comments when he was still in Nice, in May–June 1935. Someone might one day try to check if anything is written on the back of the picture either by raising it or by using some other technique to scan the back of the picture. But an analysis of the glue used could prove very revealing and indicate where (and when) the photo was pasted in. If the glue used for this picture would prove to be the same as that used for the picture of the grave in the guestbook, ánd there is *no* date on the back, then this would be further convincing evidence that Giese did indeed have some of the later Hirschfeld diaries in Brno. Without these diaries, he could not have known the exact date that Hirschfeld visited the Gordon couple in Nice in January 1935. Unless, of course, he obtained the date of the visit from another source, like a letter that the Gordons may have sent to Hirschfeld or Giese referring to the Nice visit.

168 Archiv MHG, Berlin, fonds Ernst Maass, letter (dated Jul. 13, 1939) from Ernst Maass to Françoise Lafitte-Cyon. We will return to Maass' (mistaken) mention of "German authorities" in his letter. See below pp. 390-91.

wrote that he was the "material and spiritual heir" of Magnus Hirschfeld.[169] This may explain why he obtained the greater or more important part of the lot when he, Maass, and Li Shiu Tong decided who would take what. Of all the materials Giese ended up with in Brno, only the Hirschfeld guestbook survives. In what follows we will show how this possibly came to be. In hindsight, it would have been wise to divide the remaining Hirschfeld archives in three equal parts in the weeks after Hirschfeld's death. The parts entrusted to Li Shiu Tong and Ernst Maass mostly survived while, again, Giese's part was most likely almost completely lost.

Maass' misconception, that the materials were in jeopardy in 1939, because they had been confiscated shortly after Giese's March 1938 suicide, apparently prompted him, then already living in New York, to intensify his efforts to safeguard other archival documents related to Hirschfeld. In the same letter to Françoise Lafitte-Cyon, Maass asked if they would be willing to entrust him with some of the letters Hirschfeld sent to Havelock Ellis: "As I try my best to collect all papers and documents, pictures and books relating to my uncle's work, I would herewith ask you whether it would be possible for you to let me have those documents in Dr. Ellis' possession which have been written by my uncle, especially letters".[170] But it seems that Maass never obtained any Hirschfeld letters either from the English sexologist or his secretary. Presumably, Maass' initial optimism about safeguarding Magnus Hirschfeld's epistolary heritage quickly faded after that. Later, we will return a few more times to the items Giese had in his possession when he lived in Brno, in the years 1936–38.

THE INSTITUTE MATERIALS IN SAARBRÜCKEN, WIESBADEN AND BERLIN

What happened to the Institute materials that, according to article 5 in Hirschfeld's will, were left in Berlin and Wiesbaden and in Saarbrücken? Article 5 also states that Giese knew exactly where and with whom these Institute materials were stored in these cities.[171] On this point particularly, nothing is very clear about the fate of these Institute materials, but a few elements can be elucidated here. The typed copy of Hirschfeld's last will – which Hirschfeld most likely used as the basis for his final handwritten version – contains an interesting difference from the final handwritten version dropped off at Demnard's office, in February 1935. In order to bring out this minimal but significant difference, we reproduce the two versions here.

> **Typed (draft) version:**
> "1. I bequeath to Mr. Karl Giese all objects, in particular manuscripts, documents, questionnaires, pictures, books and works, most of which are currently at the garde-meuble Bedel, Paris, 18 Rue St-Augustin, and some of which are in Berlin and Wiesbaden in places known to him" [ill. 12].[172]
>
> **Handwritten (final) version:**
> "I. I bequeath to Mr. Karl Giese the objects rescued with his help from the Berlin Institute of Sexual Science, in particular all documents, manuscripts, questionnaires, pictures, books, etc., etc., which are at present partly in the garde-meuble of Bedel & Co. in Paris

[169] MZA, Brno, fonds B 40, Zemský úřad Brno (Landesbehörde in Brünn), kart. n° 2138, sign. 5274/38, f. 6b: "Magnus Hirschfeld ustanovil mne [*sic*, mne ustanovil] totiž ve své závěti, jelikož jsem byl svou mnoholetou spoluprací nejlépe obeznámen s jeho dílem a jeho ideami, výslovně svým hmotným a duchovním dědicem." (Since I was the most familiar with his work and ideas, from my many years of collaboration with him, Magnus Hirschfeld named me his material and spiritual heir in his will).

[170] Archiv MHG, Berlin, fonds Ernst Maass, letter (dated Jul. 13, 1939, 1–2) from Ernst Maass to Françoise Lafitte-Cyon.

[171] Baumgardt 1984, 10.

[172] Original (dated December 1934) in Archiv MHG, Berlin, fonds Ernst Maass: "1. Herrn Karl Giese vermache ich alle Gegenstände, insbesondere Manuskripte, Dokumente, Fragebogen, Bilder, Bücher und Werke, die sich zum grössten Teil zur Zeit bei dem garde-meubles Bedel, Paris, 18 Rue St-Augus-

> 18 Rue St. Augustin, partly still in Germany (Berlin, Wiesbaden) or Saarbrücken in a place known to him".[173]

Whereas in the earlier typed version only the cities of Berlin and Wiesbaden are mentioned, in the later final handwritten version of the will, the city of Saarbrücken shows up for the first time. The word "or" between "(Berlin, Wiesbaden)" and "Saarbrücken" makes it even more intriguing. This *adding* of Saarbrücken seems to indicate that some or even all the materials (then in Berlin and Wiesbaden) were going to be moved to Saarbrücken in the near future. The word "or" might also indicate that it was still uncertain if these materials would be moved from Berlin and Wiesbaden to Saarbrücken. We have seen that Hirschfeld dated his handwritten will on January 10, 1935, and that he or Herzfelder dropped off the final version on February 23, 1935 at Demnard's office. This means that the new idea or plan to possibly store materials in Saarbrücken was in the air in the first months of 1935, likely linked to the people Hirschfeld met in Nice at that time. There is another slight difference in the two versions that might be significant. Hirschfeld claims in the typed draft that most (*zum grössten Teil*) materials were still at the garde-meuble while the hand written version says they are partly (*teils*) there. Had some materials been moved to Nice already by the time Hirschfeld wrote the final version of his will ?

A good candidate to have played a role here was Dr. Leo Klauber. Klauber was still working and living in Nice when Hirschfeld settled down there at the end of 1934. We have seen that Klauber wrote a sick note for Karl Giese, shortly after his arrival in Nice from Brno, at the end of December 1933.[174] In *Testament: Heft II*, Hirschfeld wrote that he met Klauber when he went to Nice in the first months of 1934.[175] Klauber also attended the funeral ceremony for Hirschfeld in May 1935. So it is far from improbable that Hirschfeld met Klauber again in Nice, in December 1934 or January 1935, and that they might have broached the idea of storing some Institute materials in Saarbrücken, possibly even of moving the materials still in Berlin and Wiesbaden to Saarbrücken.

Leo Klauber was an Alsacian, born in Forbach, and his brother Jules Klauber kept a wholesale men's clothing business in nearby Saarbrücken.[176] Saarbrücken (or in French Sarrebruck) and the Saarland (or in French la Sarre) was still under French and British occupation in 1934 but was restored to Germany after a local referendum on January 13, 1935, in which ninety percent of the population voted to return to Germany. When he used the German name of the city in the final handwritten version of his last will, Hirschfeld must have been well aware that the most likely outcome was a big majority opting to change Sarrebruck to Saarbrücken again. Hirschfeld

tin, zum anderen Teil in Berlin und Wiesbaden an ihm bekannter Stelle befinden". Article 5 of the will is on p. 2 of that document. The date "December 1934" is written on the envelope which contained the typed copy. Also note the question mark added by Hirschfeld right next to the passage concerned, see illustration n° 12 in this chapter.

173 I have used Baumgardt's transcription (Baumgardt 1984, 10) of Hirschfeld's will as the main source but adapted that version minimally, thus closely following the handwritten original of Hirschfeld's will deposited in the ADAM, Nice, Archives notariales, minutes notariales étude Pierre Demnard, May 22, 1935, n° 563, cote 03E 148 011, f. 1b (p. 2): "I[.] Herrn Karl Giese vermache ich die mit seiner Hülfe aus dem Berliner Institut für Sexualwissenschaft geretteten Gegenstände, insbesondere alle Dokumente, Manuskripte, Fragebogen, Bilder, Bücher etc. etc., die sich zur Zeit teils auf dem garde-meuble von Bedel u. Co. in Paris 18 Rue St. Augustin, teils noch in Deutschland (Berlin, Wiesbaden) oder Saarbrücken an ihm bekannter Stelle befinden". See addenda (n° 17).

174 See AN, site de Pierrefitte-sur-Seine, Ministère de l'intérieur, Service central des cartes d'identité d'étrangers, Direction de la Sûreté Générale, Service central des cartes d'identité d'étrangers, file Karl Giese, file number 198379, cote 19940506/68, certificat médical Léon [*sic*] Klauber dated Jan. 26, 1934. The partially visible letterhead on that sick note reads: "Docteur KLAUBER, médecin-spécialiste pour les maladies internes, interne [?] de la clinique universitaire". Klauber is also mentioned in *Annuaires des Alpes-Maritimes* 1935, 836; but he does not appear in the 1934 volume. He and his wife lived at 3 Boulevard Gambetta (in a building called Le Forum).

would have known, in other words, that the Institute materials would be stored in a German city, even if one on the French border. The case and location of Sarrebruck/ Saarbrücken are of course particular. When it became German again, in February 1935, it was adjacent to the French border. Forbach was (and still is) the first French city on the other (French) side of the border.

The choice of Saarbrücken seems to say: depending on the political situation, we will move the materials quickly to the safe side of the border. And in that sense, Saarbrücken was a better location than Wiesbaden, located deeper inside Germany, 150 kilometers from the French border. The Marxist Rudolf Hilferding, a good friend of Magnus Hirschfeld, might have had similar ideas. He decided to settle down in the French city of Saint-Louis, located exactly at the meeting point of three countries: France, Switzerland, and Germany. Hilferding apparently wanted to be able to move quickly if a quickly evolving political situation forced him to decide between three countries. That the Klaubers lived in Forbach and Saarbrücken is of course in this regard intriguing. Had Hirschfeld relied on Leo Klauber and his brother Jules Klauber? This possibility could be quickly dismissed, at least in part. Jules Klauber had indeed a wholesale men's clothing business in Saarbrücken, but the business ceased operation in the beginning of the 1930s. Jules Klauber left Saarbrücken with his family around 1931–32. Presumably, the family moved to Paris.[177] I managed to contact the current relatives of Jules Klauber in the summer of 2020 but one of his two daughters, Jacqueline Cunow (née Klauber, 1925–), had never heard of Magnus Hirschfeld.[178] But then, she was only an eight-year-old child in the beginning of 1934. Leo and Jules Klauber also had a sister named Marie Rénee Luft (née Klauber, 1897–1981) since their mother Eugénie Horvilleur (1861-1930?) had remarried a certain Ernst Klauber (1865–1940). But despite some effort, I did not manage to gain contact with this American branch of the Klauber family.[179]

The location of the border cities of Saarbrücken and Forbach, and Hirschfeld mentioning Saarbrücken in the final handwritten version of his will, remains of course intriguing. The idea to move things quickly to the French side of the border, depending on the evolution of the political situation in Germany, might indeed have

[175] Hirschfeld & Dose 2013, f. 86/184.

[176] The further destiny of Leo Klauber's immediate family remains a bit unclear. He and his wife Erna Peiser (1895–?) had a son named Alfred Klauber (1919–2007), who was active in the resistance in the years 1943–44 under the pseudonym Gaston Féral. After the war, Alfred Klauber lived in Marseille, where he was a school teacher in the lycée Thiers. See Ministère des armées, Service historique de la Défense, Vincennes, fonds GR 16 P, Dossiers individuels du bureau Résistance, cote GR 16 P 320522, Alfred Klauber (1919–2007), alias Gaston Féral. A letter was sent on September 10, 2021 to Alfred Klauber's last known address, 28 Rue de Crémone in Marseille. On September 16, 2021, Vincent A., resident at this address, sent me a friendly email saying he neither knew nor was related to Alfred Klauber, but would ask his older neighbors if they knew anything about the man. But I did not hear anything from him afterwards.

[177] Email (dated Jun. 10, 2020) from Peter Wettmann-Jungblut (Landesarchiv Saarland, Saarbrücken-Scheidt) to the author. The wholesale textile business was located at 24 Friedrich-Ebert-strasse. Their private residence and property was located at 61 Petersbergstrasse. See *Einwohnerbuch der Stadt Saarbrücken* 1929/30, 177, 586, 715. See also the two *Gewerbekarten* (trade cards) (Handelsregister-Eintragungen, n° A 2162) of the several different businesses Jules Klauber had in Saarbrücken, kindly sent to me by Kathrin Schmidt (Stadtarchiv Saarbrücken) on June 18, 2020, which also contain mention of "Paris umgezogen" (moved to Paris) under the years 1931–32.

[178] Email (dated Jul. 13, 2020) from Yves Cunow (1954–), the son of Jacqueline Klauber, to the author. I also contacted Pierre-Olivier Monceaux, one of the two sons of Jules Klauber's other daughter, Denyse Monceaux (1927–2022), but he did not reply.

[179] Marie Rénee Klauber married the psychiatrist Lothar Luft (1891–1941) and moved to the USA in 1939. For unclear reasons, the German writer Joachim Maass (1901–1972) lived with the couple in their Manhattan flat. See National Archives and Records Administration, Washington D.C., Bureau of the Census, sixteenth Census of the United States, 1940, New York, roll m-t0627-02668, f. 11b, enumeration district 31-1819; available online at Ancestry.com, 1940 United States Federal Census. René Klauber had a relationship with Joachim Maass after her husband died. See https://de.wikipedia.org/wiki/Joachim_Maass_(Schriftsteller) (accessed Oct. 22,

played a role. That Leo Klauber's brother was no longer living in Saarbrücken by 1935 does not necessarily undermine this possible set-up completely. Leo Klauber might have relied on his or his brother's acquaintances living in Saarbrücken. Hirschfeld's idea of storing items in Saarbrücken, possibly concocted with Klauber, may have been still tentative when Hirschfeld finalized his will in January 1935, explaining the presence of the "open" phrase in article 5: "(Berlin, Wiesbaden) or Saarbrücken". So the possible arrangement with Klauber may have fallen through, just as, in 1934 the planned cooperation with Klauber to start up a new Institute in Paris did not come about. On the other hand, one could think that Klauber owed Hirschfeld a favour precisely *because* the Paris project was abandoned.

But we have already seen that Hirschfeld found another Alsatian candidate to start up a new practice in Paris, Edmond Zammert, whose family lived in Wiesbaden. Zammert sometimes visited Wiesbaden to see his family. When he was still active as a doctor, he had a practice in the French city of Creutzwald (in German, Kreuzwald), twenty-five kilometers away from Forbach, next to the German border.[180] Hirschfeld certainly stored some Institute materials with Zammert or his family in Wiesbaden. The choice of Wiesbaden may have been part of the initial idea to store Institute materials as close to the French border as possible. If so, then the choice of Saarbrücken would represent a further refinement of that idea. That, in the 1980s, the Magnus-Hirschfeld-Gesellschaft managed to recover a few Institute materials from the unmarried daughter of Edmond Zammert, Jeanne Zammert, living in Wiesbaden, seems to confirm that items from the Institute were indeed stored in Wiesbaden and that the possible plan to move them from Wiesbaden to Saarbrücken was never realized. One of the items the Magnus-Hirschfeld-Gesellschaft managed to buy back from Edmond Zammert's daughter was a box of Japanese dildos (called Harikata).[181] Unfortunately, Jeanne Zammert had earlier sold several Institute objects to an antiquarian book dealer named Valentiner, whom the Magnus-Hirschfeld-Gesellschaft was not able to locate, since he had moved to South America.[182]

So it remains possible that Leo Klauber was never the man with whom Hirschfeld planned moving Institute materials to Saarbrücken. But it may have been that an agreement was reached with someone else. Before the 1935 referendum, the Saarland was a special place where many German left-wingers sought refuge, since the Nazis could not persecute them there (like they persecuted other opponents in Germany) as long as the region was under French/British occupation.[183] That means that it had a great many left-wing candidates with whom Hirschfeld might have stored (or intended to store) a part of the Institute materials.[184]

2020). Joachim Maass does not seem to have been related to Ernst Maass. Marie Renée and Lothar Luft had one son, Albert Paul Luft (1922–2001), who changed his name to Bert Powell in order to work as a broadcaster for US propaganda radio during the war years. He had two children with his wife Florence Jacko (1925–1976) but I was not able locate the son Joseph Powell (?–?) or an unknown sister (?–?). Bert Powell Luft's obituary says that the family emigrated to the USA with an uncle. See the obituary for Bert Powell (Luft) in *Needles Desert Star*, Oct. 24, 2001. I thank Don McLeod for sending me a copy of this obituary on May 30, 2020. It might be useful one day to check Joachim Maass' archives in the Deutsches Literaturarchiv in Marbach for his relationship with the Klauber and Luft families. Marie Renée Klauber-Luft was painted by Hans Reichel (1892–1958). See https://webmuseo.com/ws/musee-unterlinden/app/collection/record/72?expo=7&index=16&lang=fr (accessed Nov. 10, 2020).

180 *Journal officiel de la République, lois et décrets*, Oct. 3, 1941, 4260.

181 A photo of the dildos can be seen in Hirschfeld & Linsert 1930c: the third and fourth images on the page facing p. 282.

182 Dose & Herrn 2006, 46–47; Dose 2019, 17; Dose 2012; emails (dated Jun. 6 and 13, 2020) from Ralf Dose to the author.

183 I thank Ralf Dose for pointing this out to me.

184 One of the figures I looked at was Heinrich Cunow (1862–1936), another important left-wing German politician, who had one unidentified child with Elisabeth (Lizzie) Lamb Cornelius (1885–?). See Lane 1995, 1: 235–36. Yves Cunow wrote to me that

Another good ally in the region might have been Hirschfeld's friend, Rudolf Hilferding, who was the editor of the newspaper *Die Freiheit,* based in Saarbrücken. Hirschfeld published two articles in that newspaper in 1933 and 1934.[185] Hilferding's ex-wife, Margarete Hilferding (1871–1942), would have been at least acquainted with Hirschfeld since she lectured at the fourth WLSR congress in Vienna in 1930.[186] If Hilferding himself was not directly involved, he might have known people who were able and willing to help Hirschfeld with his storage problem.

Another possible Saarbrücken candidate was a certain Erich Messing, to whom we shall return later. Messing was the brother of Herta Messing, who, in 1939, would marry the brother of the younger Karl Fein, Gustav Fein. Erich Messing, an engineer and literary figure, lived in Saarbrücken. He had moved there from Vienna in February 1925 and would stay there until May 1939. It is possible that Karl Fein suggested his name to Magnus Hirschfeld. But Messing is merely another hypothetical candidate and there is no proof of his involvement. Erich Messing would have been a very discreet candidate for storing Institute materials since there was virtually no way to link him to Hirschfeld's entourage.[187] But then again, Hirschfeld may have sought out still other people in the large pool of left-wingers who settled in the Saarland between 1933 and 1935.[188]

There was another city named in article 5 of Hirschfeld's last will as holding materials: Berlin. We are completely in the dark about who might have been involved in this case, but Giese had possibly chosen some of his Communist friends or even some members of his own family to store and hide Institute materials. But still other Berlin friends or acquaintances of Hirschfeld or Giese could also have been involved.

his father said that Heinrich Cunow had no direct link ("pas de rapport direct") with the Cunow family we have been looking at. See email (dated Jul. 10, 2020) from Yves Cunow to the author.

185 I thank Ralf Dose for informing me that Hilferding was the editor-in-chief of *Die Freiheit*. See email (dated Jun. 6, 2020) from Ralf Dose to the author. For a mention of Hirschfeld's 1934 article, see also Hirschfeld & Dose 2013, f. 85/182 n. 471. For Hilferding, see http://www.dasrotewien.at/seite/hilferding-rudolf (accessed Feb. 9, 2023).

186 The couple divorced in 1922. See http://der-rote-blog.at/frau-dr-margarete-hilferding-x-favoriten strasse-67 and https://ub.meduniwien.ac.at/blog/?p=37159 (both accessed Feb. 9, 2023). The couple had two children, Karl Hilferding (1905–1942) and Peter Milford-Hilferding (1908–2007).

187 There are two reasons that speak against Messing being a good candidate. Firstly, Gustav Fein might not even have known Herta Messing in 1934. She only divorced her previous husband, a man named Jirásko (or Jirasek), in October 1938. Gustav Fein, on the other hand, divorced his first wife, Alice Hanna Weill, in May 1932. Gustav Fein married Herta Messing in 1939 in Prague. This does not preclude, of course, that the two might have had an extramarital affair in 1935. Fein lived in Vienna before he returned to Czechoslovakia in 1938. The second reason has to do with Eric Messing himself. At first, he sympathized with the German and Nazi cause, as stated in a letter (dated beginning of July 1965) from one of his friends, the engineer Karl Stephan, to Birgit von Schowingen-Ficker. See Forschungsinstitut Brenner-Archiv, Universität von Innsbruck, Innsbruck, Nachlass Herta Fein-Erich Messing, Kassette 151, folder Stephan, Karl, p. 2.

188 There is one more person that we could mention in this regard, whom Hirschfeld met in Nice, and who seems to have had a link to Saarbrücken, though after the war. This is the German artist Hermann Henry Gowa (1902–1990), who survived the war in France thanks to his knowing members of the resistance. Immediately after the war, he was the director of the "centre de métiers d'art" in Saarbrücken. Hirschfeld owed a small debt to the painter at the time of his death. See Soetaert 2014, Table 10, Feb. 14, 1936, 54. Gowa worked in Nice in the atelier once belonging to Rosa Bonheur (1822–1899), located at 9 Route de Bellet (very close to the Avenue Rosa Bonheur) in Nice. See Archives Municipales, Nice, folder Gowa (note et coupures de presse). Hirschfeld was an admirer of the lesbian painter Bonheur and possibly met Gowa this way. But Gowa was also a friend of Walter Hasenclever (1890–1940), who was a friend of Hirschfeld. See Soetaert 2014, 54 n. c; and also Hirschfeld & Dose 2013, 106 n. 302. The Jüdisches Museum, Frankfurt, has the personal archives of Henry Gowa. See https://www.juedischesmuseum.de/en/collection/fine-arts/detail/ludwig-meidner-archive/ (accessed Aug. 12, 2021); but the archival fonds is currently not available for consultation. See email (dated Aug. 16, 2021) from Erik Riedel (Ludwig Meidner-Archiv, Frankfurt am Main) to the author.

1. "Helena Antonia / born in the archdiocese of Lüttich [Liège, Belgium] / raised until she was eighteen years old in Graz [Austria] / 1622" (Helena Antonia / Gebohrene in Ertzbistum Littich [sic] / ihres alters 18. Iahr [sic] ertzogen / zu Gratz / 1622). Copy of a seventeenth-century painting of a woman suffering from hirsuteness (aka "the bearded lady"), hanging in the Velké Losiny castle in the Olomouc region in Czechia.

2. Participants in the 1930 WLSR Vienna conference at the makeshift exhibition set up in the concert hall (Konzerthaus), with items from Hirschfeld's Institute. On the right wall, at the top, hangs a copy of an oil painting (originally by Joshua Reynolds) of the French transsexual diplomat and spy Chevalier d'Éon. The participants are, from left to right: Josef Karl Friedjung (1871–1946), Jonathan Leunbach, Norman Haire, Magnus Hirschfeld, Pierre Vachet, Paul Krische (1878–1956), unidentified person, Kommerzialrat (Business and trade councilor) R. Ludwig Assinger (1877–?), unidentified person. September, 16, 1930. Josephinum – Ethics, Collections and History of Medecine, MedUni Vienna.

3. Photobooth picture of the painter Victor Bauer. October 1937.

4. Henri Nouveau (né Henrik Neugeboren). 1932.

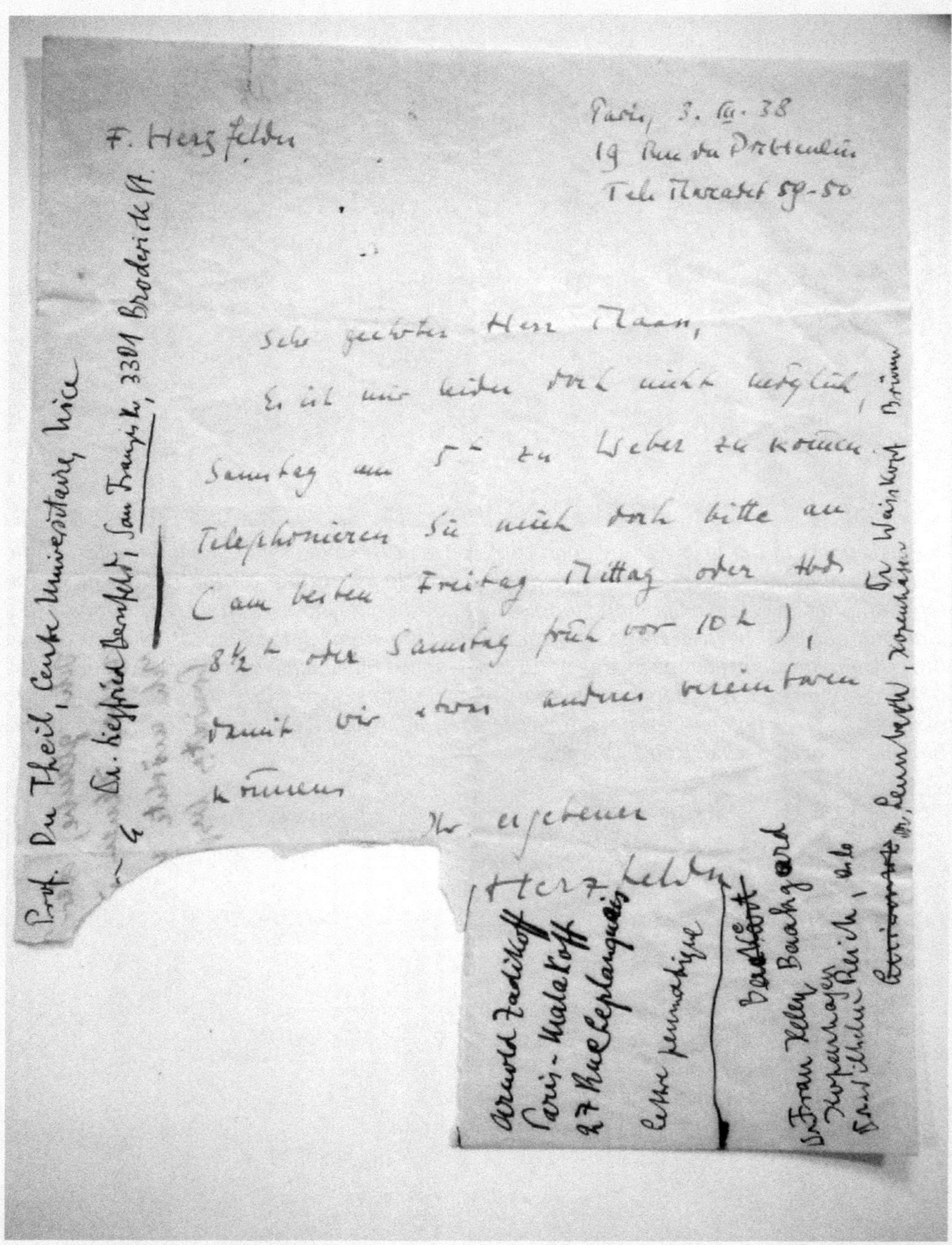

F. Herzfelder

Paris, 3. III. 38
19 Rue du [illegible]
Tel. Marcadet 89-50

Sehr geehrter Herr Maass,

Es ist mir leider doch nicht möglich, Samstag um 5h zu Weber zu kommen. Telephonieren Sie mich doch bitte an (am besten Freitag Mittag oder Abd 8½h oder Samstag früh vor 10h), damit wir etwas anderes vereinbaren können.

Ihr ergebener
Herzfelder

Prof. Du Theil, Centre Universitaire, Nice
Dr. Siegfried Bernfeld, San Francisco, 3301 Broderick St.

Arnold Zadikoff
Paris-Malakoff
27 Rue Leplanquais
Lettre pneumatique

5. Partly torn letter sent by Franz (François) Herzfelder to Ernst Maass on March 3, 1938. The letter dealt with a planned Paris appointment, but the names added by Maass constitute its main interest.

6. Photobooth passport picture of Ewa Stross. Ca. 1938.

8. Cover of Hans Giese's L'homosexualité de l'homme, published in translation in 1959 in France. The German original, Der homosexuelle Mann in der Welt, was published the year before.

7. Contemporary picture of Villa Antoinette in Nice, at 5 Allée du souvenir, a dead end street (near 37 Boulevard de Cessole), whose third (top) floor Victor Bauer occupied with some close friends in 1936.

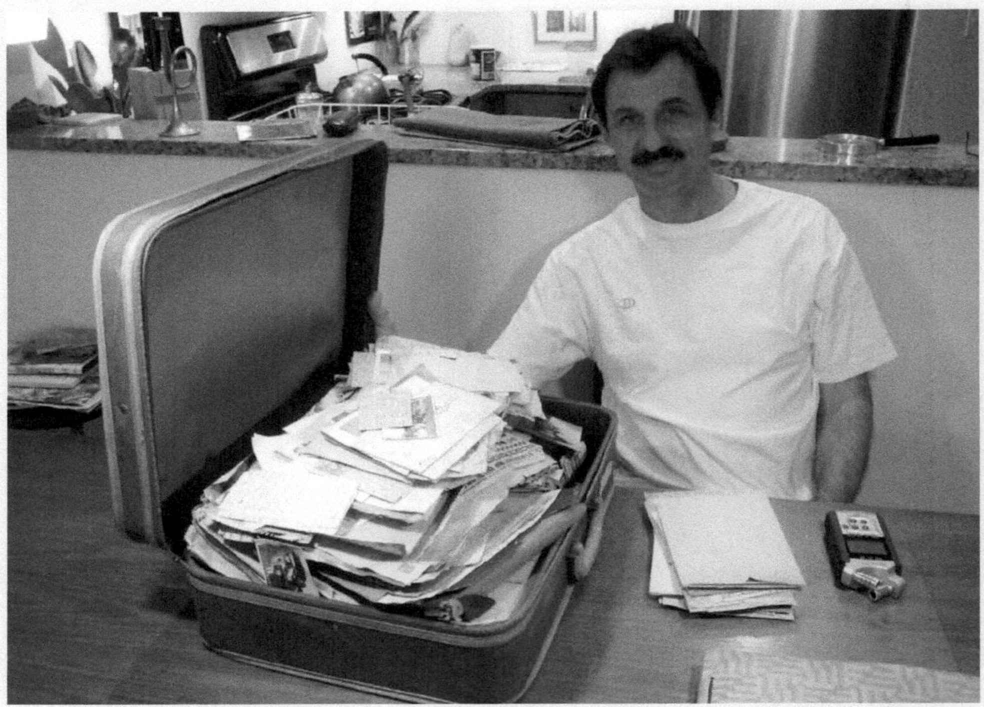

9. Robert Maass and the Maass-Mann family papers, brought to the USA by his father Ernst Maass. Photo taken at Robert Maass' home in Brooklyn (New York). February 5, 2010.

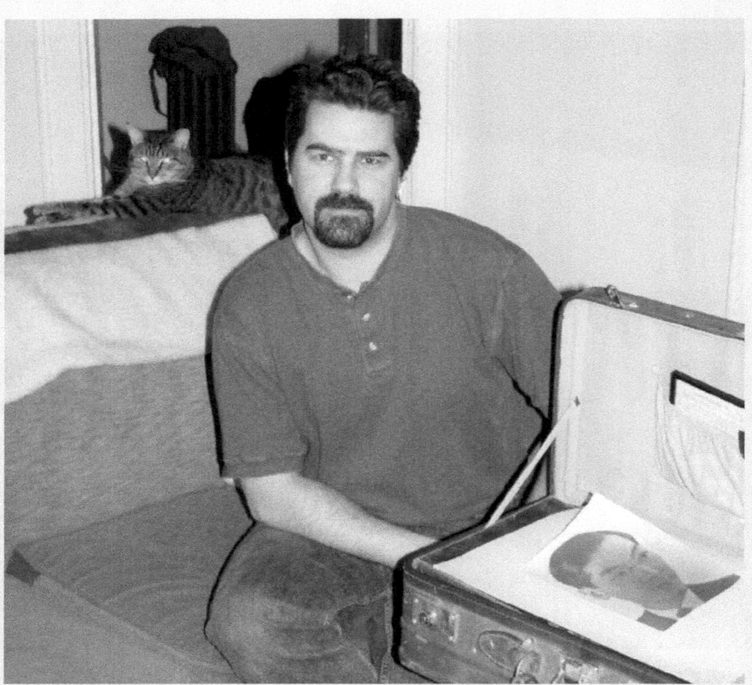

10. Adam P. W. Smith (and cat Jamie) in his Toronto flat with Li Shiu Tong's materials, which Smith saved from a dumpster in 1993. 2003.

11. Magnus Hirschfeld's finished grave in Nice in the Caucade cemetery. Photo dated August-September 1936. Most likely, this picture was sent by Li Shiu Tong to Giese in Brno in 1936. Giese then glued the picture in the Hirschfeld guestbook in his possession.

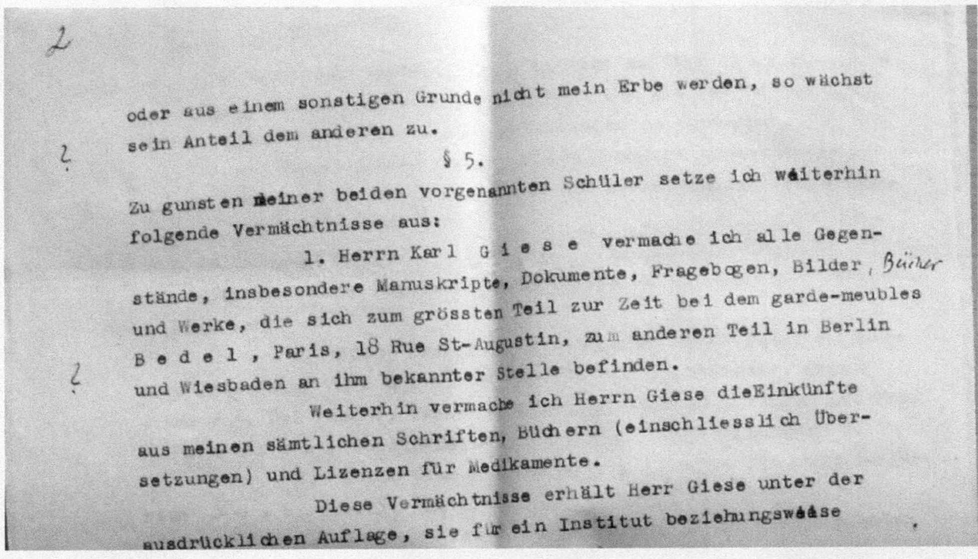

2

oder aus einem sonstigen Grunde nicht mein Erbe werden, so wächst sein Anteil dem anderen zu.

§ 5.

Zu gunsten meiner beiden vorgenannten Schüler setze ich weiterhin folgende Vermächtnisse aus:

1. Herrn Karl G i e s e vermache ich alle Gegenstände, insbesondere Manuskripte, Dokumente, Fragebogen, Bilder, Bücher und Werke, die sich zum grössten Teil zur Zeit bei dem garde-meubles B e d e l , Paris, 18 Rue St-Augustin, zum anderen Teil in Berlin und Wiesbaden an ihm bekannter Stelle befinden.

Weiterhin vermache ich Herrn Giese dieEinkünfte aus meinen sämtlichen Schriften, Büchern (einschliesslich Übersetzungen) und Lizenzen für Medikamente.

Diese Vermächtnisse erhält Herr Giese unter der ausdrücklichen Auflage, sie für ein Institut beziehungsweise

12. Typed (draft) version of Hirschfeld's last will, p. 2 (top part of page only). December 1934.

DOPZ
KAVARNA BIBER KAFFEEHAUS
Charlie CHAPLIN
"CITY LIGHTS"
RESTAURACE
RESTAURANT
MORAVIA
BIO
SVĚTLA
VELKOMĚSTA
CHARLIE
GROSSTADT
LICHTER
CHAPLIN
DOPZ
TEL.
34.056

11. Karl Giese Settles Down in Brno for the Third and Last Time

HAVING SOME FINANCIAL SECURITY, GIESE MOVES TO BRNO

On June 7, 1935, two and a half weeks after he arrived in Nice to attend Hirschfeld's funeral ceremony, Giese left. He returned to Vienna where, since October 1934, he had taken residence shortly after being expelled from France. While in Vienna, Giese often went to Brno to inquire with Karl Fein about progress in the Hirschfeld inheritance case. Around the time that the more considerable sums from the Hirschfeld estate were finally being paid to him, Giese moved to Brno. It would be his third and final stay there.[1] Giese received a first significant amount of approximately FF6,500 around the middle of March 1936.[2] On May 22, 1936, he traveled from Vienna to Brno to sign a financial agreement worked out in Nice, which anticipated his getting an extra amount (FF31,500) from Hirschfeld's estate to make up for Bækgaard, Hirschfeld and Haire's falling away.[3] Another significant amount of money, around FF20,000, was paid out to him at the end of June 1936.[4]

On May 29, 1936, one week after the signing of this final financial agreement, Giese moved from Vienna to Brno, ready for a new beginning.[5] Let us remember here that Giese was also expected to move from Vienna to Brno since, as we have seen, the May 1936 financial settlement stipulated – about the approximately FF31,500 extra that Giese obtained (in addition to the FF15,000 to which he was already entitled) – that Giese would *solely* use the money to work with Dr. Weisskopf in Brno to start up a new Institute there: "Mr. Karl Giese and Mr. Li Shiu Tong engage themselves to use all the sums they will receive from Dr. Hirschfeld's estate exclusively for the purposes of sexology in the spirit of Dr. Hirschfeld's ideas, work, and efforts on sexology in accordance with the terms of his will. In particular, Mr. Giese undertakes to use his share of the said sums, including the amount of 31,500 francs stated above, for a sexological archive which he engages to found in BRNO (C.S.R.) with the assistance of Dr. WEISSKOPF, resident in Brno".[6] François Herzfelder did not take this financial

[1] That is also why, in 1948, Kurt Hiller could write in the Swiss gay magazine *Der Kreis – Le Cercle*: "Wien oder in Brünn, den Städten, in denen er [Karl Giese] sich abwechselnd aufhielt" (Vienna or Brno, the cities in which he [Karl Giese] alternated) (Hiller 1948, 353).

[2] Soetaert 2014, 51, Table 7, Mar. 16, 1936. FF = French francs.

[3] The financial agreement was signed by Giese in Brno on May 22, 1936. See ADAM, Nice, Archives notariales, minutes notariales étude Pierre Demnard, May 29, 1936, n° 727, cote 03E 148/036.

[4] Soetaert 2014, 51, Table 7, Jun. 27, 1936. It is possible, and even likely, that the entry date given by the employees of the Demnard notary office for this payment is mistaken and that the money was already paid out on May 27, 1936. I think he was paid in May rather than June, since Giese moved from Vienna to Brno two days later, on May 29, 1936. A final amount of approximately FF15,000 was paid out to him in August 1936.

[5] Email (dated Dec. 10, 2010) from Wiener Stadt- und Landesarchiv to the author: "Am 29.05.1936 ist die Abmeldung nach Brünn vermerkt." Bestand WStLA, Bundespolizeidirektion Wien, Historische Meldeunterlagen. Another Czech archival file says that Giese lived in Brno starting from June 2, 1936. See MZA, Brno, fonds B 40, Zemský úřad Brno (Landesbehörde in Brünn), kart. n° 2138, sign. 5274/38, letter (dated Jun. 18, 1936) from Brno police to the Zemský úřad v Brně (Landesbehörde in Brünn), f. 19. Later, Giese would return to Vienna only a few times – and only for short visits – as indicated by the Breclav border stamps in his passport: Jul. 21, 1936 (day return), Jul. 23, 1937 (day return) and Jul. 28, 1937 (no return date stamp).

[6] ADAM, Nice, Archives notariales, minutes notariales étude Pierre Demnard, May 29, 1936, n° 727, cote

agreement lightly and had apparently talked the matter through with Josef Weisskopf before Giese put his signature to the agreement at the end of May 1936. At least that is how Herzfelder recalled Weisskopf's engagement in 1938, in a letter to Ernst Maass: "Dr. Weisskopf (who had assumed responsibility to me for the use, in accordance with the will, of all values and objects legated to Mr. Giese from the estate of Dr. Hirschfeld)."[7] Giese may then have still believed, or simply made others believe, in the whole cooperative project with Weisskopf. When Eugen Wilhelm visited Giese in July 1936 in Brno, the latter noted in his diary: "Giese wants to collect books on sexuality and form a library, possibly creating a kind of gay center together with a doctor from Brünn. I fear he will not succeed".[8] Wilhelm would prove to be right. But we have also seen that, in reality, Weisskopf did not have the opportunity or the will or the ambition to start up a new Institute in Brno, nor did he wish to associate himself all too publicly to the cause of sexology. Weisskopf's great reluctance was already clear in 1933, when Giese first went to Brno to ask Weisskopf if he was interested in starting a new Institute there.[9] Yet Giese repeated this same false claim again and again. In June 1936, for example, Giese declared his motive for moving from Vienna to Brno to the Czechoslovak authorities in this way: he intended to work with Dr. Weisskopf and both intended to publish their scientific findings in various languages.[10]

Another likely reason for Giese likely choosing Brno over Vienna was that it was cheaper to live there. Giese must have been well aware that, after the settlement of the inheritance in Nice, he had only received, in the end, around FF47,000, or less than 13 percent of the total amount Hirschfeld had in his bank safe and bank accounts at the time of his death. But it is almost certain that, if he could have chosen himself, Giese would have preferred to stay in Vienna. Vienna offered plentiful city delights whereas Brno simply could not compare, a situation that has not changed. Not coincidentally, many Brno gay men continue to this day to go to Vienna or Prague – both three hours away from Brno – to have some "real fun".

GIESE'S APARTMENT ON STŘELECKÁ (SCHÜTZENGASSE)

On May 30, 1936, Giese moved in with his lawyer and friend, the younger Karl Fein, at 7c U dětské nemocnice (Kinderspitalgasse). As in Vienna, Giese identified professionally on the document certifying his arrival as an archivist (*Archivar*).[11]

03E 148/036: "Monsieur Karl Giese et Monsieur Li Shiu Tong prennent l'engagementd'utiliser [*sic*, l'engagement d'utiliser] toutes les sommes qu'ils recevront de la succession du Dr. Hirschfeld, exclusivement aux fins de la sexologie dans l'esprit des idées, travaux et efforts sur la sexologie du Dr. Hirschfeld conformément aux termes de son testament. Spécialement Monsieur Giese s'engage à employer sa part dans lesdites [*sic*, les dites] sommes y compris le montant de 31.500 frs ci-dessus énoncé, pour des archives sexologiques qu'il s'engage à fonder à BRNO (C.S.R.) avec le concours de Monsieur le Docteur WEISSKOPF demeurant à Brno". See also Soetaert 2014, 44, 50.

[7] Archiv MHG, Berlin, fonds Ernst Maass, letter (dated Aug. 31, 1938) from François Herzfelder to Ernst Maass: "Dr. Weisskopf (der mir gegenüber die Verantwortung für die testamentsgemässe Verwendung aller Herrn Giese aus dem Nachlass Dr. Hirschfelds zukommenden Werte und Gegenstände übernommen hatte)".

[8] Diary of Eugen Wilhelm, carnet 39, entry dated Jul. 25, 1936–Sep. 26 1936 and Oct. 3, 1936: "Giese veut recueillir des livres sur la sexualité et former une bibliothèque év.[entuellement] créer avec un médecin de Brunn [*sic*, Brünn] une sorte de centre pour les homos. Je crains fort qu'il ne réussisse pas".

[9] Archiv MHG, Berlin, fonds Adelheid Schulz, letter (dated Aug. 6, 1933) from Karl Giese to Adelheid Schulz.

[10] MZA, Brno, fonds B 40, Zemský úřad Brno (Landesbehörde in Brünn), kart. n° 2138, sign. 5274/38, letter (dated Jun. 18, 1936) from Policejní ředitelství Brno to Zemský úřad v Brně.

[11] AMB, Brno, fonds Z 1, resident registration card for Karl Giese. Karl Fein signed as *Wohnungsgeber* (landlord) and Giese was the *Untermieter* (subtenant). Fein had been living at this address since November 1932. In another document, the house number is given as 7, which is another building. See MZA, Brno, fonds B 40, Zemský úřad Brno (Landesbehörde in Brünn), kart. n° 2138, sign. 5274/38, f. 18. However, I think that house number 7c is right since this is how it is expressly typed on the resident registration card documenting Giese's arrival. In 1934, the 7c U dětské nemocnice apartment building was

From the rear of the apartment building where they lived, they could look into the vast garden and terrace of the magnificent and now famous modernist villa of the Jewish Tugendhat family [ill. 1].[12]

But Giese only stayed in Fein's apartment for the summer. By mid-September 1936, he moved to his own three-room apartment at 8 Střelecká (Schützengasse), in the suburb of Královo Pole (Königsfeld) in northern Brno.[13] The apartment block into which Giese moved had just been built.[14] It is a bit unclear why Giese chose this location but, again, it may have had to do with the mentioned financial agreement: Josef Weisskopf lived a few blocks north of Giese's address in Královo Pole.[15] Another reason that may have played a part was that, like with his former apartment in Vienna, the new one was located just opposite a military barracks.[16] Apparently, the sexual availability of soldiers – always considered more reliable than male prostitutes – was as common in Brno as in Vienna and Berlin.[17] Giese lived in apartment 7 on the second floor of the building. The three-room apartment had a hallway (*Vorzimmer*), a kitchen, and a bathroom.[18] He would stay in this modern apartment until his untimely death in March 1938 [ill. 2].[19]

owned by a certain Karel Koschalek. See *Adreßbuch von Groß-Brünn* 1934, 811. The street name refers to a children's hospital in the immediate vicinity. This hospital still exists but has now been replaced by a modern building.

[12] The Tugendhat Villa has an important place in Brno history. The modernist villa was designed by Mies Van der Rohe, commissioned by the very well-off Jewish Tugendhat family. The 1993 negotiations which resulted in the dissolution of Czechoslovakia took place there. For several years, the villa was closed for restoration, opening to the public again in March 2012. In 2001, it was recognized as a UNESCO world heritage site. See https://whc.unesco.org/en/list/1052/ (accessed Nov. 27, 2021).

[13] The current name of the street is Domažlická. During the German occupation, the street was renamed Asperngasse (Aspernská). A few weeks later, in the beginning of October 1936, Karl Fein moved from his Kinderspitalgasse (U dětské nemocnice) apartment to 35 Koliště (Glacis).

[14] Email (dated Sep. 26, 2018) from Lea Oškerová (Odbor územního a stavebního řízení, OUSŘ, Brno) to the author. She wrote me that the building was erected in 1936. When I went to visit the apartment building, in December 2009, the building still had its original look but was quite dilapidated. In 2011, the facade and interior were completely renovated and lost a lot of its original characteristics. For example, the wooden front door was replaced by an aluminum one.

[15] Weisskopf lived at 15 Serbische Gasse (Srbská) in Královo Pole, a suburb that was already part of greater Brno. Weisskopf moved from his initial address, 2 Tyršgasse (Tyršova) to Serbische Gasse (Srbská) around 1934–35. See MZA, Brno, fonds B 40, Zemský úřad v Brně, presidiální registratura, kart. N° 175, sign. 553/32, protocol Dec. 15, 1931; *Adreßbuch von Groß-Brünn* 1934, 599; and *Nezávislá politika*, May 18, 1935, 5.

[16] The old name of the street where Giese lived, Střelecká (Schützengasse), refers to the Artilleriekaserne (artillery barracks, Dělostřelecká kasárna). The Jaselská kasárna, built in 1903, became the Adolf-Hitler-Kaserne II or III during the German occupation. See Filip, Břečka & Schildberger et al. 2012, 170, 278. To this day, it is still a Czech military building, nowadays known as Krajské vojenské velitelství Brno. Behind the block where Giese lived, there was another, even larger barracks, the Neue Kavalleriekaserne (Nová jezdecká kasárna) that today houses the veterinary and pharmaceutical faculties of Masaryk University. See Filip, Břečka, Schildberger et al. 2012, 171, 278.

[17] Seidl 2017, 81–82. Beachy also mentions this common Berlin phenomenon (Beachy 2014, 9, 65, 200ff.). For two other examples, revealing that this was a widespread (though today hardly comprehensible) European phenomenon, see Dubout & Wolfert 2013; Apitzsch & Artières 2006. Elledge 2023, 112, depicts the same practice for 1920s and 1930s New York.

[18] Judging from the handwritten deletion in the lease, Giese was initially to take apartment 5 on the first floor, but he ended up in apartment 7 on the second floor. The same floor and apartment number can be found in both the rental booklet and the rental agreement. See MZA, Brno, fonds C 107, Německý úřední soud Brno (Deutsches Amtsgericht Brünn), kart. n° 256, sign. 5aV 3/41, f. 4 and f. 6. We find the same apartment 7 also on the back of an envelope of a letter (dated Oct. 31, 1937) from Karl Giese to Adelheid Schulz, Archiv MHG, Berlin, fonds Adelheid Schulz.

[19] The apartment was owned and rented out by the Vladimír Stavíček Baumeister firm, located at 6 Sirotčí (Waisenhausgasse). See MZA, Brno, fonds C 107, Německý úřední soud Brno (Deutsches Amtsgericht Brünn), kart. n° 256, sign. 5aV 3/41, f. 6. Possibly, at the time of Giese's death, in March 1938, the building became property of the Sonnenschein family. See ibid., f. 29.

GIESE'S RELATIVELY CAREFREE LIFE IN BRNO

We hardly know anything about Giese's activities in Brno since only very few sources documenting Giese's life at that time remain. As we will see later, his personal archive has most likely been completely lost. The main source for Giese's life in Brno are (the surviving) letters that he sent to friends and acquaintances. First of all, we need to mention that, in a repetition of the story in Vienna, Giese never started medical studies at Masaryk University in Brno.[20] "The plan to become a doctor was – with good reason – abandoned by Giese", Eugen Wilhelm wrote in his diary after visiting Giese in the summer of 1936.[21] In Nice, Pierre Demnard and François Herzfelder were also aware that Giese had given up on his medical studies. Giese never took a job in Brno because immigrants simply were not allowed to work.[22] The money from the Hirschfeld estate meant that he did not need one.[23]

Apparently, Giese kept himself busy with all kinds of – unpaid – activities he liked. In an October 1937 postcard to Adelheid Schulz, he wrote that he was working on a fairy tale (*Märchen*) called "The Lover's Fairy Tale" (*Märchen von den Liebesleuten*) and that three quarters of it was written. Giese added that the story was based on an unidentified Brno couple, Gustl and Livia. He was well-acquainted with the couple, who also taught Giese how to cook.[24] Did Giese have writing ambitions? In a document that Karl Fein wrote together with Giese, Giese was presented as an archivist and a writer (*archivař a spisovatel*).[25] Giese was also perfecting his basic English and apparently mainly read English-language books.[26] He had already been relatively proficient in English when still living in the Institute in Berlin, from which he wrote letters to Norman Haire. When he was in Vienna, Giese also read English-language

[20] Emails (dated Oct. 24, 2010 and Nov. 1, 2010) from Jitka Krylová (Archiv Masarykovy univerzity, Brno) to the author.

[21] Diary of Eugen Wilhelm, carnet 39, entry dated Jul. 25, 1936–Sep. 26, 1936 and Oct. 3, 1936: "Le projet de devenir médecin a été – avec raison – abandonné par Giese".

[22] For immigrants not being allowed to take on paid work, see Kämper 2015, 93; Ondrichová 2000, 22.

[23] MZA, Brno, fonds B 40, Zemský úřad Brno (Landesbehörde in Brünn), kart. n° 2138, sign. 5274/38. Giese also signaled a certain lethargy in a letter he sent to Ernst Maass in December 1937, in which he also appears evasive on the subject: "Mit der Arbeit als Aequivalent für alles Verlorene ist es beides (?) nicht (?) viel (?) (?) Von einer produktiven Tätigkeit muss mann absehen und die andere ist auf die Dauer höchst unbefriedigend. Vielleicht werde ich mich noch einmal wieder umstellen müssen" (With work as an equivalent for all the losses, it is both ... not ... much ... You must refrain from any productive activity and anything else is highly unsatisfactory in the long run. Maybe I will have to adjust once again.) See Archiv MHG, Berlin, fonds Ernst Maass, letter (dated Dec. 27, 1937, 8) from Karl Giese to Ernst Maass.

[24] See Archiv MHG, Berlin, fonds Adelheid Schulz, letter (dated Oct. 31, 1937, 2) from Karl Giese to Adelheid Schulz, which says that the couple would get married the next year. I checked the Jewish registers (Židovské matriky, Judische Matriken) in the NA, Praha, fonds n° 167, for the years 1937–41, and also the Brno městská rada marriage registers for the years 1937 until 1939 at http://actapublica.eu/ but did not find any Gustav married to a Livia there. I did find one Livia Colucci (1913–?), of Italian descent, who was married to Bořivoj Král (1909–?). This was also the only mention of the first name Olivia that I found for that time period. They married on April 21, 1938. See http://actapublica.eu/matriky/brno/prohlizec/10773/?strana=50 (accessed Jun. 16, 2020). But, of course, there is no way to link Gustl (Gustav) with the first name Bořivoj. Olivia's father, František Colucci (*c.* 1866–1938), on the other hand, worked for the cement factory Leo Czech & Co. in Maloměřice (Malomierschütz or also Malmeritz) and we have already seen that Karl Fein had ties with the owner of this big company and the Brno building industry in general. See also n° 3 in the addenda. In April 1938, in an explosion on the company premises, caused by the use of dynamite, František Colucci was wounded and four workers were killed. See "Hrozné neštěstí v Malomeřické Dynamitový cementárně", *Moravská orlice*, April 28, 1938, 1. This article says that František Colucci came from San Demetrio in Italy, had worked for the company for thirty years, and was the father of two other children. I did not follow up on these two, but Livia's mother, Elisabeth Colucci, still lived in Brno after the war. See *Adresář zemského hlavního města Brna* 1948, 42.

[25] MZA, Brno, fonds B 40, Zemský úřad Brno (Landesbehörde in Brünn), kart. n° 2138, sign. 5274/38, f. 6.

[26] Archiv MHG, Berlin, fonds Adelheid Schulz, letter (dated Oct. 31, 1937) from Karl Giese to Adelheid Schulz.

[27] Giese mentioned the author's name (spelling it "Muntsche") in a letter (dated Oct. 20, 1935) to Max Reiss, Archiv MHG, Berlin, fonds Max Reiss. For the

books. One of these, sent to him by a friend in the USA, was the bestseller *The Story of San Michele* by the Swedish doctor and psychiatrist Axel Munthe (1857–1949) about his villa and its famous guests in Capri.[27] Is this an indication that Giese was still planning or hoping to emigrate to an Anglo-Saxon country one day? That he might at least have considered emigrating to the USA – maybe seeing the country as a place where he would not have to worry about his personal freedom – is attested by a touching letter, most likely the very last, that he wrote to Ernst Maass: "If I had a talent for envy [...], I would now envy your journey through France and especially to the U.S.A., still the 'New World'".[28] Lastly, Eugen Wilhelm's diary mentions that, apart from the money he received from the Hirschfeld estate, Giese had "no other means of existence than to publish occasional articles in German newspapers".[29] To my knowledge, nothing is known about any texts that Giese may have written after 1935, and presumably published in German-language exile newspapers. Of course, he may have published these pseudonymously.

It is generally assumed that Giese lived in poverty in Brno. For a long time, many thought that Giese never touched the money he inherited from the Hirschfeld estate.[30] The records of the 480 Czech crowns (Koruna česká, Kč) paid monthly in the rental booklet for his apartment show that Giese never had a problem paying the rent.[31] Giese had received around FF47,000 from the Hirschfeld estate, but since he had borrowed money here and there and had also received a few advance payments, totaling around FF11,500, he started out his new life in Brno, in May–June 1936, with approximately FF35,500, which amounts to 56,000 Czech crowns.[32] We also know that Giese still had 38,000 Czech crowns in his Czech bank account in June 1937, one year after he arrived in Brno.[33] That means that he had spent around 20,000 Czech crowns in one year. If we look at the monthly rent of 480 Czech crowns, recorded in the rental booklet, from mid-September 1936 until June 1937, Giese would have paid 4,620 Czech crowns in rent. We may presume that Giese paid Karl Fein some rent

novel itself, see Munthe 1931. While on his world tour, in November 1931, Hirschfeld planned to go to Capri with Giese on his return, but this never happened. See Hirschfeld & Dose 2013, f. 60/132; Hirschfeld 2003, 37. At the top of a letter from Norman Haire to Ernst Maass, there is written "Giese" and the titles of two books. See Archiv MHG, Berlin, fonds Ernst Maass, letter (dated May 29, 1935, 1) from Norman Haire to Ernst Maass. Are these books that Giese recommended to Maass or rather books that were recommended to him by Ernst Maass? The handwriting seems to be Maass's. The titles were Geoffrey Gorer's *The Marquis de Sade: A Short Account of His Life and Work* (Gorer 1934b, American edition) and Cesare Giardini's *Lo strano caso del cavaliere d'Éon: 1728–1810* (Giardini 1935). The Italian title would seem to indicate that Maass was the one responsible for the (perhaps only intended) recommendations, since he was working for an Italian publisher in 1935.

[28] Archiv MHG, Berlin, fonds Ernst Maass, letter (dated Jan. 21, 1938) from Karl Giese to Ernst Maass: "Wenn ich Talent zum Neid hätte [...], so wurde ich Sie nun Ihre Reise durch Frankreich und vor allem nach U.S.A., der immer noch "Neuen Welt", beneiden".

[29] Diary of Eugen Wilhelm, carnet 39, entry dated Jul. 25, 1936–Sep. 26, 1936 and Oct. 3, 1936: "pas d'autres moyens d'existence que de publier de rares articles dans des journaux allemands".

[30] Sigusch wrote that Giese lived in Brno "in großer Armut" (in great poverty) (Sigusch 2008, 356). Hergemöller even claimed that Giese was on the verge of dying from hunger ("Dem Hungertod nahe") (Hergemöller 1998, 279). Even Herrn, Taylor and Timm continue to repeat that Giese and Li Shiu Tong never received their part of the Hirschfeld inheritance, despite my text on the handling and settlement of the Hirschfeld estate published in 2014 (Herrn, Taylor & Timm 2017, 69, fig. 36; see Soetaert 2014).

[31] MZA, Brno, fonds C 107, Německý úřední soud Brno (Deutsches Amtsgericht Brünn), kart. n° 256, sign. 5aV 3/41, rental booklet (*knížka nájemní, Zinsbüchel*) Karl Giese. A monthly fee of ten Czech crowns was added to this monthly rent for the *Hausbesorger* (housekeeper) Jaroslav Vysekal.

[32] See Soetaert 2014, 51, Table 7. Eugen Wilhelm visited Giese in Brno, in July 1936, and heard about the amount paid out to Giese: "Giese a enfin reçu sa part d'héritage de Hirschfeld 30.000 f.[rancs] dont il vit". See diary of Eugen Wilhelm, carnet 39, entry dated Jul. 25, 1936–Sep. 26, 1936 and Oct. 3, 1936.

[33] The money was deposited in an account of the Anglo-české banky v Brně. See MZA, Brno, fonds B 40, Zemský úřad Brno (Landesbehörde in Brünn), kart. n° 2138, sign. 5274/38, f. 13. I have used the 1935 conversion rate according to which FF1 = 1.58 Czech crowns, as in Soetaert 2014, 51, Table 7.

when he was living with him in the summer months of 1936. If we assume a total of 6,000 Czech crowns in rent, this means that Giese had 14.000 Czech crowns left. In other words, he spent a little more than 1,000 Czech crowns a month on average on other expenses. We also do not see any distress about material conditions in any of the postcards or letters Giese wrote to Adelheid Schulz either. Every day some fresh buns and milk were delivered to his door.[34]

We have already seen that, when he was living in the Institute in Berlin, Giese was fond of cats. For his birthday, in October 1936, he was given a young white angora kitten by his friends.[35] These "friends" suggest that Giese was not living a secluded life. He likely also frequented the Café Biber, located in the DOPZ building, the main meeting point for Brno social democrats as well as many German exiles. It is also possible that Giese attended one of Klaus Mann's lectures there [ill. 3].[36] Probably, Giese also visited the gay bars in the city. The best known where "die Warmen" (German slang for gay men) congregated was the buffet on the first floor of the modernist Passage Hotel in the Neugasse (Nová). It was likely no coincidence that Klaus Mann stayed in this hotel specifically when he was in Brno [ill. 4].[37] Another gay venue was the nearby Museumscafé.[38]

Friends also came to visit him from abroad. Two months after he arrived in Brno, the Alsatian gay activist and Hirschfeld follower, Eugen (Eugène) Wilhelm, visited with a friend named Albert Bastian and other friends of Wilhelm. Giese went to pick them up at the main Brno railway station and introduced them to Karl Fein and to one of Giese's best friends in Brno, Willi Bondi. The troupe took long walks in the wooded countryside around Brno. A young Alsatian man named Kurt or Karl Barbie especially enamored Eugen Wilhelm, and this quickly ended in his having sex with the young man.[39] Wilhelm also reported on the cruising going on in the evenings in one of the Brno parks, presumably the Augarten (Lužánky) park, which was (and still is) quite near to the two gay bars just mentioned.[40] I have argued elsewhere that Karl Giese (and his Brno gay friends) likely also met the twenty-six years old – and later French writer – Jean Genet (1910-1986) when the latter was in Brno, from March to June 1937.[41]

[34] MZA, Brno, fonds C 107, Německý úřední soud Brno (Deutsches Amtsgericht Brünn), kart. n° 256, sign. 5aV 3/41, f. 12, in which a certain Ludmila Purová, after Giese's death, had an outstanding bill for the half liter of milk and three *Brötchens* (buns) delivered daily.

[35] Archiv MHG, Berlin, fonds Adelheid Schulz, postcard (dated Oct. 20, 1936) from Karl Giese to Adelheid Schulz. See also Schulz 2001, 33.

[36] Klaus Mann lectured in the DOPZ building on December 6, 1935 and April 16, 1937. See Bečvová 2007, 17–18 and *Licht ins Volk!*, Jg. 8, Heft n° 2, 1935/1936, 4–5. Giese was certainly living in Brno in April 1937. It is less likely, but nevertheless possible, that Giese went to see Erika Mann's cabaret performance *Die Pfeffermühle* in the DOPZ building. Giese was not living in Brno when it was performed in February 1935, September 1935, and February 1936. Of course, he could have traveled from Vienna to Brno to see it. After all, Giese often went from Vienna to Brno to see his lawyer Karl Fein about the handling of the Hirschfeld inheritance in Nice in 1935–36. After 1933, and until 1937, the cabaret was only performed in Switzerland, the Benelux and Czechoslovakia. See Bečvová 2007; *Licht ins Volk!*, Jg. 8, Heft n° 2, 1935/1936, 6.

[37] Bečvová 2007, 26.

[38] MZA, Brno, fonds C 43, Německý zemský soud Brno (Staatsanwaltschaft bei dem Landgericht Brünn), file Wilhelm Sponer & Helmuth Holdau, kart. n° 184, sign. 4 K Ls 24/41, Kripo-testimony (dated Mar. 18, 1941) Franz Seebauer (1902–?), f. 70. The Passage-Büffett (Passage-buffet) is also mentioned as a place where gay men gathered in Wilhelm Sponer's testimony (dated Mar. 18, 1941). See MZA, Brno, fonds C 43, Německý zemský soud Brno (Staatsanwaltschaft bei dem Landgericht Brünn), file Wilhelm Sponer & Helmuth Holdau, kart. n° 184, sign. 4 K Ls 24/41, f. 73b. The Passage Hotel was later renamed Hotel Slovan and exists to this day.

[39] Diary Eugen Wilhelm, carnet 39, entry dated Jul. 25, 1936–Sep. 26, 1936 and Oct. 3, 1936.

[40] Diary of Eugen Wilhelm, carnet 39, entry dated Jul. 25, 1936–Sep. 9, 1936: "Dans un des parcs le soir grand strich" (In one of the parks, in the evening, busy cruising area). Cf. Valtus 2015, 12, 97, 99.

[41] Soetaert 2024.

[42] Schulz 2001, 88, 116–17, 122.

Giese had a strong aversion to transvestites and transsexuals, apparently calling them "a terrible lot" (*ein schreckliches Volk*).[42] Despite this dislike, in Brno he was in contact with a former resident of the Institute, Toni (Arno, Anna) Ebel (1881–1961), and her lover Charlotte Charlaque (1892–1963), both transsexuals. Ebel arrived in Brno at the beginning of November 1936 and stayed there until March 1939.[43] Toni Ebel was operated on at the Institute by Ludwig Levy-Lenz.[44] In the correspondence between Giese and Adelheid Schulz, they sometimes speak about "Toni", but this was rather Giese's sister, Toni Mertens.[45] It was likely also Toni Mertens (and not his other sister, Martha Thal) who visited Giese in Brno, in March or April 1937.[46]

It is not known if Giese ever kept a diary. As already mentioned, the main source for his life are the surviving letters that he sent to friends and acquaintances. He was an avid letter writer, often noting in his letters – as we saw earlier – that he had "Briefschulden".[47] He wrote a lot of letters to his sister Toni Mertens and also several letters and postcards to Adelheid Schulz. But the current relatives of his siblings, especially those of his sister Toni Mertens, have still not been identified. It seems unlikely to me, though, that Giese's letters to his sister Toni could have survived. Let's now turn to the two most important people in Karl Giese's life when he lived in Brno between 1936 and 1938, Willi Bondi and Walter Lukl.

GIESE'S GOOD FRIEND WILLI BONDI

Very probably, Karl Giese often went to the theater since his best friend in Brno was Willi (Wilhelm) Bondi (1897–1941) [ill. 5].[48] It was most likely Karl Fein who introduced Bondi to Giese. Bondi was the son of the Jewish Gustav Bondi (1860–1941) and his non-Jewish wife Marie Windner (1871–1952). Gustav Bondi was the long-serving secretary and deputy director (*stellvertretende Direktor*) of the German Theater (Deutsches Theater) in Brno.[49] Brno had three theaters in Giese's time: the main city theater (currently the Mahenovo divadlo) in the Krapfengasse (Kobližná), the Redoute (Reduta) on Krautmarkt (Zelný trh), and the Deutsches Haus (Německý dům) on Lazanskyplatz (Lažanského náměstí). Theater was one of the main venues in which the cultural wars between Czechs and Germans were fought out in Brno.[50]

Through his friendship with Willi Bondi, Giese was able satisfy his lifelong love of the theatre. The two would have had easy access to all kinds of theatrical

[43] See the resident registration cards for Ebel in the AMB, Brno, fonds Z 1, where (s)he is clearly sometimes perceived by the Brno police (or presented her/himself when filling out the form) as a man and sometimes as a woman. See also Schulz 2001, 18-19. I thank Raimund Wolfert for spelling out Ebel's many first names for me. See also Wolfert 2015a, 2021.

[44] Schulz 2001, 75.

[45] Wolfert 2015a; Schulz 2001, 15–17.

[46] Archiv Kurt Hiller Gesellschaft, Neuss, letter (dated Apr. 27, 1937, 1) from Karl Giese to Kurt Hiller.

[47] See above, chapter 2, p. 34.

[48] Willi Bondi is not to be confused with the Prague Jewish psychiatrist, Hugo Bondy (1897--1939). Hugo Bondy, who also worked as a court expert in sexual pathology, played a pivotal role in the Czechoslovak homosexual emancipation movement of the First Republic. See, for example, Bondy 1925. Giese knew Hugo Bondy as he had visited Hirschfeld's Institute in Berlin, see Seidl 2007a, 73. Giese also spoke to Bondy (about the thwarted gay activist agenda in Czechoslovakia) in Prague, in the beginning of 1937, see Archiv Kurt Hiller Gesellschaft, Neuss, letter (dated Apr. 27, 1937, 1) from Karl Giese to Kurt Hiller. Bondy was also present at the 1928 Copenhagen WLSR conference, where he reported on the proposal to reform the penal code in the Czechoslovak Republic. See Sigusch 2008, 100. For the text of the lecture he gave, see Bondy 1929. Bondy was married and committed suicide shortly after the Reichsprotektorat Böhmen und Mähren (Protectorate of Bohemia and Moravia) was installed, in April 1939. His wife and children perished in a concentration camp. See Seidl 2007a, 74.

[49] *Adreßbuch von Groß-Brünn* 1934, 876.

[50] Wessely 2011, 116–18. Gustav Bondi also published on the Brno theater, another testimony to his lifelong passion for it. See, for example, Bondi 1907 and Bondy 1924. Hans Demetz (1894–1983) was one of Brno's theater directors (1926–32). See Wessely 2011, 122–25. He was also the father of the writer Peter Demetz (1922–), who has published several books on Prague under Nazi rule. I contacted Peter Demetz in February 2012 to ask him several things about Brno, a city where he had lived when he was a young man.

performances thanks to Gustav Bondi's high-ranking position in Brno's theatrical world. The Bondi family had their own box in the city theater and must have surely invited acquaintances and friends on occasion.[51] That the son of the deputy director of the main theater was a gay man was more than a happy coincidence. At the time, the theater was for a large number of gay men a central part of their identity. Several 1941 testimonies make it clear that many gay men worked for the Brno theater. A singer named Hans Drabek (1913–?) once even argued in his defense that, just *because* he worked for the Brno theater, this did *not* automatically mean that he was gay.[52] Many gay men likely also attended the theater performances. One of the people from Brno whom I interviewed, Helga Sikora, told me that she went at least once a month to the Mahen Theater with her mother, recalling above all the extraordinary performances of one male dancer – whose name she could not remember – and the "many men" attending his performances.[53]

The Bondi family was thoroughly well-established and lived on one of the posh streets of Brno, at 18 Legionärenstrasse (třída Legionářů).[54] Willi Bondi lived with his parents, who "accepted his homosexuality and welcomed his German- and Czech-speaking male friends into their flat".[55] So we may assume that Giese visited the Bondis once in a while, or even quite often. Willi Bondi had apparently "a wonderful sense of humor" and was very good at mimicry.[56] This vision of a fun guy to be around, with a love of theater, and Communist-leaning politics must have appealed to Giese. As we have seen, Giese's parents, and also his sister Toni Mertens, were Communists. Bondi's atheist conviction might have also attracted Giese. When, in 1934, Giese was imprisoned in France and asked to name his religion, he let the civil servant note: "none". That was an explicit declaration since we know Giese was baptized a Protestant (*Evangelisch*) in the church near his birth house in Berlin.[57] Willi Bondi and Karl Giese were also close in age, Bondi being one year older.

[51] Email (dated Sep. 20, 2012) from Judy M. King to the author.

[52] MZA, Brno, fonds C 43, Německý zemský soud Brno (Staatsanwaltschaft bei dem Landgericht Brünn), file Wilhelm Sponer & Helmuth Holdau, kart. n° 184, sign. 4 K Ls 24/41, testimony of Hans Drabek (dated Mar. 20, 1941), f. 74 and f. 74b: "Wenn ich in diesen [homosexuelle] Kreisen verkehre, dann ist dies auf meine Tätigkeit beim Theater zurückzuführen, nicht aber, weil ich homosexuell veranlagt bin". Many names mentioned in this same file were indeed professionally linked to the Brno theater: the actor Paul Mentos (stage name), f. 18b and f. 71b; Balletmeister Anton Wojanitsch, f. 18 and f. 66b; Hans (Johann) Drabek, f. 75 and f. 47b; Wilhelm Sponer, f. 70b; Jan Kiveron, f. 75; and, finally, a German man named Bergmann who was originally from Frankfurt am Main, f. 71b.

[53] Author's interview with Helga Sikora (dated Feb. 7, 2016).

[54] The Brno address books consistently mention the same 18 Legionärenstrasse (třída Legionářů) address for Gustav and Wilhelm Bondi throughout the years.

[55] Email (dated Sep. 20, 2012) from Peter Barber to the author.

[56] Email (dated Sep. 20, 2012) from Judy M. King to the author.

[57] Archives départementales du Val-de-Marne, Créteil, Etablissement pénitentiaire de Fresnes, registre d'écrou, cote 2Y5 277, JO22, mention Karl Giese in the *rubrique* (section) "Allemagne".

[58] Hermine Bondi and her daughter Helga Wolfenstein (1922–2003) were deported on transport "G" from Brno to Terezín on December 2, 1941. Hermine, who was married to (and later divorced) Bernhard Wolfenstein (1887–1942?), was head of the nursery in Terezín. She died on typhus on the day Terezín was liberated by the Russians, in May 1945. As a twenty-year-old in Terezín, Helga Wolfenstein had an intense love affair with the artist Peter Kien (1919–1944). See Serke 2006. It was thanks to this story that I was able to trace the current relatives of the Bondi family. Hermine's other daughter, Renate Wolfenstein (1918–1987), managed to reach Palestine with her husband Frederick Barber in September 1940. After the war, the couple settled down in England. I was lucky to find and speak to the current relatives of the surviving Bondi/Wolfenstein/Barber family. I want to express my sincere gratitude to Judy M. King (1959–), the only child of Helga King (née Wolfenstein) and Eric King; and to Peter M. Barber (1948–), the oldest of Renate Barber's (née Wolfenstein) four sons. Judy and Peter were very quick to talk to me and helpfully shared photographs and archival documents related their family's past and their gay great-uncle. I have used information, and quoted from the emails they wrote me in September and October 2012, in order to complete the portrait of the Bondi family. The Brno Jewish cemetery

Willi Bondi was the youngest child of the Bondi family and had three older sisters, Hermine (1893–1945),[58] the eldest, then Julia (Ully) (1895–1982),[59] the youngest being Elisabeth (Aesche) (1896–1941?).[60] Elisabeth's husband, Leopold Fleischer (1891–1941?), lent Giese a considerable sum when Giese was still living in Vienna and waiting for money from the Hirschfeld estate. After the settlement of Hirschfeld's estate, Giese repaid him in 1936.[61] That the Bondi-Fleischer family lent Giese money seems to attest to a real friendship between Giese and Willi Bondi and his family. I also think it quite likely that, in April 1934, the Leopold Fleischer moving firm transported some of the Institute materials bought back from Nazi Germany in 1933 from Brno to Paris. In that case, lending Giese money was maybe also a favor after a prior lucrative business deal. Willi Bondi worked as a secretary in the law office of his brother-in-law, Bernhard Wolfenstein (1887–1942), the (divorced) husband of Bondi's sister Hermine.[62] At some point during Giese's stay in Brno, in 1936–38, Bondi must have started to work for the Leopold Fleischer moving firm, then run by Leopold Fleischer's brother, Bruno Fleischer.[63] After the death of her husband Bruno, in July 1939, Julia Fleischer took over the management of the company until it was Aryanized during the war. We will return to this moving firm and its history later.

Willi Bondi's life ended in tragedy. One evening, in mid-March 1941, around 9 p.m., along with several other gay men, his sister Julia Fleischer, his brother-in-law Leopold Fleischer, and others, among them a lesbian friend or even lover of Julia Fleischer, Kamila Gregor (1896–?), Bondi was arrested by the Gestapo in Julia Fleischer's apartment at 21 Ponawkagasse (Na Ponávce) in Brno.[64] It was known to

houses the grave of Gustav Bondi, who died in May 1941, to which Hermine Wolfenstein's ashes were added. See Condell 2005, 223. The grave is in parcel 19, row 7, grave 4. The stone contains an error in the date: the month of Hermine Bondi's death is mistakenly given as March 9, 1945. Peter Barber wrote to me that this was likely due to a misunderstanding between the Czech-speaking stonemason and Julia Bondi, who only spoke German. A small white marble grave plaque (placed there on the initiative of Julia Fleischer), mentioning Gustav, Willi, and Hermine Bondi, has been added to the grave plot. The plaque makes no mention of Elisabeth Fleischer because Julia Bondi at first tried to conceal the news of her death from their mother, Maria Windner. See email (dated Oct. 22, 2012) from Peter Barber to the author; Condell 2005, 223. See http://www.hohenemsgenealogie.at/en/genealogy/getperson.php?personID=I16838&tree=Hohenems (accessed Jan. 12, 2017) for more genealogical information on the Bondi family (a few dates are mistaken).

[59] Julia Fleischer was deported with her son Karl Heinz (1925–1945) from Brno to Terezín on transport "Ai" on April 8, 1942. Julia Bondi, who was a nurse in Terezín, survived and lived in Brno after the war, where she died in 1982. Her son Karl Heinz was further transferred from Terezín to Auschwitz-Birkenau on transport "Ek", on September 28, 1944. See Kárný et al. 1995, 466, 476. Julia Fleischer is buried, together with her husband Bruno Fleischer (1888–1939), in the Jewish cemetery in Brno in parcel 26B, row 2, grave 8. In front of the grave there is a commemorative stone with the following Czech inscription: "v konc. táborech zahynuli [died in the concentration camps] Arnoštka, Karel, Alois, Leo, Alžběta, Sylvia a Harry Fleischerovi". The names Leo, Sylvia and Harry were members of Elisabeth (Alžběta) Fleischer's immediate family, who all perished in the Holocaust. The seven names on this commemorative stone are not mentioned in the Brno Jewish cemetery database. One can find the inscription of the names in the database in the entry for Leopold and Bruno Fleischer's father, Hermann Fleischer (1853–1927).

[60] Elisabeth, her husband Leopold Fleischer, and their two children, Sylvia (1925–1941?) and Hermann (Harry) (1927–1941?), were deported on transport "F" from Brno to Minsk on November 16, 1941.

[61] Soetaert 2014, 50 and n. 122.

[62] Handwritten note (dated Aug. 25, 2001) by Judy King in the personal archives of Peter Barber.

[63] Willi Bondi's working for the Leopold Fleischer moving firm can also be inferred from Karl Giese's last will. See MZA, Brno, fonds C 107, Německý úřední soud Brno (Deutsches Amtsgericht Brünn), kart. n° 256, sign. 5a V 3/41, f. 9.

[64] Some uncertainty remains about the exact identity of Kamila Gregor. Presumably, she was the unmarried seamstress (*Schneiderin*, *švadlena*), born in 1896 in Kyjov (Gaya). In the beginning of November 1941, she applied successfully for Deutsche Volkszugehörigkeit (German ethnic) status. By February 1946, she was living in Vienna. See AMB, Brno, fonds Z 1. Peter Barber possibly met her in Vienna in the early 1970s, see email (dated Oct. 29, 2021) from Peter Barber to the author. Kamila Gregor invested 30,000 Czech crowns in the Leopold Fleischer company. See the list "Verzeichnis der Gläubiger" (dated Sep. 9, 1940) in NA, Praha, fonds n° 375, Arizačni spisy, kart. n° 205, sign. 1268, liquidation file firm Leopold Fleischer, not foliated. There was also an unmarried gynecologist of the same name, Kamila

the Bondi family that Julia, despite having been married, had lesbian tendencies. Especially after World War II, she was known to partner with a few women. Julia Fleischer herself was apparently rather discreet about her sexual preference [ill. 6].[65] Among the gay men present at the gathering, there was also a German soldier named Franz Helmuth Holdau (1916–?). For our later story, it is important to stress that the gathering raided was to a great extent a gay and also lesbian social affair.[66]

The Gestapo raid was the result of a denunciation. On March 14, 1941, Wilhelm Sponer (1915–?), a young Czech man, was arrested at work.[67] Based on correspondence found by the German Criminal Police (Kriminalpolizei, Kripo) in Sponer's home that revealed him to be gay, the Gestapo decided to pay an unannounced visit to the home of Julia Fleischer, that evening or the next.[68] Several people in the gathering were arrested. Julia and Leopold Fleischer were later released but Willi remained imprisoned for several months, first in the Sušil college (Sušilova koleje) at 2 Stiftergasse (Stifterova), then in the Kaunitz college (Kounicovy koleje) at 45 Husgasse (Husova).[69] Willi Bondi was tortured. During his imprisonment, Bondi managed

Gregor (1910–?), who lived and had her practice in Prague. See NA, Praha, fonds Policejní ředitelství Praha II, všeobecná spisovna, 1941–1951, kart. n° 2586, sign. G 833/2, Kamila Gregorová 1910. Several other people lived in Julia Fleischer's apartment for certain periods during the war years. These were her sister Elisabeth, with her husband Leo and their children; the family friends Rega Neubauer and, starting in July 1941, the single (or divorced?) Dr. Leo Allerhand (1874–1942); and, briefly, Leo's brother (?), Max Allerhand (1890–1944?) and his wife and children. See their resident registration cards in AMB, Brno, fonds Z 1. I found "bei Fleischer" (living with Fleischer) mentioned and the address "Ponavká-gasse [*sic*] 21" in a document referring to goods stored by Dr. Leo Allerhand with the Morava storage company. See MZA, Brno, fonds G 427, Německá správa zabaveného majetku Brno, kart. n° 11, f. 59. This would also be Leo Allerhand's last address before he was deported on March 23, 1942, from Brno to Terezín on transport "Ad". See his death certificate at https://www.holocaust.cz/en/database-of-digitised-documents/document/78543-allerhand-leo-death-certificate-ghetto-terezin/ (accessed Nov. 2, 2021). Leo Allerhand moved into the Julia Fleischer apartment in the summer of 1941 and thus cannot have attended the predominantly gay and lesbian gathering that was assaulted by the Gestapo.

[65] Emails (dated Sep. 21, 2012; Oct. 25, 2020; and Oct. 29, 2021) from Peter Barber to the author.

[66] A German Kripo (Criminal Police) report (dated Mar. 27, 1941) says: "Dabei hat sich herausgestellt, dass sich die Personen, die meist aus Homosexuellen bestanden, aus letztgenannten Gründen dort getroffen haben" (It turned out that the people, who mostly consisted of homosexuals, met there for the reasons last named). See MZA, Brno, fonds C43, Německý zemský soud Brno (Deutsches Landgericht), Staatsanwaltschaft bei dem Landgericht Brünn, file Wilhelm Sponer & Helmuth Holdau, kart. n° 184, sign. 4 K Ls 24/41, f. 100.

[67] MZA, Brno, fonds C 43, Německý zemský soud Brno (Deutsches Landgericht), Staatsanwaltschaft bei dem Landgericht Brünn, file Wilhelm Sponer & Helmuth Holdau, kart. n° 184, sign. 4K Ls 24/41, f. 121.

[68] There is a lack of clarity in the archival sources regarding the exact date of the Gestapo's arrest of the group of people at the 21 Ponawkagasse (Na Ponávce) apartment. Some sources say the raid took place on March 14, 1941, others say it was on March 15, 1941. See MZA, Brno, fonds C43, Německý zemský soud Brno (Deutsches Landgericht), Staatsanwaltschaft bei dem Landgericht Brünn, file Wilhelm Sponer & Helmuth Holdau, kart. n° 184, sign. 4 K Ls 24/41, f. 18, f. 100; and, for comparison, f. 116. See also NA, Praha, fonds n° 375, Arizačni spisy, kart. n° 205, sign. 1268, liquidation file firm Leopold Fleischer, letter (dated Mar. 16, 1941) from Walter Prochaska to the Oberlandrat (Arisierungsabteilung), not foliated. In the last archival file we also read that Julia Fleischer lived on the first floor of the corner building with her – sick – sister Elisabeth (and presumably also her two children, Sylvia and Harry), her husband Leopold Fleischer, and possibly also his mother. According to the resident registration cards in the AMB, Brno, fonds Z 1, Leopold Fleischer and his imediate family first lived at 12 Ponawkagasse (Na Ponávce) and then moved to 46 Ponawkagasse (Na Ponávce) in November 1937. A third resident registration card shows that he and his family moved to 21 Ponawkagasse (Na Ponávce) in March 1940, which means that Leopold Fleischer moved in with his sister-in-law Julia. A resident registration card for Julia Fleischer in the AMB, Brno, fonds Z 1, shows that she moved to 21 Ponawkagasse on July 31, 1939. In an undated letter (but presumably from 1948 or 1949) addressed to the engineer Willi Neubauer (1900–?), living in London, Julia Fleischer wrote that her sister and brother-in-law had moved in with her because Leopold Fleischer had lost his company and his income. See Condell 2005, 220. This letter, and some photos of the Bondi family reproduced in the same book, are now part of the family archive of Peter Barber. Willi Neubauer was married to Rega Neubauer (née Teller, 1904–1942?) and had a daughter named Ruth. Willi Neubauer and his daughter managed to escape but Rega was deported on transport "K" on December 5, 1941 from Brno to Terezín and then on transport "P" on

to smuggle out messages to his family about how he was doing, sometimes using operatic language as a code. His last message "simply bore the name Cavaradossi – the painter who was tortured and shot in the opera *Tosca.* It was a work with which the whole family, who went to the opera two or three times a week, was very familiar [...] and they [immediately] grasped what he meant".[70] On August 29, 1941, the forty-four-year-old Willi Bondi was taken from Brno to Auschwitz where he was registered as inmate number 20.271. He was most likely shot to death the next day, at 8:45 in the morning [ill. 7].[71] Other than the letters sent from or smuggled out of prison, no other of Willi's personal papers – a diary, for example, or other letters – are present in the Bondi family archive.[72] In November 2012, a stumbling stone (*Stolperstein*) commemorating Willi Bondi was unveiled in front of 18 Legionärenstrasse (currently třída Kapitána Jaroše), the house where the Bondis had lived.[73]

January 15, 1942 from Terezín to Riga. Finally, in the same letter, Julia Fleischer wrote that the Germans cited "support for the Communist party" as the reason for arresting the group and, later, for imprisoning Willi Bondi. See Condell 2005, 220.

[69] The word "college" is understood here as "residence hall". For Bondi's imprisonment in the two former student colleges, see the postcard (dated Mar. 20, 1941) addressed to Gustav Bondi, and the postcard (dated Jul. 16, 1941) addressed to Marie Bondi, both in the personal archives of Peter Barber. According to Barber, Bondi was also held in Špilberk (Spielberg) castle. See email (dated Sep. 20, 2012) from Peter Barber to the author. However, there is no other source confirming this, and most of the written documents sent by Willi Bondi from prison are quite illegible. One handwritten note (dated Jul. 23, 1941) makes it clear he was still in the Kaunitz college five weeks before being transferred to Auschwitz, on Jul. 29, 1941. The Sušilova koleje (Sušil college) was initially a Catholic student dormitory built in 1923, and known for German atrocities during the war. The college was named after P. František Sušil (1804–1868), a Catholic Moravian priest. See http://encyklopedie.brna.cz/home-mmb/?acc=profil_osobnosti&load=368 (accessed Jul. 7, 2020). At first, the building housed the Gestapo, but they eventually moved to the Kaunitz college. See https://encyklopedie.brna.cz/home-mmb/?acc=profil_domu&load=1028, http://cikrle.cz/studenti.htm (all accessed Sep. 7, 2020). See also Černý 2006, 41; Filip, Břečka, Schildberger et al. 2012, 57; and *Adressbuch der Landeshauptstadt Brünn* 1942 (1943 Behörden: 6). For more information on Kounicovy koleje (Kaunitz college), built in 1922, see Vašek, Černý, & Břečka 2015 and https://www.bam.brno.cz/objekt/c019-susilovy-koleje (accessed Sep. 29, 2020).

[70] Email (dated Sep. 20, 2012) from Peter Barber to the author. In the already mentioned letter that Julia Fleischer wrote to Willi Neubauer, Julia used an operatic scene to describe the very first deportation in the family: "Act One of Kuhreigen". See Condell 2005, 221. *Der Kuhreigen* (The Cow Round) is an opera by the Austrian composer Wilhelm Kienzl, which premiered in Vienna in 1911. However, Condell mistakes the year: it was in November 1941, not 1942, that Elisabeth, Leopold Fleischer, and their two children were deported.

[71] See the prisoner's database of the Auschwitz concentration camp, http://auschwitz.org/en/museum/auschwitz-prisoners/ (accessed Feb. 12, 2021). See also the three name cards on Wilhelm Bondi in the Central name index in the digital copy of the ITS archive database, consulted in the Brussels Rijksarchief/Archives de l'État. The exact cause of death remains a bit uncertain. Peter Barber wrote to me that Julia told him that, "according to family legend", after the war, Willi's clothes, with bullet holes in them, were sent to his mother. And yet, the official cause of death mentioned in a telegram, sent to Willi's mother, was *Myocardinsuffizienz* (cardiac arrest). From her letter to Willi Neubauer, we learn that, in the years following the war, Julia Fleischer thought that her brother Willi had been gassed in Auschwitz. See Condell 2005, 220. Referring to Rees, Peter Barber pointed out to me that systematic gassing in Auschwitz started only after Willi Bondi arrived there (Rees 2005, 57). In his time, people were sent to the *Stammlager* (also known as Auschwitz I) mainly for political "crimes" and not for being Jewish. See email (dated Sep. 20, 2012) from Peter Barber to the author. Indeed, the construction of Auschwitz-Birkenau, also known as Auschwitz II, infamous for its gas chambers and crematoria, only started operation in October 1941. Perhaps Julia's mother suppressed the story of the clothes and their bullet holes, only informing her daughter about them later. Julia Fleischer may have thus generalized the shocking news about the mass gassing of people in Auschwitz-Birkenau when it became public knowledge immediately after the war.

[72] The Bondi family archive was assembled by Helga Wolfenstein and is now in the possession of her daughter Judy M. King, while other parts of the family archive are in London with Peter Barber. The family archive contains several pictures of Willi Bondi, from his youth to the fortysomething he ended up being.

[73] In September 2012, I contacted Peter Barber and Judy M. King. Some time later, the Czech acdemic Jan Seidl also contacted Peter Barber. Seidl later published on Willi Bondi, claiming that Willi was one of the very early Czechoslovak Nazi victims (perhaps even the only one) deported *because* of homosexuality. See Seidl 2013, 225–26, 241, 250; and Seidl et al. 2012, 222. On November 18, 2012, Seidl organized a presentation on his findings in Brno. On the

GIESE'S LAST LOVE, WALTER LUKL

It was Willi Bondi and a man named Walter Lukl (1907-1967) who lent Giese furniture for his Brno apartment. Giese mentioned this kind gesture in his handwritten last will, which referred to Bondi and Lukl together. For a while, this made me think that Lukl might have been Willi Bondi's lover or boyfriend.[74] To my great surprise, I later found out that Walter Lukl was rather Karl Giese's Brno boyfriend. Many things suddenly fell into place. The main reason that this information did not surface was a typo made by the court clerk who transcribed Giese's handwritten last will. He typed "Walter Linke" instead of Walter Lukl in his transcript.[75] It was not until a few years ago, when I encountered the name of Walter Lukl, that it suddenly occurred to me that Lukl could have been misspelled as Linke in the transcription. When I checked Giese's original handwritten last will, I saw that this had indeed been the case. At the end of May 1936, a few days before moving from Vienna to Brno, in a letter to Adelheid Schulz, Karl Giese wrote that he had fallen in love with a man in Brno: "On top of all that, I have now lost my heart in Brno. And how! There is not a crumb of it left for me. Your Hans cannot be that lovely. And yet I know that that was already quite a lot".[76] "Hans" was Adelheid Schulz's husband, Hans Schulz, whom she married in 1933.[77]

For a while, I thought that the man Giese had fallen in love with might have been Karl Fein, since, as we have seen, Giese moved in with him when he arrived in Brno from Vienna. Had Giese maybe fallen in love with the man who had saved him from financial disaster? Had Fein become, in some way, Giese's new "Papa"? The idea did not seem incredible. Since Giese moved out of Fein's apartment, at the end of the summer of 1936, I presumed the love affair had ended then. But the truth suddenly surfaced when, as said, I looked more closely at the life of Walter Lukl. I first noticed his name when I looked at the employees of the Leopold Fleischer moving firm, the company owned by Willi Bondi's brother-in-law, to which we shall return later in much more detail. Willi Bondi also worked for this company during the last years of his life. Walter Lukl took employment in the company in early 1936. I quickly assumed that the youth was hired because he was young and attractive, reason enough, or so I thought, for Willi Bondi to pressure his brother-in-law, Bruno Fleischer, who

same day, a *Stolperstein* (stumbling stone) for Willi Bondi was unveiled. See http://www.mezipatra.cz/en/program/off-program/lectures-bondi.-cruelty-stone (accessed Mar. 30, 2013). More information on Bondi's *Stolperstein* can be found at https://de.wikipedia.org/wiki/Liste_der_Stolpersteine_in_Br%C3%BCnn (accessed Dec. 12, 2016). Curiously, but probably not coincidentally, the Bondis' house was for some time the home of the Gender Information Center NORA. See http://www.gendernora.cz/?lang=en (accessed Jan. 7, 2016). Stud Brno, občanské sdružení gayů a leseb (http://www.stud.cz/) was one of the three organizations behind the foundation of NORA in 2004. For more on the treatment of homosexual behavior in the Protectorate, and specifically in Brno (as well as for a photo of the young Willi Bondi), see Brummer & Konečný 2013, 86–89.

[74] MZA, Brno, fonds C 107, Německý úřední soud Brno (Deutsches Amtsgericht Brünn), kart. n° 256, sign. 5a V 3/41, handwritten last will Karl Giese (dated Mar. 16, 1938), f. 9. In reality, Willi Bondi's boyfriend was a Czech working-class boy, a *Schlosser* (metalworker) by profession, named Jan Příborský (1910–?). He was Bondi's main (Saturday night) bed partner from *c.* 1932–33 until 1941, when Bondi was arrested by the Gestapo. See Bondi's testimony (dated Mar. 28, 1941) in MZA, Brno, fonds C 43, Německý zemský soud Brno (Deutsches Landgericht), Staatsanwaltschaft bei dem Landgericht Brünn, file Wilhelm Sponer & Helmuth Holdau, kart. n° 184, sign. 4 K Ls 24/41, f. 94b. For his part, Příborský did not deny being Bondi's friend for all these years, but denied that anything sexual had consciously or voluntarily happened between them when they slept in the same bed. See his testimony (dated Mar. 28, 1941) in ibid., f. 95 and 95b.

[75] See MZA, Brno, fonds C 107, Německý úřední soud Brno (Deutsches Amtsgericht Brünn), kart. n° 256, sign. 5a V 3/41, f. 9, for the typed version; and MZA, Brno, fonds C 152, Okresní soud civilní Brno (Bezirksgericht für Zivilsachen Brünn), rubber stamp (dated Mar. 23, 1938), ad DV 206/38/2, sign. s.l. 69/38, for the original handwritten version. Since I only saw the handwritten original of the will later, I was looking for men named Walter Linke. I found three people with that name in the AMB, Brno, fonds Z 1, all married working-class men.

[76] Archiv MHG, Berlin, fonds Adelheid Schulz, letter (dated May 26, 1936) from Karl Giese to Adelheid Schulz: "Zu alledem habe ich jetzt noch mein Herz in Brünn verloren. Und wie! Es ist nicht mehr ein Krüm-

then managed the Leopold Fleischer company, to hire him. By then, it was known to me that Willi Bondi was gay, and often on the prowl for handsome young men. Walter Lukl, though, looked perfectly heterosexual, having married his Berlin-born Jewish wife Milli (Milada) Tabatznik (1902–1963) on August 8, 1936.[78] On a November 1936 document, she described herself as a stenographer.[79] But when I saw that Willi Bondi, along with another unmarried Brno resident and journalist named Eduard Homolatsch (1901–1970), was a witnesses at the wedding, I sensed something was going on.[80] When I looked up Lukl's resident registration cards, everything fell into place. On one, I could clearly see that Lukl moved in with Karl Giese on September 26, 1936, only one week after Giese had moved into his new Střelecká (Schützengasse) apartment. Giese signed the card as a landlord sub-renting to Lukl [ill. 8].[81] That also meant that Lukl had taken a job with the Leopold Fleischer company around the time

mel davon für mich übrig geblieben. So lieb kannst du deinen Hans gar nicht haben. Und dabei weiss ich doch dass das schon eine ganze Menge war".

77 Adelheid Schulz mentioned the name of her husband in Schulz 2001, 101. See also Dose 2021, 12.

78 Matriky uložené v Moravském zemském archivu v Brně, Brno (městská rada), marriage registers, year 1936, číslo knihy n° 17882, entry n° 604 (dated Aug. 8, 1936), f. 123. Accesible online at http://actapublica.eu/matriky/brno/prohlizec/10509/?strana=176 (accessed Aug. 26, 2019). Milli Lukl's parents were Isaak (?–?) and Berta (1872–1934) Freedman or Friedman. An Isak Tabatznik, a businessman, is indeed mentioned in the *Berliner Adreßbuch* 1934, 846. This profession is also mentioned on Milli's marriage certificate; however, the certificate also makes it clear that, by 1936, Isak had died. Milli Lukl later consistently repeated that she was married in Brno on August 3, 1936 (instead of the correct date of August 8, 1936). See U.S. Department of Homeland Security, US Citizenship and Immigration Services, Lee's Summit (Missouri), USCIS Genealogy Program, certificate n° 7269065, Naturalization Certificate File C007269065 (dated Jul. 25, 1955), Milada Vandernald.

79 NA, Praha, fonds Policejní ředitelství Praha II, evidence obyvatelstva sheet, Milada Luklová, 1902.

80 Except for a brief interval in 1937, Homolatsch lived with his parents at 19 Na kopečku (am Bergl), see *Adreßbuch von Groß-Brünn* 1927, 194. In the 1920s he had lived in Buenos Aires. See his resident registration card in AMB, Brno, fonds Z 1. The Hamburg Passenger Lists (1850–1934) in the Ancestry.com database show that he took a ship from Hamburg to South America in June 1926 and July 1933, four months after his father Franz Homolatsch (1873-1926) died. Though it is unclear when, the Roman Catholic Homolatsch eventually moved to Coyoacán in Mexico where, around 1950, he married Pearl (Perla) B. Fagan (1917–2003) and adopted a daughter named Suzan (Suzi) (?-?). Other than his being a witness, along with Willi Bondi, at the counterfeit marriage of Walter and Milada Lukl, I have encountered a few other elements that would suggest that Homolatsch may have been a gay man while living in Brno. In March 2022, I tried to contact the current relatives of Homolatsch through Ancestry.com. In September 2023, I received an email from Lenny Husen, the daughter-in-law of Carol Husen (née Fletcher, 1943-2023). The latter was a daughter of Pearl Fagan within her first marriage. Lenny Husen and her daughter Sarina M. kindly provided me with some more information on Eduard's life in Mexico and also some photos and other documents, see our email correspondence (dated September 2023). Unfortunately, they had no idea about the exact whereabouts (but likely Mexico), nor the exact surname, of the adopted daughter Susan, who married around 1970 and also had a son. Homolatsch also befriended the German journalist and writer Will Schaber (1905–1996), who fled with his wife to Brno and stayed there in the years 1933–38, before emigrating to the USA. In Brno, Schaber was a collaborator of the periodical *Měsíc = Der Monat: illustrierte Zeitschrift* (1933–1940) and also wrote articles for *Tagesbote*, the local newspaper. From 1967 until 1972, he was the president of the PEN-Zentrum deutschsprachiger Autoren im Ausland. Schaber and Homolatsch were both music lovers. In 1937, together with a certain Fritz Deutsch (?–?), they brought out a literary-musical program that also aired on Brno German-language radio as "Durch die Blume gesprochen". See *Volksfreund*, May 15, 1937, 6; May 21, 1937, 6; and *Tagesbote*, May 15, 1937, 8; Jul. 17, 1937, 8; Oct. 30, 1937, 8. In Brno, they also collaborated on a movie screenplay about the composer Haydn. The archives of the journalist Will Schaber contains some correspondence between the two men. See Institut für Zeitungsforschung, Dortmund, Nachlass Will Schaber, correspondence between Eduard Homolatsch and Will Schaber (1939, 1957–1969 [?]), sign. II AK 2003/75-13. Finally, in Brno, Homolatsch also befriended the musician Edith Barber (1914–1992), who after the war married the psychoanalyst Victor B. Kanter (1918–1984) in the UK. The couple had one daughter, Hannah Kanter (1955-), whom I contacted in April 2022 through her daughter Nina Kanter. Hannah Kanter did not have any further information on Homolatsch, or his friendship with her mother Edith, since she did not have any of her mother's pre-war correspondence or diaries. See emails between Hannah Kanter and the author (dated April–May 2022). Eduard Homolatsch had no siblings.

81 On the resident registration card in the AMB, Brno, fonds Z 1, Giese signs as Lukl's subtenant. On

Giese arrived in Brno from Vienna to make his new start, at the end of May 1936.[82] In a way, giving Lukl a job in the Fleischer company was Willi Bondi's "wedding present" to Giese and his new love. Lukl moving into Giese's apartment likely also explains why Giese asked his landlord for a second house key, in December 1936 or January 1937.[83]

Walter Lukl was born in Vienna but, like the rest of his family, lived most of his life in Brno. He was an electrician (*elektromontér*). Giese's old friend, Günter Maeder, knew about this love affair. He mentioned it several times in his correspondence with Charlotte Wolff, Hirschfeld's first biographer. Maeder claimed that, in 1937, Giese had fallen in love with the owner of a cinema and that Giese's love for the man was unrequited.[84] Lukl was likely not a cinema owner but, being an electrician, might have worked in a cinema; however, I have not found any conclusive evidence for this.[85] It is not known when exactly Giese and Lukl met, but it might have been during one of the many trips Giese made to Brno from Vienna, where he then lived, to follow up on the Hirschfeld inheritance case with his lawyer Karl Fein in the years 1935–36. Giese might also have met Lukl as early as 1932, when Giese was in Brno to attend the WLSR conference. It is possible that the person who placed one of the few classified ads in the first and last issue of *Kamarád*, a gay magazine published in 1932 in Brno, was Walter Lukl. In the ad, he mentioned that he was twenty-three and an electrician; Lukl's actual age at the time was twenty-four, differing by only a single year.[86] This would indicate that, by 1932, Lukl was already homosexually active. In the years 1929–31, Lukl did his military service in Bzenec (Bisenz), near Kyjov (Gaya), and it seems that Lukl started to live his life as a twenty-four-year-old gay man shortly after he returned to Brno.[87]

September 26, 1936, Lukl moved from 6 or 8 Josefa Švece (Josef-Švec-Gasse) (two resident registration cards give different house numbers) to Giese's address at 8 Střelecká (Schützengasse).

[82] MZA, Brno, fonds D 25, Celní pátrací služebna, pobočka Brno, Julia Fleischer, Brünn, Adlergasse 34, kart. n° 51, sign. E 535/39, testimony Walter Lukl, f. 21: "seit Frühjahr 1936" (since the spring of 1936).

[83] See the December 1936 handwritten addition "(+ II. Hausschlüssel)" (+ second house key) in Giese's rental booklet (*knížka nájemní, Zinsbüchel*), MZA, Brno, fonds C 107, Německý úřední soud Brno (Deutsches Amtsgericht Brünn), kart. n° 256, sign. 5a V 3/41.

[84] See, for example, Wellcome Library, London, fonds Charlotte Wolff (1897–1986), correspondence II, 1981–1986, PSY/WOL/6/8/2, letter (dated Dec. 28, 1984, 1) from Günter Maeder to Charlotte Wolff; and ibid., letter (dated Oct. 26, 1984, 3) from Günter Maeder to Charlotte Wolff. In the latter, Maeder claimed he knew Giese's boyfriend. This perhaps means that Maeder visited Giese at least once when he was in Vienna or Brno. But it also remains possible that Giese simply had written about his new love to Maeder. This, I think, lines up much better with Erhart Löhnberg's claim that Maeder never went to Brno with Giese to start up a new Institute. See Wellcome Library, London, fonds Charlotte Wolff, correspondence with Erhart Löhnberg, letter (dated Mar. 28, 1985, 1–2) from Erhart Löhnberg to Charlotte Wolff. That Giese's boyfriend was the owner of a cinema was not mentioned in Wolff's Hirschfeld biography (nor in part three of her book, "Memories of Hirschfeld's Contemporaries"). See Wolff 1986.

[85] Because there was a cinema named Elektra on Střelecká (Schützengasse), the street where Giese lived, I tried my luck and checked if Lukl might have worked there. The cinema was opened around 1911 and was located in the corner building at 2 Střelecká (Schützengasse) (where the entrance was) and 145 Neugasse (currently the corner of 55 Stefánikova/2 Domažlická). In Giese's time, the main street address was 55 Pražská (Prager Strasse). The cinema was run by Johanna (Jana) Szpaková (1889–1944) between 1933 and 1948; after the war, her grandson Roman Szpak (1942–), whom I interviewed in Brno on January 30, 2020, took over. He had not heard of anyone named Walter Lukl. The cinema went through several changes of name, starting as Vitagraf, then Illusion in the 1920s, Elektra in the 1930s, and Květen after the war, keeping this last name until its demise in 1950. See https://encyklopedie.brna.cz/home-mmb/?acc=profil_domu&load=352 and https://encyklopedie.brna.cz/home-mmb/?acc=profil_udalosti&load=3140 (both accessed Jan. 17, 2020). For the location of the cinema, see also *Lidové noviny*, Mar. 11, 1921, 6; *Adreßbuch von Groß-Brünn* 1925, 301, under Franz Schimmera; *Adressbuch des Protektorates Böhmen und Mähren für Industrie, Gewerbe, Handel und Landwirtschaft = Adresář Protektorátu Čechy a Morava pro průmysl, živnosti, obchod a zemědělství* 1939, II: 1421.

[86] *Kamarád*, May 28, 1932, 25.

[87] MZA, Brno, fonds B 252, Zemský prezident Brno, správa z příkazu říše, kart. n° 462, index card Deutsche Volkszugehörigkeit, application Walter Lukl. See also chapter 16, p. 659, where we will bring up one more time the gay magazine Kamarád and

Something peculiar is going on with Walter Lukl's father. Lukl's real father is unknown and that is why Lukl's family chose to add this "unlawful" child to the long list of the children of his maternal grandfather, Wenzel (Václav) Lukl (1844–1916?).[88] In this way, Walter Lukl's mother, Emma Lukl (1884–1945), was, biologically speaking, Wenzel Lukl's youngest child and at the same time also officially Walter Lukl's sister. Walter Lukl thus became, at least officially, the ninth child of Wenzel Lukl, with no less than twenty-two years between him and his mother (and sister) Emma.[89] Lukl seems to have been attached to his mother. When I checked the places where he lived before he moved in with Giese, I discovered that he lived not far or even next door to her.[90]

But what about Walter Lukl's marriage then? When looking at the resident registration cards of Walter and Milli Lukl, I noticed that the couple never lived together in Brno. After moving three times within Brno, in the three months following her marriage to Walter Lukl, Milli Lukl moved to Vienna in the beginning of November 1936, armed with a Czechoslovak passport. She would only stay there a month before going to Prague where she stayed at the local YWCA from December 1936 until April 1937. Paris was her next stop. Apparently, she had been to France before. In the summer of 1931, she spent two months in Boulogne-sur-Mer learning French, and also claimed to have spent two years in Paris in the years 1933–35. Was it perhaps there that Giese and/or Hirschfeld got to know her? She might have applied to be Hirschfeld's secretary. When she returned to Paris, in 1937, Milli Lukl would have been in contact with Chinese Communists, who promised her a job in China [ill. 9]. In the autumn of 1937, she left for Saigon, in then French Indochina (currently Ho Chi Minh, Vietman), on the *Jean Laborde* sailing from Marseille. On the ship, she apparently stayed with a man in the entourage of the captured Chinese Kuomintang general Yang Hucheng (1893–1949). She later went to Hong Kong and afterwards flew to Hankow (Hankou, currently known as Wuhan) where she apparently did not get the job promised to her by the Communists. After returning to Hong Kong, she headed to Shanghai, in the first half of 1938, where she presumably stayed until 1948. The Czech and French authorities both kept an eye on her because they thought the adventurous woman a spy, even a woman of ill repute.[91]

Lukl's possibly having inserted a contact advertisement in it. All archival traces relating to Lukl's military service, even the *Grundsbuchblatt* (basic registers) of men born between 1887 and 1910, were largely destroyed in the 1970s and 1980s. See email (dated Nov. 26, 2021) from Jan Chleboun (Vojenský ústřední archiv, Praha) to the author.

[88] The wife of Václav Lukl was Viktoria Dvořak (1848–?).

[89] AMB, Brno, fonds B 1/39, home certificates for Wenzel (Václav) Lukl and Walter Lukl. On Walter Lukl's 1936 marriage certificate, his father's name is not mentioned. On the record of Walter Lukl's Vienna baptism (dated Jun. 13, 1907), the name of the father was not filled out. See Archiv Erzbischöfliches Ordinariat, Wien (Österreich), Niederösterreich (Osten), Rk. Erzdiözese Wien 08, Alservorstadtkrankenhaus, Taufbuch, year 1907, sign. 01-206, f. 723, entry n° 4368 , Walther [*sic*] Lukl 07-13/06/1907, available online at https://data.matricula-online.eu/de/oesterreich/wien/08-alservorstadtkrankenhaus/01-206/?pg=399 (accessed Jan. 28, 2021).

[90] In 1934, they virtually lived next to each other, Walter Lukl at 6 Am Rasen (Trávníky) and his mother at 10 Am Rasen (Trávníky). See Walter Lukl's resident registration card in AMB, Brno, fonds Z 1; *Adreßbuch von Groß-Brünn* 1934, 323.

[91] According to a resident registration card in the AMB, Brno, fonds Z 1, Milli Lukl moved to Vienna on November 1, 1936. On November 27, 1936, she arrived in Prague, leaving it again on April 27, 1937. See NA, Praha, fonds Policejní ředitelství Praha II, evidence obyvatelstva sheet, Milada Luklová, 1902. I use two sources for this account. One is a French intelligence report on her whereabouts in her police file in: Shanghai Municipal Police Files, 1894–1949, n° 9360, box 95, 16W4 12/9/E, Mme (Mrs.) Milli Luklová née Milida [*sic*] Tabatznikova, alias Milli Tabank. The collection is currently housed in the Military Archives Division of the National Archives, Washington, DC, as Record Group 263. I thank Don McLeod for his help in obtaining a digital copy of her microfilmed file in the University of Toronto library in September 2020. The inventory list of this archival fonds can be found at https://www.virtualshanghai.net/Asset/Source/bnBook_ID-2712_No-01.pdf (accessed Aug. 7, 2020). The second source is NA, Praha, fonds n° 225, Ministerstvo vnitra I. Praha, prezidium, kart. n° 1312, sign. 225-1312-1/40-45, file Milada Luklová.

That her marriage with Walter Lukl was indeed a counterfeit is also suggested by the fact that at least one, possibly both of the witnesses were gay men. From a May 1937 letter that Milli Lukl wrote in Paris to the Committee for Assistance to Refugees (Comité d'assistance aux réfugiés, CAR), we learn that the local Brno authorities themselves saw it as a counterfeit marriage and contested it. It went to trial, with Karl Fein acting as the defending lawyer (apparently the couple won).[92] What is not really clear is why the marriage was contracted in the first place. At first, I thought that concocting a heterosexual cover was Giese's idea since, aware that he was watched by the Czechoslovak authorities and German intelligence, he may not have wanted to jeopardize either Lukl or himself in any way. A Jewish woman who fled Nazi Germany, perhaps with almost no income, might have seemed a good candidate for a lucrative trade-off. But in a May 1937 letter, Milli Lukl wrote that it was to her advantage to marry a Czechoslovak man, and this means that Lukl, who was born in Vienna, had been naturalized as Czechoslovak at some point.[93]

[92] NA, Praha, fonds n° 658, Pomocný výbor pro uprchlíky v Paříži (1936–1942) (Comité d'assistance aux réfugiés [CAR], Paris), kart. n° 191, inv. n° 2, Lu-Ly, ff. 792, letter (dated May 3, 1937) from Milada Lukl to Comité d'assistance aux réfugiés; and ibid., letter (dated May 25, 1937) from CAR to Milada Lukl. It is clear from the file that CAR was also suspicious about Milada Lukl's marital status. Milada Lukl gave Dr. Bruno Altmann (1878–1943?), who also lived in Brno for a while before he left for Paris, as a reference. See NA, Praha, fonds n° 225, Ministerstvo vnitra I. Praha, prezidium, kart. n° 1312, sign. 225-1312-1/40-45, file on Milada Luklová. Altmann wrote her a small (undated) reference letter when he was in Paris, saying that he had come to know her in Brno and confirming the truth of her claim. See NA, Praha, fonds n° 658, PVU, Pomocný výbor pro uprchlíky v Paříži (1936–1942) (Comité d'assistance aux réfugiés [CAR], Paris), kart. n° 191, inv. n° 2, Lu-Ly, f. 793, undated letter from Bruno Altmann to CAR. Bruno Altmann has a file in AN, Pierrefitte-sur-Seine, Direction générale de la sûreté nationale (fonds de Moscou), Bruno Altmann 1878, file n° 12246, cote 19940432/128. See also https://de.wikipedia.org/wiki/Bruno_Altmann (accessed Feb. 8, 2020). According to three resident registration cards in the AMB, Brno, fonds Z 1, Altmann arrived in Brno from Berlin in May 1934, and left Brno for Paris in December 1936. Unfortunately, the court file of the counterfeit marriage case could not be located by the staff of the MZA, Brno, in the civil law cases registers of the fonds C 11, Krajský soud civilní Brno (Kreisgericht für Zivilsachen), or in the fonds C 152, Okresní soud civilní Brno (Bezirksgericht für Zivilsachen Brünn-Stadt). See email (dated Jan. 31, 2020) from Jana Fasorová (MZA, Brno) to the author. That court file could possibly contain details about Karl Giese and Walter Lukl living together in Giese's apartment.

[93] On the form stating his Deutsche Volkszugehörigkeit (German ethnic) status (in the AMB, Brno, fonds A 1/53, Německý národností katastr), Walter Lukl wrote "ČSR" under "nationality [*Staatszugehörigkeit*] before March 15, 1939". When Milada Lukl was in Paris, in September 1937, her nationality was indeed stated as Czechoslovak. See AN, site de Pierrefitte-sur-Seine, Ministère de l'intérieur, Direction générale de la sûreté nationale (fonds de Moscou), fichier central de la Sûreté nationale, *fiche* (index card) Milada Luklová (née Tabatznik), cote 19940508/1534.

[94] Coming from Shanghai, she arrived in San Francisco on the *General William H. Gordon*. See the National Archives, Washington, D.C., Records of the Immigration and Naturalization Service, 1787–2004, Record Group Number 85, Passenger Lists of Vessels Arriving at San Francisco (California), NAI Number 4498993, M1410, San Francisco, 1893–1953, NARA Roll number 399, list 32, image 296. She entered the USA on a Quota Immigration Visa (QIV) (file number 6(a)(3)QIV2115). Her passage was paid by the American Jewish Joint Distribution Committee (AJJDC), see columns 6 and 20 on the passenger list. Her AJJDC file (dated Jan. 1, 1950) is known to exist, but it is in China and inaccessible. See AJJDC, New York, JDC Shanghai Refugee Client List, year 1950, box n° 5, file n° 4733, under the name Milena [*sic*] Luklová. In Shanghai, she lived at 24/13 Ward Road. See U.S. Department of Homeland Security, US Citizenship and Immigration Services, Lee's Summit (Missouri), USCIS Genealogy Program, certificate n° 7269065, Naturalization Certificate File C007269065 (dated Jul. 25, 1955), Milada Vandernald, p. 36.

[95] The National Archives, Washington D.C., Records of the Immigration and Naturalization Service, Passenger Lists of Vessels Arriving at San Francisco (California), M1410, San Francisco, 1893-1953, roll 399, list 32, 15 June 1948. Available online in the Ancestry.com database, California, Passenger and Crew Lists, 1882–1959.

[96] In Seattle, she lived at 1326 7th Avenue. See email (dated Sep. 8, 2020) from Jewell Lorenz Dunn (Washington State Archives, Southwest Regional Branch, Olympia, Washington) to the author.

[97] U.S. Department of Homeland Security, US Citizenship and Immigration Services, Lee's Summit (Missouri), USCIS Genealogy Program, certificate n° 7269065, Naturalization Certificate File C007269065 (dated Jul. 25, 1955), Milada Vandernald, pp. 31–35.

WHAT HAPPENED TO MILADA LUKL?

We have seen that, after Paris, Vienna, and Prague, Milli Lukl turned up in Shanghai where she survived the war, along with many other Jewish citizens who had also fled there. On June 30, 1948, she arrived in San Francisco after two weeks aboard a ship. The American Jewish Joint Distribution Committee (AJJDC), familiarly known as the Joint, sponsored her passage.[94] Upon arrival she filled out a form stating that she was a music teacher.[95] In October 1948, she was resettled to Seattle by the United Service for New Americans (USNA), which had also financially supported her since her arrival in San Francisco. In Seattle, Milli Lukl started work for the Swedish Hospital but, a month later, took employment as a sander for the Northwestern Furniture Sales company.[96] In her first years in the USA, she worked as a maid, a waitress, and kitchen help in hotels and restaurants. She also suffered from poor health. In 1948–50, the Jewish Family & Child Service of Seattle helped her out financially.[97]

On April 20, 1952, in Spanaway (Pierce County, Washington), she married the Dutch carpenter Rudolf Vandernald (1909–1989).[98] From Groningen in the Netherlands, Rudolf had emigrated to the USA in 1929. It was not Rudolf's first marriage, his first wife Beatrice having died in 1943.[99] In a June 1952 letter to this mother in Groningen, Rudolf wrote: "Also got married a month ago, she is a nice girl or woman 35 [or 38?] years old[,] has been all over the world France, Germany – China etc., plays the piano

[98] Washington State Archives, Olympia Branch, Olympia, Thurston County Auditor (dual county with Pierce), Marriage certificate n° 29844, issued Apr. 20, 1952; and Washington State Archives, Olympia Branch, Thurston County Auditor, Application for Marriage License, Application issued Apr. 14, 1952. I thank Jewell Lorenz Dunn (Washington State Archives, Southwest Regional Branch, Olympia, Washington) for her help in obtaining a digital copy of these two documents, see her email (dated Sep. 8, 2020) to the author. It remains unresolved why Milada Lukl, on her arrival in San Francisco in 1948, stated on the ship manifest (column 6) that she was married (as Luklová), whereas on the marriage license she declared that she was divorced. On her January 1949 declaration of intent to be naturalized, she stated that she had no children, arrived in the USA without her husband, and had no idea where her husband now resided. See National Archives Seattle, RG 21, United States District Court (USDC), Western District of Washington (WDW), Seattle, declaration of intention n° 51780, dated Jan. 8, 1949, Milada Luklová. Did the authorities simply accept this as true? Later in this chapter, we will see that her husband Walter Lukl was in Germany after the war, where he died in 1967. It thus remains unclear how Milli Lukl resolved this issue before she married her second husband Rudolf Vandernald in Seattle in 1952. Jewell Lorenz Dunn (Washington State Archives, Southwest Regional Branch) believes that no one would have scrutinized very closely her marital status before her marriage to Rudolf Vandernald. I also inquired with the Archives of the County of San Francisco, on September 9, 2020, as it was possible that she settled her marital status while still in San Francisco. In her emigration file, which I ordered in September 2020 and obtained in May 2021, in her application to file a petition for naturalization (dated May ?, 1955), Milli Lukl stated that she divorced Walter Lukl in 1938. But on the application for her immigration visa and alien registration (dated May 24, 1948), that she completed in the American consulate in Shanghai, she stated that she was married to Walter Lucklova [*sic*], likely also adding her marriage certificate. See U.S. Department of Homeland Security, US Citizenship and Immigration Services, Lee's Summit (Missouri), USCIS Genealogy Program, certificate n° 7269065, Naturalization Certificate File C007269065 (dated Jul. 25, 1955), Milada Vandernald, pp. 6–7 and pp. 36–37. In any case, there is no divorce file for Walter and Milli Lukl in MZA, Brno, fonds C 11, Krajský soud civilní Brno. See email (dated Jun. 17, 2021) from Tereza Dlesková (MZA, Brno) to the author. For her USA naturalization procedure, Milada Vandernald was represented by Clark R. Belknap, a Seattle lawyer, and had also received assistance from Mary Castleman Cavenaugh, a social worker. In addition to Rudolf, who was born Roelof J. Van der Nald in Groningen (the Netherlands), his brother Wobbe (1900–1983) and, likely also an uncle Ben (who changed his last name to Van der Niedle) (1884–1968) also emigrated to the USA (and lived in Hammond, Indiana). Both brothers wrote letters to their parents, Rink van der Nald (1872–1943 or 1953) and mother Geertruida Scheringa (1875–1954), in Groningen, and to Hilda Hesling (1913–2008), a sister also living in the Netherlands. These letters have survived (as photocopies) in the "Dutch Immigrant Letters" collection in the Hekman library of Calvin University (Grand Rapids, Michigan). It is not known how photocopies of these letters arrived in this collection. See email (dated Jul. 21, 2020) from Will Katerberg (Hekman library) to the author.

[99] On Aug. 1, 1936, Rudolf Vandernald married Beatrice Tiger (1912–1943). I found the name of his first wife mentioned in the description of the "Dutch Immigrant Letters" collection in the Hekman library of Calvin University (Grand Rapids, Michigan).

and a pretty good housekeeper, somewhat high strung but that will wear off".[100] Milli Vandernald was not thirty-five (or thirty-eight) but forty-nine years old, turning fifty that very month. Rudolf was seven years her junior. In June 1955, Milli Vandernald, who started using the first name Estelle in the USA, petitioned to be naturalized [ill. 10].[101] In the summer of 1961, Milli made a trip to Paris, presumably curious to see once again the city where she had lived a few times before the war.[102] Milli seems to have had a regular life in the USA. We only find traces of her being active in the local Seattle chapter of the Ladies Auxiliary of the carpenters' trade union, the United Brotherhood of Carpenters and Joiners of America, of which her husband Rudolf was a member.[103] Milli Vandernald died on December 16, 1963. The next year, in November, Rudolf Vandernald married Mary Virginia Harrington (1907–1993).

My attempts to locate the current relatives of Milada Vandernald were quite successful. My great hope was that the current relatives would have a picture of the wedding of Milli and Walter Lukl in Brno in their family archive, but this was not the case. I wished, of course, to see many familiar faces in such a picture: besides the bride and groom, the two witnesses, Eduard Homolatsch and Willi Bondi, and maybe also Karl Giese and Karl Fein. In my quest to find the current relatives, I focused first on Milada's three siblings: her older brother Leopold (1900–?), who moved to the USA, and her two sisters Hanni and Beth, who both moved to Palestine before World War II. I managed to contact the current relatives of Milada in the USA and Israel, but the younger generation of the Tabatznik family in the USA apparently had not even been aware that there was a third Tabatznik sister.[104] I also concentrated on the current relatives of Rudolf Vandernald's third wife, Mary Virginia Hamilton, but received no

[100] Calvin University (Grand Rapids, Michigan), Hekman library, fonds Dutch Immigrant Letters, letter (dated Jun. 15, 1952, 2) from Roelof Vandernald to his mother Geertruida Vandernald. I thank Will Katerberg (Hekman library, Grand Rapids, Michigan) for sending me scans of the Van der Nald family letters in July 2020. In the same letter, Vandernald claimed that he married Milli or Estelle "a month ago", but in reality he married her on April 20, 1952, almost two months earlier.

[101] As early as December 1948, Milada Lukl declared she wanted to be naturalized as a US citizen, see the National Archives, Washington D.C., Naturalization Records of the U.S. District Court for the Western District of Washington, 1890–1957, microfilm serial M1542, microfilm roll n° 3, dated Dec. 1, 1948, declaration n° 51780, available online in the Ancestry.com database, Naturalization Records, 1840–1957. On January 8, 1949, she filled out the declaration of intention to become a US citizen. See National Archives Seattle, RG 21, United States District Court (USDC), Western District of Washington (WDW), Seattle, declaration of intention n° 51780, dated Jan. 8, 1949, Milada Luklová. I thank Brita Merkel (National Archives Seattle) for her kind and patient assistance in obtaining a copy of this document. The petition for naturalization for Milada Vandernald, n° 48647, dated Jun. 24, 1955 can be found in the National Archives at Seattle (Washington), Petitions for Naturalization, 1890–1991, NAI Number 592779, Records of District Courts of the United States, 1685–2009, Record Group n° 21, volume 178, petitions 48631-48790, 1955–1956, f. 36, available online in the Ancestry.com database, Petitions for Naturalization, 1860–1991. I also saw Milli Vandernald's Naturalization Certificate File ("C-File"), kept at the U.S. Department of Homeland Security, US Citizenship and Immigration Services, Lee's Summit (Missouri), USCIS Genealogy Program, certificate n° 7269065, Naturalization Certificate File C007269065 (dated Jul. 25, 1955), Milada Vandernald. I thank Aaron Seltzer (National Archives at San Francisco, San Bruno) for his great assistance in setting up the complicated online inquiry with US Citizenship and Immigration Services in September 2020. I obtained a paper copy of the file eight months later, on May 31, 2021. Due to privacy regulations stipulated in §552 of the Freedom of Information Act, 6.5 pages of her C-file were withheld. Presumably, these pages held information about the medical condition of Mrs. Vandernald. The other pages of the file contain a few hints that her health was unstable.

[102] The National Archives at Washington D.C., Records of the Immigration and Naturalization Service, 1787–2004, Record Group n° 85, Series n° A3998, NARA Roll n° 535, New York State, Passenger and Crew Lists, 1917–1967, A3998, New York, 1957–1967, image n° 261, available online at Ancestry.com, Passenger and Crew Lists, 1917–1967 (accessed Jan. 26, 2021). Milada S. Vandernald returned to New York on August 12, 1961, on an Air France flight. It is not known if she also visited other European countries on this trip.

[103] On the activities of the Ladies Auxiliary no. 703, see *West Seattle Herald*, May 17, 1962, 7.

[104] Milli Lukl's older brother, Dr. Leopold Tabatznik (1900–1990), migrated to the USA in August 1940. He took a ship from Finland to New York. He was naturalized in December 1940 and, on April 19, 1948, married the US citizen Gertrude Damsker (1917–2010).

response to the several letters I sent to her relatives in the USA in the beginning of 2020.[105] After that, I looked at the relatives of the Rudolf Vandernald's Dutch siblings. The current relatives replied in a courteous and helpful way, but also told me that

When in Germany, he was married twice, in 1927 and 1938. It is unclear what happened to his second wife in Germany, and her identity is unknown. In 1942, he was drafted by the US Army and worked in a New York hospital. The couple had a son named Robert A. Tabatznik (1950–). I wrote him a letter on March 29, 2020, in the middle of the Covid crisis. He telephoned me on June 9, 2020, to say that he received my letter but that he knew nothing about Milli other than that she had lived in Seattle. From a letter Milli wrote in 1937, I knew that she had two sisters who lived in Palestine (with their father Isaak?) at the end of the 1930s, Johanna Tabatznik (1904–?) and Beth Tabatznik (?–?). According to the same letter, Johanna was a pianist and lived in Ramat Gan (Tel Aviv), while Beth kept a poultry farm in Jerusalem and married as Greiner (?). See NA, Praha, fonds 658, PVU, Pomocný výbor pro uprchlíky v Paříži (1936–1942) (Comité d'assistance aux réfugiés [CAR], Paris), kart. n° 191, inv. n° 2, Lu-Ly, ff. 792, letter (dated May 3, 1937) from Milli Lukl to CAR. For Hanni/Johanna, see also the immigration record in the Israel State Archives (Jerusalem), fonds ISA-MandatoryOrganizations-Naturalization-000a0b5, file dated Jan. 1, 1939, accessible online at https://www.archives.gov.il/en/archives/#/Archive/0b07170680034dc1/File/0b071706806cebfd, Hanni Tabatznik (accessed May 11, 2020). On March 29, 2020, I sent eight letters to people with the last name Greiner living in Israel. I received one reply by someone who was not a relative. On June 14, 2020, Robert A. Tabatznik wrote to me that he had contacted Hanni's three grandchildren and that they were not even aware that there had been a third sister named Milli. Several weeks later, not having made any real progress myself, I wrote to him again asking him to put me in contact with the current relatives of Milli's two sisters. That resulted in a prompt and very friendly and helpful email (dated Jul. 22, 2020) from Tal Shohamy (1974–), the grandson of Lucy (or Beth) Tabatznik. Tal's last name is explained by his grandfather changing his name from Mojsiej Finkelsztejn to Moshe Shohamy (1914–?) when he emigrated from Poland to Palestine. See the immigration record in the Israel State Archives (Jerusalem), fonds ISA-Mandatory-Organizations-Naturalization-0010j8k, dated Apr. 1, 1938, file Moshe Shohamy https://www.archives.gov.il/en/archives/#/Archive/0b07170680034dc1/File/0b0717068106398c (accessed Jul. 28, 2020). This means that Beth did not marry as Greiner (or maybe this was a first marriage?), as Milli said in her letter, but as Shohamy. Tal Shohamy suggested that I contact Yoram Shohamy, one of the two sons of Moshe Shohamy and Beth Tabatznik. But my two emails to Yoram Shohamy went unanswered. Tal Shohamy also gave me the email address of Benni Kahn's wife, Madlen Kahn. Benni Kahn was the only son of Johanna Kahn (née Tabatznik) and her husband Alfred Kahn (?–?), who lived in Tel Aviv until the 1990s. Madlen Kahn's email address was unfortunately no longer valid (the email sent bounced back). Then, at the end of July 2020, Tal Shohamy put me in contact with the grandson of Alfred Kahn, Eyal Kahn, who wrote to me that his grandfather was a collector, very well organized, and had a closet full of family items that ended up in the house of Eyal's elderly mother, Madlen. See email from Eyal Kahn (dated Jul. 30, 2020) to the author. The Covid crisis meant that he was – understandably – not prepared to check the contents of this closet. So there is still a chance that a photo of the marrying couple Walter Lukl and Milli Tabatznik in Brno might be there. Tal Shohamy also sent me two emails (dated Jul. 22, 2020 and Jul. 29, 2020) saying that he found out that Milli and her two sisters had a rift, some time after World War II, because Milli did not want it known in the USA that she was Jewish. It is even possible that her husband Rudolf Vandernald did not know she was Jewish, and this was why Milada did not want her sister to visit her in the USA. This quarrel seems to explain why the younger relatives were not aware of a third sister. On the other hand, an obituary in the *Seattle Times* by Milli's family indirectly indicates that Milli's Jewish background was actually known and not suppressed, since it referred to her two sisters Honey [*sic*] and Beth who were living in Israel. See *Seattle Times*, Dec. 18, 1963, 69, column 1. Lastly, Isaak and Berta Tabatznik had two other daughters: Greta Tabatznik (1907–1907), who lived only two days, and Helene Tabatznik (1896–?), who presumably also died shortly after birth. I want to thank Robert A. Tabatznik, Tal Shohamy, and Eyal Kahn for their friendly help in 2020 and 2021 with my inquiries on Milli Vandernald (née Tabatznik) and her ancestral family.

[105] In a genealogical database, I found a Virginia Vandernald (1973–) who at some point lived at the same Seattle address as the one I found for Rudolf Vandernald; however, it is impossible she might have been a natural daughter of Rudolf and Mary Virginia Vandernald (née Harrington), since this would mean that Mary Virginia had a child at the age of 66. The name and above all the birth date are likely the result of a database glitch. Indeed, on three separate occasions, the current family confirmed to me that Rudolf's three marriages were childless. The last possibility is that the younger Virginia Vandernald (1973–) was an adopted daughter. In the beginning of July 2020, I sent some letters to the person named as informant (Mary Murphy, Seattle) on the death certificate for the elder Mary Virginia Vandernald (1907–1993). Was she a daughter of Mary Virginia by a previous marriage? Mary Murphy's address was likely no longer the same by then, and "Murphy" is also not an easy name to track. I sent a letter to the funeral company that took care of Mary Virginia Vandernald's cremation, and to the old age home where she spent the last years of her life, both in Seattle. No one replied. In February 2021, I finally identified Mary Virginia Vandernald's two siblings: Donald M. Dickinson (1904–1973) and Samuel K. Dickinson (1909–1999). On February 4, 2021, I sent

many things had been thrown out and also that, unlike Rudolf Vandernald, they did not live in Seattle, but in the Chicago region.[106]

WALTER LUKL BREAKS UP WITH KARL GIESE

Walter Lukl moved out of Giese's flat on January 5, 1938. Lukl moved to 4–6 Mlýnská (Mühlgasse), not far from the office and even closer to the storage facilities of the Leopold Fleischer firm where Lukl continued to work.[107] Giese was heartbroken. The shattered love affair marked the start of or may even have been the main cause of Giese's subsequent downfall. Two and a half months later, on March 16, 1938, Giese committed suicide. According to Giese's childhood friend, Günter Maeder, the unhappy love affair was the main reason.[108] That Giese was at the very least seriously depressed after the break up appears clearly in a letter Giese wrote to Ernst Maass on January 21, 1938, in which Giese literally says "farewell" to Ernst Maass, who was then preparing to move to the United States after returning from Palestine to France. Several other features of that letter can also be interpreted as the symptoms of a man suffering from depression. Unlike the young Ernst Maass, Giese no longer had either the courage or the energy to flee to a better and freer world. In the letter, one can also perceive a man looking back at his life and drawing up the balance: he had had a good life and had always been aware of his limited capacities and the situation he was in.[109] Giese's soured love affair was likely not the sole reason he took his own life.

a letter to a grandson of Donald M. Dickinson, N. E. Dickinson, and also left a message on his Facebook page. He did not respond. It was unknown to me if his father, Jeffrey L. Dickinson (1940–), was still living. I assumed that Mary Virginia Vandernald was the best candidate to preserve the things of her late husband Rudolf, who died in 1989, four years before her own death. My final initiative was to contact the son of Sam and Louise Angell, the witnesses to the wedding of Virginia and Rudolf Vandernald, married in the Chapel of the Chimes in Seattle in November 1964. That a certain bond existed between the Angells and Vandernalds is indicated by the fact that the then unmarried Virginia Dickinson was one of the witnesses at the Angell wedding in February 1938. A letter (dated Feb. 3, 2021) was sent to the surviving son of the Angells, Charles L. Angell (1940–). He replied with an email (dated Feb. 17, 2021), recalling that he often stayed in the home of Rudi and Dicky (Rudolf and Virginia Vandernald) and that the couple had indeed been his parents' close friends. But he could not help me in determining who Virginia Vandernald's relatives were. The couples lost touch around the 1970s, presumably due to an age-related disease of Rudolf Vandernald.

106 I contacted the current relatives of Rudolf's brother Wobbe (Walter) and his three children, Walter (1940–), Karen (1934–) and Nancy (1938–). I also sent a Facebook message to the four people with the names Van der Nald and Vandernald on July 22, 2020. The nephew of Rudolf Vandernald, Walter Vandernald Jr. (1940–), the son of Wobbe Vandernald, told me over the phone (on Jul. 24, 2020) that his uncle's three marriages were childless. This was also confirmed by Jean Graf-Teterycz, a granddaughter of Wobbe Vandernald. See email (dated Jul. 27, 2020) from Jean Graf-Teterycz to the author. Walter Vandernald Jr. told me that many things had been thrown out after the death of his mother, Johanna Vandernald (1906–1996) (phone conversation [dated Jul. 24, 2020] between Walter Vandernald and the author). I also sent a letter to Mabel Tuinman-Hesling (1947–) on November 26, 2020. She is a daughter of Hilda Hesling (née van der Nald, 1913–2008), who was one of Rudolf Vandernald's three sisters. Mabel Tuinman-Hesling wrote to me that she would look in the family archive, and kindly found some photos of Milli and Rudolf Vandernald. I also think it probable that it was her mother, Hilda Hesling, who donated copies of the letters her USA family sent to the Netherlands to Calvin University's Hekman Library (Grand Rapids, Michigan), where these letters became part of the Dutch Immigrant Letters archival fonds. Rudolf Vandernald's other two sisters were Dora Hein (née van der Nald, 1901–?) and Gesina Wolthouse (née van der Nald, 1899–1932). Gesina and her husband Rudolph Wolthouse (1899–1974) had a daughter, Lorraine A. Graf (née Wolthouse, 1926–2015). Gesina died in 1932, and her husband Rudolph abandoned the child. Wobbe Vandernald and his wife Johanna Schaper raised her. On July 8, 2020, I sent letters to the relatives of Lorraine A. Graf. There was also another son, Hein van der Nald (1904–1930), who died in Calcutta in 1930. So, in total, Rudolf Vandernald had five siblings. The one trace that I did not follow was that of Dorothea van der Nald (1901–?), another sister of Rudolf Vandernald.

107 AMB, Brno, fonds Z 1, resident registration card (dated Jan. 5, 1938) Walter Lukl. His home certificate indicates that Lukl still lived 4–6 Mühlgasse in 1939–40. See AMB, Brno, fonds B 1/39.

108 "Zu allem Überfluß beging Karl Giese kurz darauf wegen einer Liebesgeschichte Selbstmord" (To make matters worse, Karl Giese committed sui-

Several other factors also probably worsened the pain of his broken heart and made it seem insurmountable.

NO LONGER WELCOME IN BRNO

Around the middle of June 1937, the Czechoslovak Ministry of the Interior issued a drastic and unpleasant ordinance/measure that impacted German exiles in Brno. Dora Müller, a key figure in the history of Brno's exiles, writes: "In June 1937, the Ministry of the Interior decreed, under pressure from the Third Reich, that emigrants had to leave Brno within 24 hours and go to certain places on the Bohemian-Moravian Heights".[110] Kateřina Čapková and Michal Frankl have shed light on this still partly unexplained matter in their book on German and Austrian refugees in pre-war Czechoslovakia. They argue that the idea to move German refugees in Czechoslovakia to the countryside of the Bohemian-Moravian Highlands was likely the product of – undocumented – secret negotiations with the German National Socialist government.[111] The Bohemian-Moravian Highlands (Böhmisch-Mährischen Höhe, Českomoravská vysočina) are a string of hills and mountains marking a natural border between Bohemia and Moravia.[112] The German-Jewish gymnast Fredy Hirsch, who fled to Czechoslovakia, also fell under this measure. In the summer of 1937, he moved to Brumov (Brumow), "in the middle of nowhere" (*am Rande von Nirgendwo*), as one of his biographers puts it.[113]

The National Socialists were of course keenly aware of the many German exiles who vehemently criticized their politics in all kinds of exile publications in Czechoslovakia and other European countries. Moving these exiles out of the big cities and into the countryside had the express purpose of cutting off these politically active emigrants from all the modern amenities and advantageous networks that cities offered. Their banishment would degrade their political activity. One tactic used by the Czechoslovak authorities to make the transfer of German emigrants to the countryside look less drastic was to only take action when an emigrant's residence permit had expired. In this way, since not everyone would be transferred at the same time, it was hoped that the new measure would cause less upheaval.[114] It is clear that many emigrants tried to get out of Czechoslovakia after this largely failed attempt to transfer them to the countryside. The measure made it clear to them that they were no longer welcome in Czechoslovakia.[115]

cide shortly after because of a love story) (Maeder [1993], 7).

[109] Archiv MHG, Berlin, fonds Ernst Maass, letter (dated Jan. 21, 1938, 3) from Karl Giese to Ernst Maass: "Wenn ich Talent zum Neid hätte, was mir, nicht zuletzt [word unreadable, wohl ?] insfolge meines wundervollen Vorlebens, aber auch auf Grund mangelnder Veranlagung (Sie wissen, "Anlage und Lage" !) abgeht[,] so würde ich Sie [...], beneiden". This "Anlage oder Lage" expression (which Giese learned from Hirschfeld) can also be seen in Giese 1927, 133. Giese wrote about the Abteilung für seelische und nervöse Sexualleiden (Department of Mental and Nervous Sexual Disorders) in the Institute, adding, in parenthesis, that this or that kind of sexual suffering was usually caused by the conflict between "Konstitution und Milieu" (heredity and environment). In a July 1932 interview, Hirschfeld said that the importance of *Lage* and *Anlage*, *Konstitution* and *Milieu* was indeed one of the central themes of his work. See Spielmann, Jul. 28, 1932, 4; see also Dobler 2020, 81.

[110] "Im Juni 1937 verfügte das Innenministerium, auf Druck des Dritten Reiches, daß die Emigranten binnen 24 Stunden Brünn zu verlassen und sich nach bestimmten Orten auf der Böhmisch-Mährischen Höhe zu begeben hätten" (Müller 1997, 91–92). See also "Emigranten-Ausweisung aus Brünn", *Prager Tagblatt*, Jun. 23, 1937, 4.

[111] Čapková & Frankl 2012, 220, 238.

[112] See https://en.wikipedia.org/wiki/Bohemian-Moravian_Highlands (accessed Apr. 4, 2017).

[113] This measure left one of Hirsch's biographers at a loss for an explanation. See Kämper 2015 93–94. Hirsch's other biographer is Ondrichová 2000. For more details on Hirsch's gay love and sex life, see Hájková, May 2, 2019.

[114] Čapková & Frankl 2012, 222. Refugees had a permit that allowed them to stay in Czechoslovakia, but which needed to be renewed annually with the provincial authorities. See Čapková & Frankl 2012, 52–53, 55.

[115] Čapková & Frankl 2012, 238, 257, 277.

In July 1937, Giese received a letter from the Brno Provincial Authority (Zemský úřad v Brně, Landesbehörde in Brünn), which instructed him to leave Brno, allowing him only to live in certain prescribed villages.[116] Giese and his legal counselor and friend Karl Fein took the matter very seriously and wrote an appeal (*odvolání*) in an attempt to reverse the decision.[117] Giese's reaction reflected precisely the intention of the measure: he could not imagine how he could function living in a much smaller city. The long defense – written in Czech – includes several convincing, and some less convincing arguments to persuade the Moravian provincial authorities that this summons would prove disastrous for Giese. For starters, it was noted that Giese was unjustly perceived as a danger to the Czechoslovak state because of his German nationality. He and Fein stressed that Giese did not side with the National Socialists but was rather their victim. Giese and Fein used all the rhetorical and less-than-rhetorical ammunition at their disposal: Hirschfeld had been an admirer of Mendel (the Brno-based discoverer of the laws of heredity); Hirschfeld considered Mendel as a precursor; Hirschfeld had always thought that Brno was the best place for Giese to continue Hirschfeld's research; President Masaryk had shown his great interest in the 1932 WLSR conference by sending a telegram on September 6, 1932; Giese needed the intellectual environment of Brno (people with a shared interest in Hirschfeld's ideas) and the university library to continue his work; he was working with the Institute materials in his possession; and, finally, (re)packing the 2,000 kg of these materials in twenty-three boxes would simply be too costly.[118] Giese also stressed that his livelihood was intimately dependent on the stipulations in Hirschfeld's will. He was only entitled to money from Hirschfeld's estate if he fulfilled these stipulations: "I would also like to point out that, according to the express terms of Hirschfeld's will, I am appointed heir only on condition that I devote all my effort to scientific activity."[119] And he concluded, rather dramatically, that Hirschfeld's death had made him a sort of shareholder of Magnus Hirschfeld's fate.[120]

The measure was revoked in October 1937, though not completely.[121] The initial motivation of the measure, an entente with Nazi Germany, apparently faded away as an argument for the Czechoslovak authorities. But the measure seems nevertheless to have marked the start of a much less tolerant attitude to emigrants by the Czechoslovak authorities.[122] The Czechoslovak Ministry of the Interior grew wary, as Nazi Germany became more and more of a threat, that the German emigrants could be German spies.[123] The Czechoslovak authorities hoped that a forceful transfer to the isolated countryside would be an incentive for the emigrants to leave the country voluntarily and quickly.[124] In 1938, the Czechoslovak authorities even made a plan to

[116] On October 30, 1937, Giese was ordered to move to any of the following towns: Jihlava (Iglau), Velké Meziříčí (Großmeseritsch), Třebíč (Trebitsch), or Nové Město na Moravě (Neustadl in Mähren). See MZA, Brno, fonds B 40, Zemský úřad Brno (Landesbehörde in Brünn), kart. n° 2138, sign. 5274/38, f. 6.

[117] The file and the seven-page-long appeal, titled "Odvolání do výměru zemského úřadu v Brně ze dne 8. července 1937 jedn. čís. 2224/I-7 k Ministerstvu vnitra v Praze" can be found in MZA, Brno, fonds B 40, Zemský úřad Brno (Landesbehörde in Brünn), kart. n° 2138, sign. 5274/38, f. 6-11. It is also reproduced in the addenda (n° 9). Since it is undated and only refers to the July 8, 1937, decree in its title, it is unclear when exactly Giese and Fein wrote and sent the appeal. However, other documents in the same archival file seem to suggest that the appeal was written and also sent in July 1937.

[118] MZA, Brno, fonds B 40, Zemský úřad Brno (Landesbehörde in Brünn), kart. n° 2138, sign. 5274/38, f. 8. We will return later to the issue of what exactly Giese had in his possession in Brno.

[119] MZA, Brno, fonds B 40, Zemský úřad Brno (Landesbehörde in Brünn), kart. n° 2138, sign. 5274/38, f. 8: "Poukazuji ještě k tomu, že jsem podle výslovného nařízení Hirschfeldovy závěti ustanoven dědicem jen s tou podmínkou, že všechnu svou pracovní sílu věnuji vědecké činnosti".

[120] Ibid., f. 8 – f. 8b: „nýbrž stal jsem se, [...] a v zájmu další společné práce jaksi podílníkem na jeho osudu ještě přes jeho skon [*sic*, skonem]".

[121] "Kurz darauf wurde der ungesetzliche Erlaß zurückgenommen" (Müller 1997, 91–92). On the partial revocation of the measure, see also Čapková & Frankl 2012, 231–34.

put German refugees in camps, as would later be done in other European countries (France, for example).[125] Contrary to the general assumption, romantically rendered in post-war Communist historiography, Czechoslovakia was not a true paradise for German refugees after all. Other than a small circle with enough financial resources, the outlook for an emigrant in Czechoslovakia was generally not very bright.[126] The Ministry of the Interior always hoped that emigrants who had come to Czechoslovakia would leave the country again quickly. This was also one of the main aims of the strict policy against emigrants working.[127]

In the archival file documenting Giese's case, there are several traces that the claims in Giese's defense, drawn up with Karl Fein, were checked by the Brno police. In a report the Brno police sent to the Brno Provincial Authority in February 1938, they wrote that Giese's claims were rather exaggerated: he was not doing any research, but was looking for a job. This assessment was used as a reason against Giese's staying much longer in Brno. If he found work, so the police reasoned, he would take a job away from a Czech person. The police report also presented the following "argument" in an attempt to further discredit Giese: "Giese, as we found, is in contact with sexually deviant people here".[128] As a consequence, the authors of the report proposed not to extend Giese's permit to stay in the country, suggestively noting that his passport would expire on May 5, 1938. The Provincial Authority followed their advice and sent a letter to Giese on March 1, 1938, informing him that his permit was valid until the day his passport expired.[129] In other words, Giese was allowed to stay another two months before he had to leave the country. Many other exiles in Czechoslovakia headed to France after the 1937 summer measure but, as we have seen, that option was not available to Giese, since he had been expelled from France in October 1934.

On September 14, 1937, President Tomáš Garrigue Masaryk died. The death of this important figure, a symbol of liberal democracy and justice, likely added to the precarious situation of political refugees in Czechoslovakia, or, at least, foreshadowed a gloomy future. In 1935, Hugo Iltis could still write of the Deutsche Volkshochschule (German adult education center), renamed the Masaryk Volkshochschule in 1934: "As long as Masaryk is alive, we feel safe. His life is a protection for all who struggle for freedom and peace".[130] In a memoir written long afterwards, the Jewish man Charles Ticho, who was ten years old when Masaryk died, said that it felt like the death of a father.[131]

MONEY MATTERS

We have seen that Giese could live comfortably from the money from the Hirchfeld estate and did not have to resort to paid work. Yet he must have been aware that he was walking on the edge of a volcano. The money would run out one day. Of course, in theory, Giese was also entitled to royalties from Hirschfeld's books. When, in June 1935, he returned to Vienna from Nice, he was still optimistic that continuing

[122] See "Emigranten-Umsiedlung nur ausnahmsweise" (Emigrant relocation only in exceptional cases), *Prager Tagblatt*, Oct. 24, 1937, 4.

[123] Čapková & Frankl 2012, 220–34.

[124] Čapková & Frankl 2012, 222, 231.

[125] Čapková & Frankl 2012, 235–36, 293. The French internment camps were Gurs, Camps des Milles, Schirmeck, Pithiviers, Saint-Cyprien, etc.

[126] Čapková & Frankl 2012, 84, 98–99.

[127] Čapková & Frankl 2012, 36, 49, 56, 181, 233.

[128] MZA, Brno, fonds B 40, Zemský úřad Brno (Landesbehörde in Brünn), kart. n° 2138, sign. 5274/38, letter (dated Feb. 10, 1938) from Brno police to Zemský úřad Brno, f. 2: "Giese, jak bylo zjištěno, stýkáse zde s osobami sexualně úchylnými".

[129] MZA, Brno, fonds C 107, Německý úřední soud Brno (Deutsches Amtsgericht Brünn), kart. n° 256, sign. 5aV 3/41, letter (dated Mar. 1, 1938) Zemský úřad v Brně to Karl Giese, f. 4.

[130] "Solange Masaryk lebt, fühlen wir uns geborgen. Sein Leben ist ein Schutz für alle, die um Freiheit und Frieden kämpfen" (Iltis 1935, 1).

[131] Ticho 2001, 3 (The gathering storm).

to publish Hirschfeld's books was one of his tasks. An Austrian journalist who spoke to Giese in Vienna wrote: "Karl Giese tells of the work that lies ahead for him. New editions in English and French of the works of the famous sex researcher".[132]

It is indeed possible that Giese received some royalties for one book especially, the publication in January 1938 of Hirschfeld's *Racism*.[133] The book was written as early as 1934–35, but it would take another three years before the English translation was finally published. In January–February 1934, in Nice, Giese had assisted Hirschfeld by typing the manuscript as it was being written.[134] This is probably when Giese met the Paul couple who would translate Hirschfeld's book into English.[135] That Giese was in fact involved in the later operations to publish this book after Hirschfeld's death can be gleaned from the fact that, in January 1938, he received the first author copies (*Belegexemplare*) from the London publisher. Giese wrote to Ernst Maass: "Finally, Dr Hirschfeld's last work, '*Racism*' [underlining in original] has appeared, albeit in English translation. I received the first copies this week [illegible]".[136] *Der Racismus: ein Phantom als Weltgefahr* (*Racism: a phantom as world threat*) was the title of the German original but no German edition of the book ever saw the light of day due to the evolving political situation in the years 1935–38.[137] It is possible that, by participating in the publication of Hirschfeld's last book, Giese had ensured that one of Hirschfeld's final explicit wishes was fulfilled: publish the book that was very critical of the racist Nazi ideology that destroyed Hirschfeld's life work. Maybe Giese also thought that, this wish honored, a debt to Hirschfeld had been paid.

Following another stipulation in Hirschfeld's will, Giese was also entitled to income from Titus Pearls licenses. But here things did not run as smoothly. Giese had a conflict with a Russian-Jewish man, Lazare Tcherniak (also spelled as Tscherniak), living in Belgium, who held the license for selling the "sex pills" in Belgium and France, but he refused to pay Giese. We will look again at Giese's dispute with Tcherniak in the next chapter.

WALKING ON THE EDGE OF A VOLCANO

When the Germans finally annexed Austria, on March 12, 1938, Giese likely saw no other way out. In the evening (or night) of March 16, 1938, the day after Hitler gave a grand public speech on the Heldenplatz in Vienna, Giese took his own life. But was Giese's panicked reaction somewhat unwarranted? That Czechoslovakia would be next on Germany's expansionist list indeed seeped through in the local newspapers. The headlines in the March 16 edition of the pro-German Brno *Morgenpost* – which

[132] See "Magnus Hirschfelds Erbe in Wien", *Der Morgen – Wiener Montagblatt*, Jun. 24, 1935, 10: "Karl Giese erzählt von der Arbeit, die ihm bevorsteht. Neue Ausgaben in englischer und französischer Sprache von den Werken des berühmten Sexualforschers".

[133] Hirschfeld 1938a.

[134] Frischknecht 2009, 27; Hirschfeld & Dose 2013, 86.

[135] Frischknecht 2009, 31–32.

[136] Archiv MHG, Berlin, fonds Ernst Maass, letter (dated Jan. 21, 1938, 2) from Karl Giese to Ernst Maass: "Endlich ist das letzte eigene Werk von Dr. Hirschfeld, der "*Racismus*" [underlining in original] erschienen, allerdings in englischer Übersetzung. Ich erhielt diese Woche [unreadable] die ersten Belegexemplare". Giese also promised to send Maass the book as soon as he received more copies from the publisher.

[137] Frischknecht 2009, 25–27, 32–34; Herrn 2003. To this day, the book has not been published in German.

[138] *Morgenpost*, Mar. 16, 1938, 2, 1, 3: "Wenn Deutschland die Tschechoslowakei angriffe" / "Frankreich leistet der Tschechoslowakei Waffenhilfe. Im Falle eines Angriffes" / "Deutsche Zusicherungen an die Tschechoslowakei". The same worry surfaced the day before in *Morgenpost*, Mar. 15, 1938, 1: "Die Frage im englischen Unterhaus: Nichteinmischung oder Beistand ? Wenn Deutschland die Tschechoslowakei angriffe" (The question in the English House of Commons: non-intervention or assistance? When Germany attacks Czechoslovakia).

[139] Čapková and Frankl refer to a political cartoon of a map in the social-democrat weekly *Neuen Vorwärts* depicting an animalistic head, labeled Berlin, swallowing Prague (Čapková & Frankl 2012, 274, 276; *Neuen Vorwärts*, Mar. 27, 1938).

Giese possibly still saw – were indeed quite ominous and hinted that Czechoslovakia was next in line after the fait accompli of the Anschluss: "When Germany attacks Czechoslovakia" / "France will provide arms assistance to Czechoslovakia. In case of attack" / "German assurances to Czechoslovakia".[138] But even a simple look at the map of Europe, after the annexation of Austria, was enough [ill. 11].[139] Immediately after the Anschluss, many Jewish and left-wing emigrants indeed left Czechoslovakia. The country had ceased to be a safe haven for them.[140] Giese must have felt the same despair but drew a more drastic conclusion. Three days after the invasion of Austria, a newspaper reported on the "suicide epidemic" among emigrants in Prague.[141] A similar report on a suicide epidemic in Vienna appeared the next day.[142]

With the invasion of Austria, the National Socialists came physically closer to Czechoslovakia. Vienna is only three hours from Brno by train and Giese likely also feared the very real, meticulously prepared lists of people to be arrested as soon as the Germans invaded new territory. Such lists were indeed used when the Sudetenland and, later, the rest of Czechoslovakia (Rest-Tschechoslowakei, also Rest-Tschechei) were annexed.[143] Once Czechoslovakia and Brno were finally invaded, on March 15, 1939, the Gestapo immediately started work; they had already headed for Brno police headquarters the night before the invasion.[144] "Immediately after March 15, [1939], the so-called 'Gitter' action began, the preventive mass arrest of potential opponents – in Moravia almost 6,000 people were arrested, among them about 3,300 Communists and about 1,000 German emigrants, as well as Legionnaires. Of these, about 1,500 were sent to Buchenwald concentration camp (e.g. Communist functionaries), the rest were released after barely a month in prison". And: "The Gestapo was most interested in Jews, Communists and members of the German opposition who had arrived earlier in the Czechoslovak Republic".[145]

We have already noted that Giese lost his passport in September 1935, when he was still in Vienna, and that he obtained a new one from the passport department (*Passabteilung*) of the German embassy (*Deutsche Gesandtschaft*) there. His new passport was valid for one year, starting on November 5, 1935. His passport would be extended (*verlängert*) two more times after that at the German consulate in Brno, the

[140] Čapková & Frankl 2012, 257, 277.

[141] See "Epidemie sebevražd emigrantů", *Moravské Slovo*, Mar. 18, 1938, 3. The article is dated March 17, 1938.

[142] See "Epidemie sebevražd ve Vídni", *Moravské Slovo*, Mar. 20, 1938, 1. The article is dated March 19, 1938.

[143] The occupiers, hunting for Communists, leftists, and foreign-based German opponents of the Nazi regime, made use of the so-called "Kartei M", *Fahndungslisten* (wanted persons lists) prepared by the Sicherheitsdienst (SD) and the Gestapo in advance. See Filip, Břečka, Schildberger, et al. 2012, 54–55, 57. Sládek also refers to the so-called Mobilmachungskartei (M-Kartei) prepared by the SD in June 1938 (Sládek 2000, 317). See also document 241 ("Ein unbekannter Verfasser beschreibt die Situation der jüdischen Bevölkerung im Protektorat bis Ende März 1939") in Löw 2012, 583: "Die Gestapo erschien mit fertigen Verhaftungslisten in ihren Aktentaschen, so daß schon eine Stunde nach ihrer Ankunft mit den Verhaftungen begonnen werden konnte. [...] Im ganzen sollen in der Tschechoslowakei 13 000 Personen verhaftet worden sein". See also Gruner 2010, 149; Oprach 2006, 89 n. 379. In the years before the invasion, German spies were sent to Czechoslovakia. Some, for example, tried to infiltrate committees that helped out refugees. See Čapková & Frankl 2012, 125–26. Before the annexation of the Sudetenland, German murder commandos were also sent ahead.

[144] Filip, Břečka Schildberger et al. 2012, 54.

[145] Filip, Břečka, Schildberger et al. 2012, 55ff: "Gleich nach dem 15. März [1939] begann die so genannte Aktion "Gitter", die präventive Massenverhaftung potenzieller Gegner – in Mähren wurden fast 6000 Personen festgenommen, darunter etwa 3300 Kommunisten und etwa 1000 deutsche Emigranten, des weiteren Legionäre. Von ihnen kamen etwa 1500 in das Konzentrationslager Buchenwald (z. B. kommunistische Funktionäre), die übrigen wurden nach knapp einem Monat Haft freigelassen". And: "Die Gestapo interessierte sich am meisten für Juden, Kommunisten und Angehörige der deutschen Opposition, die schon früher in die Tschechoslowakische Republik angekommen waren". See also Potthast 2002, 63–64; Kárný 1999, 55. Potthast also mentions that someone in the German embassy in Prague had prepared lists of the addresses of undesirables in advance (Potthast 2002, 56).

first time for one year, until November 1937, and the second time for only six months, until May 5, 1938.[146] This was likely another factor that contributed to Giese's suicidal thoughts: wherever he looked, he must have felt that the net was tightening.

We have seen that the Czech authorities allowed him to stay in the country as long as he had a valid passport. When the consulate in Brno initially extended his passport, they first consulted with the Gestapo in Berlin if they had any objections. Although, the second time, they appeared to be ready to extend his passport for one year, this was cut in half.[147] The German consulate in Brno thought it suspect that Giese could survive financially in Brno without a job. They inquired with the Gestapo whether Giese had lost his civil rights as a German expatriate (*ausgebürgert*) or whether such a decision was maybe pending.[148] The Gestapo in Berlin was well aware of Giese's whereabouts in Brno. In December 1936, the Gestapo wrote to the consulate in Brno: "He [Giese] is the former private secretary of Prof. Dr. Magnus Hirschfeld. Although he never particularly stood out, there should be no doubt about his attitude".[149] In February 1937, the consulate in Brno replied to the Gestapo that Giese's return to Germany, however short, was undesirable due to his connection with Hirschfeld.[150] A copy of every decision by the German consulate in Brno regarding the extension of Giese's passport was sent to the office of the Gestapo in Berlin, at the latter's explicit request.[151] A clipping of a small article in the evening edition of the local Brno newspaper *Tagesbote*, announcing Giese's death, in March 1938, sat on top of his consulate file.[152] So Giese's fears were not as unwarranted as one might think. Despite him keeping a low profile in Brno, it is very likely that Giese would have appeared on one of the wanted persons lists, and be arrested as soon as the Germans arrived in Brno a year later. Otto Schütz, a left-wing lawyer and friend of Karl Fein, was already searched by the Gestapo on March 16, 1939, the day after the Germans invaded Czechoslovakia. Luckily, Schütz managed to escape abroad in time.[153]

Another thing that may have weighed on Giese's no doubt troubled mind was Hirschfeld's *Racism*, published only a few months before. As already said, this book was a clear criticism of Nazi racist ideology. We may assume that the National Socialists in Berlin were well aware of its publication and resented that Hirschfeld

[146] Giese's final passport has survived in MZA, Brno, fonds C 107, Německý úřední soud Brno (Deutsches Amtsgericht Brünn), kart. n° 256, sign. 5aV 3/41, see pages 2, 4, and 5.

[147] Politisches Archiv des Auswärtigen Amts, Berlin, Akten des früheren Deutschen Konsulats in Brünn, Bündel 42, Passangelegenheiten, Einzelfälle gebündelt, Buchstabe G, 1935–1939, file Carl [*sic*] Giese. No reason is given in the file for why the second extension was for only six months.

[148] Ibid., letter (dated Oct. 8, 1936) from the German consul in Brno to the Gestapo in Berlin: "Das Konsulat bittet um gefl. [gefällige] Mitteilung, ob Giese noch die deutsche Reichsangehörigkeit besitzt, ob gegen ihn ein Verfahren auf Widerruf der Einbürgerung oder auf Ausbürgerung schwebt und ob Tatsachen bekannt sind, die eine Versagung des Passes geboten erscheinen lassen".

[149] Ibid., letter (dated Dec. 2, 1936) from the Gestapo Berlin to the German consul in Brno: "Er [Giese] ist der ehemalige Privatskretär des Prof. Dr. Magnus Hirschfeld. Obwohl er nie besonders hervorgetreten ist, dürften über seine Einstellung keine Zweifel bestehen".

[150] The German authorities' concern that Giese might return to Germany was possibly linked to the fact that, in 1935, Giese obtained from the Berlin Polizeipräsidium an "Unbedenklichkeitsbescheinigung" (clearance certificate). See letter (dated Oct. 8, 1936), sent by the German consul in Brno to the Gestapo in the Albrechtstrasse in Berlin, in ibid. In 1937, Giese also obtained a "Heimatschein (für den Aufenthalt im Ausland)" (certificate of nationality [for foreign stays]) valid from Februay 25, 1937 until February 25, 1942. See MZA, Brno, fonds C 107, Německý úřední soud Brno (Deutsches Amtsgericht Brünn), kart. n° 256, sign. 5aV 3/41, f. 5. I do not know why Giese deemed it necessary to procure these two documents from the police in Berlin. Had he maybe learned his lesson from the problems with Hirschfeld's residence issue encountered during the Hirschfeld inheritance case in Nice? For more information on German citizenship issues and their complicated history, see Gosewinkel 2003.

[151] Politisches Archiv des Auswärtigen Amts, Berlin, Akten des früheren Deutschen Konsulats in Brünn, Bündel 42, Passangelegenheiten, Einzelfälle gebündelt, Buchstabe G, 1935–1939, file Carl [*sic*] Giese.

[152] See "Selbstmord eines deutschen Emigranten in Brünn", *Tagesbote*, Abendblatt, Mar. 17, 1938, 2.

[153] That is at least what Otto Schütz himself claimed in a letter. See NA, Praha, fonds n° 1007, Ministerstvo

managed to slap them in the face from beyond the grave. It is very likely that Giese was also thinking of this dangerous book, and had even seen or received indications that the National Socialists were looking into the matter [ill. 12].

Despite all these factors, undoubtedly pressing upon Giese with great stress, we now know, with the advantage of historical hindsight, that all still depended on the Munich Agreement, imposed on Czechoslovakia by the Allied states, in September of 1938. This was immediately followed by the annexation of the Sudetenland. In March 1939, the Germans effectively annexed what remained of the already dismantled Czechoslovakia, the so-called "Rest-Tschechoslowakei". Strategically speaking, the immediate invasion of Czechoslovakia, after the "easy" Anschluss of Austria, was not an option for the Germans. It would take another year, almost to the day, after Giese's suicide for Hitler to drive in an open car on the Freiheitsplatz (náměstí Svobody) in Brno, renamed the Adolf-Hitler-Platz for the occasion (only for the one day). But who could have known for sure, in the middle of March 1938, when the Germans would make their next expansionist move?

Both Adelheid Schulz and Erhart Löhnberg mentioned that, shortly before his suicide, Giese threw a party at his Brno flat, which he decorated for the occasion. On the evening of the party, a (gay?) couple in attendance wanted to get married and staged a mock (gay?) marriage. Giese gave away many of his personal belongings that night.[154] This likely explains the bizarre happenings in Giese's bank account. The Brno police reported that, in June 1937, Giese had 38,000 Czech crowns in his account; however, by February 10, 1938, only 1,000 Czech crowns remained.[155] Did Giese give the money away here and there? All this seems to be confirmed by a letter, written in the summer of 1938, by François Herzfelder to Ernst Maass: "Upon enquiry, Dr. Weisskopf informed me that Mr. Giese committed suicide, after having gone through all the money he received from Dr. Hirschfeld's estate. The reason for the suicide was apparently despair over his economic situation and Hitler's invasion of Vienna".[156]

Every other onlooker abroad had their own ideas for why Giese had taken this fatal decision. Hirschfeld's housekeeper Adelheid Schulz said that Giese had already been depressed because the Institute was looted, because he had been imprisoned in France, and, most of all, because Hirshfeld died.[157] "Yes, Karl Giese was imprisoned twice until he [...] was so exhausted, Sanitätsrat [Hirschfeld] was perhaps already

sociální péče, Londýn (Ministry of Social Welfare, London), letter (dated Mar. 17, 1943) from Otto Schütz to Dr. [Marie] Fischer-Ascher, kart. n° 1007/43, inv. n° 1/659, microfilm 4299, f. 427.

[154] Schulz read about this party in a letter Giese sent to her afterwards. Giese's sister, Toni Mertens, also told her about this farewell party. See Schulz 2001, 103: "Ja mit seinem [Hirschfeld's] Tod ist dann alles vorbei gewesen. Karl Giese war todunglücklich, er hatte denn noch ein paar Freunde, der hat dann auch sehr sehr nett gefeiert mit diesen Freunden, und da war ein Pärchen, daß sich da verheiraten wollte, das schrieb er mir noch [...] Und da hat er noch mit denen gefeiert und Toni [Mertens, Giese's sister] erzählte mir, daß er die noch so halb eingerichtet hat die Wohnung, er hat ja viel Talent gehabt, mit Dekorieren und da hat [er] noch sehr viel von sich geschenkt, und dann hat er sich das Leben genommen" (Yes, it was all over when he [Hirschfeld] died. Karl Giese was very miserable, he still had a few friends, and he had a very very nice party with these friends, and there was this cute little couple who wanted to get married, he still wrote me [...] And then he celebrated with them and Toni [Mertens, Giese's sister] told me that he still had the apartment half decorated, He had a lot of talent for decorating and [he] still gave away a lot of his things, and then he took his own life). Erhart Löhnberg heard the same story about a party thrown shortly before Giese's suicide from Kurt Hiller in London. See Wellcome Library, London, fonds Charlotte Wolff (1897–1986), correspondence II, 1981–1986, PSY/WOL/6/8/2, letter (undated [1985?], 9) from Erhart Löhnberg to Charlotte Wolff.

[155] MZA, Brno, fonds B 40, Zemský úřad Brno (Landesbehörde in Brünn), kart. n° 2138, sign. 5274/38, letter (dated Feb. 10, 1938) from Brno police to Zemský úřad v Brně, f. 2.

[156] Archiv MHG, Berlin, fonds Ernst Maass, letter (dated Aug. 31, 1938, 1) from François Herzfelder to Ernst Maass: "Auf Anfrage teilte mir dann Herr Dr. Weisskopf mit, dass Herr Giese durch Selbstmord geendet habe [*sic*], nachdem er die ganzen ihm aus dem Nachlass Dr. Hirschfelds zugeflossenen Geldmittel aufgebraucht hatte. Grund des Selbstsmords offenbar die Verzweiflung über seine wirtschaftliche Lage und über den Hitlereinmarsch in Wien".

[157] Schulz 2001, 74, 82, 103, 115.

dead, what else could he do, no? That was his life, Papa was his life".[158] Schulz also stressed what a happy fellow Giese was but claimed, at the same time, that Giese suffered more than others when life did not go as he wanted: "But as cheerful as he [Giese] could be, he could also take one thing so seriously. [...] [W]hat Hirschfeld did not take as very tragic, Karl Giese took as doubly tragic".[159]

GIESE'S SUICIDE

Some time in the evening or night of Wednesday March 16, 1938, Giese tried to hang himself in his apartment. Because this apparently proved "unsuccessful", he then tried and succeeded to suffocate himself with gas from a gas lamp (*Leuchtgas*) or a coal or gas stove.[160]

Alarmed by the smell of gas, the apartment building superintendent prompted the discovery of Giese's lifeless body the next morning.[161] The glass in the front door of Giese's apartment was broken to open the door that must have been locked from the inside.[162] A newspaper article reported: "On Thursday morning, while descending the stairs, the superintendent in 8 Střelecká smelled coal gas [*Leuchtgas*] leaking from

[158] Schulz 2001, 94: "Ja, Karl Giese ist zweimal eingesperrt gewesen, bis er denn, er war so fertig, Sanitätsrat [Hirschfeld] war vielleicht schon tot, was soll er noch, nich ? Das war sein Leben, Papa war sein Leben".

[159] Schulz 2001, 115: "Aber so fröhlich wie er [Giese] sein konnte, so schwer konnte er auch eine Sache nehmen. [...] [W]as Hirschfeld nicht so tragisch nahm, daß Karl Giese das doppelt tragisch nahm."

[160] See the *ohledací list* (coroner's report or medical examiner's sheet) in MZA, Brno, fonds C 107, Německý úřední soud Brno (Deutsches Amtsgericht Brünn), kart. n° 256, sign. 5aV 3/41, f. 13: "19. Základní nemoc: Otrava plynem uhelným ze svítiplynu" (Underlying disease: Coal gas poisoning from lamp gas). And: "20. Komplikace (nemoci sdružené a pod.): Stav po pokusu sebevraždy oběšením" (20. Complications (associated diseases, etc.): Condition after attempted suicide by hanging). See also the mention in *Reichenberger Zeitung*, Mar. 19, 1938, 3: "mit Leuchtgas vergiftet" (poisoned with illuminating gas). The Brno local newspaper mentioned "Selbstmord durch Einatmen von Leuchtgas" (Suicide by inhalation of illuminating gas) (*Tagesbote*, Mar. 17, 1938, 2). Adelheid Schulz also knew about how Giese committed suicide: "Mit Gas vergiftet" (poisoned with gas). See Schulz 2001, 74.

[161] There is quite some confusion in the archival sources on the exact date of Giese's death. It is in fact somewhat uncertain if Giese died on March 16, 1938, or after midnight and thus on March 17. In any case, he was found dead in the morning of March 17, 1938. As we will see later, one newspaper explicitly stated that he had died in the evening of March 16, 1938. Another newspaper noted that he killed himself early in the morning of March 17, 1938 (*Tagesbote*, Abendblatt, Mar. 17, 1938, 2). Giese's last will, left on a table in his flat, was dated March 16, 1938. François Herzfelder also wrote to Ernst Maass that "Herr Giese hat sich am 16. März das Leben genommen" (Mr. Giese took his own life on March 16). See Archiv MHG, Berlin, fonds Ernst Maass, letter (dated Aug. 13, 1938) from François Herzfelder to Ernst Maass. See also the letter Herzfelder wrote in 1965 to the Landgericht in Berlin where the same March 16, 1938 date is repeated and where Herzfelder states that he obtained this information from Dr. Josef Weisskopf (who lived near Giese's flat). See Herzer 2001, 242 n. 21. On the other hand, Karl Fein consistently declared in all subsequent documents that March 17, 1938, was the date of Giese's death. At least one court, the Brno District Civil Court (Okresní soud civilní Brno, Bezirksgericht für Zivilsachen Brünn), mentions this date as well. And yet many official documents give the official death date as March 18, 1938, mainly because the coroner stated this date in his report. The official coroner, a certain Prof. Dr. Berka, made things even worse by adding several other nonsensical dates. He stated, for example, that Giese's burial took place on March 17, 1938. So the coroner was clearly frivolous in his use of dates, making it even uncertain that he actually examined Giese's body on the morning of March 18, 1938. See the *ohledací list* (coroner's report or medical examiner's sheet) in MZA, Brno, fonds C 107, Německý úřední soud Brno (Deutsches Amtsgericht Brünn), kart. n° 256, sign. 5aV 3/41, f. 13. This document also served as the official death certificate (or was simply an added form) since a stamp was added stating "umrtní protokol v Brně" (Brno death certificate), to which there was added the handwritten numbers "1156, [year] 1938". One can also find this same (clearly incorrect) death date, March 18, 1938, in AMB, Brno, fonds A 1/3, Sbírka rukopisů a úředních knih, 1333–1958, Úmrtní protokol z roku 1938, book n° 8226, entry n° 1156 (dated Mar. 22, 1938), Karl Giese (born October 18, 1898). Lastly, some Brno central cemetery administration documents in Giese's file even claim that he died on March 19, 1938. See the cemetery file on Karl Giese, obtained from the cemetery administration and kindly sent to me by Markéta Jančíková (AMB, Brno) on September 27, 2010. Christopher Isherwood proved even more frivolous, stating that Giese committed suicide in 1936. See Isherwood 1988, 137. I must point out this

the flat of the 40-year-old Karl Gize [*sic*], archivist. The superintendent immediately called the police, who broke into Gize's [*sic*] flat and found Gize [*sic*] dead, lying on the bed in his bedroom. The flat was contaminated by coal gas and a further search of the flat revealed that Gize [*sic*] had committed suicide in the evening of the preceding day. The body was examined by the police doctor and then transported to the Institute of Forensic Medicine. It is not known why Gize [*sic*] was in such despair".[163] Another newspaper article added: "The members of the Voluntary Rescue Society could only confirm the death. A prepared suicide note was retrieved by the police".[164]

One cannot help but notice that virtually all of the local newspapers were rather discreet, or maybe simply ignorant, about Giese's past. This might indeed suggest that Giese was keeping a somewhat low profile in Brno, as the Gestapo in Berlin also noticed. He was simply an archivist, not a gay activist. On the other hand, it could also be that Brno newspaper ethics (or simply local custom?) preferred to be discreet about "private" matters. One newspaper gave the impression that it knew a little bit more, but in the end did not name names: "Gize [*sic*] was a German emigrant. He used to work as an archivist in a Berlin library which he fled after Hitler came to power".[165] Only the *Prager Tagblatt*, which kept good contacts with Magnus Hirschfeld during his lifetime, told the complete truth, together with a plain mistake: "Giese, who lived in Brno for five years, had been Magnus Hirschfeld's secretary in Germany and the administrator of the Sexological Archive in Berlin". They were mistaken about the term of Giese's residence. Giese had only lived in Brno on and off starting in 1933, moving there permanently only in the summer of 1936.[166]

mistake because Isherwood's novel is, alas, treated as authoritative on the lives of Hirschfeld and Giese.

162 The Giese inheritance file contains a bill for the mending of a door window pane. See MZA, Brno, fonds C 107, Německý úřední soud Brno (Deutsches Amtsgericht Brünn), kart. n° 256, sign. 5aV 3/41, f. 29.

163 P. K., "Sebevražda archiváře v Brně" (The suicide of an archivist in Brno), *Moravská orlice*, Mar. 18, 1938, 3: "Brno 17. března. Ve čtvrtek v ranních hodinách, když šel po schodišti domovník ve Střelecké ulici čís. 8 v Brně, pocítil, že z bytu 40letého Karla Gize, archiváře, vychází svítiplyn. Přivolal proto rychle stráž, která byt Gizův násilím otevřela a v ložnici v posteli nalezla Gizu, který byl již však mrtev. Byt byl zamořen svítiplynem a při ohledání bytu bylo zjištěno, že Giza spáchal sebevraždu již ve večerních hodinách. Mrtvola jeho byla po prohlídce policejním lékařem převezena do ústavu pro soudní lékařství. Proč si zoufal, není známo". A German-language newspaper confirmed that Giese's dead body was found "gestern früh" (yesterday, early in the morning) of March 17, 1938. See "Selbstmord eines deutschen Emigranten in Brünn", *Morgenpost*, Mar. 18, 1938, 3. However, another newspaper reported that Giese was found in the afternoon: "The housekeeper of 8 Střelecká in Brno noticed a strong smell of coal gas this afternoon in the corridors of the house" (*Moravské Slovo*, Mar. 18, 1938, 2; the article itself was dated Mar. 17, 1938).

164 See "Selbstmord eines deutschen Emigranten in Brünn", *Tagesbote*, Abendblatt, Mar. 17, 1938, 2: "Die Mitglieder der Freiwilligen Rettungsgesellschaft konnte nurmehr den Tod feststellen. Ein vorbereiteter Abschiedsbrief wurde von der Polizei übernommen". Inspired by the original Vienna *Verein* (association), founded in 1881, the German Voluntary Rescue Society (*Německá dobrovolná ochranná společnost, Brunner Freiwillige Rettungsgesellschaft*) started in 1891. See "Tochtergesellschaften" in https://de.wikipedia.org/wiki/Wiener_Freiwillige_Rettungsgesellschaft, and https://www.senat.cz/informace/z_historie/tisky/1vo/stena/080schuz/prilohy/priloh05.htm (both accessed Apr. 1, 2020). The archival fonds R 8, Brünner freiwillige Rettungsgesellschaft des Brünner Turnvereines, in the AMB, Brno, covers only the years 1901–28 and was thus not consulted.

165 See "Smrt německého emigranta" (Death of a German emigrant), *Moravské Slovo*, Mar. 18, 1938, 2: "Býval archivářem v jedné knihovně v Berlíně, odkud utekl po nastolení hitlerovského režimu".

166 See "Emigrantendrama in Brünn" (Emigrant drama in Brno), *Prager Tagblatt*, Mar. 19, 1938, 6: "Giese, der seit fünf Jahren in Brünn lebte, war in Deutschland Sekretär Magnus Hirschfelds und Verwalter des Sexualwissenschaftlichen Archivs in Berlin gewesen". Almost the same brief text, with a similarly vague title, was also printed in the exile newspaper *Pariser Tagesblatt*. See "Emigrantenselbstmord in Brünn", *Pariser Tagesblatt*, Mar. 23, 1938, 2; https://portal.dnb.de/bookviewer/view/1026584663#page/2/mode/1up (accessed Apr. 15, 2021). The North Bohemian *Reichenberger Zeitung* (*Organ für die deutsch-nationale Partei in Böhmen*) also copied, almost word for word, the *Prager Tagblatt* (*Reichenberger Zeitung*, Mar. 19, 1938, 3) but added a more explicit title: "Magnus Hirschfelds Sekretär begeht Selbstmord" (Magnus Hirschfeld's secretary commits suicide). Another (minor) mistake reported in most newspaper articles was that Giese was forty. Strictly counting the days and months, Giese was thirty-nine at the time

March 16, 1938, the date of Giese's suicide, was presumably etched for some time in Ernst Maass' mind as a tainted, as it also the date that he and his mother arrived in New York. On the very day that Maass set foot on American soil, having escaped a continent sliding into war, the last remaining guardian of the Institute and the Hirschfeld materials, Giese, had given up. Knowing Maass' real, heartfelt concern for the preservation of the Hirschfeld estate, this must have been a real shock to him. But the news that Giese committed suicide may possibly have reached Maass only in August 1938, in a letter from François Herzfelder: "Mr. Giese took his own life on March 16th".[167]

GIESE'S LAST WILL

Giese left a handwritten will on a table in his apartment [ill. 13]. He wrote it in blue fountain pen ink, on the same light yellow letter paper he had used for numerous letters in his lifetime.[168]

This is what he wrote:

> *My last will* [underlining in original]
> I hereby bequeath all my books, writings and objects in my flat, Brno, 8 Střelecká (with the exception of the furniture and economic objects belonging to Mr. Willi Bondi, Brno, Orlice [Orlí][169] and to Mr. Walter Lukl, of same, which are listed in an inventory kept by Dr. Fein) to my legal friend Dr. Karl Fein, Brno, 35 Koliště.
> Likewise, I bequeath to him all claims from the proceeds of the books and medicines to which I am entitled according to the will of Dr. Magnus Hirschfeld.
> I ask him to accept this bequest and to preserve and administer it, as far as is at all possible, in the spirit of the deceased, who was also dear to him.
> Brno, March 16th, 1938 Karl Giese.

> *Mein letzter Wille* [underlining in original]
> Hiermit vermache ich alle meine Bücher, Schriften und Gegenstände, die sich in meiner Wohnung, Brno, Střelecká 8, befinden (mit Ausnahme der Herrn Willi Bondi, Brno, Orlice [Orlí] und Herrn Walter Lukl ebendaselbst gehörigen Möbel und Wirtschaftsgegenstände, die in einem bei Dr. Fein befindlichen Inventar verzeichnet sind) meinem Rechtsfreund Dr. Karl Fein, Brno, Koliště 35.
> Desgleichen vermache ich ihm alle Ansprüche aus den Erträgnissen der Bücher und Medikamente, die mir nach dem Testament Dr. Magnus Hirschfelds zustehen.

of his death. He would not have turned forty until October 1938.

[167] Archiv MHG, Berlin, fonds Ernst Maass, letter (dated Aug. 13, 1938) from François Herzfelder to Ernst Maass: "Herr Giese hat sich am 16. März das Leben genommen". Herzfelder wrote in another letter (dated Aug. 31, 1938) to Ernst Maass that he was answering Maass's letter (dated Aug. 24, 1938). It is conceivable that Maass contacted Herzfelder in August because his letters to Giese went unanswered. That Maass only sought to renew contact with Giese in Brno only several months after his arrival in the USA is possibly an indication that he did not go to Brno to pick up more materials in the weeks or months before he left France for the USA. Otherwise, he would have likely kept in closer contact with Giese, if only to report briefly that he had arrived safely with the materials in the USA. On the other hand, Maass might simply have had other things on his mind in the first months after arriving in the USA, like finding a job and a place to stay.

[168] A typed transcription of Giese's last will is in MZA, Brno, fonds C 107, Německý úřední soud Brno (Deutsches Amtsgericht Brünn), kart. n° 256, sign. 5aV 3/41, f. 9. The original handwritten will can be found in MZA, Brno, fonds C 152, Okresní soud civilní Brno, rubber stamp (dated Mar. 23, 1938), ad DV 206/38/2, sign. s.l. 69/38. I have slightly emended the text of the typed version after a close examination of the handwritten original will, and, in the case of illegible or unclear words, based on my research. Other small changes are confined to diacritics. The Mar. 16, 1938 date added at the end of the letter seems indeed to confirm that Giese committed suicide the evening of that day.

[169] "Orlice" is the word in Giese's handwriting and it is transcribed in the typed copy. But Giese meant the address of the Leopold Fleischer expedition firm where both Bondi and Lukl worked, located at 34 Orlí (Adlergasse). Most likely, Giese mixed up the name of the street, Orlí, with the Czech word for street, *ulice*.

Ich bitte ihn, dieses Vermächtnis anzunehmen und es soweit es ihm irgend möglich ist im Sinne des auch ihm teuren Verstorbenen zu erhalten und zu verwalten.
Brno, den 16. März 1938 Karl Giese.

When the police arrived in Giese's apartment the following morning, they quickly noticed that there were strange objects present in the apartment of a man whom they "suspected" – as the police document states – of being a homosexual.[170] On Sunday, March 20, 1938, on the order of the police inspector, Dr. Jindřich Procházka (1903–1942), three boxes of (for the Brno police) "problematic" materials were seized (*beschlagnahmt*) in one of the rooms of the apartment.[171] The apartment building superintendent, Jaroslav Vykesal, was called by the police as a witness. "Found and confiscated items: 3 boxes of materials, various pornographic photographs, vinyl records, 1 brass tray, 8 boxes of film reels, 1 wooden carving, 9 casts of genitals".[172] These were most likely some of the wax genital casts described in May 1935 by the appraiser Giauffer in the Gloria Mansions I apartment in Nice. All of Giese's other belongings in the living room of the apartment, including the two bookcases filled with 535 books, were left untouched.[173] An inventory made by the Brno police of the things found in Giese's apartment can be found in the addenda section of this book.[174]

Karl Giese was buried on March 23, 1938, in Brno's central cemetery (*Zentralfriedhof, ustředním hřbitov*), a few kilometers southwest of the city center.[175] He was buried in parcel 23, row 6, grave 416 in the southwest quarter of the cemetery.[176] Brno's central cemetery is known for its modernist crematorium, designed by Ernst Wiesner (1890–1971), located on the northeast edge of the cemetery. The cemetery includes the graves

[170] MZA, Brno, fonds C 107, Německý úřední soud Brno (Deutsches Amtsgericht Brünn), kart. n° 256, sign. 5aV 3/41, f. 5: "pro podezření homosexuelních styků" (for suspicion of homosexual relations). Giese's police file in fonds B 26 (Policejní ředitelství v Brno, Polizeidirektion Brünn) could not be retrieved from the MZA, Brno, archives due to a lack of access index lists. I was also told that most police archives for 1938 were simply missing. See email (dated Sep. 6, 2012) from Miroslava Kučerová (MZA, Brno) to the author. The following police file reference numbers that I also saw in Giese's inheritance file were thus not found in fonds B 26 by the MZA, Brno, staff either: Okresní policejní komisařstvi Brno – vnitřní město: n° 13091 Kl (f. 3), and Policejní ředitelství v Brně (Polizeidirektion in Brünn): n° 14.301 (f. 15) and n° 13666/38 (f. 15). I did not ask the MZA, Brno, staff for the following police file reference numbers found in the archival file in MZA, Brno, fonds B 40, Zemský úřad Brno (Landesbehörde in Brünn), kart. n° 2138, sign. 5274/38: 82.496/II (dated Feb. 10, 1938), 34.476/I-7 (dated Oct. 19, 1937 and Nov. 5, 1937) (f. 2), 78.804/II (dated Aug. 27, 1937), 26190/I/7 (dated Aug. 20, 1937), 22241/I-7 (dated Jul. 8, 1937) (f. 5), 97067/II (dated Jun. 10, 1937), 23739/I-7 (f. 13), 19245/II (dated Jun. 18, 1936) (f. 19).

[171] The staff at MZA, Brno, wrote to me that they were quite certain of the identity of this man (born Dec. 12, 1903) since he was the only Procházka (a very common name in Czechoslovakia and current Czechia) in the Brno police staff files with the title of doctor. According to the name label on the cover of his staff file, Procházka was "tortured to death in Auschwitz". I found his name in Kopečný, where he is reported dying in Mauthausen on February 7, 1942 (Kopečný 2006, 207). I also found his name in the Mauthausen victims database, https://raumdernamen.mauthausen-memorial.org/?L=1 (accessed Jul. 26, 2020). His wife, Eugenie (Evženie) Procházková (née Triegerová, 1907–1942?), was deported on October 24, 1942, on transport "Ca" from Prague to Terezín and then further transferred to Auschwitz-Birkenau on transport "By" on October 26, 1942. She was a Jewish lawyer with international contacts and, clandestinely, politically active. See MZA, Brno, fonds B 26, Policejní ředitelství Brno, kart. n° 2120, file Jindřich Procházka.

[172] MZA, Brno, fonds C 107, Německý úřední soud Brno (Deutsches Amtsgericht Brünn), kart. n° 256, sign. 5aV 3/41, f. 5: "Nalezené a zábavené předměty: 3 bedny materiálu, různých fotografií pornografických, desek, 1 mosazný tác, 8 krabic filmů, 1 řezba, 9 odlitků pohlavních údů". These items were found in *pokoj* (room) II, according to the inventory of Giese's apartment drawn up on March 18, 1938. See ibid., f. 4.

[173] These books were found in *pokoj* (room) III, according to the inventory of Giese's apartment drawn up on March 18, 1938. See MZA, Brno, fonds C 107, Německý úřední soud Brno (Deutsches Amtsgericht Brünn), kart. n° 256, sign. 5aV 3/41, f. 4.

[174] See n° 7 in the addenda.

[175] AMB, Brno, fonds A 1/3, Sbírka rukopisů a úředních knih, 1333–1958, Úmrtní protokol z roku 1938, book n° 8226, entry n° 1156 (dated Mar. 22, 1938), Karl Giese (born Oct. 18, 1898).

[176] Email (dated Sep. 24, 2010) from Eva Holoubková (Správa hřbitovů města Brna, Brno) to Markéta Jančíková (AMB, Brno), forwarded to the author.

of several Brno luminaries, the most famous being the grave of Georg Mendel. Since there was likely no money to pay for a long permit, certainly not a perpetual one, as with Hirschfeld's grave in Nice, Giese's grave was removed in the decades following the war. There is no way of knowing now where exactly in parcel 23 the grave was located as at some point all the grave plots in the parcel were renumbered.[177]

WALTER LUKLS'S FURTHER FATE

After he had moved out of Giese's apartment, in the beginning of January 1938, Lukl moved to 4–6 Mühlgasse (Mlýnská) in Brno. He continued to work for the Fleischer company, which would later be Aryanized. According to his own statement after the war, until 1939 he had worked for the company as a truck driver.[178] In June 1939, he was temporarily held in the police prison in the Adlergasse (Orlí) because he was caught up, in his capacity as an employee of the Leopold Fleischer firm, in a case of fraud involving sending valuables abroad for a Jewish customer. While in prison, Lukl sent a letter to the Brno Gestapo, asking for a daily copy of the local German national newspaper *Volksdeutsche Zeitung* (*Tagblatt der deutschen Volksgruppe in der Tschecho-Slowakei*).[179]

Presumably shortly after his release, Lukl stopped working for the Leopold Fleischer firm. In February 1940, Lukl requested to be added to the German ethnicity (Deutsche Volkszugehörigkeit) register. This request was approved in April 1940 and the very next month Walter Lukl was a Wehrmacht artillery soldier in Brno.[180] It is unclear if Lukl volunteered or was conscripted, but most likely his enrollment was linked to his application for German ethnic status and his search for a new or more reliable source of income. He would remain under arms until the end of the

[177] Email (dated Sep. 24, 2010) from Eva Holoubková (Správa hřbitovů města Brna, Brno) to Markéta Jančíková (AMB, Brno), forwarded to the author: "tyto hroby byly zrušeny a skupina přečíslovaná" (these graves were removed and the parcel renumbered).

[178] LKAN, Nürnberg, Archiv Diakonie Herzogsägmühle, Personenakte n° 15265, Walter Lukl (born 1907), text (undated but presumably March 1966) Lebenslauf – Aufenthaltsverhältnisse.

[179] MZA, Brno, fonds D 25, Celní pátrací služebna, pobočka Brno, kart. n° 51, sign. E 535/39, Julia Fleischer, Brünn, f. 25, 25-26. The client that the Leopold Fleischer tried to help was Otto Glückselig (1907–1942?). Glückselig was deported on transport "Ae" on March 27, 1942 from Brno to Terezín and further transferred to Rejowiec on transport "Ap" on April 18, 1942.

[180] Lukl's request was made on February 23, 1940, and his status was approved on April 1, 1940. See the handwritten addition on his home certificate in AMB, Brno, fonds B 1/39; and the index card for the status application itself in AMB, Brno, fonds A 1/53. Cf. the index card in MZA, Brno, fonds B 252, Zemský prezident Brno, správa z příkazu říše, kart. n° 462, Deutsche Volkszugehörigkeit application index card Walter Lukl. There the same date is given for the application and approval, February 23, 1940. The index card also mentions his Jewish wife (*Jüdin*) Mili [*sic*] Tabatznik and includes a rather illegible handwritten added comment that seems to say "lebt seit 3 Jahren nicht mehr mit d.[ieser] Frau zusammen" (has not lived with this woman for 3 years), which was factually correct. I thank Rainer-Joachim Siegel for his assistance in reading the handwriting. Lukl's mother also applied for Deutsche Volkszugehörigkeit status, but as early as November 1939. She was also a member of three Nazi organizations: Bund Deutscher Osten (BDO), Deutsche Krankenversicherung (DKV) and Deutsche Frauenwerk (DFW). Her son Walter was not a member of any Nazi organizations.

[181] The first archival mention shows he reported to the Wehrmacht in May 1940 (Einheit 2. leichte Artillerie-Ersatz-Abteilung 260). See Bundesarchiv, Berlin, signatur B 563/ Band 58161, p. 218. His fourth and final transfer within the Wehrmacht artillery is dated June 29, 1944, when he was assigned to Einheit Stabsbatterie II, Artillerie-Regiment 43. See Bundesarchiv, Berlin, signatur B 563/ Band 52203, p. 99. In the end, he was transferred to Artillerie Ersatz- und Ausbildungs-Abteilung 63. See email (dated Apr. 23, 2020) from Mr. Rettig (Bundesarchiv Berlin, Abteilung Personenbezogene Auskünfte, formerly Deutsche Dienststelle-WASt) to the author. A death notice for his mother Emma Lukl, in the beginning of April 1945, makes it clear that he was still in Brno and "im Felde" (enlisted) at that time. See *Volksdeutsche Zeitung*, Apr. 3, 1945, 2. There is no information about Lukl's military career in the heavily war-damaged, remaining military archives of the Bundesarchiv-Militärarchiv in Freiburg im Breisgau. See email (dated Mar. 27, 2020) from Roman Zimmermann (Bundesarchiv, Abteilung Militärarchiv, Freiburg im Breisgau) to the author.

[182] Bundesarchiv, Berlin-Lichterfelde, NSDAP Mitgliederkartei.

war.[181] Walter Lukl never became a member of the NSDAP.[182] If we are to believe his own statements, he was imprisoned by the Russians at the end of the war for half a year and then returned to Brno as a prisoner of war. In the summer of 1946, he was presumably driven out of Czechoslovakia as a German national.[183]

On December 7, 1946, he arrived, without official papers, in Weilheim in Oberbayern (Bavaria, Germany) where he stayed for a while in the refugee camp there.[184] That he arrived without papers is not unimportant. He stated that his mother, whose name he claimed he could not remember, had died "when the Czechs invaded" (*beim Einmarsch der Tschechen*). That his mother died near the end of the war, on March 29, 1945, is true; but she died a natural death, from heart problems, a month before Brno was liberated on April 26, 1945 by the Russian, Romanian, and Ukranian armies.[185] He was however simply right, as we have seen, in stating that his father was unknown. But he did not mention that he had been married to Milli Lukl (née Tabatznik), nor even that he, at least officially, was still a married man, on documents that he completed [ill. 14].

For the first ten years after the war, Walter Lukl moved a lot in the village of Weilheim in Oberbayern.[186] He later claimed that he worked for several moving firms until 1956.[187] In a local 1955 telephone directory, he is listed as truck driver (*Kraftfahrer*), living at 8 Steinlestrasse.[188] Starting in July 1957, he settled at 1 Schießstattsiedlung.[189] At some point, he started working for the Oskar Bormann radio cabinetmaking (*Radiogehäusebau*) firm.[190] In March 1965, he had a heart attack and spent six weeks in hospital. After his release, he was apparently not able to work anymore and, since he had no income, was housed in a wooden shed owned by the Bormann firm. His former boss then sought a solution for Lukl with the local Church authorities. It was agreed that, in the beginning of March 1966, Lukl would move to a religiously inspired community for homeless people in the village of Herzogsägmühle (Ortsteil

[183] LKAN, Nürnberg, Archiv Diakonie Herzogsägmühle, Personenakte n° 15265, Walter Lukl (born 1907) text (undated but presumably March 1966) Lebenslauf – Aufenthaltsverhältnisse. An index card for Lukl from the Kirchliche Suchdienst, on the other hand, states that Lukl fled from (or was driven out of) Brno on May 8, 1945. See Bundesarchiv, Bestand B-530-Karteien, Kirchlicher Suchdienst, Digitalisat, SID 3452, Vertriebenenausweis n° 3122 (dated Jan. 9, 1955), index card (Karteikarte) Walter Lukl (born Jun. 7, 1907).

[184] After the war, Lukl did not return to Vienna, the city where he had been born and baptized. See email (dated Feb. 11, 2020) from Elisabeth Mauser (Wiener Stadt- und Landesarchiv, Wien) to the author; and, for the baptisimal record, Archiv Erzbischöfliches Ordinariat, Wien (Österreich), Niederösterreich (Osten), Rk. Erzdiözese Wien 08, Alservorstadtkrankenhaus, Taufbuch, year 1907, sign. 01-206, f. 723, entry n° 4368, Walther Lukl 07-13/06/1907, available online at https://data.matricula-online.eu/de/oesterreich/wien/08-alservorstadtkrankenhaus/01-206/?pg=399 (accessed Jan. 28, 2021). See also emails (dated Apr. 29, 2020) from Joachim Heberlein (Stadtarchivar Weilheim in Oberbayern) to the author. The archival documents consulted by Mr. Heberlein are in Stadtarchiv Weilheim i.OB (StadtA WM), OA Meldekarten and OA 13-0144. For more information on the approximately 3,000 postwar refugee camps in Germany, housing around twelve million so-called ethnic Germans, see Bispinck & Hochmuth 2014. When he arrived in Germany, Lukl also declared that he had lost his identity papers. See LKAN, Nürnberg, Archiv Diakonie Herzogsägmühle, Personenakte n° 15265, Walter Lukl (born 1907), Personalbogen (dated Mar. 8, 1966).

[185] AMB, Brno, fonds A 1/3, Sbírka rukopisů a úředních knih, 1333–1958, Úmrtní protokol z roku 1945, book n° 8233, entry n° 1130, dated Mar. 30, 1945, Emma Lukl (born Aug. 22, 1884–died Mar. 29, 1945).

[186] Emails (dated Apr. 29, 2020) from Joachim Heberlein (Stadtarchivar, Weilheim in Oberbayern) to the author.

[187] LKAN, Nürnberg, Archiv Diakonie Herzogsägmühle, Personenakte n° 15265, Walter Lukl (born 1907), text (undated but presumably March 1966) Lebenslauf – Aufenthaltsverhältnisse.

[188] *Adressbuch der Stadt Weilheim* 1955, 37.

[189] Emails (dated Apr. 29, 2020) from Joachim Heberlein (Stadtarchivar Weilheim in Oberbayern) to the author. According to information from the Bundesarchiv in Berlin, in 1964, Lukl lived at 19b Trifthofstrasse. See email (dated Apr. 23, 2020) from Mr. Rettig (Bundesarchiv Berlin, Abteilung Personenbezogene Auskünfte) to the author.

[190] LKAN, Nürnberg, Archiv Diakonie Herzogsägmühle, Personenakte n° 15265, Walter Lukl (born 1907), text (undated but presumably March 1966) Lebenslauf – Aufenthaltsverhältnisse. The firm was located at 19 Trifthofweg. See *Adressbuch der Stadt Weilheim* 1955, 21.

von Peiting, Landkreis Weilheim-Schongau), twenty kilometers away, which to this day has a center that takes care of the poor and unhoused.[191] The doctor who examined Lukl in March 1966 described him as a man who "generally gives a somewhat disturbed impression, his details are very imprecise and nothing can be ascertained about his previous history".[192]

On April 30, 1966, in the Herzogsägmühle community center, a certain doctor O. Weiß from Schongau decided that Lukl needed to be transferred to the psychiatric hospital (*Nervenkrankenhaus*) in Kaufbeuren, thirty kilometers away.[193] Lukl died in this hospital eighteen months later, on November 6, 1967 [ill. 15].[194] Lukl was buried in the hospital cemetery the next day. In the 1980s, the cemetery graves marked by simple wooden crosses were removed. Nowadays, the parcel that contained the former graves is a meadow and has a plaque (*Erinnerungstafel*) commemorating the graves that were once there.[195] In his Herzogsägmühle community file, it says that Lukl was "completely on his own" (*völlig alleinstehend*). His only contact seems to have been with some soldiers in Weilheim in Oberbayern.[196]

[191] The exact date of his arrival in Herzogsägmühle was March 4, 1966. See emails (dated Apr. 29, 2020) from Joachim Heberlein (Stadtarchivar Weilheim in Oberbayern) to the author. The archival documents consulted are in Stadtarchiv Weilheim i.OB (StadtA WM), OA Meldekarten and OA 13-0144. See also email (dated Jun. 29, 2020) from Babette Gräper (Lernort Sozialdorf Herzogsägmühle) to the author. I thank Annette Eberle (Katholische Stiftungshochschule München) for her assistance in establishing contact with the person responsible for the archive of the Diakonie Herzogsägmühle, Babette Gräper. See email (dated Jun. 26, 2020) from Annette Eberle to the author. For the Herzogsägmühle worker's colony, started in 1894, see https://de.wikipedia.org/wiki/Herzogsägmühle (accessed Apr. 29, 2020); Eberle 1994. Lukl has a file in the LKAN, Nürnberg. I thank Mrs. Babette Gräper for ordering and sending me a digital copy on July 8, 2020. See LKAN, Nürnberg, Archiv Diakonie Herzogsägmühle, Personenakte n° 15265, Walter Lukl (born 1907).

[192] LKAN, Nürnberg, Archiv Diakonie Herzogsägmühle, Personenakte n° 15265, Walter Lukl (born 1907), doctor's medical report (dated Mar. 7, 1966): "[m]acht allgemein einen etwas verstörten Eindruck, seine Angaben sind sehr ungenau und es ist über seine Vorgeschichte nichts zu ermitteln".

[193] LKAN, Nürnberg, Archiv Diakonie Herzogsägmühle, Personenakte n° 15265, Walter Lukl (born 1907); email (dated Jun. 29, 2020) from Babette Gräper (Lernort Sozialdorf Herzogsägmühle) to the author. The hospital is currently called Bezirkskrankenhaus Kaufbeuren: Fachkrankenhaus für Psychiatrie, Psychotherapie, Psychosomatik und Neurologie, and is located at 16 Kemnater Straße. See https://www.bezirkskrankenhaus-kaufbeuren.de/kliniken/klinik-fuer-psychiatrie-psychotherapie-und-psychosomatik.html (accessed Jul. 9, 2020).

[194] First communication of Lukl's death date in email (dated May 14, 2020) from Marlene Habersetzer (Einwohnermeldeamt Markt Peiting) to the author; and death certificate for Walter Lukl from the Stadtarchiv Kaufbeuren. I thank Dr. Peter Keller (Stadtarchiv Kaufbeuren, Kaufbeuren) for his assistance in obtaining a copy of the death certificate in July 2020. I was allowed to see the Bezirkskrankenhaus Kaufbeuren patient file of Walter Lukl in 2020 under the strict condition that I not disclose any medical details it contained. I can say that Lukl died of natural causes, linked to his bodily decrepitude and ailments; unlike Karl Giese, he did not commit suicide. I thank Petra Schweizer-Martinschek (Historisches Archiv Bezirkskrankenhaus, Klinik für Psychiatrie, Psychotherapie und Psychosomatik, Kaufbeuren) for her patient and kind assistance in this regard. An email was sent on April 30, 2020, to the Lastenausgleichsarchiv, Bayreuth, and I was told that a search would be made to ascertain if Lukl had made a request for war damage compensation. After a long wait and two reminder emails, I finally received an answer in June 2021, saying there was no *Lastenausgleichakte* (burden equalization file) request for Lukl. See email (dated Jun. 2, 2021) from Maximilian Krogoll (Lastenausgleichsarchiv, Bayreuth) to the author. For more information on the *Lastenausgleichsgesetz* (Burden equalization law) and its consequences for war compensation for Jewish people and German *Volkszugehörige* (nationals), see, for example, Nachum 2013.

[195] Emails (dated Oct. 15, 2020 and Oct. 20, 2020) from Petra Schweizer-Martinschek (Historisches Archiv Bezirkskrankenhaus, Klinik für Psychiatrie, Psychotherapie und Psychosomatik, Kaufbeuren) to the author.

[196] LKAN, Nürnberg, Archiv Diakonie Herzogsägmühle, Personenakte n° 15265, Walter Lukl (born 1907). On June 17, 2020, I sent approximately ten letters to people with the last name Lukl in Czechia. Two people responded, one of them unrelated. Markéta Lukl was related but only distantly. She kindly sent me a family tree where I saw Walter Lukl's father (biologically, his grandfather), Wenzel Lukl (1844–1916?). See email (dated Apr. 23, 2021) from Markéta Lukl to the author.

1. The apartment building at 7c U dětské nemocnice (Kinderspitalgasse) where Karl Giese lived with Karl Fein in the summer of 1936. January 2011.

2. The apartment building at 8 Střelecká (Schützengasse, currently Domažlická) in the northern Brno suburb of Královo Pole where Karl Giese lived in apartment n° 7 on the second floor, from September 1936 until March 1938. January 2011.

3. Café Biber, located in the art deco-style DOPZ building at 3 Lažanského náměstí (Lažanský-Platz, currently Moravské náměstí). This building was an important meeting point for Brno social democrats and German exiles. Ca. 1931–32.

4. One Brno café where gay men gathered in the 1930s was the buffet on the first floor of the art deco-style Passage (Pasáž) Hotel on Neugasse (Nová). Ca. 1933.

5. Willi (Wilhelm) Bondi. 1930s.

6. From left to right: Julia Fleischer, Elisabeth Fleischer, Kamila Gregor. 1916.

7. Gustav Bondi, Willi Bondi and Hermine Wolfenstein's grave stone in the Jewish cemetery in Brno. January 2011.

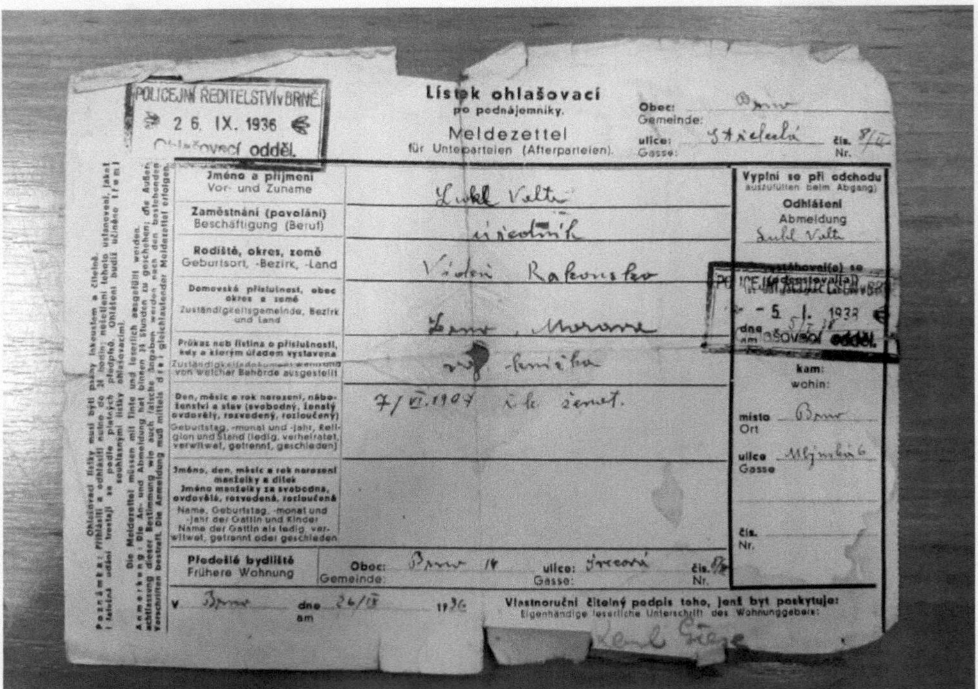

POLICEJNÍ ŘEDITELSTVÍ v BRNĚ
26. IX. 1936
Ohlašovací oddíl.

Lístek ohlašovací
po podnájemníky.
Meldezettel
für Unterparteien (Afterparteien).

Obec: / Gemeinde: Brno
ulice: / Gasse: Strělecká čís. / Nr.

		Vyplní se při odchodu / auszufüllen beim Abgang)
Jméno a příjmení / Vor- und Zuname	Lukl Valtr	Odhlášení / Abmeldung: Lukl Valtr
Zaměstnání (povolání) / Beschäftigung (Beruf)	úředník	
Rodiště, okres, země / Geburtsort, -Bezirk, -Land	Vídeň Rakousko	POLICEJNÍ ŘEDITELSTVÍ v BRNĚ — 5. I. 1938 — dne / am 5/I 38 — Ohlašovací oddíl.
Domovská příslušnost, obec okres a země / Zuständigkeitsgemeinde, Bezirk und Land	Brno, Morava	
Průkaz neb listina o příslušnosti, kdy a kterým úřadem vystavena / Zuständigkeitsdokument wann und von welcher Behörde ausgestellt	… knížka	kam: / wohin:
Den, měsíc a rok narození, náboženství a stav (svobodný, ženatý, ovdovělý, rozvedený, rozloučený) / Geburtstag, -monat und -jahr, Religion und Stand (ledig, verheiratet, verwitwet, getrennt, geschieden)	7/VI. 1907 … žen.	místo / Ort: Brno
Jméno, den, měsíc a rok narození manželky a dítek / Jméno manželky za svobodna, ovdovělá, rozvedená, rozloučená / Name, Geburtstag, -monat und -jahr der Gattin und Kinder / Name der Gattin als ledig, verwitwet, getrennt oder geschieden		ulice / Gasse: Mlýnská 6 — čís. / Nr.
Předešlé bydliště / Frühere Wohnung	Obec: / Gemeinde: Brno 14 — ulice: / Gasse: — čís. / Nr.	

V Brně dne / am 26/IX 1936

Vlastnoruční čitelný podpis toho, jenž byt poskytuje: / Eigenhändige leserliche Unterschrift des Wohnunggebers: Karl Giese

8. Walter (Valtr) Lukl's resident registration form (dated September 26, 1936), signed by Karl Giese as Lukl's sublessor.

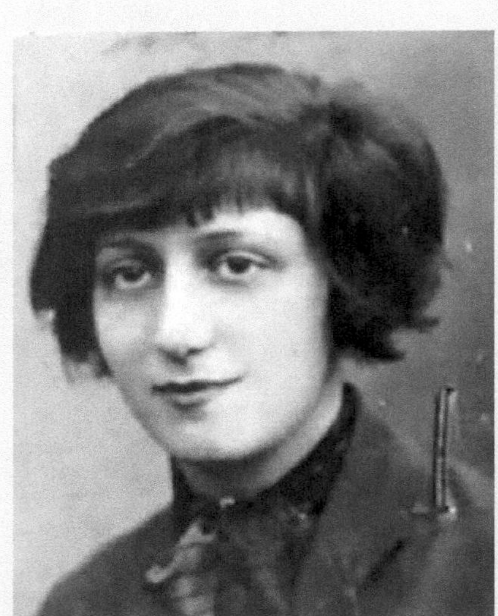

9. Milada Lukl (née Tabatznik). 1937.

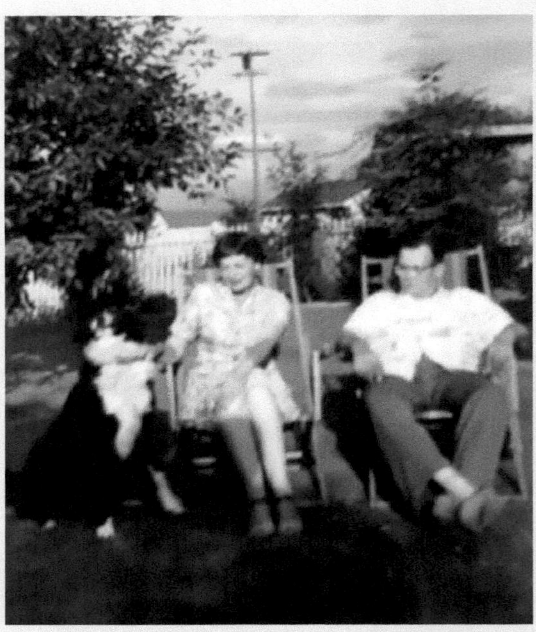

10. Milada Vandernald (Lukl's former wife) and her husband Rudolf Vandernald in the garden of their Seattle home. 1957.

11. "Germany after the annexation of Austria" (Deutschland nach der Eingliederung Österreichs). Map printed in the Brno newspaper Morgenpost, dated March 20, 1938.

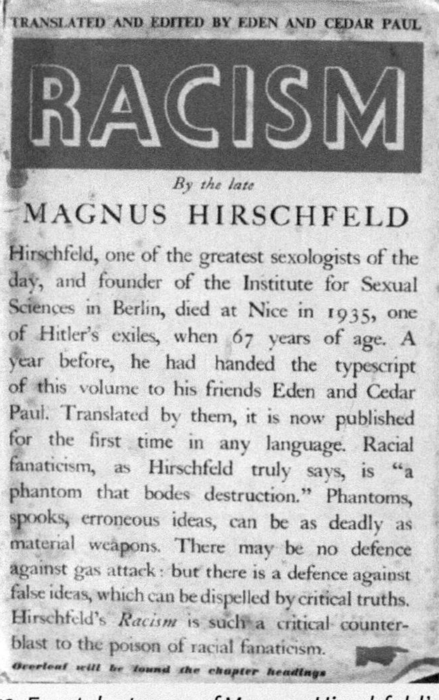

TRANSLATED AND EDITED BY EDEN AND CEDAR PAUL

RACISM

By the late

MAGNUS HIRSCHFELD

Hirschfeld, one of the greatest sexologists of the day, and founder of the Institute for Sexual Sciences in Berlin, died at Nice in 1935, one of Hitler's exiles, when 67 years of age. A year before, he had handed the typescript of this volume to his friends Eden and Cedar Paul. Translated by them, it is now published for the first time in any language. Racial fanaticism, as Hirschfeld truly says, is "a phantom that bodes destruction." Phantoms, spooks, erroneous ideas, can be as deadly as material weapons. There may be no defence against gas attack: but there is a defence against false ideas, which can be dispelled by critical truths. Hirschfeld's *Racism* is such a critical counter-blast to the poison of racial fanaticism.

Overleaf will be found the chapter headings

12. Front dustcover of Magnus Hirschfeld's Racism, published in English in 1938.

S. 1. 69/38 Mein letzter Wille ad Dv 206/38 / 2

Hiermit vermache ich alle meine Bücher, Schriften und Gegenstände die sich in meiner Wohnung Brno, Střelecká 8, befinden (mit Ausnahme der Herrn Willi Bondi, Brno, Orlice und Herrn Walter [illegible] ebendaselbst gehörigen Möbel und Wirtschafts=gegenstände, die in einem bei Dr. Fein befindlichen Inventar verzeichnet sind) meinem Rechtsfreund Dr. Karl Fein, Brno, Koliště 35.

Desgleichen vermache ich ihm alle Ansprüche aus den Erträgnissen der Bücher und Medikamente die mir nach dem Testament Dr. Magnus Hirschfelds zustehen.

Ich bitte ihn, dieses Vermächtnis anzunehmen und es soweit es ihm irgend möglich ist im Sinne des auch ihm teuren Verstorbenen zu erhalten und zu verwalten.

Brno, den 16. März 1938 Karl Giese.

13. Karl Giese's handwritten last will (dated March 16, 1938), found on a table in his apartment after his suicide.

14. Walter (Valtr) Lukl. October 8, 1946.

15. The newly built psychiatric hospital (Nervenkrankenhaus) in Kaufbeuren (Bavaria, Germany), ca. 1962-1970.

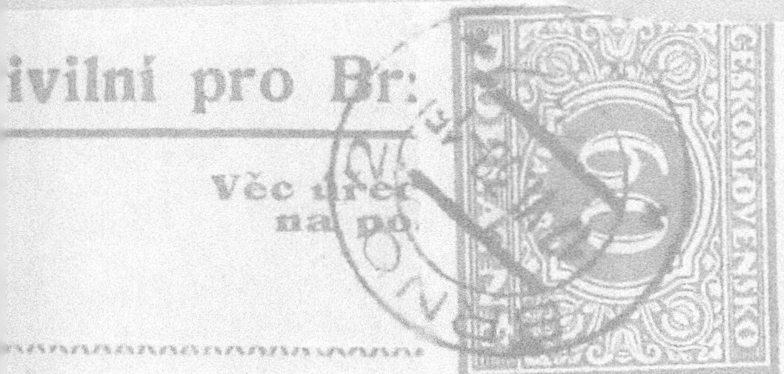

ivilní pro Br:

Věc úřed...
na po...

Doplat. známky
lepiti na
zadní stranu!

(Místo pro doporuční nálepku a úřední
podávacího pošt. úřadu).

Zpáteční lístek

okresního soudu civilního pro Brno-město.

Místní
a denn
razítko
podávací
poštovní
úřadu

Adresát (Příjemce): us

Pan Dr.Karel Fein, advokát

v Brně

D V 206/38 v

Jed. č. 19.

Pošta

Potvrzuji svým vlastnoručním podpisem, že jsem shora označenou zásilku dnes obdržel

dne 19

Doručeno oprávněným pracovatelem:

18. VI. 1938

podpis.

12. The Giese-Fein Inheritance Case

KARL FEIN TAKES MATTERS IN HAND

On Tuesday March 22, 1938, the day before Giese's burial, Karl Fein sent a letter to the Brno District Civil Court (Okresní soud civilní Brno, Bezirksgericht für Zivilsachen Brünn) in which he urged the court to appoint a trustee (*Nachlasskurator, Verlassenschaftskurator*) for the Giese estate.[1] That Fein moved quickly can be explained by his worries regarding items confiscated by the police in Giese's apartment: "Mr. Karl Giese ended his life by suicide on March 17, 1938. He left a last will and testament, which is at the Brno police headquarters. In this last will and testament, of which I had only a glimpse, I, the undersigned Dr. Karl Fein, attorney in Brno, was considered by the testator, and perhaps even appointed as universal heir. In particular, he bequeathed to me the scientific inventory of the sexual-scientific institute in Berlin at that time. Now, on Sunday, March 20, 1938, the Brno police headquarters, as I was subsequently informed, somehow made seizures. Since it will be necessary to take the necessary steps as soon as possible to safeguard the heirs' rights, and since certain measures under private law will also have to be taken, it is necessary that an interim trustee be appointed."[2]

The District Civil Court acted quickly. The very next day, the district court's Supreme court counselor (*Obergerichtsrat*) Ernst Hogenauer sent a letter to the Brno police (Policejní ředitelství Brno), asking if they would object to handing over the keys to Giese's apartment to Karl Fein. Three days later, the police answered the court, saying they had no objections to the request.[3] But a package containing Giese's last will, personal documents, apartment keys, the inventory of items present in the apartment, and a copy of the protocol stating what had been confiscated had already

[1] The Brno District Civil Court (Okresní soud civilní Brno, Bezirksgericht für Zivilsachen Brünn) functioned in this case as a probate court. The inheritance procedure in Czechoslovakia was then modeled on the Austro-Hungarian legal model, going back to the 1854 Verlassenschaftspatent. The beginning of the inheritance procedure (*Verlassenschaftsverfahren*, in German) has not changed much since: "Ein Verlassenschaftsverfahren Ablauf sieht in der Regel wie folgt aus: Das Standesamt hält die Sterbeurkunde für die Angehörigen eines Verstorbenen bereit. Gleichzeitig meldet das Standesamt dem Bezirksgericht den Todesfall. Dieses leitet das Verlassenschaftsverfahren ein. Um die rechtmäßigen Erben sowie den Vermögensstand zu ermitteln, wird vom Gericht ein Gerichtskommissär (Notar) bestellt. Alle potenziellen Erben und Angehörigen werden frühestens zwei bis drei Wochen nach dem Tod einer Person vom Gerichtskommissär eingeladen, um den Todesfall aufzunehmen", https://www.erbrechts info.at/verlassenschaftsverfahren/ (accessed Jul. 20, 2016). For a better understanding of the Czechoslovak inheritance procedure, I have also consulted https://www.uibk.ac.at/zivilrecht/buch/pdf/zivilrecht2004_kapitel17.pdf and https://www.oesterreich.gv.at/themen/dokumente_und_recht/erben_und_vererben/4/Seite.793020.html (both accessed Aug. 1, 2020).

[2] MZA, Brno, fonds C 107, Německý úřední soud Brno (Deutsches Amtsgericht Brünn), kart. n° 256, sign. 5aV 3/41, f. 1: "Herr Karl Giese hat am 17. März 1938 durch Selbstmord seinem Leben ein Ende gemacht. Er hinterliess eine letzwilligen Verfügung, die sich bei der Polizeidirektion Brünn befindet. In dieser Verfügung, die ich allerdings nur flüchtig Einsichtigen [?] konnte, bin ich unterzeichneter Dr. Karl Fein, Advokat in Brünn von dem Erblasser bedacht worden, möglicherweise sogar zum Universalerben eingesetzt worden. Insbesondere hat er mir das wissenschaftliche Inventar des seinerzeitigen sexualwissenschaftlichen Institutes in Berlin vermacht. Nun hat am Sonntag den 20. März 1938 die Polizeidirektion Brünn, wie mir nachträglich mitgeteilt wurde, irgendwie Beschlagnahmungen vorgenommen. Da es notwendig sein wird, sofort zur Wahrung der Rechte der Erben die erforderlichen Schritte einzuleiten und ausserdem gewisse privatrechtliche Massnahmen zu treffen sein werden, ist es notwendig, dass einstweilen ein Kurator bestellt wird".

[3] MZA, Brno, fonds C 107, Německý úřední soud Brno (Deutsches Amtsgericht Brünn), kart. n° 256,

been sent to the district court by the district police commissariat Brno-inner city (Okresní policejní komisařstvi I, Brno-vnitřní mesto, Bezirkspolizeikommissariat I, Brünn, innere Stadt) on March 22, 1938, the day Fein had made his request.[4] Which means that the letters crossed, that Fein had panicked, and that he must have quickly obtained the keys to Giese's apartment from the district court.

"GERMAN AUTHORITIES"

What exactly unfolded in Brno, in the days after Giese's death, only reached François Herzfelder in France in a distorted way. In an August 1938 letter to Ernst Maass, Herzfelder wrote: "After Mr. Giese's death, most of the materials in his apartment (coming from the estate of Dr. Hirschfeld) were confiscated by the local police. Apparently, these materials are still at police headquarters. The police have reportedly stated that they would only release the material if an appropriate scientific institute was established in Brno or elsewhere, either in Czechoslovakia or abroad".[5] A year later, that mistaken information was passed on by Ernst Maass in a letter to Françoise Lafitte-Cyon: "Many papers have been lost because they were given to Mr. Karl Giese, formerly secretary of the 'Institut für Sexualwissenschaft' in Berlin, who lived in Brno, Cechoslovakia [*sic*], where they were taken by the German authorities".[6] There are two mistakes here: only a tiny part of the Institute materials had been confiscated by the Brno police and the "German authorities" had nothing to do with it, since the Germans had not yet invaded Czechoslovakia in March 1938. Or did Ernst Maass think that there were separate Czech-language and German-language police in Brno and in Czechoslovakia?

We have just seen that Karl Fein had the keys to Giese's apartment in his hands at the end of March 1938. Presumably, he then acted quickly to secure the Institute materials and Giese's belongings in his Střelecká (Schützengasse) apartment.[7] Likely, Fein emptied the Giese apartment some time in April, since the cost of the April rent is included in the final settlement of the inheritance. As for the already mentioned three boxes of items confiscated by the Brno police in the days after Giese's suicide, it looks as if some or even all of these "suspicious" goods were later returned to Fein, Giese's lawful heir. Some of these confiscated items reappear in the inventory of what Fein obtained from the Giese estate.[8] So, things did not look as bleak as suggested

sign. 5aV 3/41, f. 15. For Hogenauer's legal title, see *Adreßbuch von Groß-Brünn* 1934, 69.

[4] MZA, Brno, fonds C 107, Německý úřední soud Brno (Deutsches Amtsgericht Brünn), kart. n° 256, sign. 5aV 3/41, f. 3, letter (dated Mar. 22, 1938) Okresní policejní komisařství Brno-vnitřní město to Okresní soud civilní Brno. The District police headquarters of the inner city of Brno I (Okresní policejní komisařství I, Brno, vnitřní mesto, Bezirkspolizeikommissariat I, Brünn, innere Stadt) was located at 32 Adlergasse (Orlí). See *Adreßbuch von Groß-Brünn* 1934, 58. But so was the Brno police headquarters (Policejní ředitelství v Brně, Polizeidirektion in Brünn), which means there were some communication problems. See *Adreßbuch von Groß-Brünn* 1934, 57.

[5] Archiv MHG, Berlin, fonds Ernst Maass, letter (dated Aug. 31, 1938) from François Herzfelder to Ernst Maass: "Nach dem Tode Herrn Gieses wurde der grösste Teil des in seiner Wohnung befindlichen (aus dem Nachlass Dr. Hirschfeld stammenden) Materials von der dortigen Polizei beschlagnahmt. Es befindet sich offenbar heute noch auf der dortigen Polizeidirektion. Die Polizei soll erklärt haben, dass sie das Material nur herausgebe, wenn in Brünn oder an anderem Ort, sei es in der Tschechoslowakei, sei es im Ausland, ein entsprechendes wissenschaftliches Institut gegründet worden sei".

[6] Archiv MHG, Berlin, fonds Ernst Maass, letter (dated Jul. 13, 1939) from Ernst Maass to Françoise Lafitte-Cyon.

[7] The registration of death (*úmrtní zápis*, *Todesfallsaufnahme*) (dated Mar. 30, 1938) in the Giese inheritance file also mentions that Karl Fein had already received the keys. See MZA, Brno, fonds C 107, Německý úřední soud Brno (Deutsches Amtsgericht Brünn), kart. n° 256, sign. 5aV 3/41, f. 5 and 17b.

[8] MZA, Brno, fonds C 107, Německý úřední soud Brno (Deutsches Amtsgericht Brünn), kart. n° 256, sign. 5aV 3/41, f. 29, list Místpřísežně seznámí jmění, point n° 11: "různý vědecký materiál různé fotografie, filmy a negativy, 12 odlitků anatomických edlitků" (various scientific materials, various photographs, films and negatives, 12 casts of anatomical parts).

[9] Archiv MHG, Berlin, fonds Ernst Maass, letter (dated Aug. 31, 1938, 1) from François Herzfelder to Ernst Maass: "Von Herrn Dr. Fein erhielt ich auf

in Herzfelder's and Maass' letters. Herzfelder apparently got his information from Josef Weisskopf, complaining in the same letter to Maass that he had not managed to contact Karl Fein: "To my astonishment, I have still not received any reply at all from Dr. Fein to several letters".[9] Such distorted information makes one wonder if Fein and Weisskopf were even on speaking terms. That Josef Weisskopf communicated Fein's old professional address to Herzfelder, 6 Masarykova (Masarykstrasse), inactive since October 1936, seems a quite clear indication that indeed Fein and Weisskopf were not in contact in the years 1936–38.[10]

APPOINTING AN ESTATE TRUSTEE

In Karl Fein's initial March 22, 1938, letter to the District Civil Court, he also recommended his friend, the lawyer Otto Schütz as someone the court should appoint as trustee.[11] In the same letter, Fein added that he had been Giese's mandated legal representative, including the power of attorney (*Vollmacht*) attesting to this, signed by Giese.[12] The next day, Ernst Hogenauer of the District Civil Court indeed appointed Otto Schütz as the estate trustee.[13] The case was then transferred to the Brno notary Dr. Otokar Kříž (1877–1946), operating as the court commissioner (*Gerichtskommissär*), for the preparation of a document known as the registration of death (*úmrtní zápis, Todesfallsaufnahme*). This document was drawn up on March 30, 1938. It summed up the legal situation consequent on Giese's death, and also stated the basic tenets and possible beneficiaries of the estate. This legal document was signed by Karl Fein and Karl Giese's youngest sister, the then widowed Toni Mertens (née Giese), representing the two legal parties involved.[14] The court then asked for the estate to be submitted, allowing four months for this.[15]

On May 5, 1938, Fein informed the district court of the following: "I was appointed universal heir by the testator in the last will. I hereby make an unconditional declaration of inheritance. Furthermore, I declare that I want to carry out the probate

mehrere Schreiben bis heute zu meinem Erstaunen überhaupt keine Antwort". This was also the last in a series of several letters between Herzfelder and Maass, written in 1935–38. Yet, of course, it is never certain that all letters from a correspondence survive. Herzfelder getting the information from Josef Weisskopf is also stated in a letter (dated Jan. 25, 1965) from Herzfelder to the Landgericht Berlin, found by Manfred Baumgardt in a postwar *Wiedergutmachungs* (restitution) file. This letter is quoted in Herzer 2001, 242–43 n. 21. This letter also reveals that Herzfelder's (incorrect) views of what happened in Brno shortly after Giese's death never altered.

[10] 6 Masarykova (Masarykstrasse) was also mentioned in Hirschfeld's will, drawn up in January 1935, as Fein's professional contact address. At that time it was correct. On reflection, maybe Josef Weisskopf had a copy of Hirschfeld's will and gave Herzfelder Fein's address from the document? In October 1936, Karl Fein's professional address changed to 35 Koliště (Glacis), where he would stay until October 1938. See the resident registration card (dated Oct. 8, 1936, home and work address) for Karl Fein in the AMB, Brno, fonds Z 1. Cf. *Seznam advokátů dle stavu koncem roku 1936* 1937, 28), which indeed lists his professional address as 35 Koliště (Glacis). The registration of death (*úmrtní zápis, Todesfallsaufnahme*) (dated Mar. 30, 1938) in the Giese inheritance file also gives Karl Fein's address as 35 Koliště (Glacis). See MZA, Brno, fonds C 107, Německý úřední soud Brno (Deutsches Amtsgericht Brünn), kart. n° 256, sign. 5aV 3/41, f. 16b.

[11] MZA, Brno, fonds C 107, Německý úřední soud Brno (Deutsches Amtsgericht Brünn), kart. n° 256, sign. 5aV 3/41, letter titled Antrag auf Bestellung eines Kurators (dated Mar. 22, 1938) from Karl Fein to Okresní soud civilní Brno (Bezirksgericht für Zivilsachen Brünn), f. 1. Since the rubber stamp on the letter is very faint, there is a slight doubt about the exact date of the letter. Otto Schütz also signed the document.

[12] MZA, Brno, fonds C 107, Německý úřední soud Brno (Deutsches Amtsgericht Brünn), kart. n° 256, sign. 5aV 3/41, undated power of attorney document, signed by Giese, f. 2. Not dating the document may have been a deliberate choice.

[13] MZA, Brno, fonds C 107, Německý úřední soud Brno (Deutsches Amtsgericht Brünn), kart. n° 256, sign. 5a V 3/41, f. 11, 14.

[14] Ibid., f. 16-17.

[15] Ibid., f. 17b. The notary Otokar Kříž returned the inheritance file to the court on May 23, 1938, and, on July 20, 1938, sent them a detailed list of his expenses. See MZA, Brno, fonds C 107, Německý úřední soud Brno (Deutsches Amtsgericht Brünn), kart. n° 256, sign. 5aV 3/41, f. 22-23.

myself *and request that the administration of the estate assets be granted to me as heir"*.[16] This phase in the (Austro-Hugarian) inheritance procedure is called the unconditional declaration of inheritance (*unbedingter Erbserklarung* or *Erbantrittserklarung*). In an unconditional declaration of inheritance, the heir accepts any and all debts – even unknown – the deceased might have had at the time of his death. Opting for the longer conditional declaration of inheritance requires a thorough preliminary investigation of the financial situation of the deceased.[17] It is not known why Karl Fein wanted to be the estate trustee from that point or why Otto Schütz fell out. It is also unclear how the person inheriting (Fein) would be legally allowed to spell out what he would inherit, as the new estate trustee.

INHERITANCE DISPUTE?

Despite Giese's will appointing Karl Fein as the universal heir of Giese's worldly goods, the Brno District Civil Court seems to have decided, on November 14, 1938, that Giese's relatives – and not Fein – were lawfully Giese's heirs. A December 30, 1938, letter from Karl Fein indirectly reveals that the court must have taken this decision shortly before. In this letter, Fein objected to the November 14 decision *not* to accept Giese's handwritten last will, and asked them to rectify the matter. He informed the court that the inheritance should be executed according to Giese's will: "The testator Karl Giese did not die intestate, but left a will. I have therefore made an unconditional declaration of inheritance on the basis of this will and not through the law. In this sense, I request that the enclosed November 14 decision DV 206/38 be corrected".[18]

Unfortunately, the documents in the inheritance file do not allow us to determine exactly what happened in this regard between May and November 1938. Did Karl Giese's siblings maybe contest the will, as foreseen by Karl in his last will, or was it a simple oversight by the court?[19] By then, however, the legitimacy of Giese's handwritten will had long been confirmed, in a court hearing on March 23, 1938,

[16] "Ich wurde vom Erblasser laut Testament zum Universalerben eingesetzt. Ich gebe hiemit [*sic*, hiermit] die unbedingte Erbserklärung ab. Weiters erkläre ich, dass ich die Verlassenschaft selbst durchführen will *und ersuche mir als Erben die Verwaltung des Nachlaßvermögens zu bewilligen*". The text in italics was a handwritten addition to the typed text. I thank Rainer-Joachim Siegel (Germany) for helping me decipher the added handwriting in February 2012. MZA, Brno, fonds C 107, Německý úřední soud Brno (Deutsches Amtsgericht Brünn), kart. n° 256, sign. 5aV 3/41, letter (dated May 5, 1938), titled "[tritt (?)] Erbserklärung ab und stellt weitere Anträge", from Karl Fein to Okresní soud civilní Brno (Bezirksgericht für Zivilsachen Brünn), f. 18.

[17] See https://www.erbrechtsinfo.at/verlassenschaftsverfahren/ (accessed Aug. 1, 2020).

[18] See MZA, Brno, fonds C 107, Německý úřední soud Brno (Deutsches Amtsgericht Brünn), kart. n° 256, sign. 5aV 3/41, letter (dated Dec. 30, 1938) from Karl Fein to Bezirksgericht für Zivilsachen Brünn, titled "ersucht um Berichtigung des Beschlusses und um Fristverlaengerung", f. 26: "Der Erblasser Karl Giese ist nicht ohne Hinterlassung eines letzten Willens, sondern mit Hinterlassung eines letzten Willen gestorben. Ich habe daher die unbedingte Erbserklaerung auf Grund dieses Testamentes und nicht aus dem Gesetze abgegeben. Ich bitte in diesem Sinn den beiliegenden Beschluss DV 206/38 vom 14. November zu berichtigen".

[19] I did not find any court document in the Giese inheritance file attesting to the court decison (dated Nov. 14, 1938) to which Fein referred in his letter. This is one of several unclear elements in the Giese inheritance file. These interpretive issues can be partly explained by the fact that essential and clarifying documents are missing from the file. This results from a structural problem: with the exception of one letter (f. 14), the inheritance file does not hold *any* copies of the letters the court itself sent regarding the Giese inheritance case. Therefore, I asked the MZA, Brno, if there maybe existed a parallel or remnant file in the archives of the Okresní soud civilní Brno (District Civil Court). After all, the file was later transferred later to the Deutsches Amtsgericht (German District Court). Maybe some documents had been removed before it was transferred? The MZA, Brno, let me know that there was no such "remnant file" in the archives of the District Civil Court. Another unexplained, but most likely minor detail of the Giese inheritance file is that the archival documents provide no explanation why the file temporarily ended up, in mid-May 1938, in the hands of another Brno notary, Jaroslav Podlipný (1885–1949). Had the file been sent to him by mistake? See MZA, Brno, fonds C 107, Německý úřední soud Brno (Deutsches Amtsgericht Brünn), kart. n° 256, sign. 5aV 3/41, f. 19.

[20] MZA, Brno, fonds C 107, Německý úřední soud Brno (Deutsches Amtsgericht Brünn), *zápis* (record)

a week after Giese's suicide.[20] The court then apparently agreed to Fein's request to alter their previous decision and accepted Giese's last will.[21]

KARL FEIN IS OUSTED AS A JEWISH LAWYER

In the December 30, 1938 letter, Fein also asked the court to extend the term to settle the inheritance by three months. Fein alluded to the tumultuous political situation that prevented him taking up the inheritance case: "I have been preoccupied by family matters for the last few months / [*sic*] my brother was in protective custody for 10 weeks, my 82-year-old mother had to leave her residence in Vienna and move to Brünn, my sister and her husband have lost their livelihood in Vienna /, [*sic*] and I have had to travel to Vienna very frequently, which is why it has not been possible for me to deal with this probate matter properly up to now. I therefore ask you to extend the deadline to March 30, 1939".[22]

When first accepting the inheritance (*Erbserklärung* or *Erbantrittserklärung*), at the beginning of May 1938, Fein had already asked the court to extend the term allotted to settle the inheritance to July 1, 1938. Since his letter asking for an extension is dated December 1938, he must have asked the court for at least one other extension; however, the letter requesting this second extension is not present in the archival inheritance file. On March 30, 1939, Fein requested the court, for the fourth time, to extend the term (*Fristverlängerung*) by another month: "Due to extraordinary circumstances, it has not been possible for me to devote myself to the probate work. I therefore request that the deadline be extended to April 30, 1939".[23] Every time, the court agreed to Fein's request to extend the agreed-upon term.

But what were these "extraordinary circumstances" (*ausserordentlichen Verhältnisse*) to which Fein referred ? At first, Fein had to deal with his brother and mother, who returned from Vienna to Brno after the Germans annexed Austria, in March 1938. The acute housing problems in Brno were caused by an influx of Austrian refugees, and later on also by refugees from the annexed Sudetenland.[24] As we have seen, Giese's suicide was clearly linked to the invasion and annexation of Austria. This means that Fein had to deal with Giese's inheritance and the distress of his immediate family at the same time. But a year later, two weeks before Fein requested yet another extension,

(dated Mar. 23, 1938), kart. n° 256, sign. 5aV 3/41, f. 8. The two witnesses heard by the court were Rudolf Palzer and Arnold Schneider. Palzer was an employee of the District Civil Court. See *Adreß-buch von Groß-Brünn*, 1934. 68. Arnold Schneider was likely an employee of the Vrchní soud v Brně (Obergericht Brünn, Brno High Court). See *Adreß-buch von Groß-Brünn* 1934, 68, 427. I erroneously supposed that at least one of the men heard in court would have been a part of the police contingent that entered Giese's apartment on March 17, 1938, and found Giese's last will on a table.

[21] The day after Karl Fein's letter (dated Dec. 30, 1938), the court completed a pre-printed, bilingual form (*Usnesení, Beschluss*) (dated Dec. 31, 1938), where, in the Czech column alone, it clearly says: "bez podmínečně podle poslední vůle" (unconditionally on the basis of the last will). See MZA, Brno, fonds C 107, Německý úřední soud Brno (Deutsches Amtsgericht Brünn), kart. n° 256, sign. 5aV 3/41, f. 25.

[22] See MZA, Brno, fonds C 107, Německý úřední soud Brno (Deutsches Amtsgericht Brünn), kart. n° 256, sign. 5aV 3/41, f. 26: "Ich bin durch Familienangelegenheiten, die mich die ganzen letzten Monate in Anspruch genommen haben / [*sic*] mein Bruder war 10 Wochen in Schutzhaft, meine 82 jaehrige Mutter musste ihren Wohnsitz in Wien verlassen und nach Bruenn uebersiedeln, meine Schwester und deren Gatte haben in Wien ihre Existenz verloren /, [*sic*] sodass ich sehr haeufig nach Wien reisen musste, weshalb es mir bisher nicht moeglich war, mich mit dieser Verlassenschaftssache gehoerig zu bescheftigen [*sic*, beschäftigen]. Ich bitte daher mir die Frist bis 30. Maerz 1939 zu verlaengern". We will return in chapter 13 to the stories about the members of Fein's immediate family fleeing from Vienna to Brno after March 1938.

[23] See MZA, Brno, fonds C 107, Německý úřední soud Brno (Deutsches Amtsgericht Brünn), letter (dated Mar. 29, 1939) from Karl Fein to Okresní soud civilní (Bezirksgericht für Zivilsachen), titled "ersucht um Fristverlaengerung", kart. n° 256, sign. 5aV 3/41, f. 28: "Infolge der ausserordentlichen Verhaeltnisse war es mir bisher nicht moeglich, mich den Verlassenschaftsarbeiten zu widmen. Ich ersuche daher mir die Frist bis 30. April 1939 zu verlaengern".

[24] On Jewish and German refugees fleeing the Sudetenland, see Gruner 2010, 144.

the Germans annexed the so-called "rest of Czechoslovakia" (*Rest-Tschechei*) as well. On March 15, 1939, almost exactly one year after Giese's suicide, German troops marched into Brno, putting Fein and his immediate family in even greater distress.

With this annexation, another grave problem raised its ugly head, touching directly on Fein's livelihood. As early as the second day after the invasion, Nazi Germany's intentions regarding Jewish lawyers and doctors in the newly created so-called "Protectorate of Bohemia and Moravia" were clear: "On 16.3.1939 the Reich Bar Association first banned Prague Jewish lawyers, and a little later those in Brno, from practicing their profession".[25] On the same day, in a meeting of the Brno Moravian Bar Association (Mährische Advokatenkammer in Brno, Advokátni komora Moravská v Brně), a decision was made about who would liquidate the law practices of the Jewish lawyers in Moravia.[26] It is important to note here that this discriminatory ruling against Jewish lawyers was a very hostile and dramatic measure imposed by the new people in power but was not completely a top-down decision. The Moravian Bar Association was given some leeway: it needed to decide for itself who would liquidate whose law practice. The draconian measure was thus somewhat moderated by a sort of gentleman's agreement between Jewish and non-Jewish lawyers within

[25] See document n° 241 ("Ein unbekannter Verfasser beschreibt die Situation der jüdischen Bevölkerung im Protektorat bis Ende März 1939") in Löw 2012, 583 n. 12: "Am 16.3.1939 verbot die Reichsanwaltskammer erst den jüdischen Anwälten in Prag, wenig später auch in Brünn die Ausübung ihres Berufs". For these official measures, see also Gruner 2010, 150. Czechoslovakia was peculiar in that Hitler at first decided that the Protectorate government should deal with the Jewish question, something that the Czechoslovak government was indeed at first willing to do: "Die Protektoratsregierung hatte aus eigener Initiative schon bei ihrer ersten Sitzung am 17. März 1939 Maßnahmen zur Ausschaltung der Juden aus dem öffentlichen Leben genehmigt. Diese betraf besonders die Stellung der ärzte und Rechstanwälte. Aber auch weitere, die wirtschaftliche Tätigkeit der Juden betreffende Maßnahmen wurden genehmigt" (The Protectorate government had already approved measures to eliminate Jews from public life on its own initiative at its first meeting on March 17, 1939. This particularly concerned the position of doctors and lawyers. However, other measures affecting the economic activities of Jews were also approved) (Oprach 2006, 42). It needs to be noted that Jewish lawyers (and doctors) were already under scrutiny in the last years of the so-called Second Republic. See document n° 260 ("Die Jüdische Kultusgemeinde Prag berichtet am 21. August 1939 über die katastrophale Lage der Juden und Eichmanns Herrschaft im Protektorat"): "Es wurde immer klarer, daß das benachbarte Deutschland schon in die Sphäre des vorläufig noch unabhängigen Staates immer stärker eingriff, um eine Lösung der Judenfrage im Sinne der nationalsozialistischen Gründsätze zu erreichen. Unter dem Einfluß dieser Grundsätze trat innerhalb des tschechischen Volkes eine Anderung in der Haltung einiger Schichten ein, die im Antisemitismus ein Mittel zur persönlichen Bereicherung erblickten. Es waren dies hauptsächlich die Advokaten und Arzte, die sich in den ersten Monaten des Jahres 1939 ihrer jüdischen Kollegen entledigen wollten" (It became increasingly clear that neighboring Germany was already intervening more and more in the sphere of the temporarily still independent state in order to achieve a solution to the Jewish question in line with National Socialist principles. Under the influence of these principles, there was a change in the attitude of some sections of the Czech people, who saw anti-Semitism as a means of personal enrichment. These were mainly lawyers and doctors who wanted to get rid of their Jewish colleagues in the first months of 1939.) (Löw 2012, 625–26). See also Gruner 2010, 151; Kárný 1996, 34; Krejčová 1999, 182–83. For a detailed chronology of the defining events in the history of the so-called *Protektorat* (Protectorate), see Padevět 2021.

[26] The publication of the Mährische Advokatenkammer (Moravian Bar Association) stated the following: "Z podnětu avokátní komory v Praze a po ujištění o souhlasu ministerstva spravedlnosti usneseno vyzvati nearijské členy komory, aby zastavili výkon advokátní praxe a navrhli substitute" (On behalf of the Lawyers' Chamber, headquartered in Prague, and confirmed by the Ministry of Justice, a resolution was passed to ask non-Aryan members of the Chamber to cease their practice and suggest a substitute) (*Věstník Moravské advokátní komory v Brně*, year 2, n° 2, April 1939, 2, Schůze výboru 16. března 1939 [Committee meeting March 16, 1939]). Cf. Kárný 1998, 11. Kárný claims rather that the decision was taken by the Protectorate government on March 17, 1939. Later, as communicated by the Moravian Bar Association on July 3, 1940, to the Protectorate authorities, a partial list containing only twenty-six liquidated law practices from Brno, in which Fein's name is mentioned, was published in the *Amtsblatt des Protektorates Böhmen und Mähren = Úřední list Protektorátu* Čechy *a Morava*, year 1940, n° 155, Jul. 6, 1940, n° 1710, 4984–85. Only the names of the liquidated law practices were published, not the names of the lawyers who performed the liquidations. The message also refers to *Regierungsverordnung* (Government Order) 136/140 on the "Rechtsstellung der Juden im öffentlichen Leben" (legal status of Jews

the Chamber. When examining several of the names of the unfortunate Jewish lawyers, I noticed that they often chose the lawyer with whom they had done their apprenticeship with as the one to liquidate their practice.[27] In the March 16, 1939, report on the meeting of the Brno Moravian Bar Association, for the city of Brno alone, there is a list of no fewer than ninety-four Jewish lawyers whose law offices were liquidated. Next to their names appear the names of the lawyers responsible for liquidating their colleagues' practices. Next to Karl Fein's name, we see Franz Nawratil (1889–1942). Nawratil also liquidated two other Brno Jewish law practices, the offices of Richard Freund (1879–1953)[28] and Ludwig Goldmann (1882–1942?).[29]

in public life) of July 4, 1939 that only became law after significant amendments on April 24, 1940, due to discussions between the Protectorate government and the German occupation authorities. See *Sammlung der Gesetze und Verordnungen des Protektorats Böhmen und Mähren = Sbírka zákonů a nařízení Protektorátu Čechy a Morava*, n° 44, April 1940, 337–42. This likely explains why the names of the ousted Jewish lawyers were only officially acknowledged more than a year after the measure was actually taken. On the complicated history of this postponed *Regierungsverordnung*, see Kárný 1994–1995; Kárný 1998; and, for an analysis of the *Verordnung*, see Petrův 2000, 97–113. For a brief mention of the issue, see also Löw 2012, 24.

[27] I checked the following years of *Seznam advokátů dle stavu koncem roku*: 1904, 1908, 1910, 1926, 1928–37.

[28] Nawratil's liquidation of the law practice is mentioned in *Věstník Moravské advokátní komory v Brně*, April 1939, 2. Richard Freund started out as a lawyer in Brno in 1910. See *Amtsblatt zur Brünner Zeitung*, Jan. 5, 1917, n° 4, n.p.. His last pre-war Brno address was 5 Schwarze Gasse (Černá). See NA, fonds PR 1841–1951, kart. n° 2321, sign. F 1557/8, file Richard Freund 1879; his address is confirmed in *Adreßbuch von Groß-Brünn* 1934, 196. He and his family managed to escape Czechoslovakia, since his police file in Prague contains one page saying that Richard Freund lost his Protectorate citizenship. This is a certain sign that he left the country, possibly illegally. In Brno, he was politically involved with the German social democrats. See NA, Praha, fonds n° 828, Ministerstvo vnitra, Londýn, 1940–1945, kart. n° 236, sign. 2-56/3. Two documents state that he went to France before moving to England. The back of the resident registration card of his son Gerhard Freund (1913–?) (in AMB, Brno, fonds Z 1) notes that Richard Freund moved to Paris on January 6, 1939. So, he would have been in Paris, in August 1939, when he worked for the Národní výbor (National Committee). See NA, Praha, fonds n° 828, Ministerstvo vnitra, Londýn, 1940–1945, kart. n° 236, sign. 2-56/3. In Paris, he prepared a memorandum on the German autonomy cause in Czechoslovakia for a Mr. W.[enzel] Jaksch (1896–1966). See NA, Praha, fonds n° 828, Ministerstvo vnitra Londýn, 1940–1945, kart. n° 13, sign. 2-1/259/15. For Wenzel Jaksch, see https://de.wikipedia.org/wiki/Wenzel_Jaksch (accessed Feb. 10, 2017). Once in London, Richard Freund spent the war years working for the Československý studijní ústav (Czechoslovak Research Institute) reporting on the political situation in Czechoslovakia. See NA, Praha fonds n° 1007, Ministerstvo sociální péče, Londýn, kart. n° 6, sign. 24079/2016. Briefly, I assumed that this Richard Freund was the author of two pre-war books on Czechoslovakia, *Zero Hour* (1936) and *Watch Czechoslovakia* (1937). But the real author of these books was Richard Fry, who used the pen name Richard Freund. See Rothenberg 2001, 11. Another document mentions Richard Freund's wife and son: Olga Minichová (1897–?) and Gerhard (1913–?). See NA, Praha, fonds n° 828, Ministerstvo vnitra, Londýn, kart. n° 236, sign. 2-56/3, f. 26. His son would have joined the Czechoslovak army. See NA, Praha, fonds n° 828, Ministerstvo vnitra Londýn, 1940–1945, kart. n° 236, sign. 2-56/3. A registration document in the AMB, Brno, suggests that Richard Freund returned to Brno in January 1948 but went back to London a year later, in January 1949. His wife Olga joined him in London, as a resident registration card (in the AMB, Brno, fonds Z 1) makes clear. Gerhard Freund also returned to Brno after the war, together with his wife Elisabeth Spatzová (1908–?), and was still living in Brno in 1949. It is unclear if, like his father, he also went back to England. Richard Freund died in London in October 1953. His last London address was 28 Blomfield Road, W9, London Paddington. I ordered Richard Freund's death certificate from the General Register Office on December 21, 2016. Richard Freund's father was Alois Freund (1848–1927), married to Rosa Freund (née Poláková, 1851–1923). They are buried in the Jewish cemetery in Brno in parcel 25c, row 1, grave 21. The couple had two other children: Martha (1882–?) and Egon (1887–1970). Egon Freund is mentioned in Richard Freund's 1953 probate record. Egon Freund emigrated to Australia in 1950 with his wife Marie (1896–1967). They died in Sydney (Australia) in 1970 and 1967, respectively. See Cemetery Headstone Transcriptions Sydney (Australia), 1837–2003, Sydney Metropolitan Cemetery Records, Society of Australian Genealogists (Sydney), retrieved record for Egon Freund on Macquarie Park cemetery and National Archives of Australia, Inward passenger manifests for ships and aircraft arriving at Fremantle, Perth Airport and Western Australian outports (1897–1963), series n° K 269, reel n° 107 (both retrieved from the Ancestry.com database Dec. 21, 2016). The grave stone for Marianne Freund says "Frau, teure Mutter und Grossmutter" (wife, dear mother and grandmother). See Cemetery Headstone Transcriptions Sydney (Australia), 1837–2003, Sydney Metropolitan Cemetery Records, Society of Australian Genealogists (Sydney), record for Marianne Freund on Macquarie Park cemetery (retrieved from the Ancestry.com

Despite the Moravian Bar Association's immediate response to the new ruling, it is unclear when exactly the liquidation of Fein's law office (*Kanzlei*) took effect or how exactly it was carried out. But it looks as though matters were settled in the most pleasant way possible by former colleagues. It remains uncertain why Fein and Nawratil paired up, but it is likely, as we have seen, that Karl Fein had been an apprentice for some years in Nawratil's law office.[30]

FRANZ NAWRATIL

Franz Nawratil (1889–1942) was a Brno-based lawyer who had his law office at 1 Schlossergasse (Zámečnická), a side street giving onto the Náměstí Svobody (Freiheitsplatz) in Brno. He was a Roman Catholic, and married Wilma Naplawa (1907–?) in March 1938.[31] Curiously, Nawratil married only a few days after the Germans invaded Austria, on March 19, 1938.[32] Franz Nawratil's marriage was childless and the couple rented a ground-floor apartment in a large and very pleasant uphill house with a garden [ill. 1].[33] Franz Nawratil's father, Kaspar Nawratil (1849–1928), had been a high-ranking police official.[34] Kaspar Nawratil was twice married and Franz Nawratil was the first of three children of Kaspar Nawratil's second marriage, to Klara Zimek (1858–1935). During the war, Franz Nawratil was one of nineteen lawyers admitted to plead in the Brno German Regional Court (Deutsches Landgericht).[35]

database Dec. 23, 2016). This means that there had to be relatives. On December 22, 2016, I wrote a letter to the ten people with the last name Freund in an Australian online phonebook, but no one replied. I was not able to determine the further fate of the son of Egon and Mariane Freund, Jiří Freund (1924–?). On a home certificate in the AMB, Brno, fonds B 1/39, it states that he obtained Palestinian nationality, which indicates that he moved to Israel.

[29] The liquidation of Goldmann's law practice by Nawratil is mentioned in *Věstník Moravské advokátní komory v Brně*, April 1939, 2. Ludwig Goldmann was married to Markéta Beamtová (1894–1942?). The couple had two children, Hana (1936–1942?) and Terezie (1928–1942?). The family was put on transport "G" from Brno to Terezín on December 2, 1941. On October 26, 1942, Goldmann and his family were transferred from Terezín to Auschwitz-Birkenau on transport "By". See the www.holocaust.cz database; Kárný et al. 1995, 178. More information on Ludwig Goldmann's parents, Josef (1845–1908?) and Regina (1854–?), who moved to Brno in 1900, can be found in the digitized Brno census data for the year 1900 (inventory n° 2723, volume D-G, p. 167a, lines 6-9). The family lived at 13 Schmerlingstrasse (currently třída Kpt. Jaroše), on one of Brno's poshest streets. Ludwig's older sister was named Gisela (1880–?).

[30] See chapter 6, p. 168 and n. 73.

[31] Wilma Naplava's parents, Otmar Naplava (1880–1928) and Berta Musil (1880–1930) lived in the posh address of 23 Legionärenstrasse (třída Legionářů) until their deaths in 1928 and 1930, respectively. See *Adreßbuch von Groß-Brünn* 1927, 353; Bundesarchiv, Berlin-Lichterfelde, Reichsjustizministerium, Personalakten N (1877–1945), Nawratil, Franz, geb. 4.8.1889, sign. BArch, R 3001/69402, f. 12. Otmar Naplava was an accountant and also the *Zeitungsverwalter* (publication manager) of the periodical *Mährisch-schlesische Blätter für Stenographie*. See *Adreßbuch von Groß-Brünn* 1927, 93.

[32] The marriage date of March 19, 1938 can be found in Franz Nawratil's staff file in the Bundesarchiv, Berlin-Lichterfelde, Reichsjustizministerium, Personalakten N (1877–1945), Nawratil, Franz, geb. 4.8.1889, sign. BArch, R3001-69402, f. 3. I was not able to find Nawratil's marriage certificate at the Brno city hall. Neither his name nor that of his wife figures in the 1938 volume of the marriage register of the Brno *městská rada* (city council) or in the register of that volume available at https://www.mza.cz/actapublica/matrika. This possibly indicates that Nawratil married outside of Brno. However, another document states that he was married in Brno. See MZA, Brno, fonds C 107, Německý úřední soud Brno (Deutsches Amtsgericht Brünn), kart. n° 282, sign. 5bV146/14, inheritance file Franz Nawratil, f. 3. Like Nawratil, his wife was born in Brno, so the tradition of marrying in the bride's birth city does not resolve the matter either.

[33] The Nawratil inheritance file mentions properties he owned outside of Brno, but not the house at 79 Talgasse (Údolní). See MZA, Brno, fonds C 107, Německý úřední soud Brno (Deutsches Amtsgericht Brünn), kart. n° 282, sign. 5bV146/14, inheritance file Franz Nawratil. See also p. 407 for more information on this house.

[34] He had been *Oberpolizeirat* (senior commissioner) in the police hierarchy, a title and position in the *höherer Dienst* (command ranks). See Bundesarchiv, Berlin-Lichterfelde, Reichsjustizministerium, Personalakten N (1877-1945), Nawratil, Franz, geb. 4.8.1889, sign. BArch, R 3001/69402, f. 10.

Although Franz Nawratil likely never officially changed the spelling of his very Czech surname, he preferred to spell it in the German way as "Nawratil".[36] He also applied for German ethnic (Deutsche Volkszugehörigkeit) status on November 18, 1939. It was granted to him on March 11, 1940.[37] Some, but not all, of his siblings applied for the same status, indicating that the family was, at least to the outside world, pro-German.

Nawratil was also clearly involved in at least one Aryanization of a Jewish firm in Brno, the Schindler & Stein Exportmalzfabriken AG, which owned three factories and was one of the biggest malt factory companies in the Protectorate. Nawratil was appointed as its trustee (*Truehänder*) by the Reich Protector in Bohemia and Moravia (Reichsprotektor in Böhmen und Mähren) on December 7, 1940. This earned him 800 German marks a month until at least December 1941.[38] A 1942 obituary for Franz Nawratil, paid for by former colleagues, shows that his employment as a trustee eventually got Nawratil a seat on the governing board (*Aufsichtsrat*) of the newly formed company, the Böhmisch-Mährischen Exportmalzfabriken-Aktiengesellschaft, which merged the former Jewish Schindler & Stein firm and a similar malt factory in Austria [ill. 2].[39] Franz Nawratil died in the morning of May 10, 1942, presumably of a heart attack after a short sickness.[40] Nawratil was a well-off man. He left considerable capital and some properties to his wife Wilma.[41]

[35] See *Seznam advokátů v Protektorátu Čechy a Morava = Verzeichnis der Advokaten im Protektorate Böhmen und Mähren* 1940, 77; and ABS, Praha, SÚMV, fonds n° 134, Německé soudy v Protektorátu Čechy a Morava, Vrchní zemský soud Praha, personální spisy justičních zaměstnanců (Akten über die Dienstverhältnisse), file Franz Nawratil, sign. 134-909-12.

[36] His father Kaspar also sometimes spelled his name the German way. One can see that some Czech-German language battles were fought out in the administrative documents for Kaspar Nawratil now kept in the AMB, Brno. The nationality preference of the civil servant determined the spelling of his last name, and even altered it in administrative documents. Because Franz Navratil (or even Navrátil) preferred to spell his name as Nawratil, I have chosen to follow this spelling of his name in his text. It is unknown to me if he ever made an official request to the Brno city authorities to actually change one letter in his name. It may or may not be significant that the Deutsches Amtsgericht in Brünn (Německý úřední soud Brno) consistently spelled his last name as "Navratil".

[37] See AMB, Brno, fonds A 1/53, Německý národností katastr (Deutsche Volkszugehörigkeit), index card Dr. Franz Alfred Navrátil [*sic*].

[38] See the two Aryanization files for Schindler & Stein in NA, Praha, fonds 375, Arizačni spisy, kart. n° 42, file n° 438 and kart. n° 441, file n° 3240.

[39] See *Brünner Tagblatt*, May 13, 1942, 6. At the top left corner of this newspaper obituary, there is the usual *Runen-Zeichen* (runic character) – three prongs pointing down (instead of up for a birth) – used by some National Socialists to mark someone's death. The same runic character can also be found in Nawratil's Deutsche Volkszugehörigkeit registration index card. See MZA, Brno, fonds A 1/53, Německý národností katastr. See also the newspaper article announcing the new enterprise, "Neue AG. in Brünn: Südosteuropäische Getreide-Handels-AG. übernimmt Schindler & Stein," *Tagesbote*, Jun. 12, 1941, 6. Richard Stein (1883–1942?), one of the former Jewish directors of Schindler & Stein, was not the Richard Stein who owned (along with his wife Jenny Stein) the house at 35 Koliště, where Karl Fein lived for a few years. For more information on Richard Stein's company, see Smutný 2012, 419. The director Richard Stein and his wife Vilma Nerber (1897–1942?) were deported on transport "Af", on March 31, 1942, from Brno to Terezín, and then transferred to Rejowiec on transport "Ap", on April 18, 1942. Stein's two sons, Alexander Morris Stein (1923–2010) and Paul Gustav Stein (1925–), spent the war in Panama. After the war, they requested war reparations at a claims resolution tribunal. See http://www.crt-ii.org/_awards/_apdfs/Stein_Richard.pdf (accessed Aug. 7, 2020).

[40] See MZA, Brno, fonds C 107, Německý úřední soud Brno (Deutsches Amtsgericht Brünn), inheritance file Franz Nawratil, kart. n° 282, 5bV 146/42, f. 3, where *Thrombose* (?) (thrombosis [?]) is mentioned as the *Grundkrankheit* (underlying condition) and *Herzembolie* (embolism) as the direct cause of death (under the heading "Welche von den genannten Krankheiten hat unmittelbar den Tod herbeigeführt?"). I thank Marita Keilson-Lauritz for checking the handwriting with me. See email (dated Jun. 29, 2017) from Marita Keilson-Lauritz to the author. See also the mention "Thrombo ... [illegible]" in AMB, Brno, fonds A 1/3, Sbírka rukopisů a úředních knih, 1333–1958, Úmrtní protokol z roku 1942, entry n° 1936, dated May 10, 1942, Dr. Franz Nawratil.

[41] See MZA, Brno, fonds C 107, Německý úřední soud Brno (Deutsches Amtsgericht Brünn), kart. n° 282, 5bV 146/42.

THE INHERITANCE PROCEDURE IS NOT HINDERED IN ANY WAY

We will look in a moment at the details of the final settlement of the Giese inheritance, i.e. the final balance of assets and liabilities (activa and passiva) handled by Karl Fein himself and presented to the district court on May 25, 1939, fourteen months after Karl Giese killed himself.[42] This date indicates that Fein presented the final settlement of Giese's estate *after* Jewish lawyers had been forbidden to practice, and *after* Fein's law office (*Kanzlei*) had officially been liquidated by Franz Nawratil. So it comes as no surprise that Giese's inheritance file actually contains three registered mail reply stubs, related to Fein's incoming mail, from the end of April 1939, signed for by an employee of Franz Nawratil's law office [ill. 3] [ill. 4].[43] The final settlement was presented one month later. A November 1939 letter from Fein's medical insurance company, asking for Fein's correct address, shows that Fein's then last known official address was indeed Nawratil's law office.[44] It is also clear that Karl Fein did not respect the likely fourth agreed-upon extension (*Fristverlängerung*) of April 30, 1939, since the final settlement of the inheritance was dated May 25, 1939. Which of course raises the question if Fein or Nawratil was the one who asked the district court for yet another extension.[45]

[42] This final part of the inheritance procedure is called "certificate of inheritance" in English, *Verlassenschaftseinantwortung* or *Einantwortungsbeschluss* in German and *rozhodnutí o vypořádání dědictví* (decision on the settlement of the succession) in Czech. Karl Fein titled it "písemné pozůstalostní projednání" (written estate hearing). To this was also added a detailed list of assets and liabilities (activa and passiva) under the title "Místpřísežně seznámí jmění". See MZA, Brno, fonds C 107, Německý úřední soud Brno (Deutsches Amtsgericht Brünn), kart. n° 256, sign. 5aV 3/41, f. 29-31.

[43] The registered mail reply stub (dated Apr. 27, 1939) is loose between f. 27 and f. 28 in the Giese inheritance file. See MZA, Brno, fonds C 107, Německý úřední soud Brno (Deutsches Amtsgericht Brünn), kart. n° 256, sign. 5aV 3/41. An employee of Franz Nawratil, Kubek (?), signed the acceptance of a registered letter addressed to Fein and sent by the Brno Civil Court in Brno (Okresní soud civilní Brno, Bezirksgericht für Zivilsachen Brünn). Nawratil's law office stamp was added to the signature. It is unclear why the stub sits between f. 27 and f. 28 in the archival file, and if its position is meaningful or not. It is also unclear to which letter, sent to Fein by the district court, the postal stub refers. Possibly, it was one letting Fein know that his final extension (until April 30, 1939) was approaching and no further extension would be granted. As already stated, one of the things that makes the interpretation of the Giese inheritance file quite difficult is that it does not contain any copies of the letters sent by the district court. Nawratil's employee signed a second time for a letter sent by the district court on June 19, 1939. This stub seems to refer to a court decision of June 15, 1939, likely informing Fein and Nawratil that the inheritance procedure would only come to a definitive end once the inheritance tax was paid. See MZA, Brno, fonds C 107, Německý úřední soud Brno (Deutsches Amtsgericht Brünn), kart. n° 256, sign. 5aV 3/41, f. 31. This reply stub is one of four loose stubs in the back of the inheritance file. A final registered mail reply stub, signed by the same employee, is dated October 29, 1940, and follows f. 35. Most of these reply stubs do not mention an address for Fein. Presumably, this official mail had to be collected from the post office where the reply stub was stamped and sent back to the court as proof of receipt. So it is likely that Nawratil, or an employee in his office, had an official document stating that the bearer, as the liquidator of Fein's law office, could accept registered mail addressed to Karl Fein. A total of five registered mail reply stubs, both fixed and loose, attest to the existence of these letters or messages sent by the district court to Karl Fein. They bear the following dates (in chronological order): March 24, 1938 (f. 11), November 24, 1938 (after f. 37), January 18, 1939 (f. 27), April 27, 1939 (f. 28) and June 19, 1939 (after f. 37). The two other reply stubs concern letters or messages addressed to Fein by the Brno German District Court (Deutsches Amtsgericht Brünn, Německý úřední soud Brno), dated October 29, 1940 (after f. 35) and January 3, 1941 (after f. 37). The latter reply stub was signed by Karl Fein himself who was then, as we shall see later, already in Prague. An eighth reply stub, finally, is addressed to the notary Otokar Kříž and is dated November 24, 1938 (the stub follows f. 37). The March 24, 1938 reply stub was signed by Kurt Brammer, an intern and nephew of Karl Fein to whom we will return later.

[44] NA, Praha, fonds Policejní ředitelství Praha II, všeobecná spisovna, 1931–1940, kart. n° 5661, sign. F 271/9, Fein Karel JUDr 1894, f. 5, letters (dated Nov. 9, 1939 and Dec, 22, 1939) Okresní nemocenská pojišovna v Brně to Policejní ředitelství Praha. The street address given is 1 Zámečnická (Schlossergasse).

[45] To be completely clear: while there are two letters in the inheritance file in which Fein asks the district court for an extension, no letter in the file, by either Fein or Nawratil, asks the district court for another extension at the end of April 1939.

[46] Fein's choice to spell his name as "Karel" is intimately related to the German invasion of Czechoslovakia in March 1939. In all the documents of the Giese inheritance file before that date, Fein used a

One particular feature, related to the documents of the final settlement, betrays that, despite his own year-long procrastination, Fein was getting more and more nervous about the still unsettled Giese inheritance. Until then, all Fein's outgoing correspondence with the district court had been conducted in German, but he composed the final text of the settlement in Czech. This was most likely done in an effort to conceal the Giese inheritance file from any German scrutiny or from eyes sympathetic to the German invaders. In this document, Fein spelled his first name as Karel and used the same Czech spelling in his signature as well.[46] Even Giese's first name was spelled as "Karel" on the title page of the final settlement.[47]

But did Karl Fein, and the Giese inheritance case in which he was involved, have anything to fear? In strictly legal terms, there was no reason why the inheritance could not be finalized properly. In June 1939, the infamous Decree of the Reich Protector in Bohemia and Moravia on Jewish Property (Verordnung des Reichsprotektors in Böhmen und Mähren über das jüdische Vermögen), expropriating the Jewish population, was proclaimed. The twelve-paragraph-long ordinance (*Verordnung*) stipulated that Jewish people could no longer sell their belongings or buy property, assets, etc. Jewish people also had to register all their belongings before July 31, 1939.[48] On December 8, 1939, article 5 of a second executive order, dealing with the handling of inheritances (*Verlassenschaftsabhandlungen*), clearly stated that the court or a court commissioner needed to determine, *before* the start of an inheritance procedure, if one or more of the beneficiaries was Jewish. If so, the inheritance procedure could not be initiated. Paragraph 8 also stipulated that a lawyer or notary had to announce if a Jewish person was involved.[49] The Giese-Fein inheritance case started in March 1938

stamp with his name spelled "Karl Fein"; however, after that date, he used a stamp with "Karel Fein". See MZA, Brno, fonds C 107, Německý úřední soud Brno (Deutsches Amtsgericht Brünn), kart. n° 256, sign. 5aV 3/41, f. 1, 18, 26, 28 and 29. We see the same spelling of "Karel Fein" in a letter (dated May 27, 1939) from Karl Fein to Editions Montaigne in IMEC, Abbaye d'Ardenne, Saint-Germain-la-Blanche-Herbe, fonds Aubier-Montaigne, P 7.1., Service éditorial. One can also see the same name change already on pre-printed envelopes and letterheads from 1937, when Fein was still living at his 35 Koliště (Glacis) address. See, for example, the pre-printed envelope, sitting loose in MZA, Brno, fonds B 40, Zemský úřad Brno (Landesbehörde in Brünn), kart. n° 2138, sign. 5274/38. Of course, one could argue that Fein simply used the two different spellings for his professional correspondence, choosing one or the other depending on the language of his clients. I think that one rather sees here that Fein "Czechized" his first name to "Karel" to seem less German when he thought it more opportune. "Karel Fein" also appears in Fein's clear signature in the protocol (dated Sep. 8, 1941) in NA, Praha, Policejní ředitelství Praha II – všeobecná spisovna, 1941–1950, kart. n° 2034, sign. F 277/3, Feinová Helena roz. Brecherová 1856. Since, after 1939, Fein continued to spell his first name in the Czech way, even on occasions when doing so had no clear reason or benefit, I think it is also possible that Fein was conspicuously and consciously turning his back on the German-ness that had developed in Germany, and which threatened to flood the rest of Europe. Possibly, he expressed his new attitude by deliberately using the Czech version of his name more and more. Cf. Sapák 2000, 12. Sapák sees a similar "bilingual state of mind" in the Jewish architect Arnošt Wiesner (1890–1971), whose position Sapák describes as "on the fence". Wiesner consciously chose to use the Czech version of his first name, Arnošt, instead of the German Ernst. I think one clearly sees Karl Fein opportunistically playing with this double identity. Initially, for all these reasons, in the first texts presenting my work, I chose to spell Fein's name as "Karel Fein"; however, later on, I changed my mind. Karl Fein was after all also German-speaking, most of his life writing his name as "Karl Fein", and his name at birth was "Carl Fein". It is clear that Czech researchers who mention Fein usually also spell his name as "Karl Fein". See, for example, Seidl et al. 2014a, 118–19; Seidl et al. 2014b, 189–90.

47 MZA, Brno, fonds C 107, Německý úřední soud Brno (Deutsches Amtsgericht Brünn), kart. n° 256, sign. 5aV 3/41, f. 30. In July 1937, Karl Fein also advised Karl Giese to spell his name as "Karel Giese" in a document where Giese and Fein tried to convince the Czechoslovak authorities to waive a disadvantageous decision. The stamp Karl Fein used on a document spelled his first name as "Karel". See MZA, Brno, fonds B 40, Zemský úřad Brno (Landesbehörde in Brünn), kart. n° 2138, sign. 5274/38. The document is reproduced in the addenda (n° 9).

48 See "Verordnung des Reichsprotektors in Böhmen und Mähren über das jüdische Vermögen", *Verordnungsblatt des Reichsprotektors in Böhmen und Mähren*, Jul. 7, 1939, 6: 45–49. See also Potthast 2002, 65–66.

49 See "Zweiter Durchführungserlaß des Reichsprotektors in Böhmen und Mähren zur Verordnung über das Jüdische Vermögen", *Verordnungsblatt des*

and thus did not, strictly speaking, fall under the later Protectorate rules concerning Jewish property and inheritances. The June 1939 Decree of the Reich Protector in Bohemia and Moravia on Jewish Property was declared retroactive (*rückwirkend*) only from March 15, 1939, the day of the German invasion of the rest of Czechoslovakia.[50]

So why then did Fein deem it necessary to undertake the concealment of starting to write in Czech, and spelling his first name the Czech way? I think that Fein acted circumspectly for fear that the National Socialists might have been tempted to disrupt or even abort the inheritance procedure. By presenting the final step in the procedure in Czech, Fein tried to stay under the radar and hoped that he would bring the inheritance procedure to a definitive end. Directly related to Fein's precaution and fear was the introduction of a new judicial procedural rule introduced by the German invaders. This new rule stated that the involvement of a German citizen in a law case was sufficient to transfer the file to a German court. And Karl Giese had definitely been a German citizen in his lifetime. This new policy was already adopted in March 1939, with the installment of the Protectorate of Bohemia and Moravia (Protektorat Böhmen und Mähren), and was officially sanctioned in April of that year.[51]

With the annexation of the rest of Czechoslovakia, Czechoslovak citizens became "members of the Protectorate" (*Protektoratsangehörige*).[52] This also entailed that a case involving a Czechoslovak citizen, now called a member of the Protectorate, would continue to be heard by a Czech court since "[t]he [Nazi Protectorate] citizenship decrees created two legal worlds, [...] Protectorate nationals, most of whom were Czechs, were subject to Czech laws and were tried in Czech courts, [...] Germans were tried in German courts".[53] But despite this new ruling, the Giese inheritance case *was not* immediately transferred to the German District Court. It was only in December 1939, nine months after the introduction of the new rule, that the file was transferred to the German court.[54]

Reichsprotektors in Böhmen und Mähren, Dec. 13, 1939, 39: 318–23. Article 5 on *Verlassenschaftsabhandlungen* (probate treatises) appears in §12 on p. 321: "Im Verfahren zur Abhandlung des Nachlasses hat das Verlassenschaftsgericht oder der Gerichtkommissar *vor Beginn der Abhandlung* [my italics] die Frage zu stellen, ob der Erblasser oder einer der am Verfahren beteiligten Personen Juden sind. § 13 Ist der Erblasser oder eine der am Verfahren beteiligten Personen Jude, so steht dies der Abhandlung und Einantwortung des Nachlasses nicht entgegen". Cf. Friedmann, Jul. 31, 1942/1997, 238–39.

[50] See §12 (2), "Verordnung des Reichsprotektors in Böhmen und Mähren über das jüdische Vermögen", *Verordnungsblatt des Reichsprotektors in Böhmen und Mähren*, Jul. 7, 1936, 6: 48.

[51] See document n° 240 ("Im Reichsinnenministerium werden am 25. März 1939 die Rechtsstellung des Protektorats und Richtlinien für die Behandlung der jüdischen Bevölkerung besprochen") in Löw 2012, 574: "Es wird ferner festgestellt, daß nach Auffassung des Führers die deutsche Gerichtsbarkeit für die deutschen Staatsangehörigen nicht nur im Strafrecht, sondern auch auf dem Gebiete des Zivilrechts, und zwar auch dann zur Anwendung kommen soll, wenn nur *ein* Teil (Kläger oder Beklagter) deutscher Staatsangehöriger ist". The measure was officially sanctioned in the Verordnung über die deutsche Gerichtsbarkeit im Protektorat Böhmen und Mähren (Ordinance of German Jurisdiction in Bohemia and Moravia) of April 14, 1939 and was made public in the *Reichsgesetzblatt* (RGBl. 1939 I: 752–54). See also Löw 2012, 574 n. 6; Löw 2012, 597 n. 3.

[52] A day after the annexation of the Rest-Tschechoslowakei (rest of Czechoslovakia), Hitler made the following clear in the „Erlaß des Führers und Reichskanzlers über das Protektorat Böhmen und Mähren" (Decree of the Fuhrer and Reich Chancellor of the Protectorate of Bohemia and Moravia), published in the *Reichsgesetzblatt* (RGBl. 1939 I, 485): "Den dort [Protektorat Böhmen und Mähren] lebenden Deutschen verleihe er umgehend die deutsche Staatsbürgerschaft, sie unterständen künftig ausschließlich der deutschen Gerichtsbarkeit. Tschechen und Juden, auch jene deutscher Herkunft, blieben als Protektoratsangehörige Staatsbürger zweiter Klasse". See also Gruner 2010, 145 n. 30, 152.

[53] Bryant 2007, 53.

[54] MZA, Brno, fonds C 107, Německý úřední soud Brno (Deutsches Amtsgericht Brünn), kart. n° 256, sign. 5aV 3/41, f. 33. According to the indications of the respective rubber stamps, the file was transferred from the district court on December 18, 1939 and arrived at the Deutsches Amtsgericht (German District Court) on December 23, 1939. This also explains why the Giese inheritance file was preserved for posterity in the archives of the German District Court and not in those of the Czechoslovak Brno District Civil Court (Okresní soud civilní Brno, Bezirksgericht für Zivilsachen Brünn).

It is clear that Fein, and possibly even people working for the district court and Nawratil, tried to profit from this temporary gray area in which new ideas and procedures were (presumably) only slowly introduced, needing time to settle in. So, apparently, the new legal regulation did not take effect overnight and, in the first months of the occupation, the relatively independent Czech courts probably had some maneuvering space in which to act. Furthermore, the Protectorate remained, at least in theory, an autonomous state and former Czechoslovak civil servants were not German civil servants (*Reichsbeamte*). The Czech courts maintained a certain degree of autonomy.[55] So the district court in Brno must have known that, since strictly speaking a German citizen was involved, they should have handed the case over to the German court as early as April 1939. Did Fein, or even Nawratil, intervene with people working for the district court to prevent this? Fein may have also tried to obtain some good will from the Czech court by redacting his final settlement in Czech. Before that, the letters and texts he addressed to them had been exclusively in German.

It is hard to determine what exactly was at play as concerns the cooperation of the Czech courts with the newly created German District Court (Deutsches Amtsgericht). The complicated new legal situation in the Protectorate, which needed time to settle in, might explain the delay in transferring the Giese inheritance file to the German District Court. But it is also possible that the Czech courts passively resisted by waiting for the German District Court to order them to transfer the files of cases involving Germans. Possibly, these Czech courts turned a blind eye to sensitive facts in some of the cases, knowing very well that transferring the file to the German District Court would be disadvantageous to the people involved [ill. 5].

INHERITANCE TAX

When Karl Fein presented the final settlement of the Giese inheritance to the district court, at the end of May 1939, the inheritance procedure had still not been concluded. It would take another five months for the Brno Fee Assessment Office (Gebührenbemessungsamt in Brünn, Úřad pro vyměřování poplatků v Brně) to determine an inheritance tax (*Erbgebühren*) of 218 Czech crowns.[56] When, at the beginning of October 1939, the Brno tax office communicated the amount due to the district court, Fein had already left Brno and was in Prague.

Two months later, in December 1939, seven to eight months after the establishment of the Protectorate, the German District Court finally took the Giese inheritance file out of the hands of the district court "because the deceased was a German national".[57] The file had finally arrived at its lawful place, as determined as early as

[55] See also document n° 240 ("Im Reichsinnenministerium werden am 25. März 1939 die Rechtsstellung des Protektorats und Richtlinien für die Behandlung der jüdischen Bevölkerung besprochen") in Löw 2012, 579: "5. Die Beamten des Protektorats werden nicht Reichsbeamte. […] 6. Eine reichseigene Verwaltung wird im Protektorat nur in beschränktem Maße eingerichtet werden. Neben Wehrmacht und Luftfahrt wird die Zollverwaltung, die Sicherheitspolizei, der Rundfunk, die Devisenbeschaffung und für die volksdeutschen Bewohner die Justizverwaltung in reichseigene Verwaltung zu übernehmen sein".

[56] See the note (dated Oct. 19, 1939, received on Oct. 24, 1939) from the Úřad pro vyměřování poplatků v Brně (Gebührenbemessungsamt in Brünn) to the Bezirksgericht für Zivilsachen Brünn (Okresní soud civilní Brno) in MZA, Brno, fonds C 107, Německý úřední soud Brno (Deutsches Amtsgericht Brünn), kart. n° 256, sign. 5aV 3/41, f. 32. It is unclear if this possible delay was "normal" or rather exceptional, but one may suppose that it could have been linked to the new political situation. In this connection, one can think of the Germans reorganizing the city administration, but also this department's great amount of work since a lot of Jewish people were forced to sell their belongings, properties or businesses through a *Treuhänder* (trustee).

[57] MZA, Brno, fonds C 107, Německý úřední soud Brno (Deutsches Amtsgericht Brünn), kart. n° 256, sign. 5aV 3/41, f. 33, handwritten working note (dated Nov. 18, 1939) from the District Civil Court to the German District Court (received on Dec. 23, 1939): "weil der Verstorbene [Karl Giese] der deut-

April 1939 by the new people in power. At first, the Giese inheritance file led a quite inconspicuous life in the German District Court. In January 1940, likely following the normal procedure, a member of the German court simply noted in the file that the inheritance tax in the Giese inheritance case (*Verlassache Karl Giese*) had yet to be paid.[58] As pointed out already, by the time the German District Court took over the file from the District Civil Court, in December 1939, the inheritance tax had already been known for some time and awaited payment. But it was likely that the term in which the tax had to be paid was not heeded. A handwritten note in the Giese inheritance file, dated November 16, 1939, tersely stated in Czech: "term passed" (*lhůtou prošla*).[59] That Fein was then already in Prague likely also explains why it would take him another half year to finally pay the inheritance tax. As we will see later, Fein faced an even more tumultuous housing situation in Prague than in Brno. He also had severe financial problems in Prague, having lost his income as a lawyer in March 1939. And most of all, and as we will again see later, Fein probably had other things on his mind at the time. Getting out of the country was likely his main concern then.

It is unclear if it was Nawratil or the German District Court that informed Fein in Prague about the amount he needed to pay to the Brno tax office. It would also have taken any individual or organization operating from Brno time to locate him in Prague. But the tax was eventually paid by Fein. On June 5, 1940, the Brno Fee Assessment Office informed the German District Court that the sum of 218 Czech crowns had finally been paid.[60]

THE GERMAN DISTRICT COURT TAKES ACTION

Surprisingly, it was only then that alarm bells started to go off in the German District Court. Until then, it had apparently not been clear to the officers of the court who "Dr. Fein" was. Suddenly, they also felt compelled to check whether Fein was Jewish.[61] The German District Court apparently only then noticed Franz Nawratil's name and sent him, in the beginning of July 1940, a letter asking him who he was and whether he could shed some light on the case. A seemingly reluctant (or typically very concise) Nawratil answered only the question(s) asked by the German District Court: "In response to your enquiry of 8 July, I would like to inform you of the following: I am a substitute appointed by the Chamber [Moravian Bar Association] and liquidator of the law firm of Dr. Karl Fein, after he, as a Jew, was not allowed to continue the law firm. I hope this has served you and sign with Heil Hitler!"[62]

sche Reichsangehörige [*sic*, deutscher Reichsangehöriger] war".

[58] The handwriting says: "Verlegen und Bezahlung der Erbgebühren. (12.01.1940)". MZA, Brno, fonds C 107, Německý úřední soud Brno (Deutsches Amtsgericht Brünn), kart. n° 256, sign. 5aV 3/41, f. 33.

[59] This possibly shows that the German District Court also employed Czechs. See MZA, Brno, fonds C 107, Německý úřední soud Brno (Deutsches Amtsgericht Brünn), kart. n° 256, sign. 5aV 3/41, f. 32b.

[60] See note (dated Jun. 5, 1940) from the Fee Assessment Office to the German District Court, confirming the payment of 218 Czech crowns. A German District Court stamp on the document makes it clear the message was received or processed on June 26, 1940. See MZA, Brno, fonds C 107, Německý úřední soud Brno (Deutsches Amtsgericht Brünn), kart. n° 256, sign. 5aV 3/41, f. 34.

[61] On the back of one of the papers in the Giese inheritance file it states that Fein suddenly needed to declare under oath that he was not a Jew or married to a Jewish woman. See MZA, Brno, fonds C 107, Německý úřední soud Brno (Deutsches Amtsgericht Brünn), kart. n° 256, sign. 5aV 3/41, anonymous handwriting on a letter (dated Jul. 11, 1940) from Franz Nawratil to the German District Court, f. 35: "Wer ist Dr. Fein? 29.7.[19]40 [unidentified signature]" (Who is Dr. Fein? 29.7.[19]40 [unidentified signature]); ibid., f. 34: "Dr. Fein auffordern nachzuweisen, bezw. [beziehungsweise] eine eidesstattliche Erklärung abzugeben, daß er kein Jude ist u.[nd] mit einer jüdischen Gattin nicht verheiratet ist. 2 Wochen. 8/7/1940. [unidentified signature]" (Summoning Dr. Fein to prove, or respectively make an affidavit, that he is not a Jew and is not married to a Jewish wife. 2 weeks. 8/7/1940 [unidentified signature]).

[62] MZA, Brno, fonds C 107, Německý úřední soud Brno (Deutsches Amtsgericht Brünn), kart. n° 256, sign. 5aV 3/41, f. 35, letter (dated Jul. 11, 1940) from Franz Nawratil to the German District Court: "In Erledigung Ihrer Anfrage vom 8. Juli teile ich Ihnen nachstehendes mit: Ich bin von der Kammer [Mähri-

So, it was only in July 1940 that the German District Court suddenly started to realize exactly who Fein and Nawratil were, and decided to summon Nawratil to look more closely into the matter and hear his opinion on who should further handle the Giese-Fein inheritance.[63] But, strictly speaking, the case had legally been concluded with Fein paying the inheritance tax in June 1940. Apparently, the German District Court then insisted on trying to get hold of Nawratil, who seemingly procrastinated. It is not known if Nawratil's procrastination had anything to do with the fact that the German District Court itself was not in a real hurry, only picking up the case again in November. But another handwritten fragment in the Giese-Fein inheritance file, by the people handling the file in the German District Court, gives us a clue that the relationship between Nawratil and the German District Court had grown far less relaxed. In November 1940, they summoned Nawratil for questioning: "Summoning Dr. Navratil on 5.11.1940 – 10 ½ with *disciplinary consequences* [emphasis added]. 24.10.40 [unidentified signature]".[64] Apparently, Nawratil answered the summons a few days before that date. A certain B. in the German District Court concluded in a handwritten note on November 2, 1940: "Dr. Navratil [*sic*] has no objections to issuing the inheritance final document [?] [...], since it is neither real estate nor cash or [papers?] but old rubbish which is in any case already in the custody of the Jew Fein[.] Fein lives in Prague. Address will be announced within 1 week".[65]

It is of course strange that the German court still had doubts about whether to issue an inheritance certificate (*Erbschaftsurkunde*). As we have seen, the new Protectorate law concerning inheritances in which a Jew was involved only applied to inheritances initiated after March 15, 1939. But six months after the second executive order, issued by the Reich Protector in December 1939, the idea of a Jew inheriting anything, even "old rubbish" (*alten Kram*), was likely unthinkable for the German District Court. The Giese inheritance file appears to show that Nawratil succeeded in convincing the court that all this fuss was much ado about nothing. In all likelihood, he pointed out that the inheritance procedure had anyway come to a close with the payment of the inheritance tax. But it remains strange that Nawratil could get away with claiming that the "assets" of Giese's estate were nothing but worthless "old rubbish", and that neither he nor the district court knew anything about the materials that had belonged to Karl Giese.

FRANZ NAWRATIL'S ROLE

Judging from all these details, found in the Giese inheritance file, it looks as though Franz Nawratil, directly or indirectly, helped Karl Fein bring the Giese inheritance procedure to a satisfactory conclusion. This is one of the surprising features of the Giese inheritance case. Nawratil's professional letterhead bore a Nazi emblem,

sche Advokatenkammer in Brno, Advokátni komora Moravská v Brně] bestellter Substitut und Liquidator der Kanzlei des Dr. Karl Fein, nachdem dieser als Jude die Kanzlei nicht weiterführen darf. Ich hoffe, Ihnen damit gedient zu haben und zeichne mit Heil Hitler!"

[63] MZA, Brno, fonds C 107, Německý úřední soud Brno (Deutsches Amtsgericht Brünn), kart. n° 256, sign. 5aV 3/41, f. 35: "Dr. Franz Nawratil auffordern zur Akteneinsicht. Es ist zu klären, wer die Erbschaft übernehmen soll u.[nd] auf welche Weise. [...] 29.7.1940" (Summon Dr. Franz Nawratil to inspect the court files. It must be clarified who is to take over the inheritance and in what way. [...] 29.7.1940).

[64] MZA, Brno, fonds C 107, Německý úřední soud Brno (Deutsches Amtsgericht Brünn), kart. n° 256, sign. 5aV 3/41, f. 35b: "Laden Dr. Navratil zum 5.11.1940 – 10 ½ *unter Disziplinarfolgen* [emphasis added]. 24.10.40 [unidentified signature]". This was possibly the one and only time that the German District Court invited Nawratil to discuss the matter.

[65] MZA, Brno, fonds C 107, Německý úřední soud Brno (Deutsches Amtsgericht Brünn), kart. n° 256, sign. 5aV 3/41, f. 35: "Dr. Navratil [*sic*] hat keine Einwendungen gegen die Herausgabe der Erbschaftsurkunde [?] [...], da es sich weder um Liegenschaften noch um Bargeld oder [Papiere?] handelt sondern um alten Kram, der sich jedenfalls schon in der Verwahrung des Juden Fein befindet[.] Fein wohnt in Prag. Anschrift wird binnen 1 Woche bekanntgegeben".

indicating that he was a member of the National Socialist Association of Legal Professionals (Nationalsozialistische Rechtswahrerbund, NSRB), which rather curiously had its premises in the former Hirschfeld Institute in Berlin some time after 1933. Nawratil also dutifully signed his letters with "Heil Hitler". But one cannot help but notice that Nawratil kept silent when he should have spoken out.

Minimally, he seems to have been a passive witness as the Giese-Fein inheritance procedure unfolded. And he continued in this role until the summer of 1940, when the German District Court started asking questions about the Giese inheritance case. Nawratil certainly could have been a more "dutiful" Nazi lawyer. It is clear that both Fein and Nawratil operated in a gray and dangerous zone in the months after the German invasion of Czechoslovakia. But it remains difficult to gauge Nawratil's exact input and stance. Was he indeed actively protecting a former colleague from further harassment? Or, less heroically, had Franz Nawratil simply ignored the case at first in a desire to save him the extra work? Or, judging from Nawratil's relative wealth, was he only interested in much more lucrative undertakings? Or, another possibility, was he simply pragmatically trying to stay out of trouble when the German District Court started asking him questions? This could also explain why he procrastinated in giving answers to their questions. Lastly, one may also wonder if Nawratil possibly resented the newly created German District Court and, like the Czech courts, resisted their intrusion. That said, let us also remember that, starting in 1940, Nawratil was one of the approved lawyers able to plead in the German Regional Court (Deutsches Landgericht) in Brno.[66] Some more information on Nawratil's life will likely help shed more light on the matter.

[66] The long approval process to be admitted as a lawyer pleading in the court finally ended in March 1941. See *Seznam advokátů v Protektorátu Čechy a Morava = Verzeichnis der Advokaten im Protektorate Böhmen und Mähren* (1940, 77) and ABS, Praha, SÚMV, fonds n° 134, Německé soudy v Protektorátu Čechy a Morava, Vrchní zemský soud Praha, personální spisy justičních zaměstnanců, Akten über die Dienstverhältnisse, file Franz Nawratil, sign. 134-909-12, f. 16.

[67] See *Seznam advokátů dle stavu koncem roku 1936* 1937, 50.

[68] Piowatý left Brno in May 1939. See AMB, Brno, fonds Z 1, resident registration card (stamp dated May 14, 1938). Kurt Piowatý changed his name to Anthony George Vernon when he arrived in the USA after a short stay in Panama. In 1940, in London, he married Helga Weiner (1920–?), whom he divorced in 1954. He went to live in Georgia (USA) and, in 1960, married Evelyne Goldberg. He died in Atlanta in 2010. In 1947, he briefly went back to Czechoslovakia to try to find out more about family members who did not survive the Holocaust. See http://www.legacy.com/obituaries/atlanta/obituary.aspx?n=anthony-vernon&pid=143571883 (accessed Nov. 28, 2016). I sent a letter to Kurt Piowatý's son, Andrew Vernon, on November 30, 2016, as well as an email (dated Dec. 12, 2016). Kurt Piowatý's parents, Sigmund Piowatý (1879–1944?) and Elsa Piowatá (née Rothschildová, 1890–1944?) were deported from Brno to Terezín on March 31, 1942 on transport "Af", and then transferred to Auschwitz-Birkenau on transport "Et" on October 23, 1944. In 2011, at the instigation of relatives currently living in the USA, four *Stolpersteine* (stumbling stones) for Sigmund, Elsa, Kurt and Greta Piowatý were placed in front of the house at 3 Stephansgasse (Štěpánská) in Brno that had belonged to the family. See http://encyklopedie.brna.cz/home-mmb/?acc=profil_objektu&load=1066 (accessed Nov. 28, 2016). For pictures of the *Stolpersteine*, see https://de.wikipedia.org/wiki/Liste_der_Stolpersteine_in_Br%C3%BCnn (accessed Dec. 12, 2016). The fourth *Stolperstein* was for Elsa Piowatá's sister, Greta Piowatá (née Rothschildová, 1896–1976), the widow of Richard Piowatý, a brother of Sigmund Piowatý. Greta was deported to Terezín but survived the war. The fifth *Stolperstein* is for Rosa Rotschildová (1866–?), the mother of Greta and Elsa Piowatý, who also survived Terezín. See emails (dated Dec. 12, 2016 and Dec. 28, 2016) from Andrew Vernon to the author. The house that Elsa and Sigmund Piowatý owned at 3 Stephansgasse (Štěpánská) was forcefully sold in April 1941 to the Auswanderungsfonds für Böhmen und Mähren (Emigration Fund for Bohemia and Moravia). In January 1943, the latter sold the property to the Nationalsozialistischen Volkswohlfart e. V. (Berlin) (National Socialist People's Welfare). See MZA, Brno, fonds B 392, Vystěhovalecký fond, úřadovna Brno, kart. n° 9, sign. n° 189, Elsa and Zikmund Piowaty, f. 8-12, 25-26.

[69] *Seznam advokátů dle stavu koncem roku 1933* 1934, 45; *Seznam advokátů dle stavu koncem roku 1934* 1935, 45. Her law office was liquidated in 1939. See *Věstník Moravské advokátní komory v Brně*, Apr. 1939, 3. She was deported from Olomouc to Terezín on transport "AAm" on July 4, 1942, and then transferred to Treblinka on transport "Bx" on October 22, 1942. She lived in Brno until at least 1937, as her resident registration cards in the AMB Brno, fonds Z

FRANZ NAWRATIL AND JEWISHNESS

Franz Nawratil was certainly a somewhat uncommon Nazi sympathizer. Earlier, we mainly highlighted his unmistakable Nazi features. Yet one can also see that, without being Jewish himself, Franz Nawratil chose to immerse himself in Jewishness. He never had many interns in his law office but, when he did, many happened to be Jewish. One of the last interns in his law office was a young Jewish man named Kurt Piowatý (1911–2010), who stayed for a year in 1936.[67] The young man later started a law practice in Prague but also worked for private firms in Brno. He managed to escape Czechoslovakia shortly after the Germans invaded.[68] Franz Nawratil also took on a Jewish woman named Berta Seliger (1906–1942?) as an intern in 1933–34.[69] In other words, in the very period when younger Jewish lawyers had already lost their jobs in Nazi Germany.[70] Such relations with Jewish people were not new for Nawratil. As a young man, Nawratil did his internship with the Jewish lawyer Wladimir Lustig (1867–1925) and Nawratil likely also took over Lustig's law office after the latter's suicide in February 1925.[71]

Nawratil's brother, the lawyer Adolf Navratil (1891–?), was not exactly allergic to Jewishness either. He married the Jewish woman Lily (Liliane) Hauser (1903–1941), who committed suicide by poison in March 1941 after being questioned and tortured by the Gestapo.[72] And as if this was not enough, Franz Nawratil's sister, Marie Subák

1, testify. Before being deported, she lived in Prostějov (Prossnitz). See http://www.vets.cz/vpm/mista/obec/970-prostejov/n%C3%A1m%C4%9Bst%C3%AD%20Edmunda%20Husserla/ (accessed Apr. 24, 2017).

[70] Ladwig-Winters 2007.

[71] The address of Lustig's law office, 18 Freiheitsplatz (náměstí Svobody), was also later the address of Nawratil's law office. See *Adreßbuch von Groß-Brünn* 1920, 682. Lustig is buried in the Brno Jewish cemetery in parcel 28D, row 3, grave 3. He was married to Josefa Schnabl (1877–1942?), who was deported from Brno to Terezín on transport "U" on January 28, 1942, and then transferred to Treblinka on transport "Bv" on October 15, 1942. The couple had three children: a son named Walter (1902–?), who became a lawyer, Konrád (1904–1939), and a daughter Hanna (1912–?) who was possibly deported. The further fate of Walter Lustig, who fought in the Czechoslovak Legion during the war, is unknown. See https://encyklopedie.brna.cz/home-mmb/?acc=profil_osobnosti&load=16696&f_search=true&q=lustig (accessed Feb. 2, 2021).

[72] See MZA, Brno, fonds C 12, Krajský soud trestní Brno, kart. n° 1620, sign. Tk III 2809/45, file on Adolf Navrátil (born Feb. 18, 1891), f. 6 and f. 6b and MZA, Brno, fonds C 12, Krajský soud trestní Brno, kart. n° 2698, sign. Tk XXI 7617/46, file on Adolf Navrátil (born Feb. 18, 1891), f. 56 and f. 56b. There is no Gestapo file on Lily Navratil in the MZA, Brno. For the self-poisoning, see the death certificate in AMB, Brno, fonds A1/3, Sbírka rukopisů a úředních knih 1333–1958, Úmrtní protokol z roku 1941, entry n° 1985, dated Mar. 26, 1941. The couple married on January 21, 1933 in Brno and had a son named Robert (1934–?). We know that Adolf Navratil survived the war because one of his home certificate cards bears a postwar Brno address, dated 1947. See AMB, Brno, fonds B 1/39. In 1950, he was living in Vienna. See *Brünner Heimatbote*, 8, August 1950, 37. For this reason, on January 9, 2019, I sent a letter to the ten people in Vienna with the name Nawratil, found in an online Austrian phonebook. I did the same for the twenty-seven Nawratils living outside of Vienna on May 9, 2019. I inquired if they were relatives of the Nawratils from Brno and, if they were, whether they knew more about their family history. No one responded. I did not look into the lives of the two children from the first marriage of Kaspar Nawratil, Franz Nawratil's father, to Karoline Kritsche (?–?): the engineer Emil Navratil (1884–?), who died by 1942, and Erwin Navratil (1887–?), who lived in Italy. The search for Franz Nawratil's current relatives was, of course, also in great part curtailed by the fact that he and his wife had no children. However, even if I had found current relatives of the Nawratils, it seems unlikely they would have been willing to talk about this past. Last but not least, I realized of course that Nawratil, or more correctly, Navrátil, is not exactly an uncommon Czech name … It is not clear if Wilma Nawratil, Franz Nawratil's wife, was chased out of the country after the war, along with so many other German-speaking citizens, but this seems very likely as she and her husband Franz applied for Deutsche Volkszugehörigkeit (German ethnic) status in November 1939. See the Deutsche Volkszugehörigkeit application index card for Franz Navrátil [*sic*] in AMB, Brno, fonds A 1/53. There was no postwar trial for or prosecution of Nawratil's heirs in Czechoslovakia. According to Miroslava Kučerová (MZA, Brno), Franz Nawratil's name was not found in the following two archival fonds: MZA, Brno, fonds C 141, Mimořádný lidový soud Brno (Sondervolksgericht in Brünn); MZA, Brno, fonds C 130, Veřejný žalobce u Mimořádného lidového soudu Brno (Öffentlicher Ankläger beim Sondervolksgericht in Brünn). See email (dated Sep. 6, 2012) from Miroslava Kučerová (MZA, Brno) to the author. For more information on the postwar retribution trials in Czechoslovakia, see Frommer 2005.

(1900–?), was married to a Jewish man named Paul Tandler (1898–1925).[73] Because of all this, I started to wonder about when Nawratil became a member of the NSDAP. It came as no real surprise that he became a member on April 1, 1939, only two weeks after the Germans invaded Czechoslovakia.[74] That Franz Nawratil's allegiance to National Socialism was possibly opportunistic was also raised by Eugen Buchta, a fellow lawyer, who resented that Nawratil, and not he, had been appointed at one point as a trustee (*Treuhänder*), despite Nawratil's only joining the NSDAP after March 1939. An argument which was factually true.[75]

[73] MZA, Brno, fonds C 12, Krajský soud trestní Brno, kart. n° 2698, sign. Tk XXI 7617/46, file on Adolf Navrátil (born Feb. 18, 1891), f. 40-41, 59. This file deals with the postwar trial of Adolf Navratil, Franz Nawratil's brother, for threatening to denounce a lady, who owed him a considerable sum of money, to the Gestapo. He was sentenced to six months in prison; however, on appeal, the term was increased by another two months. See also http://encyklopedie.brna.cz/home-mmb/?acc=profil_osobnosti&load=30234 (accessed Jul. 6, 2017). Paul Tandler is buried in the Brno Jewish cemetery in parcel 26B, row 1, grave 14. Marie Navratilová remarried and took the name Subáková, but her new husband was not the Jewish lawyer Emil Subak (1886–1944) who lived at 7 Sadova (Parkstrasse) in 1934.

[74] Franz Nawratil (NSDAP membership number 7,064,153) and his wife Wilma Nawratil (NSDAP membership number 7,064,152) both became members of the NSDAP on April 1, 1939. See email (dated Jan. 13, 2017) from Heinz Fehlauer (Bundesarchiv Berlin) to the author; Fehlauer refers to fonds R 3001/69402 and the NSDAP-Gaukartei, respectively. The fonds G 637, NSDAP místní skupina Brno, in the MZA, Brno, does not contain any documents other than lists of names and so was not useful. See email (dated Mar. 9, 2017) from Michaela Růžičková (MZA, Brno) to the author. Nawratil had memberships in other National Socialist organizations: Nationalsozialistschen Volkswohlfart (National Socialist People's Welfare, NSV), Sudetendeutschen Partei (Sudeten German Party, SdP) and Nationalsozialistische Rechtswahrerbund (National Socialist Association of Legal Professionals, NSRB). It was not compulsory for jurists and lawyers to join the NSRB but not being a member was likely disadvantageous. Nawratil's membership in the NSRB was declared on his letterhead. See, for example, MZA, Brno, fonds C 107, Německý úřední soud Brno (Deutsches Amtsgericht Brünn), kart. n° 256, sign. 5aV 3/41, f. 37. For more information on the NSRB, see Sunnus 1990.

[75] See NA, Praha, fonds n° 375, Arizačni spisy, kart. n° 441, file n° 3240, letter (dated Oct. 7, 1940), Aktz. III 79 21: "Dr. Buchta bemerkte dann noch, dass es seltsam erscheine, wenn Leute, die erst nach dem März 1939 ihr nationales Herz entdeckten, auf einmal derartig umfangreiche Treuhänderschaften bekommen und dass er nicht wisse, warum seine Kanzlei bezw. die Kanzlei Dr. Tauschinsky übergangen werde. Dr. Buchta fühlte sich benachteiligt" (Dr. Buchta then remarked that it seemed strange that people who had only discovered their national heart after March 1939 were suddenly given such extensive trusteeships and that he did not know why his office or the office of Dr. Tauschinsky was passed over. Dr. Buchta felt disadvantaged.) To which someone added the handwrittern comment: "Neid!" (envy!).

[76] Franz Nawratil's resident registration card (dated Jul. 1, 1938) is signed by a certain Jellenik as the homeowner. This was Dr. Hermann Jellenik (1897–1975), who indeed owned the house since 1936. Jellenik was one of the three children of the Jewish doctor Berthold Jellenik (1863–1936). See http://encyklopedie.brna.cz/home-mmb/?acc=profil_osobnosti&load=19431 (accessed Jun. 1, 2017). Berthold Jellenik was married to Leontine Grünbaum (1870–1940). Hermann Jellenik was married to Božena Hanzlová (1903–1989) and the couple had a son named Jiří (1943–2020). All three survived the war but it is not known exactly how. Hermann, Božena and their son Jiří Jellenik returned to their home at 79 Talgasse (Údolní) by mid-July 1945. Hermann and Božena Jellenik are buried in the family grave plot in the Brno Jewish cemetery in parcel 28D, row 1, grave 18. The Brno land register shows that Hermann Jellenik bought the house (built in 1902) in 1936. See Katastrální úřad pro Jihomoravský kraj, katastrální pracoviště Brno-město, Katastralgemeinde Křížová (Kreuzgasse), land register entry 713 (Zahl der Grundbuchseinlage, číslo vložky knihovní), Údolní n° 79/354. It is important to note that the house currently falls under the Katastrální obec (Katastralgemeinde) Stránice and that the house numbers on the street have changed since 1942. What before the war was 79/354 Údolní has now become 61/550 Údolní. (The current house with number 79/557, a little further uphill, is thus not the house we are considering.) The previous owner of 79 Údolní was Emanuel Kaloud (1860–1935), a pensioned bank director. See *Adreßbuch von Groß-Brünn* 1934, 223, 814. The Brno land register shows that, in the beginning of November 1941, a *Treuhänder* (trustee) named Ladislaus (last name uncertain: Berdierek?) was appointed to sell the house, but there is no information on what happened afterwards since the next entry is dated 1946. According to a resident registration card in the AMB, Brno, fonds Z 1, Hermann Jellenik left his house on October 29, 1941 to move in with the engineer Bedřich Weiner (1892–1944?), who lived at 39A Alleestrasse (V aleji, currently třída Kpt. Jaroše). Weiner was deported on April 8, 1942 on transport "Ai" from Brno to Terezín, and later died in Auschwitz-Birkenau. See https://encyklopedie.brna.cz/home-mmb/?acc=profil_osobnosti&load=15437 (accessed Dec. 16, 2018). His wife Olga Weinerová (née Gottlob, 1898–?), survived deportation from Terezín to

THE HOUSE WHERE NAWRATIL LIVED

Another indication that Franz Nawratil was sympathetic to Jewishness is the fact that he lived in the house of a Jewish man, Dr. Hermann Jellenik (1897–1975), starting in July 1938, three months after his marriage.[76] It is unclear why Franz Nawratil moved to this address.[77] The house was located in the posh so-called civil service quarter (*Úřednická čtvrť, Beamtenviertel* or also *Beamtenheim*), a Brno neighborhood where the Brno upper classes continue to live today.[78] One of the most famous Czechoslovak sexologists, Antonin Tryb, lived in the same neighborhood.[79] The Jelleniks lived on the second floor of the house they owned and Nawratil rented the apartment on the first floor. In May 1940, Hermann Jellenik's brother, the bachelor Ludwig Jellenik (1899–1942), took up residence in the house and lived on the first floor, which means he must have moved in with Franz Nawratil.[80] Nawratil intended to buy the house, in mid-March 1942, but this never happened as he died in the beginning of May 1942.[81]

Auschwitz-Birkenau in October 1944. See https://encyklopedie.brna.cz/home-mmb/?acc=profil_osobnosti&load=15438 (accessed Dec. 16, 2018) and Kárný et al. 1995, 477. Their child, Leo Weiner (1923–?), survived the war in Denmark. See https://encyklopedie.brna.cz/home-mmb/?acc=profil_osobnosti&load=15439 (accessed Dec. 16, 2018). Berthold Jellenik's third child was Marianne Leimdörfer (1894–1990), who married Dr. Alfred Leimdörfer (1885–1956). The couple and their daughter Fritzie Demsetz (née Leimdörfer 1930–2018) survived the war. On February 2, 2021, I sent a letter to Freda Demsetz (1959–), one of the two daughters of Alfred and Fritzie Demsetz. Fritzie Demsetz's sister, Tina Herpe, sent me an email on February 28, 2021, saying that neither she nor her sister Fritzie had any information about the house in Brno, and that they had no contact with the current relatives in Brno. A family picture showing Berthold Jellenik, his wife and their two sons Hermann and Ludwig, can be seen at https://www.geni.com/people/Ludwig-Jellenik/6000000033079700645?through=6000000033079685302 (accessed Sep. 23, 2018). I also tried to contact the current relatives in Czechia of the younger Jiří Jellenik (1943–2020), the son of the elder Hermann Jellenik. Jiří Jellenik had two daughters and was married twice. See https://www.geni.com/family-tree/index/6000000033079874922 (accessed Mar. 4, 2021); and email (dated Feb. 28, 2021) from Tina Herpe to the author. No mention of the surname Jelenik or Jellenik was found in an online Czech phonebook. An email in English was sent to Dr. Jiří Jeleník [*sic*] from Brno, whose address and doctor's office I found online; he lived in the same house at 61 Údolní (79 before and during the war). I did not know his exact relation but presumed he was most likely the younger Jiří Jellenik since the man with this name lived and practiced medicine at the same 61 (79) Údolní house. There was no response to my email. On May 15, 2021, I then sent a letter – this time written in Czech – to Dr. Jiří Jeleník, which was returned as undeliverable (addressee unknown or letter expressly refused). Lucie Tuzová then called the phone number that appeared online but the number was no longer in service. Lucie then called a company located at the same address, and was told that the doctor was no longer living at that address. On July 7, 2021, I sent another email to the email address given for Dr. Jeleník, this time in Czech, but there was no response. On July 9, 2021, Lucie Tuzová let me know that Dr. Jeleník (1943–2020) had died in 2020 but that his wife, the medical doctor I. Jeleníková, was still alive and practicing medicine. I sent her an email on August 15, 2021. On August 22, 2021, J. Jeleník, the daughter of Jiří Jellenik (Jeleník) and I. Jeleník, sent me a friendly and informative email, confirming that her father had indeed died in December 2020. She had heard of Franz Nawratil, and knew that he was a Nazi who had lived in the house of her father and grandfather, but she knew nothing more on the matter.

77 AMB, Brno, fonds Z 1, Franz Nawratil resident registration card (dated Jul. 1, 1938). In 1934, Nawratil was still living in his parents' house, 46 Talgasse (Údolní) (*Adreßbuch von Groß-Brünn* 1934, 353). See the listing for Kaspar Nawratil [*sic*] and Franz Navratil [*sic*] in *Adreßbuch von Groß-Brünn* 1927, 301.

78 From 1925 on, the neighborhood was also known as the Masaryk quarter (Masarykova čtvrť, Masaryk-Viertel). For more information on this neighborhood, see http://www.bam.brno.cz/de/weg/4-masaryk-viertel (accessed May 8, 2015).

79 The address of the house where Tryb lived was 17 Šeříková (currently Heinrichova).

80 MZA, Brno, fonds B 392, Vystěhovalecký fonds, úřadovna Brno (1939-1945), kart. n° 10, inv. n° 223, house 79 Talgasse (Údolní) (currently 61 Údolní). The second son of Berthold Jellenik was Ludwig Gottlieb Jellenik (1899–1942). The business index card in AMB, Brno, fonds B 1/16, shows that, from December 1935 on, he traded in wool textiles. On February 28, 1940, on his own initiative, he asked the Oberlandrat (Supreme District Council) to liquidate his business. The request was accepted and the liquidation completed in October 1940. See NA, Praha, fonds n° 375, Arizačni spisy, kart. n° 263, sign. 1874, file Jellinek Ludwig. Curiously, his firm could not be located in the "Branchen Verzeichnis der jüdischen Firmen in Brünn", listing the 881 Jewish firms liquidated in Brno alone. See NA, Praha, fonds Arizačni spisy, kart. n° 338, folder n° 2392. Ludwig Jellenik was deported on transport "Ae" from Brno to Terezín on March 27, 1942, and further transferred to Piaski on transport "Ag" on April 1, 1942. Like his brother Hermann, Ludwig Gottlieb Jellenik moved

WAS FRANZ NAWRATIL A GAY MAN?

However unlikely it may seem, we need to consider one more thing regarding Franz Nawratil. Was he maybe a closeted gay man? We saw that he, a bachelor who lived with his parents until the age of forty-eight, only married a few days after the Germans annexed Austria. His wife Wilma Naplawa was eighteen years younger. Did he maybe marry his housekeeper? Wilma Naplawa's deceased father, Otmar Naplawa (1880–1928), had been a factory accountant. Her sister, Edith Hradský, who worked in a law office, married an architect and lived with him at 23 Legionärenstrasse (třída Legionářů), a very posh address. Both these facts weigh heavily against the idea that Nawratil's wife had been his maid. Or was Edith Hradský perhaps a secretary in Nawratil's law office, and did she suggest that Nawratil marry her sister?

In relation to previous years, the marriage rate in Brno peaked in 1938 (1,167 marriages) and 1939 (1,194 marriages).[82] It is not easy, of course, to explain these surges in marriage. But I do think it possible that some gay men and lesbian women decided to hide their sexual preference, putting up the facade of a heterosexual marriage of convenience, also called a "lavender marriage". But the heightened marriage rate could also be explained by the threat of German occupation and the fear that unmarried people would be more likely to be drafted or summoned to do forced labor than married people. This latter possibility is indicated by the fact that the sister of Nawratil's wife, Edith Naplava (Naplawa) (1913–?), married František Hradský (1907–?) in May 1938. And yet, it remains curious that Franz Nawratil's widow married Dr. Helmut Barta (1918–?), eleven years her junior, in February 1944. Another rather uncommon marriage.[83]

Karl Fein's possibly having been Nawratil's intern at the beginning of his career could perhaps also be explained this way. Maybe two gay men were helping each other out? Despite all these not-so-Nazi traits, Nawratil never seems to have aroused any suspicion in the Nazi establishment. When, in 1941, he was appointed as a lawyer in the Brno German Regional Court, he was thoroughly screened for his political reliability (*politische Zuverlässigkeit*) by the Prague German Higher Regional Court

in with Bedřich Weiner on Alleestrasse (V aleji) at the end of October 1941. A memorial inscription for him has been included on the above-mentioned stele for his father, mother and brother Hermann in the Brno Jewish cemetery. See https://www.holocaust.cz/databaze-dokumentu/dokument/440365-jellenik-ludvik-nezpracovano/ (accessed Sep. 23, 2018), which clearly states that Ludwig was living at the same address as Franz Nawratil in May 1940. A resident registration card for Ludwig in the AMB, Brno, fonds Z 1, seems to suggest that he only arrived in the villa on August 7, 1941; however, a closer look at the document reveals that it was rather seeking confirmation of an existing address. In any case, the back of the resident registration card shows that Ludwig left the villa on October 31, 1941, two days after his brother, to go and live with Bedřich Weiner. Lastly, another Jewish widow, Rosa Fischerová-Piraková (née Grünbaum, 1878 or 1876–1942?), possibly a sister of Berthold Jellenik's wife, Leontine Grünbaum, also lived in the Talgasse (Údolní) house and herself moved in with Weiner at the end of October 1941. She was deported on transport "U" from Brno to Terezín on January 28, 1942; then, depending on the source, further transferred either on transport "Ar" to Zamošč on April 28, 1942 (www.holocaust.cz [accessed Feb. 12, 2020]) or on transport "Ab" to Izbica on March 17, 1942. See Kárný et al. 1995, 306.

81 MZA, Brno, fonds B 392, Vystěhovalecký fonds, úřadovna Brno, kart. n° 10, inv. n° 223, f. 2-3.

82 I checked the annual number of marriages in the marriage registers for the city of Brno in the 1930s. See Matriky uložené v Moravském zemském archivu v Brně, Brno (městská rada), marriage registers, years 1930–1945, available online at: http://actapublica.eu/matriky/brno/ (accessed Aug. 26, 2019).

83 AMB, Brno, fonds Z 1, resident registration card (dated May 15, 1942) for Wilma Nawratil (Naplawa); NSDAP-membership card for Helmut Barta (1918–) in Bundesarchiv Berlin, NSDAP-Mitgliederkartei, NSDAP-Zentralkartei, BArch R 9361-VIII Kartei / 771023.

84 Franz Nawratil's staff file is located in ABS, Praha, SÚMV, fonds n° 134, Německé soudy v Protektorátu Čechy a Morava, Vrchní zemský soud Praha, personální spisy justičních zaměstnanců (Akten über die Dienstverhältnisse), file Franz Nawratil, sign. 134-909-12. At first, the ABS, Praha, had denied they had these Prague Higher Regional Court files, even though I had seen another staff file from this court for a lawyer named Walter Süss (whom Karl Fein had known) in the archives of the ABS. This initiated, in 2017, an unnecessary merry-go-round

(Deutschen Oberlandesgericht Prag, Vrchní zemský soud Praha).[84] Nawratil's file contains no trace of any perceived risk, irregularity or reported incident.[85]

However the matter may have stood regarding Nawratil's precise (non-)involvement and his actual motivations in the handling and settlement of Giese's estate, in mid-December 1940, the German District Court reached a final conclusion and declared that the Giese inheritance case was accepted, adding: "the property [illegible] of the heir is fully Jewish (*Volljüde*). This declares the probate proceedings closed".[86] A copy of this decision also reached Karl Fein in Prague. On January 3, 1941, he signed a reply stub confirming that he received a copy of the final decision.[87] It was Nawratil who gave the German Regional Court Fein's most recent Prague address, at the court's explicit request. On November 2, 1940, Nawratil promised to give them Fein's address within a week.[88] But Nawratil procrastinated and the court had to prod him on November 23, 1940. Nawratil then answered in his usual terse and assertive style: "With regard to the court summons of 23 November 1940, I give the address of Dr. Fein in the inheritance case of Karl Giese: Dr. Karl Fein, Prague X., Erbenova 11. Heil Hitler!"[89] It is remarkable that this Brno German court had to turn to Nawratil to get Fein's most recent Prague address. Yet this also indicates that, in November 1940, Nawratil was still in contact with Karl Fein in Prague.

Finally, an anonymous judicial inspector (*Justizinspektor*), working for the German District Court, took a final look at the Giese-Fein inheritance file on April 28, 1941, deciding that there were no further costs, and that all thirty-seven pages of the court file needed to be preserved for posterity.[90]

with me inquiring with two other Czech archives – MZA, Brno, and NA, Praha – where these court files might be found. The problem seems to have been that these archives were not yet ordered and accessible in the ABS, Praha, and, for this reason, or so it appears at least, I was told they did not have these archives. See email (dated Aug. 22, 2017) from Jitka Bílková (ABS, Praha) to the author.

[85] The Prague Higher Regional Court staff file for Nawratil is also clearly incomplete – Nawratil's resumé and picture are missing, for example – but this does not necessarily suggest that documents were taken out of the file because they indicated irregularities. I also checked other staff files for lawyers who were appointed to the Brno German Regional Court in the same Prague Higher Regional Court archival fonds and saw that they all had missing components, like a picture or a completed questionnaire. All files showed traces of torn-out pages. It is possible that these files were reviewed toward the end of the war and that any useful, compromising information was pulled out by individuals intending to prosecute these Nazi lawyers in a war crimes tribunal. I looked at the files of Franz Schindler (sign. 134-909-13), Fritz Cermak (sign. 134-909-6), Karl Schwabe (sign. 134-909-14), Josef Pavlak (Pawlak) (sign. 134-910-7) and Walter Süss (sign. 134-908-11). In the files for Süss and Pavlak, there are traces of a summer 1941 incident involving both lawyers. Inside the court building, they had given food to the people they were defending. This shows that irregularities were indeed reported in these files. We will return to this incident later.

[86] MZA, Brno, fonds C 107, Německý úřední soud Brno (Deutsches Amtsgericht Brünn), kart. n° 256, sign. 5aV 3/41, f. 37b: "Eigentum [illegible] der Erbe ist Volljüde. Damit wird die Verlassenschaftsabhandlung für beendet erklärt".

[87] MZA, Brno, fonds C 107, Německý úřední soud Brno (Deutsches Amtsgericht Brünn), kart. n° 256, sign. 5aV 3/41, reply stub (dated Jan. 3, 1941) from the German District Court, inserted after f. 37. Giese's inheritance file contains no letters sent by the Brno district court or by the German District Court. One has to work with the scribbles added by court employees and magistrates throughout the file documents.

[88] MZA, Brno, fonds C 107, Německý úřední soud Brno (Deutsches Amtsgericht Brünn), kart. n° 256, sign. 5aV 3/41, f. 35.

[89] Ibid., f. 37, letter (dated Nov. 28, 1940) from Franz Nawratil to German District Court: "Zur hiergerichtlichen Aufforderung vom 23. November 1940 gebe ich in der Verlassache nach Karl Giese die Anschrift des Dr. Fein bekannt: Dr. Karl Fein, Prag X., Erbenova 11. Heil Hitler!" As we will see later, Fein had been living at this Prague address with his immediate family and a couple since July 1940.

[90] "Aufzubewahren: – dauernd –". See MZA, Brno, fonds C 107, Německý úřední soud Brno (Deutsches Amtsgericht Brünn), kart. n° 256, sign. 5aV 3/41, first page of protective cover sheet and note and stamp on back side of cover sheet. On the protective cover sheet of the file there is the somewhat contradictory "Weggelegt 1940" (put away 1940), but we have already seen that an employee was still looking at the file in April 1941. On the cover page the old file number 5 a VI 478/39 was crossed out and changed to the file number that the file still bears today: 5a V 3/41. The numbers 39 and 41 in the file numbers refer to the years 1939 and 1941.

NO WRINKLE?

It is quite intriguing that no one in the Brno German District Court seems to have realized who Karl Giese, or even Magnus Hirschfeld, was. Magnus Hirschfeld's name was clearly mentioned in Karl Giese's handwritten (and transcribed) last will and this document was, after all, *the* centerpiece of the inheritance file. It also remains quite intriguing that Nawratil managed to explain all of that (away) in the German District Court when summoned by them. Can we conclude from this that Karl Giese was not really perceived as an enemy of the Third Reich when he was in Brno, and that his suicide was to this extent possibly unwarranted? We have seen that, at the very least, the Gestapo was updated about Giese's whereabouts by the German consulate in Brno. But, with Hirschfeld's death in 1935 in Nice, and Giese's death in Brno in 1938, was the Magnus Hirschfeld and Karl Giese chapter maybe considered closed by the Nazis? Did the Nazis have more pressing priorities? Or were the people working for the German District Court that handled the Giese inheritance locals, simply unaware of Hirschfeld's renown in Germany before the war? The German District Court started looking at the Giese inheritance file in December 1939 and put it away for good in April 1941. Whether this was indeed the very last time that the Third Reich looked, with some degree of awareness or even none at all, at the last meanderings of the inheritance proceedings of Giese's (and Hirschfeld's) legacy is something that will have to be determined by further research.[91]

WHAT WAS SPELLED OUT IN THE FINAL SETTLEMENT DRAFTED BY KARL FEIN?

Let us now look at two elements in the final settlement of the Giese inheritance as drafted by Karl Fein at the end of May 1939.[92] On the asset side (activa), valued at a total sum of 2,720 Czech crowns, we find, among other things, mention of "around" 400 books "that were old and used". It is not known why this number does not match the Brno police's precise count of 535 books in room II of Giese's Schützengasse (Střelecká) apartment. In addition, the Brno police apparently found more books in a cabinet with three doors in room III, but apparently did not count these.[93] This means that there were clearly more books in Giese's apartment than the approximately 400 books Karl Fein mentions in his final settlement. If we add the books in the three-doored cabinet to the 535 books found in room II, there may have been around 800–900 books from the Berlin Institute in Giese's apartment. Let us also recall that, according to Magnus Hirschfeld at least, around 2,200 kg of materials had been bought back from Nazi Germany at the end of 1933.[94] Also, the November 1933 Berlin auction announcement mentioned that 3,000 books were being auctioned.[95] This could mean that Hirschfeld managed to buy back around a third of the books for auction in Berlin in November 1933. One of the many arguments Giese and Fein invoked in their plea

[91] Given the great many annotations, the scribbles, the different handwriting, the underlining in several styles and in different colors of pens and pencils found throughout the Giese inheritance file, one nevertheless has the impression that the file was looked at by quite a few people at the time.

[92] MZA, Brno, fonds C 107, Německý úřední soud Brno (Deutsches Amtsgericht Brünn), kart. n° 256, sign. 5aV 3/41, f. 29, document titled "Místpřísežné seznání jmění" (sworn statement of assets), dated May, 25-26 1939. The text of the final settlement is reproduced in the addenda (n° 8).

[93] MZA, Brno, fonds C 107, Německý úřední soud Brno (Deutsches Amtsgericht Brünn), kart. n° 256, sign. 5aV 3/41, f. 4: "2 regály s knihami / 535 kusů" (2 shelves with books / 535 pieces) in room II and "1 tříkřídlová skříň s knihami" (1 three-door cabinet with books) in room III.

[94] Hirschfeld & Dose 2013, f. 87/186.

[95] For mention of 3,000 books, see *12 Uhr Blatt* (noon edition of the newspaper *Die Neue Zeitung*), Jg. 27, Folge 53, Nov. 15, 1933, 2. For the 2,200 kg, see Hirschfeld & Dose 2013, f. 87/186.

[96] MZA, Brno, fonds B 40, Zemský úřad Brno (Landesbehörde in Brünn), kart. n° 2138, sign. 5274/38, f. 8.

[97] MZA, Brno, fonds C 107, Německý úřední soud Brno (Deutsche Amtsgericht Brünn), kart. n° 256, sign. 5a V 3/41, f. 4: "prázdných beden" (empty boxes). Cf. the letter Giese wrote to Ernst Maass in January 1938, which also mentions *Kisten* (wooden boxes) containing Institute materials. See Archiv

that Giese not be deported from Brno, in the summer of 1937, was that packing 2,000 kg of materials in twenty-three boxes would simply cost too much.[96] In the inventory they made of Giese's apartment, the Brno police also mentioned ten empty cases in room III. Possibly these were the original wooden boxes (*Kisten*) containing the material sent from Berlin to Brno, presumably in December 1933.[97]

Most likely, the bulk of the materials that Giese had in his possession in Brno formed part of the materials bought back in November 1933 from Nazi Germany with the help of Karl Fein. In a July 1937 letter sent to the Moravian provincial authorities through his lawyer Karl Fein, Giese was clear on the matter: "Hirschfeld's scientific views completely contradicted the racist views adopted by the current ruling regime in Germany, and this contradiction led to the dissolution of the institute, whose scientific material was partly burned and partly destroyed in May 1933 during the burning of books. Part of it could be saved and is in my possession".[98]

As we have already suggested, only a part of the materials bought back were sent from Brno to Paris in April 1934. The questionnaires and presumably also some thematic folders (*Mappen*) that were also bought back were part of the lot sent to Paris. Most likely, the 800–900 books in Giese's apartment at the time of his death had remained in Brno when Giese left for France in December 1933. That the books had been left in Brno could be tied to the idea repeated by Giese, until at least mid-1937, that he intended to start a new Institute in Brno with Josef Weisskopf. This would make leaving the books behind in Brno a good decision. This also meant that someone in Brno, possibly Karl Fein or Josef Weisskopf, looked after these books until Giese moved for the third and last time to Brno at the end of May 1936. It is also possible that the books were stored in the Leopold Fleischer moving firm, the company owned by Willi Bondi's brother-in-law. The company did indeed have a plot with a storage building on it, to which we will return later.

In a July 1937 letter to Kurt Hiller, Giese wrote that he kept materials other than books from the Institute collection in his Brno apartment: "When I wrote [in a previous letter to Hiller] that I had only glanced through the material, I meant in relation to its quantity. After all, it is not just a few folders of [Magnus Hirschfeld's] correspondence from the last years of his emigration, but a very extensive, though unfortunately mostly not proportionately as important, collection of writings and documents that goes back to the beginning of this century".[99] However, all in all, Giese had never been very positive about the bulk of the Institute materials: "Among the repurchased material is much that had some value in our Institute but is less

MHG, Berlin, fonds Ernst Maass, letter (dated Jan. 21, 1938, 1) from Karl Giese to Ernst Maass.

[98] MZA, Brno, fonds B 40, Zemský úřad Brno (Landesbehörde in Brünn), kart. n° 2138, sign. 5274/38, Odvolání do výměru zemského úřadu v Brně ze dne 8. července 1937 jedn. čís. 2224/I-7 k Ministerstvu vnitra v Praze, f. 6b: "Vědecké názory Hirschfeldovy [*sic*, Hirschfelda] byly v naprostém rozporu s názory o rasismu, jež si osvojil nynější vládnoucí režim v Německu, a tento protiklad názorů vedl k zrušení uvedeného ústavu, jehož vědecký materiál byl v květnu 1933 při pálení knih dílem spálen, dílem zničen. Část mohla býti zachráněna a je v mém držení."

[99] Archiv Kurt Hiller Gesellschaft, Neuss, letter (dated Jul. 12, 1937, 1) Karl Giese to Kurt Hiller: "Wenn ich seinerzeit schrieb [in a previous letter to Hiller], dass ich das Material nur flüchtig durchgesehen hätte, so war das im Verhältnis zu seiner Menge gemeint. Es handelt sich nähmlich nicht nur um ein paar nachgelassene Korrespondenzmappen [of Magnus Hirschfeld] aus den letzten Jahren der Emigration, sondern um ein höchst umfangreiches, allerdings meist leider nicht im selben Verhältnis dazu wichtiges Schriften- und Dokumentenmaterial das bis in die Anfänge dieses Jahrhunderts zurückreicht". Marita Keilson-Lauritz thinks that the "wichtiges Schriften- und Dokumentenmaterial das bis in die Anfänge dieses Jahrhunderts zurückreicht", that Giese mentions, might well be the materials that make up the Hirschfeld scrapbook, now in the Kinsey Institute Library & Special Collections, Bloomington (Indiana). Yet Giese was writing this in 1937 and a part of the materials that were in Brno had been sent to Paris in April 1934 already.

valuable when torn out like this".[100] The impressive lot of books stored in Giese's Brno apartment was in any case the priciest asset – estimated at 1,400 Czech crowns – of the twelve items in total included on the asset side of the balance sheet.

The second intriguing element from the final settlement of the Giese inheritance is the eleventh on the list: various scientific materials, various photographs, films and negatives, twelve casts of anatomical parts, old photo materials, a lot estimated at 500 Czech crowns.[101] We have seen that these wax casts were recorded by Gaston Giauffer, the certified appraiser, in Hirschfeld's apartment in Nice shortly after his death. How these ended up in Brno remains unexplained, above all since, as we have also seen, Li Shiu Tong was the one entitled to the objects in Hirschfeld's Nice apartment.

Possibly, this can be related to another important element in Fein's final settlement list, which included mention of three large oil paintings and around forty smaller paintings or reproductions. In March 1938, in the days following Giese's suicide, the Brno police counted around eighty-five pictures and paintings in room II.[102] How did these pictures end up in Brno? At first, I thought it unlikely that any Institute materials were sent from Nice to Brno after Hirschfeld's death, but the many pictures, and especially the wax casts of genitals in Giese's flat, seem to indicate that some of the objects in Nice were indeed sent to Giese in Brno. This would also explain the three mysterious bills from two Nice moving companies in the financial settlement of the Hirschfeld estate in 1935–36. There were two bills from Reboul & Co., dated May 20, 1936, and June 15, 1936, and a smaller bill from Martini et Cie on July 7, 1936. These may well have been for the removal and packing of objects from storage coming from the Hirschfeld estate in Nice, which were then sent to Giese in Brno.[103] One of these bills could have been for the (outstanding) rent for a storage room. After all, once the Gloria Mansions I apartment was vacated, its furnishings had to be stored somewhere. These might have gone into a storage room until a part was sent to Brno, around May 1936. The bill dates seem very telling.

In the last days of May 1936, Giese moved from Vienna to Brno, firmly intending to start anew in Brno. Even if it was after a long wait, Giese certainly knew that he would receive a monetary income from the Hirschfeld estate and could finally make plans. This may also explain why Herzfelder asked the notary Pierre Demnard for a copy of the inventory of the furnishings of Hirschfeld's apartment at the end of May 1936.[104] Did Giese intend to furnish his Brno apartment with items from the Gloria Mansions I apartment? Herzfelder might have sent the copy of the inventory to Brno, for Giese to decide what he wanted from that furniture lot then, as we have suggested, most likely in storage in Nice. It is also not improbable that Li Shiu Tong

[100] Arbetarrörelsens arkiv och bibliotek, Stockholm, Max Hodann samling, vol. 15, letter (dated Sep. 24, 1935, 1) from Karl Giese to Max Hodann: "Unter dem zurückgekauften Material befindet sich vieles, was zwar in unser[e]m Institut einen gewissen Wert hatte, aber so herausgerissen weniger wertvoll ist".

[101] MZA, Brno, fonds C 107, Německý úřední soud Brno (Deutsches Amtsgericht Brünn), kart. n° 256, sign. 5aV 3/41, f. 29: "různý vědecký materiál různé fotografie, filmy a negativy, 12 odlitků anatomických odlitků, zápisky" (various scientific materials, various photographs, films and negatives, 12 casts of anatomical parts).

[102] MZA, Brno, fonds C 107, Německý úřední soud Brno (Deutsches Amtsgericht Brünn), kart. n° 256, sign. 5aV 3/41, f. 4. The three oil paintings are singled out as items 5, 6 and 7 in the final settlement list. Forty other paintings and reproductions are listed as item 9.

[103] Soetaert 2014, 58, Table 13; Soetaert 2014, 54, Table 10. Here, I am clearly stepping back from my earlier suggestion that these three bills were possibly connected with the moving and storage of the materials obtained by Victor Bauer and his troupe. See Soetaert 2014, 57–60. These expedition or storage companies usually also specialized in (international) transport.

[104] See the handwritten inscription, "Extrait [copy] remis à M. Herzfelder le 29 mai 36. [signature Herzfelder]", on the reverse side of the brown cover sheet in ADAM, minutes Demnard, May 24, 1935, n° 569, cote 03E 148/011. See addenda (n° 17), p. 763.

let Giese know that he was not interested in these furnishings, of which he had legal title according to Hirschfeld's will. The young man was too much of a world traveler to wish to hold on to them. On the other hand, I do not think that any furniture was sent to Brno. This would likely have been too expensive, and we have already seen that Giese borrowed furniture from Willi Bondi and Walter Lukl which, as stipulated in Giese's own will, had to be returned to them. Possibly around this period, May–June 1936, the remaining furniture from Hirschfeld's apartment might have been auctioned in Nice. I observed that two lots were put on sale in Nice by Martini et Cie at the auction house (*hôtel de ventes*) of the Nice auctioneers Giauffer & Terris, in May and June 1936.[105]

So, it is quite possible that the pictures that hung on the walls in Giese's Brno apartment were largely the same as those that hung on the walls of Hirschfeld's Nice apartment. Giese clearly saw how Hirschfeld had decorated his Nice apartment when he went there for Hirschfeld's funeral, in May–June 1935, and it might have consoled him to see the same pictures on the walls of his own apartment in Brno. Whether this means that the oil painting of the bearded lady ended up in Brno is not known. In the inventory list made of Giese's Brno apartment after his suicide, there is mention of pictures and paintings in almost every room and no less than 85 pieces of various paintings on the walls of room n° II.[106] In a text from July 1937 Giese also explicitly mentions paintings coming from the Institute that were in his apartment in Brno.[107] There is mention only of an "older" and a "newer" oil painting in Fein's final settlement list.[108] It is of course tempting to think that the painting of the bearded lady might have ended up in the Velké Losiny castle in the Olomouc region of Czechia; however, we saw in chapter 10 that the latter's copy of the painting had been hanging on the walls of that castle for centuries already.[109]

As already suggested, it is possible that Giese saw himself as the most trustworthy person to care for what remained of the Hirschfeld estate, even though, in hindsight, this turned out to be a deeply unfortunate misjudgment. Most likely, he simply clung onto the Hirschfeld and Institute artifacts for emotional and sentimental reasons. Li Shiu Tong's not having an interest in the furnishings of the Nice apartment might have strengthened him in this conviction that he was the one true and trustworthy guardian of Hirschfeld's estate. Giese did indeed take some of Hirschfeld's diaries from the Nice apartment when he returned to Vienna in June 1935; but, in all likelihood, he also obtained items from the furnishings of the Hirschfeld apartment despite Li Shiu Tong being entitled to them, according to Hirschfeld's last wishes. The wax casts of genitals, found in Giese's Brno apartment, are the clearest proof of this. To that were also added the Institute books, in Brno since their arrival from Berlin in December 1933. But it is important to separate these Institute and Hirschfeld materials that Giese had in Brno from the Institute materials entrusted to Bauer and his troupe in Nice.

105 ADAM, Nice, Archives privées, fonds des commissaires priseurs Rue Gioffredo à Nice, procès-verbaux des ventes du commissaire-priseur Jean-Joseph Terris, Etude Roustan et successeurs (1906–2002), May 1, 1936–June 30, 1936, cote 185J 0088, sale "divers" 66 (dated May 8–9, 1936) and sale "divers" 82 (dated June 22, 1936). See also Soetaert 2014, 57 n. 139. Since, in 2014, I still thought that January–February 1936 was a crucial time period in the handling and settlement of the Hirschfeld estate, and that Victor Bauer was the main or sole actor in Nice, the details of the public sales requested by Martini et Cie in May and June 1936 should be checked again in the ADAM, Nice. These public sales records should be compared to the inventory of the furniture in Hirschfeld's apartment made by Giauffer in May 1935. See ADAM, Nice, Archives notariales, minutes notariales étude Pierre Demnard, May 24, 1935, n° 569, cote 03E 148/011.

106 See n° 7 in the addenda, p. 733.

107 See n° 9 in the addenda, p. 740 [p. 4, f. 7b].

108 See n° 8 in the addenda, p. 736.

109 MZA, Brno, fonds C 107, Německý úřední soud Brno (Deutsches Amtsgericht Brünn), kart. n° 256, sign. 5aV 3/41, f. 29, points 5 and 6. See chapter 10, pp. 305-06 and n. 8.

As we have seen, the Institute materials sent from Brno to Paris in April 1934 were presumably moved by Hirschfeld from storage with the Bedel company in Paris to a storage facility in Nice in the beginning of 1935. Presumably, the many ethnological items that ended up with Bauer and his troupe, in the first months of 1936, had been taken out of the Institute before it was looted in 1933 and were eventually also brought to Nice. We have already shown that Giese was somewhat circumspect about "these ethnological materials", which were "still not available" for unknown reasons in Nice in September 1935.[110] I think that these were the Institute materials stored in Nice that ended up with Bauer. We also saw that there was possibly some sort of conflict between Giese and Bauer about this lot because Giese and Li Shiu Tong apparently had nothing to say regarding its further destiny.

Another striking feature of the final settlement is that there is no mention of any cash found in Giese's apartment or of money in his bank account. This seems to be consistent with the already mentioned fact that, by February 1938, there was virtually no money left in Giese's bank account. Not even the refund of the deposit (*Kaution*) of 480 Czech crowns that Giese paid in September 1936, when he started to rent his Brno apartment, is mentioned.[111] All in all, one has the impression that Fein's final settlement was done in a very summary and superficial way. But he got away with it, apparently.

THEODOR TICHAUER

On the liabilities side of the balance sheet (also named expenses, or passiva), amounting to 1,243 Czech crowns, we see the Brno central cemetery bill, rent for Giese's apartment for the month of April, a bill for mending the broken window pane in the front door of Giese's apartment (broken to be able to open the door from the outside, the morning after his suicide) and also a last, still unpaid bill for a month and a half of milk and bread deliveries to Giese's door by a certain Ludmila Purová. It also includes a paid bill for the Paris-based Jewish lawyer Theodor Tichauer (1891–1942).[112] Tichauer was a German lawyer and notary who had a practice in Berlin-Charlottenburg during the Weimar Republic. In June 1933, shortly after the Nazis seized power, he was disbarred for his Communist activities. He fled to Paris on July 26, 1933. In France, it was not possible for him to employ his German professional title but he was allowed to work under the title "conseil juridique". Tichauer counted many German antifascist immigrants among his clients. According to his daughter, Eva Tichauer, he was also the president of the Association des Emigrés Israélites d'Allemagne en France (ASSO).[113]

Hirschfeld probably knew Tichauer through Bernd Götz (1891–?) with whom he had coauthored a few books.[114] According to Rainer Herrn, Hirschfeld may have briefly

[110] Arbetarrörelsens arkiv och bibliotek, Stockholm, Max Hodann samling, vol. 15, letter (dated Sep. 24, 1935) from Karl Giese to Max Hodann.

[111] For the deposit of one month's rent paid by Giese, see p. 1 of the rental booklet (*Knížka nájemní, Zinsbüchel*) for Giese's apartment, MZA, Brno, fonds C 107, Německý úřední soud Brno (Deutsches Amtsgericht Brünn), kart. n° 256, sign. 5aV 3/41.

[112] The bill (dated Jun. 12, 1937) was for FF150 or 132 Czech crowns. In comparison, Giese's monthly rent was 480 Czech crowns. See MZA, Brno, fonds C 107, Německý úřední soud Brno (Deutsches Amtsgericht Brünn), kart. n° 256, sign. 5aV 3/41, f. 31b. Most of the information in what follows was communicated to me by Eva Tichauer (1918–2018), the late daughter of Theodor and Erna Tichauer (1892–1942), in a series of emails in December 2010. Unlike her mother and father, Eva Tichauer survived her deportation to Auschwitz-Birkenau and wrote two books on her concentration camp experience. See Tichauer 1988; Tichauer 2017. She retired from medical practice and resided in Marseille and Argenteuil. She used to work for the Éducation Nationale (Ministry of National Education) and Ministère de la Santé Publique (Ministry of Publich Health). For more information on Eva Tichauer, see http://www.lamarseillaise.fr/soci-t-quartiers/num-ro-20832.html (accessed Apr. 1, 2013).

[113] Email (dated Dec. 16, 2010) from Eva Tichauer to the author.

[114] Hirschfeld's co-authorship was often only a pro forma matter. See Herzer 2001, 216: "So kam es,

considered Götz a worthy successor at the Institute.[115] Tichauer and Götz had been the best of friends as students.[116] In the 1920s, Tichauer published three texts in *Die Ehe*, one of the sexual reform magazines launched by Hirschfeld.[117] On August 16, 1934, Theodor and Erna Tichauer made an entry in the Hirschfeld guestbook.[118] Judging by the date of the latter, we may suppose that the meeting between Hirschfeld and the Tichauers may have been connected to the problems associated with Giese's Paris bathhouse affair. On the other hand, we have no real idea what the June 1937 bill, which appears in Giese's estate documents, was for. Unfortunately, Eva Tichauer, knew barely anything about her father's professional relations as she spent the 1934–36 school year in Orléans, only spending the holidays with her parents in Paris.[119] It seems likely, in any case, that Giese and Tichauer met in Paris some time in 1934 and that Giese later relied on the Paris lawyer.

Erna and Theodor Tichauer perished in the Holocaust. Theodor Tichauer was arrested, together with other Jewish notables, on December 12, 1941, and imprisoned in Compiègne (France). He was deported to Auschwitz-Birkenau on March 27, 1942, and died there on April 6, 1942. Erna Tichauer and her daughter Eva were rounded up on July 16, 1942, during the infamous, so-called "Vel' d'Hiv Roundup" (*rafle du Vel' d'Hiv* [an abbreviation for "Vélodrome d'Hiver"]). This was the Paris sports arena where Jewish people were gathered in the summer of 1942 to be deported. Mother and daughter were put on the 36th convoy to Auschwitz-Birkenau. Eva Tichauer's mother died upon arrival in the camp, on September 23, 1942, the date of her fiftieth birthday. Eva Tichauer was exactly one hundred years old when she died in 2018.

GALLIMARD & MONTAIGNE

Fein's final settlement also contained information concerning the royalties of Hirschfeld's books. According to Hirschfeld's will, these were to go to Giese. In his own will, Giese transferred them to Karl Fein. Fein added the following sentence in the final settlement: "I reserve the right to amend this list in case the deceased has any right to a share of profits from the sale of books published in Paris by the publishers Gallimard and Montaigne".[120] We have already seen that Hirschfeld struck (at least) two publishing contracts in France with Gallimard and made contracts for two books with Montaigne.

On May 27, 1939, two days after Fein worked out the final settlement, he sent a letter, as Giese's heir, to Montaigne asking if royalties were pending from the two

dass damals mehrere Werke erschienen, bei denen Hirschfeld offensichtlich nicht als Autor beteiligt war, sondern nur seinen Namen zur Verfügung stellte. Bei zwei Werken des Arztes und Schriftstellers Berndt Götz scheint dies der Fall gewesen zu sein (Das erotische Weltbild, Dresden 1929; Sexualgeschichte der Menschheit, Berlin 1929)". See also Herrn 2022, 403.

115 Herrn 2022, 404.

116 Email (dated Dec. 18, 2010) from Eva Tichauer to the author. See also email (dated Dec. 17, 2010) from Eva Tichauer to the author: "Der beste Studenten Freund meines Vaters war der bekannte Dr. Bernd Götz (Autor einer Sexualgeschichte der Menschheit). Er ass koscher bei meiner Grossmutter. So wurde mein Vater mit meiner Mutter bekannt". Tichauer also told me that Tichauer and Götz ended their long friendship in Paris after a serious quarrel "shortly before the war", when Götz, after a stay in Prague and Palestine, left for Harvard with a woman other than his wife. However, there are no traces in the Harvard University archives of Götz ever arriving there. See email (dated Mar. 1, 2011) from Robin Carlaw (Harvard University Archives, Cambridge) to the author.

117 Tichauer, Jul. 1, 1926; Oct. 1, 1926; Feb. 1, 1927.

118 Bergemann, Dose, Keilson-Lauritz, & Dubout 2019, f. 53/97.

119 Email (dated Dec. 16, 2010) from Eva Tichauer to the author: "J'ai terminé ma scolarité lycéenne au pair dans une famille juive de médecins à Orléans de 1934 à 1936 et ne revenais à Paris que pour les vacances: d'où mon ignorance!" She did remember Rudolph Breitscheid (1874–1944) and her father working with Leonhard Auerbach who, hidden by his German wife, survived the war.

120 MZA, Brno, fonds C 107, Německý úřední soud Brno (Deutsches Amtsgericht Brünn), kart. n° 256, sign. 5aV 3/41, f. 29b: "Vyhražuji si doplniti tento seznam po případě, že by tu bylo nějakých nároků pozůstavitele z výtěžků knih, vydaných v Paříži u nakladatelství Gallimard a Montaigne".

books they published. The publisher Fernand Aubier replied three days later and was, to put it mildly, not impressed: “We owe Mr. Hirschfeld nothing since April 1936, when everything was settled. Since that date we have not made any printing of Mr. Hirschfeld’s works nor will we ever make any more”.[121] As we have seen, the publisher lost a considerable sum of money on *Education sexuelle*, published in 1934, because Hirschfeld’s coauthor, Ewald Bohm, demanded more payment. Even three years later, the publisher had clearly not forgotten this. According to Editions Montaigne, all contractual dues had been completely fulfilled, even for the second Hirschfeld book they published, *Le sexe inconnu*. This claim was repeated in 1956 when François Herzfelder asked for an update about possible royalties for Hirschfeld’s books.[122]

Fein likely wrote a similar letter to Gallimard in May 1939. By then he would have realized that, having lost his income as a Jewish lawyer, any income from the royalties of Hirschfeld’s books would be useful. But it is not known if any money came from Gallimard either. We have also seen that many of Hirschfeld’s French books were only published after his death in 1935. The book *Le Tour du monde d’un sexologue* was actually published after Giese’s death, in the summer of 1938.[123] Two excerpts from *Le Tour du monde d’un sexologue* were also published in March 1938 in the magazine *Voilà* as part of the “Eros en voyage” series.[124] It is not known whether Giese had any say in this publication of Hirschfeld’s last book, or if he or Fein ever received any money for it, but it seems not.[125] As the settlement of the Hirschfeld estate shows, Gallimard actually claimed money back in 1935–36 because they viewed the contract as breached because of Hirschfeld’s death. Lastly, it is interesting that, in the final settlement, Fein only mentioned income from Hirschfeld’s French books. Does this mean that he thought all the accounts with other foreign publishers were settled, or had he simply overlooked them? Another reason for Fein’s focusing exclusively on French publishers might have been the fact that he spoke no English, or only very little.

[121] IMEC Abbaye d’Ardenne, Saint-Germain-la-Blanche-Herbe, fonds Aubier-Montaigne, P 7.1. Service éditorial, folder Magnus Hirschfeld, cote 658ABM/16/18, letter (dated May 30, 1939) Editions Montaigne to Karl Fein: “Nous ne devons plus rien à M. Hirschfeld depuis le mois d’avril 1936 où tout a été réglé. Depuis cette date nous n’avons fait aucun tirage des ouvrages de M. Hirschfeld et nous n’en ferons jamais d’autres”.

[122] IMEC Abbaye d’Ardenne, Saint-Germain-la-Blanche-Herbe, fonds Aubier-Montaigne, P 7.1. Service éditorial, folder Magnus Hirschfeld, cote 658ABM/16/18, letter (dated Jul. 23, 1956) François Herzfelder to Editions Montaigne. Did Herzfelder hope to use these royalties to help finance his ongoing concern in the Hirschfeld estate? Strictly speaking, he was not entitled to any royalties. That said, the avalanche of pirated editions of Hirschfeld’s books after the war is simply astounding, as though publishers thought them out of copyright. Furthermore, it is quite striking that Hirschfeld’s French books, especially, were widely translated abroad after the war. It would require further study to determine if the publisher Gallimard was in any way involved. See, for example, the Spanish translation of *L’Âme et l’amour* that came out in Argentina in 1946 (published by Partenón) under the title *El alma y el amor*; and the Romanian translation of the same book under the title *Trupul si dragostea* in 1947 (published by Forum). Cf. Steakley 2021, 149, who missed the Romanian translation. For more information on some pirated English-language editions (including one that appeared in 1932, when Hirschfeld was still alive), see Dose 2014, 9.

[123] The book was printed on June 15, 1938. See Hirschfeld 1938b, [257]. The book was advertised in some French newspapers, e.g. *Le Populaire*, Aug. 17, 1938, 6; *L’Œuvre*, Sep. 25, 1938, 6; *L’Homme libre*, Oct. 1, 1938, 2.

[124] *Voilà* 364, Mar. 11, 1938; *Voilà* 365, Mar. 18, 1938.

[125] We have already noted that Gallimard’s more benevolent cooperation in opening its company archives on this (long ago) matter would be helpful.

[126] Hirschfeld & Dose 2013, f. 70/152; f. 71/154 n. 413; Herrn 2022, 367. In 1932–33, Bernhard Schapiro intended to oust Hirschfeld from this agreement or sue him.

[127] MZA, Brno, fonds C 107, Německý úřední soud Brno (Deutsches Amtsgericht Brünn), kart. n° 256, sign. 5aV 3/41, f. 17: “Pohledávka proti panu Tscherniakovi [*sic*] z Brusselu [*sic*] o níž vede se spor[nch?] (cca 5.000 Frs. belgických)”.

[128] Diary of Eugen Wilhelm, carnet 39, entry (dated Jul. 25, 1936–Sep. 26, 1936 and Oct. 3, 1936): “Giese

LAZARE TCHERNIAK

Another element on the income side of the inheritance was not mentioned by Karl Fein in his sworn affidavit of assets and liabilities. This concerned the income from licenses for the distribution of the Titus Pearls potency pills, a lucrative benefit that Giese had also inherited from Hirschfeld, and whose not insignificant income he transferred to Fein in his own will. In 1926–27, Hirschfeld agreed a shared, licensed income from Titus Pearls.[126]

The April 1934 registration of death (*úmrtní zápis, Todesfallsaufnahme*) did mention an unresolved dispute about money, tied to the sex pills, with a man living in Brussels named Lazare Tscherniak [*sic*]: "The claim against Mr. Tscherniak from Brussels, which is the subject matter of a dispute (ca. 5,000 Belgian Fr.[ancs])".[127] Eugen Wilhelm, who visited Giese in Brno in the summer of 1936, gave the best account of what was at stake here: "Giese has finally received his share of Hirschfeld's inheritance [...], Hirschfeld having also bequeathed his license rights to him. Giese is claiming fees from a man named Tscherniak in Brussels, who holds them for Belgium. He nevertheless refuses under all kinds [of] pretexts. Extensive correspondence has already taken place between him and the executor [Herzfelder]. Fein, the lawyer, is also taking care of the case. I am offering to write to this Tscherniak and, if the transaction does not succeed, to entrust a Brussels lawyer to take it to trial".[128] It is not known if this actually ever went to trial. In a December 1937 letter to Ernst Maass, Giese mentioned a court hearing in France, likely planned for some time in 1938, regarding the Hirschfeld inheritance, to which Li Shiu Tong was invited to be heard as co-heir. The hearing possibly never took place since, by December 1937, Li Shiu Tong refused all contact with Giese and the people working on the Hirschfeld estate.[129] This hearing may have been related to the financial dispute with Tcherniak, since he owned the license for France as well. It is possible that Theodore Tichauer's above-mentioned unexplained June 1937 bill may have been related to this dispute. Li Shiu Tong's refusal to help Giese in his attempt to make Tcherniak pay was likely another reason why Giese experienced more and more despair in Brno.

Lazare Tcherniak (sometimes also spelled "Tscherniak") was born in 1895 in the Russian city of Smolensk, where he also began his schooling. He left Smolensk in 1912 to continue his business studies in Antwerp (Belgium). When the war broke out, in 1914, he tried to join the Belgian armed forces, but the authorities would not allow him. He then decided to go to London where he worked for two years as a secretary for the Old Strand Chemical and Trading Company, Inc. In 1916, he returned to Russia

a enfin reçu sa part d'héritage de Hirschfeld [...], Hirschfeld lui ayant aussi légué ses droits de licence. Giese réclame les tantièmes d'un nommé Tscherniak à Bruxelles qui les détient pour la Belgique. Celui-ci néanmoins refuse sous toutes sortes [de] prétextes. Grande correspondance a déjà eu lieu avec lui et l'exécuteur testamentaire [Herzfelder]. L'avocat Fein s'occupe aussi de l'affaire, je m'offre à écrire à ce Tscherniak et si une transaction n'intervient de charger un avocat de Bruxelles du procès". The search for further information about Tcherniak and his company in Belgian archives proved impossible. The archives of the Rechtbank van Koophandel and the Handelsregister Brussels were destroyed when the retreating Germans, in September 1944, set fire to the immense building of the Palace of Justice (*Justitiepaleis, Palais de Justice*) in Brussels. See https://www.belgiumwwii.be/nl/belgie-in-oorlog/gebeurtenissen/1944-09-03-brand-in-het-justitiepaleis.html (accessed Aug. 10, 2020). In the Federale Overheidsdienst (FOD) Economie, K.M.O., Middenstand en Energie – Algemene leiding Regulering en Organisatie van de Markt – Dienst voor de Intellectuele Eigendom / SPF Economie, P.M.E., Classes Moyennes et Energie – Direction générale Régulation et Organisation du Marché – Office de la Propriété intellectuelle, staff was only prepared to go to the basement of the building (where the relevant archives were located) if I had a certain and precise date for a Belgian license agreement (visit, July 2011). At present, only a part of these archives, the Uitvindersbrevetten (inventors' patents), have been transferred to the Rijksarchief-Archives de l'État in Brussels. See email (dated Aug. 5, 2020) from Luc Vandeweyer (Rijksarchief Brussel-Archives de l'État à Bruxelles) to the author.

129 We will return to Li Shiu Tong's explicit refusal to cooperate with Karl Giese later. See chapter 14, p. 511.

to join the military. In 1918, because of the aggravated political situation brought about by the Bolshevik Revolution, he left his home country once again. He returned to London where he worked again for his old firm. In 1921, he returned to Belgium where he was head of the Belgian branch of the Old Strand Chemical and Trading Company, Inc. That same year, he married his first wife, Yvonne Williame (1900–?), whom he divorced in 1935. In 1927, Tcherniak was naturalized as a Belgian citizen [ill. 6].[130] In Brussels, he started to work for Santonine, an auxiliary Belgian branch (*succursale*) of his British firm. Later on, one finds mention of presumably his own business in the Belgian phonebook: "Tcherniak Elazer, produits pharmaceutiques", a firm listed under this name until 1969 and located at 63 Rue du Houblon (Hopstraat), Brussels 1000.[131] After 1969, Tcherniak's name disappears from the phonebook.[132]

"Lazar Tcherniak Brussels" also appears in an online list of the Holocaust Era Insurance Registry of the California Department of Insurance,[133] which, of course, shows that Tcherniak was Jewish. Since his name did not show up in any Holocaust deaths database, I realized he must have fled the European continent during the war. After some searching, I found that he lived and worked in Argentina during the war.[134] In 1945, Tcherniak was the vice president of the Chemotecnica-Sintyal S.A. factory in Buenos Aires.[135] Judging from travel records on Ancestry.com, Tcherniak traveled between Argentina and England until 1958 at the latest, in the company of his second, German-born wife Lucie Tillmanns (1902–?) whom he married in 1937 and with whom he lived on and off in London after the war.[136]

Tcherniak was not the first Titus Pearls distributor in Belgium. I found the first advertisement for Titus Pearls, distributed by the Pharmacie de la Paix in Brussels, in a January 1931 newspaper.[137] Later that year, in November 1931, Tcherniak reached a licensing agreement with the Titus GmbH factory in Berlin-Pankow (which produced the powder for the sex pills) that he would be the sole Titus Pearls distributor in Belgium and France.[138] Judging from the newspaper advertisements alone, Tcherniak took over the distribution of the sex pills in Belgium, in February 1934 at the earliest.[139]

130 Most of the information on Tcherniak's life was taken from Rijksarchief Brussels, Ministerie van Justitie, Bestuur der Openbare Veiligheid, Dienst Vreemdelingenpolitie, file on Lazare Tcherniak (born 1895), individueel dossier nr. 1.194.274; and the file on Yvonne Williame (1900–?) from Archief van de stad Brussel, Administratief Archief, Burgerlijke stand en Bevolking, Vreemdelingenbureau, file number 136.86. There is mention of one child, Raphaela Williame (1934–?), whom Tscherniak did not recognize, probably not unjustifiedly, as his daughter. Tcherniak divorced Yvonne Williame on June 21, 1935 in Schaarbeek.

131 Until 1934, Tcherniak's business address had been 6 Rue Alsace Lorraine in Ixelles/Elsene (Brussels). Starting in 1938, we also find the address 50 Rue des commerçants (Koopliedenstraat) in Brussels.

132 *Annuaire du commerce et de l'industrie de Belgique*, I, Bruxelles et son banlieue 1969: 977.

133 See http://www.insurance.ca.gov/0100-consumers/0300-public-programs/0100-holocaust-insur/upload/T.pdf and http://www.insurance.ca.gov/0100-consumers/0300-public-programs/0100-holocaust-insur/ (accessed Apr. 1, 2013). That his name was not in the database of the Archief- en documentatiedienst Oorlogsslachtoffers van de F.O.D. Sociale Zekerheid (Service des Victimes de la Guerre, S.P.F. Sécurité Sociale) in Brussels (http://warvictims.fgov.be/nl/) was further indication that Tcherniak escaped the Holocaust. See email (dated Jun. 13, 2011) from Sylvie Vander Elst (Archief- en documentatiedienst Oorlogsslachtoffers, F.O.D. Sociale Zekerheid, Brussels) to the author.

134 His name, spelled as Lazaro Tcherniak, shows up in a 1942 issue of *Boletín Oficial de la República Argentina*, 14.407, Sep. 9, 1942.

135 *The Chemist and Druggist*, Oct. 20, 1945, 401.

136 Lucie Tillmanns, born in Remscheid (North Rhine-Westphalia, Germany), was the daughter of Ernst Tillmanns and Helene Hasenclever. Her mother's family was probably not related to Walter Hasenclever (1890–1940), Hirschfeld's good friend, a writer born in Aachen.

137 *Het Laatse Nieuws*, Oct. 25, 1935, 10. When researching Titus Pearls in Belgium, I only checked the main Belgian newspapers available in the digital repository of the Belgian National Library in Brussels in 2012.

138 Dose 2019, 17 n. 36.

139 I found the first advertisement for the product distributed by Tcherniak (63 Rue du Houblon) in the newspaper *La Wallonie*, Feb. 17, 1934, 9. Starting in 1936, advertisements for the product in the Flemish newspapers provided a new contact address: 50 Rue des commerçants (Koopmanstraat), Brussels.

It is noteworthy that advertisements for the sex pills in Belgium (and thus also their distribution?) seems to have come to a complete halt in January 1939, less then a year after Giese's death, when a final advertisement for Titus Pearls appeared in a Walloon newspaper.[140]

I also found advertisements for Titus Pearls in four 1930 Czechoslovak periodicals and newspapers, but these were initiated by the Titus GmbH factory in Berlin-Pankow that produced the pills. Those interested could order the brochure "New Life" (*Neues Leben*) for 5 Czech crowns [ill. 7].[141] One advertisement claimed that the pills were sold in all pharmacies in Czechoslovakia.[142] This shows, at the very least, that Czechoslovakia was viewed as another possible market for the sex pills. Whether or not this is reliable information, the Brno police claimed, in February 1938, that Giese intended to work as a commercial representative in Czechoslovakia for Tcherniak's firm. Most likely, Giese had told them that.[143]

The sum of the assets and liabilities in the final settlement of the Giese inheritance (*Abhandlung*) meant that, in the end, Karl Fein received goods with an estimated value of 1,477 Czech crowns, approximately three times the monthly rent for Giese's Brno apartment. So, all in all, Fein did not receive much from Giese's estate.[144]

GIESE'S DECISION TO MAKE KARL FEIN HIS HEIR

Let us now take a brief look at Karl Giese's decision to will the Institute materials, the royalties from Hirschfeld's books and the licensed potency pills to Karl Fein. Was Fein's procrastination in drafting the final settlement – it took him a full year – an indication that he found the Giese inheritance a real burden? We have seen that Giese clearly sensed that he was increasingly in danger, with Germany's March 1938 annexation of Austria as the dramatic high point. A fear that was not without basis. We have mentioned the Gestapo document that reveals that the National Socialists were clearly aware that Giese was living in Brno and that he had served as Hirschfeld's personal secretary. His name might indeed have been on a list of people to be arrested in the event of a German invasion of Czechoslovakia. But Giese must also have been quite aware that, as a Jewish man, Karl Fein would have faced mounting problems caused by Nazi ideology, and that keeping the Hirschfeld materials would be a difficult and risky matter for him. Since Fein was a key figure in the buy-back operation that recovered some of the Institute materials, in the last months of 1933, he must have known that Magnus Hirschfeld was a showpiece enemy of the Nazis and that anyone associated with Hirschfeld could be in jeopardy. Did Giese saddle Fein with a thankless task that he could not perform himself? A clause in Giese's will is perhaps telling in this regard: "I [Karl Giese] ask him [Karl Fein] to accept this bequest and to preserve and administer it, *as far as possible* [my italics], in the spirit

However, the phonebook continued to list Tcherniak's firm at the Rue du Houblon address until 1969. Of course, it's possible that Tcherniak used two addresses. The Rue du Houblon address was given in the advertisements in the Walloon French-language newspaper *La dernière heure* until December 1938. After that, the 50 Rue des commerçants (Koopmanstraat) address was used there as well.

140 *La dernière heure*, Jan. 23, 1939, 3.

141 The advertisement appeared in issues of *Salon*, Jun. 15, 1930, 1h; Jul. 15, 1930, 37; Aug 15, 1930, 1d. The same advertisement also appeared in 1930 in the Czechoslovak magazines *Letem světem* and *Domov a svět*. I also saw advertisements in the newspaper *Der Tag* for the years 1932 and 1934.

142 See, for example, *Der Tag*, Mar. 31, 1932, 3.

143 MZA, Brno, fonds B 40, Zemský úřad Brno (Landesbehörde in Brünn), letter (dated Feb. 10, 1938) Policejní ředitelství v Brně to Zemský úřad Brno, kart. n° 2138, sign. 5274/38, f. 2: "Šetřením bylo však zjištěno, že Giese se vědeckou prací nezabývá, nýbrž hledá si zde zaměstnání a již navázal jednání s fou. L. Tcherniak, továrna na léčiva v Bruselu a tuto míní zde zastupovati" (The investigation has confirmed that Giese is not pursuing scientific research here [Brno] but he is looking for work and has already begun dealing with a firm called L. Tcherniak, a pharmaceutical factory located in Brussels, which he intends to represent here).

144 The final settlement of the Giese inheritance is reproduced in the addenda (n° 8).

of the deceased, who was also dear to him".[145] Giese seems to have been aware that he was burdening Fein – to some extent at least – by bequeathing him the remainder of Hirschfeld's estate.

What remains unclear is whether Fein had somehow seen Giese's suicide coming. Had Giese spoken about or even hinted his intention to Karl Fein or did it come as a complete surprise? Fein's first reaction on quickly viewing Giese's will suggests that the suicide caught him by surprise and that he had no idea that Giese had bequeathed everything he owned to him alone. So we do not really know whether Fein was happy about Giese appointing Fein as the sole custodian of Hirschfeld's materials. Of course, Fein could simply refuse the bequest. But it also seems clear that Fein would never have even contemplated this option and that Giese was well aware of this. Giese's will beseeched Karl Fein to accept the Hirschfeld/Giese legacy "in the spirit of the deceased, who was also dear to him" (*im Sinne des auch ihm teuren Verstorbenen*).[146] In a text from 1937, Giese mentions that Fein, in turn, also had the favour and confidence of Hirschfeld.[147] Giese entrusted Fein with the materials, the royalties from Hirschfeld's books and the medical licenses, knowing that he and Fein shared an affection for Hirschfeld and the cause of sexual liberation. Some would call this emotional blackmail. We may also suppose that Giese had good reasons to bequeath these materials specifically to Karl Fein and not someone else. Why did he not choose Josef Weisskopf or Li Shiu Tong, for example? In Giese's eyes, the Brno lawyer apparently represented the best guarantee that the materials would be in good hands and taken care of. That Giese saddling him with an unwanted burden did not make Karl Fein suddenly averse to Hirschfeld's gay liberation cause seems to be shown by one of Fein's subsequent actions.

145 MZA, Brno, fonds C 152, Okresní soud civilní Brno (Bezirksgericht für Zivilsachen Brünn), stamp (dated Mar. 23, 1938), ad DV 206/38/2, sign. s.l. 69/38: "Ich [Karl Giese] bitte ihm [Karl Fein], dieses Vermächtnis anzunehmen und es *soweit es ihm irgend möglich ist* [my italics] im Sinne des auch ihm teuren Verstorbenen zu erhalten und zu verwalten".

146 See the text of Karl Giese's last will in chapter 11, p. 376-77.

147 See n° 9 in the addenda, p. 741 [p. 4, f. 7b].

148 *Hlas* was restarted in October 1936 and lasted until January 1937, when seven further issues were published. I count this as the third attempt to launch a gay magazine in pre-war Czechoslovakia. For a long time, these issues were misplaced in the racks of the Klementinum in Prague and were not consultable. The Danish researcher Harald Hartvig Jepsen was still able to see these, somewhat irregularly published seven issues in the Klementinum when doing research in the 1990s. I inquired with him about this in an email sent on February 6, 2021, but he refrained from replying. One issue of the 1936–37 run is known and in private hands, see Seidl et al. 2012, 190. In January 2024, on initiative of Esra Paul Afken und Raimund Wolfert of the MHG, Berlin, a website was launched, giving further context on these precursor Czech gay magazines (authors, contents, context, illustrations), see https://hlas-queermagazin.de/, accessed 23/01/2024. They managed to retrieve the "lost" issues of the years 1936 and 1937 in their dealings with the Klementinum in Prague. It is very probable that there was only a single issue of *Hlas přírody* since there is a letter from František Jelínek (a member of the editorial staff) pasted inside the copy of the Klementinum, which states that there was only one issue. That said, until February 2021, the online Souborný katalog ČR (Union Catalogue of the Czech Republic) noted that in the (inaccessible) Národní konzervační fonds in the Prague National Library (Klementinum) there were two issues from the magazine's first year, while the Klementinum's online catalogue noted that (publicly accessible) copies had only one issue. I inquired about this discrepancy with the Klementinum in February 2021 and they replied to me this was a mistake. The Národní konzervační fonds contains only one issue. See emails (dated Feb. 8, 2021 and Feb. 9, 2021) from Karolína Košťálová (Klementinum, National Library of the Czech Republic, Prague) to the author. See also Seidl et al. 2012, 190. Only the Vědecká knihovna Olomouc (Olomouc Research Library) has another copy of this single *Hlas přírody* issue. Since Karl Giese was in Brno at the time when *Hlas* was restarted, in 1936–37, I wondered whether he contributed to some issues. After all, we have seen that, in 1934, Hirschfeld and Giese had a conflict with the Czech gay magazine *Nový hlas* and Karl Meier. I checked the contents of *Hlas* for the years 1936 and 1937 but saw that Giese's name was not there.

149 *Hlas přírody*, Sep. 1938, 2.

150 Archiv Kurt Hiller Gesellschaft, Neuss, letter from Karl Giese to Kurt Hiller (Apr. 27, 1937, 1–2) and Bondy, Oct. 13, 1922, 4. For an example of Bondy's (partial) compassion for homosexuals, see Bondy 1921, 23.

KARL FEIN AND KURT HILLER: THE LAST HIRSCHFELD MEN STANDING

Six months after Giese's death, in September 1938, there was a fourth attempt to establish a gay magazine in Czechoslovakia, during the so-called Second Republic. After *Hlas,* in 1931–32, *Nový hlas,* in 1932–34, and another attempt to relaunch *Hlas,* in 1936–37, the first and most likely last issue of *Voice of Nature: Organ of the "League for Sexual Reform"* (*Hlas přírody: orgán "Ligy pro sexuální reform"*) was published [ill. 8].[148] Here again, there was an appeal to German-speaking "comrades and like-minded fellows" (*Kameraden und Artgenossen*) to subscribe to the magazine. If enough did so, then they would consider inserting a "German supplement" (*deutsche Beilage*), even that an "extra German edition of the magazine" (*deutsche Extra-Ausgabe des Blattes*) would eventually become an option.[149]

We already suggested that Giese had been in contact with some gay activist protagonists in Czechoslovakia in the early 1930s. He certainly knew Hugo Bondy, a straight man who was sometimes dubbed "the Czechoslovak Magnus Hirschfeld" and who described himself as a pupil of Hirschfeld.[150] In an April 1937 letter to Kurt Hiller, Giese wrote that he knew that some people were already intending to have a fourth go at another gay magazine.[151]

Karl Fein wrote a piece for *Hlas přírody.* Fein wrote on the same subject as in his first two *Nový hlas* articles: the influence of the Czechoslovak penal code on the lives of homosexuals. On this occasion, he was commenting on paragraph 10 of a proposal drafted by the Ministry of Justice to reform regulations relating to (homo) sexual offenses.[152] He was not happy about the proposed amendments, which only proposed a slightly less harsh punishment of consensual gay sex. Karl Fein wrote: "Is this what Krafft-Ebing, Magnus Hirschfeld, Forel and others fought for? Is this the goal of the 50-year-old movement to move the scientific acceptance of homosexuality into practical life? Who will be helped if the law confirms that voluntary sexual intercourse between two people of the same sex is still an offense and therefore an anti-social act? By using the words 'abuse' and 'fornication', the law itself expresses the lawmakers' clear moral disapproval of sexual intercourse between two people of the same sex. So the old prejudices are embedded in the text of the law itself. However, the most important thing is that any legal system which deems voluntary sexual intercourse between two people of the same sex illegal provides fertile ground for the growth of blackmail".[153] He also felt that the anti-gay stance of Nazi Germany had reached Czechoslovakia: "It seems that the evil wind blowing from abroad has swept away the more progressive findings and scientific opinions".[154] He ended this text by implicitly referring to Hirschfeld's well-known adage "through science to justice": "We plead with all enlightened and truth-loving people across the whole of our republic to raise their voices and show the world that human moral values are still alive and that the rule of darkness cannot and will not be the fate of our culture and civilization".[155] Did Fein have the impression that, now that Giese and Hirschfeld

[151] Archiv Kurt Hiller Gesellschaft, Neuss, letter from Karl Giese to Kurt Hiller (Apr. 27, 1937, 1).

[152] Fein 1938, 6–7.

[153] Fein 1938, 7: "Pro to bojoval Krafft-Ebing, Magnus Hirschfeld, Forel a j., k tomu existovalo posledních 50 let hnutí, jež mělo za úkol dopomoci vědeckému poznání stejnopohlavnosti k tomu, aby se uplatnilo v životě praktickém? Komu se poslouží tím, jestliže zákon prohlásí dobrovolný pohlavní styk osob stejného pohlaví jako dříve za trestný, a tím za nesociální čin? Již ve formulaci zákona, ve slově "zneužije" a potom ve slově "smilstvo" dává se na jevo, že zákonodárce projevuje oproti pohlavnímu styku osob téhož pohlaví svůj mravní nesouhlas. Jsou tedy staré společenské předsudky zakotveny dokonce v textu zákona. Co však z hlediska praktického jest nejdůležitější: každé zákonodárství, které prohlašuje dobrovolný pohlavní styk osob téhož pohlaví za trestný, skýtá nejúrodnější půdu pro plevel vyděračství".

[154] Fein 1938, 7: "Zdá se, že zlý vítr, vanoucí z jiného kraje, odvanul i v tomto směru lepší poznatky a věděcké názory".

[155] Fein 1938, 7: "Vy všichni osvícení a pravdymlovní lidé v celé republice, prosíme Vás, pozvedněte svůj hlas a ukažte světu, že lidské morální hodnoty ještě

were dead, he was one of the last carrying on Hirschfeld's legacy? His text (and his willingness to contribute to the issue) clearly shows that he had not lost his belief in the gay emancipation cause. The onerous task Giese imposed on him may have been something of a burden but clearly did not affect his ideological convictions. So Giese was right to count on Fein being equally enamored with Hirschfeld and his gay activist cause.

The same *Hlas přírody* issue also contains an article written by Kurt Hiller, translated into Czech.[156] Hiller similarly appealed to Hirschfeld, reminding his readers at the beginning of his text that Hirschfeld would have turned seventy in 1938. But, given how things were evolving, especially in Nazi Germany, he asked rhetorically if Hirschfeld's activist life had been a wasted effort: "Did he live in vain?" (*Žil nadarmo?*).[157] In his short article, Hiller basically denounced the hypocrisy and double standards in Nazi Germany, where high-ranking, closeted homosexuals were immune, but homosexuality itself was harshly persecuted. The persecution of ordinary homosexuals acted as a smoke screen for these high-ranking homosexuals [ill. 9].[158]

It is tempting to think that Hiller and Fein met because of the *Hlas přírody* issue, but Hiller already knew Fein. In a 1936 letter to the gay writer Bruno Vogel, Hiller wrote about a "boy" (*Burschen*) who visited him when he was living as an exile in Prague, naming this boy "Koliste". It seems likely this was indeed Karl Fein who, as we have seen, lived at 35 Koliště (Glacis) starting in October 1936.[159] Hiller was then around fifty years old and Fein was only nine years younger ... Hiller also sent a letter to Karl Fein in April 1937.[160] The fact that Hiller and Fein were both jurists may have helped them get along. Maybe it was also no coincidence that the first three articles in the September 1938 issue of *Hlas přírody* were all written by jurists. The first was written by the long-time Czechoslovak gay activist and lawyer František Čeřovský, the second and third were by Hiller and Fein, respectively.[161]

Kurt Hiller was also in contact with the German-speaking left-wing intellectual elite of Brno.[162] In November 1934, the month after he began his exile in Czechoslovakia, he gave a lecture titled "What Will Save Us from War?" (*Was rettet uns vor dem Krieg?*) in Brno, at the invitation of the German Society for Science and Art (Deutsche Gesellschaft für Wissenschaft und Kunst). The latter association was founded in 1919, and had its offices in Hugo Iltis's Volkshochschule, starting in 1930. Iltis, Hans Tugendhat and Lothar Spielmann, one of the organizers of the 1932 WLSR

žijí a že vláda tmy nemůže být a není definitivní osud naší kultury a civilisace".

[156] Hiller 1938, 5–6. The original German text was published earlier in 1938 in the Paris-based exile periodical *Sozialistische Warte*. I thank Siegfried Tornow for alerting me to this. Lützenkirchen's Hiller bibliography includes the German text, but not the Czech translation in *Hlas přírody*. See Lützenkirchen 2000, 175, 197.

[157] Hiller 1938, 5. In German: "Hat er umsonst gelebt?" Hiller already asked the same despairing question in 1935, in a memorial text for Hirschfeld: "War unsere Arbeit, war seines Lebens Arbeit vergeblich?" See Hiller 1935, 8. The latter Hiller text is not mentioned in Lützenkirchen's Hiller bibliography. See Lützenkirchen 1992.

[158] Hiller 1938. A similar ideological mechanism is at work in the Catholic Church, whose usual professed anti-homosexuality policy acts as a cover for the daily homosexual activities of a significant part of the church hierarchy. For a recent example of this view, see Martel 2019.

[159] I thank Raimund Wolfert for alerting me to the existence of Kurt Hiller's letter to Bruno Vogel. See email (dated May 27, 2013) from Raimund Wolfert to the author.

[160] Archiv Kurt Hiller Gesellschaft, Neuss, letter (dated Apr. 27, 1937, 1) from Karl Giese to Kurt Hiller.

[161] Čeřovský 1938, 3–4. One factor possibly indicates that, by 1938, Fein and Hiller were no longer in contact. In a text written after the war, Hiller said that Giese committed suicide in "Vienna or Brno". See Hiller 1948, 353. If Hiller and Fein had indeed known each other well (or were at least in correspondence), then it is very strange indeed that Hiller was not more precise about the city where Giese killed himself. In addition, in March 1938, Hiller was in Prague and must have read about Giese's suicide in Brno in one newspaper or another. This matter remains unresolved.

conference, were its leading members.[163] In 1927, the Emil-Waelsch-Fonds, named after the husband of Marianne Waelsch, Elise Brecher's sister, was set up within the association. At least two of the association's publications were published by the L. & A. Brecher bookstore.[164] It seems reasonable to suppose that Hiller and Karl Fein may have spoken as early as November 1934.

Contact between Karl Giese and Kurt Hiller, on the other hand, was not very good. In April 1937, Hiller tried to get in touch with Karl Giese (through Karl Fein) because an overseas contact (who had heard it from Hirschfeld) informed him that the Institute in Berlin had "recorded statements" (*protokollarischen Aussagen*) about Hitler's supposed homosexuality.[165] Hiller was intent on bringing this knowledge out into the open, and even wrote to Giese that doing so would secure him (Giese) a place in world history. But Giese deflected Hiller's request, offering counterarguments in two letters. He did not have these records, nor was he aware that they actually existed; they were just rumors. Even if Hiller could find the information somewhere, Giese maintained that it could not hurt Hitler, who had been accused of so many things already that any new charge would be meaningless. The Nazis used derogatory information when it suited them, as the case of Ernst Röhm proved. Finally, what good would it do the gay movement to bring out such information? Giese additionally made it clear to Hiller, who insisted on Giese looking more thoroughly through the papers he had in Brno to find these records, that he had no ambition to figure in world history as Hiller proposed.[166] We have already seen that Giese preferred to keep a low profile in Brno. The Gestapo itself observed that Giese did not act like a fully committed gay activist in Brno, even though, it also claimed, he certainly was one in his heart and soul. On the last letter that Giese sent in reply, in July 1937, Hiller added a handwritten note that he had not replied to Giese's previous letter.[167] Likely, this was the very last contact between Giese and Hiller before Giese's suicide in March 1938.[168]

Hiller's forceful article for the 1938 issue of *Hlas přírody* showed him choosing a more radical path than Giese's, deciding on a frontally attack against the hypocritical gay Nazi notables. Had Magnus Hirschfeld, whom Hiller invoked at the very beginning of his text, not fought all his life to lift the taboo on male homosexuality, pleading for

[162] See Soetaert 2024.

[163] See "Die ordentliche Jahres-Vollversammlung der Deutschen Gesellschaft für Wissenschaft und Kunst in Brünn – Deutschmährische Blätter n° 72", in *Tagesbote*, May 26, 1935, 2. For the announcement of the Hiller lecture held on November 26, 1934, see *Tagesbote*, Nov. 22, 1934, 7. This and other lectures were organized (and financed) by the Deutschen Frauenliga für Frieden und Freiheit (German Women's League for Peace and Freedom), the Deutschen Journalisten- und Schriftstellerverein Mährens und Schlesiens (German Journalists and Writers' Association of Moravia and Silesia) and the Individualpsychologischen Arbeitsgemeinschaft (Individual Psychological Working Group), the latter relying on Alfred Adler's work. As early as 1924, the far-right *Brünner Montagsblatt* complained that the German Society for Science and Art was mainly Jewish ("verjudeten Gesellschaft für Wissenschaft und Kunst"). See *Brünner Montagsblatt*, Nov. 1, 1924, 6.

[164] Soffé 1922; Kreisler 1922. See also the advertisement in *Tagesbote*, Jun. 6, 1937, 12.

[165] Archiv Kurt Hiller Gesellschaft, Neuss, letters (dated Apr. 27, 1937 and Jul. 12, 1937) from Karl Giese to Kurt Hiller; and letter (dated Apr. 29, 1937) from Kurt Hiller to Karl Giese. Hitler's name is not mentioned once in these three letters, but one can easily deduce that they were specifically referring to Adolf Hitler and his presumed homosexuality.

[166] Archiv Kurt Hiller Gesellschaft, Neuss, letter (dated Jul. 12, 1937, 1) from Karl Giese to Kurt Hiller: "Ganz privat bemerke ich noch, dass ich nicht genügend ambitionös [*sic*] bin, um mich durch solche Veröffentlichungen in das grosse weltgeschichtliche Geschehen einzuschalten".

[167] Archiv Kurt Hiller Gesellschaft, Neuss, letter (dated Jul. 12, 1937, 1) from Karl Giese to Kurt Hiller. To this day, and especially since the 2001 publication of Lothar Machtan's book on Hitler's presumed homosexuality, most people in the LGBT movement have found it unwise even to raise the subject of Hitler's possible homosexual orientation, and also consider the matter simply unproven. Like the UFO phenomenon, it has become a rather phantasmatic topic with both believers and nonbelievers. See also Beachy 2014, 243.

[168] Possibly, and being aware that Kurt Hiller's letters archive is incomplete, these are the only two letters that Giese sent to Hiller in the period between Hirschfeld's death, in 1935, and Giese's own death, in 1938.

its free expression and freedom from persecution? I consider Kurt Hiller's article one of the last key gay texts before the outbreak of World War II. Hiller's harsh outing tactics, indirectly describing (and thus publicly identifying) two gay Nazi notables, are reminiscent of Michelangelo Signorile's 1990s outing practices and of the fierce texts of Larry Kramer (1935–2020) in the gay newspaper *New York Native* during the AIDS crisis. Yet outing had already been practiced in Germany at the beginning of the twentieth century. I have analyzed Kurt Hiller's brief but dense text elsewhere.[169]

It is also important to note that the single issue of this magazine may have drawn notice in Berlin because of Hiller's fierce anti-Nazi text. Because Karl Fein was another of the periodical's contributors, openly critical of Nazism in his own text, this might have (further?) tainted his name for the Nazi intelligence services. Two months after the publication of the single issue of *Hlas přírody*, in November 1938, the Munich Agreement, reached between Nazi Germany and several European states, signed Czechoslovakia's death warrant. The Sudetenland was annexed by Germany immediately after. Kurt Hiller fled from Prague to London in December 1938.[170] The Czechoslovak League for Sexual Reform on a Sexual Scientific Basis (Československá liga pro sexuální reformu na sexuálně vědeckěm podkladě), the association that published *Hlas přírody*, was disbanded in April 1940, in accordance with a regulation issued by the National Socialists in 1939.[171]

169 For an analysis of this extraordinary text of Hiller, Soetaert 2015, 21-23, 41-43.

170 Soetaert 2015, 23.

171 NA, Praha, Ministerstvo vnitra I, Praha, nová registratura (Interior ministry), 1936-1953, kart. n° 5059, folder Ceskoslovenská liga pro sexuální reformu na sexuálně vědeckěm podkladě v Praze.

1. Franz Nawratil. August 1940.

Wir geben hiemit geziemend Nachricht von dem Ableben des

Pg. JUDr. Franz Nawratil, Rechtsanwalt

Mitglied des Aufsichtsrates

Wir verlieren in dem Verstorbenen einen treuen, bewährten Mitarbeiter, dem wir stets ein treues Andenken bewahren werden.

Aufsichtsrat,
Betriebsführung und Gefolgschaft der
Böhmisch-Mährischen Exportmalzfabriken-
Aktiengesellschaft.

2124

2. May 1942 obituary for Franz Nawratil, paid for by former colleagues. In the top left corner, there is the typical Runes symbol (Runen-Zeichen) used by some National Socialists to mark someone's death: three prongs pointing down (the symbol is inverted for a birth).

náměstí 18 svobody
V.DRESL
RADIO

3. Postcard of Liberty Square (Náměstí svobody, Freiheitsplatz) in Brno. Franz Nawratil's law office was at 1 Schlossergasse (Zámečnická) (corner building, far left), a side street issuing into the square. Špilberk (Spielberg) castle appears in the background. Postmarked June 23, 1940.

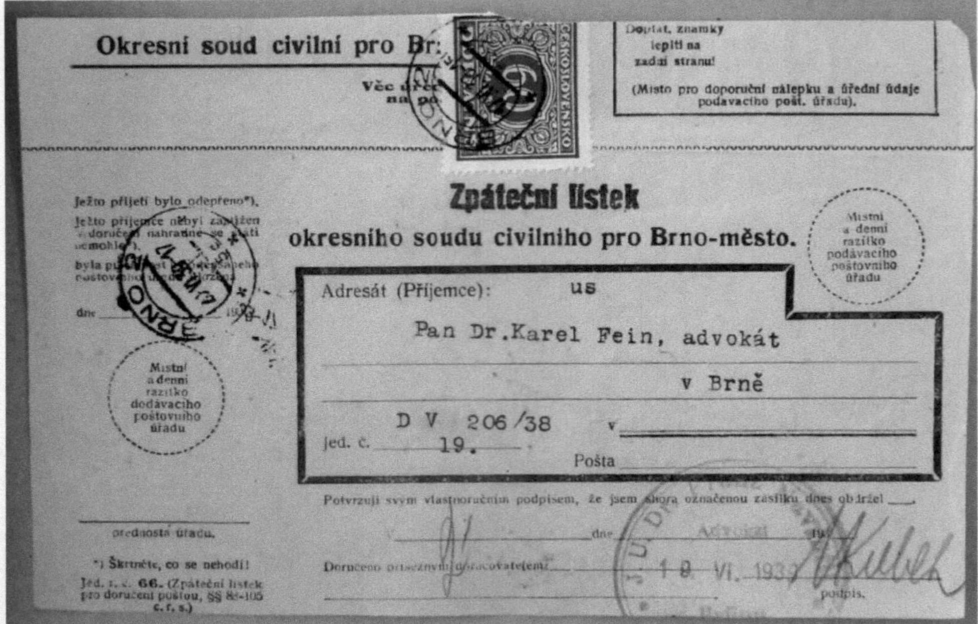

Okresní soud civilní pro Br:

Věc ... na po...

Doplat. známky lepiti na zadní stranu!

(Místo pro doporuční nálepku a úřední údaje podávacího pošt. úřadu).

Ježto přijetí bylo odepřeno*).

Zpáteční lístek

okresního soudu civilního pro Brno-město.

Místní a denní razítko podávacího poštovního úřadu

Adresát (Příjemce): us

Pan Dr.Karel Fein, advokát

v Brně

D V 206/38

Jed. č. 19.

v

Pošta

Místní a denní razítko dodávacího poštovního úřadu

Potvrzuji svým vlastnoručním podpisem, že jsem shora označenou zásilku dnes obdržel

dne 19

přednosta úřadu.

*) Škrtněte, co se nehodí!

Jed. č. 66. (Zpáteční lístek pro doručení poštou, §§ 86-105 c. ř. s.)

Doručeno oprávněným doručovatelem

19 VI. 193

podpis.

4. A registered mail reply stub sent by the Brno District Civil Court (Okresní soud civilní Brno, Bezirksgericht für Zivilsachen Brünn), dated June 17, 1939. It bears the stamp of Franz Nawratil's law office and is signed by one of his employees to confirm receipt.

5. The Palace of Justice in Brno, erected by Josef Nebehosteny's building company. 1920s–1930s.

6. *Lazare Tcherniak (sometimes also spelled Tscherniak). Ca. 1924.*

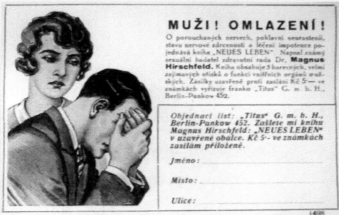

MUŽI! OMLAZENÍ!

O porouchaných nervech, pohlavní neurastenii, stavu nervové zdrcenosti a léčení impotence pojednává kniha „NEUES LEBEN". Napsal známý sexuální badatel zdravotní rada Dr. **Magnus Hirschfeld.** Kniha obsahuje 5 barevných, velmi zajímavých otisků o funkci vnitřních orgánů mužských. Zásilky uzavřené proti zaslání Kč 5·— ve známkách vyřizuje franko „Titus" G. m. b. H., Berlin-Pankow 452.

Objednací list: „Titus" G. m. b. H., Berlin-Pankow 452. Zašlete mi knihu Magnus Hirschfeld: „NEUES LEBEN" v uzavřené obálce. Kč 5·- ve známkách zasílám přiložené.

Jméno: ……

Místo: ……

Ulice: ……

1498

7. *"Men! Rejuvenation!" (Muži! Omlazení!). In 1930s Czechoslovakia as well, advertisements for Titus Pearls could be found in the press. In this case, the New Life (Neues Leben) brochure could be ordered from the Titus factory in Berlin-Pankow for 5 Czech crowns (paid for in stamps).*

HLAS PŘÍRODY

ORGÁN „LIGY PRO SEXUÁLNÍ REFORMU"

OBSAH

Český úvod.
Deutsche Einleitung.
Dr. Frant. Čeřovský: Boj o reformu tr. z.
Dr. Kurt Hiller: Případ tenisty Cramma.
Dr. Karel Fein: § 10. osnovy min. spravedlnosti.
Antonín Skládal: In memoriam Vojty Černého.
Frant. Jelínek: Dosti nás...
Jaroslav Hašek: Muž a žena v manželství.
Elaios: O žárlivosti. — Naše desatero.
Antinous: Všem, kteří obdrželi letáky Ligy.
Všelicos. — Literární koutek.
Provolání.

Ročník I. Září 1938. Číslo 1.

8. *Cover page of the September 1938 issue of Voice of Nature: Organ of the "League for Sexual Reform" (Hlas přírody: orgán "Ligy pro sexuální reformu"), the last Czechoslovak gay magazine to appear before World War II.*

9. *Photobooth picture of Kurt Hiller. December 1934.*

RUDOLF SCHNEIDER

13 The Holocaust Fates of Karl Fein and His Immediate Family

THE TUMULTUOUS POLITICAL SITUATION IN MARCH 1938

On March 16, 1938, only a few days after the annexation (*Anschluss*) of Austria, Giese committed suicide in Brno. In December 1938, Karl Fein informed the Brno District Civil Court that he had not been able to work on the final settlement of the Giese inheritance because of the tumultuous political situation after the *Anschluss*. Hitler's invasion of his native country prompted many Czechoslovak Jewish citizens in Vienna to flee home to Czechoslovakia. Among them were Karl Fein's older brother Gustav, his older sister Greta and their mother Helena Brecher, but only Gustav Fein (1889–1944?) and his mother, who lived with him in Vienna, actually returned to Brno in October 1938.[1] Karl Fein's older sister Greta Fein (1891–1942?) and her husband Rudolf Polatschek (1883–1942?) stayed in the Austrian capital.[2] It is unclear if this was of their own choice or because legal hurdles prevented them returning to Brno. In any case, the Czechoslovak authorities closed the border to Austrian refugees immediately after the annexation of Austria.[3] Since Rudolf Polatschek was a Jewish doctor, the couple lost their income soon after the annexation.[4]

We should not underestimate the immense pressure of this new wave of people flocking from Austria into Brno on the housing situation. It was the second such wave. The first, starting around 1933, was the influx of left-wing and Jewish immigrants from Germany, of which Karl Giese was a part. In October 1938, when the Germans annexed the Sudetenland, a third wave of refugees, this time Czechoslovaks, put even greater stress on the Brno housing market.[5]

[1] Gustav Fein lived with his mother at 10 Blechturmgasse, Vienna IV. See *Wiener Adressbuch – Lehmanns Wohnungsanzeiger* 1935, I: 258. He had married Alice Hanna Weill on March 19, 1922, and divorced her on May 25, 1932. Most likely the couple had no children. See email (dated Jun. 18, 2012) from Wolf-Erich Eckstein (Abteilung Matriken Israelitische Kultusgemeinde Wien/Vienna Jewish Records Office) to the author; however, the divorce date given, April 29, 1930, is incorrect. See also the certified German translation of the Czech marriage certificate for Gustav Fein and Herta Jirasková, Forschungsinstitut Brenner-Archiv, Universität von Innsbruck, Innsbruck, Nachlass Herta Fein-Erich Messing, Kassette 152. See also the Fein-Weill divorce file in MZA, Brno, fonds C 11, Krajský soud civilní Brno, kart. n° 433, sign. Ckla 572/1932. Karl Fein represented his brother in the divorce case. In 1909, Gustav Fein worked for the k.k privilegierten Österreichischen Länderbank in Vienna. See MZA, Brno, fonds C 152, Okresní soud civilní Brno (Bezirksgericht für Zivilsachen in Brünn), kart. n° 1817, sign. IV 1581/96, inheritance file Albert Fein, f. 32.

[2] Margarethe Polatschek lived with her Czechoslovak husband, Dr. Rudolf Polatschek, at 71 Margarethenstrasse in Vienna. They married on December 16, 1923 and most likely had no children. In a legal affidavit, issued at a Brno notary office, Karl Fein declared that he would look after his sister and her husband financially during their temporary stay in Brno. This document seems to indicate that some legal hurdles had to be overcome before the couple could move to Brno. See MZA, Brno, fonds C 156, Soukromí notáři Brno (1851–1951), archive of notary Otokar Kříž, protokol legalisační (dated Jun. 17, 1938) Karl Fein, sign. 16.107.

[3] Čapková & Frankl 2012, 60, 253–54; and the chapter titled "Nachtzug aus Wien". Briefly, I thought that her marriage meant that she might have lost her Czechoslovak citizenship, but her husband was born in Czechoslovakia as well. Rudolf Polatschek was born in Litomyšl (Leitomischl), located in the Pardubice region. See the Shoah-Opfer database at https://www.doew.at/ (accessed Feb. 6, 2021). In the database, the village is spelled Libomisl. For now the matter remains unresolved.

[4] Kater 1989, 199–200.

[5] On these Sudeten-Flüchtlinge (Sudeten refugees), see, for example, Čapková & Frankl 2012, 286.

Fein's claim that family matters left him with no time to work on the inheritance case was at least in part an excuse, since his brother's resident registration cards show that Gustav had arrived in Brno on October 1, 1938 already. He moved in with his brother Karl at his 35 Koliště address.[6] Their mother, Helena Brecher, arrived in Brno on October 10. She moved in with her younger sister, the widow Josefina Kohn (née Brecher, 1860-1942?),[7] but only stayed a few weeks with her.[8] At the end of October 1938, Helena Brecher moved in with her two sons at a new address, 2a Akademická (Akademiegasse). In order to be with his immediate family, Karl Fein left his 35 Koliště address where he had lived since 1936.[9] Karl Fein would move one more time – this time by himself – to another address in Brno on July 1, 1939, 9 Jesuitská (Jesuitengasse). He was living on his own earlier already, in May–June 1939, since his mother and brother had moved to Prague by then.[10] Three months later, on October 6, 1939, Karl Fein also left Brno, the city where he had spent most of his life.[11]

KARL FEIN AND THE BRNO GESTAPO

Fein had to deal with the Gestapo at least once in the preceding months but it is not known if he was imprisoned or even tortured by the Gestapo. It is unclear if the Nazis were aware of Karl Fein's writing for the gay magazines *Nový hlas* and *Hlas přírody*, his involvement in organizing the 1932 WLSR conference, or even of his homosexuality.

[6] AMB, Brno, fonds Z 1, resident registration card (dated Oct. 1, 1938) for Gustav Fein.

[7] Like Karl Fein's mother Helene, Josefina Kohn (née Brecher, 1860–1942?), was born in Prossnitz (Prostějov). She was the widow of Siegfried (Vítězslav) Kohn (1865–1931), her second husband, who is buried in the Brno Jewish cemetery in Brno in parcel 12, row 9, grave 9. For more information on Kohn's alimentation company, see Smutný 2012, 221. The couple had two children, Ida Kohn (1894–1942?) and Leo Kohn (1900–1941?), the latter becoming a lawyer who changed his name to Konrad in 1923. Leo Konrad married Gertruda Konradová (née Adlerová, 1908–1941?). She was deported together with her husband to Minsk on November 16, 1941, on transport "D", the very first Jewish transport from Brno. Ida Kohn married a lawyer named Alfred Pollak (1877–1942?). On March 23, 1942, both were sent from Brno to Terezín on transport "Ad", and from Terezín to Izbica on transport "Aq" on April 1, 1942. Less than two weeks later, on April 4, 1942, Josefina Kohn was sent to Terezín on transport "Ah" and, on October 19, 1942, further transferred from Terezín to Treblinka on transport "Bw".

[8] For a while, I mistakenly thought that Karl Fein's mother had moved in with another Brno family member, Truda Khanová (née Fein, 1890–1944). I thank Marianna Becková, Truda Khanová's daughter, for pointing out my error. The rather obvious family connection, the partly hidden signature (under an ink spot), and a barely legible house number on a resident registration card in the AMB, Brno, fonds Z 1, made me think that I saw "Truda Kahnová" on the resident registration card when in reality it was "Josefa Kohnová" who lived a little further along the same street, ulice Dra Bedřicha Macků (Dr-Bedřich-Macků-Gasse). Gertruda (or Truda) Kahnová was a sister of the elder Karl Fein, Karl Fein's cousin. See AMB, Brno, fonds Z 1, resident registration card (dated Oct. 10, 1938) for Helena Brecher.

[9] AMB, Brno, fonds Z 1, resident registration cards (all three dated Oct. 31, 1938) for Helena Brecher, Gustav Fein and Karl Fein. Curiously, until 1926, Karl Fein's aunt, the bookseller Elise Brecher, lived with her daughter Anna and her son Fritz in the house next door to Fein's new address, at 4 Akademická (Akademiegasse). But the archival sources also reveal an unexplained fact. According to another resident registration card, we can see that, before moving to the Akademická (Akademiegasse) address, Karl Fein lived (alone?) at 2a Falkensteinerova (Falkensteinergasse) from October 15, 1938 until October 31, 1938. See the resident registration card (dated Oct. 17, 1938) for Karl Fein in the AMB, Brno, fonds Z 1. There is no resident registration card for Gustav Fein showing that his brother or mother also moved to this Falkensteinerova (Falkensteinergasse) address.

[10] According to the resident registration cards for Gustav Fein and Helena Brecher in the AMB, Brno, fonds Z 1, Helena Brecher and Gustav Fein left Brno on June 6, 1939. However, other archival sources provide different dates for their arrival in Prague, in May and June 1939. This seems to indicate that mother and son did not move together from Brno to Prague.

[11] AMB, Brno, fonds Z 1, resident registration card (dated Jul. 1, 1939) for Karl Fein. See also NA, Praha, Policejní ředitelství Praha II, všeobecná spisovna, 1931–1940, kart. n° 5661, sign. F 271/9, Fein Karel JUDr 1894, f. 5, letter (dated Nov. 9, 1939 and Dec. 22, 1939) Okresní nemocenská pojišovna v Brně to Policejní ředitelství Praha. We mentioned in the note above that, according to a Brno archival record, Gustav Fein and/or Helena Brecher left Brno on June 6, 1939. That Karl Fein left Brno on October 6, 1939 may indicate that their departure dates were tied to an expiring rental contract.

If the Gestapo had access to Fein's Prague police file, then they would surely have been aware of the latter fact at least.

In September 1935, Karl Fein gave a radio talk titled "The New Race Law" (*Das neue Rassengesetz*). This was most likely very critical of the Nuremberg Race Laws issued by the National Socialist government in Germany in September 1935.[12] News of Fein's radio talk may have reached, by one channel or another, the German intelligence services. The simple fact that Fein was a lawyer was in any case reason enough for the Gestapo to arrest him. The Gestapo in Brno certainly took such measures, for example in the case of the apprentice lawyer Kurt Steel (whose name was then Otto Steklemacher) from Boskovice (Boskowitz), in the spring of 1939.[13] Artur Feldmann Sr., a lawyer and a good friend of Karl Fein, not only saw his house and art collection confiscated in the first days following the German invasion, but was also imprisoned for three months in 1940 and died the next year.[14] Lawyers, especially left-wing lawyers, were a harshly persecuted group. Karl Fein's former intern, Otto Schütz, fled Brno following the arrival of the Germans. Not coincidentally, and quite provocatively, in December 1940, the Gestapo made its headquarters in the former law faculty of Masaryk University [ill. 1].[15] As we have seen, the gay architect Otto Eisler, whom Fein likely knew, was tortured by the Gestapo in the summer of 1939.[16] That Eisler had sheltered Thomas Theodor Heine (1867–1948), the well-known founder and caricaturist of the German magazine *Simplicissimus*, was likely reason enough for the Germans to go after Eisler.[17] Willi Bondi, one of Giese's best Brno friends, and also a friend of Fein, suffered torture in the summer of 1941. Whether Fein himself experienced torture or not, its growing threat was surely sufficient incentive for him to leave Brno.

Karl Fein's documented encounter with the Brno Gestapo took place in April 1939.[18] The archival source reveals that Fein was interrogated and informed the Gestapo that he wanted to emigrate. At the time, the Gestapo and the Security

[12] The talk was broadcast on Brno radio on September 15, 1935. See the announcement in the radio programming bulletin, *Radio Wien*, Sep. 13, 1935, Heft 51, 46; and repeated in *Volksfreund*, Sep. 14, 1935, 6. In both publications, the radio talk was erroneously announced as "Das neue Ratengeseß [*sic*, Rassengesetz]". On March 19, 1936, Karl Fein and Willi Bondi's sister Aesche (Elisabeth) briefly appeared on Brno radio on the topic of divorce. See "Dr. Karl Fein und Elsa Fleischer-Bondi: Eine Frau will sich scheiden lassen" (Dr. Karl Fein and Elsa Fleischer-Bondi: a woman wants a divorce), *Prager Tagblatt*, Mar. 18, 1936, 36. Another Karl Fein radio talk was titled "Rechtsberatung für den Rundfunk: Der Schutz der Ehre" (Legal advice on the radio: the protection of honor) and lasted fifteen minutes. It was broadcast on Jul. 20, 1938. See the announcement in *Volksfreund*, Jul. 16, 1938, 8. For a chronological overview of German-language radio in Czechoslovakia from 1923 to 1990, see Krupička 2017. The Brno German radio program started broadcasting in 1927.

[13] See his testimonial in the USC Shoah Foundation Visual History Archive (http://sfi.usc.edu/), testimony 22902.

[14] Caruso 2015, 36.

[15] A commemorative plaque inside the main entry hall of the building reminds visitors of the many faculty members who lost their lives in World War II. The law faculty of Masaryk University is even today located at 70 Veveří (Eichhorner Strasse). See https://encyklopedie.brna.cz/home-mmb/?acc=profil_domu&load=641 (accessed Aug. 10, 2020).

[16] Two of Otto Eisler's brothers were imprisoned by the Nazis for six weeks. See Wladika 2009, 7; and http://encyklopedie.brna.cz /home-mmb/?acc =profil_osobnosti&load=3188 (accessed Jan 10, 2015).

[17] Malt & Juříčková 2016, 79.

[18] MZA, Brno, fonds D 25, Celní pátrací služebna, pobočka Brno, kart. n° 58, sign. 849/39, file Karl Fein. I did not see Karl Fein's name in MZA, Brno, fonds B 340, Gestapo Brno. This does not preclude that Fein was arrested or even tortured. Only some of the Gestapo files in this archival fonds have survived. In the inventory list for this archival fonds, for example, I did not find the names of Willi Bondi or any of the Eisler brothers. There is one small, yet rather indeterminate, indication that Fein was arrested by the Gestapo for his publishing activity (but not his homosexuality). The typed (!) letterhead of a letter the Brno Gestapo sent in April 1939 to the Devisenschutzsonderkommando (Foreign Exchange Special Unit) reads "Geheime Staatspolizei / Einsatzkommando VI. / D, II B 3". The Gestapo was organized in *Referaten* (departments). Department II A was concerned with left-wingers, Communists, Marxists, people returning from Spain or Russia, etc. Department II B focused on Jews, Freemasons, emigrants, pacifists, while Department II B M focused

Police (Sicherheitspolizei) were not yet much in favor of the idea of Jewish people emigrating.[19] If his emigration was ever to happen, one needed first to check whether Fein had sinned against the foreign exchange protection laws (*Devisenschutzgesetze*) introduced by the Germans. In an April 21, 1939 letter, the Gestapo inquired with the Brno Foreign Exchange Special Unit: "The above-mentioned Jew [Karl Fein] has reported his emigration here. Have any violations of the foreign exchange laws become known there?" There were no objections.[20]

Despite the good news, Fein was not able to emigrate. Perhaps he simply did not have the financial means. In a letter of early July 1939, addressed to the Brno Foreign Exchange Special Unit, Fein asked for the release of money owed to him by a former Jewish client, the veterinarian Leo Weisz (1888–1950), for past services.[21] It is unclear whether Fein did obtain this money but it seems very unlikely. Weisz had left for

on right-wing resistance. *Sachgebiet* (administrative unit) "II B 3" dealt with "Beobachtung und Überwachung des Emigrantentums" (observing and monitoring emigration). But in the reply letter (dated May 6, 1939) from the Okresní finanční ředitelství Brno to the Gestapo, the precise codes used – "Ref. II B, II P, Sachgebiet II B 3" – for the department within the Brno Gestapo differ. See ibid., f. 3. Department "II P" referred to "Politisch-polizeiliche Behandlung der Presse" (Political police treatment of the press). Department "II S", which cannot be found here, stood for *Homosexualität* (homosexuality). See Filip, Břečka, Schildberger et al. 2012, 234–37; Vašek, Černý & Břečka 2015, 108–14. This indirect indication that Fein was possibly under Gestapo scrutiny for his publishing activity (and not his sexual orientation) is nevertheless uncertain. I saw the code "Ref. II B, II P, Sachgebiet II B 3." in a Foreign Exchange Special Unit file for Leopold Fleischer, Willi Bondi's brother-in-law. It is difficult to see how this businessman could have been arrested for undesirable publishing activities. Or was he also involved in anti-Nazi publications? We have seen that Leopold Fleischer was arrested in March 1941 by the Gestapo at a gathering at which his brother-in-law, Willi Bondi, and other gay men were present, but that does not mean that Fleischer was himself a gay man. It is also possible that the Okresní finanční ředitelství Brno (Brno District Finance Directorate) made a mistake when adding the Gestapo organization codes. See MZA, Brno, fonds D 25, Celní pátrací služebna, pobočka Brno, Leopold Fleischer, kart. n° 34, sign. E 45/39, letter (dated May 4, 1939) from the Okresní finanční ředitelství Brno to the Gestapo Brno, f. 6. Another Gestapo department mentioned in Leopold Fleischer's file is Department II E, responsible for *činnost proti ekonomice* (*politická*) (activities against the economy [political]).

19 For the Gestapo policy on this before the summer of 1939, see Löw 2012, 627, document n° 260 ("Die Jüdische Kultusgemeinde Prag berichtet am 21. August 1939 über die katastrophale Lage der Juden und Eichmanns Herrschaft im Protektorat"): "Etwas bis Mitte Juli 1939 lehnten die deutschen Behörden beziehungsweise die Geheime Staatspolizei (weiterhin Gestapo genannt), der diese Agenda übertragen wurde, die Bewilligung von Auslandsreisen an Juden ab" (Some time before mid-July 1939, the German authorities, or rather the Geheime Staatspolizei (later called the Gestapo), assigned this agenda, refused to grant Jews permission to travel abroad). See also Gruner 2010, 152, 172.

20 MZA, Brno, fonds D 25, Celní pátrací služebna, pobočka Brno, kart. n° 58, sign. 849/39, file Karl Fein, letter (dated Apr. 21, 1939) from Gestapo Brünn (Einsatzkommando VI, D, II B 3) to the Devisenschutzsonderkommando bei der Finanzlandesdirektion Brünn, f. 1: "Der obengenannte Jude [Karl Fein] hat hier seine Auswanderung angezeigt. Sind dort Verstösse gegen die Devisengesetze bekannt geworden?" The file also contains the answer (dated May 15, 1939) from the Brno District Finance Directorate simply bearing the stamp "Není námitek" (no objection). Some handwritten notation in this letter refers to a specific file in the Brno District Finance Directorate archives with the signature Tr 621/39/206, now in the fonds D 19 in the MZA, Brno, but this file could not be located there. For files with the signature "Tr", the MZA, Brno, only has a name index for 1946–50 (book 59). The only 1939 file that survived bore the number 44. Presumably, all other files from 1939 (and other war years) were discarded at some point. That Karl Fein's file appeared under the signature "Tr" (abbreviation for *trestní*, criminal) is intriguing since the Brno District Finance Directorate's very brief response indicated that there was no sign of any offense in Karl Fein's case. See email (dated Oct. 19, 2016) from Daniel Štaud (MZA, Brno) to the author.

21 Leo Weisz may have been a veterinarian but also owned Karoseria [*sic*], a garage located at 20 Dornich (Dornych), together with Heinrich Březa (1908–?). During the first days of the occupation, in March 1939, Weisz fled to the USA, still owing Karl Fein 3,641.22 Czech crowns, as Fein's own very detailed, fifteen-page June 1939 bill makes clear. The Brno Foreign Exchange Special Unit allowed for some outstanding bills to be paid from Leo Weisz's blocked bank accounts. But no such permission was given in the case of Fein and another Czech company. Leo Weisz's father, Albert Weisz (1856–1942), had financial problems himself because of his son fleeing the country. When he requested a monthly allowance of 1,000 Czech crowns from his son's capital, this was granted by the Foreign Exchange Special Unit. Weisz's father was deported on transport "Ae" on March 27, 1942 from Brno to Terezín, where he died on August 2, 1942. A search inquiry left on

the USA in April 1939, and the Germans informed Fein that they needed Weisz's authorization to transfer money from his account.[22] That Fein received a negative answer from a Foreign Exchange Special Unit official named "Hirschfelder" may have struck him as an absurd twist of fate: in German, "Hirschfelder" could suggest a Magnus Hirschfeld supporter, i.e., a sexual liberation proponent or, more narrowly interpreted, a gay activist.[23] Another indication that Fein was trying to find money to emigrate lies in the letters Fein sent to the two publishers of Hirschfeld's French books. We have already seen that, on May 27, 1939, two days after concluding the final settlement of the Giese inheritance, Fein optimistically inquired with Editions Montaigne about possible royalties from Hirschfeld's books for the years 1937 and 1938.[24] It is even possible to argue that Fein suddenly decided to redact the final settlement of the inheritance because he needed money. Fein left Brno for Prague in October 1939 to go to the Central Office for Jewish Emigration (Zentralstelle für jüdische Auswanderung), created in the Czech capital in the summer of 1939. Once this organization was installed, every Jewish person wanting to emigrate had first to move to Prague.

CENTRAL OFFICE FOR JEWISH EMIGRATION

The Central Office for Jewish Emigration was created by Adolf Eichmann in Vienna in August 1938. One year later, in July 1939, Prague installed the same organization. The Prague Central Office was modeled on the one in Vienna. Instead of running around endlessly to different places and administrations, in 1938 the Jewish Community (Jüdische Kultusgemeinde, JKG) in Vienna proposed making the whole emigration procedure easier by centralizing all services in one place.[25]

In Prague also, Jewish representatives considered that the creation of the Central Office could only be beneficial for Jewish people wanting to emigrate. But the creation of the Prague Central Office also made it clear that it was *only* through this office that one could get out of the country. As a text by Oskar Singer attests, the decision to create the Central Office apparently took the remaining Jewish population, who were still debating whether emigration was a good option, by surprise: "In a single stroke, the overall situation became clear. The question of the emigration of all Jews was immediately thrust to the fore, no longer as a subject of discussion, but as a categorical imperative".[26] By suddenly making the exit a lot narrower and more

the message board of Ancestry.com ("Family Weisz of Austria/Hungary") on February 24, 2004, by Leo Weisz's daughter, Rosemarie Weisz Heinegg, states that Leo Weisz "taught at Middlesex Veterinary Medicine near Boston and had a vet[e]rinary practice in Natick, MA". See MZA, Brno, fonds D 25, Celní pátrací služebna, pobočka Brno, kart. n° 65, sign. 1177/39, file Dr. Leo Weiss, Tierartz Brünn, Dornych 20. There is also a file on the garage company in NA, Praha, fonds n° 375, Arizačni spisy, Březa a Weisz, kart. n° 182, file n° 1043.

[22] MZA, Brno, fonds D 25, Celní pátrací služebna, pobočka Brno, kart. n° 58, sign. 849/39, file Karl Fein, handwritten draft of letter (dated Aug. 16 or 17, 1939) from the Devisenschutzsonderkommando Brünn to Karl Fein, f. 6b. The handwriting says: "Aus dem Sperrkonto des Dr. Leo Weiß [*sic*] kann ich Beträge nur auf dessen [gestrichen und ersetzt durch] seinen persönlichen Antrag freigeben. Ich stelle daher anheim, sich mit dem Genannten in Verbindung zu setzen" (I can only release amounts from the blocked account of Dr. Leo Weiß [*sic*] at his [crossed out and replaced by] personal request. I therefore request that you contact the aforementioned person). I thank Marita Keilson-Lauritz for her November 2016 help in reading the handwriting.

[23] MZA, Brno, fonds D 25, Celní pátrací služebna, pobočka Brno, kart. n° 58, sign. 849/39, file Karl Fein.

[24] IMEC, Saint-Germain la Blanche Herbe, fonds Aubier-Montaigne, letter (dated May 27, 1939) from Karl Fein to Editions Montaigne.

[25] Oprach 2006, 61 and n. 245: "Im Sommer 1938 arbeiteten Funktionäre der Kultusgemeinde an einer Vereinfachung der bürokratischen Modalitäten durch Gründung einer Zentralstelle" (In the summer of 1938, officials of the religious community worked on simplifying bureaucratic modalities by establishing a central office). See also document n° 273 ("Jüdisches Nachrichtenblatt vom 8. März 1940: Interview mit Franz Weidmann über die Aufgaben der Jüdischen Kultusgemeinde Prag") in Löw 2012, 666.

[26] Löw 2012, 684, document n° 283, "Jüdisches Nachrichtenblatt: Oskar Singer schreibt am 26. Juli 1940 über die Bedeutung der Zentralstelle für jüdische Auswanderung in Prag": "Mit einem Schlage

concrete – directing all requests for emigration to the single authority of the Central Office – many Jewish people started to rush for the exit. Although initially the Gestapo discouraged Czech Jews from emigrating, it adopted the very opposite position after the creation of the Central Office in the summer of 1939.[27] Only people legally resident in Prague could apply to the Central Office.[28] News that one had to move to Prague if one wanted to emigrate reached Brno through the leaders of its Jewish community.[29] Most likely this was the first and most important reason why, in October 1939, Fein moved in with his close relatives in Prague. The creation of the Central Office was of course also a Nazi effort to bring all Jewish people to one central location, the capital of the Protectorate, in order to make this population more controllable.

Another factor that certainly played a role, and likely contributed to the panic caused by the creation of the Central Office, was the Decree of the Reich Protector in Bohemia and Moravia on Jewish Assets (Verordnung des Reichsprotektors in Böhmen und Mähren über das jüdische Vermögen), issued on June 21, 1939, just a month before the creation of the Central Office, which basically stipulated that Jewish people lost control of their belongings, assets and property. This June 1939 decree was a watershed for many reasons. Not only did it abrogate many of the half-hearted measures taken in the preceding months,[30] but signaled that the Germans were going to manage the "Jewish problem", and not the Protectorate officials as Hitler had first suggested. Indirectly, the decree also very clearly defined, for the first time, who was considered a Jewish person in the Protectorate.[31] With the National Socialists' blatant approval of the expropriation of Jewish people, there were not many reasons left to stay in the Protectorate.

The Central Office in Prague was located in the former Dutch embassy in Prague-Střešovice, at 11 Dělostřelecká (Schillstrasse).[32] Requests to emigrate could be made

klärte sich die Gesamtlage. Die Frage der Auswanderung aller Juden trat sofort in den Vordergrund, aber nicht mehr als Diskussionsgegenstand, sondern als kategorischer Imperativ".

27 Löw 2012, 661, document n° 270, "Washington Post: Artikel vom 11. Februar 1940 über die Verschärfung der antijüdischen Politik im Protektorat": "Druck zur Auswanderung wird auch noch mit anderen Mitteln ausgeübt, vor allem durch ein im Reich wohlbekanntes: Verhöre durch die Gestapo. [...] Alle Verhöre endeten mit der Mahnung zu verschwinden. Wenn nötig auf illegalem Weg" (Pressure to emigrate is also exerted by other means, above all by one well-known in the Reich: interrogations by the Gestapo. [...] All interrogations ended with the injunction to disappear. If necessary, by illegal means).

28 Anderl & Rupnow 2004, 307. Oprach 2006, 74: "Da keine Zweigstellen eingerichtet wurden, war jeder aureisewillige Jude gezwungen nach Prag umzuziehen, bevor er ins Ausland auswandern konnte, da die Zentralstelle nur Anträge von Ausreisewilligen bearbeitete, die in Prag ansässig und polizeilich gemeldet waren" (Since no branches were set up, every Jew wanting to emigrate was forced to move to Prague before he could go abroad, since the Central Office processed applications only from residents of Prague who were registered with the police there). See also document n° 252 ("Reichsprotektor von Neurath ruft am 15. Juli 1939 die Zentralstelle für jüdische Auswanderung in Prag ins Leben") (Löw 2012, 610). As early as January 1940, the *Zuständigkeit* (jurisdiction) of the Central Office was extended to the whole of the Protectorate. See Gruner 2010, 158. See also the anonymous article, "Prager Zentralstelle für jüdische Auswanderung für das ganze Protektorat zuständig", *Jüdisches Nachrichtenblatt* [Prag edition], Jg. 2, n° 7, Feb. 16, 1940, 1.

29 Löw 2012, 622, document n° 259, "Die Jüdische Kultusgemeinde Prag skizziert in ihrem Wochenbericht vom 19. August 1939 ihre Bemühungen, die Auswanderung aus dem Protektorat zu organisieren": "Für Sonntag, den 13. August 1939, waren die [jüdischen] Vorsteher der Provinzgemeinden mit Bewilligung der Geheimen Staatspolizei nach Prag berufen, und wurde ihnen klargelegt, daß sie über Weisung der Zentralstelle für jüdische Auswanderung Prag ihren Gemeindemitgliedern mitzuteilen haben, daß sie ihren Wohnsitz nach Prag zu verlegen haben" (On Sunday, August 13, 1939, the [Jewish] leaders of the provincial congregations were summoned to Prague with the approval of the Gestapo. It was made clear to them that they had to inform their congregations, through instructions from the Central Office for Jewish Emigration, that they had to transfer their residence to Prague).

30 Gruner 2010, 150–51, 153–54.

31 Tauchen 2015.

32 The Prague-Střešovice neighborhood is to this day a diplomatic quarter; however, the building that housed the Central Office (opposite the current Swiss consulate) appeared abandoned when I went to see the building in Prague during one of my research trips. See also Milotová 1997, 14.

by going through an elaborate admission process. The JKG in Prague played a crucial role in helping applicants to fill out the forms, which contained over 600 questions. The JKG also ensured that the daily quota of appointments for the "optimal functioning" of the Central Office was met.[33] For the German occupiers, the Central Office operated in the first place as a way to further strip Jews of their last belongings before being allowed to leave the country. A percentage of what one owned, the so-called emigration tax (*Auswanderungssteuer*), or also Jewish tax (*Judensteuer*), had to be paid at the start of the emigration procedure, regardless of the outcome of the procedure.[34] Visitors beginning the procedure had to pass eleven desks (*Schalter*). An oppressive atmosphere pervaded the building. Jews were ordered by German staff to denigrate themselves aloud, using offensive and insulting antisemitic language.[35]

The possibility to emigrate through the Prague Central Office lasted until July 1943, but many sources make it clear that, with the invasion of Poland and the official start of the war, in September 1939, the chances of emigrating diminished considerably since many countries stopped issuing visas. Another problem, also linked to the progress of the war, was that more and more transport routes (*Verkehrsmöglichkeiten*) gradually proved impassable.[36] This means that, by the time Karl Fein moved to Prague, in October 1939, it was basically already too late. Not surprisingly, the highest number of requests at the Central Office, of the 10,319 made between the end of July 1939 and the end of June 1940, took place in August 1939, when 3,504 people visited the Central Office to start the procedure.[37] Half of the 10,000 total procedures were completed by the end of November 1939.[38]

[33] See Löw 2012, 628, document n° 260, "Die Jüdische Kultusgemeinde Prag berichtet am 21. August 1939 über die katastrophale Lage der Juden und Eichmanns Herrschaft im Protektorat". What added to people's dependency on the JKG was the requirement that all documents be typed, at a time when all typewriters had been forbidden to Jews. Seventeen questionnaires in total had to be filled out, containing a total of around 600 questions. See Löw 2012, 651, document n° 266, "Heimann Stapler berichtet nach seiner Emigration im Oktober 1939, wie sich die Lage der Juden im Protektorat seit Kriegsbeginn verschärft hat". The thick brown binder holing one's personal file papers was nicknamed, after Hitler's bestseller, *Mein Kampf* (My Struggle), due to its color and thickness. See Löw 2012, 639, document n° 263, "Eine in die Niederlande emigrierte Jüdin schildert die Situation im Protektorat bis Anfang Oktober 1939". For the reproduction of a very interesting contemporary flow chart, titled "Abfertigungsvorgang für auswandernde Juden" (clearance procedure for emigrating Jews), showing the long process Jewish would-be emigrants had to undertake, see Veselská 2012b, 56. The nineteen hurdles to be surmounted in the Central Office, shown on the chart, nearly correspond to the seventeen questionnaires that had to be completed.

[34] Löw 2012, 652, document n° 266, "Heimann Stapler berichtet nach seiner Emigration im Oktober 1939, wie sich die Lage der Juden im Protektorat seit Kriegsbeginn verschärft hat": "Diese Fragebogen sind in erster Reihe dazu bestimmt, das Gesamtvermögen des Auswanderers zu erfassen, wobei das Steuerbekenntnis der letzten drei Jahre zur Grundlage genommen wird" (These questionnaires are primarily designed to record the emigrant's total assets, based on the tax returns of the last three years). There exists a – presumably rare – duplicate copy of one of these Central Office *Quittungen* (receipts) (dated Aug. 5, 1941) for the so-called Jewish tax paid by the couple Friedrich Mosauer (1878–1942) and Rosa Mosauer (1884–1942) in the amount of 3,500 German marks. Despite payment, we know that the couple did not manage to emigrate since they ended up in the Łódź ghetto. See APL, Łódź, fonds Przełożony Starszeństwa Żydów, signature 1218, microfilm L-19835, [Dokumenty osobiste Żydów wsiedlonych z zagranicy], 1939–1942, pencil number 141. The couple was deported on the third Prague transport, transport "C", which left Prague on October 26, 1941. The bottom of the document reveals that the couple never went to pick up their approved travel documents from the Central Office. Cf. Milotová 1997, 17–19, 21. Milotová stresses that successful applicants still had to obtain visas from consulates or embassies in Prague. This means that, despite a Central Office approval, things could still go wrong.

[35] Černý 1997, 78–80. Černý also cites Jan Wiener's personal experience of the Central Office (Černý 1997, 80). See also Wiener 1992, 17–18. Hanuš Zvi Weigl, a Brno lawyer who managed to emigrate to Palestine, also experienced the harsh treatment of Jewish people in the Central Office. See Weigl 2008/2009, 109–10.

[36] Oprach 2006, 75 n. 317; Milotová 1997, 22–23, esp. 29 n. 72. Von zur Mühlen mentions that both sea and land routes fell out of use (Von zur Mühlen 1998, 339). Cf. Černý 1997, 71–74.

[37] Oprach 2006, 75, esp. 75 n. 315. For the analogous case of people trying to emigrate to Shanghai, see Altman & Eber 2000, 27ff.

[38] Milotová 1997, 21–22.

Karl Fein clearly visited the Central Office. As a document in his Prague police file indicates, he intended to emigrate to Shanghai.[39] It is tempting, of course, to associate this Asian choice with Li Shiu Tong, Hirschfeld's second life partner, and, indeed, it cannot be excluded that contacts between Li Shiu Tong and Fein took place. Had Li Shiu Tong offered him substantial help if he managed to reach Shanghai? We can safely assume that Fein met Li Shiu Tong during the 1932 WLSR conference. They met again in Nice in September 1935, when Fein went to France to try to unblock the Hirschfeld inheritance case.[40] Since the wife of Giese's Brno boyfriend, Milli Lukl, ended up in Shanghai in 1938, she and Fein may also have been in contact. Yet, the principal or perhaps sole reason for choosing Shanghai was simply that it was one of the most popular and frequently chosen destinations for many Jewish people wanting to emigrate.[41] Shanghai's popularity as a destination can be explained by its complicated political situation. Passports were not checked and visas were not really required either. Apparently, the simple authorization of the Shanghai International Settlement authorities sufficed for entry to the city. Eventually, only around 20,000 European Jews in total would emigrate to Shanghai. Most of them, around 12,000, arrived in 1939.[42]

The available archival traces suggest that Fein decided only rather late to undertake the lengthy procedure at the Central Office – in the summer of 1940, almost a year after his arriving in Prague.[43] Fein's lateness may raise the suspicion that it was due to the lengthy process, but the Central Office was rather known for "quick" procedures that lasted a maximum of forty days.[44] There are two possibilities: either Fein did indeed try his luck quite late, or it was his second attempt.[45] One also wonders what Fein recorded on the ten-page-long declaration of assets form (*Vermögenserklärung*) during the arduous Central Office administrative procedure, which usually took from four to five hours.[46] In the section on assets (*Aktiven*), in contrast to the section on liabilities or debts (*Passiven*), candidates seeking to leave the country were asked, under "claims" (*Forderungen*), if they had received an inheritance and if they owned any patents or licenses under their name.[47] Did Fein fill out this form truthfully and state that he had inherited from the Giese estate and that he was entitled to income from the Titus Pearls? It seems unlikely that he would have done so. Karl Fein was

[39] NA, Praha, Policejní ředitelství Praha II, všeobecná spisovna, 1931–1940, kart. n° 5661, sign. F 271-9, Fein Karel 1894. In the document (dated Aug. 22, 1940) Fein asked the Prague police for testimony of his good conduct and morality (*Leumundszeugnis*, *Vysvědčení zachovalosti*) to complete his Central Office file.

[40] Arbetarrörelsens arkiv och bibliotek, Stockholm, Max Hodann samling, vol. 15, letter (dated Sep. 24, 1935, [2]) from Karl Giese to Max Hodann. See also Soetaert 2013, 13.

[41] Shanghai was the most popular destination noted by the *Paßabteilung* (passport administration) of the Prague police. See Milotová 1997, 23 n. 72, 29; Altman & Eber 2000, 2.

[42] For the complicated administrative and political situation in Shanghai, see Altman & Eber 2000; von zur Mühlen 1998, 338–39.

[43] NA, Praha, Policejní ředitelství Praha II, všeobecná spisovna, 1931–1940, kart. n° 5661, sign. F 271-9, Fein Karel 1894.

[44] Milotová 1997, 18.

[45] Milotová mentions a certain Leonard Heinrich who applied in 1939 and 1940 (Milotová 1998, 45). She writes that, for several reasons, it became more and more difficult to leave the country. She also mentions the case of Viktor Abel (1892–?) who, like Fein, applied in August 1940. Abel's papers were in order in December of that year. Nevertheless, Abel did not manage to emigrate but was put on transport "B", with Fein, which transported them from Prague to Łódź.

[46] Sedláková 2003, 277, esp. 277 n. 3; Anderl et al. 2004, 307–8.

[47] The Jewish Museum in Prague has digitized a small part of the many forms that had to be filled out in the Central Office. See the Formuláře dokladů k tzv. Vystěhovaleckým mapám: http://collections.jewishmuseum.cz/index.php/ Detail/Object/Show/object_id/173556 (accessed Jan. 26, 2017). I thank Lucie B. Petrusová (Židovské muzeum v Praze) for her assistance in locating these documents in the museum's digitized collection. The digital scan of the "Vermögenserklärung" is missing pages 5–6. The formulation in German goes as follows: "7. Ist Ihnen eine *Verlassenschaft* [bold in original] oder ein *Legat* [bold in original] angefallen? [...] 9. Welche Ansprüche stehen Ihnen aus *Lizenzverträgen, Patent-Urheber-Marken und Musterschutzrechten* zu? [bold in original]" (7. Have you accrued an *estate* [bold

most likely not even aware that, from 1939 on, income from Titus Pearls went directly to the Prussian state, on the order of the Berlin police director.[48]

A "DESIRE" TO EMIGRATE

Very indirectly, the (second) marriage of Gustav Fein – Karl Fein's brother – in Prague, in April 1939, before Gustav Fein and his mother moved from Brno to Prague, tells us a little about the very difficult situation of Jewish people [ill. 2].[49] The name of Gustav Fein's second wife was Herta Fein (née Messing, 1902–1981). She was a classically-trained draftswoman (*akademische Malerin*).[50] Like Gustav Fein, Herta Messing had been married before.[51] The couple likely got to know each other when Gustav was living in Vienna, the city of Herta's birth.

Other than a mutual affection, the exact reasons for their marrying in Prague are not known; however, marrying Gustav Fein, a Czechoslovak citizen, may have been the only way for Herta Fein – who was Austrian – to legally stay in the Protectorate.[52] Pragmatic considerations may have played a part, since it was rumored that mixed marriages would not face prosecution. When the couple married, the June 21, 1939 Decree of the Reich Protector in Bohemia and Moravia on Jewish Assets, had not yet seen the light. This decree also stipulated the National Socialists' definition of "Jewish". Even if one did not consider oneself as Jewish, a Jewish ancestor might decide the matter differently. On her identity papers, Herta Fein was indeed described as Protestant (*Protestantisch/Evangelisch*).[53]

Herta Fein was the sister of the engineer and literary figure Erich Messing (1895–1942), who lived in Saarbrücken.[54] Because Erich Messing was part of the circle

in original] or a *legacy* [bold in original]? [...] 9. What claims are you entitled to from *license agreements, patent-copyright-trademarks and design protection rights*? [bold in original]). I obtained a complete version of the document from YIVO Archives (New York). The digital scan of the document was found in YIVO Archives, New York, RG 116, Czech folder 2.3. I thank Gunnar Berg (YIVO, New York) for sending it to me. See his email (dated Oct. 29, 2019) to the author.

48 Dose & Herrn 2005, 19–20.

49 The couple married on April 8, 1939 in Prague. The original marriage certificate can be found in Forschungsinstitut Brenner-Archiv, Universität von Innsbruck, Innsbruck, Nachlass Herta Fein-Erich Messing, Kassette 152. Friedrich Landesmann (1881–1942) was one of the witnesses. He was deported on transport "AAt" on July 23, 1942, from Prague to Terezín, then on transport "AAz" from Terezín to Maly Trostinec. His wife, Margareta Treusch (1900–1978), was already in Paris in 1939. She survived the war and married Heinrich Fasal. Friedrich and Margareta Landesmann had one daughter, Ruth Felicie Adler (1924–1945), who was in London in 1939. See the Prague police file on Friedrich Landesmann, https://www.holocaust.cz/en/database-of-victims/victim/103942-bedrich-landesmann/ (accessed Apr. 1, 2021); further genealogical information is available at Geni.com (accessed Apr. 1, 2021). On April 1, 2021, a message was left for Nicole Adler on www.myheritage.com, inquiring about Friedrich Landesmann. There was no response. The other witness was Captain Lev Astl (?–?). Herta's brother, Erich Messing, attended the marriage in Prague. See Forschungsinstitut Brenner-Archiv, Universität von Innsbruck, Innsbruck, Nachlass Herta Fein-Erich Messing, Kassette 153, Tagebuchaufzeichnungen Erich Messing, 1932–1942: "22/04/1939: Abreise aus Prag" (22/04/1939: Departure from Prague).

50 Her parents were Heinrich Richard Messing (1865–?) and her mother was Emma Maria Schück (1874–1956). Herta's father died shortly before the war, but her mother survived and lived in England and Switzerland.

51 She divorced her first husband, a man named Jirásko (or Jirasek), in October 1938. See the certified Czech-to-German translation of the marriage certificate of Gustav Fein and Herta Jirásková in Forschungsinstitut Brenner-Archiv, Universität von Innsbruck, Innsbruck, Nachlass Herta Fein-Erich Messing, Kassette 152.

52 Čapková & Frankl 2012, 61–62.

53 "In memoriam Erich Messing", probably written by Birgit von Schowingen-Ficker, reveals that, despite their Jewish ancestry, the Messings were baptized as Protestants for two generations. After the war, Herta Fein continued to be close to the Protestant church in Switzerland. See Forschungsinstitut Brenner-Archiv, Universität von Innsbruck, Innsbruck, Nachlass Herta Fein-Erich Messing, Kassette 151.

54 *Einwohnerbuch (Adressbuch) der Stadt Saarbrücken* 1934–35, II, 227. Messing moved to Saarbrücken from Vienna in February 1925, and lived at 21 Im Heimgarten with the engineer Joseph Mahlberg, for whom he worked from 1933 until September 1939. The company (Askania-Werke A.G., Bamberg-Werk, Ingenieur-Büro Saarbrücken, Jos. Mahlberg) was located at the same address. The other person living there was Anton Schneider, Stadt-Oberamtmann. See email (dated Nov. 30,

around the Austrian literary periodical *Der Brenner*, led by Ludwig (von) Ficker, some correspondence between Erich Messing and the Fein family has survived.[55] This correspondence shows that, in June 1939, Erich Messing, Gustav Fein, his new wife Herta and also Karl Fein's sister, Margarethe Polatschek and her husband, Dr. Rudolf Polatschek, were investigating several emigration options. They had bound their fates by exchanging as much information as possible on the latest possibilities and requirements for emigration. Messing's letters show that each country had different rules for emigrants, resulting in an administrative jungle of practices. Or at least, this was the situation in Prague, one month before the creation of the Central Office for Jewish Emigration. Messing seems to have been the one who took matters in hand. He typed his letters using carbon so he could send the information to his close relatives. Through these multiple copies, the relatives joined in a communal conversation. Starting on June 1, 1939, during his first week in Hamburg, Messing typed and sent a long letter crammed full of technical details about emigration issues nearly every day, the information interspersed with his humorous and sometimes sarcastic views on the extraordinary aspects of the Jewish emigration crisis he saw around him. Apparently, Messing had gone to Hamburg to look into the possibility of emigrating to South America by ship with the HAPAG-Reederei, a German shipping company.[56] Messing's first, four-page letter, dated June 1, 1939, was addressed to Rudolf Polatschek and his wife Margarethe, Karl Fein's sister, then still living in Vienna. Messing described in meticulous detail how the couple could take the night train from Austria to Hamburg and which hotels would accept Jews.[57] Another letter

2020) from Michael Jurich (Stadtarchiv Saarbrücken) to the author. Until September 1933, Messing taught at the Höheren Technischen Lehranstalt (higher technical college) in Saarbrücken. Afterwards, he gave private lessons. Starting in July 1937, he lived at 10 An der Trift (also Anderstrasse). It remains unclear exactly when Messing left Saarbrücken for Frankfurt. However, this was possibly in the second half of May 1939 since Messing shows up, as we will see, in Hamburg at the beginning of June 1939. The evacuation of people from the Saar district to German cities was instigated by the German authorities as a precaution, and with war imminent. From November 1941 until June 1942, Messing was registered in Frankfurt where he was subject to forced labor (street cleaning). In Frankfurt, he lived at 23 Unterlindau, 16 Hohenzollernstrasse, 24 Jahnsstrasse, 42 Oberweg and 57 Rohrbachstrasse. See email conversation between the author and Michael Lenarz (Jüdisches Museum Frankfurt); the information on Erich Messing in the "biographies" database of the Memorial Neuer Börneplatz of the Jüdisches Museum Frankfurt (document ID 6524); and especially Hessisches Hauptstaatsarchiv, Wiesbaden, Bestand 518, Regierungspräsidien als Entschädigungsbehörde, Regierungspräsidium Wiesbaden, 1958–1972, Akte n° 41623, Erich Messing (°25/12/1895)/Herta Fein (°19/03/1902) and Hessisches Hauptstaatsarchiv, Wiesbaden, Bestand 519/3, Akten der Devisenstellen Frankfurt und Kassel, Devisenstelle Frankfurt, 1940-1942, JS 10429, Erich Messing (°25/12/1895).

55 This correspondence, together with some other documents and photos relating to Herta Fein and Erich Messing, is now located in the Nachlass Herta Fein-Erich Messing in the Forschungsinstitut Brenner-Archiv at the Universität von Innsbruck. The archival fonds in Innsbruck mainly revolves around the literary figure of Erich Messing. Since she was Messing's surviving sister, Herta Fein was first contacted in 1964 by Birgit von Schowingen-Ficker (1911–2001), the daughter of Ludwig von Ficker (1880–1967). Contact between Birgit and Herta was most intense in 1964 and 1965. The documents in the Nachlass Herta Fein-Erich Messing were donated by Herta Fein in 1973. The two women kept in touch until at least 1981, the date of the last letter (dated Jul. 21, 1981) sent by Herta Messing to Birgit present in Forschungsinstitut Brenner-Archiv, Universität von Innsbruck, Innsbruck, Nachlass Herta Fein-Erich Messing, Kassette 151. Birgit von Schowingen-Ficker was also likely intrigued by Erich Messing since he wrote to her in 1932 that he had fallen in love with her. See letter (dated Feb. 5, 1932, 1) from Erich Messing to Birgit von Schowingen-Ficker in Forschungsinstitut Brenner-Archiv, Universität von Innsbruck, Innsbruck, Nachlass Ludwig (von) Ficker, n° 41, Kassette 70, M023, Messing Erich.

56 The acronym stands for Hamburg-Amerikanische Paketfahrt Aktien-Gesellschaft.

57 Forschungsinstitut Brenner-Archiv, Universität von Innsbruck, Innsbruck, Nachlass Herta Fein-Erich Messing, Kassette 153, letter (dated Jun. 1, 1939) from Erich Messing to [Rudolf] Polatschek. The other letters sent from Hamburg were dated June 2, 1939 (four pages), June 3, 1939 (two pages), June 5, 1939 (three pages) and July 19, 1939 (one page).

58 See the undated letter, written in rather poor English, by Erich Messing to an unknown addressee in Australia (likely a diplomatic office) in which Messing refers to a previous letter by Gustav Fein. See Forschungsinstitut Brenner-Archiv, Universität

indirectly indicates that Gustav Fein also took emigration to heart and helped where he could. For example, he wrote a letter in English to an institution in Australia to help find Erich Messing a job that met his qualifications.[58]

It is likely that there were difficult discussions about emigration issues within the Fein family. It is possible that Helene Brecher, the mother of Karl, Margarethe and Gustav Fein, who was over eighty years old, urged the newlyweds Gustav and Herta Fein to leave without her. Her great age probably did not allow demanding travel. She already needed help walking, as we will see later. In addition, the Prague address where she and her oldest son Gustav stayed after moving from Brno in June–July 1939 was a Jewish home for the elderly. In one of his letters, sent from Hamburg in June 1939, Erich Messing asked Gustav Fein what Karl Fein and his mother were planning to do, as though they were less involved in Messing's sudden but short-lived burst of activity.[59] Had Karl Fein and his mother still not decided whether they would leave? The impossible choice to leave one's parents behind was one many Jewish people had to grapple with. It is also possible that they agreed to try to get the newlyweds out first. A striking aspect of the letters is the clear intent to confuse the possible enemy reader. For example, Messing says "the cousin" (*die Cousine*) when he meant his sister Herta. His mother Emma Messing, who was already in London, was consistently described as "the aunt" (*die Tante*). Messing's mother helped when she could from abroad, informing those still in Czechoslovakia about her inquiries regarding possibilities of and requirements for emigration.

Herta Fein eventually managed to leave the Protectorate, likely some time in mid-July 1939. It is possible, but not very likely, that Herta Fein went through the newly created Central Office, which started operations on July 21, 1939. Curiously, she left for Belgrade (Serbia) the next day.[60] For unexplained reasons, she had already been in Belgrade in January 1939. From there, she went to Switzerland to settle money matters.[61] Apparently, Herta Fein cited professional reasons when obtaining a visa to travel to England where, as already noted, her mother resided. Her husband Gustav Fein stayed behind.[62] Erich Messing stopped writing letters and sending the carbon copies almost as suddenly as he had started them. The impression given by these remaining letters is that, in June 1939, Messing suddenly assertively decided "to make it happen". In a June 2, 1939 letter, he writes: "We need to figure out what we are going to do soon".[63] But, judging from the available letters, Messing's initial intense concern

von Innsbruck, Innsbruck, Nachlass Herta Fein-Erich Messing, Kassette 153.

59 Forschungsinstitut Brenner-Archiv, Universität von Innsbruck, Innsbruck, Nachlass Herta Fein-Erich Messing, Kassette 153, letter (dated Jun. 3, 1939, 2) from Erich Messing to "Meine Lieben!": "Wie geht es Karl? und der Mutter Fein? was haben sie für Aussichten und für Pläne?" (How is Karl doing? and mother Fein? what are their prospects and plans?).

60 See the mention "ona Bělehrad" (she [went to] Belgrade [Serbia]), NA, Praha, fonds Policejní ředitelství Praha II, evidence obyvatelstva sheet for Gustav and Herta Fein. Herta Fein's Prague police file contains a ripped red coupon attached to one of the papers. See NA, Praha, Policejní ředitelství Praha II, všeobecná spisovna, 1931–1940, kart. n° 5661, sign. F 271/14, Herta Feinová 1902, f. 4. Was this the red coupon that was used in the Central Office for Jewish Emigration? Cf. Černý's explanation of what happened at *Schalter* (counters) 10 and 11 in the Central Office (Černý 1997, 79–80).

61 Schweizerisches Bundesarchiv, Bern, Personenkartei der Personenregistratur der Eidgenössische Fremdenpolizei (1912–1997), FEIN, HERTA, 1902.03.19, GB; JIRASKO, HERTA, 1902.02.19 [*sic*], A (1954-1962), sign. E4301#1992/36#3570*, Légation de Suisse, Belgrade, demande d'entrée en Suisse (dated Jan. 21, 1939), Herta Jirasko.

62 See the letter (dated May 5, 1939, 3) from Erich Messing to his mother in London; and letter (dated Jul. 19, 1939) from Messing to several people: "Zuerst muss Kusine [*sic*: Herta Fein] die Uebersiedlung gemacht haben." (First, the cousin [*sic*: Herta Fein] must have successfully emigrated). See also the handwritten (love) letter (dated Jul. 18, [1939]) from Gustav Fein to Herta Fein. All three letters are in Forschungsinstitut Brenner-Archiv, Universität von Innsbruck, Innsbruck, Nachlass Herta Fein-Erich Messing, Kassette 153 (the first two letters) and Kassette 151 (the third letter).

63 Forschungsinstitut Brenner-Archiv, Universität von Innsbruck, Innsbruck, Nachlass Herta Fein-Erich Messing, Kassette 153, letter (dated Jun. 2,

about the Fein family's emigration issues evaporated as soon as his sister had safely arrived in England.[64] It would be incorrect, however, to conclude that Messing was only concerned about the Fein family because his sister was married to Gustav Fein. As we will see later, Erich Messing would send the Fein family considerable sums of money when they were in Prague.

It is of course possible that, as soon as Herta Fein joined her mother in London, some attempts were still made to help the Fein family from abroad. But, soon, emigrating to England became virtually impossible for the Fein family members still stuck in Czechoslovakia and Vienna. The main reason for this was probably the United Kingdom's policy towards Czechoslovak refugees. First of all, the British Committee for Refugees from Czechoslovakia (BCRC), created in October 1938, issued visas to "political" and not "economic" refugees. Secondly, British Jewish organizations were opposed to the immigration of Czechoslovak Jews.[65] The third reason for British reticence was their unwillingness to accede to the sudden (changed) wish of the Gestapo for Jews in the Protectorate to emigrate *en masse*. They hoped that this firm stance would persuade the Germans to revoke that decision.[66] This meant that, in practice, hardly any Czechoslovak Jews reached England. Jewish people from the Sudetenland and Germany itself mainly obtained visas to emigrate to England.[67] The well-known so-called Children's Transports (*Kindertransporte*) were an exception. It is also possible that, after his wife successfully fled to England, Gustav Fein changed his mind. He would stay behind and take care of his mother, not Karl Fein.[68] Let us recall that Gustav Fein lived with his mother in Vienna in the 1930s. As we will see later, Gustav Fein was indeed the one who took care of his mother, until mid-December 1943, the day he was deported from Terezín to Auschwitz-Birkenau.

What happened to Herta's brother, Erich Messing? Despite managing to obtain an entry permit (*Einreisegenehmigung*) for Shanghai, issued by the Shanghai Municipal Council in May 1940,[69] Messing did not leave Europe. There may have been other insurmountable obstacles preventing people from emigrating, one of the most im-

1939, 4) from Erich Messing to Fein family members: "Wir müssen uns nun bald klar werden, was wir machen".

[64] It is possible that the carbon copies, also sent to Messing's mother and his sister Herta Fein, who had by then managed to escape, simply ceased at some moment to reach England. Yet it also remains possible that the letters in the Forschungsinstitut Brenner-Archiv in Innsbruck are only part of a larger correspondence. This may be connected to Herta Fein herself: maybe she did not keep all the letters or did not donate them all to the Brenner-Archiv in Innsbruck? The archival fonds of the Forschungsinstitut Brenner-Archiv also contains photos of Herta and Gustav Fein's wedding day (and a few other pictures) and one wonders if there were not more documents in Herta Fein's personal archives. Maybe the documents that *were* given by Herta Fein to the university archive in Innsbruck were deliberately chosen to convey a certain image or impression? In the archival fonds, one finds only a single letter of Gustav Fein written to Herta Fein, shortly after she managed to escape Czechoslovakia. Did Gustav Fein write only one letter to his wife? Were there other letters that she possibly did not donate to the archive because they were simply too painful to her? Is it only a coincidence that the *only* letter (dated Jul. 18, [1939]) from Gustav Fein in the archival fonds is a love letter? Let us also not forget that Birgit von Schowingen-Ficker contacted Herta Fein regarding Erich Messing, the literary figure. Herta Fein may have used the occasion to tell the story about her own fate and that of her husband Gustav, even as she realized that she was contacted because of her brother. One also senses in Herta Fein's correspondence with Birgit von Schowingen-Ficker that she struggled with survivor's guilt.

[65] London 2000, 151, 160.

[66] Ibid., 159–60, 168.

[67] Ibid., ch. 6, "Refugees from Czechoslovakia". This also explains why I did not consider it useful to look at some relevant archival fonds in the National Archives in Kew (England).

[68] The one letter (dated Jul. 18, 1939) from Gustav Fein to Herta Fein, written shortly before she left Czechoslovakia, is clearly a touching love letter by a man saying goodbye. There is no police file on Gustav Fein in the NA, Praha, so we cannot determine, as we could in the case of Karl Fein, if he ever applied at the Central Office. The police file for Fein's mother certainly contains no documents that indicate her ever visiting the Central Office. As we have seen, Karl Fein applied at least once at the Central Office, in the summer of 1940. This may be a further indication that Gustav indeed decided, after his wife managed to emigrate, to bind his destiny to his mother's.

[69] Forschungsinstitut Brenner-Archiv, Universität von Innsbruck, Innsbruck, Nachlass Herta Fein-

portant being that, as time wore on, fewer and fewer transportation routes out of the country were left.[70] There is also the possibly dubious view, suggested by some documents in the Messing-Fein archival fonds in Innsbruck, that Messing did not want to flee, but deliberately accepted his "fate" as a Jew. Erich Messing died in July 1942 in the Lublin-Majdanek prisoner-of-war camp (*Kriegsgefangenenlager*).[71]

LIFE IN PRAGUE

The Fein family clung to each other when in Prague. Karl Fein stayed in Prague for two years until he was deported to occupied Poland in October 1941. His brother and mother would stay three years and nine months in Prague until they were also deported. Karl Fein lived at three different addresses, his brother and mother at four different addresses.

When Gustav Fein and his mother arrived in Prague, in May–June 1939, they moved into 3 U Půjčovny (Leihamtsgasse) in the Nove Město (Neustadt) district, together with Gustav's new wife Herta Messing. This street is very close to the main Prague railway station and even closer to the Jerusalem Synagogue (Jeruzalémská synagoga) [ill. 3].[72] Their new residence was in a home for the elderly owned by the Jewish community.[73] They stayed in the apartment belonging to a couple, Siegfried Tausik (1876–1943) and Ida Kohn (1886–1944?),[74] whose daughter Valerie Tausik (1914–?) had moved to Austria in 1938.[75] Karl Fein joined his brother and mother in September or October 1939 at this address.[76] Approximately one year later, in mid-July 1940, Karel, Gustav, their mother Helene and the Tausik couple all moved to 11 Erbenstrasse (Erbenova) in the

Erich Messing, Kassette 153, beglaubigte Einreisegenehmigung (certified entry permit) for Erich Messing.

[70] Messing was not alone in obtaining authorization to enter Shanghai without making use of it. See Altman & Eber 2000, 31.

[71] See the September 2011 email conversation between Michael Lenarz (Jüdisches Museum Frankfurt) and the author. See also the information on Erich Messing in the "biographies" database of the Memorial Neuer Börneplatz of the Jüdisches Museum Frankfurt (document ID 6524).

[72] The complete house number is 969/3. See *Strassenverzeichnis der Hauptstadt Prag* 1941, 94, 187; *Tabulky popisných čísel všech katastrálních obcí Velké Prahy* 1938, 22; *Orientační plán hlavního města Prahy s okolím* 1938, part 39. The street was then located in Praha II (now Praha I). The resident registration cards for Gustav Fein and Helene Fein in the AMB, Brno, fonds Z 1, give June 6, 1939 as their departure date from Brno, but the evidence obyvatelstva sheet in the NA, Praha, fonds Policejní ředitelství Praha II, gives May 2, 1939 as Gustav Fein's arrival date and June 21, 1939 as the arrival date for Helene Fein.

[73] See the undated document n° 3, titled "Soziale Fürsorge", by the Prague JKG (Krejčová, Svobodová & Hyndráková 1997, 76) which describes the *Altersheim* (home for the elderly) as having eighty-five beds. It would later be used as one of the storage buildings (having numbers 17, 17a, 17b, 17c, 17d) for confiscated Jewish goods. A photo of the building can be found in the (unpaginated) depositories photo section (under the heading "Prague II") in Krejčová 2008. The Jerusalem Synagogue lies at the northeast end of the street, at 7 Jeruzalémská (Siebenburgengasse). It would later also be used to deposit confiscated goods. The synagogue and its colorful oriental-style facade exist to this day.

[74] The police files on the Tausiks are in NA, Praha, Policejní ředitelství Praha II, všeobecná spisovna, 1931–1940, kart. n° 11452, sign. signatura T 214/14, Tausiková Ida 1886; and NA, Praha, Policejní ředitelství Praha II, všeobecná spisovna, 1941–1951, kart. n° 11506, sign. T376/1, Tausik Vítězslav 1876. According to his police file, Siegfried Tausik was a driver by profession. I also found mention of a certain Vitězslav Taussig, a lawyer in the 1930s in Prague (at 5 Dlážděná ulice). Eventually an examination of the police files present in the NA, Praha, fond Policejní ředitelství Praha, should be made to check if this is the same Vítězslav Tausik we are looking at. I also noticed that the couple's name was commonly misspelled "Taussik" in several documents. See, for example, the evidence obyvatelstva sheet for the Tausiks in NA, Praha, fonds Policejní ředitelství Praha II.

[75] NA, Praha, fonds Policejní ředitelství Praha II, evidence obyvatelstva sheet for Valerie Tausigová (also Tausiková). Starting in October 1935, and before moving to Austria, she lived with her parents at 3 U Půjčovny. See *Pražský adresář* 1937–38, 1446. According to her evidence obyvatelstva sheet, she left for Austria at the end of May 1938. Her further fate is unknown. Neither her name nor her birth date can be found in the www.holocaust.cz database, or in the Austrian Shoah-Opfer database at https://www.doew.at/ (accessed Feb. 8, 2021), or in the Yad Vashem Holocaust victims database.

[76] Karl Fein's new 3 U Půjčovny address can be seen in two documents. The first is the evidence obyvatelstva sheet for Karl Fein in NA, Praha, Policejní

Prague-Karlín (Karolinenthal) district. The Feins paid thirty Reichsmark (or around 300 Czech crowns) for a room they rented, possibly from the Tausiks.[77] This is also the address that Franz Nawratil communicated to the Brno German District Court as Fein's Prague address.[78] The Feins would stay at this address for almost a year. It was shortly after this move that Karl Fein first tried his luck at the Central Office, or perhaps for the second time already.[79] Almost a year later, in June 1941, the three members of the Fein family moved a third time, this time without the Tausiks, to 4 Gödinger Gasse (Hodonínská), also in the Karlín (Karolinenthal) district.[80] It is important to remember that the German occupiers changed both the name of the street and the house numbers in 1941, when 2A Pobřežní became 4 Hodonínská (Gödinger Gasse).[81] The Hodonínská building was almost right beside the railway station, Praha Denisovo nádraží (Prag Denisbahnhof).[82]

If the Fein and the Tausik families chose the first two Prague addresses in relative freedom, the Fein family's move to a third address was likely semi-compulsory since, in the beginning of 1941, the Nazis started a campaign of gathering Jewish people together in so-called "Jewish houses" (*Jüdenhäuser*).[83] This cramming together of more

ředitelství Praha II. This document dates Fein's arrival in Prague as September 8(?), 1939. See also the handwritten remark added to the lower half of a letter in NA, Praha, Policejní ředitelství Praha II, všeobecná spisovna, 1931–1940, kart. n° 5661, sign. F 271/9, Fein Karel JUDr 1894, f. 5, letter (dated Nov. 9, 1939 and Dec. 22, 1939) Okresní nemocenská pojišovna v Brně to Policejní ředitelství Praha. On Karl Fein's home certificate in the AMB, Brno, fonds B 1/39, the house number is given as 3. However, Fein's exact departure date from Brno, as given on a resident registration card in the AMB, Brno, fonds Z 1, is October 6, 1939; and this card gives Fein's Prague address as 2 U Půjčovny. That building is located across the street from 3 U Půjčovny. Does this indicate that Karl Fein moved to a house near to his relatives after spending several weeks with them or was this a simple mistake? I further checked whether Karl Fein may have known the Tausiks through his Brno acquaintances but found no indication of this, I only encountered a Max Tausik (1881–1942?) who was deported from Brno to Terezín in March 1942. However, more candidates are possible since Tausik is consistently misspelled "Taussik" in, for example, the www.holocaust.cz database. There are four people named Taussik who were deported from Brno: Josef Taussik (1888–1942?), Oskar Taussik (1882–1942?), Helena Taussik (1890–1942?) and Klára Taussik (1882–1942?). Oskar Taussik and his wife Klara Taussik could very possibly have been related to Siegfried and Ida Tausik, from Prague, since Klara Taussik was born Klara Weiss, one of the daughters of Leopold Weiss (1848–1930), who had a family link to Karl Fein. But I did not find any family link between Siegfried Tausik (Prague) and Oskar Taussik (Brno). I entered the address "U půjčovny 3" as a search term in the www.holocaust.cz database; but, of the seventy-six names listed, I encountered none from my research. I also entered the search terms "U půjčovny" and "Leihamtsgasse" in the same database with the same negative result.

77 Hessisches Hauptstaatsarchiv, Wiesbaden, Bestand 519/3, Akten der Devisenstellen Frankfurt und Kassel, Devisenstelle Frankfurt, 1940–1942, JS 10429, Erich Messing (°25/12/1895), letter (dated Aug. 21, 1940) from Gustav Fein to Devisenstelle Saarbrücken, unpaginated.

78 The full house number is 448/11. The arrival date of July 16, 1940 for Karel, Gustav and Helene Fein and the Tausiks can be found in the evidence obyvatelstva sheets in NA, Praha, fonds Policejní ředitelství Praha II. The original street name was Riegrova. The Germans renamed it Erbenova (Erbenstrasse) during the war. The current street name (and address) is 448/2 Urxova, Praha VIII. See *Orientační příručka: soupis popisných a orientačních dat a čísel domů ve Velké Praze* 1941, 1263; *Tabulky popisných čísel všech katastrálních obcí Velké Prahy* 1938, 123; *Orientační plán hlavního města Prahy s okolím* 1938, part 40. For a while, I thought that the names of two of the streets in which the Fein family lived corresponded to the *current* street names, initially giving me the impression that, with each move, the Fein family were further and further removed from the center of Prague. See Soetaert 2013, 88. A visit to the Prague city archives (Archiv hlavního města Prahy) fortunately helped me see this was a mistake. Through their several moves, the Feins remained in the city center. Over a number of study trips to Prague, I have seen and photographed all four addresses where the Feins lived.

79 NA, Praha, Policejní ředitelství Praha II, všeobecná spisovna, 1931–1940, kart. n° 5661, sign. F 271/9, Fein Karel JUDr 1894, f. 9.

80 The full house number is 370/4.

81 *Strassenverzeichnis der Hauptstadt Prag* 1941, 59, 135. It was possible to determine the old street numbers by a synergetic use of http://web2.mlp.cz/mapa1938/list_39 (accessed Dec. 13, 2018); the 1938 *Tabulky popisných čísel všech katastrálních obcí Velké Prahy*, https://digitalniknihovna.mlp.cz/mlp/view/uuid:bb6e1ad0-80a4-11dd-ba63-000d606f5dc6?page=uuid:d6156b50-c5ea-11dd-83cc-0030487be43a (accessed Dec. 13, 2018); and Google Maps. Jana Brantová (Katastrální úřad pro hlavní město Prahu) confirmed that the house numbers

and more people in fewer homes had a clear goal: "Herr [Adolf] Eichmann takes the view that it is not his business to worry about what these people will live on and where they will live. If there will be 10 to 15 Jews living in one room in Prague, they will try harder to emigrate".[84] By worsening the already miserable living conditions of Jewish people, the Germans sought to provoke a desire to emigrate (*Auswanderungslustigkeit*), making people think it the greatest blessing if they could emigrate, even abandoning their belongings and property: "Mr. Eichmann's intention is to spread a mood among the Jews, such that they would already be happy if he allowed them to emigrate at

were changed in 1941. See her email (dated Dec. 28, 2018) to the author. The original confusing house numbering 1, 1A, 2, 2A, 2B, 3, 3A, 4, 4A, 4B, etc. was changed to, 1, 2, 3, 4, 5, etc. One can also infer the house number change from the fact that the second house number – known as a conscription number (in Czech: *číslo popisné*, abbreviated as "ČP" in a column of the evidence obyvatelstva sheets in the NA, Praha, fonds Policejní ředitelství Praha II) – stayed the same: 370. (In Czech, the regular house number is *číslo orientační*, abbreviated as ČO.) After the war, the new house numbers were accepted but the street name was restored to Pobřežní. Knowledge of this change helps remove unnecessary confusion in the Prague police files on several people. In some cases, a personal file contains both street names with a different house number. This does *not* mean that the person moved to another house in another street. Both street names are contained, for example, in the evidence obyvatelstva sheet for Marie Neumann, who also lived at this address. On April 17, 1941, her address "changed" from 2A Pobřežní to 4 Hodonínská (while retaining the same conscription number 370). Official documents for three other people at this address – Zdeňka Neumannová, Anna Kummermann and the owner of the building, Josef Schneider – show that they were deported from 2A (not 4) Hodonínská. They lived at this address before the house numbers were changed and this explains the use of the old house number 2A. The official papers of everyone who took up residence in the house around 1941 showed the German name of the street, Gödinger Gasse, and also the new house number: 4.

[82] This railway station no longer exists. The tracks have been replaced by a large highway. The buildings of the northern wing of the Denis Railway Station (Praha Denisovo nádraží, Prag Denisbahnhof) – known after the war as Praha-Těšnov – were torn down in 1972 to make room for the construction of the north-south axis of Wilsonova Street, also known as the Magistrale (Magistrála). Even though they were not, strictly speaking, in the way of the north-south axis of Wilsonova Street, the building of the southern wing, along with its impressive neo-Renaissance entrance hall, were torn down in 1985. See https://de.wikipedia.org/wiki/Bahnhof_Praha-Těšnov, and the map http://web2.mlp.cz/mapa1938/list_39 (both accessed Nov. 29, 2019). Other important buildings near 4 Hodonínská (Gödinger Gasse) were the Muzeum hlavního města Prahy (The City of Prague Museum), still at the same location, and the former ministries of transport and agriculture.

[83] Gruner 2010, 162: "Zugleich drängte die Zentralstelle – in Erwartung der Deportationen – auf Kontrolle in mehr Bereichen und konnte dabei auch Erfolge verbuchen. Seit Herbst 1940 überwachte sie den 'jüdischen Wohnungsmarkt'. Deshalb wurden im September in Prag und im Oktober in Brünn alle 'jüdischen' Wohnungen besichtigt und verzeichnet. Die Konzentration der Mieter in sogenannten Judenhäusern betrieben in Prag künftig Stadt, Zentralstelle und NSDAP gemeinsam. Ab dem Frühjar [1941] begannen sie, die jüdische Bevölkerung Prags in 'Judenhäusern' zu konzentrieren". (At the same time, the Central Office – anticipating the deportations – pushed for control in more areas and was successful in doing so. Starting in the autumn of 1940, it monitored the 'Jewish housing market'. Consequently, in September in Prague, and in October in Brno, all 'Jewish' flats were inspected and recorded. In Prague, the concentration of tenants in so-called Jewish houses was thereafter carried out jointly by the city, the Central Office and the NSDAP. From the early part of the year [1941] they began to concentrate the Jewish population of Prague in 'Jewish houses'). Cf. Krejčová, Svobodová & Hyndráková 1997, 227, document n° 14, "Sonderaktionen: Erfassung Jüdischer Wohnungen in Prag, 10–13 September 1941". The Germans further issued regulations stipulating that, starting at some moment, some city areas were off limits for Jews. See Potthast 2000, 159 n. 18. On the topic of the so-called *Judenhäuser*, see Löw 2012, 42–43; also documents n° 181 and n° 215 (Löw 2012, 108–9, 459–60, 527–29). Even more specific measures were introduced. See document n° 289, "Der Schrifsteller Jiří Orten zählt am 27. Oktober 1940 auf, welchen Einschränkungen Juden unterliegen": "Ich darf nirgendwohin übersiedeln außer nach Prag I oder Prag V, und dann nur als Untermieter" (I am not allowed to move anywhere, except to Prague I or Prague V, and then only as a subtenant) (Löw 2012, 697). Then, in October 1940, Jews were simply not allowed to leave the greater Prague (Groß-Prag) city district. See Löw 2012, 697 n. 6.

[84] In document n° 260, "Die Jüdische Kultusgemeinde Prag berichtet am 21. August 1939 über die katastrophale Lage der Juden und Eichmanns Herrschaft im Protektorat": "Herr [Adolf] Eichmann vertritt die Ansicht, daß es nicht seine Sache sei, sich darum zu bekümmern, wovon diese Leute leben und wo sie wohnen werden. Wenn in Prag in einem Raum 10 bis 15 Juden leben werden, so werden sie

all, even if they were almost naked".[85] In the Prague *Jewish News Journal* (*Jüdisches Nachrichtenblatt*), there was a notice that, starting in September 1940, Jews were not allowed to enter new rental leases, but had to move in with people on an existing lease.[86] Presumably, then, the Feins rented from the Tausiks for one year and were not able to extend their lease. This meant that they had to look elsewhere and had to go to the housing department (*Wohnungsreferat*) of the JKG to be assigned a new place. The Tausiks stayed behind at the Erbenstrasse (Erbenova) address.[87]

Despite the imposition of these compulsory measures, and the Feins' being forced to turn to the JKG housing department, two factors indirectly indicate that the Fein family looked on their own for other places to live in Prague. Siegfried and Ida Tausik's daughter, Valerie Tausik, lived at 4 Hodonínská, from March 1934 until January 1935.[88] So it seems quite likely that the Feins heard of this address because of her. Very possibly, they checked the location and then decided, most likely in cooperation with the JKG housing department, to move there. Yet another element was probably quintessential for the Fein family ending up in this building in June 1941. Since 1918, the owner of the house at 2A Pobřežní (which became 4 Hodonínská in 1941) was the Jewish wholesale wine merchant Rudolf Schneider (1886–1941?), who was married to Marie Kummermann (1887–1941?). At their new 4 Hodonínská address, the Feins stayed in the apartment of the widow Anna Kummermann (1879–1942?), the sister of Marie Kummermann.[89] Likely, Anna Kummermann was paying little rent, or no rent at all, since she was the sister-in-law of the building's owner, Rudolf Schneider [ill. 4]. Schneider was one of three children of Josef Schneider (1855-1942), who also

sich kräftiger um die Auswanderung bemühen" (Löw 2012, 630). See also Potthast 2002, 75.

[85] In document n° 260, "Die Jüdische Kultusgemeinde Prag berichtet am 21. August 1939 über die katastrophale Lage der Juden und Eichmanns Herrschaft im Protektorat": "Herr Eichmann hat nämlich die Absicht, unter den Juden eine Stimmung zu verbreiten, in der sie schon glücklich sind, wenn er ihnen nur überhaupt erlaubt, auszuwandern, sei es auch fast nackt" (Löw 2012, 629).

[86] See the anonymous "Kundmachung: Neuregelung jüdischer Wohnungsmietung in Prag" (Announcement: New Regulation for Jewish Housing Rentals in Prague), *Jüdisches Nachrichtenblatt* [Prague edition], Jg. 2, n° 37, Sep. 13, 1940, [1]: "hat der Jüdischen Kultusgemeinde Prag mitgeteilt, daß Juden in Prag freie Wohnungen nicht mehr mieten dürfen. Es dürfen somit Juden nur in bereits von Juden benützte Wohnungen einziehen" (The Jewish Community in Prague has announced that Jews are no longer allowed to rent vacant flats in Prague. Jews are consequently only allowed to move into flats already occupied by Jews). Following the Reichsprotektor's ordinance, this also meant that, starting in October 1940, leases for flats rented to Jews that were coming to an end could only be renewed with the explicit approval of the Central Office. See Oprach 2006, 71; Potthast 2000, 159 n. 18. In October 1940, the Prague police also forbade Jews to move on their own initiative. See Oprach 2006, 74 n. 313. All this seems to confirm my proposition that the Feins' first two Prague addresses were indeed still chosen in relative freedom, since they had moved to their second Prague address by July 1940. Their third move, to 4 Hodonínská (Gödinger Gasse), took place in June 1941.

[87] This would also turn out to be the last Prague address of Ida Tausik and her husband Siegfried Tausik before they were deported to Terezín on transport "Aan" on July 6, 1942. Siegfried died in Terezín on April 20, 1943. Ida was further transferred from Terezín to Auschwitz-Birkenau on transport "Er" on October 16, 1944.

[88] NA, Praha, fonds Policejní ředitelství Praha II, evidence obyvatelstva sheet, Valerie Tausik (Tausig). The address was then still 2A Pobřežní.

[89] In 2012, for Karl Fein, there was the mention "c/o Kummermann" (currently removed) in the victims database of www.holocaust.cz. The same name also recurs on his evidence obyvatelstva sheet in NA, Praha, fonds Policejní ředitelství Praha II. The name "A. Kummermannová" also appears in one of his police file documents in NA, Praha, Policejní ředitelství Praha II, všeobecná spisovna, 1931–1940, kart. n° 5661, sign. F 271/9, Fein Karel JUDr 1894. Before the war, the widow Anna Kummermann lived at the same 2A Pobřežní address. See the *Pražský adresář* 1937–38, 727. She was deported to Terezín on May 15, 1942 on transport "Au 1" and transferred further to Malý Trostinec on transport "Bc" on August 25, 1942. Her late husband was Adolf Kummermann (1869-1928). The couple had six children. Child 1: Valerie Klinger (née Kummermann, 1903–1928) died in 1928 and her husband Otto Klinger (1891?–1934) in 1934. Their child Vally Liliane Adler (1928–1941?) was deported from Prague to Łódź on transport "C" on October 26, 1941 and perished in the Holocaust. Child 2: Stefanie Adler (née Kummermann, 1900–1942?) died during deportation along with her two children Yvetta Jitka Adler (1925–1942?) and Alexander (1927–1942?). They were deported on transport "R" on January 18, 1942 from

lived at 4 Hodonínská.[90] Josef Schneider's wife, who died in 1884, was Žofie Stránská (1855–1884), originally from Boskovice, the ancestral village of the Fein family. Karl and Gustav Fein's father, Albert Fein, was born in Boskovice (Boskowitz) in 1854. Žofie Stránská was born in 1855. Since both had lived in the Boskovice Jewish ghetto, the Feins and the Schneiders would at least have known each other's last names. It seems probable to me that this common ancestral village was a second factor that helped the Feins obtain their new place in Prague. Let us not forget that it was likely not easy to find a place, with fewer and fewer houses and apartments available to Jewish people. Any argument that would help find a place that suited one's standards was most welcome.

SALOMON SABOVIČ

Except for one other person, the twenty-seven-year-old mechanic Salomon Sabovič (1914–1942?), it looks like the Feins were the only ones staying in Anna Kummermann's apartment.[91] Salomon Sabovič may have been Karl Fein's lover or (gay?) friend.[92] Since Jewish people in the whole of the Protectorate could no longer visit cultural and leisure centers, and since there was an evening curfew, it does not seem illogical

Pilsen (Plzeň) to Terezín and then on transport "Bc" on August 25, 1942 from Terezín to Maly Trostinec. Anna Kummermann was deported on the same transport "Bc" as her daughter Stefanie, indicating that there was a good bond with this daughter. Stefanie Adler's husband, Leo Adler (1894–1939), died in 1939. Child 3: The fate of Eugenie Evza Eisler (née Kummernann, 1905–1942?) and her husband Anton Eisler (1896–1942?) was also fatally determined by the Holocaust. They were both deported on transport "Bg" from Prague to Terezín on September 12, 1942, and further transferred to Treblinka on transport "Bu" on October 8, 1942. Child 4: Milan Kummermann (1918–1945?) was deported to Terezín on transport "Ck" on December 22, 1942. He was further transferred to Auschwitz-Birkenau on September 28, 1944 on transport "Ek". He survived the war but his further fate is unknown. Children 5 and 6: The fate of František Kummermann (1902–?) and Marie Kummermann (1897–?) is not known. It is unclear what happened to Marie Elhenicky (née Kummermann, 1897–?) (and what happened to her husband Franz Elhenicky), the daughter born to Adolf Kummermann's first marriage with Hermine Bondy (1871–1899). More genealogical information on Anna Kummermann can be found at https://www.geni.com/people/Anna-Kummerman/6000000022971012350#name=Anna%20Kummerman? (accessed Jul. 26, 2015). See also NA, fond Policejní ředitelství I, konskripce 1850–1914, kart. n° 329, f. 441, available online at http://digi.nacr.cz/ prihlasky2/index.php?action =link&ref=czarch:CZ-100000010:874 &kart.=329&folium=441 (accessed Jan. 24, 2019). Interestingly, a certain Max Kummermann (1902–?) was on transport "D" on which most of the Schneider family was deported. He survived the war and was liberated from Friedland (Germany). See Kárný et al. 1995, 126; NA, Praha, fonds n° 375, Arizačni spisy, company Rudolf Schneider, kart. n° 43, invent. n° 443.

[90] NA, Praha, fonds n° 375, Arizačni spisy, company Rudolf Schneider, kart. n° 43, invent. n° 443. Josef Schneider was deported on July 20, 1942 on transport "AAs" from Prague to Terezín where he died on November 11, 1942. Josef and Žofie Schneider had three children: their oldest son was Viktor Schneider (1882–?) whose further fate, other than that he moved to Hungary, is unknown. See NA, Policejní ředitelství I, konskripce 1850–1914, kart. n° 608, f. 158, available online at http://digi.nacr.cz/prihlasky2/index.php?action=link&ref=czarch:CZ-100000010:874&kart.=608&folium=158 (accessed Jan. 24, 2019). Another child was Olga Gross (1884–1942?). She was deported on transport "N" on December 17, 1941 from Prague to Terezín and then on transport "P" from Terezín to Riga on January 15, 1942. For her police file in NA, see https://www.holocaust.cz/en/database-of-victims/victim/90339-olga-grossova/ (accessed Apr. 10, 2019). I was not able to identify her husband nor what happened with him. The third and youngest child was Rudolf Schneider (1886–1941?).

[91] Salomon Sabovič's evidence obyvatelstva sheet, in NA, Praha, fonds Policejní ředitelství Praha II, stated that he was also staying with Anna Kummermann. It is unknown why the same sheet reconfirmed that Sabovič was staying at 4 Hodonínská on August 31, 1941. I checked all the other Jewish people who lived at 4 Hodonínská and found no mention that other people stayed with Mrs. Kummermann. In addition to the victims database on www.holocaust.cz, I checked existing police files and the evidence obyvatelstva sheets of most other persons listed as living at 4 Hodonínská.

[92] NA, Praha, fonds Policejní ředitelství Praha II, všeobecná spisovna, 1941–1950, kart. n° 9761, sign. S38/1, Salomon Sabovič 1914. Sabovič's police file gives no clues that the young man may have engaged in homosexual activities or was ever condemned for such. His date of birth is given as April 11, 1914 by www.holocaust.cz and Kárný et al. 1995, 155. However, all official documents on him that I have seen give February 1, 1914. Salomon Sabovič was originally from Slatinské Doly (okres Rachov) in the Carpathian Ruthenia region (in German, Karpatenukraine), part of Czechoslovakia in the interwar

that Fein who, as Giese suggested, devoted a good deal of time to his love and sex life, sought the company of a steady friend. That Jewish and gay social relations took place indoors in the evenings may explain why Fein may have preferred to have a good friend or even a lover close by.[93]

As far as I can tell, Jewish people were well aware of class differences before the deportations started and, presumably, did what they could to lodge with people in their own social circle. Most likely, the JKG in Prague also took this into consideration when assigning people to new locations. That the upper classes later mingled with the "common folk" in Jewish ghettos like Łódź and Terezín would be, in addition to hunger and other miseries, one of the great cultural shocks they had to deal with after deportation. For these reasons, it is hard to explain how a working-class boy like Salomon Sabovič ended up in the apartment of an upper-class widow, Anna Kummermann, the sister-in-law of Rudolf Schneider, the owner of the building, where the Feins also lived. An intervention on Salomon Sabovič's behalf by Karl Fein may indeed offer a good explanation. Judging from the photobooth picture in his police file, Sabovič was indeed a handsome working-class boy [ill. 5]. The one factor that speaks against this interpretation is that Sabovič arrived at 4 Hodonínská on March 18, 1941, and Karl Fein not until June 19, 1941.[94] These differing arrival dates may in fact suggest that the new policy of concentrating people in so-called Jewish houses, started in the autumn of 1940, nevertheless entailed total strangers being randomly brought together in Prague apartments. But I think it possible that Fein's later arrival was linked to the expiry of the lease for the Feins' previous address. That lease ran from July 1940 to June 1941.[95]

"FEASTING WITH PANTHERS"

Let us briefly return to upper-class gay men being attracted to young working-class boys and young men, an important form of sexual expression, even a homoerotic norm, for many homosexual upper-class men in most Western countries before the war, and also afterwards.[96] That this was indeed a longstanding gay tradition is attested by the essential Oscar Wilde, who in 1897 famously described his sexual

period, now the Ukrainian urban-type settlement of Solotvyno. Sabovič arrived in Prague in 1929, at the age of 15, where he worked as a mechanic. His parents were Lazar Sabovič and Ester Lebovičová. Their fate is unclear. However, the Yad Vashem Shoah database mentions a "Lazar Sabovich" from the town of Salomon Sabovič's birth (Solotvina). See http://db.yadvashem.org/names/nameDetails.html?itemId=6452720&language=en (accessed Aug. 10, 2015). The information was retrieved by Yad Vashem from record group M 33, Records of the Extraordinary State Commission to Investigate German-Fascist Crimes Committed on Soviet Territory, document ID 6421109, List of survivors and perished from Selo Slatina, prepared by the Soviet Extraordinary State Commission, April 8, 1946, 225–316. The original document is in the State archive of the Russian Federation in Moscow. The digitized list can be found on the Yad Vashem website (accessed August 10, 2015). I checked the ninety-two-page-long handwritten list but did not see the last name Sabovich/ Sabovič there.

[93] An overview of several anti-Jewish measures can be found in Kárný et al. 1996, 35–37.

[94] It also remains unexplained why Gustav Fein arrived in the apartment on June 16, 1941, three days before his brother Karl Fein. Their mother followed two days later, on June 21, 1941. See their evidence obyvatelstva sheets in NA, Praha, fonds Policejní ředitelství Praha II. For unclear reasons, Gustav Fein is listed in the www.holocaust.cz database at 18 Hodonínská. This is likely a mistake since the database mentioned "c/o Kummermann" (now removed). No other people in the www.holocaust.cz database were found at 18 Hodonínská.

[95] I have no explanation for why the Erbenstrasse (Erbenova) apartment lease was for only eleven months. The Erbenstrasse (Erbenova) lease started in mid-July 1940, and the Gödinger Gasse (Hodonínská) lease in June 1941. Yet the fact that the moves both occurred around the 15th of the month does indicate that they were indeed linked to (expiring) leases.

[96] Barry Reay has shown that this fluid sociological complex, which linked sexuality and (earning) money, lasted well after World War II in, for example, New York. See Reay 2010, chapter 1, esp. 16–17.

[97] McKenna 2005, 216–25; the chapter, "Feasting with Panthers". Curiously, the expression is recalled

encounters with working-class boys and young men as "feasting with panthers".[97] Robert Beachy has recently, in the context of prewar Berlin, described this thwarted complex of prostitution, class difference, remuneration, sexual desire and love.[98]

We have also seen this same homoerotic complex in the case of Willi Bondi. During a 1941 Criminal Police (Kriminalpolizei, Kripo) hearing, Bondi stated that he had sex with "rent boys and other young men",[99] either paying them or covering their expenses.[100] Berta Gottwald, a maid who worked in the Fleischer-Bondi household, confirmed that Bondi had sex only with young men and boys.[101] Bondi met many of his sexual partners in swimming pools.[102] One young man he encountered this way was Wilhelm Sponer, whom he met in the Central Bathhouse (Zentralbad, also known as Charlottenbad) in Brno where they had sex in a changing room.[103] Sponer also prostituted himself. Bondi also had a steadier partner, Jan Příborský (1910–?), whom he met in 1933. The young working-class man was financially supported by Bondi; both he and Příborský slept in Bondi's bed on weekends.[104] Most likely, Karl Fein's love and sex life greatly resembled Willi Bondi's. Fein knew most of Bondi's gay friends.[105]

THE RUDOLF SCHNEIDER COMPANY

The building in Gödinger Gasse (Hodonínská), where the Feins lived, was built in the 1890s. It had two wings. The street-facing wing had four floors. Behind it, there was an inner courtyard with a larger wing housing apartments in another four floors. We do not know exactly where the Feins lived, but it may have been in a street-facing apartment. Anna Kummermann was a close member of the family and presumably had one of the best street-facing apartments. The owner of the building, Rudolf Schneider, lived elsewhere in the city with his wife and children. Schneider additionally owned a wholesale company, founded in 1913, trading in wine and spirits

in the title of the biography of the gay Austro-Hungarian army officer, Colonel Alfred Redl (1864–1913), *The Panther's Feast*. See Asprey 1959. Better known is the 1985 movie on Redl's life, *Oberst redl* (*Colonel Redl*). More recently, an American novelist has given a contemporary rendering of this tenacious homosexual tradition. See Greenwell 2016. For a good analysis of the structural entanglement of the fates of gay men and male prostitutes in 1920s Berlin, see Marhoefer 2015, ch. 4, esp. 124–27.

[98] Beachy 2014, 188–89, 192–96, 200–12, 218–19, and esp. 202, 219. In many parts of the world, all kinds of sexual practices, imbricated with material and/or financial dependency, are still common. The more egalitarian, Western ideal of sexual and emotional bonding, developed mostly after World War II, is still rare elsewhere or just one cultural form in which homosexual behavior finds expression. For a recent reconsideration of this topic on a global scale, see Navratil & Remele 2021.

[99] See his testimony (dated Mar. 28, 1941) in MZA, Brno, fonds C 43, Německý zemský soud Brno (Deutsches Landgericht), Staatsanwaltschaft bei dem Landgericht Brünn, file Wilhelm Sponer & Helmuth Holdau, kart. n° 184, sign. 4 K Ls 24/41, f. 94b: "z.[um] Teil Strichjunge und andere jüngere Männer" (partly hustlers and other younger men). The German word for rent boy is *Strichjungen*, a term used for a male prostitute, for example, by a Kripo Kriminal-Oberassistent (Senior Detective Assistant) named Hofmann to describe Wilhelm Sponer (1915–?). See MZA, Brno, fonds C 43, Německý zemský soud Brno (Deutsches Landgericht), Staatsanwaltschaft bei dem Landgericht Brünn, file Wilhelm Sponer & Helmuth Holdau, kart. n° 184, sign. 4 K Ls 24/41, f. 76b.

[100] Ibid., f. 14. Cf. f. 94b.

[101] Ibid., f. 82: "Er hat sich nach meinen Wahrnehmungen immer nur an junge Männer, bezw. Burschen gehalten" (According to my observations, he only hooked up with young men, or boys, respectively).

[102] Ibid., f. 86.

[103] For more information on this swimming pool, see https://encyklopedie.brna.cz/home-mmb/?acc = profil_udalosti&load=3665 (accessed Nov. 11, 2021).

[104] MZA, Brno, fonds C 43, Německý zemský soud Brno (Deutsches Landgericht), Staatsanwaltschaft bei dem Landgericht Brünn, file Wilhelm Sponer & Helmuth Holdau, kart. n° 184, sign. 4 K Ls 24/41, f. 13b, 14, f. 94-95. Peter Barber wrote to me that the young man had good contact with the Bondi family during and after the war. See email (dated Nov. 2, 2021) from Peter Barber to the author.

[105] MZA, Brno, fonds C43, Německý zemský soud Brno (Deutsches Landgericht), Staatsanwaltschaft bei dem Landgericht Brünn, file Wilhelm Sponer & Helmuth Holdau, kart. n° 184, sign. 4 K Ls 24/41, f. 82b.

under his own name, operating from 4 Hodonínská,[106] its offices occupying the first floor and a part of the second floor on the street-facing side.[107] Vast cellars under the building stocked the merchandise and this may also have played a part in the Feins choosing this building: in the case of bombardment, they would have robust shelter.[108]

Schneider's wine and spirits business was one of the main dealers in foreign wines in Prague, employing around thirty people, and did a turnover of around 400,000 liters of wine and spirits per year.[109] In obedience to paragraph 9 of the Decree of the Reich Protector in Bohemia and Moravia on Jewish Assets of June 21, 1939, Rudolf Schneider's building and business were sold below market value in November 1941 to the Austrians Matthias (?–?) and Franz Mielacher (1909–1943).[110] Schneider and his father, Josef Schneider, who also worked for the wine business, were fired at the end of 1940.[111] In order to profit from its renown, the company continued to operate during the war under Rudolf Schneider's name.

Rudolf Schneider and his wife Marie Kummermann were deported on transport "D" on October 31, 1941, from Prague to Łódź. Three of their four children, Jiří (1914–1944), Petr (1922–1941?) and daughter Eva (1924–?) were deported with them.[112] Only Eva Schneider survived the war, being liberated from Kudowa Zdrój (Poland).[113] She married and took the name Weinberg, but continued her father's wine business after the war, preserving Rudolf Schneider as the company name. Later, the company was nationalized, continuing to trade in wine at the same location under the name Czechoslovak State Wineries (Československý stat – vinařské závody).[114]

[106] See https://www.holocaust.cz/en/database-of-victims/victim/ 121747-josef-schneider/ (accessed Dec. 28, 2018); *Adresář hlavního města Prahy* 1936, 380.

[107] NA, Praha, fonds n° 375, Arizačni spisy, company Rudolf Schneider, kart. n° 43, invent. n° 443.

[108] It turned out that Prague was only bombed twice, in 1945.

[109] NA, Praha, fonds n° 375, Arizačni spisy, company Rudolf Schneider, kart. n° 43, invent. n° 443.

[110] For more on Franz Mielacher, see https://www.findagrave.com/ memorial/140370994 (accessed Dec. 28, 2018). Franz Mielacher lived in Arnbruck (Austria). Landesrat Matthias Mielacher was active in the NSDAP in Linz (Gauwirtschaftsberater für den Gau Oberdonau [Gau Economic Adviser for the Upper Danube]) and survived the war. Mielacher's name appears in the US Holocaust Memorial Museum, Washington DC, Robert M. W. and Ruth Benedicta Kempner papers, Series 5, Subseries 4: Prosecution & Defense Document Books, Case XI, box n° 312, folder n° 17. Robert Kempner (Oct. 17, 1899–Aug. 15, 1993) was the deputy US chief counsel on the International Military Tribunal in Nuremberg; however, the file on Mielacher was only accessible on the US Holocaust Memorial Museum site. See email (dated Feb. 10, 2021) from Vincent Slatt (US Holocaust Memorial Museum, Washington DC) to the author. No fewer than six different *Treuhänder* (trustees) were appointed before the sale of the wholesale wine business: Wilhelm Triska, Paul Huhn, Erhard Gauba (who was arrested by the Gestapo in June 1941), Alois Nožička (who held the post for five weeks), Franz Philipp (from Brno) and the *Verkaufstreuhänder* (sales trustee) and Prague lawyer Wilhelm Magerstein. See NA, Praha, fonds n° 375, Arizačni spisy, company Rudolf Schneider, kart. n° 43, invent. n° 443.

[111] NA, Praha, fonds n° 375, Arizačni spisy, company Rudolf Schneider, kart. n° 43, invent. n° 443. They were fired by the *Treuhänder* (trustee) Erhard Gauba. Rudolf Schneider's son, Georg Schneider, who worked as a *Kellermeister* (cellarmaster), and a certain unidentified Jewish man named Karl Taussig (?–?), continued to work for the company, though it is unclear until when. I could not determine if this Karl Taussig was in any way related to the couple Siegfried and Ida Tausik.

[112] The third son, Kamil Schneider (1917–1944?), was deported on November 20, 1942 on transport "Cc" from Prague to Terezín and then, on May 15, 1944, on transport "Dz" from Terezín to Auschwitz-Birkenau. See his police file at https://www.holocaust.cz/en/database-of-victims/victim/121752-kamil-schneider/ (accessed Dec. 28, 2018).

[113] Kárný et al. 1995, 126.

[114] Email (dated Dec. 28, 2018) from Jana Brantová (Katastrální úřad pro hlavní město Prahu) to the author. On my behalf, Jan Škoda (Archiv hlavního města Prahy) consulted the file of the Josef Schneider firm, founded in 1913, with license n° 229130 in Referátů II.A and II.B (referát živnostenský), the Prague business register (*živnostenském rejstříku, Handelsregister*). Due to the fragile state of this archival fonds, its documents are not accessible to researchers in the Prague city archive research room. See email (dated Nov. 22, 2019) from Jan Škoda (Archiv hlavního města Prahy, Praha) to the author. See also email (dated Dec. 28, 2018) from Jana Brantová (Katastrální úřad pro hlavní město Prahu, Praha) to the author.

[115] When I entered "Hodonínská 4" in the www.holocaust.cz database, around 2012–13, eight names

THE NEUMANN FAMILY

Hoping to find the testimony of a Holocaust survivor who had stayed at 4 Hodonínská, I looked at all the other Jewish people who lived at this address. Other than the Fein family and Salomon Sabovič, who lived in Anna Kummermann's apartment, I found several other names of Jewish people living on the same 4 Hodonínská address.[115]

In a December 1941 postcard sent from the ghetto in Łódź, Karl Fein asked his mother, who was still in Prague, how Mrs. Kummermann (Frau Kummermann) was doing and also how a certain Mrs. Neumann (Frau Neumann) was faring. This shows, of course, that Fein had been in contact with the Neumann family, also living at 4 Hodonínská.[116] Again, the eight p.m. curfew only makes it likely that, in the evenings, people sought out each other's company in the safety of a building that contained several apartments. The engineer Richard Neumann (1881–1942) and his wife Sidonie (Zděnka) Propper (1889–1944?) had indeed been living at 2A Pobřežní (which later became 4 Hodonínská) since June 1935.[117] But by 1940, Richard Neumann was ill with a kidney disease (nephrosclerosis) and was staying in a Jewish hospital in Prague. That Fein specifically inquired about Mrs. Neumann only appears to confirm that Richard Neumann was no longer living with his wife at 4 Hodonínská.

The Neumann couple had two daughters. Josefina Neumann (1919–1944?) lived with her mother at the same address. Zděnka Neumann and her daughter Josefina were deported from Prague to Terezín on transport "AAu" on July 27, 1942.[118] Zděnka's husband Richard died a month later. It seems probable that his death was linked in some way to the deportation of his wife and daughter.[119] The other daughter was Marie Lotte Neumann (1915–1972), who married Jiri Kot'átko (1914–?), a man studying to be a doctor. The couple had lived at 4 Hodonínská since mid-June 1936, moving out in October 1942.[120] The couple survived the war because they had a so-called "mixed marriage". Marie Lotte was nevertheless deported to Terezín in February 1945 on the mixed breed (*Mischlingen*) transport "AE". My attempts to make contact with the Kot'átko couple's current relatives in Prague led nowhere.[121]

came up. Not counting Karl Fein, his mother and Salomon Sabovič, that gave five new names. A sixth name came up when manually checking the eighty-five names retrieved after entering "Hodonínská" in the www.holocaust.cz database.

[116] APŁ, Łódź, fond Przełożony Starszeństwa Żydów, signature 2316, microfilm L-20930, [Karty pocztowe przeznaczone dla krewnych i znajomych w Generalnej Guberni, Rzeszy i w innych krajach, które nie zostały wysłane z getta przez pocztę], number 1668, postcard (dated Dec. 8, 1941) from Karl Fein to Helena Fein.

[117] See the evidence obyvatelstva sheet for the couple in NA, Praha, fonds Policejní ředitelství Praha II. The Neumann couple were married on June 8, 1913 in Slaný, Zděnka Neumannová's home town. Information on their marriage can be found in NA, Praha, fond n° 167, Jewish registers (Židovské matriky, Judische Matriken), Slaný, category O [marriages], 1841–1944, inv. nr. 1861, f. 123, reproduction n° 130, available online at: http://www.badatelna.eu/fond/1073/inventar/ (accessed Nov. 20, 2015). The marriage register records that Rudolf Neumann, Richard Neumann's brother, was one of the two witnesses. I was not able to determine with certainty who he was since sixteen people with this name are mentioned in Kárný et al. 1995.

[118] On October 12, 1944, both were transported from Terezín to Auschwitz-Birkenau on transport "Eq". Curiously, and likely erroneously, the evidence obyvatelstva sheets in NA, Praha, fonds Policejní ředitelství Praha II, for Zděnka Neumann and her daughter Josefina give September 28, 1942 as the date that they were transported. But there was no transport from Prague on that date. See Kárný et al. 1995, 67.

[119] Richard Neumann died in August 1942. See the - hard to decipher - death certificate (*Totenschein, úmrtní lístek*) date in NA, Praha, fonds Policejní ředitelství II, všeobecná spisovna, 1941–1951, kart. n° 7897, sign. N 951/5, Richard Neumann 1881. In the Prague death index for 1942, there is only a reference to the death register (XXIII/201/584), see http://www.badatelna.eu/fond/1073/reprodukce/?zaznamId=3763&reproId=24213 (accessed Aug. 11, 2016).

[120] NA, Praha, fonds Policejní ředitelství Praha II, evidence obyvatelstva sheet Jiri Kot'átko.

[121] The couple had one daughter named Magdalena, presumably born after the war, but her birth year was redacted for privacy reasons on the evidence obyvatelstva sheet for Jiri Kot'átko in NA, Praha, fonds Policejní ředitelství Praha II. The couple's police file is in NA, Praha, Policejní ředitelství Praha II, všeobecná spisovna, 1941-1950, kart. n° 5688, sign. K 4434/5, Koťátko Jiří MUDr. 1914 and Marie 1915. On October 15, 2016, I sent a letter to the eleven people named Kot'átko in Prague. Regretta-

ZDENĚK KÖNIG

Zdeněk König (1921–1943) was another resident at 4 Hodonínská whom I identified. He was born in the small Bohemian village of Hřiměždice, 50 kilometers south of Prague, to well-off parents, Hugo and Božena König.[122] Presumably in an attempt to emigrate, the eighteen-year-old Zdeněk König left his parents' house in Smolotely and moved to Prague on October 12, 1939. He arrived in Prague around the same time as Fein did from Brno. König stayed for a year and a half with a sister of his mother, Irma Saxlová (1890–?), then living at 9 Písecká in Prague's Vinohrady (Weinberge) district.[123]

König arrived at 4 Hodonínská on April 4, 1941, and lived in the apartment of Richard Neumann and his wife Sidonie.[124] König would stay at this address for quite a long time, until May 1942. Here, we see a young man from the countryside ending up in the capital in a flat of people of his own class. Since he lived with the Neumann family, whom Karl Fein knew, Fein would have known König also.[125] Starting in

bly, no one responded. On January 19, 2017, I sent nineteen letters to the people named Kot'átko living outside of Prague. Several people replied but none of them was related. See also https://www.geni.com/people/Marie/6000000036950002466?through=6000000036949346686#/tab/overview (accessed Nov. 20 2015); the evidence obyvatelstva sheet for Marie Lotte Neumann in NA, Praha, fonds Policejní ředitelství Praha II.

[122] Hřiměždice (Wermeritz) is located in the Středočeský kraj (Central Bohemian) region and in the Příbram (okres Příbram) district. Zdeněk König's parents, Hugo König (1878–1943) and Božena (née Lüftschitz, 1888 or 1889–1944?), lived in the village of Smolotely, also in the Příbram district. Both parents were deported on transport "Bz", from Tábor to Terezín, on November 12, 1942. The father died in Terezín in September 1943. The mother was transferred further on transport "Eq" to Auschwitz-Birkenau on October 12, 1944. The family had three members of their serving staff living in the household, indicating they were well off. See Státní okresní archiv Příbram, fonds Okresní úřad Příbram, census reports (sčítání lidu), year 1921, kart. n° 12. Later, the couple owned a property and an agricultural business in the village of Smolotely.

[123] The widow Irma Saxl (née Lüftschitz, 1890–1959), a sister of Zdeněk's mother Božena, had been married to the engineer Viktor Saxl (1886–1930). She was deported on transport "Bf" from Prague to Terezín on September 8, 1942. She was liberated from Terezín and after the war lived in Prague where she died in 1959. Vera Konig, the daughter of Viktor König, Zdeněk's older brother, confirmed to me that Irma Saxl was indeed a sister of Božena König. See email (dated Dec. 9, 2018) from Vera Konig to the author. Viktor König also stayed with his aunt Irma Saxl in 1935–36. See the evidence obyvatelstva sheets for Viktor and Zdeněk König in NA, Praha, fonds Policejní ředitelství Praha II; and Irma Saxlová's police file in NA, Praha, Policejní ředitelství II, všeobecná spisovna, 1941–1950, kart. n° 9796, sign. file S 210/21, Irma Saxlová 1890.

[124] See his evidence obyvatelstva sheet in NA, Praha, fonds Policejní ředitelství Praha II and the note (dated Apr. 6, 1941) of the četnická stanice Smolotely to the Polizeidirektion in Prague in NA, Praha, Policejní ředitelství Praha II, všeobecná spisovna, 1941–1950, kart. n° 5522, sign. K 3666/1, Zdeněk König 1921, f. 5.

[125] Zdeněk König had three siblings. Pursuing their surviving traces led me to some pictures of Zdeněk König as a young boy and of his parents. Zdeněk's younger brother František (1924–1943?) was put on transport "Bg", bringing him from Prague to Terezín on September 12, 1942. František stayed with his aunt Berta Lüftschitz (1863–1943) in the Prague suburb of Velká Chuchle before he was deported. Zdeněk's older brother, the engineer Viktor König (1913–2005) managed to emigrate with his wife Hanna Spitz (1917–2008) to South America in 1938. The couple had two daughters, Vera Konig (1942–) and K. H. M. (1945–), both born in Ecuador. After a brief return to Czechoslovakia after the war, the couple moved to the USA in 1948 and eventually became US citizens. Both died in New York. Lastly, Zdeněk also had an older sister, Irma (1911–2001), who survived the Holocaust. She, her son Richard Milan (1938–2018), and her first husband, Viktor Fleischmann (1906–1945), were deported on transport "Di" from Prague to Terezín on July 13, 1943, five days after her brother Zdeněk. Her husband was eventually further transferred to Auschwitz-Birkenau on October 1, 1944. He perished in Dachau in January 1945. Irma and her son survived Terezín. After the war, Irma married Kurt Arje (1914–1971). She became a British citizen in 1975. The couple had one son, Dan Arje (1950–). Her son Richard Milan and his wife Milena left Czechoslovakia in 1968 and emigrated to Canada. See email (dated Dec. 10, 2018) from Vera Konig to the author. On December 5, 2018, I received a friendly email from K. H. M. containing some pictures of Zdeněk, his brother and their parents. She also kindly forwarded my letter to her sister Vera and her cousin Dan. Vera Konig replied one more time by email on December 5, 2018 and sent me another family photo and the names of two people I could contact.

[126] Her late husband was Rudolf Klemperer (1878–1918). The couple had four sons: Ernst Klemperer (1904–?), whose fate is unknown; Paul Klemperer (1905–1943?) and Franz Klemperer (1907–1943), who both died in Terezín; and Karl Klemperer (1909–194?), who was deported from Terezín to

the autumn of 1942, Zdeněk König worked for the Prague Jewish Central Museum (Jüdisches Zentralmuseum). That he obtained this job shows that he was protected. Possibly, he got his position thanks to Gustav Fein, Karl Fein's brother, intervening with the JKG. In any event, the job temporarily protected him from being deported.

The widow Cecilie Klemperer (née Neumann, 1883–1944) also lived at 4 Hodonínská. She was likely related to Richard Neumann, but was not his sister.[126] The other five people living at the same address were Gerta Benedikt (1905–1942?),[127] the widow Hedwig Lokesch (1874–1942),[128] the widow Ríza Weil (1888–1942?)[129] and Elisabeth Freund (1860–1942?).[130] All perished in the Holocaust.

Auschwitz-Birkenau on September 6, 1943. Cecilie Klemperer was deported to Terezín on December 14, 1941 on transport "M", together with her son Franz and other family members. She was further transferred to Auschwitz-Birkenau on transport "Ep" on October 9, 1944. Markéta Klemperer (1910–?) was the wife of Paul Klemperer (1905–1941?) and was put on transport "M" from Prague to Terezín on December 14, 1941 with her two children, Jan (1932–1944?) and Hana (1937–1944?). She and her two children were transferred further to Auschwitz-Birkenau on transport "Dz" on May 15, 1944. Markéta Klemperer was liberated from Stutthof in 1945 but her two children perished in Auschwitz. See NA, Policejní ředitelství Praha II, všeobecná spisovna, 1921–1930, kart. n° 1553, sign. K 1049/24, Cecilie Klempererová; Kárný et al. 1995, 239, 247; and the entry for Markéta Klemperer at https://www.geni.com/people/Mark%C3%A9ta-Klempererov%C3%A1/6000000034928909117 (accessed Jan. 18, 2017). I wish to thank Olda Poživil for further clarifications about his family tree. See her email (dated Feb. 20, 2017) to the author. Paul Klemperer had been deported three weeks earlier, on November 24, 1941, on transport "Ak" to Terezín, where he was arrested by the Gestapo on December 20, 1942. Likely, his earlier transport was tied to an unpaid fine of 20,000 Czech crowns for which he was convicted. For his Prague police file, see https://www.holocaust.cz/databaze-obeti/obet/99373-pavel-klemperer/ (accessed Feb. 12, 2019). Paul Klemperer's mother's maiden name was Neumann and this could be the reason why Cecilie Klemperer, ended up in the apartment of Richard Neumann. See also the evidence obyvatelstva sheet for Rudolf Klemperer in NA, Praha, fonds Policejní ředitelství II.

127 According to the evidence obyvatelstva sheet in NA, Praha, fonds Policejní ředitelství Praha II, Gerta Benedikt arrived at 4 Hodonínská on April 22, 1941. Presumably, she was a widow or divorced from her husband Alfred Benedikt. She was deported on transport "X" on February 12, 1942 from Prague to Terezín and then transferred on transport "Aai" from Terezín to an unknown destination on June 13, 1942. Her police file can be found at https://www.holocaust.cz/en/database-of-victims/victim/76603-gerta-benediktova/ (accessed Mar. 23, 2012). See also http://www.jewishhistory.cz/cz2/eng/victims/person/1321516/ (accessed Mar. 23, 2012). Gerta Benedikt's daughter, Ruth Renée Benedikt (1930–?), is on a list of about 13,400 people who managed to escape to England thanks to the efforts of the British Committee for Refugees from Czechoslovakia (BCRC) and the later Czech Refugee Trust Fund (CRTF). She was possibly one of the children on the so-called *Kindertransporte* (children's transports). See the alphabetical list, "Names of registered individuals and associated persons", at http://sh1.webring.com/people/fc/czechandslovakthings/WW2_CRTF_regind.htm and also http://www.holocaust.cz/databaze-obeti/obet/76603-gerta-benediktova/ (both accessed Dec. 16, 2015). On December 16, 2015, I sent an email inquiring about the fate of Ruth Benedikt to the British Association of Jewish Refugees (AJR), who referred me to the World Jewish Relief Archives (London), the current name for the Fund for German Jewry (CBF), founded in 1933. However, they have no file on Gerta Benedikt (other than a 1947 registration slip likely indicating that she applied but was eventually not allowed to enter the UK) nor on her daughter Ruth Benedikt. See emails (dated Jan. 26, 2016 and Jun. 7, 2016) from Tanya Fox (World Jewish Relief Archives, London) to the author. On June 11, 2016, an email was also sent to the Kindertransport Association (USA) and the Association of Children of Jewish Refugees (ACJR, UK) to inquire about the further fate of Ruth Renée Benedikt (and František Fuchs). A search query for the Benedikts was kindly made by Oliver Walter (former chairman of the ACJR) in an issue of the ACJR Newsletter (357, July 2016) but only a few people responded to let me know they were not related. Karen Lindenbaum (the Kindertransport Association, New York) posted the same search query on the "ktgenerations" Yahoo group (a mailing list for descendants of Kindertransport children) on October 13, 2016. A certain Wendy Henry (New York) responded, claiming to have known Ruth's deceased sister. See emails (dated Oct. 14, 2016 and Oct. 15, 2016) from Wendy Henry to the author; however, Mrs. Henry did not answer my further emails. Pictures of Gerta and Ruth can be found at http://www.holocaust.cz/databaze-obeti/obet/76603-gerta-benediktova/ (accessed Jun., 11, 2016). It is unclear what happened to Gerta Benedikt's husband Alfred Benedikt.

128 Hedwig Lokesch (née Adelberg) moved to 4 Hodonínská on September 30, 1940. She was deported on June 20, 1942 on transport "AAe" from Prague to Terezín where she died exactly one month later, on July 20, 1942. (The evidence obyvatelstva sheet in NA, Praha, fonds Policejní ředitelství II, claims she was put on transport on August 7, 1942. But, around this date, only transport "Ba" left Prague, on August 10, 1942. I found nothing to explain the different information on this document.) She married

FINANCIAL PROBLEMS

On the basis of several available archival sources, we can conclude that the Fein family had serious financial problems shortly after they moved to their second Prague address on Erbenstrasse (Erbenova). In August 1940, the Feins had only 5,400 Czech crowns (or 540 Reichsmark). Erich Messing, the brother of Gustav Fein's wife Herta, tried to gain approval from the Foreign Exchange Department (Devisenstelle), a part of the Higher Finance Authority (Oberfinanzpräsidium) in Frankfurt am Main, to send six payments of 300 Reichsmark, over six months, to the Feins from his blocked German bank account (*Sicherungskonto*).[131]

But things only got worse. In September 1941, following a decision applicable to the German Reich as a whole, Jewish people in the Protectorate were also compelled to wear the yellow star.[132] Very shortly after the introduction of this degrading measure, Karl Fein's mother walked in the street without wearing a yellow star. For this misdemeanor she was sentenced to pay the enormous fine of 1,000 Czech crowns. To put this in perspective, the rent for Karl Giese's Brno apartment in 1938 was 480 Czech crowns (or 48 Reichsmark) a month. Karl Fein appealed this fine in vain, only managing to obtain permission to pay it off in four installments of 250

and divorced Karl Lokesch (1869–1934) in 1898. The couple had three children: Eduard Erich Lokesch (1899–1942?), Hans Herbert Lokesch (1900–1943?) and Paul Lokesch (1905–1942), who all perished in the Holocaust. See http://www.holocaust.cz/databaze-obeti/obet/107655-hedvika-lokeschova/ and https://www.geni.com/people/Hedwig-Lokesch/6000000010930637893 (both accessed Jun. 11, 2016). See also NA, Policejní ředitelství Praha II, všeobecná spisovna, 1931–1940, kart. n° 8490, sign. L 1503/11, Hedvika Lokeschová and the evidence obyvatelstva sheet for Karl Lokesch in NA, Praha, Policejní ředitelství II.

[129] Ríza Weil (née Elfer) was the widow of Otto Weil (1875–1931). She moved to 4 Hodonínská on February 22, 1941. See the evidence obyvatelstva sheet in NA, Praha, Policejní ředitelství II. She was deported on transport "Am" on April 24, 1942 from Prague to Terezín and was further transferred to Izbica three days later, on April 27, 1942, on transport "Aq". The evidence obyvatelstva sheet in the NA, Praha, Policejní ředitelství II, however, claims she was deported on July 2, 1942. There was indeed a transport "Aal" from Prague that day but I do not know how to explain this possible mistake. It is not known what became of her daughter Magda Erika Weil (1921–?). Magda Erika Weil's name is not mentioned in Kárný et al. 1995. For Ríza Weil's police file, see https://www.holocaust.cz/en/database-of-victims/victim/132399-riza-weilova/ (accessed Apr. 11, 2019).

[130] Elisabeth Freund (née Herrmann) seems to have lived initially in the house next door (2 Hodonínská) but her police file in the NA in Prague indicates that she lived at 4 Hodonínská in April 1941. See NA, Praha, Policejní ředitelství Praha II, 1941–1950, sign. F 1563/1, Freundová Alžběta, available online at https://www.holocaust.cz/en/database-of-victims/victim/85795-alzbeta-freundova/ (accessed February 9, 2021). She does not appear to be related to the Brno lawyer Robert Herrmann, one of Karl Fein's interns in his law office. She was transported on July 9, 1942, from Prague to Terezín on transport "AAp" and transferred further to Treblinka on transport "Bw" on October 19, 1942. She can be found under the name Alžběta Freundová in Kárný et al. 1995, 748.

[131] In order to obtain these sums, Gustav, Karl and Helene Fein filled out each with the JKG in Prague an affidavit stating they were *mittellos* (without means). The tight financial situation was confirmed by the city of Prague as well through a so-called destitution certificate (*Mittellosigkeits-Zeugnis*, *Vysvědčení chudoby*) that all three family members filled out in August 1940. See Hessisches Hauptstaatsarchiv, Wiesbaden, Bestand 519/3, Akten der Devisenstellen Frankfurt und Kassel, Devisenstelle Frankfurt, 1940-1942, JS 10429, Erich Messing (°25/12/1895), f. 9-13. Messing's request to the Foreign Exchange Department was approved (though only for five times 300 Reichsmark) on November 21, 1940, which means that the money was wired to the Fein family of three in Prague. See ibid., not foliated, last folio.

[132] See the September 1, 1941, "Polizeiverordnung über die Kennzeichnung der Juden" (Police regulation on the labeling of Jews), *Verordnungsblatt des Reichsprotektors in Böhmen und Mähren*, Sep. 12, 1941, n° 44, 497–98. See also Löw 2012, 522–23, document n° 212, "Polizeiverordnung vom 1. September 1941 über die Kennzeichnungspflicht für Juden"; Löw 2012, 664 (and 664 n. 6), document n° 272, "Der Befehlshaber der Sicherheitspolizei lehnt am 5. März 1940 die Kennzeichnung der Juden im Protekorat ab".

[133] Karl Fein argued that his mother was too old, and did not know about the recent regulation to wear a Jewish star. See NA, Praha, Policejní ředitelství Praha II, všeobecná spisovna, 1941–1950, kart. n° 2034, sign. F 277/3, Feinová Helena roz. Brecherová 1860, police investigation document (dated Jul. 11, 1941), f. 9-11. This police file also mentions that the Fein family indeed had to rely on their brother-in-law, Erich Messing, to pay the fine.

[134] Hessisches Hauptstaatsarchiv, Wiesbaden, Bestand 519/3, Akten der Devisenstellen Frankfurt und Kassel, Devisenstelle Frankfurt, 1940-1942, JS

Czech crowns.[133] We know Karl Fein must have spent a considerable amount of money already simply by going through the application process at the Central Office, and in paying the so-called Jewish tax beforehand. This contestation of the fine was in any case the last time that Karl Fein would be able to help his approximately 86-year-old mother deal with unwelcome administrative paperwork. It is striking to note that the next payment, likely made by Gustav Fein, was for 500 Czech crowns. Karl Fein had already been deported. Was this done in an attempt to mollify the authorities? Maybe they also had the idea that Karl was deported because he dared to challenge the fine imposed on his mother?

In August 1940, Fein's brother Gustav wrote that he and Karl Fein were both looking for a job and were registered at the JKG employment bureau (*Arbeitsamt*), adding that most positions were taken by younger men.[134] It is not known if Karl Fein was called on to do forced labor (*Arbeitseinsatz*) during his stay in Prague. The new forced labor measure for Jews, which started in January 1941, affected a significant number of people. In December 1941, 13,623 men were doing forced labor in Prague.[135]

KARL FEIN'S DEPORTATION TO THE ŁÓDŹ GHETTO IN POLAND

At the end of September 1941, Konstantin von Neurath (1873–1956) was dismissed as Reichsprotektor for being too soft on an increasingly resilient Czech population, and replaced by the younger and certainly more ruthless Reinhard Heydrich (1904–1942). Under Heydrich, Prague and the Protectorate experienced a terror regime.[136] In August 1941, it was decided by the Reich Security Main Office (Reichssicherheitshauptamt, RSHA) in Berlin that the voluntary Jewish emigration had to be stopped. Forced deportation would be the new order of the day.[137] Soon afterwards, in October 1941, and after the failure of the so-called Nisko experiment,[138] the transportation of 20,000 Jews from several European cities began.[139]

In total, twenty transports were planned to the Polish city Łódź, then German territory known as the Warthegau. It was anticipated that the five transports leaving Prague would each carry 1,000 people. The first Prague transport "A" left on October 16, 1941, the fifth and last transport "E" on November 3, 1941. Not coincidentally, a Decree of the Reich Protector in Bohemia and Moravia on the Supervision of Jews and Jewish Organizations (Verordnung des Reichsprotektors in Böhmen und Mähren über die Betreuung der Juden und jüdischen Organisationen) was issued on October 12, 1941, ensuring the definitive expropriation (*Enteignung*) of the Jewish population, intimately linked to their deportation from the country.[140]

10429, Erich Messing (°25/12/1895), letter (dated Aug. 21, 1940) from Gustav Fein to Devisenstelle Saarbrücken, not foliated. That Karl Fein and Gustav Fein had both lost their jobs and thus had no income is also mentioned in NA, Praha, Policejní ředitelství Praha II, všeobecná spisovna, 1941-1950, kart. n° 2034, sign. F 277/3, Feinová Helena roz. Brecherová 1860. Karl Fein's unemployment is also mentioned on his evidence obyvatelstva sheet in NA, Praha, Policejní ředitelství II.

135 See the introduction in Löw 2012, 42; Löw 2012, 726–27, document n° 305, "Der Reichsprotektor erläutert dem Ministerium für soziale und Gesundheitsverwaltung am 17. April 1941 das Verfahren beim Arbeitseinsatz von Juden". On the basis of this document, we can safely conclude that, if Karl Fein had been called for forced labor, this would have likely happened at the earliest in August or at the latest in October of 1941. See Löw 2012, 726 n. 5. See also Gruner 2010, 159–60, 163. Gruner writes that the first group of forced labor workers had to assist with burning Prague city waste. See also Landré 1982.

136 Gruner 2010, 166–67; Wildt 2003, 617–22.

137 Milotová writes: "die Zentralstelle für jüdische Auswanderung in Prag [schloß] die 'Auswanderungsetappe' ab und leitete die 'Evakuierungsetappe' ein" (the Central Office for Jewish Emigration in Prague [concluded] the 'emigration stage' and initiated the 'evacuation stage') (Milotová 1998, 52).

138 Oprach 2006, 101–6.

139 Oprach 2006, 121–23. On the decision making immediately before these deportations, see also Milotová 1998, 51–52.

140 Milotová 1998, 58–59. The Decree appeared in *Verordnungsblatt des Reichsprotektors in Böhmen und Mähren* 51, Oct. 14, 1941, 555–56. Jančík et. al. speak of the fourth and final stage in the process of curtailing Jewish property rights that had started on March 15, 1939: "Stage 4: October 12, 1941 – [until] war's end. Forfeiture of Jewish property in favor

It was in October 1941, when living at his third Prague address in Gödinger Gasse (Hodonínská), that Karl Fein was summoned to be deported to the Łódź ghetto in Poland. Of all the Jewish people living at the Hodonínská (Godinger Gasse) address, Fein was the only person deported to Łódź that day.[141] That they were going to be deported to that Polish city was not known to those being deported.

The literature on the particular "genesis" of these massive Jewish transports in Europe is already quite extensive and I will not develop this – fiercely debated – theme here.[142] However the exact etiology and intentional situation around this first phase of the Holocaust can be interpreted and explained, the harrowing facts are there: starting in October 1941, twenty transports carrying approximately 1,000 persons each, from several European cities as diverse as Berlin, Düsseldorf, Köln, Frankfurt am Main, Hamburg, Luxembourg, Vienna and Prague, set off to Łódź (Litzmanstadt) in the Warthegau, as that part of annexed Poland was then called.[143] The Łódź ghetto was created between February and April 1940 as a slave labor camp where Jewish inmates worked mainly for the clothing industry. When the ghetto was created, the considerable local Polish Jewish population in Łódź was grouped together in the impoverished city district still known as Bałuty. When the ghetto was completely closed off from the rest of the city, it already counted more than 140,000, perhaps as many as 160,000 inhabitants.[144] Łódź was the second largest Jewish ghetto in Poland after the much better-known one in Warsaw. The tumultuous story of the always overpopulated ghetto (with an area of only four square kilometers) has already been

of the German Reich in connection with the mass deportations of the Jewish population" (Jančík et. al. 2001, 11).

[141] As we have seen, Rudolf Schneider, the owner of the 4 Hodonínská building, and his wife and three children (who were not living there) were deported from Prague to Łódź on the fourth transport, transport "D", on October 31, 1941, ten days after Karl Fein. Of the eighty-seven people listed in Hodonínská, another ten were eventually deported to Łódź. Only two other people from Hodonínská were on Fein's transport "B": Dr. Bedřich Pollak (1890–?) and his wife Ella Pollaková (née Berger, 1893–?) who lived next door at 6 Hodonínská. See http://www2.holocaust.cz/en/victims/PERSON.ITI.2090596 and http://www2.holocaust.cz/en/main#birth_date_day= --&language=en&last= Pollakov%C3%A1%20&birth_date_month=--&first=Ella%20&birth_date_year=--&victims=1 (both accessed Dec. 30, 2014).

[142] See, for example, Potthast 2002, 128–33. Peter Witte calls it the "Genesis-Diskussion" (Witte 1995, 45). The debate tries to determine how Hitler and other Nazi officials came to decide on these first transports of around 20,000 people. It asks whether or not the Nazis had precise ideas about what they were going to do with the deported people, why the decision was made then (and not at another moment), who or what events played a part in making this decision, etc. That the Nazis were intent on settling "the Jewish question" once and for all, even before the war started, is certain. But it is also clear that the concrete implementation and timing of this pernicious idea was actually determined by many contextual factors, principal among these being the realities of the war situation. The ever-changing plans of what needed to be done with the Jews were intimately related with the progress of the war. For example, Witte writes: "[d]er 'Madagaskar-Plan' war ausgearbeitet worden im Vorgriff auf einen Friedensvertrag mit Frankreich und einen militärischen Sieg über England" (the 'Madagascar plan' was conceived in anticipation of a peace treaty with France and a military victory over England) (Witte 1995, 40). The invasion of Poland and the creation of the Generalgouvernement was another war-related factor that allowed further development of the idea of moving the Jews "further East". So, in mid-September 1941, when Hitler decided, suddenly, to go against his earlier stance, and opted for the "Teilevakuierung der größeren Städte" (partial evacuation of major cities) (Witte 1995, 42), this decision was informed by another war reality: the growing *Wohnungsmangel* (housing shortage) caused by increased enemy bombings (Witte 1995, 43–44). The former dwellings of Jews could help ameliorate the housing shortage for Germans. Finally, another non-negligible contextual factor in decisions about how to settle the "Jewish problem" was the chronic competiton between different power factions in the Third Reich and their different and clashing ideas on the matter.

[143] For a good overview of these twenty transports, see: http://www.centrumdialogu.com/en/getto/history/western-jews/list-of-transports-of-european-jews (accessed Dec. 19, 2014).

[144] For the different numbers, see, respectively, Löw & Feuchert 2007, 1941, 15; and https://encyclopedia.ushmm.org/content/en/article/lodz (accessed Jul. 12, 2021).

[145] Oprach 2006, 53. The original, however, says "Dezimierungsgehoot". Witte uses that term and quotes a Nazi source (Witte 1995, 53 n. 77).

[146] Gruner 2010, 157–58, 164; Oprach 2006, 101–6; Moser 2012.

quite extensively researched. The Nazis were quite aware that Łódź (or Litzmanstadt, as they renamed it) would be a "decimation ghetto" (*Dezimierungsgetto*) where many people would work and starve to death.[145]

Karl Fein was deported from Prague to Łódź on October 21, 1941, on the so-called "B" transport, which was also known, because it was the second mass transport leaving from Prague, as the "Prague II" transport. Fein's transport was the seventh of the twenty transports sent to Łódź. Whether these mass transports were indeed the first phase of the Holocaust, as most of the literature seems to suggest, is of course debatable. Before, in October 1939, there was a first attempt at organizing Jewish transports to Nisko in the Generalgouvernement (as that part of occupied Poland was renamed). That experiment, involving no fewer than 100,000 deported Jews, was abandoned in April 1940 and considered a failure.[146] Also, the so-called deployment groups (*Einsatzgruppen*) who, starting in 1939, killed Jewish people in Poland, and continued during the Russian campaign of 1941, were even earlier. A quarter of the six million Jewish people killed during World War II were victims of these Einsatzgruppen.[147]

That this first considerable wave of deportations to Łódź was nevertheless a kind of "tryout" is indicated by the fact that "only" around 20,000 of the 60,000 initially planned were deported.[148] The Germans saw the Łódź scenario as only a temporary solution. The Czechoslovak "Jewish problem" would be solved otherwise. Starting in 1942, most Czechoslovak Jews would be deported to Terezín (Theresienstadt), as was the case for Karl Fein's brother, mother, and most other members of his immediate family.

On October 18, 1941, Fein was ordered to go to the Prague exhibition grounds (*Výstaviště, Messegelände*) in Prague-Holešovice where around 1,000 Jewish people were gathered in a wooden building then known as Radio Mart (Radiotrhu). "Those called up were sent to a makeshift wooden building that had served as an annex of the Trade Fair Palace and, because it had been used for an exposition of radios during the last trade fair, was known as the Radio Mart. The building had not been in use for several years and lacked plumbing, ventilation, and heat. Here Jews scheduled for transport were 'processed', a procedure that usually lasted three or four days" [ill. 6].[149] Heda Margolius remembered the continuous and unbearable noise and chaos inside the building.[150] Deportees were allowed to take along luggage not exceeding a total weight of fifty kilograms. Before boarding the transport, they had to sign a declaration of assets (*Vermögenserklärung*), consenting to the confiscation of their remaining properties.[151] "A conveyor belt was set up for the administrative processing

[147] See https://www.britannica.com/topic/Einsatzgruppen (accessed Aug. 11, 2020).

[148] Witte 1995, 52; Kárný 1996, 41.

[149] Kisch et al., 1984, vol. III, qtd. by Růžena Kovaříková in Weil 1990, [IX–]X, translator's note. For more information on the Radio Mart building (and many other aspects of the Czechoslovak Holocaust), see http://www2.holocaust.cz/web_data/pdfs/jom_ha_soa2012_brozura.pdf (accessed Dec. 19, 2014). I deduced the date of Fein's *Anmeldung* (registration) to be October 18, 1941, based on the testimony of Bernard Heilig, who was on Fein's transport. Heilig would later become one of the so-called Łódź ghetto chroniclers. He writes about three days spent in the exhibition grounds. See Heilig 2007, 11–12. This accords with Milotová 1998, 60; and a contemporary JKG text, which gives the dates of October 13 (arrival in the exhibition grounds) and October 16 (departure from Prague) for the very first transport "A" leaving Prague for Łódź. See Krejčová, Svobodová & Hyndráková 1997, 170, esp. 172, document n° 10, "Evidenz der Juden. Registrierung. Transporte". The first list of 5,000 people to be deported initially met with resistance from the JKG. Two people in the JKG *Auswanderungsabteilung* (emigration department), who informed the Germans that they were not able to provide so long a list in such a short time, were both promptly deported to Mauthausen. See Ondrichová 2000, 24–25. The current address of the still existing Prague Holešovice exhibition hall grounds is 67 Výstaviště.

[150] Margolius Kovály, Třeštíková & Margolius 2018, 33.

[151] It remains uncertain if this was the same ten-page-long *Vermögenserklärung* (declaration of assets) that was used in the Central Office when emigration was still an option. Potthast appears to

of the transport participants in the collection camp. The transportees had to hand in the completed property declarations, listing all the assets they left behind in detail; they handed over the keys to their flats, [...] cash, jewelry or objects made of precious metal, personal documents; they received an identity document marked 'ghettoized on ...'"[152] Here again, we may ask what Fein may have included in his declaration of assets in the Radio Mart now that he was being forcibly deported. From Giese, as we have seen, he inherited all income from Titus Pearls, even though this income was confiscated by the Prussian state in 1939. Presumably, he left the section on possible licensing or patent rights blank or answered "no".

On October 21, 1941, starting at 5:30 a.m., the 1,000 people on the second Prague transport, the so-called transport "B", were escorted from the Prague-Holešovice exhibition grounds to the nearby Bubny railway station in Bubenská street, escorted by thirty Czech policemen. That day, the passenger train with forty-three carriages left the station around 11 a.m. The train stopped once in the middle of the night to refill barrels of drinking water, each carriage having one.[153] The transport arrived the next day in the Radegast (Radogoszcz) railway station of the Łódź (Litzmannstadt) ghetto at 3:30 p.m., after a twenty-eight-hour journey. The train was emptied in half an hour.[154]

Those who were able walked through heavy hail (*Hagelschlag*) from the Radegast (Radogoszcz) station, on the outskirts of the ghetto, to the center of the ghetto.[155] The decrepit houses that the new arrivals saw as they approached the center of the ghetto did not make things look very promising. People from the first Prague transport, who had arrived five days earlier, came to greet the newcomers and told them about the

say that it was indeed the same list. He writes that the declarations of assets that had to be filled out in the Radio Mart and in the Central Office were both ten pages long (Potthast 2002, 144, 204–6, 298 n. 66).

[152] Krejčová, Svobodová & Hyndráková 1997, 171, document n° 10, Evidenz der Juden. Registrierung. Transporte: "Für die administrative Abfertigung der Transportteilnehmer im Sammellager wurde ein laufendes Band eingerichtet. Die Transportteilnehmer haben dort die ausgefüllten Vermögenserklärungen, in welchen ihr gesamtes zurückgelassenes Vermögen detailliert verzeichnet ist, abzugeben, sie übergeben die Schlüssel zu ihren Wohnungen, [...] Bargeld, Schmuckgegenstände oder Gegenstände aus Edelmetall, Personaldokumente; ein mit dem Aufdruck 'ghettoisiert am ...' versehenes Ausweispapier erhalten sie zurück".

[153] Margolius Kovály, Třešťíková & Margolius 2018, 34.

[154] Karl Fein's name is included in a transport list in APŁ, Łódź, fonds Przełożony Starszeństwa Żydów, sign. 997, microfilm L-19621, [Wykazy imienne Żydów zagranicznych wsiedlonych do getta], f. 257. Fein is 49th in the list of 100 people under "F". Color reproductions of this list of this transport (and all other transports) can be found at the memorial site of the former Radegast (Radogoszcz) railway station in the north of Łódź, in the binders inside the wooden building and also on the north wall inside the memorial concrete tunnel building. Fein's name is missing in another – incomplete – list of that transport (starting from number 16 and running to 996). See APŁ, Łódź, fonds Przełożony Starszeństwa Żydów, sign. 1176, microfilm L-19793, [Imienne wykazy transportów wsiedlonych z Pragi czeskiej], 1941. On a postcard that Fein tried to send from the Łódź ghetto in 1941 (see also pp. 463-65), he wrote that his transport number was 343. This number is confirmed by the www.holocaust.cz database and also accords with the information on the ITS database. According to Kárný et al., there were 1,002 (and not 1,000) people on Fein's transport, eighty of whom would survive the war (Kárný et al.1995, 91–102). This number is also given in Kárný 1996, 100. The first Prague transport to Łódź of exactly 1,000 people left Prague on October 16, 1941. Only twenty-four people on that transport survived the war. See Kárný et al. 1995, 79–90. For the transport's time of arrival and deboarding, and the number of people it carried, see APŁ, Łódź, fonds Przełożony Starszeństwa Żydów, sign. 19, microfilm L-18637, [Wsiedlanie Żydów zagranicznych do getta łódzkiego], X 1941-VI 1942, 186 (in pencil), "Aufstellung der Neueingesiedelten"; and ibid., list (dated Nov. 5, 1941), 200 (in pencil), "Aufstellung der Transports vom 16.X. – 4.XI.1941". For information on the Radegast (Radogoszcz) railway station, see Milotová 1998, 61. For the number of carriages on the train, see Klein 2009, 419.

[155] In her memoir, Heda Margolius Kovaly describes a fierce snow storm: "Upon our arrival in Łódź, we were greeted by a fierce snowstorm. It was only October, but in the three years I spent there I never again saw such a blizzard". See Margolius Kovaly, Epstein & Epstein 1988, 9; repeated in Margolius Kovály, Třešťíková & Margolius 2018, 34.

[156] Heilig 2007, 10. The source writes it without diacritics: "nemohlo to byt horsi [*sic*]".

"unimaginable hunger" (*unvorstellbaren Hunger*) in the ghetto, adding ominously: "it couldn't be worse" (*Nemohlo to být horší*).[156]

The approximately 1,000 people from the second Prague transport were all taken to the three-story former children's hospital at 37 Łagiewnicka street (Hanseatenstrasse) in Łódź.[157] For most other transports carrying so-called Western Jews to Łódź, school buildings were requisitioned since there was no more room in the houses of the ghetto where around 143,000 Polish Jews had been herded together in 1939–40, and which had been sealed off from the outside world at the end of April 1940. As we have seen, the Germans initially intended to bring 60,000 Western Jews to the ghetto but apparently that total was reduced to one third of that number.[158]

There was no furniture in the children's hospital and every square centimeter was used to lay people on mattresses and straw sacks. One document states that the second Prague transport did not bring enough clothes and sheets to meet the urgent initial need.[159] The very real problem of how to fit as many people as possible in one room for the night – Heilig dubbed it the "land question" (*Bodenfrage*) – was unbearable: "Lying on one's side, upper body and feet tightly pressed by various neighbors, this produced the feeling of already being in a mass grave and led to anxiety, shortness of breath, nightmares and the like".[160] Karl Fein likely stayed, like most others from his transport, at this Łagiewnicka address for several months before moving to another address in the Łódź ghetto.[161]

[157] Searching for archival traces of Karl Fein's forced six-month stay in the Łódź ghetto, I did extensive research during two one-week sessions (in August 2011 and June 2012) in the Archiwum Państwowe w Łodzi (Łódź State Archives) in Łódź (Poland). This endeavor was quite frustrating since the surviving, microfilmed archive of the Łódź ghetto is, to put it mildly, not very well ordered. It is also very incomplete. When examining specific parts of the archive, one all too often encounters documents that are clearly not in the right place. Very often, chronological boundaries were not sufficiently respected. Even simple alphabetical order cannot be relied upon. There are many reasons for this unfortunate situation. First of all, the cause is the disorder of the archive that survived the war. Secondly, the Łódź ghetto archive was donated to different competing institutions after the war and thus divided up. A third reason for the archive's disorderly state is the choices made by post-war Polish archivists. Whatever the exact causes for the disorder of this archival fonds, it leaves the researcher with the feeling that finding something about a specific person is largely a matter of being lucky … or not. Indeed, finding traces of Karl Fein's presence in the Łódź ghetto archive proved quite difficult. I did of course see his name in a few places but I simply did not see it in the many more "obvious" places where I would have expected to see it. In what follows, I will mention where I saw his name as well as the many more instances where I did not. Fein's name is for example absent in two archival fonds that a researcher looking for somebody in Łódź would certainly examine: the alphabetically arranged registration cards (APŁ, Łódź, fonds Przełożony Starszeństwa Żydów, sign. 1011, microfilm L-21111, [Karty meldunkowe I karty pracy], letter F) and the workers' cards (APŁ, Łódź, fonds Przełożony Starszeństwa Żydów, sign. 1011, microfilm L-21086, [Karty meldunkowe I karty pracy], letter F). Account must also be taken that these workers' cards are not dated, meaning that it is not known when exactly they registered a person's work situation. Because I quickly learned that the alphabetical arrangement was not very reliable, I checked all the names under "F". Karl Fein's name is also missing from the Łódź residents list available online at www.jewishgen.org. In general, Fein's arrival in the ghetto and his death there, six months later, are the only events that can be said to be well documented.

[158] Feuchert et al. 2007, 5, 11, 14–15.

[159] APŁ, Łódź, fonds Przełożony Starszeństwa Żydów, sign. 19, microfilm L-18637, [Wsiedlanie Żydów zagranicznych do getta łódzkiego], "Aufstellung der Transports vom 16.X. – 4.XI.1941" (dated Nov. 5, 1941), 200.

[160] Heilig 2007, 15: "Auf der Seite liegend, Oberkörper und Füsse von verschiedenen Nachbarn eng gepresst, erzeugte dieses Liegen das Gefühl, sich bereits in einem Massengrabe zu befinden und führte zu Angstzuständen, Atemnot, Alpdruck und dergleichen".

[161] Heilig stayed at this address for nine weeks: "Was für Menschen waren es, die unter diesen Umständen neun Wochen lebten?" (What kind of people were they who lived in these circumstances for nine weeks?). See Heilig 2007, 15. During one of my two research trips to Łódź, I noticed that many doctors and nurses from the "B" or "Prague II" transport continued to stay at 37 Hanseatenstrasse (Łagiewnicka). Likely this had to do with the fact that the main ghetto hospital was right across the street from this building. Both were still standing in June 2012 when I visited Łódź. The hospital was in a sorry state, however, and up for sale. Quite a number of documents in the APŁ archive in Łódź attest to the fact that most people from the second Prague transport stayed in the 37 Łagiewnicka

WAS KARL FEIN BLACKLISTED?

It is rather astounding, and simply tragic, that Karl Fein got tangled up in what is now considered the first crucial phase of the Holocaust: the first wave of systematic deportations of Jewish people "to the East", starting in October 1941.[162] Fein may have been on one or another German blacklist. We saw that, on Brno radio in 1935, he presumably commented critically on the Nuremberg race laws and somebody may have taken note.[163] We have also mentioned that he contested the high fine his mother had to pay for not wearing the mandatory yellow star. That he was single and did not have a wife and children to take care of might have been another factor to his disadvantage. The train on which Fein was taken to Łódź from Prague was also known as "the lawyers' train" (*Advokatentransport*).[164] Bernard Heilig, who was also on transport "B", estimated that the majority of the 700 academics on the train were indeed lawyers.[165] A second source seems also to confirm the impressive number of

until at least December 10, 1941. A list of bills exists, ordered by transport. The earliest bill for the "Prague II" transport at 37 Łagiewnicka is dated December 10, 1941. See APŁ, Łódź, fonds Przełożony Starszeństwa Żydów, sign. 1219, microfilm L-19836, [Rachunki wystawione przez różne wydziały], 1941–1942, "Aufstellung der Rechnungen", f. 259. Karl Fein sent a postcard to his sister and mother from this Łagiewnicka address on December 8, 1941. See APŁ, Łódź, fonds Przełożony Starszeństwa Żydów, sign. 2316, microfilm L-20930, [Karty pocztowe przeznaczone dla krewnych i znajomych w Generalnej Guberni, Rzeszy i w innych krajach, które nie zostały wysłane z getta przez pocztę], two postcards numbered 1667–1668 and 1669–1670. A final factor that shows that, at the beginning of December 1941, the people of the "B" or "Prague II" transport were still at 37 Łagiewnicka are typed cards (the earliest of which is dated December 1, 1941) sent by the Litzmannstadt ghetto *Verwaltung* (administration) responding to inquiries about the condition of family members in Łódź (and confirming receipt of money sent to them). See, for example, the cards for two engineers from the "B" transport, Artur Steinhauer (1897–?) and Franz Fischmann (1901–1943), APŁ, Łódź, fonds Przełożony Starszeństwa Żydów, sign. 301, microfilm L-18920, [Korespondencja z osobami w różnych krajach w sprawie informacji o Zydach zamieszkałych w getcie łódzkim], f. 104-105. The same cards are in sign. 300, microfilm L-18919 as well. The leader of the second Prague transport was Dr. Karel Bondy (1882–?). The www.holocaust.cz database mistakenly gives his birth year as 1889. His police file can be found at http://www.holocaust.cz/databaze-obeti/obet/142051-karel-bondy/ (accessed Jan. 17, 2016). Bondy's *Stellvertreter* (deputy) was Dr. Jan Menzel (1902–?), originally from the third Prague "C" transport. See Kárný et al. 1995, 114. Menzel survived the war.

162 Milotová 1998, 40: "Die Entscheidung über Judendeportationen aus Deutschland, Oesterreich, Luxemburg und aus dem Protektorat Böhmen und Mähren in das 'Gau-Ghetto' in Łódź im Herbst 1941 war eines der Schlüsselmomente der Holocaust-Geschichte" (The decision on deportations of Jews from Germany, Austria, Luxembourg and the Protectorate of Bohemia and Moravia to the 'Gau-Ghetto' in Łódź in the autumn of 1941 was one of the key moments in Holocaust history). Milotová also quotes Adolf Eichmann, who wrote in January 1942: "Die in der letzten Zeit in einzelnen Gebieten durchgeführte Evakuierung von Juden nach dem Osten stellen [*sic*] den Beginn der Endlösung der Judenfrage im Altreich, der Ostmark und im Protektorat Böhmen und Mähren dar" (The recent evacuation of Jews to particular areas in the East mark the beginning of the final solution of the Jewish question in the Old Reich, the Ostmark [Austria] and the Protectorate of Bohemia and Moravia). The original Eichmann quote is in Adler 1974, 188. Marc Oprach, who has written the best and most comprehensive German-language text on the Protectorate and the evolution of the Jewish Holocaust in Czechoslovakia, agrees: "Die ersten Deportationen Prager Juden nach Łódź im Oktober 1941 stellen einen für das Gesamtverständnis des Holocaust entscheidenden Faktor dar" (Oprach 2006, 19) (The first deportations of Prague Jews to Łódź in October 1941 constitute a decisive factor for the overall understanding of the Holocaust).

163 See chapter 13, p. 433 and n. 12.

164 Heilig 2007, 11, 16. If one looks at the list of 1,002 deportee names in Fein's transport (Kárný et al. 1995), one indeed sees many instances of "Dr.". In Czech, a lawyer usually is indicated by the suffix "JUDr". By comparing the deportation list to another list, I discovered that this particular suffix was not consistently used for lawyers in the former, and that quite a number of "Dr." titles were applied to jurists.

165 Heilig stressed the wealth of the second transport, dubbing it the "Prager Kapitalisten- und Akademikertransportes" (Prague capitalists and academics transport), estimating its – former – wealth "sächverständigerweis auf 1 1/2 Miliarden Kronen" (as a matter of fact, 1 1/2 billion crowns). See Heilig 2007, 11. For a fictionalized account of this aspect of the second Prague transport, see Weil 1990, 94–95.

166 Frank Schlomo (1902–1966), a former journalist, wrote in his Łódź diary: "Today another 1000 persons arrived from Prague. All deportees were in good shape. Among them are 300 lawyers, 26 physicians, 30 engineers, and many other professionals" (qtd. in Adelson & Lapides 1989, 175). Though there are some serious problems with the reliability of the two published editions of Schlomo's diary (they dif-

approximately 300 lawyers on the transport.[166] Apparently the first transport from Prague had been full of paupers. Because this displeased the Germans, the second transport – Fein's transport – was a train of mainly rich people.[167]

Jan Björn Potthast mentions the protocol of a meeting of all the main Protectorate Nazi officials (Heydrich, Eichmann, Frank, Böhme, etc.), in the beginning of October 1941, where it was said that 5,000 of the most "troublesome" (*lästigsten*) Jews would be sent on these first transports.[168] It is unclear to what extent the JKG could independently decide the names that ended up on the transport lists or how exactly these lists were assembled.[169] That Karl Fein was listed on the second transport from Prague shows that neither he nor his family had the means or network in the Prague Jewish community to challenge the decision. It also looks as though Karl Fein's brother, Gustav Fein, started to work for the JKG in Prague shortly after his brother was deported. Apparently, his brother realized he would have to make himself useful if he did not want to be deported as well. On October 13, 1941, the day the first thousand people on transport "A" were ordered to the exhibition grounds in Prague, the JKG received orders from the Germans to set up a massive trustee office (*Treuhandstelle*) to manage the enormous operation of Jewish expropriations.[170] It was for this organization that Gustav Fein ended up working.

Around the end of December 1941, the "Prague II" collective (*Prag II Kollektiv*) moved to a school building at 15 Franciszkańska (Franzstrasse).[171] Karl Fein also moved to this address [ill. 7]. Until his death, on May 2, 1942, Fein was also administratively tied to the Prague II collective.[172] Living conditions in these buildings must have been

fer significantly from the Yiddish original), there is no reason to believe that, in this particular instance (the arrival of the Western Jews), Schlomo would have intentionally distorted information. For more on the reliability issue, see Shapiro 1999, 101–2.

167 Gruner 2005, 47.

168 Potthast 2002, 136.

169 Krejčová, Svobodová & Hyndráková 1997, 171, document n° 10, "Evidenz der Juden. Registrierung. Transporte": "Von der Zentralstelle für jüdische Auswanderung Prag erhält die Jüdische Kultusgemeinde Prag jeweils ein Verzeichnis der zur Abwanderung bestimmten Personen. Diese sogenannte Vorliste wird in der Kultusgemeinde abgeschrieben und vervielfältigt" (From the Central Office of Jewish Emigration in Prague, the Jewish Community in Prague receives a list of persons who are to emigrate. This so-called preliminary list is copied and duplicated in the Jewish Community). It is possible but unproven that Fein's name was also on a list of undesirables drawn up by the Germans.

170 For an idea of the gigantic bureaucratic task imposed on the JKG, having to empty out the evacuated Jewish apartments, around 500 per transport, see Krejčová, Svobodová & Hyndráková 1997, 166–73, document n° 10, "Evidenz der Juden. Registrierung. Transporte", a text by the JKG. For a summary report on the organization and operation of the Prague Central Office for Jewish Emigration (Zentralstelle für jüdische Auswanderung), see Potthast 2000, 161–62.

171 In a list (dated Feb. 9, 1942), the address given for the "Prague II" collective is 15 Franciszkańska (Franzstrasse). See APŁ, Łódź, fonds Przełożony Starszeństwa Żydów, sign. 19, microfilm L-18637, [Wsiedlanie Żydów zagranicznych do getta łódzkiego] Liste der Kollektive, deren Leiter und Stellvertreter, nach dem Stande vom 9. Februar 1942 [illegible word]. Today, a commemorative plaque on the building (13–15 Franciszkańska) states: "Site of a school until October 1941. It then became the quarters of deportees from Prague (collective 'Prague II')". This is not completely correct since the "Prague II" collective did not move there until around the end of December 1941 at the earliest. We have already mentioned that Fein's name does not appear very often in the archives of the Łódź ghetto, even where one would expect his name to show up. For example, his name is missing from the messy and incomplete lists of residents of 13–15 Franzstrasse (Franciszkańska). See APŁ, Łódź, fonds Przełożony Starszeństwa Żydów, sign. 1021, microfilm L-19644, [Książka meldunkowa domów]. For Fein's stay at 37 Hanseatenstrasse (Łagiewnicka), see APŁ, Łódź, fonds Przełożony Starszeństwa Żydów, sign. 1028, microfilm L-19650, [Książka meldunkowa domów]. I also checked APŁ, Łódź, fonds Przełożony Starszeństwa Żydów, sign. 845, microfilm L-19643, [Alfabetyczny spis mieszkańców getta. Litera F] but did not find Fein's name there either. The main source confirming that Fein did live at 15 Franciszkańska (Franzstrasse) is APŁ, Łódź, fonds Przełożony Starszeństwa Żydów, sign. 962, microfilm L-19581, [Kopie dziennych wykazów zgłoszonych zgonów] [Copies of the daily lists of reported deaths], f. 269. Fein is mentioned in the list dated May 7, 1942. The exact title at the top of the page is "wykaz zgonów zgłoszonych" (list of deaths reported).

172 APŁ, Łódź, fonds Przełożony Starszeństwa Żydów, sign. 962, microfilm L-19581, [Kopie dzien-

harsh. As the name states, it was a collective in which there was no privacy. Sleeping quarters, meals, toilets and basic washing amenities were shared with the other people in one's transport.

CULTURE CLASH IN THE GHETTO

The influx of 20,000 new arrivals, coming from all over Europe, in a ghetto that had initially harbored impoverished Polish Jews, was of course deeply disruptive for the ghetto. The newly arrived were perceived as a clear burden by the Polish Jews. How to feed 20,000 new mouths suddenly arriving in the ghetto in a time span of less than three weeks (from October 17 to November 4, 1941)? Most of the Western Jews (*Westjuden*), as the new arrivals were called, were placed in school buildings, which caused Łódź schools to close and the education of the Polish children in the ghetto to come to a definitive halt, earning them the further scorn of the original so-called Eastern Jews (*Ostjuden*). The newbies, mainly middle-class people, also had a hard time accepting being forced to live near and with Polish Łódź Jews, who were mainly textile industry workers. Not without reason, before the war, Łódź was called the "Manchester of Poland". One can still see many factory buildings in the city, but many have been transformed into trendy office buildings, shopping malls and hotels. The impressive Manufactura shopping mall is a prime example of such a modern conversion.

So there was certainly a culture clash between the more prosperous and educated, mainly German-speaking new arrivals and the more traditionally religious Polish Jewish residents: "Under the cruel conditions of the ghetto, in the fall of 1941, people who had nothing in common except that they were Jews were forced to live together – [...] The 'Western Jews' were older than average, which is why it was difficult for the Jewish Elder to integrate them into the work process. They came from a completely different culture – consequently, first perceptions were marked by prejudice and mutual distrust".[173] The "Western Jews" were frowned upon and mocked as luxury birds by the original Polish ghetto residents because they appeared well-fed and, in the days and weeks following their arrival, tried to buy their way out of their first hunger by selling their expensive clothes. This moral condemnation had a gendered character. The newcomers were also named *joupe* or *jukiel*. *Joupe*, possibly derived from the French *jupe* (skirt), referred to the newcomers wearing coats (rather than kaftans). *Jukiel* meant penis, and was also a term for a despised, inexperienced person.[174]

nych wykazów zgłoszonych zgonów] [Copies of the daily lists of reported deaths], f. 269.

[173] Feuchert et al. 2007, 1941: 15: "Unter den grausamen Bedingungen des Gettos waren nun im Herbst 1941 Menschen gezwungen, miteinander zu leben, die nichts gemeinsam hatten, außer dass sie Juden waren – (...) Die »Westjuden« waren überdurchschnittlich alt, weswegen es dem Judenältesten schwerfiel, sie in den Arbeitsprozess zu integrieren. Sie entstammten einer völlig anderen Kultur – von Vorurteilen und gegenseitigem Misstrauen waren folglich die ersten Wahrnehmungen geprägt". See also Rosenfeld 1994, 25, 27, 108, 194.

[174] Bopp et al. 2020, 98–99.

[175] APŁ, Łódź, fonds Przełożony Starszeństwa Żydów, sign. 2316, microfilm L-20930, [Karty pocztowe przeznaczone dla krewnych i znajomych w Generalnej Guberni, Rzeszy i w innych krajach, które nie zostały wysłane z getta przez pocztę], two postcards numbered 1667-1668 and 1669-1670, both dated Dec. 8, 1941. The postcards survived in the archive of the Łódź ghetto because they were not sent out but held by the ghetto authorities. I thank Ewa Wiatr (Centrum Badań Żydowskich, Łódź University, Łódź) for helping me to retrieve these cards in a heartbeat (with the help of a database that she and her team set up cataloguing the ghetto mail that was not sent out) during the first day of my second visit to Łódź in June 2012. It saved me a lot of time.

[176] De Buton 2007, 20.

[177] De Buton 2007, 21: "Die vielen Prager, die im Amte waren, hatten es leicht, ihre tschechische Zunge ist der polnischen Sprache nicht so fremd gegenüber und ihr Ohr versteht fast alles. Aber die Deutsche!"

[178] Rosenfeld 1994, 57.

[179] Brechelmacher 2015, 186, 196.

[180] Feuchert et al. 2007, Anhang und Supplemente: 181.

[181] For more information on Bernard Heilig, see, for example, http://www.getto-chronik.de/de/dr-

TWO POSTCARDS WRITTEN IN ŁÓDŹ

Other than that his living conditions must have been extremely harsh and that he must have run out of money sooner or later, we know hardly anything about Karl Fein's almost six months in the Łódź ghetto. From two surviving postcards that he tried to send to his family, on December 8, 1941, we know that he clearly perceived, in the first month and a half in the ghetto, that finding a job was crucial for his survival.[175] There were many reasons for this. Not only did a job mean more food, but also exempted one from deportation, thus providing one the right to live. Manual workers clearly had a greater chance of getting work than "desk people" (*Büromenschen*). Very soon after their arrival, the skills of the newly settled individuals (*Neueingesiedelten*) were scrupulously recorded.[176]Another precondition for finding work seems to have been knowledge of Polish. Apparently, people from Prague had a slight advantage here: "The many Prague people who were in the office had it easy, their Czech tongue was not so foreign to the Polish language and their ear understood almost everything. But the Germans!"[177] Oskar Rosenfeld also claimed that, of all the so-called Western Jews, the ones from the five Prague transports had the best chance of getting jobs in Łódź.[178] However, Fein did not possess any manual skills, so it must have proved very difficult for him to find a job. In addition, the positions in the privileged ghetto administration were of course limited and highly desired. Knowing the "right people" to get a white-collar job was another survival factor.[179] The Łódź ghetto researchers around Sascha Feuchert correctly speak of a "favoritism economy" (*Günstlingswirtschaft*) in this regard.[180] Bernard Heilig (1902–1943), an economic historian who was on transport "B" with Fein, had more luck in finding a job in the ghetto administration, though it took him some time to obtain the position. Three months after he arrived, in February 1942, he got a job in the ghetto archive. He would become one of the writers of the so called "ghetto chronicle", a document that survived the war and is now one of the primary sources for all historians studying life in the Łódź ghetto.[181]

In Fein's two surviving postcards, both written on December 8, 1941, he wrote that he had received some mail from his family and started to write immediately after the postal ban (*Postsperre*) was lifted, on December 4, 1941 [ill. 8].[182] He also wrote that he had received the money they had sent and updated them on who had written to whom and what expected mail had not arrived.[183] These postcards that Fein mailed in Łódź survived in the Łodź State Archives (Archiwum Państwowe w Łodzi) paradoxically … because they were never sent. The archive has around 22,000 such postcards which were taken to the ghetto post office but never left the ghetto [ill. 9]. Likely there were many more such postcards but they were possibly discarded at some point.[184] There are several factors why some were sent, and others not. To start with, there were too many, the postal and the censorship services could not handle so many postcards.[185] The daily limit of 20,000 postcards able to leave the ghetto was exceeded on the

bernard-heilig (accessed Dec. 20, 2014). See also Feuchert et al. 2007, Anhang und Supplemente: 180 n. 56. The best critical edition of the famous Łódź chronicle is the extended 2007 German edition. See Feuchert et al. 2007. The earlier English edition (Dobroszycki 1984) is incomplete. For a fictionalization of the situation in Łódź, see *The Emperor of Lies* by the Swedish author Steve Sem-Sandberg (Sem-Sandberg 2011).

182 For more on the lifting of the postal ban on November 4, 1941, see, for example, Steinert 2015, 165.

183 I would like to express my deepest gratitude to Rainer-Joachim Siegel for his gracious and very capable assistance in deciphering most of Karl Fein's virtually illegible handwriting. I also thank Els Snick for putting me in contact with him.

184 Steinert 2015, 185. In June 2012, Ewa Wiatr told me that, besides the mail already microfilmed, there is still more from the Łódź inhabitants that has been held back and not microfilmed (or digitized) yet. Piotr Zawilski, then director of the Łódź state archives, on the other hand, claimed that all surviving postcards have been microfilmed. See email (dated Aug. 12, 2016) to the author. So it is unclear if still other postcards from Karl Fein – not sent – might yet surface in the future.

185 Steinert 2015, [167], 173, 175.

first day that the postal ban was lifted. According to the ghetto chronicle, around 600,000 postcards were mailed in the Łódź ghetto in the one month that mail was allowed.[186] Secondly, the postcards had to meet certain criteria (word count, content restrictions, adding "Israel" or "Sara" to the name of the addressee, no crossed-out words, etc.) before they could actually be sent.[187] Postcards had also to be written in clearly legible capital letters and could not exceed the maximum of thirty words. Karl Fein's very difficult handwriting was likely enough to prevent his postcards from being sent: the censor was unable to read what he wrote.[188]

From Fein's two postcards, we also learn that his sister, Greta Polatschek, who had been deported with her husband from Vienna to Poland in March 1941, possibly asked, somewhat naively, if her brother could inquire "officially" (*an offizieller Stelle*) whether he could join her in the Polish ghetto where she was staying.[189] Karl Fein also asked how certain people were doing: the landlady at his last Prague address, Frau Kummermann, an aunt in Boskovice, Frau Neumann, the wife of the engineer Richard Neumann whom he knew from his last Prague address, Gerda[190] and Gustav and Lizzy.[191] But most of all Fein wanted to know how his mother and older brother Gustav were doing. He also mentioned he "had company in the Prague collective" (*habe im Kollektiv Gesellschaft*). It is of course not clear if Fein meant by this a gay friend or even a boyfriend, but his cryptic and clearly prudent "had company" would surely have been understood by his family as referring to a male companion – had the postcard reached them. Fein also mentioned that he intended to send more postcards to his brother and mother in Prague, that he could eat in the evenings, against payment (in German marks), with a certain Mrs. Bloch. Other than this, as far one can make out Fein's handwriting, the two postcards do not say much more.

The lifting of the ban on outgoing mail was very short-lived. On December 13, 1941, all mail, except postcards to the Protectorate and Germany, was forbidden again.[192] And starting on January 5, 1942, no mail at all was allowed to be sent from the ghetto.[193] Most likely, this new postal ban was linked to the planned mass deportations from the ghetto in the first half of 1942, to avoid the risk of any information about these

[186] Ibid., [167], 181.
[187] Ibid., 166, 170, 176.
[188] Beneš & Tošnerová 1996, 28–30, 61, 66–69.
[189] In the postcard (dated Dec. 8, 1941), Karl Fein wrote about his sister's *Einladung* (invitation). In the address box of the postcard to his sister, he wrote only his sister's name and the name of the city, "Tarnogród b.[ei] Bilgoraj" (Tarnogród near Bilgoraj), a city in Poland a little less than 200 kilometers southeast of Łódź. As we will see later, Karl Fein's sister and her husband had already been deported to Poland from Vienna on March 5, 1941, two months before Fein was deported from Prague. This also means, of course, that his sister, and presumably also his brother-in-law, were still alive in December 1941.
[190] A good candidate for the Gerda mentioned here is Gertrude Brecher (née Laufer, 1910–1989), who fled with Karl Fein's cousin, Heinrich Brecher (1904–1955), to Uruguay in June 1938. See below, pp. 674-79. It seems unlikely that this was Fein's aunt, Gertruda Fein, given what was said in the interview I had with Marianna Becková, see chapter 6, pp. 174-75.
[191] These two names are unidentified. As we have seen, the couple Giese knew in Brno were Gustl and Livia but Lizzy (from Elisabeth) is, of course, not Livia. See Archiv MHG, Berlin, fonds Adelheid Schulz, letter (dated Oct. 31, 1937, 2) from Karl Giese to Adelheid Schulz. "Lizzie" could also be Fein's aunt, the former bookseller Elise Brecher (née Löw, 1869–1943) then still in Brno. Was Gustav maybe her new partner or a code name for her son Fritz? One might also think that Gustav and Lizzy were Gustav and Herta Fein, but this seems unlikely since Karl Fein later mentions Gustav on his own when asking how a list of individuals were doing. And Herta Fein had already escaped to England in 1939.
[192] Feuchert et al 2007, 1941, 300: "*Briefverkehr für Neueingesiedelte* [underlining in original]. An den Schulgebäuden, in denen die mit den letzten Transporten ins Getto Eingesiedelten gemeinsam untergebracht worden sind, ist heute folgende Verfügung des Judenältesten plakatiert worden: 'Es ist mir gelungen, das Verbot des Briefverkehrs für Neueingesiedelte zu annullieren, doch werden trotz mehrfacher Mahnungen immer noch zu viele Postsendungen weggeschickt. Aus diesem Grund habe ich die Annahme der Postsendungen ins Reich sowie ins Protektorat Böhmen und Mähren einstellen lassen. Die Verfügung gilt bis auf Widerruf. Dies macht es mir möglich, die in großen Mengen rückständigen Postsendungen ins Deutsche Reich und ins Protektorat über mein Postamt abzufertigen. Trotz der vorübergehenden Sperre werden die Briefkästen

operations leaving the ghetto. In December 1941, the ghetto administration sent out only typed cards in answer to inquiring family members, stating that the person asked about was living in the ghetto and that the wiring of money was allowed.[194] The postal ban meant that one lost all contact with one's family abroad. This must have been very hard on the newcomers to the ghetto and added to the despair of an already hopeless and awful situation.[195] Most likely, Fein's closest family members kept sending him money in the following months. His older brother Gustav and his mother were at that point still in Prague.[196]

THE DEATH OF KARL FEIN

From January 16, 1942, until April 2, 1942, fifty-four transports deporting around 44,500 people to Chełmno (Kulmhof), around seventy kilometers northwest of Łódź, were arranged. One month later, a large part of the so-called "newly resettled people" (*Neueingesiedelten*), who arrived in the ghetto in the autumn of 1941 would follow suit.[197] Twelve transports in total were planned between May 4 and 15, 1942.[198] Around 10,900 of these newly resettled people were deported and gassed to death in

nach und nach wieder geleert, sobald die Einschränkung rückgängig gemacht werden kann. Um die Bestätigung von Geldschecks zu ermöglichen, werden an den Schaltern meiner Postämter am Plac Kościelny 4-6 und in der ul. Rybna 1 ausnahmsweise nur Postkarten entgegengenommen. Der Versand von Telegrammen wurde ebenfalls eingestellt" (*Correspondence for newly resettled persons* [underlining in original]. The following order by the Judenälteste [Jewish Elder] was posted today on the school buildings where those resettled from the last transports to the ghetto were housed: "I have succeeded in cancelling the ban on mail for newly resettled persons, but despite repeated reminders, too many mail items are still being sent. For this reason I have stopped accepting mail to the Reich as well as to the Protectorate of Bohemia and Moravia. The order is valid until revoked. This will enable me to process the large quantities of overdue mail to the German Reich and the Protectorate via my post office. Despite the temporary block, the letterboxes will gradually be emptied again as soon as the restriction can be reversed. In order to permit the confirmation of money checks, postcards alone are exceptionally accepted at the counters of my post offices at 4-6 Plac Kościelny and 1 ul. Rybna. The sending of telegrams has also been discontinued).

[193] Feuchert et al. 2007/1942, 17–18. See also Steinert 2015, 175–76; http://www.japhila.cz/hof/0476/index0476a.htm (accessed Aug. 8, 2015).

[194] Feuchert et al. 2007/1942, 616 n. 18: "Die Wienerin Alice de Buton etwa musste in dem Buro, in welchem sie zuerst arbeitete, Postkarten mit behordlich vorbereitetem Text maschinenschriftlich versehen: 'Wir teilen Ihnen mit, dass Herr und Frau Soundso sich wohl befinden und in Litzmannstadt-Getto, an der Siegfriedstrasse 7, Wohnung 23, wohnen. Geldsendungen sind erlaubt'" (The Viennese Alice de Buton, for example, had to type officially prepared text on postcards in the office where she first worked: 'We inform you that Mr. and Mrs. So-and-so are well and living in Litzmannstadt-Getto, in flat 23, 7 Siegfriedstrasse. Money transfers are permitted'). See also the mention of these *Vordruckkarten* (preprinted cards) (dated Nov. 4, 1942) and *Drucknachrichten* (print messages) (dated Dec. 8, 1942) in Feuchert et al. 2007/1942, 537, 591. I saw many examples of these typed cards scattered through several parts of the Łódź ghetto archive on my two research trips to Łódź.

[195] Feuchert et al. 2007/1942, 66: "Zu den schwersten Sorgen der Eingesiedelten gehöre die Postsperre" (One of the most serious concerns of the resettled is the postal ban). See also Feuchert et al. 2007/1942, 67, 71. Poznański wrote in his Łódź diary that the postal ban was indeed "eine schwere Strafe" (a heavy punishment) (Poznański 2011, 168, entry dated Oct. 26, 1943). See also Steinert 2015, 176–77.

[196] For more information on sending money to the ghetto, see the entry "*Von der Post*" [underlining in original] (dated Nov. 4, 1942) in Feuchert et al. 2007/1942, 537. See also Steinert 2015, 176.

[197] Steinert & Genger 2010, 153.

[198] Steinert and Genger refer to two very informative sheets in APŁ, Łódź, fonds Przełożony Starszeństwa Żydów, sign. 1299, microfilm L-19916, [Wysiedlenia resortów, transportów, pojedynczych osób. Działalność Komisji Międzyresortowej], f. 38 and f. 41 (Steinert & Genger 2010, 153 n. 3), now available at http://szukajwarchiwach.pl/39/278/0/20/1299/-skan/full/_vBcWIMUk3IdJcn80fU6RA and http://szukajwarchiwach.pl/39/278/0/20/1299/skan/full/H2ICSJxBfaTBRsClmKt2hQ (both accessed Aug. 2, 2016). The authors add: "Die Listen finden sich im Bestand 'Aussiedlungswesen'" (The lists can be found in the archival fonds "Aussiedlungswesen"). This is incorrect since the sheets are part of the Bestand Komisja Międzyresortowa (Zwischen-Ressort-Komitee). But it is correct to think that they *should have been* part of the Bestand Komisja Wysiedleńcza (Aussiedlungs-Kommission). In other words, this is yet another example of the already mentioned disorder that is a structural characteristic of the Łódź ghetto archival fonds.

Chełmno (Kulmhof) in trucks over a period of two weeks.[199] One also needs to add to these sixty-six transports the 4,300 Sinti and Roma deported between January 5 and 12, 1942.[200] This means that likely a total of around seventy transports left the Łódź ghetto for Chełmno (Kulmhof) in the first half of 1942. If we include the Sinti and Roma transports, a total of 59,292 people were deported from Łódź in the first half of 1942. After the departure of these transports, the total population of the ghetto sank to around 100,000 people.[201]

The announcement of the eastward deportation of the "Western Jews" came on Wednesday April 29, 1942, printed on the yellow poster "Announcement n° 380" (*Bekanntmachung n° 380*), put up that afternoon across the ghetto: "At the behest of the authorities, the President [Chaim Mordechai Rumkowski] announces that as of Monday, May 4, the resettlement of Jews from the Old Reich, Luxembourg, Vienna and Prague settled in the ghetto will begin".[202] It is clear that mainly non-working ghetto residents were being targeted, since they were of no use to the ghetto whose well-known motto, advanced by the – contested – Jewish Elder (*Judenälteste*) in Łódź, Chaim Mordechai Rumkowski (1877–1944) was: "Our only way is work" (*Unser einziger Weg ist Arbeit*). Most likely, like most of the newly settled people, Karl Fein was still without a job. The "ghetto chronicle" tells us that, of the 20,000 Western Jews taken to the ghetto six months earlier, approximately 17,000 survived the harsh winter months.[203] And of these survivors, only 3,000 were employed.[204]

[199] Neubauer, Nov. 9, 2011. See also Feuchert et al. 2007/1942, 144; and Feuchert et al. 2007/1942, 645 n. 10: "Zwischen dem 4. und dem 15. Mai 1942 deportierten die Nationalsozialisten 10 914 Menschen aus dem Getto Litzmannstadt in das Vernichtungslager Kulmhof [Chełmno] und ermordeten sie dort. Fast alle Opfer gehorten zu den „Neueingesiedelten" vom Herbst 1941, lediglich 416 der Betroffenen waren polnische Juden. In der Zeit von Januar bis Mai 1942 wurden insgesamt 54 990 Menschen aus dem Getto Litzmannstadt im Vernichtungslager Kulmhof getotet" (Between May 4 and 15, 1942, the National Socialists deported 10,914 people from the Litzmannstadt ghetto to the Kulmhof [Chełmno] extermination camp and murdered them there. Almost all of the victims belonged to the "newly resettled" from autumn 1941, only 416 of those targeted being Polish Jews. In the period from January to May 1942, a total of 54,990 people from the Litzmannstadt ghetto were killed in the Kulmhof extermination camp). The 10,914 exactly matches the number in a source from the Łódź ghetto archive: http://szukajwarchiwach.pl/39/278/0/20/1299/skan/full/H2ICSJxBfaTBRsClmKt2hQ (accessed Aug. 2, 2016). Cf. Witte 1995, 59. Witte says twelve trains transported a total of 10,993 so-called "Western Jews" between May 4 and May 15, 1942.

[200] Steinert & Genger 2010, 153 n. 2.

[201] Feuchert et al. 2007/1942, 141.

[202] "Auf Geheiß der Behörden gibt der Präses [Chaim Mordechai Rumkowski] bekannt, dass ab Montag, dem 4. Mai, die Aussiedlung der ins Getto eingesiedelten Juden aus dem Altreich, aus Luxemburg, Wien und Prag beginnen werde". The first version of this poster is reproduced in Steinert & Genger 2010, 155. The second, slightly adapted version can be found at http://www.jewishgen.org/databases/holocaust/JG0194_img1.jpg (accessed Aug. 7, 2016).

[203] That the winter of 1941-42 was indeed long and harsh is confirmed by Rosenfeld 1994, 65–66, 70.

[204] Feuchert et al. 2007/1942, 136. See also Feuchert et al. 2007/1942, 135, under the heading "*Arbeitslose westeuropäische Juden werden das Getto verlassen* [underlining in original]" (*Unemployed Western European Jews will leave the ghetto* [underlining in original]). In his diary, Singer also writes about the unemployment situation of the newly settled people, and seems to imply that the "Western Jews" were, starting at a certain moment, deliberately blocked from taking the jobs of local Poles (qtd. in Feuchert et al. 2007/1942, 643 n. 120). See also Feuchert et al. 2007/1942, 139: "Im Allgemeinen dominierte die Auffassung, dass man die hiesige Bevölkerung in Ressorts und Büros versteckt habe, um sie vor der Aussiedlung zu retten, stattdessen habe man die westlichen Juden in den Vordergrund geschoben. In gewissen Kreisen der Neueingesiedelten herrschte eine gewaltige Verbitterung" (In general, the dominant view was that the local population had been hidden away in work places (resorts) and offices in order to save them from resettlement; instead, the Western Jews were pushed to the fore. Among certain circles of the newly resettled there was tremendous bitterness). As already noted, I did not find an *Arbeitskarte* (work permit) for Karl Fein, but this is only very relative evidence given the only partial survival of the Łódź ghetto archives. The JewishGen "Lódz Ghetto Work Identification Cards" database does not mention Fein's name either. See http://www.jewishgen.org/databases/holocaust/0147_Łódź_work_cards.html (accessed Aug. 7, 2016).

[205] At least five sources – three of them in the archival fonds of the Łódź ghetto – confirm Fein's exact death date. The main source is APŁ, Łódź, fonds Przełożony Starszeństwa Żydów, sign. 962, microfilm L-19581, [Kopie dziennych list zgonów] [Copies

Karl Fein's death occurred just a few days before this new wave of deportations of the newly settled "to the East" started, on May 2, 1942.[205] This was also the day when those chosen for the first of these transports had to go to the central prison (*Zentralgefängnis*) of the ghetto, where the deportees were gathered to await their actual deportation on May 4, 1942.[206] When news of the deportations was announced, the rate of suicides among the newly settled in the camp exploded "for fear of being deported".[207] Oskar Singer wrote in his diary: "The panic is indescribable".[208] The ghetto chronicle reported that on May 4, 1942, the newly settled counted for almost half of the approximately seventy ghetto deaths that day.[209]

It was possible to appeal a deportation decision in the Department for the Newly Settled (*Abteilung für Eingesiedelte*), located at 8 Rybna (Fischgasse). Apparently,

of the daily lists of reported deaths], list dated May 6, 1942, f. 269, entry n° 8121, Fein Karel. Now available online at https://szukajwarchiwach.pl/39/278/0/13.2/962/skan/full/5k9aah3vsNutyGHVKbu5zA (accessed Feb. 19, 2021). Besides the death registry number (8121), the list includes the first and last name, the arrival transport, address(es) in the ghetto, the cards (work, ration, etc.) the deceased possessed, and several other columns whose contents are not clear. The barely legible handwriting added (in Polish) says "z Pragi, zmarł", which means "from Prague, deceased". I thank Marcin Piotr Wojciechowski for his assistance in reading these few words in February 2021. The exact title of the list found at the top of the page is "wykaz zgonów zgłoszonych" (list of reported deaths). This list recorded those who had died in the ghetto since its inception. Fein was the 8,121st death registered. Fein's name also shows up in a list organized alphabetically, by month, of people who had died. It appears under the letter "F" for May 1942, again numbered 8,121. See APŁ, Łódź, fonds Przełożony Starszeństwa Żydów, sign. 2460, L-21074, [Alfabetyczny spis osób], f. 104. Curiously, the list ends at the letter "F". Among secondary sources, there is, of course, the very reliable reference work *Terezínská pamětní kniha – Theresienstädter Gedenkbuch* (Kárný et al. 1995), which notes Karl Fein's Prague "Transport B" and his death date in volume I, p. 93. The very useful booklet that gives an English translation of the long introduction to this work (Kárný et al. 1996, 89–98) provides the exact sources used to compile the register. The same death date is given on an ITS index card of the "ústřední kartotěka – transport" database, which also mentions the same *Matriken* (register) number 8,121. Lastly, Fein's name appears on a list of deaths (also present in the I.T.S archives) produced for or by the Łódź Getto-Verwaltung (Łódź ghetto administration): "Namentliche Aufstellung der verstorbenen Zugewiesenen aus dem Altreich u.a. [...] gemeldet von 1. bis einschl.[ießlich] 21 Mai 1942" (List by name of deceased, allocated persons from the Old Reich and others [...] reported from May 1 to 21, 1942, inclusive). In the list "Prag II", Karl Fein's name appears under number 3,177. In the same month (May 1942), thirty people from the "Prague II" transport died. Despite these many sources confirming Fein's death on May 2, 1942, his name is absent from the death register in APŁ, Łódź, fonds Przełożony Starszeństwa Żydów, sign. 959a, [Akta zgonów], II-V 1942. This was one of the rare items in the Łódź ghetto archive not microfilmed in 2012, necessitating consultation in another reading room of the APŁ on the other side of the city. It is now available online at https://szukajwarchiwach.pl/39/278/0/13.2/959a?q=Akta+zgon%C3%B3w+XARCHro:39+XNRZESPro:278+XCDNUMERUro:0&wynik=1&rpp=15&page=1#tabJednostka (accessed Feb. 18, 2021). This is where I probably need to mention a novel published in Switzerland in 2011. The novel, whose author received financial assistance in the form of two subventions, imagines Karl Fein surviving the war and working for the Mossad. In an afterword reflecting on the various true elements in his work of fiction, the author claims that Fein's death is not certain, because three of his consulted contacts in Czechia could not confirm it. See Verdan 2011, 289. I think it sufficient, for a start, to simply look up the information on Fein's certain death in Łódź in the very reliable printed reference work Kárný et al. 1995.

206 Steinert & Genger 2010, 157. Cf. Feuchert et al. 2007/1942, 650 n. 33: "In einer anderen, undatierten Notiz halt Oskar Rosenfeld fest: 'Am 2. Mai fullte sich das Zentralgefangnis zum erstenmal mit den Ausgewiesenen. Sie bekamen vom Getto Suppe und Brot. Am 4. Mai gings zum Bahnhof'" (In another undated note, Oskar Rosenfeld writes: "On May 2, the central prison filled up with those expelled for the first time. They received soup and bread from the ghetto. On 4 May they went to the railway station"). See also Feuchert et al. 2007/1942, 146: "*Erster Tag der Aussiedlung.*" [underlining in original] dated Monday, May 4, 1942. Quite consistently, we see that the newly settled had to register two days before being deported. See Steinert & Genger 2010, 158, 164–65, 167.

207 Feuchert et al. 2007/1942, 147: "Ursache: Angst vor der Aussiedlung".

208 Quoted in Feuchert et al. 2007/1942, 642 n. 117: "Die Panik ist unbeschreiblich". See also Feuchert et al. 2007/1942, 139.

209 Feuchert et al. 2007/1942, 145–46, date May 4, 1942. See also Feuchert et al. 2007/1942, 148, date May 5, 1942: "*Sterbefälle und Geburten.* [underlining in original] Heute starben: 72 Personen, davon 34 Eingesiedelte" (*Deaths and births.* [underlining in original] Today, 72 persons died, 34 of them resettled persons).

one had two days to do so.[210] While some people sought to be spared from further transportation, others thought that things could not get any worse and made their "peace" with being transported.[211] Some in the ghetto suspected that the transports were up to no good: "There existed different ideas and preconceptions in the ghetto about the fate of the 'expelled'".[212] We have already seen that deportations of the newly arrived, in May 1942, were preceded by several other deportation waves. People noticed the luggage being taken away, in the Radegast (Radogoszcz) station, from those being deported.[213]

Even though Fein likely did not have a job, it is nevertheless possible that he was in contact with people who worked for the ghetto administration (*Ghettoverwaltung*). It cannot be excluded that he learned from such a contact that these transports "further East" ended in death. This rumor may have also spread among the lawyers, who had been so numerous on the "Prague II" or "B" transport. One may also wonder if Fein's homosexuality may have played a role in his possibly being better informed than others. An informal gay information network, connecting men with very different backgrounds and positions in the ghetto, may have been a conduit through which the secret information about what happened in Chełmno (Kulmhof) nevertheless passed. It is certain in any case that all people deported from Łódź, in the first half of 1942, ended up in the gas trucks of Chełmno (Kulmhof).[214]

The available archival sources did not allow me to determine whether Karl Fein received a deportation summons. Nor, if he did, when he received it. And if he did,

[210] Steinert & Genger 2010, 158: "Die Verantwortlichen des Düsseldorfer Transportes organisierten sofort nach dem Eintreffen der "Ausreise-Aufforderungen" das Schreiben von Widersprüchen gegen die Aussiedlung. Um keine Zeit zu verlieren – zwischen der Zustellung der Karten und der Meldung an der Sammelstelle lagen häufig nur 48 Stunden – verfassten wohl zwei Angehörige des Kollektivs ab 1. Mai 1942 handschriftlich die Anträge auf Rückstellung ihrer Miglieder" (The people in charge of the Düsseldorf transport organized the writing down of objections against the deportation orders immediately after they were received. In order not to lose time – often there were only 48 hours between the delivery of the cards and reporting at the collection point – probably two members of the Düsseldorf collective wrote their members' applications for revocation by hand from May 1, 1942 onwards). See also Steinert & Genger 2010, 164.

[211] Feuchert et al. 2007/1942, 139–40: "Andererseits beabsichtigen sehr viele, auf das Privileg, bleiben zu dürfen, zu verzichten; diese haben beschlossen, ihre Auszeichnungen überhaupt nicht preiszugeben. Mehr als fünf Monate auf nacktem Fußboden, in Hunger und Kälte, spornen sie gar nicht zum Kampf um solch ein Dasein im Getto an. Sie sagen, wo auch immer sie sich befinden werden – schlimmer kann es ihnen nicht ergehen, und deshalb wollen sie die bisherige Bleibe gerne verlassen. Unter ihnen gibt es viele Menschen, die einst nicht nur sehr vermögend waren, sondern auch eine hohe gesellschaftliche Stellung bekleideten. Im Getto leisten die meisten von ihnen schwere körperliche Arbeit, sehr viele sind sogar bei der Abfuhr von Müll und Fäkalien beschäftigt und die Verbitterung darüber ist unermesslich! In den einzelnen Transporten ist die Lage geradezu katastrophal" (On the other hand, a great number intend to give up the privilege of staying; they have decided not to renounce their distinction. More than five months on a bare floor, hunger and cold, does not in the least spur them to struggle for such an existence in the ghetto. They say that wherever they find themselves – they cannot do worse, and that is why they are eager to leave their present abode. Among them there are many people who were once not only very wealthy but also held high social positions. In the ghetto, most of them do hard physical labor, a large number are even employed to remove waste and feces, and the bitterness this causes is immeasurable! In the individual transports the situation is downright catastrophic).

[212] Feuchert et al. 2007/1942, 645 n. 10: "Uber das Schicksal der 'Ausgesiedelten' gab es im Getto unterschiedliche Vorstellungen und Vorahnungen".

[213] Feuchert et al. 2007/1942, 146 n. 33: "Vorläufig konnte als wichtigstes, mit dem Abgang des ersten Transports zusammenhängendes Detail festgestellt werden: Allen abreisenden Personen / der Transport bestand aus tausend Menschen/ wurde das Gepäck, die Rucksäcke und auch das Handgepäck, abgenommen. Diese Nachricht hatte im ganzen Getto eine deprimierende Wirkung zur Folge" (For the time being, the most important detail connected to the departure of the first transport can be established: all departing persons / the transport consisted of a thousand people/ had their luggage, backpacks and also hand luggage, taken away. This news had a depressing effect throughout the ghetto). See also Feuchert et al. 2007/1942, 148, 650 n. 33; Rosenfeld 1994, 27, 306 n. 2, 309 n. 19.

[214] Witte 1995, 59, 67 n. 75. Witte also shows that the October–November 1941 transports had been planned as a first *Stufe* (stage), and that the second deportation wave "further East", in the first half of 1942, had been planned along with the first wave.

did he appeal? Thousands of letters asking for an exemption have survived, but Fein's name is not among them. So what presumed orders from the Department for the Newly Settled Karl Fein had to deal with in the days before his death remains unresolved.

The fact that Fein's known death date – Saturday, May 2, 1942 – was so close to the planned deportations further East, which must have undoubtedly caused great stress, made me think for a long time that there was a possibility that Fein committed suicide. But I found no archival trace for this possibility.[215] Later, I found a source that said that Fein died of undernourishment and heart failure.[216] These two causes of death were quite common in the Łódź ghetto, but we also have to consider the possibility that other causes may have been involved in his death. Presumably, poor health from undernourishment, combined with the great stress caused by the announcement of the deportations, contributed to his dying shortly before the deportations started.[217]

First they would see how many would survive their first Polish winter (1941–42). Although many scenarios about what to do next with the deported Jews were entertained at the same time, there is a chance that the murderous intent of the second wave was known all along but kept in limbo. See also Witte 1995, 53–54.

[215] I have checked several parts of the Łódź ghetto archive in my attempt to find hard proof of Fein's possible suicide but have found none. For example, I looked at the daily *Meldungen* (notifications) from the *Ordnungsdienst* (order service) of the neighborhood where Fein was living. Fein's neighborhood Ordnungsdienst district building (at 24 Franzstrasse) is even now a police station. See APŁ, Łódź, fonds Przełożony Starszeństwa Żydów, sign. 131-134, microfilms L-18749 until 18752. I checked the latter for traces of Fein's possible suicide in the period from the end of April until the beginning of May 1942. Especially sign. 132, microfilm L-18750 was very informative. Its daily reports provide the total daily deaths and sometimes also report specific suicide cases. Suicides in Łódź were mainly by jumping off buildings, hanging or taking poison (Luminal or Veronal). I was surprised to discover that many ghetto residents died by poison and that poison was apparently relatively easy to obtain in the ghetto. Rosenfeld claims that the Western Jews had brought poison when they were deported. See Rosenfeld 1994, 168. I also checked the rather meager and very disorderly Kripo archives of the Łódź ghetto. See APŁ, Łódź, fonds 203, Kriminalpolizeistelle Litzmannstadt 1939-1944, sign. 59, microfilm L-15120, Ermittlungen der Kripo über Totschlagen u.[nd] Selbstmorde der Juden im Getto 1940-1942. In addition, I checked the Tages- und Tätigkeitsberichte Kriminalkommissariats Getto 1941-1942, APŁ, Łódź, fonds 203, Kriminalpolizeistelle Litzmannstadt 1939-1944, sign. 60, microfilm L-15121, but only found notes on deaths, suicides, house searches, etc., out of chronological order. A day report for May 2, 1942 was missing. The other microfilms I examined in this same Kripo archival fonds were sign. 38, microfilm L-15099, sign. 39, microfilm L-15100, sign. 40, microfilm L-15101 and sign. 41, microfilm L-15102. Especially interesting was sign. 38, microfilm L-15099, which mentioned several suicides, the most repeated motive being "Angst vor die Aussiedlung" (fear of being deported). Here as well, the lack of chronological order of the archival documents stood out. It also occurred to me that Fein's possible suicide may have escaped the reports that I saw because some poisonings were considered "natural deaths". These may not have been reported as suicides, either out of ignorance of the medical symptoms of poisoning or else to prevent further upheaval in the ghetto because of intentional deaths.

[216] APŁ, Łodz, Akta miasta Łodzi, fonds Zarząd Getta (Gettoverwaltung), Meldungen über Sterblichkeit im Getto, sign. 29207, microfilm L-21291, f. 301, Aufstellung der in der Zeit vom 4.-10. Mai 1942 gemeldeten Todesfälle, n° 142, Fein Karel: "Herzmuskelschw.[äche] Unterern.[ährung]" (myocardial insufficiency [and] undernourishment).

[217] I also looked at the other people from the Prague II transport who died around the same time as Fein. A list of these deaths can be found in APŁ, Łodz, Akta miasta Łodzi, fonds Zarząd Getta (Gettoverwaltung), sign. n° 29208, microfilm L-21292, Meldungen über Sterblichkeit im Getto, f. 74. I was intrigued by a certain Artur Koretz (1892–1942) who died on May 1, 1942, the day before Fein died. A bachelor, Koretz was a lawyer from Prague who was with Karl Fein on transport "B" (the "Prague II" transport) from Prague to Łódź in October 1941. For Koretz's police file, see https://www.holocaust.cz/databaze-obeti/obet/142408-artur-koretz/ (accessed Aug. 29, 2019). For his death date, see APŁ, Łodz, Akta miasta Łodzi, fonds Zarząd Getta (Gettoverwaltung), Meldungen über Sterblichkeit im Getto, inv. n° 29207, microfilm L-21291, f. 322, n° 388, Koretz Arthur. The latter says that Koretz died of Unterernährung and Herzschwäche (undernourishment and mycordial insufficiency), just like Karl Fein. Koretz did not live at 15 Franciszkańska (Franzstrasse) – Fein's building – but at 12 R Strasse, which was the Pieprzowa ulice or Pfeffergasse. See the Strassenbezeichnung im erweiterten Wohngebiet der Juden map, https://www.kestenbaum.net/auction/lot/auction-62/062-184/ (accessed Feb 19, 2021). Another intriguing name was Wilhelm Heller (1913–1942), a philosophy professor, who also arrived in Łódź on the "Prague II" transport, and who died the day after Fein did, on May 3, 1942. That Heller died so young makes

KAREL JELÍNEK

Fein did not die all alone. Most likely, a Czech family of three took care of him in the weeks or even days before his death. One of the primary sources that recorded Fein's death date shows that he did not die in the "Prague II" collective building, where he officially lived, but in a building slightly north on the same street, at 34 Franciszkańska (Franzstrasse).[218] When looking into who lived in this building, I came upon a bachelor named Karel Jelínek (1894–1942), who resided there with his half-brother Anton Jelínek (1884–?) and his wife Hermine Alter (1888–?). Their "apartment", 10c, consisted of one room and no kitchen.[219] Together with the couple's son, František Jelínek (1920–?), all four were deported to Łódź on the fourth Prague transport, transport "D", on October 31, 1941.

Initially, Karel, Anton and Hermine lived in the "Prague IV" transport building, but on March 5, 1942, they moved to their new address at 34 Franciszkańska (Franz-

his death more conspicuous. For his police file, see https://www.holocaust.cz/en/database-of-victims/victim/142292-vilem-heller/ (accessed Feb. 19, 2021). He died of entiritis. See APŁ, Łodz, Akta miasta Łodzi, fonds Zarząd Getta (Gettoverwaltung), Meldungen über Sterblichkeit im Getto, inv. n° 29207, microfilm L-21291, f. 297, n° 22, Heller Wilhelm. The address given there is 13 4 Strasse. This "4 Strasse" was Młynarska (Mühlgasse). See the Strassenbezeichnung im erweiterten Wohngebiet der Juden map, https://www.kestenbaum.net/auction/lot/auction-62/062-184/ (accessed Feb. 19, 2021). Of course, all that can be determined here is that these two people died immediately before and after Fein's death. It is not known if Fein knew them, or if their deaths were in any way related.

218 APŁ, Łódź, fonds Przełożony Starszeństwa Żydów, sign. 962, microfilm L-19581, [Kopie dziennych list zgonów], list dated May 6, 1942, f. 269, entry n° 8121, Fein Karel. Available online at https://szukajwarchiwach.pl/39/278/0/13.2/962/skan/full/5k9aah3vsNutyGHVKbu5zA (accessed Feb. 19, 2021). After the handwritten note (in Polish), "z Pragi, zmarł" (from Prague, deceased), there is the address where he died (in German): "Franzs.[trasse] 34". That this is indeed where Fein died can be inferred, to name just one example, from another death recorded in the same folio. Josef Pels (1892–1942) from the Duesseldorf collective, located at the 21 Fischstrasse (Rybna), also died at this address since the address of his collective is repeated again after the note "z Duesseldorf, zmarł" (from Düsseldorf, deceased).

219 APŁ, Łódź, fonds Przełożony Starszeństwa Żydów, sign. 1025, L-12682, [Książka meldunkowa domów], f. 195. Of the approximately fifty-five units in this four-story apartment building, only apartment 10 was divided into three smaller units: 10a, 10b and 10c. However, apartments 1, 6, 14 and 30 were also divided into 1a, 6a, 14a and 30a. The only people I found also living in apartment 10c were the Gol(d)szstajn family: Szewach Golszstajn (1906–?), his wife Perla Golszstajn (1906–?) and their son Wolf (1936–?). Most likely, they occupied the room before the Jelíneks moved in. See APŁ, Łódź, fonds Przełożony Starszeństwa Żydów, sign. 1025, microfilm L-12682, [Książka meldunkowa domów], f. 185. Karel Jelínek's parents were Leopold (1854–?) and Hermine Jelínek (née Weiss, 1863–?). Hermine Jelínek's birth year is incorrectly given as 1898 in Kárný et al. 1995, 121; and www.holocaust.cz. The second child from Leopold Jelínek's second marriage was Anna Marie Jelínek (1896–?), who was married to Franz Kraus (1892–?). They had one son, Jerzy (1925–1945), who followed an astounding itinerary: after Łódź, he was deported to Ujazdów, Minsk, Terezín, dying in Mauthausen in March 1945, shortly before his twentieth birthday. See http://archive.pamatnik-Terezín.cz/vyhledavani/Aghetto/detail.php?table=ghetto&col=id&value=2103739 and https://raumdernamen.mauthausen-memorial.org/ index.php?id=4&p=27405&L=1 (both accessed Feb. 23, 2021). The Kraus family was on the "Prague III" transport to Łódź. They lived in apartment 40, 16 Brunnenstrasse (Berka Joselewicza). See APŁ, Łódź, fonds Przełożony Starszeństwa Żydów, sign. 1020, microfilm L-12677, [Książka meldunkowa domów], f. 263. That Karel Jelínek was a witness at the Kraus couple's marriage in 1920 shows that brother and sister got along. See http://katalog.ahmp.cz/pragapublica/permalink?xid=6D33FBA99FCD4877A3ECE78258B87041&scan=252#scan252 (accessed Feb. 24, 2021). Leopold Jelínek's first wife was Anna Dub (1854–1891). There were five children from this marriage: Klara Bloch (1882–1944?), Ernestine (1877–?), Emil (1878–?), Anton (1884–?) and the engineer Rudolf (1886–?). Rudolf Jelínek arrived late to the Terezín ghetto but it is unclear if he survived the war. See his index card in the online ITS database. His wife was Beatrix (1901–?) but nothing more is known about her. Emil Jelínek's widow, Adele Bergstein (1885–1942), and her son Franz Jelínek (1921–1943?), were deported from Prague to Terezín on transport "Aal" on July 2, 1942. Adele died two months later. Franz was further transferred from Terezín to Auschwitz-Birkenau on transport "Cu" on February 1, 1943. The fate of Emil and Adele Jelínek's other son, Hans Jelínek (1910–?), is not known.

220 APŁ, Łódź, fonds Przełożony Starszeństwa Żydów, sign. 1011, microfilm L-21090, [Karty meldunkowe i karty pracy], f. 8897 and 8917. They moved on March 5, 1942, notifying the civil registry office on March 10, 1942.

221 APŁ, Łódź, fonds Przełożony Starszeństwa Żydów, sign. 1025, L-12682, [Książka meldunkowa domów], f. 184-198. I looked especially at the new

strasse).[220] They were probably able to move out of their transport collective building because, as we have seen, deportations out of the ghetto started at the beginning of 1942, making more places to live available. For three reasons, I think that Karl Fein spent the last days or weeks of his life with this Czech family of three. Most of the other surnames of people living in the approximately fifty units in the building were Polish-Jewish. Jelínek was one of the only Czech-sounding names.[221] Secondly, Karel Jelínek was unmarried and may have been a gay man and friend of Karl Fein.[222] But the strongest argument is that, before being deported to Łódź, Karel Jelínek lived in Prague at 11 Ve Pštrosce (Pštrossgasse), the very last Prague address where Karl Fein's brother Gustav and mother lived before they were deported to Terezín. This could mean that Karl Fein knew Karel Jelínek when he was still living in Prague [ill. 10]. But the acquaintance could also be explained in the other direction: Karl Fein may have contacted the Jelíneks in Łódź because his mother and brother had lived in the same building where the Jelíneks had lived before they were deported from Prague. Let us be clear: this possible link through the Ve Pštrosce (Pštrossgasse) building is not conclusive and could still be a coincidence of sorts, despite 1940s Prague having a population of around 900,000.[223]

In the beginning of May 1942, Karel, Anton and Hermine Jelínek received a letter ordering their further deportation on transport "X", leaving Łódź on May 13, 1942. In their letter trying to obtain exemption from the transport, the couple mentioned their son Franz (František), who had volunteered to work in a labor camp in Poznań (Posen) in mid-November 1941. They also referred to their daughter Helene (1916–?), not knowing where she had been deported.[224] In his own letter, Karel Jelínek mainly referred to the fact that he had had a job in the ghetto since his arrival. All three

people moving into this address (from f. 193 on) since the Western Jews arrived in the ghetto only at the end of 1941. I found the name of Karel Jelínek when looking up the "Franzstr. 34" address in the "Last letters from the Łódź ghetto" database (database ID: 20817) at https://www.ushmm.org/ (accessed Feb. 20, 2021). But let us be clear: several other people lived in the 34 Franciszkańska (Franzstrasse) building. The "Holocaust survivors and victims" database at https://www.ushmm.org/ returns no fewer than 477 name entries when the term "Franzstrasse 34" is entered in the "all fields" search bar. So it cannot be excluded that Karl Fein was staying here with another person or family at the time of his death.

222 It is not certain that Fein was referring to Karel Jelínek when, in his two December 1941 postcards, he wrote that he "had company" in the "Prague II" collective. Karel Jelínek arrived on the "Prague IV" transport and, until March 1942, lived in the "Prague IV" collective building at 29 Franciszkańska (Franzstrasse). This likely indicates that Fein was *not* referring to Karel Jelínek. Judging from his surviving passport, Karel Jelínek traveled extensively around Europe in his late twenties and visited Germany, Italy, Austria, Belgium and France. We are not claiming this as typical of a gay man – Karl Fein himself did exactly the opposite – but it does not contradict that this was Jelínek's possible sexual preference. See NA, Praha, Policejní ředitelství Praha II, všeobecná spisovna, 1941–1950, kart. n° 4481, sign. J 1141/7, Jelínek, Karel (May 26, 1894).

223 There were several apartments in the building at 11 Ve Pštrosce (Pštrossgasse) in Prague. Gustav Fein and his mother lived with a Mrs. Pick. Since May 1937, Karel Jelínek lived with his half-sister Klara Bloch in another apartment. See the evidence obyvatelstva sheets for both in NA, Praha, fonds Policejní ředitelství Praha II, and for the family relationship, https://www.geni.com/people/Karl-Jelinek/6000000041013310210 (accessed May 4, 2021). There is another suggestion that the shared address was not a coincidence. Karl Fein's mother and brother moved to 11 Ve Pštrosce only in October 1942, several months after Fein's death in May. But it is also possible that Karl Fein's mother and brother ended up at this Prague address *because* Karl Fein had mentioned it (and the owner of the apartment) in a postcard sent from Łódź, or because Fein's relatives knew Karel Jelínek through Karl Fein when the latter was still in Prague. This would also mean that Karl Fein's mother and brother were able to choose even their very last Prague address in relative freedom, and communicated their wish to be housed at 11 Ve Pštrosce to the JKG in Prague (who then sent them a letter ordering them to move there). See also p. 476 for this later address.

224 Helene Poláková (née Jelínek), a medical doctor, was in Terezín, Auschwitz, Hamburg and Bergen Belsen and survived the war but I did not follow up on her further post-war itinerary. For more information on the recruitment of workers for factories in Poznań (Posen), where the working and living conditions were worse than those in Łódź, see Genger & Jakobs 2010, 269–72.

were exempted from the transport.[225] Despite having a job in the ghetto, which was always a means to more food, thereby assuring survival, Karel Jelínek also died of undernourishment on July 7, 1942, two months after Karl Fein.[226] The further fate of Anton and Hermine Jelínek is unknown but they may have been deported when the Łódź ghetto was liquidated, in mid-1944, and killed in Chełmno (Kulmhof) or Auschwitz-Birkenau.

Other of Karel Jelínek's family members were also deported to the Łódź ghetto. His half-sister, the widow Klara Bloch (1882–1944?) and her daughter Ida Bloch (1912–1944?), were deported on the "Prague IV" transport.[227] Karel Jelínek had lived with Klara Bloch in Prague before he was deported.[228] Just like the Jelíneks, the

[225] APŁ, Łódź, fonds Przełożony Starszeństwa Żydów, inv. n° 1290, microfilm L-19907, [Podania Żydów zagranicznych o zwolnienie z wysiedlenia lub o odroczenie terminu, załatwione pozytywnie], letter (dated May 7, 1942) from Anton Jelínek to Aussiedlungs-Kommission, f. 1385-1386. The letter is stamped UWZGLĘDNIONE (approved). Their exemption letter also proposed letting the Wilder family of four go in their place. Clearly, they knew this family wanted to leave the ghetto: "Do Komisji Wysiedleniowej w Getto. Podanie. Niżej podpisany uprzejmie prosi o wysłanie go wraz z żoną i 2 dzieci w zastępstwie pana Antona i Herminy Jelínek, zam.[ieszkałych] Franciszkańska 34. Za co zgodę dziękuję" (To the Ghetto displacement commission. Application. The undersigned kindly requests to be sent with his wife and 2 children in lieu of Mr. Anton and Hermina Jelínek, residing at 34 Franciszkańska. For which I thank you). See ibid., f. 1387. I thank Marcin Piotr Wojciechowski for his help in reading and transcribing these documents in February 2021. For Karel Jelínek's letter, asking to be exempted from the May 1942 transports deporting Western Jews further East, see APŁ, fonds Łódź, fonds Przełożony Starszeństwa Żydów, inv. n° 1288, microfilm L-19905, [Podania Żydów zagranicznych o zwolnienie z wysiedlenia lub o odroczenie terminu, załatwione negatywnie], f. 937-941. The added stamp UWZGLĘDNIONE (approved) appears on the bottom of f. 937. Jelínek's two letters requesting exemption to the Aussiedlungs-Kommission (Resettlement Commission) (one undated and the other dated May 9, 1942) were thus wrongly added to the folder of denied exemption applications. These letters also reveal that Karel Jelínek spoke German. For Anton and Hermine Jelínek's letter requesting exemption, see APŁ, Łódź, fonds Przełożony Starszeństwa Żydów, inv. n° 1290, microfilm L-19907, [Podania Żydów zagranicznych o zwolnienie z wysiedlenia lub o odroczenie terminu, załatwione pozytywnie], f. 1385-1387.

[226] For Karel Jelínek's death date, see APŁ, Łódź, fonds Przełożony Starszeństwa Żydów, invent. n° 962, microfilm L-19581, [Kopie dziennych list zgonów], f. 204, entry number 11857, Jelínek Karel and APŁ, Łódź, Akta miasta Łodzi, fond Zarząd Getta (Gettoverwaltung), sign. 29207, microfilm L-21291, Meldungen über Sterblichkeit im Getto, f. 180, n° 262, Jelínek Karel.

[227] For further genealogical information on Klara Bloch, see p. 470, n. 219. Klara Bloch was the widow of Robert Bloch (1877–1933). They had one son, Jiří (Georg) Bloch (1911–?), but his further destiny is unknown. He may have died at a young age since he is not mentioned in the evidence obyvatelstva sheet for Robert and Klara Bloch in NA, Praha, fonds Policejní ředitelství Praha II, which only mentions Georg's younger sister Ida. In February 1947, a certain Dr. Max Bloch, living in Jerusalem, replied to a search notice placed in a post-war Czech Jewish periodical by an engineer named Slavíčka, inquiring about the current address of Klara and Ida Bloch, who had lived at 11 Ve Pštrosce (Pštrossgasse) in Prague before the war. See *Věstník Židovské obce náboženské v Praze*, Feb. 15, 1947, 44. Dr. Max Bloch (1874–later than 1942) was born in Netolice (Nettolitz) in Czechoslovakia and married Dr. Olga Bermann (1879–1969). Klara Bloch was Max Bloch's sister-in-law since she was the widow of Robert Bloch (1877–1933), one of his two brothers. Max and Olga Bloch had two children: Dr. Clementine Zernik (whose first married name was Bern) (1905–1996) and Ernestine Salzberger (1903–1974). Max and Olga Bloch emigrated to Palestine with their eldest daughter Ernestine in 1939. Ernestine presumably married Marc or Michael Salzberger (?–?). Clementine emigrated to the USA with her first husband Oscar Bern (1890–1948) in August 1938. In 1947, Clementine married her second husband Herbert Zernik (1899–1981?). See https://jwa.org/encyclopedia/article/bern-zernik-clementine (accessed Apr. 30, 2021); the Ancestry database New York, State and Federal Naturalization Records, 1794-1943. For Max Bloch's naturalization file in the Israel State archives, see https://www.archives.gov.il/archives/Archive/0b07170680034dc1/File/0b07170680bf9dc5 (accessed Apr. 30, 2021). I thank Avi Haimovsky for his assistance in locating the archival file in the database. I did not check the archive of Clementine Zernik in the DNB, Leipzig. See https://exilarchiv.dnb.de/DEA/Web/EN/Navigation/MenschenImExil/zernik-clementine/zernik-clementine.html (accessed Apr. 30, 2021). See also the oral history interview "'Man liebt nicht, man haßt nicht' – Ein Gespräch mit Dr. Clementine Zernik", https://www.youtube.com/watch?v=oNQm4trzkLY (accessed Apr. 30, 2021). I could not determine if Max and Olga Bloch's two daughters had any children. Robert and Max Bloch's father, Jakob Bloch (1842–1912), married Filipinne Weiss (1853–?) and had another three children from this second marriage: Ernst Bloch (1881–?), Gustav Bloch (1882–?) and Hermine Samuely

mother and her daughter first lived in the Prague IV collective building (located at 29 Franciszkańska/Franzstrasse). In the beginning of March 1942, however, they moved to apartment 28a at 34 Cranachstrasse (also known as T street), quite close to the building where most of the "Prague IV" people were still living. A total of seven people lived in this one-room apartment with no kitchen.[229] In November 1942, Klara and Ida Bloch moved to 34 Franciszkańska (Franzstrasse) where their relatives Anton and Hermine Jelínek were living.[230] Mother and daughter both survived in the ghetto until at least mid-May 1944. Both worked in a ghetto factory as seamstresses making feminine lingerie.[231] Presumably, they were deported on one of the ghetto liquidation transports, taking them to either Chełmno (Kulmhof) or Auschwitz-Birkenau.

When, in his two unsent postcards of December 1941, Karl Fein said that he was eating in the evenings (against payment) with a "Mrs. Bloch", I presumed for a moment that this might be Klara Bloch. However, she was then still living in the "Prague IV" collective building and it seems very unlikely that she would have been able cook there, let alone have a private kitchen. It is more likely that, in December 1941, Fein was buying his food when he still had the money to do so, presumably from a Polish woman by the name of Bloch. In most cases, the initial Polish residents of the ghetto were then still living in the better private houses and apartments. Again, the Łódź ghetto was mainly run by Polish Jews who lived there before the so-called "Western Jews" arrived in the autumn of 1941. Along with the Jewish Elder (*Judenälteste* or also *Präses*) of the ghetto, Mordechai Chaim Rumkowski (and several of his close family members), many other leading people, mentioned in the so-called ghetto Encyclopedia (*Enzyklopädie*), confirm this. Most were born in Poland, specifically in Łódź itself.[232]

If, on the other hand, we maintain the possibility that Mrs. Bloch was one of the Western Jews anyway, then the second and likely best candidate would have been Louise Bloch (née Landesmann, 1881–1942). She was the mother of Helene Herrmann (née Bloch, 1904-1965), the second wife of the Brno lawyer Robert Herrmann. In the early 1920s, the latter was an intern in the Karl Fein's law office in Brno. We have also seen that, at the beginning of his career, Karl Fein briefly worked in the law office of Robert Herrmann's father, Friedrich August Herrmann. Louise Bloch arrived with her husband Felix Bloch (1873–194?) in Łódź on the "Prague IV" transport. In December 1941, she moved from the "Prague IV" collective building to the senior home (*Greisenheim*), located at 26 Bolzengasse/Gnesener Strasse (Gnieźnieńska),[233]

(1883–?). Hermine married an Emil Samuely –?). The couple had three sons but there the trail ends: Max Selby (Samuely) (1909–1977), Ernst Samuely (1911–1939) and Hans Samuely (Henry Santon) (1913–1977). Max Selby married Charlotte Zuckerberg (1911–1994) but it is not known if they had any children. Finally, Olga Bermann seems to have been in no relation to Wilhelm and Anna Bermann. The latter was the daughter of Elise Brecher, Karl Fein's aunt.

[228] See p. 477.

[229] APŁ, Łódź, fonds Przełożony Starszeństwa Żydów, sign. 1011, microfilm L-21107, [Karty meldunkowe i karty pracy], f. 19031. The building in which they lived was located at the corner of 22 Franciszkańska (Franzstrasse) and 34 Cranachstrasse. Interestingly, they moved to this address on the same day (March 5, 1942) that Karel, Anton and Hermine Jelínek moved from the "Prague IV" collective building to their new 34 Franciszkańska (Franzstrasse) address.

[230] APŁ, Łódź, fonds Przełożony Starszeństwa Żydów, sign. 1025, microfilm L-12682, [Książka meldunkowa domów], f. 197 and APŁ, Łódź, fond Przełożony Starszeństwa Żydów, sign. 1022, microfilm L-12679, [Książka meldunkowa domów], f. 273. See also APŁ, Łódź, fonds Przełożony Starszeństwa Żydów, sign. 1011, microfilm L-21107, [Karty meldunkowe i karty pracy], f. 19029, which says that they lived at this address with four other people.

[231] APŁ, Łódź, fonds Przełożony Starszeństwa Żydów, sign. 1051, microfilm L-12707, [Książka meldunkowa domów], f. 161. They moved on May 17, 1944 to apartment 7, 6 Rubensstrasse. See APŁ, Łódź, fonds Przełożony Starszeństwa Żydów, sign. 1011, microfilm L-21107, [Karty meldunkowe i karty pracy], f. 19027.

[232] Bopp et al. 2020.

[233] She arrived at this new address on December 22, 1941. See APŁ, Łódź, fonds Przełożony Starszeństwa Żydów, inv. n° 1011, microfilm L-21107, [Karty meldun-

where she was joined by her husband.[234] Louise Bloch committed suicide by taking Veronal in August 1942, a few days after her sixty-first birthday.[235] Her husband's fate is not known. But in this case, the same counterargument surfaces: Fein wrote his two postcards on December 8, 1941, when Louise Bloch was still living in the "Prague IV" collective building.

So it is indeed quite possible that Karl Fein lived for some time with Karel, Anton and Hermine Jelínek in their one-room Franciszkańska (Franzstrasse) apartment when he got sick or grew weak. Minimally, one can say that the Jelíneks presumably looked after him in their "home" as he was dying. Fein was so weak that "he could no longer cross the bridge", as they used to say in the Łódź ghetto. The reference was to two wooden bridges in the ghetto with stairways for pedestrians, which one had to cross to reach another part of the ghetto.[236] We have seen that one author actually suggested that Karl Giese died of hunger in Brno, but, in reality, it was Karl Fein who died in the Łódź ghetto from the lack of decent or simply sufficient food.[237] As one Polish survivor of the Łódź ghetto characterized the place: "The ghetto was hunger, getting worse all the time".[238]

We do not know where Karl Fein is buried in the so-called "ghetto field", the southernmost part of the immense, still existing Jewish cemetery in Łódź, but we do know that that is the only place where he could be buried.[239] It is not known with absolute certainty if Fein's family was ever informed of his death, though this seems probable.[240] It is also possible that the news reached them indirectly. Since outgoing mail was suspended most of the time in Łódź, many family members continued to send letters to the Łódź ghetto, asking how their relatives were doing and if they had received the money they had sent. I have seen several examples of typed and even pre-printed cards from the ghetto administration, very briefly stating that the money had been received and confirming that their relatives were still living in the ghetto. Presumably, similar cards saying someone had died were sent out as well.

kowe i karty pracy], index card n° 19090, Luise Sara Bloch.

[234] APŁ, Łódź, fonds Przełożony Starszeństwa Żydów, inv. n° 1024, microfilm L-12681, [Książka meldunkowa domów], f. 393 and APŁ, Łódź, fond Przełożony Starszeństwa Żydów, inv. n° 1011, [Karty meldunkowe i karty pracy], index card n° 18987, Felix Israel Bloch.

[235] APŁ, Łódź, fonds Przełożony Starszeństwa Żydów, inv. n° 962, microfilm L-19581, [Kopie dziennych list zgonów], f. 160, death registration n° 14162 and APŁ, Łódź, Akta miasta Łodzi, fond Zarząd Getta (Gettoverwaltung), inv. n° 29207, Meldungen über Sterblichkeit im Getto, n° 231, f. 131.

[236] Margolius Kovály, Třešťíková & Margolius 2018 39–41.

[237] For Hájková's considerations that it was *not* literally "dying of hunger" (Hájková 2020, 115–17) but rather from a lack of essential nutrients, as well as for some lemmas on avitaminosis, see Bopp et al. 2020, 28–30. Heda Margolius Kovály described the death of her twenty-year-old cousin, Jindříšek Löwy, who lived with them in the Łódź ghetto, and who also died of undernourishment in January 1943. See Margolius Kovály, Třešťíková & Margolius 2018, 42–43, 157.

[238] See Claude Lanzmann's interview with Paula Biren (née Pawa Sara Szmajer, 1922–2016) in the "Baluty" part of the four-part documentary *Les quatre soeurs* (2017). One needs to add that Mrs. Biren was mainly a witness of this great hunger, as she was herself better nourished than most people in Łódź.

[239] The grave cannot be exactly located because the cemetery documentation for the year 1942 is not extant. See email (dated Aug. 19, 2011) from Dana Rothschild (representing Mr. Marek Szukalak, director and board member of the Fundacja Monumentum Iudaicum Łódźense, Łódź) to the author. For more information on the Łódź Jewish cemetery, see http://www.jewishŁódźcemetery.org/ (accessed Dec. 31, 2014). Oskar Rosenfeld claims that the Łódź ghetto dead were buried according to their chronological death date, not by name (Rosenfeld 1994, 180).

[240] We will return to this matter a few times later. See chapter 15, pp. 591-93; chapter 16, p. 637.

[241] See http://db.yadvashem.org/deportation/transportDetails.html?language=en&itemId=6996699 (accessed Dec. 31, 2014).

[242] See the "Shoah-Opfer" database of the Dokumentationsarchiv des österreichischen Widerstandes (DöW), http://www.doew.at.html (accessed Dec. 17, 2014). See also email (dated Jun. 18, 2012) from Wolf-Erich Eckstein (Matriken Israelitische Kultusgemeinde Wien) to the author.

[243] Tarnogród is approximately sixty-five kilometers southeast from Modliborzyce. For more information on Tarnogród as a Jewish site through the centuries, see http://www.jewishgen.org/yizkor/pinkas_poland/pol7_00250.html (accessed Dec. 31, 2014).

GRETA POLATSCHEK (NÉE FEIN)

What happened to Karl Fein's other close family members? Karl's sister, Margarethe (or Greta) Fein, and her husband Rudolf Polatschek, were deported on transport n° 4 from Vienna to the Modliborzyce ghetto in Poland on March 5, 1941. In the days preceding their deportation, they were gathered into a Jewish school next to the Augarten park (35 Castellezgasse), and taken on trucks to the Aspang railway station on the day of their transport.[241] There were 999 people deported; their transport numbers were 547 and 548.[242] At some point, they must have been transferred from Modliborzyce to the Jewish ghetto created in May 1942 in the nearby village of Tarnogród, not far from the city of Biłgoraj in Lublin province.[243] Judging from the postcard that Karl Fein tried to send his sister in December 1941, she was already living in Tarnogród by then. If the couple survived the harsh conditions of the Tarnogród ghetto, they were possibly killed when the ghetto was liquidated, in the autumn of 1942, when most inmates were transported – via Biłgoraj – to the Bełżec extermination camp (*Vernichtungslager*). This was the first camp erected by the National Socialists in which most people were gassed to death upon arrival.[244] This could mean that Karl Fein's sister, three years his elder, outlived her brother by a few months in the year 1942.

We have seen that, in June 1939, the couple was included in the epistolary conversation set up by Erich Messing, informing the Fein family about emigration possibilities and tactics. Messing helped out the couple financially, sending them 600 Reichsmark twice, in May and August 1939.[245] Apparently, Karl Fein's sister and her husband continued to try to find a way to escape Austria after that.

They also received financial help from the USA to fund their efforts. In April 1941, on behalf of Leopold Pilzer, a Lisa Allina twice deposited $500 in the bank account of the Jewish Transmigration Bureau, set up in 1940 by the American Jewish Joint Distribution Committee (JDC). The money was intended for Dr. Rudolf Polatscheck [*sic*] and his wife Grete (8 Biberstreet, Vienna 1).[246] The sum was held in escrow by the Jewish Transmigration Bureau until the emigrants were able to procure all the necessary documents to emigrate from Europe. But Greta and Rudolf Polatschek had been deported from Vienna the preceding month, in March 1941. This is why, in June 1941, the two sums of $500 were refunded to the depositors. It is not known if the Polatscheks knew the Allinas or the Pilzers; and, if they did, how. Leopold Pilzer (1871–1961) was certainly a very wealthy entrepreneur – born in Auschwitz – to whom these sums were utterly insignificant. Pilzer also forced the bentwood furniture industry competitors, Thonet and Kohn, to merge with his own company (Mundus). Thanks to this merger, his company became a multinational. "By 1922, Thonet-Kohn-Mundus AG became the world's largest furniture manufacturer, with over 10,000 workers and 20 production sites in German-speaking Europe".[247] In October 1938, Leopold Pilzer emigrated with his wife Laura Spielmann (1870–?) from Zürich to the USA.[248] After the war, Pilzer became a US citizen. Laura Weill (née Spielmann) was the first

[244] Bełżec is approximately sixty km east of Tarnogród. For more information on the Bełżec Vernichtungslager, see https://de.wikipedia.org/wiki/Vernichtungslager_Belzec (accessed Feb. 10, 2021).

[245] Hessisches Hauptstaatsarchiv, Wiesbaden, Bestand 518, Regierungspräsidien als Entschädigungsbehörde, Regierungspräsidium Wiesbaden, 1958-1972, Akte n° 41623, Erich Messing (°25/12/1895)/Herta Fein (°19/03/1902), f. 81.

[246] Lisa Allina was the wife of Joseph Allina, who lived at 105 Parkway Road, Bronx, New York. The address given for Leopold Pilzer was 1 Park Avenue, New York. See the two Jewish Transmigration Bureau deposit cards for case 6044, benefiting Dr. Rudolf and Grete Polatscheck [*sic*] in the names index database of the JDC, available online at http://archives.jdc.org/archives-search/?s=archivestopnav (accessed Mar. 24, 2013).

[247] Lourie de la Belleissue 2008, 69. See also von Vegesack 1987.

[248] National Archives at Philadelphia, Philadelphia (Pennsylvania), Declarations of Intention for Citizenship, 1842-1959, Records of District Courts of the United States, 1685-2009, U.S. District Court for the Southern District of New York, year 1939, roll 553, declaration 338167 (dated May 9, 1939), available online at the Ancestry.com database, State and Federal Naturalization Records, 1794-1943 (accessed

wife of Rudolf Weill (1863–1938?), one of Pilzer's main business partners.[249] The two stepsons, Bruno and John (or Hans) Weill, would later take leading positions in the newly merged company in Vienna and Paris. The first wife of Karl Fein's older brother Gustav was named Alice Hanna Weill. Gustav divorced her in 1932. Most likely, she was Rudolf Weill's daughter. The financial intervention could then be explained as a compassionate response to an appeal for help from (ex-)relatives. Since there was a Thonet store in Brno, not very far from the house on Rennergasse (Běhounská) where Karl Fein and his sister were raised, this could explain the USA support as well.[250] Judging from the small Aryanization file that exists for the bentwood furniture business, the National Socialists considered, though only for a short time, that Jewish influence in the company was significant enough to consider the Aryanization of the company suitable.[251] The third and last possibility – that Leopold Pilzer provided financing to other people seeking help to emigrate – can be excluded since his name only shows up in relation to the Polatschek couple in the JDC database.

GUSTAV FEIN

Almost one year to the day after Karl Fein was deported from Prague, on October 24, 1942, his mother and older brother Gustav moved from 4 Hodonínská (Gödinger Gasse) to yet another house in the center of Prague.[252] Anna Kummermann, the sixty-two-year-old woman in whose apartment they had been staying for almost a year and a half, had been deported in May 1942. Gustav and Helene Fein moved to the apartment of a widow named Anna Picková (1883–1943?), located at 11 Pštrossgasse (Ve Pštrosce).[253] Anna Picková's husband Gustav Pick (1875–1921) died in 1921 and her daughter Hana (1917–1943?) lived with her.[254] It was the fourth Prague address in three years for Helene and Gustav Fein [ill. 11].

Feb. 10, 2021). That said, Leopold Pilzer twice returned to Europe after October 1938, returning to New York in September 1939 to pass the war years there.

249 Laura Pilzer (née Spielmann) said in her declaration of intention (for naturalization as a US citizen) that she divorced Rudolf Weill in 1914. Rudolf Weill was the father of her three children: Bruno (1892–1962), John L. (Hans) (1896–1967) and Alice (1900–?). See National Archives at Philadelphia, Philadelphia (Pennsylvania), Declarations of Intention for Citizenship, 1842-1959, Records of District Courts of the United States, 1685-2009, U.S. District Court for the Southern District of New York, year 1939, roll 554, declaration n° 432738 (dated May 9, 1939), available online at the Ancestry.com database, State and Federal Naturalization Records, 1794-1943 (accessed Feb. 10, 2021).

250 See the record under the heading "Möbelhändler" (furniture dealers) in *Adreßbuch von groß-Brünn* 1934, 609: Thonet-Mundus, Vereinigte čsl. Bugholz-Möbel-Fabriken, A.-G., 9 Rennergasse. The corner building on the Jakobsplatz (Jakubské náměstí) where the company was located was built in 1891 by the Viennese architects Ferdinand Fellner & Hermann Helmer, and was long known as Thonet-Hof. Two of the five sons of bentwood furniture pioneer Michael Thonet (1796-1871) commissioned it. Starting in 1929, it was more famous as the modernist Savoy café, designed by the local architect Jindřich Kumpošt (1891–1968). In 2008 it became a café again, bearing the same name, but with a changed interior and façade. See http://www.bam.brno.cz/en/object/c095-savoy-cafe?filter=code and http://www.savoy-brno.cz/historie/ (both accessed Jan. 15, 2015); Zatloukal 2006, 119.

251 NA, Praha, Arizační spisy, fonds n° 375, kart. n° 241, sign. 2242B, firm Thonet & Mundus.

252 NA, Praha, fonds Policejní ředitelství Praha II, evidence obyvatelstva sheets for Gustav and Helene Fein.

253 The full house number was 1680/11. The building is located in the Prague Vinohrady district, then Prague XII, now Prague II. The street is currently named Anny Letenské, named after the actress Anna Letenská (née Svobodová, 1904–1942). Letenská hid a doctor who took care of the wounded Jan Kubiš, one of Heydrich's assassins. She was later executed for her involvement. Sometimes, the old street name is also spelled as Ve Pštrosse. See https://encyklopedie.praha2.cz/ulice/6-anny-letenske (accessed Aug. 13, 2020). Anna Picková was living at this address since May 1914. See her evidence obyvatelstva sheet in the NA, Praha, fonds Policejní ředitelství Praha II; *Pražský adresář* 1937–38, 1051. See also http://www.holocaust.cz/databaze-obeti/obet/113061-anna-pickova/ (accessed Apr. 30, 2016) for her Prague police file. Pštrossgasse (Ve Pštrosce) is not to be confused with the current dead-end Pštrossova. During the war, the latter was named Wankagasse (Vaňková). See *Strassenverzeichnis der Hauptstadt Prag* 1941, 144, 191. Looking at Anna Pick's close family tree on Geni.com and the evidence obyvatelstva sheets for both her and her hus-

As we have seen, their previous move to 4 Hodonínská (Gödinger Gasse) appeared to be freely chosen. This time, mother and son were explicitly ordered by the JKG in Prague to move to a so-called "Judenhaus", as it was known in Germany and also Vienna.[255] But it remains possible that they ended up at this address because of Karl Fein's possible and even likely acquaintance with Karel Jelínek in Łódź. That could mean that their last Prague address was also mainly their own choice. Before Karel Jelínek was deported from Prague to Łódź, he lived at this same Pštrossgasse (Ve Pštrosce) address, though in his half-sister Klara Bloch's apartment. During the war years, no fewer than thirty-four people had this address as their last temporary address before they were deported.[256]

Approximately four months after they arrived at their last Prague address, on March 6, 1943, Helene and Gustav Fein were deported from Prague to Terezín (Theresienstadt) on transport "Cv", Gustav being number 339 and Helene number 340. Anna Picková and her daughter were on the same "Cv" transport. They were the last four Jewish people to be deported from 11 Pštrossgasse (Ve Pštrosse), indicating that Gustav Fein and his mother had acquired a certain "privileged" status within the Prague Jewish community.[257] This privileged position can be explained by the fact that Gustav Fein was employed by the JKG in Prague as a clerk (*Sachbearbeiter*) for the control service (*Kontrolldienst*) of the trustee office (*Treuhandstelle*), which had no fewer than twenty departments.[258] As a member of the control service, Gustav Fein had control over the people who assessed and emptied the abandoned apartments of

band Gustav in the NA, Praha, it does not seem that Gustav Pick was related to Rudolf Pick, the sender of a key postcard in our story. See further in chapter 16.

[254] Anna Picková had another daughter named Susanna (Suse) (1915–1979), who married Rudolf Taussik (1907–1977). (It is not known if Rudolf Taussik was in any way related to Siegfried and Ida Tausik, the couple with whom the Feins stayed with when they arrived in Prague.) In 1939, Rudolf Taussik was in England for business purposes and managed to bring over his wife before disaster struck. The couple had a daughter named Sonja (who married with Nahum Tovy, and now lives in Israel) and also a son, Richard John Taussik (1947–2021), who married Judith E. Posen (1948–2024) in 1971, and married Genevieve Khander (née Talbot, 1946–2010) in 1979. Richard J. Taussik and his second wife had two children: Marc Rudolph Taussik (1981-) and daughter D. Taussik (1983-). I sent an email to Richard J. Taussik on August 13, 2020, followed later by a letter, in August and September 2020, to the two postal addresses found online for the same man. There was no reply. On August 13, 2020, I also sent a Facebook message to his son, Marc R. Taussik, and there was an unexpected reply in May 2024. Marc kindly shared with me more details on his family members but also wrote me that his father had been reluctant to talk about the war experience of his parents (who had been, in turn, as reluctant to do so). This reluctancy was likely linked to the fact that most other family members had perished in the Holocaust. As a starting point for the search on this family branch, I used https://www.geni.com/-people/Suse-Taussik/6000000033868791657?through=6000000013405389971 (accessed Aug. 13, 2020). I also sent a message to Leo Pick on August 13, 2020, on Geni.com asking for information about current relatives, but there was no reply. For the daughter Hana's Prague police file, see https://www.holocaust.cz/en/database-of-victims/victim/113284-hana-pickova/ (accessed Dec. 16, 2018).

[255] See the Prague JKG letter (dated Oct. 23, 1942), reporting the order for this move, sent to the Prague police, NA, Praha, fonds Policejní ředitelství Praha II, všeobecná spisovna, 1941-1951, kart. n° 2044, sign. F 277/3, Feinová Helena roz. Brecherová, 1860, f. 17.

[256] See the thirty-two names that come up in the database www.holocaust.cz when entering "Pštrosce 11" in the "address before" search bar. Since, as we have seen, the last address (before deportation) given in this database for Gustav Fein (18 Hodonínská) and Helena Fein (4 Hodonínská) is wrong, we can add two more people to this group of thirty-two.

[257] That most of the people who recorded this as their last Prague address had already been deported in 1941 and 1942 is further clear indication that Gustav and Helene Fein, as well as Anna and Hana Picková, were "privileged". Curiously, the evidence obyvatelstva sheet for Anna Picková shows "25/03/1943" as the date of her deportation transport, but there was no transport from Prague that day. On the list for transport "Cv", Anna and Hana Picková's numbers were 773 and 772, respectively. In addition, several sources give a different birth year for Anna Picková. The evidence obyvatelstva sheet has this as 1887. According to Kárný et al. 1995, no fewer than twenty-two people named Anna Picková were deported. The database www.holocaust.cz even records twenty-eight people with that name.

[258] See the "Mitarbeiter der Jüdischen Kultusgemeinde in Prag, Stand zum 21.9.1942" list in Krejčová, Svobodová & Hyndráková 1997, 428. This list was retrieved from NA, Praha, Ministerstva vnitra České republiky (Interior Ministry of the Czech Republic), sign. 425-365-11.

deported Jews and also controlled the doubtless many registers recording these and related operations.[259]

It is unclear when exactly Gustav Fein's employment with the JKG in Prague began. Since he was not able to prevent his brother Karl being deported, a matter in which the JKG's influence was quintessential, we may presume that it was some time after November 1941.[260] The trustee office for which Gustav Fein worked only began in mid-October 1941. In Terezín also, Gustav Fein, as a former collaborator (*Mitarbeiter*) of the JKG in Prague, probably held a somewhat privileged position.[261] There is a chance that he obtained his Terezín position – and possibly also the one in Prague – through Terezín's first leader, the so-called Jewish Elder (*Judenälteste*), Jakob Edelstein (1903–1944).[262] Edelstein attended the same Brno business school as Gustav Fein.[263] This shared past possibly served as an essential or additional leverage point for Gustav Fein in Terezín's protection economy (*Protektionswirtschaft*).[264] One may even wonder if Gustav Fein would have survived the war had the Germans not discovered that some people working for Jacob Edelstein manipulated the numbers of detainee lists in Terezín.[265] This discovery led to Edelstein's dismissal as Terezín's Jewish Elder in November 1943. He was replaced by the German-Jewish Paul Eppstein.[266] One month later, on December 12, 1943, Edelstein and his family, and many of his former

[259] See document n° 12, titled "Treuhandstelle", in Krejčová, Svobodová & Hyndráková 1997, 192–93. Gustav Fein was number 1017 and his mother Helene Fein number 1018 in the list of JKG collaborators. This does not indicate that his mother was also working for the JKG. Rather, it means that she was protected from deportation because her son had this job. Gustav Fein's name (and his handwritten paragraph) can also be found in a document (dated Feb. 27, 1942) where fourteen people in charge of (unspecified) JKG departments confirm (and sign to this effect) that they understood a regulation as communicated in *Rundschreiben* (circular) n° 182, issued by Franz Weidmann (1910–1944), the leader of the JKG. See Židovské muzeum v Praze, Praha, fonds Jewish Religious Community in Prague under the occupation, I. Board of Directors, Central Secretariat, Contact with Superior Authorities, Circulars and provisions of the Jewish Religious Community in Prague leadership governing contact with the *Zentralamt* (central office) and other offices, document JMP.ARCHIVE/312/I/3/a/015/001, available online at http://collections.jewishmuseum.cz/index.php/Detail/Object/Show/object_id/173393 (accessed Aug. 8, 2015).

[260] Potthast 2002, 143.

[261] ITS database, Ghetto Theresienstadt, 1.1.42.1., Listenmaterial, "Transport "Ds" am 18.12.1943 zum KL-Auschwitz", sequence n° 3792, document id n° 118500833. It is uncertain if the acronym on the unclear microfilm is "JKG" or "JKO". See also Mändl Roubicková, Springmann & Schellenbacher 2007, 222: "Vor Transporten geschützt waren lange Zeit Personen, die für das Funktionieren des Ghettos wichtig waren" (For a long time, people who were important for the functioning of the ghetto were protected from transports).

[262] Jacob Edelstein was chosen as one of the Protectorate deportees for the failed Nisko experiment. After being deported from Ostrava (Ostrau), he was forced by the Germans to supervise this project. This additionally shows that Edelstein was indeed a key figure in the history of the Holocaust. See Bondy 1989, 159–64; Kämper 2015, 123; Moser 2012, 92.

[263] Bondy 1989, 14. Gustav Fein attended Kaiser Franz Joseph Handelsakademie in Brno, located at 10 Husova třída (Husstrasse), finishing his studies in 1907. See the *Dreiundzwanzigster Jahresbericht der k. k. deutschen Kaiser Franz-Joseph Handelsakademie in Brünn* 1918, 90. Gustav Fein was a banker and financial specialist when living in Vienna. Until March 1938, he worked for the Treuhand, Vereinigung für Wirtschaftsprüfung und -Beratung in Vienna. See Hessisches Hauptstaatsarchiv, Wiesbaden, Bestand 519/3, Akten der Devisenstellen Frankfurt und Kassel, Devisenstelle Frankfurt, 1940-1942, JS 10429, Erich Messing (°25/12/1895), letter (dated Aug. 21, 1940) from Gustav Fein to Devisenstelle Saarbrücken, unpaginated; *Compass, Kommerzielles Jahrbuch* 1938, 169.

[264] Mändl Roubicková, Springmann & Schellenbacher 2007, 79, 222. Such solid reliance on a Brno link seems to have been common practice. Consider, for example, what Hanka Wertheimer's mother, also imprisoned in Terezín, said before being transported to Auschwitz-Birkenau in May 1944: "She [Hanka Wertheimer's mother] had always hoped that Jacob Edelstein, the chief Jewish elder, would help to keep her off the transports. She knew him personally, from Brno, through her membership in Blue-White, the Zionist organization. But he [Edelstein] had long since left the ghetto". See Brenner-Wonschick 2009, 207. See also Hájková 2020, 28.

[265] Mändl Roubicková, Springmann & Schellenbacher 2007, 160 n. 211; Bondy 1989, 319; Rothkirchen 2005, 244; Ondrichová 2000, 78; Hájková 2020, 34–35, 209.

[266] Mändl Roubicková, Springmann & Schellenbacher 2007, 122, 233 n. 179.

[267] Bondy 1989, 396–400. See also Mändl Roubicková 2007, 122, 163, 234 n. 214; Kárný 1997, 152. Of the 2,504 people on this transport, Edelstein's number was 2492.

collaborators, were deported to Auschwitz-Birkenau on transport "Dr".[267] Edelstein was put in Block 11 in Auschwitz I, the so-called "main camp" (*Stammlager*).

Three days after Edelstein's deportation, on December 18, 1943, Gustav Fein, then fifty-four, was deported to Auschwitz-Birkenau on transport "Ds".[268] It is unclear if Gustav Fein survived the two-day journey. All we know is that, of the 2,503 people transported, somewhere between twenty-three and one hundred people died on the way.[269] Contrary to the well-known Auschwitz-Birkenau practice, none of the newly arrived were gassed to death upon arrival. All the people on the Terezín transports of December 15 and 18, 1943, were resettled in the so called "Czech camp" (*Tschechenlager*) in Auschwitz-Birkenau, also known as the "family camp" (*Familienlager*) and "Construction segment BIIb" (*Bauabschnitt BIIb*). Also, unlike all the other Auschwitz inmates, the newly arrived did not have their hair shaved off and were allowed to keep their own clothes. In September 1943, two previous transports had taken around 5,000 Terezín inmates to the "family camp".[270] Possibly, these Czech prisoners were kept "in reserve" if there was a chance, as the Nazis suspected, that the Red Cross might visit Auschwitz.[271] Like the later ruse the Germans concocted in June 1944 for Red Cross inspectors in Terezín, a coverup operation was possibly being prepared in Auschwitz with the Terezín prisoners as "actors", held in readiness for a deceptive enactment.[272] As soon as the possibility of a Red Cross disappeared, the denizens of the "family camp" were doomed.

What makes the story of the "family camp" so extraordinary, and also unbearable, is that these people knew what was really happening in Auschwitz, and lived in constant fear that the same fate of being gassed to death awaited them. With the help of the camp's underground resistance, there was also an attempt to organize a revolt as soon as there was a sign that gassing was planned.[273] In March 1944, around 3,700 of the September 1943 arrivals were separated from the "family camp" and were gassed to death. The story of the young German-Jewish Fredy Hirsch (1916–1944), who had arrived with the September 1943 transports in Auschwitz-Birkenau, and was responsible for the education of the "family camp" children, is now well

[268] Gustav Fein's position was the second-highest on a reserve list of around 170 people (he had number "R3", "R2" was not listed). He was added to the transport of 2,503 people. The "only" two transports from Terezín to Auschwitz-Birkenau in December 1943, within a span of three days, were also known as the "December transports". More information on the totals of people transported from Terezín to Auschwitz-Birkenau can be found in Dokumentationsarchiv des österreichischen Widerstandes & Steinhauser 1987. For more information on features of the reserve list, see Hájková 2020, 204–5.

[269] Czech 1990, 551. There seems to be a problem with one of Czech's calculations. She seems to have miscounted the total number of women and girls given a prisoner number in Auschwitz-Birkenau: the number of new female prisoners should be 1,266, not the 1,336 she mentions ((73,700 – 72,435) + 1 = 1266). This would bring the number of people who did not survive the journey to exactly one hundred (2,503 – 1,137 – 1,266 = 100). Kárný infers, on the basis of Czech's faulty numbers, that thirty people died en route (Kárný 1997, 152). It is also possible that the forty-four male and thirty-three female prisoners (Czech 1990, 551), whom the original Auschwitz documents (Archiwum Państwowe Muzeum Auschwitz-Birkenau, APMO, Dpr.-Hd/6, 255) list under the same (arrival) date of December 20, 1943, were also part of transport "Ds". They may have been former collaborators of Jacob Edelstein, who were counted separately and held in Block 11. If this is correct, the transport's number of deaths upon arrival needs to be adjusted to twenty-three (100 - (44 + 33) = 23). Gustav Fein was on the same December 18, 1943 "Ds" transport as Ruth Elias (née Huppertová, 1922–2008), later famous for her autobiography about her Holocaust destiny. See Elias 1998. See also Kárný et al. 1995, 462, 1173.

[270] The approximately 7,500 European Jews on the three May 1944 mass transports to Terezín also ended up in the "family camp". See Hájková 2020, 209–10.

[271] Kárný 1997, 135–36. All these prisoners' names were accompanied by the initials "SB", which stood for "Sonderbehandlung" (special treatment).

[272] Kárný 1997, 224–37; Hájková 2020, 172. For an implied critique of this interpretation that the Germans were preparing for a possible Red Cross visit as in Terezín, see Kämper 2015, 42–43. How, he argues, would the Nazis explain the crematoria chimneys or would these not be in operation during the presumed visit of the Red Cross delegation? Cf. Ondrichová 2000, 68–69.

[273] Kárný 1997, 194 ff.

known. He "escaped" the unthinkable by poisoning or simply sedating himself in the hours before he was gassed to death.[274] The planned uprising never took place.[275] Yet there was an even more terrible amount of fear and horror. The approximately 5,000 people of the two December 1943 transports suddenly realized that the people who had preceded them in the "family camp", in September 1943, had all been gassed to death exactly six months after arriving. Would the same thing happen to them, six months after their arrival? The emotional stress experienced during the long months of waiting must have been unbearable.[276] Again, plans were made for an uprising.[277] When, in July 1944, the Germans decided to exterminate the last Terezín prisoners in the "Czech camp", they employed several misleading tactics to prevent people who knew they had nothing to lose from fomenting a revolt. Between 3,000 and 3,500 members of the "family camp" were sent to other work camps or facilities, but most, six to seven thousand people, were gassed to death anyway.

This also suggests that if Gustav Fein had survived the December 1943 train journey to Auschwitz-Birkenau, he might have survived in the concentration camp for an unknown period of time. It is possible that Gustav Fein was in the "Czech camp"; however, as one of Edelstein's inner circle, he may also have been, imprisoned in Block 11, like Edelstein himself. In her *Auschwitz Chronicle*, Danuta Czech records that, according to the surviving archival papers of the camp resistance movement, the group of collaborators shot with Edelstein numbered fifty people.[278] If, despite a mortality rate of 35 percent, Gustav Fein survived the six months that the December transports stayed in the "Czech camp", then he was possibly gassed to death on July 10 or 11, 1944.[279] If he was imprisoned, then he was possibly shot on June 20, 1944. That was the day that Edelstein, the group of his former collaborators, his wife Miriam and their twelve-year-old son (who had mostly lived in the "family camp") were shot to death.[280]

HERTA FEIN (NÉE MESSING)

Unlike her husband Gustav Fein, Herta Fein managed to escape abroad before disaster struck, in July 1939 [ill. 12]. She fled to London and joined her mother, Emma Messing. When Herta Fein and Gustav Fein married in Prague, in June 1939, her mother was already in England. While her daughter was in Czechoslovakia, Emma Messing tried to pull strings for the Fein family and her daughter from her place of safety. In 1951, Herta Fein, then a British citizen, moved to Switzerland to take care of her sick mother.[281] Her mother died in 1956.[282] At the end of the 1950s, Herta Fein taught drawing at a private boarding school for the wealthy, the American School in Switzerland (TASIS), at first briefly located in the Villa Verbanella Alta in Minusio-

[274] Dirk Kämper gives a more nuanced treatment of the poisoning story. It was likely that Hirsch took sleeping pills and was gassed as he slept. See Kämper 2015, 209 n. 286. Cf. Kárný 1997, 197. To this day, many Czechs speak about the young man without once mentioning his sexual orientation. See http://www.holocaust.cz/en/history/people/alfred-fredy-hirsch-2/ (accessed Jan. 18, 2017). Kämper's biography clearly shows that his sexuality was an important part of his life that clearly determined its itinerary (Kämper 2015). Anna Hájková has recently published a text on Hirsch's homosexuality and one of his last lovers (Hájková, May 2, 2019).

[275] On the many unrealistic plans for an uprising, see Kárný 1997, 194–212.

[276] Ibid., 183–84, 208–23.

[277] Ibid., 208–12.

[278] Czech 1990, 649, entry for June 20, 1944. If the number of seventy-seven women and men that we mentioned in n. 269 on p. 478 were indeed Edelstein's former collaborators, then this would mean that a third died since their arrival. This also corresponds with the already mentioned mortality rate of 35 percent in the "Czech camp".

[279] Kárný 1997, 176 n. 99, 222–23.

[280] Bondy 1989, 441–42; Kárný 1997, 217 n. 166; Rothkirchen 2005, 260–61; http://www.holocaustresearchproject.org/ghettos/edelstein.html (accessed Jan. 2, 2015).

[281] Schweizerisches Bundesarchiv, Bern, Personenkartei der Personenregistratur der Eidgenössische Fremdenpolizei (1912-1997) FEIN, HERTA, 1902.03.19,

Locarno. In the 1960s, she taught English at the Humanitas School in Minusio-Locarno.[283] Until her death, Herta Fein lived at 33 Via del Sole in a building called Casa Solatia in Muralto, bordering the Lago Maggiore. Recall that, in 1933, Magnus Hirschfeld, Li Shiu Tong and Karl Giese had briefly stayed in Casa Werner, a villa with a view of Lago Maggiore.

It is unlikely that Herta Fein remained in contact with Gustav Fein and the Fein family once she was in England. England was an enemy country and no mail exchange was allowed. On the other hand, there was limited postal service to Terezín and even the "family camp" in Auschwitz-Birkenau – where Gustav Fein possibly ended up – received some mail.[284] It is not known if Herta Fein had other documents in her personal archives other than the letters and papers she donated to the Forschungsinstitut Brenner Archiv in Innsbruck. It cannot be excluded that she lived in denial and tried to forget the matter once she arrived in England. Her correspondence with Birgit von Schowingen-Ficker suggests she suffered from survivor's guilt after the war.

In 1958, Herta Fein inquired about what happened to her husband Gustav Fein with the International Tracking Service (ITS) in Bad Arolsen. Gustav Fein's central name index card mentions her name and a number (CNI 312 329) referring to an inquiry tracing document (TD).[285] In June of 1958, she also made inquiries in Prague about the precise Holocaust fate of her husband.[286] Then she hired a lawyer in Germany to obtain financial compensation for the war crimes committed against her husband and brother. The judicial proceedings took years but ended in her receiving money from the German state.[287]

I attempted to reach out to people in Ascona/Locarno who might have known Herta Fein, but this did not lead to any results.[288] Eventually, I found Herta Fein's death date in a memorial booklet published by her friends after her death. From this publication, I learned that she died in July 1981.[289] Obtaining a death certificate for

GB; JIRASKO, HERTA, 1902.02.19 [*sic*], A (1954-1962), sign. E4301#1992/36#3570*, Ufficio degli stranieri del Cantoni Ticino, Rilascio di un permesso di domicilio (dated Mar. 2, 1962), Herta Fein. The document gives May 30, 1951 as the exact date of Herta Fein's arrival in Switzerland.

282 See the Principal Probate Registry, Probate Register London, 1958, Emma Maria Messing, death date Oct. 29, 1956, probate date Jan. 10, 1958, available online at the Ancestry.com database, England & Wales, National Probate Calendar (Index of Wills and Administrations), 1858-1995 (accessed Mar. 17, 2021).

283 The American School in Switzerland (TASIS), founded by Mary Crist Fleming (1910–2009), started in 1956. See https://switzerland.tasis.com/page.cfm?p=1587 (accessed Mar. 17, 2021). Herta Fein's name is indeed mentioned twice in the American School in Switzerland Class of 1958 yearbook. I thank Yvonne Procyk (TASIS, Montagnola) for her kind assistance in digging up this and other documents related to the school in March 2021.

284 Kárný 1997, 164; Kämper 2015, 56, 136–37.

285 The oldest date of the many handwritten dates on the back of the index card is April 15, 1958. This was presumably the date of Herta Fein's first inquiry with ITS.

286 See the *Bestätigung* (acknowledgment) (dated Jun. 11, 1958) from Rada židovských náboženských obcí v krajích českých to H. Fein in Forschungsinstitut Brenner-Archiv, Universität von Innsbruck, Innsbruck, Nachlass Herta Fein-Erich Messing, Kassette 152, n° E 10283 A.

287 Hessisches Hauptstaatsarchiv, Wiesbaden, Bestand 518, Regierungspräsidien als Entschädigungsbehörde, Regierungspräsidium Wiesbaden, 1958-1972, Akte n° 41623, Erich Messing (°25/12/1895)/ Herta Fein (°19/03/1902) and Landesarchiv Nordrhein-Westfalen, Abteilung Rheinland, Düsseldorf, Bestand BR 3002 (Bezirksregierungen/staatliche Aufsichtsbehörden, Regierung Düsseldorf), Entschädigungsakten, Verfahren nach §§150/160 Bundesentschädigungsgesetz (Sonderzuständigkeit BR Köln), Akte n° 769082, Herta Fein/Gustav Fein.

288 I have spelled out this search in the addenda, see n° 15.

289 Rüegg et al. 1981, [17]. The very last letter (dated Jul. 21, 1981) that Herta Fein sent to Birgit von Schowingen-Ficker was mailed five days before Herta Fein's death date. See Forschungsinstitut Brenner-Archiv, Universität von Innsbruck, Innsbruck, Nachlass Herta Fein-Erich Messing, Kassette 151. An email (dated Sep. 7, 2011) sent to Archivio della città di Locarno went unanswered. A new attempt was made on February 11, 2021. I obtained an answer (email dated Feb. 15, 2021) from Rodolfo Huber (Archivio della città di Locarno) saying that Herta Fein lived in Muralto, not Locarno. On the other hand, I found no mention of a city archive on the city of Muralto's website. See https://www.muralto.ch/ (accessed Jul. 10, 2021).

her or her mother proved impossible.[290] I think it would be interesting to determine if Herta Fein left a will. I think she was quite prosperous. Being childless, she likely anticipated that her estate would be administered according to her own wishes. Judging from her strong interest in the Locarno evangelical-reformed church community (*evangelisch-reformierte Kirchgemeinde*), it cannot be excluded that her will included a bequest to this church community. Maybe her will also left instructions about what to do with her personal archives and her artistic work. Her will would of course also help to locate any of her surviving relatives. But even if such a will exists, the archives of notary acts are closed for one hundred years in Switzerland.[291]

HELENE FEIN

In Terezín, Gustav and Karl Fein's mother, Helene Fein, was at one point housed with approximately forty-five other people of various ages from her arrival transport "Cv" in sick bay n° 1 (*Marodenzimmer n° 1*) of the Aussiger barracks (building J IV).[292] She died in Terezín on December 22, 1943, four days after her eldest son Gustav was deported from Terezín to Auschwitz-Birkenau. Without her son, the eighty-eight-

[290] Emma Messing died in Muralto (Switzerland) in 1956. Her daughter Herta Fein was the principal heir of her estate. See England & Wales, National Probate Calendar (Index of Wills and Administrations), 1858-1995 at Ancestry.com. My attempts to obtain death certificates for both women started in 2013, but led to a merry-go-round with several Ufficio Controllo Abitanti (residents' registration offices) in Locarno, leaving me empty-handed in the end. Possibly, my not knowing Italian might have been a major handicap. That I only had Herta Fein's presumed death year at that point may have been a further hindrance. A collaborator of the Brenner Archiv in Innsbruck informed me that they had also attempted to obtain this same information from the Swiss authorities with the same negative result. See email (dated Oct. 27, 2011) from Ursula Schneider (Forschungsinstitut Brenner-Archiv, Innsbruck) to the author. In 2020, I made another attempt. A first email sent on August 11, 2020 (with a reminder email on Sep. 2, 2020) to the Muralto residents' registration office, asking for a copy of Emma Messing's death certificate, was ignored. Later, the Sezione della popolazione, Servizio circondariale dello stato civile di Locarno refused to share a digital copy of the death certificate as I was not related to Herta Fein. Further communication with the Ufficio Circondariale di Stato civile di Locarno proved frustrating and rather unpleasant, all the more so because they refused to reply in a language other than Italian. Later, I learned that, by law, Swiss death certificates are not made available for one hundred years after a person's death. See email (dated Mar. 29, 2021) from Stefano Anelli (Archivio di Stato del Cantone Ticino, Bellinzona) to the author. Eventually, in March 2021, I managed to order online a transcribed and certified copy of the information on Emma Messing's death certificate, but this was not an exact copy of the original death certificate. The transcribed copy did not reveal, for example, who reported Emma Messing's death to the *Standesamt* (civil registry). From this, I learned that it was no use to try to obtain (and pay in advance for) a copy of Herta Fein's death certificate as well.

[291] Email (dated Mar. 29, 2021) from Stefano Anelli (Archivio di Stato del Cantone Ticino, Bellinzona) to the author. I did not attempt to ask for an exception from the Ticino region's Commissione per il notariato (notary commission), as suggested by Stefano Anelli. Herta Fein also had her brother Erich Messing's diary in her possession. This may be yet one more reason why the search for her estate should continue.

[292] Památník Terezín (Terezín Memorial), Terezín, undated list of forty-six persons from transport "Cv", who were put on sick leave in *Marodenzimmer n° 1* (sick bay n° 1) in the Aussiger barracks (building J IV), sign. n° A 11011-4. I thank Tomáš Fedorovič (Památník Terezín, Terezín) for sending me a digital copy of this list on February 10, 2022. "Marodenzimmer" is the military term for a sick bay meant for soldiers unfit for combat. It makes sense that this term was used to describe the room. Terezín had been a garrison town before it was transformed into a Jewish ghetto by the Germans. It is unclear if the people in this room, who clearly varied in age, were actually (very) sick or not. It might be tempting to think that *Marodenzimmer n° 1* was not the worst place to stay in Terezín, since one third (34 percent) of its residents survived the Holocaust. Helene Fein's son Gustav might indeed have had a hand in lodging his elderly mother there. To provide even more context, the survival rate of Helene and Gustav Fein's quite late March 1943 transport "Cv", which carried 1,021 deported people, was 30 percent.

[293] Brenner-Wonschick 2009, 93–94, 98.

[294] Terezín index card for Helena Feinová (07/16/55) at https://collections.arolsen-archives.org/search/ (accessed Feb. 11, 2021); NA, Praha, fond n° 1077, Okupační vězeňské spisy, Krematorium Ghetto Theresienstadt, Cremation Book, file no. 19/7, Ofen n° III + IV, dated Dec. 23, 1943, Sarg n° 20.867, Fein Helene. I thank Tomáš Fedorovič (Památník Terezín, Terezín) for sending me a digital copy of the latter document on February 10, 2022. According to Mr. Fedorovič, two of the four cremation ovens were usually operational in 1942–43, the other two serv-

year-old woman was most likely no longer able to care for herself. The elderly had the lowest chance of surviving in Terezín, especially if they were on their own.[293] A decent diet, enough to allow one's survival, largely depended on who you knew. With the deportation of her son, this essential support might have fallen away. Or maybe Helene Fein reflected that she may have survived all three of her children, that her life no longer had purpose now that her sole remaining and surviving child, Gustav, had been taken away from her. Undernourishment, presumably combined with great despair, may explain her death or even suicide. At 11:25 a.m., on the day after her death, Helene Fein was cremated in cremation oven III in the Terezín crematorium. Her body was the ninth cremated in that oven in a period of half an hour that morning. Cremation oven IV, in the same location, would be used to cremate eighteen corpses that day [ill. 13].[294] Her ashes, along with the ashes of approximately 30,000 others cremated in Terezín, were thrown into the Eger (Ohře) River in mid-November 1944.[295]

SALOMON SABOVIČ

What happened, in the end, to Salomon Sabovič, the young man who lived with Karl Fein in the Hodonínská (Gödinger Gasse) flat? On November 24, 1941, approximately one month after Karl Fein was deported from Prague, Sabovič was deported on a relatively small transport "Ak" (also "Ak I") of 342 people to Terezín. This transport was also known as the first of two "construction detail" (*Aufbaukommando*) transports.[296] This first "precursor transport" was sent to Terezín to do preparatory construction work for the planned ghetto. The later pre-eminent scholar of the Czechoslovak Holocaust, Miroslav Kárný (1919–2001), was deported on this "Ak" transport.

That the young Salomon Sabovič left or, more likely, was forced to leave the 4 Hodonínská apartment a month after Fein was deported may further indicate that he and Fein had some kind of relationship. One may suppose that Gustav Fein and his mother were suddenly stuck with a stranger in Mrs. Kummermann's apartment after Karl Fein was deported. Mother and son may have pushed some buttons to make the young man go. Or was he the one who wanted to leave the apartment? The real conundrum about the young man lies elsewhere: three months after his arrival in Terezín, on March 11, 1942, Salomon Sabovič was further transferred to Izbica (Poland) on mass transport "Aa", carrying around 1,000 people. This was only the third mass transport (of a total of sixty-five) deporting people *from* Terezín to annexed Polish territory. Sabovič's exact further fate after this, and his exact death date, is not known. We only know that there was a Jewish ghetto in Izbica and that the first mass deportations from this ghetto to the Bełżec extermination camp, where people were gassed to death upon arrival, started in mid-March 1942. Exactly when Sabovič arrived in Izbica, in other words.[297]

What needs explanation is why he was deported to Poland so soon after his arrival in Terezín. The mostly young people on the two "construction detail" transports formed the elite of the Terezín ghetto for the duration of its existence. They got the best jobs in the ghetto and this greatly helped them survive.[298] That they were shielded from deportation is revealed by the fact that 75 percent of those from the "construction detail" transports were deported to Auschwitz-Birkenau only very late,

ing as backups. See email (dated Mar. 7, 2022) Tomáš Fedorovič (Památník Terezín, Terezín) to the author.

[295] Brenner-Wonschick 2009, 317–20.

[296] 'Detail' is understood and used here as a military term for a small group who were assigned a special task.

[297] See https://en.wikipedia.org/wiki/Izbica and https://en.wikipedia.org/wiki/Belzec_extermination_camp (both accessed Apr. 5, 2021).

[298] Hájková 2020, 74, 179 and passim. A Terezín cabaret show titled "Why We Laugh" mocked the two main Terezín elites: "the Aufbaukommando aristocracy of the ghetto founders and then the French aristocracy – that is, the functionaries of the Prague Jewish Community who arrived much later than everyone else" (Hájková 2020, 177).

in the second half of 1944.[299] Eighty-six people in total (or 25 percent) of transport "Ak" survived the Holocaust. So what happened with Salomon Sabovič that he was apparently *not* thus privileged?

Ten people who arrived in Terezín with Sabovič on the first "Ak" transport were also transferred further with Sabovič on the same mass transport "Aa" to Izbica.[300] A small assumption was made that Salomon Sabovič might have been a gay young man, or a straight young man willing to make some extra money by granting men sexual favors. That this working-class young man lived with Karl Fein in Prague, an upper-class gay man, leads me to think that at least some of the eleven people deported from Terezín to Izbica in March 1942 may have been gay men or men with a flexible sexual life. Anna Hájková's characterization of the Czech social elite of the "construction detail" transportees as Terezín's "golden youth" (*jeunesse dorée*) clearly *also* hints at the sexual aura conferred on them.[301] Is it possible that men who were perceived as

[299] The initial "Ak" "construction detail" transport carried 342 people to Terezín. Forty-two people in total, or 12 percent of the November 1941 arrivals, were deported from Terezín before the bulk – almost 90 percent – of the first "construction detail" was sent to Auschwitz-Birkenau in 1944. Of the 342 people on the first transport, 258 were sent to Auschwitz-Birkenau. To determine these numbers, I used the "Ak" transport list in Kárný 1996, 152–55; however, I looked at its first section, which lists those who perished. A second, much shorter, section lists the survivors.

[300] These eleven people formed the second group of the first "Ak" transport deported from Terezín. In what follows, I detail the eleven men (including Salomon Sabovič) from the "construction detail", who arrived in Terezín on transport "Ak", and who were transferred to Izbica on transport "Aa" (which included, in total, 991 people). I arrange the names from youngest to oldest. I also add "PF" to a name if a part of or a complete Prague police file is added to the www.holocaust.cz database. Jiří Löwy (February 17, 1920), Vilém Tabak (August 20, 1919, PF), Evžen Preiss (December 12, 1918, PF), Julius Neuhauser (February 18, 1915, PF), Salomon Sabovič (April 11, 1914, PF), Arnošt Müller (December 10, 1912, PF), František Weisel (April 30, 1911, PF), Samuel Aškaneza (December 31, 1909, PF), Farkaš Braun (April 3, 1909, PF), Josef Schwarz (February 3, 1907, PF) and Ludvík Moravec (October 4, 1906). It needs to be added that another five people from the same "construction detail" had been deported earlier from Terezín to Riga: four people on January 9, 1942, on transport "O", and one person on January 15, 1942, on transport "P". The men deported were Alois Fried (July 19, 1907, PF), Abraham Klein (January 31, 1915, PF), Jindřich Josef Proskauer (July 30, 1904, PF), Valtr Stern (April 20, 1904, PF) on transport "O", and Arnošt Grünberger (January 26, 1912, PF) on transport "P". Very curiously, the day after the first four people were deported, one of the leaders and another man of the first "construction detail" transport, along with seven other people, were hanged in the ghetto. It is not known if there is any link between the January 9, 1942 deportations and the January 10, 1942 executions. The first executed man was number 2 on the first "construction detail" transport, the married mathematician Dr. Jaroslav (Jaroslaus) Stránský (November 21, 1902–January 9, 1942). (The fates of his first wife, Josefa Stránská [?–?] and his second, Blanka Martinovičová, are not known.) The other person executed from the same "construction detail" transport was Jindřich Jetel (April 6, 1920–January 9, 1942). See https://web.math.muni.cz/biografie/jaroslav_stransky.html, (accessed Apr. 6, 2021) and https://newsletter.pamatnik-terezin.cz/the-story-of-jindrich-jetel-one-of-the-executed-man-in-the-ghetto-terezin/?lang=en (accessed Dec. 26, 2022). Both died of "strangulation" on the same date, as their Terezín death certificates, both issued by Dr. Erich Munk, state. Their names also appear on a list of "Popravy v Terezíne" (executions in Terezín) with seven other people, who were all executed on January 10, 1942. See https://collections.jewishmuseum.cz/index.php/Detail/Object/Show/object_id/130487#fullscreenandhttp://www.ghetto-theresienstadt.de/pages/h/hinrichtungen.htm (both accessed Apr. 6, 2021). The executions are also confirmed in "Denní rozkaz Rady starších č. 23 ze dne 10.1.1942" (Daily Order of the Council of Elders n° 23 of 10.1.1942). See https://collections.jewishmuseum.cz/index.php/Detail/Object/Show/object_id/135545 (accessed Apr. 6, 2021). The man given number 1 on the first "construction detail" transport was Egon Popper (February 28, 1906–1944?). He was deported on transport "Ev" on October 28, 1944 from Terezín to Auschwitz-Birkenau.

[301] Hájková 2009.

[302] It is enough to take a closer look at some of the numbers and aspects of the "construction detail" transport to see where this could be headed. Firstly, all 342 people on the first "Ak" transport from Prague to Terezín, in November 1941, were men and almost 90 percent of them were unmarried. To reach this rough percentage, I used the www.holocaust.cz database, which only lists the names of those who perished in the Holocaust (the survivors are left out of this database). So I looked at the 256 people of the "construction detail" transport who died in the Holocaust and also had a quick look at the Prague police file of these names in the same database. I noticed that, of these 256, around thirty people, or 12 percent, were married. That means that around 88 percent were unmarried. (I also extrapolated this number to the eighty-six men who survived. I could

gay in the months after their arrival in Terezín clashed with the heteronormativity there and were expelled? To be sure, this hypothesis of a homophobic motive for deporting Salomon Sabovič (and possibly some or all of the ten people from the "Ak" transport who were deported on transport "Aa") definitely requires further research before anything can be stated with certainty.[302]

not determine if the members of this group were married or not because, as noted, survivors are not registered in the www.holocaust.cz database and their marriage records could not be checked online.) This status could be partly explained by the fact that many of them were still young men; however, the number of older and unmarried men that I found in the "Ak" transport list was nevertheless considerable. This also means that, statistically speaking, a considerable number of men on this transport may have been gay. We do need to point out that these young and mostly unmarried men had been selected for the "Ak" transport in large part *because* they were not married. The people from the JKG in Prague who assembled the list likely reasoned that such men were not breadwinners having to take care of a wife and children. Even if no more than the known and accepted minimum percentage of gay men in a regular male population (3 percent) is taken into consideration, one still arrives at ten gay men, at least, as part of the "Ak" transport. I therefore think it a real possibility that a considerable number of the men from that transport who ran into discredit in Terezín may have been gay and were possibly transferred because they were gay. The eleven men, including Sabovič, sent from Terezín to Izbica on transport "Aa", were all between twenty-one and thirty-six years old. The Prague police files in the NA, Praha, should be checked for any traces of homosexual behavior related to them before the war broke out. I checked the Prague police files of Arnošt Müller (1912–1942?) and Farkaš Braun (1909–1942?) and did not see any such traces there. See https://www.holocaust.cz/en/database-of-victims/victim/110190-arnost-m-ller/ and https://www.holocaust.cz/en/database-of-victims/victim/79103-farkas-braun/ (both accessed Jul 11, 2021). Arnošt Müller was deported to Izbica with his young wife Frederika (1916–1942). Assuming that the transport numbers handed out were not determined on a list in advance, I looked at consecutive numbers to determine who might have befriended whom. Ludvík Moravec (1906–1942?), Salomon Sabovič and Farkaš Braun (1909–1942?) may have been friends since they had transport numbers 10, 11, and 12, respectively, on transport "Aa" to Izbica. Ludvík Moravec's police file was missing from the Prague police fonds in the NA, Praha. (Arnošt Müller had number 13 and his wife Frederika was number 14 on the "Aa" transport.) I performed the same exercise for the numbers on transport "Ak" to Terezín. Sabovič had number 280. Zdeněk Svoboda (1911–1944?) had number 279 and Vladimír Saxl (1922–?) had number 281. Svoboda's police file can be found at https://www.holocaust.cz/en/database-of-digitised-documents/document/391841-svoboda-zdenek-nezpracovano/ (accessed Jul. 11, 2021). Zdeněk Svoboda took the last name of his mother's second husband, Josef Svoboda. His surname at birth was Fröhlich. His deceased father, Hugo Fröhlich (?–?), had been a lawyer. Vladimír Saxl was liberated from Terezín. See Kárný et al. 1995, 157. Saxl was imprisoned in a concentration camp in Uherský Brod from March 24, 1941 to July 9, 1941. See his index card in the Ghetto Theresienstadt Card File on the ITS database. No Prague police file was found for Vladimír Saxl in the NA, Praha. Vladimír Saxl was most likely not related to Zdeněk König (whose aunt, as we have seen, was Irma Saxl). See email (dated Jun. 22, 2021) from K. H. M. to the author.

1. Postcard photo of the Faculty of Law building of Masaryk University in Brno, provocatively chosen by the Gestapo as its main headquarters in December 1940. Postmarked July 30, 1942.

2. Marriage of Gustav Fein and Herta Messing in Prague. April 8, 1939.

3. Prague Main Railway Station (Hlavní nádraží). 1939.

4. The third building where Karl Fein lived in Prague, from June until October 1941 (his brother and mother living there longer still), 4 Gödinger Gasse (Hodonínská) (currently Pobřežní) in Prague-Karlín (Prag-Karolinenthal). The building belonged to Rudolf Schneider, a Jewish wine wholesaler. Today the street terminates in a dead end, but not in 1941 when it ran immediately by the Prague Denis Station (Praha Denisovo nádraží, Prag Denisbahnhof). The street extended through a tunnel under the railway tracks. After the war, the station was demolished. The railway tracks were removed to make room for a wide highway. January–February 1941.

5. Salomon Sabovič lived with the Fein family in their apartment at 4 Gödinger Gasse (Hodonínská) (currently Pobřežní). He may have been Karl Fein's friend or even his lover. February–March 1941.

6. Postcard showing the Prague exhibition grounds (Výstaviště, Messegelände) in Prague-Holešovice. This is where Jewish people were assembled a few days before their deportation, in a wooden building known as Radio Mart (Radiotrhu). Likely, this was one of the buildings in the top left in the picture. 1924.

7. Photo of the former school building (left) at 15 Franciszkańska (Franzstrasse) in Łódź (Litzmannstadt) where most of the approximately 1,000 deportees on the "Prague II" transport were lodged. August 2011.

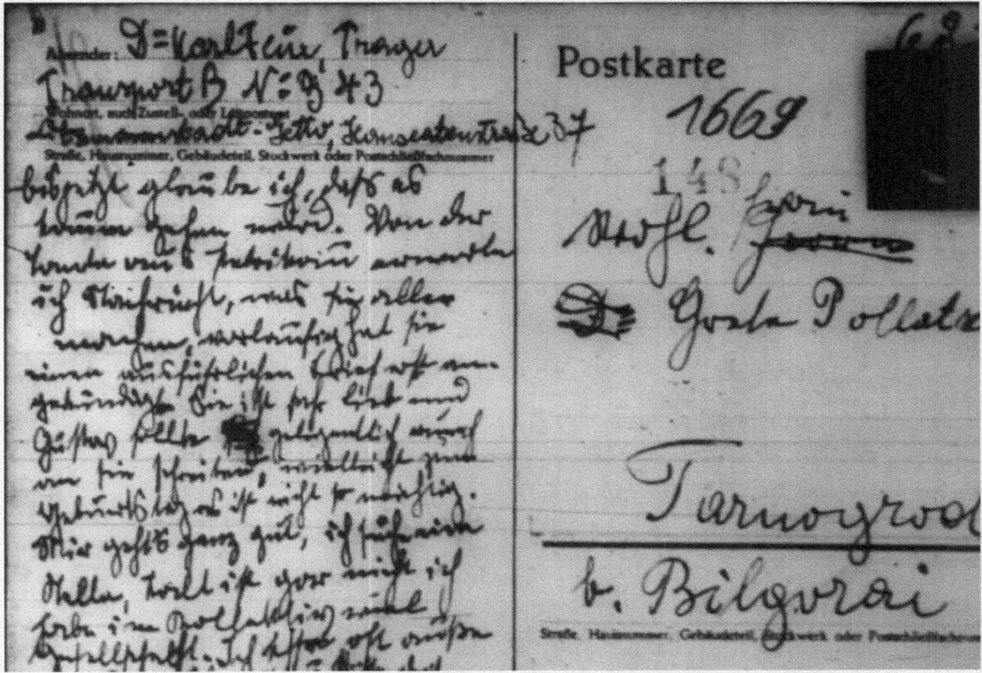

Postkarte

1669

Tarnogrod

b. Bilgorai

8. A postcard Karl Fein attempted to send from the Łódź (Litzmannstadt) ghetto to his sister Greta Polatschek, on December 8, 1941. She was then in the Tarnogród ghetto, also in Poland. Microfilm.

9. 4 plac Kościelny in Łódź, the corner building that housed, among other offices, the Łódź ghetto Post Office, the Registration Office, the Statistics Division and Archive. It was in this building that the Chronicle of the Łódź ghetto was written by the Statistics Division staff. June 2012.

10. Karel Jelínek, a presumably gay friend of Karl Fein in the Łódź ghetto. Ca. January 1939.

11. Gustav Fein, Karl Fein's brother. Undated photo.

12. Photobooth picture of Herta Fein. Ca. 1939.

13. The crematorium in Terezín. May 2017.

14. What Did Karl Fein Do (and Not Do) with the Hirschfeld and Institute Materials in Brno? One Lead, and a First Approach.

LACKING SOURCES

We now know more about the mostly fatal Holocaust destinies of Karl Fein and his immediate family. But what happened to the materials from the Berlin Institute that Magnus Hirschfeld bought back from the National Socialists, and which Giese kept in his Brno apartment? Besides these Institute materials, mainly books, we have seen that Giese's Brno apartment contained parts of the private archives and correspondence of Magnus Hirschfeld, and presumably also Giese's own private archive, which grew in the three years following Hirschfeld's death. We also now know that Giese's handwritten will bequeathed these materials, along with the income from Hirschfeld's books and medical licenses, to Karl Fein.

But what did Karl Fein do with these materials when he left for Prague in October 1939? The question becomes even more poignant in the light of Fein's deportation to the Łódź ghetto in October 1941. Was Fein still concerned about the Institute and Hirschfeld materials when he was in Prague in 1940 and 1941? After all, he was one of the far too many Jewish people in distress, harassed by the ever-increasing oppressive measures imposed by the Nazis. Wasn't his mind, very understandably, rather concerned with escaping the country, even with his simple survival as someone who had lost his income? Fein's procrastination in concluding the Giese inheritance procedure, when still in Brno, could be linked to his simply having other worries. But we also know that, in entrusting what he had of the Hirschfeld estate to Fein, Giese's will appealed to Fein's affection for Hirschfeld and his cause. That Fein (and possibly also his aunt) had been instrumental in buying back the materials from Nazi Germany in December 1933 may have been another reason for Giese determining that Fein was the right man to entrust with the materials. Giese knew or believed that the materials would be in good hands with Fein.

Presuming that Fein did whatever was necessary to safeguard the remaining Institute materials does not tell us, of course, what exactly he did in this regard. Karl Fein did not leave an estate. His possessions were officially taken from him by the Nazis when he was deported from Prague. Six months later, he lost his life in the Łódź ghetto. A similar fate befell the lives and belongings of his immediate family. As we have seen, only one of Fein's immediate relatives managed to escape the Holocaust, Herta Fein. There are, in other words, no surviving first-hand archival sources in the estates of Fein's immediate family that could tell us what happened. This is the principal reason why, in the following chapters, there will be a good deal of unavoidable conjecture in trying to determine what may have happened to the Institute materials after Fein went to Prague in October 1939. The following three chapters should thus be read as a very detailed research report from an ongoing investigation.

THE HIRSCHFELD GUESTBOOK RESURFACES IN BRNO

When I began my research, more than ten years ago, I was almost completely in the dark about what happened in Brno. There was no certainty even about the basic question: did Fein take the Institute materials when he went to Prague or did he leave them behind in Brno? In the introduction, we mentioned that the guestbook, which Hirschfeld kept in France in 1933–35, was found in Brno in a container for old papers in 1942. This was a strong first indication that Fein did not take the Hirschfeld and Institute materials to Prague. That was also the one and only factual clue I had at the start of my research project. So, let us first take a closer look at the details of this initial lead.

In 1995, Marita Keilson-Lauritz (1935–), one of Europe's foremost gay literature scholars, decided to undertake a thorough analysis of the guestbook that Hirschfeld kept from his return from his world tour until his death in May 1935. The Hirschfeld guestbook was housed in the Literaturarchiv in Marbach (Germany).[1] Hirschfeld invited the people he met to make all kinds of entries in the guestbook: simple signatures – dated and undated – or just their names, quotes, wishes, poems, thoughts, drawings, etc. Hirschfeld added comments himself, here and there, pasting photos of those he met, as well as newspapers clippings of his public activities. The approximately 260 contributors made their entries randomly in the guestbook; everyone did as he or she pleased.[2] The guestbook thus looks rather varied but also a little chaotic. Hirschfeld did not call it a guestbook but spoke instead of "memory books" (*Erinnerungsbücher*).[3] From the many entries, one gets a glimpse into the troubled minds of the often homesick (mainly) German emigrants whom Hirschfeld met in France. When publishing the Hirschfeld guestbook in 2019, the editors tried to introduce a little structure into this deliberately created anarchy, mainly attempting to identify the many contributors. They were able to identify around 160 of the approximately 260 people who contributed to the guestbook.[4]

But how did the guestbook end up in the Literaturarchiv in Marbach? In 1985, the archive bought the guestbook from a Czech-born lady, Milena Baumgarten (née Johanová, 1946–), who had married a German national in 1973 and moved from Czechoslovakia to West Germany.[5] According to Milena Baumgarten, she was given the guestbook by a Brno doctor and good family friend, Dr. Stanislav Kaděrka (1906–1986), with the clear purpose of selling it in the West. This interest in a financial reward will prove important for our further interpretation of the 1942 discovery of

[1] Keilson-Lauritz 2004a, 71. Marita Keilson-Lauritz has written two texts on her finding and initial dealings with the Hirschfeld guestbook. See Keilson-Lauritz 2004a; Keilson-Lauritz 2008. The guestbook was splendidly transcribed and edited in 2019. See Bergemann, Dose, Keilson-Lauritz & Dubout 2019.

[2] Bergemann, Dose, Keilson-Lauritz & Dubout 2019, 27. The guestbook has a little less than 160 unnumbered pages and measures 20 x 13 centimeters.

[3] Bergemann, Dose, Keilson-Lauritz & Dubout 2019, 27 n. 1.

[4] Bergemann 2019, 29. The addition of an index and other research instruments makes it much easier for researchers to draw more and different information from the guestbook. Since the 2019 publication of the guestbook, a small supplement containing additions and corrections has also been published. See Bergemann, Dose, & Keilson-Lauritz 2021.

[5] The marriage allowed Milena Baumgarten to legally leave Czechoslovakia and move to West Germany. In 1950, Mr. Baumgarten had himself moved with his mother from East Germany to West Germany. See Keilson-Lauritz 2004a, 73, 89 n. 7; Keilson-Lauritz 2008, 36. I wish to thank Marita Keilson-Lauritz for her help in contacting Milena Baumgarten in 2012, and for sharing her work notes of her earlier contact with Mrs. Baumgarten. Many thanks also to Milena Baumgarten for talking to me a few times on the telephone in the summer of 2012, and for the email exchange we had in October–November 2012, and from January 2015 to 2016. Some of the information that I present here is taken from this email exchange. We also spoke to each other "live" in Frankfurt in February 2016.

[6] Email (dated Mar. 7, 2016) from Milena Baumgarten to the author and Kamila Kratochvílová (née Orlová) questionnaire. Mrs. Baumgarten knew the Kaděrkas because her mother was a good family friend of theirs. Their friendship started only after the war. As Keilson-Lauritz notes (and heard from Mrs. Baumgarten?), the guestbook was given to

the guestbook.[6] Kaděrka and his wife were childless and apparently regarded Milena Baumgarten and her brother a little like their own children.[7] After their marriage, the Baumgarten couple visited the Kaděrkas every summer in Czechoslovakia. Kaděrka entrusted the guestbook to Milena Baumgarten in the beginning of the 1980s, thus a few years before she sold it to the Marbach archive.[8]

The next question, of course, is how the Hirschfeld guestbook ended up in the hands of Dr. Kaděrka. The answer to that question can be found in the salvaged guestbook itself. On one of its last pages, there is the following affidavit, handwritten in Czech [ill. 1]:[9]

> Památník tento zachráněn
> byl ze sběru starého papíru
> u fy. [firmy] J. Růžičková, Brno,
> Křenová 68 v r.[oce] 1942.
> i s některými jinými
> sexuol.[ogickými] knihami a
> mnou předán jako vědecká
> pomůcka Dr. Kaděrkovi
>
> [illegible signature 1]
>
> Pravdivost zápisů
> stvrzuje jako svědek
>
> [illegible signature 2][10]
>
> This memorial book was saved
> from the container for old papers
> at [or near] the f.[irm] J. Růžičková, Brno,
> 68 Křenová in the y.[ear] 1942
> together with some other
> sexol.[ogical] books and
> I gave it to use for research purposes
> to Dr. Kaděrka
>
> [illegible signature 1]
>
> The veracity of the description is confirmed by
>
> [illegible signature 2][10]

Milena Baumgarten to help finance her journey to the West (Keilson-Lauritz 2004, 73). This seems questionable to me. Milena Baumgarten told me that she had been entrusted with the guestbook in the beginning of the 1980s, but she was already married in 1973. Mrs. Baumgarten wrote me, in fact, that Kaděrka gave her the guestbook with the clear intention of making some money out of it "in the West". By the time Milena Baumgarten was ready to give Kaděrka the money paid by the Literaturarchiv in Marbach, he had died. See email (dated Nov. 5, 2012) from Milena Baumgarten to the author.

[7] Emails (dated Nov. 5, 2012 and Nov. 25, 2012) from Milena Baumgarten to the author.

[8] Email (dated Jan. 12, 2015) from Milena Baumgarten to the author.

[9] This handwritten text appears on (the unnumbered) p. 163 of the Hirschfeld guestbook. See Bergemann, Dose, Keilson-Lauritz & Dubout 2019, 163. Milena Baumgarten, a professional translator, has provided a German-language rendering of the Czech text: "Dieses Gedenkbuch wurde gerettet aus einer Sammlung Altpapier aus dem Müll/Makulatur von Altpapier aus der Wohnung/Firma (?) von Frau Ruzicková [*sic*], Brünn, Kröna 68, im Jahre 1942 und mit einigen anderen sexuol.[ogischen] Büchern von mir als wissenschaftliches Hilfsmittel Dr. Kadĕrka übergeben. / Die Echtheit der Unterschrift bestätigt als Zeuge". I thank Marita Keilson-Lauritz for sharing Milena Baumgarten's translation with me. See email (dated Apr. 6, 2012) to the author. Mrs. Baumgarten is uncertain about the Czech abbreviation for company, "fy." (= *firmy*), and leaves out some of the Czech diacritics in Růžičková.

[10] I was not able to determine the identity of the two signatories of the affidavit. Judging by the handwriting, the longer explanatory text was written and signed by the same person (the first illegible signature), and "Pravdivost popisu stvrzuje jako svědek", saying that the first part is true, was added by another person (the second illegible signature).

Let us now take an extensive look at the elements that can be discerned in this affidavit and also at some of its attendant problems and ambiguities.

STANISLAV KADĚRKA

According to the affidavit, the guestbook, as well as some sexology books, were given to Dr. Stanislav Kaděrka. Kaděrka, a Roman Catholic, was born in 1906 in the northern Brno suburb of Královo Pole (Königsfeld).[11] He graduated as a doctor from Masaryk University in Brno in 1933 and practiced medicine in Královo Pole all of his life.[12] Kaděrka married Zdeňka Grošovová (1907–1986) and had one sister, Pavla Kaděrka (1902–?). Stanislav Kaděrka moved several times within the same Královo Pole suburb.[13] After the war, around 1950, he and his wife rented the art nouveau-style house at 84 Palackého třída where they lived until 1986 [ill. 2].[14] Stanislav Kaděrka died after an operation on October 19, 1986, and Zdeňka died five days later of heart failure. His wife had been sick for a long time and depended on her husband.[15] Milena Baumgarten told me that the couple's urns were added to the family plot belonging to one of the Kaděrkas' former housekeepers (*Haushälterin*), Anna Kratochvílová (née Hrozková, 1894–1982) and her husband Tomáš Kratochvíl (1888–1968), a policeman [ill. 3].[16] When Anna Kratochvílová died in 1982, her daughter-in-law, Kamila Kratochvílová (née Orlová, 1933–) took over as the Kaděrkas' housekeeper. In 1952, Kamila married Jaroslav Kratochvíl (1925–?), one of the two sons of Tomáš Kratochvíl. I managed to trace her in 2016 but, unfortunately, she could provide barely any answers to most of the questions I asked her in a long questionnaire.[17]

Since the Kaděrka couple did not have any children, their belongings were confiscated by the Czechoslovak Communist state after their death in 1986. Milena Baumgarten also told me that she and her brother visited the Kaděrkas' art nouveau-

[11] AMB, Brno, fonds Z 1, resident registration cards Stanislav Kaděrka. Stanislav Kaděrka's parents were Jindřich Kaděrka (?–1925) and Marie Trávníčková (1881–?).

[12] For his graduation year, see the "Recover an alumnus" database of Masarykova Univerzita Brno, https://is.muni.cz/absolventi/oziveni?fakulta=1422;lang=en (accessed Aug. 19, 2020).

[13] Starting in April 1936, he resided at 17 Chorvatská (Kroatische Gasse), but during the war he lived at 35 Josef-Pekař-strasse (třída Josefa Pekaře, currently Palackého třída), having his medical practice at number 20 in the same street. See *Adressbuch der Landeshauptstadt* Brünn 1942, 2, 118. A different address, 5 Palackého, is recorded in *Adressbuch der Ärzte im Protektorat Böhmen und Mähren* 1942, 71.

[14] Milena Baumgarten informed me that the Kaděrkas did not own the house at 84 Palackého třída. She also told me that the Kaděrkas owned a Datscha (holiday cottage) in the village of Hluboké, about 45 kilometers west of Brno, where the Kaděrkas went during the weekends and holidays. See her email (dated Nov. 5, 2012) to the author.

[15] AMB, Brno, fonds Magistrátu města Brna, Majetkový odbor, I 1/17, sign. Rp-E-1974/87 and email (dated Mar. 13, 2017) from Jana Čermáková (AMB, Brno) to the author.

[16] On October 10, 1986, the two urns containing the ashes of the Kaděrka couple were added to a plot in the Královo Pole suburb cemetery on Myslínova in parcel 3B, grave 171. See email (dated Nov. 20, 2012) from Eva Holoubková (Správa hřbitovů města Brna, Brno) to Gabriela Patriková, and Milena Baumgarten's friendly confirmation of this information. The other people buried in the same plot are Josef Brach, Emanuel Morávek, Bedřich Rišlínek and Anděla Rišlínková. See https://gis.brno.cz/mapa/hrbitovy/ (accessed Feb. 12, 2021). Tomáš Kratochvíl was married in Brno on September 6, 1926. See https://www.mza.cz/actapublica/matrika/detail/8448?image=216000010-000253-003381-000000-017872-000000-VR-B02945-02340.jp2 (accessed Mar. 7, 2021). Tomáš Kratochvíl and Anna Hrozková had two sons, Tomáš (1923–?) and Jaroslav (1925–?), but the couple married only after the children were born. I was not able to determine anything about Milada Kratochvílová (1914–?), also mentioned on Tomáš Kratochvíl's citizenship certificate in the AMB, Brno, fonds B 1/39. She may have been Tomáš Kratochvíl's daughter from another marriage. During the war years, Tomáš Kratochvíl and his family lived at 18 Hinterm Gärtchen (Za zahrádkou) (number 16 before the war). See *Adreßbuch von Groß-Brünn* 1932, 293; and *Adreßbuch von Groß-Brünn* 1943, 148. After the war, only the sons are listed as living at this address. See *Adresář zemského hlavního města Brna* 1948, 206, 207.

[17] In October of 2015, the Brno cemetery administration (SHMB, Správa hřbitovů města Brna, Brno) sent me a small list of the people responsible for the grave plot containing the urns of Dr. Kaděrka and his wife. Until 1951: Marie Colová: 1951–74: Bedřich Rišlinek; 1974–88: Aglaia Hrušková; 1988 to the present: Kamila Kratochvílová. In February 2016, the

style house at 84 Palackého třída in the summer of 1987, in the company of a civil servant from the Brno branch of the National Committee (Národní výbor, Nationalausschuss). They were allowed to buy what interested them and did indeed make a few purchases. It was a sad experience for her to see the looted house, approximately nine months after the Kadĕrkas died: "On entering the flat, the scenario was very sad, as though there had been a search: all the cupboards and drawers were open and empty". When I inquired about Kadĕrka's library, she added: "I saw his books the last time I sadly entered the flat. They did not look like reference works and there were not very many of them".[18]

KADĚRKA'S LIBRARY

The affidavit's claim that, besides the Hirschfeld guestbook, some sexological books were also fished out of the old paper container in 1942 seems supported by an archival source. I managed to locate the list of the books found in (the remains of) Kadĕrka's library after his death.[19] This list contained at least two higly specialized sexology books, which could well have been part of the Berlin Institute's collection: Victor Areco's *The Love Life of Gypsies* (*Das Liebesleben der Zigeuner*) (1914), and Nikolaj Nikolaevič Evreinov's *Corporal Punishment in the Russian Justice System and Administration* (*Die Körperstrafen in der russischen Rechtspflege und Verwaltung*), published by the Verlag für Sexualwissenschaft Schneider & Co. in Vienna in 1931 [ill. 4].[20] There were a few other sexology titles in Kadĕrka's library but these were rather more common at the time and therefore possibly not from the Hirschfeld lot saved from the old paper container. For the sake of completeness, I here note three additional sexology or erotica titles in the list compiled by the bookseller in 1987: one unnumbered volume (of three) of Eduard Fuchs' *Geschichte der erotischen Kunst*, one unnumbered

SHMB kindly forwarded a letter from me to Kamila Kratochvílová. On November 23, 2016, I received a reply from the engineer Stanislav Herodes, who wrote that he was Kamila Kratochvílová's grandson and invited me to email the questions I had for her. Shortly afterwards, I emailed a long questionnaire, in Czech. In May 2017, after repeated requests, the sparsely completed questionnaire was returned. Kamila Kratochvílová stressed that she was not a paid housekeeper but rather a good family friend of the Kadĕrkas who helped the couple. Since the Kadĕrka urns were added to the grave in 1986, this meant that Aglaia Hrušková (née Morávková, 1901–1988?) was responsible for adding the urns to the plot. Her husband was Josef Hruška (1894–?). In January 2016, a letter was sent to the nine men having the name Hruška in Brno, which I obtained from the online Czech phonebook http://www.1188.cz/ (accessed Jan. 16, 2016). No one answered. It must be added that the April 22, 1987 cemetery bill for the placement of the Kadĕrka couple's two urns was sent to Kamila Kratochvílová. See AMB, Brno, fonds Magistrátu města Brna, Majetkový odbor, I 1/17, sign. Rp-E-1974/87, f. 14, [15].

[18] Email (dated Nov. 5, 2012) from Milena Baumgarten to the author: "Das Szenario nach dem Betreten der Wohnung war sehr traurig, wie nach einer Durchsuchung: alle Schränke und Schubladen offen und leer". And: "Seine Bücher habe ich bei dem letzten traurigen Betreten der Wohnung gesehen, die sahen nicht nach Fachbüchern aus und es waren auch nicht so viele".

[19] AMB, Brno, fonds Magistrátu města Brna, Majetkový odbor, I 1/17, sign. Rp-E-1974/87. I thank Jana Čermáková (AMB, Brno) for her help in retrieving this file. See her email (dated Mar. 13, 2017) to the author. The quest to find a source documenting the settling of the Kadĕrka estate was not easy. In 2012, Markéta Jančíková (AMB, Brno) let me know that the fonds B 1, Národní výbor města Brna (1945-1990) in the AMB, Brno, would remain closed for thirty years (1987–2017). See her email (dated Nov. 16, 2012) to the author. Of course, it was not clear at first exactly which administrative level of the National Committee monitored the settlement of Kadĕrka's estate. The omnipresent Czechoslovak Communist National Committee had no less than eight hierarchical administrative levels (provincial, municipal, municipal district, etc.). See http://de.wikipedia.org/wiki/Nationalausschuss (accessed Jan. 11, 2015).

[20] AMB, Brno, fonds Magistrátu města Brna, Majetkový odbor, I 1/17, sign. Rp-E-1974/87. Evreinov's *Die Körperstrafen in der russischen Rechtspflege und Verwaltung* was on the long list of banned books in Germany. See the list "Verbannte Bücher" on https://www.berlin.de/berlin-im-ueberblick/geschichte/berlin-im-nationalsozialismus/verbannte-buecher/#headline_1_2 (accessed Nov. 28, 2020). An interest in corporal punishment intersects the sexological topic of flogging and sadomasochism. That the latter was dear to Hirschfeld can be seen from the more than thirty pages on the topic in the image volume of his *Geschlechtskunde*. See Hirschfeld 1926–1930, 1930, vol. IV, Bilderteil, 162–98.

volume (of six) of Eduard Fuchs' [*Illustrierte*] *Sittengeschichte* [*vom Mittelalter bis zur Gegenwart*] and an unspecified copy of *Das Kamasutram*.[21] Of course, that only one volume is listed from each of two multi-volumed series possibly indicates that only these scattered, single volumes were retrieved from the presumed chaos of the old paper container. Owning an incomplete run of a series is not something one would expect from a book lover.[22]

After local people were able to pick and buy items from the Kaděrka house, the approximately 750 remaining books in Kaděrka's collection – the greater part in the Czech language – were sold as a lot to a Brno antiquarian bookstore with the generic name "Books" (*kniha*) in April 1987. An antiquarian bookstore is found at the same address today. Of course, I checked whether the online book catalogue of the current store included Victor Areco and Nikolaj Nikolaevič Evreinov's titles but, as was only to be expected thirty years later, it did not.[23] I also checked whether the few copies of these titles in Czech libraries bore the typical Institute stamps but they did not.[24]

[21] It must be noted that Hirschfeld wrote an introduction to an edition of this famous book in 1929. See Leiter & Thal 1929. However, the list of titles in Kaděrka's library only mentions the (German) "Kamasutram", and there were no fewer than four German editions of the Indian sex technique manual published before 1933. In January 2022, Marita Keilson-Lauritz and I took another look at this list and she told me that several other titles may have been Institute books. Two novels were especially intriguing. Demonstrating again her extraordinary expertise in early European gay literature, Keilson-Lauritz identified a novel by the Swiss writer John Knittel (1891–1970), *Via mala*, which originally appeared in 1934. Knittel was married but was also emotionally involved with the writer Robert Hichens, who in 1939 published a novel based on Li Shiu Tong. See Hichens 1939; and ch. 9, p. 265, n. 46. But the Knittel book was most likely a Czech translation since I found at least one title in the Kaděrka library list with "německy" (i.e., [book] in German language) next to the title, indicating that this book was an exception. A second Knittel title on the list is certainly a Czech translation of one of his novels, *Hakim*. One could argue that, since they were Czech translations, these titles could not have originated from the Institute collection, which would mean that the Knittel trail could be relegated. The German translation of another novel was intriguing. This was the just-mentioned title with the "německy" tag, Herman Melville's *Taipi*, which first came out in German translation in 1927. See Melville 1927. (Czech translations of *Typee* only appeared after the war.) Although Melville was never a weighty figure in the German gay canon (see Keilson-Lauritz 1997, 287), this title could still have been a good candidate to come from the Institute. But here again, the trail was too weak to mount a hypothesis, since another Melville title, *Bílá velryba* (*Moby-Dick; or, the Whale*), in the Kaděrka library list came out in Czech translation in 1933. So Kaděrka may have bought the German translation of Melville's *Typee* himself… because he may have liked the author and wanted to read that novel as well. On the whole, it proves impossible to determine with any degree of certainty – with the possible exception of the two books we have advanced, *Das Liebesleben der Zigeuner* and *Die Körperstrafen in der russischen Rechtspflege und Verwaltung* – whether another book from the library list came from the Institute collection. Lastly, one might add that the Kaděrka library list contained several French-language titles. This is not surprising. Kaděrka studied in France in 1925–28, where he obtained his *baccalauréat* in philosophy. The lycée Carnot in Dijon had a Czech section that was supported by the Czechoslovak state. See email (dated May 11, 2015) from Jocelyne Carminati (Archives départementales de la Côte-d'Or) to the author; Archives départementales de la Côte-d'Or, fonds du Lycée Carnot, série SM 17546, élèves: résultats scolaires, examens et concours, états annuels, 1912-1940, année 1928 and Ibidem, série SM 17524, élèves: livre journal des entrées et sorties des élèves, Oct. 1, 1922–Oct. 1, 1930, 1925–1926. See also ABS, Praha, SÚMV, fond n° 305, Ústředna Státní bezpečnosti, sign. 305-865-1, f. 269. For more information on Czech citizens' still persistent interest in the French language and their desire to learn it, see Raková 2011.

[22] Still other books on the Kaděrka library list stand out because the bookseller placed a high valuation on them, and also because most are in German: three (out of a total of fourteen) volumes of Adolfo Venturi's *Storia Dell'Arte Italiana* by Adolfo Venturi (Milano: Ulrico Hoepli, 1901–1940); Paul Kristeller's *Kupferstich und Holzschnitt in vier Jahrhunderten* (Berlin: Bruno Cassirer, 1905 or later); Richard Hamann's *Geschichte der Kunst von der altchristlichen Zeit bis zur Gegenwart* (Berlin: Knaur, 1932); and three volumes of Heinrich Meng and Karl August Fießler's *Das ärztliche Volksbuch* (publisher and year unknown). Almost all other books on Kaděrka's library list were of lesser value.

[23] The antiquarian bookstore located at 1 Rašínova now goes by the name of Antikvariát Sobotková, U jakubské věže v Brně. In 1987, the street was still called ulice 9. května. See https://www.antikvariat-sobotkova.cz (accessed Jan. 10, 2018). On September 6, 2019, I sent an email to the bookseller asking if their stock included either of the two titles mentioned so far, but no answer was received. A Czech email sent by Lucie Tuzová to the bookseller was also ignored. When I visited the store with Lucie Tuzová in January 2020, an employee told her at the entrance (the shop was closing an hour earlier than

We also need to consider that people who, like Mrs. Baumgarten, visited the Kaděrka house accompanied by a National Committee (Národní výbor) civil servant may have bought some Institute books. This would mean that Kaděrka's library possibly contained more titles from the Institute and that the book dealer only bought up what was left in April 1987.[25]

JINDŘIŠKA RUŽIČKOVÁ'S COMPANY

The J. Růžičková company mentioned in the affidavit traded in scrap (*Altmaterialen*), and would nowadays be called a recycling company. The business was owned by Jindřiška (Jindra) Ružičková (née Fikesová, 1905–1964).[26] As early as April 1937, Jindra obtained a trade permit from the Council of Free and Licensed Trades of Greater Brno (Gremium der freien und konzessionierten Handelsgewerbe Groß-Brünns, Gremium obchodních živností svobodných a koncessovaných velkěho Brna) [ill. 5].[27] But Růžičková's business seems to have really taken off in December 1939, very soon after her marriage to Jaroslav Růžička (1905–1978).[28] Their marriage and the starting of the company seem intimately linked. We will return to this subject later. During the war years, the couple lived at 51 Falkensteinergasse (Falkensteinerova), a posh address in Brno.[29] On the basis of my interview with the couple's living relatives (who preferred to remain anonymous) it seems that Jaroslav did most of the work in the company, Jindra being mainly the company owner in name.[30] In a 1942 phonebook, there is a rare record of the company: "Ružičká J. Purchase and collection point

usual) that they never answered emails about book titles. I then proceeded to check myself if the four titles mentioned in the previous note, and the three other sexology titles mentioned in the main text, appeared on the bookseller's website. They were not there. Finally, on October 15, 2021, I was able to go into the bookstore myself. I examined the few shelves of German-language books but did not find any of the titles. I thank Lucie Tuzová for her assistance and patience in this endeavor.

[24] I consulted the Union Catalogue of the Czech Republic (CASLIN) to determine where copies of the two books could be found in the Czech Republic. There are three copies of Evreinov's book. The copy in the Knihovna Historický ústav Akademie věd České republiky (Institute of History of the Czech Academy of Sciences) in Brno was inspected by Lucie Tuzová. It bore no German-language stamps from Hirschfeld's Berlin Institute. See email (dated Jul. 6, 2018) from Lucie Tuzová to the author. The other two copies were also checked but neither bore the typical stamps of the Berlin Institute. See email (dated Sep. 20, 2018) from Helena Houfková (Knihovna muzeum města Ústí nad Labem) and email (dated Sep. 24, 2018) from Tomáš Batěk (Knihovna Historický ústav Akademie věd České republiky, Praha) to the author. Oddly, the MZK Brno lists Evreinov's book in their online catalogue but the book is physically missing. According to an MZK collaborator, the book went missing in 1963 which means that that copy cannot be the one we are looking for. See email (dated May 9, 2017) from Michal Škop (MZK, Brno) to the author. The Knihovna Ústavu etnologie (Institute of Ethnology) of Charles University in Prague is the only Czech library with a copy of Areco's book, but it is also without the usual stamps of the Berlin Institute. See email (dated Feb. 4, 2020) from Kamila Remišová (Univerzita Karlova Praha, Knihovna Filozofické fakulty UK, Ústav etnologie, Praha) to the author.

[25] The April 1987 date of the sale of the remaining lot of books possibly explains (or contradicts) Milena Baumgarten's statement that she saw Kaděrka's library in the summer of 1987 and that it did not have many books then. Perhaps the bookseller did not buy all of the remaining books?

[26] Jindřiška Ružičková was originally from the Královo Pole district in Brno. Her father was Jan Fikes (1872–1924) and her mother was Marie Minaříková (1881–1939). She had a brother and a sister: Ladislav Fikes (1900–1948) and Marie Fikesová 1901–1939).

[27] Private archive Brno (soukromý archiv Brno). The archival fonds F 34 of the Gremium obchodních živností svobodných a koncessovaných velkěho Brna in the AMB, Brno, does not contain any other information on her company. See email (dated Oct. 29, 2019) from Petr Houzar (AMB, Brno) to the author.

[28] The couple was married on December 23, 1939. See http://actapublica.eu/matriky/brno/prohlizec/10776/?strana=1 (accessed Aug. 13, 2019).

[29] *Adressbuch der Landeshauptstadt Brünn* 1942, 258. Jaroslav Růžička is listed as a businessman ("Kfm-obch", *Kaufman, obchodník*). After the war, the couple moved to number 58 in the same street (baptized Titova in 1946, a name that would last for three years), directly opposite to the earlier, prewar location at number 51. In 1949, the street was renamed again, becoming Gorkého, the name that it still bears today.

[30] See the author's interview (dated Oct. 10, 2019, in Brno) with a living female relative (and her husband) of Jindřiška Ružičková and Jaroslav Ružička (Jindřiška Ružičková was the interviewee's great aunt). She had heard a lot of stories about Jindra from her father and, until the age of fourteen, had

of old [or "all"?] waste products".[31] The exact kind of scrap that Ružičková and her husband traded changed often.[32] The history of the company is a bit tumultuous but it survived the war and was nationalized in 1948.[33] In December 1939, the Czech authorities in Prague tried, presumably on the order of the Germans, to regulate the market in old iron and other recyclable materials by issuing new trade permits to existing companies. In 1940, Jindra Ružičková's firm obtained a new permit from the Ministry of Industry, Trade and Commerce (Ministerstvo průmyslu, obchodu a živností, Ministerium für Handel und Industrie) in Prague to trade in scrap as a medium-sized company (*Mittelhändlerin*), with permission to retrieve materials from Brno's inner city (*Innere Stadt*).[34]

Following the handwritten affidavit, it was initially unclear to me why the Hirschfeld guestbook and some sexological books ended up with this particular company. Since the items were found in 1942, my first hunch was that Ružičková's company was possibly a player in the Jewish expropriating process set up by the Germans. Was her company maybe involved in clearing out the furnishings of the houses and flats abandoned by Jewish deportees in 1941 and 1942? Or, even more specifically, did her company possibly deal with whatever was left over after the valuable items had been identified and removed by people working for the JKG in

known Jaroslav Ružička herself. When I asked her and her husband how they wanted me to refer to them, they told me they preferred to remain anonymous. In what follows, I will quote their family archive as "private archive Brno" (soukromý archiv Brno). I thank the couple for their generous hospitality, granting me access to their family archive, and for their friendly cooperation afterwards. I thank Lucie Tuzová for her help translating during the interview and for making the appointment for the interview with the couple.

[31] *Amtliches Fernsprechbuch für Mähren* 1941, 66: "Ružičká J. Einkauf und Sammelstelle alter [or "aller"?] Abfallstoffe". The Germans were clearly unwilling to adopt the Czech-language practice of adding a suffix to women's family names and did not add "ová" to them in this phonebook.

[32] There are three company registration cards for Ružičková's company in the AMB, Brno, fonds B 1/16. On each of these cards the description of the kind of scrap Ružičková traded changed a bit, but the main focus seems to have been on textiles of all qualities: from refuse to finer clothes. One card says that she traded in old iron, old machinery and expensive metals; another one simply mentions generic "waste products". She is listed as a machine trader ("maschhdlg - obch stroji") at the same 68 Kröna address in *Adressbuch der Landeshauptstadt Brünn* 1942, section Maschinen/Stroje, 70, 258.

[33] According to the three already mentioned registration cards, the company ceased operations (due to bankruptcy?) in January 1944. A stamp supplemented by handwriting on one of the three – rather confusing – registration cards says: "Erlöschen gemäß § 1 der Reg. Vdg. [Regierungs(?) Verordnung(?)] vom 28.4.1943, / N° 121 Slg. d. G. u. V. [Sammlung der Gewinn und Verlust]/ (Zl. [?] 12/46850/43 vom 10.1.1944" (Terminated pursuant to §1 of the Government [?] Ordinance [?] of 28.4.1943, / N° 121 Collection of Profit and Loss/ (Zl. [?] 12/46850/43 of 10.1.1944). Yet the company survived the war years. We find advertising for the company in June 1945. See *Slovo národa*, Jun. 20, 1945, 4. Another registration card states that in 1948 the company was nationalized and generically named "Sběrné suroviny" (scrap material, *Schrott*). Růžičková's business was not registered (*nicht protokolliert, Einzelunternehmen*) in the *Handelsregister* (trade register) of the Krajský soud civilní Brno (Brno regional civil court), which implied there was no file for her company in fonds C 11 in the MZA, Brno. See emails (dated Aug. 28, 2018 and Aug. 29, 2018) from Jana Fasorová (MZA, Brno) to the author. There is no specific file on Růžičková's company in fonds n° 903, Ministerstvo průmyslu, obchodu a živností (Ministerium für Industrie, Handel und Gewerbe, Ministry of Industry and Trade) in the NA in Prague. See email (dated Jul. 30, 2018) from Eva Drašarová (NA, Praha) to the author.

[34] That Jindřiška Ružičková's company obtained such a permit in 1940 was reported by Eduard Kaiser, the *Treuhänder* (trustee) of a Jewish scrap iron company named Josef Pollak. The latter obtained a permit from the same Prague Ministry of Commerce to trade as a *Großhandlung* (wholesale company) dealing in scrap iron (permit 449, dated Mar. 13, 1940). See NA, Praha, fonds n° 375, Arizačni spisy, company Josef Pollak, kart. n° 249, inv. n° 1706, message (dated Nov. 13, 1940) from Eduard Kaiser to Oberlandrat, not foliated. In another May 1940 message, the trustee Eduard Kaiser referred to a regulation decision of December 21, 1939, published on January 30, 1940 in *Sammlung der Gesetze und Verordnungen des Protektorats Böhmen und Mähren = Sbírka zákonů a nařízení Protektorátu Čechy a Morava*, year 1940, Jan. 30, 1940, n° 29, Vládní nařízení ze dne 21. prosince 1939 o hospodaření odpaky (Government order of 21 December 1939 on waste management), 12–13. After an evaluation process, following this decision, companies obtained a definite status and business permit as either a small, medium-sized or large company, dealing in scrap. In another archival file, I found the exact file number (44008-40-IV) and

Brno?[35] After all, Ružičková's company was located in a part of Brno always known to be a typical Jewish neighborhood.[36] We will see later on that this was not the case. Jaroslav and Jindra Ružička were never pro-German.[37]

THE NEBEHOSTENY HOUSE

Jindřiška Ružičková's scrap company was located behind the imposing and splendid Nebehosteny family "city palace" in Brno at 68 Křenová (Kröna) [ill. 6]. Josef Nebehosteny (1852–1921) was an architect and a building contractor who erected many important buildings in Brno, the best known being the main railway station (*hlavní nádraží*) that still stands to this day.[38] Nebehosteny also built the well-known Mahen Theatre, the Palace of Justice and the mourning ceremonial hall (*Trauerzeremonienhalle*) in the Jewish cemetery.[39] When the entrepreneur died, in January 1921, the *Brünner Zeitung* succinctly noted: "His name is intimately linked with the history of Brno's architectural development".[40]

Nebehosteny's son, the engineer Karl Nebehosteny (1888–?) took over his father's business and inherited his father's share of the Křenová house.[41] Karl Nebehosteny married his second wife Hildegarda Janotta (1907–1983), nearly twenty years his junior, in 1927. The intriguing fact for our story is that Karl Nebehosteny and his wife left Brno for Berlin in September 1938.[42] When they were in Germany, they rented out the apartments in their Kröna (Křenová) house. After the war, the couple did not return to Czechoslovakia, nor did Karl Nebehosteny ever reclaim his property. In 1946, the building was confiscated and nationalized.[43] In post-war Germany, Hildegard Fidel Nebehosteny was known as an illustrator of children's and other

date (Apr. 4, 1940) of the newly obtained permit for Ružičková's company. See MZA, Brno, fonds G 115, Obchodní a živnostenská komora Brno (Geschäfts- und Gewerbekammer in Brünn), II. series, kart. n° 194, inventory n° 50, company file Jindra Ružičková.

[35] In his memoir, Arnold Hindls wrote that the task of inventorying and emptying Jewish apartments and homes was carried out by people working for the JKG on orders of the Germans. See Hindls 1966, 139.

[36] Tomková 2010, 18. At least eleven Jewish citizens living on Kröna (Křenová) were deported. See the www.holocaust.cz database (entering the street name in the street search bar).

[37] Neither Jindra Růžičková nor her husband Jaroslav Růžička ever applied for Deutsche Volkszugehörigkeit (German ethnic) status during the war. See email (dated Nov. 1, 2012) from Markéta Jančíková (AMB, Brno) to the author.

[38] Zatloukal 2006, 145.

[39] For more information on the Palace of Justice and the ceremonial hall, see Zatloukal 2006, 182, 197.

[40] *Brünner Zeitung*, Jan. 13, 1921, 4: "Sein Name ist mit der Geschichte der baulichen Entwicklung Brünns innig verknüpft". Josef Nebehosteny was also active in the local association of building entrepreneurs and the Verein der Baumeister in Mähren und Schlesien (Association of Master Builders in Moravia and Silesia). See Zatloukal 2006, 229. Josef Nebehosteny was buried in Reichenberg (currently Liberec). His resident registration card in the AMB, Brno, fonds Z 1, gives the letter "k", which stands for "kein" (none), for his religion. His first wife (whom he divorced) was Karoline Bichler or Bieler (1865–?). His second wife, Emilie Oplustil (1865–?), survived him. For Josef Nebehosteny, see http://encyklopedie.brna.cz/home-mmb/?acc=profil_osobnosti&load=10500 (accessed Jan. 10, 2015).

[41] MZA, Brno, fonds C 11, Krajský soud civilní Brno, kart. n° 740, sign. Jd V. 243, company file Josef Nebehosteny. In 1930, Karl Nebehosteny bought the other half of the property from Wilhelm Schimpersky.

[42] AMB, Brno, fonds Z 1, resident registration card Karl Nebehosteny. In Berlin, they lived at 5 (and later 7) Halenseestrasse in Berlin-Halensee. In April 1959, the couple moved from Berlin to Stuttgart. See email (dated Nov. 26, 2015) from Axel Schröder (Landesarchiv Berlin) to the author. At my request, Schröder checked the Berlin Einwohnermeldekartei (EMK) 1875-1960, Bestand B Rep. 021. Karl Nebehosteny is listed in *Amtliches Fernsprechbuch für den Bezirk der Reichspostdirektion Berlin* 1939, 854. He and his wife are also listed in *Amtliches Fernsprechbuch für Berlin (West) 1959/60* 1960, 518.

[43] See Katastrální úřad pro Jihomoravský kraj, katastrální pracoviště Brno-město, cadastral municipality Obrowitz/Zábrdovice (Katastralgemeinde Obrowitz, Katastrální obec Zábrdovice), volume 1, entry number land register (*Zahl der Grundbuchseinlage, číslo vložky knihovní*) n° 282, Kröna/Křenová n° 68/194. After the war, the land plot became part of the cadastral municipality (*Katastralgemeinde/Katastrální obec*) of Trnitá and was assigned new cadastral numbers, Kröna/Křenová 68/235. I thank Terezie Tenorová (Katastrální pracoviště Brno-město, Brno) for assisting me in obtaining certified extracts of the land register in November 2015. The cadastral document also bears the stamp "konfiskováno" (confiscated) at the top.

books published from the mid-1950s to the mid-1970s.[44] It is not definitively known whether the couple had any children but it looks like they did not.[45]

THE COMPANY SITE BEHIND THE NEBEHOSTENY HOUSE

We can safely assume that Ružičková's company was indeed situated *behind* the Nebehosteny house. It is simply unimaginable that semi-industrial activity would have been conducted inside the Nebehosteny family's very posh street-facing "city palace". Jindřiška Ružičková or her husband must have rented the space behind the imposing Nebehosteny house from the Nebehostenys' property manager. Looking at the Nebehosteny city palace from Kröna (Křenova) street, the building has a gated passage on the right-hand side. To this day, this grand entrance and passage, with its elaborate and artistic stucco work, serves as the main entrance to the immense house, but it also gives access to the space behind. It is wide enough for a car or horse-drawn cart, and nowadays cars use it to reach the small closed off parking lot currently behind the house. However, as we will see later on – a matter that will prove important – this passage was possibly not the only way to reach Ružičková's company.

A post-war cadastral drawing gives a better idea of what the site of Ružičková's company looked like [ill. 7].[46] It marks the main building behind the Nebehosteny house, having an area of 672 square meters, with the letter "b".[47] This was built in 1928 and still stands today. The building had twenty-four individual garage spaces

This document also leaps from July 1930 to June 1946, indicating that the Nebehosteny couple continued to receive income from the rents in Berlin during the war. See also NA, Praha, fonds n° 981, fonds Národní obnovy Praha (National restoration fonds, Prague), confiscation of the house Křenová n° 194/68, Brno-Zábrdovice, sign. VZ 11073/III/1, žadost o konfiskováný majetek, nezpracovaný fond (unprocessed fonds). The latter says that the house was confiscated because Nebehosteny had registered as a German national before the war.

[44] At some point, Hildegard Nebehosteny added the first name "Fidel" to her own in the books that she published. Possibly, this addition could be viewed as a clear political statement regarding the contemporary military and political activities of Fidel Castro in Cuba. On April 6, 2016, I left a message on the website of a Stuttgart publisher that frequently published her, Boje Verlag, https://www.luebbe.de/boje (accessed Apr. 6, 2016). There was no response. The other two publishers that frequently published her were Franckl Verlag (Stuttgart), which merged with Kosmos, and Herold Verlag, which passed through many hands and was ultimately taken over by Beltz Verlag in 2004. See https://de.wikipedia.org/wiki/Levy_%26_M%C3%BCller (accessed Apr. 6, 2016).

[45] Finding the exact death dates of the couple proved challenging. The last address we have for Hildegard Nebehosteny – who likely survived her husband, born in 1888 – was 30 Supperstrasse (Stuttgart-Rohr). See *Adressbuch Stuttgart* 1984. To this day this is a *Seniorenheim* (home for the elderly), the Hans-Rehn-Stift. See http://www.leben-und-wohnen.de/einrichtungen/hans-rehn-stift.html (accessed Jan. 5, 2016). The current management claimed to have no further information on their former patient since it was "to[o] long ago". See email (dated Jan. 7, 2016) from Aylin Akgün (Verwaltung Hans-Rehn-Stift, Stuttgart) to the author. Hildegard Nebehosteny's previous address was 6a Orionweg, Stuttgart Vaihingen. The *Adressbuch Stuttgart* indicated that Mrs. Nebehosteny died around 1983–85. Relying on this extra information, Rita Eckmann (Bezirksamt Vaihingen) more exactly determined that the date of her death occurred in December 1983. Mrs. Nebehosteny was buried in the Pragfriedhof on January 2, 1984. See *Stuttgarter Nachrichten / Stuttgarter Zeitung* 302, Dec. 31, 1983, 27, Bestattungen section. No obituary was published. I thank Natascha Hauer (Württembergische Landesbibliothek Stuttgart) for her very constructive help. See her emails (dated Dec. 22, 2015 and Jan. 8, 2016) to the author. The grave has already been removed. See email (dated Jan. 26, 2016) from Mark Ramsaier (Ramsaier Bestattungen Stuttgart) to the author. Mrs. Nebehosteny's death certificate did not contain any information regarding other relatives. I was not able to find the exact death date of Karl Nebehosteny.

[46] NA, Praha, fonds Národní obnovy Praha (National restoration fonds, Prague), file confiscation of house 194/68 in Křenová, Brno-Zábrdovice, sign. VZ 11073/III/1.

[47] A comparison of the map in the fonds Národní obnovy Praha (National restoration fonds, Prague), in the NA, Praha, with current Google Maps satellite images reveals that, in the 1940s, the northern side of building "b" was closer to the rear of the Nebehosteny house. This means that part of building "b" was demolished at some point after 1948, likely to make space for the current private parking lot behind the Nebehosteny house. The south side of building "b" was extended, probably to compensate for the space lost space by the partial demolition of its northern side. One can see this old disposition, with the garage closer to the Nebehosteny building,

in it.[48] Since it does not appear on the cadastral drawing of 1948–50, the other, much larger, yellowish beige garage building, which now faces the site from Křenová, must have been built in the decades after the war. The other smaller buildings that figure on the cadastral drawing, and which must have been there before the war, are the buildings marked with the letters "d", "f" and "g".[49] These must have been the three buildings used by Ružičková's company, measuring ninety-two, sixty-two and eighty-five square meters in area, respectively. They were grouped together in the extreme rear of the site. A post-war file also states that most of these buildings were in very poor condition. Building "f" was a horse stable and building "g" was where the groom lived.[50] On the basis of current satellite images on Google maps, one must conclude that buildings "d", "e", "f" and "g" must have been torn down after the war, and this also means that none of the three buildings used by Ružičková's company are still there.

AMBIGUITY: IN OR NEAR

The Czech language of the affidavit in the Hirschfeld guestbook also contains an ambiguity. The affidavit says that the guestbook was found "in" or "near" Ružičková's company.[51] This ambiguity led me for some time to consider the possibility that the Institute items had maybe been found, against all odds, not on the premises of Jindra Ružičková's company but only *near* it. In addition, what if the writers of the affidavit had only *assumed* that the old paper container where they found the items belonged to the recycling company having the same street number as the Nebehosteny house? Maybe the materials found were rather linked somehow or other to the Nebehosteny house? This is why I also had a thorough look at Ernst Fischer (1904–1980 or 1988), the Nebehostenys' Jewish neighbor, who lived at 66 Křenová.[52] That there was (and still is) a passage between the two buildings on Kröna (Křenová), numbers 66 and 68,

on an aerial photo from the year 1948, see Letecké měřické snímky, LMS 1948-03416 (dated Sep. 27, 1948), https://ags.cuzk.cz/archiv/openmap.html?typ=lms&idrastru=WMSA08.1948.BRNO90.03416 (accessed Mar. 7, 2021). Building "c" would then seem to be another compensatory southward extension of the garage. A comparison of the structure of the building "b" roof in the 1948 aerial photo (chapter 16, p. 608, n. 3) with the current (not homogeneous) roof structure on Google Maps satellite view further confirms this postwar remodeling.

48 According to a newspaper article, which however speaks of only fourteen garage boxes, the garage was built in 1927–28. See "Městská rada brněnská" (Brno city council) (dated Sep. 13, 1927), *Lidové noviny*, Sep. 14, 1927, 4. In December 1928, there was an advertisement for garage rental at this address. See *Tagesbote*, Dec. 22, 1928, 14. In an interview I conducted with her on February 7, 2016, Helga Sikora, a former Nebehosteny house resident, spoke of a "grosse Garage mit viele Einzelboxen" (big garage with many boxes for one car). Her only other childhood memories of the things she saw behind the house were scaffolding materials.

49 In addition, the Národní obnovy fonds drawing in the NA, Praha, clearly states in a note that buildings "c" and "e" were not there before the war and must have been added afterwards: "přístavby postavené novým majitelem" (additions built by the new owner). The 1948 aerial photo also shows that building "h" was not yet in existence.

50 NA, Praha, fonds Národní obnovy Praha (National restoration fonds, Prague), file confiscation of house n° 194/68 on Křenová, Brno-Zábrdovice, sign. VZ 11073/III/1.

51 The Czech "u" (in "u fy. [firmy] J. Růžičková") can be translated as both "near" or "in", and "u firmy" is therefore ambiguous. In a February 15, 2015 conversation in Brno, the Brno academic Jana Nosková told me that this ambiguity could have been avoided in Czech, implying that it may have been an intentional feature of the affidavit. Instead of "u fy. [firmy] J. Růžičková", meaning "in or near the J. Růžičková company", other alternatives were possible: "ve firmě" ("in the firm") and either "blízko firmě" or "nedaleko firmě" ("near the firm").

52 The house at 66 Křenová was owned by Ernst Fischer, who was Jewish and listed in the Brno phonebook as "Beamter" (civil servant). See *Adreßbuch von Groß-Brünn* 1930, 193. Fischer fled to France during the war years. See NA, Praha, fonds n° 375, Arizačni spisy, liquidation file B. Friess (Spediteur), Brno, kart. n° 206, sign. 1274. There is some uncertainty about the exact year of Fischer's death. The Brno Jewish cemetery database gives his death date as July 6, 1988, while Fischer's headstone itself gives 1980 as the year of his death. In 1932, Ernst Fischer inherited the house from his deceased mother Regine Fischer (1869–1931). His father was Moritz Fischer (1855–1924). The Fischer family has a grave stone in the Brno Jewish cemetery in parcel 25c, row 2, grave 2. There is another name on

leading directly to the vast site behind these buildings, was another reason to look at Ernst Fischer's property.

Why the Ružička couple chose to rent company space there, or specifically from the Nebehosteny family, remains unexplained. We have already seen that Karl Fein knew the building industry promoter Arthur Eisler and presumably also his gay brother, the architect Otto Eisler. I found that Fein had another – family – connection to important people in the Brno building industry.[53] That the house at 68 Křenová (Kröna) was owned by Nebehosteny, a pivotal figure in that industry, certainly struck me in the first years of my research. That this was an immense house, from which the couple moved out in September 1938, was a first promising lead that the building was a good candidate for storing materials. The small circle of Brno building entrepreneurs, so I reasoned, must have known that its owners had left for Germany. The house would indeed have served as a good safe location for storing the Hirschfeld and Institute materials. Another factor was likely also of crucial importance here: Karl Nebehosteny was not Jewish.

I also conducted a search for the residents of 68 Křenová (Kröna) during the war years. This is how I found Helga Sikora (1927–), who spent her childhood in the house, in Germany. I interviewed her in 2016. Mrs. Sikora was not even aware that Jindra Ružičková's company had been located behind the house. She did tell me that the people who sewed the costumes for the Brno theater apparently lived in the house's *souterrain* (semi-basement). This seemed to me another possible reason why Karl Fein may have gone to this house. He might have heard about the seamstresses through his friend Willi Bondi, who of course had links to the Brno theatre through his father, Gustav Bondi.[54] All in all, during my first years of research, I was likely somewhat

the headstone: Margarete Fischer (1904–1992). This was Ernst Fischer's second wife, whom he married in 1948 or 1949. In 1993, the urns of Ernst and Margarete Fischer were added to the grave of his parents. Since Ernst Fischer was Jewish, he lost his property very soon after the arrival of the National Socialists. On May 28, 1942, the building was sold to a certain Erich Endlich. Fischer's moving company was also sold to Endlich. See NA, Praha, fonds n° 375, Arizačni spisy, liquidation file B. Friess (Spediteur), Brno, kart. n° 206, sign. 1274. After the war, Ernst Fischer reclaimed the building but the property was ultimately nationalized. See the cadastral document for the building in Katastrální úřad pro Jihomoravský kraj, Brno, katastrální pracoviště Brno-město, cadastral municipality, Gerichtsbezirk Stadt Brünn (Soudní okres město Brno), Katastralgemeinde Obrowitz (Katastrální obec Zábrdovice), volume 1, Zahl der Grundbuchseinlage (číslo vložky knihovní) n° 142, Kröna (Křenová) n° 145/66. In November 1940, Max Pokorný (1902–?), a trustee and lawyer, was appointed to find a non-Jewish owner for this property. Max Pokorný ended up in Germany after the war, where he worked as an *Angestellte* (office worker) for the German authorities and at one point lived in a Wohnheim für heimatlose Ausländer (residence for displaced foreigners) in Ludwigsburg-Grünbühl. Max Pokorný is an intriguing figure. He can be linked to the Jewish community in Brno and may have been, like Franz Nawratil, a gray figure. Either alone or with his father, Max Pokorný senior, he liquidated the law firm of Robert Herrmann and Felix Gallia. See *Věstník Moravské advokátní komory v Brně*, April 1939, 2. As we have seen, Robert Herrmann can also be linked to Karl Fein, having been an intern in Karl Fein's law office. Because Max Pokorný was so closely involved in the forced sale of a building adjacent to the premises where the Hirschfeld guestbook was found in 1942, I reasoned that I needed to look at this person as well.

[53] See n° 3 in the addenda.

[54] Helga Sikora (also spelled Sykora or Sýkora) (1927–) was the daughter of the engineer Raimund Sikora (1888–1956) and Therese Sikorová (1889–?). The couple married in 1917 and had one other child, Erich (1919–?). All four family members applied for Deutsche Volkszugehörigkeit (German ethnic) status, which was granted in April 1940. I discovered that Therese Sikora and her daughter Helga lived in Frankfurt am Main after the war. See *Brünner Heimatbote*, Jg. 16, 1964, no. 8, 223; and ibid., Jg. 16-18, Sep. 2, 1964-Folge, 512. Thanks to some internet luck, I then found out that in 2016 the eighty-seven-year-old Helga Sikora was living in a home for the elderly near Frankfurt am Main. See http://www.usinger-anzeiger.de/lokales/usingen/greifvoegel-einmal-ganz-hautnah-erleben_14409328.htm (accessed Jan. 26, 2016). Since this was a unique chance to speak to somebody who had lived in the house, I went to interview Helga Sikora on February 7, 2016. I thank Helga Sikora for her hospitality and her willingness to be interviewed. She, her brother Erich and her parents had lived on the second floor of the building at 68 Křenová. Her father had his company office in the same apartment. I had supposed that Sikora's company was also located behind the

"starstruck" by the impressive 1890s Nebehosteny family city palace, whose facade was painted a beautiful red a few years ago.[55] In the end, both the house and its prestigious owners were likely distracting and false leads. But when I first undertook my research, still groping in the dark, I had to look at every factor that may have played a role in our story. The Nebehosteny house and its owners were definitely such a factor.

Nebehosteny house; however, a company file made it clear that only Sikora's office and living quarters were at the Kröna (Křenová) address, his company workplace being in Brno-Černovice (Brünn-Czernowitz). See MZA, Brno, fonds C 11, Krajský soud civilní Brno, company file Raimund Sikora, kart. n° 169, sign. A XVII.131. Helga Sikora had vivid memories of her playmates as a child and teenager but knew nothing about Jindra Ružičková's company. Helga Sikora also remembered that two older Jewish women must have been living in hiding in the house (since she never saw them) and that they were arrested one day. Their discovery likely explains why all the residents of the house whom I was able to identify had to confirm their address with the Brno authorities on June 15, 1942. See AMB, Brno, fonds Z 1. In 1942, Otmar Lutz (1886–?) was the new *Hausverwalter* (property manager), likely appointed on the order of the Germans after the discovery that Jewish people had been living in hiding in the house. Lutz's resident registration card states that he took up residence at 68 Křenová on March 23, 1942, and that he arrived in Brno in September 1941 from the Sudeten German city of Bílina (German Bilin). The sparsely typed index card for Lutz's application for German ethnic status seems to suggest that this was automatically granted in December 1942 by the German authorities. See AMB, Brno, fonds A 1/53. Hildegarde Nebehosteny's father, the engineer and widower Franz Janotta (1874–?), had lived in the house since the 1930s. See *Adreßbuch von Groß-Brünn* 1934, 249. It is unclear if he lived in the house continuously or if he returned to the house in mid-June 1942, as his resident registration card seems to suggest. See AMB, Brno, fonds Z 1. If the latter, it could be linked to the discovery of the Jewish people. Mrs. Sikora also told me that the house was hit by a bomb, presumably in 1944. The damage caused is mentioned in NA, Praha, fonds Národní obnovy Praha (National restoration fonds, Prague), file confiscation of house 194/68 on Křenová, Brno-Zábrdovice, sign. VZ 11073/III/1. However, the bomb is not recorded in the "Bombardování Brna" database. See https://gis.brno.cz/ags/bomby/ (accessed Mar. 8, 2021). A further attempt to communicate with Helga Sikora was unsuccessful because, apparently, the senior home where she resided withheld her letter mail. A second letter did not reach her either. Lastly, I found a Jewish couple who lived in at 68 Křenová in 1941. See the citizenship certificate for Berthold Löw in AMB, Brno, fonds B 1/39. Berthold Löw (1876–1942?) was married to Ida Löw (née Marburg, 1880–1942?). Both were deported from Brno to Terezín on transport "U" on January 28, 1942 and further transferred on transport "Ar" to Zamošč on April 28, 1942. Their two children, Hansi Fischer (1909–?) and Wilhelm Löw (1903–?), seem to have survived the Holocaust since their birth dates do not appear in either the holocaust.cz database or in Kárný et al. 1995. Wilhelm Löw fought with the Czechoslovak armed forces active in France. See https://encyklopedie.brna.cz/home-mmb/?acc= profil_osobnosti&load=16277 (accessed Aug. 21, 2020). Hansi Löw married the already mentioned Ernst Fischer (1904–1980), who lived at 66 Křenová, on August 9, 1931. This may explain why the parents wanted to live close to their married daughter, next door in the Nebehosteny house. Hansi and Ernst Fischer both survived the war but divorced in 1948. See http://www.badatelna.eu/fond/1073/reprodukce/?zaznamId=173&reproId=150372 (accessed Aug. 21, 2020). I did not manage to find any living relatives of this family. On August 7, 2020, I sent letters to the Fischers living in Brno and to people with the last name Scholz in Czechia. Several people replied but none were related.

[55] The year 1895 is carved into a stone above the building's main entrance gate. In Zatloukal, the house is named the Rudolf Karger Tenement, which Zatloukal claims was built in 1890 (Zatloukal 2006, 117). Today, a passerby is impressed not only by the abundant ornamentation and the sheer scale of the building. The house must have been restored some time after 1989 and painted a showy red. In the 1940s, the house did not have this color, as was confirmed to me by Helga Sikora, who lived in the house in those years. Until its restoration, which must have taken place in the 1990s, the house was unpainted and rather grimy. Older versions of Google Street View reveal the rather derelict condition of the house before it was restored and painted, blending better into the general atmosphere of utter destitution common for a city emerging from Communism. If I have learned one thing from my visits to former Communist countries in the past decade, it is that Communist regimes seldom cared about the material upkeep of houses and apartment buildings. Many buildings were left untouched for more than forty years until the collapse of the Communist regimes in the early 1990s. Visiting these countries was therefore often like going through a time warp. One could still see how buildings looked just after the war. I remember, for example, that many buildings in former East Berlin still bore World War II bullet holes when the Berlin Wall came down in 1989. The dire state of buildings was also noticed by Horst Morawek when he returned to Brno: "alles so heruntergekommen" (everything is so run-down), see Morawek 2021, 68.

WHAT DIDN'T FEIN DO?

Let us return to the question that began this chapter: what did Karl Fein do with the Institute materials before he left for Prague? When I started on this research, I saw four possible hypothetical courses of action: he sold the lot; he entrusted the lot either to a person or an institution; or he stored the materials in a storage room in anticipation of better times. Let us now take a closer look at these four possibilities. This will already allow us to exclude some of their variations before we look, in the two following chapters, at two – or even three – more plausible options regarding what Fein eventually did. I believe that going through the less likely accounts of what Fein did with the Institute materials will put the choices he did eventually make into better perspective.

WAS THE INSTITUTE LOT SOLD?

I will start by considering the least likely option and entertain for a moment the idea that Karl Fein may have sold some materials coming from the Berlin Institute either in whole or in part. As we have already seen, Fein lost his position as a lawyer and with it his income in March–April 1939. So, starting in the summer of 1939, Fein's financial situation, as an economically persecuted Jewish citizen, may not have been very secure. It was likely not a coincidence that, after he settled the Giese inheritance, Fein immediately inquired with some French publishers if he was owed any money from Hirschfeld's French books. We have also seen that, in August 1940, the Feins started to panic when they realized that they were slowly using up their last savings. Finally, we determined that the bulk of the Institute materials Giese had in Brno were books. Because we also know that Fein's aunt owned one of the German-language bookstores in Brno, L. & A. Brecher, I checked the last two catalogues (numbers 34 and 35) it issued before it was Aryanized. Neither included any sexological books for sale.[56] Since Giese committed suicide in March 1938, and the bookstore's last catalogue was issued in November 1938, it was in this last catalogue (number 35) that

[56] The L. & A. Brecher catalogues seem to have been issued at irregular intervals, and their numbering included no mention of the publication year or any time marking. Thirty-five numbered catalogues were issued during the existence of the L. & A. Brecher bookstore. On the basis of the surviving copies, and the issues that I have seen, I was able to conclude that, generally speaking, at least for the period 1931–38, the catalogues were on average published annually. Catalogue number 31, for example, bears the temporary address of 8 Náměstí Svobody on its cover. It can be dated "end of 1933" since it is included in the list of catalogues received in the January 1934 issue of the periodical *Philobiblon* (p. 72). The Prague National Library, on the other hand, dates the oldest Brecher catalogue in its holdings (number 29) to 1929. Counting backwards, one could deduce that the series of thirty-five numbered catalogues started around the time that L. & A. Brecher moved to its new Náměstí Svobody address, in 1907. On the other hand, I found mention of free catalogues from the bookstore in a 1906 directory, when it was still located at 4 Johannesgasse: "Grosses Lager aus allen Wissenschaften. Kataloge gratis" (Large stock of all the sciences. Free catalogues). See *Internationales Adressbuch der Antiquar-Buchhändler* 1906, 47.

[57] I was able to determine the date of catalogue number 35 (November 1938) from an arrival stamp of the Czech National Library (22/XI/1938), and from an advertisement for the catalogue in *Philobiblon*, Heft 9, November, 1938, 456. Generally speaking, only catalogues from the last years of L. & A. Brecher can be located in the holdings of a few libraries around the world. The Grolier Club library in New York is a happy exception, having several older catalogues, going back to number 10 from 1896. See http://www.grolierclub.org/ (accessed Dec. 17, 2014). It is unclear if this indicates that there was a more international focus – or perhaps that more catalogues were sent to different libraries – only in the last years of the bookstore's existence. In the final catalogue, number 35, we find the injunction to "Buy in Czechoslovakia!" (unnumbered verso of front cover, underlining in original) that seems to confirm this greater international orientation. Most likely, it was simply a desperate effort to sell more in a time of political crisis. What one also learns from this last November 1938 catalogue is that Fritz Brecher, Elise Brecher's son, quickly adapted to the new political situation following the annexation of the Sudetenland to Germany on October 1, 1938. After describing the practical steps to order a book, the catalogue states: "Diese Vorschriften gelten desgleichen für die Ostmark und die Sudetengebiete." (These stipulations likewise apply to the Ostmark and Sudeten territories).

the books would have been on offer, had they been put up for sale.[57] Just to be safe, I also checked the previous catalogue (number 34), which could plausibly be dated "May 1938".[58]

The absence of the Institute books or materials from the last, November 1938 L. & A. Brecher catalogue does not prove, of course, that these books or materials were not sold. They could have been offered in other venues or bookstores. However, I had another idea associated with L. & A. Brecher. Was it not possible that Fein stored the many Institute books in his aunt's store? It would have made sense to keep the materials in the bookstore given that Fein moved several times following his mother and brother's return from Vienna, shortly after Giese's suicide. There may have been no space to store these materials in the apartments where they lived. If the books were indeed stored in his aunt's bookstore, what happened when, starting in mid-March 1939, Ludmilla Schaal and another employee forcibly took over L. & A. Brecher? Schaal changed the locks shortly after March 15, 1939, when Fritz Brecher left on a short trip to Prague. When he returned to Brno, on March 17, 1939, nobody in the Brecher family had access to their family-owned bookstore.[59] I did not find any catalogues under Ludmilla Schaal's name nor that of Ostland-Buchhandlung (Ostland bookstore), as Schaal renamed the store. Were the Institute books held hostage in the L. & A. Brecher bookstore, starting in March 1939? Luckily, there was a post-war file on the liquidation of the Aryanized Ostland Buchhandlung store.[60]

Determining exactly how long Ludmilla Schaal carried on with her Ostland Buchhandlung proved difficult. She possibly left Brno and the Protectorate as early as 1944. That the Alfa Passage was struck by a US bomb, in November 1944, may have been a deciding factor.[61] In the months before the liberation of Brno, Karel Liška (1912–?), a man who had previously worked in many other bookstores, tried in vain to acquire the store from the Brno authorities intending to make it a bookstore again. Remarkably, he began his attempt in August 1944. This could indicate that Schaal's store was already closed by then. Brno was liberated by the Soviet army on April 26, 1945. The store did not reopen in May 1945.[62] In July 1945, the remaining contents of the bookstore were transferred to the Brno Regional and University Library (Zemská a universitní knihovna v Brně) at 1 Kounicova, to this day (though now at another location) one of the main academic libraries in the country.[63] Using a horse-drawn

[58] The undated catalogue number 34 was added as a *Beilage* (supplement) to the May 1938 issue of *Philobiblon*, the book collector periodical (*Philobiblon*, Jg. X, Heft 5). Starting in 1928, this periodical was published by the press of the Jewish man Herbert Reichner (1899–1971) that bore his name. Reichner fled to the USA in September 1938. See Dickinson 1998, 172–73. From 1938, *Philobiblon* was issued by the *völkische* (fascist-oriented) Rudolf M. Rohrer Verlag in Brünn until the autumn of 1939, when it was taken over by Asmus Verlag in Leipzig, starting with Heft 7/8.

[59] MZA, Brno, fonds D 23, Souhrnná likvidační správa, kart. n° 490, sign. Lž 1545/2938-51, letter (dated Aug. 8, 1939) from Ludmilla Schaal to the Oberlandrat.

[60] MZA, Brno, fonds D 23, Souhrnná likvidační správa, kart. n° 490, sign. Lž 1545/2938-51. Most of the information about post-war events was taken from this file.

[61] See the Poštovská address in the "Bombardování Brna" database, https://gis.brno.cz/ags/bomby/ (accessed Oct. 2, 2020). The neighboring JEPA building (where L. & A. Brecher was earlier located, and which also provided one of the entrances to the Alfa Passage) was almost completely destroyed by the same November 1944 bombing. See the Náměstí Svobody address in the "Bombardování Brna" database, https://gis.brno.cz/ags/bomby/ (accessed Oct. 2, 2020).

[62] The store in the Alfa Passage was eventually bought by Adolf Machač (1880–?), who had a gun business and was looking for a new premises since his own shop had been bombed during the war. Adolf Machač was then living at 11 Tůmova (Tůmagasse) in Brno-Žabovřesky (Brünn-Sebrowitz).

[63] The library is currently called Moravská zemská knihovna (Mährische Landesbibliothek, MZK). Since 2001, it has been housed in a new building at 65a Kounicova. See http://www.mzk.cz/ (accessed Dec. 17, 2014). For more information on the library's previous location, see https://www.bam.brno.cz/objekt/c277-zemsky-dum-iii (accessed Aug. 22, 2020). The 1932 WLSR conference held its opening evening in the semi-basement of this building.

cart, five to six carts full of books were taken from the deserted store to the library. There are no traces of this massive book transfer in the archives of the current Moravian Regional Library (Moravská zemská knihovna) since the deposition lists were apparently discarded.[64] So this is where our hypothetical research question comes to a halt.

Schaal was denounced as an "enemy of the state" in 1945 by a woman living at 12 Janska. The whole case was finally settled and closed in 1951.[65] Selling the Hirschfeld materials was likely never an option for Karl Fein. His admiration and affection for Magnus Hirschfeld, alluded to by Giese in his handwritten will, certainly seems to indicate this. But his financial worries may have forced him to sell off some or several books anyway.

ENTRUSTED TO AN INSTITUTION?

Karl Fein most likely did not entrust the Institute materials to an institution. I requested the Masaryk University archive in Brno, for example, to check possible donations by Fein made around 1939. They found none.[66] I also asked a collaborator at the Moravian Regional Library (Moravská zemská knihovna, MZK) to check the few books by Hirschfeld in their collection for the typical "Institut für Sexualwissenschaft" and "Bibliothek des Instituts für Sexualwissenschaft" stamps or markings. There were none.[67] I also looked at the possibility that Fein entrusted the Hirschfeld lot to the medicine faculty of the Brno university. I did so mainly because I came across Růžena Kaderková's name in a 1934 Brno address book: she had worked there as a clerk at one time.[68] We now know that at least some of the Institute materials ended up with Dr. Stanislav Kaděrka from the Královo Pole suburb. Was there a possibility that Růžena Kaderková played the role of intermediary in getting the Giese materials to

[64] Email (dated Jan. 23, 2013) from Ludmila Ondráčková (MZK, Brno) to the author.

[65] I also investigated the following possibility. Starting in June 1939, Fein and his family stayed in Prague with the couple Ida and Vítězslav Tausik. This prompted me to look at the Taussig & Taussig Akademisches Antiquariat bookstore in Prague. For a moment, I speculated that maybe a deal was struck with the bookstore in exchange for Fein's lodging with his relatives. This Prague bookstore would indeed have been an excellent choice for the sale of the Institute's book lot. The ten-page-long inventory in the very meticulous Aryanization file for this bookstore makes it clear that "Medizin" was one of its best-stocked academic subjects. See NA, Praha, fonds n° 375, Arizačni spisy, kart. n° 533, sign. 626, firm Taussig. But I quickly perceived that the spelling of the family names simply was not the same. It was Ida and Vítězslav "Tausik", not "Taussig". That said, I noticed that the somewhat careless spelling of that family name in Czechoslovakia (and present-day Czechia) caused, and continues to cause, confusion. I discovered that at least two different spellings of the surname are used interchangeably, both being considered correct. The www.holocaust.cz database, for example, consistently misspells "Tausik" as "Taussik".

[66] Email (dated Mar. 23, 2011) from Jaroslava Plosová (Archiv Masarykovy university, Brno) to the author: "Die Archivalien des Archivs der Masaryk Universität enthalten wahrscheinlich kein Testament Karl Feins über die Bücher für die Bibliothek der Philosophischen Fakultät. Ich suchte die Materalien von der Bibliothek aus der Kriegszeit und Nachkriegszeit durch" (The archival records of Masaryk University probably contain no will by Karl Fein for books for the Faculty of Philosophy library. I searched library materials from the war and the post-war period).

[67] For pictures of the (in this case, missing) stamps in books from the Berlin Institute, see Dose & Herrn 2006, 43. See also chapter 6, ill. n° 1. I asked Ludmila Pohanková of the MZK, Brno, to check the few Hirschfeld publications I found in their online catalogue since bringing up these rare books from storage required a (very) long wait. She checked a few volumes of the *Jahrbuch für sexuelle Zwischenstufen mit besonderer Berücksichtigung der Homosexualität*, a copy of *Die Homosexualität des Mannes und des Weibes* (1914) and the five volumes of *Geschlechtskunde auf Grund dreißigjähriger Forschung und Erfahrung*. See email (dated Mar. 21, 2011) Ludmila Pohanková (MZK, Brno) to the author.

[68] See the record of Růžena Kaderková as a clerk of the medicine faculty ("úřed.[ník] lék.[ařské] fak.[ultní]", medicine faculty clerk) and her address in Královo Pole (11 Masarykova) in *Adreßbuch von Groß-Brünn* 1934, 259.

[69] The death date of Růžena Kaderková (1909–1933) was confirmed to me by Markéta Jančíková (AMB, Brno). See email (dated Nov. 14, 2012) to the author. It looks like Růžena Kaderková and Stanislav Kaděrka were not in fact related. Neither the name of Růžena Kaderková's father or grandfather (both

Dr. Kadĕrka? That Kadĕrka is not a very common Czech name strongly supported the possibility at first. Yet I quickly discovered that Růžena Kadĕrková died in 1933. That Růžena Kaderková and Stanislav Kadĕrka did not seem related was a further reason to dismiss this possibility.[69]

ENTRUSTED TO A PERSON?

Did Fein entrust the Institute materials to a person? Well aware that Jewish people were increasingly persecuted by the German invaders, it seemed likely to me, at least at first, that Karl Fein would entrust the Hirschfeld materials to someone who was not Jewish. This was my first intuition. Yet, at the time, Jewish people simply did not know what lay ahead and certainly not the horrific details of the Holocaust that we now know. According to Oskar Rosenfeld, who was deported on the fifth and last transport from Prague to Łódź, the mass deportations at the beginning of November 1941 came as a surprise. Almost no one thought that they were heading towards certain death: "There was not a single Jew who resigned himself once and for all to losing his life".[70] In Brno also, Jewish citizens did not grasp that deportation would take them to their deaths.[71] So it was quite possible that Fein left Brno convinced that he would return when the nightmare was over. That most Jewish people could not imagine that their persecution would in most cases end soon afterwards in death possibly explains why Fein most likely did not draw up a will. Since Karel Fein's last Prague address before his deportation was located in the Karlín neighborhood, a collaborator at the Prague City Archives (Archiv hlavního mĕsta Prahy) checked on my behalf, in 2010, for any record of Fein's name in the registers of the Prague-East District Civil Court (Pražské okresní soudy civilní – Prahu-východ) for 1941–48, but there was none.[72] A not insignificant question was thus answered very early in my research.[73]

František Kadĕrka) matched the name of Dr. Stanislav Kadĕrka's father (Jindrich Kadĕrka). However, this lead, which proved to be false, nevertheless opened my eyes to something at that point in my research (2012). Following through on this Růžena Kaderková lead, however briefly, meant that I had to question the validity of the affidavit, added at the end of the Hirschfeld guestbook, that claimed that the guestbook was found "in or near" Růžičková's company. Looking at this false trail for a short time did make me realize that the veracity of the affidavit's claims simply could not be taken for granted.

[70] Rosenfeld 1994, 38; ibid., 41: "Es gab keinen einzigen Juden, der sich ein für allemal mit dem Verlust seines Lebens abfand".

[71] Interview with Marie Hlaváčková (1926–) in Nosková & Čermáková 2013, 395–96.

[72] Emails (dated Nov. 29, 2010 and Dec. 13, 2010) from Miroslav Veselka (Archiv hlavního mĕsta Prahy, Praha) to the author. There were then five Prague district courts in total: vnitřní Prahu, Prahu-západ, Prahu-sever, Prahu-východ and Prahu-jih. According to Mr. Veselka, the official declaration of death and the related initiation of the inheritance procedure may not have taken place since Karl Fein had no children. As there was still a slight chance that the procedure might have been undertaken after 1948, Mr. Veselka referred me to the Centrální spisovna mĕstského soudu v Praze (Central Registry Office of the Prague Municipal Court). Communications in this case proved quite difficult and frustrating, and the resulting answer was likely negative. See email (dated Mar. 3, 2011) from a collaborator at the Centrální spisovna mĕstského soudu v Praze to Gabriela Patriková, one of the students then assisting me with Czech translations. The reason this organization's answer was somewhat frustrating is that it mentioned looking (under heading "M"?) for records of Gustav Fein, Greta Fein and Helena Fein in 1949–50 ... but possibly not Karl Fein, since his name was not present in the reply sent by the Centrální spisovna mĕstského soudu v Praze. Their message ended with: "The Central Registry Office in Prague does not have any other data that could be used to answer your request". Gabriela Patriková also informed me that she had read on the registry office's website that access to documents related to inheritances before 1960 was severely hindered as a consequence of the 2002 Prague flood. See http://portal.justice.cz/Justice2/Soud/soud.aspx?j=36&o=26&k=422&d=11262 (accessed July 28, 2011). Eventually, Gabriela Patriková telephoned the central registry office, only to learn that the person who had initially helped us no longer worked there, and the person on the phone had no knowledge of the matter. Later, Gabriela Patriková sent a fax to the office, but the faxed inquiry went unanswered.

[73] After the war, François (Franz) Herzfelder, the executor of Hirschfeld's estate, also wondered if Fein had drawn up a will. See the letter (dated Jan. 25, 1965) from François Herzfelder to the Landgericht Berlin: "Herr Dr. Fein soll nach Mitteilungen,

Possibly, then, Fein imagined that the Institute and Hirschfeld materials were safe in Brno. The idea was not outrageous. We know that Karl Fein returned to Brno at least a few more times after moving to Prague, in the autumn of 1939.[74] Since Jewish citizens living in Prague were forbidden travel, starting in November 1940, we may assume that Fein returned to Brno a few more times in 1940[75] – unless, of course, Fein managed to obtain the special travel permit exempting him from this prohibition, but this seems unlikely.[76] Here, we need to mention the Feins' financial problems starting in August 1940. Was there, after that date, sufficient money for a roundtrip train ticket to Brno?

It is not known whether Fein's trips to Brno involved any further dealings with the Hirschfeld and Institute materials. Maybe Fein only came to visit the Brecher family, and other Jewish and non-Jewish friends and acquaintances who had decided to stay in Brno. It is also not known if Fein sent any letters or postcards to Brno (or telephoned) in the days before he was deported from Prague. Although restrictive regulations applied to Jewish people in Prague, allowing them to use certain post offices only during specific and limited hours, writing letters was possible.[77] Did Fein make arrangements for or give instructions on what should be done with his belongings in Brno? We do not know. It should also be remembered that the censor was always active and possibly excluded any last instructions.

die ich nach dem Kriege erhielt, in der Deportation umgekommen sein. Seine Erben konnten seinerzeit nicht ermittelt werden" (According to information I received after the war, Dr. Fein died in the deportation. His heirs could not then be found). The letter is quoted in Herzer 2001, 243 n. 21.

[74] In the March 1941 transcript of a Kripo (Kriminalpolizei, Criminal police) hearing, a woman named Anna Baum (1900–?), who had already worked for several years for Willi Bondi's sister, Ully (Julia) Fleischer, stated the following: "Ich bin beinahe 7 Jahre bei Fleischer in Stellung. Frau Fleischer ist eine Schwester von [Willi] Bondi. Bondi jun.[ior, Willi Bondi] kam täglich zu uns zum Nachtessen, d.h. seit zwei Jahren, seit der Mann der Fleischer [Bruno Fleischer] gestorben ist. Vor etwa 3 Jahren kam ein gewisser Bergmann, der durch Bondi bekannt war, zu uns. Er kam auch täglich zum Nachtessen. Er führte auch den Rechtsanwalt Fein aus Prag bei uns ein. Fein war früher in Brünn und ist jetzt in Prag. Seit er in Prag ist, kommt er selten, vielleicht einmal in halben Jahr zu uns" (I have been in Fleischer's service for almost seven years. Mrs. Fleischer is a sister of [Willi] Bondi. Bondi jun.[ior, Willi Bondi] came every day for dinner, that is, for the two years since Fleischer's husband [Bruno Fleischer] died. About 3 years ago, a certain Bergmann, whom Bondi knew, came to us. He also came every day for dinner. He also introduced the lawyer Fein from Prague to us. Fein used to be in Brno and is now in Prague. Since he has been in Prague, he rarely comes to us, maybe once in six months). See MZA, Brno, fonds C 43, Německý zemský soud Brno (Deutsches Landgericht), Staatsanwaltschaft bei dem Landgericht Brünn, file Wilhelm Sponer & Helmuth Holdau, kart. n° 184, sign. 4 K Ls 24/41, f. 10b.

[75] Since the new ruling took effect in November 1940, and the transcript of Anna Baum's hearing is dated March 1941, we may presume that Fein did not return to Brno in 1941. See the announcement (dated Oct. 25, 1940) "Reisen im Inland" (Domestic travel) by the Prague police in Krejčová, Svobodová & Hyndráková 1997, 139–48, document n° 8. The document was reproduced from NA, Praha, fonds Archiv Ministerstva vnitra České republiky, AMV ČR (Prague Ministry of the Interior), Židovské organizace, sign. 425-220-4. The ruling was ultimately imposed on the whole of the Protectorate in September 1941, a few months before the first deportations started. See Krejčová, Svobodová & Hyndráková 1997, 139. See also Friedmann, Jul. 31, 1942/1997, 249, esp. 262; Kárný et al. 1996, 36: "A temporary absence from the district of Prague or other place of abode without summons or consent of the relevant authority was also forbidden". The ruling was thereafter binding for the whole of the German Reich and was imposed together with the requirement to wear the Jewish star. Nevertheless, the Reich Protector in Bohemia and Moravia issued his own version of the regulation. See Löw 2012, 537–41, document n° 222, "Der Reichsinnenminister beschränkt am 15. September 1941 die Freizügigkeit für Juden und knüpft die Nutzung von Verkehrsmitteln an Bedingungen".

[76] A travel permit issued by the JKG's Abteilung für Inlandreisen (Domestic travel department) in Prague and further approval from the Zentralstelle für jüdische Auswanderung (Central Office for Jewish Emigration) were required. Jewish citizens were in fact granted such travel permits. Between January 1941 and May 1942, on average 1,660 were issued every month; however, it is clear that more than half were meant for people who had to do forced labor outside of Prague. See Krejčová, Svobodová & Hyndráková 1997, 146–47. The fact that Karl Fein was deported from Prague to Łódź quite early on – the implication being that he was not shielded from deportation – suggests that neither he nor his brother Gustav had sufficient influence, if any, with

Early on in my research, oral history interviews with Brno Holocaust victims informed me that many Jewish people forcefully deported from Brno deposited their belongings with non-Jewish friends and acquaintances, even though, as we will see later, this was strictly forbidden, starting in the autumn of 1941. This was done on the assumption that they would be able to reclaim their possessions once the Nazi nightmare was over.[78] Did Karl Fein entrust the Hirschfeld materials to people he knew well before he left Brno for Prague in the autumn of 1939? Apparently he did. But before we look at the two most likely candidates in the following two chapters, I first want to provide an overview of the people Fein seems to have disregarded.

LI SHIU TONG

The most obvious person to whom Fein could (and even should) have turned was Hirschfeld's young Chinese pupil, Li Shiu Tong. Along with Karl Giese, Li Shiu Tong was after all one of the two universal heirs (*légataires universels*) of the Hirschfeld estate. In article 4 of Hirschfeld's will, it was stipulated that one universal heir would inherit the other's share of Hirschfeld's estate if, for any reason, he did not accept it. Could it not be said that, in a way, Giese's suicide reneged on his part of the deal to continue Hirschfeld's life work? Of course, as Giese's friend and lawyer, Karl Fein was probably well aware of the stipulation in Hirschfeld's will. He may have tried to contact Li Shiu Tong some time after Giese's death. But we should also remember that, when the Hirschfeld inheritance was being settled in Nice in 1935, Li Shiu Tong expressed serious doubts about accepting his part. We have also seen a frustrated Giese complaining that Li Shiu Tong had stopped cooperating with him, soon after the completion of Magnus Hirschfeld's grave in the summer of 1936.[79] Things only got worse with time. For example, in a December 1937 letter to Ernst Maass, Giese wrote that Li Shiu Tong expressly refused to accept a registered letter sent to him by Karl Fein.[80] Li Shiu Tong's adamant refusal to have anything to do with Hirschfeld and his estate extended into the post-war period, when he resolutely refused to answer any and all inquiries from the German restitution authorities (*Wiedergutmachungsbehörden*).[81]

the JKG in Prague to obtain a travel permit for Karl Fein. We have already suggested that Gustav Fein may only have started working for the JKG in Prague after his brother had been deported, in the fall of 1942.

[77] Beneš & Tošnerová 1996, 28–30, 61, 66–69.

[78] As was to be expected, and as recounted in some of these Shoah interviews, this caused dramatic scenes in post-war Czechoslovakia. It was very sadly true that most Jewish people never returned to their homes, but some people had counted on their former acquaintances and friends not returning, and sold the belongings entrusted to them. Yet some Jewish friends and acquaintances did indeed appear on the doorstep of the people to whom they had entrusted their belongings, shortly after end of the war. I heard such a story from Marianna Becková during my interview with her, in the summer of 2013. See also Elias 1998, 39, 44, 60, 217–18; Rosenfeld 1994, 41.

[79] One can infer this from an April 1937 letter from Giese to Kurt Hiller, in which he complains that Li Shiu Tong's failure to cooperate lasted "seit beinahe einem Jahr" (since almost a full year). Li Shiu Tong refused to answer letters "mit wichtigem Inhalt und dringenden Fragen" (containing important content and urgent questions). See Archiv Kurt Hiller Gesellschaft, Neuss, letter (dated Apr. 27, 1937, 1) from Karl Giese to Kurt Hiller. The letter is also quoted in Dose 2003, 18 n. 21. See also Soetaert 2014, 55.

[80] Archiv MHG, Berlin, fonds Ernst Maass, letter (dated Dec. 29, 1937, 5) from Karl Giese to Ernst Maass: "daß er [Li Shiu Tong] wie es letzlich geschah einen Einschreibbrief Dr. Feins, in dem dieser nach der Richtigkeit der Adresse fragte, weil Tao [Li Shiu Tong] sich evtl. [eventuell] in einem Prozess als Miterbe außern sollte, audrücklich verweigert anzunehmen" (that he [Li Shiu Tong], as recently happened, emphatically refused to accept a registered letter from Dr. Fein, asking whether the address was still correct, because Tao [Li Shiu Tong] would maybe eventually have to appear as co-heir in a lawsuit).

[81] In a 1958 letter to Günther Hauck, a relative of Magnus Hirschfeld, Franz Herzfelder wrote that Li Shiu Tong had explicitly forbidden him to communicate his whereabouts to anyone. See Archiv MHG, Berlin, fonds Ernst Maass, letter (dated Apr. 15, 1958) from François Herzfelder to Günther Hauck. See also Dose 2003, 10. Li Shiu Tong's express refusal to cooperate with the *Wiedergutmachungsamt* (restitution office) in Berlin in 1958 is revealed in a letter (dated Jan. 25, 1965) from François Herzfelder to the

Li Shiu Tong's lack of cooperation likely made Giese feel that the burden of honoring Hirschfeld's testamentary intentions fell heavily on his shoulders. Possibly, it was yet another reason that contributed to his suicide. Like Karl Giese, Li Shiu Tong seemed gripped by fear of the Nazis, even though, unlike Giese, a well-off Chinese citizen with a valid passport like Li Shiu Tong could move around more easily in Europe. We have also noted Ralf Dose's suggestion that Li Shiu Tong's evasiveness was likely due to a growing fear of the National Socialists and a plain, somewhat paranoid "persecution motive" (*Verfolgungsmotiv*).[82] So it is quite unlikely that Li Shiu Tong – who was then residing in Zürich – would have gone to Brno in 1939 to collect the materials that Fein had inherited from Giese.[83] All of these factors make it more understandable that Giese bequeathed his part of the Hirschfeld estate to Karl Fein and not to Li Shiu Tong. When Ralf Dose was in Vancouver, in February–March 2003, and saw several sexology titles owned by Li Shiu Tong, he noticed that, with the exception of two books, they all lacked the typical Institute library stamps.[84] We have shown that most of the books in Giese's Brno apartment were likely bought back from Nazi Germany at the end of 1933, and the majority most likely bore the typical Institute stamps. We may conclude from all this that Fein never entrusted any of the books (or other materials) he inherited from Giese to Li Shiu Tong. The most obvious candidate, legally speaking, to take over the estates of Hirschfeld and Giese was simply unwilling to do so.

JOSEF WEISSKOPF

I also looked at a group of people as likely candidates for Karl Fein to entrust with the Institute materials. These were the members of the organizing committee of the 1932 WLSR Brno conference, most of whom were doctors. We have seen that Karl Giese continually invoked a possible future cooperation with Dr. Josef Weisskopf. This cooperation was even a precondition for the extra financial support worked out for Giese in the settlement of the Hirschfeld inheritance in Nice.[85] We have already mentioned a newspaper article that reported that, in addition to Karl Fein, Weisskopf played a role in the 1933 buy-back operation. But Giese knew, possibly as early as 1933, when he first approached Weisskopf, that there would never be any cooperation. Weisskopf had his own demons to deal with in Brno. We have also seen that Josef Weisskopf informed François Herzfelder about the events in Brno in the weeks following Giese's death, but the fact that Weisskopf provided him with an old address for Fein clearly showed that he was not in direct contact with the latter. So it is likely that Karl Fein did not attempt to make contact with Weisskopf either. Yet it is striking that Karl Fein left for Prague the same month that Weisskopf left the country. Did Fein work out something with Weisskopf after all? In 2012, I was in email contact with Josef Weisskopf's current family in the USA. A grandson of Josef Weisskopf informed me, among other things, that Josef Weisskopf was "on the Board of Directors for the National Library of Medicine".[86] Though this claim was flatly denied by a staff member of the History of Medicine Division of the prestigious library in Bethesda (Maryland, USA), the information is rather intriguing and likely

Landgericht Berlin. The letter is quoted in Herzer 2001, 243 n. 21.

[82] Dose 2003, 21.

[83] It is unclear if any of Li Shiu Tong's passports have survived. A passport could confirm or refute a 1939 Brno visit. In an email (dated Jan. 21, 2015) Ralf Dose told me that he did not ask for Li Shiu Tong's passports when he visited his Chinese family in Vancouver. Safeguarding the Hirschfeld and Institute materials was then, understandably, his first priority.

[84] Dose 2003, 16.

[85] ADAM, Nice, Archives notariales, minutes notariales étude Pierre Demnard, May 29, 1936, n° 727, cote 03E 148/036.

[86] Email (dated Jun. 5, 2012) from Joe Weisskopf – Josef Weisskopf's grandson – to the author.

[87] Email (dated Jul. 6, 2012) from Stephen Greenberg to the author: "NLM [National Library of Medicine] does not have a board of directors; it has a board of regents, but I do not see Dr. Weisskopf's

needs further close scrutiny.[87] If there was indeed a link between Weisskopf and the National Library of Medicine, was this tied in any way to the Hirschfeld and Institute materials? Josef Weisskopf was certainly an ardent and faithful admirer of Magnus Hirschfeld, but did he also play some role in the further fate of Hirschfeld's legacy? The question remains open.

SIEGFRIED FISCHL

Besides Weisskopf, there were two other doctors with whom Fein collaborated in organizing the 1932 WLSR conference. Karl Fein was at least acquainted with Dr. Siegfried (Vítězslav) Fischl, since the two are recorded as speakers at a tumultuous public reunion of the Moravian Animal Welfare Association (Mährische Tierschutzverein) in the summer of 1935.[88] Fischl was elected a co-opted board member of the association in June 1935.[89] Fein was hired for his legal services, or worked pro bono, to help with the association's problems.[90] That Fischl was Jewish, like Fein, makes him an unlikely candidate for Fein to have chosen to safeguard the Hirschfeld materials. That said, we will briefly mention Dr. Fischl again, in chapter 16, since it cannot be conclusively stated that he did *not* play a part in our story.

VLADIMÍR ZAPLETAL

Dr. Vladimír Zapletal was likely a much better candidate since he was not Jewish. Zapletal was involved in the resistance and survived the war, dying in 1983. I was rather intrigued to discover during my research that Zapletal was known as an ardent collector of materials mainly connected to local medical history. This impressive collection is now in the possession of the Mendelianum in Brno (a department of the Moravian Museum, Moravské zemské museum); however, the folder on Magnus Hirschfeld listed in the inventory of Zapletal's collection could not be located.[91] My attempts to obtain clarity about the existence, contents and even the location of Zapletal's other personal archives proved challenging. Apparently, (some of?) these archives are located in Budišov Castle (zámek Budišov), fifty kilometers west of Brno, but these are not accessible.[92] That Karl Fein possibly stayed for two weeks at

name on the list of former board members. Moreover, I see no evidence of any major donation of books to NLM from Dr. Weisskopf. In fact, the only time his name comes up in our databases is as the author of a single 16 page pamphlet on hygiene and sex education, published in Brno in 1932". See also Soetaert 2014. 66–67 n. 176–77.

[88] "Mährischer Tierschutzverein", *Morgenpost*, Aug. 8, 1935, 3.

[89] MZA, Brno, fonds B 26, Mährischer Tierschutzverein Brünn, kart. n° 3154, sign. 1703/746, f. 187.

[90] Ibid., undated letter from Karl Fein to Brno police, f. 188b.

[91] Moravské zemské muzeum, Mendelianum, library and archive, Brno, fonds F 99, Vladimír Zapletal, písemný a obrazový materiál, folder Magnus Hirschfeld, inv. n° 6262, sign. GM 7/83. The library and archive are located at 76B Hudcova, Dům Jiřího Gruši, Brno.

[92] In my efforts to locate the Zapletal archives, I faced difficulties that I encountered a few times when contacting Czech archives. Under the postwar Communist regime, many archival collections were divided up and moved here and there, to this day causing disputes between agencies about what is located where. Even a simple inquiry about the matter seems to annoy some archive staff members. The following (anonymised) email (from October 2015) is an example: "We have NO information on your topic. Our institution is not an archive. The depository at Budišov Castle is NOT open for [*sic*] the public and the funds deposited there are NOT acessible [*sic*] to researchers". Neither was anyone able to give me even a minimal idea of the types of Zapletal's documents in Budišov Castle. The castle is actually a part of the Moravské zemské museum (Moravian Museum). See http://www.mzm.cz/en/castle-of-budisov/ (accessed Aug. 23, 2020). I thank Márta Mrazová (Center for 20th-Century Cultural-Political History, Moravian Museum, Brno) for her mediation. See email (dated Oct. 5, 2015) to the author. The Encyklopedie dějin města Brna (Encyclopedia of Brno history) website (managed by AMB, Brno), on the other hand, states that part of Vladimír Zapletal's personal archives are now kept in the MZA, Brno: "Zapletalův archiv spravuje Zemský archiv Brno (dlouho byl uložen v Budišově)" (Zapletal's archive is managed by the Brno Regional archive [previously stored for a long time in Budišov]). See http://encyklopedie.brna.cz/home-mmb/?acc=profil_osobnosti&load=5368 (accessed Jan. 27, 2015). However, these archives are not in

Zapletal's home in October 1938 is intriguing.[93] So whether Vladimír Zapletal played a relevant part in our story remains for now an open question.

JESUITSKÁ (JESUITENGASSE) LAWYERS

Since Karl Fein was a lawyer, I also supposed for a long time that Fein might have reached out to someone from his (former) professional network. Moreover, I think that the liquidation of ninety-four Jewish lawyers' practices in Brno, in March 1939, likely provoked a wave of solidarity among the outlawed Jewish lawyers, and possibly compassionate concern from at least some of their non-Jewish colleagues.

I also observed that, in the summer of 1939, when his brother and mother were already in Prague, Karl Fein moved to 9 Jesuitská (Jesuitengasse), an address in a modernist building called Typos Passage (Pasáž Typos), which still stands today [ill. 8].[94] From a 1934 address book, I learned that the lawyers Jaromír Appel (1900–1958),[95] Otto Löffler[96] (who was also Jewish), Rudolf Tížek[97] and Weiner Václav were listed at the same address. In the 1942 telephone directory, I saw that – "logically", because he was Jewish – Löffler's name disappeared and the name of the lawyer Franz Tomášek was added.[98] I could find no further clues there other than that, during the war, Jaromír Appel became the president of the Bar Association (*Advokatenkammer*) and apparently managed to passively resist the Germans from this position. His personal archives do not contain any letters to or from Karl Fein.[99] So, despite the fact that several lawyers had their offices in the Typos building, I did not really find a useful clue.

I also looked at two other lawyers whom Fein knew and who may have played a part in our story: Karel Růžička and Franz Nawratil. Both died in 1942, the year when, at least according to the guestbook affidavit, the Hirschfeld materials were saved. What if some materials from Karl Fein's estate were stored in their office, I wondered? Maybe these materials were thrown into the old paper container because their law offices had to be emptied in 1942?

the MZA. See email (dated Aug. 23, 2012) from Jiřina Kalendovská (Archiv Masarykovy univerzity Brno) to Gabriela Patriková (forwarded to the author). The same email also says that there is a small fonds of Vladimír Zapletal's texts, fonds B 48, donated to Masaryk University's archive in 1968.

93 See AMB, Brno, fonds Z 1, inhabitant registration card for Karl Fein for the address 2a Falkensteinergasse (Falkensteinerova) and *Adresář Protektorátu Čechy a Morava pro průmysl, živnosti, obchod a zemědělství = Adressbuch des Protektorates Böhmen und Mähren für Industrie, Gewerbe, Handel und Landwirtschaft* 1939, II: 1417 for Zapletal's address 2 Falkensteinergasse (Falkensteinerova). That Dr. Siegfried Fischl lived at the neighboring address, 4 Falkensteinergasse (Falkensteinerova), is another interesting fact.

94 The modernist building, completed in 1931, was designed by the Brno architect Václav Roštlapil (1901–1979). In Fein's time, it was known as the Pasáž Typos (Typos Passage) because of the gallery of shops in the building (now closed off). If one walked into the gallery from Jesuitská (Jesuitengasse), one emerged into Běhounská (Rennergasse). Today, the part of the gallery giving out into Běhounská is a "cul-de-sac" of shops. Until 2016, the Jesuitská-side gallery served as the private entrance to the building wing that housed some divisions of Česká televise Brno (Czech television, Brno). The building façade on Jesuitská still bears the legend "Typos". See http://encyklopedie.brna.cz/home-mmb/? acc = profil_osobnosti&load=14218 and http://www.bam.brno.cz/en/architect/26-vaclav-rostlapil (both accessed Jan. 28, 2015). I thank Milena Baumgarten for her help in establishing the building's construction year and architect. See her email (dated Jan. 28, 2015) to the author. House numbers on Jesuitská were renumbered after the war. That is why the Typos building is now at 7 Jesuitská, whereas it was number 9 in Fein's time.

95 See http://encyklopedie.brna.cz/home-mmb/?acc=profil_osobnosti&load=12941 (accessed Jul. 3, 2016 and Krčál 2011.

96 Interestingly, in 1933, Otto Löffler settled the deal between Leopold Fleischer and Bruno Fleischer, making the latter the sole owner of the Leopold Fleischer company and Leopold Fleischer becoming a partner in Gerstmann & Lindner. See MZA, Brno, fonds C 11, Krajský soud civilní Brno, firemní agenda, Rudolf Siegmund, zasilatelství a komisionářství, Brno (dř. Leopold Fleischer, zasilatelství a komisionářství, Brno, 1920-1942), 1920-1955, kart. n° 68, sign. A VI 121. Later in this chapter, we will return to the history of these two companies.

97 Rudolf Tížek liquidated the law practice of H. Friedmann in 1939. See *Věstník Moravské advokátní komory v Brně*, April 1939, 2.

KAREL RŮŽIČKA

As we have indicated, it is not certain that Fein and Růžička ever worked together, but they certainly practiced law in the same building on Masarykstrasse (Masarykova) in 1932–36 and both were also left-wing.[100] We have seen that Růžička was active in the resistance and was murdered in Mauthausen in January 1942. The question occurred to me: had Marie Vavrouch, Karel Růžička's surviving partner, maybe relied on another Růžička family member to empty out her husband's law office after his death? So one of the first things that I immediately checked was whether Karel Růžička had any connection to Jindra Růžička's scrap company. Was Jindra Růžička's husband, Jaroslav Růžička, related in any way to Karel Růžička? Realizing that Růžička is a very common Czech name, it required a time-consuming email conversation with two regional Czech archives before I could conclude that the two men were not related. Jaroslav and Karel Růžička were not brothers or cousins.[101]

FRANZ NAWRATIL

As we have already shown, Nawratil's exact attitude to Karl Fein could not have been one of complete hostility. We have seen that Nawratil was apparently somewhat instrumental in helping Fein to bring the Giese-Fein inheritance case to a good conclusion. Nawratil died on May 10, 1942, five days after Karl Fein died in Łódź. His premature death, at the age of fifty-two, is a bit troubling.[102] Nawratil drafted his will on December 1, 1941. Was he aware of what could happen to him or was he prompted to do so by life-threatening health issues? We have also seen that, in the handling of the Giese-Fein inheritance case, Nawratil's relationship with the German District Court did not run as smoothly as expected. And we have also shown that Nawratil was certainly not allergic to Jewish people. His landlord, Dr. Hermann Jellenik, was Jewish. The Jewish wife of his brother, Lily Navratil, committed suicide by poison after being questioned and tortured by the Gestapo in March 1941. Which begs the question: was Nawratil also maybe questioned and possibly even tortured by the Gestapo because of his ties to members of the Jewish community? Does this help explain the sudden illness and premature death of a man of fifty-two? Or was Nawratil a severely conscience-stricken National Socialist, realizing that Karl Fein was deported to Łódź in October 1941, and that the lawyer Ludwig Goldmann (1882–1942?) and his immediate family were deported from Brno in December 1941? In addition to Karl Fein's law practice, Nawratil also liquidated Goldmann's in 1939.[103] Nawratil

[98] Otto Löffler's law practice was liquidated by K. Křepelka. See *Věstník Moravské advokátní komory v Brně*, April 1939, 2. See also *Adressbuch der Landeshauptstadt Brünn 1942* 1943, 1. In 1939, Franz Tomášek liquidated Karl Sonnenfeld's law practice. See *Věstník Moravské advokátní komory v Brně*, April 1939, 3.

[99] MZA, Brno, fonds G 465, JUDr. Jaromír Appel, kart. n° 1, sign. 23.

[100] The slight objection to the idea that they may have worked together is the fact that Karl Fein moved out again, in October 1936, to his new 35 Koliště (Glacis) address, while Růžička kept his law office on Masarykstrasse (Masarykova). For 35 Koliště (Glacis) as Karl Fein's professional address, see *Seznam advokátů dle stavu koncem roku 1936* 1937, 28. That the two seemingly went their separate ways in 1936 does not, of course, necessarily mean that they no longer got along.

[101] The family roots of Jaroslav Růžička (1905–1978) were in Brtnice (Jihlava district). He was the son of Franz (František) Růžička (1871–?) and Magdalena Otta/Ottová (1867–?). The couple had six children: Josef (1899–?), Antonín (1901–?), Růžena (1903–?), Jaroslav (1905–?), Alžběta (1907–?) and Ludmila (1909–?). Petr Dvořák (Státní okresní archiv Jihlava) checked the information about Jaroslav Růžička's ancestry. See his email (dated Feb. 18, 2015) to the author. See also Jaroslav Růžička's home certificate in AMB, Brno, fonds B 1/39. The family roots of the lawyer Karel Růžička (1895–1942) were in Dědice (Vyškov district). His parents were Josef Růžička (1857–?) and Marie Baňar (1863–?), Josef Růžička's second wife. Michaela Zemánková (Státní okresní archiv Vyškov se sídlem ve Slavkově u Brna) checked the information about Karel Růžička's ancestry for me. See her email (dated Feb. 11, 2015) to the author.

[102] An obituary states that his death was *unerwartet* (unexpected), *nach kurzem Leiden* (after a brief illness) (*Brünner Tagblatt*, May 12, 1942, 8).

[103] *Věstník Moravské advokátní komory v Brně*, April 1939, 2.

would also have known that his Jewish neighbor, Marie Wagner (née Feldmann, 1881–1942?), who lived in the house she owned at 77 Údolní (Talgasse), was deported from Brno in the beginning of December 1941.[104] In the month before Nawratil died, in April 1942, the last Jewish mass transport "Ai", carrying 923 people, also left Brno. Did these persecutions of Jewish people trouble Nawratil?

Nawratil's dying one week after Karl Fein is curious, but likely a coincidence. It is even possible to ask: were the National Socialists aware that, in liquidating Karl Fein's law practice, Nawratil indirectly dealt with materials belonging to their archenemy, Magnus Hirschfeld? That Nawratil himself was not a wholly reliable National Socialist is, I think, also indicated by the fact that, only a few days after his death, in mid-May 1942, his wife, Wilma Naplawa, gave her sister, Edith Hradský (née Naplawa, 1913-?), power of attorney (*Vollmacht*). This allowed her sister to look after all the requisite proceedings and actions related to the inheritance procedure. Wilma Naplawa drew up the power of attorney the day after she confirmed her last address to the Brno authorities, perhaps indicating that she was either expecting a Gestapo visit (or other German police instance) or summoned for questioning.[105] I think this act shows that she was quite uncertain about the outcome. Most likely, she was well aware that her husband was not the ideal National Socialist he outwardly had claimed to be.[106]

With all that in mind, and remembering that Nawratil liquidated Fein's law office, it seemed to me that Nawratil, however implausible it might appear, could have been another good candidate to take care of parts of Fein's estate. After all, another relevant question is what happened to Karl Fein's client files after his law practice was liquidated in April 1939? We do not really know exactly how the liquidation of a Jewish law practice was carried out. Did the liquidation "merely" entail Karl Fein simply ceasing all professional activities at a certain moment? Or did it also mean that he lost all control of the files of his former clients? Was the procedure to be followed in the liquidation of a law office strictly laid out beforehand? And was the liquidation procedure – whether strict or not – controlled by another agent other than the liquidator?

To see how the procedure was followed, I looked at the liquidation file of one Jewish law practice in the Sudetenland. In the liquidation of the Jewish law practice of Karl Löwy, of Komotau (currently Chomutov), Karl Mocker, a local lawyer, was appointed as the second and final "handler" (*Abhandler*). Initially, in July 1942, the Aussig (Ústí nad Labem) *Regierungspräsident* (district president) stipulated that Karl Löwy had four weeks to collect his files (*Akten*) before they would be destroyed. However, it was eventually decided that Karl Mocker would first go through the files and place advertisements in newspapers to allow clients to retrieve their personal files. The whole operation was time-consuming and the remaining files were finally discarded as waste paper (*Altpapier*), though only in the beginning of 1944.[107] Of course, we cannot extrapolate from this one case that the same or similar practices applied to all liquidated Jewish law practices in the so-called Südetenland and in the Protectorate. Indeed, in Franz Nawratil's inheritance file, I found a letter stating that the law

[104] MZA, Brno, fonds B 392, Vystěhovalecký fonds, úřadovna Brno (1939-1945), kart. n° 10, inv. n° 222, Údolní n° 348/77, Maria Wagnerová. The current house number is 814/59. Maria Wagner was deported on transport "K" from Brno to Terezín on December 5, 1941 and further transferred to Riga on January 15, 1942 on transport "P". Her name was added to the grave of her husband Philipp Wagner (1872–1934) in the Brno Jewish cemetery, section 28D, row 1, grave 23.

[105] See the single (!) resident registration card (dated May 15, 1942) for Wilma Nawratil in AMB, Brno, fonds Z 1.

[106] MZA, Brno, C 107, Německý úřední soud Brno (Deutsches Amtsgericht Brünn), kart. n° 282, sign. 5bV146/14, inheritance file Franz Nawratil, f. 4.

[107] NA, Praha, fonds n° 375, Arizačni spisy, liquidation file Karl Löwy, kart. n° 90, sign. 73.

[108] See the anonymous letter (dated Jul. 7, 1942) to the lawyer Alfred Wehowski (1886–?) in MZA, Brno,

stipulated preserving law office files for five years after a lawyer died. The same letter states that German officials were the ones who clearly dealt with the matter, and records that Nawratil's widow informed them that she had nowhere to store her husband's client files after he died.[108] Interestingly, the client files and personal library of the Jewish lawyer Robert Herrmann – who, as we have seen, interned with Karl Fein – survived the war and had been safeguarded by Max Pokorný (either senior or junior), the Nazi lawyer who liquidated Herrmann's law office.[109] We have seen that a Jewish law practice was usually liquidated by a known and trusted lawyer. This would mean that Karl Fein's client files were likely not immediately discarded in 1939. There is a good chance that Nawratil, as the liquidator of Fein's law office, took them into his charge. Had Nawratil not died in 1942, Fein's client files may have survived the war. The file on Karl Giese, one of his clients, would have been among them. This raises another question: if, besides the client files, Nawratil may have had other private papers belonging to Karl Fein, or even Institute materials. But because Nawratil died in 1942, it seems that Fein's client files were likely discarded at some point during the war.

Nothing much can be said with certainty about the exact nature of the relationship between Fein and Nawratil, but I have already demonstrated that Nawratil was likely more involved in our story than his Nazi outlook would suggest. Later, in chapter 16, we will return one more time to Franz Nawratil's possible close involvement in our story.

OTTO SCHÜTZ

I also want to bring up a lawyer whom we have already encountered. This is Otto Schütz, whom Fein initially proposed as trustee of the estate (*Nachlasskurator*) to the Brno district civil court, for the Giese inheritance procedure. I do not believe that Schütz was at all involved with safeguarding the Institute materials, but he certainly would have known a lot about the whole Hirschfeld-Giese-Fein case – just for starters because he was an intern in Karl Fein's Brno law office in 1931–36. This most likely also means that Otto Schütz ran Fein's law office while Fein spent several weeks in Nice in the summer of 1935 to oversee the slow proceedings of the Hirschfeld inheritance. Like Karl Fein and Karel Růžička, Otto Schütz's work address, until 1936, was 6 Masarykova (Masarykstrasse).[110] And, again like Fein and Růžička, Schütz was a left-wing lawyer.[111] He was the president of the Brno branch of the League for Human Rights (Liga für Menschenrechte, Liga pro lidská práva). In 1938, he also established a committee to assist German (and mainly Jewish) exiles in Brno, the Central Support Office for Refugees in Brno (Zentralhilfstelle für Flüchtlinge in Brünn, Pomocné ústředí pro uprchlíky v Brně). Schütz also knew Kurt Hiller, Karl Giese and the elder Karl Fein, the nephew of the younger Karl Fein.[112] Schütz may also have mediated

fonds C 107, Německý úřední soud Brno (Deutsches Amtsgericht Brünn), inheritance file Franz Nawratil, kart. n° 282, sign. 5bV 146/42, f. 16.

[109] Library and Archives Canada/Bibliothèque et archives Canada, Ottawa, manuscript division, fonds Stephen S. Barber, MG 31, H 113, Personal records and correspondence, vol. 12, file n° 1, letter (dated Jul. 1, 1945, 1) from Stephen Barber to Robert Herrmann. Stephen Barber (1911–1983) was an intern in Herrmann's law office from 1935 to 1939. Both men remained very good friends after the war. Stephen Barber was the brother of Edith Barber, who was in turn a friend of Eduard Homolatsch, one of the witnesses at the marriage of Walter Lukl, Giese's Brno boyfriend.

[110] See, for example, the index card for Otto Schütz in NA, Praha, fonds n° 1420/6 (AMV 200), Policejní ředitelství Praha II, Zpravodajská ústředna od roku 1930, 1930-1934 při Policejním ředitelství Praha, kart. n° 47, sign. 200-47-3. In 1937, when Schütz started working for himself, he moved to 3 Divadelní (Theatergasse). See *Seznam advokátů dle stavu koncem roku 1937* 1938, 32.

[111] In a December 1933 article Schütz wrote for the Brno newspaper *Tagesbote*, he clearly stated the he was not on the side of Hitler, then in power in Germany. See Schütz, Dec. 5, 1933, 3.

[112] Archiv Kurt Hiller Gesellschaft, Neuss, letter (dated Apr. 29, 1937, 3 [2]) from Kurt Hiller to Karl

the publication of one of Magnus Hirschfeld's texts on the Ernst Röhm case in *Der Aufruf*, the magazine of the German-language branch of the Czechoslovak League for Human Rights.[113] Schütz himself published several articles in the magazine.[114]

The Gestapo were already searching for Schütz the day after the invasion of Czechoslovakia. He managed to flee to Sweden where he was very active in assisting Czechoslovak emigrants as much as he could during the war years. In Sweden, he was likely concerned about the fate of Karl Fein and I think it likely that they corresponded. I have looked closely at this man because I think he was a good (possibly gay) friend of Karl Fein and because he may have been very well informed about Fein's intentions for the Institute materials. But the long search for his living relatives and personal archives ended with my hearing from his current family in the USA that his many files were likely lost when the ship carrying them to the United States sank. More on this "indefatigable" Otto Schütz – as two Czech historians call him – can be found in the addenda.[115]

ROBERT HERRMANN

Noticing that many young Jewish lawyers in Brno – unlike Fein – managed to flee abroad in time, I also looked at Robert Herrmann (1899–1995), the very first intern in Karl Fein's law office in 1923.[116] I must add that I was also intrigued by Herrmann because the lawyer Max Pokorny Jr. (1902–?) liquidated Herrmann's law office in 1939. Pokorny was also the trustee (*Treuhänder*) of the Jewish-owned house at 66 Křenová (Kröna), the house (owned by Ernst Fischer) that neighbored the Nebehosteny city palace.[117] I also looked at Robert Herrmann because I learned that the wealthy Brno local Anna Bloch (née Scherbak, 1904-1991) had good contacts with Kurt Hiller and presumably also Magnus Hirschfeld in the early 1930s. Anna Bloch married Erwin Bloch (1902-1986) in 1925. Robert Herrmann's later wife, Helene Bloch (1904-1965), was a sister of Erwin Bloch.[118] My very long search for any of Robert Herrmann's remaining personal archives left me, at least for the time being, partly empty-handed. The matter is explained further in the addenda.[119]

KURT BRAMMER

There was one more young lawyer who interned with Karl Fein. One of the postal reply stubs in the Giese inheritance file was signed by Kurt Brammer (1914–1944?), a nephew of Karl Fein.[120] Kurt Brammer's mother was Irma Brammer (née Fein, 1883–1944), a daughter of Adolf Fein, who was a brother of Karl Fein's father Albert. This family tie likely explains why the young man was able to intern with Karl Fein.[121]

Giese: " mein Freund Dokter Otto Schütz, den Sie ja wohl auch kennen" (my friend Doctor Otto Schütz, whom you probably also know). Otto Schütz wrote a piece in *Tagebote*, the local newspaper, on Karl Fein Sr. shortly after the latter's death. See Schütz, Oct. 14, 1932, 3–4. In October 1935, three years after Karl Fein Sr.'s death, an anonymous donation of 50 Czech crowns was made to the League for Human Rights, in honor of Fein's memory. See *Tagesbote*, Oct. 12, 1935, 8. See also Soetaert 2024.

[113] Hirschfeld, Jul. 15, 1934, 512–15.

[114] See, for example, Schütz 1932a, 1932b, 1932–33 and Sep. 15, 1934. Kurt Hiller also wrote a text for *Der Aufruf* (in the issue that included Schütz's article), further indicating that Hiller was in contact with Otto Schütz. See Hiller, 1932–33, 6–7. When Hiller was arrested and imprisoned for a second time in Germany, in July 1933, the matter was reported in *Der Aufruf*. See *Der Aufruf* 16, Sep. 15, 1933, 12.

[115] Čapková & Frankl 2012, 279. See also n° 5 in the addenda.

[116] *Seznam advokátů dle stavu koncem roku 1923* 1924, 36. For Robert Herrmann, see http://encyklopedie.brna.cz/home-mmb/?acc=profil_osobnosti&load=20621 (accessed Jan. 8, 2016).

[117] *Věstník Moravské advokátní komory v Brně*, April 1939, 2; and chapter 14, pp. 503-04, n. 52.

[118] See Soetaert 2024.

[119] See n° 6 in the addenda.

[120] The reply stub, dated March 24, 1938, signed by "Dr. Brammer" for a letter from the district civil court can be found in MZA, Brno, fonds C 107, Německý úřední soud Brno (Deutsches Amtsgericht Brünn), kart. n° 256, sign. 5aV 3/41, f. 11. For Brammer's internship, see *Seznam advokátů dle stavu koncem roku 1937* 1938, 50. The database www.holocaust.cz consistently misspells his and his mother's name as "Bramer". A later resident registration card, in AMB,

Until 1932, Irma Fein and her husband, the engineer Lipmann Brammer (1886–1941), lived at 62 Kröna (Křenová), only a few houses down from the Nebehosteny city palace, located at 68 Kröna (Křenová).[122] This, of course, got my attention. That Kurt Brammer signed for a letter while working in Karl Fein's law office, in March 1938, reveals that he most likely knew about the Giese-Fein inheritance case. This was reason enough to follow his trail.

Kurt Brammer's father, Lipmann Brammer, was tried by the first court martial on October 3, 1941. He was handed over to the Gestapo, losing all claim to his belongings. He was killed in Mauthausen in October 1941.[123] Kurt Brammer went to Prague in November 1939; however, likely seeing no possibility of emigrating, he returned to Brno in February 1940.[124] Kurt Brammer and his mother were deported from Brno to Terezín on transport "Ad" on March 23, 1942. In Terezín, Kurt Brammer played the piano with The Ghetto Swingers, a jazz group.[125] On September 28, 1944, he was deported on transport "Ek" from Terezín to Auschwitz-Birkenau. On October 6, 1944, a week after her son, Irma Brammer was transported to Auschwitz-Birkenau on transport "Eo", which carried 1,550 people. Most likely, shortly after her arrival, she and most others on her transport suffocated to death in one of the Auschwitz-Birkenau gas chambers.[126]

IMRICH MATYÁŠ

The Slovak gay militant Imrich Matyáš, who was befriended by Magnus Hirschfeld and Kurt Hiller, was another good candidate to safeguard the materials. Matyáš was not Jewish and survived the war. He died in Bratislava in 1974, at the age of seventy-eight. Yet Matyáš does not seem to have been in contact with Karl Fein when he was in Brno and before he moved to Prague in 1939. Moreover, when Kurt Hiller inquired with Matyáš, after the war, about the fate of Karl Fein, Matyáš wrote that he did not know anything about what had become of Fein.[127]

DID KARL FEIN HAVE A STORAGE ROOM IN BRNO?

We have just considered the possibility that Karl Fein may have sold all or only some of the Institute materials. We have also reviewed the possible candidates, both institutions and individuals, Fein may have entrusted with these materials. A final hypothetical question occurred to me when I started my research project: did Karl Fein store his belongings and the Institute materials with a Brno storage company

Brno, fonds Z 1, reveals that Kurt Brammer did not become a lawyer since it describes him as a civil servant (*úředník, Beamte*). His name does not appear in the list of liquidated Jewish law offices. See *Věstník Moravské advokátní komory v Brně*, April 1939, 2-3.

[121] The young man's academic grades were not sufficient for him to start out as an *Auskultant* (trainee). See the investigation into the matter, in January 1939, by the Disciplinární rada moravské advokátní komory, Disziplinarrat des mährischen Advokatenkammer (Disciplinary Council of the Moravian Bar Association) in MZA, Brno, fonds C 7, Vrchní státní zastupitelství Brno, 1850-1948, kart. n° 67, folder E 1939, 4789/80, n° 86, DR 52/37, disciplinary case Karl Fein/Kurt Brammer.

[122] *Adreßbuch von Groß-Brünn* 1932, 140; and for their later 1 Dolní ulice (Untere Gasse) address, see *Adreßbuch von Groß-Brünn* 1934, 144.

[123] Lipmann Brammer was a Freemason, a member of the Moravian lodge in Brno, sent to Mauthausen after being sentenced by the first court martial on October 3, 1941. He died in Mauthausen on October 31, 1941. See MZA, Brno, fonds B 340, Gestapo Brno, n° 667, kart. n° 292, sign. 100-292-21, file Lipmann Brammer and https://www.mauthausen-memorial.org/ (accessed Jul. 25, 2017). Until July 25, 2017, when I suggested a correction, the latter database spelled Lipmann Brammer's name as "Bramer". Lipmann Brammer is also mentioned in an antisemitic book published in 1938. See Rys 1938, 188.

[124] NA, Praha, fonds Policejní ředitelství Praha II, všeobecná spisovna, 1931-1940, kart. n° 4898, sign. R2637/49, Kurt Brammer 1914.

[125] See http://www.holocaust.cz/databaze-obeti/obet/78960-kurt-bramer/ (accessed Mar. 25, 2016).

[126] For details on transport "Eo", see http://www.holocaustresearchproject.org/othercamps/Terezíntransport.html (accessed Mar. 10, 2021).

[127] Archiv Kurt Hiller Gesellschaft, Neuss, letter (dated Apr. 24, 1957) from Imrich Matyáš to Kurt Hiller.

before he left for Prague in 1939? In what follows we will suggest that it was indeed possible that Fein did so, though only for a limited time. The idea of renting a storage room was surely not unfamiliar to Karl Fein. As Giese's friend and legal counsellor, he must have known that Hirschfeld had rented storage rooms in Paris, and likely also in Nice, for Institute materials. Since the looting of the Institute in May 1933, Hirschfeld and Giese were likely convinced that the Institute materials were much safer in storage rooms than in their residences.[128] Fein may have had similar ideas. We may also wonder if Fein was willing to move the several hundred books received from Giese's estate every time he changed residence in Brno in 1938 and 1939. Fein lived at three or as many as four different addresses during his last two years in Brno.[129]

Moreover, the idea of finding a storage room for one's belongings was not uncommon among the general Jewish population of Brno. Storing household belongings with storage companies was not forbidden to Jewish people.[130] In his memoir of occupied Brno, the Jewish engineer Arnold Hindls (1885–1977) recorded that many Jewish people rented storage rooms once they were forced to leave their residences and had to move in with other Jewish people. There was simply no room in these very crowded houses or apartments for their household effects. As in Prague, the JKG in Brno, on the order of the Germans, gathered together many families in so-called "Jewish houses" (*Judenhäuser*). The Germans also influenced where Jews could live by disallowing the automatic extension of leases.[131]

In April 1941, Arnold Hindls and his wife Hedvika Bondy (1894–1941) had to move to a "Jewish house" when their own house was taken from them. It was the Supreme District Council (Oberlandrat) in Brno, the local administration representing the German occupiers, that distributed the vacated Jewish houses to new German owners; however, it was up to the JKG in Brno to relocate their former owners to more modest "Jewish houses".[132] Hindls and his wife were forced to move from their comfortable home, with a garden, to another house already occupied by fourteen other Jewish people. There was no room for their household goods. Arnold Hindls and his sick wife were given three days and nights to pack up all their belongings and needed to figure out in that short time where to store everything: "In addition, there was the great worry of where to put our household goods. The warehouses of the many moving companies were already completely full. So where to put it all? Then I remembered

[128] Soetaert 2014, 59 n. 144. Interestingly, whenever Hirschfeld or Giese mentioned these storage rooms in a document or a letter, they were always rather vague and evasive. Such caution was understandable as one could never be sure into whose hands letters or documents might fall. But this caution now frustrates the historian looking for clues. See, for example, Ralf Dose's disappointment mentioned in chapter 18, p. 700, n. 16.

[129] He lived at the following addresses in 1938–39: 35 Koliště (Glacis), 2a Falkensteinerova (Falkensteinergasse) (uncertain because he only stayed two weeks there), 2a Akademická (Akademiegasse), and 9 Jesuitská (Jesuitengasse).

[130] Hindls 1966, 141: "obgleich damals eine Einlagerung von Möbeln und Hausrat, wo immer, nicht verboten war" (although at that time, storing furniture and household effects, wherever it might be, was not forbidden.)

[131] Potthast 2000, 159 n. 18; see also ch. 13, pp. 444-45 for a similar situation in Prague.

[132] Hindls 1966, 137–40. For more information on the history and organization of the Oberlandräte (Supreme District Councils, led by directors or councilors, also called Oberlandräte), which initially administered twenty Oberlandratsbezirke, see Kokošková, Zdeňka, Pažout, Jaroslav & Sedláková 2019; https://cs.wikipedia.org/wiki/Oberlandrat (accessed Nov. 2, 2021). In April 1939, the Oberlandrat Brünn-Stadt (Brno-město) was responsible for the 270,000 citizens of greater Brno alone. Moravia initially had eight Oberlandräte and Bohemia had twelve. From 1940 on, the Oberlandrat Brünn governed the 750,000 citizens of Brünn-Stadt (Brno-město), Brünn-Land (Brno-venkov), Boskowitz (Boskovice), Tischnowitz (Tišnov) and Wischau (Vyškov). See Kokošková, Zdeňka, Pažout, Jaroslav & Sedláková 2019, 229–31, 234–37.

[133] Hindls 1966, 140–41: "Dazu kam noch die grosse Sorge, wohin mit dem Uebersiedlungsgut. Die Lagerhäuser der vielen Versandhäuser waren schon vollkommen überfüllt. Wohin also damit? Da erinnerte ich mich an einen mir bekannten Möbeltischler, der uns vor Jahren einige Möbelstücke angefertigt hatte. Auf meine Bitte erklärte er sich bereit unsere Wohnungseinrichtung, Kisten und Bilder in seinen

a carpenter I knew who had made some furniture for us years earlier. At my request, he agreed to store our furnishings, boxes and pictures on his premises".[133] Since their belongings were apparently not safe from theft at the carpenter's company, Hindls eventually managed to store everything with the Morava moving company in Brno.[134] In 1934, Brno had no fewer than forty-five moving and storage firms.[135] Several were Jewish-owned and were Aryanized in the first years of the war.[136] Almost all the moving companies in Brno rented out storage rooms.[137]

AN UNDER-RESEARCHED TOPIC

The question of how the National Socialists dealt with storage rooms rented by Jewish people in the Protectorate is, as far as I was able to determine, under-researched.[138] The matter of Jewish expropriation and restitution has clearly been ascendant in the academic research and scholarly literature of the past few decades. But today the focus seems to apply mainly to the theft of objects of great value: money and other financial capital, property, Aryanized companies, art works, library collections and other costly cultural artifacts. The fate of less valuable household furnishings is overlooked. Of course, this can be partly explained by the more numerous traces the robbery of valuable Jewish assets has left in the archives ... while the theft of more modest belongings has left hardly any.[139] Surviving relatives' quest for the restitution of the more valuable belongings stolen from the murdered is certainly another driving factor.

Räumen einzulagern". This passage (and many other passages) from this typescript cannot be found in the commercial edition of Hindls' memoirs. See Hindls 1965. I thank Hermann Teifer (head archivist of the Leo Baeck Institute, New York) for sending me the undigitized verso page (140a) of the document on June 29, 2016, which allowed me to complete the quotation. The date of the event, April 1941, can be found on p. 138.

[134] Hindls misspells the name of the company as "Moravia" in his text. See *Adreßbuch von Groß-Brünn* 1934, 649; *Adressbuch der Landeshauptstadt* 1942, 99. The company was founded in 1921 and its shareholders all lived in Prague. Only one of them was Jewish, but this meant that the company was Aryanized. The name of the Jewish shareholder was Gustav Klauber (1882–1941?). He was deported, with his wife Berta Leiner (1889–1941?) on transport "C" on October 26, 1941, from Prague to Łódź. Their daughter Lilly (1917–1942?) was deported six months later, on April 24, 1942, on transport "Am" from Prague to Terezín. Four days later, on April 28, 1942, she was further transferred on transport "Ar" to Zamošč. Arnold Hindls was deported from Brno on transport "Ah" on April 4, 1942. He was liberated from Lublin. His wife died in October 1941. Both Hindls and his wife are buried close to each other in the Brno Jewish cemetery, Arnold in parcel 27B, row 2, grave 3, and his wife Hedvika in parcel 27B, row 2, grave 7.

[135] These moving and storage companies were listed under several headings in the *Adreßbuch von groß-Brünn*: Lagerhauser (skladiště), Speditionsgeschäfte (Spediční obchody), Transporte, Internationale [*sic*] (Mezinárodní dopravy) and Möbeltransport- und Uebersiedlungsgeschäfte (Nábytková přeprava a přesídlení). The Speditionsgeschäfte (Spediční obchody) section includes the most companies, forty-five in total. See *Adreßbuch von Groß-Brünn* 1934, 649. The 1942 *Adressbuch der Landeshauptstadt Brünn* changed the indexing terms. Under "Möbeltransporte und Einlagerungen" (Přepravy a uskladnování nábytku) there are only three companies: Hermann Neisser, Jaroslav Černil and the company belonging to a certain Franz Zigmund located at 25 Křenová. See *Adressbuch der Landeshauptstadt Brünn* 1942, 78. A total of forty-nine companies are listed under the sections "Spediteure" (Zasilatelé) and "Spedition und Lagerei" (Stěhování a uskladnění). See *Adressbuch der Landeshauptstadt Brünn* 1942, 99–100.

[136] I looked at a great many wholly or partly Jewish-owned Brno moving firms that were eventually Aryanized. These files are in NA, Praha, fonds n° 375, Arizačni spisy. I looked at the files of the following companies: Leopold Fleischer, kart. n° 205, sign. 1268; Eger & Co., kart. n° 214, sign. 1348; F. Deutsch, kart. n° 187, sign. 1076; Morava, kart. n° 242, sign. 1641; Schück & Skutezky, kart. n° 420, sign. 2990; Philipp Frischauer, kart. n° 209, sign. 1299; Hermann Liebschütz, kart. n° 216, no sign. n°; Ja[c]ques Pollak, kart. n° 249, sign. 1705; Gerstmann & Lindner, kart. n° 267, sign. 1913 and kart. n° 266, sign. 1913; Wilhelm Gärtner, kart. n° 445, sign. 5009; Alfred Wolf, kart. n° 434, sign. 3162; Mautner & Co., kart. n° 255, sign. 1778; B. Friess, kart. n° 206, sign. 1274.

[137] Hindls 1966, 140–41, 155.

[138] The staff of the Židovské muzeum v Praze (Jewish Museum in Prague) had no idea that these storage places even existed or that they were used by Jewish people. See email (dated Aug. 22, 2016) from Daniela Bartáková (Židovské muzeum v Praze, Shoah History Department, Praha) to the author.

[139] Anderl et al. 2004, 11, 173.

I found some relevant research for Austria only, but the focus there is rather on the moving firms themselves, called "Spediteure" in German.[140] There is also a tendency in this research to focus on the Jewish people who had stored their belongings (known as "Umzugsgut") in these firms either awaiting imminent emigration or already abroad. And here again, the writing is mainly about the handling of valuable objects in these storage rooms.[141] In Vienna, starting in September 1940, the contents of storage rooms rented by Jewish people abroad (thus losing all rights of ownership of the stored goods) were irregularly auctioned off by the Gestapo Office for the Clearing of the Property of Jewish Emigrants (Verwertungsstelle für jüdisches Umzugsgut der Gestapo), better known by the acronym VUGESTA.[142] This organization represented the interests of both the moving companies (mostly fearful of unpaid rent for the storage rooms) and the National Socialists who wanted to make money from the stolen Jewish goods.[143] To take one example, the art collection belonging to the Brno-born theater artist Fritz Grünbaum (1880–1941) was deposited in a storage room at the Schenker moving company in Vienna before mysteriously disappearing.[144] Although Gabriele Anderl and her team focused specifically on the stored belongings left behind by Jewish people already abroad, she also includes a chapter on what happened to the possessions of those who were not able to escape Austria in time. In Vienna, the expropriation of the contents of Jewish apartments and houses was taken care of by the Furniture Clearing Office (*Möbelverwertungsstelle*) in the Krummbaumgasse, also known as the VUGESTA 2.[145] Approximately 180 Jewish people, used as forced labor, emptied the apartments.[146] In Austria, the moving companies were obligated to report to the VUGESTA if non-Aryans rented storage space from them. When, around 1940–41, the Germans decided to confiscate all remaining Jewish "Umzugsgut", moving companies had to provide detailed lists of the items stored with them.[147] In other words, the Austrian case shows – who could have expected anything different? – that the National Socialists, and especially the Gestapo, were well aware of the existence of storage rooms rented out to Jewish people. It also makes it clear that the Nazis were very keen to rob them.

[140] See, for example, Fischer-Defoy & Nürnberg 2011; Kuller 2004.

[141] In Germany itself, Jewish people also made use of these storage rooms for their furnishings. See, for example, document n° 93 ("Julian Kretschmer aus Emden schildert die Auflösung seiner Arztpraxis im Spätsommer 1938") and document n° 212 ("Paul Fürstenberg erinnert am 24. Dezember 1938 die Reichs-Kredit-Gesellschaft an ihre Zusagen in Zusammenhang mit der 'Arisierung' seiner Firma") in Heim 2009, 288, 579.

[142] For more information on the Vienna VUGESTA, see Holzbauer 2000. See also document n° 160 ("Das Reichssicherheitshauptamt erweitert am 5. März 1941 die Möglichkeiten, das Umzugsgut von jüdischen Auswandern zu versteigern") and document n° 179 ("Die VUGESTA informiert in einem Merkblatt über die Modalitäten der Versteigerung jüdischen Eigentums in Wien am 3. Mai 1941") in Löw 2012, 413, 456–57.

[143] Alexander Schröck, Einbringungen der Verwaltungsstelle für jüdisches Umzugsgut der Gestapo (VUGESTA), qtd. in Niederacher, June 30, 2010, 15 n. 33: "Die Vugesta verwertete, d. h. verkaufte die formal beschlagnahmten aufgrund von offenen Forderungen in Bezug auf die Lagerkosten bzw. [beziehungsweise] die zu Gunsten des Deutschen Reiches eingezogenen Güter, die in Folge des Kriegsausbruches in den Speditionen liegen geblieben waren. Die Vugesta war eine Schnittstelle zwischen Gestapo und den Spediteuren und war privatwirtschaftlich organisiert" (Vugesta made use of, i.e. sold, the goods formally confiscated for outstanding claims related to storage costs, or of the goods confiscated for the German Reich, which had been left in moving firms as a result of the outbreak of war. The Vugesta was an interface between the Gestapo and the moving firms and was organized as a private company). The interests of the moving companies were also safeguarded by the Austrian branch of the Reichsverkehrsgruppe Spedition und Lagerei (Reich Transport and Storage Group), the Landesgeschäftsstelle Ostmark. See Anderl et al. 2004, 17, 179.

[144] Arnbom & Wagner-Trenkwitz 2005, 148, 153–54; Niederacher, Jun. 30, 2010.

[145] Anderl et al. 2004, 134–46, chapter 5.6. Gabriele Anderl's team thinks that the VUGESTA 2 started operating around 1940–41. See Anderl et al. 2004, 12 n. 3, 175.

[146] Ibid., 144.

[147] Ibid., 115, 172, 175.

[148] See the anonymous article "Auswanderung: Nachbeförderung von Umzugsgut durch Speditionsfirmen" (Emigration: subsequent transport of house-hold effects by moving companies), *Jüdi-*

The Austrian situation gave me a first inkling of how things likely proceeded in the Protectorate. An article published in the Prague edition of the *Jüdisches Nachrichtenblatt* (Jewish news journal), clearly shows that, as early as August 1939, the National Socialists instructed moving companies on the procedures to be followed when dealing with the so-called Jewish "Umzugsgut".[148] In addition, there was the already mentioned ten-page-long declaration of assets (*Vermögenserklärung*), which needed to be completed by Jewish people in the Central Office for Jewish Emigration,[149] and also in the Radio Mart at the exhibition hall in Prague. Point VII of the main "Aktiven" section, the counterpart to the "Passiven" or debts section, asked if any belongings were kept in others' custody: "Are your belongings in the care of others?" If answered in the affirmative, their name, race and address had to be provided.[150] But especially point VI, "Art Objects" (*Kunstgegenstände*), seemed to point to storage rooms where valuables – Persian carpets, porcelain, paintings, etc. – may have been stored. The form added: "Custody receipts must be enclosed". But, all in all, no specific reference to a storage room or moving company can be found on the form.[151] In this case, too, the impression is that the German occupier was mainly after valuable objects and not the regular furnishings that may have been stored in a storage room. And yet, section IV of the form, "Furnishings and household effects" (*Wohnungseinrichtung und Hausrat*), asked Jewish people to record in minute detail both the valuable objects and more common items they had left behind.[152]

ARCHIVAL FONDS ON BRNO STORAGE ROOMS

In the Protectorate itself, there was close cooperation between the National Socialists and moving and storage companies. A letter from the owner of one moving firm in Brno says that they had to inform the Gestapo if their companies had any Jewish storage rooms.[153] Yet it took me a long time to uncover any relevant archival sources for the Protectorate. In April 1945, many of the index cards (*Karteikarten*) used by the JKG (known as the Jewish Council of Elders [Altestenrat der Juden] starting in February 1943) and by the administration of the Central Office for Jewish Emigration (renamed the Central Office for the Solution of the Jewish Question in Bohemia and Moravia [Zentralamt für die Regelung der Judenfrage in Böhmen und Mähren] in August 1942) were deliberately destroyed.[154] Presumably, the questionnaires that

sches Nachrichtenblatt [Prague edition], Jg. 1, n° 3, Dec. 8, 1939, 2. For further instructions about and definitions of "Umzugsgut", see also the anonymous article "Auswanderung: Umzugsgut" (Emigration: household effects), *Jüdisches Nachrichtenblatt* [Prague edition], Jg. 1, n° 6, Dec. 29, 1939, 2.

[149] See the anonymous article "Stempel und Gebühren beim Einreichen der Mappe" (Stamps and fees when submitting the folder), *Jüdisches Nachrichtenblatt* [Prague edition], Jg. 1, n° 4, Dec. 15, 1939, 2.

[150] A digital copy of the "Umzugsgutverzeichnis" form can be found in the "Formuláře dokladů k tzv. vystěhovaleckým mapám" section at http://collections.jewishmuseum.cz/index.php/Detail/Object/Show/object_id/173556 (accessed Jan. 26, 2017): "VII. Sind Ihnen gehörige Sachen bei Anderen in Verwahrung ? Name, Rasse und Anschrift des Verwahrers und genaue Beschreibung und Bewertung der Sachen sind anzuführen".

[151] "Depotscheine sind beizufügen", Point VIII ("sonstiges Vermögen", other assets) could also be linked to the rental of storage facilities.

[152] "1. Möbel und Einrichtungsgegenstände [to be described room by room], 2. Gemälde, Kunst, Antiquitäten, Schmuck, Goldwaren, Juwelen, 3. Tafelgeschirr, Bestecke, Kristall, 4. Wäsche, 5. Kleidungsstücke, 6. Sonstiges" (1. furniture and furnishings [to be described room by room]; 2. paintings, art, antiques, jewelry, goldware, jewels; 3. tableware, cutlery, crystal; 4. Linen; 5. Clothing; 6. miscellaneous).

[153] MZA, Brno, fonds G 427, Německá správa zabaveného majetku Brno (1939–1944), letter (dated Mar. 23, 1943) from Walter Prochaska to Gestapo Brno, kart. n° 10, folio n° unknown: "In meinen Lagerräumen ist eine stattliche Menge von Einrichtungsgegenständen jüdischer Herkunft, welche Ordnungsgemäss gelagert und gemeldet sind, untergebracht" (In my storage rooms there are considerable amounts of furnishings of Jewish origin, which are properly stored and declared).

[154] Hájková 2000, 343. The forty "Holocaust-related" archives in the NA, Praha, mentioned in the EHRI database, do not record any archival fonds where this information could be found. See https://

people had to complete prior to their deportation, and the administrative paperwork regarding their expropriation afterwards, shared the same fate.

In Brno there was a Protectorate counterpart of the Viennese VUGESTA 2, the Brno (Brünn) and Ostrava (Ostrau) auxiliary branch (*Zweigstelle*) of the Prague-based Treuhand- und Revisionsgesellschaft m.b.H. (Trust and Auditing Association), in charge of expropriations,[155] whose offices were located at 4 Beethovenstrasse (Beethovenova) in Brno.[156]

While no administrative papers of the Prague Treuhandstelle (for which Gustav Fein worked) have survived, a very tiny part of this organization's archives in Brno were not destroyed, giving us a glimpse into the liquidation of the storage rooms in the years after their Jewish renters had been deported.[157] Essentially, the archival fonds consists mostly of the administrative paperwork from a vast storage place in

portal.ehri-project.eu/institutions?country=cz (accessed Aug. 26, 2020).

155 MZA, Brno, fonds G 427, Německá správa zabaveného majetku Brno (1939–1944). In German, "m.b.H." stands for *Gesellschaft mit beschränkter Haftung* (limited liability company).

156 *Adressbuch der Landeshauptstadt Brünn 1942* 1943, 111.

157 It is not known why this small portion (though still amounting to 11.5 linear meters of archives) was not destroyed. Did someone (maybe ordered to destroy the archival lot?) intentionally safeguard a small part of this archival fonds as a sample of testimony? After a more close study of some parts of this archival fonds, it would seem that a large part of the remaining archives relates to the expropriation of the more prosperous Brno Jewish families. My search for archival traces of the liquidation of Jewish storage rooms in Brno by the National Socialists was long and bumpy. In a 1944 issue of the Moravian and Bohemian moving companies' branch industry magazine, I read that in the case of cities within the Protectorate (excepting Prague), the local *Bezirkshauptmann* (district chief) was responsible for the liquidation of these storage rooms. See *Anzeiger der Verkehrsgruppe Spedition und Lagerei im Zentralverband des Verkehrs für Böhmen und Mähren = Véstník dopravni skupiny zasilatelství a skladovaní v Ústředním svazu dopravy pro Čechy a Moravu*, Jg. 4, n° 7, Apr. 1, 1944, 2: "Die Verwertung der bei Spediteuren eingelagerten Fahrnisse [the German term for "movables"] von Juden, deren Vermögen vom Auswanderungsfonds abgewickelt wird, erfolgt durch die örtlich zuständigen geschäftsführenden Bezirkshauptmänner. Nur im Stadtgebiet von Groß-Prag wird die Verwertung von dem Zentralamt für die Regelung der Judenfrage in Böhmen und Mähren selbst durchgeführt" (The valuation of Jews' movable property kept in storage companies, whose assets are administered by the Auswanderungsfonds (Emigration Fund), is conducted by locally responsible and managing district chiefs. Only in the municipality of Greater Prague is the liquidation conducted by the Central Office for the Solution of the Jewish Question in Bohemia and Moravia itself). No information on this topic was to be found in the archives of the Bezirkshauptmanschaft Brünn-Land. See email (dated Jun. 15, 2018) from Ivo Durec (Státní okresní archiv Brno-venkov, Rajhrad) to the author. Mr. Durec examined the inventory list of the fonds A-1, Okresní úřad Brno-venkov (Bezirkshauptmanschaft Brünn-Land, District office Brno-venkov 1850-1945), and found no traces of the liquidation of these storage rooms. During the war years, the Bezirkshauptmanschaft Brünn-Land (Brno-Country District Authority) was located at 7 Waisenhausgasse (Sirotčí) and was led by a W. Schmälzlein. See *Adressbuch der Landeshauptstadt Brünn* 1942, 8. In addition, the archival fonds B 254, Oberlandrát Brno, 1939-1945, in the MZA, Brno, which survived the war years only very partially, contains no traces of these operations, to judge from the online inventory. See http://www.mza.cz/oberlandrat-brno-1939-1945-okresni-hejtman-brno-sprava-z-risskeho-prikazu (accessed Jul. 16, 2018). It was then that I finally discovered that the MZA, Brno, also contained the archival fonds G 427, Německá správa zabaveného majetku Brno (1939–1944). This turned out to be the fragmentary archival fonds of the Brno and Ostrava branch of the Treuhand- und Revisionsgesellschaft (Trust and Auditing Association). In an email conversation about this archival fonds with Michaela Růžičková (MZA, Brno), in November–December 2019, I slowly started to realize that it might contain something on the liquidation of the Jewish storage rooms in Brno. It must be said that the very poor and confusing description of the title of this archival fonds, despite being created by a German organization (in Czech language only!), is astonishing and provided no assistance in finding this archival fonds. The least that one could expect is that the German name of the organizational archive creator be added to the archival description, in parentheses if necessary. EHRI, the Holocaust research website, also failed to describe this archival fonds adequately. G 427, the MZA Brno archival code of the archival fonds, for example, is not even mentioned in the description; however, EHRI *does* mention the archive creator, the Treuhand- und Revisionsgesellschaft. See https://portal.ehri-project.eu/units/cz-002230-collection_surv_mza_brno_898 (accessed Aug. 26, 2020).

158 The building at 10 Zeile (Cejl) is still standing. Satellite images of the premises behind the street-facing building reveal that the site in the rear is indeed quite vast and also very long (stretching all the way to the railroad tracks). Even today, the site has many warehouses. The extensive storage facil-

Brno, set up by the Germans, located at 10 Zeile (Cejl), where Jewish belongings from storage rooms across Moravia ultimately ended up.[158] This storage place also housed the furnishings from the apartments of Jewish people who had been deported from Brno. This building is one of the most important in the history of Jewish Brno, yet totally unrecognized [ill. 9].[159] In what follows, we will refer several times to this unique and largely unknown archival fonds.

THE HISTORY OF THE LEOPOLD FLEISCHER COMPANY

When trying to determine where Karl Fein might have rented a storage room to keep his belongings, the first and best candidate that came to mind was of course the Leopold Fleischer moving company that, as we know, was owned and operated by Willi Bondi's family. Leopold Fleischer was the husband of Willi Bondi's sister Elisabeth. We have proposed that, in April 1934, it was most probably this company that transported some of the Institute materials bought back from Germany, from Brno to Paris. Leopold Fleischer was also the one who lent Karl Giese money when he was in dire straits after Hirschfeld's death in 1935. Giese and Fein were both good friends with Willi Bondi. In 1933 or 1935, Willi Bondi started to work for his family's moving company.[160]

The "Leopold Fleischer" company was founded in 1919 by Leopold Fleischer himself. Because of the poor economic conditions in the early 1930s, Fleischer eventually left the company he founded, becoming the second partner in another, much bigger moving company in Brno, Gerstmann & Lindner.[161] In 1933, Leopold Fleischer transferred the management of his company to his brother Bruno Fleischer

ities would have been necessary to store the many Jewish furnishings arriving from moving company storage rooms across Moravia.

[159] The building is not even mentioned in Klenovský 2002 or Brummer & Konečný 2013, for example. A detailed view of the organization of the storage space can be found in MZA, Brno, fonds G 427, Německá správa zabaveného majetku Brno, kart. n° 2, Protokoll (dated Jun. 19, 1943), f. 5-7. This fonds also records that a factory belonging to Weinberger was used for additional storage. Presumably this was the factory that belonged to Hans Weinberger (1904–1985), located at 8 Zeile (Cejl). The premises at 10 Zeile (Cejl) belonged to Alfred Weinberger (1872–1946?), who was not related to Hans Weinberger. Alfred Weinberger had inherited this textile factory from his father, Adolf Weinberger. See Ryšková & Mertová 2014, 230, 233, 277. See also MZA, Brno, fonds G 427, Německá správa zabaveného majetku Brno, kart. n° 10, f. 473. Cf. Klenovský 2002, 72, 75. Alfred Weinberger and his wife Valery (née Ende, 1892–?) first fled to London, then to Brazil, later going to New York. The Weinbergers appeared on the German occupiers' priority expropriation list, as attested by many documents in MZA, Brno, fonds G 427, Německá správa zabaveného majetku Brno.

[160] Previously, Willi Bondi had worked as a secretary in the law office of his brother-in-law, Bernhard Wolfenstein (1887–1942), the (ex-)husband of Willi Bondi's sister Hermine. See the handwritten note by Judy King (dated Aug. 25, 2001), personal archives Peter Barber (London). It was presumably in 1939, when all Jewish law offices were liquidated, that Willi started to work for the moving company managed by his sister, Julia Fleischer. Yet, according to Willi Bondi himself, he started working for the moving firm in 1933. His brother-in-law, Bruno Fleischer, claimed Willi Bondi started to work for the company around 1935. See MZA, Brno, fonds D 25, Celní pátrací služebna, pobočka Brno, Julia Fleischer, Brünn, Adlergasse 34, kart. n° 51, sign. E 535/39, f. 27, 29.

[161] *Adreßbuch von Groß-Brünn* 1934, 693. The Gerstmann & Lindner company, founded in 1869, was led by Samuel Gerstmann (1842-1919) until his death in 1919. His son, the lawyer Hugo Gerstmann (1874–1931) took over the company, but died twelve years later, in May 1931. (The Bayerische Staatsbibliothek has two letters from Hugo Gerstmann to Thomas Mann from the year 1922.) Towards the end of 1931, Leopold Fleischer signed an agreement with Hugo Gerstmann's widow, Frieda Popper, to jointly lead the company. In 1932, Frieda Gerstmann married the paper industrialist Alfred Friedmann, later fleeing with her husband and son Herbert (1919–2006) to London at the end of March 1939. After the war, she made an attempt to regain the firm, which in June 1941 had been sold to the Berlin-born Erich Bogdan (1906–?). See MZA, Brno, fonds C 11, Krajský soud civilní Brno, firemní agenda, Bogdan a syn, mezinárodní zasilatelství, Brno (dř. Gerstmann a Lindner), zasilatelství, Brno, 1871-1942), kart. n° 33, sign. A III 162; and NA, fonds n° 375, Arizační spisy, kart. n° 266; and kart. n° 267, file n° 1913, Gerstmann & Lindner Brno. See also MZA, Brno, fonds D 25, Celní pátrací služebna, pobočka Brno, Leopold Fleischer, Gesellschafter der Fa. Gerstmann u. Lindner, Brünn, V Mezirce 4/10, ev. 10/4, kart. n° 34, sign. E 45/39.

(1888–1939).[162] When Bruno Fleischer died, in July 1939, his wife, Julia Fleischer, better known as Ully, Willi Bondi's sister, became the new head of the company.[163] Willi Bondi worked for the Leopold Fleischer company until his arrest by the Gestapo, on March 15, 1941, exactly two years after the Germans invaded Czechoslovakia.

Because we are examining the possible reasons that Fein may have had for turning to the Bondi and Fleischer families' company specifically for his storage needs, I think it important to recall a fact that we have already noted: Julia Fleischer was an at least partly closeted lesbian or bisexual woman who was having an affair with Kamila Gregor in March 1941, when the Gestapo raided the gathering of mainly gay men that took place at her home. This could mean that, as well as Willi Bondi, Julia Fleischer may have taken an interest in the safe storage of the Institute and Hirschfeld materials. As the head of the moving firm, Fleischer may have made it clear to Karl Fein that she wanted to help him wherever she could. The very least that one can say is that Julia Fleischer, and possibly also her lover Kamila Gregor, were most likely well aware of Hirschfeld's pioneering work for LGBT minorities. Certainly, Julia Fleischer was helping her brother's two gay friends, Wilhelm Sponer and Franz Helmuth Holdau, by keeping their correspondence, revealing their homosexual activities, at her home.[164]

Starting in January 1940, several other Brno moving companies started to show an interest in the Leopold Fleischer company, hoping that it would be quickly Aryanized, enabling them to buy it at a low price.[165] However, it was in the summer of 1940 – quite late when compared to other Aryanizations – that a Catholic trustee (*Treuhänder*) named Walter Prochaska (1882–?), resident at 33 Kröna (Křenová), was appointed.[166] Yet, despite Prochaska's trusteeship, Julia Fleischer continued to run the company. Several clues point to this. Firstly, Ully Fleischer told Peter Barber that this was the case when he visited her in Brno in the 1970s.[167] Secondly, a picture survives, taken in the company offices, showing Ully Fleischer with her arm on the shoulder of

[162] MZA, Brno, fonds C 11, Krajský soud civilní Brno, firemní agenda, Rudolf Siegmund, zasilatelství a komisionářství, Brno (dř. Leopold Fleischer, zasilatelství a komisionářství, Brno, 1920-1942), 1920-1955, kart. n° 68, sign. A VI 121.

[163] His new position with the Gerstmann & Lindner firm enabled Leopold Fleischer to procure extra business for the family firm. See NA, Praha, fonds n° 375, Arizačni spisy, anonymous report of the Leopold Fleischer company, dated Jan. 8, 1940, kart. n° 205, sign. 1268, liquidation file Leopold Fleischer firm.

[164] MZA, Brno, fonds C 43, Německý zemský soud Brno (Deutsches Landgericht), Staatsanwaltschaft bei dem Landgericht Brünn, file Wilhelm Sponer & Helmuth Holdau, kart. n° 184, sign. 4 K Ls 24/41, f. 100.

[165] The very first company to show and interest in buying the Leopold Fleischer firm was the moving firm of Gerold Schwarz. See NA, fonds n° 375, Arizačni spisy, liquidation file firm Leopold Fleischer, letter (dated Jan. 2, 1940) from Reichsprotektor in Böhmen und Mähren to Oberlandrat Brünn, kart. n° 205, sign. 1268, not foliated.

[166] Walter Prochaska moved to 33 Kröna (Křenová) in 1938. He was married to Adele Kollmann (1882–?). Starting out as a *Zollassistent* (customs employee), he eventually became a moving firm businessman (*Spediteur, zasílatel*). Prochaska was also appointed by the Oberlandrat (Supreme District Council) as the trustee for two other Jewish moving companies in Brno, the first of these being the Franz Deutsch firm, a company that he eventually bought. See NA, Praha, fonds n° 375, Arizačni spisy, kart. n° 187, file n° 1076, F. Deutsch. He was also appointed trustee for the Jacques Pollak firm. See NA, Praha, fonds n° 375, Arizačni spisy, file n° 1705, kart. n° 249, firm Jacques Pollak, Internationale spedition. Finally, he also acted as the *Verwaltungstreuhänder* (managing trustee) in selling Gerstmann & Lindner. See NA, Praha, fonds n° 375, Arizačni spisy, kart. n° 266, file n° 1913, Gerstmann & Lindner, Brno.

[167] Email (dated Jan. 15, 2017) from Peter Barber to the author.

[168] As communicated to Peter Barber by his aunt Julia Fleischer. Three other men appear in the picture. The one on the far right is certainly Willi Bondi, which indicates that the picture was taken at some point between the summer of 1940 (when Prochaska was appointed as trustee) and March 15, 1941, the day of Willi Bondi's arrest by the Gestapo. The offices of the company were located at 34 Adlergasse (Orlí), two houses down from the main Brno police station. The corner building housing the company offices, which suffered heavy bombardment in 1944, no longer exists. See also chapter 14, p. 540, n. 234. (It has since been replaced by a new building.) This is also the 34 Orlí (Adlergasse) address to which Karl Giese referred (misspelling its name) in his handwritten last will.

– presumably – Walter Prochaska [ill. 10].[168] This seemingly friendly gesture seems to suggest that the office atmosphere was not necessarily one of complete enmity.

From Prochaska's correspondence with and reports for the Oberlandrat in Brno, we also learn that he was well aware that the Leopold Fleischer company thrived and relied on its Jewish clientele, all of whom knew Julia Fleischer or one of her employees personally.[169] The company also actively often advertised its services in the local *Jüdisches Nachrichtenblatt* under the "Mitteilungen der Israelitischen Kultusgemeinde Brünn" (Announcements of the Jewish Community in Brno) section.[170] Prochaska further assessed that the business could not function properly without Julia Fleischer. The situation was the same for several other Aryanized Jewish moving firms in Brno, bringing the trustees or the new owners into a catch-22 situation. On the one hand, they wanted to appropriate the Jewish firms but, on the other, they also realized that these firms depended on their Jewish customers and on the latter's relationship or acquaintance with the (initial) Jewish owner. There was the further paradox that Jewish customers' transactions with these moving firms ballooned due to emigration and forced displacement. Furthermore, complicating matters even more, the Oberlandrat wanted to remove the Jewish staff as quickly as possible from their positions in the Aryanized company.[171] Prochaska noticeably clearly procrastinated when letting go the company's four Jewish employees. Was it indeed impossible to find replacements for the Jewish employees, as Prochaska claimed in several of his monthly reports? It would rather appear that Prochaska tried to keep the Jewish employees in the company as long as possible. Two of them would continue to work for the company even several months after its sale.[172]

In an attempt to hold on to their company, the Bondi family tried, in the first half of 1941, to trick the German authorities by putting forward a gay German friend of Willi Bondi, Helmuth Holdau, as a prospective buyer of the Fleischer company,

[169] NA, Praha, fonds n° 375, Arizačni spisy, firm Leopold Fleischer, kart. n° 205, sign. 1268, not foliated, letter (Übernahmsbericht [*sic*]) (dated Oct. 9, 1940) from Walter Prochaska to Oberlandrat Brünn, 3.

[170] When consulting the Klementinum Kramerius database, I found no fewer then thirty-six mentions of "zasílatel Leopold Fleischer" (Leopold Fleischer moving company), which shows that they advertised in almost every issue of the *Jüdisches Nachrichtenblatt*. See, for example, *Jüdisches Nachrichtenblatt*, Jg. 2, n° 24, Jun. 14, 1940, 8. Its last advertisement appeared in *Jüdisches Nachrichtenblatt*, Jg. 3, n° 43, Oct. 24, 1941, 2. The short advertisement includes the mention: "Stěhování, naskladněné, bezplatná porada" (moving, storage, free consultation). It needs to be said that a few other (Aryanized) Jewish Brno storage and moving companies also advertised in this Jewish weekly (for example, Jacques Pollak's company and Schück & Skutezky), though not as frequently. Shortly before the death of Jacques Pollak (1850–1933), his company was taken over by his sons Otto and Ludwig Pollak. See MZA, Brno, fonds C 11, Krajský soud civilní Brno, firemní agenda, Jaques [*sic*] Pollak, Speditions- und Kommissionsgeschäft, Brünn, 1884–1944, kart. n° 105, sign. A X 118, f. 27-28. Jacques Pollak's wife Terese (1857 or 1856–1922) died in 1922. Husband and wife are buried in the Brno Jewish cemetery in parcel 25B, row 2, grave 15. Until 1934, the offices of Jacques Pollak's company were located at 34 Adlergasse (Orlí), the same building that housed the offices of the Leopold Fleischer moving company. The "Intercontinentale", another moving company, also had its offices in 34 Adlergasse (Orlí). See *Adreßbuch von Groß-Brünn* 1934, 649.

[171] This can be seen very clearly, to name just one example, in the Aryanization file for the Schück & Skutezky firm where the trustee Franz Schmeiser had to keep the Jewish manager Robert Kulka (1890–1942?) at his post. The company's business doubled in 1939 and 1940. Robert Kulka was fired on January 1, 1941. See NA, Praha, fonds n° 375, Arizačni spisy, kart. n° 420, sign. 2990, file Schück & Skutezky. Kulka, his wife Elsa Skutezky (1902–1942?) and their son Tomas (1934–1942?) were deported on December 5, 1941 on transport "K" from Brno to Terezín. They were further transferred on transport "Ax" to Sobibór on May 9, 1942. A memorial inscription, stating that they perished in the Holocaust, was added to the tomb of the father of Elsa Kulková (née Skutezky), Eduard Skutezky (1873–1937) in the Brno Jewish cemetery in parcel 28G, row 2, grave 5.

[172] Walter Prochaska's claim, in one of his monthly reports, that Julia Fleischer was only periodically allowed to visit the company office, seems to have been made to dispel the idea ... that the opposite was the case. See NA, Praha, fonds n° 375, Arizačni spisy, liquidation file Leopold Fleischer firm, letter (Übernahmsbericht [*sic*]) (dated Oct. 9, 1940) from Walter Prochaska to Oberlandrat Brünn, p. 3, kart. n° 205, sign. 1268, not foliated.

in part because he had been the co-owner (*Miteinhaber*) of another moving firm in Germany before the war.[173] This practice was not all that uncommon in the war years. In December 1941, before there was even talk of forced Aryanizations in the occupied Netherlands, Otto Frank (1889–1980), the father of the now world-famous Anne Frank (1929–1945), managed to transfer the assets of Opekta, his Amsterdam pectin and spice company, to some of his most trusted employees. In this way, Frank's company thus became Gies & Co. Miep Gies (1909–2010), along with several other of Otto Frank's employees, were also the people who actively helped hide the Frank family in the famous annex (*het achterhuis*) behind Frank's company building on Prinsengracht. However, the German occupiers in Brno quickly discovered that Helmuth Holdau, who served in the Wehrmacht during the war years, was a gay man who had had sex with the German national Wilhelm Sponer. This immediately excluded Holdau as a possible buyer.[174]

Despite the fact that several other Brno moving companies were interested in acquiring the Leopold Fleischer company, the latter was eventually sold to the Sudeten-German Rudolf Siegmund (1898–?) on September 30, 1941 [ill. 11].[175] Like Walter Prochaska, Rudolf Siegmund was also active as a trustee in the Aryanization of another Jewish moving firm.[176] He also bought the moving company belonging to Philipp Frischauer (1872–1942?).[177] In August 1939, Siegmund also let the German authorities know that he intended to buy Gerstmann & Lindner (for whom Leopold Fleischer worked); however, the company was eventually sold to someone else.[178] Siegmund was in contact with Leopold Fleischer for twelve weeks, trying to arrange the sale of the company to him through the younger Max Pokorný, the lawyer.[179] We

[173] See Franz Helmuth Holdau's testimony (dated Mar. 25, 1941) in MZA, Brno, fonds C 43, Německý zemský soud Brno (Deutsches Landgericht), Staatsanwaltschaft bei dem Landgericht Brünn, file Wilhelm Sponer & Helmuth Holdau, kart. n° 184, sign. 4 K Ls 24/41, f. 102b, 103, 117.

[174] NA, Praha, fonds n° 375, Arizačni spisy, liquidation file Leopold Fleischer firm, letter (dated May 20, 1941) from an Oberlandrat employee to Fr. Schindler, Kreisleiter NSDAP Brünn, kart. n° 205, sign. 1268, not foliated. To be precise, Franz Helmuth Holdau, born in Elberfeld (Wiesbaden), was a *Reichsdeutsch* (German citizen) while Wilhelm Sponer was a *deutscher Staatsangehöriger* (German national). See MZA, Brno, fonds C 43, Německý zemský soud Brno (Deutsches Landgericht), Staatsanwaltschaft bei dem Landgericht Brünn, file Wilhelm Sponer & Helmuth Holdau, kart. n° 184, sign. 4 K Ls 24/41, f. 121. Holdau and Sponer both knew Willi Bondi. On July 22, 1941, they were tried and convicted by the *Erste Strafkammer* (first trial chamber) of the German District Court for homosexual offences. See MZA, Brno, fonds C 43, Německý zemský soud Brno (Deutsches Landgericht), Staatsanwaltschaft bei dem Landgericht Brünn, file Wilhelm Sponer & Helmuth Holdau, kart. n° 184, sign. 4 K Ls 24/41, f. 130-165. According to Willi Bondi's living relatives, one of the young men was then sent to the Russian front. See the undated handwritten note "Helga on Willi" in family archive Peter Barber. That this was Holdau seems to be confirmed by a note (dated Oct. 2, 1941) in MZA, Brno, fonds C 43, Německý zemský soud Brno (Deutsches Landgericht), Staatsanwaltschaft bei dem Landgericht Brünn, file Wilhelm Sponer & Helmuth Holdau, kart. n° 184, sign. 4 K Ls 24/41, f. 173.

[175] Rudolf Siegmund was born in Reichenberg (Liberec), an important city in the history of the Sudeten-German cause. For some time, he served with the Wehrmacht. See his resident registration card in AMB, Brno, fonds Z 1. He was married to Anna Spaček (1903–?), with whom he had three children: Edeltraute (1923–), Kurt (1930–) and Eva (1944–). Rudolf Siegmund's father, Adolf Siegmund (1871–1910), also born in Reichenberg, owned another moving firm in Brno. Rudolf Siegmund was the second businessman, after Gerold Schwarz, to show an interest in buying the Leopold Fleischer company. See NA, Praha, fonds n° 375, Arizačni spisy, liquidation file firm Leopold Fleischer, letter (dated Jan. 10, 1940) from Rudolf Siegmund to Oberlandrat Brünn, kart. n° 205, sign. 1268, not foliated.

[176] He was appointed as the trustee for the firm Eger & Co. See NA, Praha, fonds n° 375, Arizačni spisy, kart. n° 214, sign. 1348, file Eger & C°.

[177] In March 1942, Rudolf Siegmund also started living in Philipp Frischauer's house at 11 Lösselgasse (Lösselová) (also known as Töpfergasse). See NA, Praha, fonds n° 375, Arizačni spisy, kart. n° 209, file n° 1299, file Philipp Frischauer, and *Adreßbuch von Groß-Brünn* 1934, 197, 626, 649. According to the *Adreßbuch von Groß-Brünn*, the Lösselgasse (Lösselová) house was owned by Frida Frischauer (1882–1942?), Philipp Frischauer's sister (*Adreßbuch von Groß-Brünn* 1934, 754). On Rudolf Siegmund's resident registration card in the AMB, Brno, fonds Z 1, one can see that the Zentralstelle für Jüdische Auswanderung (Central Office for Jewish Emigration) later became the owner of the house.

[178] The company was sold in June 1941 to Erich Bogdan (1906–?), the owner, along with his father Emil

have seen that Pokorný liquidated the law practice of Karl Fein's very first intern, Robert Herrmann. The same names keep showing up, partly indicating that Jewish traders preferred to work only with certain people from the German camp. Walter Prochaska acted as the managing trustee (*Verwaltungstreuhänder*) until the conclusion of the Gerstmann & Lindner sales deal. The lawyer Walter Süss settled the sales agreement in June 1941. Walter Süss was the lawyer to whom Karl Fein's aunt, Elise Brecher, turned in 1939, when trying to save her bookstore from being Aryanized.

I think this all shows that there was an attempt to settle unpleasant Aryanization matters with acquaintances or people one knew, people who were – covertly – trying to get the best out of an enforced business deal. As in the case of Franz Nawratil, we see here again that matters were not black and white but rather gray. I think that Rudolf Siegmund, and especially Walter Prochaska and the Fleischers were at the very least on speaking terms and possibly tried to settle unpleasant but unavoidable matters with people with whom they felt an affinity or at least got along. In this way the Fleischers hoped to mitigate the unwelcome consequences of the enforced sale of their business as much as possible.

Walter Prochaska and Rudolf Siegmund got along well in any case since, starting in 1942, their offices were on the same street, at 4 and 6 Neutorgasse (U Nové brány), respectively, just around the corner from where the offices of the Leopold Fleischer company used to be.[180] After he had officially bought the Leopold Fleischer company, Rudolf Siegmund made use of its assets but decided to run the firm under his own name.[181] He (and his company) remained in Brno until 1947; however, shortly afterwards, he fled to Germany where he lived in Neufürstenhütte Grosserlach (Baden-Württemberg).[182] The postwar Czechoslovak authorities wanted to prosecute Rudolf Siegmund for war crimes, but the case was dismissed because the accused

Bogdan, of a company having the same name in Berlin, Bogdan & Sohn. See NA, Praha, fonds n° 375, Arizačni spisy, kart. n° 266, file n° 1913 (vol. one) and kart. n° 267, file n° 1913 (vol. 2), Gerstmann & Lindner, Brno; and MZA, Brno, fonds C 11, Krajský soud civilní Brno, firemní agenda, Bogdan a syn, mezinárodní zasilatelství, Brno (dř. Gerstmann a Lindner), zasilatelství, Brno, 1871–1942, kart. n° 33, sign. A III 162.

179 NA, Praha, fonds n° 375, Arizačni spisy, kart. n° 266, file n° 1913, file Gerstmann & Lindner.

180 *Adressbuch der Landeshauptstadt Brünn 1942* 1943, 100; also according to several Aryanization files of Jewish moving firms that I consulted. The Franz Deutsch moving company purchased by Walter Prochaska was also at 4 Neutorgasse (U Nové brány). For this firm's Aryanization file, see NA, Praha, fonds n° 375, Arizačni spisy, kart. n° 188, sign. 1093, file Franz Deutsch. Franz Deutsch (1892–?) was deported on transport "Ad" from Brno to Terezín on March 23, 1942. He was liberated from Terezín. His wife was probably the engineer Hedvika Deutsch (1900–?), who also survived Terezín. Interestingly, the *Amtsstelle Brünn* (Brno office) of the Verkehrsgruppe Spedition und Lagerei im Zentralverband des Verkehrs für Böhmen und Mähren (Transport Group, Shipping and Storage in the Central Transport Association of Bohemia and Moravia) was located at 3 Neutorgasse (U Nové brány) in 1942, but moved to number 10 by 1943. See *Adressbuch der Landeshauptstadt Brünn 1942* 1943, 25; and, for the organization letterhead on a letter (dated May 12, 1943), see NA, Praha, fonds n° 375, Arizačni spisy, file B. Friess (Spediteur), Brno, kart. n° 206, sign. 1274, not foliated. In 1939, the management office of the B. Friess moving firm was located next door at 12 Neutorgasse (U Nové brány). See *Adresář Protektorátu Čechy a Morava pro průmysl, živnosti, obchod a zemědělství = Adressbuch des Protektorates Böhmen und Mähren für Industrie, Gewerbe, Handel und Landwirtschaft* 1939, II: 1406, 2257. Furthermore, 10 Neutorgasse (U Nové brány) also initially belonged to B. Friess. See NA, Praha, fonds n° 375, Arizačni spisy, liquidation file B. Friess (Spediteur), Brno, kart. n° 206, sign. 1274, f. 145. As we have seen, B. Friess' logistical company site was located at 66 Kröna (Křenová), situated right next to the Nebehosteny building and Jaroslav and Jindra Růžička's company.

181 The Leopold Fleischer company was dissolved in January 1942, its name changing to "Rudolf Siegmund" that same month. See MZA, Brno, fonds C 11, Krajský soud civilní Brno, firemní agenda, Rudolf Siegmund, zasilatelství a komisionářství, Brno (dř. Leopold Fleischer, zasilatelství a komisionářství, Brno, 1920-1942), 1920-1955, kart. n° 68, sign. A VI 121. The new company name appears in the "Spediteure" (hauliers) section, *Adressbuch der Landeshauptstadt Brünn 1942* 1943, 100.

182 MZA, Brno, fonds C 11, Krajský soud civilní Brno, firemní agenda, Rudolf Siegmund, zasilatelství a komisionářství, Brno (dř. Leopold Fleischer, zasilatelství a komisionářství, Brno, 1920-1942), 1920-1955, kart. n° 68, sign. A VI 121.

was no longer in the country.[183] Walter Prochaska was still living in Brno in December 1945, but was most likely forcibly deported to Germany in the beginning of June 1946.[184]

The year 1941 was a very difficult year for the Bondi and Fleischer family. Willi Bondi was the first member to fall victim to the Nazis. Willi Bondi was arrested in March 1941 and never returned home again. This was before the massive Jewish transports in the autumn of that year started. Willi was murdered in Auschwitz in August 1941. Earlier, on May 11, 1941, Gustav Bondi, the father of the three Bondi sisters and Willi Bondi, died of cancer,[185] likely increasing the pressure on Julia Fleischer when she signed the enforced sales contract handing over the family company to Rudolf Siegmund. But the bitterness must have become even deeper when Leopold Fleischer and his immediate family – who were living with Julia Fleischer – were deported six weeks later. On November 16, 1941, they were deported on the very first Jewish mass transport from Brno, transport "F", carrying exactly 1,000 people to Minsk.[186] This transport must have come as a real shock to the Bondi-Fleischer family and the Jewish community in Brno generally. So it was likely no coincidence that the last advertisement for the Leopold Fleischer company appeared in the October 1941 issue of the local *Jüdisches Nachrichtenblatt*. The family probably felt betrayed by the leaders of the Jewish community, since it was the Brno JKG who compiled, on the orders of the Germans, the lists of those to be deported.[187] But it also seems likely that the Germans had themselves composed a list of first-level undesirables.

DID KARL FEIN RENT A STORAGE ROOM FROM THE LEOPOLD FLEISCHER COMPANY?

The Leopold Fleischer Aryanization file contains four records of Karl Fein's changing debt to the company. A first debt of 1062.60 Czech crowns is from 1939, and the client transaction number (347) seems to suggest that it was for a service late that year.[188] Was it a bill for Karl Fein's move to Prague, in the autumn of 1939, or perhaps for moving his brother and mother's furnishings to Prague earlier that year? Most likely, Gustav Fein and his mother had a storage room in Prague. In at least two of Erich Messing's June 1939 letters, he refers to the handling and further disposition of the

[183] A note on this subject, by the *Staatsanwalt* (public prosecutor), can be found in MZA, Brno, fonds C 130, Veřejný žalobce u MLS Brno. See email (dated Mar. 8, 2017) from Jana Fasorová (MZA, Brno) to the author. In addition to the retribution tribunals operating under the so-called Velký retribuční dekret (Great retribution decree), the Czechoslovak state launched another wave of persecutions, where the national honor was at stake, operating under the so-called Malý retribuční dekret (Small retribution decree) of October 1945. There, people were judged by Mimořádný lidový soudy (Special People's Tribunals). The archival fonds of the penal commissions falling under the Okresní národní výbory (ONV, National District Committees) have not been processed and are not accessible to researchers. See email (dated Apr. 21, 2017) from Jana Dosoudilová (AMB, Brno) to the author. For more information on Czech postwar retribution justice, see Frommer 2005.

[184] Prochaska's last two Brno addresses in 1945 and 1946 were 7 Bratislavská (living with a certain Kudlmayer) and 15 Vranovská. See his resident registration cards in AMB, Brno, fonds Z 1. Curiously, his name and Rudolf Siegmund's both appear under "Zasilatelství" (hauliers) in *Adresář zemského hlavního města Brna* 1948, 123.

[185] Death notice published in *Jüdisches Nachrichtenblatt* 20, May 16, 1941, 10. After the war, Julia Fleischer said that Gustav Bondi died of grief over Willi Bondi's imprisonment. See Condell 2005, 220.

[186] The date of this transport is consistently given by www.holocaust.cz as November 26, 1941, probably in error. The likely correct date, November 16, is found in Kárný et al. 1995; and in NA, Praha, fonds n° 1077, Okupační vězeňské spisy, card index of those deported from the Protectorate to Terezín, index card for Leopold Fleischer. Interestingly, on Leopold Fleischer's index card, Łódź is crossed out as the destination city and replaced by Minsk.

[187] Filip, Břečka & Schildberger 2012, 92.

[188] In 1939, the highest number found in the list of creditors is 369. See NA, Praha, fonds n° 375, Arizační spisy, liquidation file firm Leopold Fleischer, kart. n° 205, sign. 1268, not foliated, list Schuldner 1939, n° 347.

[189] Forschungsinstitut Brenner-Archiv, Universität von Innsbruck, Innsbruck, Nachlass Herta Fein-Erich Messing, Kassette 153, letter (dated Jun. 1, 1939, 2) from Erich Messing to Rudolf Polatschek and

Feins' furniture if they managed to emigrate.[189] Most if not all of their furniture was presumably in storage since the Feins had no room for most of their furnishings in their Prague apartments. Several documents in the Leopold Fleischer Aryanization file reveal that the firm mainly handled "Jewish relocations or resettlements" (*jüdische Uebersiedlungen*) and also filled carriages with Jewish household belongings on trains to Prague.[190] So we do not really know if Karl Fein's outstanding bill was for transporting his belongings, or those of his mother and brother, or for the rent of a storage room in Brno, or for all of these.

At the end of 1939, this debt was reduced by half, to 531.05 Czech crowns.[191] But thereafter, the debt appears to have grown until December 1940, when Karl Fein owned 2,278.10 Czech crowns. On average, the debt increased by approximately 145 Czech crowns per month.[192] (Let us also recall that, starting in August 1940, when they were already in Prague, Karl, Gustav and Helene Fein had financial problems. They had to rely on their brother-in-law Erich Messing in Germany to make ends meet. So paying for storage must have been an issue.) It is tempting to think that this mounting debt was for the monthly rent of storage space; however, there is simply no hard evidence that Fein ever arranged for a storage room in the Leopold Fleischer company. Nine months later, in September 1941, the debt went down to 571.90 Czech crowns.[193] As is common with almost all company archives, the complete day-to-day administration of the Leopold Fleischer company was not preserved. Any hope of ever locating the Leopold Fleischer shipping log (*Speditionsjournal*) is likely in vain. So it is extremely unlikely that we will ever be able to ascertain whether Karl Fein had a storage room in this or another moving firm in Brno.

The archival fonds G 427 – German Administration of Seized Property Brno (Německá správa zabaveného majetku Brno) – in the MZA, Brno, contains a small number of alphabetically arranged personal files, with details of the liquidation of storage rooms rented by Jewish people, but Karl Fein's name is not present.[194] I was able to find in that archival fonds two files regarding the handling of the estate of Lipmann Brammer, an uncle of Karl Fein.[195] The same archival fonds also contains the file on Karl Fein's very first intern, the lawyer Robert Herrmann.[196] These exceptions only serve to demonstrate that most files in this archival fonds were not

letter (dated Jun. 2, 1939, 3–4, point 20, Möbel [furniture]) from Erich Messing to "Meine Lieben".

[190] Around July 1941, the Central Office for Jewish Emigration, *Verbindungsstelle Brünn* (Brno auxiliary office), stipulated that only three expedition companies in Brno would thereafter be allowed to carry out these "jüdische Uebersiedlungen". The Leopold Fleischer company was not among the three selected. This decision was successfully contested by the trustee Walter Prochaska, intervening through the Oberlandrat. See NA, Praha, fonds n° 375, Arizačni spisy, liquidation file firm Leopold Fleischer, letter (dated Jul. 4, 1941) from an Oberlandrat employee to the Central Office for Jewish Emigration, Brno auxiliary office; and letter (dated Jun. 17, 1941) from Walter Prochaska to the Oberlandrat, Arisierungsabteilung, kart. n° 205, sign. 1268, not foliated. The Central Office for Jewish Emigration, Brno auxiliary office was located in the Masaryk *Viertel* (quarter) at 11a Karl-Wawra-Gasse (Karla Wawry). See *Adressbuch der Landeshauptstadt Brünn* 1942, 6. This surprised me. This was the only mention I encountered in my research that such a subsidiary office existed in Brno. However, the *Adressbuch der Landeshauptstadt Brünn* records the "Auswanderungsfonds für Böhmen und Mähren, Verwaltungsstelle Brünn" (Emigration Fund for Bohemia and Moravia, Brno administrative office) at the same address, adding, next to number 11a, number 15 on the same street. Both houses were clearly built in the same style and are still physically adjacent.

[191] NA, Praha, fonds n° 375, Arizačni spisy, liquidation file Leopold Fleischer firm, kart. n° 205, sign. 1268, not foliated, Debitoren-Reserve (undated but likely end of 1939).

[192] Ibid., list Stand der Gläubiger per 31. Dezember 1940.

[193] Ibid., Aufstellung der Gläubiger per 30. September 1941, list of *Speditionsgläubiger* [opposed to another list of *Geldgläubiger*].

[194] MZA, Brno, fonds G 427, Německá správa zabaveného majetku Brno, kart. n° 11-17.

[195] The detailed files of Lipmann Brammer (spelled "Bramer"), his son Kurt Brammer, an intern in Karl Fein's law office, and wife (and mother) Irma Fein, are in MZA, Brno, fonds G 427, Německá správa zabaveného majetku Brno, kart. n° 11 and kart. n° 22.

[196] MZA, Brno, fonds G 427, Německá správa zabaveného majetku Brno, kart. n° 38.

saved for posterity. If Karl Fein ever had a storage room in Brno, it is in this archival fonds that we would find the details of its handling and liquidation. Besides details on the contents of the storage rooms and their value, these files also include paperwork related to the expropriation of individuals' financial property.

This archival fonds also makes it clear that, in Brno, the Nazis only started liquidating Jewish storage rooms and personal property in the summer of 1942 at the earliest, shortly after most Jewish people had been deported from the city. One also observes that the Gestapo kept a close watch on the liquidations, which means that they would certainly have noticed the Institute materials in Karl Fein's storage room – if, of course, we suppose that Fein kept them in one.[197] It is important to grasp this. In the following chapters, it will help us better understand the two main scenarios we present regarding what happened to the Institute materials. Yet this fragmentary archival fonds also reveals that the Germans were only interested in storage rooms containing items of great value. For example, in an October 1943 letter to Walter Prochaska, the Treuhand- und Revisionsgesellschaft in Brno stated: "In the case of the Jewish properties of Jaques [*sic*] Waldman [and three other names], there was no profit made, since they consisted of soiled and worn laundry, old paper, pictures of Jews, etc., and other equally worthless items".[198]

THE LEOPOLD FLEISCHER COMPANY'S STORAGE PREMISES

The Leopold Fleischer company premises at 38 (also 38a) Mühlgasse (Mlýnská), which housed its logistical materials (trucks, carts and horses), were also where customers' goods were stored. The company had rented this site since at least 1919.[199] There is one archival indication that the Leopold Fleischer company stored goods for individuals (*Einlagerungen*).[200] As Arnold Hindls' memoir makes clear, there was a lot of theft in these Brno storage places during the war. Thieves were well aware that these storage places were crammed with mainly Jewish belongings. Walter Prochaska's addition of an extra cost for security staff, in October 1940, suggests that the company's Mühlgasse (Mlýnská) premises likely included storage facilities.[201] Yet the extent of Leopold Fleischer's storage capacity remains questionable due to the limited space of the plot at 38 Mühlgasse (Mlýnská).[202] At present, the site where the company was

[197] Ibid., kart. n° 10, letter (dated Feb. 5, 1943) from Gestapo Brno to Hauptzollamt Brünn, f. 523.

[198] Ibid., letter (dated Oct. 1, 1943) from Treuhand- und Revisionsgesellschaft Brünn to Walter Prochaska, f. 286: "Bei den Judenmassen Jaques [*sic*] Waldman [and three other names] wurde überhaupt kein Verkaufserlos erzielt, nachdem es sich um schmutzige und zerrissene Wächse, Altpapier, Judenbilder u.ä. [und ähnliche] wertlose Fahrnisse handelte". The man in question here was the jurist Jacques Waldmann (1877–1943?). He was deported on transport "Ae" on March 29, 1942, from Brno to Terezín and further transferred on December 15, 1943, on transport "Dr" to Auschwitz-Birkenau.

[199] An advertisement for Leopold Fleischer says that the *stáje* (stables) were located at 38a Mühlgasse. See *Lidové noviny*, Jul. 6, 1919, 8. Possibly the 38a house number belonged to the two buildings behind the street-facing building, which was presumably number 38. The location is also mentioned in the Aryanization file of the Leopold Fleischer company in NA, Praha, fonds n° 375, Arizačni spisy, and in MZA, Brno, fonds C 11, Krajský soud civilní Brno, firemní agenda, Rudolf Siegmund, zasilatelství a komisionářství, Brno (dř. Leopold Fleischer, zasilatelství a komisionářství, Brno, 1920-1942), 1920-1955, kart. n° 68, sign. A VI 121.

[200] One letter from the Treuhand- und Revisionsgesellschaft to Walter Prochaska, from October 1943, reveals that Prochaska had a Jewish client who stored items in his company. See MZA, Brno, fonds G 427, Německá správa zabaveného majetku Brno, letter (dated Oct. 1, 1943) from Treuhand- und Revisionsgesellschaft Brünn to Walter Prochaska, kart. n° 10, f. 286. It is necessary to add that, in addition to the Leopold Fleischer moving company, Walter Prochaska also bought the F. Deutsch firm. In 1942, he joined the two companies under his own name. The client mentioned in the letter could therefore have been a client of F. Deutsch.

[201] NA, Praha, fonds n° 375, Arizačni spisy, liquidation file Leopold Fleischer firm, report on the Leopold Fleischer firm made by the Brno accountant Ernst Hübner, p. 3, kart. n° 205, sign. 1268, not foliated: "6/ Bewachung: ab 15/10.1940 gegen monatliche Vergütung von K [Czech crowns] 180,- auf unbestimmte Zeit bei der Brünner Wach- und Schliess-Anstalt in Brünn./Lager Mühlgasse [Mlýnská] 38a/[.] Letztere Versicherung wurde seitens des Treuhänders neu eingeführt" (6/ Security: from 15/10/1940 against

located still has two rather small buildings, but several old maps show two buildings near the street that no longer exist [ill. 12]. The latter were bombed by the US air force on November 11, 1944, and torn down afterwards. This means that, in the best-case scenario, if Karl Fein's possible storage room in the Fleischer company had not been confiscated as Jewish property, or had been simply overlooked, it would nevertheless have been completely destroyed during the bombardment [ill. 13].[203]

THE LEOPOLD FLEISCHER COMPANY UNDER GERMAN SCRUTINY

Assuming that Fein did indeed rent storage space from the Leopold Fleischer company, it is also possible that, at a certain point, Fein stopped renting. One such possible moment could have been March 1941, when Willi Bondi, along with some of his immediate family and gay friends, was arrested. But even earlier, in the beginning of 1940, Willi Bondi and his immediate family had already clashed with the Foreign Exchange Protection Commando (Devisenschutzkommando). Willi Bondi was denounced by a Prague woman, Josefa Kučerová, for helping a Jewish friend (Franz Guempl) smuggle foreign currency (*Devizen*) and golden and silver valuables (*Schmuck*) out of the country through the Leopold Fleischer export company. After a few inquiries and hearings, Willi Bondi was convicted of smuggling. He was jailed in the Brno police prison from the end of January until mid-March 1940. He was released after the payment of an immense fine of 12,000 Czech crowns, ten percent of which was given to Kučerová as a reward.[204] It may well have been then that Fein possibly saw that very little was certain any longer where the safe storage of one's belongings was concerned. Especially during Willi Bondi's first imprisonment, Fein may have feared that Bondi could be questioned by the Germans and talk under pressure about things he should not. We have also seen that a female servant of the Fleischer family stated

monthly remuneration of K [Czech crowns] 180.- for an indefinite period by the Brno guard and lock company in Brno./Storage premises 38a Mühlgasse [Mlýnská]/[.] The latter insurance was newly introduced on the part of the trustee). In Vienna as well, storage places were overstuffed and theft was common. See Anderl et al. 2004, 174, 187.

[202] Documents contained in its Aryanization file make it clear that the land and building were rented by the Leopold Fleischer company. Later, the Oberlandrat in Brno advised the company's new owner, Rudolf Siegmund, to purchase the land plot. See NA, Praha, fonds n° 375, Arizačni spisy, liquidation file Leopold Fleischer firm, letter (dated Nov. 28, 1941) from an unknown employee of the Oberlandrat Brno to Rudolf Siegmund, kart. n° 205, sign. 1268, not foliated. At present, the company's site still has two small buildings. A 1907 map shows two buildings near the street that no longer exist. See the Katastrální plán Brna z roku 1906 map at http://www.vilemwalter.cz/mapy/ (accessed Aug. 26, 2020). From examining a 1929 cadastral map in the collection of the MZA, Brno (sign. MOR248719290), I was able to conclude that the plot on which the Leopold Fleischer company kept its logistical assets was not very extensive. The whole of the rear of the plot borders a large building at 19 Tschechnergasse (Čechyňská), known before the war as the Pestalozzi Knabenbürgerschule. See *Adreßbuch von Groß-Brünn* 1934, 93. Today this building houses the Brno Archeologický ústav (Institute of Archaeology) and the Brno branch of the Akademie věd ČR (Czech Academy of Sciences). To the right of 38 Mühlgasse (Mlýnská) (looking at the site from the street side), there was a house (at 15 Tschechnergasse (Čechyňská)), similar in size to the house still standing at 17 Tschechnergasse (Čechyňská). That house can be seen on the 1929 cadastral map, located at the corner of Mühlgasse (Mlýnská) and Tschechnergasse (Čechyňská). The existence of this corner house, before the war, was also confirmed to me by Horst Morawek. See his email (dated Jan. 27, 2017) to the author. After the war, the corner was a barren space; however, a few years ago, a new residential building was raised on the corner site. No resident for 38 Mühlgasse (Mlýnská) is given in *Adreßbuch von Groß-Brünn* 1934, 776.

[203] On the "Bombardování Brna" database, one can indeed see that the corner building at 15 Tschechnergasse (Čechyňská) and the street-facing 38 Mühlgasse (Mlýnská) were bombed during the war. See the photos of 15 Čechyňská at https://gis.brno.cz/ags/bomby/ (accessed Aug. 27, 2020). The photo is also reproduced here, see illustration n° 13 in this chapter. It is clear that these bombs were meant to strike the nearby Brno *hlavní nádraží* (central railway station) and its infrastructure. For an extensive photographic overview of the November 1944 bombings of Brno, see Filip & Schildberger 2013, 56–165.

[204] The woman who handed the valuables over to Willi Bondi in Brno testified about the matter to the Foreign Exchange Protection Commando in Prague in the beginning of January 1940. See MZA, Brno, fonds D 25, Celní pátrací služebna, pobočka Brno,

in March 1941 that Fein came to Brno from Prague approximately twice a year. Likely, Fein did not return to Brno after November 1940, when traveling was forbidden for Jewish citizens. That Fein's debt to the Leopold Fleischer company diminished after December 1940 could indicate that he stopped renting storage space from them after that date.

Although the storage rooms leases were unaffected by the company changing owners in the Aryanization proceedings, the forced sale of the Leopold Fleischer company, in September 1941, may have been another moment when Fein deemed it more prudent to transfer his stored belongings somewhere else. He was deported from Prague the next month. But the opposite may have been the case, and the Fleischers may have asked Fein to remove his belongings because the forced sale meant they no longer had any say. The two Foreign Exchange Protection Commando files for Leopold and Julia Fleischer also make it clear that their two companies, Gerstmann & Lindner and Leopold Fleischer, were under intense scrutiny from the Germans early on. The smallest irregularity was thoroughly investigated. The files show that Leopold and Julia Fleischer tried to adhere to all the strict export regulations issued by the Germans.[205] Willi Bondi's two arrests, and his death in Auschwitz, in the summer of 1941, may have influenced them not to take any more risks by storing the Institute materials in their companies. We may assume that they knew the particular story behind the Institute materials. This is also why it seems unlikely to me that Fein would have turned to Gerstmann & Lindner to store his goods after possibly moving his belongings out of the Leopold Fleischer firm.[206]

PAYMENTS FOR A STORAGE ROOM

Circumstances compelled Jewish people to make an arrangement regarding these storage rooms. How could they continue to pay rent after they had been deported? People therefore paid some months in advance, a practice that was also common in Austria.[207] But people were away much longer than they could ever have imagined. There is an explicit reference to insufficient advance payment in the memoir of Charles Ticho, from Brno, whose family was driven out of their apartment: "Much of the furniture remained in the apartment and the rest was packed in 67 crates and was stored in a warehouse. Later, we learned that all the crates were seized by the authorities for nonpayment of storage fees. All our belongings were gone".[208] These payments that dropped off, sooner or later, were also a real problem for the storage companies, which noticed that many payments ceased after their Jewish clients were deported.[209] The storage and moving companies sometimes had difficulties obtaining payment from the Brno branch of the Treuhand- und Revisionsgesellschaft for these outstanding bills. This problem is recorded everywhere in the remaining archives of

1939-1945, kart. n° 98, sign. E117/40, file on Wilhelm Bondi.

[205] MZA, Brno, fonds D 25, Celní pátrací služebna, pobočka Brno, file Julia Fleischer Brünn, Adlergasse 34, kart. n° 51, sign. E 535/39; and MZA, Brno, fonds D 25, Celní pátrací služebna, pobočka Brno, Leopold Fleischer, Gesellschafter der Fa. Gerstmann u. Lindner, Brünn, V mezírce 4/10, ev. 10/4, kart. n° 34, sign. E 45/39.

[206] Leopold Fleischer continued to work for Gerstmann & Lindner until March 1940. See NA, Praha, fonds n° 375, Arizačni spisy, kart. n° 267, file n° 1913, Gerstmann & Lindner Brno, f. 6. The Aryanization file in the NA, Praha makes it clear that the company also offered *Einlagerungen* (storage) and had as many as six different storage locations in Brno. The one closest to the Leopold Fleischer storage premises on Mühlgasse (Mlýnská) was likely at 46 Offermanngasse (Offermannova). (At the start of the occupation, in March 1939, the street's name was Ponawkagasse [Na Ponávce]. In July 1939, it was changed to Offermanngasse [Offermannova].) The building was the property of Frieda Gerstmann. See *Adressbuch von Groß-Brünn* 1934, 783. It still stands today, but many buildings in the vicinity were bombed during the war and have disappeared. See NA, Praha, fonds n° 375, Arizačni spisy, kart. n° 267, file n° 1913, Gerstmann & Lindner, Brno, f. 3-4.

[207] Anderl et al. 2004, 118.

[208] Ticho 2001, "The flood", 9.

[209] As in Vienna, moving firms' business interests in the Protectorate were guarded by an imposed

the Brno branch of the Treuhand- und Revisionsgesellschaft. For example, there is an October 1943 letter from Walter Prochazska in which he requests payment for an unpaid bill of around 45,500 Czech crowns.[210] Once again, we can wonder whether and how Fein settled these matters for the longer term – supposing, of course, that he *continued* to rent a storage room in Brno.

ELISE BRECHER'S STORAGE ROOM

The archival fonds of the Brno branch of the Treuhand- und Revisionsgesellschaft contains several lists, arranged by moving firm, of Jewish storage rooms that had not yet been liquidated. In the Morava company list, I found the name of Elise Brecher, Karl Fein's aunt [ill. 14].[211] Dr. Leo Allerhand (1874–1942), who lived with Julia Fleischer in her apartment at 21 Ponawkagasse (Na Ponávce), also had a storage room at the Morava company.[212] I think it is interesting and likely telling to observe here that Elise Brecher and Leo Allerhand did not rent a storage place from the Leopold Fleischer company (led by Julia Fleischer) or the Gerstmann & Lindner company (where Leopold Fleischer was a manager).[213] The storage buildings of the Morava company were located at two different addresses in Brno. These two extensive land plots were adjacent to each other, forming a single large site with storage buildings.[214] Both are also very close to the Mühlgasse (Mlýnská) premises of the Leopold Fleischer firm (about 150–200 meters away).

I was surprised to learn that Elise Brecher still had a storage room shortly before she was deported. By that time, July 1943, one year after the Jewish mass transports from Brno had come to an end, it must have been known that the Germans were liquidating these storage rooms and selling their contents. In August 1942, the month after the last large Jewish transport, "Dg", left Brno, the Prague Property Office of the

berufsständischen Dachorganisation (professional umbrella organization). A branch of the Berlin-led Reichsverkehrsgruppe Spedition und Lagerei (Reich Carrier Group for Shipping and Storage), which moving companies were forced to join, also existed in the Protectorate. The Office of the Transport Group, Shipping and Storage (Amtstelle der Verkehrsgruppe Spedition und Lagerei, Uřadovna dopravní skupiny zasilatelství a skladováni) in Brno was located at 3 Pilgramgasse (Pilgramova). See *Adressbuch der Landeshauptstadt Brünn* 1942, 25. The Protectorate branch of the professional umbrella organization issued a monthly magazine, *Anzeiger der Verkehrsgruppe Spedition und Lagerei im Zentralverband des Verkehrs für Böhmen und Mähren = Věstník dopravni skupiny zasilatelství a skladovaní v Ústředním svazu dopravy pro Čechy a Moravu*, published from 1941 to 1945. Štemberk's work focuses on the broader professional interest group Ústrední svaz dopravy (1940–1948) (Central Transport Union), which extended well beyond shipping and storage (Štemberk 2007). Their archival fonds can be found in NA, Praha, fonds n° 1159, Ústřední svaz československé dopravy (ÚSČD); but I did not consult it. Similarly, Bestand R 4320, Reichsverkehrsgruppe Spedition und Lagerei, in the Bundesarchiv, Berlin-Lichterfelde, would not have given us any further help.

[210] MZA, Brno, fonds G 427, Německá správa zabaveného majetku Brno, letter (dated Oct. 19, 1943) from Walter Prochaska to Vermögensamt beim Reichsprotektor für Böhmen und Mähren, kart. n° 10, f. 285.

[211] MZA, Brno, fonds G 427, Německá správa zabaveného majetku Brno, Verzeichnis der Lagerlisten u.[nd] Rechnungen der eingelagerten jüdische Möbel und Effekten bei der Firma Morava, kart. n° 10, f. 571. Elisabeth Brecher's storage room was n° 559, and she had an outstanding debt of 227 Czech crowns. The undated list includes the names of approximately 140 Jewish storage room renters. During the war, the main office of the Morava company was located at 6 Basteigasse (Na hradbách). See *Adressbuch der Landeshauptstadt Brünn 1942* 1943, 99. See illustration n° 14.

[212] He rented storage unit n° 725. See MZA, Brno, fonds G 427, Německá správa zabaveného majetku Brno, Verzeichnis der Lagerlisten u.[nd] Rechnungen der eingelagerten jüdische Möbel und Effekten bei der Firma Morava, kart. n° 10, f. 572; and also MZA, Brno, fonds G 427, Německá správa zabaveného majetku Brno, kart. n° 11, folder Leo Allerhand, f. 56, 59-60.

[213] Leo Allerhand was deported from Brno to Terezín on transport "Ad" on March 23, 1942. Two weeks after arriving in Terezín, he died.

[214] NA, Praha, fonds n° 375, Arizačni spisy, kart. n° 242, file n° 1641, firm Morava, Brno. On the basis of the "Bombardování Brna" database, the building at 16 Cyrillsgasse (Cyrilská) was completely destroyed in the November 20, 1944 bombardment. The second building at 35 Dornich (Dornych) was also in a dire state after the bombing and was eventually torn down. For both locations, see https://gis.brno.cz/ags/bomby/ (accessed Aug. 26, 2020). None of these buildings are still standing. See also ch. 16, ill. n° 9.

Reichs Protector of Bohemia and Moravia (Vermögensamt beim Reichsprotektor in Böhmen and Mähren) explicitly ordered the Brno auxiliary office of the Treuhand- und Revisionsgesellschaft to sell all Jewish stored goods (*Umzugsgüter*) as quickly as possible. The same notice reveals that the Gestapo had provided a list of all the Jewish storage rooms in Brno to both the Prague Property Office and the Brno auxiliary office of the Treuhand- und Revisionsgesellschaft.[215] At the same time, the Germans were careful not to liquidate the contents of a storage room prematurely, that is, before its Jewish owner was deported. One example is the case of Franz Perlsee (1909–?), who rented a storage room in Brno from the Bitschovský firm, but was living in Prague by 1943. He was deported from Prague to Terezín on transport "Cy" on April 9, 1943. In May 1943, one month later, orders were given to liquidate his storage room in Brno. Possibly, Perlsee was aware that this would happen soon after his deportation, since he only paid one month's rent in advance for the storage room.[216] By the summer of 1942, it was most likely no longer possible for Jewish people to move the belongings they kept in storage rooms.[217]

Elise Brecher's position is of further interest because she and her son Fritz Brecher were among the last to be deported from Brno, a fact that clearly reveals their privileged status. This also implies that they were the last to have control over their storage rooms and possibly the rooms of their immediate family. Since Karl Fein's aunt decided to stay behind in Brno, it is possible that Karl Fein eventually decided to keep his belongings in her storage room. After all, it would have been very easy for the Germans following Fein's trail to find his storage room simply by looking up his name. This is interestingly reminiscent of Elise Brecher's possible decoy involvement in the November 1933 buy-back operation. It is also possible that Elise Brecher continued to pay rent for Fein's storage room after he was deported from Prague.

So, it cannot be excluded that Fein may have kept some or all of the Institute materials in his aunt's storage room. One certain fact is that, in 1943, the Brno Provincial and University Library (Landes- und Universitätsbibliothek, Zemská a univerzitní knihovna) acquired 450 books from liquidated Jewish storage rooms. These books were kept at 10 Zeile (Cejl), the already mentioned vast extensive storage place belonging to the auxiliary office of the Treuhand- und Revisionsgesellschaft in Brno.[218] This also suggests that, if Fein had indeed relied on his aunt to watch over his belongings while he was living in Prague, it is possible that some Institute books may have eventually ended up in the collection of the current successor of the Municipal and University Library, the Moravian Library in Brno (Moravská zemská knihovna v Brně, MZK).

[215] MZA, Brno, fonds G 427, Německá správa zabaveného majetku Brno, kart. n° 2, letter (dated Aug. 8, 1942) from Vermögensamt beim Reichsprotektor in Böhmen and Mähren to Treuhand- und Revisionsgesellschaft in Brno, f. 488. But even one week after the "Dg" transport left Brno, the office of the Reichsprotektor in Prague let the Neisser moving firm know that its Jewish storage rooms had to be liquidated and that it had to buy a truck for this purpose. See MZA, Brno, fonds G 427, Německá správa zabaveného majetku Brno, kart. n° 2, letter (dated Jul. 9, 1942) from the office of the Reichsprotektor, Prag III, to moving firm Hermann Neisser in Brno, f. 354. Some uncertainty about the sender of the letter remains. It may have been the Treuhand- und Revisionsgesellschaft in Prague (which also sent a copy of the letter to the office of the Reichsprotektor).

[216] MZA, Brno, fonds G 427, Německá správa zabaveného majetku Brno, kart. n° 2, f. 138, letter (dated May 22, 1943) from Oberbürgermeister der Landeshauptstadt Brünn, Wirtschaftsamt-Möbelaktion to the Treuhand- und Revisionsgesellschaft in Brno.

[217] Jan Björn Potthast makes it clear that, in 1942, *Speditionsfirmen* (moving firms) refused to accept any Jewish property without an official permit (Potthast 2002, 227, 231–32).

[218] MZA, Brno, fonds G 427, Německá správa zabaveného majetku Brno, kart. n° 10, f. 561, letter (dated Jan. 22, 1944) from the auxiliary office of the Treuhand- und Revisionsgesellschaft in Brno to Landes- und Universitätsbibliothek Brünn, Landhaus II.

[219] MZA, Brno, fonds G 427, Německá správa zabaveného majetku Brno, kart. n° 9, f. 662-665: "Mehr als die Hälfte dieser Bücher wurden sofort von einem

The Gestapo certainly always kept an eye on what was happening in these storage rooms. It seems to have had the right to intervene directly and confiscate books arbitrarily, as was the case, for example, with the book collection of a certain Jewish doctor named Dr. Friedrich Werner (1878–1941). More than half of his book collection, stored with the Neisser moving firm in Brno, was seized by the Gestapo, presumably some time in the second half of 1942, because they were "hostile to the state" (*staatsfeindlich*).[219] The Institute materials that Fein may have kept in his aunt's storage room could just as easily have ended up at some point in the hands of the Gestapo.

In my efforts to find out exactly what happened with the contents of the storage rooms belonging to Elise Brecher and her close family, I also tried to follow the trail of a valuable collection of twenty-eight medieval manuscripts from Admont Abbey, the Austrian monastery, acquired by Fritz Brecher before the war. A few years before it was Aryanized, in March 1939, Fritz Brecher had taken over the L. & A. Brecher bookstore from his mother. He did not manage to sell all these manuscripts beforehand, so he must have kept some and possibly put them in storage. My long quest, in which I tried to follow the itinerary of the remaining sold and unsold manuscripts, ultimately led to no useful conclusion about a storage room liquidated by the Germans, nor did it indicate someone to whom Brecher might have entrusted these manuscripts.[220]

As part of the same undertaking, I also tried to follow the trail of the paintings of one of Elise Brecher's sisters, Dorette Löw (1873-1933), a local Brno painter who lived on Talgasse (Údolní) and never married. Occasionally, she exhibited her work with the Brno Society of Friends of the Arts (Brünner Gesellschaft der Kunstfreunde) or the Moravian Art Association (Mährischer Kunstverein) in the 1910s and 1920s.[221] I assumed that Elise Brecher would have kept some of her sister's paintings after her death in 1933, and inquired with the Moravian Gallery in Brno (Moravská galerie v Brně) whether they had any of Dorette Löw's paintings in their collection and, if they did, if they had any information about their acquisition. The gallery informed me that their archives contained no traces of Dorette Löw, Elise Brecher or Fritz Brecher ever having contacted the Moravian Gallery.[222] I further inquired with a few Vienna museums but none had any paintings by this thoroughly local and minor painter in their collections.[223] We will return to Elise Brecher's storage room at the Morava

Beamten der Geheimen Staatspolizei als staatsfeindlich sichergestellt", f. 662.

[220] However, one intriguing detail persuaded me that the matter needs further scrutiny. Nine of the manuscripts that Fritz Brecher bought from the monastery ended up with the Czechoslovak engineer, industrialist and bibliophile Otokar Kruliš-Randa (1890–1958). There is no trace in the remaining Kruliš-Randa archives of any correspondence between Brecher and Kruliš-Randa related to the sale of any of these Admont manuscripts, even though some of their correspondence on other book transactions has survived. Because Kruliš-Randa collaborated, at least to some extent, with the occupying Germans, I think it possible that he acquired a few or even all nine of Brecher's manuscripts unscrupulously. They may have come from a liquidated storage room that Fritz Brecher or his mother Elise Brecher had rented in Brno. It is conceivable that the Germans may have policed like this a passionate, well-known manuscript collector with an eye to new medieval manuscript acquisitions. For further analysis of this matter, see Soetaert forthcoming.

[221] See, for example, the catalogue of the VI. *Ausstellung* (sixth exhibition) of the *Brünner Gesellschaft der Kunstfreunde 1900–1910* 1910, 5; as well as other catalogues for the exhibitions of Brno art circles, 1890–1940, in the library of the Moravské galerie (Moravian Gallery). Exhibitions of the work of Dorette Löw and others sometimes took place in the beautiful *Künstlerhaus* (House of the Artists) in Brno. See, for example, *Brünner Zeitung*, Dec. 24, 1917, 3. A memorial exhibition of Dorette Löw's work was mounted in 1935, two years after her death. See *Deutschmährische Heimat*, Jun. 5, 1935, 186.

[222] Email (dated Mar. 11, 2021) from Svatava Hájková (Archiv Moravské galerie v Brně) to the author. Hájková informed me that they checked the Obrazárna Moravského zemského muzea archival fonds.

[223] Email (dated Apr. 7, 2021) from Julia Eßl (Leopold museum, Vienna) to the author; and email (dated Apr. 8, 2021) from Susanne Hehenberger (Kunsthistorisches Museum, Vienna) to the author. I also

company one more time, in chapter 16, reconsidering it when new factors, further altering the final appearance of things, will be added to our story.

THE LEOPOLD FLEISCHER FIRM'S JEWISH EMPLOYEES

Because of the possibly quintessential role of the Leopold Fleischer company in our story, I also decided to pursue the further traces of its known employees. We have already considered the destiny of Karl Giese's boyfriend, Walter Lukl, who worked for the company until 1941.

Of the firm's four Jewish employees, three are known by name: Erwin Waldapfel (Valecký) (1901–?), Ernst Wiener (1898–1945) and, of course, Willi Bondi. It is possible that Julia Fleischer, the owner of the company, was considered a fourth Jewish employee. In a letter she wrote after the war, Julia Fleischer said that she was forced to work for the company until at least December 1941, despite the sale of the company in September 1941.[224]

We already know that Willi Bondi never returned to his home or workplace after being arrested by the Gestapo at Julia Fleischer's home in March 1941. The firm's last two Jewish employees were possibly dismissed in January 1942, shortly after the Oberlandrat in Brno received a letter from the Prague Omnia Treuhandgesellschaft (Trust association), claiming the discovery of fraud at another Brno company. Investigations revealed that two Leopold Fleischer company employees were clearly involved in this fraud.[225] This fraud was most likely the proverbial last straw, leading to the removal of the two employees from the company, then already renamed after its new owner, Rudolf Siegmund. Once again, we see that some Jewish employees kept their positions for quite some time at Aryanized companies.

Julia Fleischer was deported on the last Brno Jewish mass transport "Ai" to Terezín, along with her son Karl Heinz (1925–1945), on April 8, 1942. One week earlier, on March 31, 1942, Erwin Waldapfel (Valecký) was deported on transport "Af" to Terezín. On September 29, 1944, he was further transferred to Auschwitz-Birkenau. He was liberated from Auschwitz. His was one of the eight Czech names (out of almost 1,100) on the now famous "Schindler's list".[226] Erwin Waldapfel changed his German-sounding name to Ervín Valecký in December 1945, when he was again living in Brno.[227] He still gave "freight forwarder" (*zasílatel*) as his occupation. He

sent an inquiry on to Verena Gamper of the Leopold Museum on April 1, 2021, but received no reply. Additionally, I checked the database of the Belvedere museum in Vienna but it did not include anyone with the last name Löw. See https://sammlung.belvedere.at/ (accessed Apr. 8, 2021).

[224] For Julia Fleischer's letter to Willi Neubauer, see Condell 2005, 221.

[225] NA, Praha, fonds n° 375, Arizačni spisy, Leopold Fleischer firm, kart. n° 205, sign. 1268, not foliated, letter (dated Jan. 12, 1942) from Omnia Treuhandgesellschaft m.b.H. Prague to Dr. Krampf of the Oberlandrat in Brünn. The company in which the fraud was discovered was the Jewish Semina Samenversand (wholesale seed company) in Brno, owned by Ignaz Schön (1894–1942). The Leopold Fleischer company generated more business for Semina than its *Speditionsjournal* (company register) recorded. The letter also claimed, erroneously, that there were still four Jewish clerks working for the moving firm. In reality, only two were left at that point. For more information on Semina, see MZA, Brno, fonds C 11, Krajský soud civilní Brno, firemní agenda, "Semina" semenářský závod Hynek Schön, Brno, 1931-1951, kart. n°117, sign. A XI 81. As early as 1939, a trustee was appointed for the firm. In May 1942, the decision was made to liquidate the company, not because of the fraud, but rather as a consequence of general dissatisfaction with the work of the trustee Franz Hendlinger (1894–?). Complaints about his poor management (and favoring of Jews) were made as early as February 1941. In October 1941, a thorough investigation of the company was undertaken, at which point the three remaining Jewish employees, including Ignaz Schön himself, were fired. See NA, Praha, fonds n° 375, Arizačni spisy, kart. n° 246, file n° 1684, "Semina" Brno (Ignaz Schön).

[226] Kárný et al. 1995, 448; https://en.wikipedia.org/wiki/Schindlerjuden (accessed Jan. 12, 2017).

[227] On May 11, 1945, Waldapfel arrived in Brno where he lived with the widow Miloslava Tuschnerová (?–?) at 52 Hans-Kudlich-Gasse (ulice Hanse Kudlicha). See Valecký's home certificate and resident registration card in AMB, Brno, fonds B 1/39 and fonds Z 1; and *Adressbuch der Landeshauptstadt Brünn* 1943, 321.

never married. Was he maybe another gay man whom Willi Bondi had brought into the company?

Ernst Wiener was a bookseller, an intriguing profession when we think of the book collection Fein inherited from Giese, which he may have stored at some point at the Leopold Fleischer company. He was deported with his second wife Hermine Lax (1913–1974?), on January 28, 1942, on transport "U" from Brno to Terezín.[228] Curiously, Wiener and Erwin Waldapfel were on the same transport "El", from Terezín to Auschwitz-Birkenau, on September 29, 1944, while Wiener's wife was transferred to Auschwitz-Birkenau one week later on transport "Eo". Wiener's sisters, Olga and Grete, followed on transport "Em" two days after him, on October 1, 1944. The exact fate of Ernst Wiener remains a little unclear, but it seems that he died in May 1945, shortly after being liberated from the Flossenbürg concentration camp.[229] His wife Hermine survived and remarried after the war.[230]

Julia Fleischer was liberated from Terezín but was deeply traumatized. Above all the loss of her nineteen-year-old son, Karl Heinz Fleischer, who had been deported to Auschwitz-Birkenau on transport "Ek" on September 28, 1944, was too much for her to bear.[231] Her sister Hermine died of typhus in Terezín around the time that the camp was liberated, in the beginning of May 1945.[232] In 1948 or 1949, sitting in the office of her former moving company, she wrote a letter to the engineer Willi Neubauer

[228] Ernst Wiener and Hermine Lax, both Jewish, married in Brno on November 29, 1941, two months before they were deported from Brno. Ernst Wiener's first wife was Anna Adler (1911–?), whom he divorced in May 1930. Her further fate is unknown.

[229] According to one source, Wiener arrived in Plattling, a subcamp of the Flossenbürg concentration camp, on February 20, 1945. He was assigned prison number 47093. See the Flossenbürg Concentration Camp Records, 1938–1945 on Ancestry.com (accessed Jan. 14, 2017). According to Yad Vashem, he died on May 18, 1945 in Eggenfelden (Bavaria, Germany). The Flossenbürg concentration camp was liberated by the Americans in April 1945. See the Yad Vashem central database of Shoah victims, Prisoner database Flossenbürg concentration camp, item ID 7233342, which mentions Ernst Wiener, born on August 20, 1898, and gives Eggenfelden as his place of death. Eggenfelden, located between Munich and Passau, was one of the camps for "displaced persons" after the war, but only started operations in late 1945. See http://dpcamps.ort.org/camps/germany/us-zone/us-zone-iii/eggenfelden/ (accessed May 31, 2017).

[230] Hermine and Ernst Wiener are erroneously reported as dying in Auschwitz-Birkenau by both the www.holocaust.cz database and Kárný et al. 1995, 315. Ernst Wiener's home certificate – AMB, Brno, fonds B 1/39 – reveals that he officially divorced his second wife in 1947 so that she could marry the engineer Richard Farský (1897–1950). This legal maneuver was likely motivated by the fact that Ernst Wiener did not come back after the war and had not been officially declared dead. Hermine Farská and Richard Farský are buried in Brno's Ústřední hřbitov (central cemetery), in parcel H 2, grave 51. Interestingly, the testimony about Ernst Wiener (item ID 902697) deposited on June 26, 1956 at Yad Vashem by a certain Mr. Mandelbaum, who claimed to be Wiener's brother-in-law, contains several factual mistakes (the wrong birth town, his death in Dachau in 1944) but gives the correct first names for Wiener's parents – Albert (1865-1935), a doctor, and mother Anna Levi (1876–?) – and accurately mentions the city of Brno and Wiener's profession as a *Buchhändler* (bookseller). It is also interesting that a second Yad Vashem testimony of May 31, 1956 (item ID 654968) contains more correct information about Ernst Wiener and also confirms that he was a bookseller. The latter was written in Hebrew by a certain Ferenc (Ferentz) Wiener (Viner), claiming to be Ernst Wiener's brother. This was in reality Franz Wiener (1903–?), who was deported from Brno to Terezín on the same transport "U" as his brother Ernst and his wife, on January 28, 1942. Their mother, Anna Levi, was on the same transport. She was liberated from Terezín while Franz Wiener was liberated from Flossenbürg. See Kárný et al. 1995, 318; and USHMM, alphabetical list of Flossenburg inmates, RG-30.005M, reel 2, page 1193, image nr. 366. Franz Wiener arrived in Flossenbürg on February 6, 1945. He also made a testimony for his other brother, the lawyer Walter Wiener (1907–1944?) who was deported on transport "Ai" on April 8, 1942, from Brno to Terezín and further transferred on transport "Eq" to Auschwitz-Birkenau. He was married to Margareta (Markéta) Pollak (1907–?), who was liberated from Terezín. The fate of their son Michael (1944–?), born in Terezín, is unknown. Since I observed that the grave of Hermine Lax and Richard Farský still exists in the Brno central cemetery, I sent a letter to the two people with the name Farský living in Brno on April 12, 2021. Neither answered.

[231] Condell 2005, 220, 222.

[232] Ibid., 220.

(1900–?), who fled to England in 1939,[233] saying that ownership of the company should be restored to her [ill. 15]. Most likely, her moving company was nationalized soon after.[234] She died in Brno in 1982.

GAY AND JEWISH CIRCLES

If indeed Karl Fein rented a storage room from the Leopold Fleischer company, if only for a limited amount of time, then I think we can conclude that he seems to have relied on his gay and Jewish network for a solution to store the Hirschfeld and Institute materials, and maybe also his own belongings. Fein turned to Willi Bondi and his sister, Julia Fleischer. As we have seen, Julia Fleischer, a bisexual or lesbian woman, seems to have gotten along quite amicably with Bondi's circle of gay friends. Her husband, Bruno Fleischer, even offered Walter Lukl, Karl Giese's boyfriend, a job in the Leopold Fleischer company in 1936, and also lent Lukl 3,000 Czech crowns at some point.[235] Karl Fein's reliance on gay friends and Jewish acquaintances seems to accord with the events explained in the following two chapters.

233 Ibid., 223. The letter was undated but I deduced from one of its sentences that it was written on August 25, 1948 or 1949.

234 This office could not have been the one of the former Leopold Fleischer company at 34 Adlergasse (Orlí), since the building was bombed on November 20, 1944 and later torn down. See 6 Benešova (street address) in the "Bombardování Brna" database. See https://gis.brno.cz/ags/bomby/ (accessed Sep. 10, 2020). Possibly then, she was in Rudolf Siegmund's (or even Walter Prochaska's) nearby office at 6 U Nové brány (Neutorgasse) or at 11 Cejl (Zeile). Julia Fleischer's name does not appear in *Adresář zemského hlavního města Brna* 1948, 123, under the "Zasilatelství" (moving firms) section. But, curiously, as already pointed out, the names of Walter Prochaska and Rudolf Siegmund do.

235 NA, Praha, fonds n° 375, Arizačni spisy, liquidation file Leopold Fleischer firm, kart. n° 205, sign. 1268, not foliated.

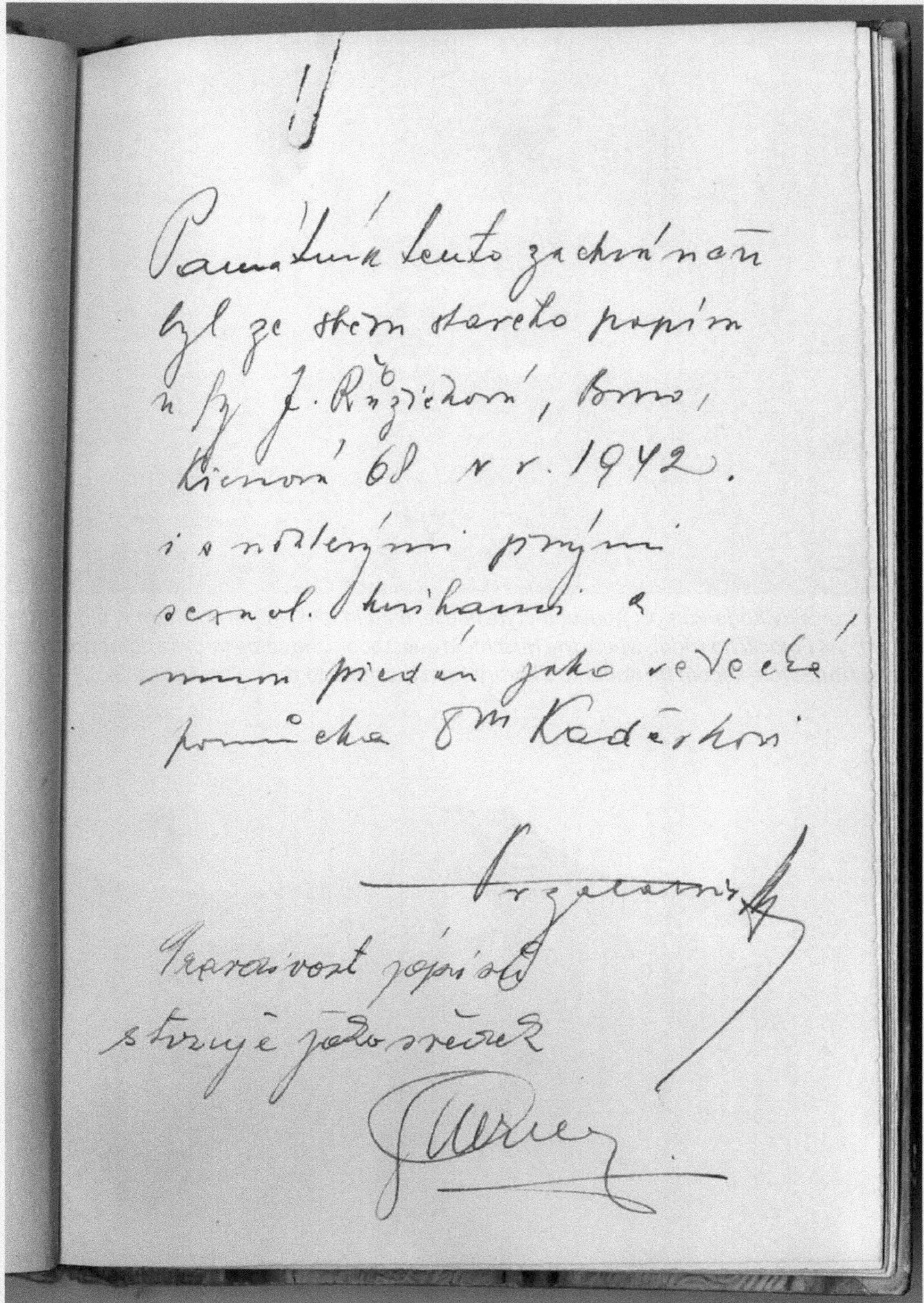

1. Anonymous affidavit in Czech, by two different people, written by hand on one of the last blank pages in the Hirschfeld guestbook.

2. Dr. Stanislav Kaděrka's art nouveau-style house, built in 1905, in the northern Královo Pole suburb (84 Palackého třída), where the Hirschfeld guestbook and some books originating from the Institute were kept in Dr. Kaděrka's library from the 1950s to the 1980s. April 2015.

3. The two urns holding the ashes of Dr. Stanislav Kaděrka and his wife Zdeňka Grošovová in the Královo Pole cemetery in Brno. April 2015.

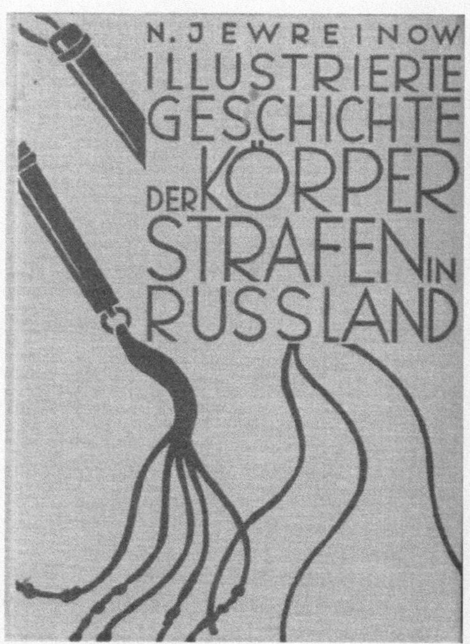

4. Cover of Nikolaj Nikolaevič Evreinov's Die Körperstrafen in der russischen Rechtspflege und Verwaltung, published by the Verlag für Sexualwissenschaft Schneider & Co. in Vienna in 1931.

5. Jindřiška (Jindra) Ružičková (née Fikesová) and her dog. Undated.

6. The building erected and once owned by the Nebehosteny family in Brno, at 68 Křenová (Kröna). January 2020.

8. The building at 9 Jesuitská (Jesuitengasse), erected in 1931, showing the former entrance to the shopping gallery named Typos Passage (Pasáž Typos). April 2016.

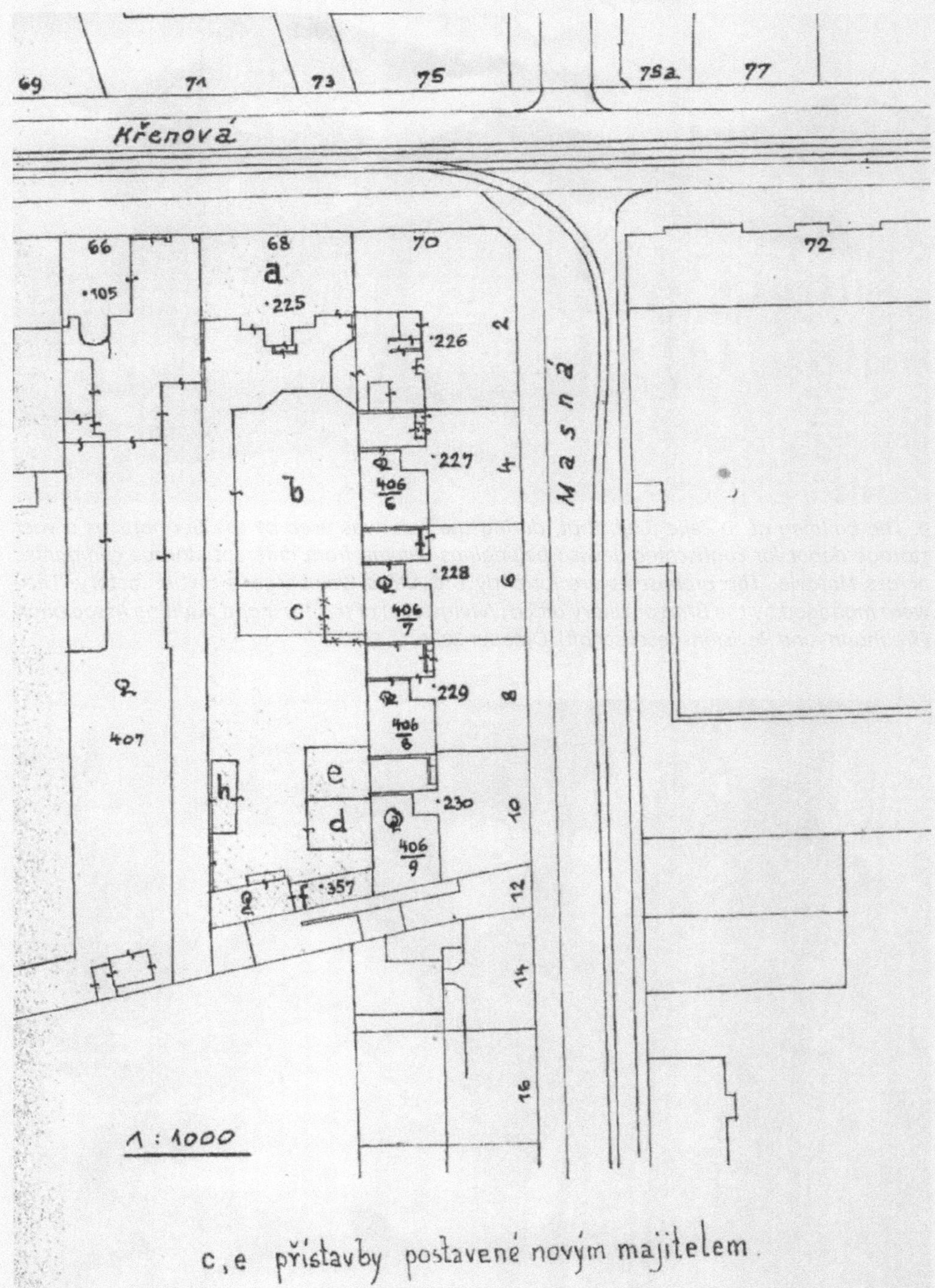

7. Postwar, schematic cadastral drawing of the site behind the Nebehosteny building, showing some company buildings rented by the Růžičkas (buildings marked with the letters "d", "f" and "g").

9. The building at 10 Zeile (Cejl) that, during the war, was used by the Germans as a vast storage depot for confiscated Jewish belongings coming from different storage companies across Moravia. The premises were formerly the Alfred Weinberger's textile factory. They were managed by the Brno auxiliary office (Zweigstelle) of the Trust and Auditing Association (Treuhand- und Revisionsgesellschaft). October 2021.

10. The Leopold Fleischer company office at 34 Adlergasse (Orlí). Standing in the rear, Julia Fleischer is putting her arm around the shoulders of – presumably – Walter Prochaska, the trustee (Treuhänder). The man sitting on the far right is Willi Bondi. Ca. Summer 1940–March 1941.

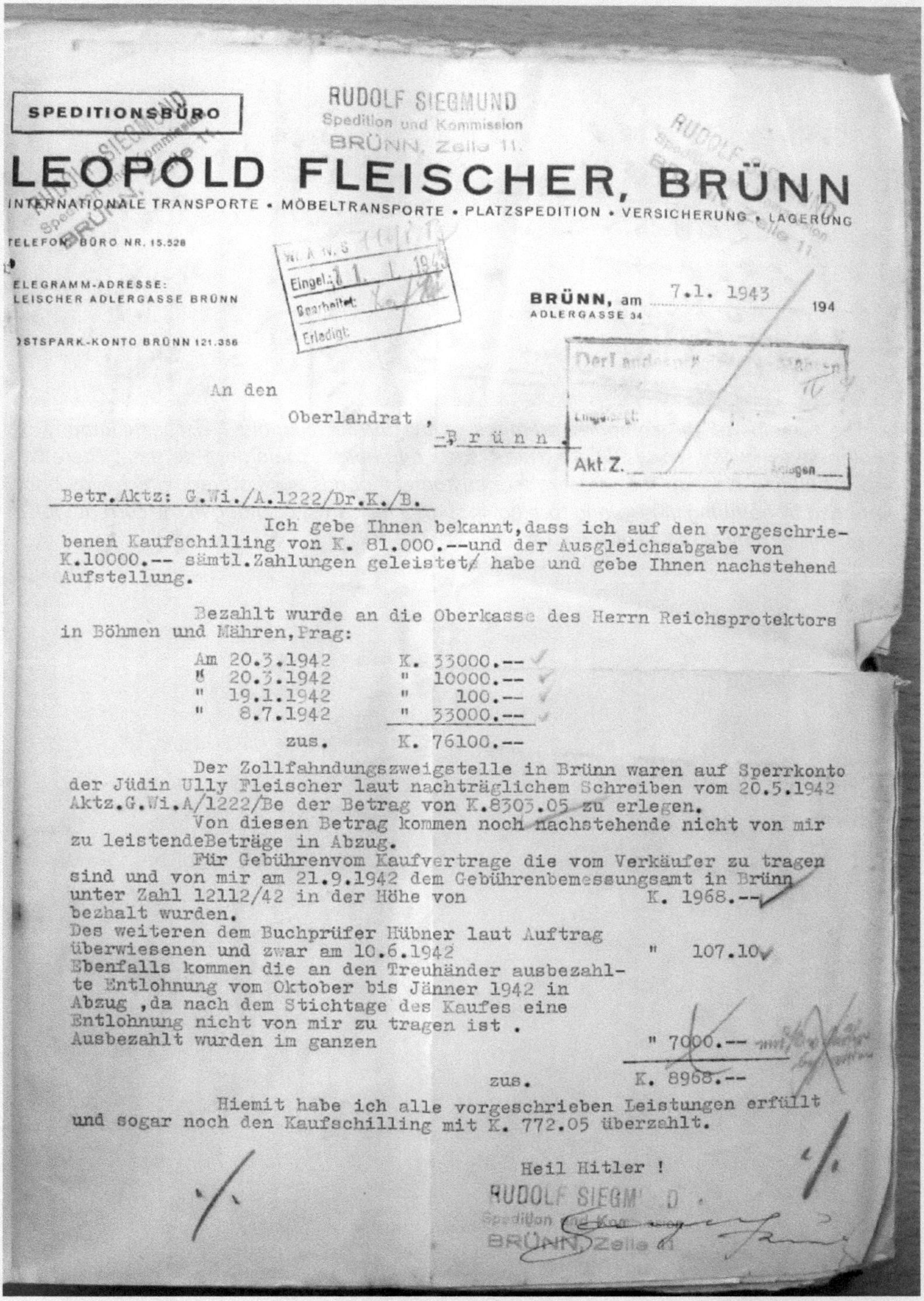

SPEDITIONSBÜRO

RUDOLF SIEGMUND
Spedition und Kommission
BRÜNN, Zeile 11.

LEOPOLD FLEISCHER, BRÜNN

INTERNATIONALE TRANSPORTE • MÖBELTRANSPORTE • PLATZSPEDITION • VERSICHERUNG • LAGERUNG

TELEFON: BÜRO NR. 15.528

TELEGRAMM-ADRESSE:
FLEISCHER ADLERGASSE BRÜNN

POSTSPARK-KONTO BRÜNN 121.356

Eingel.: 11. 1. 1943
Bearbeitet:
Erledigt:

BRÜNN, am 7.1. 1943
ADLERGASSE 34

An den

Oberlandrat,

-Brünn.

Aktz. Z.

Betr. Aktz: G.Wi./A.1222/Dr.K./B.

Ich gebe Ihnen bekannt, dass ich auf den vorgeschriebenen Kaufschilling von K. 81.000.--und der Ausgleichsabgabe von K.10000.-- sämtl. Zahlungen geleistet habe und gebe Ihnen nachstehend Aufstellung.

Bezahlt wurde an die Oberkasse des Herrn Reichsprotektors in Böhmen und Mähren, Prag:

Am 20.3.1942	K. 33000.--
" 20.3.1942	" 10000.--
" 19.1.1942	" 100.--
" 8.7.1942	" 33000.--
zus.	K. 76100.--

Der Zollfahndungszweigstelle in Brünn waren auf Sperrkonto der Jüdin Ully Fleischer laut nachträglichem Schreiben vom 20.5.1942 Aktz.G.Wi.A/1222/Be der Betrag von K.8303.05 zu erlegen.

Von diesen Betrag kommen noch nachstehende nicht von mir zu leistende Beträge in Abzug.

Für Gebühren vom Kaufvertrage die vom Verkäufer zu tragen sind und von mir am 21.9.1942 dem Gebührenbemessungsamt in Brünn unter Zahl 12112/42 in der Höhe von K. 1968.-- bezahlt wurden.

Des weiteren dem Buchprüfer Hübner laut Auftrag überwiesenen und zwar am 10.6.1942 " 107.10

Ebenfalls kommen die an den Treuhänder ausbezahlte Entlohnung vom Oktober bis Jänner 1942 in Abzug, da nach dem Stichtage des Kaufes eine Entlohnung nicht von mir zu tragen ist.

Ausbezahlt wurden im ganzen " 7000.--

zus. K. 8968.--

Hiemit habe ich alle vorgeschrieben Leistungen erfüllt und sogar noch den Kaufschilling mit K. 772.05 überzahlt.

Heil Hitler!

RUDOLF SIEGMUND
Spedition und Kommission
BRÜNN, Zeile 11

11. *Letter to the Oberlandrat by Rudolf Siegmund, the new owner of the Leopold Fleischer moving and storage company. January 7, 1943.*

12. The remains of the company premises of the former Leopold Fleischer company, 38 Mühlgasse (Mlýnská). This is where trucks, carts and horses could once be seen. There was also a building close to the street where customers' goods were stored, which was badly damaged by bombing in 1944 and torn down soon afterwards, resulting in the current look of the premises. May 2017. See also photo n° 13.

13. The bombed-out street-facing building (left) of the storage and logistical company premises of the Leopold Fleischer storage company at 38 Mühlgasse (Mlýnská). (The address of the corner building on the right was 15 Čechyňská [Tschechnergasse].) By Courtesy of Museum of the City of Brno.

14. Postcard showing the representative office of the Morava moving firm (Zasilatelství, Spedition) at 6 Basteigasse (Na hradbách) (center right). The building facade is adorned with a banner bearing the letter "V", standing for "Viktoria" (in Czech, Vítězství). In the first years of the war, Germany claimed victory, using the motto "Germany wins on all fronts for Europe" (Deutschland siegt an allen Fronten für Europa). Two of these banners also appear on the modernist Bat'a building on the left. The main city theater can be seen on the right of the picture. Postmarked April 20, 1942.

15. Passport photo of Julia Fleischer. 1945

I. ročník. V Brně, dne 28. května 1932. Číslo 1.

Časopis věnovaný zájmům přátelství uznaným vědou a kulturními státy.

Cena Kč 2·—.

15. *Kamarád* and the Discarding of the Institute Materials

THE GAY PERIODICAL *KAMARÁD*

In May 2017, I found a decisive factor that, at first sight, seemed to identify whom Karl Fein had entrusted with the Institute materials he inherited from Karl Giese. (As I will show in the next chapter, some doubts about that breakthrough quite unexpectedly arose later.) This part of our story begins in 1932, ten years before the Hirschfeld guestbook was found in an old paper container in Brno.

On May 28, 1932, a group of gay men in Brno published the first (and likely last) issue of a gay periodical, *Kamarád*. Possibly, the idea sprang from a café society that met in the Café Bellevue in Brno at 8 Lažanský náměstí (Lažanskýplatz) [ill. 1].[1] Exactly one month before, under the leadership of Vilém Drexler-Hlubocký, a founding meeting of approximately thirty supporters gathered in the café.[2] The following day, April 29, 1932, the two principal figures behind the initiative to publish a new magazine – Drexler-Hlubocký and the Slovak artist Štefan Leonard Kostelníček – informed the Brno police printed matter department by letter of their intention. The letter was handwritten by Drexler-Hlubocký and signed by him and Kostelníček, naming the other five people supporting the initiative: Stanislav Černil, Jaroslav Růžička, Jakub (or possibly Josef) Uher, Jaroslav Očadlík, and Bohdan Hájek.[3]

It is rather difficult to determine exactly who pulled the strings to set up the periodical, but Drexler-Hlubocký seems to have been the instigator and spiritual leader. Kostelníček, who is mentioned as owner and publisher of the magazine, probably financed the whole operation.[4] The magazine's editorial office was in Kostelníček's four-room, second-floor apartment at 10 Kobližná (Krapfengasse) where Kostelníček had only recently taken up residence, on May 17, 1932.[5] Stanislav Černil's poem "Kamarád", dedicated to Drexler-Hlubocký, featured in the magazine. The poem praises Drexler-Hlubocký's heroic endeavor in starting up the magazine.[6] Kostelníček wrote the issue's editorial (in Slovak) appearing on its first two pages. Stanislav Černil and Vilém Drexler-Hlubocký were named as editor-in-chief (*odpovědný redaktor*) and editor (*redaktor*), respectively. The latter wrote no fewer than four articles for the issue.[7] The Slovak LGBT militant Imrich Matyáš showed his sympathy for the new initiative by publishing the longest article in the issue, the first in a promised series of two, on a historical topic [ill. 2].[8]

[1] The café was located on the ground floor of the building of the Vzájemně pojišťovací banka Slavia (Slavia Mutual Insurance Bank). For more on Café Bellevue between the wars, see Altman 2008, 100–101, 106–7. The title may have been partly inspired by a soldiers' magazine, *Kamarádství: list válečných a současných dějů* (Camaraderie: A Journal of War and Current Events), since the café also served as a meeting place for military personnel.

[2] *Kamarád*, May 28, 1932, 21–22. The meeting took place on April 28, 1932. Cf. Seidl et al. 2012, 184.

[3] MZA, Brno, fonds C 12, Krajský soud trestní Brno, III. manipulace, kart. n° 539, sign. TK XI 1687/32, letter (dated Apr. 29, 1932) to Policejní ředitelství v Brně (tisk ref.[erat]), f. 17. There remains some uncertainty about the exact identity of Jakub (or Josef) Uher, see n° 14 in the addenda.

[4] Michal Mako thinks that Štefan Kostelníček was the principal figure behind the magazine because he wrote the editorial (Mako, May 29, 2020, 48).

[5] *Kamarád*, May 28, 1932, 24–25.

[6] Černil, May 28, 1932, 11.

[7] Hlubocký, May 28, 1932, 6, 12–13, 15–16, 17–19.

[8] Matyáš, May 28, 1932, 7–10.

In the summer of 1932, Štefan Kostelníček told the Brno police that he was a member of the Czechoslovak League for Sexual Reform (Československá liga pro sexuální reformu, ČLSR) in Prague.[9] The group in Brno wanted to join with the Prague gay movement, which had found new life that year with its own launch of a new gay magazine. The first issue of *Nový hlas* came out on May 1, 1932. Page seven of the *Kamarád* issue stated what the two periodicals had in common. However, despite the Brno initiative receiving letters of recommendation from Prague, the editors of *Nový hlas* were apparently not very pleased with the Brno undertaking; they never, not once, mentioned the new periodical in their own publication.[10]

MEETING MAGNUS HIRSCHFELD

The Brno group's enthusiasm to publish the magazine was also fired by Magnus Hirschfeld's May 20, 1932 visit to Brno with the Slovak gay activist Imrich Matyáš. Hirschfeld went to Brno for his first meeting with the local organizers of the WLSR conference to be held in September, lecturing that evening in the DOPZ building. The group around the *Kamarád* initiative attended the lecture, as did Karl Fein and Dr. Josef Weisskopf.[11] Afterwards, the gay clique presented Hirschfeld with a bouquet of lilacs, explaining that they were the color "of their flock."[12] The group then accompanied Hirschfeld to the nearby garden at the German House (Deutsches Haus, Německý dům) [ill. 3]. Hirschfeld asked his Brno admirers to sign his guestbook. Since the guestbook – published in 2019 – that survived in Giese's estate contains no trace of this meeting, Hirschfeld must have had at least one other guestbook, now most likely lost.

The next day, the group met Hirschfeld again, possibly in a room in Kostelníček's Kobližná (Krapfengasse) apartment. These May 1932 meetings certainly impressed the *Kamarád* group. They felt that Hirschfeld took a genuine interest in their complaints and in the stories of their personal lives [ill. 4].[13] One week later, the first and most likely last issue of *Kamarád* came out, bearing the subtitle "A journal dedicated to the interests of friendship recognized by science and cultural states" (Časopis věnovaný zájmům přátelství uznaným vědou a kulturními státy).[14] And, as in almost every issue of the Prague gay magazine *Nový hlas*, Hirschfeld was lauded, praised on two of the twenty-four pages of *Kamarád*.[15]

The issue also included "Truth and Justice" (*Wahrheit und Recht*), an article in German (and Czech translation) by a Dr. J. Schwarz.[16] There was no lawyer or

[9] MZA, Brno, fonds C 12, Krajský soud trestní Brno, III. manipulace, kart. n° 539, sign. TK XI 1687/32, f. 10b.

[10] Seidl et al. 2012, 182–83.

[11] *Kamarád*, May 28, 1932, 15.

[12] *Kamarád*, May 28, 1932, 15: "Kytice fialového šeříku ve znamení naší barvy."

[13] *Kamarád*, May 28, 1932, 15. An issue of *Nový hlas* (Jg. 1, n° 5, Sep. 1, 1932, picture following p. 8) includes a picture of a group of six unidentified men with Hirschfeld and Weisskopf in what seems to be a park. This possibly shows the meeting with the *Kamarád* people in the front garden of the German House (Deutsches Haus, Německý dům) in Brno on May 20 or 21, 1932. The date under the picture is "spring 1932", accompanying the description: "taken in Brno with friends". Imrich Matyáš is the fourth man from the right, according to Seidl 2012, 186. The fifth man next to him is Hirschfeld himself. This brightly-lit photo may not depict the May 20, 1932 meeting: the light would have been more dim by the end of Hirschfeld's evening lecture, even if the solstice was only one month away. The photo might have been taken the next day, when Hirschfeld met the group again.

[14] Hirschfeld made the argument that tolerance of homosexuality is an aspect of civilized countries (*Kulturstaten*) in *Nový hlas*. This theme recurs in a slogan printed in the magazine: "Kämpft mit uns gegen Schande und Unrecht, gegen den in einem Kulturstaate unmöglichen § 129!" (Fight with us against shame and injustice, against paragraph 129, which is impossible in a civilized country!). See *Kamarád*, May 28, 1932, 8. Only one physical copy of the magazine has survived, in the Vědecká knihovna v Olomouci (Olomouc Research Library). A partial digital version can be found at https://www.queer-pamet.cz/soubor/kamarad-1932 (accessed Sep. 3, 2020).

[15] *Kamarád*, May 28, 1932, 6, 15.

[16] Schwarz, May 28, 1932, 3–5.

medical doctor by that name in Brno, so this was most likely a pseudonym, possibly adopted by Karl Fein.[17] Although it is quite different in style from Karl Fein's article, "Homosexuals and the Law" (*Die Homosexuellen und das Gesetz*), which later appeared in two parts in the May and June 1934 issues of *Nový hlas*,[18] they share the same subject and an analogy. In both articles, gay men are "like ostriches" (*Der Vogel Strauß*), sticking their heads in the sand when arrested for homosexual conduct, hoping that the "bad thing" will go away on its own. The pseudonymous writer identifies as gay, speaking of "we homosexuals" (*Wir Homosexuellen*).

All in all, the *Kamarád* issue was an editorial mess, and its layout was very rudimentary. The next issue of the anticipated bi-monthly was announced for June 15 but likely never happened.[19] Let us take a closer look at the lives of the two main people behind *Kamarád*.

VILÉM DREXLER-HLUBOCKÝ

Vilém Drexler-Hlubocký (1913–1961 or later) was a Brno local who led the foundational meeting of *Kamarád* at Café Bellevue in 1932. Drexler-Hlubocký was a practicing Roman Catholic from a working-class background, and a bachelor before the war.[20] His parents were Vilém Drexler (1876–1934) and Aloisie Hauserová (1881–1939). Drexler-Hlubocký held jobs as a clerk, trader, and manager, but posterity knows him mainly for his modest literary efforts.[21] He self-published several literary pamphlets and chapbooks under the pseudonym V. D. Hlubocký.[22] One, the 1937 *Letters from a Diary* (*Listy z deníku*), includes a possibly partly autobiographical story about an unrequited gay love between Harry and Jindřich [ill. 5].[23] Although his legal surname was Drexler (sometimes also spelled Drechsler), Vilém started experimenting with

[17] The contents list on the cover page abbreviates the author's initials to "Dr. J. F.", whereas the full names of all the other authors are given. Does the "F" maybe stand for Fein? The inconsistency does seem to indicate minimally that someone was using a pseudonym.

[18] Fein 1934a; Fein 1934b.

[19] *Kamarád*, May 28, 1932, 9. Cf. MZA, Brno, fonds B 26, Policejní ředitelství v Brno, kart. n° 2736B, inv. n° 3893, sign. 846, f. 4b, 5, 6, 15. On f. 6, it is noted that the magazine had not been published since June 1932. Since the next issue was planned for mid-June 1932, it is indeed likely that the first issue was also the last.

[20] Drexler-Hlubocký did his military service, but there is no military file on him. See Hlubočky 1939, 8; and email (dated Aug. 7, 2018) from Peter Kralčák (Vojenský historický archív, Praha) to the author. Drexler-Hlubocký was drafted again in the summer of 1938. See Hlubočky 1939, 11.

[21] See his resident registration cards in AMB, Brno, fonds Z 1: *úředník, obchdoník, disponent firmy*. The name Vilém Drexler-Hlubocký is curiously absent from Brno address directories. The only Vilém Drexler listed is another person. From 1934 to 1936, Vilém Drexler-Hlubocký lived in Královo Pole. On January 2, 1935 (or 1936), he moved from 8 Komenského (Comeniusgasse) to 73 Svatopluka Čecha (Svatopluk-Čech-Gasse). In June 1936, he moved to 4 V černých polích (Schwarzfeldgasse), the residence of his mother, Aloisie Drexler, in the Černa Pole (Schwarzfeld) district. In May 1939, he moved to the Husovice suburb, where he stayed for most of the war. On May 30, 1939, he moved to 43 Cacovická (Zazowitzer Gasse), and on December 11, 1941, he moved to 1108 Soběšická (Obeschitzer Gasse) in Husovice (staying with a certain Rudolf Hájek). Then, curiously, on March 26, 1943, he went for treatment in the central Bohemian spa city of Poděbrady (Poděbrady na léčení), whose healing baths were reputed to help with heart and blood circulation problems. See https://de.wikipedia.org/wiki/Pod%C4%9Bbrady (accessed Jun. 28, 2017). Drexler-Hlubocký returned to Brno in November 1943. The name of the street he moved to was then K jízdní aleji (Kon. Z. Reitallee). I have been unable to identify its current name. On November 10(?), 1943, he moved in with a certain E. Plch. Presumably this was Eman Plch, a typographer. See *Adressbuch der Landeshauptstadt Brünn 1942* 1943, 230. It is unclear when he moved to yet another address in Brno-Husovice, 4 Hlaváčkova (Hlaváčekgasse), but he seems to have stayed there for some time in 1944. He lived with Ludmila Štastná at this address. In July 1944, he briefly moved to Lelekovice, a village ten kilometers north of Brno, most likely prompted by fear of potential Allied bombing, especially as he lived close to a vast railway network in the northeast of Brno. For the US bombing of Brno in 1944, see Noskova 2016, 462, 564. Drexler-Hlubocký returned to 4 Hlaváčkova (Hlaváčekgasse) in July 1945.

[22] See the eight titles by Hlubocký in the bibliography. Vilém Drexler-Hlubocký also published a play, *Zapomenutý život: Drama o třech jednáních* (Forgotten life: A play in three acts) with another author. See Císař & Hlubocký 1933 (?).

[23] Hlubocký 1937, 14–22, story n° III.

the pseudonym Hlubocký in *Kamarád*. He may have wanted to distance himself from his father, Vilém Drexler.[24] That he chose the new surname Hlubocký is most plausibly explained by the fact that his mother was born in the village of Hlubočky (a similar spelling to Hlubocký) near Olomouc (Olmütz). Drexler-Hlubocký was very attached to his mother. In the year of her death, he wrote a small text about her, and he did the same in another literary pamphlet of 1947.[25] At one point, he calls her the "golden mother".[26] She died on March 19, 1939, after a long illness.

Another theme that recurs in Vilém Drexler's writings is his working-class Catholic background. Most likely the Karel Hlubocký who published a few texts in *Kamarád* was indeed Vilém Drexler-Hlubocký, given that the Brno police identified "Vilém Drechsler" as one of the periodical's collaborators.[27] In 1946, Vilém Drexler officially changed his last name to Hlubocký; however, complicating matters, Vilém Drexler-Hlubocký also started publishing under the name Luděk Hlubocký in 1945.[28] In January 1948, Vilém Hlubocký moved to Opava, where he worked for a health insurance company. In 1949, he let the Communist authorities know he intended to marry and needed a bigger flat.[29] In August 1961, he inscribed one of his poetry chapbooks, but I lost track of him after that.[30]

ŠTEFAN LEONARD KOSTELNÍČEK

The elaborate, ornamental title on the cover of *Kamarád* was most likely designed by Štefan Leonard Kostelníček (1900–1949). Elaborate ornamentation was the main characteristic of his art and craft, and he had briefly studied at a decorative arts school in Prague.[31] But Kostelníček had also studied theology and was even a

[24] It remains unexplained how the prominent Brno jurist Ludwig Drechsler (1876–?) may have been related to Vilém Drexler-Hlubocký's working-class family, if indeed he was. Ludwig and Vilém Drechsler senior were not brothers. However, according to one source, in 1930, Ludwig Drechsler lived at the same address as Vilém Drexler-Hlubocký's mother: 4 Černopolní (Schwarzfeldgasse). See *Adreßbuch von Groß-Brünn* 1930, 67. (V černých polích and Černopolní were both used for the Schwarzfeldgasse.) Drechsler's judicial career rose rapidly. In 1920, he was *erste Staatsanwalt* (first public prosecutor). See *Adreßbuch von Groß-Brünn* 1920, 190. By 1930, along with Arnost Hogenauer, he was Chief Councilor (*Obergerichtsrat*, *Vrchní soudní radové*) in the Brno District Civil Court (Bezirksgericht für Zivilsachen Brünn, Okresní soud civilní pro Brno-město). See *Adreßbuch von Groß-Brünn* 1930, 67. As we have seen, the Brno District Civil Court handled the Giese-Fein inheritance case; we encountered Hogenauer's name there. Ludwig Drechsler was also active in the Verein deutscher Juristen in Brünn (Brno German Bar Association). See, for example, *Adressbuch von Brünn* 1904, 78. He applied for Deutsche Volkszugehörigkeit (German ethnic) status on July 27, 1939. See AMB, Brno, fonds A 1/53.

[25] Hlubocký 1939, 1947.

[26] Hlubocký 1939, 17, 19.

[27] See, for example, Hlubocký, May 28, 1932, 15–16. The Brno police identified those behind *Kamarád* by checking each person's most recent resident registration card. See the five loose, handmade copies of the resident registration cards with these names (containing further handwritten notes on two other names on the back of one of them) in MZA, Brno, fonds B 26, Policejní ředitelství v Brno, kart. n° 2736B, inv. n° 3893, sign. 846. Why Vilém Drexler-Hlubocký chose to publish under the name of Karel Hlubocký remains unexplained, but we have also seen that the J. Schwarz, who also published in *Kamarád*, was most likely also a pseudonym. This indicates that some had reservations about publishing in the magazine under their own names. However, Jan Seidl believes that Karel Hlubocký's four articles in *Kamarád* were possibly by a partner of Vilém Drexler-Hlubocký. See Seidl 2012, 183 n. 396. The last name Hlubocký is not in either the 1934 *Adreßbuch von Groß-Brünn* or the *Adressbuch der Landeshauptstadt Brünn 1942*.

[28] See, for example, Hlubocký & Šafránek 1945; Hlubocký & Palma 1947. It is unknown whether Hlubocký also officially changed his first name. In 1961, contrary to his habitual pre-war "V. D. Hlubocký", Vilém Hlubocký signed a copy of his poetry chapbook *Balada o ženách* (1938), which I own, "V. L. Hlubocký". This is further proof that Vilém D. Hlubocký and V. Luděk Hlubocký were indeed one and the same person.

[29] He was the director of the (presumably) state-led health insurance company Nemocenské pojištovny n.p. In Opava, he first lived at 30 Tyršova, moving in 1949 to a bigger flat at 17 Gottwaldova třída (currently Hrnčířská). See email (dated Sep. 17, 2018) from Beata Sosnová (Státní okresní archiv Opava) to the author.

[30] I own a copy of one of Hlubocký's self-published poetry chapbooks, the 1938 *Balada o ženách*, inscribed with the date August 27, 1961 by the author.

Franciscan monk for a while; hence his middle name, Leonard.[32] Kostelníček was of Slovak origin and moved to Brno around 1931.[33] Kostelníček decorated pottery for a living, employing people in an atelier to paint flower motifs.[34] On a May 1932 resident registration card, Kostelníček described himself as an artistic painter and writer.[35]

With clearly sexual intent, Kostelníček attempted to lure lower-class men in their twenties using favors, promises of employment, and the offer of a place to sleep. His apartment was a kind of shelter where young, destitute working-class men could earn a little extra money, or get a meal and a bed for the night. Sexual interactions with these young men were always possible, even though Kostelníček denied most of the Brno police's accusations, in the summer of 1932, that he had sex with his guests.[36] One of these young men arrived at Kostelníček's flat with some money in hand one day, claiming that he was coming from a cruising area (*štrych*). He also used the Czech slang word for "gay", *teplý*, implying that the young man was indeed active in gay circles.[37] Czech here borrows the German words *Strich* (cruising area) and *warm* (German slang for "gay").

In February 1932, the Brno police were closely watching Kostelníček for homosexual behavior.[38] The publication of *Kamarád* prompted them to step up their investigations. Several young men interrogated by the police stated that Kostelníček was sexually abusing them. Kostelníček was remanded in custody (*Untersuchungshaft*) on July 23, 1932.[39] On September 15, 1932, he was released for a little less than two months. This means that Kostelníček could have attended the WLSR conference in September 1932; however, I think that Magnus Hirschfeld and Karl Fein would have taken care to keep clear of the case so as not to compromise the conference in any way. Certainly, Karl Fein was not the lawyer who defended Štefan L. Kostelníček or Stanislav Hudec (1911–?), one of Kostelníček's young partners, at their February 1933 trial.[40] Kostelníček was imprisoned again on November 9, 1932.[41] On February 27, 1933, the Slovak artist was convicted and sentenced to one year in prison for fraudulent business transactions with ceramics as well as for homosexual behavior according to paragraph 129b of

On September 13, 2020, I sent six letters to people in Czechia with the last name Hlubocký, found in an online phonebook. A few people replied, but none were related.

31 MZA, Brno, fonds C 12, Krajský soud trestní Brno, III. manipulace, kart. n° 539, sign. TK XI 1687/32, f. 14.

32 For more information on Kostelníček's period in the cloister, see Seidl et al. 2012, 187. For more on his year studying theology in Bratislava (Pressburg), see MZA, Brno, fonds C 12, Krajský soud trestní Brno, III. manipulace, kart. n° 539, sign. TK XI 1687/32, f. 14. Another source says that he studied theology for three years. See "Věznice v Prostějově a v Litovli plní se účastníky homosexuelních afér" (Prisons in Prostějov and Litovel are filled with those engaged in homosexual affairs), *Polední list*, Jan. 25, 1935, 2.

33 Štefan Leonard Kostelníček's last name is spelled Kostelníčák in Slovak. He was born in a small Slovak village, Spišská Stará Ves, on the Polish border. His father was Antonín Kostelníček (?–?) and his mother Marie Reiterová (?–?).

34 See, for example, the statement of Stanislav Hudec, who claimed he was paid 200 Czech crowns per month to work as a ceramics painter. See MZA, Brno, fonds C 12, Krajský soud trestní Brno, III. manipulace, kart. n° 539, sign. TK XI 1687/32, f. 28.

35 AMB, Brno, fonds Z 1, resident registration card Štefan Kostelníček: "umělecký malíř a redactor". Elsewhere, Kostelníček was described as "malíř a žurnalista" (painter and journalist), *Adreßbuch von Groß-Brünn* 1934, 286,

36 MZA, Brno, fonds C 12, Krajský soud trestní Brno, III. manipulace, kart. n° 539, sign. TK XI 1687/32, f. 10, 11, 12. Cf. Valtus 2015, 46–47.

37 Ibid., f. 12.

38 MZA, Brno, fonds C 12, Krajský soud trestní Brno, III. manipulace, kart. n° 539, sign. TK XI 1687/32, f. 6.

39 See "Aus dem Gerichtssaal" (From the courtroom), *Tagesbote*, Feb. 28, 1933, 6; MZA, Brno, fonds C 12, Krajský soud trestní Brno, III. manipulace, kart. n° 539, sign. TK XI 1687/32, f. 1. A resident registration card dated May 16–17, 1932, in the AMB, Brno, fonds Z 1, indeed lists his December 1932 address as 71 Cejl (Zeile), the address of both the Brno *Staatsanwaltschaft* (public prosecutor) and the Moravsko-slezská trestnice (Moravian-Silesian Penitentiary). See https://encyklopedie.brna.cz/home-mmb/?acc=profil_domu&load=118 (accessed Apr. 3, 2023).

40 The defense lawyers were Dr. [Artur] Kladivo and Dr. [Václav] Pirchan. See MZA, Brno, fonds C 12, Krajský soud trestní Brno, III. manipulace, kart. n° 539, sign. TK XI 1687/32, f. 26.

41 Ibid., f. 29b, f. 40.

the Czechoslovak penal code. Stanislav Hudec was sentenced to six months.[42] Two other suspects vanished, and their prosecution was abandoned.[43] Court proceedings were held behind closed doors.[44] The *Kamarád* police file clearly shows that the police combined Kostelníček's activities with *Kamarád*, his sexual behavior, and his crooked dealings with the pottery business.[45] Kostelníček had a prior May 1930 embezzlement conviction in Košice (Slovakia) involving dealings with a pawn shop.[46]

During his stay in prison, the police authorities apparently wanted Kostelníček to make a statement that he would not publish any more issues of *Kamarád*. Kostelníček at first adamantly insisted that he would continue to publish the magazine, but abandoned this firm stance after his release. At the end of September 1933, Kostelníček was a free man again,[47] moving between several addresses in Brno before settling in Prostějov (Proßnitz) in 1934,[48] where he reverted to his usual habits of luring young men with money and making crooked deals.[49] In 1936, Kostelníček moved back to the Slovak part of the country. In 2008, a family member wrote Kostelníček's biography, but did not mention his homosexuality once in a book that mainly presented his artistic achievements.[50] The Slovak national archives (Slovenský národný archív) in Bratislava preserve several police reports on Kostelníček from the war years, but these archival files are not yet accessible.[51]

[42] Ibid., f. 26–27 and f. 39.

[43] See the newspaper clippings "Vydavatel Kamaráda" (The publisher of *Kamarád*) from *Lidove noviny* (Feb. 28, 1933, 9) and "Aus dem Gerichtssaal" (From the courtroom) in *Tagesbote*, Feb. 28, 1933, 6 in MZA, Brno, fonds C 12, Krajský soud trestní Brno, III. manipulace, kart. n° 539, sign. TK XI 1687/32, f. 1–2. The two boys who had fled were Jan Motl (1914–?) and Antonín Rosche (1913–?), see MZA, Brno, fonds C 12, Krajský soud trestní Brno, III. manipulace, kart. n° 539, sign. TK XI 1687/32, f. 22b.

[44] See the newspaper clipping "Aus dem Gerichtssaal" from *Tagesbote*, Feb. 28, 1933, in MZA, Brno, fonds C 12, Krajský soud trestní Brno, III. manipulace, kart. n° 539, sign. TK XI 1687/32, f. 1: "Der Senat verurteilte nach geheim durchgeführter Verhandlung den Maler" (After a secret hearing, the Senate sentenced the painter).

[45] MZA, Brno, fonds C 12, Krajský soud trestní Brno, III. manipulace, kart. n° 539, sign. TK XI 1687/32, f. 13.

[46] Ibid., f. 20. Cf. MZA, Brno, fonds B 26, Policejní ředitelství v Brno, kart. n° 2736B, inv. n° 3893, sign. 846, f. 13.

[47] MZA, Brno, fonds B 26, Policejní ředitelství v Brno, kart. n° 2736B, inv. n° 3893, sign. 846, f. 4b, f. 6, f. 11b. The release date indicates that his time in custody was subtracted from his one-year prison sentence.

[48] A newspaper article from 1935 claims that Kostelníček was expelled from Brno in November 1934. See "Věznice v Prostějově a v Litovli plní se účastníky homosexuelních afér" (Prisons in Prostějov and Litovel are filled with those engaged in homosexual affairs), *Polední list*, Jan. 25, 1935, 2. Kostelníček had three Brno addresses after his release in September 1933: 27 Jeronýmova (Jeronymgasse), in the Brno-Židenice suburb; two weeks later, in mid-Oct. 1933, he lived with the Jewish Windholz family until mid-January 1934, at 65 Kröna (Křenová); and, after this three-month residence, he moved again to 27 Jeronýmova (Jeronymgasse), where he stayed for only two weeks. Presumably he left this address on February 1, 1934; however, his resident registration card in the AMB, Brno, fonds Z 1, states that his later whereabouts were unknown.

[49] A 1935 newspaper report about a homosexual network in the cities of Prostějov (Proßnitz) and Litovel claimed that Brno police warned the police in Prostějov (Proßnitz) about Kostelníček. Kostelníček was certainly not the only gay man involved in the numerous (uncovered) homosexual affairs in Prostějov (Proßnitz) and Litovel, but his name was prominent nevertheless. See "Věznice v Prostějově a v Litovli plní se účastníky homosexuelních afér" (Prisons in Prostějov and Litovel are filled with those engaged in homosexual affairs), *Polední list*, Jan. 25, 1935, 2. For the affairs in Prostějov (Proßnitz) and Litovel, see also "Velká homosexuální aféra v Prostějově a Litovli" (The great homosexual affair in Prostějov and Litovel), *Moravská orlice*, Jan. 23, 1935, 3; "Hnusná aféra v Prostějově" (An ugly affair in Prostějov), *Hlas Lidu*, Jan. 24, 1935, 4; and "Die peinliche Sittenaffäre in Proßnitz" (The painful vice affair in Proßnitz), *Morgenpost*, Jan. 24, 1935, 1.

[50] Kostelničáková 2008; cf. Seidl et al. 2012, 188.

[51] The files are in the fonds of the Odbočka spravodajskej ústredne Policajného riaditeľstva v Bratislave (Central Intelligence branch of the Bratislava/Pressburg Police Directorate). I was not allowed to consult these files because I am not related to Kostelníček, or so I was told. Archive staff invoked a ninety-year archival access term. See the letter of Ivan Tichý (Slovenský národný archív, Bratislava), sent by Mariá Zsigmondová (idem) via email (dated Nov. 20, 2018) to the author; and email (dated Dec. 3, 2018) from Marek Púčik (Slovenský národný archív, Bratislava) to the author, referring to article 13/5 in Zákon (Act) 395/2002 Z.z. o archívoch a registratúrach a o doplnení niektorých zákonov, as support for the invoked archival access term. On the basis of this archival access term of ninety years, these archives should become public around 2035. The same restriction applied to Kostelníček's 1945

JAROSLAV RŮŽIČKA

Kostelníček's preying on young men in their twenties likely explains one of the seven names on the list of those starting *Kamarád*: Jaroslav Růžička (1905–1978).[52] As a young boy in 1910, Růžička moved with his parents and five siblings from Brtnice, his birthplace, to Brno.[53] In a 1952 letter, Jaroslav Růžička stressed that he was from a very poor background, something confirmed by his living relatives.[54] In the summer of 1932, he informed the Brno police that he did not complete his military service.[55]

Judging from his many completed resident registration cards in the AMB, Brno, one cannot but notice that Jaroslav Růžička was a bit of a vagabond; he moved constantly, sometimes just staying two weeks at an address. In a ten-year period, starting in 1925, he moved at least twenty-three times, possibly indicating that he did not always pay the rent.[56] In 1932, the year that *Kamarád* was launched, he moved at least six times, perhaps because of his collaboration with *Kamarád* and to escape potential police visits connected to the Kostelníček case. In July 1931, Růžička was conditionally sentenced for fraud in Velké Pavlovice (Groß Pawlowitz), a southern Moravian village, suggesting some familiarity with petty crime.[57] When interrogated in 1932, he said that he was unemployed but occasionally worked at a stall near the railway station.[58]

Štefan Kostelniček told the Brno police how he picked up one of his young lovers, Antonín Rosche (1913–?), in the entrance hall of Brno's main station.[59] Railway stations often operated as cruising areas where young men in need of cash were on the lookout for male clients [ill. 6].[60] Since Růžička claimed he was unemployed but sometimes worked near the station, we have to ask if he was possibly also lured by Kostelníček. I think it likely. Given his difficult economic position, Růžička would have been susceptible to the "easy money" to be made in Kostelníček's flat, exchanging sexual favors for shelter and food. Růžička must at least have known about the goings-on in and around the railway station. Yet, in 1932, Jaroslav Růžička told the Brno police that he was not a homosexual himself, but only helped the circle around Štefan L. Kostelníček and *Kamarád*.[61] An archival prosecution file for Jaroslav Růžička related

application for membership in Demokratická strana na Slovensku (Democratic Party of Slovakia).

[52] MZA, Brno, fonds B 26, Policejní ředitelství v Brno, kart. n° 2736B, inv. n° 3893, sign. 846, f. 24.

[53] Státní okresní archiv Jihlava, fonds n° 379, national school Brtnice, class catalogue sixth class (1910?); and email (dated May 22, 2017) from Petr Dvořák (Státní okresní archiv Jihlava, Jihlava) to the author.

[54] Private archive Brno, appeal letter (dated Oct. 20, 1952) from Jaroslav Růžička to Okresní soud civilní v Brně and interview (dated October 10, 2019) with two living relatives of Jaroslav Růžička and Jindra Růžičková. See chapter 14, p. 499, n. 30 for a first mention of this interview.

[55] MZA, Brno, fonds C 12, Krajský soud trestní Brno, III. manipulace, kart. n° 539, sign. TK XI 1687/32, f. 12.

[56] Jaroslav Růžička's many resident registration cards in the AMB, Brno, fonds Z 1, indicate that Růžička's landlords were often the ones who informed the police that he had moved out, since his new address is rarely listed. This possibly also indicates that he left without notice and without paying the rent.

[57] MZA, Brno, fonds B 26, Policejní ředitelství v Brno, kart. n° 2736B, inv. n° 3893, sign. 846, f. 22b, 24.

[58] MZA, Brno, fonds C 12, Krajský soud trestní Brno, III. manipulace, kart. n° 539, sign. TK XI 1687/32, f. 12: "udal[,] že je t.č. bez zaměstnání a prodává v jedné budce poblíže nádraží" (he reported that he is unemployed and sells at a kiosk near the station).

[59] MZA, Brno, fonds C 12, Krajský soud trestní Brno, III. manipulace, kart. n° 539, sign. TK XI 1687/32, f. 10b. See also Valtus 2015, 46.

[60] See Valtus 2015, 12. This economic motive of the young men who prostituted themselves is clearly seen in Willi Bondi's March 28, 1941 testimony, stating that he always footed the bill when out with these young men. Bondi also often invited them along when he went to dine in the home of his sister, Julia Fleischer. See MZA, Brno, fonds C 43, Německý zemský soud Brno (Deutsches Landgericht), Staatsanwaltschaft bei dem Landgericht Brünn, file Wilhelm Sponer & Helmuth Holdau, kart. n° 184, sign. 4 K Ls 24/41, f. 94b.

[61] MZA, Brno, fonds C 12, Krajský soud trestní Brno, III. manipulace, kart. n° 539, sign. TK XI 1687/32, f. 12 and f. 13: "Sám prý není homosexuélně založen, pomáhá však Kostelníčkovi v redakci časopisu 'Kamarád.'" In 1941, when a group of men were questioned about their homosexual activities by the German Kriminalpolizei (Kripo), most simply denied any such activity, or even that they were homosexuals. We know with certainty that some lied. See the testimonies in MZA, Brno, fonds C 43, Německý zemský soud Brno (Deutsches Landgericht), Staats-

to homosexual conduct existed, but it was either lost, misfiled, or shredded.[62] During a search of Štefan Leonard Kostelníček's flat in July 1932, the police discovered that Jaroslav Růžička had removed a list of addresses of people interested in *Kamarád*. It is unclear if the police recovered the list, but Růžička stated that he had hidden it to protect those named.[63] There is little use, nor any real moral or other relevance, in trying to establish whether Jaroslav Růžička was a gay man, but it seems certain that offering (homo)sexual services for money was certainly not uncommon for some young unemployed Czechoslovak men in the 1930s.

In May 2017, completely out of the blue, I discovered that Jaroslav Růžička married Jindřiška Fikes, who became Jindra Růžičkova, in December 1939.[64] Jindra Růžičkova was none other than the owner of the Brno business dealing in scrap, where the Hirschfeld guestbook was found in 1942 [ill. 7]. All of a sudden, many things seemed to fall into place. This implied, first of all, that Jaroslav Růžička, a member of the *Kamarád* clique, saw to it that the Institute materials were discarded in the old paper container owned by his wife's company in 1942. This discovery also seemed to strongly suggest that Karl Fein entrusted the Institute lot either to the non-Jewish group of people behind *Kamarád* as a whole or to a specific member of the *Kamarád* clique. The surprising discovery seemed further to show that Jaroslav Růžička remained in contact with some or all of the *Kamarád* group ten years after the very short-lived 1932 gay magazine venture.

anwaltschaft bei dem Landgericht Brünn, file Wilhelm Sponer & Helmuth Holdau, kart. n° 184, sign. 4 K Ls 24/41. In his *Schlussbericht* (conclusion) to the investigation, Kripo Kriminal-Oberassistent Hofmann wrote: "Es ist eine allgemein bekannte Tatsache, dass Homosexuelle bei Vernehmungen alles wegleugnen und nur das zugeben, was man ihnen beweisen kann" (It is a well-known fact that homosexuals deny everything during interrogations and only admit what can be proved to them). See ibid., f. 76b. That said, it is also possible that some young men whose sexual orientation or preference was heterosexual prostituted themselves to men.

62 The file Tk V 1694/32 for Jaroslav Růžička in the C 12 fonds (Krajský soud trestní Brno) of the MZA, Brno, is unfortunately missing. See Valtus 2015, 53; and email (dated May 11, 2017) from Jana Fasorová (MZA, Brno) to the author.

63 MZA, Brno, fonds C 12, Krajský soud trestní Brno, III. manipulace, kart. n° 539, sign. TK XI 1687/32, f. 12–13: "Bylo zjištěno, že dne 22. července 1932 odpoledne, bylo v bytě Štěpána Kostelníčka známo, že Rosche [...] byl zatčen a tu jistý Jaroslav Růžička, bytem v Zábrdovicích č. 14 z bytu odnesl seznam homosexuélních osob a jíné písemnosti" (It has been established that on the afternoon of July 22, 1932, in the apartment of Štěpán Kostelníček, it was known that Rosche [...] was arrested and that a certain Jaroslav Růžička, residing at 14 Zábrdovice, had taken a list of homosexual persons and other documents from the apartment). A June 1932 resident registration card in the AMB, Brno, fonds Z 1, lists one of Růžička's addresses as 14 Obrowitz (Zábrdovice); however, the house number was actually 12.

64 That Jaroslav Růžička was indeed Jindra Růžičková's husband was not immediately ascertainable, Růžička being a very common family name in Czechoslovakia and, today, in Czechia. There was also some confusion regarding Růžička's identity in the *Kamarád* police file. A copy of one of Jaroslav Růžička's resident registration cards (used by the police to identify him) indicated that the Jaroslav Růžička who worked with *Kamarád* was born in Brtnice on May 15, 1905, whereas the Jaroslav Růžička who married Jindra Fikes was born on May 4, 1905. See MZA, Brno, fonds B 26, Policejní ředitelství v Brno, kart. n° 2736B, inv. n° 3893, sign. 846, f. 22; and the marriage certificate dated December 23, 1939. http://actapublica.eu/matriky/brno/prohlizec/10776/?strana=1 (accessed Mar. 13, 2019). Was there maybe another Jaroslav Růžička born in the same year in the same village? It was possible. I checked with the Státní okresní archiv Jihlava, and there were indeed two Jaroslav Růžičkas born in the small village of Brtnice in 1905. An idea of its size then is given by the fact that, in 2012, the village had 3,700 residents (see https://cs.wikipedia.org/wiki/Brtnice [accessed Jun. 16, 2017]). There was a Jaroslav Růžička born in Brtnice on May 4, 1905 (to František Růžička and Magdalena Ottová), corresponding to the Jaroslav Růžička who married Jindra Růžičková. The second Jaroslav Růžička was born on April 10, 1905 (to Josef Růžička and Marie Hrdličková), but the baby died on January 21, 1906. The Brtnice 1905 birth registry was checked by Petr Dvořák (Státní okresní archiv Jihlava). See his email (dated May 22, 2017) to the author. This still did not explain the troubling variance in the birth date on the copy of the resident registration card in the police file. In the AMB, Brno, fonds Z 1, I also looked up Jaroslav Růžička's original resident registration card, dated March 18, 1932, and compared it with the copy made in pencil by an officer for the *Kamarád* police file, to see if the erroneous birth date was on the original as well. It was. I then realized that the birth date on this card was incorrect simply because the card was

GENERAL FEAR: REINHARD HEYDRICH

But this great leap forward in my research project immediately raised a new research question: why would the people around *Kamarád* discard the books, materials, and some of the archives of Hirschfeld, a man they so admired and whom they had gone to meet in person in Brno in May 1932? To understand this better, it is important to restore the fraught war context of the year 1942 in the Protectorate.

For being too soft on the resisting Czech population, Konstantin von Neurath (1873–1956), the first Reich Protector of Bohemia and Moravia (Reichsprotektor in Böhmen und Mähren), was replaced by Reinhard Heydrich (1904–1942). Heydrich immediately set up the first summary court martial (*1. Standgericht*) in the Protectorate, which ran from September 28, 1941, until January 20, 1942. Many Czechs were summarily tried and either deported to a concentration camp or executed.[65] In Brno alone, approximately 1,200 people were arrested in October 1941, around 250 of whom were executed and another 800 sent to concentration camps.[66] Verdicts could not be appealed. The Brno lawyer Karel Růžička, a colleague of Karl Fein, was a victim of the first summary court martial, being deported to Mauthausen where he was killed soon after his arrival. One of the organizers of the 1932 WLSR conference, Dr. Karel Hora, was also tried by this court in January 1942. He too was sent to Mauthausen, where he died in May 1942. Another organizer of the WLSR conference, Dr. Siegfried Fischl, died in Auschwitz in February 1942 (sent there before the better-known mass transports to the gas chambers).

Terror was also part and parcel of Gestapo practice.[67] "The SS and Gestapo spread fear and terror wherever they went", wrote Arnold Hindls, a Jewish Brno resident, in his wartime memoir.[68] Starting in January 1940, Brno's Kaunitz College (Kounicovy koleje) was used as a prison and site of torture and execution. The building has a tragic reputation as a consequence. Roughly 30,000 prisoners passed through the facility during the war years.[69] Defiantly, the Gestapo headquarters in Brno (*Gestapoleitstelle Brünn*) also installed their headquarters in Masaryk University's former Faculty of Law building at 70 Veveří (Eichhorner Strasse).[70] Today, the entrance hall of the building bears a plaque commemorating the faculty and staff who died during the German occupation.[71] When the Gestapo first arrived in Brno, in 1939, it counted about 200 staff members. By August 1941, 638 people were working for them.[72] The main focus of the German counterattack under the leadership of Heydrich were the increasing activities of the main Czech resistance organization, National Defense (Obrana národa, ON; also translated as Defense of the Nation); to be a legionnaire, a Communist, a Jewish person, a member of Sokol (the banned gymnastic organization), or a leftist was reason enough to be arrested. The terror regime's executions were made public to frighten potential Czech patriots.

filled out, not by Jaroslav Růžička, but by the person renting him the room. Růžička moved a lot and likely often skipped out without paying the rent. The person who signed the resident registration card, Růžena Frolová (last name uncertain), was possibly uncertain about his exact birth date and chose (or was persuaded by the police to choose) a day in the middle of the month, thus the fifteenth. Both the original resident registration card and the pencil copy show Růžička's old address, 6 Na pískách (Sandstätte), where he had stayed only two weeks.

65 Nosková 2016, 318.

66 Filip et al. 2012, 65.

67 Filip et al. 2012, 61.

68 Hindls 1966, 137: "SS — und Gestapo verbreiteten, wohin sie kamen, Angst und Schrecken".

69 Filip et al. 2012, 64; Vašek, Černý & Břečka 2015.

70 Filip et al. 2012, 64, 77. For more information on this 1928 building, see Vrabelová, Svobodová, & Šlapeta 2016, 180; and Pelčák & Šlapeta 2015, 204–5. See ch. 13, ill. n° 1.

71 The main *aula* (auditorium) of the building has a mural by Antonín Prochazka, who was closely related to the lawyer Karel Růžička, a colleague of Karl Fein. I thank Jana Nosková for facilitating my viewing of this impressive mural in April 2015.

72 Filip et al. 2012, 55. The Brno *Gestapoleitdienststelle* was also responsible for areas outside of Brno. See Filip et al. 2012, 57, 237.

A second summary court martial (*Standgericht*) started immediately after Heydrich's assassination, on May 27, 1942, and lasted until July 3, 1942. It was known as the "Heydrichiade".[73] "The atmosphere in Berlin [immediately after Heydrich's assassination] can only be described as murderous", according to one of Heydrich's biographers.[74] During the second summary court martial, a little under 400 people were executed in Brno alone.[75] Many more people from all social backgrounds and every part of the Protectorate were arbitrarily arrested and shot. The idea that *anyone* could be arrested pervaded the Protectorate, instilling general fear in the Czech population as a whole in the months after Heydrich's assassination.[76] This fear was amplified by the horrific fate of the Bohemian village of Lidice (Liditz). On Hitler's own orders, it was largely arbitrarily selected to exact retribution for Heydrich's assassination. In June 1942, all of its approximately 170 adult male residents were shot, and its women and children deported. The village itself was completely razed after the massacre.

Also in June 1942, the Prague hiding place of the two parachutists who assassinated Heydrich, Josef Gabčík (1912–1942) and Jan Kubiš (1913–1942), was betrayed by Karel Čurda (1911-1947). The two men (and their fellow parachutists) succumbed when the Orthodox Church of St. Cyril and Methodius was stormed by German troops. The siege lasted for hours. Immediately afterwards, the Germans started to hunt down all members of the local Czech network that helped the parachutists. In early July 1942, when this network was uncovered and all involved were arrested, the second summary court-martial concluded.[77] Later, in early September 1942, several leaders of the Orthodox Church in Prague, obviously aware of the hiding place, were convicted and executed.

The search for the network behind the assassination also led to Brno. One member, Jan Sonnevend (1880–1942), lived in Brno in the 1930s, working in insurance. He was sentenced to death in the Gestapo headquarters in Prague's Petschek Palace on September 3, 1942, and executed the next day.[78] Sonnevend's residence in Brno and his death sentence was reported in some newspapers, indicating that the Germans' retaliatory actions had not yet come to an end.[79] At the time of Sonnevend's trial, most of the 257 relatives of the parachutists and of those who had helped them were still held in Terezín (Theresienstadt). They were sent to Mauthausen in Austria on October 23, 1942, and executed the next day. Marie Lorková (1888–1942), the wife of Jan Sonnevend, and their daughter, Ludmila Ryšavá (1908–1942), and her husband, Josef Ryšavý (1896–1942), were among them. A second and final group of thirty-one people were shot in Mauthausen on January 26, 1943.[80] After seeing how the Germans responded to Heydrich's assassination, it required even greater courage and conviction for the Czech citizens of the self-styled Protectorate to join the resistance.[81]

[73] Vašek & Štěpánek 2002 and Filip et al. 2012, 65, 72, 191.

[74] Gerwarth 2011, 280.

[75] Filip et al. 2012, 191.

[76] Crowhurst 2013, 145, 147. Crowhurst also gives a good overview of the retaliations implemented by the Germans after Heydrich's death. See Crowhurst 2013, 140–48.

[77] Gerwarth 2011, 285.

[78] Šmejkal & Padevět 2016, 50, 95, 150–51; Burian et al. 2002, 90–91; http://encyklopedie.brna.cz/home-mmb/?acc=profil_osobnosti&load=3583 (accessed Jan. 9, 2018).

[79] See, for example, "Zločin biskupa Gorazda a společníku" (The crime of bishop Gorazd and associates), *Lidové noviny*, Sep. 6, 1942, 1, 3; "Apostel ohne Heiligenschein" (Apostle without a halo), *Mährisches Tagblatt*, Sep. 6, 1942, 3; and, though it does not mention Brno, "Kněz jako ochránce vrahů: Přechovavatelé vrahů SS-Obergruppenführera Heydricha před stanným soudem" (The priest as protector of murderers: the SS-Obergruppenführer Heydrich's murderers on trial under martial law), *Venkov: orgán České strany agrární*, Sep. 6, 1942, 1–2.

[80] Burian et al. 2002, 48, 58, 60, 61, 92–93. For a list of the people executed, see Šmejkal & Padevět 2016, 189–99.

[81] Filip et al. 2012, 228.

[82] Ticho 2001, "The flood", 1–2.

[83] Qtd. in Wildt 2003, 619–20. See also Potthast 2002, 91–92, 124–25, 134, 140–41; Kárný 1999, 52; Gerwarth 2011, 287–88. For a collection of primary

The regime of terror installed by Heydrich – which only intensified after his death – is the first significant factor that needs to be recognized to appreciate the general atmosphere of fear in which the citizens of the Protectorate lived in 1941 and especially 1942. The Czech population had been subject to ruthless Nazi terror even before the arrival of Heydrich, of course, but fear intensified with news of the Germans' ruthless retaliations against Czech citizens.[82]

At that time, the Czech population also held the belief that once the deportations of the Jewish population came to an end, they would be next. The anti-Czech stance of the Germans was no fiction. Consider, for example, an October 1941 speech by Reinhard Heydrich, in which he boldly stated that the Czechs would no longer have a place in the Germanized Protectorate.[83] Karl Hermann Frank (1898–1946), Heydrich's second-in-command, had his own ideas about how the National Socialists would deal with the Czechs in his "Memorandum on the treatment of the Czech problem and the future organization of the Bohemian-Moravian area" (*Denkschrift über die Behandlung des Tschechen-Problems und die Zukünftige Gestaltung des böhmisch-mährischen Raumes*),[84] proposing that, after the Jews, the Czechs were next, and this idea lives on in Czechia even today. Most Czech perceive Operation Anthropoid, the code name for the assassination attempt on Heydrich by the Czech Kubiš and the Slovak Gabčík, as necessary to halt, or at least delay, Heydrich's ruthless plans for the Czech population. In a 2012 BBC interview, Alois Denemarek, a surviving family member of those who helped the parachutists, said: "If it wasn't for Jan [Kubiš, who threw the grenade at Heydrich's car], I wouldn't be here today. Half the Czech nation wouldn't be here today. Heydrich had terrible plans for us Czechs".[85] The May 2009 dedication of the Operation Anthropoid Memorial (Památník Operace Anthropoid) in Prague-Libeň, on the spot where Heydrich was assassinated, is further evidence of this conviction.[86]

By June 1942, virtually all Jewish people were deported from Brno. This likely meant that the Brno Gestapo's sizable staff started to focus on new tasks and population groups. Czech citizens expected they would be next in line. In particular, Czech gay men, aware of what had happened to the gay subculture in Germany, were likely to believe – or simply feared – that they would be investigated and targeted as the Nazis' next category of victims.

These two factors shaped the general environment in which the Czech population and the *Kamarád* people had to operate. Besides a general atmosphere of terror that reigned in the Protectorate, and the new German focus on solving the Czech problem (and potentially also targeting gay Czech men), another probable factor explains why the *Kamarád* people would have been afraid to hold onto the Hirschfeld and Institute materials, deciding to discard them [ill. 8].

THE OCTOBER 1941 EXPROPRIATION ORDINANCE

Starting as early as June 1939, the National Socialists were after the "big money" in their expropriation of the Jewish population. Shortly before the first mass transports of Jewish people left the Protectorate, in the autumn of 1941, another expropriation ordinance was issued. The Central Office for Jewish Emigration (Zentralstelle für jüdische Auswanderung) in Prague decreed that *no* valuable assets (*Vermögenswerte*) belonging to Jewish people could be sold, donated (gifted), lent, pawned, entrusted,

sources on this very real anti-Czech sentiment and attitude, see Celovsky 2005.

[84] In Kral 1964, 417–21, n° 315. A few texts following Frank's memorandum in this volume deal with the same topic.

[85] See http://www.bbc.com/news/world-europe-18183099 (accessed Sep. 4, 2020).

[86] See https://cs.wikipedia.org/wiki/Památník_Operace_Anthropoid (accessed Sep. 13, 2020).

or transferred by any other means without the Central Office's prior authorization.[87] This ordinance was issued on October 25, 1941, clearly in anticipation of the impending deportations. In fact, the first two transports had already left from Prague to Łódź, on October 16 and 21, a little before the ordinance was issued. Karl Fein was deported on the second Prague transport to Łódź, meaning that he would not have been aware of this ordinance. The third Prague transport to Łódź left the day after the ordinance was issued, on October 26, 1942.

The ordinance tried to forestall the anticipated – or already observed – efforts of Jewish people summoned for transport to entrust their furnishings and other household belongings to non-Jewish neighbors, friends, and acquaintances. As we have already seen, people continued this practice in the following months and years despite the ordinance. However, after October 1941, it was a dangerous, punishable matter. As a consequence, many Jewish families summoned for deportation left at least some of their belongings behind because an empty house or apartment would indicate a breach of the new ordinance. This allowed the National Socialists to make money even from these simple everyday items when clearing the homes of the deported.

This ordinance is one more factor that helps us better understand the situation in the Protectorate in 1941 and 1942. If the Germans had found the Institute materials in the home of a *Kamarád* member (or anyone else), they would have presumed that these Jewish artifacts had been received from a Jewish person. Furthermore, all of the *Kamarád* people would most likely have known about the May 1933 Berlin book burnings, the buy-back operation conducted with the help of Karl Fein (and Josef Weisskopf), Karl Giese's bequest of the Institute materials to Karl Fein and, most of all, that Magnus Hirschfeld was a Jewish archenemy of the National Socialists. Possession of these materials therefore carried a real risk.

But even before the ordinance was issued in October 1941, there was already a deep-seated fear of holding onto goods that (had) belonged to Jewish people. The reader may remember that the Brno engineer Arnold Hindls succeeded in storing his household furnishings in a carpentry shop in April 1941. After three months, however, the shop owner changed his mind:

> Although I paid him the high rent that he demanded on time, after only three months he urged me to remove everything again; he was afraid of storing Jewish property under his roof. He had been forced to take on a German partner in his company and feared serious consequences if Jewish property was discovered. Finally, he recommended another cabinetmaker's shop in his neighborhood, which agreed to store Jewish property. How

[87] Friedmann, Jul. 31, 1942/1997, 243: "Am 25. Oktober 1941 wurde es durch die Bekanntmachung der Zentralstelle für jüdische Auswanderung Prag den Juden ausnahmslos untersagt, irgendwelche Vermögenswerte [...] zu veräussern, soferne nicht im einzelnen eine behördliche Bewilligung vorliegt. Insbesondere ist es verboten: a/ Wohnungseinrichtungen und Hausrat zu veräussern, zu verschenken, zu verpfänden, anderen Personen in Verwahrung zu geben oder ähnliche Verfügungen zu treffen" (On 25 October 1941, the Central Office for Jewish Emigration in Prague announced that, without exception, Jews were prohibited from transferring any assets [...] unless an individual official permit had been issued. In particular, it is forbidden to sell, give away, pawn, place in other people's custody, or make any similar dispositions of residential furnishings and household effects). See also Potthast 2002, 206–7. For a similar instruction to people who received a deportation order, cf. Klementová 2010, 27: "Zákaz dispozic majetkem: Je zakázáno prodat, darovat nebo zapůjčovat předměty, které máte nyní ve svém majetku. Neuposlechnutí se trestá" (Prohibition regarding the disposition of property: it is forbidden to sell, give, or lend items that you now have in your possession. Failure to comply shall be punished).

[88] Hindls 1966, 140–41: "Obwohl ich ihm pünktlich die von ihm verlangte hohe Miete bezahlte, forderte er mich schon nach drei Monaten auf, alles wieder abzuführen, da er sich fürchte jüdisches Eigentum unter seinem Dache aufzubewahren. Er sei gezwungen worden in sein Unternehemen einen deutschen Kompagnon aufzunehmen und fürchte bei Entdeck-

difficult it was then to relocate Jewish property, and the general fear of coming into conflict with the Gestapo, can hardly be imagined today.[88]

The October 25, 1941 ordinance issued by the Central Office for Jewish Emigration only confirmed what was already obvious: non-Jewish Protectorate citizens needed to stay away from all Jewish belongings at all times.

THE DANGER OF (CERTAIN) BOOKS

One may also wonder, in this connection, if keeping certain books – Jewish-owned or not – might have been dangerous during the war years. Let us look at the case of Karel Kulka (1892–1956), the trade unionist who at one point lived in the same building as Karl Fein (and Karl Giese), at 7c U dětské nemocnice (Kinderspitalgasse or Beim Kinderspital). In a testimony for the Shoah Foundation, his daughter, Alice Rosenberg, said that her convinced social-democrat father burned his controversial books when the Nazis invaded Czechoslovakia. Kulka was questioned and held in the Brno police prison on Adlergasse (Orlí) for several months. The Gestapo also searched the apartment where Rosenberg lived with her parents several times. For a very short time, Alice Rosenberg herself was active in the resistance and hid onion-leaf propaganda pamphlets behind the bathroom toilet tank in their apartment.[89]

Rosenberg's testimony indirectly reveals that keeping Institute materials or other Hirschfeld papers was a very tricky business. Finding someone who was prepared to safeguard the Institute lot was most likely a difficult problem for Karl Fein, one he may have had to confront early on, possibly as early as 1938–39. At the end of the interview, Alice Rosenberg was asked how so many of her family photos were saved since she said that they left "everything" behind in their last apartment in Královo Pole, leaving Brno with only one suitcase. She explained that these photos were left with one of her father's non-Jewish acquaintances, who had a dairy in the countryside.[90] But even in this location, their belonging apparently had to be moved several times, to evade discovery by the Germans. She added that they picked up their belongings when the war was over.

WAS THE GUESTBOOK AFFIDAVIT A DECOY?

This October 1941 ordinance was my second reason to consider that the affidavit in the Hirschfeld guestbook may have been some kind of hoax. Was it maybe a way to circumvent the prohibition against holding Jewish belongings? Maybe, I thought, the affidavit sought to make it clear, in case someone asked nosy questions, that the guestbook and sexology books were *not* entrusted by a Jewish person to Dr. Kaděrka but were fortuitously discovered in the old paper container of a scrap company? "We found it in the trash" would have severed any link to the person entrusting the materials and made the whole situation look much more innocent. The affidavit's curious self-justifying appeal to science may have been another decoy. What speaks strongly against this interpretation, I think, is not only that so few items were recovered from the old paper container in 1942, but also that, in most cases, there were only a few volumes from each of the several multi-volume titles in Kaděrka's library. Were the affidavit truly a decoy, more books (and more complete series) from

ung schwerwiegende Folgen wegen Einlagerung jüdischen Eigentums. Schliesslich empfahl er mir eine andere Möbeltischlerei in seiner Nähe, die sich zur Einlagerung bereit erklärte. Wie schwierig es damals war, eine solche Uebersiedlung jüdischen Eigentums durchzuführen, bei der allgemeinen Angst mit der Gestapo in Konflikt zu geraten, kann man sich heute kaum mehr vorstellen".

[89] Visual History Archive (USC Shoah Foundation), interview 12303, interview Alice Rosenberg (née Kulka), dated Feb. 21, 1996.

[90] The acquaintance is possibly explained through her maternal grandparents, who had a dairy.

the Institute would have ended up in Kaděrka's home. All this quickly restored my relative acceptance of the veracity of the affidavit.

So, it is indeed possible that Karl Fein entrusted the Institute materials to someone in the *Kamarád* group. Is it possible to determine who specifically? And did that person also discard the materials in 1942? In contrast to the case of Jindra and Jaroslav Růžička's scrap business, where some, presumably even all, of the other Institute materials were intentionally discarded, it is much less certain who in the *Kamarád* group might have watched over the materials until then. The available archival sources seem to point to two *Kamarád* people we have not yet met: Stanislav Černil and Jaroslav Očadlík. Let us now take a closer look at the lives of these two men before developing the argument for their possible involvement in safeguarding and discarding the Institute materials.

STANISLAV ČERNIL

After Kostelníček and Drexler-Hlubocký, Stanislav (Standa) Černil (1908–1979) was the most important man in the *Kamarád* group.[91] Like most of the other *Kamarád* founders, he was a Brno local. He studied at the Czech Higher School of Business (Česká vyšší obchodní škola) for two years, from 1925 to 1926, and was also a member of the Protestant Evangelical Church of Czech Brethren (Českobratrská církev evangelická).[92] He was the third son of Josef Černil (1870–1942) and Maria Vlašínová (1874–1948). Josef Černíl was a carpenter, specializing in miniature wooden model work late in his career. Stanislav Černil had five siblings: František Černil (1896–1970),[93] Josef František Černil (1900–1974),[94] Marie Žamberský (1902–1983), Hedvika Skácel (1903–1993), and Jaromir Černil (1914–1984).

[91] In the *Kamarád* issue, Černíl's first name is spelled "Standa". See Černíl, May 28, 1932, 11. This same first name reappears in *Adressbuch der Landeshauptstadt Brünn 1942* 1943, 32. Černíl's daughter, Dagmar, told me that her father was indeed commonly called Standa.

[92] As far as I was able to determine, training usually lasted four years, which indicates that Černíl did not finish his schooling. See *Roční zpráva české vyšší obchodní školy v Brně za školní* 1925, 46; 1926, 30.

[93] See https://encyklopedie.brna.cz/home-mmj/?acc=profil_osobnosti& load=8200 (accessed Dec. 3, 2018). František Černil had three children with his wife, Valerie Magdová (1897–1988), two sons and one daughter: Miroslav (1919–1989), Miloň (1923–?) and Blanka (1924–1995). František, Valerie, and Blanka Černil are buried in the Brno central cemetery, in parcel 99, graves 76–77. When I visited on October 16, 2021, I found a notice attached to the gravestone of a rather neglected gravesite, requesting the family to contact the cemetery administration. Presumably, the license for the grave would expire soon. If the administration was not able to contact the person responsible for the grave directly, it would certainly be impossible for me to do so. The next day, however, I saw the grave of one of František Černil's two sons, Miroslav Černil, buried with his wife Jarmila (1922–2012) and daughter Miroslava Reková (1943–1993) in parcel 45, grave 79. On November 9, 2021, I sent a letter to the person paying for the grave permit but received no reply.

[94] Josef František Černil was married to Květoslava Kantová (1893–1977) and the couple had two children: a daughter, Ester (Květa) (1933–), and a son, Pravdomil (1926–?). The couple is buried in the Brno central cemetery, in parcel 86, grave 117. I sent a letter to the relative, presumably Ester Černilová, responsible for the grave on October 27, 2021, but did not get a reply. In the 1930s, Josef František Černil served as the vice president (deputy chairman) of the Brno Esperanto Association. See https://encyklopedie.brna.cz/home-mmb/?acc=profil_udalosti&load=332 (accessed Nov. 5, 2020). Because Esperanto was the fourth official language at the WLSR conference, I wondered if the Brno Esperanto Association might have played a part in translating the conference texts into Esperanto. The WLSR conference was reported in *La Progreso*, nos. 7–8, 1932, 92, which also mentioned that Leunbach delivered his lecture in Esperanto. The still active association had no information about Josef Černil's membership or on any contacts between the Brno Esperanto Association and Hirschfeld or the WLSR. See the Facebook Messenger message (dated Apr. 16, 2019) from Miroslav Malovec (Klub esperantistů Brno) to the author. Stanislav Černíl's daughter, Dagmar, remembered that her cousin, Ester, still had the Esperanto dictionary her father gave her. See letter (dated Mar. 15, 2019, 7) from Dagmar Černilová to the author. The website of the Klub esperantistů Brno can be found at http://esperantobrno.cz/ (accessed Apr. 17, 2019). On October 7, 2021, I left a message on the message board of Geni.com, the genealogical website, for Evžen Černil (1951–), presumably a grandson of Josef František Černil. There was no reply.

Stanislav Černil married three times and was twice divorced. His first wife, Marie Břoušková (1911–1999), was an office employee. They married in 1929 and divorced in February 1935.[95] In October 1935, Černil married his second wife, Ludmila Sucháneková (also spelled Suchánková, 1893–?) in Třebíč. They divorced in 1942.[96] Černil's third wife was Helene Müller (1917–1988), whom he married in April 1944. This last marriage lasted until he died.

Stanislav Černil and his first wife had a daughter, Dagmar [married name known to author] (née Černilová, 1930–2022). A son, Stanislav (1946–2015), from his third marriage, was born after the war. In October 2018, I interviewed Černil's daughter and corresponded with her afterwards by letter.[97]

Stanislav Černil had several different jobs. On one of his post-war resident registration cards, he was identified as a warehouse employee; on another, from 1948, he was a store manager.[98] In the 1930s, Černil worked as a representative for Star, the Brno sweets and chocolate manufacturer.[99] He also worked, although it is unclear when exactly, for the Czech joint-stock veneer factory (Česká akciová továrna na dyhy) at 36 Cejl (Zeile) in Brno. Initially, he worked in the company's warehouse, but eventually became their representative in Moravská Ostrava (Mährisch-Ostrau).[100] Černil spent the working week in Ostrava, but returned to Brno on weekends. According to his daughter Dagmar, Černil lived with a Jewish family on Biskupská Street when in Ostrava. She also wrote that the son of the family was a rabbi, adding that her own father "was like a son to this family".[101] We will return to this Moravská Ostrava (Mährisch-Ostrau) Jewish family later.

Outside of work, Černil's real passion was the theater. He wrote a five-act play entitled *Why?* (*Proč*), which was performed in April 1932 by Bojmír, an amateur traveling theater company led by a man named Karničky-Litovského.[102] A short review of the play appeared in *Kamarád*.[103] The protagonist, Ernest O'Benn (played

[95] MZA, Brno, fonds C 11, Krajský soud civilní Brno, divorce file Černil/Břoušková, year 1935, kart. n° 445, sign. Ck Ia 27/35. Černil's daughter Dagmar told me that her parents broke up the "first time" when she was three years old. As she was born in 1930, this would have been in 1933.

[96] MZA, Brno, fonds C 11, Krajský soud civilní Brno, divorce file Černil/Sucháneková, year 1942, kart. n° 358, sign. Ck Ia 226/42.

[97] I interviewed Dagmar Černilová in Brno on October 23, 2018. In addition, I sent her several lists of questions afterwards. I wish to thank her for always dutifully answering them in handwritten letters. At her request, I have not given here her married name. She is referred to as "Dagmar Černil(ová)" hereafter. I thank Ondřej Tuza for his excellent and patient assistance in translating the October 2018 interview.

[98] Resident registration cards for Stanislav Černil in AMB, Brno, fonds Z 1, and *Adresář zemského hlavního města Brna* 1948, 49: "skladník" and "obchodvedoucí."

[99] The company was owned by Vojtěch Brázda. Some other Černíl family members, like Josef František Černil and Hedvika Skácel, Stanislav Černíl's elder sister, were also working for this company. See, for example, the mention of the *Prokura* (procuration) for Stanislav's brother, Josef František Černíl in *Adreßbuch von Groß-Brünn* 1932, 705. See also the interview with Dagmar Černilová; letter (dated Mar. 15, 2019) from Dagmar Černilová to the author.

[100] For the Česká akciová továrna na dyhy (Böhmische Aktien Fournier Fabrik), see *Adressbuch der Landeshauptstadt Brünn* 1942, 34. Stanislav's father was a carpenter, and this may have played a part in his son getting or choosing this job.

[101] Letter (dated Mar. 15, 2019) from Dagmar Černilová to the author. In January 2021, I inquired about this matter with Daniel Baránek (Židovské muzeum v Praze, Praha), one of the main authorities on the history of Ostrava Jewry. See Baránek 2017. He suggested that this may have been the Schön family, but pointed out that Biskupská Street was created after the war. See email (dated Dec. 17, 2020) from Daniel Baránek (Židovské muzeum v Praze, Praha) to the author. I further inquired with the Ostrava city archive and learned that the Schön family (whose son Albert was indeed a rabbi) lived at 13 Kostelní (Kirchengasse). See email (dated Jan. 7, 2021) from Šárka Glombíčková (Archiv města Ostravy, Ostrava) to the author. Google Maps Street View shows that the building where the family lived is located on the corner of Biskupská and Kostelní (or at least so it appears, since Street View shows no houses to its right). This most likely explains why Dagmar gave the building's street as Biskupská and not Kostelní.

[102] MZA, Brno, fonds C 11, divorce file Černil/Sucháneková, year 1942, kart. n° 358, sign. Ck Ia 226/42, f. 21b.

[103] The review of the play was by Karel Hlubocký (most likely Vilém Drexler-Hlubocký). See Hlubocký, May 28, 1932, 17–19.

by Stanislav Černil), feels pressured by his mother to marry a countess, but has a relationship with the countess's brother. The gay couple are blackmailed by a French man, whom O'Benn shoots. The mother dies, and, in the end, O'Benn commits suicide. Despite its many deaths, the play's title suggests it had homo-emancipation as its goal, like the plays championed by Hirschfeld and Giese in Berlin. The passport-like picture of Stanislav Černil next to the *Kamarád* review is especially remarkable. Černil's eyebrows appear plucked and contoured with a rounded mascara line, possibly documenting the part he plays [ill. 9].[104] That his picture was included in apparently the very first gay magazine ever to be published in Brno seems a testament of his great courage. Yet a little more than a week after the first issue of *Kamarád* came out, Stanislav Černil resigned from its editorial board.[105]

As a very young child, Stanislav Černíl lived with his mother and father in the Trnitá neigborhood near the Brno railway station. In 1908, the year Černíl was born, his parents lived at 12 Cyrillsgasse (Cyrilská).[106] Josef Černíl ran his carpentry business from 6 Cyrillsgasse (Cyrilská) until the beginning of World War I.[107] Marie Černíl seems to have opened a furniture business of her own, located at 12 Cyrillsgasse (Cyrilská), which operated from 1913 until at least 1922.[108] Around 1920, the family moved to 23 Kreuzgasse (Křížová) and later to number 16 on the same street.[109] From entries in the Brno address books, however, one can deduce that his parents lived apart, on and off, when Černil was a young boy. Nevertheless, Marie Černíl's last child, Jaromir Černil, was born in 1914 and Josef Černil was registered as his father. It is certain that, until 1929, when Stanislav Černíl married, he lived with his mother at 16 Kreuzgasse (Křížová) on the first floor of the building.[110] It is not known whether his first wife was also living with them. It was at this address, the couple's daughter Dagmar told me, that Černíl held a very informal gathering of theater enthusiasts every Saturday. Around 1938 or 1939, Černil also briefly tended a tiny grocery store on the ground floor of the building.[111]

104 Černil's name was printed under the photo, but his daughter Dagmar also confirmed that it was indeed a picture of her father, adding that the signature beneath the photo was her father's. See interview (dated Oct. 23, 2018) with Dagmar Černilová.

105 MZA, Brno, fonds B 26, Policejní ředitelství v Brno, kart. n° 2736B, inv. n° 3893, sign. 846, f. 28.

106 The Černil-Broušková couple's November 17, 1929 marriage certificate includes the address where he was born. See the *matriky* (registers, *Matriken*) at https://www.mza.cz/actapublica/matrika/ under Město Brno, kniha oddaných, year 1929, českobratrská církev evangelická, f. 195.

107 *Adressbuch von Brünn* 1912, 197; 1918, 230. See also the many advertisements for his carpentry business placed by Josef Černíl in *Rovnost*, Jan. 30, 1907, 8.

108 *Adressbuch von Brünn* 1912, 197; 1919, 608; *Adreßbuch von Groß-Brünn* 1922, 451.

109 Josef and Marie still lived together in 1909 at 12 Cyrillsgasse (Cyrilská), but seem to have lived apart from around 1912. See *Adressbuch von Brünn* 1909, 167. Josef Černíl then lived at 23 Bürgergasse or Měšťanská (later this was renamed Kreuzgasse or Křížová). See *Adressbuch von Brünn* 1912, 197; 1918, 230. From *ca.* 1912 until at least 1919, Marie seems to have lived on her own at 42 Erzherzog-Friedrich-Strasse (Arcivévody Bedřicha), currently Křenová (Kröna). Her new residence was in the same (housing) block as her store and Josef Černíl's carpentry business. The house at 42 Erzherzog-Friedrich-Strasse (Arcivévody Bedřicha) was bombed on November 20, 1944. See the northern most location on Čechyňská street in the "Bombardování Brna" database, https://gis.brno.cz/ags/bomby/ (accessed Sep. 10, 2020).

110 See the Černil-Broušková couple's November 17, 1929 wedding certificate at https://www.mza.cz/actapublica/matrika/ under kniha oddaných, Město Brno, českobratrská církev evangelická, f. 195; and the 1932 information (about Černil's most recent address) copied in pencil by a police officer (from the original) on a blank resident registration card, in the *Kamarád* police file, MZA, Brno, fonds B 26, Policejní ředitelství v Brno, kart. n° 2736B, inv. n° 3893, sign. 846, f. 20. In 1931 or 1932, after his daughter was born, Stanislav Černíl also briefly lived at 24 Kreuzgasse (Křížová), likely with his father. See *Adreßbuch von Groß-Brünn* 1932, 151. The owner of 24 Kreuzgasse (Křížová) was the glassblower Vilém (Wilhelm) Fabin. See *Adreßbuch von Groß-Brünn* 1934, 639, 770. The owner of 16 Kreuzgasse (Křížová) was a certain Paul Weeger. See *Adreßbuch von Groß-Brünn* 1934, 769.

111 The grocery shop is included in the "Gemischtwaren" (mixed products) section, *Adresář Protektorátu Čechy a Morava pro průmysl, živnosti, obchod a zemědělství = Adressbuch des Protektorates Böhmen und Mähren für Industrie, Gewerbe, Handel und Landwirtschaft* 1939, II: 1470. However, Černil's

The building was located next to the city hall (*Rathaus, radnice*) at the end of Kreuzgasse (Křížová). Its corner tower was a well-known sight in Old Brno (Staré Brno, Altbrünn). In early 1965, even-numbered buildings on Křížová were demolished to expand Mendlovo náměstí (Mendelplatz) [ill. 10].[112] In May 1938, two months after Giese's suicide, Černíl moved with his mother, Marie Vlašín, and his daughter, Dagmar, into a new apartment building at 68 Bäckergasse (Pekařská). He lived there through the war [ill. 11].[113] Stanislav Černil's father, Josef Černíl, was not living with his wife at that point.[114] (The reasons for providing such detail about where Stanislav Černil lived as a child and adult will become clear later on.) Černil did not have a spotless record. In 1930, he was convicted for assaulting a woman.[115] There is no military file on him in the Central Military Archives (Vojenský ústřední archiv) in Prague.

In our interview, Dagmar Černilová stressed that she was born into a family with very strong Czech nationalist convictions. František Černil, Stanislav's brother, was an accountant and a virulently anti-German veteran of World War I. In January 1933, František Černil was involved in putting down a revolt in Brno-Židenice by a group of seventy to eighty members of the National Fascist Movement (Národní obec fašistická, NOF), who tried, in the wake of Hitler's ascent to power in Germany, to organize a fascist coup d'état in Czechoslovakia. František Černil drew up a list of people who were then arrested. Apparently he tortured some of these men.[116]

surname is misspelled as Černík. See also interview (dated Oct. 23, 2018) with Dagmar Černilová.

112 The (then still) uneven-numbered buildings not demolished now form the southern border of Mendlovo náměstí (Mendelplatz). Judging from the map AMB – K86 Brno VIII, year 1934 (available at http:// www.mapy.brna.cz/bin/ [accessed Dec. 12, 2018]), the building at 16 Kreuzgasse (Křížová) was still standing in 1934. See also *Adreßbuch von Groß-Brünn* 1934, 769. Three photos of the house and neighborhood can be seen at http://www.foto-historie.cz/Jihomoravsky/Brno-mesto/Brno_-_Stare_Brno/Brno_-_Mendlovo/Default.aspx and https://encyklope die.brna.cz/home-mmb/?acc=profil_ulice&load=3338 (both accessed Dec. 13, 2018). See also the postcards of Bürgergasse (Měšťanská), as the street was called before World War I (Filip n.d., 48–50). Since 1921, there was a café called (Eduard) Turetschek (in Czech, Tureček) on the ground floor of the building where Stanislav Černíl lived. See *Adreßbuch von Groß-Brünn* 1921, 489; *Adreßbuch von Groß-Brünn* 1923, 489. After the Černíls moved out, in 1938, the name of the café changed to Švýcarský dvůr (Schweizer Hof, Swiss Court).

113 See the resident registration cards for Stanislav Černíl in AMB, Brno, fonds Z 1, and *Adreßbuch von Groß-Brünn* 1934, 156. Dagmar told me (interview dated Oct. 23, 2018) that the family later moved from an apartment on the top floor to one on the third floor in the same building.

114 See interview, dated Oct. 23, 2018, with Dagmar Černilová, in which she mentioned in passing that the couple were no longer living together by the time they moved to the modernist apartment building on Bäckergasse (Pekařská). See the resident registration cards for Josef Černíl in AMB, Brno, fonds Z 1. These show that, presumably starting in 1934 (the resident registration card does not allow us to determine the exact year), he was living at 2A Trnitá (Dörnrössel). This is likely correct, as he was still living at 16 Kreuzgasse (Křížová). See *Adreßbuch von Groß-Brünn* 1934, 156. Afterwards, he moved to 29 Zeile (Cejl), where he died in 1942. See his death certificate in AMB, Brno, fonds A 1/3, Sbírka rukopisů a úředních knih, 1333–1958, Úmrtní protokol z roku 1942, n° 1287, March 28, 1942.

115 MZA, Brno, fonds B 26, Policejní ředitelství v Brno, kart. n° 2736B, inv. n° 3893, sign. 846, f. 24b: "Stanislav Černil zaměstnanec u města Brna, bytem v Brně, Křížová úl. 16/I pod čís. 7037/V 26/5 30, byl oznámen soudu pro nebezpečné vyhrožování a čin proti bezpečnosti těla" (Stanislav Černil, employee of the city of Brno, living in Brno, in Křížová n° 16/I[,] under number 7037/V 26/5 30, was brought to the attention of the courts because of dangerous threats and actions against the security authorities). There is a mention in a name index in MZA, Brno, fonds C 11, Krajský soud Brno (Kreisgericht Brno), of this – or yet another? – case concerning Stanislav Černil, case n° Tk XI 1514/30; however, the case was transferred to the Okresní soud trestní Brno (Brno criminal district court). See MZA, Brno, fonds C 152, Okresní soud trestní Brno, case n° T VI 1817/30. Stanislav Černil was tried and convicted of the physical assault (*leichte Körperverletzung*, minor bodily harm) of a woman named Marie Růžičková. Černil had to pay two fines (one of 100 Czech crowns and the other of fifty Czech crowns). No further information on the incident is available because of a lack of archival files. See email (dated Jul. 28, 2017) from Jana Fasorová (MZA, Brno) to the author.

116 The document pamětní knihy II. národního odboje v letech 1938–1945 v Brně-Židenicích (inv. n° 152 875) can be found in the Muzeum města Brna, Brno. František Černil was one of its authors. I thank

František Černil was also active in the resistance during World War II and a political prisoner at the end of the war.[117] In June 1945, a month after the liberation of Brno, František Černil wrote a short but passionately anti-Nazi article in which he attacked several local Nazis, including the wartime Brno mayor Oskar Judex (1894–1953), along with lesser cronies like the jurist Leopold Karafiat (1890–1971), calling them "misfits and murderers" and adding that "capable Czech hands" defending "Czech blood" would leave nothing of them. His text was published in (at least) two newspapers.[118] František Černil further provided written testimony in the post-war (1945–1946) trial of Oskar Judex by the Brno Special People's Court (Mimořádný lidový soud Brno, MLS Brno; Sondervolksgericht in Brünn).[119] In the 1950s, he was a member of the Brno-Židenice branch of the Union of Anti-Fascist Fighters (Svaz protifašistických bojovníků, SPB).[120] Based on his daughter's remarks, we may assume that Stanislav Černil shared some of his brother's strong Czech nationalist feelings. After her divorce from Stanislav Černil, Dagmar's mother, Marie Břoušková, married a German national, opening another rift between her and the Černil family. Dagmar saw her mother once a week, but, after her remarriage, she was no longer allowed to see her mother. After the war, Dagmar located her mother and met her in secret so as not to offend her father. We will see later that Stanislav Černil was also involved in resistance activities during World War II.

STANISLAV ČERNIL AS THE BEST CANDIDATE

If the Institute and Hirschfeld materials once owned by Giese and Fein were indeed entrusted to someone in the *Kamarád* group, then I think that Stanislav Černil is the best candidate, for four strong reasons.

First, our main man, Jaroslav Růžička, stayed twelve days at the 16 Kreuzgasse (Křížová) apartment of Černil and his mother Marie, which means that, in May 1932, both men were more than just acquaintances. Curiously, Růžička arrived at the Černil home the day before the first issue of *Kamarád* came out, on May 27, 1932. It seems probable that this date was linked to the launch of the magazine. It looks as if Růžička was looking for shelter in advance of the launch. So here, as with the *Kamarád* address list that Růžička tried to make disappear, we seem to see a man who was cautious and thought ahead. Both men had a clearly friendly relationship and were ready to help each other out.[121]

Dana Olivová (Muzeum města Brna, Brno) for digging up this document for me. See her email (dated Dec. 7, 2018) to the author. I thank Lucie Tuzová for referring me to the right source and explaining what this 1933 fascist revolt was about. See https://cs.wikipedia.org/wiki /Židenický_puč (accessed Dec. 15, 2018).

[117] František Černil mentions his wartime resistance activities in a protocol regarding a certain Jan Plechatý, dated February 4, 1946. See ABS, Praha, SÚMV, fonds n° 304, Různé bezpečnostní spisy po roce 1945, sign. 304-9-3. There, he says that he was arrested in 1945 after joining a second resistance group around Gabriela Riedrana, Tomáš Hasala (1895–1944), and General Vojtěch Luža (1891–1944) on March 17, 1943. His code name was "major žoržick". He also mentions General Bohuslav Všetička (1893–1942), but Všetička had died in 1942. František Černil's name does not appear in *Brněnští občané v boji proti fašismu*, a book on Brno antifascists. See Adámek, Kroutil & Kučerová, 1981.

[118] Černil, Jun. 29, 1945.

[119] Trkan 2014, 46, 68 and MZA, Brno, fonds C 141, Mimořádný lidový soud Brno (1945–1949), kart. n° 195, file Oskar Judex, sign. Lsp 1143/46, protokol dated December 1, 1945, František Černil.

[120] See https://encyklopedie.brna.cz/home-mmb/?acc=profil_osobnosti& load= 8200 (accessed Dec. 8, 2018).

[121] AMB, Brno, fonds Z 1, resident registration card for Jaroslav Růžička (dated May 27, 1932). Růžička's registration card states that he moved out again on June 7, 1932, but that it was not known to what address. Three days later (on June 15, 1932) he showed up at 12 Zábrdovice (Obrowitz) where he stayed until October 12, 1932. His address before moving in with Černil and his mother was 6 Sandstätte (Na pískách). See the resident registration card dated March 18, 1932, AMB, Brno, fonds Z 1; and the pencil copy made by a police officer bearing the same house number, MZA, Brno, fonds B 26, Policejní ředitelství v Brno, kart. n° 2736B, inv. n° 3893,

Second, Černil seems to have been the bravest member of the *Kamarád* group. He was the only one of the seven founders whose photograph was printed in the issue.[122] As we have suggested, Vilém Drexler was seemingly much less courageous, resorting to a different first name and a partial pseudonym when signing three texts and a poem in *Kamarád* as Karel Hlubocký. Černil's bravery is also indicated by the fact that he was active in the resistance during the war – a subject on which we will say more later.

Third, Černil was a man of the theater, and the theater was one of Giese's soft spots. Did Karl Giese ever attend the Saturday gatherings of theater enthusiasts at Černil's home at 16 Kreuzgasse (Křížová)? We do not know. One thing struck me. When I showed Černil's daughter, Dagmar, pictures of people I had dealt with in my research, she thought only one familiar: a 1932 photobooth picture of Karl Giese.[123] Against the idea that Giese might have attended Černil's theater meetings, it could be asserted that they were most likely made up of Czech-speakers. I therefore asked Dagmar if her father spoke German, and she said that he did.

Fourth, Černil also was on very good terms with the Jewish Schön family in Moravská Ostrava (Mährisch-Ostrau). Their son, Albert Schön, who became a rabbi, was in Brno during the war. We will return to Albert Schön later. This bond with the Schön family may have given Černil compassion for Jewish people suffering persecution under the Nazis. Later in this chapter, I will provide a few more details that lend further support for Černil as the most likely – or at least the most intriguing – candidate whom Karl Fein might have chosen to safeguard the Institute materials.

JAROSLAV OČADLÍK

Jaroslav Očadlík (1894–1950) was the fifth name on the April 1932 letter announcing the launch of *Kamarád*. He may have played a part in our story as well. Očadlík was a Roman Catholic, the son of a farmer from the village of Hulín (Hullein) in Moravia.[124] Očadlík's parents were František Očadlík (1861–?) and Františka Regentíková (1867–?). The couple had three other sons, August (1888–?), Josef (1891–?), and Karel (1898–?). Jaroslav was the second youngest. All four children were born in Hulín. In February 1921, Očadlík, then twenty-seven, was still living with his parents and his younger brother Karel in Hulín. The two brothers were likely helping out on the farm.

In mid-August 1921, Jaroslav moved from the village of his birth to Brno to work for the locally well-known First Brno Joint-Stock Brewery and Malt factory (Erste Brünner

sign. 846, f. 22. The letter announcing the startup of the gay magazine, written by Drexler-Hlubocký, names the same street where Růžička lived, but gives 5 as the house number. See MZA, Brno, fonds B 26, Policejní ředitelství v Brno, kart. n° 2736B, inv. n° 3893, sign. 846, f. 12. This seems to indicate that Růžička possibly gave a false house number on purpose. Růžička would move back to Sandstätte (Na pískách) several times but to different addresses: 4, 5, 6, and 40 Sandstätte (Na pískách).

[122] *Kamarád*, May 28, 1932, 17.

[123] I also showed her a long list of names, but with the exception of one last name (which she probably confused with another person with the same name), she did not recognize any. The ability to recognize faces and remember them over time is the subject of serious scientific research. So-called "super-recognizers" can indeed recognize people's faces decades later, but I was not able to determine from these studies if an eighty-eight-year-old person could remember a face only seen at age six or seven.

[124] See Jaroslav Očadlík's birth certificate at http://actapublica.eu /matriky/brno/prohlizec/ 8897/?strana=346 (accessed Jul. 22, 2017). According to Jaroslav Očadlík's extant school records, it would seem he only finished elementary school, at the age of twelve. See Státní okresní archiv Kroměříž, fonds B-e 25, Národní škola chlapecká Hulín, třídního katalogu obecné školy v Hulíně, school years 1900–1905; Státní okresní archiv Kroměříž, fonds A-9, Okresní úřad Kroměříž, census records města Hulín, February 1921, record Pravčická n° 244; and email (dated Jul. 19, 2017) from Jitka Zezulová (Státní okresní archiv Kroměříž) to the author. An agricultural company is still at this address (now 242 Pravčická). See http://www.pravcickaas.cz/ (accessed Jul. 22, 2017). Jaroslav Očadlík's name can be found in *Adreßbuch von Groß-Brünn* 1934, 365. However, he is absent from the address books of previous years, which were, until recently, available for online consultation.

Aktienbrauerei und Malzfabrik, První brněnský akciový pivovar a sladovna), which later became the Starobrno Brewery, still operating today.[125] Interestingly, a Josef Očadlík from Olomouc (Olmütz) was a shareholder in the brewery. Was he possibly related to Jaroslav? Did he maybe get the young man a position in the brewery?[126] Jaroslav Očadlík worked for the brewery until his death in 1950. In one of the archival documents, he is described as a barrel writer (*Fassschreiber*).[127] Starting in May 1932, at the latest, Očadlík lived in a brewery building at 80 Bäckergasse (Pekařská),[128] where he may have worked as a warder in exchange for free or reduced rent.[129] Thus, around May 1938, Očadlík did not live far from Stanislav Černil's new address at 68 Bäckergasse (Pekařská), just across from St. Anne's Hospital (currently St. Anne's University Hospital).[130] Some time between 1938 and May 1940, Očadlík then moved to 4b Stephansgasse (Štěpánská) with a young man named Jan Vacek (1913–?) [ill. 12].

Jan Vacek was born in Brno-Útěchov, a district integrated into Brno-City District (okres Brno-město) only in 1980. Before and during the war, he worked as a servant and a hairdresser, but mostly as a plumber. In 1932, he was employed by the Bat'a shoe factory in Zlín (Zlin) for a month. After the war, he was a laboratory assistant (*laborant*).[131] It is not known whether he and Očadlík, nineteen years his senior, were friends or lovers. Like Jaroslav Růžička, Vacek seems to have lived a little like a

[125] MZA, Brno, fonds H 613, První brněnský akciový pivovar a sladovna, Brno, kart. n° 11, kniha n° 20, seznam dělnictva (list of workers). Erste Brünner Aktien-Brauerei und Malzfabrik is the name under which the Starobrno Brewery operated before World War I. See http://www.fa.vutbr.cz /home/zemankova/pivovary/04.htm (accessed Jul. 16, 2017). The centuries-old factory is now part of the Heineken brewing group. See http://en.wikipedia.org/wiki/Starobrno_Brewery (accessed Jul. 23, 2021).

[126] MZA, Brno, fonds C 11, Krajský soud civilní Brno, firemní agenda, První brněnský akciový pivovar a sladovna (Erste Brünner Actien-Brauerei und Malzfabrik), Brno-Hlinky, 1913–1951, kart. n° 201, sign. B I 173, list of shareholders for the year 1937.

[127] MZA, Brno, fonds H 613, První brněnský akciový pivovar a sladovna, Brno, kart. n° 11, kniha n° 20, seznam dělnictva (list of workers).

[128] *Adreßbuch von Groß-Brünn* 1934, 790. The brewery at 80 Bäckergasse (Pekařská) was initially the property of a Jewish man, Isak Lamberg (1821–1877). See *Neues Orientirungs-Schema für die Landeshauptstadt Brünn, verfasst auf Grund der neuen Strassenbezeichnung und Häusernummerirung* 1877, 41, 92; *Mährischer Correspondent*, Jul. 17, 1877, 8. After Lamberg's death, in July 1877, it became the J.[ulius] & E.[mil] Brauner Brewery. In 1903, like many other smaller breweries, it was bought up by the Erste Brunner Aktien-Brauerei und Malzfabrik. The building is not currently owned by Starobrno Brewery. See *Adressbuch von Brünn* 1903, 326, 435; MZA, Brno, inventory list H 613, První brnenský akciový pivovar a sladovna, Brno, 1840, 1889–1945, 1952, p. 3. See also email (dated Jan. 29, 2018) from Zdeňka Tvrdoňová (pivovar Starobrno Heineken, Brno) and email (dated Feb. 1, 2018) from Jiřina Tomková (pivovar Starobrno Heineken, Brno), both to the author.

[129] Several other people working at the brewery likely also lived in this building. See, for example, Karl Hausgenoß (1874–?) and Karl Hütter or Hüter (?–?), both identified as "Brauereibeamter" (brewery employee), *Adreßbuch von Groß-Brünn* 1927, 185, 199; and, for Karl Hausgenoß alone, *Adreßbuch von Groß-Brünn* 1922, 138; 1934, 218. In a list of brewery employee salaries, the note "byt" (home) appears next to Očadlík's name. See MZA, Brno, fonds H 613, První brněnský akciový pivovar a sladovna, Brno, n° 92, kart. n° 4. This note appears next to several other employees' names as well, suggesting that they were also living on company property.

[130] Both the 1929 Brno cadastral map and a satellite image available through Google Earth show the house at 80 Bäckergasse (Pekařská) as having an exceptionally large footprint. A large plot of land in the back still shows one or two storage places, most likely used by the brewery. For a photo of the building's current facade, see https://commons.wikimedia.org/wiki/File: Brno,_Peka%C5%99 sk%C3%A1_80.jpg (accessed Jul. 24, 2017). In October 2017, I visited the site. The inner court in particular seemed not to have changed much from its pre-war state.

[131] See *Adresář zemského hlavního města Brna 1948*, 451; and Jan Vacek's resident registration cards in AMB, Brno, fonds Z 1: "skuha", "holič" and "klempíř." The resident registration card showing the date that Očadlík's moved to 4b Stephansgasse (Štěpánská) is unfortunately missing; however, one of Jan Vacek's cards shows that he moved there on May 18, 1940, indicating that Očadlík was already living there in May 1940. Or did they move in together ? Starting in 1935, Vacek often went for long periods to Prague, where he stayed with a certain Alois Čížek (at 7 Krakovská), and a person named (Štefan or Štěpán?) Buchlovský or Bučkovský (at 5 Gerstnerová). After the war, he continued to go to Prague often. He returned to Brno (for good?) in August 1947. See his evidence obyvatelstva sheet in NA, Praha, fonds Policejní ředitelství Praha II, evidence obyvatelstva; *Pražský adresář 1937–1938* 1937, 113, 165.

[132] Vacek often returned to the same addresses after his stays in Prague. He moved so many times

vagabond.[132] For a while, he also lived in the Trnitá neighborhood near Brno's main railway station.[133] Was he a rent boy for a while, spending a lot of time around the main railway station?[134] In September 1937, Vacek was suspected of the theft of a wallet (containing 600 Czech crowns) belonging to Jan Ducheck from Pilsen (Plzeň), with whom he had spent the night at the Orel hotel in Prague. Vacek took the wallet and left the hotel without a trace.[135]

Vacek also lived with Očadlík at 80 Bäckergasse (Pekařská) a few times in the 1930s.[136] During the war, Vacek apparently took refuge in Očadlík's new apartment on Stephansgasse (Štěpánská). At the end of the war, on the same day in July 1945, both moved to 9/11 Starobrněnská (Altbrünnergasse).[137]

Jaroslav Očadlík was unmarried and known to the Brno police for homosexual conduct.[138] In April 1932, a local Brno newspaper reported that Očadlík was robbed of personal belongings, valued at 5,290 Czech crowns, by Jan Tylč (1913–?), an

that the dates on the Prague resident registration card sheet are actually contradictory. See Jan Vacek's evidence obyvatelstva sheet in NA, Praha, fonds Policejní ředitelství Praha II. Vacek may have returned to Brno from Prague on July 15, 1937 or Jan. 19, 1938.

[133] AMB, Brno, fonds Z 1, resident registration cards Jan Vacek. The two Brno addresses where he stayed were 13 Kröna (Křenová) and 4 Leopoldshof (Skořepka).

[134] I looked up Jan Vacek's name in Ondřej Valtus's 2015 study of prosecutions for homosexual conduct in the Krajský soud trestní Brno (Brno Regional Criminal Court) in the 1930s. There were many Jans, and even a Jan V. born in 1910, but no Jan V. born in 1913. Valtus anonymized most of the surnames in the 146 prosecution cases that he examined.

[135] NA, Praha, fonds Policejní ředitelství Praha II – všeobecná spisovna, 1941–1950, kart. n° 11702, sign. V 24/21, Jan Vacek 1913, f. 1. There are also three prosecution files on Vacek, documenting minor and more serious crimes, in MZA, Brno, fonds C 153, Okresní soud trestní Brno, III. manipulation, kart. n° 1786, sign. TV 383/1935, kart. n° 1458, sign. T IV 2577/1937 and kart. n° 1487, sign. T IV 455/1939. One case involved him stabbing someone with a knife. However, one also gets the impression that Vacek was more ruthless before the war and calmed down during the war years.

[136] In the summer of 1934 (possibly until May 1935), he lived with Očadlik at his Backergasse (Pekařska) address. See Vacek's resident registration cards in the AMB, Brno, fonds Z 1.

[137] At 9/11 Starobrněnská (Altbrünnergasse), their roles were reversed. Jan Vacek was subletting to Jaroslav Očadlík. Their resident registration cards are in the AMB, Brno, fonds Z 1. The house on Starobrněnská (Altbrünnergasse) was Jewish property before the war, jointly owned by Baruch Paul Ticho (1889–1940) and Nathan Ticho (1886–1975). See *Adressbuch von Brünn* 1934, 803. The Ticho brothers were imprisoned in Dachau on May 25, 1940. Nathan Ticho was released on July 18, 1940, and fled a few months later, in October, via Lisbon to the USA (Chicago) with his wife Fege Ticho (née Klein, 1893–1968) and two of their sons, Stephen Felix (1931–1978) and Charles (1927–). Their third son, Harold Ticho (1921–), traveled to Chicago earlier, in September 1939. Baruch Ticho died in Dachau on July 19, 1940, the day after his brother was released. See the "Dachau Concentration Camp Records" database at https://stevemorse.org/da chau/dachau.html (accessed Nov. 18, 2020). Most likely, they were forced to sell their property under pressure from the National Socialists, but there are no files on their two properties at 9/11 Starobrněnská (Altbrünnergasse) and 5 Erbenova (Erbengasse) in MZA, Brno, fonds B 392, Vystěhovalecký fonds, úřadovna Brno. For the sake of completeness, I note that Dr. Robert Ticho (1883–1957), a lawyer born in Brno but practicing in Vienna, published a poetry chapbook with the L. & A. Brecher bookstore. See Ticho 1907. He was the brother of the better-known Anna Ticho (1894–1980), an artist who emigrated to Israel. See https://www.kraus.wienbibliothek.at/person/robert-ticho (accessed Nov. 19, 2020). Nathan Ticho's son, Charles Ticho, played a decisive role in putting up a plaque for Anna Ticho in Brno in 2015. See https://encyklopedie.brna.cz/home-mmb/?acc=profil_objektu&load=1636 (accessed Nov. 18, 2020). The plaque was stolen and has not been replaced. On the history of the Ticho family, and especially Anna and Robert Ticho's father, Avraham (Albert) Ticho (1883–1960), see Reifler 2015. Charles Ticho left a Holocaust testimony (conducted by Ina Navazelskis) with the United States Holocaust Memorial Museum on September 21, 2019, accession n° 2019.410.1, RG n° RG-50.030.1053. See https://collections.ushmm.org/search/catalog/irn709457 (accessed Nov. 18, 2020). Charles Ticho additionally wrote an unpublished memoir about his family's Holocaust experience. See Ticho 2001. I contacted Charles Ticho in November 2020, and we conversed by email. We determined that Robert Ticho was the oldest son of his uncle David Ticho (1881-1942?) who upset his father with his Communist sympathies. See email (dated Nov. 24, 2020) from Charles Ticho to the author. I thank Nancy Cooey (USHMM, Washington) for facilitating my contact with Mr. Ticho in November 2020.

[138] MZA, Brno, fonds B 26, Policejní ředitelství v Brno, kart. n° 2736B, inv. n° 3893, sign. 846, f. 24: "Jaroslav Očadlík je jako úředník zaměstnán ve Star. brněnském pivovaru, bydlí v Brně Pekařská čís. 80, má sklon k homosexuelním činnům a takovéto výstupy, stížnosti jíž na něho byly" (Jaroslav Očadlík

unemployed man whom Očadlík had met by chance and with whom he had slept three times. Tylč claimed that he had not stolen the goods but rather received them in exchange for sex.[139] Like Jaroslav Růžička and Jan Vacek, Jan Tylč was a young vagabond who moved around a lot.[140] We know hardly anything more about Očadlík's personal life. Očadlík was born in 1894, the same year as Karl Fein. He turned forty-eight in 1942.

TWO MORE *KAMARÁD* FOUNDERS

Before taking another step, let us first briefly mention two final members of the *Kamarád* founding group, neither of whom seem to have played a part in our story. Bohdan (Theodor) Hájek (1898–?) was married to Marie Machová (1897–?) and belonged to the Protestant Moravian Church (Moravští bratři, also Moravská církev). The couple had one daughter, Eva (1929–?).[141] There is some confusion about the exact identity of the seventh founding member of *Kamarád*, who may have been either Jakub Uher (1878–1937) or Josef Uher (1883–1963). Both were Catholics from Brno-Židenice. The presumed reason for the confusion is more amply explained in the addenda.[142] What is remarkable about both men is that, unlike most of the other *Kamarád* founding members, they were relatively prosperous business associates of the company Josef Uher and Associates (Josef Uher a spol.), a screw factory, in Brno-Židenice. The factory employed more than one hundred people. Yet it must be stressed that both were self-made men. Josef Uher had been a factory worker himself, and Jakub Uher initially worked as a clerk at the nationalized Czech Railways (Česke drahy). Jakub Uher died in 1937, so he could not have been involved in discarding the Institute materials. Josef Uher died in 1963.

IMMEDIATE CAUSE

We know that, most likely, the Institute materials were rather drastically discarded at Jindra Růžičková and Jaroslav Růžička's scrap company. The decision to do so was possibly taken by members of the *Kamarád* group. If this was the case, their decision was likely driven by very real fears arising from the very tense general atmosphere of the Protectorate of 1942. I also tried to determine if there might have been an *immediate cause* behind the decision. After all, why wait until the very fraught year

is employed at the Old Brno brewery, lives in Brno at Pekarska 80, is prone to homosexual activities, and there have been complaints about him already). There is no military file on him in the Vojenský ústřední archiv (Central Military Archives) in Prague. Military files on men born between 1887 and 1900 were discarded. See email (dated Jul. 25, 2018) from Josef Žikeš (Vojenský ústřední archiv, Praha) to the author.

[139] See "špatná odměna za nocleh" (poor remuneration for overnight stay), *Lidové noviny*, Apr. 30, 1932, 3; which spells Tylč's last name as "Tyll". See also MZA, Brno, fonds C 12, Krajský soud trestní Brno, III. manipulace, kart. n° 511, indictment n° 739/32, invent. n° Tk V 1454/32, court file Jan Tylč and Jaroslav Očadlík. Tylč was a cinema operator in Brno-Střelice. (It is intriguing, of course, that Giese's Brno boyfriend, Walter Lukl, also may have worked for a cinema). His resident registration cards indicate that he was imprisoned from July 2 to November 1, 1932. He was also imprisoned in 1938–39. See AMB, Brno, fonds Z 1. Another name mentioned in the Tylč-Očadlík court file, named by the public prosecutor as eligible for prosecution for homosexual behavior, is Antonín Macík (1910–?). Macík was most likely a partner, friend, or simply a work colleague of Jaroslav Očadlík since he was, like Očadlík, born in Hulín. He moved from Hulín to the brewery building in Brno at 80 Bäckergasse (Pekařská) on April 12, 1931. He also worked for the brewery. Macík seems to have moved again around 1934. See his resident registration cards in AMB, Brno, fonds Z 1. It is unclear how Květoslava Chlubnová, an otherwise unidentified woman also mentioned in the same archival file, was linked to Tylč, Očadlík, or Macík.

[140] See his many resident registration cards in AMB, Brno, fonds Z 1.

[141] The family lived at 22 Rokycanagasse (Rokycanova) in Brno-Židenice, and their address stayed the same after the war; see *Adresář zemského hlavního města Brna* 1948, part B: 99. Professionally, he was a *kontrolor* (controller). See MZA, Brno, fonds C 12, Krajský soud trestní Brno, III. manipulace, kart. n° 539, sign. TK XI 1687/32, f. 23.

[142] See n° 14 in the addenda.

1942 to discard the Institute and Hirschfeld materials when these had presumably been safeguarded for at least a few years? What happened in 1942 to provoke such a drastic decision? There is no definite answer here, but the archival sources consulted seem to point to Stanislav Černil and Jaroslav Očadlík as the two *Kamarád* founders directly involved. In what follows, I develop this argument in extenso.

The September 1942 resident registration cards for Stanislav Černil, Jaroslav Očadlík, and Jan Vacek, the young man living with Očadlík, constitute the most relevant archival indication regarding the decision to discard the materials. A Brno citizen had to complete a resident registration form when moving to a new address. Indeed, a Brno citizen was obliged to report a change of residence to the local police station within twenty-four hours.[143] Upon request by the police authorities, this resident registration form was also (less commonly) used to confirm an address.[144]

In September 1942, Stanislav Černil, Jaroslav Očadlík, and Jan Vacek filled out this form to confirm their current address. During the war years, a request to confirm one's current address typically signified that a police agency, usually the Gestapo or the Kripo, planned to pay a visit. Such a request provoked real fear in its recipients.[145] People simply did not know what to expect when thus summoned, but suspected that it was nothing good. We have already mentioned the case of Franz Nawratil's wife, Wilma Naplawa, who had to fill out the form to confirm her current address five days after her husband died. Since she knew she might not return home soon, she gave her sister, Edith Hradský, her power of attorney (*Vollmacht*) as her late husband's inheritance procedure was still in process.[146] My argument is that either Černil or Očadlík or the two together may have decided to discard the Institute materials when asked to use the form to confirm their current address. The foreboding that the Gestapo, or another German police agency, would pay them a visit may have caused them to panic.

Stanislav Černil's daughter, Dagmar, told me that, during the war, she had overheard her father say one day that he expected a visit from the Gestapo any moment. She also said that her father had told her he had hidden guns in the sofa in the Bäckergasse (Pekařská) apartment.[147] Initially, she could not say if the Gestapo actually visited. Later she wrote to me that it did, but just to gather information. She could not remember the year of the visit.[148] One feature of the resident registration

[143] See, for example, *Adressbuch von Brünn* 1918, 872–73; also the *Belehrung* (instruction) on the back of a May 12, 1944, resident registration card for Ervín Waldapfel (1901–?) in AMB, Brno, fonds Z 1.

[144] See, for example, the resident registration cards for Josef Laufer (1904–?), Gustav Wilhelm Neumann (1904–?), Franziska Oppenheimer (1898–?), Bedřiška Bondyová (1889–?), Otto Weiss (1917–?), and Vinzenz Laufer (1875–?). Laufer, a retired professor who had been at the same address since 1912, was asked to confirm his residence in August 1943. In response to the question, "Schon einmal hier gewohnt?" (Have you lived here before?), he wrote "immer" (always).

[145] Another interesting example of a resident registration card used to confirm an existing address is offered by Božena Kulková (1890–?). Her husband, Josef Antonín Kulka (1894–1940), had been active in the Obrana národa (Defense of the Nation) resistance group and perished in Špilberk Castle in January 1940. See http://encyklopedie.brna.cz/home-mmb/?acc=profil_osobnosti&load=1492 (accessed Jan. 15, 2018). In this case, we see that the whereabouts of the wife of a resistance fighter were confirmed with the aid of a resident registration card, likely prior to questioning.

[146] MZA, Brno, fonds C 107, kart. n° 282, sign. 5bV146/14, inheritance file Franz Nawratil, f. 4.

[147] Interview (dated Oct. 23, 2018) with Dagmar Černilová. The fact that Stanislav Černil's father was a carpenter suggests that the guns were hidden quite inconspicuously.

[148] It is also possible that Dagmar was referring to events that took place in 1943, when Stanislav Černil's older brother, František, was imprisoned in the infamous Kounicovy koleje (Kaunitz College). Only one archival source refers to František Černil's imprisonment there: there is a grafitto of his name (that he wrote on it himself) on the wall of cell 44 in Block B. See Zatloukal 1946, 56. There is no surviving Kaunitz College prisoner register in either the B or C fonds of the MZA, Brno. See the email (dated Jan. 30, 2019) from Jana Fasorová (MZA, Brno) to the author. Presumably, František Černil was imprisoned shortly after filling out a July 30, 1943, resident registration card to confirm his current address. See AMB, Brno, fonds Z 1. On the preprinted Czech-German resident registration form,

form filled out by Stanislav Černil seems to confirm that it had to have been in September 1942. This was the only time during the war that Stanislav Černil was summoned to confirm his address, and hence the only time he faced questioning by a German police agency.[149]

Stanislav Černil and his mother, Marie, were asked to confirm their address on September 1, 1942, but, very surprisingly, Stanislav Černil did not deliver the completed forms to the police station until Saturday, September 5 [ill. 13].[150] A change of address had to be registered within twenty-four hours of the move. After examining several resident registration cards used to confirm an existing address, I concluded that registration within twenty-four hours was indeed required as well. Occasionally, a form would be completed one day and handed in at the police station the next day, where it was stamped. The different dates on Černil's form were, in other words, very unusual and also unlawful. I have not seen such a blatant discrepancy in dates on any other resident registration card, confirming a current address, and on my research trips to the AMB in Brno I saw many. For his part, Jaroslav Očadlík completed his form on September 8 and submitted it at the police station on the same day.[151] Očadlík also completed the form for Jan Vacek, the young man living with him at 4b Stephansgasse (Štěpánská). He even signed the form on behalf of the young man, who was presumably subletting from him.

Why was there such a great difference between the two dates, the one Černil wrote on the form and the one stamped by the local police station? Was Stanislav Černil maybe trying to stall before confirming his address? Did he need time to remove the Institute materials from his Bäckergasse (Pekařská) flat or somewhere else? Or did he know where the materials were and feared questioning (possibly under torture) about the matter? If this scenario is realistic, then it is possible that the Institute materials were discarded between September 1 and 5, 1942. According to the affidavit, the guestbook was found in 1942, and this does not contradict the scenario offered here. Further, I checked whether other residents and owners in Černil's building received a summons to confirm their address on September 1, 1942, but that does not seem to be the case. So, we cannot say that everyone in the apartment building was

he tried to appear as German as possible (by giving Franz as his first name, for example), something that must have been hard for him as a Czech national. It clearly did not help. In a few January 2020 interviews with two Czech newspapers, Dagmar Černilová focused mainly on her harsh and traumatizing post-war clashes with the Communist authorities, but also briefly mentioned the resistance activities of her father and uncle during the war. She was more specific about her uncle being imprisoned in 1943. Since Dagmar insisted (in October 2018) that her testimony should be partly anonymized, using only her first name and maiden name (and not her married name), I have opted to be discreet about these interviews as well (since her married name is mentioned there). The websites and specific URLs featuring these 2020 interviews are known to the author.

149 On Stanislav Černil's completed September 1942 resident registration form, the name of his third wife, Helene Müller (whom he married in April 1944), was added as well. The name of his second wife, Ludmila Suchánecková (whom he divorced in 1942), was simply crossed out. It makes sense that this was rectified only on the *last* resident registration form that he completed, and which the police kept on file. That this September 1942 form was indeed the last one he completed during the war is further indicated by the fact that the name of his son, Stanislav Mario Černil (1946–2015), who was born in 1946, was added to it after the war.

150 The date of the police station stamp on Stanislav Černil's resident registration card is unclear, showing either a 5 or a 6. I think it is in fact a 5, since Stanislav Černil's mother, Marie Černilová, also had to complete a form to confirm her latest address and the stamp on hers clearly shows September 5, 1942. On her form, we also find September 1, 1942, as the date that it was completed.

151 Three copies of the resident registration card had to be completed. The forms were for sale in local shops. Precise directions on how to correctly complete a resident registration card could be found on the back of some of these cards.

152 I checked three other people at random (their names selected from the 1934 *Adreßbuch von Groß-Brünn*) living at 68 Bäckergasse (Pekařská), but none had to confirm their previous address nor did the back of their registration cards have a 1942 Kripo *Fahndungsabteilung* (Kripo investigation department) stamp. For more information on

under scrutiny. As the only residents summoned that day, Stanislav Černil and his mother stand out.[152]

However, there is one possible explanation for Černil's procrastination. Stanislav Černil completed his and his mother's forms on September 1, 1942, a Tuesday, only delivering them to the police station on the following Saturday. Was he still working in Moravská Ostrava (Mährisch-Ostrau) at that point, returning home only for the weekend? But, in that case, did his working week start on a Tuesday, the date he completed the forms? Very regrettably, Černil's daughter, Dagmar, could not remember whether her father was still working in Ostrava during the war.[153] What weighs against the Ostrava explanation is that Černil's mother, who was also summoned to confirm her previous address, could easily have taken the completed resident registration forms herself to the police station during the week. On the other hand, if Stanislav Černil was indeed working in Ostrava, he would have had a (partly) valid excuse for submitting the forms on the weekend, when he was back home.

THE (PERSONS) INVESTIGATION DEPARTMENT STAMPS

There is a second significant factor. There were two stamps on the backs of the completed resident registration cards of Černil, his mother, and the two men, Očadlík and Vacek: "(persons) investigation department" (*Fahndungsabteilung*) and "no wants or warrants" (*wird nicht gesucht*) [ill. 14a] [ill. 14b].[154] What did these stamps mean? *Fahndungsabteilung* refers to a specific department within the Criminal Police Headquarters (Kriminalpolizeileitstelle) based in Prague. Both the Prague headquarters and its subordinate Brno Criminal Police Headquarters (Kriminalpolizeistelle Brünn) were local Protectorate departments of the German Criminal Police (Kriminalpolizei, Kripo), also known, in September 1939, as Department 5 (Amt V). The better-known Gestapo was formed as Department 4 (Amt IV) in the overarching and centralized Nazi police headquarters, the Reich Security Main Office (Reichssicherheitshauptamt, RSHA) led by Heinrich Himmler in Berlin.[155] The Kripo, and other German police agencies, like the Gestapo, started operating in the Sudetenland in 1938 and in the Protectorate in 1939.[156]

this *Fahndungsabteilung* stamp, see below. Marie Šoustalová (née Moráveková, 1906–?), a *domkářka* (homeowner), was likely the owner of the apartment building and was living in Brno-Starý Lískovec in 1942. She was married to Arnošt Šoustal (1901–?), an employee of the Brno District Civil Court (Bezirksgericht in Zivilsachen Brünn, Okresní soud civilní Brno). See *Adreßbuch von Groß-Brünn* 1934, 69; and Šoustal's resident registration card in the AMB, Brno, fonds Z 1. The couple had two sons (born in 1931 and 1940), but I did not follow up on them. Neither Marie nor Arnošt Šoustal had a Kripo investigation department stamp on the back of their resident registration cards. The couple did not appear in the German nationals register in the AMB, Brno, fonds A 1/53.

[153] I tried to find other inroads to help Dagmar remember if her father still worked in Ostrava (Ostrau) during the war. I asked, for example, if she remembered picking up her father at the railway station in Brno during the war, after his week away at work in Ostrava (Ostrau); but to no avail.

[154] AMB, Brno, fonds Z 1, inhabitant registration cards for Stanislav Černil, Marie Černilová, Jaroslav Očadlík, and Jan Vacek.

[155] Wagner 2002, 76.

[156] For an overview of the structure of the Deutsche Kriminalpolizei (German Criminal Police) within the Protectorate, see NA, fonds n° 1799, Státní tajemník u říšského protektora v Čechách a na Moravě, Praha, (1853) 1939–1945 (1948), inv. n° 2123, sign. n° 109-8/6, f. 1–19; a digitized archival fonds is available at http://www.badatelna.eu/fond/959/zaznam/339830/reprodukce (accessed Jan. 20, 2018). For an overview of all the German and Czech police forces in the Protectorate, see Macek & Uhlíř 2001. It is not easy to precisely spell out the organization of all the different German and Czech police forces active in the Protectorate, and especially their forced cooperation, which evolved as the war progressed. The Brno Kriminalpolizeistelle, for example, worked closely with the regular Protectorate police and Czech gendarmerie on criminal matters that fell under the jurisdiction of the German Kriminalpolizei. On the compulsory cooperation of Czechoslovak police forces, starting in 1939, with the German Kriminalpolizei, see Černý 2006, 40: "Podle nařízení z 1. září 1939 měla kriminální policie vykonávat odborný dozor nad kriminální policií Protektorátu pokud to vyžadují společné úkoly. Protektorátní úřady mají v tomto rámci zajistiti pomoc německé kriminální policii" (According to a September 1,

It is unclear why this stamp appears on our four subjects' resident registration cards. It is possible that their names were checked because they showed up on reports of incidents (*Meldungen*). Three different local police agencies were responsible for incoming reports: the municipal police (Gemeindepolizei, Obecní policie), the gendarmerie (Gendarmerie, Četnictvo), and the municipal criminal police (Gemeinde-Kriminalpolizei, Obecní kriminální policie).[157] These local police agencies had twenty-four hours to submit reports to the Brno Kriminalpolizeistelle, above them in the hierarchy.[158] The latter stamped the back of a resident registration card one or two days after the local police station stamped the front side of a resident registration card detailing a current address. This entailed that checking surnames in the Kripo repositories usually took one or two days. The German Kripo name-search organizational flow chart demonstrates that a local lead was checked not only in Prague but also in the Berlin RHSA index card repository (*Kartei*). This is why the process took a few days.[159] The Kripo investigation department stamps on Stanislav Černil's and his mother's resident registration cards clearly show the date as September 8, 1942. The stamp on Jaroslav Očadlík's card is less clear, but likely September 9 or 10. The more legible stamp on Jan Vacek's card seems to show September 9.[160]

The supplementary stamped "no wants or warrants" should not diminish the importance of the prior *presence* of the Kripo investigation department stamps on the

1939 decree, the Kripo were to exercise professional supervision over the criminal police of the Protectorate to the extent that common tasks demanded. The Protectorate authorities were to provide assistance to the German Kripo in this regard). Vladimír Černý is here quoting from an unpublished manuscript by František Vašek, *Německá kriminální policie v letech 1938–1945 na území východních Čech*. See also Nebe & Werner 1941, 48/2: "Die Deutsche Kriminalpolizei im Protektorat übt die fachliche Aufsicht über die Kriminalpolizei des Protektorats aus, soweit es die gemeinsamen Aufgaben erfordern. Die Polizeibehörden des Protektorats haben in diesem Rahmen den fachlichen Weisungen der Deutschen Kriminalpolizei zu entsprechen" (The German Kriminalpolizei [Kripo] in the Protectorate shall exercise professional supervision over the criminal police of the Protectorate to the extent required by common tasks. Within this framework, the police authorities of the Protectorate shall comply with the technical instructions of the German Kripo). Kárný states that forced cooperation began or grew more strict after Heydrich's assassination: "Diese zweite 'Heydrichiade' umfaßte [...], die Unterstellung der Regierungspolizei und -gendarmerie unter deutsche Führung" (This second "Heydrichiade" included [...] the subordination of the government police and gendarmerie to German leadership) (Kárný 1999, 52).

157 A contemporary flow chart makes this clear (Nebe & Werner 1941, 265).

158 On the *24 [Uhr]-Stundenfrist* (24-hour term) for reports, see Nebe & Werner 1941, 62–64; and Wagner 2002, 78: "Was die Aufklärung von Straftaten betraf, so bildete den Kern der Tätigkeit der Reichskriminalpolizei [...] die Datensammlung, Datenweitergabe und zentralisierte Datenauswertung, [...] Die örtlichen Polizeiorgane, [...], hatten binnen 24 Stunden eine Fülle von in einem Erlaß vom 16. Juli 1937 aufgelisteten Vorkommnissen zu melden, [...]. Die Kripostellen hatten die bei ihnen eingehenden Meldungen in ihre Modus operandi-Karteien einzuspeisen, um durch Vergleich mit dort bereits registrierten Taten und Menschen Zusammenhänge aufzuklären" (Where the investigation of criminal offences was concerned, the core activities of the Reich Kriminalpolizei (Kripo) [...] were the collection, transmission and centralized evaluation of data. [...] Local police agencies [...] had to report a plethora of incidents listed in a decree of July 16, 1937 within 24 hours [...]. The Kripo departments had to add the reports they received to their modus operandi index cards, in order to elucidate connections through comparison with acts and people already recorded there). See also Wagner 1996, 239.

159 For one organogram detailing the information transfer procedure followed when something suspicious was detected at the *ortliche Aussendienststelle* (local field office) level, see NA, fonds n° 1799, Státní tajemník u říšského protektora v Čechách a na Moravě, Praha, (1853) 1939–1945 (1948), inv. n° 2118, sign. n° 109-8/1, Organizační struktura a služební pokyny a předpisy německé kriminální policie v protektorátu vydané řídící úřadovnou v Praze; digital reproduction n° 345, available at http://www . badatelna.eu/fond/959/ reprodukce/ ?zaznamId=339825&reproId=379951 (accessed Jan. 20, 2018).

160 The stamp on the back of Očadlík's card shows the same month (September) and year (1942), but one can only "approximate" the day. It could be 8 or 9 or 10. Since Očadlík filled out his resident registration card on September 8, 1942, it likely was 9 or 10 since the Prague and Berlin Kripo investigation departments usually took one or two days to check a name.

resident registration cards. The latter show that there must have been a particular reason compelling the Kripo employees to follow a special procedure and crosscheck their names in Prague and Berlin. A report of an incident (*Meldung*) received at a local police station was one possible reason to initiate the procedure. The normal administrative procedure was for the Kripo to conduct a search to determine whether a name was connected to prior incidents or crimes ... but this means that a new criminal act, whether actual or suspected, prompted this procedure. Moreover, these Kripo investigation department stamps only start to appear in 1942, most likely linked to the intensified information gathering about criminal matters that followed the assassination of Heydrich. Most of the resident registration cards that I have seen with such stamps, indeed, are from the last five months of 1942.

At the very least, Kripo investigation department stamps on resident registration forms indicate that *names were checked* in the index card repository of the Prague Criminal Police Headquarters (and in the Berlin RHSA index card repository) at the request of the subordinate Brno Criminal Police Headquarters.[161] We do not know which police agency supplied the first lead (*Meldung*) on Stanislav Černil, his mother, Jaroslav Očadlík and his roommate Jan Vacek, or why exactly their names were checked.[162]

It is important to point out that Kripo investigation department stamps do not appear on all or even most 1942–45 resident registration cards in the AMB, Brno. In fact, they appear only rarely. So, the Kripo procedure that we have described was not standard for all resident registration cards of that period.[163] Significantly, one does not find these stamps on any of the surviving wartime resident registration cards of the other founding members of *Kamarád*. These investigation department stamps are further reason for me to think that, of the *Kamarád* circle, Stanislav Černil and Jaroslav Očadlík are the strongest candidates to have had a leading role in deciding the fate of the Institute materials. They are the only ones who seem to have been under close observation in 1942.[164]

[161] We cannot ascertain if the investigation (*Fahndung*) of our subjects ever reached the RSHA in Berlin, or the Kriminalpolizeistelle in Prague, since most of these archives of the German occupiers were destroyed. See Boberach 1991, 121, 124.

[162] I asked the MZA, Brno, to check their archival fonds for traces of criminal records regarding Černil, but none were found in fonds B 321 (Protektorátní kriminální policie — kriminální ředitelství Brno) or in fonds B 26 (Policejní ředitelství Brno). See email (dated May 14, 2018) from Leoš Pecha (MZA, Brno) to the author. The MZA did not check the archive of the Czech Gendarmerie (Četnictvo), fonds B 52.

[163] After 1942, the highest number of these stamps appeared in 1943. I have seen no resident registration cards from 1939–41 with these stamps and only a handful from 1944 and 1945.

[164] Nevertheless, at some point, one other *Kamarád* member (possibly two) was also required to confirm his address. Bohdan (Theodor) was summoned to confirm his current address on November 4, 1942. In the blank space (move-in date, *Tag des Zuzuges, Den příchodu*) on his resident registration card, Hájek wrote that he had lived at his current address "from birth". Since there was no Kripo investigation department stamp on the back of Hájek's card, his summons was likely unrelated to the summons of Černil and Očadlík, or it may be that a different German police agency issued the summons. On March 27, 1939, two weeks after the German invasion of Czechoslovakia, Vilém Drexler-Hlubocký (then living with his mother) also had to use a resident registration card to confirm his address. This likely explains why he moved out of his mother's home, on May 30, 1939, to 43 Cacovická (Zazowitzer Gasse) in Brno-Husovice. But it appears that Vilém Drexler-Hlubocký's summons was meant for another man, a Communist, with the same name: Vilém Drexler, born on November 8, 1900, who lived on Trávníčekgasse (Trávníčkova) in Brno-Zábrdovice. See *Rudá Rovnost*, Jan. 1, 1938, 11. However, even if they were indeed targeting the Vilém Drexler-Hlubocký of the *Kamarád* group, the 1939 date is three years away from our 1942 riddle. I found no more archival indications that Vilém Drexler-Hlubocký was traced later during the war. Of course, I do not assume that knowledge of his possible involvement can only be gained from the archives. We can only rely on the *surviving* documents of an archive, and, as I have noted, on sheer luck. It thus remains possible that yet other founding members of *Kamarád* had to confirm their address around the same time as Černil and Očadlík.

TARGETING HOMOSEXUAL CONDUCT?

It is tempting to connect this local police and Kripo inquiry to the fact that both Černil and Očadlík were homosexual or bisexual men. Indeed, homosexuality was among the felonies that fell under the Kripo's jurisdiction.[165] In the ten criminal categories in its scope, homosexuality had its own subcategory "B.1." under "Klasse VII" (class VII) (*Triebverbrechen*, sex crimes) (hence VII.B.1).[166] In March 1941, when a homosexual ring – with Willi Bondi and two German men, Wilhelm Sponer and Helmuth Holdau at its center – was uncovered by the Gestapo's surprise visit to a private gathering in the home of Julia Fleischer, the Gestapo later *returned* the case to the Kripo.[167] The two German men were tried according to paragraph 175 of the German Criminal code (*Strafgesetzbuch*).

As already mentioned, Czech gay men at the time may have thought, and intensely feared, that homosexuals would be next (after the deportation of most Jews). It is indeed possible that Černil and Očadlík may have *believed and feared* that they had been summoned because of their earlier activities with *Kamarád* or simply for their homosexual behavior. Starting in 1937, to keep Nazi society free of crime and criminals, the Kripo adopted a "crime prevention" (*Vorbeugende Verbrechensbekämpfung*) strategy, which meant preventively locking up known or suspected criminals before they could commit a crime. So-called "sex offenders" (*Sittlichkeitsverbrecher*, lit. "moral offenders") were one of the categories rounded up. Sometimes, they were even sent to concentration camps without being convicted.[168] Were Černil and Očadlík fearful that they could be imprisoned simply for being gay? Yet this pre-emptive locking up of gay men was practiced in Germany, not the Protectorate. The question of whether homosexuals were persecuted as actively in the Protectorate as in Germany has been addressed by the Czech historian Jan Seidl,[169] who claims that, for Czech men, the wartime situation was not very different from the situation before the war. According to Seidl, the only Czech person prosecuted for homosexuality per se by the National Socialists in Brno was Karl Giese and Karl Fein's mutual good friend, Willi Bondi.[170]

[165] Cf. Wagner 1996, 248–50; Wagner 2002, 83–84.

[166] NA, Praha, fonds n° 1799, Státní tajemník u říšského protektora v Čechách a na Moravě, Praha, (1853) 1939-1945 (1948), inv. n° 2118, sign. n° 109-8/1, Organizační struktura a služební pokyny a předpisy německé kriminální policie v protektorátu vydané řídící úřadovnou v Praze; digital reproduction n° 345, available at http://www.badatelna.eu/fond/959/reprodukce/?zaznamId=339825&reproId=379975 (accessed Jan. 20, 2018). This accords with Nebe & Werner 1941, 86–87. See also Wagner 1996, 240. Starting in 1943, Brno citizens' resident registration cards began to receive a new stamp, "K I/2-Fahndungskartei" (K I/2-Index of wanted persons) replacing "Fahndungsabteilung". The "K" stood for Kriminalinspektion (Criminal Inspectorate), which had three sections (I, II, and III) in the Prague Criminal Police Headquarters. Every Kriminalinspektion had three subdivisions, each responsible for specific felonies. The Fahndungskartei (FK) (index of wanted persons) fell under the Kriminalkommissariat I/2 (Criminal Investigation Department 1/2). See http://www.badatelna.eu/fond/959/reprodukce/?zaznamId=339834&reproId=381839 (accessed Sep. 6, 2020). "Sittlichkeits(Trieb)verbrechen" (moral [sex] crimes), including homosexuality, fell under Kriminalinspektion K II/3. See NA, fonds n° 1799, Státní tajemník u říšského protektora v Čechách a na Moravě, Praha, (1853) 1939–1945 (1948), inv. n° 2127, sign. n° 109–8/10, Organizační struktura řídící úřadovny německé kriminální policie v Praze; digital reproduction n° 24 and n° 30, available at http://www.badatelna.eu/fond/959/reprodukce/?zaznamId=339834&reproId=381845, and http://www.badatelna.eu/fond/959/reprodukce/?zaznamId= 339834&reproId=381860 (both accessed Jan. 20, 2018).

[167] MZA, Brno, fonds C 43, Německý zemský soud Brno (Deutsches Landgericht), Staatsanwaltschaft bei dem Landgericht Brünn, file Wilhelm Sponer & Helmuth Holdau, kart. n° 184, sign. 4 K Ls 24/41, f. 82 and f. 100: "Handlungen, die die Staatspolizei [Gestapo] interessierte, konnten nicht festgestellt werden" (Acts of interest to the Gestapo could not be identified).

[168] Roth 2011, 49–50. On *Schutzhaft* (protective custody) and *Vorbeugungshaft* (preventive detention) applied to gay men in Germany during the Nazi era, see Angrick & Hesse 2010, 102.

[169] Seidl 2013. For a comparative overview of the legal situation in the "Großdeutschen Reich" (Greater German Reich), see also Klatt 2005.

[170] Seidl 2013, 250; Seidl 2017, 80.

[171] Seidl 2017, 83–84.

[172] Seidl 2017, 76.

For Protectorate citizens during the war, gay life pretty much went on as before.[171] Protectorate citizens were tried according to paragraph 129b of the Czechoslovak criminal code, the number of convictions increasing only slightly.[172] Citizens having German nationality were tried in German courts and according to paragraph 175 of the German criminal code (*Strafgesetzbuch*). The latter, infamous paragraph was thus applied only to Sudeten-Germans and Germans living in the Protectorate, or in cases involving a German national. There are very few indications in the surviving Gestapo files in the MZA, Brno, of prosecution for homosexuality per se.[173] One of the few cases in these Gestapo files of someone prosecuted for homosexuality concerned a youth born in Metz (then French-controlled Alsace), (Renatus) Karl Cuny (1920–?), who was drafted as a German soldier and stationed in Olomouc (Olmütz). While in the Protectorate, in February 1943, Cuny was apprehended for homosexual relations with a local married baker and NSDAP-official, Hermann Späthy, from the German city of Saarburg, which was very close to the French border.[174] Since, of course, the Alsace region was annexed by Germany and considered genuine German soil, German law applied. The young man was prosecuted in the Protectorate but under German law.

Nevertheless, Czech gay men were apparently more careful about not getting caught for homosexual activities during the war years. Resorting to intercrural intercourse (between the thighs), and avoiding anal intercourse, was one tactic.[175] Furthermore, the Gestapo's interest in homosexuality seemed mainly confined to incidents involving politically active subjects, or those guilty of other crimes.[176]

All in all, then, the summons given to Stanislav Černil and Jaroslav Očadlík do not seem linked to their homosexuality or their pre-war *Kamarád* activity. That Černil's mother was also summoned could be viewed as further support for this interpretation. One thing at least cannot be doubted: a specific reason – either a crime or a suspicion of a crime – was necessary to summon four people to confirm their current address in September 1942, and for the Kripo criminal investigation department to cross-check their names.

DIVORCE

We have just seen that a report of an incident (*Meldung*) at the local police level prompted the Kripo's name-checking procedure in Prague and Berlin. It is possible that the lead followed by the local police came from a denunciation. To name only one possible source, Czech fascists active in the Protectorate may have thought it useful to report gay men living on their street or in their building to the police.[177] The Gestapo terror regime was only able to function as well as it did by heavily relying on the input of the so-called "V Männer" they hired,[178] some of whom were recruited under pressure. Tortured by the Gestapo, potential informants were offered a chance to save their lives if they assisted the Gestapo by identifying enemies of the Third Reich.[179] But leads also came spontaneously from individual denunciations. Someone

[173] The MZA, Brno, fonds B 340 (Gestapo Brno) inventory list index includes only three names for the crime of homosexuality. See p. 3585. Not all Gestapo records survived the war; however, the few files of cases of homosexuality that *did* survive appear to indicate that such cases were rare. The archival fonds lists a total of 13,781 name files.

[174] MZA, Brno, fonds B 340, Gestapo Brno, n° 907, kart. n° 349, sign. 100-349-32, file Karel Cuny.

[175] Seidl et al. 2014a, 40. Cf. several 1941 testimonies from men engaged in homosexual sex, almost all stating that they did not have *Afterverkehr* (anal) or *Schenkelverkehr* (intercrural) sex. See MZA, Brno, fonds C 43, Německý zemský soud Brno (Deutsches Landgericht), Staatsanwaltschaft bei dem Landgericht Brünn, file Wilhelm Sponer & Helmuth Holdau, kart. n° 184, sign. 4 K Ls 24/41.

[176] Seidl 2013, 250–52; Seidl 2017, 78–80.

[177] Filip, Břečka, Schildberger et al. 2012, 82. For an introduction to the subject of Czech fascists in Brno, see Filip, Schildberger & Břečka 2011, 114–21; Filip, Schildberger & Břečka 2012, 130–35.

[178] See Sládek 2000, 327–29 and Filip, Schildberger & Břečka 2012, 212–17.

[179] Filip, Schildberger & Břečka 2012, 61, 185, 187, 189, 212–17.

may have decided to remind the new people in power of the 1932 scandal around *Kamarád,* and especially around Kostelníček.

One candidate especially may have deemed it necessary to inform the authorities about Černil's sexual preferences, his involvement with *Kamarád,* or other matters. On October 28, 1935, Černil married his second wife, Ludmila Sucháneková. He joined her in Lesonice (Lessonitz) and tried to run Sucháneková's shop with her. But the marriage was soon in trouble. Sucháneková claimed Černil returned to Brno alone as early as the spring of 1936. They tried to make a new start, but there was a final break in September 1937, according to Sucháneková, or September 1939, according to Černil. In October 1942, Černil filed for divorce.

The couple's divorce file reveals that Černil's wife experienced real sexual frustration. For his part, Černil told the court that the main reason for his wanting a divorce was Ludmila Suchánková's sexual voracity, which he found physically and mentally destructive. Černil also declared that he was unwilling to have oral sex with his wife. For her part, she complained about Černil's shameful conduct with adolescents on their outings, adding that he was the one who made weird, indecent requests during sex, having learned these unnatural ways in bars.[180] Most likely, she was discreetly referring to anal intercourse and gay bars.[181] The other points of disagreement were: who would take care of Dagmar (Černil's daughter from his first marriage), their different ideas of hygiene, concerns about spending money, and conflicting ideas on how to run a shop. Suchánková claimed, in her defense, that Černil only married her for her money and that she had known from the start that she was fifteen years his senior. The age difference, on its own, had initially been an impediment for her. Yet Černil had insisted when they met that the age gap was not a problem for him. They apparently met when Bojmír, the itinerant theater company of which Černil was a member, visited Lesonice.

The divorce proceedings were initiated by Stanislav Černil on October 8, 1942. A final verdict confirming the divorce was delivered in January 1943.[182] As the couple was no longer living together since 1937 or 1939, depending on the source, it is remarkable that Černil would suddenly initiate divorce proceedings one month after being summoned to confirm his current address.[183] Although Sucháneková may have informed the authorities about Černil's homosexuality, or some other aspect

[180] MZA, Brno, fonds C 11, kart. n° 358, sign. Ck Ia 226/42, f. 12: "když se ve společnosti opíjel, pak se držel s různými výrostky kolem krku, vyváděl různé nepřístojnosti, takže jsem se musela za jeho chování hanbiti" (When he was drunk in company, he would put his arms around the necks of various adolescents, and he would commit all sorts of indecencies, making me ashamed of his behavior).

[181] MZA, Brno, fonds C 11, kart. n° 358, sign. Ck Ia 226/42, f. 13: "V pohlavních stycích neměla jsem žádních zvláštních nároků a naopak se mi žalobce sám brzy zprotivil, tím, že žádal různé nepřirozené způsoby ukájení a tu jsem mu vytýkala, že si na takové věci snad zvykl v barech" (I made no special demands regarding sexual intercourse. On the contrary, the plaintiff himself quickly antagonized me, asking for various unnatural ways of displaying myself, and here I reproached him for perhaps becoming accustomed to such things in bars).

[182] The verdict was declared by the Krajský soud civilní Brno (Brno Regional Court) on January 18, 1943. See MZA, Brno, fonds C 11, Krajský soud civilní Brno, kart. n° 358, sign. Ck Ia 226/42; and emails (dated Oct. 5, 2018, and Oct. 8, 2018) from Jana Fasorová (MZA, Brno) to the author.

[183] The final rift between the couple likely happened somewhere in 1939. The 1942 divorce file mentions that Černil's second wife gave or lent him money at one point to start his own grocery shop in Brno. See MZA, Brno, fonds C 11, kart. n° 358, sign. Ck Ia 226/42. Černil's daughter, Dagmar, confirmed the existence of this rather tiny shop, also telling me that it did not last long. The shop was located on the ground floor of 16 Kreuzgasse (Křížová), where Černíl lived with his mother and some other family members on the first floor. The shop appears in *Adresář Protektorátu Čechy a Morava pro průmysl, živnosti, obchod a zemědělství = Adressbuch des Protektorates Böhmen und Mähren für Industrie, Gewerbe, Handel und Landwirtschaft* 1939, II: 1470. Nevertheless, the 1939 date remains a bit uncertain since Černíl and his mother moved to the Bäckergasse (Pekařská) apartment building in May 1938.

[184] Of course, it is difficult to make any definitive statement about Černil's (or anyone else's) sexual preference or orientation. One could certainly argue

of Černil's life that was considered unwholesome, it is also possible that Černil only *suspected* that Suchánecková had denounced him. Černil's timing seems to indicate that he was intent on utterly severing himself from anyone he thought had possibly denounced him the month before. There was some risk in Černil initiating the divorce during the war years since his homosexual behavior may have come to light in court. Luckily for him, the stigmatizing word "homosexual" did not appear even once in the divorce file.[184]

STUDIO PHOTOS

Another factor, which I think possibly indicative of the importance of September 1942 in Černil's life, is the pair of wartime pictures of him that his daughter, Dagmar, showed me when I interviewed her in October 2018. She showed me two photographs taken in a professional studio, dated September 15, 1942.[185] What I found most striking was this date and the fact that they were taken by a professional photographer. Were these portraits perhaps making a statement? Boldly saying, "I am still alive", or "these may be my very last photographs"? The latter could explain Černil's decision to ensure their quality by hiring a professional. Dagmar confirmed that the dates added in pencil to the backs of the pictures were in her father's handwriting.[186] Remember that, ten days earlier, on September 5, Černil confirmed his address with the Brno police. By September 15, Černil may have known the reason for his summons and believed the threat to have subsided. Alternatively, he may have thought the summons a possible omen of greater, life-threatening trouble ahead; and this, as we have suggested, moved him to have quality pictures of him taken by a professional photographer, for posterity [ill. 15].

A SECOND LOOK AT JAROSLAV OČADLÍK

Let us now take another look at Jaroslav Očadlík before adding another detail to Stanislav Černil's case. I think that Očadlík could also be a good candidate involved in the safeguarding and then discarding of the Institute materials.[187] Očadlík was one of the more inconspicuous *Kamarád* members, not writing a single text for the one and only May 1932 issue. On September 8, 1942, Očadlík was summoned to confirm his current address, as was his roommate (or lover) Jan Vacek. Their completed forms were submitted to the local police station that same day.

We have seen that Stanislav Černil procrastinated and handed in his and his mother's resident registration cards on Saturday, September 5, 1942, four days after being summoned to confirm their current address. The information about Černil's current address would have reached the Kripo, the Gestapo, or yet another German police agency through the Brno police on Monday, September 7. Is it just a coincidence that Jaroslav Očadlík and Jan Vacek were summoned to confirm their address on Tuesday, September 8? Was Černil maybe questioned on Monday, September 7, and did he maybe mention Očadlík's name? We have no idea what, if any, relationship there was between Očadlík and Černil, but when Černil moved to Bäckergasse

that no judgment could be based on the mutual mud-flinging in a divorce case.

185 There were actually three studio photos, but the third was only an enlargement of one of the other two.

186 Dagmar also showed me another studio picture (dated September 1940) of her father wearing a hat, a 1934 picture of a younger Černil, and an April 29, 1944 wedding photograph of Černil's third marriage. The back of the latter photo bore the date April 29, 1944, which indeed accords with the official marriage date. This seems to suggest that the date added in pencil to the two studio portraits (September 15, 1942) is as accurate. That September 15, 1942, was a Tuesday possibly indicates that Černil was no longer working in Ostrava (Ostrau) then.

187 I wrote to the eight people with the last name Očadlík I found in two current online Czech phonebooks on July 25, 2017. No one replied.

(Pekařská), in May 1938, he lived only a few houses away from Očadlík.[188] As we have seen, Očadlík moved to his new address at 4b Stephansgasse (Štěpánská) in the Trnitá neighborhood in May 1940 at the latest.[189] He had lived almost two decades in the building at 80 Bäckergasse (Pekařská) owned by his employer.[190] Očadlík could only have moved to his new address after 1937–38, when 4a and 4b Štěpánská were built.[191] Apparently, not all of Jaroslav Očadlík's resident registration cards survived in the AMB, Brno. One of these missing cards could have told us exactly when he moved to Stephansgasse (Štěpánská).[192] What I found most troubling was Očadlík's move from a place where he possibly lived rent-free for almost two decades to a new apartment building where the rent was presumably considerable.

There is a possible answer: soon after the Germans invaded the country in March 1939, they took over control of the brewery, started in 1888 by mainly Jewish shareholders, where Očadlík worked. By 1942, the Germans had thrown out all remaining Jewish shareholders on the company board. They also inserted seventeen Germans into the company to oversee the brewery's five hundred employees.[193] Many employees were handed over to the Gestapo, two male employees even perishing

[188] It remains unclear why Černil and his mother moved to Bäckergasse (Pekařská) in May 1938. They had lived at their previous address since the early 1920s. In our interview, Černil's daughter told me that the move was connected with planned construction works at their previous address. See also chapter 15, p. 594.

[189] The question of who owned the apartment building at 4b Štěpánská (in which Očadlík lived) remains somewhat unresolved. In 1937, Alois and Adolf Hladil became the owners of the plot. See Katastrální úřad pro Jihomoravský kraj, katastrální pracoviště Brno-město, cadastral municipality (*Katastralgemeinde, Katastrální obec*) Kröna / Křenová, land registry entry number (*Zahl der Grundbuchseinlage, číslo vložky knihovní*) 150, Stephansgasse (Štěpánská) n° 4b / 25/5. In the early 1940s, the parcel became a part of the Trnitá cadastral municipality, land registry entry number (*Zahl der Grundbuchseinlage, číslo vložky knihovní*) 675, Stephansgasse (Štěpánská) n° 4b; 676, Stephansgasse (Štěpánská) n° 4a. The two Hladil brothers (cousins?) lived in Královo Pole (at 48 Smetanova , currently Berkova) and co-owned a construction company. After work was completed, Adolf Hladil sold the 4a Štěpánská apartment building, which he owned; he and Alois Haladil possibly also sold 4b Štěpánská, the building they jointly owned. Rudolf and Marie Hostovské purchased 4a Štěpánská in October 1937. See Katastrální úřad pro Jihomoravský kraj, katastrální pracoviště Brno-město, cadastral municipality (*Katastralgemeinde, Katastrální obec*) Kröna / Křenová, land registry entry number (*Zahl der Grundbuchseinlage, číslo vložky knihovní*) 151, Stephansgasse (Štěpánská) n° 4a / 25/6. There is no trace in the *Grundbuch* (cadastral register) of the sale of 4b Štěpánská to Emilie Hartvichová (née Kulmanová, 1905–?) and her husband František Hartvich (1905–?). The cadastral records for land plot 4b jump from 1937 to 1961, and contain no mention of Hartvich. This possibly indicates that the Hartvich couple were rather custodians of some kind employed by the actual owners of the apartment building. According to their resident registration cards, the Hartvich couple moved into the building in September 1937. I also found wartime resident registration cards belonging to (at least) five different people living in 4b Štěpánská in the AMB, Brno, fonds Z 1, which were signed by either František or Emilie Hartvich as the house owner. Očadlík's resident registration card was signed by Emilie Hartvich, indicating that Očadlík was renting an apartment and not subletting a room from someone else. František Hartvich was still listed at this address in *Adresář zemského hlavního města Brna 1948* 1948, B: 106. However, in June 1945, he (and possibly also his wife) had moved to 5 Zvěřinova. See the resident registration card in AMB, Brno, fonds Z 1. I sent a letter to the only person with the surname Hartvich in Czechia on December 8, 2020, but received no response.

[190] The 80 Bäckergasse (Pekařská) address also appears in the 1932 *Kamarád* police file. See MZA, Brno, fonds B 26, Policejní ředitelství v Brno, kart. n° 2736B, inv. n° 3893, sign. 846, f. 17b, 24. This address also appears in *Adreßbuch von Groß-Brünn* 1934, 365. Očadlík started working for the brewery in 1921.

[191] Emails (dated Sep. 10, 2018 and Sep. 26, 2018) from Lea Oškerová (Odbor územního a stavebního řízení, OUSŘ, Brno) to the author. The building torn down for the new apartment complex was 4 Štěpánská. See *Adreßbuch von Groß-Brünn* 1932, 805. The new, two-winged apartment building was assigned house numbers 4a/309 and 4b/310, which it still has today. Očadlík lived in 4b, in the south wing (on the left when viewed from the street).

[192] Because the question was crucial, I asked the AMB, Brno, to make certain that there were no other resident registration cards for Jaroslav Očadlík. See email (dated Jan. 22, 2018) from Blanka Plánská (AMB, Brno) to the author. The 1938 phonebook, *Seznam telefonních ústředen, hovoren a účastníků pro zemi Moravskoslezskou 1938*, does not record Očadlík's name. Having seen in the Archiv města Ostravy, Ostrava, that a tax return could be used to obtain an individual's address in Ostrava, I asked the AMB, Brno, about whether their archival fonds

in a concentration camp.[194] Presumably, either the new management told Očadlík to live elsewhere or he thought it wise to find new lodgings. If the latter option was indeed the case, then Očadlík may have thought it better to move because he was a gay man – or, perhaps, because he had stored Institute materials in his residence at 80 Bäckergasse (Pekařská).[195]

As we did for Stanislav Černil, we should consider the possibility that Očadlík may have watched over the Institute materials. We have seen that Arnold Hindls first stored some of his belongings and furnishings in a carpentry shop. Storing one's belongings in a local business was not uncommon. In 1903, the building on Bäckergasse (Pekařská), where Očadlík lived, was purchased by the Erste Brünner Aktienbrauerei und Malzfabrik, which used it as a warehouse. So, it would indeed have been a good place to keep the Institute materials. Očadlík likely paid very little rent when living at this address, or possibly even none, by acting as a warder. If the latter was the case, then Očadlík would have had some control over items and their location in the building.

We have also seen that Očadlík may have been related to one of the brewery's shareholders. I also found legal proceedings from 1923 for the brewery's incorporation of a malt factory, in which it was represented by the Jewish lawyer Artur Feldmann Sr.[196] As we have seen, Karl Fein was a very good friend of the Feldmann family, starting his career in the law office of Artur Feldmann's brother, and also working in the Brno law office of Artur Feldmann Sr. Lastly, Karl Fein lived across from the main building of the Erste Brünner Aktienbrauerei und Malzfabrik brewery as a child. His two uncles, Moriz and Adolf Fein, and his grandfather were active in the brewing industry. So, there may well have been a connection between the brewery and Karl Fein that inclined them to help with his storage problem. On reflection, storing the materials in an off-site building belonging to the brewery was likely also the least expensive option for Karl Fein – who lost his income in March–April 1939 – to store the Institute materials. It was likely also one of the safest. As we saw, storage rooms rented by Jewish people were under intense observation by the Germans, especially the Gestapo. Also, of all the Kamarád founding members, Očadlík lived, after he moved to his new address in Stephansgasse (Štěpánská), the closest (270 m) to the Leopold Fleischer storage company – where Karl Fein might have had a storage room for a while – and also the closest to the place where the guestbook was retrieved from the old paper container, the company of Jindra Růžičková (450 m).[197]

D1, D2, and D4 could be used for this purpose. I was informed that the city of Brno mostly discarded these kinds of archives. See email (dated Feb. 1, 2021) from Petr Houzar (AMB, Brno) to the author. The available Brno address books and phonebooks could not help me either.

[193] See the introduction to the MZA, Brno, inventory list, fonds H 613, První brněnský akciový pivovar a sladovna, Brno; and MZA, Brno, fonds C 11, Krajský soud civilní Brno, firemní agenda, První brněnský akciový pivovar a sladovna (Erste Brünner Actien-Brauerei und Malzfabrik), Brno-Hlinky, 1913–1951, kart. n° 201, sign. B I 173.

[194] MZA, Brno, inventory list H 613, První brnenský akciový pivovar a sladovna, Brno, (1840) 1889–1945 (1952), 4.

[195] I found at least one brewery employee, Jul.[ius?] Lažan (?–?), living at 80 Bäckergasse (Pekařská) in 1927 and still resident in 1942 (and even 1948). So it remains unclear if some employees were compelled to leave or decided to do so on their own. See *Adreßbuch von Groß-Brünn* 1927, 269; *Adreßbuch von Groß-Brünn* 1943, 168; *Adresář zemského hlavního města Brna 1948* 1948, 234.

[196] For the 1923 settlement between the Erste Brünner Aktienbrauerei und Malzfabrik and the Mährische Gersten-Malzfabrik Wilhelm Umgelter, see MZA, Brno, fonds C 11, Krajský soud civilní Brno, kart. n° 805, sign. Sp V 237. It is not known if Artur Feldmann was the usual lawyer representing the Erste Brünner Aktienbrauerei und Malzfabrik, but it is nevertheless remarkable that, of the 170 lawyers active in Brno in 1923, it was Artur Feldmann Sr., and not anyone else, who represented the company. See *Adreßbuch von Groß-Brünn* 1923, 443.

[197] In order to visualize this better, see the map on pp. [664-65] (illustration n° 9 in chapter 16).

WASTE COLLECTION REGULATION OF FEBRUARY 1940

There was another intriguing factor associated with Jaroslav Očadlík's new living quarters on Stephansgasse (Štěpánská). During the occupation, there were strict regulations for trading in scrap. According to a February 1940 regulation issued by the Ministry of Industry, Trade and Commerce (Ministerium für Industrie, Handel und Gewerbe, Ministerstvo průmyslu, obchodu a živností), individual salvage operators and small businesses trading in scrap metal and other materials could only operate within a city district specifically allocated to them, and only for the first ten days of every month. For the rest of the month, they could inspect areas outside their assigned territory. These small traders and individual operators then transferred the items they collected to medium-sized companies. Růžička's business obtained a permit as a medium-sized company.[198] That the Ministry of Industry, Trade and Commerce controlled the trade in scrap is further indicated by a 1944 Brno newspaper article announcing the Ministry's organization of an extraordinary collection of old paper, for which it appointed seven dealers. The article also confirms that Růžičková's company, which employed smaller traders and individual salvage operators, traded in old paper.[199] It would seem, then, that Jindra Růžičková's company could operate exclusively in the Trnitá city district for the first ten days of every month. Očadlík lived in Trnitá and this meant that the Růžičková couple's company, or those it employed, would have been able to collect old paper from his apartment without anyone asking questions. Since Černil, Očadlík and Vacek were summoned within the first ten days of September, they would have been able to discard the materials smoothly without violating the ministry's regulation.

It is important to recognize that discarding the Institute materials could not have been an easy venture. That the business operated by Jindra Růžičková, and not another, took the matter in hand meant that few or even no uncomfortable questions would be asked. Other traders would surely have noticed the discarding of valuable books and objected to such vandalism. When considering all of these factors related

198 See paragraphs 2–5 in the Kundmachung des Ministeriums für Industrie, Handel und Gewerbe über die Organisation der Sammlung von Abfällen, dated Feb. 12, 1940, Z. 10.385/40, *Amtsblatt des Protektorates Böhmen und Mähren = Úřední list Protektorátu Čechy a Morava*, Jg. XXI, [1940], n° 36, Feb. 13, 1940, [973]–76. The announcement distinguished between individual salvage operators and small, medium, and large companies. Confusingly, there was even a separate category of "specialized companies" engaged in waste collection, whose activities did not seem to be geographically limited. Růžička's business was a medium-sized company. See NA, Praha, fonds n° 375, Arizačni spisy, company Josef Pollak, kart. n° 249, inv. n° 1706, message (dated Nov. 13, 1940) from Eduard Kaiser to Oberlandrat, not foliated. The *Kundmachung* (announcement) makes it clear that all companies needed a new official trade permit issued by the Ministry of Industry, Trade and Commerce, classifying and deeming them as eligible. I attempted to find more information about Růžičková's company (and its permit) in NA, Praha, fonds n° 903, Ministerstvo průmyslu, obchodu a živností, 1919–1942, archive of the Ministry of Industry, Trade and Commerce. However, I finally had to conclude that the mentions of the company in several ministry registers did not lead to the permit Růžičková obtained. As a consequence, I could not determine exactly what it stipulated. Presumably, these files were shredded after or even during the war. I thank Pavel Dufek (NA, Praha) for his assistance and for showing me several of these registers in January 2020. Permits were constantly revoked and new ones issued during the war years, as shown by the company index cards in the AMB, Brno, fonds B 1/16; and the file in MZA, Brno, fonds G 115, Obchodní a živnostenská komora Brno (Geschäfts und Gewerbekammer in Brünn), II. series, kart. n° 194, inventory n° 50, company file Jindra Ružičková.

199 See "Mimořádný sběr starého papíru v Brně" (Extraordinary collection of old paper in Brno), *Lidové noviny*, Tmb, Mar. 22, 1944, 4. This newspaper article is the only source that explicitly states that Růžička dealt in old paper. Other sources only mention other scrap materials, like old iron. Curiously, when looking at the appointed traders' locations, one cannot say that they were assigned in a rational geographical way, according to the *Rayonierung* (zoning) of the old paper hunting grounds. The traders Käthe Hermann (1 Trnitá), Vinzenz Wals (37 Plotní) and Eduard Vorel (9 Cejl) were all located quite close to the business premises of Jindra Ruzicková. See *Adressbuch der Landeshauptstadt Brünn* 1942, 4, 339, 344. For Käthe Hermann (formerly Käthe Koschik), see *Volksdeutsche Zeitung*, Aug. 15, 1943, 10. But then again, the extraordinary collection of old paper occurred in 1944, not 1942.

to Očadlík, I think it possible that this escape route for the Institute materials, when faced with a threat to one's life, may have even been thought out beforehand. Did Očadlík possibly move to Stephansgasse (Štěpánská) with this very purpose in mind? This may seem far-fetched but it cannot be wholly excluded. The waste collection regulation was issued in February 1940. Očadlík was living at Stephansgasse (Štěpánská) by May 1940 at the latest. We have also seen that Karl Fein returned to Brno from Prague a few times in 1940, which would mean that, if there was such a thought-out escape plan, Fein might have known about it.

We should also not underestimate, in this regard, the fierce competition between businesses dealing in scrap or their constant scrutiny of whether competitors abided by the rules and respected their allotted trading zones. In some company files that I have seen, there were indeed heated discussions about the transgressions of other traders. The chronic paper shortage during the war years made things even more tense [ill. 16].[200] Finally, the sheer weight of the Institute and Hirschfeld papers must have represented a considerable amount of money for the Růžička couple. After all, as we have seen, approximately 3,000 kg of materials were bought back from Nazi Germany in November 1933.

PRELIMINARY CONCLUSION

The close proximity of the dates when Černil and Očadlík had to confirm their current addresses is hard to dismiss as coincidental; however, the summons that Očadlík, Vacek, and Černil and his mother received in September 1942 may well have been unconnected. Maybe Očadlík (and Vacek?) were being observed by a German police agency for possible links with the resistance, perhaps even unrelated to Černil's resistance or clandestine activities.[201] It is certain, however, that something happened in September 1942 that involved Očadlík and possibly also Vacek. Stanislav Černil may have mentioned their names when he was questioned, but there may have also been an occurrence linked to their residence. Interestingly, Očadlík's neighbor, Josef Martinkowitsch (1895–1945?), living at 4 Stephansgasse (Štěpánská), was also summoned to confirm his address on the same date as Očadlík and Vacek.[202] Did the Germans ask a pro-German neighbor if he had seen anything suspicious? Martinkowitsch applied for German ethnic (Deutsche Volkszugehörigkeit) status in September 1939, and this may have caused the Germans to view him as a reliable

[200] For more on the shortage and the old paper trade in wartime Germany, see Kohlmann-Viand 1991, 56–63; Schmidt-Bachem 2011, 281–309. See also *Anzeiger der Verkehrsgruppe Spedition und Lagerei im Zentralverband des Verkehrs für Böhmen und Mähren = Véstník dopravni skupiny zasilatelství a skladovaní v Ústředním svazu dopravy pro Čechy a Moravu*, Jul. 1, 1943, 4; Mar. 16, 1944, 1.

[201] A certain Alois Fiala (1859–1942), also living at 4b Stephansgasse (Štěpánská), hosted meetings of the Obrana národa resistance group in his apartment. See Kopečný 2003, 161; and https://encyklo pedie.brna.cz/home-mmb/?acc=profil_osobnosti&load =13365 (accessed Jan. 21, 2021). He moved into the apartment building on December 12, 1939. See his resident registration card in AMB, Brno, fonds Z 1. He died, presumably of old age, in mid-August 1942. On Fiala's death, see "Poslední ze 'Súchovské republiky': smrt Aloise Fialy" (The Last of the "Republic of Suchov": The Death of Alois Fiala), *Moravská orlice*, Aug. 19, 1942, 2. Two of his sons, Vlastimír Fiala (1904–?) and Mojmír Fiala (1894–1942), were also involved in resistance activities. See https://encyklope die.brna.cz/ home-mmb/ ?acc=profil_osobnosti&load= 8161 and https://encyklopedie.brna.cz/home-mmb/ ?acc=profil_osobnosti&load=37791 (both accessed Apr. 9, 2021). His wife, Anna Fialová (née Molnárová, 1866–1945), and eldest daughter, Květa Fialová (1896–?), also lived in the same apartment. The wife and daughter were summoned to confirm their address on Aug. 20, 1942, four days after Alois's death. At least one person living at 4b Stephansgasse (Štěpánská) applied for deutsche Volkszugehörigkeit (German ethnic) status, Amalie Buchta (1901–?). She moved into the building on September 1, 1941, with her brother (?) Henri Buchta (?–?).

[202] For the sake of clarity, it should be pointed out that, in addition to house numbers 4a/309 and 4b/310, there was a separate house, numbered 4/308. When seen from the street, 4/308 was (and still is) to the right of the two apartment blocks 4a/309 and 4b/310. See illustration n° 12 in this chapter.

witness.[203] We have seen that the Kripo and the Gestapo were not very interested in the lives of Czech gay men. According to some authors, the Kripo in Brno mainly dealt with crimes against the war economy (*Vergehen gegen die Kriegswirtschaft*).[204] This presents a final possibility: were Očadlík (and Vacek?) maybe questioned or even arrested because of unsanctioned physical handling of the Institute materials, related to the old paper trade, which was considered a criminal act?[205] Had someone maybe noticed Jaroslav Růžička or one of his employees collecting the Institute materials at 4b Stephansgasse (Štěpánská), finding it suspect, and notified the German occupiers? And was that someone maybe Josef Martinkowitsch?

All of this makes one wonder, of course, whether, in September 1942, the Germans had possibly stumbled, even inadvertently, upon the remaining paper trail of their former archenemy, Magnus Hirschfeld. Here again, there is no surviving archival source that indicates this.[206] But if they did, it would have been the second time the Germans encountered the estate of the man whom they had so thoroughly despised when alive. The first possible moment occurred in 1940, when the German District Court (Deutsches Amtsgericht) asked Nawratil about what to do with the Giese inheritance. In that encounter, the name of Magnus Hirschfeld (and his estate, transferred first to Giese and later to Fein) presumably went unnoticed or was deemed unimportant.

203 AMB, Brno, fonds Z 1, resident registration card Josef Martinkowitsch. Martinkowitsch applied for deutsche Volkszugehörigkeit (German ethnic) status on September 22, 1939, and was approved on April 1, 1940. See AMB, Brno, fonds A 1/53. A September 9, 1942, *Fahndungsabteilung* (Kripo investigation department) stamp appears on the back of his resident registration form. Martinkowitsch was married to Margarete Philipp (1898–?). The couple had one daughter, Helga (1936–?), who lived in Linz after the war. In December 2018, I wrote approximately ten letters to people with the surname Martinkowitsch in Austria, inquiring in the same letter about Mathilde Martinkowitsch (1903?–2002), a well-known figure in Brno who was likely related to Josef Martinkowitsch. A Viktoria Martinkowitsch, whose great-grandparents fled Czechoslovakia after the war, replied, but the email exchange fell silent after a while for unknown reasons.

204 Filip, Břečka, Schildberger et al. 2012, 55, 124.

205 I checked whether Stanislav Černil and Jaroslav Očadlík were named in the court registers of fonds C 152 (Okresní soud trestní v Brně) and fonds C 12 (Krajský soud trestní v Brně) for 1940–1943 with the MZA, Brno. They were not. See email (dated Sep. 21, 2018) from Tereza Broncová (MZA, Brno) to the author. I also checked whether they and the other founding members of *Kamarád* had been imprisoned during the war in one of the three Gestapo prisons – Prague-Pankrác, Cheb (German, Eger), Mírov (German, Mürau) – but this was not the case. A check for the names of Stanislav Černil, Vilém Drexler-Hlubocký, Bohdan Hájek, Štefan Kostelníček, Stanislav Očadlík and Josef Uher was also made in NA, Praha, fonds n° 1077, Okupační vězeňské spisy. See email (dated Oct. 12, 2017) from Helena Uchytilová (NA, Praha) to the author.

206 There was only one, quite intriguing handwritten date added in a small archival file concerning Jaroslav and Jindra Růžička. The archival fonds of the Prague police contains a document on Jaroslav Růžička, issued by the Všeobecné kriminální ústředna (General criminal control center), a Prague police department established in 1929. See http://www.policie.cz/clanek/okenko-do-dejin-krim inalistiky.aspx (accessed Jan. 16, 2017). The document seems to be an innocuous identity check of Jaroslav Růžička carried out in Prague, likely requested by the Brno police in September 1939. See NA, Praha, fonds n° 1420, Policejní ředitelství Praha II, PŘ II 1931–1940, kart. n° 10.238, sign. R2369/38, file Jaroslav Růžička (born May 4, 1905). This document contains a reference to Brno police file n° 23960/1939. This number refers to a September 25, 1939, record in the Brno police registry, in which both Jaroslav Růžička and Jindra Fikes reported, two months before their December 23, 1939 marriage, the theft of their home certificate ("krád domovský list"). See MZA, Brno, fonds B 26, Policejní ředitelství v Brno, book n° 1312, Podací protokol bezpečnostní a kriminální, year 1939, reference n° 23958 (J. Fike[s]), and reference n° 23959 (J. Růžička). (The number on the document in NA, Praha, seems to be mistaken, stating n° 23960/1939 and not n° 23959.) Both their home certificate was required to get married. Perhaps they reported it stolen because they were not able to find this vital document. A collaborator at MZA, Brno, wrote to me that, despite the reference number, no physical file on the matter could be found in the Brno police archives. See email (dated Jul. 11, 2019) from Tomáš Černušák (MZA, Brno) to the author. In one of the columns of the aforementioned Brno police registry, recording further events, the word "published" was added. Tomáš Černušák (MZA, Brno) thinks that more information could be found in an issue of *Československý policejní věstník* (during the occupation, this became *Polizeianzeiger für das Protektorat Böhmen und Mähren = Policejní věstník*

THE MILAN KRATOCHVÍLA CASE

As we have seen, it is unlikely – yet cannot be definitively excluded – that Černil and Očadlík were summoned because of their homosexual behavior or their involvement with *Kamarád*. Incomplete archival sources, especially belonging to the German police authorities, prevent us from determining exactly why they were summoned in September 1942. But we have uncovered a factor that possibly explains why the Kripo or the Gestapo were after Stanislav Černil.

We have already mentioned Aktion Gitter, the "mass arrest action" that started immediately after the invasion of the remainder of Czechoslovakia (Rest-Tschechei), in mid-March 1939.[207] Thousands of Communists and many German immigrants were arrested using the so-called Mobilization Card Index (*Mobilmachungskartei, M-Kartei*), a list drawn up by the Security Service (Sicherheitsdienst) and the Gestapo. Arrests did not cease with this first wave of repression. In the summer of 1939, the occupiers started compiling another list of people to be arrested, this time using the so-called A-Card Index (*A-Kartei*).[208] In September 1942, the month that Černil and Očadlík completed their resident registration cards, the German invaders' so-called Aktion E started to focus on family members of Czechs active in the resistance abroad. The "E" in Aktion E stood for emigrants (*Emigranten*).[209] It seems to me that Černil, his mother, and possibly also Očadlík came under scrutiny in September 1942 as part of this campaign.

In her 2018 interview, Dagmar told me that an uncle of hers, a school director named Stanislav Kratochvíla (1890–1975), lived at 35 Kreuzgasse (Křížová), just across the street from their home at 16 Kreuzgasse (Křížová).[210] Stanislav Kratochvíla was married to Marie Vlašínová (1885–1963). The couple had two children: Milan (1918–1977) and Zora (1922–1999) [ill. 17] [ill. 18]. Stanislav Kratochvíla was not strictly speaking Dagmar's uncle, but distantly related through Stanislav Černil's mother, Marie Vlašínová.[211] Dagmar knew a lot of intimate details about the lives of Stanislav

pro Protektorát Čechy a Morava). Unfortunately, this title is very hard to find, even in Czechia. Only the library of the Muzeum Policie ČR, Praha (Czech Police Museum, Prague), has the complete series, and they adamantly refused to answer two emails (in English) asking about access to the title and the library's opening hours. Other than a few stamps and unclear references to several administrative police services, the same Všeobecné kriminální ústředně document contains a date added in thick blue pencil on the top right-hand corner: "11/10/42". This October date falls in the month after Stanislav Černil and Jaroslav Očadlík were summoned to confirm their latest address. Why this date was added two years after the presumed loss of the couple's home certificate remains, for now, a mystery.

[207] Filip et al. 2012, 55.

[208] The A-Kartei had two parts. The first was a list of people belonging to city elite, who were to be arrested once war officially broke out in September 1939. This mass arrest action was known as Albert I. See Filip et al. 2012, 57, 60, 78. The other part contained the names of people who were to be arrested later.

[209] Filip, Břečka, Schildberger et al. 2012, 192.

[210] Many Czechs understandably believe that the spelling of this name is incorrect, the more common form being Kratochvíl, but it was indeed Kratochvíla. Milan Kratochvíla, a grandson of Stanislav Kratochvíla, noticed that several Černil, Vlašín, and Kratochvíla family members lived within a stone's throw of each other in the Staré Brno neighborhood. See email (dated Jun. 29, 2019) from Milan Kratochvíla to the author.

[211] When I asked Dagmar about the exact family relationship, she avoided the question, perhaps because she did not know the answer. Stanislav Kratochvíla was certainly not her uncle, but a great-uncle by marriage. Marie Kratochvílová (née Vlašínová) was the niece of her grandmother Marie Černilová (née Vlašínová). Stanislav Černil's maternal grandparents were Jan (Johann) Vlašín (1846–?) and Marie (Mariè Anna) Vlašínová (née Klímová, ?–?). The parents of Stanislav Kratochvíla's wife, Marie Kratochvíla (née Vlašínová, (1885-1963), were Vilém Vlašín (1853–1904) and Maria (née Čubra or Čuberna, 1857–1925). Both Jan Vlašín and Vilém Vlašín were born in Jedov (in the Třebíč district), the sons of Joseph Vlašín (Wlaschin, 1819–?) and Francisca (Františka) Rousová (1817–?). See http://actapublica.eu/matriky/brno/prohlizec/6461/?strana=156 and http://actapublica.eu/matriky/brno/prohlizec/6461/?strana=160 (both accessed Jul. 10, 2019); and MZA, Brno, fonds G 212, Osobní a penzijní spisy, kart. n° 2811, sign. 49134, pension file Stanislav Kratochvíla, f. 62. As Milan Kratochvíla explains, "uncle" and "aunt" were often used by Czechoslovak children as terms of endearment for unrelated (or far related) adults. See email (dated Jun. 29, 2019) from Milan Kratochvíla to the author.

Kratochvíla and his family. What is more, Stanislav Černil's second wife, Ludmila Suchúneková, lived with the Kratochvíla couple for a few weeks prior to their marriage in September 1935, further indicating that Stanislav Kratochvíla was related to the Černils.[212]

Dagmar also told me that their son, Milan, was active in the resistance but was denounced and fled abroad in February 1940, pretending to go on a ski trip to the Beskid mountains.[213] Milan Kratochvíla's war diary does mention that he skied with friends from Střelná in the Protectorate to Púchov in Slovakia during the "dark night" of February 28–29, 1940.[214] Traveling through a large number of countries for months, Milan Kratochvíla arrived in Liverpool in mid-July 1940. In England, he joined the Czech military operating from abroad.[215] In August 1944, as part of the 1st Czechoslovak Independent Armored Brigade under American command, Milan landed in Normandy, and went with the 3rd US Army to the Czech border in April 1945.[216] While in England, Milan married Barbara Joyce Gumb (1923–2000), and the couple had a son, Peter F. Stanley Kratochvíla (1944–). Another son, Milan (?–), was born some time after the war.[217] Also after the war, Milan Kratochvíla returned to Czechoslovakia where he died in Brno in 1977. His two sons, Peter and Milan, emigrated from Brno to the UK in the early 1960s.[218]

Milan Kratochvíla's war diary also mentions that, shortly before escaping the country, in 1940, he hid in a house on Pekařská (Bäckergasse). There is a possibility that this may have been the flat of Stanislav Černil and his mother.[219] However, there is clear proof that Milan's sister, Zora, did stay in their flat for a few days before moving

[212] AMB, Brno, fonds Z 1, resident registration card Ludmila Suchúneková.

[213] One of his resident registration cards in the AMB, Brno, fonds Z 1, records that he went skiing in the Beskid mountains and that his exact address was unknown. The Radhošť mountain and possibly also the city of Frenštát (pod Radhoštěm) are also mentioned on the same resident registration card, completed and signed by Milan's father, Stanislav, on March 30, 1940. On another post-war resident registration card (dated Jan. 2, 1946), completed by Milan himself, he declares February 28, 1940, to be the date he left his paternal home, though it was rather the date he left the country.

[214] Milan Kratochvíla's war diary (dated between Feb. 8 and 28, 1940). See email (dated Jun. 6, 2019) from Milan Kratochvíla to the author.

[215] In the interview, Dagmar said that Milan Kratochvíla was a pilot with the RAF, but this was firmly denied by his son, Milan Kratochvíla Jr., who sent me a detailed account of his father's military career during World War II. Milan joined the Czechoslovak Forces in the UK and was a Lance Corporal as part of Tank Battalion I, 1st Armoured Regiment. See email (dated Jun. 9, 2019) from Milan Kratochvíla to the author. Milan studied medicine from December 1937 to June 1939 at Masaryk University in Brno. A record at the university briefly notes that he was a member of a foreign army in a state of demobilization ("Přísl. Zahr. armády ve stadiu demob."). See email (dated May 2, 2019) from Luděk Navrátil (Archiv Masarykovy University Brno) to the author. The same documents also show that the anatomist Karel Hora was one of his professors. Hora was an organizer of the 1932 WLSR Brno conference who also interviewed Hirschfeld. As we have seen, he was killed in Mauthausen.

[216] Email (dated Nov. 10, 2021) from Milan Kratochvíla to the author.

[217] Milan Kratochvíla Jr. preferred not to share his birth year with me, something that I of course respected. See email (dated Jul. 7, 2019) from Milan Kratochvíla to the author.

[218] Email (dated Jul. 7, 2020) from Milan Kratochvíla to the author. Stanislav and Marie Kratochvíla and their two children are buried in the Brno central cemetery in parcel H 36, grave 387.

[219] Email (dated Jul. 7, 2019) from Milan Kratochvíla to the author. I infer that this took place in early 1940 since Milan fled the country at the end of February 1940, and the war diary passage mentioning the safe house on Bäckergasse (Pekařská) lies in the section dated 1940. No house number is given, so it remains possible it was not Černil's flat. We also need to consider the possibility that Milan stayed with Jaroslav Očadlík in the brewery-owned building on Bäckergasse (Pekařská). The Bäckergasse (Pekařská) address was apparently used as a safe house, or simply for meetings, more than once since it was referred to as "the office" in Milan Kratochvíla's war diary. In 1940, it ceased to be reliable. See email (dated Jul. 7, 2019) from Milan Kratochvíla to the author. This also raises the question of whether Očadlík's 1940 move to Stephansgasse (Štěpánská) was related to these resistance activities that had become too risky.

[220] AMB, Brno, fonds Z 1, resident registration card (dated May 28, 1942) Zora Kratochvíla.

[221] At least at first sight, what speaks against the possibility that Stanislav Černil was under scrutiny because of the Kratochvíla family is that Aktion E,

to Svatoslav, her father's ancestral village, at the end of July 1942.[220] I think it possible, even probable, that the September 1, 1942 summonses issued to Stanislav Černil and his mother were linked to Stanislav Černil's involvement with the Kratochvíla family.[221] Zora Kratochvíla was summoned to confirm her address on May 28, 1942, meaning she could expect to be questioned.[222] On July 9, 1942, Stanislav Kratochvíla had to confirm his address as well. It is unclear if both were actually questioned, but we can assume that the summons was related to Milan Kratochvíla's fleeing abroad.[223] The last summons for Stanislav Kratochvíla likely also explains why Zora's parents decided that she would be safer in the countryside. She was sent to Svatoslav later that month.

I think it possible that Zora Kratochvíla spent a few days in Stanislav Černil's flat because there was a (failed?) attempt to get her out of the country, following Milan's example. The arrest on September 17, 1942, of Stanislav Kratochvíla, his wife, Marie Vlašínová, and his daughter, Zora Kratochvíla, was consistent with the official September 1942 launch of Aktion E. Mother and daughter were imprisoned in the Svatobořice (Swatoborschitz) internment camp (*internační tabor*) near Kyjov, in southern Moravia. This camp was specifically designated for family members of people who had fled abroad. Mother and daughter were released at the end of January 1943 and returned to their home at 35 Kreuzgasse (Křížová).[224] Five months later, in June 1943, Zora Kratochvíla was sent alone to the same internment camp again.[225] Stanislav Kratochvíla remained imprisoned for the rest of the war, but in

which targeted family members of people who had fled abroad, did not officially start until mid-September 1942. See https://www.svatoborice-mistrin.cz/internacni-tabor/ (accessed Jul. 4, 2019): "Dne 17. září 1942 vydal Reichssicherheitshauptamt [*sic*] v Berlíně a velitel Sicherheitspolizei a Sicherheitsdients [*sic*] v Praze (bezpečnostní policie a bezpečnostní služba) rozkaz zatknout jisté příslušníky a příbuzné uprchlých Čechů a předběžně je umístit v internačním táboře až do dalšího rozhodnutí úřadů. To byl základ tzv. akce 'E' (Aktion Emingranten [*sic*]). Tímto úkonem byl zřízen ve Svatobořicích internační tábor (Internierungslager Swatoborschitz Bez. Gaya)" (On September 17, 1942, the Reichssicherheitshauptamt [RSHA] in Berlin and the commander of the Sicherheitspolizei [Sipo, Security Police] and Sicherheitsdienst [SD, Security Service] in Prague, issued an order to arrest certain family members and relatives of escaped Czechs and put them provisionally in an internment camp pending a further decision by the authorities. This was the basis of the so-called Aktion E [Aktion Emigranten]. With this action, an internment camp [Internierungslager Swatoborschitz Bez. Gaya] was established in Svatobořice [Swatoborschitz]). Nevertheless, we must presume that inquiries into and investigations of relatives of foreign fighters began before that date.

222 AMB, Brno, fonds Z 1, resident registration card (dated May 28, 1942) Zora Kratochvíla.

223 AMB, Brno, fonds Z 1, resident registration card (dated Jul. 9, 1940) Stanislav Kratochvíla. The back of his card has no Kripo *Fahndungsabteilung* (investigation department) stamp but it is rubber stamped July 17, 1940.

224 MZA, Brno, fonds B 292, Internační tábor Svatobořice, kartotéka integrovaných (digitized), index cards for Zora Kratochvílová and Marie Kratochvílová (née Vlašínová), kart. n° 3, sign n° 11. The exact date of the mother and daughter's release was January 29, 1943. These dates are confirmed in a letter (dated May 27, 1945) written by Marie Kratochvílová's husband. See MZA, Brno, fonds G 212, Osobní a penzijní spisy, kart. n° 2811, sign. 49134, pension file Stanislav Kratochvíla, f. 264. Dagmar wrote that the mother (alone) was imprisoned in Svatobořice. See letter (dated Mar. 15, 2019, 3–4) from Dagmar Černilová to the author, but this is clearly mistaken. For more information on the Svatobořice (Swatoborschitz) internment camp, see https://www.svatoborice-mistrin.cz /internacni-tabor/ and https://www.pametnaroda.cz/cs/ internacni-ta borsvatoborice-u-kyjova (both accessed Jul. 3, 2019); Padevět 2018, 373–79.

225 See the index card for Zora Kratochvíla in MZA, Brno, fonds B 292, Internační tábor Svatobořice (1942–1945), kart. n° 3, which gives two arrival dates: September 17, 1942 and June 17, 1943. The card also mentions a release date, January 29, but the year is illegible. It seems that she was temporarily released at the end of January 1943. A resident registration card for Zora Kratochvíla in the AMB, Brno, indicates that she returned home again in early February 1943. On that card, however, June 21, 1943, is the *only* arrival date at the internment camp. In addition, she confirmed her new address in Brno in April or May 1945 and listed the internment camp as her previous address. Another file indicates that she was interned from September 17, 1942, until the end of the war. See MZA, Brno, fonds B 22, Zemská školní rada, B 22, II. serie, kart. n° 28. The latter clearly indicates that the reason for her internment was her brother's service in the 1st Czechoslovak Independent Armored Brigade.

different locations. Unlike his wife and daughter, he was first sent to Kaunitz College (Kounicovy koleje), where he stayed until December 9, 1942.[226] From there he was transferred to the Pod Kaštany concentration camp (*koncentračního tábora*) in Brno.[227] On February 17, 1943, he was further transferred to Svatobořice (Swatoborschitz), where he remained until April 30, 1943.[228] At the end of June or July 1943, after another stay of two or three months in Pod Kaštany, Stanislav Kratochvíla was sent to Dachau,[229] where he was imprisoned until May 21, 1945.

Silvestr Kratochvíla (1913–1942), another member of the family, an uncle of Milan's, was also active in the resistance as a member of Obrana národa. He was caught and tried by a court martial on October 1, 1941, expropriated, and sent to Mauthausen, where he died in July 1942.[230] This may have been another reason that the Germans deemed it necessary to scrutinize the Kratochvíla family's broader social network. That Silvestr Kratochvíla worked and lived in Moravská Ostrava (Mährisch-Ostrau) may be another possible link to Stanislav Černil, who had worked there for several years, and perhaps also during the war. The Balkan escape route that Milan apparently took when he fled the Protectorate was known in Ostrava (Ostrau) Obrana národa circles.[231]

Let us now briefly return to Stanislav Černil's divorce from his second wife in October 1942 and the denunciation that perhaps preceded it. We suggested that Ludmila Suchánekovà might have denounced Černil for homosexuality, or for some other reason. Does Černil's possible involvement with the Kratochvíla family not exclude the possibility that his October 1942 divorce was connected to Černil's September 1942 summons? Why would Černil have initiated divorce proceedings the month after the summons if, after presumably being questioned by the Gestapo or some other German police agency, he realized that he was summoned because of

[226] For these dates, I mainly rely on two letters (dated May 27, 1945, and Jul. 17, 1945) by Stanislav Kratochvíla. See MZA, Brno, fonds G 212, Osobní a penzijní spisy, kart. n° 2811, sign. 49134, pension file Stanislav Kratochvíla, f. 18 and f. 264. See also the dates given by Stanislav Kratochvíla in MZA, Brno, fonds B 22, Zemská školní rada, kart. n° 28, Stanislav Kratochvíla.

[227] For more information on the Pod Kaštany *koncentračního tábora* (concentration camp), see https://encyklopedie.brna.cz/home-mmb/?acc=profil_domu&load=898 and https://encyklopedie.brna.cz/home-mmb/?acc=profil_objektu&load=296 (both accessed Feb. 12, 2020). Curiously, this Brno concentration camp is not mentioned in Padevět 2018. See also Filip & Schildberger 2013, 42–43.

[228] This means that he was imprisoned when his wife and daughter were at liberty. See MZA, Brno, fonds B 292, Internační tábor Svatobořice, kartotéka integrovaných (digitized), index card for Stanislav Kratochvíla, kart. n° 3, sign n° 11.

[229] Stanislav Kratochvíla gives June 30, 1942, as his arrival date in Dachau; however, the Dachau database entry gives this as July 30, 1943. He was liberated from Dachau at the end of the war. See https://stevemorse.org/dachau/da chau.html (accessed Apr. 9, 2019). In the database, Stanislav Kratochvíla's name is spelled "Kratochwil", identified as prisoner 50037. (Kratochwil's birth date and Brno address make it clear that he is indeed Stanislav Kratochvíla.) It is unclear if František Černil was imprisoned in 1943 in connection with Kratochvíla's or his own resistance activities. For now, it seems merely a coincidence that František Černil, Stanislav Černil's brother, received a summons to confirm his address on the day that Stanislav Kratochvíla arrived in Dachau.

[230] Silvestr Kratochvíla was the son of Karel Kratochvíla (1879–?) and Františka Kratochvílová (1882–?) See email (dated Jul. 11, 2019) from Ivo Durec (Státní okresní archiv Brno-venkov se sídlem v Rajhradě) to the author. Durec referred to 1921 census information for the address 111 Svatoslav. Karel was the brother of Jan Kratochvíla (1859–1913), the father of Stanislav Kratochvíla and grandfather of Milan Kratochvíla. Jan Kratochvíla was married to Katarina Kratochvílová (née Mikešová, 1859–1943?). Karel and Jan Kratochvíla's parents were František (Franz) (1835–1885) and Josefa Kratochvílová (née Musil, 1837–1916). See MZA, Brno, fonds G 212, Osobní a penzijní spisy, kart. n° 2811, sign. 49134, pension file Stanislav Kratochvíla, f. 61. I thank Milan Kratochvíla for help in elucidating their exact family relations and, most of all, for showing me that Jan and Karel were, indeed, born twenty years apart. See emails (dated Jun. 22, 2019; Jun. 24, 2019; and Nov. 15, 2019) from Milan Kratochvíla to the author. For Silvestr Kratochvíla's court martial sentence and imprisonment, see MZA, Brno, fonds B 340, Gestapo Brno, sign. 100-287-9; and the Mauthausen database, https://www.gedenkstaet ten.at/raum-der-namen/cms/index.php?id=4&p=6064&L=1 (accessed Aug. 1, 2019).

his involvement with the Kratochvíla family and not for being gay or involved with *Kamarád*? Here, we need to recall that Černil's second wife briefly stayed with the Kratochvíla family shortly before marrying Černil. She may have remained in contact with them and known about Černil's supposed involvement with Milan Kratochvíla's flight. Here as well, in other words, Černil may have known, or merely *suspected*, that Ludmila Sucháneková had deliberately informed the Germans about Černil's involvement in the stratagems around Milan and Zora Kratochvíla. That might have been reason enough for him to set divorce proceedings in motion shortly afterwards.

THE EXACT REASON FOR THE SUMMONS DOES NOT MATTER

However probable it may seem that Stanislav Černil and his mother were summoned on September 1, 1942, because of their involvement in the case of Milan Kratochvíla and possibly also his sister, Zora Kratochvíla, it cannot be definitively established.[232] The strange, nearly synchronous summons for Černil and Očadlík (and Vacek) leaves open the possibility that their being gay, their 1932 *Kamarád* adventure, their possible involvement with the discarding of the Institute materials in the beginning of September 1942, or still some other matter, was the real reason for the Germans tracking down these men. But, all in all, it does not really matter *why* Stanislav Černil, his mother, and Očadlík (and Vacek) were summoned in September 1942. Whatever the reason, the summons likely induced devastating panic.

The general atmosphere of terror reigning in the Protectorate in 1942, combined with the regulation completely forbidding possession of Jewish materials and belongings, was likely reason enough *not* to risk one's safety and take drastic, potentially life-saving measures as soon as it was clear that the Kripo or Gestapo would pay a visit. *Not knowing* exactly why they were summoned and expecting such a visit, Černil or Očadlík (or the two in tandem) may have decided that it was better not to take any chances and to discard the Institute materials possibly stored in the home of Černil or Očadlík, or somewhere else still. If the Institute materials were indeed stored in one of their homes, a simple visit from the Gestapo or Kripo would have got them in serious trouble. They would have had to explain why they had the Institute materials and where and from whom they had got them. Working-class men keeping a collection of hundreds of scholarly books in their home would certainly not go unnoticed.

DID SOMEONE KNOW KARL FEIN HAD DIED IN ŁÓDŹ?

Yet, despite the difficult, extremely tense, and even panicked situation in 1942, it is still difficult to understand how the people around *Kamarád*, so inspired by Hirschfeld when they met him in 1932, would have suddenly given up on their hero – if Karl Fein had indeed entrusted them with the Institute materials, of course. Another possibly significant factor may explain why the *Kamarád* group might have felt less obligated to safeguard the Institute materials at all costs. The news that Karl Fein died in Łódź

[231] Sýkora 2013, 8; https://moravskoslezsky.denik.cz/zpravy_region/cedule-v-ostrave-nove-bele-vysvetluji-nazvy-ulic-20190311.html (accessed Sep. 18, 2020). I thank Milan Kratochvíla for these two references. See his email (dated Jun. 26, 2019) to the author. See also https://encyklopedie.brna.cz/home-mmb/?acc=profil_osobnosti&load=1128 (accessed Sep. 18, 2020).

[232] I had hoped to overcome the uncertainty by looking at the stamps on the backs of the resident registration cards belonging to Stanislav and Zora Kratochvíla, and those on the cards belonging to Stanislav Černil and Jaroslav Očadlík. There is no Kripo *Fahndungsabteilung* (investigation department) stamp on the backs of the Kratochvílas' resident registration cards, but they *have* date stamps not seen on most other resident registration cards. I thought that these different stamps perhaps indicated a separate investigation by another German police agency and, consequently, that the two cases were unrelated. Yet the stamps do not solve the riddle. It is possible that Zora and Stanislav Kratochvíla's names were indeed checked in the Kripo repository in both Prague and Berlin, but that the typical

in May 1942 may have reached Brno by September 1942. But *did* it? Here too, we are consigned to uncertainty.

Oskar Rosenfeld, one of the Łódź ghetto chroniclers, wrote in his private diary that, despite the suspension of mail privileges (*Postsperre*), the ghetto post office sent anonymous pre-printed postcards – likely to people inquiring about the fate of their relatives in Łódź, or simply to inform outsiders that the money they sent had been received, thus implying that their relatives were still alive. However, it is unclear if the ghetto administration explicitly informed the outside world of the death of an inmate when a relative sent them money.[233] There is also a January 1942 note from Hans Biebow (1902–1947), the leader of the German ghetto administration, the so-called *Gettoverwaltung*, to a Mr. Otto Luchterhandt, stating that he needed monthly lists of the names of dead ghetto newcomers (*Neueingesiedelten*) in case their relatives asked if they could send money.[234] Until 1943, the Gestapo also notified the local Jüdische Kultusgemeinde (JKG, Jewish Religious Community) of the deaths of Jewish inmates in prisons and concentration camps.[235] Yet one wonders if this practice of informing Jewish relatives of the deaths of their loved ones did indeed continue until 1943. Would an avalanche of Jewish death notifications following the mass deportations of 1941–42 not have alarmed those not yet deported?[236]

In the first half of 1941, a death notice was sent for Ruth Elias's father-in-law, Heinrich Elias (1890–1941), who perished in Mauthausen.[237] Charles Ticho, who lived in Brno, wrote in his memoir: "One day the bad news hit home. We learned that Uncle

Fahndungsabteilung rubber stamp was *not yet in use* in May and July 1942. As noted above, the typical *Fahndungsabteilung* stamp only began to appear in the last five months of 1942. I encountered only one resident registration card – completed on June 8, 1942 by a certain Zikmund Bondy (1893–?) – with the *Fahndungsabteilung* stamp on the back of the form, curiously and inexplicably dated July 17, 1942. The last Jewish community leader in Brno, Rudolf Hirsch (1895–1944?), completed a resident registration card on August 17, 1942. This did have the typical *Fahndungsabteilung* stamp bearing the following day's date on the back of the card. Oskar Szpak (1911–?) completed a resident registration card to confirm his address on August 14, 1941, but this card only bears the same generic stamps on the back of his card, dated August 15, 1942, that also appears on Zora and Stanislav Kratochvíla's cards. Does this mean that the *Fahndungsabteilung* stamp was used consistently only starting in mid-August 1942? Or does a different stamp indicate that a different police department was at work? The question of whether Černil and Očadlík were summoned by the same police agency as the Kratochvílas cannot, for the present, be solved on the sole basis of registration cards. Future research should try to establish whether the generic date stamps on the backs of Zora and Stanislav Kratochvíla's cards were issued by the Kripo *Fahndungsabteilung* or some other German (or even Czech) police agency.

233 Rosenfeld 1994, 218: "Die Grußkarten 'bin gesund' eingestellt [at the beginning of August 1943]. Auch Geld darf nur bestätigt werden von 20 Mark aufwärts. Warum? Weil Menschen an ihre Angehörigen ins Getto ein paar Mark schicken, um sich zu überzeugen, ob [ihre Angehörigen noch] leben" (The greeting cards 'am healthy' discontinued [at the beginning of August 1943]. Also, money may only be confirmed if more than 20 marks is received. Why? Because people send a few marks to their relatives in the ghetto to convince themselves that [their relatives are still] alive). See also Rosenfeld 1994, 45, 171, 273.

234 APŁ, Łodz, Akta miasta Łodzi, fonds Zarząd Getta (Gettoverwaltung), inv. n° 29208, microfilm L-21292, Meldungen über Sterblichkeit im Getto, 1943 (!), document reference 027/1/B/R, f. 165: "Litzmannstadt, den 24.1.1942. Herrn Luchterhandt! Mitgehend Unterlagen über die im Getto verstorbenen, welche aus dem Reichsgebiet und aus Prag ins Getto eingesiedelt worden sind. Der Älteste der Juden soll diese Listen monatlich einmal ergänzen. Die Aufstellung soll uns als Unterlage dienen, wenn bei der Gettoverwaltung angefragt wird, ob der Betreffende hier verstorben ist oder ob es möglich ist, über die Gettoverwaltung an ihn Liebesgaben, Geldsendungen und sonstiges gelangen zu lassen. gez. Biebow" (Litzmannstadt, 24.1.1942. Mr. Luchterhandt! Including documents on those who died in the ghetto, resettled from the Reich territory and from Prague to the ghetto. The Eldest of the Jews is to complete these lists once every month. The list is to serve us as a document when inquiries are made to the ghetto administration about whether the person in question has died here or whether it is possible to have modest donations, money and other things, sent to him through the ghetto administration. is signed Biebow); available online at https://szukajwarchiwach.pl/39/221/0/5.1.10/29208/skan/full/gXlwdolc6se09HXHyaxolA (accessed Mar. 15, 2021).

235 Hájková 2000, 346, 351 n. 15.

236 I also inquired with the Židovské muzeum v Praze, Praha (Jewish Museum in Prague). According to Daniela Bartáková (Židovské muzeum v Praze,

Paul [Baruch Ticho, 1889–1940] had died in Dachau. The death certificate stated that he had died of 'natural causes'. However, some time later, Father told me that a guard had hit Uncle Paul in the head with his rifle when Uncle Paul failed to bend down fast enough to pick something up from the ground. Since Jews were not allowed any medical services in the camp, Uncle Paul died of his injury a few days later. The Germans cremated his body and a few days later a box, supposedly containing his ashes, arrived. Our concern for Father's safety now reached a desperate stage".[238] In August 1941, a telegram was sent from Auschwitz to Brno, informing Willi Bondi's family that he had died.[239] When Dr. Siegfried Fischl died in Auschwitz, in February 1942, this was recorded in German (thus most likely during the war) on his final resident registration card (pre-printed in Czech), along with the registry entry number (56886/II/42) issued by the Auschwitz civil registry office (*Standesamt*).[240] In other words, the information about Fischl's death was sent to Brno and registered in Brno.

I found no mention of Fein's death date in any of the documents for Karl Fein in fonds Z 1 and fonds B 1/39 in the AMB, Brno. I discovered that some death notices, from a few different concentration camps, reached Brno and were noted in the Jewish registers (Židovské matriky, Judische Matriken) by the JKG, but I did not find Fein's name in them.[241] Looking at all of these examples, I think there is in fact a good chance that Karl Fein's immediate family were notified of his death months after the fact, but absolute certainty about this is simply not possible. If indeed this news reached Brno, it may well have played a significant role in the decision to discard the Institute materials. The moral obligation owed to Karl Fein to safeguard the Institute materials elapsed.

WAS THE DISCARDING PLANNED BEFOREHAND?

Thus far, the only thing that is truly certain is that the Institute materials, presumably in their entirety, ended up in an old paper container owned by the scrap company belonging to Jaroslav Růžička and his wife in 1942. That Černil or Očadlík (or both) played a significant role in safeguarding and discarding the Institute materials is much less certain. At the same time, I have shown that several factors indicate that "something", which the Germans deemed criminal, was happening in September 1942 in the lives of these two men, both members of the *Kamarád* founding group; and that the Germans thought it necessary to inquire about or investigate supposedly transgressive events linked to both men.

I further argued that the upheaval caused by the simple summons to confirm their latest address, in September 1942, may have prompted the fatal decision to adopt drastic measures regarding the Institute materials. Because of the history between Magnus Hirschfeld and the Nazis, the *Kamarád* people must have been aware from the very beginning that holding onto the Institute materials entailed real risk. Indeed, the Czechoslovak gay magazines of the 1930s gave full details of the clash between Hirschfeld and the National Socialists. This led me, as already said, to the idea that the

Shoah History Department, Praha), the JKG in Prague was not systematically informed of individual deaths of Jewish prisoners in ghettos and concentration camps abroad. See her email (dated Aug. 8, 2016) to the author.

237 Elias 1998, 222: "A short time later the announcement of his death, dated 1941, was sent to Brno."

238 Ticho 2001, "The Flood," 18.

239 The telegram sent to Marie Bondi, presumably dated Aug. 31, 1941, is in the family archive of Peter Barber. The telegram added that for further information on the matter, the family needed to inquire with the local Gestapo.

240 AMB, Brno, fonds Z 1, resident registration card (stamped Feb. 14, 1942) Siegfried (Vítězslav) Fischl.

241 For the death notices received by the JKG in Brno from the *Standesämter* (civil registry offices) in Dachau, Grossrosen, Auschwitz and especially Mauthausen in 1942, see NA, Praha, fonds n° 167, Jewish registers (Židovské matriky, Judische Matriken), inv. n° 142, Brno, Z, 1942, and inv. n° 143, Z, 1942 (prosinec)-1944 (koncentrač. tábory); avail-

smooth 1942 "escape route" for the Institute materials through Růžičková's company may have been planned all along. Maybe Očadlík went to live on Stefansgasse (Štěpánská) in 1940 (or earlier still) *because* this would bring him much closer to Růžičkas' company, *and* within the district stipulated by the aforementioned waste collection regulation of February 1940. This could also explain then why a working-class man would rent a probably expensive flat in a newly built apartment building.

As we have seen, after living for two decades at the same address, Stanislav Černil moved, in May 1938, two months after Germany's annexation of Austria and Giese's suicide, to a new apartment complex, consisting of two individual, but connected, high-rise buildings containing at least sixty-four apartments. This made me think for a moment that Očadlík's move as well may have been a deliberate choice. Can one live more anonymously than in a new apartment building with many tenants who hardly know each other? Where is it more difficult for nosy neighbors to check who is visiting whom than in an apartment building? Let us recall here that, starting in 1936, Karl Fein and Karl Giese also moved into newly built apartment buildings in Brno. Did Karl Fein perhaps suggest to Černil and Očadlík that they do the same? The striking resemblance of these living quarters may well also suggest that Fein turned to Černil and Očadlík to solve his problem what to do with the Institute and Hirschfeld materials. Jaroslav Očadlík also lived very close to the storage premises of the Leopold Fleischer company on Mühlgasse (Mlýnská), where Karl Fein may have first stored the Institute materials. At the very least, the *Kamarád* members would have been quite aware that, should things get too dangerous, Jaroslav Růžička was the one most likely to allow them to make the materials disappear without any – or the least – probing questions being asked.[242]

POSSIBLE COUNTERINDICATIONS OF THE INVOLVEMENT OF THE KAMARÁD GROUP

If Karl Fein did entrust the Institute materials to people from the *Kamarád* circle, we also need to ask – with the advantage of historical hindsight, of course – whether this was a wise decision. One crucial factor, which from the beginning of my research I expected to play an essential role in Karl Fein's decision was met by the *Kamarád* group: none of its seven men were Jewish. They were all either Catholic or Protestant, and six of them, as far as I was able to determine, survived the war. (As we have seen, Jakub Uher had already died in 1937.) But was this reason enough for Fein to choose the *Kamarád* clique when seeking a safe haven for the Institute materials? Recall that Kostelníček's conviction indicates that the reputation of the group of people around *Kamarád* was already tarnished in 1932. Karl Fein must have been well aware of Kostelnícek's misdemeanors and possibly distanced himself from the group as a consequence. It was likely no coincidence that Fein did not represent Kostelnícek when the latter was prosecuted for homosexual conduct and fraud in 1932. I have already suggested that Magnus Hirschfeld might have also stayed away from the

able online at http://www.badatelna.eu/fond/1073/zaznam/182/reprodukce (accessed Aug. 11, 2016). The indexes of these registers (*matriky, Matriken*) do not include Fein's name. See ibid., inv. n° 151, indexy Brno, Z, 1926–1938, 1940–1949; available online at http://www.badatelna.eu/fond/1073 /reprodukce/?zaznamId=181&reproId=174773 (accessed May 15, 2016). Because Fein spent his last years in Prague, I also tried to check the Jewish registers (Židovské matriky, Judische Matriken) in the NA, Praha, fonds n° 167, for Prague-Karlín (Fein's last neighborhood), but the 1940–45 registers are missing. See http://www.badatelna.eu/fond/1073/inventar/ (accessed Aug. 11, 2016). Confusingly, the Prague registers are not in the alphabetical order of cities, and are listed at the very end of the online collection of Jewish registers.

[242] This "maximalist" position can go far, perhaps too far. Was providing an escape route for the Hirschfeld materials perhaps one reason that Růžička started a scrap business with his wife in December 1939? Was this, too, part of a thoroughly thought-out plan?

convicted Kostelnícek and his *Kamarád* following during the September 1932 WLSR conference.[243]

I think that there are two further counterindications. Six members of the group spoke Czech as their mother tongue, while Kostelnícek spoke Slovak, whereas Karl Fein was raised in a German-speaking Jewish family. Indeed, that a considerable part of the Jewish population in Czechoslovakia spoke German was sometimes held against them by the Czech population. This socio-cultural divide continued to operate in Terezín, where young, Czech-speaking inmates were in charge of the ghetto.[244] One's language group was a crucial marker in pre-war Czechoslovakia. Here, let us recall that Stanislav Černil had a strong Czech-nationalist, and thus anti-German, background. What is more, all seven *Kamarád* founding members were working class. Only Josef Uher was a factory owner (*továrník, Fabrikant*); however, as we have seen, he was a factory worker who had worked his way up. The same can be said of Jakub Uher, his business partner. Despite his artistic ambitions, Štefan Kostelnícek also came from a working-class background.[245] We saw that Karl Fein stayed close to people of his own social class when in Prague and even in the Łódź ghetto.

On the other hand, there is a factor that could easily have overridden these three counter-indications. The *Kamarád* group was deeply inspired by Hirschfeld when he visited Brno in May 1932, and Fein had personally witnessed their admiration. It was conceivable that they would care for the remaining estate with a zeal equal to Giese and Fein's. Initially, Fein might have relied on his good gay friend Willi Bondi to find somewhere to store the Institute materials. And that solution could have lasted until the storage of these materials became more difficult and dangerous with the Aryanization of the Leopold Fleischer moving and storage company. Afterwards, Fein may have reached out yet again to his gay network to find another way to safeguard the Institute materials, contacting the *Kamarád* group. To this day, other gay men, and their friendship, are a crucial and central part of the lives of most gay men. Many things are lived, experienced, accomplished, and settled through gay friendships.[246] This is an unignorable factor which certainly could have led Fein to entrust the Institute materials to the *Kamarád* group.

INTERVIEW WITH DAGMAR

The greatest difficulty I experienced during the research into the Czech part of our story was the almost complete lack of sources from the people directly involved, whether those around *Kamarád* or the Fein and Bondi-Fleischer families. I was confronted with a lot of loose threads. I had hoped that the interview with Stanislav Černil's daughter, Dagmar Černilová, would offer the opportunity for a breakthrough.[247] I also had the rather uncomfortable task of raising the topic of her father's involvement with *Kamarád*, thus also making it clear that her father had been a gay (or at least bisexual) man with contacts in the Brno gay community in 1932. As we have seen, Černil published a poem in *Kamarád* praising Štefan Kostelníček's bravery in starting a gay magazine, and also wrote a gay play, *Proč?*, in which Černil also played the lead.

243 As we have seen, Fein's law practice did not avoid clients prosecuted for homosexual conduct. He wrote at least one article that made it clear that he had experience with gay clients. Fein also acted as a lawyer in an affair affecting a theater company in Olomouc (Olmütz), involving a tenor named Adolf Hradečný. This requires further investigation, but it is possible that the affair revolved around homosexual conduct in a theatrical milieu. See "Afěra v olom. divaldelní společnosti" (Affair in the Olomouc Theater Society), *Moravský večerník*, Aug, 20, 1935, 2; and "Die Sittlichkeitsaffäre eines Operettentenors" (The Vice Affair of an Operetta Tenor), *Tagesbote*, Apr. 16, 1936, 6.

244 Hájková 2020, 187–91.

245 Kostelničáková 2008, 14.

246 Nardi 1999.

247 Interview (dated Oct. 23, 2018) Dagmar Černilová with the author.

At one point in the interview, I asked Dagmar if she was aware that her father had contributed to a magazine for gay men. I then showed her a digital copy of the short article on *Proč?* in *Kamarád* that makes her father's involvement very obvious. After reading the short article, she told me that she had not known and offered no further reaction. At the end of the interview, unprompted, she repeated that she had not known about her father's involvement with the magazine. But did this mean that she had not known that her father was a gay or bisexual man? Because I intended to ask her more questions after the interview (something I did in several letters in the following months), I decided not to insist on the subject so as not to forfeit the good relations I had established with her. I simply did not want to lose a unique source on pre-war Brno.

When, around December–January 2020, I sent Dagmar a letter signaling that I wanted to talk with her in person once more, adding that I would also bring up the topic of her father having been gay or bisexual, she suddenly insisted that, in my work, I only use her father's first name, Standa or Stanislav. When I had agreed to do an interview with her, in October 2018, it was on the condition (stated in the oral history contract that she signed) that, when referring in my work to what she said in the interview, I would use her first and maiden name and not give her married name. But I could not agree to her later demand that I also not mention her father's last name, for two reasons. First, in 1932, her father clearly seems to have been a brave LGBT activist *avant la lettre*, one unafraid that his picture appeared in the first gay magazine ever published in Brno. And secondly, the information that her father had contributed to *Kamarád* had already been made public in Czechia. Prior to my interviewing Dagmar, a Czech book on the country's LGBT history published her father's *Kamarád* picture along with his name. A (partial) digital copy of the *Kamarád* issue can be found on the internet as well.[248]

Did Dagmar know more, even much more, about her father's gay life and simply did not want to talk to me about it? Or had her father's involvement with *Kamarád*, and even the revelation that her father had been gay or bisexual, been totally unknown to her before I interviewed her? Was I dealing with discomfort, anxiety, or even shame (which some would call homophobic) over her father being gay or bisexual? I don't have answers here.[249] Also, the whole *Kamarád* adventure took place in 1932, when she was only two years old ... and it is simply not known whether her father ever informed his daughter about his sexual preference.

During the interview, I also asked Dagmar what happened to her father's library after his death – and he certainly had a library, she told me – but she claimed not to know what happened to it. It is perhaps important to note here that Černil's third wife, Hélène Müller, died in 1988, ten years after Stanislav Černil's death in 1979. So, it may well be that it was Černil's third wife who played the more decisive role in the handling or even discarding of her deceased husband's personal archives and/or library. Dagmar also told me that her father had a study which she was not allowed to enter as a young girl, except when he was home. Interestingly, she told me that, one day, she looked briefly at the text of a play written by her father, knowing she was not allowed to do so. Was this play maybe *Proč?* Did Dagmar know more about the fate of the Institute materials that her father, or another *Kamarád* founding member, had possibly stored somewhere, possibly even at home? And must we conclude that

[248] Seidl et al. 2012, 184; https://www.queerpamet.cz/soubor/kamarad-1932 (accessed Sep. 8, 2020).

[249] At the very beginning of our interview, I noticed that Dagmar intended to keep silent about her father's second marriage. When I insisted that there had indisputably been three marriages, she quickly said she suddenly remembered her father's second wife. That alerted me to be prudent about what she said to me.

her not knowing anything about a discarded library means that her father was never involved in discarding the Institute materials?

When Dagmar asked me, at the end of the interview, why exactly I wanted to interview her, I briefly related the story of the Hirschfeld Institute, the Berlin book burning, Karl Giese and Karl Fein, and why I ended up sitting with her at her home in Brno. I told her that it was possible that her father had discarded the Institute materials or played a part in that operation. Her immediate reaction, which somewhat surprised me, was that discarding of the Institute materials would have been a very understandable action, given the circumstances of the war. She proposed exactly the argument about the difficult year 1942 that I have been developing here.

After a good year of intensive correspondence, I intended to visit Dagmar again in January 2020. However, she let me know in another letter that she had been hospitalized and could not see me. A few months later, the Corona respiratory virus had the world in its grip and travel to Czechia was suddenly not an option. In February 2021, I found out that Dagmar had moved in with her daughter because of her health. Finally, in May 2021, and at my request, Lucie Tuzová spoke with Dagmar one last time over the phone, giving Lucie the impression that Dagmar preferred to be left alone. Dagmar repeated and emphasized that she had been too young to know much about the things I inquired about, adding that her father had almost never let her in on most of these adult matters. Dagmar died in 2022.[250]

[250] See Brněnské hřbitovy database, https://gis.brno.cz/mapa/hrbitovy/ (accessed May 13, 2024).

1. In April 1932, the meeting to found the gay magazine Kamarád took place in Café Bellevue, on the ground floor of the Slavia Bank building at 8 Lažanského náměstí (Lažanskýplatz). Postmarked March 18, 1939.

I. ročník. V Brně, dne 28. května 1932. Číslo 1.

88287

Kamarád

časopis věnovaný zájmům přátelství uznaným vědou a kulturními státy.

Štefan I. Kostelníček: Aby bolo jasno. — Dr. J. F.: Wahrheit und Recht. — Standa Černil: Kamarád. — Imrich Matyáš: Jeden homosexuální mučedník. Vzpomínáme. — Karel Hlubocký: Pohádka málé. Oskaru Wildeovi. Zoltán Škréta: Našim matkám. — Kulturní hlídka. — Redakční a spolkové zprávy. — Naše korespondence. — Odkazy redakce. — K informaci.

Cena Kč 2·—.

2. Cover of the first (and last) issue of the gay magazine Kamarád, published in Brno on May 28, 1932. It cost 2 Czech crowns. The ornamental design was most likely drawn by Štefan Kostelníček.

3. *Undated postcard showing the German House (Deutsches Haus, Německý dům) and its front garden. The not yet refurbished corner building housing Café Bellevue is on the left. Presumably 1920s.*

4. *"Professor Dr. M. Hirschfeld in a circle of Brno friends in the spring of 1932" (Profesor dr. M. Hirschfeld v kruhu brněnských přátel na jaře 1932). Photo of Magnus Hirschfeld, seemingly surrounded by several members of the Kamarád founding group. In the middle, with both hands resting on his midsection, stands Magnus Hirschfeld. The second person from the right is Josef Weisskopf. The third person from the right might be Imrich Matyaš. The fourth person from the right might be Stanislav Černil. May 20 or 21, 1932.*

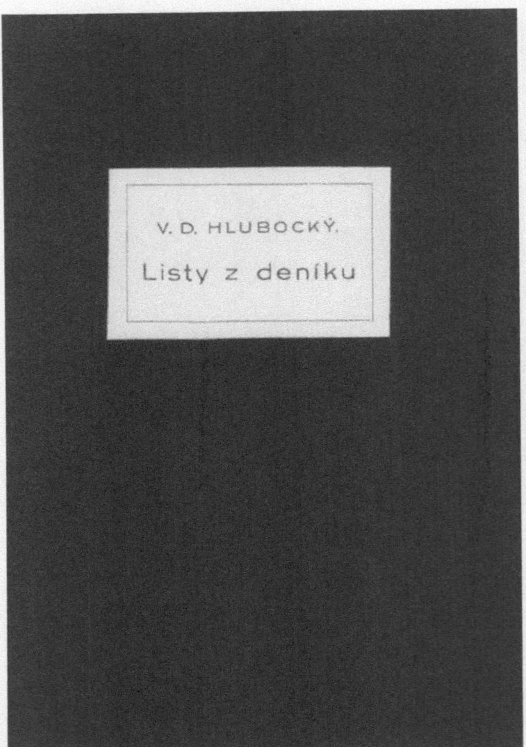

5. Cover of the literary pamphlet Listy z deníku (Letters from a Diary), published by Vilém Drexler-Hlubocký in 1937. It contains a perhaps partly autobiographical story about an apparently unrequited gay love between two men, Harry and Jindřich.

6. Postcard showing the square in front of the main Brno railway station. Postmarked September 26, 1937.

7. Jaroslav Růžička. Undated, presumably 1930s.

8. Postcard showing the Lazanskyplatz (Lažanského náměstí, currently Moravské náměstí) adorned with swastika-emblazoned banners. Postmarked March 15, 1941.

9. "Stáňa Černil, author and director of the tragedy 'Why?'" (Stáňa Černil, autor a režisér tragedie "Proč"?). Signed picture of Standa (Stanislav) Černil.

10. Photo of the house at 16 Kreuzgasse (Křížová). Until May 1938, Stanislav Černil lived with his mother on the first floor of the building, which also housed a cafe (Kavárna), Swiss Court (Švýcarský dvůr, Schweizer Hof), on the ground floor. For a little while, Stanislav Černil kept a grocer's in the small shop beside the café (to the right of the arched entrance). The bell tower of Brno's Old Town Hall (staré Brno radnice) is visible on the left. The corner tower building was once a familiar neighborhood sight known as "Old Brno" (staré Brno). The buildings were all demolished in 1965 to expand Mendel Square (Mendlovo náměstí, Mendelplatz). April 1963.

11. In May 1938, Stanislav Černil moved with his mother to a new apartment building at 68 Bäckergasse (Pekařská). 1945.

12. Contemporary view of the 4b/310 Stephansgasse (Štěpánská) apartment building (left) where Jaroslav Očadlík and Jan Vacek lived ca. 1940–45. The unrenovated 4a/309 Stephansgasse (Štěpánská) building on the right shows what 4b/310 used to look like. On the right of these two apartment blocks, the house, numbered 4/308, where Josef Martinkowitsch lived. January 2020.

Polizeiliche Anmeldung. — Policejní přihláška.

1. Name: / Příjmení: ČERNIL
   Vorname: / Jméno: STANISLAV
   geborene (Mädchenname): / rozená (příjmení dívčí):
2. Neue Wohnung: / Nové bydliště: Ort: / Místo: Brno; Bezirk (Stadtteil): / Okres (čtvrť): Staré Brno; Straße: / Ulice: Pekařská; Nr.: / č.: 68
   Wenn in Untermiete, bei: / Je-li v podnájmu, u: Marie Černilové
3. Tag des Zuzuges: — Den příchodu: 18.5.38.
4. Wird alte Wohnung beibehalten? — Podrží starý byt? ne
5. Schon einmal hier gewohnt? — Bydlel zde již? ano
6. Vorige Wohnung: / Předchozí bydliště: Ort: / Místo: Brno; Bezirk (Stadtteil): / Okres (čtvrť): Staré Brno; Straße: / Ulice: Úvoz; Nr.: / č.: 16
7. Bei Zuzug aus dem Ausland, von Reisen, Wanderschaft, RAD oder Wehrmacht letzte Wohnung im Inland: / Při příchodu z ciziny, z cest, říš. prac. služby n. branné moci poslední bydliště v tuzemsku: Ort: / Místo: Bezirk (Stadtteil): / Okres (čtvrť): Straße: / Ulice: Nr.: / č.:
8. Ich besitze die Kraftfahrzeuge Nr.: / Jsem majitelem motor. vozidel č.: nemá
9. Verwendung im Luftschutz (als was?): / Činný v protiletecké ochraně (jako?):
10. Religionsbekenntnis:
11. Staatsangehörigkeit: / Státní příslušnost: Protektorát
12. Beruf: / Povolání:
13. Geburts- / Narození: Tag / Den 8; Monat / Měs. 11; Jahr / Rok 1908; Ort / Místo: Brno; Bez. - Kreis / Okr. - Kraj
14. Jude? / Žid? ne
15. Kinder unter 15 Jahren, die mit der meldepflichtigen Person zusammen leben: / Děti do 15 let, která žijí s osobou hlášením povinnou: 1. Dagmar H. geb.: / nar.: 18.4.1930; 2. Stanislav 17.1.1936; 3.; 4.; 5.
16. Familienname und Vorname / Příjmení a jméno: des Vaters: / otce: Černil Josef †; der Mutter: / matky: Černilová Marie
17. Der Ehefrau: / Manželky: Vorname: / Jméno: Helena; Mädchenname: / Dívčí příjmení: Müllerová; Geburts- / Narození: Tag / Den; Mon. / Měs.; Jahr / Rok
18. Bei Ausländern und Staatenlosen / U cizinců a bezdomovců: Paß-Nr. und Datum: / pas č. a datum: Ausstell. Beh.: / vydal úřad:
19. Unterschrift d. Meldepflichtigen: / Podpis osoby hlášením povinné: Stanislav Černil
20. Unterschrift des Wohnungsinhabers: / Podpis majitele bytu: Marie Černilová
21. Unterschrift des Hauseigentümers: / Podpis majitele domu: Soustalová Mocé
22. Ort / V Brno den / dne 1. září 42.

13. *In September 1942, Stanislav Černil completed a resident registration card to confirm his current address. He dated his form September 1, 1942 by hand, but only submitted the form to the police station on Saturday, September 5. The back of the card bears two stamps: "Fahndungsabteilung" ([persons] investigation department) and "wird nicht gesucht" (no wants or warrants).*

14a and 14b. Two different versions of the Fahndungsabteilung (persons investigation department) stamp, one used in 1942 and the other from 1943 onwards. The notations "wird nicht gesucht" and "Suchvermerke bestehen nicht" mean "no wants or warrants".

15. Studio portrait photo of Stanislav Černil. September 15, 1942.

16. "Do not throw away paper! Waste paper is an important raw material" (Papier nicht wegwerfen! Altpapier ist wichtiger Rohstoff). This notice exhorting people to save old paper appeared in Volksdeutsche Zeitung. There was a chronic shortage of paper during the war.

17. Milan Kratochvíla. 1937.

18. Zora Kratochvíla. December 1947.

16. Dr. Stanislav Kaděrka, Elise Brecher and the Jewish Hospital in Brno

RETRIEVAL OF THE HIRSCHFELD GUESTBOOK – HAPPY ACCIDENT OR ORCHESTRATED MISSION?

In 1942, the Hirschfeld guestbook in Karl Giese's possession in Brno was retrieved from an old paper container, along with some sexology books that were in all likelihood part of the Institute lot bought by Hirschfeld in November 1933. The items were found on the premises of a scrap company associated, via Jaroslav Růžička, to a group of gay men who founded and published the gay magazine *Kamarád* in Brno. These men greatly admired Magnus Hirschfeld and his cause, twice meeting him in person in May 1932, shortly before the release of the first issue of their magazine. Karl Fein may have entrusted the Institute materials to some members of this group in anticipation of better times. If he indeed did so, then some of the *Kamarád* group may also have taken the decision to discard the materials in 1942. However, was the retrieval of the Hirschfeld guestbook and some sexology books, that same year, a happy accident or rather the result of an orchestrated mission? In the Introduction, we noted that Hirschfeld's *Testament: Heft II* was saved from a dumpster, along with several items belonging to Hirschfeld's pupil Li Shiu Tong, by Adam P. W. Smith in Canada in 1993. So it is entirely possible that, in 1942, Hirschfeld's guestbook and the few remaining Institute materials were also found "by chance" in Brno, and that their retrieval amounted to a first and quite miraculous rescue. Yet, a few factors also hint that the Brno rescue was not quite an accident. Let us examine these factors.

THE SITE BEHIND THE NEBEHOSTENY HOUSE

One of the weightier factors is that the site behind the Nebehosteny city palace, where Růžičková's company was situated, was not easily accessible to outsiders. Today, a passageway between the house at 68 Kröna (Křenová) and the much more modest building beside it, at 66 Kröna (Křenová), is still visible from the street [ill. 1]. Back then, the site behind the latter was occupied by the B. Friess moving firm. Ernst Fischer, who lived at 66 Kröna (Křenová), owned both the building and the firm.[1] Nowadays, the site behind the Nebehosteny house and the building owned by Ernst Fischer is not divided into two separate plots, as one would expect, but instead consists of a single open terrain. A cadastral drawing made in the 1940s, shortly after the war, shows that the site was still divided, one part situated behind the Nebehosteny house and the other behind 66 Kröna (Křenová).[2] In the 1930s and 1940s,

[1] MZA, Brno, fonds B 392, Vystěhovalecký fond, úřadovna Brno (1939–1945), kart. n° 24, inv. n° 525; NA, Praha, fonds n° 375, Arizační spisy, company B. Friess, spediteur, Brno, kart. n° 206, file n° 1274. In 1934, the official company address of the B. Friess company was 10 Palackýstrasse (Palackého třída). See *Adreßbuch von Groß-Brünn* 1934, 649, 609, 692. It had moved to 12 Neutorgasse (U Nové brány) by 1939. *See Adresář Protektorátu Čechy a Morava pro průmysl, živnosti, obchod a zemědělství = Adressbuch des Protektorates Böhmen und Mähren für Industrie, Gewerbe, Handel und Landwirtschaft* 1939, II: 1406, 2257.

[2] The map, also reproduced in chapter 14, ill. n° 7, can be found in NA, Praha, fonds Národní obnovy Praha (National restoration fonds, Prague), confiscation file of 194/68 Kröna (Křenová), Brno-Zábrdovice, sign. VZ 11073/III/1, nezpracovaný fond (unprocessed fonds). The many cadastral plots behind 66 and 68 Kröna (Křenová) are indeed clearly tied to their respective street-facing houses. Plots 406/10, 406/11, 406/2, behind house 68 Kröna (Křenová), are linked to each other and to the street-facing plot 225 (also 9234/41). Plots 407, 404/4, 406/4 and 404/5, behind house 66 Kröna (Křenová), are also linked to each other and to the street-facing plot 105

these two rectangular plots were physically separated, mostly by narrow company buildings and warehouses. There was likely also a small dividing wall closer to the street, but its existence is not certain; or, if not a wall, perhaps a small gate.[3] This also means that the passageway between the two buildings seen today mainly (or even exclusively) gave access to the plot behind 66 Kröna (Křenová) where the premises of the B. Friess company were located. The already mentioned postwar cadastral drawing also shows that the two plots' southern edge did not extend to Mühlgasse (Mlýnská), a street parallel to Kröna (Křenová), meaning that the two plots could not be reached from Mühlgasse (Mlýnská). That is still the case today.[4] So, the only way to reach the plot behind the Nebehosteny house may have been via its posh-looking main entrance. However, as previously suggested, it is *also* possible that the site behind the Nebehosteny house could be reached through a small gate between the two plots behind 66 and 68 Kröna (Křenová).

This may look trivial, but is in fact important for our story. If, during the war, the site was indeed as open and accessible as it is now, anyone would have been able to gain access to Růžičková's company. In all likelihood, however, in the 1930s and 1940s, one would have had to pass through either the Nebehosteny building's large wooden entrance door or the passageway between the two plots to reach Růžičková's company. The Nebehosteny house's massive wooden entrance door was presumably closed most of the time, as it still is today. In our own time, the door only opens to allow cars into the small parking lot behind the building, and also, since the passageway doubles as a posh vestibule for the building, to admit someone into the Nebehosteny house. The delicacy of the passageway's ornamental work, bearing cherubs, likely explains why the wooden gate was only opened when vehicles or carts carrying scrap had to enter or leave [ill. 2]. The gate possibly lying between the two plots would have been closed most of the time as well to protect the private apartments in the Nebehosteny building, as such a side entrance would have clearly made them more vulnerable to intruders. Finally, it is also safe to assume that another, communal street-facing gate also existed at the time, preventing nighttime access to the premises of the B. Friess company (behind 66 Kröna [Křenová]) and also, indirectly, to the premises of the Růžička company (behind 68 Kröna [Křenová]).

A MAN OR A WOMAN ON A MISSION?

All this implies that somebody gaining access to the Růžička company's premises outside of the company's daytime working hours must have an explanation, making it much less probable that the discovery of the Institute materials was an accident. We may also assume that Jindra and Jaroslav Růžička would simply not have allowed anyone access to their company premises and the scrap they stored outside of business hours. Old paper and old metal were sources of revenue – above all in wartime when raw materials were scarce – and had to be safeguarded. In addition, Jaroslav Růžička, and possibly also his wife Jindra Růžičková, would surely not have wanted any prying eyes when the Institute materials were deliberately discarded in

(also 9241/41). Cf. another (digitized) cadastral map from 1929 (signature MOR 248719290) that I consulted at http://www.mza.cz/indikacniskici/index.php (accessed Nov. 19, 2015). See also, for 66 Kröna (Křenová), MZA, Brno, fonds B 392, Vystěhovalecký fond, úřadovna Brno, kart. n° 24, inv. n° 525, file Ernst Fischer.

[3] See the aerial photo Letecké měřické snímky, LMS 1948-03416 (dated Sep. 27, 1948), https://ags.cuzk.cz/archiv/openmap.html?typ=lms&idrastru=WMSA08.1948.BRNO90.03416 (accessed Mar. 7, 2021). Depending on how it is rotated, and taking into account drop shadows that increase the distortion of the already blurred picture, the photo shows either a small building, a thin wall, no wall at all, or a gate between the two plots on the side closest to the two street-facing buildings.

[4] Its southern side then bordered (and still borders) the elongated plot of the building at 12 Masná (Fleischmarktgasse).

1942 on their company land.[5] The relative inaccessibility of the Růžička company site is my main reason for thinking that the retrieval of the Institute items and the Hirschfeld guestbook was less a happy accident than the result of a planned rescue operation. This rescue was possibly furtive, involving trespassing on a company's private property, an ad hoc operation, as indicated by its meager result: only a few books, including the Hirschfeld guestbook, were salvaged. Perhaps this was all that a single person was able to carry. Or perhaps there was the need to act quickly so as not to arouse suspicion or get caught in the act. The successful salvage of only a few items could also be explained by the fact that most of the Institute materials had been discarded by the time the individual got to the materials in the old paper container on the Růžička company premises. Perhaps the rescued items were all that remained. If so, this small trove is a sad reminder of the many materials – likely several tons of paper – deliberately discarded and now lost.

There are two other indications that the guestbook may have been retrieved by someone on a mission. The affidavit in the Hirschfeld guestbook states that both the guestbook and a few sexology books were "saved" (*zachráněn*) from an old paper container. Why not speak more neutrally of their being "found", which would indicate an accidental discovery? Secondly, that both sexology books *and* the Hirschfeld guestbook were retrieved at the same time from the container (or even heap) in Růžičková's company may also indicate that someone was deliberately looking for specific items. The Hirschfeld guestbook does not contain a title page or other clear indication explaining its exact character. It is necessary to leaf through the guestbook to find the few indications that it had belonged to someone interested in sexology.[6] If the find was indeed accidental, the guestbook *may* have escaped notice. Only the presumably heavy hardcover sexology books would have been selected, for their obvious or supposed value. Furthermore, the guestbook looks like a family photo album. A treasure hunter randomly looking for something valuable would not have retrieved it, as family pictures usually only have value for the family. That the sexology books *and* the guestbook were given together to Dr. Kaděrka is therefore likely significant. The individual possibly knew what he or she was looking for or had specific instructions to search for items belonging to Magnus Hirschfeld or bearing Institute stamps. The affidavit being added to the guestbook and (presumably) not to any of the retrieved sexology books perhaps provides further support for this view.

WHO RETRIEVED THE INSTITUTE MATERIALS FROM THE OLD PAPER CONTAINER?

In 2012, I was informed by Milena Baumgarten, the woman who sold the guestbook to the Literaturarchiv in Marbach, that Dr. Kaděrka once told her that a cleaning lady (*Putzfrau*) saved the guestbook (and the other books) from the old paper container and gave it to him.[7] Mrs. Baumgarten sent me an email in which she said: "If I may allow myself to assess the 'story' about the guestbook, really it was only what Dr. Kaděrka told me: a cleaning lady found a guestbook on a rubbish heap in the postwar chaos and took it 'to the doctor'. He kept it lying around for many years and then

[5] It remains possible that Jindra Růžičková knew nothing about the matter. On July 1, 1941, she gave her husband power of attorney, declaring that he could make all necessary decisions related to the company and lead it in her place. In the same document, she claimed to have long been sick and expected her sickness to continue. However, it is not certain that she was still sick in 1942. See the power of attorney (*Plná moc*) in private archive (Brno). The document also bears a stamp (dated Oct. 21, 1949) from the Okresní soud civilní Brno (Brno District Civil Court). This document may also explain why it was Jaroslav, rather than Jindra, who was prosecuted by the Communist regime after the war for "economic crimes".

[6] See especially the clippings pasted into the Hirschfeld guestbook, bearing words like "Sexual-Institut", "la science sexologique" and "pathologie sexuelle". See Bergemann, Dose, Keilson-Lauritz & Dubout 2019, 7, 32, 94.

[7] Phone conversation (dated Jul. 6, 2012) between Milena Baumgarten and the author.

wanted to 'sell it off'".[8] The timing, "in the postwar chaos" (*in dem Nachkriegschaos*), seems mistaken since it plainly contradicts the affidavit's claim that the guestbook was found in 1942.[9] However, despite this discrepancy, the assertion that a cleaning lady found the guestbook seems plausible and may indeed have happened.

However, this scenario has its own issues and questions. First of all, given the relative inaccessibility of the Růžička company premises, if a cleaning lady was indeed involved, one would imagine that she worked for one of the well-to-do families living in the Nebehosteny house apartments at 68 Kröna (Křenová).[10] While taking out the trash, for example, curiosity may have led a cleaning lady to look around behind the Nebehosteny house and even to rummage in the old paper container there. Her going through the Růžička company container, during or after working hours, may even have been a daily or weekly habit. Afterwards, she may have given, or even sold, the items she found to her local doctor. At the same time, without being condescending, would a cleaning lady pick up the quite peculiar Hirschfeld guestbook, along with "some sexological books", *and* take them to a physician, knowing beforehand that he would be interested? Or was the simple wartime prospect of a possible financial reward for discovering or rescuing potentially valuable materials the true motive?

I remain skeptical of the cleaning lady story. After all, most cleaning ladies – unlike Magnus Hirschfeld's housekeeper, Adelheid Schulz, who worked in the Berlin Institute – did not pass their days in the company of a world-famous sexologist.[11] I presume that, generally speaking, the majority of Czechoslovak housekeepers were not aware of the importance or value of sexological documents and books. Unless, of course, the name of Magnus Hirschfeld *did* ring a bell for some Brno cleaning ladies in 1942. And this may well have been the case. The fifth and last WLSR conference, held in Brno in September 1932, received almost daily coverage in several local newspapers. So, a bold or at least adventurous cleaning lady might be a possible candidate.

WHO WROTE THE AFFIDAVIT?

Determining who wrote the affidavit would obviously seem the most direct lead to the rescuer(s) of the Institute materials, even in the unlikely case that the authors and finders turned out to be different people. However, we simply do not know the writers of the affidavit. I was not able to match the handwriting of the persons who wrote the affidavit, the note attesting to its veracity, or the signatures below the text, with any of the many names and signatures I encountered in my research. The signatures on the affidavit are quite illegible, making it impossible to make out either last name. This led me to the idea that maybe these signatures were *deliberately* illegible, thus preventing any link to a real name or person. In any case, one person wrote the text of the affidavit and signed it. A second person then – rather clumsily – added a note saying that the statement above was true, and also undersigned. For the moment, it

[8] Email (dated Nov. 5, 2012) from Milena Baumgarten to the author: "Wenn ich mir eine Einschätzung der 'Geschichte' mit dem Gästebuch erlauben darf, dann war es wirklich nur das, was mir Dr. Kaděrka erzählt hatte: Eine Putzfrau fand in dem Nachkriegschaos ein Gästebuch auf einem Müllhaufen und brachte es 'dem Doktor'. Der hat es viele Jahre liegen gehabt und dann wollte er es 'versilbern'".

[9] On October 1, 2020, I asked Mrs. Baumgarten about this (merely seeming?) inconsistency, but my email went unanswered. It is possible that Mrs. Baumgarten only meant that the guestbook was found in 1942 but *given* to Dr. Kaděrka only after the war.

[10] I have excluded the absurd idea that the cleaning lady may have worked for Jindra Růžičková's company. What would a cleaning lady be doing in a firm dealing in scrap?

[11] As some fragments from the MHG Berlin's 2001 interview with Adelheid Schulz reveal, she still clung to a few commonsense or folk notions about sexual (ab)normality, despite being Hirschfeld's housekeeper. See Schulz, Dose, Herrn & Ripa 2001.

[12] As suggested to me by Milena Baumgarten. See her email (dated Dec. 11, 2012) to the author.

[13] Židovské muzeum v Praze (Jewish Museum in Prague), Praha, Shoah-related collections, personal and family related materials and papers, personal

looks as though the affidavit was written by the person who found the guestbook and an associate. Judging by the fluency of the language of the affidavit, the writer must have been a native Czech-speaker.[12] In April 2015, the Brno academic Jana Nosková suggested to me that the peculiar phrasing of the affidavit and the addition "in the year 1942" may indicate that the affidavit was written at a later time. This idea is interesting because it does not assume that the affidavit was added to a page in the back of the guestbook shortly after the latter was found. However, in that case it remains unclear why adding the affidavit at a later time would have been necessary. Perhaps it was related to the postwar realities of Jewish people returning (or *possibly* returning) to their home country, reclaiming their former property.

For now, my supposition is that the affidavit was added into the Hirschfeld guestbook in 1942 to mitigate the real fear that then reigned, above all, as a defense against the prohibition on keeping Jewish belongings. As already suggested, saying that the guestbook was found by accident in the garbage was indeed a useful neutralizing claim. However, the very presence of the affidavit in the guestbook is itself problematic and requires explanation. Why was its addition felt to be necessary? What purpose did it serve? What was the fear? For now, nothing much can be said with certainty about the rescuer(s) of the Institute materials or the authors of the affidavit.

WHY DID THE INSTITUTE MATERIALS END UP WITH DR. STANISLAV KADĚRKA?

In addition to asking how and by whom the guestbook and the sexology books were retrieved from the Růžička company premises, we need to also ask: is there a reason why the Institute materials ended up with Dr. Stanislav Kaděrka and not someone else? A postcard I found in the Jewish Museum in Prague (Židovské muzeum v Praze) appears to plausibly explain why the guestbook ended up with Dr. Stanislav Kaděrka specifically – suggesting, that is, that he may have instigated a search for the discarded Institute items on the premises of the Růžička company.

On March 26, 1942, someone in Prague sent a postcard to the Terezín ghetto.[13] The postcard was addressed to someone we have already mentioned, the Jewish man and bank clerk Albert Ascher (1899–1965). Albert Ascher later married Anna Kahn (1914–2007), a niece of the younger Karl Fein.[14] The postcard mainly communicated that Ascher's brother, Fritzl – the lawyer Siegfried (Vítězslav) Ascher (1895–1942) – had been hospitalized in Brno. Siegfried Ascher became a lawyer in 1924.[15] He was married to Margarete Dukes (1909–1986), and the couple had one child, Robert Ascher (1932–1986).[16] The text of the postcard was written in all capitals with a fountain pen,

estates (osobní pozůstalosti), Albert Ascher (Jul. 22, 1899), postcard (dated Mar. 26, 1942) from Pikesler to Albert Ascher, collection identifier COLLECTION.JMP.SHOAH/PERS/OP/036.

[14] Anna Kahn and Marianne Kahn were the two children of Richard Kahn and Gertrude Kahn (née Fein). Gertrude Fein and the elder Karl Fein were the two children of Moritz Fein and Kamilla Biach. Moritz Fein was one of Karl Fein's two uncles. The other uncle was Adolf Fein. I interviewed Anna Kahn's sister, Marianna Becková (née Kahnová), in Prague in the summer of 2013. See above, chapter 6, pp. 174-75. As already mentioned in the same place, it was Mrs. Becková who informed me of this archival fonds on Albert Ascher in the Židovské muzeum v Praze (Jewish Museum in Prague). See also *Zpravodaj Židovské muzeum v Praze = Newsletter of the Jewish Museum in Prague*, 2, 2008: 6-7, new acquisitions.

[15] *Seznam advokátů dle stavu koncem roku 1935* 1936, 15. Siegfried and Albert Ascher's parents were Hermann Ascher (1867–1939) and Berta Bondy (1866–1943).

[16] Both mother and son survived transport "Ad", which took them from Brno to Terezín on March 23, 1942. Mother and son both died in 1986. Robert ("Robertl") Ascher seems to have had one descendent, judging from a life tree https://www.geni.com/family-tree/index/6000000020669477557 (accessed Jun. 10, 2024). In 2015, I contacted (Pavel) Avram Fröhlich, whose website mentioned that Margarete Ascher and Robert Jiří Ascher, the wife and son of Siegfried Ascher, were his relatives. See http://www.frohlich.eu/2013/10/necht-jsou-jejich-duse-pojaty-do-svazku.html (accessed Feb. 4, 2016). On July 29, 2015, I sent a message to his Facebook account but there was no reply. I was also intrigued

there being a wartime obligation to ensure that the censor could read postcards easily.[17] The full text of the postcard is as follows:

> DEAREST ALBERT
> FRITZL [IS] IN BETTER CONDITION [, WAS] TRANSFERRED TODAY [TO]
> INFIRMARY, MÜLLERGASSE 27.[18] HAVE SPOKEN TO KAĎERKA [*sic*: KADĚRKA][19]
> GIVES HOPE. EMIL'S MOTHER[20]
> GOES TO HIM ON THE 27 TH. LOOK AFTER LITTLE
> ROBERT. WE ARE ALL WELL.
> GREETINGS
> 26/3 1942
>
> LIEBSTER ALBERT
> FRITZL IN BESEREM [*sic*: BESSEREM] ZUSTAND HEUTE ÜBERFÜHRT
> SICHENHAUS [*sic*: SIECHENHAUS], MÜLLERGASSE 27. HABE KAĎERKA [*sic*: KADĚRKA]
> GESPROCHEN[,] GIBT HOFFNUNG. EMILS MUTTER
> GEHT AM 27 ZU IHM. SCHAUE DICH UM ROBE
> RTL.[21] WIR SIND ALLE WOHLAUF.
> GRÜSSE
> 26/3 1942[22]
>
> [ill. 3a]

The sender's name appears on the other side of the postcard: "Pikesler, Prag (Galligasse 7)" [ill. 3b]. "Pikesler" was the nickname of Rudolf Pick (1891–1944?), the husband of Siegfried and Albert Ascher's sister, Stephanie (Stěpánka) Ascher (1897–1944?).[23]

by the many stones I saw on the grave of Siegfried Ascher's brother, Albert Ascher in the Jewish cemetery in Brno. The grave is located in section 36, row 1, grave 27. I also had a look at Siegfried Ascher's in-laws. His wife, Margarete Dukes (1909–1986), was the daughter of Julius Dukes (1876–1933) and Irma Stránská (1885–1942?). The latter was deported on transport "Ah" on April 4, 1942, from Brno to Terezín. Julius and Irma Dukes also had a second daughter, Nelly Spiegel (1912–1942?). She and her husband Fritz Spiegel (1904–1942?) were deported on transport "Af" from Brno to Terezín on March 31, 1942. Less than a month later, on April 27, 1942, Fritz and Nelly Spiegel and Irma Dukes were deported on transport "Aq" from Terezín to Izbica.

[17] Beneš & Tošnerová 1996, 82.

[18] The spelling of the street name is incorrect. It was actually Mühlgasse, or Mlýnská in Czech. There was indeed, as we will see in a moment, a Jewish hospital for the elderly at 27 Mühlgasse (Mlýnská) in Brno. Mühlgasse (Mlýnska) was also known as "kleine Kröna" (little Kröna) because it ran parallel to Kröna (Křenova).

[19] The caron (*háček* in Czech) is misplaced. It should be on the "e", not the "d", making it "Kaděrka".

[20] The identity of this Emil is a little uncertain. The staff of the Židovské muzeum v Praze (Jewish Museum in Prague) identify him as Emil Rosenstein (1899–1944?). Rosenstein had previously been deported on transport "J" to Terezín on December 4, 1941, and was then transferred to Auschwitz-Birkenau on Transport "Ek" on September 28, 1944. Emil Rosenstein's mother was Amálie Rosenstein (1864–1942?). On March 26, 1942, the date of the postcard, she was still in Brno. The postcard states that she would visit Siegfried Ascher in the Jewish hospital the next day, on March 27, 1942. However, she presumably had to register for her own deportation on one of the following days, at the school on Merhautova (Merhautgasse or also Senefeldergasse), because she was deported from Brno on March 31, 1942 on transport "Af". Curiously, her name is not listed in the www.holocaust.cz database; however, her name is mentioned in Kárný et al. 1995, 440. She was transferred to Treblinka on October 19, 1942. Since there is still a little doubt regarding the identity of "Emil", I will also mention that I found a certain Emil Ascher (1900–?) who was deported to Terezín from Prague on June 20, 1942 on transport "AAe". He and his wife Anna Ascher (1906–?) survived the war.

[21] Robert, "Robe-rtl", meaning "little Robert", is on two lines due to lack of space on the postcard. The reference is to Siegfried Ascher's then nine-year-old son, Robert Ascher (1932–1986).

[22] Only thirty words in total were permitted on a postcard. See Ondrichová 2000, 41. This postcard contains approximately thirty-three words and numbers. If one leaves out the numbers, the count is indeed exactly thirty words. This also shows that the text was composed in advance.

[23] The www.holocaust.cz database lists the last Prague address for this couple as 23 Havelská (Galligasse). The evidence obyvatelstva (population registry) sheet for Rudolf Pick in NA, Praha, fonds Policejní ředitelství Praha II, shows that he

Noticeably, the name "Kadĕrka" shows up here in a medical context. Most likely, this was indeed the Brno doctor Stanislav Kadĕrka who, in the 1980s, gave the Hirschfeld guestbook to Milena Baumgarten to sell in West Germany.[24] Stanislav Kadĕrka was most likely Siegfried Ascher's physician, since Ascher moved to the Královo Pole suburb, presumably around 1941, when Jewish people were forced to move to much less comfortable dwellings.[25] During the war, Kadĕrka had his medical practice at 20 Josef-Pekař-strasse (třída Josefa Pekaře) in the Královo Pole suburb where he was based all of his life.[26] It is unclear whether the postcard's omission of his "Dr." title can be explained by the writer's anxiety not to exceed the strict limit of thirty words on a postcard or by an effort at discretion so as not to compromise Stanislav Kadĕrka for helping Jewish patients.[27] Siegfried Ascher's relatives in Terezín would have known who Kadĕrka was. The writer of the postcard, Rudolf Pick, had apparently spoken to Kadĕrka about Siegfried Ascher's health and it was this conversation that "gave hope": the patient's health was not as poor as feared or else was improving. As Rudolf Pick was based in Prague, he most likely spoke about Ascher's medical condition with the Brno-based Dr. Kadĕrka over the phone.[28]

had lived in Prague from 1914 until his deportation in May 1942. For the police file of Rudolf Pick, see https://www.holocaust.cz/en/database-of-victims/victim/113681-rudolf-pick/; for Stephanie (Stěpánka) Picková's, see https://www.holocaust.cz/en/database-of-victims/victim/113714-stepanka-pickova/ (both accessed Aug. 14, 2020). A few months later, on May 15, 1942, Rudolf and Štěpánka Pick were put on transport "Au1" from Prague to Terezín. In 1944, they were transferred from Terezín to Auschwitz-Birkenau on different transports. The couple had one daughter named, Ludmila (1921–1944?), whose married name was Kesler. She was deported from Prague on May 12, 1942, three days before her parents, on transport "Au" and further transferred to Auschwitz-Birkenau on transport "Eo" on October 6, 1944. Her husband was most likely Valter Kesler (1911–?), who was liberated from Auschwitz-Birkenau. He left a testimony in Archiv Památníku Terezín, Terezín. See https://portal.ehri-project.eu/units/cz-002302-vzpom%C3%ADnky_pro_ehri-a_3926 (accessed April 30, 2016). The fourth Ascher sibling, Helena Jenny Ascher (1904–1942?) had the married name Koblitz. She and her husband František Koblitz (1894–1942?) and their eleven-year-old son Robert (1931–1942?) were deported on transport "Au" from Prague to Terezín on May 12, 1942, three days before the Pick couple. Only five days after their arrival in Terezín, the family of three was further transferred on transport "Ay" from Terezín to Lublin.

[24] Kadĕrka was a very unusual name in Czechoslovakia, as it is in today's Czechia. The 1942 Brno address book mentions only six people with that name. See *Adressbuch der Landeshauptstadt Brünn* 1942, 118. Only one was a doctor and this was indeed Stanislav Kadĕrka. Since the postcard was sent from Prague, I also checked the Prague address book, which listed only four men named Kadĕrka. None were medical doctors.

[25] An address registration card in the AMB, Brno, fonds Z 1, for Siegfried Ascher states 25 Smetanagasse (Bedřicha Smetany) in the Královo Pole suburb as his last address before he was transferred to the Jewish hospital. He arrived in the very small Smetanagasse house on February 25, 1942, one month before the postcard was sent. His previous address (likely also that of his immediate family) was 2 Havlišgasse (Havlišova), also in Královo Pole. In 1934, Siegfried Ascher and his family still lived at 6 Hutterteich (Hutterův rybník), a very posh address with a view of the Winterhollerplatz (Winterhollerovo náměstí) park. See *Adreßbuch von Groß-Brünn* 1934, 123.

[26] He lived at 35 Josef-Pekař-strasse (třída Josefa Pekaře). See *Adressbuch der Landeshauptstadt Brünn* 1942, 2, 118.

[27] In several ways, the situation of Jewish doctors and patients in the Protectorate was similar to that in Germany. National Socialists did all they could to discourage or forbid regular Germans from visiting Jewish doctors, striving in general "to leave Jewish doctors to their Jewish patients". See Kater 1989, 189. In Germany, barring Jewish doctors from practicing was a gradual process that started as early as 1933. See Kater 1989, 185, 193, 196, 198, 200–204. In May 1939, two months after the invasion of Czechoslovakia, all Jewish doctors in the Protectorate were proscribed. Every issue of *Hadoar*, the periodical of the JKG in Brno, included a list of Jewish doctors still allowed to practice; however, these were clearly not enough to look after the whole Jewish population. Jewish people also visited non-Jewish doctors, but the latter would have been careful about too great or too open an involvement with the Jewish population.

[28] The mistaken street name on the postcard – Müllergasse instead of Mühlgasse – is another indication that the writer of the postcard, Rudolf Pick, spoke to Kadĕrka in Brno over the phone. He must have misheard the name of the Brno street, with which he was likely unfamiliar. The only problem with this interpretation is that, by March 1942, Jews in the Protectorate were not permitted telephones in their homes and were not allowed to use public telephones. There are three possibilities. Rudolf Pick

According to a Holocaust testimony given by Siegfried Ascher's son, Robert Ascher, the "little Robert" fondly mentioned in the postcard, we know that Siegfried had a stroke some time before he and his family received the notice that they were being deported from Brno. In any case, the family tried to use the father's illness as a valid reason exempting the whole family from deportation. According to Robert Ascher's testimony, the Germans nevertheless instructed the family to go the deportees' meeting-point where a decision would be made. This resulted in Siegfried Ascher staying behind in Brno while his nine-year-old son, Robert Ascher, his wife Margarete Ascher (née Dukes), and his mother, Berta Bondy, were transported to Terezín.[29] Siegfried Ascher's close relatives were put on transport "Ad", taking them from Brno to Terezín on March 23, 1942, three days before the writing of the postcard. It is possible that Siegfried Ascher's health deteriorated further due to the doubtlessly traumatizing deportation of his mother, wife and son. Possibly, this decision by the Germans caused him to have a nervous breakdown or even another stroke at the deportees' meeting-point in the school building at 37 Merhautgasse (Merhautova). It was likely that Ascher's family witnessed this and arrived in Terezín with no idea of how Ascher was doing.[30] This would explain the urgency of the message on the postcard sent three days after the family was deported: "Fritzl" – Siegfried – was doing better. Siegfried Ascher's family was possibly also conscious that their father had physically depended on them. The news that he was in a hospital or infirmary must have been a consolation. We will see in a moment that, in reality, Siegfried was taken to a sort of makeshift Jewish hospital first opened in 1941. In two other May 1942 postcards to his future wife Anna Kahn (who was at that point doing forced labor just outside of Terezín), Albert Ascher mentioned that his brother Siegfried Ascher was doing better.[31]

The main reason that I was intrigued by this March 1942 postcard sent to Terezín – mentioning Stanislav Kadĕrka, Siegfried Ascher and the Jewish hospital – was my knowledge that, on January 6, 1942, Elise Brecher, Karl Fein's aunt, went to this same hospital in Mühlgasse (Mlýnská).[32] It is conceivable that Karl Fein told his aunt about the people he had entrusted with the Institute materials and that she heard in the

either used a telephone belonging to non-Jewish friends or acquaintances, or was employed by the JKG in Prague (whose workers were exempted from the prohibition), or was a lawyer or doctor (these professions were also exempt). For the January 1941 prohibition banning Jewish people from having and using telephones, see http://www.holocaustresearchproject.org/ghettos/restrictions&roles.html (accessed Jul. 14, 2015); http://www.ghetto-theresienstadt.info/pages/p/post.htm (accessed Aug. 8, 2015); Friedmann, Jul. 31, 1942; Friedmann 1997, 249. Beneš and Tošnerová refer to a postal administration circular of February 17, 1941, about Jewish people being prohibited from using a telephone, which was likely a further executive order of a January decision (Beneš & Tošnerová 1996, 28).

[29] Archiv Památníku Terezín (Terezín Memorial Archive), Terezín, fonds Sbírka vzpomínek, inv. n° 2047, ser. n° 6585, testimony (dated April 1981) Robert Ascher (interview conducted in Czech), 1–7. I thank Eva Němcová (Archiv Památníku Terezín, Terezín) for sending me a digital copy of the typoscript in July 2015. Speaking of his time in Terezín, Robert Ascher referred to his sick father – who was still in Brno – as one of the reasons that he and his mother were not deported from Terezín.

[30] All the people summoned for previous and subsequent Jewish transports had to come to this school in Merhautgasse (Merhautova). Today, the façade of the school bears a commemorative plaque. See http://encyklopedie.brna.cz/home-mmb/?acc=profil_objektu&load=118 and https://sfi.usc.edu/news/2014/05/new-iwalk-forthcoming-brno-czech-republic (both accessed Apr. 13, 2016). For more information about this meeting-point for the Brno Jewish transports, see Klenovský 1995, 16; Klementová 2014, 71–72; Brummer & Konečný 2013, 114–17.

[31] Židovské muzeum v Praze (Jewish Museum in Prague), Shoah-related collections, personal and family related materials and papers (osobní pozůstalosti), Albert Ascher (Jul. 22, 1899), postcards (dated May 5, 1942 and May 17, 1942) from Albert Ascher to Anna Kahn.

[32] See the unnumbered A5-format page sitting between folios 3 and 4 (numbered in pencil) in MZA, Brno, fonds C 11, Krajský soud civilní Brno, kart. n° 89, sign. AVIII 191, company file L. & A. Brecher, and Elise Brecher's resident registration card in AMB, Brno, fonds Z 1. The resident registration card mentions "Jüd.[isches] Siechenheim" (Jewish hospital)

hospital about the Institute materials being discarded by the Kamarád clique. There is a real possibility that, when visiting his patient Siegfried Ascher, Stanislav Kaděrka overheard that the Institute materials had been discarded at the Růžičkas' company and that he decided to attempt to get a hold of them. This makes Kaděrka look like a treasure hunter – in line with Milena Baumgarten's suggestion – intent on eventually making money out of his discoveries, like the treasure hunters scouring the still-smoldering ashes on the Opernplatz, the day after the May 1933 Berlin bonfire.

It is possible that Kaděrka, who completed his medical studies in 1933, attended the 1932 WLSR Brno conference as a student. Or he may have simply read about Hirschfeld and the 1932 conference in the local newspapers. Kaděrka may have taken an interest or even specialized in sexological matters. In 1966, a Czechoslovak magazine published an article on the sexual question and the so-called "sexual revolution".[33] In a sidebar, under the mysterious title "Ad multos annos" (Latin, for many more years), Kaděrka's name was mentioned, together with that of Jaroslav Šindelář (1906–?), a Prague neurologist and psychiatrist.[34] Kaděrka also owned at least two books, though a work of fiction and a chapbook, by the Czech sexologist and Brno resident Antonín Trýb.[35]

Alternatively, since we know that Fein's aunt may have played a part in the November 1933 buy-back operation, thus knowing the whole story about the Institute collection's tragic and painful itinerary, Kaděrka, as a relatively harmless outsider, may have been sent on a mission by Fein's aunt to try to save something. Earlier, we mostly dismissed the idea that a cleaning lady retrieved the Institute materials from the old paper container at the Růžičkas' company. That sexological books were saved in conjunction with the Hirschfeld guestbook indicated a planned search mission looking for valuable artifacts once belonging to Magnus Hirschfeld and his Institute. Kaděrka may have been given precise instructions about what to look for in the old paper container and may even have visited the site behind the Nebehosteny house himself. However, as we have also said, this would then require explaining how he, or the person (or persons) sent by him, got into the relatively inaccessible area behind the Nebehosteny house.

TOMÁŠ KRATOCHVÍL, MAN ON A MISSION?

Let us have a look at a good candidate, possibly sent on a mission by Dr. Kaděrka. At present, the open site behind the Nebehosteny house and 66 Kröna (Křenová) constitutes a single large area housing two large garages, serving as a car park for the Brno police, a function it took on shortly after World War II. The current Brno police force took over the site and its buildings from the National Security Corps (Sbor národní bezpečnosti, SNB), the national police in Czechoslovakia from 1945 to

and bears a stamp from the Israelitische Kultusgemeinde Brünn (Jewish religious community Brno, náboženská obec židovská Brno), signing as the *Wohnungseigentümer* (home owners), which was not factually correct. In the addenda (n° 12) one can find an overview of Elise Brecher's last addresses in Brno before she was deported.

33 See the articles in *Zdravotnické noviny*, n° 2, Jan. 12, 1966, 2.

34 In 1943, Šindelář co-authored the book *Hyperkinetická a hypokineticko-hypertonická forma hepatolentikulární degenerace u dvou rodných bratří* (Janota & Šindelář 1943). In 1976, an article celebrating Šindelář's seventieth birthday appeared in *Československá neurologie a neurochirurgie*. See Svačina 1976. Between 1924 and 1930, Šindelář was enrolled at Charles University in Prague, where he obtained his medical degree. See Ústav dějin Univerzity Karlovy a Archiv Univerzity Karlovy (Institute of History of Charles University and the Archive of Charles University), Praha, fonds n° 180, Matriky univerzity Karlovy 1882–2008, Matrika doktorů Univerzity Karlovy (Registry of Charles University doctors) (1928–1931), inventory number (and kart.) n° 7, f. 3317; available online at https://is.cuni.cz/webapps/archiv/public/?lang=en (accessed Aug. 8, 2015).

35 Trýb 1946a; Trýb 1946b. For a partial list of Kaděrka's library, see AMB, Brno, fonds Magistrátu města Brna, Majetkový odbor, I 1/17, sign. Rp-E-1974/87. The list is only partial because it includes only the books that remained after people were allowed to remove

1991. When the Nebehosteny building was confiscated by the Czech state in 1945–50, it was given to the SNB.[36] I reasoned that maybe the site served as a car park for the Brno police *during* the war as well. The idea did not seem too far-fetched. After all, the arrival of the German military and police in Brno may have put pressure on the local police's available parking spaces in the city. Would it not then be possible that the Brno police had to look for new parking space further from the city center? However, I was not able to find any archival support for this idea.[37] I decided to ask Helga Sikora, who had lived in the Nebehosteny house and played on the site behind the house as a child. She told me that she had not seen any police cars parking there during the war.[38]

The idea that it served as a parking lot for the Brno police intrigued me because I knew that Tomáš Kratochvíl (1888–1968), the husband of Kaděrka's housekeeper Anna Kratochvílová, was a policeman.[39] Was Tomáš Kratochvíl the man sent on a mission by Dr. Kaděrka? The site behind the Nebehosteny house may not have been a car park for the Brno police during the war, but I think that, unlike the public at large, investigative police officers would have the authority to enter (or trespass into) relatively inaccessible areas. However, Tomáš Kratochvíl's signature did not match either of the two – rather illegible – signatures under the affidavit in the Hirschfeld guestbook.[40] Nevertheless, I continue to think Tomáš Kratochvíl an intriguing candidate to have rescued some of the Institute materials and Hirschfeld guestbook in 1942.[41]

Lastly, Kaděrka may also have asked his patients if they knew somebody doing housework in the Nebehosteny house. Or, less plausibly, did Kaděrka's own housekeeper – Anna Kratochvílová (1894–1982) – also work for a family in the Nebehosteny house? I examined Kratochvílová's signature to see if it matched either of the two signatures on the affidavit, but it did not.[42]

titles following Kaděrka's death. See chapter 14, pp. 496-98.

[36] NA, Praha, fonds Národní obnovy Praha (National restoration fonds, Prague), confiscation file of house 194/68 in Křenová Street, Brno-Zábrdovice, sign. VZ 11073/III/1, nezpracovaný fond (unprocessed fonds).

[37] Email (dated Jun. 6, 2017) from Miroslava Bělíková (MZA, Brno) to the author.

[38] Phone conversation (dated Jan. 9, 2018) between Helga Sikora and the author.

[39] There is no police staff file on Tomáš Kratochvíl in MZA, Brno, fonds B 26, Policejní ředitelství Brno, but I was told by an MZA, Brno, archivist that police staff files are not complete. See email (dated Apr. 11, 2017) from Miroslava Bělíková (MZA, Brno) to the author. Another file on the man (and his wife Anna) in the AMB, Brno, was shredded at some point. See AMB, Brno, fonds A1/26, Presidiální spisovna 1880–1932, file Tomáš Kratochvíl (1920–1921), fasc. n° 914, invent. n° 1975. The evolution of Kratochvíl's professional career is hard to determine. In the 1934 *Adreßbuch von Groß-Brünn*, one sees indeed that he was a *II. Klasse Rayonsinspektor* (second class district inspector) in the Brno Uniformed Security Guard Corps (Korps der uniformierten Sicherheitswache in Brünn, Sbor uniformované stráže bezpečnosti v Brně). This was a department inside Brno police headquarters (Policejní ředitelství v Brně, Polizeidirektion in Brno). See *Adreßbuch von Groß-Brünn* 1934, 57–58. In 1938, he was a *policejní obvodní inspektor* (district police inspector). See http://encyklopedie.brna.cz/home-mmb/?acc=profil_osobnosti&load=10930 (accessed Aug. 14, 2015). However, in *Adressbuch der Landeshauptstadt Brünn 1942* 1943, 148, he is simply mentioned as a "*Pol*[izei] St[?]*Wachm*[ann]" (police guardsman). Since it is unknown where Kratochvíl pursued his professional career after the war, I also checked his name in the ABS, Praha, but they did not have a file on him. See email (dated Oct. 15, 2015) from Jitka Bílková (ABS, Praha) to the author. I also inquired whether there were traces of the man in MZA, Brno, fonds B 327, Velitelství uniformované vládní policie Brno (1942–1945), but this archival fonds does not contain any personal files for police officers. See email (dated May 14, 2018) from Leoš Pecha (MZA, Brno) to the author. A photo of Kratochvíl can be found in *Album bývalých příslušníků a zakladatelů 6. střeleckého hanáckého pluku* 1938, 19. There is no military file on Kratochvíl in the Vojenský ústřední archiv in Prague as files of men born between 1887 and 1900 were discarded. See email (dated Jul. 17 2018) from Josef Žikeš (Vojenský ústřední archiv, Praha) to the author.

[40] I saw Tomáš Kratochvíl's signature on a 1942 resident registration card in the AMB, Brno, fonds Z 1. His very clear and legible signature (one can easily read his full name) is not at all like the signatures seen under the affidavit.

[41] In June 1942, Tomáš Kratochvíl had to confirm his current address. See his resident registration card in the AMB, Brno, fonds Z 1. As we have already

But in trying to answer why the Hirschfeld guestbook and some of the Institute collection's sexology books specifically ended up with Dr. Kadĕrka in Brno, we have accidentally stumbled upon a new possible scenario. What if Kadĕrka heard about the fatal decision to discard the Institute materials because the *decision was taken in the Jewish hospital,* possibly even by Karl Fein's aunt, Elise Brecher? Did the *Kamarád* group, in other words, play no part in any of this? In the following section, we will further develop this possibility that some of the patients in the Jewish hospital were involved, and add more details that indeed further support this second scenario of what might have happened in 1942. One factor above all – a quite surprising one – that we will consider momentarily, will further convince the reader that this second scenario *on its own* can explain how the decision to discard the Institute materials could indeed have been taken in this Jewish hospital. Subsequently, we will also review the many arguments against this scenario. Let us first take a closer look at the history of this Jewish hospital.

HISTORY OF THE JEWISH HOSPITAL

The hospital (*Siechenhaus*) where Siegfried Ascher was transferred, mentioned on the postcard to Terezín, was located at the corner formed by 27 Mühlgasse (Mlýnská) and 5 Stephansgasse (Štěpánská) in Brno. It was a recent, tiny and wholly improvised Jewish hospital, which gathered all Jewish citizens whose poor health prevented their deportation.[43] The Jewish hospital presumably opened near the end of 1941. It is interesting that the Jewish community in Brno was considering (or was instructed to consider) establishing a home for the aged and sick (*Alters- und Siechenheim*) in mid-May 1941, six months before the very first Jewish mass transport left from Brno to Minsk, on November 16, 1941.[44] It remains a little unclear whether the opening of this Jewish hospital was closely connected with the planned Jewish mass transports. Similar Jewish hospitals for people too sick to be deported were also created in five other Czech cities.[45]

seen, this was usually a prelude to a visit by one or another German police agency. However, it must be noted that in 1942, especially after the assassination of Heydrich, many people were suddenly suspects.

[42] In a questionnaire that I sent to her, I also asked Tomáš Kratochvíl's daughter-in-law, Kamila Kratochvílová (who was Kadĕrka's very last housekeeper), if she recognized either of the two affidavit signatures in the Hirschfeld guestbook, but she answered this question – like most others that I asked her – with a "no". See questionnaire (dated May 2017) from Kamila Kratochvílová.

[43] See the undated document n° 3, "Soziale Fürsorge", written by the JKG in Prague (Krejčová, Svobodová & Hyndráková 1997, 78). This document comes from NA, Praha, Archiv Ministerstva vnitra České republiky (archives of the Ministry of the Interior of the Czech Republic), fonds Židovské organizace, sign. 425-220-4. See also Brummer & Konečný 2013, 134–137 (though it contains a few factual errors).

[44] *Jüdisches Nachrichtenblatt*, May 16, 1941, 8.

[45] See the undated document n° 3, "Soziale Fürsorge", written by the JKG in Prague (Krejčová, Svobodová & Hyndráková 1997, 76, 78: "Im Jahre 1941 zeigte die geschlossene Fürsorge in der Provinz folgendes Bild: In Brünn bestanden drei Altersheime mit indgesamt [*sic*] 140 Insassen, [...] und ein neuerrichtetes Siechenheim mit 25 Insassen. [...] Im Zusammenhang mit der Abwanderung, bzw. Einweisung der Brünner Juden ins Ghetto wurden die drei Altersheime in Brünn und das dortige Waisenhaus aufgelöst, sodass in Brünn nur ein Siechenheim verblieb, in dem die transportunfähigen Personen aufgenommen wurden. Anderseits wurden nach Abwanderung der Juden aus den Aussenstellen Pilsen, Kladno, Böhm. Budweis, Trebitsch und Kolin in allen diesen Orten Altersheime für aus den Transporten ausgeschiedene Personen errichtet, sodass heute folgende Institutionen bestehen: Brünn: ein Siechenheim mit 13 Insassen" (In 1941, the closed social welfare system in the province presented the following picture: In Brno there were three old people's homes with a total of 140 residents [...] and a newly built home for the sick with 25 residents. [...] In connection with the emigration of the Brno Jews to the ghetto, the three old people's homes and the orphanage in Brno were closed down, leaving only one home for the sick remaining in Brno, where those unfit for transport were admitted. On the other hand, after the emigration of Jews from the outposts of Pilsen, Kladno, Bohem. Budweis, Trebitsch and Kolin, old people's homes were set up in all of these places for people removed from the transports, so that now the following institutions exist: Brünn: a nursing home with 13 residents). Kle-

The Jewish hospital in Brno never had many patients; numbers ranged between 13 and 25 people.[46] One author claims that the house at 27 Mühlgasse (Mlýnská) was a retirement home for the Jewish elders in the second half of the nineteenth century and also functioned as a kitchen for the poor at the time.[47] In 1902, the home for the elderly would have moved to a new building at 54 Prager Strasse (Pražská) that had been built by the Max and Johanna Rosenthal foundation.[48] This would mean that the return to the much smaller building in Mühlgasse (Mlýnská) – most likely on orders of the German authorities – was also a sort of degrading measure, even more so since the building was in a rather poor condition in 1941.[49]

NELLY STERN

Nelly Stern (1890–1945), an unmarried Jewish gynecologist, was in charge of the Jewish hospital.[50] Presumably, she started working at the hospital when it opened, in the final months of 1941.[51] Previously, she lived with her mother Elise Baeck (1866–1944), the widow of rabbi Simon Stern (1856–1930 or 1933). Elise Stern (née Baeck) was the sister of Leo Baeck (1873–1956), the rabbi in Terezín after whom the world-famous Jewish research institute in New York was named after the war.[52] Baeck was the German grand president (*Großpresident*) of the B'nai B'rith lodges between 1924 and 1937. He visited Brno in 1932 on the occasion of the thirty-fifth anniversary of the local Moravia B'nai B'rith lodge where he gave a lecture on "Revolution in Judaism" (*Revolution im Judentum*).[53] But Baeck also had relatives in Brno, closely associated

mentová refers to this document as well, but to its Czech translation (Klementová 2014, 68–69 n. 3).

46 Krejčová, Svobodová & Hyndráková 1997, 76, 78.

47 Klenovský 1995, 42–43.

48 Max Rosenthal (1827–1893) was a Jewish industrialist from Brno who married Johanna Gerstel (1834–1898). Before World War II, Brno had three Jewish retirement homes, one of them at 54 Prager Strasse (Pražská).

49 For the building being in poor condition in 1941, see NA, Praha, fonds n° 375, Arizační spisy, company Josef Pollak (obchod starým železem a kovy), kart. n° 249, invent. n° 1706. Curiously, even today an air of poverty clings to the area immediately around where the Jewish hospital stood. Poor people standing around or even lying on the sidewalks can be seen nearby. This is in part related to the Salvation Army, which is now housed in the Eisler building (currently named Dům Josefa Korbela), located just across the street, at 25 Mühlgasse (Mlýnská). See https://encyklopedie.brna.cz/home-mmb/?acc=profil_udalosti&load=2609 (accessed Aug. 26, 2019).

50 Stern studied medicine in Vienna between 1911 and 1917. See email (dated Aug. 11, 2015) from Barbara Bieringer (Archiv der Universität Wien, Vienna) to the author. See also http://encyklopedie.brna.cz/home-mmb/?acc=profil_osobnosti&load=9240 (accessed Jul. 8, 2015).

51 Nelly Stern moved to 27 Mühlgasse (Mlýnská) on January 15, 1942. See the only resident registration card for Nelly Stern (dated Sep. 12, 1941) in the AMB, Brno, fonds Z 1. In 1934, she lived with her mother Elise Baeck at 18 Na kopečku (Am Bergl) in Brno. On September 12, 1941, mother and daughter moved to 1a Gerichtsgasse (Soudní), most likely a forced move. Several index cards for Nelly Stern in NA, Praha, fonds n° 1077, Okupační vězeňské spisy, card index of those deported from the Protectorate to Terezín, also mention the Jewish hospital's address as her last address in Brno before being deported. I also noticed that, at some point, Nelly Stern lived at 35 Koliště (Glacis), one of Karl Fein's last Brno addresses. Karl Fein lived and kept his law office at 35 Koliště (Glacis) from October 1936 until October 1938. We should inquire into whether they knew each other. I could not determine exactly when Nelly Stern lived at this address.

52 Elise Stern is described as "Rabbinerswitwe" (a rabbi's widow) in *Adreßbuch von Groß-Brünn* 1934, 464. Rabbi Samuel Baeck (1834–1912), Leo Baeck's father, had eleven children, five sons (Alfred, Leo, Salo, Richard and Martin) and six daughters (Frieda, Therese [Rosa], Liese, Ernestine, Lina and Anna). Leo Baeck was the only son to become a rabbi. Three sisters (Therese Mandelová, Liese Sternová and Ernestine Levin Salomonová) married rabbis. See Bato 1965, 67. Information about the fate of Leo Baeck's sisters in Terezín is rather paltry and even distorted. One source (likely based on a publication by Leo Baeck) claims that four Baeck sisters perished in Terezín, including Nelly Stern's mother, who died in 1944. See the "Mai 1945" entry in Leo Baeck's short biography at http://www.ghetto-theresienstadt.de/pages/b/baeckl.htm (accessed Jul. 14, 2015). The truth is that three and not four of Leo Baeck's sisters died in Terezín, see Hájková 2014; Hájková 2020, 51. The two other Baeck sisters who perished in Terezín were Rosa (Růžena) Mandelová (1871–1942) and Frieda (Bedřiška) Feldmannová (1863–1942). The Baeck family tree can be consulted on Geni.com by entering "Leo Baeck" in the search bar.

53 *B'nai B'rith: měsíčník Velkolóže pro Československý stát = Monatsblätter der Grossloge für den Čechoslovakischen Staat*, vol. 11, n° 2, 1932, 70.

with the local B'nai B'rith lodge there. Walter Stern, the brother of Nelly Stern, was a Moravia lodge member. Another Moravia lodge brother was an uncle of Karl Fein, the engineer Lipmann Brammer, whom we have already mentioned. So was Dr. Siegfried Fischl, a member of the Brno WLSR conference preparatory committee. The younger Arthur Feldmann (1887–1941), a lawyer whose mother's maiden name was Baeck, was also a member. Karl Fein's nephew, the elder Karl Fein, was a member of a B'nai B'rith lodge as well, presumably in Prague. It is not known if the younger Karl Fein was also a B'nai B'rith lodge member.[54]

On April 8, 1942, Nelly Stern was deported with her mother to Terezín on transport "Ai". Her brother, Walter (Valtr) Stern (1892–1944), also a doctor, and his wife Gertruda (1900–1944), were on the same transport.[55] In Terezín, Nelly Stern and her brother continued to work as doctors.[56] Unlike her mother and brother, Nelly Stern survived her deportation to Terezín, but was killed in a road accident in Bavaria (Germany) in July 1945.[57] Because the postcard sent to Albert Ascher in Terezín mentioned both the Jewish hospital and Stanislav Kaděrka, I also considered the possibility that Kaděrka might have been the non-Jewish doctor in charge of the Jewish hospital after Nelly Stern's deportation in early April 1942, but this does not seem to have been the case.[58]

The Jewish deportations from Brno started on November 16, 1941, with a first convoy of one thousand people sent to Minsk. Nine more mass transports would

[54] Rys 1938, 274–75.

[55] NA, Praha, fonds n° 167, Jewish registers (Židovské matriky, Judische Matriken), inv. n° 142, Brno, Z, 1942 and inv. n° 143, Z, 1942 (prosinec) – 1944 (koncentrač. tábory).

[56] See, for example, the "Todesfallanzeige" (death certificate) Nelly Stern drew up for her aunt Frieda (Bedřiška) Feldmannová (1863–1942), a sister of Leo Baeck, who also lived in Brno before the war. See http://www.holocaust.cz/databaze-dokumentu/dokument/78908-feldmannova-bedriska-oznameni-o-umrti-ghetto-Terezín/ and http://encyklopedie.brna.cz/home-mmb/?acc=profil_osobnosti&load=9224 (both accessed Jul. 14, 2015). Walter Stern was responsible for building L 410 in Terezín (*Mädchenheim*, girls' home). See the two documents at http://www.holocaust.cz/databaze-dokumentu/dokument/137053-inspekce-ve-zdravotnickych-zarizenich-seznam-vedoucich-lekaru-zdravotnicka-osveta-v-Terezíne/ (accessed Jul. 14, 2015); Makarová, Makarov & Kuperman 2004, 519. Walter Stern and his wife Gertrude Reach had two daughters, Dorly Bodenheimer (née Stern) and Eva Nir (née Stern), who survived the Holocaust. Dorly Bodenheimer – whose husband is deceased – has two children, one a daughter, Shelly Bodenheimer. Nelly Stern also had a sister, Marianne Löw (Lev) (Stern) (1895–1979). She survived the war, possibly by emigrating just before it broke out. Neither her name nor that of her husband Walter Löw is listed in Kárný et al. 1995. The couple had one son (d.) and one daughter, Shoshana Alp(p)ern (Lev) (1932–?). See http://www.geni.com/people/Marianne-Loew-lev/6000000007265882391?through=6000000015263391422 (accessed Jul. 14, 2015). I also asked Ellen Weinberg Dreyfus, a retired New York rabbi and direct relative of Leo Baeck, about Nelly Stern. She initially wrote to me that she was not familiar with any of the names mentioned in my message, despite herself adding an entry on Nelly Stern on the Geni.com website in 2012. See message from Ellen Weinberg Dreyfus (dated Jul. 14, 2015) to the author via the Geni.com website. A year later, she contacted me again, with some more information about Nelly Stern and her surviving family members. See message from Ellen Weinberg Dreyfus (dated Jul. 17, 2016) to the author via the Geni.com website. I subsequently asked her to put me in contact with the surviving family members Shoshana Alp(p)ern (or Alperin) (Lev) and Eva Nir (née Stern), Dorly Bodenheimer (née Stern) and the latter's daughter Shelly Bodenheimer; however, I have not managed to contact any of these people. Here, we may also mention that Immanuel Stern (1882–1960), a Brno Jewish lawyer whose practice was liquidated in 1939, does not seem to have been related to this Stern family. See *Věstník Moravské advokátní komory v Brně*, year 2, n° 2 (April, 1939): 3. In 1939, Immanuel Stern managed to flee to England with his family, and returned to Czechoslovakia after the war. See http://encyklopedie.brna.cz/home-mmb/?acc=profil_osobnosti&load=21537 (accessed Jul. 14, 2015).

[57] See https://www.geni.com/people/Nelly-Stern/6000000015263347185#/tab/overview (accessed Jul. 21, 2015). See also a completed 2005 restitution claim by Shoshana Alp(p)ern (or Alperin) (Lev), the daughter of Marianne Löw (Lev) (Stern), Nelly Stern's sister, http://www.crt-ii.org/_awards/_denials/_apdfs/Stern_Nelly_den_1.pdf (accessed Jul. 8, 2015).

[58] See also email (dated May 15, 2015) from Alena Mikovcová and Alena Kubešová (Židovská obec Brno, Brno) to the author: "Kromě MUDr. Nelly Sternové neznáme žádné lékaře, kteří by působili ve starobinci v Mlýnské ulici" (Other than Dr. Nelly Stern, we do not know of any other doctor who worked in the retirement home on Mlýnská).

follow.[59] The tenth mass transport, "Ai", carrying 923 people, left Brno on April 8, 1942. On May 27, 1942, another much smaller transport "AAa", carrying eighty-one people, left Brno. It is clear that the last two transports together contained a little more than 1,000 people. Most likely, the JKG in Brno managed to exempt approximately eighty people from transport "Ai" by claiming that they needed a work force to organize the deportations and the emptying of the apartments of those deported.[60] The last three Jewish medical doctors in Brno most likely left on the smaller, penultimate transport "AAa" of May 27, 1942.[61] The one remaining transport, "Dg", later carried approximately thirty Jewish people and patients from Brno, along with twenty-six people from other cities. This final Jewish transport left Brno on July 1, 1943, thirteen months after transport "AAa". When reviewing the list of deportees on transport "Dg", I did not find "MUDr." (medical doctor) next to any names.[62]

A certain Dr. Otto Slovak pronounced the lawyer Siegfried Ascher dead in the Jewish hospital in December 1942.[63] Slovak lived nearby, at 3 Dornich (Dornych).[64] On the basis of the Jewish registers (Židovské matriky, Judische Matriken), this doctor pronounced all deaths at the Jewish hospital in the year before the final July 1943 Jewish transport from Brno.[65] It is unclear if this means that Dr. Slovak was appointed the non-Jewish doctor responsible for the Jewish hospital after Nelly Stern's deportation. Yet the main conclusion seems to be that Stanislav Kaděrka had no structural links at all to the Jewish hospital.

[59] For an overview of all Jewish transports starting or arriving in the Protectorate, see Kárný et al. 1995, 63–74. See also n° 13 in the addenda.

[60] Klementová 2014, 72. This text is based on Klementová's 2010 MA thesis. See Klementová 2010.

[61] They were Walter (Valtr) Auffärber (1914–1944?), Bedřich Katz (1894–1942?) and Bedřich Wessely (1908–1945). See Kárný et al. 1995, 588–89. Ernest (Arnošt) Bass (1904–1944?), Kurt Bauer (1910–1944?) and Otto König (1906–1943?), all lawyers, were on the same transport. Otto König was the president of the JKG in Brno from 1938 until 1942. See Klementová 2014, 68; Klenovský 2002, 20. König was deported, together with his wife Thea (1912–1943?), on transport "AAa" from Brno to Terezín on May 27, 1942. On September 6, 1943, both were further transferred from Terezín to Auschwitz-Birkenau on transport "Dl".

[62] Kárný et al. 1995, 1207–8. Cf. Štěpánek 2004, 191. Klementová claims that this transport also included the very first Brno "Mischlinge" (Klementová 2014, 73).

[63] Siegfried Ascher died of "essentielle Hypertonie" (high blood pressure) in the Jewish hospital on December 18, 1942. His address at the time of his death was indeed that of the Jewish hospital, 27 Mühlgasse (Mlýnská). See NA, Praha, fonds n° 167, Jewish registers (Židovské matriky, Judische Matriken), inv. n° 142, Brno, Z, 1942, http://www.badatelna.eu/fond/1073/reprodukce/?zaznamId=181&reproId=174796 (accessed Jan. 21, 2016). Siegfried Ascher is buried in the Brno Jewish cemetery in section 36, row 3, grave 40. His plot has a contemporary gravestone bearing the word "Holokaust" and a Hebrew phrase. His wife Margarete (or Markéta) and son Robert, who both died in 1986, are buried in the same cemetery but in the Du(c)kes-Ascher family plot in section 23b, row 2, grave 11. Siegfried Ascher's name was added to the stone at this family plot. However, his first name is given in its Czech form, Vítězslav.

[64] For Slovak's address, see "Branchen-, Beruf-u.[nd] Gewerbe-Verzeichnis", *Adressbuch der Landeshauptstadt Brünn* 1942, 2. For the date of Siegfried Ascher's death, pronounced by Dr. Slovak, see AMB, Brno, fonds A 1/3, Sbírka rukopisů a úředních knih, Úmrtní protokol z roku 1942, book n° 8230, entry n° 4574, dated December 18, 1942, Siegfried Ascher.

[65] Max Grünhüt (1868–1942), who died on December 19, 1942, is one case of Dr. Slovak pronouncing the death of a patient in the Jewish hospital. See NA, Praha, fonds n° 167, Jewish registers (Židovské matriky, Judische Matriken), inv. n° 142, Brno, Z, 1942, http://www.badatelna.eu/fond/1073/reprodukce/?zaznamId=181&reproId=174796 (accessed May 15, 2016). For Dr. Slovak pronouncing other deaths in the Jewish hospital in February, March, May and June 1943, see NA, Praha, fonds n° 167, Jewish registers (Židovské matriky, Judische Matriken), inv. n° 143, Brno, Z, 1942–1944.

[66] MZA, Brno, fonds C 12, Krajský soud trestní Brno, kart. n° 2381, sign. Tk XI 1852/38, file Heinrich Brecher, letter from Elise Brecher (dated June 24, 1938) to Státní zastupitelství v Brně (public prosecutor's office in Brno), f. 5. In this document, composed with her lawyer Süss, Elise Brecher stated that the embezzlement case involving her son Heinrich, and the feverish attention it provoked, combined with her age, had an adverse effect on her health.

[67] I did not review the arrival dates of all the other patients at the Jewish hospital systematically; however, all the resident registration cards that I have seen, which included the date of the patients' arrival, show that they arrived at the hospital shortly after a transport date. Many arrived at the Jewish hospital on April 10, 1942, a few days after the last mass transport "Ai" left Brno, on April 8, 1942.

ELISE BRECHER, SIEGFRIED ASCHER AND THE JEWISH HOSPITAL

In a June 1938 document, Elise Brecher, then sixty-eight years old, stated that she was sick.[66] Yet, when comparing the dates of the ten Brno Jewish mass transports and Elise Brecher's arrival at the hospital, on January 6, 1942, the latter does not seem linked to a pending transport. The fourth Jewish mass transport "U" left Brno on January 28, 1942, three weeks after her arrival. The previous transport, "K", left Brno on December 5, 1941, one month before her arrival. It is possible that Elise Brecher was one of the few patients, or perhaps the only one, whose arrival at the hospital was independent of any planned transport.[67] Maybe, after the first three mass deportations from Brno, Elise Brecher noticed or learned that the sick were exempt.[68] Was her move to the Jewish hospital a deliberate attempt to escape deportation? Was the Jewish hospital a sort of privileged safety net? It seems to have been that, at least for Elise Brecher. Most other people at the Jewish hospital were either too sick to be deported or were there because their family caregivers faced deportation. This was normal procedure. For every transport, an appointed doctor at the meeting-point decided who was too sick to be deported.[69]

It must be noted that most of the people at the Jewish hospital died rather soon after arriving. Living conditions in the makeshift Jewish hospital were most probably not very good. The 1942 Jewish registers (Židovské matriky, Judische Matriken) reveal that many deaths in the hospital occurred at the beginning of that year. This high mortality rate extended into mid-1943 when the makeshift hospital ceased to exist, clearly demonstrating its harsh conditions.[70] However, it is also true that those who did not succumb were not deported until mid-1943, more than one year after the end of the Jewish mass transports from Brno. Whether or not Elise Brecher planned her stay in the Jewish hospital, it is certain that she stayed there for a year and a half.

Some patients at the Jewish hospital belonged to the Jewish elite of Brno. The most important patient was Siegfried Ascher, elected the first deputy head of the board (*Vorstand*) of the JKG in Brno in June 1939.[71] In other words, one of pre-war Jewish Brno's main people in authority was now operating out of the Jewish hospital. So, it was also no accident that the future head of the board of the JKG in Brno, the lawyer Rudolf Hirsch (1895–1944?), personally reported Siegfried Ascher's death to his family in Terezín in December 1942.[72] Hirsch's postcard was addressed to the young Brno

[68] For the general exemption of the sick from deportation, see Krejčová, Svobodová & Hyndráková 1997, 171.

[69] For the same procedure being applied in Terezín, see also Hájková 2020, 160–161, 222.

[70] The first (?) two deaths were recorded on February 2, 1942; the last recorded death was dated June 8, 1943, the month before the remaining patients were deported. The 1941 Brno Jewish registers (Židovské matriky, Judische Matriken) are missing, making it impossible to determine more precisely when in 1941 the hospital started functioning. During an eighteen-month period, approximately thirty people died in the hospital. Many died in March and April 1942 especially. This may have been tied to the decline of support by family members deported from Brno around that time. See NA, Praha, fonds n° 167, Jewish registers (Židovské matriky, Judische Matriken), inv. n° 142, Brno, Z, 1942, f. 7 and inv. n° 143, Z, 1942 (prosinec)–1944 (koncentrač. tábory), f. 10. Since the deaths that occurred after December 1942 were added to the Jewish registers (Židovské matriky, Judische Matriken) only after the war, the JKG in Brno seems to have stopped registering deaths in December 1942.

[71] *Hadoar*, Jul. 15, 1939, 3. His exact title was *I. Vorsteher-Stellvertreter*. The then head of the board of the JKG was the lawyer Karl Sonnenfeld (1883–1944?). He was deported, with his wife Irma Löwenthal (1897–1946) and one of his two daughters, Lotte Ranon (1924–2007), from Brno to Terezín on transport "U" on January 28, 1942. On October 16, 1944, he was further transferred on transport "Er" to Auschwitz-Birkenau. His wife and daughter were liberated from Terezín. The fate of the second daughter, Ruth Sadeh (1925–?), is less clear. Presumably, she emigrated to Palestine in 1939. See https://encyklopedie.brna.cz/home-mmb/?acc=profil_osobnosti&load=29439 (accessed Mar. 31, 2021). The Židovská obec Brno (Jewish community in Brno) used pictures taken from her private archive on one of its webpages. See https://www.zob.cz/almanach-zidovskeho-gymnazia/prehled-rocniku/ (accessed Mar. 31, 2021).

[72] For Rudolf Hirsch mentioned as the *Leiter* (leader) of the *Aussenstelle Brünn* (Brno branch) in a docu-

lawyer Paul Fertig (1908–1994). He completed his internship in Siegfried Ascher's law practice in 1936.[73] Fertig was deported on transport "Ai", along with Nelly Stern.[74]

Elise Brecher's admission to the hospital as well was likely also connected to her status. We have already mentioned that, on her mother's side, she descended from the Gomperz, a notable Jewish family; and, as we will see, her uncle Heinrich Gomperz stipulated in his will that his house should become the property of the Jewish community in Brno after the death of his wife Julia. Elise Brecher's husband, Alois Brecher, who died in 1912, may also have contributed to her privileged status. A year after Alois Brecher's death, in 1913, a library in Brecher's honor was inaugurated, the Alois Brecher Library Foundation (Alois Brecher-Bibliothek-Stiftung). Brecher was also the president of the local Moravian B'nai B'rith lodge, founded in 1896.[75] The least that we can say is that the Brecher family was not in any way anti-Jewish. In 1905, the L. & A. Brecher bookstore published a portrait of the recently deceased rabbi Salomon Breier (1861–1904).[76] It also published a 1902 pamphlet on a Jewish subject by the Pohrlitz (Pohořelice) pedagogue Emanuel Bondi (1819–1908). Emanuel Bondi was the father of Gustav Bondi, Willi Bondi's father.[77]

ment from the JKG in Prague, which indicated that the names on its list were allowed to travel freely, see https://ca.jewishmuseum.cz/media/zmarch/images/3/7/9/8/59635_ca_object_representations_media_379815_large.jpg (accessed May 15, 2016). That Rudolf Hirsch was an important man in the Jewish community in Brno is further attested by the fact that he was deported from Brno on the very last (and the smallest) Jewish transport "Dg", which left Brno on July 1, 1943. His wife Gertruda Kupfelmacher or Knöpfelmacher (1904–?) survived being transported to Terezín and Auschwitz-Birkenau and was liberated from Kurzbach (Germany). It is likely (but thus far unverified) that Ruth Hirschová (1926–?) was their daughter and that she survived the war, like her mother. She was also liberated from Kurzbach. Significantly or not, Hirsch was number 2 on the "Dg" transportation list, followed by his wife and daughter (numbers 3 and 4, respectively). Otto Steiner (1893–1944) was number 1.

[73] *Seznam advokátů dle stavu koncem roku* 1937, 46. It remains unclear why Hirsch's message regarding the death of Siegfried Ascher was not sent to any of the Aschers in Terezín, given that the May 1942 postcard about Siegfried Ascher's hospitalization was sent directly to Albert Ascher, Siegfried Ascher's brother. Paul Fertig survived the war. I was in email contact with his son Jan Fertig in June 2015 and January 2016, but he had no relevant archival sources able to give us further clues. See email (dated Jun. 9, 2015) from Jan Fertig to the author. Jan Fertig did tell me about a good friend of his father's, also an intern in Siegfried Ascher's law office, Hans (Hanuš) Zvi Weigl (1912–2009). In an interview with the Czech newspaper *Dnes* (May 24, 2009), Weigl indeed says that he worked for Siegfried Ascher. See http://brno.idnes.cz/nejstarsi-student-masarykovy-univerzity-zije-v-izraeli-pex-/brno-zpravy.aspx?c=A090523_1195083_brno_krc (accessed Jan. 24, 2016). I thank Jan Fertig for drawing my attention to this interview. Weigl left Czechoslovakia in November 1939. See Weigl 2008/2009, 109. Weigl was a frequent contributor to the periodical *Židovská ročenka*, writing about his experiences in pre-war Brno. He was also a very important figure in matters related to Czech refugees fleeing to Israel. See Bondy 2003, 187. In 2010, Weigl was posthumously awarded a commemorative medal by the Czech state. See http://www.mzv.cz/telaviv/cz/kultura_a_skolstvi/archiv_akci/predseda_senatu_parlamentu_ceske$1325.html?action=setMonth&year=2016&month=1&day=1 (accessed Jan. 24, 2016). Since there was a chance of some correspondence existing between Hans Weigl and Siegfried Ascher, I tried to get into contact, in January 2016, with the son and daughter of Hans Weigl, H. Z. (Rafi) Weigl and Dina Margalit Gross-Weigl, both lawyers in Tel Aviv. Dina Gross-Weigl wrote me an email on January 24, 2016, telling me that she would look. A reminder email was sent out on April 22, 2016, but, regrettably, no further answer was received.

[74] Židovské muzeum v Praze, Praha, Shoah-related collections, collection Albert Ascher (July 22, 1899), postcard from Dr. Rudolf Hirsch (Brno) to Dr. Paul Fertig (Theresienstadt) (dated Dec. 22, 1942), document identifier COLLECTION.JMP.SHOAH/PERS/OP/036/145. The censor's stamp (dated Dec. 23, 1943), approving the postcard the next day, erroneously gives the year as "1943". Klenovský writes that the JKG in Brno was already dissolved on March 27, 1942 (Klenovský 1995, 16), that is, before the last Jewish mass transport "Ai" on April 8, 1942. However, it is clear that at least some people in Brno continued to represent the JKG after that date, as Rudolf Hirsch's postcard attests, which gives the sender's address as "c/o. Jüdische Kultusgemeinde in Brünn – Glacis 17". It is true that this was no longer the pre-war address of the JKG – at 45 Koliště/Glacis – where the New Synagogue was built in the garden, nor the JKG's later address, during the occupation, at 31 Legionärenstrasse (třída Legionářů). For more on the latter building, initially owned by the B'nai B'rith lodge, see Klenovský 1995, 29, 31, 39. Pavel Fertig was yet another Jewish lawyer from Brno whose practice was liquidated in 1939. See *Věstník Moravské advokátní komory v Brně*, year 2, n° 2 (April

FRITZ BRECHER

That Elise Brecher's family was indeed privileged and protected is further suggested by the fact that her unmarried youngest son, Fritz Brecher, was deported on the very last mass transport "Ai", which left Brno on April 8, 1942.[78] Even Fritz Brecher's last Brno address reveals that attempts were made to bring him close to the top layer of the city's Jewish elite, perhaps in the hope of saving him from deportation or at least postponing it as much as possible. Starting in November 1940, until his deportation in April 1942, Brecher lived with (or rented a room from) Julius Zwicker (1865–1947) at 74 Cejl (Zeile) in Brno.[79] Julius Zwicker was married to Rosa Stiassny (1878–1951).[80] The house at 74 Cejl (Zeile) was located next to the textile factory at 76–80 Cejl (Zeile), which Julius Zwicker co-owned with Paul Himmelreich (1899–*ca.*

1939): 2. Pavel Fertig's brother, Bedřich Fertig (1905–1991), was also a lawyer. For additional genealogical information on Pavel Fertig, see http://www.geni.com/people/Pavel-Fertig/6000000025551272943 (accessed May 15, 2015).

[75] *Jüdische Volksstimme*, Nov. 14, 1912, 5. See also n° 1 in the addenda.

[76] Breier is buried in the Jewish cemetery in Eisenstadt (Austria). See Blum 1905. On Breier, https://www.ojm.at/blog/2017/09/26/breier-samuel-13-dezember-1904/ (accessed Nov. 14, 2020). The booklet was reissued in 1907. See the online catalogue of the Österreichische Nationalbibliothek.

[77] Von Glasenapp & Horch 2005, II: 836. This also makes it apparent that the Brecher and Bondi families knew each other.

[78] A possible counterargument is that Elise Brecher's daughter, Anna Bermann, had already been transported on the fifth Jewish mass transport from Brno, transport "Ad", which left Brno on March 23, 1942.

[79] See the signature of Julius Zwicker on Fritz Brecher's resident registration card in the AMB, Brno, fonds Z 1. There are only a few resident registration cards for Fritz Brecher in the AMB, Brno, but one clearly indicates that his very last address in Brno was 74 Cejl (Zeile), moving there on November 13, 1940, and where he lived until he was deported on April 8, 1942. See also the index card for Fritz Brecher in NA, Praha, fonds n° 1077, Okupační vězeňské spisy, card index (kartotéka) of those deported from the Protectorate to Terezín. In 1934, the house where Fritz Brecher lived was owned by three sisters: Eugenie Preutz, Elsa Schwarz and Marie Porges. See *Adreßbuch von Groß-Brünn* 1934, 741. Their father was Karl Anton Löw (1849–1930), a wool industrialist who had nine children. Himmelreich & Zwicker, the textile factory, was founded in the nineteenth century by Karl Anton Löw's father, Adolf Anton (Aron) Löw (1824–1883). There seem to be no direct or indirect family ties between the Löws and Julius Zwicker. Zwicker and Himmelreich acquired the factory in 1900 in a bankruptcy auction. See Ryšková & Mertová 2014, 76. For more information on Adolf Anton (Aron) Löw, see http://encyklopedie.brna.cz/home-mmb/?acc=profil_osobnosti&load=22110 (accessed Jun. 15, 2017). When looking at the three Löw sisters, who owned the house at 74 Cejl (Zeile), I was not able to discover any family tie to Elise Brecher whose maiden name was also Löw. It seems a little strange that the factory, but not the house at 74 Cejl (Zeile), was sold in 1900. The buildings from 76 to 82 Cejl (Zeile) were in fact owned by the Himmelreich & Zwicker factory. See *Adreßbuch von Groß-Brünn* 1934, 741–42. Of course, this still does not preclude Julius Zwicker buying 74 Cejl (Zeile) between 1934 and 1939. Presumably, Julius Zwicker either rented a flat in the house from the three sisters or lived there for free. However, a direct relative wrote me that Julius Zwicker could reach the factory via a stairway leading from 74 Cejl (Zeile) and that he strongly believes the house was part of the factory. See email (dated Jun. 13, 2017) from Harry R. Kirsch to the author. Many houses in this street were Jewish-owned before the war. One of the Löw sisters, Marie Porges (1896–?), emigrated to the USA in October 1938 with her husband, Dr. Otto Porges (1879–1967), and her two children, Franziska (1919-2006) and Karl (1920–2007). See National Archives, Washington, D.C., Records of the Immigration and Naturalization Service, Passenger and crew lists of vessels arriving at New York, 1897–1957, microfilm T715, NAI 300346, roll 6241, microfilm 57, list or manifest of alien passengers, 29. Retrieved from Ancestry.com database on December 29, 2016, New York, Passenger Lists, 1820–1957. Otto Porges was a famous doctor and settled down in Chicago with his family. See also the current Porges family website, http://www.porges.net/FamilyTreesBiographies/OttoPorges1879-1967.html (accessed Dec. 30, 2016). Eugenie (Jenny) Löw (1874–?) married Josef Preutz(e?) (1859–?) in Aachen but her further fate is unknown. See http://encyklopedie.brna.cz/home-mmb/?acc=profil_osobnosti&load=22324 (accessed Dec. 29, 2016). Else (Elsa) Löw (1879–?) married Gustav Schwarz (1866–?), but the couple's further fate is also unknown. See http://encyklopedie.brna.cz/home-mmb/?acc=profil_osobnosti&load=22357 (accessed Dec. 29, 2016).

[80] One of the couple's two daughters, Suzanne (Susi) M. Kirsch (1911–2004), married the non-Jewish Richard A. Kirsch (1898–1995). The couple survived the war, half-hiding in the Slovak part of the country, emigrating to the USA afterwards. Harry R. Kirsch (1931–), their son, married Chrysanthe Frangos and the couple had two children, Gregory and Charles. On June 7, 2017, I sent a letter to Harry R. Kirsch, the grandson of Julius Zwicker, asking whether he had any information about Fritz Brecher's stay in

1970).[81] Himmelreich was married to Julius Zwicker's eldest daughter, Marie Zwicker (1900–1985).[82] The factory employed 500 workers, ceased operation in 1940, was liquidated in 1942, and was partly destroyed in wartime bombing.[83] Julius Zwicker and his wife Rosa Stiassny were deported from Brno to Terezín on transport "Ae" on March 27, 1942, approximately one week before Fritz Brecher's deportation. Rather surprisingly, despite their advanced age, the Zwicker couple were liberated from Terezín. Julius Zwicker was eighty years old at the time. The most likely explanation for his surviving Terezín at such a great age is his prestige. Zwicker was a very important Jewish man in pre-war Brno. Besides co-owning Himmelreich & Zwicker, he was also active in city politics and had a seat on the boards of several companies. Zwicker was also the president of the JKG in Brno from 1929 to 1938.[84] His pre-war prestige most likely gave him and his wife a protected status in Terezín.[85] Zwicker's high social standing supports the idea that Fritz Brecher being his tenant at 74 Cejl (Zeile) indicates Brecher's own privileged status.

Fritz Brecher's previous address is itself interesting. Until November 1940, Brecher lived at 16a Kampelíkova (Kampelíkgasse) in the posh Masaryk-Viertel neighborhood.[86] A senior police counselor (*Oberpolizeirat*), Bohumil Hromádka (1895–1942), lived at the same address.[87] The man was not unimportant: "Oberpolizeirat Bohumil Hromádka, who opposed JUDr. [Karl] Schwabe on March 15, 1939, when the latter wanted to take over the Brno police directorate, was already imprisoned on May 10, 1939. After his release, Hromádka joined the resistance (Obrana Národa). On November 8, 1941, he was arrested for a second time".[88] He was imprisoned in the

his grandfather's flat, but he did not know anything about it. He did confirm that "the Zwickers were forced to share their spacious apartment with other members of the Brno Jewish community. In fact, a distraught Jewish couple committed suicide in one of their bedrooms". See email (dated Jun. 13, 2017) from Harry R. Kirsch to the author. I was in further email contact with Mr. Kirsch in June 2017.

[81] Ryšková & Mertová 2014, 76–77, 237, 270, 277.

[82] See http://encyklopedie.brna.cz/home-mmb/?acc=profil_osobnosti&load=20915 (accessed Jun. 13, 2017). The couple divorced in 1938. In 1940, Paul Himmelreich joined the Czechoslovak army in London. Both survived the war.

[83] Ryšková & Mertová 2014, 171.

[84] Klenovský 2002, 20.

[85] Surprisingly, Julius Zwicker applied for Deutsche Volkszugehörigkeit (German ethnic) status, which was actually, inexplicably approved. See the home certificate for Zwicker in AMB, Brno, fonds B 1/39. The approval recorded on the home certificate was possibly simply a mistake. There is no index card specifically for Julius Zwicker in AMB, Brno, fonds A 1/53, Německý národností katastr (Deutsche Volkszugehörigkeit).

[86] AMB, Brno, fonds Z 1, resident registration card Fritz Brecher and AMB, Brno, fonds B 1/39, home certificate Fritz Brecher. Kampelíkgasse became Dr. Schindler-Gasse (ulice Dra. Schindlera) during the war. See *Adressbuch der Landeshauptstadt Brünn 1942* 1943, 116. In 1934, the house where Fritz Brecher lived was owned by Edmund Spitz (1873–1942?) and Josefine Spitz (1883–1942?). See the record of house number 16a in *Adreßbuch von Groß-Brünn* 1934, 456, 760. The couple was deported on March 31, 1942, from Brno to Terezín on transport "Af", and then transferred from Terezín to Auschwitz-Birkenau on transport "By" on October 26, 1942. Before 1934, Fritz Brecher lived at 40 Dr-Bedřich-Macků-Gasse (Dra Bedřicha Macků), but must have moved to 8 Stojangasse (Stojanova) in 1934. See *Adressbuch von groß-Brünn* 1934, 145, 240. Around July–September 1939, his address was 36 Lehmstätte (Hlinky), where he lived with his sister Anna Bermann and her husband Wilhelm Bermann. See NA, Praha, fonds n° 375, Arizační spisy, kart. n° 191, sign. 1119, file L. & A. Brecher. Lehmstätte (Hlinky) is where the Starobrno brewery is located and where Karl Fein also passed his childhood years. The house in which Fritz Brecher lived with his sister was owned by the Melichar family. See *Adreßbuch von Groß-Brünn* 1934, 822.

[87] "PolRat" [Polizeirat] (Police councillor) appears next to his name in *Adressbuch der Landeshauptstadt Brünn* 1943, 101.

[88] Filip, Břečka & Schildberger 2012, 193: "Oberpolizeirat Bohumil Hromádka, der sich am 15. März 1939 JUDr. [Karl] Schwabe entgegen stellte, als dieser die Brünner Polizeidirektion übernehmen wollte, kam bereits am 10. Mai 1939 in Haft. Nach seiner Entlassung schloss sich Hromádka dem Widerstand an (Obrana Národa). Am 8. November 1941 wurde er zum zweiten Mal festgenommen".

[89] Hromádka's name is mentioned in the Mauthausen victims' database. See https://raumdernamen.mauthausen-memorial.org/ (accessed Mar. 28, 2021). See also Filip, Břečka & Schildberger 2012, 53; MZA, Brno, fonds B 340, Gestapo Brno, file Bohumil Hromádka, n° 2986, sign. 100-326-26. A commemo-

Kaunitz College (Kounicovy koleje). After sentencing by a summary court martial (*Standgericht*), in December 1941, he was sent to Mauthausen where he was beaten to death in the quarry in April 1942.[89] This could mean that Fritz Brecher was in contact with the highest-ranking police official in Brno. If so, Brecher (and the rest of the Jewish community in Brno) would have had discreet access to very valuable inside information about the activities of the German invaders.

SPECIAL STATUS JEWISH HOSPITAL

The Jewish hospital in Brno was a unique place, and not just because its patients were exempt from deportation. What went through the minds of people looking at the inexorably sinking Titanic from the temporary safety of a life boat? Siegfried Ascher arrived at the Jewish hospital on March 26, 1942, only a few days after his wife, son and mother were deported from Brno on transport "Ad".[90] By the time Siegfried Ascher arrived at the Jewish hospital, half of the Jewish population of Brno had already been deported on five mass transports, each carrying exactly one thousand people. Elise Brecher's eldest child, Anna Bermann (1893–1944) and her immediate family were also summoned to transport "Ad". The shared trauma of their families being deported on the same transport could account for Elise Brecher and Siegfried Ascher speaking to and quickly bonding with each other in the Jewish hospital. It is also possible, of course, that they had known each other before the war since both belonged to the Jewish elite. (Alois Brecher, Elise Brecher's deceased husband, was the president of Moravia, the local Brno chapter of the B'nai B'rith lodge.) At the same time, the hospital was so small and the patients so few that they would certainly have met and spoken.

As time went on, and the Jewish community diminished more and more due to the ongoing mass transports that were becoming increasingly frequent, in March and April 1942, the hospital likely also functioned as a sort of repository for the latest news of Jewish Brno and for information about the Germans' future plans for the remaining Jewish people. This information and their great fear about their own possibly imminent deportation were likely the first and main concern of the patients in the Jewish hospital. Due to the hospital's small size, rumors and the latest news likely circulated intensely among the patients. It is also easy to imagine – with the mass deportations still occurring in the first half of 1942 – that some or even most of that information was warped by irrational fears and even paranoia. Rational and practical assessment of incoming news was likely rather rare. Even in terms of facts, the news in the hospital concerned a pool of people becoming smaller by the day. When the mass deportations came to an end, at the end of May 1942, the patients likely had a fairly good idea of who in Jewish Brno was still left. The patients in the Jewish hospital were themselves part of the approximately thirty Jewish people left in Brno after the departure of the penultimate transport "AAa", at the end of May 1942. As a consequence, once the deportations came to an end, most of the information about Brno's remaining Jewish community likely mainly circulated in the hospital.

rative stone for Hromádka can be found in the central cemetery in Brno.

[90] See the above-mentioned postcard (dated Mar. 26, 1942), which says that Ascher was "heute überführt" (transferred today) to the Jewish hospital. See Židovské muzeum v Praze, Praha, Shoah-related collections, personal and family related materials and papers, osobní pozůstalosti, Albert Ascher (Jul. 22, 1899), postcard (dated Mar. 26, 1942) from Pikesler to Albert Ascher, collection identifier COLLECTION.JMP.SHOAH/PERS/OP/036. The back of a resident registration card for Siegfried Ascher in the AMB, Brno, fonds Z 1, on the other hand, gives "27/IV/1942" as the date of his arrival in the Jewish hospital. This was likely the day that his arrival was registered at the police office, although it gives the month as April instead of March. The latter mistake can possibly be explained by the fact, judging by the handwriting and the red ink used, the information was not added until January 1943, shortly after Siegfried Ascher's death in December 1942.

Since Siegfried Ascher, who was second in charge of the JKG in Brno before the war, was a patient at the hospital until December 1942, it is even conceivable that some important decisions were made there.

If a decision about what to do with the Institute materials that once belonged to a Jewish sexologist was made at the Jewish hospital in Brno, then it seems likely that Karl Fein's aunt Elise Brecher introduced the topic. Karl Fein's being a fellow lawyer may have been the first element to spark Siegfried Ascher's interest in the case of Fein's belongings. Karl Fein might in fact have known Ascher since both were students at the same German-language gymnasium in Brno, although Siegfried Ascher, being a year younger, was in the year below Karl Fein.[91] Since Jewish lawyers had been banned in March 1939, it is possible that former competitors now felt a deep solidarity. The fact that Siegfried Ascher's brother, Albert Ascher, his junior by four years, had a relationship with Anna Kahn, a niece of Karl Fein (whom he later married in Terezín), may have also created a bond between Siegfried Ascher and Elise Brecher.[92]

All this makes it more conceivable that Stanislav Kaděrka may have overheard talk about the Institute materials being discarded, either as one of the many news items circulating in the Jewish hospital or as a decision actually taken there. That Kaděrka presumably did not visit the hospital every day could perhaps explain why he went to look only for the *remaining* Institute materials. By the time he heard about them, the bulk of the materials was already irrevocably lost. This could be yet another explanation for why only a few items were saved from the Růžičkas' company.

One could argue, of course, that Siegfried Ascher's being Stanislav Kaděrka's patient was simply a coincidence; that Kaděrka never got the information about the Institute materials in the Jewish hospital; and, consequently, that the Institute items were saved only by sheer chance. This remains a real possibility. However, let us also have a look at numbers and probability. In 1937, Brno was the second-largest city in Czechoslovakia (as in current Czechia) with approximately 300,000 inhabitants.[93] The city's cultural elite clearly socialized and married mainly among themselves, and this was even more true of the small Jewish community (approximately 12,000 people in 1938).[94] Karl Fein was a member of this Jewish cultural elite. The fact that Stanislav Kaděrka's name appears on the postcard presented at the beginning of this chapter and in the Hirschfeld guestbook affidavit – and not one belonging to another of the hundreds of thousands in greater Brno – bears, to my mind, great explanatory weight. That Kaděrka did not belong to the mostly German-speaking Jewish elite of the city but was a Czech-speaking Roman Catholic makes him quite conspicuous, showing up where he would not normally belong. Not insignificantly, Kaděrka was not anti-Jewish, apparently helping Jewish people a few times during the war.[95] His willingness to take risks during the war is possibly attested by his being arrested at least once by the Gestapo in 1942.[96]

[91] *Jahresbericht des Staatsgymnasiums mit deutscher Unterrichtssprache in Brünn für das Schuljahr* 1911–1912, 61. Fritz Tugendhat, the later builder of the famous Villa Tugendhat, was enrolled in the same year as Siegfried Ascher.

[92] For the marriage of Albert Ascher and Anna Kahn in Terezín, see Albert Ascher's home certificate in AMB, Brno, fonds B 1/39 and NA, Praha, Jewish registers (Židovské matriky, Judische Matriken), Terezín, category O [marriages], 1942–1943, inv. n° 2120, entry n° 1, f. 1; available online at http://www.badatelna.eu/fond/1073/reprodukce/?zaznamId=2792&reproId=73957 (accessed Apr. 5, 2021).

[93] In 1937, Greater Brno included more than 300,000 residents, half of whom lived in the inner city. See *Prager Tagblatt*, Mar. 19, 1938, 6.

[94] Alicke 2008, 699.

[95] I owe this information to Milena Baumgarten, who in turn heard it from her brother. He was aware that the Gestapo interrogated Kaděrka and his wife a few times "weil sie Juden geholfen haben" (since they helped Jewish people). See email (dated May 11, 2015) from Milena Baumgarten to the author. Kaděrka is mentioned in a December 1944 case, naming Kaděrka as one of the people who helped the attempt of a certain Jan Kotinský (1909–?) to escape forced labor. Kaděrka likely wrote a false

ROBERT POLLAK AND JAROSLAV RŮŽIČKA

We have suggested that Kaděrka may have visited the Jewish hospital a few times to see how his patient Siegfried Ascher was doing, and that this might explain why the Hirschfeld guestbook and some of the Institute sexology books ultimately ended up in his hands. Late in my research, to my utter astonishment, I found out that another person, someone we have already encountered, could also be linked to the Jewish hospital. This discovery seemed considerably to undermine my initial hypothesis of the Kamarád members' basic involvement in discarding the Institute materials. Let us turn to the prehistory of the Jewish hospital.

Before it started operation as a Jewish hospital, at the end of 1941, the building at the corner of 27 Mühlgasse (Mlýnská) and 5 Stephansgasse (Štěpánská) was privately owned by the Jewish woman Josefine Rosenbaum (1860–1942) [ill. 4] [ill. 5].[97] She inherited the building from her husband, Josef Pollak (1853–1923), who died in 1923. Josef Pollak owned a wholesale scrap iron business (*Großhändler*) located on the site behind the corner house where Pollak lived with his immediate family on the first floor.[98] The offices of the company were located on the ground floor, part of which was also rented out to another company dealing in enamel utensils.[99]

sick note stating that Kotinský's health did not allow him to do forced labor. The case is mentioned in Štěpánek 2004, 104 n. 232. Štěpánek refers to MZA, fonds G 432, Svaz národní revoluce – zemská odbocka Brno (1945–1948), kart. n° 9, sign. 1002, testimony file of Jan Kotínský (dated January 1946), n. 349; however, Štěpánek erroneously refers to kart. n° 6 (instead of kart. n° 9).

[96] There is a list showing people's names, along with sums of money transferred to the Vermögensamt beim Reichsprotektor in Böhmen und Mähren (Property Office of the Reich Protector in Bohemia and Moravia) in 1942 and 1943. Most likely, this was money confiscated when the people named on the list were arrested by the Gestapo. The seemingly random, quite various, and sometimes very small sums next to the names suggest that they were indeed taken from people when they were arrested on the spot. Dr. Kaděrka's name figures in this list next to the sum of 448 German marks. This sum was registered at the Property Office on October 15, 1942. See NA, Praha, fonds n° 114, Úřad říšského protektora v Čechách a na Moravě, Praha, seznam osob na jejichž jména bylo v pokladně majetkového úřadu v Praze založeno konto, prčemž je jako vkladatel uvedeno gestapo a to velitelství v Praze, Brně a Kladně. Tato kon byla založena v roce 1942 a každým rokem se převáděla, kart. n° 191, sign. 114-193-3, f. 9. The money was most likely in Czech crowns but the value was converted to German marks. Kaděrka's arrest must have occurred before October 1942, the date of Kaděrka's entry on the list. However, the registration dates of these confiscated sums do not seem to correspond in any way to the date of a person's arrest. For example, the registration date of the money taken from Alice Feinová (1920–1942) is clearly not linked to her death. The sum was sent to the Property Office on September 19, 1942, more than three months after her execution. See NA, Praha, fonds n° 114, Úřad říšského protektora v Čechách a na Moravě, Praha, kart. n° 191, sign. 114-193-3, f. 5. For a confirmation of her execution date, see NA, Praha, Jewish registers (Židovské matriky, Judische Matriken), inv. n° 142, Brno, Z, 1942, f. 25. Cf. http://encyklopedie.brna.cz/home-mmb/?acc=profil_osobnosti&load=4488 (accessed May 18, 2016), which gives precedence to the registration date of her death (June 5, 1942) over the actual death date (June 4, 1942). Alice Feinová was not related to Karl Fein. I checked one more name and found the same discrepancy in dates. The modest sum of 7.80 Czech crowns, belonging to Wilma Feuermann (1883–1942?), taken away from her when she was arrested by the Brno Gestapo, was sent to the Property Office on September 16, 1942. However, she was deported from Olomouc (Olmütz) to Terezín on transport "Aaf" on June 26, 1942. I found the reference to this not unimportant list of sums in the ABS, Praha, in a May 1957 archival document about it needing to be proven that Kaděrka did *not* collaborate with the Gestapo during the war. See ABS, Praha, fonds SÚMV, Mapy zpráv zpracované Studijním ústavem MV, sign. Z-10-217, f. 6. Around 1957, Kaděrka found himself entangled in a purification process, known as "lustration" (also vetting) in former Communist countries. Referring to the list of sums, the 1957 document concluded that Kaděrka had not collaborated with the Gestapo during the war since they had arrested him.

[97] *Adressbuch von Brünn* 1901, 511; *Adreßbuch von Groß-Brünn* 1934, 805.

[98] In 1900, Josef Pollak was living with his wife and four children at 3 Stephansgasse (Štěpánská), a house he owned. See census of 1900, http://digiarchiv.brno.cz/home (accessed Aug. 13, 2019); *Adressbuch von Brünn* 1901, 536. The numbering of the house was later changed from 3 to 3b and the latter corresponds to the current house. Josef Pollak also owned a house at 14 Mühlgasse (Mlynska).

[99] From 1921 until at least 1932, part of the ground floor was rented out to a certain Ferdinand Christek (?–?), who manufactured or dealt in kitchen utensils and enamel products. See *Adreßbuch von Groß-Brünn* 1921, 774; *Adreßbuch von Groß-Brünn* 1932,

Josef Pollak's company, named "Scrap Iron Trading Association" (Společnost pro obchod starým železem), was founded in June 1919. After Pollak's death, his widow Josefine continued the business with her two sons, Robert Pollak (1895–1942?) and Hugo Pollak (1885–1941).[100] Josef and Josefine Pollak also had two daughters. Cornelia Pollak (1889–1919) married the physician Hugo Deutsch (1874–1944) in 1910. The couple had two children, Alice (1911–1944?) whose married name was Jónász, and a son who never married, the student Jan (Hans) Deutsch (1917–1942).[101] When Cornelia Pollak died in 1919, Hugo Deutsch married Josef Pollak's other daughter, Rosa Pollak (1893–1926), in 1920. The couple had one daughter, Kornelie Deutsch (1921–?). Rosa Pollak died six years later, in 1926.[102] (Kornelie Deutsch will be briefly mentioned again in our story, when the war is over.)

The wholesale scrap iron company was of a considerable size. During its Aryanization in 1940, one of the trustees claimed that the Protectorate contained only seven companies of this size, three of them in Moravia.[103] The company was bought by Leopold Spielvogel (1891–?) in January 1941.[104] In March 1941, the house was sold to the Emigration Fund for Bohemia and Moravia (Auswanderungsfonds für Böhmen und Mähren). The terms of the sale included the stipulation that Spielvogel could continue to use the ground floor offices.[105] In June 1941, Robert Pollak, his wife and his mother moved out of the building.[106] Later that year, the Jewish hospital was set up on the building's first floor; Leopold Spielvogel's company offices were still on the ground floor.

On December 11, 1927, Robert Pollak married Anděla Švecová (1898–1981) in Brno's old Jewish synagogue. They divorced on May 26, 1941, as the surviving wife claimed

576. Cf. MZA, Brno, fonds C 152, Okresní soud civilní Brno, inheritance file Josef Pollak, sign. A VII 85/23, not foliated. On November 1, 2019, I sent letters to the two people with the family name Christek in an online German phonebook, but there was no reply.

[100] *Brněnské noviny, Amtsblatt zur Brünner Zeitung*, n° 156, Jul. 11, 1919, 1. For mention of Handel mit altem Eisem und Emballagegenständen, see also *Adreßbuch von Groß-Brünn* 1922, 523; *Adreßbuch von Groß-Brünn* 1927, 464; *Adreßbuch von Groß-Brünn* 1932, 637; *Adresář Protektorátu Čechy a Morava pro průmysl, živnosti, obchod a zemědělství = Adressbuch des Protektorates Böhmen und Mähren für Industrie, Gewerbe, Handel und Landwirtschaft* 1939, II: 1411.

[101] Alice Deutsch married the Slovak doctor Josef Jónász (also spelled "Jónás", 1900–1945) on March 27, 1932 in Brno. The couple was deported from Brno to Terezín on transport "Ad" on March 23, 1942, and further transferred to Auschwitz-Birkenau on transport "Es" on October 19, 1944. Josef was liberated from Dachau at the end of April 1945, but died a few days later, on May 3, 1945. According to a resident registration card in the AMB, Brno, fonds Z 1, Jan (Hans) Deutsch (1917–1942) died on the last day of May 1942, a curious date because the last sizable Jewish mass transport, "AAa", left Brno on May 27, 1942. His name could not be found in the 1942 list of Brno dead in the Jewish registers (Židovské matriky, Judische Matriken) in NA, Praha, fonds n° 167. Consequently, for now, his exact fate remains unclear. He may have been imprisoned and executed soon after the Jewish mass transports leaving Brno ended. I found approximately fourteen other Jewish people imprisoned and executed in Brno in June. Such was the case with the already mentioned Alice Feinová, who was executed on June 4, 1942. Jan Deutsch's name does not appear in the archival fonds of the Brno Gestapo in the MZA, Brno, fonds B 340.

[102] Both wives of Hugo Deutsch and their father Josef Pollak are buried in the Jewish cemetery in Brno in plot 25B, row 1, graves 9–10. I did not actively pursue the further fates of Hugo Deutsch's seven siblings. See https://www.geni.com/people/Hugo-Deutsch/6000000083760490180 (accessed Jul. 26, 2021). Most perished in the Holocaust.

[103] NA, Praha, fonds n° 375, Arizační spisy, company Josef Pollak (obchod starým železem a kovy), kart. n° 249, file n° 1706, kurzer Bericht betreffend die Firma Josef Pollak, Brünn, message trustee (Treuhänder) Eduard Kaiser (dated 1940), not foliated. Two *Treuhänders* (trustees) were appointed to sell the business and property: Josef Jahn (1913–?), appointed on December 4, 1940; and Edmund Kaiser (1876–?), who started on January 10, 1941.

[104] NA, Praha, fonds n° 375, Arizační spisy, company Josef Pollak (obchod starým železem a kovy), kart. n° 249, file n° 1706. Spielvogel is recorded as a scrap metal wholesale business (*Schrottgroßhandel, velkoobchod železným*) in *Adressbuch der Landeshauptstadt Brünn* 1942, 293.

[105] The exact date of sale was March 3, 1941, or March 13, 1941. See Katastrální úřad pro Jihomoravský kraj, katastrální pracoviště Brno-město, Katastralgemeinde Kröna / Křenová, Grundbuchseinlage n° 86, Mühlgasse / Mlýnská n° 27 and Stefansgasse / Štěpánská n° 5, conscription n° 93. In 1941, the plots were transferred (and renumbered) to the Katastral-

after the war, because the Gestapo forced them to [ill. 6].[107] In what was most likely an attempt to escape future persecution, the Pollak couple also had a Catholic marriage ceremony on April 30, 1939, six weeks after the installation of the Protectorate. Robert Pollak was deported on transport "Ah" on April 4, 1942, from Brno to Terezín and further transferred to Rejowiec on transport "Ap" on April 18, 1942.[108] Robert Pollak's brother, Hugo Pollak, was sentenced by the first court martial on October 1, 1941, his property was expropriated, and he died in Mauthausen on October 24, 1941.[109] Hugo Pollak's second wife, Solči Musafija (1897–1942?), was deported on transport "Ad" from Brno to Terezín on March 23, 1942, and further transferred to Lublin on transport "Az" on May 25, 1942.[110] Like his brother Robert, Hugo Pollak had no children. Hugo Deutsch, the surviving husband of the two Pollak daughters, was deported on transport "Ah" on April 4, 1942, and died in Terezín on November 19, 1944.[111] Of his three children, only Kornelie Deutsch survived the war, taking residence in Kenya.[112] The widow Josefine Pollak (née Rosenbaum) was deported on March 23, 1942, on transport "Ad" from Brno to Terezín, where she died three months later, on June 30, 1942.[113]

To my great astonishment, I noticed one day that Robert Pollak was one of the witnesses to the marriage of Jaroslav Růžička and Jindra Fikesová, in December 1939 [ill. 7].[114] This meant that a significant bond between Robert Pollak and Jaroslav Růžička must have existed. This fact also sheds new light on the marriage of Jaroslav

gemeinde Dornrössel / Trnitá, Grundbuchseinlage n° 651, Mühlgasse / Mlýnská n° 27 and Stefansgasse / Štěpánská n° 5, conscription n° 319.

106 On June 5 or 11, 1941, Robert Pollak and his wife Anděla Švecová moved to 56 Svatopluka Čecha (Svatopluk-Čech-Gasse) in Královo Pole. Josefina Pollak left the house a few days later, on June 16, 1941. See the resident registration cards for all three in AMB, Brno, fonds Z 1.

107 For the date of their civil marriage (December 11, 1927) and divorce (May 26, 1941), see NA, Praha, Jewish registers (Židovské matriky, Judische Matriken), http://www.badatelna.eu/fond/1073/reprodukce/?zaznamId=173&reproId=150109 (accessed Aug. 15, 2019). I thank Iva Čadková (NA, Praha) for sending me a digital scan of the page, whose digitized online version was obscured by an added note. See her email (dated Aug. 20, 2019) to the author. For the divorce file, see MZA, Brno, fonds C 11, Krajský soud civilní Brno, III. manipulace, kart. n° 610, sign. Ck IIa 209/41, divorce Robert Pollak and Anděla Švecova. A person named Anděla Švecová was prosecuted in 1916 and 1936 for pretending to be a teacher and using false names. See *Lidové noviny*, May 11, 1916, 2; *Brněnské noviny*, May 13, 1916, 3; *Venkov*, Jul. 30, 1936, 10. In 1944, a person also having the same name was convicted of stealing jewelry. See *Lidové noviny*, Mar. 28, 1944, 6. It is, of course, possible that the homonymous person(s?) mentioned here was not Robert Pollak's later wife.

108 See https://www.holocaust.cz/en/database-of-victims/victim/115205-robert-pollak/ (accessed Dec. 6, 2019).

109 MZA, Brno, fonds B 340, Gestapo Brno, file n° 100-291-21; the Mauthausen database, https://www.gedenkstaetten.at/raum-der-namen/cms/index.php?&L=1 (accessed Aug. 13, 2019). Hugo Pollak's last resident registration card in the AMB, Brno, fonds Z 1, also mentions that he died on October 24, 1942, and includes a stamp (dated Nov. 20, 1941) of the Královo Pole police station.

110 Hugo Pollak married Solči Musafija on April 11, 1920. Hugo Pollak's first wife was the engineer Melita Knöpfelmacher (née Kohn, 1892–1942?) whom he had married on March 20, 1910. Hugo Pollak's first and second wife were deported on transport "Ad", on March 23, 1942, from Brno to Terezín. On April 18, 1942, Melita Knöpfelmacherová was further deported on transport "Ap" from Terezín to Rejowiec. She was on the same transport as Robert Pollak. Solči Musafija was further deported on transport "AZ" from Terezín to Lublin on May 25, 1942.

111 See https://encyklopedie.brna.cz/home-mmb/?acc=profil_osobnosti&load=32712 (accessed Aug. 14, 2019).

112 I was not able to trace her current relatives.

113 See the entry for her on http://www.holocaust.cz/databaze-dokumentu/dokument/77196-denni-rozkazy-rady-starsich-c-163-ze-dne-2-7-1942/ (accessed Jul. 23, 2015); and email (dated May 15, 2015) from Alena Mikovcová / Alena Kubešová (Židovská obec Brno, Brno) to the author.

114 For their marriage certificate, see http://actapublica.eu/matriky/brno/prohlizec/10776/?strana=1 (accessed Aug. 13, 2019). The other witness was Alois Bulla (1896–?), a married Catholic *zubní technik* (dental technician) with three children, who lived in Královo Pole. In the late 1920s and early 1930s, Bulla's business was located at 26 and 32 Kreuzgasse (Křížová), but he lived at 32 Weinberggasse (Vinohradská). Curiously, around 1932, he started to spell his last name with only one "l", as "Bula", and this is how he also signed the Růžička/Fikesová marriage certificate in 1939. See *Adreßbuch von Groß-Brünn* 1927, 120, 575; *Adreßbuch von Groß-Brünn* 1934, 150, 675; *Adreßbuch von Groß-Brünn* 1932, 146;

Růžička and Jindra Růžičková. Jindra Růžičková officially founded her scrap company on December 12, 1939, marrying Jaroslav Růžička ten days later. Most likely, the initiation of the company was closely associated to the then-pending reorganization – by the Ministry of Industry and Trade (Ministerstvo průmyslu, obchodu a živností, Ministerium für Industrie, Handel und Gewerbe) – of the trade in scrap through the issuing of new trader permits. All companies needed to apply for a new valid permit. I think that the decision to officially found the Růžičková company and get a trade permit under the new rules was made at Robert Pollak's instigation, and this explains, at least in part, his being a witness to the Růžičkas' wedding. I think it quite likely that Robert Pollak and the Růžička couple struck a deal to help each other. In an attempt to get around the expropriation (Aryanization) of his (Jewish) business, Robert Pollak possibly proposed that the Růžička couple pay him a percentage of their profits "off the books" in exchange for the trade he could procure by sharing his contacts and knowledge of the business.[115] We have seen that the Fleischer-Bondi family also tried (and failed) to put forward Willi Bondi's gay friend, the German soldier Franz Helmuth Holdau, as a prospective owner of the Leopold Fleischer company. We have already briefly mentioned the case of Otto Frank's Amsterdam pectin and spice business, which pursued a similar path to safeguard its company assets. The likely underhand deal between Robert Pollak and the Růžičkas could help explain how a company that began with nothing eventually turned out to be very successful. Indeed, by 1942, the Růžička couple were already able to afford a posh flat in the center of Brno.[116] As we will see later, the Czechoslovak Communist state even prosecuted Jaroslav Růžička for being too successful in his scrap business.

That there existed a real business relationship, and possibly even a close friendship between Robert Pollak and Jaroslav Růžička, is further illustrated by two other incidents. In November 1940, a man named Maresch and another collaborator of the Brno Supreme District Council (Oberlandrat), made an unannounced visit to the Pollak company, where they met Robert Pollak and his brother Hugo Pollak but also two other visitors, one being Jaroslav Růžička. After being briefed and questioned about this unexpected visit, the Pollak company's Sudeten-German trustee (*Treuhänder*), Eduard Kaiser (1876–?), felt compelled to report his view on the incident. In a letter to the Oberlandrat, he stated that Růžička constantly supplied the Pollak company with scrap iron and, until recently, rented a warehouse on the company premises to store rags (*Hadern*). In the same letter, Kaiser added that, because Růžička had a Jewish-looking face and visited the Pollak company often, the Gestapo had received a denunciation by neighbors who had observed disallowed Jewish gatherings on the Pollak company premises.[117] Because Kaiser was summoned by the Gestapo regarding this incident, the trustee then strictly forbade further meetings between the Pollak brothers and Jaroslav Růžička on the premises.[118]

Adressbuch der Landeshauptstadt 1942, 27, 121, under "dental technicians" (*Zahntechniker, zubní technici*). Bulla applied for Deutsche Volkszugehörigkeit (German ethnic) status on August 10, 1939, and this was approved on February 20, 1940. After the war, he was forcibly exiled from the country and fled to Austria. See the handwritten note (and stamp dated April 13, 1950) on the back of one of his resident registration cards in the AMB, Brno, fonds Z 1.

115 In a May 1940 message, the *Treuhänder* (trustee) Eduard Kaiser referred to a December 21, 1939, regulatory decision that companies dealing in scrap had to apply for new trading permits before March 31, 1940, if they wanted to conduct business legally. See NA, Praha, fonds n° 375, Arizační spisy, company Josef Pollak, kart. n° 249, invent. n° 1706, kurzer Bericht betreffend die Firma Josef Pollak, Brünn, not foliated. The regulatory decision was published on January 30, 1940, in *Sammlung der Gesetze und Verordnungen des Protektorats Böhmen und Mähren = Sbírka zákonů a nařízení Protektorátu Čechy a Morava*, year 1940, January 30, 1940, n° 29, Vládní nařízení ze dne 21. prosince 1939 o hospodaření odpadky (Government ordinance of December 21, 1939, on the management of scrap), 12–13

116 *Adressbuch der Landeshauptstadt Brünn* 1942, 258. Jaroslav Růžička and Jindra Růžičková's current relatives have also stressed that the couple's

After the war, in 1946, Anděla Pollak tried to be recognized as the legal heir of the estate of her husband Robert Pollak, who perished in the Holocaust. She claimed at the Brno Regional Civil Court (Krajský soud civilní Brno) that their 1941 divorce was made under duress by the Gestapo and thus was not valid. The two witnesses called upon to corroborate her claim were Oldřich Kukla (1911–?)[119] and Jaroslav Růžička. In the same archival file about the annulment of the divorce, we learn that Jaroslav Růžička was at Robert Pollak's home when the Gestapo visited one day.[120] There are thus several indications that Robert Pollak and Jaroslav Růžička were likely friends or at least close business associates.

Quite unexpectedly, Jaroslav Růžička, one of the seven founding *Kamarád* members, thus shows up here as well. In addition to being a friend or close business associate of Robert Pollak, he often visited the Pollak company since, until at least November 1940, he rented space on its premises for his own company. We have also seen that Robert Pollak, his wife, mother and brother used to live in the building that would become, at the end of 1941, the Jewish hospital. Discovering that Jaroslav Růžička, our central figure, could be tied to Brno's Jewish community through the Pollak family, who owned the building of the future Jewish hospital, forced me to seriously consider a second hypothesis: the minimal suggestion that the decision of what to do with the Institute materials may have been made in the Jewish hospital. Further support for this second scenario is given by the possibility that, when visiting Siegfried Ascher in the Jewish hospital, Dr. Kaděrka may have heard about the discarded Institute materials. If this in fact happened in 1942, then Karl Fein's aunt, Elise Brecher, seems the most obvious candidate when trying to determine who decided to discard the Berlin Institute materials. She could have inquired about how to discard them safely and found Jaroslav Růžička and his wife's company through the former owners of the building housing the Jewish hospital. It is also possible that, once the Pollaks left, Růžička continued to visit their former company premises to trade with Leopold Spielvogel, the new owner of the Aryanized company. Maybe, during these visits, Jaroslav Růžička also came into contact with the patients of the Jewish hospital on the first floor of the corner building.

business clearly prospered, but it was less clear to them if this was true in its early years. See the interview (dated Oct. 10, 2019) with the current relatives of Jindra and Jaroslav Růžička.

117 On October 10, 2019, when viewing pictures of Jaroslav Růžička in the home of his current relatives in Brno, I observed that Růžička had a pronounced nose, but also that one of his eyes was misaligned.

118 NA, Praha, fonds n° 375, Arizační spisy, company Josef Pollak, kart. n° 249, invent. n° 1706, letter (dated Nov. 13, 1940) from Eduard Kaiser to Oberlandrat, not foliated. Although Kaiser writes "Josef Růžička", it is clear that he meant Jaroslav Růžička since he also mentions that Josef (Jaroslav) Růžička was in charge of the company owned by his wife, Jindra Fikes (Růžičková). Eduard Kaiser was born in Hohenelbe (currently Vrchlabí) and was married to Ottilie Effenberger (1873–?). On November 21, 1939, he applied for Deutsche Volkszugehörigkeit (German ethnic) status, which was granted on March 1, 1940. See AMB, Brno, fonds A 1/53. He lived at the posh 12 Winterhollerplatz (Winterhollerovo náměstí) address in Brno.

119 Oldřich Kukla was also a witness when the couple divorced in 1941. He was presumably a trusted (and unmarried) manager or employee of the scrap company who lived in for one year with the Pollak couple during the war. In June 1940, he moved in with the couple, moving out again in June 1941, on the same day the Pollak couple also moved out of their home (after their home and company had been sold the previous month). He was born in the town Soběslav Tábor in South Bohemia. Coming from Prague, he moved to Brno in 1938 (or earlier still). See his resident registration cards in AMB, fonds Z 1. After the war, he tended a shop in men's and women's clothes, see *Adresář zemského hlavního města Brna* 1948, 57.

120 For the date of the annulment of the divorce (May 21, 1946), see NA, Praha, Jewish registers (Židovské matriky, Judische Matriken), http://www.badatelna.eu/fond/1073/reprodukce/?zaznamId=173&reproId=150109 (accessed Aug. 15, 2019). For the postwar file on the annulment of the divorce, see MZA, Brno, fonds C 11, Krajský soud civilní Brno, III. manipulace, annulment divorce Robert Pollak and Anděla Pollak, kart. n° 620, sign. Ck IIa 337/46.

So, we must now consider the possibility that, when he sought a solution for the Institute materials as he was leaving Brno, in the autumn of 1939, Karl Fein may have approached his aunt. Of course, this completely contradicts our initial intuition that Fein likely entrusted the Institute materials to someone who was *not* Jewish, like the members of *Kamarád*. On reflection, however, possessing Jewish materials was not a problem for Jewish people. We have already introduced Elise Brecher, an educated and ethically progressive woman. She possibly played some kind of role in the buy-back operation of the Institute materials saved from the flames in Berlin in the final months of 1933. At the very least, she was most likely aware of the story behind these materials: Magnus Hirschfeld's renown in Germany and abroad, the books and other materials looted from the Institute in Berlin, the book burning on the Opernplatz, the buy-back operation in November 1933. She likely knew what was at stake and also of the scorn with which the Germans viewed their archenemy, Magnus Hirschfeld. We have also suggested that Hirschfeld possibly visited her bookstore when Karl Fein took Hirschfeld on a tour of Brno in 1932.

THE NETWORK OF PEOPLE AROUND THE LAWYERS JOSEF PAVLAK AND WALTER SÜSS

Another factor sheds further light on the rather peculiar position of the Jewish hospital and its possible part in our story. A close look at some of the Jewish hospital patients, the former owners of the building housing the hospital, and some of our main subjects reveals that they all belonged to a single network of people who relied upon each other. Two lawyers in particular seem to have been pivotal figures in this network. The first was Josef Pavlak (also spelled "Pawlak") (1890–?), whose professional life quickly adapted to the Germans' March 1939 takeover of the country and their demands.[121] He became a member of the NSDAP and the National Socialist Association of Legal Professionals (Nationalsozialistische Rechtswahrerbund, NSRB) in April 1939. He and his wife Ella Queck (1903–?) applied for German ethnic (Deutsche Volkszugehörigkeit) status.[122] For starters, in 1939, Pavlak liquidated the law practice of Siegfried Ascher, second in charge of the JKG in Brno and the most important patient staying in the Jewish hospital.[123] That Pavlak was not as anti-Jewish as one would expect can be inferred from the fact that he accepted Walter Mautner (1910–?), a young Jewish man, as an intern in his law office in 1933. Doing so in the

[121] Josef Pavlak has a staff file in the Bundesarchiv, Berlin-Lichterfelde, Reichsjustizministerium, Personalakten P (1877–1945), Pawlak, Josef, geb. 28.9.1890, sign. BArch, R 3001/70434.

[122] Pavlak married Ella Gertrude Queck (1903–?) on September 23, 1922, and divorced her on January 23, 1942. The couple had one daughter named Gertrude (1923–?). See Bundesarchiv, Berlin-Lichterfelde, Reichsjustizministerium, Personalakten, P (1877–1945), Pawlak, Josef, geb. 28.9.1890, sign. BArch, R 3001/70434 and ABS, Praha, SÚMV, fonds n° 134, Německé soudy v Protektorátu Čechy a Morava, Vrchní zemský soud Praha, personální spisy justičních zaměstnanců, Akten über die Dienstverhältnisse, file Josef Pavlak (Pawlak), sign. 134-910-7. For the January 1942 divorce, see MZA, Brno, fonds C 43, Německý zemský soud Brno (Deutsches Landgericht Brünn), kart. n° 146, divorce file Josef and Ella Pavlak. Ella Queck later married Karl Walnohn (1889–?). Curiously, by June 1942, Ella Queck appears in the Rosternitz bei Wischau (Rostěnice-Zvonovice) *Arbeitslager* (labor camp). I could not find this camp in Padevět 2018; nor was I able to determine the location of this camp's archives. Josef Pavlak's name does not appear in a postwar retribution file in MZA, Brno, fonds C 130, Veřejný žalobce u mimořádného lidového soudu Brno nor in fonds C 141, Mimořádný lidový soud Brno. See email (dated Nov. 26, 2020) from Leoš Pecha (MZA, Brno) to the author. Pavlak's name appears on a 1946 list of "removed lawyers", see *Věstník ministerstva spravedlnosti*, Mar. 31, 1946, 28.

[123] *Věstník Moravské advokátní komory v Brně*, April 1939, 2. As we have shown, the liquidator of a Jewish law practice was usually a chosen friend, and often the lawyer with whom the Jewish lawyer had interned. This would lead one to expect that Siegfried Ascher had interned with Josef Pavlak, but this was not the case. The fact that Pavlak was born in 1890 and Ascher in 1895 did not preclude this possibility. Siegfried Ascher interned with the non-Jewish lawyer Václav Javůrek (1883–1953) in 1922. See *Seznam advokátů roku 1922* 1923, 35.

[124] *Seznam advokátů roku 1933* 1934, 48. Walter Mautner's further fate is not known; however, he survived the war since a 1946 address in Buenos

year of the Nazi takeover in Germany is possibly significant. We have also seen that Franz Nawratil apparently adopted a similar stance when he accepted the Jewish woman Berta Seliger as an intern in his law office in 1933–34. Jewish and non-Jewish lawyers in Brno would have been well aware of the explicit political statement made by these two lawyers.[124] Further, Josef Pavlak settled the agreement when Josef Pollak's scrap iron company was sold to Leopold Spielvogel in 1941.[125] Pavlak also handled the divorce of Robert Pollak and his wife Anděla.

Josef Pavlak can also be clearly linked to the second pivotal figure in the network, the aforementioned lawyer Walter Süss.[126] Süss was an intern in Pavlak's law office from 1925 to 1929.[127] Elise Brecher relied upon Walter Süss when her store was threatened with Aryanization in 1939.[128] Karl Fein likely suggested Süss to his aunt when she needed to find a non-Jewish lawyer not publicly known as a leftist. Walter Süss also spoke at the aforementioned gathering of the Moravian Society for the Prevention of Cruelty to Animals (Mährischer Tierschutzverein) in 1935 at which Karl Fein was also present. It is possible that Fein and Süss knew each other through their involvement in this organization.[129] Walter Süss was also one of the two defense lawyers in the July 1941 homosexuality case against Wilhelm Sponer and Helmuth Holdau, two of Willi Bondi's gay friends.[130] Interestingly, both lawyers were apparently known for defending gay clients in court. We have mentioned the dispute between Jaroslav Očadlík and the nineteen-year-old Jan Tylč. The two met in April 1931 in the Bellevue Café, where *Kamarád* was founded a year later. In April 1932, Očadlík claimed that Tylč had robbed him, but Tylč countered that he had actually received the goods in question in exchange for sex. The case went to court, where Tylč was defended by Josef Pavlak.[131]

In addition, Walter Süss liquidated the Artur Feldmann Sr.'s law practice, and we have already pointed out several times that Fein had a close, though still somewhat unexplained, relationship with the Feldmann family.[132] Karl Fein's suggestion that his aunt Elise Brecher hire Süss as her lawyer may thus have come from Artur Feldmann Sr. Walter Süss was also the lawyer appointed by the Oberlandrat when the moving

Aires (Argentina) (308 Viamonte) is mentioned on his home certificate in the AMB, Brno, fonds B 1/39. His name is also listed in *Revista jurídica argentina "La Ley"*, vol. 8, 1947, 393. Walter's father, Leopold Mautner (1884–1926), died in 1926 and is buried in the Jewish cemetery in Brno in section 21B, row 4, grave 8. His mother, Hedvika Seidl (1888–1941?), was deported on transport "F" from Brno to Minsk on November 26, 1941. Her small laundry business was expropriated from her by the Oberlandrat in the summer of 1939 to favor a German national. In one of the Aryanization documents, she wrote that she was a widow and that her only son had emigrated. See NA, Praha, fonds n° 375, Arizační spisy, kart. n° 254, sign. 1773, Hedwig Mautner, *Gesuch* (request) (dated Jul. 26, 1939) from Hedwig Mautner to Oberlandrat Brünn.

[125] NA, Praha, fonds n° 375, Arizační spisy, company Josef Pollak, kart. n° 249, invent. n° 1706, not foliated.

[126] In the 1930s, Süss had his law office at 1 Bratislavská (Preßburgerstrasse), the building on the corner of Glacis (Koliště) and Preßburgerstrasse (Bratislavská). See *Adreßbuch von Groß-Brünn* 1934, 536. During the war, his office was located at 12–14 Herrengasse (Panská) and he lived at 26 Traubengasse (Hroznová). See *Adressbuch der Landeshauptstadt Brünn 1942* 1943, 79; ABS, Praha, SÚMV, fonds n° 134, Německé soudy v Protektorátu, sign. 134-908-11, f. 8b.

[127] *Seznam advokátů dle stavu koncem roku 1925* 1926, 38; *Seznam advokátů dle stavu koncem roku 1926* 1927, 38; *Seznam advokátů dle stavu koncem roku 1927* 1928, 40; *Seznam advokátů dle stavu koncem roku 1928* 1929, 38; *Seznam advokátů dle stavu koncem roku 1929* 1930, 38.

[128] NA, Praha, fonds n° 375, Arizační spisy, kart. n° 191, sign. 1119, file L. & A. Brecher.

[129] "Mährischer Tierschutzverein", *Morgenpost*, Aug. 8, 1935, 3.

[130] Süss was Wilhelm Sponer's defense lawyer. See MZA, Brno, fonds C43, Německý zemský soud Brno (Deutsches Landgericht), Staatsanwaltschaft bei dem Landgericht Brünn, file Wilhelm Sponer & Helmuth Holdau, kart. n° 184, sign. 4 K Ls 24/41, pink cover page and f. 57, 79.

[131] MZA, Brno, fonds C 12, Krajský soud trestní Brno, III. manipulace, kart. n° 511, indictment n° 739/32, sign. Tk V 1454/32, file Jan Tylč and Jaroslav Očadlík.

[132] *Věstník Moravské advokátní komory v Brně*, April 1939, 2. Interestingly, Artur Feldmann Sr.'s house was located on the street where Josef Pawlak and Walter Süss also lived, Traubengasse (Hroznová) in the posh Schreibwald (Pisárky) district. See also

firm Gerstmann & Lindner was Aryanized and sold to Erich Bogdan in June 1941.[133] Leopold Fleischer, Willi Bondi's brother-in-law, had been the principal manager of the Gerstmann & Lindner firm. Walter Prochaska was the appointed managing trustee (*Verwaltungstreuhänder*) in the Aryanization of Gerstmann & Lindner, a firm that Rudolf Siegmund had at first intended to buy. Presumably, Walter Prochaska played a part in the decision to appoint Süss, who then settled the sales agreement in June 1941. All this should make us wonder about the exact stance of Prochaska, Siegmund, Pavlak and Süss vis-à-vis the German occupiers and the Jewish population. We can clearly see here that there were many shades of gray, and not just the black and white opposites of Nazi sympathizers and their enemies.[134]

Yet, despite such gradations, the Catholic lawyer Süss, like Pavlak, did what was necessary to comply with the German occupation regime. Walter Süss and his wife Maria Schlesinger (1907–?) and their son Ronald Süss (1929–?) applied for German ethnic status in September 1939.[135] His law office's letterhead indicated that he was a member of the NSRB.[136] The names of Josef Pavlak and Walter Süss can also be found in a list of nineteen approved lawyers allowed to work for the German Regional Court in Brno (Deutsches Landgericht Brünn).[137] Interestingly, Franz Nawratil, who liquidated Karl Fein's law office, was another member of the relative small group of lawyers allowed to work for this court. Just like Nawratil, both Süss and Pavlak were screened for their aptitude and political trustworthiness (*politische Zuverlässigkeit*) by the German Supreme Regional Court in Prague (Deutschen Oberlandesgericht in Prag, Vrchní zemský soud Praha) before being admitted to plead in this court. All three passed.[138]

In August 1941, a complaint was made against Süss and his colleague Pavlak for repeatedly giving some of their clients food in the court building, the month before, apparently because they were in dire need.[139] They were acquitted.[140] However, it seems that Süss was eventually unable to comply with the requirements of the National Socialist order. His (incomplete) German Supreme Regional Court staff file shows that, in April 1944, Süss was harshly sentenced by the Disciplinary Chamber (Dienststrafkammer) of the Supreme Regional Court in Prague "for breach of the duties incumbent on him as a lawyer". In addition to committing some financial embezzlement, Pavlak also smuggled six letters to and from one of his imprisoned

p. 633, n. 126. Several Brno notables owned houses on this street – for example, Alfred Stiassny (1883–1961), Hugo Eisler (1884–March 1944) and Eugenie Padowetz (1857–1939), the widowed owner of the famous hotel bearing this family name near the main Brno railway station. See *Adreßbuch von Groß-Brünn* 1934, 754. The modernist Villa Stiassni was recently restored and opened to the public. See http://www.vilastiassni.cz/ (accessed Dec. 28, 2016).

133 NA, Praha, fonds n° 375, Arizační spisy, kart. n° 266 and 267, file n° 1913, Gerstmann & Lindner Brno, not foliated.

134 A similar, not-black-and-white constellation regarding the forced sale of the Leopold Fleischer company was sketched in chapter 14, pp. 528-29.

135 AMB, Brno, fonds B 1/39, home certificate Walter Süss. See also http://encyklopedie.brna.cz/home-mmb/?acc=profil_osobnosti&load=14420 (accessed Jul. 26, 2016), where Walter Süss' name is incorrectly spelled as "Süs".

136 ABS, Praha, SÚMV, fonds n° 134, Německé soudy v Protektorátu Čechy a Morava, Vrchní zemský soud Praha, personální spisy justičních zaměstnanců, Akten über die Dienstverhältnisse, file Walter Süss, sign. 134-908-11, not foliated.

137 See the "Verzeichnis der zur Vertretung und Verteidigung vor den deutschen Gerichten des Protektorates Böhmen und Mähren vorläufig und widerruflich ZUGELASSENEN RECHTSANWÄLTE" [capital letters in original], *Seznam advokátů v Protektorátu Čechy a Morava = Verzeichnis der Advokaten im tektorate Böhmen und Mähren*, 1940, 77.

138 ABS, Praha, SÚMV, fonds n° 134, Německé soudy v Protektorátu Čechy a Morava, Vrchní zemský soud Praha, personální spisy justičních zaměstnanců, Akten über die Dienstverhältnisse, file Josef Pavlak (Pawlak), sign. 134-910-7, file Walter Süss, sign. 134-908-11 and file Franz Nawratil, sign. 134-909-12.

139 The complaint was made by Dr. Bollacher, the *Amtsgerichtrat* (district court judge). It was sent to the German Supreme Regional Court (Deutsches Oberlandesgericht, Vrchní zemský soud Praha) in Prague. See ABS, Praha, SÚMV, fonds n° 134, Německé soudy v Protektorátu Čechy a Morava, Vrchní zemský soud Praha, personální spisy justičních zaměstnanců, Akten über die Dienstverhältnisse,

clients and their family. After unsuccessfully appealing to the Supreme Disciplinary Court (Dienststrafsenat beim Reichsgericht) in Berlin, in July 1944, he was barred from practicing law.[141] It would thus appear that Walter Süss, like Franz Nawratil, was not a perfect or ardent Nazi lawyer himself.

So, there was clearly a network of people who knew and depended on each other, despite their contrary political allegiances, during the early years of the war: Karl Fein, Elise Brecher, the Bondi-Fleischer family, Artur Feldmann Sr., Siegfried and Albert Ascher, the lawyers Walter Süss and Josef Pavlak, Walter Prochaska and Leopold Spielvogel, the Pollak family and Jaroslav Růžička and possibly also his wife Jindra. The lawyers Josef Pavlak and Walter Süss seem key figures here, connecting a great number of the people we have looked at.

I think that the very existence of this small network is sufficient to explain how information about the fate of the Institute materials may have circulated in the Jewish hospital, or to account for how the decision on what should be done with the materials was taken there. The information may have reached any of the people in this network. It is easy to imagine that Jaroslav Růžička may have been found by Elise Brecher via this network, spoken of as an efficient and helpful trader capable of assisting her to inconspicuously discard the Institute materials. Moreover, the Pollak family were not secular Jews who lived in conflict with the Jewish community. In May 1941, the widow Josefine Pollak (née Rosenbaum) donated 5,000 Czech crowns from her share of the Pollak company capital to the "Sacrifice – Build – Live" (Opfern – Aufbauen – Leben) fundraiser (*Spendensammlung*) set up by the Social Welfare Department (Fürsorgeabteilung) of the JKG in Prague to help the needy.[142] This seems to indicate that the Pollaks did not hesitate to show their solidarity with the Jewish community and this allegiance may have continued after they had moved out of their home in Mühlgasse (Mlýnská). This is further support for the idea that Jaroslav Růžička may have been found by Elise Brecher through the Pollak family and their contacts with the Jewish community.

THE FREQUENCY OF THE TRANSPORTS, RECONSIDERING THE STORAGE ROOMS

As with the Kamarád clique, we need to ask if there was a possible direct cause for Elise Brecher's decision to discard the Institute materials. I think that we need to look at the frequency of the Jewish mass transports to obtain an initial idea of why a decision about the fate of the Institute materials may have been taken in the Jewish hospital. We have seen that there were twelve Jewish transports from Brno in total, the first ten of which were mass transports. Except for the last mass transport, each carried exactly one thousand deported people. The first four mass transports took place between mid-November 1941 and the end of January 1942. Then, after a break of seven weeks, the frequency clearly intensified in March and April 1942 when, in less than three weeks, another six mass transports left Brno.[143] This sudden acceleration and its attendant turmoil must have caused great panic in the Jewish hospital. The fact that Nelly Stern, the head of the Jewish hospital, was herself deported on the

file Walter Süss, sign. 134-908-11, f. 36. See also Ibid., file Josef Pavlak (Pawlak), sign. 134-910-7.

140 Ibid., file Walter Süss, sign. 134-908-11, f. 40.

141 Ibid., f. 45b: "wegen Verletzung der ihm als Rechtsanwalt obliegenden Pflichten" (for breach of duties incumbent on him as a lawyer). See also Bundesarchiv, Berlin-Lichterfelde, Reichsjustizministerium, Personalakten (1877–1945), Walter Süß, 1.10.1901, sign. BArch, R 3001/77924 and Bundesarchiv, Berlin-Lichterfelde, Dienststrafsenat beim Reichsgericht (1939–1945), Walter Süß, sign. R 3015/618.

142 Curiously, the German authorities allowed Josefine Pollak to make the donation. See NA, Praha, fonds n° 375, Arizační spisy, company Josef Pollak, kart. n° 249, invent. n° 1706, not foliated. For the "Opfern – Aufbauen – Leben" fundraising campaign, see Gruner 2016, 116–17.

143 An overview of the Jewish transports from Brno can be found in the addenda, n° 13. See also Klementová 2010, 22–23; Klenovský 2002, 18.

last mass transport "Ai", on April 8, 1942, must surely have been viewed as an omen that the sanctuary of the hospital was now clearly threatened. When would the last patients be deported?

Along with thirteen other people in the Jewish hospital, Elise Brecher and Siegfried Ascher were indeed summoned at the end of May 1942 for deportation on the much smaller transport "AAa". That transport would leave Brno on May 27, 1942, carrying approximately eighty people; however, prior to its departure, the Jewish hospital patients were again exempted from the transport list.[144] This means that – for a short or long stretch of time – Elise Brecher, Siegfried Ascher and the other patients in the Jewish hospital lived in fear of being deported. Their exemption from the transport list was most likely in response to pressure from the JKG in Brno, again confirming the relatively privileged status of the patients in the Jewish hospital.

We already mentioned that Elise Brecher's daughter, Anna Bermann, was deported on transport "Ad" on March 23, 1942, along with her husband Wilhelm Bermann and their son Felix. Less than a week later, on March 29, 1942, Elise Brecher's sister, the widow Marianne Waelsch, was deported on transport "Ae". The following week, on April 8, 1942, Elise Brecher's oldest son, Fritz Brecher, was deported from Brno on the last Jewish mass transport "Ai", which carried just over 900 people. Nelly Stern, the head of the hospital, was also deported on this transport. It is not unthinkable that several drastic decisions were made between the two dates when Elise Brecher's children were deported. If the fate of the Institute materials was indeed decided in the Jewish hospital, the decision was likely made by Elise Brecher and her son Fritz between March 23, 1942, and April 8, 1942. Presumably it was Fritz Brecher who was the one able to get things done, being the last member of the Brecher family, unlike his aunt Elise Brecher, young and fit enough to settle matters before his deportation. The announcement, a few days before his actual deportation, that Fritz Brecher would not be exempted, may have constituted a decisive moment. Realizing – or at least dreading – that eventually no one would be spared deportation, urgent decisions about the Jewish storage rooms may have been taken in the Jewish hospital. Items might have been moved and agreements made for advance rent payments to the storage companies.

We have seen that there was a chance that Karl Fein had a storage room at the Leopold Fleischer company; it was certain that Elise Brecher had one at the Morava

[144] The first stirrings of this somewhat startling discovery came when I saw an index card for Siegfried Ascher in NA, Praha, fonds n° 1077, Okupační vězeňské spisy (Occupation imprisonment records), kartotéka deportovaných osob do Terezína a z Terezína (card index of persons deported to and from the Terezín ghetto). This index card includes a typed statement that Ascher was marked for transport "AAa" on May 27, 1942. Since, as we have seen, Ascher died in Brno in December 1942, I knew that he must have been exempted from this transport. Furthermore, there is a line across the text on the card, indicating that it was no longer valid. My next question was whether other people from the Jewish hospital had also been intended for transport "AAa" and then exempted. Another list found in the same fonds n° 1077, Okupační vězeňské spisy, in the NA, Praha, and titled "Verzeichnis der in den Transport AAa eingereihten Personen, die im Siechenheim in Brünn, Mühlg. 27, zurückgeblieben sind" (List of persons assigned to transport AAa who remained in the hospital in Brünn, Mühlg. 27) showed that fifteen people, all at the Jewish hospital, were exempted from transport "AAa". The list included Siegfried Ascher and Elise Brecher. Siegfried Ascher was assigned transport number AAa 88 and Elise Brecher transport number AAa 90. The fifteen names on the list were assigned transport numbers AAa 85 to AAa 99. Since the final number of people deported on transport "AAa" was eighty-one, three people not staying in the Jewish hospital were either exempt, disappeared or had died. The fonds n° 1077, Okupační vězeňské spisy, is currently being reordered by the NA, Praha, and the kartotéka deportovaných osob do Terezína a z Terezína (card index of persons deported from and to the Terezín ghetto) has no inventory number as yet. The NA, Praha, claims that these index cards were assembled after the war by an unknown party using the available transport lists; however, Ascher's card seems rather to indicate that these index cards were gathered during the war. Cf. email (dated Apr. 19, 2017) from Eva Drašarová (NA, Praha) to the author.

company. We may presume that several of their family members also had storage rooms. It is not unreasonable to think that, as the last family members still in Brno, Elise Brecher (and perhaps her son) decided – out of caution – to discard the Hirschfeld Institute materials kept either in her own or Karl Fein's storage room or in one rented by yet another person. Elise Brecher may have suspected (correctly) that the Germans would sooner or later seize the contents of storage rooms rented by Jewish people. She might also have feared that the discovery of the dangerous Institute materials would put her family in some kind of jeopardy, even after they had been deported, and that it was more prudent not to take any risks. The traumatic and certainly stressful times, which were most likely experienced with greater intensity in the little world of the Jewish hospital, might have played a part themselves. The spreading panic may have driven them to take decisions wanting in wisdom. Fear, as most of us know, is usually a poor counselor.

Unlike the scenario of the *Kamarád* group's involvement, the news of Karl Fein's death in Łódź, in May 1942, which possibly reached Brno some time later, likely did *not* play a role here given Fritz Brecher's deportation in the beginning of April 1942. Unless, that is, Elise Brecher was still able to maneuver things without the help of her son, possibly even in May, the month in which she learned that she would also be deported. The announcement of Elise Brecher's imminent deportation might have been another possible key moment for her, prompting her to take drastic decisions. If, by then, she was also aware that Karl Fein had died in Łódź in Poland, she may have realized that this left the responsibility for the Hirschfeld and Institute materials solely in her hands.

If Elise Brecher was indeed involved in any way, between March and May 1942, then the decision to discard the Institute materials would surely not have been an easy one. However, it would have been understandable and pragmatic, given the harsh and highly uncertain wartime conditions. Her main motivation might have been the protection of her close family and also her own after deportation. The fact that Elise Brecher was one of the very last Jewish people from Brno to be deported is clear testimony to her resilience and survival skills.

THE JEWISH HOSPITAL: COUNTERARGUMENTS

Of course, it is neither certain nor proven that the decision about what to do with the Institute materials was taken in the Jewish hospital and that, consequently, the people in the *Kamarád* group played no part in discarding the Institute materials. That Jaroslav Růžička was a very important business partner of Robert Pollak, and often visited the scrap iron company premises, might also be a coincidence, having no relation to our story. We simply do not have enough archival or other kinds of sources at our disposal to lead us to the effective decision makers in 1942. We can only present the case and the facts as presently known. So, after our examination of the arguments and factors that apparently support the idea that the decision to discard the Institute materials was made in the Jewish hospital, let us not neglect a few equally weighty factors that seem to speak *against* the involvement of the people staying in the Jewish hospital.

One of the main counterarguments involves the Jewish storage rooms. It is not known to what extent Jewish people were able to move things in and out of rented storage rooms in 1942. I think it likely that, especially once the Jewish mass transports from Brno ended, in April 1942, this activity was simply no longer possible. I think that the storage companies, closely scrutinized by the German occupiers, would not have allowed this and did not want any trouble with the Germans either. In addition, any initiative coming from the Jewish hospital might have brought unwanted German attention to a small group of people who had, rather miraculously, managed to (temporarily) avoid deportation. Let us also recall the November 1941 ordinance that stipulated that no Jewish belongings could be transferred to others by any means. However, if Jewish people were still able to transfer items out of storage rooms, it is probable that storage companies had to report this activity to the German authorities. On the other hand, if Jewish belongings kept in rented storage rooms could no longer be moved – a restriction possibly in effect as early as November 1941 – this would count as one of the stronger counterarguments against the idea that Elise Brecher decided the fate of the Institute materials. Unless, of course, the Institute materials were not kept in a storage room. Also, if Elise Brecher took the decision after her son Fritz had been deported, then she would have had to rely on others for help. Elise Brecher most likely did not have the physical strength to accomplish the task. Moreover, even if she did, it is not clear that she was allowed to leave the Jewish hospital – to take a walk in the neighborhood, for example.

Another objection seems to be the founding of the hospital in the final months of 1941, by which time Karl Fein had been deported from Prague to Łódź. His aunt arrived in the Jewish hospital in January 1942. This means that Fein could not have conceived a scenario in which the Jewish hospital played a role. Of course, this still does not exclude the possibility that Fein entrusted the Institute materials to his aunt and that she later acted on her own from the Jewish hospital.

A further counterargument concerns the Pollaks. They were forced to sell their company and house on the corner of Stephansgasse (Štěpánská) and Mühlgasse (Mlýnská) in the beginning of 1941. They moved out of the building in June 1941 and then lived in the northern suburb of Královo Pole, where Karl Giese also lived until his suicide in March 1938.[145] By the time the Jewish hospital was established in their former home, the Pollaks were long gone. In addition, Robert Pollak was imprisoned in the beginning of February 1942, for unknown reasons, and was likely held until his deportation from Brno on April 4, 1942.[146] The Hirschfeld guestbook was found in 1942. If its fate was tied to the ongoing Jewish deportations, then Robert Pollak was possibly not significantly involved since he was in prison. On the other hand, it could be retorted that Jaroslav Růžička was likely concerned about the fate of his presumably good friend Robert Pollak, who helped him set up his own eventually thriving business. We suggested that Pollak most likely shared his business contacts and knowledge of the trade with Růžička; if so, then they *needed* to stay in contact to pass on this trade-related information. Růžička may have visited Pollak in prison for this purpose. (In this regard, it would prove useful to determine whether Robert

[145] By June 6, 1941, Hugo Pollak, and probably also his wife, lived at 92 Purkyňova (Purkynĕgasse); Robert Pollak lived at 56 Svatopluka Čecha (Svatopluk-Čech-Gasse). Both streets are in Královo Pole. See their resident registration cards in the AMB, Brno, fonds Z 1. Also cf. Robert Pollak's police file on www.holocaust.cz, which gives June 6, 1941, as the date they moved out. The mother, Josefina Pollak, seems to have moved out on June 11, 1941.

[146] See Robert Pollak's resident registration card in AMB, Brno, fonds Z 1, which contains a handwritten note in pencil: "do zajišťovací vazby" (in provisional detention). His confinement was likely linked to an initial request to confirm his existing address (dated Dec. 3, 1941) on the front of his resident registration card. A request to confirm one's existing address usually signaled imminent questioning by the Germans. In 1946, Anděla Pollaková claimed that she lived together with her husband Robert Pollak "until he was imprisoned". See MZA, Brno, fonds C 11, Krajský soud civilní Brno, III. manipulace, kart. n° 620, sign. Ck IIa 337/46, annulment divorce Robert Pollak and Anděla Pollak. Interestingly, we also see that Anděla Pollaková mentions the date of February 4, 1942, on a postwar resident registration card in AMB, fonds Z 1, under the heading "Den příchodu přihlašovaných osob" (date of arrival of persons being registered); however, the date is crossed out and replaced by December 1, 1948. This seems to indicate that she either moved in or out of 56 Svatopluk-Čech-Gasse (Svatopluka Čecha) in Královo Pole shortly after her husband's arrest.

[147] For Artur Feldmann Sr., see http://encyklopedie.brna.cz/home-mmb/?acc=profil_osobnosti&load=9059 (accessed Jan. 28, 2016). For a more detailed account of his life, see the restitution claim filed

Pollak had legal representation during his imprisonment and if his lawyer could have been Josef Pavlak or Walter Süss.)

Another counterargument has to do with Jaroslav Růžička himself, whose "Jewish-looking face" caused him to be forbidden, in November 1940, from meeting the two Pollak brothers on their company premises. He may have realized that he would continue to be perceived as Jewish by wary neighbors, who sided with the German invaders and felt it their duty to inform the German authorities. Růžička may have decided that it would be simply better to stay away from the premises of the former Pollak company, now owned by the non-Jewish man Leopold Spielvogel. So, it is possible that Jaroslav Růžička never returned to the former Pollak company and house after November 1940.

PRESERVING JEWISH HERITAGE: THREE EXAMPLES

A final, rather solid objection to the idea that people in the Jewish hospital decided to discard the Institute materials is connected to the wish – at least among a part of the Jewish population – to preserve Jewish property and Jewish heritage in the light of German persecution of the Jews. I think that Karl Fein's aunt might have been rather inclined to safeguard the Institute materials if indeed she, or her son Fritz, took the decision to act in this matter. That Elise Brecher may have played a major or minor role in the buy-back operation already indicated such a wish to preserve rather than discard Jewish heritage. Let us now take an extensive look at three stories that further illustrate the tendency among the Czech Jewish elite to preserve Jewish cultural heritage.

ARTUR FELDMANN'S ART COLLECTION

Firstly, let us return to the Feldmann family, whom Fein knew well. The lawyer Artur Feldmann Sr. owned an important collection of Old Master drawings.[147] Quite remarkably, this collection was confiscated by the Gestapo on March 15, 1939, the day of the invasion of the remainder of Czechoslovakia. In addition, Artur Feldmann was forced to leave his villa at 13 Traubengasse (Hroznová) in the posh civil servants' quarter (*Beamtenviertel*) in Brno. Feldmann saw no other option than moving in with his son, Otto Feldmann, then living at 35 Koliště (Glacis).[148] This was also the address of the modernist apartment building where Karl Fein was then living. Feldmann was tortured in 1940 and died the following year [ill. 8]. Karl Fein would have been well aware of what happened to Artur Feldmann and to the Feldmann collection. The immediate seizure of the Feldmann art collection made it clear that the National Socialists were very well informed about important Brno art collectors before their full invasion of the country. The Gestapo was apparently also after Otto Eisler's art collection. As we have suggested, Fein may have known Otto Eisler, who was also tortured. Lenka Kudělková reports an unverified story about Otto Eisler and the Gestapo: "Otto Eisler was a talented draftsman of landscapes of his native Czech-Moravian Uplands; he designed and carved puppets, collected graphic art and books (he was supposedly ordered to burn his collection under the supervision of the Gestapo)".[149]

by Uri Arthur Peled-Feldmann (1943–), the son of Karl Feldmann (1909–1989), the brother of Otto Feldmann. Karl and Otto Feldmann were the sons of Artur Feldmann Sr. See http://www.provenienz-forschung.gv.at/wp-content/uploads/2014/04/Feldmann.pdf (accessed Apr. 3, 2016); Gnann & Schödl 2015. I thank Julia Eßl (Provenienzforschung Albertina, Wien) for putting me in contact with Uri Arthur Peled-Feldmann in June 2016.

148 Eßl 2015, 10, 16. For Otto Feldmann, see http://encyklopedie.brna.cz/home-mmb/?acc=profil_osobnosti&load=12675 (accessed Jan. 28, 2016). Otto Feldmann managed to emigrate to Palestine.

149 Kudělková 1998, 24. See also Malt & Juříčková 2016, 80 n. 46, referring to a 1967 radio interview in which Otto Eisler stated this.

All this might have inspired real fear in Karl Fein and driven him to caution. As we have already noted, the Nazis knew that Giese lived in Brno. But did they also know that Karl Fein provided essential help for the buy-back of the Berlin Institute materials? Karl Giese's handwritten will clearly states to whom Giese bequeathed the Institute and other materials. But were the National Socialists actually interested in finding the remaining Hirschfeld materials and eager to pursue former Hirschfeld allies? We have already suggested several times that this seems not to have been the case. However, the National Socialists' aggressive confiscation of the Feldmann collection, implying that the Germans had prepared the robbery well in advance, might have prompted Fein quite early on to decide to entrust the Institute materials to someone else or at least to be very cautious. The brutal seizure of Feldmann's art collection could also have provoked a sort of opposite reaction, with Fein and other Jewish citizens doing all they could to safeguard their own valuables. Elise Brecher might have shared this view since she was also the owner of a (much more modest) collection of ex libris and military commemorative coins.[150] She might have also possessed some paintings by her sister, Dorette Löw. Some of the more expensive items in her collection could potentially be confiscated by the German occupiers since all Jewish valuables (property, assets, jewels, valuable collections, etc.) had to be registered by July 31, 1939.[151] So, early on, Elise Brecher might have looked for ways to safeguard her more precious belongings.

VIKTOR OPPENHEIMER'S ART COLLECTION

Elise Brecher arrived in the Jewish hospital in the beginning of January 1942, and was joined a few weeks later by Ernestine (Erna) Oppenheimer (née Löwenthal, 1855–1942).[152] Ernestine Oppenheimer ended up in the Jewish hospital two days after her son, the engineer and artist Viktor Oppenheimer (1877–1942?), was deported.[153] In contrast to Elise Brecher, whose stay in the Jewish hospital was a kind of privilege granted to her, Ernestine Oppenheimer was there because she had been summoned for deportation with her son Victor but was presumably too sick to travel. Before being deported, Viktor Oppenheimer entrusted his oriental art collection, containing approximately 1,500 items, to the Museum of Decorative Arts (Uměleckoprůmyslové muzeum) in Brno.[154] We may safely assume that this undertaking was most likely executed in a very discreet way.[155]

[150] Elise Brecher was a collector who sometimes lent objects from her personal collection to exhibitions. See, for example, the mention of Elise Brecher as a collector, loaning parts of her ex libris and military coins collection to exhibitions in *Mitteilungen des Erzherzog-Rainer-Museums für Kunst und Gewerbe*, Jg. 36, 1918, n° 5, 42; ibid., Jg. 35, 1917, n° 2, 22. See also "Buchbild- und Exlibris-Ausstellung" (Book illustration and bookplate exhibition), *Brünner Zeitung*, May 18, 1918, 3. The Erzherzog-Rainer-Museum für Kunst und Gewerbe became a part of the Moravská galerie v Brně in 1961, when the Moravian Gallery in Brno was founded. See email (dated Aug. 19, 2015) from Petr Tomášek (Moravská galerie v Brně, Brno) to the author. For an introductory guide to the museum's history, see https://cs.wikipedia.org/wiki/Um%C4%9Bleckopr%C5%AFmyslov%C3%A9_muzeum_%28Brno%29 (accessed Mar. 24, 2015); Leisching 1913.

[151] Potthast 2002, 65–66.

[152] Ernestine Oppenheimer arrived in the Jewish hospital on January 30, 1942. See AMB, Brno, fonds Z 1. The http://encyklopedie.brna.cz/home-mmb/?acc=profil_osobnosti&load=9255 website erroneously give her address as 19 Mühlgasse (Mlýnská) (accessed Mar. 24, 2016). This mistake is copied from the document in http://www.holocaust.cz/databaze-dokumentu/dokument/78482-oppenheimerova-erna-oznameni-o-umrti-ghetto-Terezín/ (accessed Mar. 24, 2016). The Jewish hospital's address was 27 Mühlgasse (Mlýnská).

[153] For more information on Viktor Oppenheimer, see http://encyklopedie.brna.cz/home-mmb/?acc=profil_osobnosti&load=2058 (accessed Mar. 24, 2016).

[154] In 1950, the rescued Oppenheimer collection was bought by the same museum from Viktor Oppenheimer's brother. The Uměleckoprůmyslové muzeum (Museum of Applied Arts), established in 1873, is now part of the Moravská galerie v Brně (Moravian Gallery in Brno). See Sedlářová 2001, 64. For the current museum, see http://www.moravska-galerie.cz/moravska-galerie/navsteva-mg/budovy-mg/umeleckoprumyslove-muzeum.aspx?lang=cs

Elise Brecher and Ernestine Oppenheimer were most likely not complete strangers. In 1941–42, Elise Brecher's daughter, Anna Bermann, her husband, the pharmacist Wilhelm Bermann, and their son Felix were living in a house owned by Marie Oppenheimer (née Vašíček, 1894–1988), the Catholic wife of Josef Oppenheimer (1883–1933), Victor Oppenheimer's brother.[156] The grave of the parents

(accessed May 11, 2016). It is unclear where Oppenheimer's collection of medallions ended up. The Czech version of Sedlářová's article mentions that their location is unknown, while the English résumé of the article claims that "it is believed" that he hid them somewhere. See Sedlářová 2001, 64–65.

[155] I contacted Jitka Sedlářová to inquire about her research on Victor Oppenheimer (Sedlářová 2001). She wrote that she had not looked for traces of Oppenheimer's agreement in the Gewerbemuseum archives, presuming that there would be none since the operation was likely settled secretly, also giving the poor organization of the museum's archives as another reason. In addition, she wrote that she had based her claim exclusively on an oral communication from the brother who sold the collection to the museum after the war. She added that the museum's brave act of sheltering Oppenheimer's collection during the war may have contributed to the brother's benevolent attitude when selling the collection to the museum after the war. In her email, she also mentioned the German director of the museum, the engineer and architect Max Kühn (1877–1944), but implied that the act of bravery was rather performed in secret by Czech collaborators of the museum. Max Kühn is best known for his architectural work in the Sudeten German city of Reichenberg (Liberec). See email (dated Feb. 25, 2017) from Jitka Sedlářová to the author. The matter clearly deserves further scrutiny. Max Kühn is certainly also interesting because his brother, Karl Friedrich Kühn (1884–1945), was the director of the Brno Institute of Monument Conservation (Institut für Denkmalpflege in Brünn, Památkového ústavu v Brně) from 1942 onwards and, from 1937 onwards, the chairman of the Deutsche Gesellschaft für Wissenschaft und Kunst (German Society for Science and Art). See http://encyklopedie.brna.cz/home-mmb/?acc=profil_osobnosti&load=9969, http://ftp.npu.cz/biograficky-slovnik-pamatkaru-I/kuehn-karl-friedrich/ and http://www.biographien.ac.at/oebl/oebl_K/Kuehn_Karl-Friedrich_1884_1945.xml?frames=yes (all accessed Mar. 4, 2017). Many German-speaking Jewish people, Hugo Iltis among them, were active in this association before the war. There are two archival fonds on Karl Friedrich Kühn, but I did not consult them. See MZA, Brno, fonds G 177, fonds Karl Kühn and the archival fonds in Národní památkový ústav Brno. It is also possible that Rudolf Leger (1894–1945) became the director of the museum at some point during the war. See http://encyklopedie.brna.cz/home-mmb/?acc=profil_osobnosti&load=4269 and https://cs.wikipedia.org/wiki/Um%C4%9Bleckopr%C5%AFmyslov%C3%A9_muzeum_(Brno) (both accessed Mar. 4, 2017). In later emails, Jitka Sedlářová seemed surprised that she had been mistaken in thinking that one of the Kühn brothers was the director of the museum. See her emails (dated Mar. 4, 2017 and Mar. 6, 2017) to the author. The names of Victor Oppenheimer and Rudolf Leger also appear together in a 1926 article on an art exhibition in Prague. See "Pražské výstavy" (Prague exhibitions), *Lidové noviny*, Jun. 11, 1926, 7. Oppenheimer and Leger were both members of the *Kunstverein* (art association) Die Scholle, founded in 1922, which put on exhibitions in the beautiful Brno Künstlerhaus (Dům umění) located next to the Brno Mahen Theater. I owe this information about Die Scholle to Jitka Sedlářová, see her email (dated Mar. 4, 2017) to the author. This makes it more conceivable that the director of the Uměleckoprůmyslové muzeum (Museum of Decorative Arts) was aware of the deal concluded. It is also worth noting that, from 1938 until 1940, a certain Václav Richter (1900–1970) was the director of the museum. Finally, I also asked Svatava Hájková (head archivist of the Moravská galerie v Brně) whether there were any traces in their archives of the Uměleckoprůmyslové museum (or of Leger, its director). In response, on May 12, 2017, Mrs. Hájková sent an archives inventory list of the fonds of the Moravské uměleckoprůmyslové museum, requesting me to tell her where she should look. The archives of the Uměleckoprůmyslové museum were initially housed in the MZA, Brno, fonds G 412, Moravské uměleckoprůmyslové museum, but this archival fonds was transferred to the Moravian Gallery in 2008.

[156] Marie Oppenheimer survived the war. In November 1939, she applied for Deutsche Volkszugehörigkeit (German ethnic) status. The request was approved in May 1940. See the note on the home certificate (of the year 1900) for her husband Dr. Josef Oppenheimer (1883–1933) in the AMB, Brno, fonds B 1/39. Surprisingly, this application for German ethnic status was not seen as a problem by the Czechoslovak authorities after the war. See the anonymous handwriting in red ink on Josef Oppenheimer's mentioned home certificate. See also NA, Praha, fonds Ministerstvo vnitra – nová registratura (Ministry of the Interior – New Registry), 1945–1948, year 1947, sign. A-4605-21/4-47-VI/2, file Marie Oppenheimer. Marie Oppenheimer was allowed to keep her Czechoslovak citizenship since two of her relatives were victims of the National Socialists: her son Paul (Pavel) Oppenheimer (1914–1982), who was half-Jewish, and his fiancée (whose name is unknown) who died in Mauthausen. Before and after the war, the Roman Catholic Marie Oppenheimer lived at 10 Schillergasse (Schillerova) in the Masaryk quarter. See *Adreßbuch von Groß-Brünn* 1934, 799; *Adressbuch der Landeshauptstadt Brünn* 1942, 215.

of Wilhelm Bermann in the Jewish cemetery was designed by Victor Oppenheimer.[157] That the Jewish hospital was not a very reliable sanctuary is suggested by the fact that Ernestine Oppenheimer was deported from Brno to Terezín on March 23, 1942 on transport "Ad". Exactly what happened is not known. Did she volunteer to go or was she deported by force? Her son Victor and his wife were deported from Brno to Terezín two months earlier.[158] Ernestine Oppenheimer died one week after arriving in Terezín.[159]

Most of all, the Victor Oppenheimer case gives us an idea of the resilience and creativity shown by a part of the Brno Jewish population in safeguarding their most valuable belongings. These actions took place in a relatively small circle of people who knew each other and were similarly concerned about the fate of their valuables. Elise Brecher might have devised a plan similar to Victor Oppenheimer's for her own collection. Ernestine Oppenheimer may have told her about the particular settlement arranged by her son.

Let me add another consideration. Elise Brecher's maternal uncle, Heinrich Gomperz (1843?–1894), was one of Brno's most important and well-known art patrons, who bequeathed 437 paintings and drawings to the city.[160] Gomperz was also a city councilor and, in 1882, the co-founder of the Brno Moravian Art Association (Mährische Kunstverein Brünn).[161] As with so many other museum collections across

Like his mother, Paul Oppenheimer survived the war and lived with her in the house on Schillergasse (Schillerova), later renamed Jiříkovského. He also applied for German ethnic status. In 1958, he and his mother illegally moved to Vienna. See the handwritten note on the back of his resident registration card in AMB, Brno, fonds Z 1. Josef and Marie Oppenheimer also had a daughter named Elisabeth Oppenheimer (1917–2005), who later married the architect Miroslav Duchoň (1910–1988). This couple's further fate is mostly unknown. During the war, they lived in the house at 15 d'Elvertstrasse (d'Elvertova) owned by Marie Oppenheimer. This was also the last Brno address of the Bermann family. See *Adressbuch der Landeshauptstadt Brünn 1942* 1943, 51. There are several people with the name Duchoň in Brno in a current online Czech phonebook but I did not attempt to contact them.

[157] See https://cemeteries.jewishbrno.eu/cemetery/hrobovemisto/id/1037/cemetery_id/1 (accessed Nov. 4, 2020). See chapter 17, illustration n° 5.

[158] Victor Oppenheimer was deported, with his wife Elize (Elsa) Oppenheimer (1881–1942?) on transport "U" from Brno to Terezín on January 28, 1942. They were both further transferred to Warsaw on transport "An" on April 25, 1942.

[159] See her Terezín death certificate, https://www.holocaust.cz/en/database-of-digitised-documents/document/78482-oppenheimerova-erna-death-certificate-ghetto-terezin (accessed Apr. 1, 2021).

[160] Even though his tombstone gives his birth date as December 10, 1843, the exact date of Heinrich Gomperz's birth is unclear and disputed. The home certificate of his father, Jacob Moriz Gomperz (1811–1876), in the AMB, Brno, fonds B 1/39, gives the birth date of his son Heinrich as December 24, 1843. Possibly, Heinrich was an illegitimate or adopted child. See also Smutný 2004, 13–15.

[161] Heinrich Gomperz was married to Julie Kropp (1858–1928), a singer from Prague also known as Dalena, her stage name. The Gomperz couple had no children and lived in a house at 11 Jesuitengasse (Jesuitská). See Smutný 2004, 17. Gomperz inherited the house from his father, Jacob Moriz Gomperz, who was Elise Brecher's maternal grandfather. Julie Gomperz, Heinrich Gomperz's widow, who died in 1928, had arranged for the house to be bequeathed to the JKG in Brno. But the property was soon sold to the Aktiengesellschaft Volksdruckgesellschaft (Tisková společnost lidová), which would build the modernist Typos Gallery on the parcels with house numbers 9–11. In the summer of 1939, Karl Fein spent the last three months of his life in Brno in this Typos building. Heinrich Gomperz is buried, together with his wife Julie, in the Jewish cemetery in Brno. Their impressive grave monument can be found on parcel 1B, row 4, grave 1. The grave is very close to the grave of Heinrich Gomperz's parents, Jacob Moriz and Julia Gomperz, who are buried in parcel 1A, row 3, graves 5 and 6. Heinrich Gomperz was also very close to the Brno artist and businessman Eduard Sykora (1836 or 1835–1897), who was also an art collector. Sykora also bequeathed his art collection to the city of Brno. See Karkanová 2004, 54–55. Sykora provided the mise-en-scène for the art from his former art friend's collection when it was exhibited in the old (former) Landhaus (Zemský dům) at the Dominikanerplatz (Dominikánské náměstí). See Rille 1907, 6. I do not know what to make of a remark by someone who knew Gomperz intimately, who noted that Gomperz considered a seventeenth-century Italian oil painting by Carlo Dolcis, depicting an androgynous-looking Saint Sebastian, one of his more satisfying works: "In dem Zimmer zur Rechten [in Gomperz's house] hing über dem Schreibtisch am Fenster Carlo Dolcis 'Heiliger Sebastian', zu dem sein Besitzer stets mit besonderer Befriedi-

the world, this private collection formed the basis for the creation of an art museum in Brno. Disregarding the wishes of their benefactor, some postwar curators, driven by Czech nationalist sentiment and also influenced by the Communist regime, gradually transferred the collection owned by the city of Brno to the Moravian Museum (Moravské zemské museum), and later to the Moravian Gallery in Brno (Moravská galerie v Brně), opened in 1961.[162] Mentioning her uncle, the art patron Heinrich Gomperz, Elise Brecher would have had the credentials to find a refuge for her collection with one of the local museums.[163] Yet, I was told that the archives of the Moravian Gallery in Brno (Moravská galerie v Brně) and the Moravian Museum in Brno (Moravské zemské muzeum v Brně) contained no traces of Elise Brecher entrusting her collection to either of them.[164]

ZDENĚK KÖNIG: THE YOUNG MAN IN THE JEWISH MUSEUM

As a third case, we can again mention Zdeněk König (1921–1943), the young man who lived in the same building as Karl Fein in Prague (4 Hodonínská/Gödinger Gasse) and who worked for the Jewish Central Museum (Jüdisches Zentralmuseum) in the capital. On one occasion, I saw his name on a list of almost four thousand people working for the JKG in Prague.[165] Another staff list specified that König was one of the four members of the administrative section of the Jewish Central Museum.[166]

gung hinaufblickte" (In the room to the right [in Gomperz's house], above the desk by the window, hung Carlo Dolci's *Saint Sebastian*, which its owner always looked at with special satisfaction). See Rille 1907, 5. The painting is reproduced in Janás et al. 2004, [381].

[162] Karkanová 2004, 67, 69 and passim; http://encyklopedie.brna.cz/home-mmb/?acc=profil_osobnosti&load=10563 (accessed Jan. 31, 2017). Gomperz's will also provided the necessary funds to start up the Brno Municipal Museum that opened in 1904. See http://www.spilberk.cz/en/brno-city-museum/brno-city-museum-history/ (accessed Feb. 1, 2017). The people behind the 2004 exhibition, which focused on Gomperz's founding collection, were well aware that things in the past had not been handled as they should have been. Starting in 1918, museum curators were animated by anti-German, anti-Austrian and eventually Communist ideas. So it was no accident then that the 2004 exhibition was jointly organized by the Moravian Gallery and the Brno Municipal Museum, as the two introductions to the catalogue also make clear. See Janás et al. 2004, [6-7].

[163] One could counter that Elise Brecher always worked with the Erzherzog-Rainer-Museums für Kunst und Gewerbe and not, like her uncle, with the city of Brno. (After World War I, the Erzherzog-Rainer-Museums für Kunst und Gewerbe museum was known as the Uměleckoprůmyslové museum [Museum for Decorative Arts]. See https://cs.wikipedia.org/wiki/Um%C4%9Bleckopr%C5%AFmyslov%C3%A9_muzeum_%28Brno%29 [accessed Feb. 6, 2017]. In 1961, this museum joined the Moravian Gallery.) However, Gomperz also bequeathed objects to the Erzherzog-Rainer-Museum für Kunst und Gewerbe. See Smutný 2004, 17.

[164] Email (dated Aug. 18, 2015) from Marta Mrázová (Moravské zemské muzeum Brno, Brno) to the author. She also indicated that the art collection once owned by the Moravské zemské muzeum Brno (Moravian Museum in Brno) was transferred to the Moravská galerie v Brně (Moravian Gallery) when it opened in 1961. See also email (dated Oct. 12, 2015) from Petr Tomášek (Moravská galerie v Brně, Brno) to the author. Nevertheless, I believe there is reason to remain cautious about a final verdict on the matter. Petr Tomášek, the curator of the fine arts collection, wrote to me, eight months later, that the Moravian Gallery's newly appointed archivist had "neither experience nor interest" in this matter. See email (dated Jun. 6, 2016) from Petr Tomášek (Moravská galerie v Brně, Brno) to the author.

[165] The employee list "Mitarbeiter der Jüdischen Kultusgemeinde in Prag, Stand zum 21.9.1942" appears as annex n° 1 in Krejčová et al. 1997, 409–72. This list also includes the protected relatives of people working for the JKG. This list is called "Angestelltenliste der jüdischen Kultusgemeinde" in Potthast 2002, 234. The list of no more than twenty-nine collaborators of the Kultur- und Denkmalreferat – Zentralmuseum can be found in Krejčová et al. 1997, 471–72 (Zdeněk König appears on p. 472, his first name spelled in the Slovak way as "Zdenko"). Cf. Bušek 2007, 35. König's evidence obyvatelstva sheet in the NA, Praha, fonds Policejní ředitelství Praha II, states that he was an "Angestellter der J.K.G." (employee of the JKG). An index card for König – in NA, Praha, fonds n° 1077, Okupační vězeňské spisy, kartotéka deportovaných osob do Terezína a z Terezína (card index of persons deported to and from the Terezín ghetto) – shows that he was employed by the Ältestenrat der Juden (ARJ) (Jewish Council of Elders), as the JKG was later renamed.

[166] Židovské muzeum v Praze, Praha, 1906–1945 (1946), III. Personálni záležitosti, n° 38, Korespondence dr. Poláka – 1942-1943, Arbeitseinteilung in Jüdischen Zentralmuseums (Sep. 24, 1942), p. 2. In his Prague police file, Zdeněk König was initially described as an "úředník" (clerk), while later 1942

The museum in Prague officially started to function in the beginning of August 1942.[167] As early as April 1940, some Jewish notables were able to convince a few high-ranking National Socialist Protectorate officials that the JKG in Prague, since March 1940 the sole Jewish representative organization in the Protectorate, would be exempt from a measure issued by the Reich Protector von Neurath, stipulating that all valuables owned by Jewish people, Jewish companies or Jewish organizations had to be deposited in a foreign exchange bank (*Devisenbank*). This was the first crucial step towards the effective creation of the Jewish Central Museum two years later. It meant that all kinds of Jewish religious artifacts could be saved from being either sold, destroyed, or melted down in the case of precious metals like gold and silver.[168]

That this "impossible" Jewish museum was allowed to exist by the National Socialists is a source of perplexity to this day. The Nazis were after all intent on destroying the "Jewish race".[169] Jan Björn Potthast has given the hitherto most satisfying answer to the difficult "existential question" of this museum, one that considers the National Socialists' possible interests for supporting the endeavor to preserve the Czechoslovak Jewish heritage. Most likely, the museum was founded and supported by the SS because they envisioned a long-term project of so-called "enemy research" (*Gegnerforschung*). The SS, which enjoyed a certain autonomy vis-à-vis Berlin in the Protectorate, reasoned that if they wanted to destroy the enemy, they must know the enemy. Some leading SS figures in the Protectorate also thought that, after the war was won, and the Jews of Europe had been eradicated, the new younger SS generation would have to be educated about the defeated evil that could always resurface. The younger Nazi generations would need to be trained to recognize "Jewishness". Competition with other National Socialist *Gegnerforscher* factions, mostly in Germany, was another important impetus for some SS leaders in the Protectorate to support the museum.[170]

During the war, the main building of the Jewish Central Museum was located at 3 Jáchymova in Prague, a former Jewish elementary school building,[171] where objects from all over the Protectorate were recorded and prepared for storage. There were in total five "commissions" dealing with these objects: "commission a", led by Dr. Mojzis Woskin-Nahartabi (1884–1944),[172] dealt with books; "commission b" assessed "museum objects of all kinds" (*Musealgegenstände jeden Art*); "commission c" dealt with silver artifacts; "commission d", led by Prof. Dr. Alfred Engel (1881–1944),[173] was devoted to archives; and "commission e" treated "sheet music" (*Musikalien*). Zdeněk König was responsible for correctly recording the objects handled by these five

documents describe him as a student and also a worker. See NA, Praha, fonds Policejní ředitelství Praha II, všeobecná spisovna, 1941-1950, kart. n° 5522, sign. K 3666/1, Zdeněk König 1921. König did not study at Charles University in Prague. See email (dated Aug. 14, 2015) from Kateřina Schwabiková (Archiv Univerzity Karlovy) to the author.

[167] Potthast 2002, 216.

[168] Potthast 2002, 106–9, 111–12, 219–22, 407–10.

[169] In this connection, Potthast speaks of the "Widersprüchlichkeit des Museums" (contradictoriness of the Jewish Central Museum) (Potthast 2002, 13, 441). For a more extensive Czech-language source, which focuses on the history of the Jewish museum in Prague before and after the war, see Veselská 2012b (we are waiting for a translation of this book).

[170] See the concluding chapter 8.2. on the Germans' role in the creation of the Jewish Central Museum in Potthast 2002, esp. 452–54.

[171] The street was named Regnartgasse (Regnartova) during the war. For some photos and more information on the building, see Padevět 2013, 140–42; Bušek 2007, 47; Potthast 2002, 239; Potthast 2000, 166. After the war, the building also became the main administrative center and book depot for the nationalized Jewish museum.

[172] See http://www.yadvashem.org/yv/en/exhibitions/our_collections/Terezín/index.asp and http://www2.holocaust.cz/en/victims/PERSON.ITI.1998647 (both accessed May 3, 2015).

[173] See http://www2.holocaust.cz/en/victims/PERSON.ITI.1308256 (accessed May 3, 2015).

[174] Židovské muzeum v Praze, Praha, 1906-1945 1946, fonds III. Personálni záležitosti, n° 38, Korespondence dr. Poláka – 1942-1943, Arbeitseinteilung in Jüdischen Zentralmuseums (Sep. 24, 1942), p. 2: "Er ist für die richtige Uebernahme der inventarisierten und bewerteten Gegenstände von den Kom-

commissions. He apparently also ensured that the objects were then transferred to the right storage premises in Prague. König also dealt with all the correspondence related to the objects.[174] Karel Rind (1892–1944), who had been a banker before the war, was König's superior.[175]

Considering a society in which Jewish people were persecuted, where "protection" – more specifically, "protection from being deported" – played such a pivotal role, what requires explanation is how a young man, who likely had no more than a secondary-school education, was chosen to work for the Jewish museum. Most of the people who worked there had academic qualifications and expertise in the objects being assessed. The first reason I see for this privilege is that König came from a well-off family. His socio-economic background likely also explains, as we have suggested, why König was lodged with other people of his class, like the Feins, in the building in Hodonínská (Gödinger Gasse). I also think that there is a good possibility that König obtained his position through Gustav Fein, Karl Fein's brother. Likely at some point after Karl Fein's deportation from Prague, Gustav Fein gained an important position in the JKG in Prague, within the control service (*Kontrolldienst*) of the trustee office (*Treuhandstelle*).[176] Gustav Fein certainly belonged to the right Jewish network to get König a job. It is also possible that Gustav Fein's working as a financial expert in Vienna before the war may have carried some weight with the banker Karel Rind.[177] Nothing much can be established here, but it is indeed remarkable that this rather unqualified (though likely well-educated) young man ended up in the Jewish museum.

Since the number of people working for the Jewish museum was always rather small, this makes his having been chosen stand out even more. The exact number of people working for the Jewish museum varies from one source to the next. According to one source, in September 1942, twenty-nine people worked there. Another source

missionen verantwortlich, ebenso für die richtige Verteilung der Gegenstände in die Lager und die Reinigungsstube. Er ist mit der Uebernahme der Kisten und Konsignationen betraut und mit der Führung der Korrespondenz, die sich auf die eingelaufenen Sendungen bezieht" (He is responsible for the proper receipt of inventoried and appraised items from the commissions, as well as for the proper distribution of items to the warehouses and the cleaning room. He is charged with taking delivery of boxes and consignments, and with conducting correspondence pertaining to shipments received).

175 The obituary for Karel Rind's daughter, Milena Rindova Rykin Chalfin (1925-2011), mentions that he was a banker. See http://www.legacy.com/obituaries/wickedlocal-needham/obituary.aspx?n=milena-chalfin&pid=152182076 (accessed Aug. 5, 2015). Before the war, Rind was working for the Legion Banka (Legionářská banka) in Prague at 24 Na poříčí. See email (dated Oct. 10, 2015) from Carol Rykin to the author. The building (currently the ČSOB bank) was designed by the architect Josef Gočár (1880–1945) in the early 1920s and is known for its so-called "Rondo-Cubist" style. See, for example, http://fra.archinform.net/projekte/4912.htm (accessed Nov. 5, 2015). While in Prague, in October 2015, I also consulted, the archival fonds on Josef Rind (1898–1950), a brother of Karel Rind, in the digitized database of the Židovské muzeum v Praze, Praha. The archival fonds was donated by Jaroslav (Jerry) Rind (1924–?), from Australia, the son of Josef Rind. This fonds includes a picture of Karel Rind posing with Fredy Hirsch (1916–1944), the Jewish sex symbol, and Franz Weidmann (1910-1944), one of the leaders of the JKG in Prague. See the digitized archive of the Židovské muzeum v Praze, Praha, sign. n° JMP.SHOAH/F/6/56/52262. But there are no pictures of Karel Rind's immediate family from the war. When I asked Martin Jelínek, of the Židovské muzeum v Praze, Praha, about the approximately 50.000 pictures recording the work done by staff in the Jewish museum during the war, he told me that the photos were not accessible to researchers nor digitized. I had hoped that a search through the photos would yield an image of Zdeněk König. I think seeing a young man in these pictures would be rather exceptional. Most of the men in the pictures were presumably older, scholarly-looking men. One of Martin Jelínek's tasks is to try to identify the people in these pictures, but he also told me that the bulk of the photos belonged to the period *after* the deportation of the first generation of museum collaborators (which included Karel Rind and Zdeněk König) in the summer of 1943. This generation was replaced by the so-called Mischlinge Jews. See also Potthast 2002, 355.

176 "Mitarbeiter der Jüdischen Kultusgemeinde in Prag, Stand zum 21.9.1942" (Krejčová, Svobodová & Hyndráková 1997, 427–28).

177 Let us recall also that Karl Fein's nephew, the elder Karl Fein (1893–1932), worked for the Petschek bank in Prague until his death in 1932.

claims that the maximum number of people employed there at any time was a little below seventy, while yet another claims that it never exceeded fifty.[178] In comparison, the trustee office, with its forty-two different sections, was the largest Prague JKG branch and employer, giving work to a little more than 1,000 people. The whole of the JKG in Prague employed (and protected) around 3,000 people, not counting their relatives.[179] Being employed by the JKG meant that one was temporarily shielded from deportation.

That König was one of the privileged few to end up specifically in the Jewish museum was thus likely not the result of sheer luck. That none of the other Jewish people living on Hodonínská (Gödinger Gasse) got such a life-saving job with the JKG could also indirectly indicate König's exceptionality. By the time the Jewish Central Museum started operating, in the summer of 1942, most of the other Jewish inhabitants of the Hodonínská (Gödinger Gasse) building had already been deported. In May 1942, Zdeněk König moved to 11 Valentinsgasse (Valentinská), Prague I. The move was likely tied to his newly obtained employment in the Jewish museum. From his new residence it was only a five minutes' walk to his new job.[180] Karl Fein's mother and older brother Gustav Fein moved out of the apartment in Hodonínská (Gödinger Gasse) street in October 1942.

In this connection, it is important to recall the curfew that forbade Jewish people leaving their homes after 8 p.m.[181] As a consequence, Jewish people likely sought out each other's company in the evenings and spoke a lot. It cannot be excluded

[178] In the "Mitarbeiter der Jüdischen Kultusgemeinde in Prag, Stand zum 21.9.1942" list, I counted twenty-four names belonging to people who worked for the Jewish museum. See Krejčová et al. 1997, 471–72. Cf. Bušek 2007, 32 n. 12. Bušek counts thirty-four employees in the same list. According to another source, forty-seven people were working for the Jewish museum at the end of December 1942. See Židovské muzeum v Praze, Praha, 1906-1945 1946, fonds III. Personálni záležitosti, n° 38, Korespondence dr. Poláka – 1942-1943, Jahresbericht für die Zeit von 3.8.[1942]-31.12.1942, p. 4. Potthast quotes yet another source that gives the number of people working for the Jewish Museum as sixty-three (Potthast 2002, 233). Further, Potthast mentions a November 1943 document that lists forty-four people, but this was after the deportation of the first generation of employees of the Jewish museum (Potthast 2002, 289). The same is true of another October 1944 staff list that Potthast mentions, in which twenty-nine people were employed in the Jewish museum. See Potthast 2002, 373. Cf. Potthast 2000, 167, 172, 174.

[179] Bušek 2007, 32 n. 12. Referring to Krejčová, Svobodová and Hyndráková, Ondrichová cites the number of people working for the JKG in Prague as 2,102 (Ondrichová 2000, 42; Krejčová, Svobodová & Hyndráková 1997, 409). However, I did not find that number in the source given.

[180] König's boss, Karel Rind and his family, lived – literally – just around the corner at 10 Veleslavínova (Weleslawingasse), Prague I. The evidence obyvatelstva sheet for König in NA, Praha, fonds Policejní ředitelství Praha II, notes that he lived in with "Ing. Fuchs". This was Arnošt Fuchs (1883–1943?) and his wife Alice Fuchsová (1892–1943?) who were deported from Prague to Terezín on transport "AAt" on July 23, 1942. Both were further transferred from Terezín to Auschwitz-Birkenau on February 1, 1943. The Fuchs couple had two children, Jan Fuchs (1917–?) and František Fuchs (1919–?). Jan Fuchs was deported to Terezín on transport "J" on December 4, 1941. He was further transferred to Auschwitz-Birkenau in October 1944, ultimately being liberated from the Buchenwald concentration camp at the end of the war. I have tried to get into contact with the current relatives of one of Jan Fuchs's two sons, Petr Fuchs and Jiří Fuchs. In January 2016, I sent twelve letters to the twelve people with those names in an online Czech phonebook, http://seznam.1188.cz/ (accessed Dec. 16, 2015). I received only one reply, saying that he was not the person I was looking for. Arnošt Fuchs's second son, František Fuchs, was part of the so-called *Kindertransporte* (children's transports) to England. His Prague police file states that he left for England on August 22, 1939. See NA, Praha, fonds Policejní ředitelství Praha II, všeobecná spisovna, 1931-1940, kart. n° 5906, sign. F 1822/26, František Fuchs 1919. His name also figures on the list of Czechoslovak people safely reaching England. See http://sh1.webring.com/people/fc/czechandslovakthings/WW2_CRTF_regind.htm (accessed Jan. 5, 2016). His further whereabouts are unknown. An inquiry with the World Jewish Relief Archives (London) brought no further information. See emails (dated Feb. 4, 2016 and May 19, 2016) from Sharon Adler (World Jewish Relief archives, London) to the author. On June 11, 2016, I also sent an email to the Kindertransport Association (USA) and the Association of Children of Jewish Refugees (ACJR, UK) inquiring about the further fate of František Fuchs. Oliver Walter (former Chairman of the ACJR) promptly replied with an email (dated Jun. 12, 2016) and kindly proposed publishing a search message in

that, on one of the many such evenings spent together, Karl Fein spoke about Magnus Hirschfeld, the looting of the Institute in Berlin, and all the tribulations of safeguarding the vulnerable Institute materials after Giese's suicide. Zdeněk König might have heard and been influenced by the story. We have just suggested that the young man was possibly deliberately dropped into the Jewish museum, perhaps at Gustav Fein's direct suggestion. If this was the case, Zdeněk König's position in the Jewish Central Museum may have interested Elise Brecher, Siegfried Ascher and still others from the around thirty Jewish people still in Brno when König started work. It is in any case easy to imagine that the people in Brno would have been eager to know about the further fates of the confiscated Jewish artifacts from Brno (and other cities) sent to the Jewish museum in Prague. We have suggested that the Jewish hospital in Brno was likely the place where much of the relevant information regarding the Jewish community was eagerly collected and also intensely circulated. Zdeněk König may have been one of their informants.

Another good source of information on the whole massive expropriation operation taking place in Prague may have been Gustav Fein, since he was a controller in the trustee office in Prague. The already mentioned Alfred Engel, responsible for Jewish archives coming into the Jewish museum, might have been another. Starting in 1922, Engel taught at the German gymnasium in Brno for a while, the school where Karl Fein and most others in Brno's German-speaking elite received their primary education. As a teacher in this school, Alfred Engel likely had his own contacts with the mainly German-speaking Jewish elite of Brno.[182]

The artifacts collected by the Jewish Central Museum in Prague were mostly religious objects, scrolls and books. We saw earlier that, in 1913, the Alois Brecher-Bibliothek-Stiftung was inaugurated, honoring Elise Brecher's late husband Alois Brecher. The Alois Brecher-Bibliothek-Stiftung's book collection was in time added to the library of the B'nai B'rith Moravia lodge and housed at 31 Legionärenstrasse (třída Legionářů) in Brno. Learning what had happened to the Alois Brecher-Bibliothek-Stiftung book collection may have been reason enough for Elise Brecher to take an interest in the activities of the newly founded Jewish museum in Prague.[183]

So, all in all, it is possible that Zdeněk König was indeed inserted into the Jewish museum with a hidden agenda, and that his information about what was happening to the books and religious artifacts that once belonged to the Protectorate's Jewish community also reached Brno. Gustav Fein, and possibly others too, may have passed on information about what was happening in Prague. Like the employees of the JKG in Prague, the patients of the Jewish hospital in Brno were temporarily exempt from deportation and the two might indeed have been in contact with one another. There is an almost exact overlap in the period, from the summer of 1942 until the summer of 1943, that each group stayed in its location – the approximately thirty remaining Jewish people in Brno, after the Jewish mass transports ended, and the first wave of people working for the Jewish Central Museum in Prague.

the June 2016 issue of the ACJR newsletter. This was done, but no one responded.

181 Kárný et al. 1996, 35–37.

182 For information on Engel, see Veselská 2012a, 593. Engel married Emilie Wiesner (1881–1933), but the couple had no children. Someone else was involved in the effort to start up a Jewish museum in Mikulov (Nikolsburg) in the decades before the war: Richard Teltscher (1888–1974). Teltscher's family donated his very interesting library to the Center for Jewish studies at the University of Manchester after his death. See http://www.library.manchester.ac.uk/search-resources/guide-to-special-collections/atoz/teltscher-collection/ (accessed Aug. 11, 2015). The Nikolsburg Jewish museum's collection, which Alfred Engel guarded, is also mentioned in Potthast 2002, 232–33. This museum's artifacts were apparently stored in Brno. Eventually, the collection also became homeless and was sent to Prague.

183 Apart from one volume, none of the books of the Alois Brecher-Bibliothek-Stiftung or the B'nai B'rith Moravia lodge seem to have ended up in the Jewish museum in Prague.

Zdeněk König was transported to Terezín on transport "Dh" on July 8, 1943, along with his superior Karel Rind and his family.[184] Two months later, on September, 6, 1943, König was deported on transport "Dl" from Terezín to Auschwitz. That transport carried 2,479 people.[185] The entire "first generation" of Jewish collaborators of the Prague Jewish museum was deported in the first week of July 1943, and was replaced.[186] König's transport left Prague a week after the very last Jewish people from Brno were deported on the final transport "Dg" on July 1, 1943. Officially, Elise Brecher was deported on this transport as well. (More on this not-so-straightforward matter later on.)

Artur Feldmann Sr.'s confiscated art collection, Viktor Oppenheimer's protected art collection and Zdeněk König's story seem to point to the great willingness to safeguard their own valuables of some of the educated or well-off members of the Jewish community in the Protectorate. This seems to me one of the main indications that the decision to discard the Institute materials was *not* taken in the Jewish hospital in Brno. I do not think that the conscious destruction of Jewish cultural heritage was on the agenda for the Jewish cultural elite in the Protectorate, and Elise Brecher certainly belonged to that elite. Furthermore, as already suggested, she was most likely very aware of the many ordeals the remains of Hirschfeld's collection experienced after 1933 and, as also suggested, she may even have played a role in safeguarding it. Coldly discarding this collection was not really a viable option for Elise Brecher.

PRELIMINARY CONCLUSION

By asking how the guestbook could have ended up with Dr. Stanislav Kadĕrka, and after taking a close look at the Jewish hospital in Brno, we came upon an alternative scenario about who might have decided to discard the Institute materials and where this decision was made. The unexpected discovery that Jaroslav Růžička was closely associated with the family who previously owned the building housing the Jewish hospital led us to the idea that Karl Fein's relatives could have taken the decision to discard the Institute materials there. Elise Brecher and her son Fritz Brecher may have made the difficult decision about the fate of the Institute materials in March, April or even May 1942. Of course, this alternative scenario also lends further credence to the hypothesis with which we started this chapter. We suggested that Kadĕrka might have heard about the discarding of the Institute materials in the Jewish hospital when visiting his patient Siegfried Ascher, not just because the news was circulating

[184] Rind's wife was Gisela Reinish (1894–1944?). They had two children: Josef (1921–1945) and Milena (1925–2011). See the "Mitarbeiter der Jüdischen Kultusgemeinde in Prag, Stand zum 21.9.1942" (Krejčová et al. 1997, 472) where the family of four is assigned numbers 3582, 3583, 3584 and 3585. Milena Rind was liberated from Merzdorf, a subsidiary camp of Groß-Rosen (currently Rogoźnica in Poland). After the war, she took the name Milena Rindova Rykin Chalfin and moved to the east coast of the USA where she married and had a daughter, Carol Rykin Rightor. Milena Rindova Rykin Chalfin remarried after the death of her first husband and died in 2011. See http://www.legacy.com/obituaries/wickedlocal-needham/obituary.aspx?n=milena-chalfin&pid=152182076 and http://www.ancientfaces.com/person/milena-rindova-rykin-chalfin/12607558 (both accessed Aug. 5, 2015). On August 5, 2015, I sent a letter to Carol and Ned Rightor and received an answer by email (dated Aug. 21, 2015) from Carol Rykin. I want to thank her for answering my very particular questions. Although some family albums survived the war, having been left with friends before the Rind family's deportation, no pictures depicted Karel Rind's activity in the museum. See email (dated Oct. 10, 2015) from Carol Rykin to the author.

[185] At first sight, his brother František König (1924–1943?), three years his junior, followed Zdeněk König, being deported to Auschwitz the same day, though on the second mass transport "Dm", which carried 2,528 people. However, if one looks at the different number(s) of people deported on the two mass transports – each of which should have carried exactly 2,500 people – it is conceivable that František König may have initially tried to avoid deportation to Auschwitz by not showing up for the first transport that day.

[186] Potthast 2000, 172.

there but maybe also because that is where the decision itself was taken. But we need to stress that it is also possible that Stanislav Kaděrka never set foot in the Jewish hospital. Rudolf Pick ("Pikesler") had possibly simply sent a postcard to Albert Ascher, then already imprisoned in Terezín, informing him that Ascher's brother, Siegfried, was safe in the Jewish hospital in Brno, having been told this by Kaděrka over the telephone. Indeed, we may even ask why Kaděrka would need to visit a hospital that was already under the responsibility of another doctor, Nelly Stern. At the same time, however, this possible absence does not in any way invalidate our newly forged hypothesis – arrived at by considering a scenario involving Kaděrka – that the decision about what to do with the Institute materials may have been taken in the Jewish hospital.

A THIRD SCENARIO

But is there not a third possibility, one that combines involvement by the *Kamarád* group *and* a part played by the Jewish hospital? What if Karl Fein told his aunt Elise Brecher about his decision to entrust the materials to the *Kamarád* people or (though less likely) vice versa? A "hybrid explanation" of who decided to discard the Institute materials, involving both the *Kamarád* people and Elise Brecher in some way, is not all that exotic an idea. Especially some curious geographic "proximities" are maybe not to be neglected in this regard. The Jewish hospital where Elise Brecher was a patient and Jaroslav Očadlík's apartment building were on the same street. Očadlík's lived at 4b Stephansgasse (Štěpánská); the hospital's address was 5 Stephansgasse (Štěpánská), about a hundred meters away. The moving firm Leopold Fleischer had its storage premises at 38 Mühlgasse (Mlýnská), only one block away from Stephansgasse (Štěpánská), and the same is true of the storage room that Elise Brecher rented with the Morava storage company. The Růžička couple's scrap company was 500 meters' distant from Stephansgasse (Štěpánská) [ill. 9] [ill. 10]. These locations' proximity would have made a more inconspicuous transfer of the Institute materials possible. However, the small distance between the Jewish hospital and Očadlík's apartment should be viewed with some reservation. We have seen that Elise Brecher only arrived in the Jewish hospital in January 1941. Očadlík was already at his Stephansgasse (Štěpánská) address in May 1940 (at the latest), before the makeshift Jewish hospital existed. This may indicate that their geographical proximity is accidental.

Secondly, we already mentioned that Stanislav Černil and Jaroslav Růžička were very familiar with the Trnitá (Dörnrössel) neighborhood. Stanislav Černíl's parents, Josef and Maria Černíl, lived there at least until around 1920. The year that their son Stanislav was born, they briefly lived at 14 Stephansgasse (Štěpánská).[187] Marie Černíl kept a furniture shop at 12 Cyrillsgasse (Cyrilská) until at least 1927,[188] a street that ran (and still runs) parallel to Stephansgasse (Štěpánská). The furniture shop was even adjacent to the Jewish hospital. This means that Stanislav Černíl must have been very familiar with the Trnitá neighborhood until he was (at least) twelve or even eighteen. He would surely have known the hustle and bustle of the Josef Pollak scrap iron company, located behind the building where he and his parents lived. As we have seen, Jaroslav Růžička moved a lot in the 1920s and 1930s, sometimes living in this neighborhood. On three separate occasions, he lived on Tschechnergasse (Čechyňská), a street that ran parallel to Cyrillsgasse (Cyrilská), where Černíl's

[187] *Adressbuch von Brünn* 1908, 160. Earlier, the couple had lived on other streets in the same Trnitá (Dörnrössel) neighborhood, among them Arnoldgasse (Zvonařka) and Dornich (Dornych). See *Adressbuch von Brünn* 1906, 147; *Adressbuch von Brünn* 1907, 153.

[188] *Adreßbuch von Groß-Brünn* 1927, 528.

parents lived and kept their businesses.[189] But, of course, this could also be just coincidence.

Lastly, we may also mention here that Dr. Siegfried Fischl, a member of the organizing committee of the 1932 WLSR Brno conference, lived at 10 Stephansgasse (Štěpánská) until mid-February 1941.[190] Two buildings separated the house where Fischl and his wife lived and Jaroslav Očadlík's apartment building. Here again, we may wonder if this geographical proximity has any connection to our story or is simply a coincidence [ill. 11].

RABBI ALBERT SCHÖN

Beyond these intriguing geographical proximities, I think that one factor, above all, lends further credence to the third scenario of the possible involvement of both the *Kamarád* people and the Jewish community in the fate of the Institute materials in 1942. We have already briefly mentioned that Stanislav Černil was an intimate friend of the German-speaking Jewish Schön family in Moravská Ostrava (Mährisch-Ostrau), a city where Černil worked in the 1930s. Let us take a closer look at this family. Leopold (Arje) Schön (1882–1974), a plumber by trade, was married to Therese (Terezie) Rivka Jellinek (1890–1974). The couple had two sons. According to Dagmar Černil, Stanislav Černil's daughter, the couple's youngest son, Albert Schön (1913–1944?), became a rabbi in February 1936 in Prostějov (Proßnitz), at the age of twenty-two.[191] Albert Schön was a left-wing Zionist, a member of the socialist Blue and White (Thelet Lavan) youth organization.[192] In 1934–35, he was briefly in Jerusalem, and studied at the Hebrew University there [ill. 12].[193]

In October 1939, Leopold Schön was entangled in the Nisko experiment, which deported 100,000 Jews, around 900 of them Jewish men from Moravská Ostrava

189 Růžička lived at 5, 6 and 9 Tschechnergasse (Čechyňská), and also at 9 Dornich (Dornych), both streets in the same Trnitá neighborhood to which he returned a few times. See the many resident registration cards for Jaroslav Růžička in the AMB, Brno, fonds Z 1.

190 See the resident registration card (dated Feb. 14, 1941) for Siegfried Fischl in the AMB, Brno, fonds Z 1, which gives 10 Stephansgasse (Štěpánská) as his previous address. The same address appears in the Fischl-Krak couple's February 1941 divorce file. See MZA, Brno, fonds C 11, Krajský soud civilní Brno (Kreisgericht für Zivilsachen Brünn), III. manipulace, kart. n° 461, sign. Ck Ia 62/41, divorce file Siegfried Fischl and Vera Krak. The couple moved to 10 Stephansgasse (Štěpánská) in November 1939. In 1934, Siegfried Fischl was still living at 52 Neugasse (Nová). See *Adreßbuch von Groß-Brünn* 1934, 191. This was a peculiar address since it was located in the Augarten (Lužánky) park. Fischl's very last Brno address (immediately after living on Stephansgasse/Štěpánská) was 4 Quergasse (Příční). After he died in Auschwitz-Birkenau, in February 1942, his widow lived at 51 Offermanngasse (Offermannova), continuing to live there after the war, when it was renumbered and renamed 12 Vlhká. See Siegfried Fischl's home certificate in the AMB, Brno, fonds B 1/39; *Adresář zemského hlavního města Brna 1948* 1948, 82. The house at 10 Stephansgasse (Štěpánská) where Fischl used to live was bombed on November 20, 1944, so extensively damaged that it was later torn down. See the address "Štěpánská 10" in the "Bombardování Brna" database, https://gis.brno.cz/ags/bomby/ (accessed Nov. 30, 2020). There is another "proximity" linked to Fischl. Starting in November 1937, he also lived (our owned or rented an apartment) at the address 4 Falkensteinergasse (Falkensteinerova), see NA, Praha, fonds n° 1420, Policejní ředitelství Praha II, PŘ II 1931-1940, kart. n° 709, sign. F21/17, file Siegfried (Vítězslav) Fischl (born March 5, 1877). In 1938, Karl Fein lived for two weeks at the (presumably) neighboring address 2a Falkensteinergasse (Falkensteinerova).

191 GFHA, Beit Lohamei Haghetaot (Israel), Collection of the Schoen-Sima family from Czechoslovakia, documents, albums, and books, catalogue n° 30069, 1935 correspondence on clerical service, available online at https://infocenters.co.il/gfh/pdf_viewer.asp?lang=ENG&dlang=ENG&module=search&page=pdf_viewer&rsvr=4@4¶m=<pdf_path>multimedia/Files/Idea/נכנס 030069-2.pdf</><book_id>129722</>¶m2=&site=gfh (accessed Jan. 22, 2021). Most sources note that he became a rabbi at twenty-three, but he only turned that age in November 1936. Curiously, he was only officially certified as a rabbi by the Breslau (currently Wrocław, Poland) theological school in January 1937. See also emails (dated Dec. 16, 2020 and Dec. 17, 2020) from Daniel Baránek (Židovské muzeum v Praze, Praha) to the author; https://www.geni.com/people/Leopold-Sch%C3%B6n/6000000038834123429 and https://www.geni.com/people/Albert-Vojtech-Sch%C3%B6n/6000000038830049192 (both accessed Dec. 18, 2020).

(Mährisch-Ostrau), to the General Government (Generalgouvernement) in occupied Poland. When the project was abandoned, in the beginning of 1940, Leopold Schön returned to Ostrava in May 1940.[194] Together with other Jewish citizens, Leopold's son Albert Schön was arrested in Prostějov (Proßnitz) on September 1, 1939, and deported to Dachau one week later, and then transferred to Buchenwald.[195] He was released from Buchenwald in January 1940 and arrived in Brno from Prostějov on March 1, 1940. In Brno, he first lived at 12 Česká (Tschechische Gasse).[196] In 1940–42, Albert Schön was one of Brno's rabbis.[197] His Gestapo file tells us that he was released from Buchenwald on the order of the Brno auxiliary office (*Zweigstelle*) of the Central Office for Jewish Emigration (Zentralstelle für Jüdische Auswanderung). The latter was aware that, because he was himself young, Schön was popular with the Jewish youth and thus a good candidate to assist them in encouraging the emigration of Jewish youngsters from Brno.[198] Schön's parents themselves eventually moved to Brno and lived with their son.[199]

Albert Schön and his parents were deported together from Brno to Terezín on March 31, 1942, on transport "Af". In Terezín, Albert Schön officiated Jewish marriages and burials and presumably also worked in the Hebrew library, where nineteen other rabbis and additional specialists processed incoming books and

[192] On his being a left-wing rabbi and visiting Jerusalem, see "Interview with Jenny and Josef Manuel, 1997, Nahariya, Israel", Makarova, Makarov & Kuperman 2004, 384.

[193] GFHA, Beit Lohamei Haghetaot (Israel), Collection of the Schoen-Sima family from Czechoslovakia, documents, albums, and books, catalogue n° 30069, certificate for his studies at the Hebrew University of Jerusalem in 1933–1934.

[194] AMB, Brno, fonds Z 1, resident registration card (dated May 6, 1940) Leopold Schön. On Ostrava and the Nisko project, see Lawson, Salomonovičová & Šústková 2018, 225–32.

[195] MZA, Brno, fonds B 340, Gestapo Brno, file n° 8968, kart. n° 184, sign. 100-184-18, file Albert Schön, f. 1-5, 19. Schön was arrested because his name was on the so-called *A-Kartei* (see above, p. 587, n. 208). One of the leaders of the Jewish community in Prostějov (Proßnitz), Josef Holz (1876–1944?), was also arrested and deported to Buchenwald. Albert Schön was imprisoned in Buchenwald from September 27, 1939 until January 12, 1940. See Individuelle Häftlingsunterlagen KL Buchenwald at https://collections.arolsen-archives.org/archive/7053199/?p=1&s=albert%20sch%C3%B6n&doc_id=7053200 (accessed Jan. 22, 2021). His Buchenwald *Entlassungsschein* (release certificate), on the other hand, claims he was imprisoned on September 10, 1939. See GFHA, Beit Lohamei Haghetaot (Israel), Collection of the Schoen-Sima family from Czechoslovakia, documents, albums, and books, catalogue n° 30069, release certificate from the Buchenwald camp, available online at https://infocenters.co.il/gfh/pdf_viewer.asp?lang=ENG&dlang=ENG&module=search&page=pdf_viewer&rsvr=4@4¶m=%3Cpdf_path%3Emultimedia/Files/Idea/%D7%A0%D7%9B%D7%A0%D7%A1%20030069-2.pdf%3C/%3E%3Cbook_id%3E129722%3C/%3E¶m2=&site=gfh (accessed Jan. 22, 2021). See also MZA, Brno, fonds B 340, Gestapo Brno, file n° 8968, kart. n° 184, sign. 100-184-18, file Albert Schön, f. 5.

[196] The modernist building at 12 Česká (Tschechische Gasse) was erected in 1936. See Pelčák & Šlapeta 2015, 188–89.

[197] Albert Schön's file on his appointment as a rabbi in both Prostějov (Proßnitz) and Brno is included in the papers donated to the Ghetto Fighters' House in 2012 by David Shima, the son of Albert Schön's brother Kurt Schön. See GFHA, Beit Lohamei Haghetaot (Israel), catalogue n° 32911, Collection of the Schoen-Sima family from Czechoslovakia, documents, albums, and books, available online at https://www.infocenters.co.il/gfh/multimedia/Files/Idea/%D7%A0%D7%9B%D7%A0%D7%A1%20030069-2.pdf (accessed Jan. 22, 2021).

[198] MZA, Brno, fonds B 340, Gestapo Brno, n° 8968, kart. n° 184, sign. 100-184-18, file Albert Schön, f. 16-17.

[199] According to resident registration cards in the AMB, Brno, fonds Z 1, Terezie Schön arrived in Brno on March 22, 1940 and Leopold Schön on May 6, 1940. All three moved from 12 Česká (Tschechische Gasse) to 3a Hutterova (Huttergasse) on March 30, 1941. See the resident registration cards for all three in AMB, Brno, fonds Z 1. See also Leopold Schön issued's identity card in Brno on June 3, 1940, in GFHA, Beit Lohamei Haghetaot (Israel), catalogue n° 32911, Collection of the Schoen-Sima family from Czechoslovakia, documents, albums, and books, 2.2, a Czech ID card issued to Leopold Schoen for the Protectorate of Bohemia and Moravia, available online at https://infocenters.co.il/gfh/pdf_viewer.asp?lang=ENG&dlang=ENG&module=search&page=pdf_viewer&rsvr=4@4¶m=%3Cwords%3Eschoen%3C/%3E%3Cpdf_path%3Emultimedia/Files/Idea/%D7%A0%D7%9B%D7%A0%D7%A1%20032911-1%20%D7%91.pdf%3C/%3E%3Cbook_id%3E136860%3C/%3E¶m2=&site=gfh (accessed Jan. 22, 2021).

scrolls. The latter group, who sifted the Judaica and Hebraica coming into Terezín, was known as the Talmudkommando.[200] As a member of the group formed around the German Philipp Manes (1875–1944?), Albert Schön delivered more than thirty lectures in Terezin.[201] In Terezín also, on March 28, 1943, Schön married Eva Nassau (1924–1944?), then eighteen, whom he knew from Brno.[202] Jacob Edelstein was one of the two witnesses at the wedding.[203] (We have previously linked Edelstein to Gustav Fein, Karl Fein's brother.)

Albert Schön was transferred from Terezín to Auschwitz-Birkenau on transport "El" on September 29, 1944. His young wife and her parents also perished in the Holocaust.[204] Albert Schön's father, Leopold Schön, and his wife Therese, were liberated from Terezín. They returned to their home at 13 Kostelní in Ostrava (Ostrau), emigrating to Israel some time after 1948, where both died in 1974 [ill. 13] [ill. 14].[205] The couple also had another son, Kurt Schön (1920–2004), who joined the Czech military abroad during the war. Kurt changed his last name to Šíma (Simah) shortly after the war and emigrated to Israel in 1949.[206] He married Yehudit Miriam Berkovitz (1923–2013) in December 1948. The couple had one son, David Abraham Shima (1949–).[207]

When working in Moravská Ostrava (Mährisch-Ostrau) in the 1930s, Stanislav Černil was thus in close contact with the family of a young man who turned out to be the rabbi of Brno early in the war (1940–42). For her part, Elise Brecher was staying in the Jewish hospital with Siegfried Ascher, one of the former leaders of the JKG in Brno. Moreover, before moving to Brno, Albert Schön had been a rabbi for three years (1936–39) in Prostějov (Proßnitz), the ancestral city of the Brecher family. Of the eight children of the bookseller Ignaz Brecher (1813–1880) and Amalia Kurz (1818–1905), Karl Fein's maternal grandfather and grandmother, six were born in Prostějov (Proßnitz). Alois Brecher, Elise Brecher's husband, was born there.[208] Politically, like Karl Fein and his aunt, Albert Schön was a leftist.

[200] Rothkirchen 2005, 266; Makarova, Makarov & Kuperman 2004, 383. On the Hebrew library and its Judaica and Hebraica holdings in Terezín, see Bušek 2007, 38–39.

[201] For the list of Schön's lectures in Terezín, see Makarova, Makarov & Kuperman 2004, 509–10.

[202] Schön was in contact with the girl in Brno since at least November 1941. He may even have known the very young Eva Nassau in 1936–39, when he was in Prostějov (Proßnitz), where she was born.

[203] GFHA, Beit Lohamei Haghetaot (Israel), Collection of the Schoen-Sima family from Czechoslovakia, documents, albums, and books, catalogue n° 30069, marriage license from the Terezín ghetto (dated Mar. 28, 1943), available online at https://infocenters.co.il/gfh/pdf_viewer.asp?lang=ENG&dlang=ENG&module=search&page=pdf_viewer&rsvr=4@4¶m=%3Cpdf_path%3Emultimedia/Files/Idea/%D7%A0%D7%9B%D7%A0%D7%A1%20030069-3%D7%90.pdf%3C/%3E%3Cbook_id%3E129722%3C/%3E¶m2=&site=gfh (accessed Jan. 22, 2021).

[204] Four days after Albert Schön and his parents were deported, Eve Nassau and her parents, Robert Nassau (1889–1944?) and Klara Nassau (1893–1944?), were also deported from Brno to Terezín on transport "Ah" on April 4, 1942. She and her parents were further transferred to Auschwitz-Birkenau on transport "Es" on October 19, 1944. See Kárný et al. 1995, 457, where Eva's name erroneously appears under "Nasau". See also https://www.geni.com/people/Eva-Sch%C3%B6n/6000000038830284827 (accessed Dec. 18, 2020). Ruth Jokl (née Nassau, 1920–2006), Robert and Klara Nassau's other daughter, survived the Holocaust and died in Los Angeles in 2006. I was not able to determine if Ruth had any children with her husband Erich Jokl (1919–?).

[205] Kárný et al. 1995, 447.

[206] GFHA, Beit Lohamei Haghetaot (Israel), catalogue n° 32911, Collection of the Schoen-Sima family from Czechoslovakia, documents, albums, and books. In 1998, Kurt Schön left a Holocaust testimony (in Hebrew) at the USC Shoah Foundation Visual History Archive, which I did not consult. See https://vhaonline.usc.edu/viewingPage?testimonyID=41418# (accessed Jan. 3, 2020). A good amount of the information I use here also comes from the very informative email (dated Jan. 7, 2021) from Šárka Glombíčková (Archiv města Ostravy, Ostrava) to the author.

[207] See https://www.geni.com/people/David-Shima/6000000055570886837 (accessed Jan. 21, 2021). On January 23, 2021, I sent an email to the Ghetto Fighters' House Archives in Israel, requesting that an email be sent to Kurt Šíma's son, David Shima. The director of the archive informed me that the email was forwarded to David Shima. See email (dated Jan. 28, 2021) from Anat Bratman-Elhalel (GFHA,

When Albert Schön visited the Jewish hospital, all these various elements may have surfaced in conversation, setting in motion certain dynamics, possibly even co-determining the further fate of the Institute materials. Schön arrived in Brno in March 1940; he was deported from there on the last day of March 1942. That makes it very likely that, in his capacity as a rabbi, he visited the sick people of his community in the Jewish hospital, which started operation late in 1941, over a period of at least three or four months. Since, as we have just seen, Schön was part of the Talmudkommando in Terezín, he must also have had a prior concern for the preservation of Jewish heritage.

We have also seen, in relation to Jaroslav Růžička, that some people on Stephansgasse (Štěpánská) kept a close eye on who visited the Jewish hospital, or the scrap iron company, and did not hesitate to inform the Germans about anything they considered suspect. In this context, Albert Schön may have been the perfect messenger between the people residing in the Jewish hospital and the *Kamarád* clique or even Stanislav Černil alone. According to his daughter Dagmar, Černil was very close to and even lived in with the Schön family, and this shows, at the very least, that Černil had no issues with the Jewish community and may even have felt some concern about their persecution by the Germans. Also, if Černil had any issues with the Jewish community in Brno, he would easily have been able to appeal to Albert Schön's parents, who could have intervened for him through their son Albert.[209] One possible scenario can be rejected. As we have seen, Stanislav Černil may have made a drastic decision about the Institute materials in September 1942. Since Schön was deported in March 1942, he could not have imparted the news about what Černil or another *Kamarád* member had done to the people in the Jewish hospital.

So, it's possible that the *Kamarád* group, or at least some of its members, and Elise Brecher stayed in contact regarding the further fate of the Institute materials for the first three years of the war. Karl Fein's involving two very different players to safeguard the Institute materials would indeed have been wise, as more people would share the burden. In case of trouble, others would be able to take over and carry on. Fein's entrusting the Institute materials to the *Kamarád* people would at least have ensured that the task did not rest on the shoulders of just one person. Elise Brecher and the *Kamarád* clique may even have agreed together to discard the Institute materials. But group dynamics tend to have surprising outcomes. We have already pointed out that fierce discussions on what to do with the Institute materials may have occurred within the *Kamarád* group. Seized by real fear of a life-threatening situation, a single person could "infect" the whole group with his urgent desire that all respect his fear.

We have also already suggested that Černil may have feared interrogation, feeling that he simply could not guarantee that, if faced with possible torture, he would *not talk*

Beit Lohamei Haghetaot, Israel) to the author. David Shima preferred not to answer my email. I also sent a message to David Shima through www.geni.com, on January 21, 2021, but there was no reply.

[208] See the excellent Brecher family tree, started by Andreas Franck in 2019, https://www.geni.com/family-tree/index/6000000096581224821 (accessed Feb. 22, 2021).

[209] The young Albert Schön also received some rabbinical training in Berlin, but it is not known if this was before or after 1933, or if he was aware of the existence of Hirschfeld's Institute. An undated handwritten document contains notes by Schön from a course on *Jüden und Jüdentum in Aegypten* (Jews and Jewishness in Egypt) he took at the Rabbiner-Seminar zu Berlin, an educational institution that exists to this day. See GFHA, Beit Lohamei Haghetaot (Israel), Collection of the Schoen-Sima family from Czechoslovakia, documents, albums, and books, catalogue n° 30069, notebook from a rabbinical seminar in Berlin on Jewish matters and Egyptian Jewry, available online at https://infocenters.co.il/gfh/pdf_viewer.asp?lang=ENG&dlang=ENG&module=search&page=pdf_viewer&rsvr=4@4¶m=%3Cpdf_path%3Emultimedia/Files/Idea/%D7%A0%D7%9B%D7%A0%D7%A1%20030069-3%D7%90.pdf%3C/%3E%3Cbook_id%3E129722%3C/%3E¶m2=&site=gfh (accessed Jan. 23, 2021). I inquired with the Rabbinerseminar zu Berlin e.V. about König's attendance but I was told that most of the archives were lost in the war. See email (dated Feb. 15, 2021) from Debo-

about the Institute materials or his network of gay friends. We have focused mainly on Černil and Očadlík in the *Kamarád* group as the ones most likely to have taken the initiative to safeguard and/or discard the materials. But others in the Kamarád group might have strongly disagreed about what to do with the Institute materials. Maybe some panicked more than others, or maybe someone acted single-handedly without consulting the others. Let us also recall that Jaroslav Růžička seems to have been a cautious person who, on his own initiative, took the Kamarád address list from Štefan Kostelníček's apartment in the summer of 1932. Was Růžička maybe the one behind the radical idea to discard the materials in 1942? If he was, then he also immediately offered the safest solution.

In addition, the cooperation between Elise Brecher and the *Kamarád* group possibly did not go as smoothly as hoped. Maybe the *Kamarád* people, in a moment of panic, suddenly acted on their own without consulting Elise Brecher. The summons for both Stanislav Černil and Jaroslav Očadlík to confirm their current addresses in September 1942 might have constituted such a moment of extreme panic. Maybe the news that the Institute materials were discarded reached Elise Brecher because one of the *Kamarád* people felt obliged to report what they had done. Since the *Kamarád* group seems to have acted in September 1942, Elise Brecher could only have heard about their discarding the materials that month at the earliest. At that point, Siegfried Ascher was still alive and a patient in the Jewish hospital, where Dr. Kadĕrka might have visited him and heard about the discarding of the Institute materials.[210]

CONCLUSION

So, we now have not two but three main possibilities of who in Brno may have decided to discard the Institute materials in 1942. The decision might have been taken by members of the *Kamarád* founding group or by people in the Jewish hospital. As a third scenario, we considered the possibility that both groups might have been in some kind of contact about the guarding and possibly also discarding the Institute materials. Once again, the only truly certain factor in the final part of our story was and is the scrap trader, Jaroslav Růžička, and his wife Jindra, who saw to it that the Institute materials were discarded in 1942.

At present, we are still missing a few elements that would lead us to a final conclusion about who precisely took the fatal decision in 1942. Had the affidavit in the Hirschfeld guestbook, instead of only mentioning the year, also included the month that the Institute materials were retrieved from the old paper container, it would likely have enabled us to choose between scenarios. The *Kamarád* people, if indeed they were involved, would seem to have acted in September 1942, when Stanislav Černil and Jaroslav Očadlík were summoned to confirm their current addresses. If, on the contrary, the decision was taken in the Jewish hospital by Karl Fein's aunt, Elise Brecher, or her son Fritz Brecher, then action was most likely taken earlier, in March, April or even May 1942.

rah Ohayon (Rabbinerseminar zu Berlin) to the author. Mrs. Ohayon also referred me to Eliav & Hildesheimer 2008; however, it does not mention Albert Schön.

[210] In another imaginable scenario Jaroslav Růžička simply told his Jewish friend, the entrepreneur Robert Pollak, what he had done, not realizing that this news would spread like wildfire in the microcosm of the steadily shrinking Jewish community of Brno and, in particular, the Jewish hospital. But since Robert Pollak was deported in April 1942, and the Kamarád people acted around September 1942, this variant scenario seems almost excluded.

[211] I thank Marita Keilson-Lauritz for encouraging me to spell out these two "inside job" scenarios.

AN INSIDE JOB?

Let us go back to the beginning of this chapter. We asked if the 1942 retrieval of the Hirschfeld guestbook and some Institute books from an old paper container was a happy accident or rather the action of a man or woman on a mission. In either case, we saw that an explanation would be required for how someone managed to gain access to the Růžičkas' relatively inaccessible company premises. However, what if we remove this not negligible problematic element by treating the operation as an inside job? I think there are two possible *inside job* scenarios.[211]

Jaroslav Růžička's employees may have taken the initiative, independently of their employer. Strictly speaking, this would be theft, but theft is simply something to which humans are susceptible ... and all the more so during the trials of the war years. Since Jindra Růžičková was originally from Královo Pole, those working for her and her husband may have lived there as well, possibly contacting their local doctor with their booty. But in this case, we need to explain, as in the scenario involving Kaděrka's housekeeper, why two working-class people would, in addition to the hardcover Institute sexology books plausibly deemed more valuable by treasure hunters, *also* collect the Hirschfeld guestbook. Yet, the scenario of theft well accords with the reality that only a few items were taken. The possible robbers were clearly not able to take all the Institute books and, if this scenario was a reality, likely also needed to act furtively and in haste. The theft scenario does not contradict the affidavit. The thieves may have written the affidavit, possibly even at Kaděrka's request, in 1942, or after the war. As we have suggested, Kaděrka may have feared that one day he would have to explain – to returning Jewish people, or inquiring German occupiers – how he had acquired the artifacts.

There is a second possible inside job scenario. Until now, we have implicitly treated Jaroslav Růžička and (possibly) his wife Jindra as the pivotal evil geniuses in our story, since they seem to have had the final hand in making the greater part of the Hirschfeld and Institute materials disappear. But what if Jaroslav Růžička and his wife were the ones who decided in the end to save at least some of the materials? It is clear, for starters, that they would have done this in secret, that is, without the other *Kamarád* people's knowledge. We have just recalled that Jindra Růžičková was born and raised in the Královo Pole suburb where Dr. Stanislav Kaděrka also had his practice. Did the couple approach the doctor about the difficult matter of their being asked to destroy valuable materials? This second inside job scenario about how the materials may have ended up with Dr. Kaděrka in Královo Pole carries its own contradictions. If Růžička and his wife did indeed have a hand in all of this, then why did they have a change of heart all of a sudden? Remorse? And, secondly, why did they then not save more materials? Why did Dr. Kaděrka give only the Hirschfeld guestbook to Mrs. Baumgarten in the 1980s to sell in West Germany? What happened to all the other materials from Hirschfeld's private archive and Giese's personal archive? Furthermore, the affidavit in fact states that only a few books were saved – or was that just a decoy? – although, as we have seen, Karl Giese had at least 500 Institute books in his Brno apartment. If this second inside job scenario holds true, then Jaroslav Růžička and his wife Jindra would be the true, if only part-time, heroes of the last part of our story.

Like the first, this second inside job scenario does not contradict the claim made in the guestbook affidavit. The Růžičkas could have asked two of their employees to write the affidavit, making the latter the "accidental finders" of the Institute materials and the Hirschfeld guestbook. It is also possible that fear was, once again, powerfully at work and may have so constrained them that they only dared to save a *few* items. A modest rescue operation was simply a safer and more viable venture. Saving only a few items would further support the "fact" that the find was just accidental.

In an attempt to find some evidence for an inside job involving the Růžičkas' employees, I checked whether the two illegible signatures on the affidavit could have belonged to any of the twenty-seven employees of the Růžička company that I found mentioned in a June 1949 letter. They did not. Of course, this negative answer does not entirely exclude the possibility, since there may have been only partial overlap between the people working for the Růžičkas in 1942 and 1949.[212] And yet, even if I had been able to determine that the two affidavit signatures indeed belonged to two of Růžička's employees, this would not clear up the question of who exactly pulled the strings in 1942 and mounted a last-minute rescue operation on the company premises.

The possible eleventh-hour active involvement of Jaroslav Růžička and his wife Jindra (or some of their employees) does not necessarily contradict the scenario in which Dr. Kaděrka overheard about the discarding of the Institute materials while visiting his patient Siegfried Ascher in the Jewish hospital. Kaděrka may have approached the Růžička couple directly, or reached out to one of their employees, who then went to the old paper container and fished out *what they could still find.* The affidavit might have been added to the Hirschfeld guestbook then, not to take any risks. The affidavit's "we found it in the garbage" claim, which we have already mentioned, and which absolves the parties from guilt, may indeed have been both welcome and very convenient. The affidavit also defends against the somewhat pornographic and scandalous nature of the sexology books found, neutralizing any charge by safely transferring them to a medical doctor, Dr. Kaděrka, who would use them for strictly scientific purposes. This rationalization may have operated as a further precaution, offering a safe way out for materials deemed dangerous.

It is clear in any case that Kaděrka did himself not write the affidavit. His handwriting is completely different from that of the two people who signed the document.[213] However, if we examine the text of the affidavit, we perceive that it was most likely written by someone with a scientific background ... and definitely not a cleaning lady. The abbreviation "sexuol.[ogical]" is the strongest evidence for this idea. This term was likely best known to doctors, who used it for a fairly recent

[212] The list of employee names can be found in a letter that was signed by twenty-seven of the Růžičkas' employees. See private archive (Brno), typed *prohlášení* (declaration) (dated Jun. 30, 1949) of twenty-seven employees of the Růžička company sent to the Okresní soud civilní Brno (Brno District Civil Court). Since the twenty-seven names were all typed, this required checking their signatures on their resident registration cards in AMB, Brno, fonds Z 1. I thank Petr Houzar (AMB, Brno) for undertaking this laborious task in February 2022. Realizing that nosy neighbors can be good candidates as well, I also had a look at the signatures of some of the people who lived or worked on the neighboring plot of Ernst Fischer and the B. Friess company at 66 Kröna (Křenová). Otto Pestl (1911-?) was since 1937 the *Hausbesorger* and *Magazineur* (house caretaker and warehouse employee) of the Friess moving and storage firm who, together with his wife Helena (1913-?), lived on the company premises, see MZA, Brno, fonds B 392, Vystěhovalecký fond, úřadovna Brno (1939-1945), kart. n° 24, inv. n° 525, f. 4c. His signature, nor that of his wife, found on their resident registration cards, matched any of the two signatures in the affidavit, see AMB, Brno, fonds Z 1. They also had a son named Alexander (1942-) but I could not trace him. Since Ernst Fischer, the Jewish owner of the B. Friess company, already sold his company in 1939, I also looked at the main names linked to the Aryanisation of the company: Otto Lunz (*Zolldeklarant,* customs clerk), the accountant Wilhelm L. Jung (1892-?) and the later owner Erich Endlich, but their signatures did not match either. I am aware one probably needs to look, rather, for the names of the blue collar staff working for the company. Unfortunately, the B. Friess Aryanisation file mainly has the names of the administrative staff of the company, who worked in the representational office of the company, located on another address, 12 Neutorgasse (U Nové brány). A company that rented space from the B. Friess firm was the brushes factory Hanák & Spurný, owned by Josef Novák, see *Adresář Protektorátu Čechy a Morava pro průmysl, živnosti, obchod a zemědělství = Adressbuch des Protektorates Böhmen und Mähren für Industrie, Gewerbe, Handel und Landwirtschaft* 1939, II: 1406; company registration card in AMB, Brno, fonds B 1/16. I looked at Novák's signature and that of his wife Růžena but their signatures did not match either, see AMB, Brno, fonds Z 1.

[213] Dr. Kaděrka's handwriting (and signature) can be seen in MZA, Brno, fonds G 212, Osobní a penzijní spisy (Persönliche und Pensionsschrifstücke), 1860-1957, III. Manipulace, fascikul n° 333, file Stanislav Kaděrka.

medical specialization. It would not surprise me that Dr. Kadĕrka, clearly a man of science, dictated the text of the affidavit to the people who wrote and signed it. Possibly, these people were also the ones who found the materials, or, if it was an inside job scenario, the ones who rescued the Institute materials and the Hirschfeld guestbook.

THE EVASIVE MURDERER

Have we uncovered in this and the previous chapter the playing field and the main actors in the events surrounding the discarding of the Institute materials in Brno? Let us briefly return to another, though much less plausible scenario of what might have happened in Brno in the year 1942. The already mentioned emptying of Franz Nawratil's law office, and the settling and handling of his personal estate, in the year 1942, could have provided yet another occasion for the Institute materials to end up in the Růžičková company. We have suggested that Nawratil may have been a closeted gay man who possibly helped Karl Fein at the very beginning of his legal career, and who certainly liquidated Karl Fein's law office in March 1939. Did Karl Fein entrust Nawratil not only with his client files, but also the Institute materials until better times returned? This is another possible scenario that could explain what happened to the Institute materials in Brno in the year 1942, the year that Nawratil died. Nawratil's surviving family could have found a safe conduit for the dangerous Institute materials by inquiring with Franz Nawratil's gay network after his death. The path to Jaroslav Růžička's company, where these dangerous materials could safely disappear, might have been discovered this way. Like the maximalist interpretation mentioned earlier, this exit strategy for the Institute materials via the Růžičkas' company, in case of trouble, might even have been thought out beforehand by Karl Fein and Franz Nawratil.

We already broached this other possible scenario in chapter 14, but it now brings us to the rather paradoxical structural feature that haunts and also undermines our final suggestion that there are three principal scenarios for the discarding of the Institute materials. I think that if Jaroslav Růžička had been a more conventional heterosexual man, his explanatory force would be much less diffuse. Straight men, one assumes, stick mainly to a core family, consisting of a wife, children and close relatives, for their emotional and social needs. The social and sexual network of a rent boy, on the other hand, extends in many, sometimes vastly different directions. This makes it virtually impossible to make a well-grounded assessment about the *limited* circle of people with whom such a rent boy, or former rent boy, might have been in contact. We saw that, as a young man, Jaroslav Růžička clearly had contact with the gay scene in Brno. He also had at least one conviction for homosexual sex, despite his 1932 claim to the Brno police that he was not a gay man. Růžička was thirty-seven years old in 1942 and it is not known if his earlier lifestyle extended into his later years or after his marriage. But he may have remained in contact with the gay milieu. Contacts made through the sexual encounters of his younger years might have created a network of acquaintances on which he could rely in adult life. His gay or bisexual past, in other words, might have put him in contact with men from a very different socio-economic background. We have already suggested a few times that, prior to World War II, it was much more common for gay men's sexual encounters to cross social strata. With his past contact with the gay community, and a history of homosexual conduct, possibly even homosexual prostitution, Růžička therefore has the status of a "wild card" in our story. When still young, living in poverty through the harsh years of the Great Depression, Růžička could literally have passed through many hands.[214] As a rent boy, he could easily have made money by having sex with men. Jaroslav Růžička could have been "everywhere".

I think that the peculiar status of Jaroslav Růžička's persona structurally determines that there *may* exist yet more, still unknown possible scenarios regarding the discarding of the Institute materials. Růžička may have known other gay men in Brno, acquaintances of a decade before, who might have played a role in our story of the Institute materials. Men – women seem excluded – whose names we possibly do not even know yet ... Again, regarding Jaroslav Růžička, there is thus far only one real certainty: every possible scenario that we have suggested so far ended up in Růžička's company.

I think that this structural inability to limit the scenarios about what might have happened to the Institute materials, linked to Růžička's being gay or bisexual, or even a rent boy in his youth, accords rather well, and not coincidentally, with the analysis Karl Giese developed in his 1934 *Nový hlas* article on the Paris murder of the theater director Oscar Dufrenne. In that article, Giese claimed that police often failed to find the murderers of gay men because they usually did not belong to the same social class as the victims.[215] On the other hand, murderers of straight people were more likely to be found in their core family of wife and children, their close relatives, friends having a similar socio-economic background, or neighbors.[216] The Czech newspaper *Lidové noviny* concluded that, since they were often not found, the murderers of gay men were "privileged murderers" (*vrazi privilegovaní*). However, Jaroslav Růžička did not kill a gay man but, one could say, the library of a famous gay man named Magnus Hirschfeld. It has proved virtually impossible to determine with any certainty who may have requested the hitman Růžička to discard the Institute materials. He may simply have known too many men from all societal backgrounds, either from his past as a rent boy or, at the very least, his acquaintance with Brno's gay community. The request to discard the Institute materials could have come from still other people than the ones we have suggested. Again, had Jaroslav Růžička been a more conventional heterosexual man, the range of possible scenarios of the discarding of the Institute materials would, I think, be much narrower. As things stand, Jaroslav Růžička remains a structurally evasive man, one who, even now, plays hard to get.

KARL FEIN AND THE BRNO WORKING CLASS

But we do not have to confine ourselves to Jaroslav Růžička in this regard. We can also look at Karl Fein and his peculiar position in this rent boy constellation. One of the implicit questions in this book has been whether Fein, as a gay man, stayed within the usual habitus (*vécu*) of the Jewish bourgeoisie.[217] Did he *also* wander into to the world of working-class young men and rent boys, not only to satisfy his emotional and sexual needs, but to settle the problem about what to do with the Institute materials? Did he indeed turn to the working-class men of the *Kamarád* group, who themselves seemed a bit more, or more easily, entangled in the milieu of rent boys? Or, on the contrary, did Fein stick to and rely only on his own Jewish bourgeois flock to help with his problem?

Indeed, even though it is very likely that, by September 1932, Fein and Hirschfeld shied away from the *Kamarád* group because of Štefan Kostelníček's February 1933 conviction, Fein would nevertheless have been well aware that Kostelníček had already left Brno in 1934. Because Kostelníček was out of the picture, Fein may have

[214] For more information on the Great Depression and Czechoslovakia, see LeCaine Agnew 2004, 190–95.

[215] Giese 1934.

[216] Vermassen 2017.

[217] I use "habitus" in the sense defined by the French sociologist Pierre Bourdieu (Bourdieu 1979).

been more willing to contact Stanislav Černil and Vilém Drexler-Hlubocký two years later. As their *Kamarád* efforts clearly demonstrate, they had literary and theatrical ambitions, cultural aspirations highly valued by Fein's Jewish bourgeois social class. This may have helped Fein make the mental leap. Neither should we forget, of course, that Karl Giese himself had a working-class background, and that the *Kamarád* group, who most likely knew the details of Hirschfeld's life story, were well aware that Hirschfeld's main life partner was a working-class man. The idea that Giese was "one of us" may have been a vitally enabling factor in the *Kamarád* people's possible involvement, and partly explain their motivation to help, possibly even while Giese was still living in Brno. We have suggested, for example, that Giese may have attended some of the Saturday gatherings of theater people at Stanislav Černil's home. This class allegiance might have endured after Giese's death.

In this regard, we need to look again at Giese's working-class boyfriend, Walter Lukl, who may also have played a role in all of this. We have already suggested that Lukl was possibly acquainted with the *Kamarád* group, since he may have placed a classified ad – one of the seven in total – in the first and last issue of *Kamarád*. The fact that it was placed in the very first issue suggests that he likely personally knew at least one of the founders of the gay magazine, whom he asked to place the ad. On the other hand, one can also come up with arguments for the opposite, that Lukl played no part in our story since – outwardly, at least – Lukl seems to have distanced himself from involvement with the Jewish (and gay?) community by joining the Wehrmacht in 1940. That he lived on Mlýnská (Mühlgasse) after he broke up with Karl Giese, the street where the Leopold Fleischer firm's storage facilities were located, is not a coincidence but likely not linked to our story in any way.[218]

[218] After Lukl broke up with Karl Giese, in January 1938, he went to live in the Mühlgasse (Mlýnská) n° 4-6. He continued to work for some time for the Leopold Fleischer company after the break up. The storage facilities of the firm were located at Mühlgasse (Mlýnská) n° 38. The office of the company in the Adlergasse (Orlí) n° 34 was not far from the Mühlgasse (Mlýnská) address either. But at that point, the later and nearby Jewish hospital, located at Mühlgasse (Mlýnská) n° 27, was not there yet. Nor were Jaroslav Očadlík and Jan Vacek at that point already living in the equally nearby Stephansgasse (Štěpánská) apartment. Presumably, Lukl moved out again of the building in the Mühlgasse (Mlýnská) when he joined the Wehrmacht, in 1940.

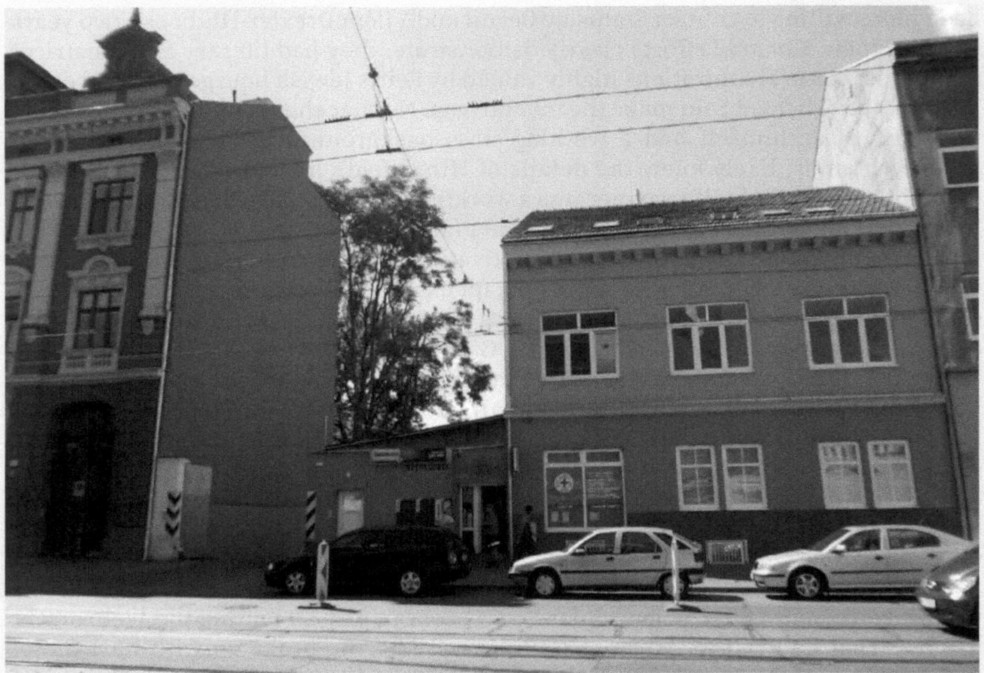

1. The passageway between the two street-facing buildings, 68 Kröna (Křenová) (Nebehosteny building, left) and 66 Kröna (Křenová) (Ernst Fischer's property, right), giving direct access to the expansive site in their rear. July 2012.

2. The immense Nebehosteny house's grand entrance with its elaborate, artful stucco work – cherubs and all. Still today, it functions as the building's main entrance, and also gives access to a small car park in the rear. July 2012.

LIEBSTER ALBERT
FRITZL IN BESEREM ZUSTAND HEUTE ÜBERFÜHRT
SICHENHAUS, MÜLLERGASSE 27. HABE KADĚRKA
GESPROCHEN GIBT HOFFNUNG. EMILS MUTTER
GEHT AM 27 ZU IHM. SCHAUE DICH UM ROBE
RTL. WIR SIND ALLE WOHLAUF.
GRÜSSE

26/3 1942

PIKESLER, PRAG
BALLIGASSE 7

U-938
BRÜNNER TRANSPORT
ALBERT ASCHER
L 136

Eingang | Datum | Nr. 1658
Expedit 6 III 1942

FUPRA 024

3a and 3b. Postcard sent by "Pikesler" (Rudolf Pick) in Prague to Albert Ascher in Terezín on March 26, 1942, back and front side.

4. The building which housed the Jewish hospital from 1941 to 1943, at the corner of 27 Mühlgasse (Mlýnská) and 5 Stephansgasse (Štěpánská). The building had belonged to the Jewish Pollak family. Ca. February 1941.

5. The longer wing of the L-shaped Jewish hospital building on Stephansgasse (Štěpánská). Ca. February 1941.

6. On December 11, 1927, Robert Pollak married Anděla Švecová in the Great Synagogue (Velká synagoga) in Brno.

7. Wedding photo of Jindra Fikesová and Jaroslav Růžička at Brno Town Hall (Rathaus, radnice). Robert Pollak was one of the two witnesses. From left to right: Alois Bula (?), Robert Pollak, Anděla Pollaková, Aunt Svobodová (family of the bride), Jindra Fikesová, unknown lady, Jaroslav Růžička, Uncle Hladký and his wife (family of the bride), Jaroslav Růžička's sister. December 23, 1939.

8. Mug shot of the lawyer Artur Feldmann Sr. when he was imprisoned and tortured. February 10, 1940.

9. Map (from 1906) of the Kröna (Křenová) neigborhood.

1. *Brno main railway station (Hlavní nádraží)*
2. *Walter Lukl's last known Brno address, 4–6 Mühlgasse (Mlýnská)*
3. *Beginning of Křenová (Kröna) Street*
4. *Great Synagogue (Velká synagoga), 3 Tempelgasse (U synagogy)*
5. *Location 1 of the Morava storage company, 35 Dornich (Dornych)*
6. *Location 2 of the Morava storage company, 16 Cyrillsgasse (Cyrilská)*
7. *Building designed by Otto Eisler for the Stiassny family and erected in 1934, 25 Mühlgasse (Mlýnská)*
8. *Dr. Siegfried Fischl's home address (until mid-February 1941), 10 Stephansgasse (Štěpánská)*
9. *The Pollak family home / makeshift Jewish hospital, corner building with street address 27 Mühlgasse (Mlýnská) and 5 Stephansgasse (Štěpánská)*
10. *Jaroslav Očadlík's apartment building, 4b/310 Stephansgasse (Štěpánská)*
11. *The house of Josef Martinkowitsch, 4/308 Stephansgasse*
12. *Church of the Immaculate Conception (Kostel Neposkvrněného Početí Panny Marie) at 21 Křenová (Kröna), built in 1914*
13. *Stanislav Černil's parental home at 12 Cyrillsgasse (Cyrilská)*
14. *The location of the premises where the Leopold Fleischer company's logistical materials (trucks, carts and horses), and also where customers' goods were stored, 38a (also 38) Mühlgasse (Mlýnská)*
15. *B. Friess company plot (owned by Ernst Fischer), 66 Křenová (Kröna)*
16. *Nebehosteny city palace, 68 Křenová (Kröna)*
17. *Jindra Růžičková's company, 68 Křenová (Kröna)*

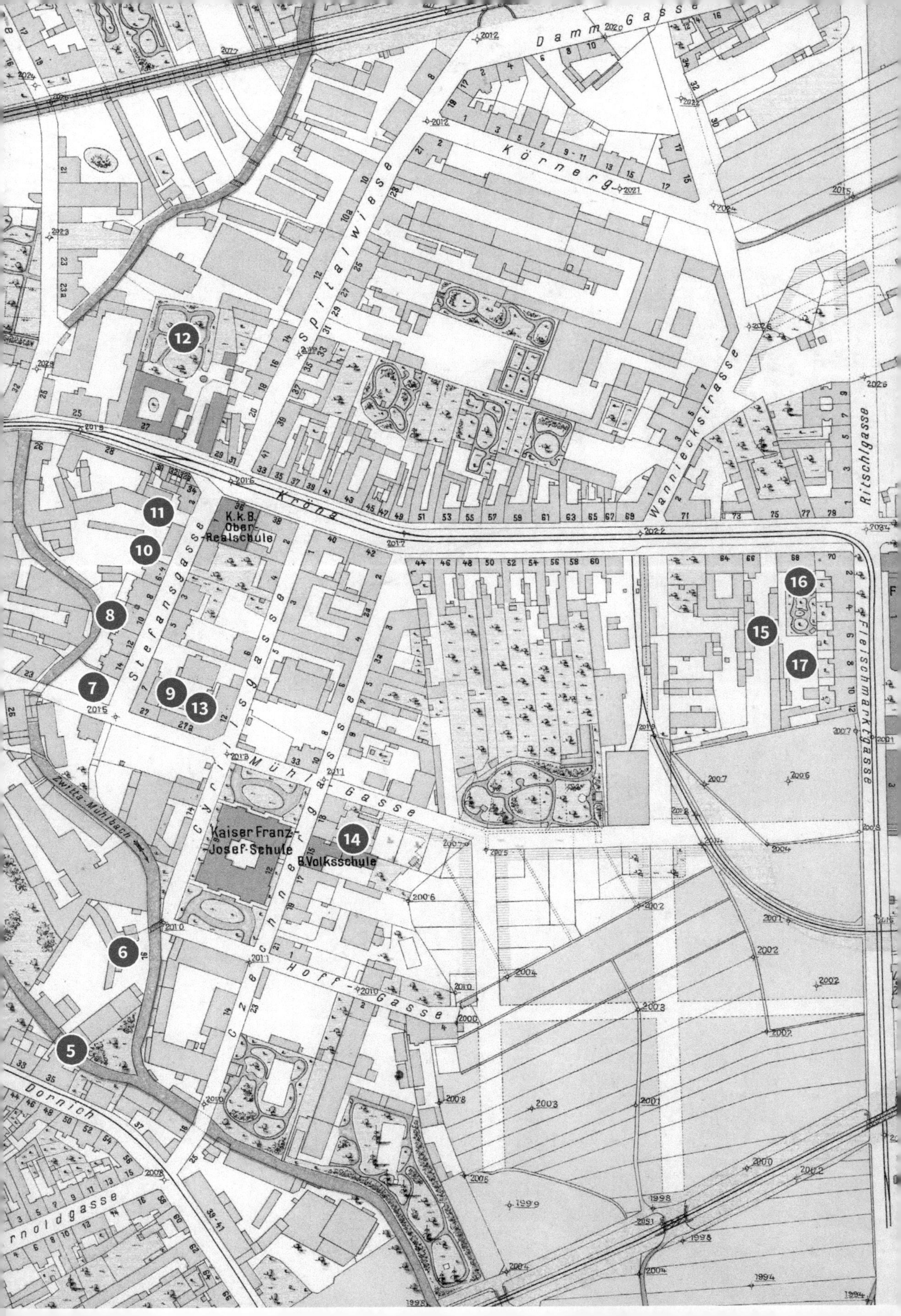
Damm Gasse
Körnerg.
Spitalwiese
Wannieckstrasse
Ritschlgasse
Kröna
K.k.B. Ober-Realschule
Stefansgasse
Cyrillsgasse
Mühlgasse
Czechnergasse
Kaiser Franz-Josef-Schule
B.Volksschule
Hoff-Gasse
Fleischmarktgasse
Zwitta-Mühlbach
Dornich
rnoldgasse
5
6
7
8
9
10
11
12
13
14
15
16
17

12
3

10. View of the Trnitá (Dörnrössel) neighborhood. 1936–37. Fourteen numbered locations from the map (ill. n° 9, p. 664) are also shown here.

11. Siegfried Fischl, the far-left and likely also affluent doctor, a member of the preparatory committee of the 1932 WLSR Brno conference, the Proletarian Freethinkers of the ČSR (Proletarische Freidenker in der ČSR) and also the Association of German Social Democratic Doctors (Verein deutscher sozialdemokratische Ärzte). He was deported to Auschwitz in mid-February 1942 where he was likely shot to death immediately after arriving.

12. The young Albert (Vojtěch) Schön, who became a rabbi in 1936. September 1934.

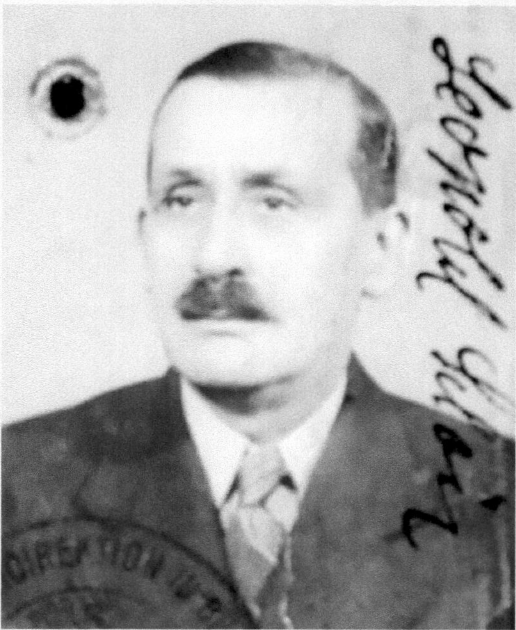

13. Photo of Leopold Schön from an ID card issued in Ostrava. 1948.

14. Photo of Terezie Schön (née Jellinek) from an ID card issued in Brno (Brünn). 1940.

17. Concluding Itineraries

THE JEWISH HOSPITAL CEASES TO EXIST

Elise Brecher's turn to be deported from Brno eventually came as well. We have already mentioned that the Jewish mass deportations from Brno ended with transport "Ai", which carried 923 people, on April 8, 1942. Another, much smaller transport of eighty-one people, "AAa", followed the next month, on May 27, 1942. This transport was apparently intended for people who were most likely exempted from the "Ai" transport. Since her name was on its official list, Elise Brecher should have been deported on the very last and smallest Jewish transport from Brno, carrying sixty people in total, in the summer of 1943.[1] And yet, as will be discussed below, she was not. This very last transport, "Dg", left Brno on July 1, 1943.[2] Rudolf Hirsch and the lawyer Leo Nitschke (1908–1944?), the last two men in charge of the JKG in Brno, were deported on this transport.[3] We can safely assume that this transport carried a good number of protected people.[4] Of the fifty-three people actually deported on transport "Dg", twenty-seven were from Brno. "Assistant" (*Hilfsarbeiter[in]*) appeared next to almost all of their names; mostly, they were also people in their early twenties. The other twenty-six people on the list of the "Dg" transport came from Uherský Brod (Ungarisch Brod), Kuřim (Gurein), Jihlava (Iglau), Polná (Polna) and Olomouc (Olmütz).[5]

In reality, things did not proceed in the manner indicated by the official list of transport "Dg". Only fifty-three people, not the sixty on the list, were deported on this transport.[6] We have already seen that it was originally anticipated that the remaining fifteen patients in the Jewish hospital would be deported on transport "AAa", on May 27, 1942. However, likely as a consequence of pressure from the JKG in Brno, the patients were removed from the list. Siegfried Ascher and Elise Brecher – who, as we have seen, were assigned transport numbers AAa88 and AAa90, respectively – were among those exempted.[7] Transport "AAa" finally carried only eighty-one people. Six

[1] Kárný et al. 1995, 1207.

[2] See http:// encyklopedie.brna.cz/ home-mmb/ ?acc=profil_osobnosti&load=14130 (accessed Jan. 10, 2015), where her name is insistently spelled the Czech way, Eliška Brecherová. The identity of the very last Jewish person deported from Brno on transport "Ez", on September 13, 1943, is not known. See Kárný et al. 1995, 70, 1241–44. Presumably, he or she was found hiding somewhere and added to this existing transport, which seems to have departed from Prague.

[3] See the untitled list of names on transport "Dg" in NA, Praha, fonds n° 1077, Okupační vězeňské spisy. Next to his name, Leo Nitschke had "Angestellter des ARJ" (employee of the ARJ). (As noted previously, this is the Altestenrat der Jüden, the Council of Jewish Elders.) "Mitarbeiter(in) des ARJ" (coworker of the ARJ) appeared next to the names of Rudolf Hirsch and his wife Gertrude Hirsch (1904–?). Leo Nitschke was deported on transport "Ev" from Terezín to Auschwitz-Birkenau on October 28, 1944. His wife Hilda (1913–?) was liberated from Terezín. She resumed her work as a dental technician after the war. See *Adresář zemského hlavního města Brna* 1948, B: 187. Laura Nitschke, also mentioned in the latter, was likely her daughter, who was living with her. Rudolf Hirsch, his wife and their daughter Ruth Hirsch (1926–?) were further transferred on transport "Er" from Terezín to Auschwitz-Birkenau on October 16, 1944. Gertrude and Ruth Hirsch were liberated from Kurzbach. See Kárný et al. 1995, 1208. Only Ruth Hirsch appears in *Adresář zemského hlavního města Brna* 1948, B: 114.

[4] Is it possible that this last transport's assigned numbers were themselves significant. Of the sixty people in total, Elise Brecher was number 59.

[5] NA, Praha, fonds n° 1077, Okupační vězeňské spisy, name list for transport "Dg". Cf. Hrubá 2008.

[6] The official list for this transport has sixty names. See Kárný et al. 1995, 1207–8.

[7] The list of the fifteen patients in the Jewish hospital started with AAa85 and ended with AAa99. Since the actual number of people deported on transport "AAa" was eighty-one, this means that an additional three people *not* staying in the Jewish hospital were either exempted, disappeared or died. See the list

patients died in the Jewish hospital in the following year, Siegfried Ascher being one of them.[8] This means that nine other patients from the Jewish hospital should have been on the very last Jewish transport "Dg" from Brno. However, an archival source shows that seven of the hospital's female patients were already deported on May 10, 1943, on a exceptional transport (*Sondertransport*), more than seven weeks before transport "Dg" left Brno. Elise Brecher was one of these seven women.[9]

It is not clear why their evacuation was so urgent that an exceptional transport was organized for them. Trying to find a possible explanation, I think that these seven elderly women patients may have been suddenly deported from Brno in May 1943 after an unannounced visit to the Jewish hospital by the Germans. Presumably, the Germans assessed these seven women as "too healthy" to be in the hospital and, in a retaliatory gesture, immediately deported them. Significantly, the transport numbers they were assigned in May 1943 were the same as those for transport "AAa" on May 27, 1942 – the transport from which they were exempted a year earlier.[10] With this symbolic gesture, the Germans clearly signaled that these seven women should have been deported as originally planned. Here again, we see that permission to stay in the Jewish hospital was definitely a way for some patients to avoid deportation. Tragically, the two remaining Jewish patients in the hospital, apparently deemed sick enough to stay, died within four weeks of the sudden deportation of these seven female patients, before the very last Jewish transport "Dg" left Brno, on July 1, 1943. Mathilde Nachod (1862–1943) died on May 19, 1943, while the very last patient, Siegmund Cohn (1863–1943), died on June 8, 1943. Judging from their death certificate,

"Verzeichnis der in den Transport AAa eingereihten Personen, die im Siechenheim in Brünn, Mühlg. 27, zurückgeblieben sind" in NA, Praha, fonds n° 1077, Okupační vězeňské spisy. The same transport numbers also appear on the individual pink index cards of the kartotéka deportovaných osob do Terezína a z Terezína (card index of persons deported to and from the Terezín ghetto), also in NA, Praha, fonds n° 1077, Okupační vězeňské spisy. At some point, the people working for the International Tracking Service (ITS) in Bad Arolsen also noticed that the sources contradicted each other here. See document n° 131446290, which says, erroneously, that Elise Brecher's transport number AAa90 should be (*správně* [correctly]) Dg59.

[8] Hugo Morgenstern, Siegfried Ascher, Marie Schwarsbartová and Magdalena Stuckhart were already dead in 1942. Gabriele Plaček (née Weigl, 1874–1943) died on March 6, 1943, and Frieda Bisenz (1898–1943) on May 7, 1943. See the typed and handwritten additions next to the names of the people who died in the Jewish hospital in the same "Verzeichnis der in den Transport AAa eingereihten Personen, die im Siechenheim in Brünn, Mühlg. 27, zurückgeblieben sind", in NA, Praha, fonds n° 1077, Okupační vězeňské spisy. See also the database of the Jewish cemetery in Brno, https:// cemeteries.jewishbrno.eu/cemetery/, and the death register for 1942 and 1943 in AMB, Brno, fonds A 1/3.

[9] See "Die Liste des Transportes DG [*sic*] vom 1.7.1943 enthält folgende 7 Personen, welche bereits am 10.5.1943 in den Stand des Ghettos genommen wurden" (The list of the transport DG [*sic*] of July 1, 1943, contains the following 7 persons, who were already added into the ghetto civil registry on May 10, 1943) in NA, Praha, fonds n° 1077, Okupační vězeňské spisy. The names of the seven women on this list were Kateřina Brüll (née Weinstein, 1859–1943), Regina Schnitzerová (née Gold, 1860–1943), Cäcilie Rosenzweig (1857–1944), Marie Spitzer (née Kapscher, 1880–1943), Olga Weiger (née Schick, 1878–1962), Elise Brecher (1869–1943) and Ella Hatschek (1879–1943). Hatschek, incidentally, was the daughter of the landlady of the house where Karl Fein's parents lived in the 1890s. Someone had added their anticipated numbers on transport "Dg" next to these seven names, from Dg54 to Dg60. The list of sixty names for transport "Dg" (in Kárný et al. 1995) is thus incorrect. Jaroslav Klenovský, an authority on Moravia's Jewish heritage, saw that the number of deportees on transport "Dg" had to be adjusted from sixty to fifty-three people, but does not accordingly modify the number on transport "AAa" from eighty-one to eighty-eight. See https:// www.brnotrails.cz/ en/ object/ 5-the-main-railway-station (accessed Nov. 25, 2020); Klenovský 2016, 23. Cf. the numbers given by Kárný et al. 1995, 588 for transport "AAa", and 1,207 for transport "Dg".

[10] See "Die Liste des Transportes DG [*sic*] vom 1.7.1943 enthält folgende 7 Personen, welche bereits am 10.5.1943 in den Stand des Ghettos genommen wurden" in NA, Praha, fonds n° 1077, Okupační vězeňské spisy. Although their earlier AAa transport numbers were "recuperated", these appeared under the heading "special admission number" (*Sondereinweisungs-Nr.*) in the list, further indicating that this transport was indeed exceptional. This separate, exceptional transport of seven people to Terezín is not mentioned anywhere in the official transport lists of Jewish deportations from the Protectorate.

we have to conclude that these last two patients in the Jewish hospital in Brno died of starvation.[11]

ELISE BRECHER IN TEREZÍN

We may assume that, soon after Elise Brecher's arrival in Terezín, she met her daughter Anna Bermann, Anna's husband Wilhelm Bermann and their teenaged son, Felix, who arrived in Terezín more than a year earlier. Her eldest son Fritz had already been transferred from Terezín to Maly Trostenets (Malý Trostinec, Maly Trostinez) in August 1942, four and a half months after his arrival in Terezín. It is likely that Elise Brecher also saw her sister-in-law, Helene Fein, Karl Fein's mother, and Helene's other son, Gustav Fein, who arrived in Terezín, from Prague, approximately four months before Elise Brecher. Elise Brecher stayed in room 214 in building H V, better known as the Dresden barracks (Dresdner Kaserne) [ill. 1]. It remains unclear if any of them were then aware that Karl Fein died in Łódź. They likely would have shared news of all the misfortunes of the preceding years.

Ten weeks after her arrival in Terezín, on August 11, 1943, at the age of seventy-three, Elise Brecher died. She died in room 207, the sick bay (*Siechenkrankenstube*) of the Dresden barracks.[12] It is striking that five out of the seven people on the May special transport (*Sondertransport*) from Brno to Terezín died in 1943, Elise Brecher and one other patient in the first few months after their arrival. A sixth person died in January 1944. We may wonder whether these women were being punished in some way by the Germans; but this was not necessarily the case. Generally speaking, the elderly died very soon after arriving in Terezín.[13] Of the seven patients suddenly taken from the Jewish hospital, one survived the war and was liberated from Terezín: Olga Weiger (née Schick, 1878–1962).[14] After the war, she first lived in Prague and then moved back to Brno in 1948. She is buried in the Jewish cemetery in Brno.[15]

[11] For Mathilde Nachod and Siegmund Cohn's dates and causes of death, see http://www.badatelna.eu/fond/1073/reprodukce/?zaznamId=182&reproId=2297 (accessed Mar. 7, 2017). Cohn's final medical diagnosis was arteriosclerosis marasmus senilis. Nachod's diagnosis says myodegeneratio cardis. kachexia. Cachexia is a disorder causing extreme weight loss and muscular atrophy. The names of the last eight patients who died in the Jewish hospital in Brno are listed in the database of the Jewish cemetery in Brno, https:// cemeteries.jewishbrno.eu/cemetery/. Siegmund Cohn's wife was Leontina Benedikt (1872–1921). She is buried in the Jewish cemetery in Brno in plot 28C, row 11, grave 5. The couple had five children: Grete (1895–?), Emma (1897–?), Olga (1899–?), Adolf (1902–?) and Pavel (1908–?). I did not follow any traces of the children. One of Mathilde Nachod's three sons, Camillo Nachod (1893–?), obtained Argentinian nationality and moved from Argentina to Brazil after the war. It is not known what became of her son Hans Nachod (1886–?). Her other son, Kurt Nachod (1890–1918), died in 1918. Mathilde Nachod's only daughter, Gertruda Feldmann (1895–1942?), was deported on the final transport "Ai" from Brno to Terezín on April 8, 1942, along with her husband Leo Feldmann (1888–1942?) and one of their twin sons, Kurt Feldmann (1921–1942?). On April 18, 1942, the family was further transferred to Rejowiec on transport "Ap". Their other twin son, Erich Feldmann (1921–1944?), was deported on September 10, 1943, on *Sondertransport* (exceptional transport) "St-Ez", from Prague to Terezín, and then from Terezín to Auschwitz-Birkenau on transport "Es", on October 19, 1944.

[12] See Elise Brecher's Terezín death certificate at https://www.holocaust.cz/en/database-of-digitised-documents/document/97892-brecherova-eliska-death-certificate-ghetto-terezin/ (accessed Dec. 3, 2021).

[13] Hájková 2020, 77–78, 136.

[14] Kárný et al. 1995, 1208; Terezín-Ghetto 1945, 504.

[15] AMB, Brno, fonds Z 1, resident registration card Olga Weiger. Olga Weiger is buried in the Jewish cemetery in plot 36, row 1, grave 14. Her husband, Moritz Weiger (1869–1943), died in Terezín in January 1943. He was transported from Brno to Terezín on transport "Ae" on March 27, 1942, along with his son Felix (1908–1944) and the latter's wife Liese (Lisa) Redlich (1917–1942?). Both Felix and Liese Weiger were further transferred to Piaki on transport "Ag" on April 1, 1942. According to www.holocaust.cz, Felix died in Auschwitz-Birkenau. See https:// www.holocaust.cz/ en/ database-of-victims/ victim/ 131953-felix-weiger/ (accessed Nov. 2, 2021). The second child and son of Olga and Moritz Weiger, Fritz Weiger (1920–1945), was deported on May 13, 1943, on transport "Db", from Prague to Terezín, and then further transferred on transport "El" to Auschwitz-Birkenau on September 29, 1944. On October 10, 1944, he was transferred from Auschwitz-Birkenau to Dachau, where he died on February 14, 1945. I was not able to further identify Markéta (Margita) Weiger (née Löw or Lev [?], 1921–?)

HEINRICH BRECHER

Because Elise Brecher may have played an important role in our story, I also took a closer look at her youngest son Heinrich (also spelled Heinz, Jindřich, Enrique) Brecher (1904–1955), since he fled abroad "in time" with his wife Gertrude Laufer (1910–1989).[16] In the beginning of June 1938, the couple were involved in a serious case of financial fraud, one that was reported nationwide in the Czechoslovak newspapers. Apparently, Heinrich Brecher tried to embezzle approximately 420,000 Czech crowns from Omnipol, a Prague company trading in spices and intestines, which worked closely with the Moriz Laufer Bros. company in Brno belonging to Brecher's in-laws.[17] Max Laufer (1878–1941), Gertrude Laufer's father, owned the Brno company; Heinrich Brecher eventually took over the management of the business.[18]

The Brecher-Laufer couple left Brno on the night of June 5–6, 1938. They managed to escape Europe with the embezzled money on a ship sailing from Cherbourg (France) to Montevideo in Uruguay, via Lisbon (Portugal), on June 10, 1938. They intended to take another ship to nearby Buenos Aires in Argentina [ill. 2] [ill. 3].[19] South America was familiar territory to Heinrich Brecher, who spent eight years there before his return to Brno in the summer of 1934.[20] In Argentina, he seems to have been involved in – or at least associated with – at least one other unscrupulous affair.[21] The family members in Brno seemed unaware that Heinrich Brecher had taken a vast sum of money until, around the end of June, alarm bells started ringing in Prague.[22] Judging

who was on the same transport "Ae" from Brno to Terezín as Felix, Liese and Moritz Weiger. Possibly, she was the one-year younger wife of Fritz Weiger. Markéta had transport number 976. Felix and Liese had transport numbers 974 and 975, respectively. Moritz's transport number was 978, leaving us to wonder who had number 977. On October 19, 1944, three weeks after Fritz Weiger, Markéta was moved from Terezín to Auschwitz-Birkenau on transport "Es". She was liberated from Auschwitz-Birkenau and later took the name Margiṭ Ben-Yitsḥaḳ. See Kárný et al. 1995, 433. She was interviewed in Israel by the USC Shoah Foundation (interview 24781) on December 12, 1996; however, I did not consult this interview. In the interview's technical index card, on the USC Shoah Foundation website, there is no mention of the surname Weiger.

[16] Gertrude Laufer married and divorced Dr. Norbert Klein (1900–1970) before marrying Heinrich Brecher. See also below, pp. 678-79 and n. 42 for more information on Norbert Klein.

[17] *Adreßbuch von Groß-Brünn* 1934, 655, 702, 761. The company was located at 4 Wannieckgasse (Wannieckova). The building was later used for storage by the *Verwaltungsstelle Brünn* (Brno administrative office) of the Auswanderungsfonds für Böhmen und Mähren (Emigration Fund for Bohemia and Moravia). See MZA, Brno, fonds B 392, Vystěhovalecký fond, úřadovna Brno, kart. n° 9, inv. n° 186, f. 38. See also MZA, Brno, fonds B 392, Vystěhovalecký fond, úřadovna Brno, kart. n° 24, sign. n° 537, Hedvika and Max Laufer.

[18] Gertrude Laufer's parents were Max Laufer (1878–1941) and Hedwig Blum (1886–1942?). They married in 1909. Max Laufer died in Mauthausen. See NA, Praha, Jewish registers (Židovské matriky, Judische Matriken), inv. n° 142, Brno, Z, 1942, f. 47. See also the Gestapo file on Max Laufer, MZA, Brno, fonds B 340, Gestapo Brno, n° 4943, kart. n° 338, sign. 100-338-10, file Max Laufer. Hedwig Laufer was deported on transport "U" from Brno to Terezín on January 28, 1942, and further transferred to Izbica on transport "Ab" on March 17, 1942.

[19] MZA, Brno, fonds C 12, Krajský soud trestní Brno, kart. n° 2381, sign. Tk XI 1852/38, letter (dated Jun. 20, 1938) from Gertrude Laufer to her parents (sent from the ship *Alcantara* sailing to Montevideo), f. 49. Cf. "Honba za Brechrem skončena?" (Is the hunt for Brecher over?), *Lidové noviny*, Jul. 9, 1938, 5.

[20] MZA, Brno, fonds C 12, Krajský soud trestní Brno, kart. n° 2381, sign. Tk XI 1852/38, f. 62.

[21] See the mention of Enrique Brecher's name in *Boletín Oficial de la República Argentina*, año XL, n° 11.412, 1932, message dated May 13, 1932, (Buenos Aires), written by Aníbal Ponce de León (secretario).

[22] In a rather curious, five-page statement of June 24, 1938, which Elise Brecher, Heinrich Brecher's mother, redacted with her lawyer, Elise Brecher sought to rescue her youngest son. She adumbrates claims, likely communicated to her by her son from abroad, that not only were Omnipol's meat products of bad quality but the Prague firm repeatedly failed to meet the delivery times agreed with the Laufer company in a contract made at the beginning of their cooperation. The money taken by Brecher was in compensation for the losses suffered by the Laufer company over a period of three years because of the supposed negligence of Omnipol. The statement includes a detailed list of the losses that this negligence caused to the Laufer company, their total sum corresponding to the amount embezzled by Heinrich Brecher. See MZA, Brno, fonds C 12, Krajský soud trestní v Brně, letter from Elise Brecher (dated Jun. 24, 1938) to Státní zastupitelství v Brně (Office of the Public Prosecutor in Brno), kart. n° 2381, sign. Tk XI 1852/38, f. 3–5. On the other hand, a Gestapo document claims a debt of 100,000 Czech crowns owed by Max Laufer to Omnipol in April–May 1938,

by the shipboard letter written by Gertrude Laufer, she did not seem aware of her husband's dealings or actual intentions.[23]

The Czechoslovak newspapers reported that the couple was arrested shortly after arriving in Uruguay or Argentina in July 1938. However, a court file makes it clear that the couple was never extradited to Czechoslovakia.[24] The file also explains why Czechoslovak newspapers almost abruptly ceased reporting on the case.[25] Despite its coming to a sudden halt, the case was not forgotten on the home front. When Max Laufer's meat and spice company and his brother Siegfried Laufer's company were Aryanized, in December 1941, Omnipol once again stepped in and clearly pointed to the amounts they were still owed by Max Laufer's company, though without specifically mentioning the embezzlement case. It is unclear exactly why Max Laufer was condemned by a summary court martial in 1941, but it is possible that he was held accountable for the upheaval that his son-in-law Heinrich Brecher and his daughter Gertrude Laufer caused three years earlier.[26] Possibly, the embezzlement case not only strengthened the National Socialist view that all Jews were thieves, but may have also led to Heinrich Brecher or Gertrude Laufer's relatives being punished or condemned for their – in any case – unproven complicity in the offence. Whatever the relation to the Heinrich Brecher embezzlement case, Max Laufer was tried by summary court martial on October 1, 1941. All his possessions were confiscated.[27] On October 16, 1941, he was killed in Mauthausen.[28] Max Laufer's brother, Siegfried Laufer (1876–1941), who was also active in the meat industry, experienced the same fate.[29] He was tried by summary court martial on September 30, 1941, two days before

that is, in the months preceding Heinrich Brecher's flight. See MZA, Brno, fonds B 340, Gestapo Brno, kart. n° 338 invent. n° 100-338-10, file Max Laufer, f. 35b. Elise Brecher was represented by Jaroslav Hromádka (1903–1967), a non-Jewish lawyer. For more information on Hromádka, see http://encyklopedie.brna.cz/home-mmb/?acc=profil_osobnosti&load=22914 (accessed Jul. 3, 2016). The parents of Gertrude Laufer, Heinrich Brecher's wife, were represented by a Jewish lawyer named Alexander Bedö (1890–1975). Bedö was a Slovak Communist, who published on judicial matters in the 1930s and fought in the Czechoslovak army in France during the war. He emigrated to the United States but his further life story there is unknown. In a May 24, 1946 travel document, he is described as working for the United Nations Relief and Rehabilitation Administration (UNRRA). See the Ancestry.com database, New York, Passenger Lists, 1820–1957, series T 715, 1897–1957, roll 7114. Bedö is likely the Alexander Kalniki Bedö who published on Hungarian legal matters in the 1950s. However, the birth year (1910) given by the Library of Congress authority record does not match the birth year (1890) found in the AMB, Brno, fonds Z 1. Bedö divorced his second wife Gertruda in 1939. He applied for Deutsche Volkszugehörigkeit (German ethnic) status when still in Czechoslovakia. He had one daughter named Eva (1937–?). See Maršálek 2014, 178 n. 442.

[23] MZA, Brno, fonds C 12, Krajský soud trestní v Brně, kart. n° 2381, sign. Tk XI 1852/38, file Heinrich Brecher, f. 49.

[24] MZA, Brno, fonds C 12, Krajský soud trestní v Brně, kart. n° 2381, sign. Tk XI 1852/38, file Heinrich Brecher. On the other hand, a newspaper article reported that the couple had been arrested in Argentina (*Lidové noviny*, Jul. 9, 1938, 5).

[25] I have tried in vain to obtain more information on the further fate of the couple by contacting the Archivo General de la Nación (National Archives) in Uruguay. Although the registers of the Dirección Nacional de Migraciones (DNM, National Migration Office) for the period concerned were indeed transferred to this archive, the information was not currently available because the names in these registers were being imported into a database. See email (dated Jul. 8, 2015) from José Luis Dati (Archivo General de la Nación) to the author. Simply contacting the DNM resulted in its Departamento Tècnico Jurìdico y Notarial sending me an email invoking a privacy clause and declining to give any information. See the scanned letter (dated Aug. 27, 2015) from Daniela Olivera and Marcela De Souza, sent in an email of that date to the author. I did not contact the Uruguayan Ministerio de Relaciones Exteriores (Ministry of Foreign Affairs). I thank Benny Gezels and his partner for their kind assistance with the necessary Spanish translations.

[26] MZA, Brno, fonds B 340, Gestapo Brno, kart. n° 338, invent. n° 100-338-10, file Max Laufer, f. 16. The *Treuhänder* (trustee) of the S. Laufer & Sohn company was a Hans Poliwka.

[27] MZA, Brno, fonds B 340, Gestapo Brno, kart. n° 338, invent. n° 100-338-10, file Max Laufer, f. 1.

[28] See http://www.badatelna.eu/fond/1073/reprodukce/ ?zaznamId=181&reproId=174649 (accessed Sep. 3, 2016); the Mauthausen deaths database, https:// raumdernamen.mauthausen-memorial.org/?L=1 (accessed Oct. 15, 2020).

[29] See the Mauthausen victims database, which lists Siegfried Laufer as Vítězslav Laufer, https://raumdernamen.mauthausen-memorial.org/index.php?&L=1 (accessed Oct. 18, 2020). See also the

his brother. He was murdered in Mauthausen, three days before his brother Max. It seems that the Nazis killed the two brothers in order more easily to get hold of their considerable possessions.[30] Meanwhile, the adventurous Heinrich Brecher quickly set up a meat products company in Uruguay, thinking that he could continue to rely on his business contacts on the Czechoslovak home front for help in starting up such a business abroad.[31]

Gestapo file on Siegfried Laufer, MZA, Brno, fonds B 340, Gestapo Brno, kart. n° 352, sign. 100-352-28, file Siegfried Laufer. Some of the papers from Siegfried Laufer's case were misplaced in Max Laufer's Gestapo file.

[30] The name of Siegfried Laufer's company was S. Laufer & Sohn, Darm- und Gewürzgrosshandlung (S. Laufer & Son, Intestines and Spices Wholesaler). Its office was at 11 Marxgasse (Marxova). In Max Laufer's Gestapo file, two of Siegfried Laufer's four children, the banker Karl (1909–?) and Herta (1919–?), are mentioned as emigrating to Palestine. See MZA, Brno, fonds B 340, Gestapo Brno, kart. n° 338, invent. n° 10, file Max Laufer, f. 7. Siegfried Laufer's home certificate indeed confirms that Herta Laufer managed to emigrate. See AMB, Brno, fonds B 1/16, mention of *Auswanderungspass* (emigration pass) issued by the police in Prague. Siegfried Laufer's Gestapo file, on the other hand, claims that his son Karl Laufer (1909–?) fled to British India with his wife Alice Goldreich (1917–?) in September 1940. See MZA, Brno, fonds B 340, Gestapo Brno, kart. n° 352, sign. 100-352-28, file Siegfried Laufer, f. 36. The database "Illegal immigration to Palestine" (RG 17) in the USHMM, Washington, indeed mentions both Karl and Alice Laufer (with their corresponding birth years), indicating that Karl Laufer (and his wife) and stepdaughter Herta Laufer (whose later married name was Pick) emigrated to Palestine. More details on their escape to Israel can be found here https:// en.wikipedia.org/ wiki/ Wikipedia:WikiProject_Stolpersteine/Stolpersteine_in_Brno#J-L (accessed Nov. 7, 2021) (for example, under the name Franz Laufer). I did not follow their further trail as there were too many Laufers in an online Israeli phonebook. I also assumed that the Laufer family's memory of the Brecher family, and more specifically of Heinrich Brecher, would not be positive. Siegfried Laufer's two other children, Erwin Laufer (1905–1945) and Franz Laufer (1903–1945?), perished in the Holocaust. Erwin Laufer was deported from Brno to Terezín with his wife Thea (1902–1944) and their two-month-old son Paul (1942–1944) on transport "Ai" on April 8, 1942. Erwin Laufer arrived in Dachau, presumably on a so-called death march to evacuate prisoners from Auschwitz-Birkenau, on October 10, 1944, where he died on March 28, 1945. See https://stevemorse.org/dachau/dachau.html (accessed Nov. 7, 2021). Dachau was liberated a month later. On September 29, 1944, one week after her husband Erwin left Terezín, Thea Laufer was also transferred to Auschwitz-Birkenau on transport "El" with her two-and-a-half-year-old son Paul. Most likely, mother and child were gassed to death upon arrival in Auschwitz-Birkenau. Franz Laufer's exact deportation fate is unknown. See https://www.holocaust.cz/ en/ database-of-victims/ victim/ 176328-franz-laufer/ (accessed October 18, 2020). For unknown reasons, his name can also not be located in Kárný et al. 1995. Presumably, he was immediately deported from Brno to Dachau, where he arrived on November 6, 1940. On May 18, 1942, he seems to have been transferred on another transport to an unknown destination. See https://stevemorse.org/dachau/dachau.html (accessed Nov. 7, 2021). On the other hand, according to two index cards in the ITS database, Franz died in Dachau on July 1, 1942. This Dachau death date is also confirmed in MZA, Brno, fonds B 340, Gestapo Brno, kart. n° 352, sign. 100-352-28, file Siegfried Laufer, f. 36. Siegfried Laufer's second wife, Helene Faltin (1881–1942?), was deported on transport "Ah" from Brno to Terezín on April 4, 1942, and further transferred on transport "Ap" to Rejowiec on April 18, 1942. On June 16, 2011, six *Stolpersteine* (stumbling stones) commemorating the Holocaust fates of Siegfried, Helene, Franz, Erwin, Thea and Paul Laufer were added to the footpath in front of Siegfried Laufer's former house at 69 Bratislavská in Brno. See https://encyklopedie.brna.cz/home-mmb/?acc=profil_objektu&load=1076 (accessed Nov. 7, 2021). See also https://en.wikipedia.org/wiki/Wikipedia:WikiProject_Stolpersteine/Stolpersteine_in_Brno#J-L (accessed Nov. 7, 2021). The initiative for the *Stolpersteine* originated from a presumed relative, Edna Gal, from Israel. See https://encyklopedie.brna.cz/home-mmb/?acc=profil_objektu&load=1073 (accessed Nov. 7, 2021). Siegfried Laufer's first wife, Selma Oppenheim (1880–1919), died in 1919, in the month following the birth of her fourth child, Herta. Selma Laufer is buried in the Jewish cemetery in Brno in plot 22B, row 6, grave 16. Yad Vashem, Jerusalem, has some correspondence between Karl and Herta Laufer and their family in Brno (1940–1942); however, I did not consult these archives, nor was I able to locate these documents in the Yad Vashem database. I found reference to these documents at https://en.wikipedia.org/wiki/Wikipedia:WikiProject_Stolpersteine/Stolpersteine_in_Brno#cite_note-4 (accessed Nov. 8, 2021).

[31] The company's name was Exportación internacional de productos animales (International Animal Products Export). As early as the summer of 1938, the company's letterhead included the following address: 290 calle 25 de mayo in Montevideo (Uruguay). See MZA, fonds C 12, Krajský soud trestní v Brně, letter (dated Sep. 3, 1938) from Gertrude Laufer to Grete [Fischl], kart. n° 2381, sign. Tk XI 1852/38, file Heinrich Brecher, p. 1. Jindrich [*sic*] Brecher, along with "Exp. Prod. Anim." and the address "Rincón n° 438", appear in the 1942 edition of *Guía telefónica oficial de la República Oriental del Uruguay*

In August 1939, when her bookstore was Aryanized, Elise Brecher's list of conditions for the people who wanted to take over her business included the demand that they pay for her travel ticket (*Reisekarte*) from Brno to Montevideo.[32] This shows that her youngest son and his wife were likely in Uruguay in the summer of 1939 and also that she was on good terms with him. Interestingly, the incoming letters seized by the Brno authorities indirectly indicate that Karl Fein operated as a useful go-between between the couple in Uruguay and the Brechers (and Laufers?) in Brno. Fein seems to have corresponded with Heinrich Brecher and his wife until at least the summer of 1938.[33] Since I suspected there being more letter traffic between the couple and their relatives in Czechoslovakia, I tried to determine the further fate of the Brecher-Laufer couple.[34] I wished to ascertain whether they survived the war in Uruguay or Argentina. In June 2016, I hired a professional genealogist in Argentina to track the couple.[35] It turned out that, after the war, Heinrich Brecher was living in Montevideo and deliberately used the Czech spelling of his first name, "Jindrich" (more correctly, Jindřich). In 1947, Jindrich Brecher divorced Gertrude Laufer.[36] In December 1949, Heinrich Brecher married the Uruguayan national Elida Visconti (1915–1976).[37]

1942, 66. I thank Claudia Weiss for her assistance in looking up this telephone directory information in the National Library of Uruguay in June 2016.

[32] NA, Praha, fonds n° 375, Arizační spisy, kart. n° 191, sign. 1119, liquidation file L. & A. Brecher bookstore, undated letter from Walter Süss to the Oberlandrat Brünn (Abteilung Arisieriungen, Aryanizations Department), received August 22, 1939.

[33] On behalf of people he knew, Karl Fein wrote in his letters to inquire if they could emigrate to Uruguay and if Brecher would intervene for them. In this regard, a certain Stadelmann, an accountant from Brno, is mentioned by Heinrich Brecher in a letter to Karl Fein. This was most likely Anton Stadlmann (1893–?), who married Hedwig Schroth (1895–?). See *Adreßbuch von Groß-Brünn* 1934, 458; MZA, Brno, fonds C 12, Krajský soud trestní Brno, kart. n° 2381, sign. Tk XI 1852/38, file Heinrich Brecher, letter (dated Sep. 7, 1938) [Heinrich Brecher] to [Karl Fein], p. II, f. 130. (In this letter, Heinrich Brecher also mentions that he was inquiring about six Viennese friends who had the same wish to go to Uruguay.) Stadlmann did the accounts for the Laufer brothers' firms, as attested by Elise Brecher in her statement given to the Brno *Staatsanwalt* (public prosecutor) in June 1938. See MZA, Brno, fonds C 12, Krajský soud trestní Brno, kart. n° 2381, sign. Tk XI 1852/ 38, file Heinrich Brecher, letter from Elise Brecher (dated Jun. 24, 1938) to Státní zastupitelství v Brně (Office of the Public Prosecutor in Brno), f. 5b. One of Stadlmann's three daughters, Anna Sla Simandl (née Stadlmann 1923–2004), moved to the USA. See Social Security Applications and Claims Index, 1936–2007, for Anna Sla Simandl (1923–2004) (retrieved from Ancestry.com, Jul. 3, 2016). Gertrude Laufer also wrote a letter (dated Sep. 3, 1938) to a Grete Fischl. It is unclear who this Grete Fischl was, but presumably she was a good friend. There was a Greta Fischl (1903–1941?) in Brno, who was deported on the very first Jewish transport "F" to Minsk on November 16, 1941. However, there was also a Margareta Fischl (1904–1942?), who was deported from Brno to Terezín on transport "Ad" on March 23, 1942, and further transferred to Lublin on transport "Al" on April 23, 1942. A *Stolperstein* (stumbling stone) was laid down for her in 2020. See https://encyklopedie.brna.cz/ home-mmb/ ?acc=profil_objektu&-load=1875 (accessed Oct. 16, 2020).

[34] I also examined the conditions imposed on postal traffic since the Germans created the Protectorate, trying to determine if the Feins or Brechers were allowed to communicate with Uruguay or Argentina during the war. The answer involves several nuances. Initially, letters and postcards could be sent to these countries, since neither was listed as an enemy country by Germany. However, a letter could only be posted under strict conditions, and could only be sent from a post office where the sender's identity could be confirmed. Every letter would also be inspected by censors, who could, for any reason, without need of justification, deem it unfit to be sent. See *Verordnungsblatt des Reichsprotektors in Böhmen und Mähren*, Jun. 24, 1940, n° 26, 239–45. Furthermore, starting in May 1942, all postal communications with the outside world ceased once the Protectorate Jews arrived in Terezín. Later, only inmates coming from Germany, Austria or the Sudetenland were allowed to send postcards. The Jewish citizens from the Protectorate, who arrived in Terezín after December 1941, were not. Since most transports carrying Protectorate Jews took place in 1942, this leniency in effect excluded most Terezín inmates. See Beneš & Tošnerová 1996, 90, 94.

[35] I thank Andres Rodenstein of vitalrecords.com.ar for his useful and prompt assistance.

[36] See the temporary visa permit issued on July 15, 1947 by the Brazilian consulate in Montevideo for Jindrich Brecher. His address was 793 Maldonado, Montevideo.

[37] Elida Visconti's parents were Francisco Visconti (likely 1888–?) and Inés Pandolfi. In November 2020, I sent fifteen letters to the people with the last name Pandolfi in Uruguay. I received three replies (dated December 2020, May and June 2021) from people who were not related.

Most likely, the couple had no children.[38] Heinrich Brecher died in Montevideo in December 1955 of a heart attack.[39]

Gertrude Laufer married Georg Reinitz (1896–1998), a Jewish man from Vienna. Both were registered as Uruguayan citizens living in Montevideo; however, they moved back to Vienna towards the end of their lives, spending their final years in Vienna. Most likely, this couple had no children either. We may also presume that the Brecher-Laufer couple's divorce was not conducive to the safekeeping of any Brecher family archives. My attempt to find the current relatives of Jindrich/Heinrich Brecher's second wife, Elida Visconti, yielded no useful results.[40] My attempt to locate the current relatives of the Laufer-Reinitz couple proved unfruitful as well.[41] The last trail that I followed was the itinerary of Gertrude Laufer's first husband, Norbert Klein (1900–1960), a radiologist who managed to escape Czechoslovakia with his

[38] Email (dated Sep. 22, 2016) from Mario Schertz (professional genealogist, Uruguay) to the author. Brecher's marriage certificate still lists his profession as "exportador" (exporter). The witnesses who signed the marriage certificate were José Fusco and Eduardo de Escarza.

[39] Death certificate n° 1631 (dated Dec. 29, 1955) provided by Andres Rodenstein. See also the death notice in *El bien publico*, Jan. 2, 1956, 7; under "informacion del registro civil, defunciones registradas el 29 de diciembre" (information from the civil registry, deaths recorded on December 29). The notice also says that Brecher was *casado* (married), and gives 2731 L.[uis B.] Cavia in Montevideo as Enrique Brecher's last address. On the other hand, his death certificate lists 2736 as the house number. In November 2020, acutely aware of the very small chance of obtaining any information, I sent seven letters to the people currently living at these two addresses. No one replied. No probate file for either Enrique Brecher or Elida Brecher (née Visconti) was found in Argentina. See email (dated Jul. 2, 2016) from Andres Rodenstein (professional genealogist, Buenos Aires) to the author. No probate file check was carried out in Uruguay.

[40] I sent a letter to the twenty-four Viscontis living in Montevideo in October 2016, receiving three replies from people (Roselen Visconti, Gaspar Catalá and Maria Noel Visconti) who either could not help me further or were not related. In October 2020, I sent letters to the fourteen people with the last name Visconti living outside Montevideo, but only a few unrelated people responded. I thank Andrés Sorin and Rubén Hernández for their help with the Spanish translations.

[41] According to online phonebooks, there is currently no one with the name Reinitz living in Uruguay or Austria. I did find some more information on Georg Robert Reinitz on Geni.com. See https:// www.geni.com/ people/ Dr-Georg-Reinitz/ 6000000013085316682 (accessed Sep. 28, 2016). I was in brief contact with one of the people managing the page, Michael Mandl, who ultimately replied on the Geni.com message board in October 2016. He wrote to me that he met Georg Reinitz once in a home for the elderly in Vienna in 1992, but knew nothing regarding the Reinitz couple. This indicates that the couple moved to Austria at the end of their lives. See message (dated Oct. 1, 2016) from Michael Mandl to the author on Geni.com. Michael Mandl's grandmother, Hedwig Mandl (née Reinitz, 1894–1982), was Georg Reinitz' sister. I also contacted the Döbling cemetery in Vienna where the Reinitz couple's urns are deposited. The name of the person responsible for the placement of Georg Reinitz' urn of could not be released to me, but an employee kindly offered to pass on a letter from me to this person. No reply was received. See email (dated Oct. 10, 2016) from Friederike Mika (Kundenservice Friedhöfe Wien) to the author. Georg and Hedwig Reinitz also had a brother, Stefan Karl Reinitz (1903–1984), who lived in Vienna. He was married to Elisabeth Gerngross (1911–1983). Both are also buried in the Wien Döbling cemetery. It is not known whether the couple had any children. See, for example, https:// gw.geneanet.org/pfdm?lang=en&pz=israel&nz=fleischmann&ocz=1&p=elisabeth+lisl&n=gerngross (accessed Jan. 21, 2021).

[42] The Klein-Laufer couple divorced early in the 1930s. One resident registration card for Norbert Klein in the AMB, Brno, fonds Z 1, gives February 19, 1931, as the date, but it is unclear that this was in fact the divorce date. The MZA, Brno, found no information on the divorce in fonds C 11, Krajský soud civilní Brno (Kreisgericht für Zivilsachen in Brünn). See email (dated Dec. 3, 2015) from Jana Fasorová (MZA, Brno) to the author. I was therefore not able to determine whether Karl Fein was one of the lawyers involved in the divorce case. Klein had his medical practice at 4 Beethovenstrasse (Beethovenova), in a building designed by the famous architect Ernst Wiesner. He likely moved to 9–11 Jesuitská (Jesuitengasse) in 1933. Norbert Klein later married a Berta Lamplová (or Lamprová?) (1910–?). He and his new wife managed to escape from Czechoslovakia and presumably fled to China. An obituary for Norbert Klein published in the *New Zealand Herald* says that he "left Europe in 1939 to work for the Chinese Red Cross. He returned to Europe the following year to fight in France with the Free Czechoslovakian Forces. After the fall of France he escaped to Spain and then served some time with the British Navy". After the war, Norbert Klein worked for a hospital in Glasgow and London. He moved to New Zealand from England – seemingly without his second wife – in June 1947 and worked as a radiologist until his death in Auckland in 1960. See http://www.birpublications.org/ doi/ abs/ 10.1259/ 0007-1285-34-

second wife. However, this venture produced nothing useful for this research project either.[42]

ANNA BERMANN (NÉE BRECHER)

In an effort to further pursue any traces of Jewish survival and, in their wake, new possible sources, I also closely examined the precise fates of Elise Brecher's two other children, Fritz Brecher and Anna Bermann (née Brecher). Anna Bermann married the pharmacist Wilhelm Bermann in 1922. In 1931, Wilhelm Bermann took over the U dobrého pastýře (At the good shepherd, zum guten Hirten) pharmacy from his father David Bermann (1855–1933). The pharmacy was located at 49 Kreuzgasse (Křížová) in Brno.[43] The Bermann-Brecher couple lived in a small nearby apartment block at 36 Lehmstätte (Hlinky). Lehmstätte (Hlinky) is the street in which the Starobrno brewery was (and is) located and where Karl Fein spent his childhood years. The Bermann couple likely lived at this address because the Melichar family, the Roman Catholic owners of the apartment block, was also a family of pharmacists [ill. 4]. I

399-186 (accessed Nov. 12, 2015), and The National Archives (Kew, Richmond, Surrey, England), Board of Trade, Commercial and Statistical Department and successors, Outwards Passenger Lists, Records of the Commercial, Companies, Labour, Railways and Statistics Departments, Records of the Board of Trade and of successor and related bodies, names and descriptions of alien passengers, ship Rimutala (New Zealand Shipping Company Limited), London to New Zealand, dated Jun. 19, 1947, BT27/ 1607; available online at the Ancestry.com database, UK Outward Passenger Lists, 1890–1960 (accessed Nov. 15, 2015). A letter sent to thirteen people with the last name Klein living in Auckland in November 2015 (retrieved from https://whitepages.co.nz/) brought several prompt and very friendly replies, but no one was related. The Archives New Zealand (Wellington office) have a record on Norbert Klein (Klien) (1947–1961) that is sealed for 100 years: Department of Internal Affairs, Head Office (AAAC), 1840–current, item ID R23436543, 1947–1961, series 489 (Alien Registration files, 1939-1949), box 219, record number AL 19804. Klein's naturalization file in Archives New Zealand (Wellington office) is accessible: Department of Internal Affairs, Head Office (ACGO), 1840?–1982?, item ID R24597199, series 8333 (Central filing system, ca 1840–ca 1982), record group IA1, box 2358, record number 115/2626. Norbert Klein is buried in the Jewish section of the Waikumete cemetery in Auckland in plot Hebrew A, row 10, plot 89. See http://waitakere.govt.nz/ cnlser/ cm/cemeterysearch/ (accessed Dec. 31, 2015). Klein's final address was 103A Remuera Road, Remuera, Auckland. See email (dated Jan. 5, 2016) from Dianne Rogers (Waikumete Cemetery, Auckland) to the author. There is no probate record on file for Dr. Klein in Archives New Zealand (Auckland office). See email (dated Jan. 6, 2016) from Natalie Vaha'akolo (Archives New Zealand, Te Rua Mahara o te Kāwanatanga) to the author. No probate file was found for Helen Klein either. See email (dated Jan. 7, 2016) from Sarah Mathieson (Archives New Zealand, Te Rua Mahara o te Kāwanatanga) to the author. Norbert Klein's death certificate indicates that his third and last wife was Helen Louise (Luise) Kennedy-Kallina. She was a cabaret artist who fled from Austria to London where she continued to perform during the war with her Viennese husband Willy Kennedy, also an actor. Willy Kennedy died in England in 1942. I thank Iris Fink (Österreichisches Kabarett Archiv, Graz) for communicating the information on Helen and Willi Kennedy-Kallina to me (taken from Veigl & Fink 2012). See her email (dated Jan. 14, 2016) to the author. Shortly after the war, Helen emigrated, possibly already as Klein's third wife, to New Zealand. In this case, too, the Archives New Zealand (Wellington office) record on Helen Luise Klein (1947–1957) is inaccessible (until 2057): Immigration New Zealand (ABKF), 1988–2012, item ID R15519365, series 6794 (Immigration Case Files, 1908–current), box 846, record number 116778. I was not able – despite extensive efforts – to determine the exact date of her birth or death, but Norbert Klein's obituary states that she survived her husband and must have therefore died after 1960. The obituary does not mention any children or other relatives, meaning that the long trail I followed ended there. For all this, see the two obituaries "Dr Norbert Klein" and "Death of Dr N. Klein" in the *New Zealand Herald* and the *Auckland Star*, respectively, both dated December 5, 1960. I thank Joanne Graves (Heritage Central Research, Auckland City Libraries, Auckland) for looking up these newspaper clippings. See her emails (dated Jan. 15, 2016; Jan. 18, 2016) to the author.

[43] The building was demolished in the 1960s. The house numbers in Kreuzgasse (Křížová) were changed at some point after World War II. The street also used to continue along what is now the southern edge of Mendlovo náměstí (Mendel Square). A cadastral plan from 1927 and 1929 allows one to determine that the house in which the pharmacy was located lay between Václavská and Mendlovo náměstí. In the 1960s, a whole strip of houses, whose house number ran approximately from 43 to 49, including Bermann's pharmacy, was demolished to allow the enlargement of Křížová. See AMB, Brno, fonds F 86, Hlavní lékárnické gremium v Brně, n° 153, Lékárna "U dobrého pastýře" Brno, Křížová 49 (1919–1950).

also followed both the traces of the Melichar family and of the Jewish Kulka family, who lived in the same building as the Bermanns. I was able to find both families' current relatives; however, they could not help me with my specific questions.[44]

[44] The house at 36 Lehmstätte (Hlinky) initially belonged to the famous entomologist Leopold Melichar (1856–1924) and his wife Antonia Růžičková (1866–1948). Leopold Melichar was educated as a doctor and had also worked as a counselor for the *Sanitäts-Section* (Sanitary Section) of the Ministry of the Interior. See, for example, *Prager medicinische Wochenschrift*, Jul. 27, 1899, 402; https://www.biographien.ac.at/ oebl/ oebl_M/ Melichar_Leopold_1856_1924.xml (accessed Nov. 24, 2020). He published on medical topics, but is best known for his work in entomology. For an example of a medical treatise, see Melichar 1905. The couple had three children: engineer Leopold Melichar (1896–?), pharmacist František Melichar (1897–1950 or 1953) and a daughter named Antonie Melichar (1899–1985). The eldest child, Leopold Melichar, married Božena Pavlíčková (1901–?). They moved to Plzeň (Pilsen) and had no children. František Melichar married Marie Strachonavá (1901–?). The couple had at least one daughter, Johanna (1928–2014). On March 9, 2016, I spoke over the phone with her son Pavel Vank, who told me that his mother had died just two years earlier. However, he had not heard her talk about the Bermann couple – who, after learning where others lived in the building, I supposed lived on the third and top floor. Vank's mother did talk about the pharmacy owned by Wilhelm Bermann. He also said that his mother had spoken to him about two other people who had lived in the building, mentioning an Edgar Kulka, who emigrated to the USA in December 1938. Paul Kulka, a civil servant and father of Leodegar (Edgar) Kulka, is indeed recorded as living at 36 Hlinky in *Adreßbuch von Groß-Brünn* 1934, 307. On Ancestry.com, I found a record of Paul Kulka (1894–1976), his wife Leontine (Lilly) (1899–?), their daughter Eva Lieselotte Kulka (1926–?) and their son Leodegar D. Kulka (1921–1998), who emigrated from Brno to the United States in December 1938 on a ship taking them from Le Havre to New York. See the Ancestry.com database, New York, Passenger Lists, 1820–1957, T 715, 1897–1957, Roll 6258. They first moved to Los Angeles. See National Archives and Records Administration Washington D.C. (NARA), Naturalization Records of the U.S. District Court for the Southern District of California, Central Division (Los Angeles), 1887–1940, Microfilm Serial M1524, Microfilm Roll 53, Declarations of Intention 147–148, 90201-91800, Jan. 30, 1939, to May 9, 1939, n° 23-69862, Declaration of Intention Paul Kulka. Leodegar Kulka married Patricia (Pat) Loewery in 1985 and they had a daughter named Lilly. I sent an email to the latter on August 30, 2016, inquiring whether there were any family archives but received no reply. See also https://en.wikipedia.org/ wiki/ Leo_De_Gar_Kulka and http:// www.aes.org/ aeshc/ docs/ jaes.obit/ JAES_V46_5_PG486.pdf (both accessed Aug. 30, 2016). I also tried to contact the current relatives of Paul Kulka's brother, Karel Kulka (1892–1956). I sent an email to David Kulka, the son of Felix Kulka (1925–1992), one of the two children of Karel Kulka. David Kulka wrote to me that his aunt, Alice Kulka (1921–2017), his father Felix Kulka's sister, was still alive. Equipped with my questionnaire, David Kulka went to talk to his aunt in Arizona in November 2016, but her health had deteriorated, meaning that she could not answer most questions. It is curious that Karl Fein lived in the same apartment building as Karel Kulka and his family during the years 1933–36: 7c U dětské nemocnice (Kinderspitalgasse or also Beim Kinderspital). The Kulkas moved into the building around 1930. This led me to think for a while that possibly a certain connection existed between the Fein, Brecher and Kulka families. However, in the interview conducted by her nephew David Kulka, Alice Kulka said that the Paul Kulka and Karel Kulka branches of the family were not on good terms. That the two families emigrated from Brno in different years (1938 and 1941, respectively) is a further indication of this family distance. Their distance also seems to stem from different political allegiances: Paul Kulka was a right-winger, Karel Kulka was a convinced social democrat and trade unionist. It is unclear whether Karl Fein and Karel Kulka knew each other, or whether Karl Fein's stay in the U dětské nemocnice apartment building had any relation to the Kulkas who were already living there, but it is certain that Karl Fein was also a leftist. The only other possibly significant factor that can be added here is that Karel and Paul Kulka's father, Rafael Kulka (1859–1939), was, like Karl Fein's father, originally from Boskovice. See Visual History Archive (USC Shoah Foundation), interview 12303, interview with Alice Rosenberg (née Kulka), dated Feb. 21, 1996. Leopold Melichar's youngest child, Antonie Melichar, was married to the pharmacist Vladimír Klein (1891–1962). Ludmila Kleinová, who now lives at 36 Hlinky, married Vladimír Klein (?–2011), a son of Vladimír Klein and Antonie Melichar. Ludmila Kleinová wrote to me that, before the war, only Leopold Melichar's wife and her son, the pharmacist František Melichar and his family, lived in the house at 36 Hlinky. She also wrote to me that she and her husband moved to the house in 1990, shortly after its restitution by the Czech state. See her emails (dated Mar. 14, 2016; Mar. 21, 2016) to the author. Dagmar Klein (1929–?) was another child of the Klein-Melichar couple. She died young. See email (dated Sep. 6, 2016) from Ludmila Kleinová to the author.

[45] The move was noted on one of Felix Bermann's resident registration cards in the AMB, Brno, fonds Z 1. During the occupation, the street was named d'Elvertstrasse (d'Elvertova). Before 1939, it was known as Lange Gasse (Dlouhá). Today, the street is called Staňkova. The impressive house was designed by Anton Jelinek (1855–1931) and erected in 1903–5. See Zatloukal 2000, 226. For a time, the couple also stayed at 4 Akademiegasse (Akademická), but the exact dates are not known. A note that may be "[19]39" appears prior to the address on Wilhelm Bermann's home certificate in the AMB,

On July 14, 1941, the Bermann couple moved with their son to 15 d'Elvertstrasse (d'Elvertova) in Brno.[45] This was most likely another forced move, after the Germans started gathering Jewish people together in so-called Jewish houses (*Jüdenhäuser*). Like the Feins in Prague, the family was lodged with someone of their own class, whom they knew. The couple lived in a room in the apartment of Gustav Wiener (1883–1943) and his wife Marie Smetiprachová (1891–?). The enormous house where the Wieners rented their apartment was owned by Marie Oppenheimer (née Vašičeková, 1894–1988), the widow of Dr. Josef Oppenheimer (1883–1933), the brother of the artist Victor Oppenheimer mentioned earlier. Josef and Victor Oppenheimer's mother ended up in the Jewish hospital with Elise Brecher.[46] So, it was most likely no coincidence that the Bermann couple moved to this house in d'Elvertstrasse (d'Elvertova). Gustav Wiener was Jewish, but his wife was listed as "non-denominational" (*konfessionslos*). He did forced labor on the railroads during the war.[47] In September 1944, he died of lung cancer.[48]

Gustav Wiener was a partner in Weiss, Schwarz & Co., a company dealing in dentist's technical materials, founded in 1922. Starting in 1939, the company was Aryanized. In the company's Aryanization file, Gustav Wiener's wife Maria is described as "a dyed-in-the-wool Marxist and reactionary!!" I think that this is yet another indication that the Brecher and Fein families moved in mainly leftist circles.[49] After the war, Marie Wiener continued to live at 15 Staňkova, but, in 1950, moved to another address in Brno.[50] The Weiss, Schwarz & Co. Aryanization file also provided the first clues to the fate of Gustav and Maria Wiener's two children, Gertrude Ulmann (née Wiener, 1919–2017) and her younger brother Hans Robert Wiener (1924–1944). The children were already abroad by 1939. After a long search, I finally located the ninety-seven-year-old former literary agent Gertrude Wiener in Paris, but she did not know anything about the people staying in her mother's apartment during the war. In February 2017, only a few days after I contacted her, she passed away. The Bermann couple and their son Felix stayed in the Wiener family's apartment until their deportation on transport "Ad", from Brno to Terezín, on March 23, 1942. Anna Bermann and her husband Wilhelm were further transferred on transport "Ea" to Auschwitz-Birkenau on May 16, 1944. On September 28, 1944, their twenty-year-old son Felix was also sent to Auschwitz-Birkenau on transport "Ek".

Wilhelm Bermann's father and mother, David Bermann and his wife Adele Chamaides (1861–1930), are buried in one of the more prestigious spots in the Jewish cemetery in Brno.[51] As mentioned earlier, their grave was designed by the Brno artist Victor Oppenheimer. After the war, the names of Wilhelm, Anna and Felix Bermann were added to the gravestone; however, it is not known who added the names [ill.

Brno, fonds B 1/39. Let us recall that Karl Fein, along with his mother and brother, stayed at 2a Akademická (Akademiegasse) from October 1938 until July 1939. That this was next door to the Bermanns' address was likely no coincidence. It is rather difficult to follow the Bermanns' precise itinerary in Brno since there are hardly any resident registration cards for the couple in the AMB, Brno, fonds Z 1.

[46] *Adreßbuch von Groß-Brünn* 1934, 744.

[47] Phone conversation (dated Mar. 23, 2017) between Pascale Paugam and the author.

[48] AMB, Brno, Sbírka rukopisů a úředních knih, 1333–1958, Úmrtní protokol z roku 1944, n° 3679, death date Sep. 26, 1944. His death was thus unrelated to the deportation of the so-called "Mischlinge", which only started in January 1945.

[49] NA, Praha, fonds n° 375, Arizační spisy, kart. n° 435, sign. 3178, Weiss, Schwarz a spol., not foliated: "eine eingefleischte Marxistin und Reaktionärin!!" The company was eventually bought by a German man named Kurt Plagge. After the war, it was nationalized and renamed Sanitas. Many similar smaller businesses were merged with this company, further indicating its importance in pre-war Czechoslovakia. See also MZA, fonds C 11, kart. n° 82, sign. A VII 287, company file Weiss, Schwarz & Co.

[50] AMB, Brno, fonds Z 1, resident registration card Marie Wiener.

[51] They are buried in plot 26C, row 1, grave 4. David Bermann's last name is spelled as "Berman" in the Jewish cemetery's database.

5].[52] The pharmacist David Bermann also had a daughter named Marie Ernestine Bermann (1890–1942?), who was married to Otto Weiss (1879–1942?), an authorized signatory (*Prokurist*) for the cement and lime company in Malmeritz (Maloměřice) (Maloměřické cementárny a vápenky).[53] We mentioned earlier that Emil Tschauner, the husband of Karl Giese's very first Brno landlord, Hedi Tschauner, as well as his elder brother, the engineer Leo Tschauner (1901–?), would later play important roles as appointed trustees in the Aryanization process of this immense cement and lime company. We suggested that Giese possibly found his first room in Brno, in the second half of 1933, through Karl Fein's family connections with the Brno building industry. Otto and Marie Weiss were deported from Brno to Terezín on transport "U" on January 28, 1942. They were further transferred later that year, but the destination is unknown. The couple had two children, who survived the Holocaust. Following their traces led me to their current relatives in Uruguay and England; however, these relatives could not tell me much about the lives of their ancestors in Brno.[54] The fate of the other son of David Bermann (and brother of Wilhelm Bermann), Anton Bermann (1888–1940?), is also known. Anton Bermann was married to Ernestine Tugendhat (1893–1961) and the couple had two children: Paul (1914–1942?) and Marianne (1921–1975). Ernestine Bermann managed to emigrate to Palestine with her daughter Marianne, but her husband Anton Bermann and their son Paul died in their arduous attempts to escape Europe.[55] At some point after the war, their names were also added to the Bermann family gravestone designed by Victor Oppenheimer in the Jewish cemetery.[56]

FRITZ BRECHER

In the summer of 1938, Fritz Brecher was still living, likely by himself, at 5a Husova třída.[57] However, around the time of the L. & A. Brecher bookstore's aggressive takeover by its employees, Ludmilla Schaal and Josef Cižek, in mid-March 1939, Fritz

[52] Their names are carved into the left-hand stone under the short phrase "zahynuli naši drazí" (died, our loved ones). They do not appear in the Jewish cemetery database, since, strictly speaking, they are not buried there.

[53] See n° 3 in the addenda for more detailed information on this company.

[54] One of Otto and Marie Weiss' two children, Fritz (Friedrich, Frederick, Federico) Weiss (1916–2003), survived the war by fleeing to England in 1939, where he joined the Czechoslovak army. After the war, he returned for a few years to Czechoslovakia. Fleeing Communism, he returned to England where he worked for a few years for his uncle. In 1957, he moved to South America and – after first living in Brazil and Argentina – finally settled in Uruguay, where he started Montelan S.A., a wool export business, in 1959. In 1953, he got married in Argentina and had two daughters, Claudia (1958–) and Diana (1959–). The Montelan S.A. / Don Baez company is currently run by his daughter Claudia Weiss. See http://donbaez.com/ (accessed Feb. 28, 2023). "Don Baez" was derived from the Spanish pronunciation of Fritz Weiss' family name when he arrived in South America (Weiss sounded like Baez). An email sent to Claudia Weiss' company on July 31, 2015, resulted in a very friendly reply the very next day. I thank Mrs. Weiss for her friendliness and the help she offered. In 1999, Fritz Weiss left two Yad Vashem testimonies for his murdered parents. See, for example, the testimony for his father: http://db.yadvashem.org/names/nameDetails.html?itemId=3943282&language=en (accessed Jul. 31, 2015). Otto and Marie Weiss' second surviving child was Liselotte Weiss (1912–?). I sent an email (dated Aug. 3, 2015) to her two children, Garry W. and Suzanne C., but received no response. The Leopold Weiss (1848–1930) family grave plot in the Jewish cemetery in Brno, located in section 26 C, row 2, grave 2, is the burial place of many of the people mentioned in this section.

[55] Marianne married Alfred Bentley (?–d.). They had one son, Mark Bentley (1959–). I was in contact with Mark Bentley on Facebook in January 2016. He was able to provide some information about his closest relatives, but did not know a lot about the oldest members of his maternal grandmother's family nor did he have many pictures of them. I learned a few things about his grandmother's other siblings from him. I thank Itai Hermelin for communicating Mark Bentley's Facebook address to me. See Geni.com message (dated Dec. 18, 2015) from Itai Hermelin to the author.

[56] The gravestone also lists their presumed death years, which could not be found in any other source: Antonín Bermann (July 6, 1888 to 1940?) and the engineer Pavel (Paul) Bermann (April 2, 1914 to 1942?).

[57] MZA, Brno, fonds C 12, Krajský soud trestní Brno, kart. n° 2381, sign. Tk XI 1852/38, file Heinrich Brecher and Gertrude Laufer, f. 49.

Brecher lived for some months with his sister Anna Bermann and her immediate family at 36 Lehmstätte (Hlinky).[58] Afterwards, he lived on Kampelíkgasse (Kampelíkova) and, in November 1940, he moved to 74 Cejl (Zeile), where he stayed with the notable Zwicker family until his deportation. Fritz Brecher was deported on the last Jewish mass transport "Ai" from Brno to Terezín on April 8, 1942.[59] On August 25, 1942, he was further transferred east on transport "Bc" to Maly Trostenets (Malý Trostinec, Maly Trostinez), near Minsk in occupied Belarus, at the time renamed Reichskommissariat Ostland by the occupying Germans. Three days later, he and 999 other Jewish people arrived at an extermination site. Most likely, very shortly after his arrival, Fritz Brecher was either shot by the pit that would serve as his grave or was gassed to death in a truck.[60]

WALTER SÜSS AND JOSEF PAVLAK

At the end of April 1945, Brno was liberated by the Red Army and several thousand German nationals were locked up by partisans in the Kaunitz College (Kounicovy koleje), the building where the Germans had tortured and murdered so many of their political enemies during the war [ill. 6].[61] The liberators of Brno also imprisoned Walter Süss in the Kaunitz College, and his name appears on a list of those who died there.[62] Süss died in one of the cells in August 1945, likely as a consequence of

[58] The pharmacist Wilhelm Bermann, Fritz Brecher's brother-in-law, mediated over the phone when Ludmilla Schaal tried to contact Fritz Brecher (who was out of town) on or after March 15, 1939, the day the Germans invaded the rest of Czechoslovakia. See NA, Praha, fonds Arizační spisy, kart. n° 191, sign. 1119, file L. & A. Brecher Brno, letter (dated Aug. 8, 1939) from Schaal to Oberlandrat, p. 1.

[59] Trying to find clues for the life of Fritz Brecher, I also researched those with whom he was deported. Quite understandably, when they were being deported, friends and family members stayed together when getting their transport numbers at the meeting point. Since a transport number was in part assigned according to the order in which people were registered, a single man like Fritz Brecher may have joined friends or people he knew when queuing up. Fritz Brecher's transportation number was 167. The two numbers preceding him were 165, Adolf Roth (1897–1942?), and 166, Lina Roth (1910–1942?), who lived at 3 Cyrillsgasse (Cyrilská), a street that ran parallel to Mühlgasse (Mlýnská), where the Jewish hospital was located. Likely, Fritz Brecher knew Adolf Roth, a bachelor, since he had briefly lived at 4 Van der Strass-Gasse (Van der Strassova), where Fritz Brecher's mother, Elise Brecher, had also lived. See Roth's resident registration card (dated Jan. 2, 1940) in AMB, Brno, fonds Z 1. One of Roths's resident registration cards bears the unique stamp of the Zentralhilfstelle für Flüchtlinge (Central Refugee Aid Office, Pomocné ústředí pro uprchlíky), led by the lawyer (and Karl Fein's friend) Otto Schütz. This organization assisted Roth when he fled from Vienna to Brno in July 1938. His resident registration card, indicating the move from Vienna and his arrival in Cyrillsgasse (Cyrilská), is signed by a certain Lustig. This was most likely Nora Lustig (née Weinreb, 1899–1943), a member of the League for Human Rights, see Soetaert 2024, 84-85. It is unclear how Lina Roth was related to Adolf Roth, but both were further transferred from Terezín to Rejowiec on April 18, 1942, and were assigned successive numbers for this transport as well. In the transport list, Fritz Brecher was followed by 168, Vítězslav Rybarsch (1886–1942?); 169, Růžena Rybarsch (née Hochsinger, 1894–1942?); and 170, their daughter, Anneliese Rybarsch (1925–1942?). They fled from Vienna in 1938, first to Bratislava and then, in the second half of 1938, to Brno, where they lived in different houses on Quergasse (Příční). Two months before they were deported, they moved to 12 Legionärenstrasse (třída Legionářů), the street where Willi Bondi and his mother lived. Like Adolf and Lina Roth, the Rybarsch family was further transferred from Terezín to Rejowiec on April 18, 1942, and were assigned transport numbers immediately succeeding those of Adolf and Lina Roth. Possibly, their first deportation from Brno to Terezín created a bond between the two families, and moved them to stay together for their next transport. I was not able to link the Rybarsch family of three with any other person mentioned in this book.

[60] For the two certain death trails of people arriving at Maly Trostenets, see https://en.wikipedia.org/wiki/Maly_Trostenets (accessed Oct. 17, 2020).

[61] Vašek, Černý & Břečka 2015; Padevět 2016, 520.

[62] Padevět 2016, 521 and n. 1343. Jiří Padevět refers to a fonds 303-50-1 in the ABS, Praha as his source, but does not specify its exact archival signature. As a result, a collaborator of the ABS, Praha was unable to retrieve the specific archival file. Fonds 303-50-1 was also, as I was told, transferred into another archival fonds A 2/1, Sekretariát (ministra národní bezpečnosti) ministra vnitra, 1945–1961. See email (dated Nov. 11, 2016) from Jitka Bílková (ABS, Praha) to the author. An email I sent to Jiří Padevět, and acknowledged by him, did not result in greater clarification. See email exchange (November 2016) between Jiří Padevět and the author. A reminder email sent on January 24, 2017 was not answered.

poorly treated diabetes.[63] He was buried the very next day, on August 21, 1945, in the central cemetery in Brno.[64] The further fate of his wife and son Ronald is not known. Presumably, they were chased out of the country shortly after the war.[65]

Approximately 19,000 German nationals were moved to the suburb of Malmeritz (Maloměřice), most of whom were sent towards Austria, more specifically to the city of Pohrlitz (Pohořelice), on the infamous so-called Brno death march (*Brünner Todesmarsch*) in the last two days of May 1945, which mainly consisted of women, children and the elderly, since able-bodied men were kept prisoner in Brno.[66] To this day, Czech retaliation against German nationals immediately after the war is a very sensitive subject in Czechia. The annual marches – conducted in the opposite direction, from Pohořelice to Brno – that commemorate this mass exodus are for many in the city an intolerable ritual.[67] The reconciliation (*Versöhnung*) that some sought remains elusive.[68] In 2015, seventy years after the event, the Brno mayor Petr Vokřál officially apologized for the vengeful acts committed in 1945 and, for the first time, invited the citizens of his city to attend the annual march that until then had been the private initiative of the Bruna Heimatverein der Brünner e.V., an association of former German-speaking citizens of Brno.[69] The further fate of Josef Pavlak, a colleague of Süss, is not known. Presumably, he fled or was chased out of the country shortly after the war.

ANDĚLA POLLAK

In 1946, Anděla Pollak (née Švecová) sought to become the legal heir of her husband Robert Pollak who had perished in the Holocaust. In the Brno Regional Civil Court (Krajský soud civilní Brno) she claimed that their divorce was made under duress by the Gestapo and was thus not valid. The two witnesses called upon to corroborate her claim were Oldřich Kukla (1911–?), and the key figure in the discarding of the Institute materials, Jaroslav Růžička. Oldřich Kukla had been a witness to the Pollak-Švecová couple's divorce in 1941, on which occasion Kukla claimed – before the same court –

[63] AMB, Brno, Sbírka rukopisů a úředních knih, 1333–1958, death registers of German nationals, year 1945, n° 13, death date Aug. 20, 1945. The cause of death is given as "diabet.[es] mell[itus]". According to German sources, approximately 300 German nationals died of disease in the unhygienic conditions of the Kaunitz College. See Padevět 2016, 520–21. Cf. the list assembled by Walter Saller (1922–2008) of German nationals who died in *Lager* (prison camps) in Czechoslovakia after the war, which includes the names of Walter Süss and his wife Mina Süss. However, Saller does not provide any information on his source(s). See *Brünner Heimatbote*, Jg. 47, n°s 9–10, September-Oktober, 1995, 127.

[64] Email (dated Feb. 13, 2017) from Eva Holoubková (Správa hřbitovů města Brna, Brno) to the author. Süss was buried in plot 34, row 11, grave 949.

[65] On December 29, 2016, I sent a letter to the three people with the name "Ronald Süss" in an online German phonebook. No one replied. The name did not appear in an Austrian online phonebook.

[66] Padevět 2016, 523–25; and, for a colored, more partisan view of these events, Hertl, Pillwein & Schneider 2000.

[67] Different sources provide other figures, ranging between 17,000 and 27,000, for the approximate number of people who were deported. See Padevět 2016, 525; https:// de.wikipedia.org/ wiki/ Br%C3%BCnner_Todesmarsch (accessed Nov. 12, 2016). There is even less consensus regarding the number of deaths connected to the German exodus.

[68] At present, Tomáš Staněk is the author of the best researched work on the *Vertreibung* (expulsion) of the German-speaking population of Czechoslovakia (Staněk 2002, 2005 and 2007). Two of his works have been translated into German. See Staněk 2002; Staněk 2007. See also http://www.radio.cz/de/rubrik/tagesecho/bruenner-marsch-der-versoehnung-zum-zehnten-mal-aber-weiter-umstritten (accessed Oct. 22, 2020). In 1995, a stone was placed in the garden of the Augustine cloister, where Mendel once had his greenhouses, to commemorate the death march that took place fifty years earlier.

[69] See http://www.tagesschau.de/multimedia/video/video-88993.html (accessed Nov. 12, 2016). The June 2021 inauguration of the Dokumentationszentrum Flucht, Vertreibung, Versöhnung (Documentation Center for Displacement, Expulsion and Reconciliation) in Berlin, commemorating the forced exile of ethnic Germans (but also other ethnic and national groups) from Poland and Czechoslovakia, took fifteen years of planning, and was greeted with dissent in Poland and Czechia. See https://www.flucht-vertreibung-versoehnung.de/de/home (accessed Nov. 10, 2021).

that the couple did not get along "for race reasons". The divorce was annulled by the court in May 1946.[70]

Once she had passed this legal hurdle, Anděla Pollaková tried to recover her deceased husband's former belongings: the Leopold Spielvogel scrap iron company, and the Pollaks' house on Mühlgasse (Mlýnská) where the Jewish hospital was located for two and a half years during the war. We have mentioned that Leopold Spielvogel bought the Pollak company in 1941, when it was Aryanized, and that Spielvogel then continued the scrap iron business under his own name. After the war, the Leopold Spielvogel company was nationalized, even having Anděla Pollak as its new director for a while. In May 1947, the company became the private property of Anděla Pollak, only to be renationalized again in 1951.[71] Anděla Pollak also managed to gain possession of the house, though only in part.[72] Kornelie Deutsch (1921–?), a granddaughter of Josefa Pollak – the original owner of the corner house – then living in Nairobi (Kenya), also tried to acquire her relatives' house through her lawyer in Prague.[73] The end result of the legal battles with the Czechoslovak state was that, in 1948, Kornelie Deutsch owned three quarters of the house and Anděla Pollak one quarter.[74] However, in 1953, the house was nationalized.

After the 1948 Communist coup, together with Oldřich Kukla, Anděla Pollak was involved in an underground ring that organized illegal crossings into Austria. They were closely watched by State Security (Státní bezpečnost, StB). Both fled to Austria in 1950 [ill. 7].[75] In the beginning of 1952, Anděla Pollak emigrated from Bremerhaven

[70] For the May 21, 1946 date of the annulment of the divorce, see NA, Praha, Jewish registers (Židovské matriky, Judische Matriken), http://www.badatelna.eu/fond/1073/reprodukce/?zaznamId=173&reproId=150109 (accessed Aug. 15, 2019). For the postwar file on the annulment of the divorce, see MZA, Brno, fonds C 11, Krajský soud civilní Brno, III. manipulace, kart. n° 620, sign. Ck IIa 337/46, annulment of divorce of Robert Pollak and Anděla Švecová.

[71] See the newspaper articles in *Slovo národa*, Jun. 15, 1945, 4; *Slovo národa*, May 13, 1947, 5; *Svobodné noviny*, Apr. 22, 1948, 10. See also MZA, Brno, fonds C 11, Krajský soud civilní Brno, firemní agenda, Josef Pollak, obchod starým železem Brno (Leopold Spielvogel), 1904–1948, kart. n° 101, sign. A X 14; and Katastrální úřad pro Jihomoravský kraj, katastrální pracoviště Brno-město, Katastralgemeinde Dornrössel / Trnitá, Grundbuchseinlage n° 651, Mühlgasse / Mlýnská n° 27 and Stefansgasse / Štěpánská n° 5, conscription n° 319, where we see that, in 1951, Československý stát – Sběrné suroviny, národní podnik v Praze became the new owner. In 1953, the property was transferred to the nationalized company Československý stát – Kovošrot Brno, národní podnik v Brně.

[72] The property was nationalized in June 1945. Anděla Pollak tried and managed to persuade the Brno court to agree that the house – whose original owner was her husband's mother – was hers since both her mother-in-law and her husband Robert Pollak (his mother's heir) died in the Holocaust. See Katastrální úřad pro Jihomoravský kraj, katastrální pracoviště Brno-město, Katastralgemeinde Dornrössel / Trnitá, Grundbuchseinlage n° 651, Mühlgasse / Mlýnská n° 27 and Stefansgasse / Štěpánská n° 5, conscription n° 319; and the following three files: NA, Praha, fonds n° 375, Ministerstvo práce a sociální péče (nezpracované, unprocessed fonds), Anděla Pollaková, no kart. n°, sign. VIIa-6521, NA, Praha, fonds n° 375, Národní správa majetkových podstat, Anděla Pollaková, kart. n° 91, sign. III/A-2763, Brno, n° 319 and MZA, Brno, fonds C 152, Okresní soud civilní Brno, inheritance file Robert Pollak, sign. M 256/46.

[73] MZA, Brno, fonds C 152, Okresní soud civilní Brno, inheritance file Hugo Pollak, sign. M V 82/46; and MZA, Brno, fonds C 152, Okresní soud civilní Brno, inheritance file Hugo Pollak, sign. D III 502/47. It is unclear why she used the name Pollak (her mother was Rosa Pollak) in the judicial files, instead of Deutsch (her father was Hugo Deutsch). It is possible that her married name was also Pollak.

[74] Katastrální úřad pro Jihomoravský kraj, katastrální pracoviště Brno-město, Katastralgemeinde Dornrössel / Trnitá, Grundbuchseinlage n° 651, Mühlgasse / Mlýnská n° 27 and Stefansgasse / Štěpánská n° 5, conscription n° 319.

[75] A handwritten note on the back of one of her resident registration cards in the AMB, Brno, fonds Z 1, says that State Security (Státní bezpečnost) notified the authorities that the woman emigrated in 1950. See also ABS, Praha, fonds Správa pasů a víz (Passports and visas department), karta emigrace (emigration index cards), Anděla Poláková (Švecová) (Jan. 1, 1898). Several investigation files on her in the ABS archive in Prague show that she was followed (and likely also harassed) by the Czech authorities who did not like her dealings with Oldřich Kukla. See ABS, Praha, SÚMV, fonds n° 302, Hlavní správa vojenské kontrarozvědky (Military counterintelligence headquarters), file Anděla Poláková (Švecová) (Jan. 1, 1898), sign. 302-208-16, sign. 302-219-5 and sign. 302-220-5. See also ABS, Praha, fonds Správa vyšetřování StB (State security investigation headquarters), vyšetřovací spis, spis arch. č. V-650

in Germany to Canada by ship.[76] Many other Czechs went to Canada in the 1940s, fleeing Communism in their home country.[77] Anděla Pollak owned a house on Major Street in Toronto, where she died in April 1981.[78] She did not remarry in Canada and bequeathed her Toronto house to Rudolf Klein (1913–1996). Rudolf Klein was the son of Angela's oldest sister, Žofie Švecová, whose married name was Klein.[79] It took some time to contact Rudolf Klein's son, Rudy Klein (1956–). He wrote an email on June 29, 2021, in reply to my April 2021 letter, sent to all the "R. Kleins" living in or near Toronto.[80] When Rudy Klein's parents visited their aunt Angela in Toronto in 1969, the couple decided not to return to Czechoslovakia. Given his still quite young age as a teenager, Rudy Klein obviously knew only a few things about his great aunt's life in Brno. However, he did have some pictures that he kindly shared with me, from a photo album belonging to his great aunt, mainly showing the happy years of Anděla and Robert Pollak as a married couple. There were also a few postwar pictures of the building that had housed the Jewish hospital, and which had once been the property of the Pollak family.

THE JEWISH HOSPITAL'S POSTWAR FATE

Only a part of the original building of the Jewish hospital, located at the corner of Mühlgasse (Mlýnská) and Stephansgasse (Štěpánská), has survived. Of the two wings of the L-shaped building, only the one on Mlýnská (formerly also Mühlgasse) still exists. The building is now a maternity school. Most of the Stephansgasse (Štěpánská) wing was demolished after the war, presumably in the 1950s, after Anděla Pollak fled the country.[81] Now there is a just wall separating the maternity school's playground

BN, Anděla Poláková [*sic*] (Švecová) (Jan. 1, 1898); and ABS, Praha, fonds Svazková agenda (Operative files), Objektové svazky (Subject files group), Brno, arch. č. OB-30 BN.

[76] See the Ancestry.com database, Africa, Asia and Europe, Passenger Lists of Displaced Persons, 1946–1971. She left by ship from Bremerhaven (Germany) on December 28, 1951. I could not find out more about her in Canadian archives, since most records were too recent and therefore sealed. See email (dated Oct. 15, 2020) from Mary Munk (Library and Archives Canada/Bibliothèque et archives Canada) to the author. The year 1952 accords rather well with a note written on the back of a picture of the Pollaks' former house, stating that it was abandoned on June 30, 1950. The picture is in the private collection of Rudy Klein.

[77] On October 23, 2020, not knowing whether other relatives of Angela Pollak might have moved to Canada, I also sent letters to the three people with the last name Svec living in Toronto. Only one person, who was not related, responded. I sent four additional letters to people with the last name Svec living outside Toronto, on November 14, 2020, but no one replied. Rudy Klein later wrote to me that he was pretty certain that no other family members, other than his mother and father, moved to Toronto or Canada. See his email (dated Aug. 19, 2021) to the author.

[78] Mary Munk (Library and Archives Canada/Bibliothèque et archives Canada) suggested to me that a widowed Angela Pollak, resident in Toronto, was on the federal voters' lists for the years 1963 and 1972. See LAC/BAC, Voters Lists, Federal Elections, 1935–1980, year 1963, Ontario, Spadina, [house number left out] Major Street, R1003-6-3-E (RG113-B), reference number M-5107, 28887, p. 2; and LAC/BAC, Voters Lists, Federal Elections, 1935–1980, year 1972, Ontario, Spadina, [house number left out] Major Street, R1003-6-3-E (RG113-B), reference number M-6176. Yet there was no way of knowing whether this Angela Pollak was indeed our subject. On October 19, 2020, I sent a Facebook message to Krishna C., who now lives in the former house of Anděla Pollak in Major Street, and who has owned the house since 1983. Mr. C. and I exchanged some information on Facebook and I thank him for his help. He suggested that Mrs. Pollak died in 1982. That was helpful since the date was close: her obituary appeared in the *Toronto Star*, Apr. 28, 1981, D14. I thank Pat and Ann Rexe (Ontario Genealogical Society, Toronto Branch) for their assistance in retrieving this obituary for me. Angela Pollak was given a Catholic ceremony at St. Wenceslaus Church in Toronto, the home church of Toronto's Czech Catholics. See https://www.archtoronto.org/ffc/Pages/109-St-Wenceslaus-Toronto.aspx (accessed Oct. 22, 2020).

[79] Email (dated Jul. 1, 2021) from Rudy Klein to the author. The *Toronto Star* obituary also says that Angela Pollak was Rudolf Klein's aunt.

[80] Krishna C. suggested to me that, when he bought Angela Pollak's house, his payment was made to Rudolf Klein. I then tried, in October 2020, to find Rudolf Klein or his son by sending letters to every "R. Klein" listed in an online Toronto phonebook. No one replied. In April 2021, I sent fifteen more letters to every "R. Klein" living near Toronto. Two unrelated people were the first to reply. Then, on June 29, 2021, Rudy Klein, Rudolf Klein's son, sent me an email.

from the street. Several buildings belonging to the Josef Pollak company, used mainly to store scrap iron, were located on the site of the current playground and were also demolished. No memorial indicates that, from 1941 to 1943, the building had been a Jewish hospital which housed the very last Jewish people in Brno for a full year after the Jewish mass deportations ended [ill. 8].

When the very last patient in the Jewish hospital died, in June 1943, the building was given a new function. On April 1, 1944, the Brno administrative office (*Verwaltungsstelle Brünn*) of the Emigration Fund for Bohemia and Moravia (Auswanderungsfonds für Böhmen und Mähren), employing approximately thirty people, moved into the building of the former Jewish hospital.[82] Previously, the Brno office was located at 11a and 15 Karl-Wawra-gasse (Karla Wawry).[83] The building on Mühlgasse (Mlýnská) was renovated prior to the move. In July 1943, when the very last Jewish transport "Dg" left Brno, renovation plans for the building had already been made.[84] There was also some conflict between the Germans and Leopold Spielvogel, who still kept his company offices on the ground floor of the corner building. In the autumn of 1944, a clearly procrastinating Spielvogel was ordered to clear the site behind the building, where he stored his scrap iron, to allow the excavation of a shelter for the Emigration Fund staff in case of bombardment.[85] That was an understandable measure. Three immediately adjacent buildings were heavily damaged by bombing in November 1944, the blasts likely shattering all the windows of the former Jewish hospital.[86]

[81] On July 30, 2021, Rudy Klein sent me some pictures of the house, likely taken by his father in 1961, showing that the Štěpánská wing was already gone. Based on one of the pictures, the partial reconstruction work on the remaining Mlýnská (Mühlgasse) wing was of a recent date.

[82] MZA, Brno, fonds B 392, Vystěhovalecký fond, úřadovna Brno, kart. n° 9, inv. n° 186, f. 59–60. See also the announcement of the move in *Tagesbote*, Apr. 2, 1944, 6. I found one letter sent to this address in December 1944. See MZA, Brno, fonds B 392, Vystěhovalecký fond, úřadovna Brno, kart. n° 24, sign. n° 537, file Hedvika and Max Laufer, letter (dated Dec. 8, 1944) Allgemeine Pensionsanstalt (Amtsstelle Brünn) to Auswanderungsfonds für Böhmen und Mähren (Zweigstelle in Brünn), Mühlgasse n° 27, f. 2b.

[83] For the earlier address, see *Adressbuch der Landeshauptstadt Brünn* 1943, I: 6. The two buildings – at 11a and 15 – are in the same style and were clearly erected together; they are physically joined. In 1940, Fritz Brecher lived on Kampelíkova (Kampelíkgasse) in a house adjacent to the house at 11a Karl-Wawra-gasse (Karla Wawry).

[84] MZA, Brno, fonds B 392, Vystěhovalecký fond, úřadovna Brno, kart. n° 9, inv. n° 186, f. 34, 70. Comparing pictures of the hospital taken during and after the war, I was not able determine if the renovations had been done. There was only one small indication that, after the war, one window on the Mühlgasse (Mlýnská) side, which was sealed off at some point, must have been reinstalled. On the Stephansgasse (Štěpánská) side, the reconstruction plan shows ten windows, whereas there are eleven windows in the wartime picture; however, one window has only a pane since its opening was walled up. Finally, on the corner opposite to Stephansgasse (Štěpánská), at 25 Mühlgasse (Mlýnská), a modernist building designed by Otto Eisler, built in 1934, still stands. See http://www.bam.brno.cz/objekt/c119-najemni-dum?filter=code (accessed Jun. 26, 2016). The building was commissioned by Alfred Stiassny (1883–1961) and his wife Hermine Weinmann (1889–1962) for their daughter Susanne Martin (née Stiassny, 1923–2005). The Stiassny family moved to the USA before the war. The contemporary alterations – mainly to the corner entrance of the building – clearly do an injustice to Eisler's original design. For a photo of this building, see Pelčák, Škrabal & Wahla 1998, 42. The Stiassny brothers Alfred, Ernst (1887–1962) and Rudolf (1880–1948), owned many buildings and plots on Mühlgasse (Mlýnská). See *Adreßbuch von Groß-Brünn* 1934, 776. Villa Stiassny (also spelled Stiassni) in the Pisárky (Schreibwald) district, located at 14 (Traubengasse) Hroznová, was where Alfred Stiassny lived with his wife. See also above, chapter 16, pp. 633-34, n. 132.

[85] The German word is *Splitterschutzgraben*. See MZA, Brno, fonds B 392, Vystěhovalecký fond, úřadovna Brno (1939–1945), kart. n° 9, inv. n° 186, f. 26–27. I did not consult MZA, Brno, fonds C 107, Německý úřední soud Brno (Deutsches Amtsgericht Brünn), sign. 5 a C 39/44.

[86] See "Štěpánská 10", "Štěpánská 12" and "Mlýnská 25" in the "Bombardování Brna" (bombing of Brno) database, https:// gis.brno.cz/ ags/ bomby/ (accessed Nov. 6, 2020). 25 Mlýnská was the address of the Eisler building mentioned on p. 687, n. 84. One of the buildings was completely demolished after the bombing. In one picture, partly showing the building of the former Jewish hospital, it indeed looks like the windows in the Mühlgasse (Mlýnská) wing were shattered by the blast of the Allied bombs.

STANISLAV ČERNIL AND HIS WIFE HELENE MÜLLER

After the war, in 1947, Stanislav Černil moved the short distance from the apartment building at 68 Pekařská (Bäckergasse) to 3 Antonína Nováka (currently Leitnerova), later moving to 9 Antonína Nováka and 5 Antonína Nováka.[87] He died in May 1979. His third wife, Helene Müller, whom he married in April 1944, died almost ten years later, in 1988. Both are buried in the same Černil family plot in the central cemetery in Brno.[88]

JAROSLAV OČADLÍK AND JAN VACEK

In March 1950, Jaroslav Očadlík moved from Brno to Kroměříž (Kremsier), a city near Hulín, where he was born. Severe illness likely moved him to return to his birth town, where he died in a hospital at the end of the same month. It is not known where he is buried.[89] The further fate of Jan Vacek, the young man who lived with Očadlík in the Stephansgasse (Štěpánská) apartment during the war, and lived with Očadlík at another address after the war, is not known.

JINDRA AND JAROSLAV RŮŽIČKA

Jaroslav Růžička was harshly persecuted by the Communist Czechoslovak state after the war. Profit-making was not a Communist ideal, and his scrap iron business thrived a little too much in the eyes of the Communists.[90] The Communist regime charged Jaroslav Růžička with black market dealings, or, more specifically, "undocumented" profitable transactions with other companies in the years 1947–1949, and, in January 1950, the Brno Regional Criminal Court (Krajský soud trestní Brno) fined him 50,000 Czech crowns and sentenced him to six months in prison.[91] In 1951, presumably charged with additional economic crimes, the same court fined him 500,000 Czech crowns. His belongings were confiscated.[92]

According to a current relative, Jaroslav Růžička employed up to fifty people after the war. When coming into conflict with the Czechoslovak state, twenty-seven employees drew up a declaration (*prohlášení*) in June 1949 stating that Růžička was

[87] AMB, Brno, fonds Z 1, resident registration cards Stanislav Černil. Cf. *Adresář zemského hlavního města Brna* 1948, B: 49. Judging from two resident registration cards for Helene Müller, we can establish that she and her husband Stanislav Černil moved on the same dates (in 1947, 1951 and 1953) to the same Antonína Nováka (currently Leitnerova) addresses.

[88] They are buried in plot 89, row 1, graves 39–40.

[89] Očadlík was not buried in either the Brno or Kroměříž cemetery, his name not appearing in their databases. See email (dated Jul. 25, 2017) from Eva Holoubková (Správa hřbitovů města Brna, Brno) and email (dated Jul. 24, 2017) from Šárka Silná (Kroměřížské technické služby, Hřbitovy) to the author. I also sent an email to the Hulín city administration on September 20, 2018, but I did not receive a reply. Očadlík's *úmrtní list* (death certificate), obtained from the Městský úřad Kroměříž on August 2, 2017, did not contain any additional information on any of his relatives.

[90] This paragraph on Jaroslav Růžička's postwar fate is in great part based on an interview I conducted with the current relatives of Jindra and Jaroslav Růžička (who preferred to remain anonymous) in Brno on October 10, 2019; and also on documents shown to me from the private archive of the couple I interviewed.

[91] See the newspaper articles in *Rudé parvo*, Jan. 18, 1950, 3; *Lidové noviny*, Jan. 31, 1950, 4. His business was incorporated into Sběrné suroviny, a nationalized company.

[92] On the basis of the documents in the archive of Jaroslav Růžička's current relatives, it is difficult to determine the fines that Růžička eventually had to pay, the number of weeks he served in prison, and the term of his hard labor. The court seems to have modified the fine several times. One appeal letter, written by Růžička in 1952, mentions the sum of 500,000 Czech crowns, fifteen months' imprisonment, six months of forced labor, and the confiscation of property valued at 238,738 Czech crowns. Although Růžička did go to jail for some time, it is unclear for how many weeks or months. However, in the just-mentioned letter, he claimed to have spent six months in prison. Nor is it clear how much of the fine he actually paid. See appeal letter (dated Oct. 20, 1952) from Jaroslav Růžička to Okresní soud civilní v Brně (private archive, Brno). In our interview, Jaroslav Růžička's current relatives told me that Růžička escaped hard labor by citing (false) medical reasons.

a good employer and not guilty of the economic crimes of which he was accused.[93] Their adversity gravely affected the Růžička couple's finances. They had to leave their apartment at 58 Gorkého (known before the war as Falkensteinerova or Falkensteinergasse) and moved into a two-room apartment at 12 Vranovská street, where, out of necessity, they rented one room to a student. Their financial worries also compelled them to sell their weekend bungalow near the water reservoir (*vodní nádrž*) in Brno-Rozdrojovice in October 1949. The Czechoslovak authorities also made it clear to Jaroslav Růžička that he had to make his living as a laborer in the Communist state. In 1951, Růžička started to work for Drukov, a new company specializing in metal kettles.[94] He obtained certification as an electrician in 1957. He also worked as a porter in a bakery. When Jaroslav Růžička received his pension in 1963, after nine years as a manual worker, it amounted to 819 Czech crowns per month.[95] His wife Jindra Růžičková died the following year, in 1964.

Despite the persistent Communist harassment, his current relatives remember Jaroslav Růžička as always having a positive attitude and a charming personality. Near the end of his life, in the 1970s, Růžička also became something of a living mascot for a local handball team (*házená*), which affectionately referred to him as "stářa", derived from the Czech for "old man". In his current relatives' photo archive, I have seen several photos depicting the older Jaroslav happily surrounded by the young men of the handball team in sports attire. A heavy smoker all of his life, Jaroslav Růžička died of throat cancer in 1978. Both Jindra and Jaroslav are buried in the Královo Pole cemetery [ill. 9].[96] In 1990, a year after the so-called Velvet Revolution, there was some discussion of Jaroslav Růžička as eligible for possible rehabilitation; however, we do not know the outcome of these discussions.[97]

[93] Private archive, Brno, statement (prohlášení) (dated Jun. 30, 1949) of twenty-seven employees of the Růžička company sent to the Okresní soud civilní Brno.

[94] For a short history of the Drukov company, see http://www.drukov.cz/ (accessed Nov. 30, 2019).

[95] Private archive, Brno, letter (dated Jul.? 10?, 1963) Státní úřad sociálního zabezpečení [unreadable] Praha to Jaroslav Růžička.

[96] They are buried in parcel 1b (the row adjacent to the cemetery wall), graves 52/53 in the Královo Pole cemetery on Myslínova street.

[97] Jaroslav Růžička's postwar case file number T VII 132/50 from MZA, Brno, fonds C 153, Okresní soud trestní Brno, was renumbered as 12 T 211/90, and is not present in the MZA, Brno. In all probability, the file is now kept at the Městský soud v Brně (Brno Municipal Court) where it is registered as rehabilitation file n° 119/90. See email (dated Dec. 9, 2019) from Tereza Mrkvičková (MZA, Brno) to the author.

1. The H V building, better known as the Dresden barracks (Dresdner Kaserne), in the Terezín (Theresienstadt) ghetto. Only women and children occupied this building. Elise Brecher stayed there from June to August 1943 in rooms 214 and 207. May 2017.

2–3. Heinrich Brecher and his wife Gertrude Laufer. 1938 or earlier.

4. The building at 36 Lehmstätte (Hlinky) (left), where, until July 1941, Anna Bermann (née Brecher) and her husband, the pharmacist Wilhelm Bermann, lived with their son Felix in an apartment on the right-hand side of the top floor. The house was owned by the Melichar family. The building in the background (lower center) is the First Brno Joint-Stock Brewery and Malt factory (Erste Brünner Aktienbrauerei und Malzfabrik, První brněnský akciový pivovar a sladovna). Above it, one can see Špilberk Castle. October 2015.

5. The Bermann family grave in the Jewish cemetery in Brno (parcel 26C), designed by Victor Oppenheimer. May 2017.

6. The infamous Kaunitz college (Kounicovy koleje) at 45 Husgasse (Husova), postmarked October 21, 1941.

REPUBLIKA ČESKOSLOVENSKÁ 20 1938 20

Běž. čís. .... platný do ....

slovy ....

Majitel(ka) ....

bytem ....

Popis osoby majitele rybářského lístku:

Rok nar. ......, postava ......, vlasy

oči ......, zvláštní znamení ....

ONV .... Magistrát ....

ONV zem. hl. města Brna

V .... dne ....

Za referenta UN

Podpis majitele:

7. Anděla Pollak. Ca. 1949.

8. The former Jewish hospital, now a maternity school. Only the shorter wing of the original L-shaped building has survived. The longer wing on Stephansgasse (Štěpánská) was demolished after the war. October 2016.

9. Memorial plaques of the graves of Jindra Růžičková (née Fikesová) and Jaroslav Růžička in the Královo Pole cemetery. October 2019.

ONGINE

18. Fear

SEXUAL KNOWLEDGE AS BASIC HISTORICAL SUBJECT MATTER

There is no doubt that Magnus Hirschfeld was one of the most important early gay activists in the prehistory of the LGBT movement.[1] Hirschfeld was a German and Jewish man, who worked in Germany most of his life, but his renown and influence had a global reach before World War II. Hirschfeld inspired many early gay activists all over Europe between *ca.* 1900 and 1940, and this book has shown that this also included Czechoslovakia. The World League for Sexual Reform (WLSR), initiated by Hirschfeld, further illustrates the cross-border ambitions he had for progressive ideas about sexual reform. Hirschfeld's world tour, which lasted from November 1930 to March 1932, extended his trademark-like name on a global scale. While on this tour, he likely also prospected new markets where he could license his profitable Titus Pearls sex pills.

Hirschfeld was a gay man who was adamant about bettering the life conditions and legal situation of "sexual intermediaries" (*sexuelle Zwischenstufen*), as he dubbed his flock. Unlike the masculinists around the German literary magazine *Der Eigene*, and its head Adolf Brand, Hirschfeld was a tolerant maximalist. He was not opposed to feminine men whom the masculinists scorned as effeminate. For this reason, in Brand's masculinist circle, but also in Hirschfeld's own, Hirschfeld was known and mocked as "Aunt Magnesia" (*tante Magnesia*).[2]

The classes and subclasses of sexual categories that Hirschfeld claimed to observe in his time continue to come to light in our own day. The great diversity of Hirschfeld's "sexual intermediaries" can be observed in the ever-expanding acronym that started with the words "lesbian" and "gay" and has since grown into LGBTQIAP, itself likely already outdated. "Transgender" has been one of the most media-covered categories added in recent years. The categories added since include queer, intersex, asexual and pansexual. Because the acronym does not seem to end, some have added an asterisk to LGBT, making it LGBT*.

Magnus Hirschfeld is part of the history of the movement of sexual minorities, or better, sexual variations that, at least in its initial stage, attached great importance to the ever-growing scientific knowledge about these sexualities. Hirschfeld believed that an ideological alliance with science was the best means to make progress in the emancipation of non-heterosexual sexual variations. His most important life motto adorns his gravestone in Nice: *per scientiam ad justitiam*, through science to justice. In Hirschfeld's view, the study and emancipation of sexual variations was closely linked to scientific knowledge about alternative sexualities and their correlative emergence from the shadows in which, supposedly, they had been hiding because they diverged from an imposed heteronormative constellation. Scientific knowledge, but also, simply, *knowing about*, and daring to know about (one's) sexuality, is therefore a central aspect of this view of sexuality. The French philosopher Michel Foucault (1927–1984) interpreted this important feature of modern Western sexualities as "the

[1] See especially Ralf Dose's attempt to make this clear to the English-speaking world in his book *Magnus Hirschfeld: The Origins of the Gay Liberation Movement*. See Dose 2014.

[2] Satirical special issue of *Der Eigene* (year 10, n° 9, April 1925) titled 'Die Tante' (The 'Aunt'). See also Herzer 2017, 232; Beachy 2014, 229; Keilson-Lauritz 1997, 130, 366–67. Its cover page is reproduced in Hohmann 1981, following p. 330.

will to know" (*la volonté de savoir*) about sexuality and, more specifically, the sexual being (and essence) of the individual. Foucault also claimed that the presumed shrouding of sexual knowledge – as well as it supposed emancipation – was a Western myth.[3] He contrasts this Western approach to sexual phenomena with practices in other cultures and times, where sexuality was more a matter of mastering sexual techniques (*ars erotica*) and of the ability to incorporate one's sexual desires into one's life in a balanced way.

In his Berlin Institute, Magnus Hirschfeld ardently collected a vast number of books, magazines and other publications that captured this new science of sexuality (named *Sexualwissenschaft* in German), which started to emerge at the end of the nineteenth century. Because of Hirschfeld's basic decision to link scientific knowledge and the emancipation of sexual variations, these books, magazines and archival materials about all aspects of sexual life form the basic raw material of this important chapter in the prehistory of LGBT. The Institut für Sexualwissenschaft in Berlin, and especially its collection, were the palpable result of a brave man on a quest for social justice. Hirschfeld did not go to Berlin or Germany after returning from his world tour. In May 1933, the Nazis assaulted his life's work in Berlin, throwing a considerable part of his enormous Institute collection into the flames. Wishing to burn the man himself at the stake, Nazi students threw Hirschfeld's bust on the pyre instead.[4] So, when writing the very last part of the history of Hirschfeld's activist accomplishment, it is no accident that a considerable part of this book has been devoted to attempts to trace the itinerary and further fate of Hirschfeld's pioneering sexology collection.

I believe that we pay our dues to Hirschfeld's precursor work by trying to write – in as detailed a manner as possible – the history of the itinerary of these materials. Because so many items were lost or deliberately destroyed, the search for any remnants of Hirschfeld's Institute rather resembles the quest for the Jewish Ark of the Covenant or King Arthur's Holy Grail. In this book, I have tried to shed more light on what happened to the Institute materials bought back from Germany, which ended up in Nice with the group formed around Victor Bauer, and especially on the materials kept by Karl Giese and Karl Fein in Brno. Hirschfeld's surviving guestbook, saved from an old paper container in Brno in 1942, and the affidavit it contained were my first and only lead. Our journey started in 1932, when Hirschfeld returned from his world tour, and ended in 1942, the year when drastic and dramatic decisions were taken in Brno regarding the further fate of the remaining materials originating from the Institute.

FEAR

When examining the itinerary of these Institute materials, a single ever-recurring central factor explains much of what happened in the ten years after Hirschfeld returned from his world tour. Many of Hirschfeld's actions can be explained by the fear instilled throughout Europe by the National Socialists. This is even more true of the people in his inner circle who took up the torch after Hirschfeld's death. As early as 1920, when he suffered an attempt on his life in Munich, Hirschfeld viscerally realized that conservative forces would rather see him dead.[5] Landing in Athens when he returned from his world tour, in March 1932, he immediately perceived that

[3] The programmatic thesis of Foucault's history of sexuality project was spelled out in his book *La volonté de savoir* (The will to know), which came out in 1976. See Foucault 1976.

[4] As suggested by Kurt Hiller in 1935. See Hiller 1945, 2.

[5] Certainly, starting around 1920, the National Socialists did not conceal their wish to see Hirschfeld dead. See In het Panhuis 2020, 66, 71–72. Manfred Herzer has shown that, as early as 1907, pamphlets were distributed close to Hirschfeld's Berlin-Charlottenburg home, warning about the per-

the old animosity against him had resumed, and decided that it was simply not safe to return to Germany [ill. 1].

The two principal beneficiaries of Hirschfeld's estate were also paralyzed by fear, though to different degrees. Karl Giese deliberately kept a low profile in Brno in 1936–38, while Li Shiu Tong's fear of Nazism bordered on paranoia and lasted long after the war. Hirschfeld's Chinese scholar also refused to reply to the German restitution (*Wiedergutmachungs*) authorities in the 1950s, and intentionally disappeared from sight. The result was that the items in Li Shiu Tong's possession, which had once belonged to Hirschfeld, only partly survived. A few are still in the hands of Li Shiu Tong's current family. The Brno lawyer Karl Fein also likely grew very prudent when, after Giese's suicide in March 1938, he realized that he was responsible for the Institute materials. Fein would have known – and feared – the real possibility that the National Socialists would pursue him as soon as they invaded Czechoslovakia in March 1939. Several of Fein's acquaintances and good friends did indeed come into conflict with the Gestapo very soon after the German takeover: Artur Feldmann Sr.'s art collection was immediately confiscated, and he himself was imprisoned from January until March 1940 in Špilberk Castle. Also suffering from an arterial disease, the lawyer Feldmann died one year after his release.[6] The gay Brno architect Otto Eisler was tortured by the Gestapo. Like many other Czechoslovak lawyers, Fein's friend and former colleague, the lawyer Otto Schütz, president of the Brno branch of the League for Human Rights, fled the country immediately after the Germans invaded, in March 1939. Josef Weisskopf and Hugo Iltis also left the country in 1939. In the first year after the invasion of Czechoslovakia, several of Fein's other left-wing friends and colleagues – for example, the lawyer Karel Růžička and the doctor Karel Hora – were tried by summary courts martial and murdered by the Nazis.

In 1939–40, Karl Fein conceivably rented a storage room from the Leopold Fleischer company under his own name or that of his aunt Elise Brecher. Later, prompted by closer scrutiny by the Nazis of the Leopold Fleischer company, Fein's caution may have led him to entrust everything he inherited from Karl Giese to the *Kamarád* group, to guard it for posterity. This possible option remains the wiser course of action and was likely the true course of events. The quintessential fact that the materials were discarded at the Růžička couple's company points to the direct involvement of the *Kamarád* clique.

If indeed some of the gay men around the gay magazine *Kamarád* decided the fate of the Institute materials, possibly in September 1942, their action could be described as driven by fear of the Nazis. If Karl Fein indeed entrusted the Institute materials to the *Kamarád* people, they understandably concluded that their lives were worth more than the preservation of a lot consisting mainly of papers. If, on the other hand, the drastic decision about discarding the Institute materials was taken in the Jewish hospital, before the deportation of the last Jewish citizens in Brno, we may suppose that it was also a desperate choice made out of utmost caution and fear of the Nazis. Elise Brecher and her son Fritz may have wished to prevent the Institute materials – possibly kept in a storage room – from compromising both their own lives and those of other family members once they were deported.

The years 1941–42 were years of real horror for many Czechoslovak people, the situation growing even worse after the assassination of Reinhard Heydrich in June 1942. Fear of death or confrontation with the dreaded Gestapo was the primary concern of many. The times were dark and complicated and difficult decisions

nicious influence of Jews and – more specifically – Hirschfeld. See Herzer 2015, 141.

6 Eßl 2015, 17; Caruso 2015, 36; NA, Praha, fonds n° 1077, Okupační vězeňské spisy, kart. n° 241, sign. 101-615/5, note (dated Mar. 2, 1940) showing the release of Artur Feldmann from Špilberk's police prison.

needed to be taken. The real, justified fear caused by the German occupiers of the so-called Protectorate in itself explains much of the occupied population's behavior during the war.

CIRCUMSPECTION AND ITS CONSEQUENCES

The May 1933 looting of the Institute left Hirschfeld and Giese traumatized and likely also painfully aware of the utter fragility of the thousands of sexuality-related materials they had both diligently collected in the Institute in Berlin over the years. We may assume that the May 1933 events left them fearful of a renewed attack on the remains of the Institute collection, bought back in part from Germany, and that this provoked them to heightened caution. Some factors seem to support this idea, but not in a straightforward way. For example, Hirschfeld and Giese may have decided against gathering the materials they had in one place. However, it is also possible that the Institute materials' scattered locations were imposed by external and undesired conditions. For example, we examined how the Institute books – bought back in November 1933 from Nazi Germany – most likely stayed in Brno while other materials, including the Institute questionnaires (*Fragebogen*), were sent to Paris. It is unclear why the books stayed in Brno. This choice may have been dictated by prudence but there may simply have not been enough money to send the books to Paris as well. Or possibly the idea to establish an Institute in Brno was never really abandoned. Other materials – likely kept in a safe location before the looting of the Institute – were stored in three German cities, as noted in Hirschfeld's last will. This could also be the consequence of last-minute decisions and not and intention to deliberately spread out the materials and thus reduce the risk.

We have also observed that, once they arrived in Paris from Brno, in 1934, the Institute materials were sorted by Karl Giese and Max Reiss in a house on Boulevard Haussmann and not in the Avenue Charles Floquet apartment where Hirschfeld lived. It is impossible to determine whether this was a conscious choice. In Giese's known letters, he almost never mentions where the materials are located; however, he is not wholly silent about the matter. In letters to Max Hodann and Ernst Maass, he does at times divulge a few details regarding the share of the collection he held onto in Brno.[7] As a consequence, it remains uncertain whether Giese suspected that his letters could be possibly intercepted by the Nazis or their informers or spies.

The same can be said about the choice to rent a storage room in Paris and possibly also Nice. Storing materials at Hirschfeld's Paris or Nice apartment could be perceived as risky; however, it is also possible that a storage room was a purely practical solution. Maybe there was not enough room to store everything in the apartment. In article 3 of his will, Hirschfeld urged that the executor of his estate (*Testamentvollstrecker*), Franz (François) Herzfelder, be as discreet as legally allowed regarding the contents of his last will.[8] In article 5, Hirschfeld did not hesitate to state that the materials in France were located in the Bedel & Co. storage facility (*garde-meuble*) at 18 Rue St. Augustin in Paris. Even here, we may observe some prudence. Hirschfeld was likely well aware that this was the address of the storage company's representative office, and not of one of the four Parisian premises where the materials were actually stored.[9] In article 5 itself, Hirschfeld was much less precise about the exact location

[7] We have mentioned Karl Giese's seemingly very discreet treatment of matters in a September 1935 letter to Max Hodann, but I think this rather a reflection of the unresolved and complicated (legal ?) situation in Nice: "Das wertvolle ethnologische Material ist zur Zeit noch immer nicht 'disponibel', wie ich mal sagen möchte. Ich kann mich da nicht näher auslassen" (The valuable ethnological material is still not "available" at the moment, I would say. I cannot be more specific about it). See Arbetarrörelsens arkiv och bibliotek, Stockholm, Max Hodann samling, vol. 15, letter (dated Sep. 24, 1935) from Karl Giese to Max Hodann.

[8] Baumgardt 1984, 145.

[9] Baumgardt 1984, 146. For the four Bedel storage places in other parts of Paris, see p. 238, n. 85.

of Institute materials still in Germany, only naming three cities – Berlin, Wiesbaden and Saarbrücken – and adding that Karl Giese knew where or with whom those materials were stored.[10] Unfortunately, Hirschfeld assumed that it was enough for his appointed successors – Karl Giese and presumably also Li Shiu Tong – to know where exactly the materials were stored. We have examined a few candidates who might have guarded some of the Institute materials stored in Germany: the Alsatian doctors and Hirschfeld's friends, Leo Klauber and Edmond Zammert.

A SELF-CENSORED COPY OF THE HIRSCHFELD DIARY

One can see that a sense of caution endured – and possibly grew even stronger – in the minds of the people from Hirschfeld's inner circle after his death in May 1935, as clearly illustrated by the following example. We have observed that Magnus Hirschfeld kept a diary. In 1927, Giese wrote that Hirschfeld already started keeping a diary in 1896 and that he had seen his diaries.[11] We have also suggested that many of Hirschfeld's earlier diaries likely ended up on the Berlin bonfire in May 1933 and that Giese took some volumes to Brno. Hirschfeld used his diary to note a potpourri of ideas and impressions, numbering these text fragments.

On the night of May 16–17, 1935, a few days after Hirschfeld's death, Ernst Maass read the last volume of Hirschfeld's diary sitting at Hirschfeld's former desk in the Gloria Mansions I apartment in Nice, copying the fragments that he found interesting or striking along with the numbers that Hirschfeld assigned them. When he finished reading the diary, at sunrise, he had filled eight pages. Maass added a tender comment of his own at the end, saying that he had listened to the murmuring of the Mediterranean sea all night through the open window as he took notes. In the diary fragments themselves, Hirschfeld philosophically pondered the importance of the sea and the sun for his mental well-being, stating, for example, that he had been born by the Baltic Sea and would likely die near the Mediterranean. Presumably, Maass also read the diary to get a better understanding of Hirschfeld's last wishes and ideas since the funeral ceremony was four days away.[12]

A typed copy was made of Maass's handwritten notes.[13] It is unclear who did the typing or why a typed copy was made. Both the typed and handwritten versions are part of Ernst Maass's estate. Interestingly, a tiny piece containing two diary fragments was cut from the typed version with scissors.[14] The excised passage contained sensitive information that someone apparently did not wish to fall into the wrong hands. One partial sentence removed was from fragment 65, in which Hirschfeld meditated that his sister, Franziska Mann (1859–1927), who died in 1927, would likely have suffered under the Nazis' terror regime. In this instance, very tellingly, the words "suffered under the horrors of the Hitler era" were cut out. The other sentence removed was fragment 71, which stated: "Indication of the locations

[10] Article 5 in Hirschfeld's last will (Baumgardt 1984, 146). See also Dose & Herrn 2006, 46–47.

[11] Giese 1927, 132. Finding and acquiring any surviving Hirschfeld diaries is one of the most cherished wishes of the staff and volunteers working for the MHG in Berlin.

[12] MHG, Berlin, fonds Ernst Maass, manuscript (dated May 16–17, 1935) of Ernst Maass consisting of fragments copied from Hirschfeld's (presumably) last diary, eight pages. Ernst Maass took this document with him when he moved to the USA in March 1938.

[13] Archiv MHG, Berlin, fonds Ernst Maass, undated typoscript of fragments (copied by Ernst Maass on May 16–17, 1935) from Hirschfeld diary, three pages. The typescript is mostly a direct copy of the original eight-page manuscript, but there are some small omissions.

[14] Another aspect of this typed version remains unexplained. The typist left a blank space for a passage, which was later filled by a note written by hand. The handwriting was identified as belonging to Ernst Maass. One possible explanation is that the typist was unable to read a passage; however, a review of both the typed and handwritten versions reveals that this could not have been the reason for the blank space.

where belongings of the institute are to be found" [ill. 2].[15] It is far from certain that Magnus Hirschfeld actually noted in his diary the names and addresses of places where Institute materials were stored, or that he simply included a reminder that he needed eventually to compile such a list.[16]

That these two fragments specifically were excised is rather remarkable. It suggests that merely mentioning that former Institute materials were stored here and there in Europe was already considered too risky. It is possible that the dangerous fragments were cut out by Li Shiu Tong, who was staying in the Gloria Mansions I apartment with Robert Kirchberger. We have already discussed Hirschfeld's favorite student's deep-seated fear of Nazism. However, it is possible that Giese, who had not yet arrived in Nice when Maass read the last volume of Hirschfeld's diary, took the initiative in this instance. Giese arrived in Nice three days after Maass copied the diary fragments. He would stay in Nice until June 6, 1935, the date of his final departure from France. Yet, on the whole, it does not truly matter who did the cutting. The important thing to observe is that there was a clear fear of Nazi Germany, one that seeped into any possible plans regarding Hirschfeld and his estate, compelling caution. The members of Hirschfeld's entourage were apparently not willing to risk these few sheets of fragments copied from Hirschfeld's diary falling into the wrong hands.[17]

Another factor also possibly indicates a degree of caution, one prompted by the events of May 1933, and perhaps intensifying after Hirschfeld's death. In a May 1935 letter to Max Reiss, Giese asked the young Dutch man to send him three copies of clippings of Dutch newspaper articles about the death of Hirschfeld.[18] It is unclear if Giese asked for three copies to distribute the clippings to three different locations, thus diminishing the risk, or if it was simply the usual practice thus to collect items related to Hirschfeld.

Maybe caution further intensified with the growing prospect of war. I am of the opinion that Karl Fein, especially, would have been very discreet about where and with whom he stored the Institute materials that he inherited after Giese's suicide. As we have seen, Fein was closely involved in counteracting the traumatic events of May 1933 by actively assisting in the operation to buy back the Institute materials. In this regard, Fein may have replicated Hirschfeld's and Giese's discretion and caution. Furthermore, Fein knew about the intimidating conduct of the Gestapo in Brno and would have realized that the fewer people who knew where and with whom the Institute materials were stored, the better. We may even wonder if Fein would have taken the risk of being denounced by someone during one of the Gestapo's feared interrogations. It cannot be excluded that only a few of the *Kamarád* group,

[15] Archiv MHG, Berlin, fonds Ernst Maass, undated typescript of fragments (copied by Ernst Maass on May 16–17, 1935) from Hirschfeld's diary: "[unter] den schrecknissen [der] Hitlerzeit gelitten haben". And: "Angabe der Orte, wo Sachen d.[es] Instituts sich [be]finden".

[16] This prompted Ralf Dose of the MHG – who transcribed this Hirschfeld diary fragment – to add a clarification in square brackets: "[...], warum hat er [Ernst Maass] das nicht abgeschrieben!" ([...], why did he [Ernst Maass] not copy this!). I'm not sure that Hirschfeld's original diary contained the names of such places. Yet, if the detailed information was indeed included in the original, then it further supports our theory that utter discretion was practiced.

[17] Ralf Dose of the MHG in Berlin, who transcribed the handwritten version of Maass's text, wondered whether the typed copy was perhaps meant to be sent to Germany, explaining the omission of the "sensitive" parts. That is indeed a possibility. However, we also need to consider the possibility that Maass assembled a purely personal choice of fragments from Hirschfeld's diary. Dose's contention would be more persuasive if Maass had copied Hirschfeld's diary in its entirety, or at least a part with no consecutive numbers missing. If he merely compiled a freely chosen potpourri of diary fragments, Maass did not need a safe copy. So, it remains unexplained why Maass deemed it necessary to make a typed copy of his selection of fragments from Hirschfeld's diary.

[18] Archiv MHG, Berlin, fonds Max Reiss, letter (dated May 1935, 4 – presumably May 28) from Karl Giese to Max Reiss.

and possibly also Elise Brecher and her son Fritz, knew where the Institute materials were when Fein left Brno for Prague in September 1939. This would mean that, of the great many people discussed in this book, the greater part likely knew nothing about the matter. This shows that fear of the Nazis, and the extreme caution it provoked, largely determined why we currently know so little about exactly what happened to the Institute materials in Brno in 1942. The many Holocaust deaths, duly recorded in this study, further explain that the few people who may have had inside knowledge took this information to their involuntary graves – if, like Karl Fein, they were lucky enough to have one.

LACKING SOURCES AND LOOKING FOR TRACES OF SURVIVAL

The National Socialists' terror regime in Europe committed the murder of six million Jewish people. In addition to taking their lives, it expropriated their property as well. In addition to their more valuable possessions, traces of their personal lives in the form of letters, diaries, identity cards, photo albums, picture frames, etc., have also largely disappeared. One of the great difficulties this research project faced was the basic absence of these personal archives. The Holocaust mostly eliminated these documents, mainly during the liquidation of the Jewish storage rooms. To make matters even worse, the administrative archives of the expropriation of the Jewish storage rooms are virtually nonexistent. In most cases, these archival traces were deliberately discarded by the Germans. This is the principal reason why, in my research, I have sought to follow *any* possible trace of Jewish survival (the family or friends of those involved), hoping that some archival traces, items or even stories or memories might have still survived. However, despite my many efforts, I think it no accident – to name just one example – that I was not able to find even one photograph of the younger Karl Fein.[19] I hope that the reader will forgive me for imparting often minute details about the lives (and deaths) of several people. My sole purpose was to prevent future researchers from duplicating work, and thus to provide a firm basis on which further historical research may hopefully build. I also hope that any readers who discover their families in these pages may be enticed to further help uncover new leads and elements.

THE BLACK HOLE OF THE HOLOCAUST

I think that the enormous, ruthless aggression of the National Socialists, which ultimately resulted in the devastation of World War II and the Holocaust, not only negatively impacted Hirschfeld and his life's project, but has had detrimental repercussions to our own day. When, in the 1980s, the founders of the Magnus-Hirschfeld-Gesellschaft (MHG) in Berlin reported that they wanted to research the then-largely forgotten Magnus Hirschfeld, people said that his legacy had been completely destroyed during the war and there was no sense in an initiative to reconstitute Hirschfeld's legacy.[20] The tireless efforts of the MHG have since proven the opposite.[21]

I also noticed that, all too often, research seems to be brought to a halt once the specter of the Holocaust is invoked. "The lawyer Karl Fein, Giese's heir, was soon after deported to a concentration camp and presumably killed there", Manfred

[19] That said, Fein likely figures in one of the pictures of the 1932 WLSR Brno conference, but the problem is that none can tell which of the people depicted is Fein. This is one reason why I also asked current relatives of the people I was tracking for family photos (some depicting people whose identities they may not have known). Perhaps I would recognize a face from the conference photos.

[20] See https://makinggayhistory.com/podcast/magnus-hirschfeld/ (accessed Nov. 5, 2020).

[21] An extensive overview of these efforts is given in Dose 2012.

Herzer succinctly writes in his first Hirschfeld biography, implicitly and indirectly suggesting that Fein's story simply ends there.[22] However, Karl Fein's life continued for six months after he was transported to the Jewish ghetto in Łódź. He wrote (at least) two postcards that have survived – because they were *not* sent. From these, we learned that Fein's still undeported family members were likely still in contact with Gertrude Laufer and her husband Heinrich Brecher, the youngest son of Elise Brecher. This made me think that letters sent from Europe to Uruguay had possibly survived in Uruguay. Investigating the Łódź address where Fein died also led me to one of Karl Fein's presumably gay friends in Łódź, Karel Jelínek, providing a new lead to follow. In May 1942, the deportation of the people in the Jewish hospital in Brno was postponed by a full year. In this case, too, I thought it important to determine who was staying in the hospital and to follow their further stories. That an important figure active in the JKG in Brno before the war, the lawyer Siegfried Ascher, was staying in this hospital was most likely significant for our story. Discussions about what to do with the Institute materials might have been made in the Jewish hospital. The May 1942 summons of the patients in the Jewish hospital for a planned transport, soon revoked, may have led to panicked and improvised decisions about the Institute materials. It made me decide to follow up on Ascher's relatives and former lawyer colleagues who survived the war.

I have the impression that the paralyzing effects of the Holocaust continue to spread even now. The Holocaust sometimes functions as a sort of black hole in which reason, rather than matter, tends to disappear or at least halt. What most likely paralyzes many is the fear of getting close, if only in imagination, to people heading to their certain death, and, all the more, to the unimaginable suffering and death struggles of those who perished in the gas chambers. People tend to shrink from these lethal, horrific Holocaust stories, preferring to shield themselves behind self-aggrandizing moral indignation about the Holocaust. We should not give in to the fear and terror spread by the Nazis, thereby becoming some kind of silent, withdrawn accomplices.

That it took until 2020 for a researcher to focus *exclusively* – in excruciating detail – on what happened to the world-famous Anne Frank and her family *after* they had been betrayed and deported is evidence of the attitude that stops and refrains from investigating once we know about the almost certain death of Holocaust victims.[23] Yet, the truth is that some of these victims lived for some time after they were deported. A very small minority even survived their horrendous deportation and incarceration. In addition, most people being deported had no knowledge of the horrible fate awaiting them. They assumed that they would be living somewhere else, though in worse conditions. I think that we contribute to the further dehumanization of the victims of the Holocaust if we lose sight of their lives after the moment of their deportation, when their Holocaust fate befell them.

In this research project, besides spelling out the transport and death dates of many, I have followed all the trails of Jewish survival that I could. Yet, despite sending out

[22] "Der Rechstanwalt Dr. Karl Fein wurde sein [Karl Giese's] Erbe, ist aber kurz darauf von den Nazis ins Konzentrationslager deportiert und dort anscheinend ermordert worden" (The lawyer Dr. Karl Fein became his [Karl Giese's] heir but was deported to a concentration camp by the Nazis shortly afterwards and apparently murdered there). See Herzer 2001, 242. An expression found in many German-language publications, which forestalls telling the rest of the story about this or that person, is "wurde ins KZ verschleppt" (was deported to a concentration camp).

[23] For the research on the Frank family, see Von Benda-Beckmann 2020. This was of course not the first book that considered Anne Frank's fate after her arrest in August 1944, but I think it the first to focus on this topic exclusively. Von Benda-Beckmann tried to determine, as far as possible, what could be gathered from archival sources and Holocaust testimonies about Anne Frank's last seven months before her death in Bergen-Belsen. See also https://www.annefrank.org/nl/over-ons/nieuws-en-pers/nieuws/2020/11/23/nieuw-boek-na-het-achterhuis/ (accessed Mar. 5, 2022). Interestingly, the

several hundred letters and emails to the current relatives of those who perished, or managed to escape Europe, I learned only a few details from the living relatives about the lives of these Holocaust victims. Often, it was rather the relatives who learned about their family history from me; in a few cases, they explicitly refused to face the subject of the Holocaust.[24] The deep rift opened by the terror regime of the Nazis continues to exert its many negative effects even today.

A CAUTIONARY TALE

This book started by mentioning the 2019 publication of the facsimile edition of the Hirschfeld guestbook and the presentation of this book at the ALMS *Queering Memory* conference, held in Berlin in June 2019, on the very premises once occupied by Hirschfeld's Institute [ill. 3]. The looting of the Institute, along with the auto-da-fé enacted by the National Socialists in May 1933, was a traumatizing and devastating blow to the life's work of Magnus Hirschfeld, one from which Hirschfeld and his circle of close friends and sympathizers never really recovered. From that moment, a justified fear guided many of their actions and omissions. That the Hirschfeld guestbook survived is nothing short of a miracle, coming to us either through sheer luck or, possibly, the more deliberate action of a treasure hunter, Dr. Stanislav Kaděrka of Brno. The history and destiny of the Institute materials, before and after 1933, constitute a cautionary tale. It is my hope that the presentation of the facsimile edition of the Hirschfeld guestbook at the ALMS Berlin conference may have served as a reminder of the extreme vulnerability of the documentary LGBT legacy, now more and more preserved in archives, libraries and museums worldwide. My wish is that the fear of possible future attacks on these LGBT documentary legacies not paralyze us; rather, it should make us wiser and empower us to do what is necessary.[25] By doing this, let our task further honor Hirschfeld's pioneering life's work. Or must we, again and again, start all over?

betrayal (and almost certain death sentence) of Anne Frank and her immediate family (and other people hiding with them) gained much more media attention in 2022. See the (contested) publication by the so-called "cold case team" on the betrayal of Anne Frank, Sullivan 2022. The greater interest in the betrayal does not contradict my claim.

[24] On the troubled constellation of Holocaust victims and their relatives in the USA, see Stein 2014.

[25] Cf. the reaction of the MHG, Berlin, to the November 2023 donation of two original Institute books by Olov Kriström, co-founder and active member of the Swedish Queer Archive and Library (Queerrörelsens Arkiv och Bibliotek, QRAB): "Olov überreichte uns die beiden Bücher mit dem Wunsch, sie mögen sich hoffentlich bei und mit ihren „alten Buchfreunden" wohlfühlen. Wir sind überzeugt, dass sie das werden. In jedem Fall werden wir sie gut behüten und alles tun, damit ihnen nichts Unvorhergesehenes widerfährt!" (Olov presented the two books to us expressing the wish that they will hopefully feel at home with their 'old book friends'. We are convinced that they will. In any case, we will take good care of them and do everything to ensure that nothing unforeseeable happens to them!). See https://magnus-hirschfeld.de/bibliothek-und-archiv/sammlungsschwerpunkte/aus-dem-institut-fur-sexualwissenschaft/ (accessed Jul. 5, 2024).

1. Magnus Hirschfeld and Karl Giese. Undated, possibly Athens in March 1932, or Nice in January–February 1934.

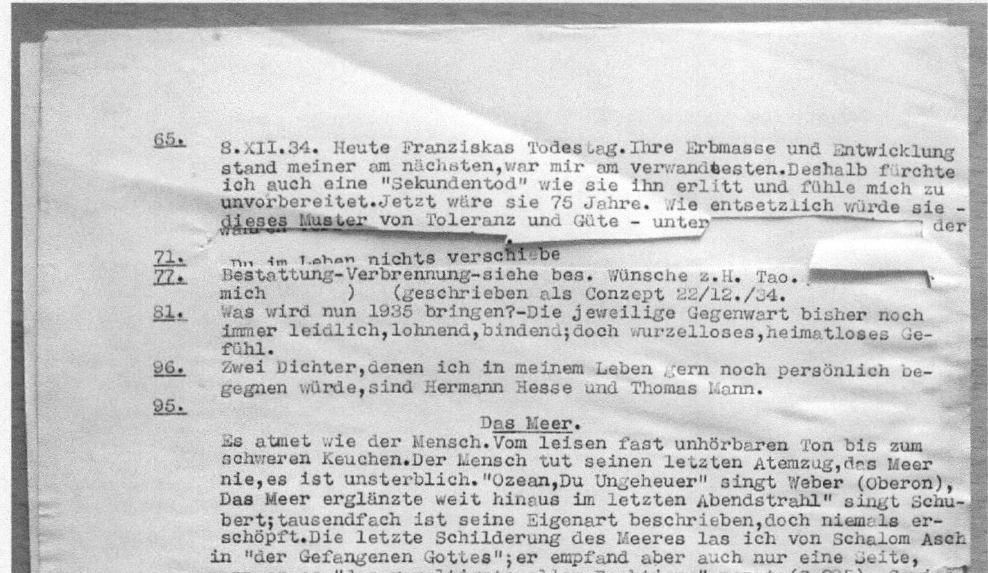

65. 8.XII.34. Heute Franziskas Todestag.Ihre Erbmasse und Entwicklung stand meiner am nächsten,war mir am verwandtesten.Deshalb fürchte ich auch eine "Sekundentod" wie sie ihn erlitt und fühle mich zu unvorbereitet.Jetzt wäre sie 75 Jahre. Wie entsetzlich würde sie - dieses Muster von Toleranz und Güte - unter der

71. Du im Leben nichts verschiebe

77. Bestattung-Verbrennung-siehe bes. Wünsche z.H. Tao. mich) (geschrieben als Conzept 22/12./34.

81. Was wird nun 1935 bringen?-Die jeweilige Gegenwart bisher noch immer leidlich,lohnend,bindend;doch wurzelloses,heimatloses Gefühl.

96. Zwei Dichter,denen ich in meinem Leben gern noch persönlich begegnen würde,sind Hermann Hesse und Thomas Mann.

95.

Das Meer.

Es atmet wie der Mensch.Vom leisen fast unhörbaren Ton bis zum schweren Keuchen.Der Mensch tut seinen letzten Atemzug,das Meer nie,es ist unsterblich."Ozean,Du Ungeheuer" singt Weber (Oberon), Das Meer erglänzte weit hinaus im letzten Abendstrahl" singt Schubert;tausendfach ist seine Eigenart beschrieben,doch niemals erschöpft.Die letzte Schilderung des Meeres las ich von Schalom Asch in "der Gefangenen Gottes";er empfand aber auch nur eine Seite,

2. In May 1935, in the days following Hirschfeld's death, Ernst Maass read Hirschfeld's last diary, copying out some fragments by hand, which were eventually typed out. At some point, someone used scissors to cut out two diary fragments from the typed version: a part of fragment 65 and fragment 71.

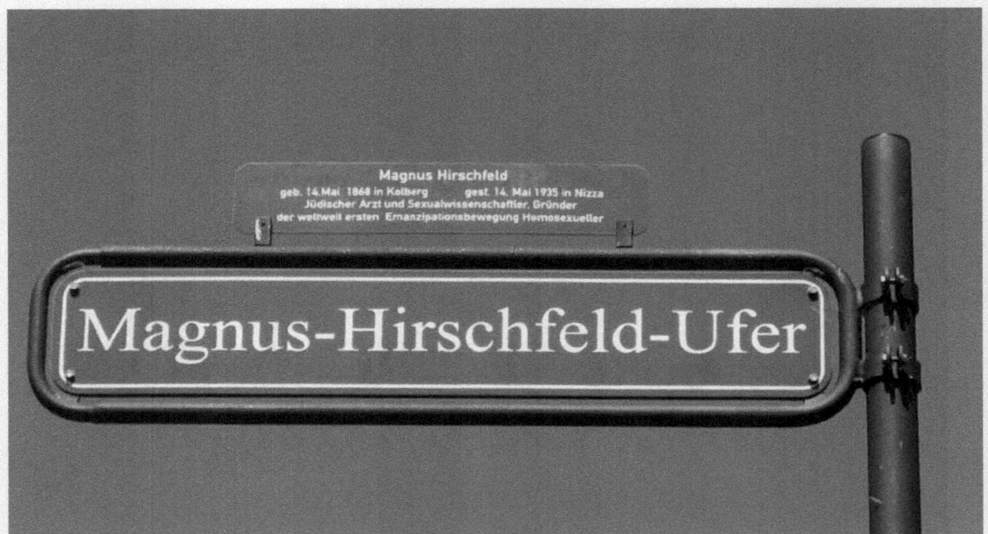

3. The signpost indicating the start of the Magnus-Hirschfeld-Ufer, the pedestrian path along Berlin's Spree River, inaugurated in 2008. The path is located just across from where the Institute once stood. The text says: "Magnus Hirschfeld / born May 14, 1868 in Kolberg / died May 14, 1935 in Nice / Jewish doctor and sexologist. Founder of the world's first homosexual emancipation movement" (Magnus Hirschfeld / geb.[oren] 14. Mai 1868 in Kolberg / gest.[orben] 14. Mai 1935 in Nizza / Jüdischer Arzt und Sexualwissenschaftler. Gründer der weltweit ersten Emanzipationsbewegung Homosexueller). May 2017.

Addenda

1. **A HISTORY OF THE L. & A. BRECHER BOOKSTORE IN BRÜNN (BRNO)**
2. **THE THREE COMMISSION AGENTS *(KOMMISSIONÄRE)* REPRESENTING THE L. & A. BRECHER BOOKSTORE ABROAD**
3. **KARL FEIN AND THE BRNO BUILDING INDUSTRY**
4. **KAREL RŮŽIČKA (1895–1942)**
5. **OTTO SCHÜTZ (1892–1970)**
6. **ROBERT HERRMANN (1899–1995)**
7. **INVENTORY (DATED MARCH 18, 1938) OF GIESE'S BRNO APARTMENT (8 SCHÜTZENGASSE/ STŘELECKÁ)**
   (ENGLISH TRANSLATION AND CZECH ORIGINAL)
8. **FINAL SETTLEMENT OF THE KARL GIESE-KARL FEIN INHERITANCE**
   (ENGLISH TRANSLATION AND CZECH ORIGINAL)
9. **KARL GIESE'S JULY 1937 APPEAL *(ODVOLÁNÍ)* TO THE MORAVIAN PROVINCIAL AUTHORITIES**
   (ENGLISH TRANSLATION AND CZECH ORIGINAL)
10. **BERLIN, BRNO, PARIS, FRESNES, NICE, VIENNA AND SWITZERLAND ADDRESSES WHERE KARL GIESE LIVED OR STAYED (1898–1938)**
11. **BRNO, PRAGUE AND ŁÓDŹ ADDRESSES WHERE KARL FEIN LIVED OR STAYED (1894–1942)**
12. **OVERVIEW OF ELISE BRECHER'S LAST ADDRESSES IN BRNO (BRÜNN) BEFORE HER DEPORTATION**
13. **OVERVIEW OF THE JEWISH TRANSPORTS FROM BRNO (1941–43)**
14. **JAKUB OR JOSEF UHER?**
15. **HERTA FEIN (1902–1981)**
16. **THE (KNOWN) LECTURES GIVEN BY MAGNUS HIRSCHFELD IN PARIS (1933-34)**
17. **LAST WILL (TESTAMENT) OF MAGNUS HIRSCHFELD**
   (GERMAN ORIGINAL AND ENGLISH TRANSLATION)

1. A HISTORY OF THE L. & A. BRECHER BOOKSTORE IN BRÜNN (BRNO)

The L. & A. Brecher bookstore started business in 1866 at earliest. It was led by Ignaz Brecher (1813–1880), Karl Fein's maternal grandfather, originally from the city of Olmütz (Olomouc).[1] A short text from 1916, written on the occasion of the bookstore's fiftieth anniversary, states: "At the instigation of his clever and energetic wife [Amalia Kurz], he [Ignaz Brecher] came [to Brno] from Olomouc at the time of the great Brno markets and, in the manner of the Parisian 'bouquinists', moved into a bookstall in a house entrance on Rathausgasse [currently Radnická], which was happily frequented by the city's book buyers. [...] In 1866 he turned this 'traveling bookshop' into a regular one, which existed for many years on Herrengasse [currently Janská]".[2] The "traveling bookshop" (*fliegenden Buchhandlung*) was started in 1860 in Olmütz (Olomouc).[3] Before he became a bookseller, Ignaz Brecher was a language teacher in Proßnitz (Prostějov).[4] Ignaz Brecher was a brother of one of the main figures of the Moravian Jewish Enlightenment (Haskalah), Dr. Gideon Brecher (1797–1873).[5]

[1] For Ignaz Brecher's death date, see NA, Praha, Judische Matriken (Jewish registers, Židovské matriky), Olomouc, Z, 1868-1901, inv. n° 1461, f. 115. His profession is given as *Buchhändler* and *Antiquar* (bookseller and antiquarian book dealer). It also mentions "grave 145", presumably his grave in the Jewish cemetery in Olomouc (Olmütz). This cemetery was closed in 1900 when some of its headstones were moved to another place that would eventually be turned into a park. The remaining headstones were later destroyed by the National Socialists. See http://kehila-olomouc.cz/rs/historie/hrbitovy/ (accessed Jan. 21, 2016).

[2] *Börsenblatt für den deutschen Buchhandel*, n° 161, Jul. 14, 1916, 928, section "Kleine Mitteilungen": "Auf Anregung seiner klugen und energischen Gattin [Amalia Kurz] kam er [Ignaz Brecher] von Olmütz zur Zeit der großen Brünner Märkte dorthin und bezog nach Art der Pariser "Bouquinisten" einen Bücherstand in einem Hauseingang der Rathausgasse [currently Radnická], der von den Bücherlaufern der Stadt gern ausgesucht wurde. [...] Im Jahre 1866 machte er aus dieser 'fliegenden Buchhandlung' eine seßfaste, die viele Jahre in der Herrengasse [currently Janská] bestand". It is interesting to compare this text with a slightly different version that appeared in *Oesterreichisch- ungarische Buchhändler-Correspondenz*, n° 30, Jul. 26, 1916, 350. The 1866 founding year is also mentioned in d'Elvert 1866, 592. On the other hand, a different starting year for the store in Brno is reported in 1892: "s.[eit, since] 5. Augustus 1884 in Brünn" (*Adressbuch des Deutschen Buchhandels* 1892, 60). (Because the latter annual publication had many, quite minimal name changes over the years of its long existence, and because this publication will be quoted fairly often, all editions hereafter will be cited as *adressbuch des deutschen Buchhandels*, with the respective year.) The extant sources contradict each other about the exact date of Ignaz Brecher's settling down. Cf. the more precise statement in *Adressbuch des deutschen Buchhandels* 1879, 35: "s.[eit, since] 22. Juli 1878". The Brecher bookstore is not mentioned in any *Adressbucher des deutschen Buchhandels* from previous years. The first bookstore was located at 20 Herrengasse (currently Janská). See *Allgemeiner Wohnungs-Anzeiger nebst Handels- und Gewerbe-Adressbuch für die Landeshauptstadt Brünn* 1881, 188, "Antiquar-Buchhändler" section. Ignaz Brecher's sons (see below) rented their store from the Erste Mährische Sparcassa [*sic*]. See section VI, titled "Haüserschema nach grundbücherlichen Aufzeichnungen revidiert bis Ende September 1891", *Adressbuch von Brünn* 1892, 233. The bank building's address was 4-6-8 Herrengasse, replaced by a new modernist building in 1939, which still houses a bank, the Česká spořitelna (Czech Savings Bank). See http://www.bam.brno.cz/de/objekt/c078-verwaltungsgebaude-der-ersten-mahrischen-sparkasse?filter=code (accessed Dec. 16, 2014). "Herrengasse", which is mentioned in different guides and address books as the location of the first store, could give rise to the confusion that the store was located on Panská and not Janská. In the eighteenth century, Herrengasse (currently Panská) and Johannesgasse (currently Janská) were known as *obere* (upper) and *untere* (lower) Herrengasse, respectively. It is likely that this older name lingered, even after the street's name change in the nineteenth century, when upper Herrengasse became simply Herrengasse, and lower (and actually descending) Herrengasse became Johannesgasse.

[3] *Adressbuch des Deutschen Buchhandels und der verwandten Geschäftszweige* 1892, 60.

[4] Heller 1892, 10, entry on Dr. Adolf Brecher. This is also confirmed in "Protokoll aufgenommen in der II. ordentlichen Sitzung der Handels- und Gewerbekammer in Olmütz am 25. Februar 1861 (Fortsetzung)", *Brünner Zeitung*, May 28, 1861, 965.

[5] Heller 1892, 10, entry on Dr. Adolf Brecher. According to the same source, Ignaz Brecher was Dr. Alois Brecher's uncle, which would mean that Gideon Brecher and Ignaz Brecher were indeed brothers. Gideon Brecher had four sons: Dr. Alois Brecher (1830–1918), Dr. Adolf Brecher (1831–1894), Gabriel Brecher (1833–?) and Moritz Brecher (1838–1905). Moritz Brecher was a professor in Brno and, like several other Brecher family members, is buried in the Jewish cemetery, in section 21B, row 2, grave 15. One of his sons was the stage and movie actor Egon Brecher (1880–1946), who emigrated to the USA. Another son was Dr. Gideon Brecher Jr. (1873–?). The

Ignaz Brecher's first brick-and-mortar bookstore was located on Janská, a side street off Ferdinandsgasse (now named Masarykova), to this day the main shopping street in Brno's city center. Shortly after Ignaz Brecher's death, his two sons, Ludwig Brecher (1852–1916) and Alois Brecher (1853–1912), took ownership of the store, in January 1881, initially keeping its original name.[6] (The two brothers had six sisters: Helene Fein (the mother of Karl Fein), Josefina Kohn, Rosa Kohn, Elise Frank, Berta Kohn and Anna Bernfeld.[7]) In 1884, the store's name included both of their first initials, L. & A. Brecher.[8] The bookstore would keep this name until its forced Aryanization in the summer of 1939 under Nazi rule. The two brothers parted ways in 1893; it is unclear if this was due to a business or some other quarrel. From that time, Ludwig Brecher independently took over the store in Olomouc (Olmütz), keeping the name L. & A. Brecher.[9] The store in Olomouc was located at 4 Denisovy ulice (Elisabethstrasse).[10] The Olomouc store disappears from bookstore lists in 1917 because Ludwig Brecher died in Olomouc in February 1916.[11]

So, from 1893 onwards, it was Alois Brecher, Karl Fein's uncle and guardian, who ran the Brno store until Brecher's death of a heart attack in November 1912.[12] Alois Brecher is buried in the Jewish cemetery in Brno. His grave monument is tall and impressive.[13] Brecher was a member and also, at one point, the president of the

composer and conductor Gustav Brecher (1879–1940), who died in Belgium, was Dr. Alois Brecher's son. Dr. Gideon Brecher Sr. was also the maternal uncle of Moritz Steinschneider (1816–1907), the man who came to be known as the father of Hebrew bibliography. The Brechers were also related to the architect Paul Engelmann (1891–1965), a friend of Ludwig Wittgenstein. See Bakacsy 2003. I thank Michael L. Miller for pointing me to some internet sources on Gideon Brecher Sr.'s children and grandchildren. I think that, in return, I have made him curious about the history of the Brecher family of booksellers in Brno. Miller's *Rabbis and Revolution* – in addition to being a book on the Jewish *Haskalah* in Moravia – is an excellent introduction to the history of the emancipation of the Jewish communities in Moravia. See Miller 2010.

[6] *Amtsblatt zur Brünner Zeitung*, n° 185, Aug. 12, 1884, 2: "Die Gesellschaft ist eine offene und besteht zum Betriebe des Antiquar- Buchhandels seit 18. Jänner 1881" (The company association is an open one and has been in existence for the operation of the antiquarian book trade since January 18, 1881). Both sons were born in Prostějov (Proßnitz).

[7] Starting in 2019, Andreas Franck (who is related to Rosa Kohn, née Brecher) has been uploading the most complete family trees of the Brecher family – and others – to Geni.com.

[8] This 1884 date is given in MZA, Brno, fonds C 11, Krajský soud civilní Brno, company file L. & A. Brecher, kart. n° 89, sign. AVIII 191, f. 10. An 1883 reference states: "Bes.[itzer]: Lud.[wig] u.[nd] Al.[ois] Brecher, s.[eit] 1880" (Owners: Ludwig and Alois Brecher, since 1880) (*Adressbuch des deutschen Buchhandels* 1883, 41).

[9] *Amtsblatt zur Brünner Zeitung*, n° 80, Apr. 8, 1893, 1: "Bei dem k. k. Kreis- als Handelsgerichte in Olmütz wurde in das Handelsregister eingetragen: Am 31. März 1893: Die Löschung der Gesellschaftsfirma: Brüder L. & A. Brecher, Zweigniederlassung in Olmütz der in Brünn befindlichen Hauptniederlassung, wegen Auflösung der Gesellschaft, und gleichzeitig wurde die Firma: Brüder L. & A. Brecher, des Ludwig Brecher, Buchhändlers und Antiquars in Olmütz, im Handelsregister für Einzelnfirmen eingetragen" (The following was entered in the Business register at the Imperial and Royal District commercial court in Olomouc: On March 31, 1893: The cancellation of the company association: Brothers L. & A. Brecher, Olomouc auxiliary of the main branch in Brno, due to the dissolution of the company association, simultaneously entered in the Business register for individual companies: the company Brothers L. & A. Brecher, owned by Ludwig Brecher, bookseller and antiquarian book dealer in Olomouc). See also *Amtsblatt zur Brünner Zeitung*, n° 185, Aug. 12, 1884, 2.

[10] *Adressbuch des deutschen Buchhandels* 1907, 57: "Seit [since] 1891. Gegr.[ündet, founded] 1860. Inh. [aber, owner]: Ludwig Brecher". This accords with the bookstore's company registration card in the AMB, Brno, fonds B 1/16, where the date of the first *Anmeldung* (registration) of the Brno store owned by Alois Brecher is given as July 5, 1892. See also the mention of the Olomouc store, owned by the brother as *Zweigniederlassung* (auxiliary office), *Wiener Zeitung*, n° 65, Mar. 19, 1893, Amtsblatt zur Wiener Zeitung, [399].

[11] *Adressbuch des deutschen Buchhandels* 1917, second part, "Erloschene und veränderte Firmen sowie geschäftliche Einrichtungen und Veränderungen", 3. Editions of the *Adressbuch des deutschen Buchhandels* cease to mention the Olomouc store after 1917. For Ludwig Brecher's death date, see NA, Praha, Jewish registers (Židovské matriky, Judische Matriken), Olomouc, Z, 1908-1919, 1925-1949, inv. n° 1462, n° 726, f. 75. The handwriting noting the cause of death is illegible, but the death seems unrelated to World War I. Ludwig Brecher is described as unmarried.

[12] *Tagesbote*, Nov. 13, 1912, 3.

[13] The grave is in parcel 4, row 3, grave 1. See chapter 6, ill. n° 9.

local Brno chapter of Moravia, the Jewish B'nai B'rith lodge, founded in 1896.[14] In 1913, a year after Alois Brecher's death, at the initiative of a Dr. Feith, the B'nai B'rith lodge decided to fund and inaugurate a library in Brecher's honor. The Alois Brecher Library Foundation (Alois-Brecher-Bibliothek-Stiftung) was housed in the Moravia lodge building at 31 Třída Legionářů (Legionärenstrasse) in Brno.[15] Alois Brecher also seems to have been a pacifist, as his membership contribution for the year 1894 of the Austrian Society of the Friends of Peace (Oesterreichische Gesellschaft Der Friedensfreunde) makes clear.[16] Finally, Brecher was also a philantropist, as his honorary membership of the Support association for destitute Jewish technicians (Unterstützungsverein für mittellose jüdischen Techniker in Brünn) in Brno makes clear.[17]

In 1907, the Brno bookstore moved to nearby 11 Grosser Platz (then named Velké náměstí), the main, central city square.[18] The new location was again inside the building of a bank, the Mährische Escompte Bank.[19] To its right, there was the then newly erected House of the Four Mamlases (Dům u Čtyř mamlasů), built between 1899 and 1902, which continues to amaze to this day.[20] The Brecher bookstore would remain at this central location until 1933, when the building, owned by the Mährische Escompte Bank, was torn down to make space for the JEPA department store building, designed by the Brno-based architect Otto Eisler (1893–1968). The bookstore then temporarily moved to 8 Náměstí svobody, to the left of the former bank building. Although the intention was apparently to return to the JEPA building (being erected in the record time of three months), in 1934, the store finally moved to the Alfa Passage shopping gallery, located just behind the L. & A. Brecher bookstore's previous location.[21] Inside the JEPA building, as it was being built, a passageway was constructed linking it to the Alfa Passage. So the store's Alfa Passage location was, all in all, quite close to its former Freiheitsplatz (Naměstí svobody) position.[22] After

[14] *Jüdische Volksstimme*, n° 32, Nov. 14, 1912, 5.

[15] See *Gedenkschrift zur Feier des 25 jähr. Bestandes des israel. Humanitätsvereines "Moravia" B'nai B'rith*, 1921, 53. My first thought was that the Alois Brecher named in the Bibliothek-Stiftung (library foundation) was possibly the more famous Dr. Alois Brecher (1830–1918) from Prostějov (Proßnitz), one of Gideon Brecher Sr.'s sons. For information about the Dr. Alois Brecher Stiftung (Dr. Alois Brecher foundation), started in Prostějov (Proßnitz) in 1869, see *Die Gegenwart (israelitische Wochenschrift für politische, sociale und religiöse Interessen)*, Oct. 15, 1869, 202; *Mährischer Correspondent*, Apr. 20, 1869, 3. The focus of the Dr. Alois Brecher Foundation was more on those in need of medical care. The Teltscher Collection at the University of Manchester contains a rare copy of the 1932 library catalogue of the Alois Brecher-Bibliothek-Stiftung, as well as an older, undated one. The Alois Brecher lending library was exclusively for Moravia lodge brothers and should not be confused with the Bücherei der Israelitischen Kultusgemeinde Brünn (Library of the Jewish religious community Brno).

[16] Third list of the *Mitgliederbeiträge* (member contributions) vom 5. März bis 5. Juni, *Die Waffen Nieder!*, vol. 3, n° 6, 1894, 234.

[17] *Jüdische Volksstimme*, Jul. 19, 1911, 5.

[18] AMB, Brno, fonds B 1/16, company registration card for L. & A. Brecher bookstore. The central square – like several Brno streets – was renamed several times, always in accord with the political situation in the Czech lands. Starting in 1915, the square was known as Kaiser-Franz-Josef-Platz. After World War I, it became Náměstí svobody (Freiheitsplatz), a name it still bears today. It is under this last address, Náměstí svobody (Freiheitsplatz), that the Brecher bookstore is most known and quoted in the sources. For the different renamings of the Náměstí svobody square, http:// encyklopedie.brna.cz/ home-mmb/ ?acc=profil_ulice&load=1277 (accessed Feb. 18, 2012).

[19] The bookstore's street number changed around 1916 but it stayed at the same location: 11 Náměstí Svobody (Freiheitsplatz) became 9 Náměstí Svobody (Freiheitsplatz). See *Adressbuch des deutschen Buchhandels* 1917, 62.

[20] For this building, also known as the Valentin Gerstbauer Foundation house, see Zatloukal 2006, 141; Vrabelová, Svobodová & Šlapeta 2016, 20–21.

[21] The official address of the bookstore in the Alfa Passage was 6 Postgasse (Poštovská).

[22] For the JEPA building see, http://www.bam.brno.cz/en/object/c084jepa-department-store?filter=code (accessed Feb. 18, 2012). The existence of a passageway between the Alfa gallery and the JEPA building (along with many other aspects of pre-war Brno) was kindly confirmed to me by Horst Morawek (1924–), who lived in Brno before the war. See his email conversation (dated Jan. 2012) with the author. Some years ago, the JEPA building was replaced by the current OMEGA shopping mall, which still gives passage to the Alfa shopping gallery. For the mod-

Alois Brecher's death, in November 1912, his widow Elise Löw (1869–1943) inherited and managed the Brno bookstore.[23] The Brecher couple had four children: Anna Bermann (1893–1944?), Fritz Brecher (1901–1942?),[24] Heinrich Brecher (1904–1955) and Ida Brecher (1895–1904). The latter died at the age of nine. Fritz, the eldest son, took over the store from his mother in January 1938.[25]

On March 15, 1939, the day of the German invasion of the so- called "rest of Tschechoslowakei" (Rest-Tschechoslowakei), the Brecher bookstore was taken over by two of its longtime employees, Ludmilla Schaal (1900–?) and Josef Cižek (1901–?).[26] Spurred on by the Germans invading the city, they exploited the situation. Schaal applied for German ethnic (Deutsche Volkszugehörigkeit) status in December 1939.[27] Ludmilla's fervent National Socialism is proven by the fact that, in April 1939, she sent a telegram to the Führer congratulating him on his fiftieth birthday.[28] Fritz Brecher, Elise Brecher's son, and the manager of the bookstore fled Brno a few days before the invasion. In the ensuing months, supported by the June 21, 1939 Decree of the Reich Protector in Bohemia and Moravia on Jewish Property (Verordnung des Reichsprotektors in Böhmen und Mähren über das jüdische Vermögen, Schaal and Cižek succeeded in appropriating the Jewish business. The store remained at the same location in the Alfa shopping gallery, but was eventually renamed Ostland Buchhandlung.[29] In July and August 1939, Elise Brecher engaged the help of the lawyer

ernist Alfa Passage, see Pelčák & Šlapeta 2015, 184–85; Vrabelová, Svobodová & Šlapeta 2016, 50–51. To this day, the Alfa Passage contains a bookstore, the "knihkupectví Michal Ženíšek". It is not known if it is on the same spot once occupied by the Brecher bookstore. When I inquired with the current bookstore owner, he was unaware of any pre-war details.

[23] In January 1914, Elise Brecher disputed the inheritance taxes she had to pay. It is unclear if this indicates that she was experiencing financial problems. See "Brünner und Provinzial- Nachrichten", *Brünner Zeitung*, n° 10, Jan. 14, 1914, 1: "15. Jänner: Elise Brecher in Brünn und Genossen wider das Finanzministerium wegen Nachlassgebühren" (15 January: Elise Brecher in Brno and associates against the Ministry of finance regarding inheritance fees).

[24] Gideon Brecher Jr. (1873–?) was one of the two witnesses mentioned in Fritz Brecher's birth and circumcision register. See NA, Praha, Jewish registers (Židovské matriky, Judische Matriken), Brno, N, 1896-1914, f. 88, entry n° 788, birth record Friedrich Brecher (Jan. 6, 1901).

[25] *Adressbuch des deutschen Buchhandels* 1938, 68; NA, Praha, fonds n° 375, Arizačni spisy, kart. n° 191, sign. 1119, company file L. & A. Brecher.

[26] NA, Praha, fonds n° 375, Arizačni spisy, kart. n° 191, sign. 1119, company file L. & A. Brecher bookstore. Ludmilla Schaal, who joined the business on December 25, 1926, worked as an employee for thirteen years; Josef Cižek, who was hired on September 1, 1918, worked for the Brecher family bookstore for twenty-one years. Ludmilla Schaal was the second wife of Viktor Schaal (1893–?). Viktor Schaal's first wife was Editha Schrutková (1892–?), whom he divorced in 1926. See Viktor Schaal's home certificate in AMB, Brno, fonds B 1/39. Viktor Schaal had three children with his first wife: Wolfgang (1921–?), Julie (1924–?) and Ingeborg (1925–?). I did not investigate the further fates of these three children.

[27] AMB, Brno, fonds A 1/53. She applied on December 27, 1939, and the status was approved on May 15, 1940.

[28] NA, Praha, fonds n° 114, Úřad říšského protektora v Čechách a na Moravě, Praha, kart. n° 166, sign. 114-168-1, f. 56.

[29] In 1940, Schaal took out six advertisements in the Brno newspaper *Tagesbote*. See, for example, *Tagesbote*, Feb. 17, 1940, 8. That same year, under the name L. & A. Brecher there appeared: "jetzt [now]: Ludmilla Schaal" (*Adressbuch des deutschen Buchhandels* 1940, 66). Further in the same volume, it says: "Schaal, Ludmilla, (Ostland-Buchhandlung u.[nd] Antiquariat), Brünn (Mähren), Alfa-Passage. – Gegr.[ündet, founded] 9 IX 1939. ([telephone symbol] 14756) w. Fernau" (ibid., 480). In the 1941 *Adressbuch des deutschen Buchhandels*, one is directed from Schaal Ludmilla to the new company name, "Ostland-Buchhandlung u.[nd] Antiquariat Ludmilla Schaal" (*Adressbuch des deutschen Buchhandels* 1941, 490, 423). Both the phone number and the Fernau *Kommissionär* (commission agent) in Leipzig remained the same; however, the bank account numbers changed. In the geographical listings of the same volume, Ostland- Buchhandlung appears under the Protektorat Böhmen und Mähren (Protectorate of Bohemia and Moravia) section, with an added "d", standing for "Deutsches Unternehmen" (German enterprise or company) (ibid., 98–99). In a 1965 phonebook, available online, I found an "L. Schaal" who kept a *Gasthaus* (pension) in Otterfing (Holzkirchen) in Bavaria (Germany), but the Gemeinde Otterfingen city hall refrained to reply when I inquired about this. See email (dated Dec. 15, 2015) from the author to Gemeinde Otterfingen. Since Schaal's name disappears from the following year's phonebook, there is a chance that Schaal died around that time. See *Amtliches Fernsprechbuch für den Bezirk der Oberpostdirektion München* 1965–66,

Walter Süss to resist this appropriation of her family business. She drew up a list of ten, quite costly conditions that needed to be met if she were to sell the business. It is remarkable that she had the audacity to try to have all the cost of her emigration paid if she indeed had to sell the business. But, after a visit from the Gestapo, she quickly understood what was expected and formally withdrew her demands through her lawyer. Since the store's total debts were evaluated as greater than the value of its stock, no money at all was paid in the final settlement between Elise Brecher's son, Fritz Brecher, and the two employees Schaal and Cižek in September 1939.

219. Josef Cižek officially changed his last name to Cischek in October 1939 and applied for Deutsche Volkszugehörigkeit (German ethnic) status on July 19, 1939. His application card in the AMB, Brno, fonds A 1/53, does not say if his request was approved but a small postwar file on him states that he was refused the status. See NA, Praha, fonds n° 1442/0/1, Ministerstvo vnitra ČSR/ČR, Praha, Vytříděné německé spisy, kart. n° 322-56-1, file Josef Cižek.

2. THE THREE COMMISSION AGENTS (*KOMMISSIONÄRE*) REPRESENTING THE L. & A. BRECHER BOOKSTORE ABROAD

A. KOMMISSIONSGESCHÄFT CURT FERNAU, LEIPZIG

The L. & A. Brecher bookstore was represented in Germany by the L.[ouis] Fernau company in Leipzig.[30] The company was founded in 1843 when, along with Friedrich Voigt, Louis Fernau (1814–1883) bought the Heinrich Franke publishing house (*Verlag*), giving birth to Voight & Fernau. In 1849, the company was divided, with Louis Fernau taking over the commissions and assortment (*Kommissions- und Sortimentgeschäft*) part.[31] In 1882, Louis Fernau left the business to his son, Curt Fernau (1851–1918). Curt Fernau was one of the founders (*Mitbegründer*) of the German National Library (Deutsche Bücherei) in Leipzig.

After his death in 1918, Fernau's homonymous son Curt Fernau (1895–1962) continued the business. He married Irene (Agnes Martha) Dittrich (?) (1894–?) in April of 1918.[32] The merger of Koehler and Volckmar, two former competitors in the intermediate book trade (*Zwischenbuchhandel*), was also decided around 1918. The resulting company, which would become a joint-stock company (*Aktiengesellschaft*) in 1921, eventually also acquired Curt Fernau's commission business (*Kommissionsgeschäft*) in 1931. By that time, Koehler & Volckmar AG already controlled 80 percent of the German intermediate book trade.[33] Curt Fernau continued to work under his own company name under the umbrella of the Koehler & Volckmar firm. He also proved to be one of the principal figures in the company's tumultuous history, roiled by a never-resolved power struggle between the Koehler and the Volckmar factions of the founding families (*Gründerfamilien*). Fernau was an expert in the company's foreign department (*Ausland-Abteilung*) and, more specifically, in relations with Austrian booksellers.[34] He was active in the Leipzig Association of Commission Agents (Verein Leipziger Kommissionäre), a subsection of the German Publishers and Booksellers Association of Leipzig (Börsenverein der Deutschen Buchhändler zu Leipzig) and also in the Leipzig Booksellers Association (Verein der Buchhändler zu Leipzig).

In 1946, shortly after the war, the Fernau couple moved to Bad Elster (Sachsen, in former East Germany). In that same year, Fernau's own company officially ceased to exist.[35] Curt Fernau likely continued to work for the Koehler & Volckmar company that rose from the ashes of the war, and managed to escape the Communist East by relocating to Stuttgart. Today, the company continues to exist under the name Koch, Neff & Volckmar GmbH. In his last years, Fernau worked for the publisher W. Kohlhammer. Curt Fernau died in 1962 in Stuttgart. A survey of the archival

[30] I have gathered most of my information about the first seven decades of the Fernau business from the "Buchhändlerische Geschäfts- Rundschreiben aus der ehemaligen Bibliothek des Börsenvereins der Deutschen Buchhändler zu Leipzig" database, managed by the Deutsches Buch- und Schriftmuseum of the Deutsche Nationalbibliothek (DNB, German National Library) in Leipzig. See http://bermudix.ddb.de/dbsm/cgi-bin/gr.pl. Some information was also taken from an anonymous piece published shortly after Curt Fernau's death in 1962. See "Curt Fernau zum Gedächtnis", *Börsenblatt für den deutschen Buchhandel*, Frankfurter Ausgabe, Jg. 18, n° 39, May 15, 1962, 825.

[31] I thank Carola Staniek (DNB, Leipzig) for the information on the division of the business. As she wrote to me, not all *Geschäftsrundschreiben* (archival materials) have been digitized and added to the database mentioned in the previous footnote. See emails (dated Oct. 24–25, 2012) from Carola Staniek (DNB, Leipzig) to the author.

[32] Meldeblatt for Curt Fernau (1895–1962) in Sächsisches Staatsarchiv, Staatsarchiv Leipzig, Polizei-Präsidium Leipzig, Bestand 20031, Sign. PP-M 216. In the "religion" *Fenster* (field), there is "ggl.", *gottgläubig* (lit., believing in God), a typical National Socialist designation for believing people who have turned their backs on organized religion. Curt Fernau's father appears on a list of Leipzig Jewish citizens in an issue of *Journal Juden in Sachsen* 2009, 40.

[33] Keiderling 2008, 22.

[34] Ibid., 244.

[35] Email (dated Nov. 2, 2012) from Hannelore Hoyer (Amtsgericht Leipzig, Registergericht) to the author.

fonds on the Koehler & Volckmar company, undertaken in the Sächsisches Staatsarchiv Leipzig (Bestand Koehler & Volckmar Leipzig 1877–1953) revealed, as more or less expected, no traces of the company's detailed commercial activities. However, it is clear that, in 1933, the company already needed to position itself vis-à-vis the new powers in Germany and specifically the Reich Chamber of Literature (Reichsschrifttumskammer). In October 1936, there were concerted Nazi attempts to undermine the company structure by further stoking the old Koehler and Volckmar feud.[36]

B. KOMMISSIONSGESCHÄFT LECHNER & SOHN, VIENNA

The L. & A. Brecher bookstore also had a representative in Vienna. A few firms represented the Brno bookstore in Austria's capital over the years. Starting in 1890, the first commission agent (*Kommissionsgeschäft*) acting on Alois and Ludwig Brecher's behalf in Austria was the company belonging to the publisher Moritz Perles (1844–1917).[37] In 1900, Sallmayer & Co. took over. Six years later, around 1906, their new partner, Lechner & Sohn, stepped in after buying Sallmayer & Co.[38] Lechner & Sohn remained the L. & A. Brecher bookstore's Viennese commission agent until its dissolution in 1939.

The Lechner family's history in the bookselling trade starts in October 1816, when Michael Lechner (1785–1843) acquired a permit for a court and university bookstore (*Hof- und Universitätsbuchhandlung*). In 1847, this mainly antiquarian bookselling business was sold by Michael Lechner's son, Rudolf Lechner (1822–1895).[39] Thereafter, Rudolf Lechner, who was also the leading force within the Association of Austrian Booksellers (Verein der oesterreichischen Buchhändler), focused principally on the commission agent business. In 1894, assisted by his son Oskar (1868–1928), the business started to operate under the name Rudolf Lechner & Sohn, Verlags- und Kommissionsbuchhandlung, and was known under this name until its dissolution in 1992. After his father's death in 1895, Oskar Lechner started buying other Austrian commission bookstores (*Kommissionsbuchhandlungen*), including, in 1905, Sallmayer & Co., Brecher's commission agent.[40] In this way, the Rudolf Lechner & Sohn Kommissionsbuchhandlung became the biggest intermediate book trader (*Zwischenbuchhandel*) in the Austro-Hungarian Empire. World War I and the subsequent dissolution of the Austro-Hungarian empire considerably diminished this monopoly.[41]

[36] Keiderling 2008, 34 and passim.

[37] For more information about the company of Moritz Perles (1869–1938), see Punkl 2002; Hall (n.d.). (For more information about the Aryanization of the company, see Bertz 2015.) However, the Brecher bookstore is not mentioned in the "Vertretung ausländischer Firmen bei Moritz Perles" list in Punkl's *Anhang* (appendix). See Punkl 2002, 131–61. Perles is mainly known for his *Adressbuch für den Buch-, Kunst-, Musikalienhandel und verwandte Geschäftszweige von Österreich*, issued between 1866 and 1937. His company also published, among other things, the *Jahrbuch deutscher Bibliophilen* (1917–1927). I consulted the memoir *Looking Back* by Paul Perles (1908–2001), Moritz Perles's grandson, who worked for the company, but did not find any useful information. I thank Murray G. Hall for bringing me in contact with Paul Perles's son, Tom Perles, who kindly sent me a rare copy of the memoir. According to Murray G. Hall, no archive of the Perles family has survived. See his email (dated May 13, 2013) to the author.

[38] The approximate time periods for these *Kommissionsgeschäfte* are derived from the year-to-year mentions of who represented the Brecher bookstore in the annual *Adressbuch des deutschen Buchhandels*.

[39] The bookselling business was sold to Eduard Müller and Alfred Werner. See *125 Jahre R. Lechner (Walter Krieg)* 1941, 2. For this short history of the Lechner & Son Kommissionsgeschäft, I have mainly relied on Lechner 1967, as well as on *"Hundertfünfundzwanzig Jahre Lechner in Wien", Börsenblatt für den deutschen Buchhandel, Bd. 108, 1941, n° 35*, 47–48.

[40] Interestingly, in 1891, Oskar Lechner also worked for the Kommissionsgeschäft K. F. Koehler in Leipzig, apparently a formative period. See Lechner 1967, [5].

[41] Lechner 1967, [6].

Because Oskar Lechner's oldest son, Rudolf, died in World War I, his younger son Oskar Wilhelm Lechner (1901–1963), together with his wife Maria Weiss, took over the business after his father's death in 1928. The couple made efforts to further grow the company by finding more publishing houses to represent. Both the National Library in Vienna and the National Library in Leipzig list a stock catalogue (*Lagerkatalog*) for Rudolf Lechner & Sohn Verlags- und Kommissionsbuchhandlung, which started in 1927 and was published until at least 1970. Oskar Wilhelm Lechner died in 1963, and his wife Maria died soon after him. In accordance with Oskar Wilhelm Lechner's own wishes, his nephew Dr. Harald Schnattinger eventually took over the business, even changing his family name to Lechner for the purpose.[42] In 1967, Harry/Harald Schnattinger/Lechner published a fifteen-page document about the history of the company.[43] Two attempts to contact him were unsuccessful.[44] In 1992, the company celebrated its 175th anniversary; however, four years later, in 1996, Lechner & Sohn Verlags- & Commissionsbuchhandlung AG went bankrupt.[45]

One must be careful not to confuse the R. Lechner bookstore, which Rudolf Lechner sold as early as 1874, with the Verlags- und Kommissionsbuchhandlung Rudolf Lechner & Sohn that went its own way. A commission bookstore (*Kommissionsbuchhandlung*) has a peculiar role in the German book trade, since it stands between the publisher and a retail bookshop.[46]

In 1938, shortly after the *Anschluss* of Austria, an Aryanization procedure enabled Walter Krieg (1901–1955), a German bookseller, to gain possession of the Universitätsbuchhandlung und Photographischen Manufaktur R. Lechner bookstore (Wilhelm Müller).[47] Walter Krieg kept the long-standing R. Lechner company name. In 1941, he issued a catalogue on the occasion of the 125th anniversary of the

[42] His dissertation on the history of Vienna publishing houses was published in 1951. See Lechner 1951. In the sources that I consulted, his first name is either Harald or Harry. Possibly, he also changed his first name when he changed his family name from Schnattinger to Lechner. I think that Harry was in fact his original first name, but this remains uncertain.

[43] Lechner 1967.

[44] A letter I sent in October 2012 to the only Harald Lechner living in Vienna went unanswered. Another letter, sent to the Vienna-based law firm Rant & Freyler (Dr. Hans Rant and Dr. Kurt Freyler), which at one point represented the Lechner company, received a reply containing only a small amount of useful information. See email (dated Oct. 30, 2012) from Rant & Freyler to the author. Their website showcases the Lechner company as one of the firms they represented. See http://www.rant-freyler.at/, tab "Philosophie" > tab "Für wen wir arbeiten" (accessed Oct. 26, 2012). Annette Lechner (no relation), from Vienna, has worked on the history of publishing in Austria. She informed me that she was still in contact with Harald Lechner in 1990, although she did not know his current whereabouts. See emails (dated Oct. 25, 2012 and Nov. 7, 2012) from Annette Lechner to the author.

[45] Anonymous 1992, 6–7. On the bankruptcy of the Lechner company, see Führing 1996.

[46] In addition, early on, the R. Lechner bookstore included an important photographic material and map department. The company played an important role in the history of photography in Austria. See *125 Jahre R. Lechner (Walter Krieg)* 1941, 3–5; http://www.photohistory.at/lechner.htm (accessed Apr. 28, 2016).

[47] See Fischer 2013, 202 n. 42. Fischer refers to Buchhas 1994, but I was not able to consult this rare dissertation. Presumably, Walter Krieg described his acquisition of the bookstore as follows: "Ein eigenartiges Geschick hat es gefügt, daß […] Walter Krieg, der alten angesehenen "Universitätsbuchhandlung […]", als Alleininhaber und Betriebsführer vorsteht" (A peculiar happenstance brought it about that […] Walter Krieg of the old prestigious 'University bookstore […]' presides as sole owner and manager of the business"). See *125 Jahre R. Lechner* (Walter Krieg) 1941, 6. For more precise details about the Aryanization procedure of the R. Lechner bookstore, see Pawlitschko 1996, 65–67, 78–81. The business had two Jewish owners. One was the Czechoslovak Max Faltitschek (1888–1975), who fled to the USA in December 1938 and changed his name to Fulton. The other was Alfred Rechnitzer (1888?–1938?). Rechnitzer's widow, Marie Sachs, came back from Shanghai in 1947. See Pawlitschko 1996, 78. Walter Krieg continued in the bookselling trade in Austria after the war and edited the bimonthly periodical *Das Antiquariat* until at least the 1950s. The 1946 postwar restitution file on the R. Lechner (Walter Krieg) bookstore (and three other book businesses acquired by Walter Krieg) is in the National Archives and Records Administration of the United States (NARA), Holocaust-era assets, Records of the Property Control Branch of the U.S. Allied Commission for Austria (USACA), 1945–1950, Cases and Reports Pertaining to Property Administered by the Vienna Area Command (VAC), PC/V/I/255 R. Lechner (Walter

founding of the company.[48] What is intriguing for our story is that, according to a January 1941 letter to Karl Hermann Frank, the state secretary of the Reich Protector in Bohemia and Moravia, prior to 1933, Walter Krieg was the head of the Berlin office of Püttmann Verlag. "Before 1933, Walter Krieg was head of the publishing house Püttmann, Stuttgart, which then published the writings of Magnus Hirschfeld. He later headed the publishing house N. Neubert, Berlin. In 1938, he became publishing director of Nibelungen-Verlag. Today, he is the owner of Herbert Stubenrauch-Verlagsbuchanstalt Berlin, R. Lechner Universitäts-Buchhandlung Vienna[,] and several other publishing houses and bookstores. [...] His main field of work has been publishing, while he has only recently become active as a retail bookseller".[49]

Julius Püttmann Verlag was indeed the publisher of Hirschfeld's magnum opus, the five-volume *Geschlechtskunde* (Hirschfeld 1926–30), and also of the proceedings of the first WLSR conference in Berlin in 1921. It also published many other works on sexology, sexual cultural history, (para)psychology, hypnosis, etc.[50] In 1923, Julius Püttmann Verlag also published the very last volume of the *Jahrbuch für sexuelle Zwischenstufen unter besonderer Berücksichtigung der Homosexualität*.[51] It is unclear when Krieg assumed direction of the publishing house; however, according to Krieg himself, he was pushed out of the company in 1933.[52] He continued to be active in his other publishing companies in Germany, Walter Krieg Verlag among them.[53] In 1938, after they had been invaded by Germany, he also tried his luck as a businessman in Austria and Czechoslovakia. It is clear that he sailed on the seas of National Socialism

Krieg) Universitätsbuchhandlung, 1-126, 1-141 1-125; this can be found on the historical military records website, https://www.fold3.com/. For an analysis of the long postwar restitution process of the bookstore, see Schwarz 2003, 139–49.

48 The 125 years refer to the start of the Hof- und Universitätsbuchhandlung in 1816. See *125 Jahre R. Lechner (Walter Krieg)* 1941; Wendt 1955.

49 Walter Krieg is mentioned in a letter regarding the Aryanization of the Jewish bookstore André in Prague, eventually taken over by Krieg and Detlev Herbst, the son of Erich Herbst, who owned the Moritz Diesterweg'schen Verlagsbuchhandlung in Frankfurt. See letter (dated Jan. 18, 1941) from Sicherheitsdienst RFSS (Leitabschnitt Prag) to K. H. Frank, the state secretary of the Reichsprotektor in Böhmen und Mähren in: NA, Praha, fonds n° 1799, Státní tajemník u říšského protektora v Čechách a na Moravě (Staatssekretär beim Reichsprotektor in Böhmen und Mähren), 1939–1945, Praha, inv. n° 1970, sign. sg.109-6/62 (Arizace židovských podniků v protektorátu), f. 38; available online at http://badatelna.eu/fond/959/reprodukce/?zaznamId=339677&reproId=370753 (accessed Apr. 2, 2016): "Walter Krieg war vor 1933 Leiter des Verlages Püttmann, Stuttgart und verlegte seinerzeit die Schriften von Magnus Hirschfeld. Er leitete später den Verlag N. Neubert, Berlin. 1938 wurde er Verlagsleiter des Nibelungen-verlages [*sic*]. Heute ist er Inhaber der Herbert Stubenrauch-Verlagsbuchanstalt Berlin, der R. Lechner'schen Universitäts-buchhandlung [*sic*] Wien und einiger anderer Verlage und Buchhandlungen. [...] Sein Hauptarbeitsgebiet war bisher der Verlag, während er sich als Sortimentsbuchhändler erst seit kurzem betätigt".

50 Hirschfeld 1926–30; Weil 1922. To get an idea of the works published by this publisher, I consulted *Die Bücher des Verlages Julius Püttmann* 1930. The publisher's main seat was in Stuttgart. Julius Püttmann (1846?–1901) started the publishing house in Elberfeld (a Wuppertal city district) in 1880, later moving to Köln. In 1905, the company was bought by Richard Ahrens and Curt Hauschild and its seat was transferred to Berlin. The publisher also had offices in Stüttgart, Leipzig and Vienna. The information on Julius Püttmann and the fate of his company was retrieved from the DNB database, http://bermudix.ddb.de/dbsm/cgi-bin/gr.pl. For more details about the history of the company (1869–1936), see also Würffel 2000, 671.

51 Previously, the yearbook was published by Max Spohr Verlag. See Lehmstedt 2002, 116–17, 284; Sigusch 2008, 108–9.

52 Würffel 2000, 471–72, 859. That Walter Krieg was indeed the head of the *Zweigstelle* (auxiliary office) of the Julius Püttmann publishing house in Berlin is indirectly confirmed by two letters he wrote to Georg Kolbe in March and April 1933. See Nachlass Georg Kolbe, Georg-Kolbe-Museum Berlin, sign. GK.485; 15; 1; 1–3: "[Walter] Krieg berichtet von seiner Totenmaskensammlung im Archivraum seines Verlages am Potsdamer Platz [in Berlin]" ([Walter] Krieg reports on his death mask collection in the archive room of his publishing house at Potsdamer Platz [in Berlin]). See http://kalliope.staatsbibliothek-berlin.de/de/ead?ead.id=DE-611-HS-1513819 (accessed Jul. 9, 2016). Würffel does not mention Walter Krieg's name in the lemma on Julius Püttmann Verlag, but does mention a certain Paul Neubert who moved from Stuttgart to Berlin in 1932 and possibly also moved the main seat of the company from Stuttgart to Berlin (Würffel 2000, 671). Krieg moved to Berlin in 1927. See Würffel 2000, 255.

53 Würffel 2000, 471–72.

before and during the war; but, in August 1945, he described this period as follows: "I suffered particularly under Nazi rule. As the owner of Julius Püttmann Verlag in Stuttgart, founded in 1865, I was the publisher of the life's work of the well-known researcher San. Rat Dr. Magnus Hirschfeld. The publishing house was expropriated from me without compensation at the beginning of 1933. After that, as a publisher of Jews, I was continuously attacked, which finally led to my German Reich ventures being closed down by the Gestapo in 1941 and to my having to go through a 19-month-long trial to assert my existence and my vocation. Given this, it goes without saying that I did not engage in National Socialist activities in Austria either. I was even called to account by the Labor Front (Arbeitsfront) for not employing party comrades".[54] It is indeed true that Walter Krieg often clashed with the Reich Chamber of Literature (Reichsschrifttumskammer), a department of the Reich Chamber of Culture (Reichskulturkammer). Yet, in 1942, Goebbels himself decided that Krieg should not be ousted from the Reich Chamber of Culture despite his many misdemeanors and the many complaints against him.[55]

It is clear that, since 1874, there was no connection between the R. Lechner (Walter Krieg) bookstore and the Rudolf Lechner & Sohn Kommissionsbuchhandlung. However, even supposing that they still communicated, Walter Krieg most likely played no part in the 1933 operation to buy back the Institute materials since he only bought the R. Lechner bookstore in 1938. In addition, the books published by Julius Püttmann Verlag (or any other publishing company [*Verlag*] where Krieg was active) were never part of the catalogue of Rudolf Lechner & Sohn Kommissionsbuchhandlung.[56] The Aryanization procedure reveals that Walter Krieg was very familiar with the bookstore landscape in Austria and Germany. His possible role in the 1933 buy-back operation cannot be totally excluded.

C. J. & E. BUMPUS, LONDON REPRESENTATION

From 1928, the L. & A. Brecher bookstore also had a British representative: Simpkin, Marshall, Hamilton, Kent & Co. (London), which became Simpkin, Marshall, Ltd. (London) in 1929. Another year later, in 1930, J[ohn] & E[dward] Bumpus (London) took over the aforementioned business and subsequently became the L. & A. Brecher bookstore's constant UK partners.[57]

[54] Letter (dated Aug. 8, 1945) from Walter Krieg to Staatsamt für Industrie, Gewerbe, Handel und Verkehr (Vienna), qtd. in Schwarz 2003, 141: "Unter der nazistischen Herrschaft habe ich besonders zu leiden gehabt. Als Inhaber des 1865 gegründeten Julius Püttmann Verlages in Stuttgart war ich der Verleger des Lebenswerkes des bekannten Forschers San. Rat Dr. Magnus Hirschfeld. Der Verlag wurde mir anfangs 1933 entschädigungslos enteignet. Seitdem wurde ich in den vergangenen Jahren als Verleger von Juden ununterbrochen angefeindet, was schließlich dazu führte, dass mir 1941 meine reichsdeutschen Unternehmungen von der Gestapo geschlossen wurden und ich einen 19 Monate währenden Prozess um die Behauptung meiner Existenz und meiner Berufung führen mußte. Daraus versteht sich von selbst, dass ich mich auch in Österreich nicht nationalsozialistisch betätigt habe. Ich wurde sogar von der Arbeitsfront zur Verantwortung gezogen, weil ich keine Parteigenossen beschäftigte".

[55] Bundesarchiv, Berlin- Lichterfelde, Sammlung Berlin Document Center (BDC), Personenbezogene Unterlagen der Reichskulturkammer (RKK), Walter Krieg (born November 28, 1901), sign. R 9361-V/25973.

[56] Put otherwise: Julius Püttmann Verlag did not act as a *Kommittent* (consignor) for Rudolf Lechner & Sohn Kommissionsbuchhandlung. I checked the *Verlegerlisten* (publisher lists) in the Rudolf Lechner & Sohn Lagerkatalog for 1933 and 1934. Julius Püttmann Verlag did not appear in these lists.

[57] See http://www.wells-genealogy.org.uk/bumpas/bumpusbooks.htm (accessed Dec. 17, 2014).

3. KARL FEIN AND THE BRNO BUILDING INDUSTRY

We mentioned in the main text that the name and stamp of the engineer Artur Eisler (1887–1944) appears on a 1938 resident registration card for Karl Fein.[58] Together with his brother Moriz Eisler (1888–1972), Artur Eisler was the owner of one of the most important construction companies in pre-war Brno. We also mentioned that Otto Eisler (1893–1968) was one of the principal Brno modernist architects. He designed the JEPA building on Náměstí svobody (Freiheitsplatz). Its 1933–34 construction forced the L. & A. Brecher bookstore to move out of the building it had occupied for thirty years, which had to be demolished to make space for the new JEPA building. I think that Karl Fein might have known Otto Eisler since the latter was, like Fein, a gay man. Because both men were part of the Jewish upper classes, and Brno's gay milieu was small, I judge it possible that they may have known each other. Both men were also close in age, separated by only one year. This would in any case help explain how, in 1938, Fein obtained a place to live from Artur Eisler when the housing pressure was great – through the intervention of his gay brother Otto Eisler. Artur Eisler (or people working for him) also managed the rental of numerous apartments in a modernist apartment building designed by his brother Otto, built by the Eislers, at 35 Koliště, another of Karl Fein's addresses, starting in 1936.[59] I think it justified to assume that Karl Fein was at least acquainted with the building industry through the Eisler family.

A few other factors further indicate that Karl Fein can be linked in some way to several people in the Brno building industry. Josef Nebehosteny, the original owner of the house at 68 Kröna (Křenová), also built the so-called Small Löw-Beer Villa in 1906 for the Brno wool industrialist Alfred Löw-Beer (1872–1939) in the town of Svitávka (Zwittawka).[60] The Löw-Beers were among the wealthiest and most renowned families in Brno before World War II. Let us recall that, until his premature death in 1896, Karl Fein's father Albert worked for the Löw-Beer family company, then known as "Aron und Jakob Löw-Beer Söhne" (Sons of Aron und Jakob Löw-Beer).

Shared school history is another indication. Karl Fein graduated from the German gymnasium in Brno in the same year as Hans Tugendhat (1894–?), the brother of Fritz Tugendhat, one year his junior.[61] Grete Tugendhat (née Löw-Beer, 1903–1970), the daughter of Alfred Löw-Beer, married Fritz Tugendhat (1895–1958). The couple is best known for the modernist Villa Tugendhat they built in Brno in 1930.[62] Villa Tugendhat was erected in the upper part of the garden of the posh Löw-Beer villa at 22 Sadová (Parkstrasse), bought by Alfred Löw-Beer in 1913.[63] Alfred Löw-Beer gave this land

[58] AMB, Brno, fonds Z 1, resident registration card Karl Fein. Exactly why Artur Eisler's name and stamp appear on Karl Fein's resident registration remains unexplained. One of Artur Eisler's own addresses was located on the same street, 59 Falkensteinerova (Grohova). See http://encyklopedie.brna.cz/home-mmb/?acc=profil_osobnosti&load=3192 (accessed Jan. 29, 2015).

[59] MZA, Brno, fonds B 392, Vystěhovalecký fond, úřadovna Brno, kart. n° 14, inv. n° 302, 35 Glacis (currently Koliště).

[60] See http://www.tugendhat.eu/en/the-low-beer-villa-in-svitavka.html (accessed Nov. 6, 2015). Alfred Löw-Beer is mentioned as "Fabrikant" (manufacturer) and "Vizepräsident d.[es] Handels- u.[nd] Gewerbekammer" (vice-president of the Chamber of Commerce and Industry) in *Adreßbuch von Groß-Brünn* 1934, 322. Alfred Löw-Beer's company was Aryanized during the German occupation. See NA, Praha, fonds n° 375, Arizační spisy, kart. n° 221, file n° 1411. For an overview of Alfred Löw-Beer's commercial activities, see Smutný 2012, 262–63.

[61] *Jahresbericht des Staatsgymnasiums mit deutscher Unterrichtssprache in Brünn für das Schuljahr* 1912–13, 35. See also http://www.geni.com/people/Hans-Tugendhat/6000000009035737061 (accessed Feb. 6, 2016).

[62] See http://www.geni.com/people/Grete-Tugendhat/6000000011491656627, http:/www.geni.com/people/Alfred-L%C3%B6w-Beer/6000000009634745995 and http://www.geni.com/people/Fritz-Tugendhat/600000007298051436 (all accessed Nov. 6, 2015). For Fritz Tugendhat's commercial activities, see Smutný 2012, 462–63.

[63] The street is currently named Drobného. This villa, facing the Augarten (Lužánky) park, was

to his daughter and also financed the construction of the now world-famous Villa Tugendhat. And Villa Tugendhat was built by the Eisler brothers, Artur and Moriz.

There are still other factors. In the main text, we mentioned Karl Giese's first landlord in Brno, Hedi Tschauner, the wife of the architect and engineer Emil Tschauner.[64] We showed that, in the second half of 1933, Karl Fein helped Giese find a room during his first six months in Brno. There is a chance that Karl Giese found this room by inquiring with a network of acquaintances. As I conceive it, Fein's building industry network looked as follows. Anna Bermann (née Brecher), the daughter of the L. & A. Brecher bookstore manager Elise Brecher, was Fein's niece. She was married to the pharmacist Wilhelm Bermann. The sister of Wilhelm Bermann, Marie Ernestine Bermann, was married to Otto Weiss (1879–1942?), an authorized signatory (*Prokurist*) for the Maloměřické cement and lime company (*cementárny a vápenky*) founded in 1906 by Leo Czech (1877–1943) and the engineer Max Kohn (1857–1943), located in the Brno suburb of Maloměřice (Malomierschütz or also Malmeritz).[65] We mentioned in the main text that Karl Fein acted as Leo Czech's lawyer in a libel case in 1926.[66] At that time, the latter's very profitable cement factory was the biggest of its kind in Czechoslovakia, employing around 500 people and producing approximately 360,000 tons of cement a year.

Emil Tschauner (1904–?), the husband of Giese's very first Brno landlord, Hedi Tschauner, was later one of the people who indirectly participated in the Aryanization of this cement and lime company.[67] Emil Tschauner's brother, Leo Tschauner, worked for the company as a manager before the Germans invaded the country.[68] For its part, the very wealthy Löw-Beer family had strong financial ties to this company.[69] Alfred Löw-Beer's sister, Cecílie Hože (née Löw-Beer, 1864–1942), was married to the lawyer Cornelius Hože (1854–1936). Their son, Max Hože (1888–1942), was a co-owner and director of the cement plant.[70] In 1940, Emil Tschauner was appointed as the trustee (*Treuhänder*) of Max Hože's capital, while his brother Leo Tschauner was appointed as the trustee of Paul and Max Kohn's capital. Leo Tschauner and a certain Josef Dostal (?–?) were appointed as the trustees (*Treuhänder*) of the cement company itself.[71]

Finally, we might also mention that Leopold Weiss, Otto Weiss' father, was the president (*Vorstand*) of the Association of Industrial Employees (Verein der Industrie-

opened to the public in 2015 after a years-long restoration. See http://www.vilalowbeer.cz/en/villa2/the-l-w-beers and http://www.vilalowbeer.cz/en/villa2/history-of-the-villa (both accessed Nov. 6, 2015).

[64] See chapter 5, p. 139.

[65] MZA Brno, fonds K 441, company file Maloměřické cementárny a vápenice, n. p., Brno, (1904) 1946–1979, sign. 2536. See also *Adreßbuch von Groß-Brünn* 1934, 546. The company ceased trading at the end of the 1990s. See Dušek 2020, 53; Černá et al. 2017, 116. Leo Czech left the company the following year. See Smutný 2012, 72. For Max Kohn, see Smutný 2012, 220; http://encyklopedie.brna.cz/home-mmb/?acc=profil_osobnosti&load=13888 (accessed Dec. 4, 2015).

[66] "Doležal auf eine Stunde wieder Kommunistischer Chefredakteur" (Doležal again a one-hour Communist editor-in-chief), *Volksfreund*, Aug. 20, 1926, 6.

[67] ABS, Praha, fonds SÚMV, n° 305-501-4, file Emil Tschauner (Dec. 1, 1904–?), f. 19, 26.

[68] ABS, Praha, fonds SÚMV, n° 305-501-4, file Emil Tschauner (Dec. 1, 1904–?), f. 19, 25.

[69] See, especially, the overview of these families' exact financial participation in the Buch- und Vermögensrevision zum 31 Mai 1940 (Audit of accounts and assets, situation on May 31, 1940), Firma Leo Czech & Comp., Zementfabrik Brünn-Malmeritz, written by Anton Stadlmann in NA, Praha, fonds n° 375, Arizační spisy, kart. n° 186, sign. 1073, cement company Leo Czech & Co., Brno. In 1933, Alfred Löw-Beer and Rudolf Löw-Beer injected new capital into the company. See Smutný 2012, 72; ABS, Praha, fonds SÚMV, n° 305-501-4, file on Emil Tschauner, f. 18.

[70] Max Hože was deported with his wife Friederike Hože (1896–1942?) on transport "Au" from Prague to Terezín on May 12, 1942. Five days later, on May 17, 1942, they were further transferred to Lublin on transport "Ay". Max Hože died in Majdanek on June 23, 1942.

[71] NA, Praha, fonds n° 375, Arizační spisy, kart. n° 186, sign. 1073, cement company Leo Czech & Co. Brno. See also http://www.tugendhat.eu/en/locality.html and http://www.tugendhat.eu/en/the-arnold-villa-and-the-first-villa-colony-nad-lu.html (both accessed Dec. 4, 2015). The Arizační spisy

beamten), of which Karl Fein's father had also been a member.[72] Leopold Weiss was an authorized signatory for a Löw-Beer firm and the cement company. Later on, Otto Weiss took over his father's function.[73] Karl Fein knew the accountant Anton Stadlmann (1893–?) who audited the cement company in 1940. On behalf of his nephew Heinrich Brecher, Fein inquired whether he could assist Stadlmann in any way with emigration to Uruguay.[74]

Max Kohn apparently strongly resisted the takeover of his company by the Germans and their local allies. As Kohn was then in his eighties, the Nazis "reasoned" that his hyperactivity could be explained (away) by the rumor that Kohn was once treated by a Viennese doctor known for etching monkey testicles.[75] The actual name of this doctor was left out of a letter by the Brno Gestapo in May 1939, but they most likely meant Dr. Eugen Steinach (1861–1944), in whose experimental work Magnus Hirschfeld took a great interest: "Kohn will be 83 years old this year. I was told, by reliable sources, that he has already been treated twice in Vienna by the professor [space left blank] (specialist for the insertion of monkey glands). [...] Dostal and Tschauner, who were once Kohn's closest collaborators, stated that they sometimes doubted Kohn's sanity. Kohn sometimes had days when he harassed his surroundings in the most vicious manner – like a monkey [...] Under any circumstances, this man ought to be eliminated. I recommend that Max Kohn's mental state be examined. On this basis, his disenfranchisement would be decided and his vote not count in the possible sale of the company".[76] The widower Max Kohn was put on transport "Ah" from Brno to Terezín on April 4, 1942. On October 19, 1942, he was further transferred to Treblinka on transport "Bw". As can be seen, Karl Fein would have known – and, to some extent, relied upon – a very dense, closely linked professional network of people in the Brno building industry. That is why I initially thought that another important player in the Brno building industry, the Nebehosteny family, and especially their magnificent house on Kröna (Křenová), may have played a more important part in our story.

fonds' inventory list in the NA, Praha, mentions three archival entities for this company: kart. n° 186, sign. 1073; kart. n° 315, sign. 2228 and kart. n° 763, sign. 435. I consulted the first two only.

72 "Der Verein der Industriebeamten in Brünn" (The association of industrial employees in Brno), *Brünner Morgenpost* (*Beilage zur Brünner Zeitung*), Jg. 29, n° 61, Mar. 16, 1894, 3.

73 ABS, Praha, fonds SÚMV, n° 305-501-4, file on Emil Tschauner (born Dec. 1, 1904), f. 18, 25.

74 MZA, Brno, fonds C 12, Krajský soud trestní Brno, kart. n° 2381, sign. Tk XI 1852/38, file Heinrich Brecher, letter (dated Sep. 7, 1938) [Heinrich Brecher] to [Karl Fein], II, f. 130.

75 See, for example, Joe Schwarcz's "Getting 'Steinached' was all the rage in Roaring '20s", https://www.mcgill.ca/oss/article/health-history-science-science-everywhere/getting-steinached-was-all-rage-roaring-20s (accessed Jul. 7, 2024).

76 NA, Praha, fonds n° 375, Arizační spisy, kart. n° 186, sign. 1073, cement company Leo Czech & Co. (Brno), letter (dated May 8, 1939) from Gestapo Brünn (Einsatzkommando VI, II E) to unknown addressee, 2–3: "Dieser Kohn wird in diesem Jahre 83 Jahre alt. Er liess sich, wie mir von verlässlicher Seite aus gesagt wurde in Wien schon zweimal von dem Professor [space left blank] (Spezialist für Einsetzung von Affendrüsen) behandeln. [...] Dostal und Tschauner, die früher die engsten Mitarbeiter des Kohn waren, gaben an, dass sie beideoft [*sic*: beide oft] an dem Verstande des Kohn gezweifelt haben. Dieser Kohn habe manchmal Tage gehabt, an denen er in boshaftester Weise – nach Affenart – seine Umgebung schikaniert [...] Dieser Mann müsste unter allen Umständen ausgeschaltet werden. Ich rege an Max Kohn auf seinen Geisteszustand hin untersuchen zu lassen. Auf Grund diesem, wäre seine Entwendung Entmünd[ig]ung [last word added by hand] gegeben und würde seine Stimme bei einem eventuellen Verkauf der Firma nicht mitzählend sein". For more information on Eugen Steinach, see Dose 2020b, 27–30.

4. KAREL RŮŽIČKA (1895–1942)

Karel Růžička was born on January 26, 1895, in the Czechoslovak city of Dědice (Dieditz). He started his career as a lawyer in Brno around 1923, and married Marie Vavrouch (1885–197?) in 1919. Marie Růžička was the daughter of Jan Vavrouch, a schoolmaster from Vážany (near Vyškov). Jan Vavrouch was apparently the decisive inspiration for the artistic career of Antonín Procházka (1882–1945). This painter and former lawyer married the artist Linka Scheithauerová (1884–1960) in Berlin Charlottenburg in 1908. The couple spent the last twenty years of their life in Brno. There was an artistic circle in Brno of admirers and collectors of Procházka's work, the Group of Visual Artists in Brno (Skupina výtvarných umělců v Brně, SVU). Karel Růžička and his wife Marie were active members of this group and also close friends of the Procházkas.[77] The Růžička-Vavrouch couple lived in a comfortable villa in a large and fashionable neighborhood known to this day in Brno as the Civil Servant Quarter (*Úřednická čtvrť, Beamtenviertel* or also *Beamtenheim*). The villa's exact address was 28 Šeříková (currently Heinrichova).[78] It was built and paid for by Marie's father, Jan Vavrough.[79]

Karel Růžička was on the left of the political spectrum, and this made him an easy target for the National Socialists. For a commemorative 1925 booklet, co-authored by the Brno philosophy professor Josef Tvrdý (1877–1942),[80] and issued on the occasion of President Masaryk's seventy-fifth birthday, Růžička wrote a piece on "Masaryk and Socialism". This text pondered an ideal socialist state where manual labor would be more appreciated, and the working class would be entitled to an education. A few years after starting his legal career, Růžička seemed to be dreaming of a sort of Communist state.[81] In 1922, he also published a short history about the separation of church and state.[82]

Being left-leaning, and possibly also a Freemason,[83] was reason enough for the National Socialists to persecute Karel Růžička. Růžička was also engaged in real resistance activities in Brno during the war. The Czechoslovak resistance movement, National Defense (or Defense of the Nation, Obrana národa), intensified its activities

[77] See Slavíček 2002; http://encyklopedie.brna.cz/home-mmb/?acc=profil_osobnosti&load=1749 (accessed May 8, 2015). Vrchlického, a street where the painter used to live, in Brno-Kohoutovice, was renamed after him in 1946, becoming Antonína Procházky. See http://encyklopedie.brna.cz/home-mmb/?acc=profil_ulice&load=142 (accessed May 8, 2015). The archival fonds Skupina výtvarných umělců v Brně (SVU) is part of the fonds R 39, Brněnské umělecké spolky, in the AMB, Brno. Jana Dosoudilová (AMB, Brno) kindly checked for me whether Karl Fein's name appeared in any of the art circle's more important documents. She checked the 1936–39 cash book, the 1933 attendance list, the correspondence of 1936–38 and records of the 1925–39 meetings. Fein's name did not appear. See email (dated May 7, 2015) from Jana Dosoudilová (AMB, Brno) to the author. For more information about the art circle, see Nováková 2014.

[78] AMB, Brno, fonds Z 1, resident registration cards of Karel and Marie Růžička. During the German occupation, the street where they lived was known as Fliedergasse and later as Grilparzergasse. On the complicated history of this street, see http://encyklopedie.brna.cz/home-mmb/?acc=profil_ulice&load=1601 (accessed May 15, 2015). That the Civil Servant Quarter was (and still is) reserved for Brno's affluent class is also indicated by the example of one of the most famous Czech sexologists, Antonín Trýb, who lived at 17 Šeříková, on the same street as Karel Růžička and his wife.

[79] Katastrální úřad pro Jihomoravský kraj, Brno, katastrální pracoviště Brno-město, Obrowitz/Zábrdovice, Katastralgemeinde Kreuzgasse, Katastrální obec Křížová (cadastral municipality Kreuzgasse/Křížová), land register entry number (Zahl der Grundbuchseinlage, číslo vložky knihovní) n° 1137, Šeříková/Heinrichova n° 213/28.

[80] Like many other academics at Brno's Masaryk University, Josef Tvrdý fell victim to the Brno Gestapo and was transported to Mauthausen. After the war, a street (Tvrdého) was renamed after him in Brno. See http://encyklopedie.brna.cz/home-mmb/?acc=profil_osobnosti&load=412 (accessed May 6, 2015).

[81] Tvrdý & Růžička 1925, 26–32.

[82] Růžička 1922.

[83] I found Karel Růžička's name on a long list of (pre-war) Freemasons, "Seznam svobodných zednářů ČSR", on a dubious fascist website: http://freeglobe.parlamentnilisty.cz/Articles/2980-seznam-svobodnych-zednaru-csr-961-clenu-prvorepublikovych-lozi.aspx (accessed May 8, 2015).

shortly after October 1939, when celebration of the founding of Czechoslovakia was forbidden. This movement was mostly led by former Czechoslovak military officers. However, the moment that this resistance group revealed itself, the Gestapo intensified its own activity and persecuted many of those active in the group, considerably damaging this first important wave of Czechoslovak resistance.[84] As early as September 1940, 5,000 National Defense members had been arrested in the Protectorate. In the wake of this serious blow, other resistance groups – where civilians played a more important role – formed. Most of these were, in some way, in contact with National Defense.[85] It is a little unclear in which resistance group Karel Růžička was active, but his name is mentioned in connection with another Brno resistance member, Jan Obořil (1900–1942).[86] This man will be treated more fully below.

Karel Růžička was caught up, along with many other Protectorate citizens, in the new and savage policy against political opponents initiated by the new Reich Protector Reinhard Heydrich. Immediately after Heydrich's appointment, in September 1941, the *Standgerichte* (summary court martial) started their work. Like so many other political opponents, Růžička was sent to the Mauthausen concentration camp, where he died on July 12, 1942, six months after his court-martial conviction in Brno.[87]

It is not known when exactly Karel Růžička was arrested and imprisoned. However, we do know that, on January 10, 1942, he was sentenced in Brno for high treason (*Hochverrat*) by a summary court martial presided by three Nazi officials. The archival file is vague on the exact nature of Růžička's crime against the German occupiers, although use of the term *Hochverrat* (high treason) indicates that it involved resistance activity of some sort: "The accused Růžička is transferred to the Gestapo for the crime of disturbing public order and security pursuant to § 3 [?] and § 4 [?] of the Reich Protector in Bohemia and Moravia's decree on the imposition of a state of civil emergency of September 27, 1941, as well as for the preparation of an enterprise of high treason (§§ 80–82 StGB) [Strafgesetzbuch, German penal code]. The assets of the accused are confiscated. The sentence cannot be appealed".[88]

[84] Kopečný 2006, 125–28; Wagner & Zarusky 2011, 497–513. However, Karel Růžička does not appear in the reference list of Brno resistance members (Seznam členů brněnské Obrany národa a jejich spolupracovníků) in Kopečný 2006, 147–235.

[85] See Wagner & Zarusky 2011, chapter E III, which gives an extensive overview of the many Czechoslovak resistance groups.

[86] For succinct information about Jan Obořil and his accomplices, see Adámek, Kroutil & Kučerová et al. 1981, 119. See also http://encyklopedie.brna.cz/home-mmb/?acc=profil_osobnosti&load=3479 (accessed May 28, 2015).

[87] A postwar inheritance file contains the official death certificate of Karel Růžička issued in Mauthausen. See MZA, Brno, fonds C 152, Okresní soud civilní Brno, Pozůstalost po Dru. Karlu Růžičkovi zemřelém Jul. 12, 1942 (inheritance file Karel Růžička, d. Jul. 12, 1942), Todfallsaufnahme (death certificate) of Karel Růžička (dated Jul. 15, 1942), sign. D XVIII 53/50. The *Amtsblatt des Protektorates Böhmen und Mähren = Úřední list Protektorátu Čechy a Morava*, year 1942, n° 37, Oct. 8, 1942, 9552, says that Karel Růžička was removed from the list of lawyers due to his death. The message also states that he was *Substitut* (replaced) by Ctibor Chytil. It is not specified if this was Ctibor Chytil Sr. (1869–1944) or Ctibor Chytil Jr. (1898–?). The latter lived at 95 Talgasse (Údolní), not very far from Karel Růžička's place of residence. Ctibor Chytil Jr. was a regular lawyer. Ctibor Chytil Sr. gained one of the highest-ranking judicial positions in Brno, and was being pensioned around that time. See *Adressbuch der Landeshauptstadt Brünn* 1942, I: 37; *Adreßbuch von Groß-Brünn* 1934, 161; Ctibor Chytil Jr.'s home certificate is in AMB, Brno, fonds B1/39; Ctibor Chytil Sr.'s staff file in MZA, Brno, fonds C 136, Krajský soud Brno, kart. n° 52, složka Ctibor Chytil (1869–1944).

[88] MZA, Brno, fonds B 340, Gestapo Brno file Karel Růžička, kart. n° 147, n° 8489, sign. 100-147-7, f. 2: "Der Angeklagte Růžička wird wegen Verbrechens der Störung der öffentlichen Ordnung und Sicherheit gem.[äß] § 3 [?] und § 4 [?] der Verordnung des Reichsprotektors in Böhmen und Mähren über die Verhängung des zivilen Ausnahmezustandes vom 27.9.1941 sowie wegen Vorbereitung eines hochverräterisches Unternehmens (§§ 80-82 StGB) [Strafgesetzbuch, German criminal code] der Geheime Staatspolizei überwiesen. Das Vermögen des Angeklagten wird eingezogen. Das Urteil ist unanfechtbar". The physically damaged Gestapo file on Růžička makes it very hard to decipher the first page of the *Standgericht* (court martial) conviction file. The transcription offered here of parts of the barely-legible carbon copies and typed text of the conviction is therefore tentative. An employee of

Court-martial convictions always had only three possibilities: a death sentence, transfer to the Gestapo, or acquittal.[89] Some material characteristics of the archival page laying out Růžička's conviction make it evident that the main part of the accusation was the carbon copy of a typed text.[90] Karel Růžička's name – along with other identifying information – was clearly added afterwards to the carbon copy using a typewriter with a black ribbon. This strongly indicates that multiple people were sentenced and that the same vague standard verdict was being reused.

A letter in Růžička's Gestapo file from a Brno bank notified the Gestapo in Brno that the bank accounts of seventeen people, including Růžička, had been blocked. Most of the seventeen names on this list were lawyers, doctors and university professors in Brno.[91] Among them was Karel Hora, one of the organizers of the WLSR Brno conference. When checking these seventeen names in the inventory list of the Gestapo fonds in the MZA in Brno, I found in the short description of their cases that (at least) five were tried on the same date as Karel Růžička, on January 13, 1942.[92] These were Dr. Tomáš Vacek (1899–1942), Dr Josef Podlaha (1893–1975),[93] Vladimír Němec (1900–1942),[94] Václav Šilhan (1898–1945),[95] and Jan Obořil (1900–1942). The latter was certainly a member of National Defense.[96] Obořil, Němec, Šilhan and Karel Růžička were arrested on the same day, December 17, 1941.[97] All five were transported to Mauthausen. Three of them were killed there.

In addition to being convicted of high treason, Karel Růžička's property was expropriated by the National Socialists. Nevertheless, it looks like his widow, Marie Vavrouch, continued to live in the house they owned in Brno's Civil Servant Quarter during the war.[98] In 1946, after the war, Růžička's widow initiated legal proceedings to reclaim the other half of the house and other assets that belonged to her late husband before the war. The awkward legal situation of living in a house that was only half hers needed rectification. The belated settlement of the Karel Růžička inheritance

MZA, Brno, told me that the only documents left in a Gestapo file on a person are often these final court martial convictions. See email (dated Apr. 14, 2015) from Jana Fasorová (MZA, Brno) to the author. For the German legal definition of *Hochverrat* (high treason), see Wagner & Zarusky 2011, 50.

89 Wagner & Zarusky 2011, chapter E. III; esp. 490–91 n. 136.

90 The original dark blue of the carbon copy has presumably faded over time, becoming a – barely legible – light blue.

91 MZA, Brno, fonds B 340, Gestapo Brno, file Karel Růžička, kart. n° 147, n° 8489, sign. 100-147-7, letter (dated Jan. 30, 1942) from Postsparkasse (Zweigstelle in Brünn) to Gestapo Brünn.

92 This recurring date in other people's Gestapo files is the main reason why I shed my initial doubts about Růžička's barely legible conviction date, January 10, 1942. This date seems further confirmed by the slightly later dates of the other documents in Růžička's file, which were added in chronological order after his conviction (for example, January 30, 1942 and February 2, 1942). Three other people named in the bank's letter to the Gestapo (mentioned in the previous note) were sentenced three days later, on January 13, 1942.

93 Josef Podlaha was arrested on November 27, 1941. See Kopečný 2006, 205. He survived the war. See Vašek, Černý & Břečka 2015, 476; https://encyklopedie.brna.cz/home-mmb/?acc=profil_osobnosti&load=3885 (accessed Apr. 23, 2021).

94 See https://encyklopedie.brna.cz/home-mmb/?acc=profil_osobnosti&load=1931 (accessed Apr. 24, 2021).

95 See Kopečný 2006, 220. Cf. http:/encyklopedie.brna.cz/home-mmb/?acc=profil_osobnosti&load=893 (accessed May 5, 2015). The bank letter uses "Wenzel", the German of his first name, instead of "Václav".

96 See https://encyklopedie.brna.cz/home-mmb/?acc=profil_osobnosti&load=3479 (accessed Apr. 23, 2021).

97 Adámek, Kroutil & Kučerová et al. 1981, 119. See also http://encyklopedie.brna.cz/home-mmb/?acc=profil_osobnosti&load=3479 (accessed May 5, 2015): "Za nacistické okupace pracoval v odboji v obnovené Obraně národa (skupina doc. dr. Vladimíra Němce, dr. Růžičky, dr. Václava Šilhana a dalších). Zatčen 17.12.1941" (During the Nazi occupation, he worked in the resistance, in the renewed Obrana národa [the group of Drs. Vladimír Němec, Růžička, Václav Šilhan, and others]. Arrested on December 17, 1941).

98 MZA, Brno, fonds C 152, Okresní soud civilní Brno, Pozůstalost po Dru. Karlu Růžičkovi, sign. D XVIII 53/50, letter (dated Oct. 19, 1942) from Vermögensamt beim Reichsprotektor in Böhmen und Mähren in Prague to Bezirksgericht für Zivilsachen Brünn (Okresní soud civilní Brno): "Eine Abhandlung der Verlassenschaft kommt nicht in Betracht" (There is no question of settling the estate).

procedure took years, and ended in 1950. Interestingly, Marie Vavrouch was assisted by Jaroslav Soukop, a lawyer and old friend of Karel Růžička, who had an office in the same building (6 Masarykova) as Marie Růžičková's husband did before the war. It is unclear whether – and to what extent – the address of Soukop's law practice was itself a symbolic gesture or if he had simply taken over Růžička's former law office. The postwar inheritance file also mentions that Karel Růžička anticipated the approach of a possible disaster since he made a will (naming his wife as his sole universal heir) on July 31, 1937.[99] He also had three life insurance policies. The inheritance case was reopened again in 2009, twenty years after the Velvet Revolution.[100] Since Marie Růžička died in the 1970s, it must have been reopened by relatives or heirs of the unfortunate lawyer. Because Karel Růžička looked like an important figure, I tried my utmost to contact the current relatives of his widow Marie Vavrouch. I managed to make contact with a son, born after the war, but did not succeed in seeing the archives that he claimed he had on Karel Růžička.[101]

There is another figure that I would like to mention here, Konstantin Raclavský (1900–1992), who was also a part of the aforementioned Brno SVU art circle around the Brno painter Antonín Procházka. An exhibition catalogue for Antonín Procházka mentions that, in his younger years, Konstantin Raclavský was a "protégé" of the painter and his wife Linka Procházková. Raclavský ultimately studied engineering, but was also the secretary of the Brno art group. Apparently, during the war, Raclavský was also active in the resistance.[102] Raclavský interested me because he survived. When Linka Procházková, Antonín Procházka's widow, died in 1960, her will revealed that she had decided that Konstantin Raclavský and Marie Růžička, Karel Růžička's wife, should be her sole heirs.[103] That means that many Antonín Procházka's paintings, and presumably some capital as well, were left to two of the painter's former intimate friends. I thought it likely that Karel Růžička's personal archives would have ended up with his widow. Since she died in the 1970s, and Konstantin Raclavský was still living, there was a chance that her archives and estate were passed down – possibly willed – to him. I tried to contact Konstantin Raclavský's surviving son, also named Konstantin Raclavský (1940–), after his father. Despite a few emails and even a registered letter in Czech explaining my interest in his father, all contact was regrettably refused. In this case, too, a chance to possibly discover more about Karl Fein from Karel Růžička's personal documents was blocked.

[99] MZA, Brno, fonds C 152, Okresní soud civilní Brno, Pozůstalost po Dru. Karlu Růžičkovi, sign. D XVIII 53/50.

[100] The case (file number 86D 363/ 2009) was reopened at the Městský soud v Brně (Brno Municipal Court), but the court refused to disclose any further information on the matter. See email (dated Apr. 14, 2015) from Jana Fasorová (MZA, Brno) to the author.

[101] I initiated the search by looking up cadastral information about the house at 28 Heinrichova. One of the house's two current owners is Jiří M.. After several attempts, I finally managed to contact him. He offered to function as a go-between between me and Quido P., the son of Marie Vavrouch. However, months of waiting and several emails yielded no results. Jiří M. claimed that Quido P. stopped answering his calls and he finally ignored calls as well. My own attempt to contact Quido P. proved unsuccessful at first. Letters to his business and home addresses went unanswered and phone numbers retrieved from online databases were not in operation. Assisted by Lucie Tuzová, I visited Quido P. in 2017. Quido P. told me that he had several boxes in his garage containing archives of his mother and Karel Růžička. Despite friendly conversations, a seeming willingness to help me, and my several attempts (each time generously assisted by Lucie Tuzová) to keep the iron hot, no more progress was made. Most of all, I had hoped to find a picture of Karl Fein, Karel Růžička's legal colleague, in these family archives. Being unable to consult these archives was one of the great frustrations of this research project.

[102] Kopečný 2006, 8, 20, 36, 52, 62, 209.

[103] Hlusicka, Holesovský, Hubatová-Vacková et al. 2002, 18, 217.

5. OTTO SCHÜTZ (1892–1970)

Otto Schütz interned in Karl Fein's law office and was initially appointed as the estate curator (*Nachlasskurator*) for the Giese-Fein inheritance procedure.[104] For several years, therefore, Schütz worked at 6 Masarykova (Masarykstrasse), the address of Karl Fein's law practice.[105] In the first years of his career, Schütz worked for a bank.

Otto Schütz was born on July 26, 1892, and received a classical education in the same gymnasium that Karl Fein attended.[106] Like Fein, Schütz lost his father when he was a child.[107] It appears that, at the very least, Fein and Schütz were colleagues, but they may also have been friends. Otto Schütz's acquaintance with Karl Giese and Kurt Hiller seems to indicate a circle of gay friends.[108] Starting in 1928, Schütz occasionally wrote a column for the Brno newspaper *Tagesbote,* his contributions revealing an intelligent man who pleaded for humanistic values.[109] Schütz was also the president of the Brno branch of the League for Human Rights (Liga für Menschenrechte, Liga pro lidská práva), modeled on the French example, La ligue des droits de l'homme, founded in 1898 in the wake of the Dreyfus affair.[110] The Czechoslovak League was founded in 1929 at the initiative of the Czech politician Edvard Beneš (1884–1948). Schütz was also the founder of a committee established in 1938 assisting German, mostly Jewish, immigrants arriving in Brno – the Central Office for the Assistance of Refugees in Brno (Zentralhilfstelle für Flüchtlinge in Brünn, Pomocné ústředí pro uprchlíky v Brně). Schütz was very actively engaged with these immigrants.[111]

[104] See the "kandidáti advokacie" (candidates for the Bar) list, *Seznam advokátů dle stavu koncem roku 1935* 1936, 47; MZA, Brno, fonds C 107, Německý úřední soud Brno (Deutsches Amtsgericht Brünn), kart. n° 256, sign. 5a V 3/41, f. 11, 14.

[105] From 1924 until 1932, Otto Schütz lived at 7 Masarykova (Masarykstrasse), just across the street from the building where Karl Fein had his law office, 6 Masarykova (Masarykstrasse). In 1937, his new work address was 3 Theatergasse (Divadelní), indicating that he had become an independent lawyer. See *Seznam advokátů dle stavu koncem roku 1937* 1938, 32. A resident registration card in the AMB, Brno, fonds Z 1, reveals that he moved to this address as early as September 1932, the month of the WLSR Brno conference. The only curious aspect is that Otto Schütz's home address on his resident registration card is the same as his work address, 3 Theatergasse (Divadelní). It is unclear whether he was reluctant to reveal where he lived or whether he indeed lived and worked at the same place.

[106] Schütz was listed as a pupil belonging to the age group of the elder Karl Fein (1893–1932), the nephew of the younger Karl Fein (1894–1942). See *Jahresbericht des Staatsgymnasium mit deutscher Unterrichtssprache in Brünn für das Schuljahr 1910–1911* 1910–11, 61; *Jahresbericht des Staatsgymnasium mit deutscher Unterrichtssprache in Brünn für das Schuljahr 1911–1912* 1911–12, 43.

[107] Otto Schütz's parents were Josef Schütz (1860?–1896) and Mathilde Schütz (1860–1935). They are buried in the Jewish cemetery in Brno in plot 5D, row 9, grave 24.

[108] Archiv Kurt Hiller Gesellschaft, Neuss, letter (dated Apr. 29, 1937, 2) from Kurt Hiller to Karl Giese. That Schütz may have been a gay man is possibly also indicated by his brief involvement with Jean Genet during the latter's three-months stay in Brno in 1937. See Soetaert 2024.

[109] His very first, quasi-philosophical contribution to the newspaper *Tagesbote* was an article titled "Von den Unentschlossenen" (On those who are undecided) (Schütz, Jan. 15, 1928, 17).

[110] NA, Praha, fonds Ministerstvo sociální péče, Londýn (Ministry of Social Welfare, London), kart. n° 1007/43, inv. n° 1/659, microfilm 4299, f. 427, letter (dated Mar. 17, 1943, 1) from Otto Schütz to Dr. [Marie] Fischer- Ascher. For more information on the Prague branch of the League for Human Rights and its links with the League in Germany, see also Čapková & Frankl 2012, 106. There is no file on the Brno branch of the League in the MZA, Brno, fonds B 26, Policejní ředitelství Brno; or in the fonds B 40, Zemský úřad Brno (Landesbehörde in Brünn). This possibly indicates that the Brno branch of the association was not officially sanctioned. See email (dated Jan. 5, 2016) from Miroslava Kučerová (MZA, Brno) to the author. See also the article "Delegace Ligy pro lidská práva vykázána z Košúty" (Human rights league delegation expelled from Košúty), *Dělnická Rovnost*, Jg. 3, n° 109, Jun. 3, 1931, 1.

[111] Čapková and Frankl consulted the archives of the "Büro des Exekutivkomitees des World Jewish Congress" (Office of the Executive Committee of the World Jewish Congress), Paris, archival fonds n° 1190, in the Archiv für Zeitgeschichte in Zürich, documenting Schütz's activity: "An der Spitze dieser Hilfsorganisation stand der unermüdliche Dr. Schütz" (At the head of this aid organization stood the tireless Dr. Schütz) (Čapková & Frankl 2012, 279). It is surprising that the authors do not mention Schütz's first name and also that his name is missing from the book's index.

According to Schütz, the Gestapo pursued him the day after Czechoslovakia was invaded; but he had left Brno the day before the invasion, on March 14, 1939.[112] Fleeing through Poland, Schütz sought refuge in Norway. When the Germans invaded Norway in April 1940, he was again pursued by the Gestapo. Hiding for some time in the mountains, Schütz managed to flee to Sweden in the final months of 1942.[113] In January 1943, Schütz was in the Nolhage Läger refugee camp in Alingsås, approximately 60 kilometers northeast of Göteborg.[114] (He eventually settled in Göteborg, not leaving Sweden until 1951.) By May 1943, he was working from his Göteborg hotel room to assist Jewish people still trying to escape from countries occupied by the Germans.[115] Even after the war was over, Schütz continued his work for Jewish refugees and named his office the Czechoslovak Refugee Office (Tjeckoslovakiska flyktingskontor, Československá uprchlická kancelář), and later simply the Refugee Office (Flyktingkontor), located at 33 Södra Hamngatan in the center of Göteborg.[116] According to a January 1946 census document, Schütz worked as a welfare officer (*socialkurator*), his address listed as 2E Sergelsgatan.[117] In its digitized archives, the American Jewish Joint Distribution Committee (AJJDC) contains 217 letters sent or received by Otto Schütz as he helped those fleeing National Socialism.[118] Schütz worked with a female secretary who translated all his letters (from German) into Swedish.[119] A January 1943 letter allows us to deduce that *at the very least* he knew who the Brno architect Otto Eisler was.[120] The same letter also indicates that Schütz was also very concerned about the fate of Jews and Jewish refugees in occupied Norway.

Schütz emigrated to the USA in 1951–52. He was listed as single on an August 1951 first-class passenger list.[121] As his New York address, he gave the address of Leon Baum

[112] AMB, Brno, fonds Z 1, handwritten date on resident registration card of Otto Schütz. Curiously, this resident registration card was not date-stamped by the Brno police until April 28, 1939.

[113] NA, Praha, fonds Ministerstvo sociální péče, Londýn (Ministry of Social Welfare, London), kart. n° 1007/43, inv. n° 1/659, microfilm 4299, f. 427, letter (dated Mar. 17, 1943) from Otto Schütz to Dr. [Marie] Fischer-Ascher. The letter requests Marie Fischer's mediation in obtaining visas for England for four people, including Otto Schütz himself. A Baum family story (see below) tells that Schütz skied his way out of Czechoslovakia. See email (dated May 18, 2016) from L. Baum to the author. We have mentioned that this also happened in the case of Milan Kratochvíla. See chapter 15, p. 588. It is possible that Schütz also skied when he fled from Norway to Sweden later in the war.

[114] AJJDC, New York, 1941–1967, Stockholm Collection, Olika Organization P-S 1941–1949, document ID 944740, letter (dated Jan. 12, 1943) [the AJJDC inventory gives the date of the letter incorrectly as Jan. 21, 1943] from Otto Schütz to Mr. [Marcus] Levin.

[115] AJJDC, New York, 1941–1967, Stockholm Collection, Olika Organization P-S 1941–1949, document ID 944682, letter (dated May 2, 1943) from Otto Schütz to Mr. [Marcus] Levin.

[116] This address is given in several letters, and confirmed by a 1947 list of residence and work permits in the archives of the Police Chamber in Gothenburg. See email (dated Jun. 5, 2015) from Per Forsberg (Landsarkivet i Göteborg) to the author. I thank Per Forsberg for his friendly help and for providing useful information on Schütz and his stay in Göteborg. I also thank Paul Epäilys (Region- och stadsarkivet i Göteborg) for consulting the Jewish community's documents on Schütz as well as his refugee file (flyktingakt). See his email (dated Jun. 17, 2015) to the author. Finally, I also thank Åke Norström (Riksarkivet, Stockholm) for checking for any additional information on Schütz in the Statens utlänningskommission (Immigrant services bureau) fonds. See his email (dated Jun. 30, 2015, reference number 2015/06246) to the author.

[117] See the scanned census document in the email (dated Jun. 5, 2015) from Per Forsberg (Landsarkivet i Göteborg) to the author.

[118] AJJDC, New York, 1941–1967, Stockholm Collection, Olika Organization P-S 1941–1949. To retrieve all the letters, one simply has to enter "Otto Schutz" in the "simple search" bar of their database. See http:// search.archives.jdc.org/ (accessed Sep. 5, 2015).

[119] AJJDC, New York, 1941–1967, Stockholm Collection, Olika Organization P-S 1941–1949, document ID 910337, letter (dated Feb. 13, 1946) from American Jewish Joint Distribution Committee in Stockholm to Mrs. [Inga] Gottfarb. The letter is written in German.

[120] Ibid. document ID 944740, letter (dated Jan. 12, 1943) from Otto Schütz to Mr. [Marcus] Levin.

[121] National Archives at Washington, D.C., Records of the Immigration and Naturalization Service, Passenger and Crew Lists of Vessels Arriving at New York, 1897–1957, manifest of in-bound passengers (aliens) first class on m.s. *Stockholm*, Gothenburg-New York, August 15–23, 1951, Microfilm serial T 715, 1897–1957, Microfilm roll 8025, 183. Retrieved from

(1885–1951?), living in New York. In October 1951, he returned by ship to Sweden.[122] Otto Schütz's emigration to the USA in January 1952 seems related to the death of Leon Baum. This Romanian man was the husband of Schütz's sister, Hermine Baum (née Schütz, 1893–1967). Leon Baum was a bank director before the war. He and his wife lived in Brno, where they were married. Baum emigrated by ship to New York in February 1942, his wife and son following later that year. Mother and son were accompanied on the same ship by Otto Schütz's youngest sister, Olga Schütz (1895 or 1896–?).[123] According to Leon Baum's naturalization record, issued in New York in December 1947, the couple indeed had one son, Thomas Baum (1931–1985), who died in February 1985.[124] In April 2016, I managed to contact Thomas Baum's daughter, L. Baum.[125] L. Baum wrote to me that the few remaining pictures of Otto Schütz were discarded when her mother moved a few years previously.[126]

L. Baum's friendly and helpful email exchange with me in May 2016 revealed that Otto Schütz married Heda Stiassny (née Fischer, 1893–?) in the United States. According to L. Baum's mother, Isabel Milstein Merritt, Schütz had a relationship with this woman when he was still in Brno. The father of Heda Stiassny's children, Emanuel Stiassny, died on March 15, 1941, and is buried in the Jewish cemetery in Brno.[127] Clearly, Schütz worked very hard to find a safe refuge in Europe for Heda Stiassny as well as for one of her children, Fränze Löwy (Bayer) (née Stiassny, 1915–2002), and for Heda Stiassny's sister, Greta Ascherová (née Fischerová, 1891–?).[128] One letter seems to show that Heda Stiassny followed Otto Schütz's trail. She also fled from Norway to Sweden in October 1942.[129] She was in the same Nolhage Läger refugee camp in Alingsås as Otto Schütz.[130] Presumably, she (and Otto Schütz) played a part in saving thirty-four Jewish children brought from Czechoslovakia to Norway in October 1939. As a first-hand witness of the operation, Stiassny reported on it in the Czechoslovak Jewish magazine *Hadoar*.[131] When Schütz went to the USA, in

the "New York, Passenger Lists, 1820–1957" database on Ancestry.com (accessed Jun. 7, 2015).

[122] See the "U.S., Departing Passenger and Crew Lists, 1914–1966" database on Ancestry.com (accessed Mar. 5, 2023). This likely explains why another source reports that he moved to the USA on January 31, 1952. See the scanned census document in the email (dated Jun. 5, 2015) from Per Forsberg (Landsarkivet i Göteborg) to the author.

[123] Olga Schütz married late in life and had no children. See email (dated Jul. 31, 2016) from L. Baum to the author.

[124] National Archives and Records Administration USA (NARA), New York City branch, naturalization records, Federal Court Eastern District of New York, petition for naturalization of Leon Baum, 453510, Dec. 16, 1947. I thank Angela Tudico (the National Archives at New York City) for her friendly help in efficiently obtaining a copy of this petition in September 2015.

[125] I owe this contact to the excellent help provided to me by Renée Stern Steinig (Jewish Genealogy Society of Long Island) in April 2016. I contacted the daughter L. Baum through her Facebook account on April 20, 2016. She replied by email on May 13, 2016. On April 21, 2016, I also sent a letter to Thomas Baum's wife, L. Baum's mother, Mrs. Isabel Milstein Merritt (1934–). L. Baum wrote to me that her mother had indeed received this letter.

[126] Email (dated May 13, 2016) from L. Baum to the author.

[127] He has a commemorative stone in the Jewish cemetery in Brno in section 26c, row 3, grave 9. There seems to be no family link between Emanuel Stiassny and Alfred Stiassny (1883–1961).

[128] NA, Praha, fonds Ministerstvo sociální péče, Londýn (Ministry of Social Welfare, London), kart. n° 1007/43, inv. n° 1/659, microfilm 4299, f. 427, letter (dated Mar. 17, 1943) from Otto Schütz to Dr. [Marie] Fischer-Ascher.

[129] NA, Praha, fonds n° 828, Ministerstvo vnitra Londýn (Ministry of Interior, London), kart. n° 52, sign. 2-1/796/2. See also NA, Praha, fonds Ministerstvo sociální péče, Londýn (Ministry of Social Welfare, London), kartotéka, kart. n° 34, sign. 1/ 489, microfilm 1007/34/1.

[130] NA, Praha, fonds Ministerstvo sociální péče, Londýn (Ministry of Social Welfare, London), kartotéka, kart. n° 34, sign. 1/489, microfilm 1007/34/ 1. The camp's name is spelled Nolgaha in the document, which also states that she was put there with nine other Czechs. The document further reveals that she was a protected person supported by a confidential Czechoslovak individual in Sweden, and that she had received money to help other Czechoslovaks in Sweden.

[131] Stiassny, Nov. 15, 1939, 2. She dated her text October 31, 1939, adding that it was written in Oslo. Otto Schütz, who was likely also there when the children arrived in Oslo on the night train, is – likely on purpose – not named.

August 1951, Heda Stiassny travelled on the same ship.[132] Only much later, when Otto Schütz was already sixty-five years old (so, around 1957), did he marry Heda, likely for financial reasons.[133]

I was told by L. Baum (who communicated my questions to her mother and reported her answers to me) that Schütz sent materials proving that he had been active in the anti-fascist movement by boat to the USA, but that this boat sank: "My mother recalled that German paperwork implicating my uncle in anti-Nazi activity was on a boat that sank and was, therefore, lost".[134] The further fate of Heda Stiassny's second daughter, Fränze Löwy (Bayer), who also moved to the USA, remains unclear. She married, but apparently had no children.[135] Heda Stiassny's youngest daughter, Rudi Stiassny (1917–1944?), stayed behind in Czechoslovakia for unknown reasons and perished in the Holocaust. Her Prague police file shows that she tried but failed to emigrate to Norway.[136] She was deported on transport "Bf" from Prague to Terezín on September 8, 1942, and further transferred to Auschwitz on transport "Eq" on October 12, 1944.[137] Edmund White claims that Otto Schütz worked for the United Restitution Organization (URO) in New York after the war.[138] Another source claims that he was a welfare worker for the United Nations in the same city.[139] Otto Schütz died in New York in November 1970. I was unable to find any further traces of relatives since I found no published obituary for Otto Schütz.[140]

[132] National Archives at Washington, D.C., Records of the Immigration and Naturalization Service, Passenger and Crew Lists of Vessels Arriving at New York, 1897–1957, manifest of in-bound passengers (aliens) first class on m.s. *Stockholm*, Gothenburg-New York, August 15–23, 1951, Microfilm serial T 715, 1897–1957, Microfilm roll 8025, 183. Retrieved from the "New York, Passenger Lists, 1820–1957" database on Ancestry.com (accessed Jun. 7, 2015).

[133] Email (dated May 18, 2016) from L. Baum to the author.

[134] Ibid.

[135] Email (dated Jul. 31, 2016) from L. Baum to the author.

[136] NA, Praha, fonds Policejní ředitelství Praha II – všeobecná spisovna, 1931–1940, kart. n° unknown, sign. S 5586/48, Stiassná Rudolfina; available online at https://www.holocaust.cz/en/database-of-digitised-documents/document/388707-stiassna-rudolfina-nezpracovano/ (accessed Mar. 5, 2023).

[137] See http://www.holocaust.cz/databaze-obeti/obet/127741-rudolfina-stiassna/ (accessed Nov. 1, 2016).

[138] White dubs it the United Restitution Office (White 1993, 134). For more information on the history of this organization, see https://www.cjarchives.ca/archives/uro/history/history.htm (accessed May 4, 2021). There is a listing for "Dr. Otto Schutz" at 777 West End Avenue (*Manhattan Telephone Directory* 1959–60, 1427).

[139] Private archive, Yvonne Oliver, "Otto Schütz, Man & doctor – on the death of Dr. Scherbak", transcript and English translation of obituary for Dr. Leopold Scherbak (1871–1936), undated [originally 1936]. See also Soetaert 2024.

[140] For Otto Schütz's death date, see Social Security Administration, Washington D.C., USA, Social Security Death Index, 1935–2014, issue state New York, issue year 1952–1953, record Otto Schütz (born Jul. 26, 1892), retrieved from the Ancestry.com database (accessed Jun. 7, 2015). Unfortunately, since I am not related to Otto Schütz, and his death record does not predate 1948, I was not legally entitled to obtain a copy of his death certificate from the New York City Department of Health.

6. ROBERT HERRMANN (1899–1995)

Robert Herrmann was the younger of the two children of Friedrich August Her(r)mann (1859–1923) and Hermine Schüller (1873–1939).[141] At the beginning of his career, Karl Fein briefly worked in the law office of Robert Herrmann's father, Friedrich August Herrmann. Likely, Fein was supposed to take over the practice. For his part, Robert Herrmann was Karl Fein's very first intern in 1924–26.[142] In his early youth, Robert Herrmann was a Communist.[143] He ran a law office jointly with the lawyer Felix Gallia (1901–1942?).[144] Max Pokorný Jr. (1902–?) or his father, Max Pokorný Sr. (1874–), liquidated Robert Herrmann and Felix Gallia's joint law office in 1939.[145] From 1932 onwards, Robert Herrmann was the president of the Brno B'nai B'rith Moravia lodge.[146] Robert Herrmann and Felix Gallia donated to a charity organization in 1935.[147]

Robert Herrmann's first wife was the engineer Lisbeth Wolf (1898–1942?). They married in 1923 and had a daughter named Agnes (1928–1942?). Presumably before the war, Lisbeth Wolf began an extramarital affair with Herrmann's law partner, Felix Gallia. Felix Gallia, Lisbeth Herrmann and Agnes Herrmann were deported on transport "Af" from Brno to Terezín on March 31, 1942. Two weeks later, on April 18, 1942, they were further transferred to Rejowiec (Poland) on transport "Ap".[148] Apparently, Felix Gallia lived with Lisbeth Wolf in Robert Herrmann's house before they were both deported.[149] Shortly before the start of the war, Robert Herrmann emigrated to England. In December 1942, when in England, Robert Herrmann tried to prevent the deportation of his wife, his daughter and Felix Gallia, but it was already too late.[150] Robert Herrmann's marriage to his first wife Lisbeth was officially dissolved in 1947 because she died in the Holocaust.[151] Robert Herrmann died in 1995

[141] Cf. Friedrich Hermann's home certificate in AMB, Brno, fonds B 1/39, mentioning only Robert Herrmann. Robert Herrmann had an older sister, Helene Herrmann (1893–?), who will be treated below.

[142] *Seznam advokátů dle stavu koncem roku 1923* 1924, 35; *Seznam advokátů dle stavu koncem roku 1924* 1925, 36; *Seznam advokátů dle stavu koncem roku 1925* 1926, 35. That Herrmann and Fein's friendship or acquaintance continued may be indicated by their both being elected as *Prüfer für Richteramtskandidaten* (examiners of candidate judges) in the Mährische Advokatenkammer (Moravian Bar Association). See *Tagesbote*, Dec. 12, 1937, 6. That same year, both men also made a donation to the Liga für Menschenrechte. See *Tagesbote*, Jun. 7, 1937, 4.

[143] "Aus der roten Häuslichkeit" (From the red domesticity), *Tagesbote*, May 10, 1921, 4.

[144] MZA, Brno, fonds G 427, Německá správa zabaveného majetku Brno, kart. n° 10, f. 741.

[145] *Věstník Moravské advokátní komory v Brně*, April 1939, 2. Since Max Pokorný Jr., Robert Herrmann and Felix Gallia – born in 1902, 1899 and 1901, respectively – might have known each other as law students, I think it likely that Max Pokorný Jr. was the one who liquidated the co-owned law office.

[146] *B'nai B'rith: měsíčník Velkolóže pro Československý stát = Monatsblätter der Grossloge für den Čechoslovakischen Staat*, vol. 11, n° 2, 1932, 70. By 1935, the lodge's president was Isidor Schulz. See Rys 1938, 274.

[147] *Tagesbote*, Jan. 17, 1935, 3.

[148] See Kárný et al. 1995 (the record for Agnes [Anežka] Herrmann is missing from the www.holocaust.cz database). In the transport "Af" list, the three had transport numbers 26, 27 (mother and child) and 33 (Felix). In the transport "Ap" list, their transport numbers were 112, 113 and 114.

[149] The index cards in the "Ghetto Theresienstadt card file" (ITS database) show that Felix Gallia and Agnes Herrmann, the daughter of Robert and Lisbeth Herrmann, were both living at 6 Alleegasse (V aleji) before being deported from Brno. See https://collections.arolsen-archives.org/en/archive/5027821/?p=1&s=felix%20gallia&doc_id=5027821 and https://collections.arolsen-archives.org/en/archive/5044477/?p=1&s=Ane%C5%BEka%20Herrmann&doc_id=5044477 (both accessed May 10, 2021). (I did not find Lisbeth Herrmann's index card in this ITS database.) The Alleegasse (V aleji) house was owned by Robert Herrmann. See MZA, Brno, fonds G 427, kart. n° 10, f. 741.

[150] USHMM, Washington, database n° 22199, List of evacuation applicants, RG-48.015M, original source is in NA, Praha, Ministerstvo sociální péče, London (Ministry of Social Welfare, London), document n° RG- 48.015M.0001.00000363.jpg, applicant Robert Herrmann (London), n° 8170, dated *ca.* Dec. 5, 1942, f. 11; available online at https:// www.ushmm.org/online/hsv/wexner/cache/1620603209-486200-RG-48.015M.0001.00000363.jpg (accessed May, 10, 2021).

[151] See https://encyklopedie.brna.cz/home-mmb/?acc=profil_osobnosti&load=20621 (accessed Dec. 12, 2016).

in London in the Heinrich Stahl House, a Jewish home for the elderly. Like Otto Schütz, during and after the war, Herrmann was actively involved in the fates of Jewish victims of National Socialism.

In 1962, Robert Herrmann wrote an article for the periodical of the British Association of Jewish Refugees (AJR) on restitution legislation.[152] At my request, a search notice was placed in the February 2017 issue of the *AJR Journal* inquiring about Herrmann's further fate.[153] Very soon after the issue came out, Erika Judge contacted me to say that her husband, Robert Judge, had worked with Robert Herrmann in a law firm. She also wrote to me that Robert Herrmann had a stepdaughter, Ruth P. Barnett, living in the USA and shared her contact information with me.[154] On February 4, 2017, I had a telephone conversation with Ruth Barnett's husband, Alan W. Barnett (1928–). I learned from him that Herrmann's second wife was Helene Panofsky (née Bloch, 1904–1965). Helene Panofsky and Robert Herrmann seemed to have known each other already in 1939.[155] It is not known if this friendship or relationship was linked to his first wife's – Lisbeth Wolf's – extramarital affair.

Helene Panofsky (née Bloch) was initially married to the German banker Alfred Panofsky (1899–1973). This marriage produced two children, Hans Eugen Panofsky (1926–2013) and Ruth P. Barnett (née Panofsky, born *ca.* 1927). Hans and Ruth Panofsky later became Robert Herrmann's stepchildren. Helene Herrmann (née Bloch) died in a car accident in 1965 while on a trip to Czechoslovakia with Robert Herrmann. Robert Herrmann entered into another relationship after the death of his second wife, but unfortunately Mr. Barnett could not remember the woman's name. Robert Herrmann's third partner seems to have inherited Robert Herrmann's estate, meaning that she also likely inherited the lawyer's personal papers.

On February 13, 2017, I was contacted by Michael Cohn, who had also seen the search ad in the February issue of the *AJR Journal*. He knew of Robert Herrmann through his professional activity in a law firm. Mr. Cohn also brought me in contact with his former colleague, David King-Farlow, who administered Robert Herrmann's estate, and whose name I remembered from Robert Herrmann's death certificate.[156] He wrote to me that Robert Herrmann's last partner was a certain Viola Vondrak (?–2003).[157] I sent a letter to her last known address on March 3, 2017. On March 16, 2017, Catrin Sammer, the current owner of the house where Mrs. Vondrak – and presumably her husband Clemens Vondrák – once lived sent me an email explaining that Mrs. Vondrak died in a car accident in 2003. She knew that the Vondrak couple had four children and gave me some indications as to where they could be found. I sent a letter to one of the sons, Thomas Vondrak, who replied by email (dated Apr. 9, 2017) that neither he nor any of his siblings had any notion of what happened to Robert Herrmann's personal archives. I later learned that Robert Herrmann knew the couple Jan (1896–1967) and Greta Vondrák (1899–?), who married in Brno in 1928.[158] One of their children was Clemens Vondrák (?–?). Finally, on the suggestion

[152] Herrmann 1962.

[153] I thank the editors Jo Briggs and Howard Spier for their kind help in this regard.

[154] Email (dated Feb. 2, 2017) from Erika Judge to the author.

[155] According to John Panofsky, there is a discussion within the current Bloch-Panofsky family about whether or not Robert Herrmann and Helene Bloch already knew each other before the war. John Panofsky's father was convinced that they did. See email (dated Aug. 1, 2018) from John Panofsky to the author.

[156] On February 6, 2017, I ordered the death certificate of Robert Herrmann.

[157] See the two emails (dated Feb. 13, 2017) from Michael Cohn to the author; email (dated Mar. 1, 2017) from David King-Farlow to the author.

[158] See the "Vienna, Austria, Catholic Church Registers, 1600–1960" database, birth registration of Johann Vondrák (born May 9, 1896), on Ancestry.com (accessed Mar. 6, 2023). For Robert Herrmann's knowing Johannes Vondrák and his wife Greta, see Library and Archives Canada/ Bibliothèque et archives Canada, Ottawa, manuscript division, fonds Stephen S. Barber, MG 31, H 113, Personal records and correspondence, vol. 12, file n° 1, letter (dated May 18, 1967, 2) from Robert Herrmann to Stephen Barber.

of Michael Cohn and David King-Farlow, on April 13, 2017, I approached another of Robert Herrmann's former colleagues, the lawyer John E. Rhodes, and inquired whether he had any idea where Herrmann's personal papers may have ended up. He contacted Andrew Kaufman, another former colleague of Robert Herrmann, who mainly contacted Erika Judge again, with the same negative result.

On July 31, 2018, I received an email from John Panofsky (1962–), a relative of Helene Herrmann (née Bloch). Helene Bloch's first marriage was to Alfred Panofsky, and John Panofsky is Alfred's grandchild. Mr. Panofsky kindly sent me a copy of Herrmann's last will. This will stated that, among other things, all of Herrmann's "personal chattels" (moveable properties) were to be given to Countess Sylvia des Fours Walderode zu Mont und Athienville (née Gallia, 1922–2017), an English artist living in Leatherhead (Surrey, UK) who, in 1981, married the Catholic writer and businessman Peter Francis Askonas (1919–2007).[159] In December 2018, I identified the countess's son, the jeweler and businessman Charles Alfred Arthur des Fours-Walderode (1949–), who had a business in Aberdeen, but I was initially unable to reach him due to inaccessible UK contact information.[160] On May 6, 2021, I phoned Mr. des Fours-Walderode and we had an amicable conversation about his mother's friendship with Robert Herrmann. In the email conversation that followed, I learned that Felix Gallia, the lover of Robert Herrmann's first wife, was Charles des Fours-Walderode's maternal grandfather.[161] This explains the special postwar bond between Robert Herrmann and Sylvia des Fours Walderode, one likely conditioned by (broken) family relationship dynamics, whether acknowledged or not.

At present, I do not think that there is much chance of Robert Herrmann's archival estate ever being found, supposing, of course, that this part of his estate still exists. However, Charles des Fours-Walderode promised me that, as soon as the Covid crisis subsided, he would check his UK house to see if it contained any documents once belonging to Robert Herrmann.

Felix Bloch (1873–?) and Louise Landesmann (1881–1942) – the parents of Robert Herrmann's second wife, Helene Herrmann (née Bloch) – were deported to Łódź on the Prague transport IV. There is a chance that Karl Fein and this couple met in Łódź. Helene Herrmann was also the sister of Erwin Bloch (1902–1986), who was married to Anna Bloch (née Scherbak, 1904–1991). The couple lived in Brno before the war, emigrating to England in time. Anna Bloch knew Kurt Hiller, Hugo Iltis, Otto Schütz and most likely also Magnus Hirschfeld.[162]

I also researched Robert Herrmann's sister, Helene Herrmann (1893–?), but was not able to determine her further itinerary. Like her brother Robert, she may have emigrated to England.[163] She married Rudolf Kraus (1888–1941), but the couple divorced. Rudolf Kraus was convicted by a summary court martial on October 3, 1941, and died in Mauthausen in October or November 1941.[164] The couple had one

[159] I thank John Panofsky for his friendly help in sending me a copy of Robert Herrmann's will. For more information on Peter Francis Askonas, see https://www.independent.co.uk/news/obituaries/peter-askonas-433860.html (accessed Dec. 2, 2018). Sylvia Gallia's first husband was *Graf* (Count) Carl Friedrich Theodor des Fours-Walderode zu Mont und Athienville und von Eckhausen (1904–2002).

[160] See http://vat-search.co.uk/RbEn_Charles+Alfred+Arthur+Des+Fours+Walderode+%7C+Local+Talent+Jewels, accessed Dec. 2, 2018. For more genealogical info on the des Fours-Walderode family, see http://patricus.info/Rodokmeny/Desfours.txt (accessed May 10, 2021).

[161] Felix Gallia's wife, Dr. Irene Mihelis (?) (1898–1987), died in 1987 in Vienna. I owe this information to Charles des Fours-Walderode. See his email (dated May 10, 2021) to the author.

[162] Soetaert 2024.

[163] Robert Herrmann's will bequeathed some money to a certain Elisabeth Kraus, who also lived in Heinrich Stahl House, but she was probably not Helene Kraus (née Herrmann).

[164] MZA, Brno, fonds B 340, Gestapo Brno, kart. n° 288, sign. 100-288-7, file Rudolf Kraus. Kraus was tried and convicted by summary court martial, his belongings confiscated and handed over to the Gestapo. Rudolf Kraus's home certificate in the

son, Ernst Konrad Kraus (1914–1941), who died in Auschwitz. Ernst Kraus divorced his wife Cecilia Holoubková (1915–?) in March 1941, presumably because of his being Jewish.[165] Cecilia then married Heinz Münz (1921–?) in March 1946. Rudolf Kraus married Regina Heiligová (1889–?) in 1920, but they divorced in January 1938.[166] They had one son, Heinz Peter Kraus (1921–?). Heinz Peter fought in the Czechoslovak army during the war and returned to Brno in 1946.

AMB, Brno, fonds B 1/39, states that Kraus died in Mauthausen on November 1, 1941. However, this was most likely the date that the news of his death reached Brno. The October 20, 1941 date of death was retrieved from the Mauthausen deaths database, https://raumdernamen.mauthausen-memorial.org/ (accessed May 12, 2021).

165 AMB, Brno, fonds B 1/39, home certificate Ernst Kraus.

166 On Rudolf Kraus's home certificate in the AMB, Brno, fonds B 1/39, it says that Heiligová received a passport (in 1940?) from the Prague police so that she could emigrate. She is not listed in the www.holocaust.cz database or in Kárný et al. 1995.

7. INVENTORY (DATED MARCH 18, 1938) OF GIESE'S BRNO APARTMENT (8 SCHÜTZENGASSE/STŘELECKÁ) (ENGLISH TRANSLATION AND CZECH ORIGINAL)[167]

ENGLISH TRANSLATION:

[p. 1, f.4]

Copy.
List of items.

Hallway:
1./ 1 three-door wardrobe with 3 men's suits and linen,
2./ 1 hanger with 2 winter coats, 3 hats, 1 light winter hat and 3 scarves,
3./ 1 carpet,
4./ 11 pictures on the walls, 1 mask and 1 plate

Kitchen:
1./ 3 cupboards with kitchen equipment,
2./ 1 kitchen table,
3./ 1 upholstered chair,
4./ 3 pairs of men's shoes, 1 pair of rain boots,
5./ 1 empty box,
6./ 1 painting,
7./ 1 "Norma" stove.

I. Room:
1./ 1 ottoman,
2./ 2 blankets and 1 pillow,
3./ 1 iron bed warmer,
4./ 1 drawing board,
5./ gas stove.

II. Room:
1./ 2 boxes with straw and various prints,
2./ 1 big empty suitcase,
3./ 10 empty boxes,
4./ 1 box with photographic negatives,
5./ 1 three-door cabinet with books and 11 wax models of men's and women's genitals,
6./ 1 suitcase with paintings,
7./ 1 chair,
8./ iron stove,
9./ 85 pieces of various paintings on the walls of the room,
10./ 1 wall cabinet with birth instruments,

III. Room:
1./ 1 French sofa,
2./ 1 table,
3./ 5 upholstered chairs,
4./ 1 iron stove,

[167] Source: MZA, Brno, fonds C 107, Německý úřední soud Brno (Deutsches Amtsgericht Brünn), kart. n° 256, sign. 5aV 3/41, f. 4.

5./ 2 bookcases / 535 pieces/,
6./ 1 radio table,
7./ 1 desk,
8./ 1 iron stove shield,
9./ 1 dresser,
10./ 1 water bucket,
11./ 1 litter bin,

[p. 2, f. 4b]

12./ 1 gray men's suit and 1 blue men's shirt,
13./ 1 Chinese table cover,
14./ 1 carpet,
15./ 2 pillows,
16./ 1 small leather briefcase,
17./ 4 painted wall hangings,
18./ 19 pieces of various paintings,
19./ 1 desk lamp,
20./ 1 nickel men's watch,
21./ 1 fountain pen with gold tip,
22./ 1 vase on the table.

Bathroom.
4 dirty towels and dirty laundry.

In Brno on March 18, 1938.

CZECH ORIGINAL:

[p. 1, f. 4]

Opis.
Seznam věcí.

Předsíň:
1./ 1 tříkřídlová skříň – v níž jsou 3 pánské obleky a prádlo
2./ 1 věšák, na němž jsou 2 zimní kabáty, 3 klobouky, 1 čepice, barvy světlé a 3 nákrční šály,
3./ 1 koberec,
4./ 11 obrazů na stěnách předsíně, 1 maska a 1 talíř

Kuchyně:
1./ 3 skříně s náčiním pro kuchyň,
2./ 1 kuchyňský stůl,
3./ 1 čalouněná židle,
4./ 3 páry černých pánských bot, 1 pár gumových galoší,
5./ 1 prázdná bedna,
6./ 1 obraz,
7./ 1 sporák „Norma".

I. Pokoj:
1./ 1 otoman,
2./ 2 přikrývky a 1 polštář,

3./ 1 železná vložka do postele,
4./ 1 rýsovací prkno,
5./ plynová kamna.

II. Pokoj:
1./ 2 bedny se slámou a různými tiskopisy,
2./ 1 prázdný velký kufr,
3./ 10 prázdných beden,
4./ 1 bedna s fotogr. negativy,
5./ 1 tříkřídlová skřín s knihami a 11 voskových odlitků mužských a ženských pohlavních orgánů,
6./ 1 kufr s obrazy,
7./ 1 židle,
8./ železná kamna,
9./ 85 kusů různých obrazů visících na stěnách pokoje,
10./ 1 nástěnná skřínka s náčiním pro pomoc při porodu,

III. Pokoj:
1./ 1 francouzská pohovka,
2./ 1 stůl,
3./ 5 čalouněných židlí,
4./ 1 železná kamna,
5./ 2 regály s knihami / 535 kusů/,
6./ 1 radio-stolek,
7./ 1 psací stůl,
8./ 1 železné chránítko ke kamnům,
9./ 1 prádelník,
10./ 1 kbelík na vodu,
11./ 1 koš naodpadky [*sic*, na odpadky],

[p. 2, f. 4b]

12./ 1 šedý pánský oblek a 1 modrá pánská košile,
13./ 1 čínská pokrývka na stůl,
14./ 1 koberec,
15./ 2 polštáře,
16./ 1 malý kožený kufřík,
17./ 4 nástěnné plachty malované,
18./ 19 kusů různých obrazů,
19./ 1 stolní lampa,
20./ 1 niklové pánské náramkové hodinky,
21./ 1 plnicí pero se zlatou špičkou,
22./ 1 váza na stole.

Koupelna.
4 špinavé ručníky a špinavé prádlo.

V Brně dne 18. března 1938.

8. FINAL SETTLEMENT OF THE KARL GIESE-KARL FEIN INHERITANCE (ENGLISH TRANSLATION AND CZECH ORIGINAL)[168]

ENGLISH TRANSLATION:

[p. 1, f. 31]

Sworn acknowledgement of assets:

I solemnly swear that I have inherited the following assets from Karl Giese of Brno, deceased March 17 in Brno, 8 Střelecká:

I. Active assets:

1./ old linen and clothes	K 200.-
2./ 1 large white wardrobe	
3 bookcases	50.-
3./ 1 watch with leather strap	80.-
4./ 1 larger hand-embroidered mat	20.-
5./ 1 older painting / oil / portrait damaged / in frame	100.-
6./ 1 newer oil painting / portrait / in frame	200.-
7./ 1 watercolor portrait in frame	50.-
8./ *ca.* 400 various scientific and belletristic books / old, worn,	1400.-
9./ *ca.* 40 smaller paintings / reproductions, some in frames	100.-
10./ several pieces of medical equipment, practically worthless	20
11./ various scientific materials, various photographs, films and negatives, 12 casts of anatomical parts	500.-
transfer ...	K 2,720.-

[p. 2, f. 31b]

transfer of active assets	K 2,720.-

II. Passive assets:

1./ cost of the funeral according to receipts from March 18, 1938, and January 18, 1939, received from the Brno Cemetery Management	K 520.-
2./ April rent according to the receipt from April 7, 1938, received from Mr. Sonnenschein, the owner of the house in Brno at 8 Střelecká	K 480.-
3./ glazing according to the bill from April 3, 1938[,] from František Heger[,] and according to the receipt from May 4, 1938	32.-
4./ milk from Mrs. Purová, paid by postal order	79.-
5./ debt to the advocate, Mr Tichauer in Paris according to the letter from June 12, 1937, 150 French francs, which means, according to the exchange rate on the date of death (March 17, 1938) 88 : 100, i.e.	132.-

[168] Source: MZA, Brno, fonds C 107, Německý úřední soud Brno (Deutsches Amtsgericht Brünn), kart. n° 256, sign. 5aV 3/41, f. 31.

K 1,243.-

The net worth of all assets is K 1,477.-

I reserve the right to amend this list in case the deceased has any right to a share of profits from the sale of books published in Paris by the Gallimard and Montaigne publishers.

In Brno, on May 25, 1939.

[signature of Dr. Karel (*sic*) Fein]

CZECH ORIGINAL:

[p. 1, f. 31]

Místopřísežné seznání jmění:

Přiznávám místopřísežně pozůstalostní jmění po Karlu Giese – evi z Brna, zemřelém dne 17. března 1938 v Brně, Střelecká ul. 8 takto:

I. Aktiva:

1./ staré prádlo a šaty K 200.-

2./ 1 velká bílá skříň

3 stojany na knihy 50.-

3./ 1 náramkové hodinky s koženým řemínkem 80.-

4./ 1 ručně vyšívaná větší dečka 20.-

5./ 1 starší obraz /olejový / portrét poškozený / v rámci 100.-

6./ 1 novější olejový obraz / portrét / v rámci 200.-

7./ 1 portrét Akvarel v rámci 50.-

8./ asi 400 různých vědeckých a benestrických [*sic*, beletrických] knih / starých, opotřebovaných / 1400.-

9./ asi 40 menších obrazů / reprodukce, částečně v rámci 100.-

10./ několik kusů lékařského nářadí skoro bezcenné 20.-

11./ různý vědecký materiál, různé fotografie, filmy a negativy, 12 odlitků anatomických odlitků [*sic*, údů?], zápisky 500.-

převod ... K 2720.-

[p. 2, f. 31b]

převod aktiv K 2720.-

II. pasiva:

1./ útraty pohřbu dle stvrzenek ze dne 18. 3. 1938 a 18. 1. 1939 hřbitovní správy města Brna K 520.-

2./ nájemné za duben podle potvrzení p. Sonnenscheina, majitele domu Brno, Střelecká 8, ze dne 7. dubna 1938 K 480.-

3./ za sklenářské práce podle účtu Františka Hegra ze dne 3. 4 1938 a dle st[v]rzení ze dne 4. 5. 1938 32.-

4./ za mlého pí. Purové, zaplaceno poštovní poukázkou 79.-

5./ pohledávka avokáta Tichauera v Paříži podle dopisu ze dne 12. června 1937 franc. frs. 150.- t.j. dle kursu ku dni úmrtnímu/ 17. 3. 1938 / 88 : 100, t.j. 132.-

K 1243.-

zůstává tudíž čistém jmění K 1477.-

Vyhražuji si doplniti tento seznam po případě, že by tu bylo nějakých nároků pozůstavitele z výtěžků knih, vydaných v Paříži u nakladatelství Gallimard a Montaigne.

V Brně, dne 25. května 1939.

[podpis Dr. Karel (*sic*) Fein]

9. KARL GIESE'S JULY 1937 APPEAL *(ODVOLÁNÍ)* TO THE MORAVIAN PROVINCIAL AUTHORITIES (ENGLISH TRANSLATION AND CZECH ORIGINAL)[169]

ENGLISH TRANSLATION:

[p. 1, f. 6]

[rubber stamp:]

Dr. Karel [*sic*] Fein
Lawyer
BRNO

[end rubber stamp].

To the Provincial office in Brno

Karel [*sic*] Giese, archivist and writer in Brno, 8 Střelecká
Dr Karel [*sic*] Fein, attorney at law in Brno, 35 Koliště

[signature Dr. Fein]

Appeal

to the decree of the Provincial Office in Brno of 8 July 1937, Unit n° 22241/I-7, to the Ministry of the Interior in Prague.

Once, power of attorney.

[p. 2, f. 6b]

By the decision of the Provincial Office of July 8, 1937, Unit n° 22241/I- 7, my application for residence was only granted in the political districts of Jihlava, Vel. Meziříčí, Třebíč, Nové Město na Mor. effective until October 30, 1937. I hereby submit the following in response to this decree, as I have not been granted residence in Brno or in the whole of the Czechoslovak Republic

appeal

to the Ministry of the Interior in Prague for the following reasons:

I was born in Berlin on October 18, 1898. I lived in Berlin until May 7, 1933 and worked for 18 years as secretary and archivist at the Institute of Sexual Science of the world-famous sex researcher Professor Dr. Magnus Hirschfeld, who died in Nice on May 13 [*sic*: 14], 1935. The said Institute of Sexual Science, as is well known, is the work of Magnus Hirschfeld, and he took upon himself the task of dealing on a scientific basis with sexual questions and reforms in the fields of sexual biology, pathology, sociology and ethnology. During my long years of activity, I gained a keen scientific knowledge of this field, which made me one of Magnus Hirschfeld's closest collaborators. Hirschfeld's scientific views completely contradicted the views on racism adopted by the present ruling regime in Germany, and this contradiction of views led to the dissolution of the Institute, whose scientific material was partly destroyed in the book-burning in May 1933. Part of it was saved and is in my possession. Since I was the most familiar with his work and ideas, from my many years of collaboration

[169] Source: MZA, Brno, fonds B 40, Zemský úřad Brno (Landesbehörde in Brünn), kart. n° 2138, sign. 5274/ 38, Odvolání do výměru zemského úřadu v Brně ze dne 8. července 1937 jedn. čís. 22241/I-7 k Ministerstvu vnitra v Praze, f. 6-11.

with him, Magnus Hirschfeld named me his material and spiritual heir in his will. Already in his lifetime, he stipulated that I should settle in Brno, as he considered the Czechoslovak Republic, and Brno in particular, the most suitable

[p. 3, f. 7]

soil where he could continue his scientific work. Already in his early lectures, Dr. Hirschfeld was in favor of the Czechoslovak Republic, finding warm understanding from the authorities, the public and the press. He also saw in the research work of Brno's Gregor Mendel the scientific precursor of his ideas. All of these circumstances, along with the personal relationships he cultivated with local figures, led him, as president of the World League for Sexual Reform, to propose, in 1932, that its 5th Congress – the earlier having been held in Copenhagen, Vienna, Berlin and London – be held in Brno. This 5th Congress was indeed held in Brno, in the rooms of Masaryk University. President Masaryk expressed his interest in this congress and validated it with a telegram with the following message:

> "The Office of the President of the Republic
>
> Number: D 5887/32
>
> In Prague, 6 September 1932.
>
> Mr.
> Josef Weisskopf, MD,
> Secretary General of the 5th International Congress of the World League for Science-Based [*sic*] Sexual Reform
> in Brno-Král.[ovo] Pole
>
> To your letter of 6 July 1932, n° O 1137/32, the Office of the President of the Republic informs you that the President is unable to register as a participant in the Fifth International Congress of the World League for Sexual Reform on a Scientific Basis in Brno or to attend the Congress in person and asks you to kindly excuse him.
> The President sends his greetings to all the participants of the Congress and wishes your proceedings every success.
>
> On behalf of the Office of the President of the Republic
>
> illegible signature."

The congress has aroused the liveliest interest both in this country and abroad among eminent scientists. The Brno scientists, professors Bělohlávek [*sic*: Bělehrádek], Trýb, Iltis, Norman Haire from London, Leunbach from Co-

[p. 4, f. 7b]

penhagen, D'Alsace [Dalsace] from Paris, Lewandovski [*sic*: Lewandowski] from Amsterdam, and many other foreign scientists took an active part in the congress and spread the reputation of Brno and the Czechoslovak Republic as the focus of scientific and spiritual endeavors.

When Professor Dr. Magnus Hirschfeld died in May 1935, it fell to me, according to his express wish, to continue his scientific life's work. His material arrangements allowed me to transport the remains of his Institute's scientific material to Brno. Since last year, I have been busy going through, organizing and compiling this material – books, newspaper clippings, scientific discussions, disease papers, manuscripts, scientific objects and paintings – in order to restore what was destroyed for research and science, and to rebuild the foundations for further scientific investigation. I stand in the midst of these undertakings and, at great material sacrifice, have rented a two-room apartment in which to establish this archive. I am happy to have found a home in Brno where I can devote myself to this scientific work. Here I can use the university library and encounter people with the greatest insight into the scientific and world views of Hirschfeld's works.

Allow me to point out that the late Magnus Hirschfeld entrusted all his legal affairs, for as long as he lived in exile, to my present attorney, the undersigned Dr. Karel Fein, who is thus best informed about all my legal affairs as Hirschfeld's successor. Consequently, I have in him, and thanks to his practical experience, a firm support, and this contributes to my peace of mind, since I know that my legal representative enjoyed Hirschfeld's favor and confidence. If the decision of the provincial authority is that I am to leave Brno and move

[p. 5, f. 8]

II.

to one of the places mentioned, I would lose every condition necessary to my existence and the possibility of continuing Hirschfeld's scientific work. Conditions for scientific work in the small towns mentioned do not exist. They have no scientific libraries and insufficient journals and newspapers. I am a complete stranger there, I know no one, and I cannot associate with people with the same scientific and spiritual interests to work on Hirschfeld's legacy. On top of that, I would suffer grievous material damage. It would cost a considerable amount of money to move twenty-three boxes weighing 2,000 kg, to say nothing of the fact that many of the objects are difficult to transport or that I could hardly accommodate all the items. I would have to dispose of these items, which, assembled and sorted by an expert hand, are of considerable value, completely against the will of the testator. I would also like to point out that, according to the express terms of Hirschfeld's will, I am appointed heir only on condition that I devote all my effort to scientific activity. I would not have this opportunity in any of the places mentioned and would thus be deprived of the material basis of my existence.

I do not know what considerations have induced the celebrated provincial authority to restrict my stay to these places, so I am perhaps not stating my conclusions correctly if I point out to the high ministry these other circumstances.

Neither before nor during my emigration was I in any way politically active or interested. Nor can I be regarded as a political émigré. However, as I have already stated, in connection with my collaboration with Magnus Hirschfeld, and in the interest of further joint work, I have somehow become a participant in his fate,

[p. 6, f. 8b]

despite his death. I am aware that in enjoying the hospitality in a foreign country I must be very careful and conscientious about its regulations, interests and fundamental opinions. This thought is so far from my mind that I cannot think that my actions could somehow be in contradiction with the state of the Czechoslovak Republic. During the whole period of my stay in Brno, now three years, with brief interruptions, I have lived in the greatest seclusion, devoting myself to my scientific work, and only seeking rest in the exchange of ideas with the circle of people who, united with me by the memory of Hirschfeld, seek to continue his scientific life work.

From the above it is obvious that the provincial authority's measure would destroy not only my modest existence, but also the life's work of the world-famous scientific researcher Dr. Magnus Hirschfeld, entailing that this scientific activity – which is also of great importance for Czechoslovak science's research work – would be lost, all the more completely because the name of Brno has been associated around the world with this scientific field as an effect of the last scientific congress.

I therefore ask that my appeal be accepted and the contested decree be amended to the effect that I am permitted to reside in the Czechoslovak Republic without local restrictions, with permanent residence in Brno.

If this appeal cannot be granted, I hereby respectfully

request,

that I be allowed to reside in the Czechoslovak Republic without local restriction, with permanent residence in Brno.

I ask that this appeal of mine be allowed to have suspensive effect until a final decision has been taken,

[p. 7, f. 11 (!)]

if any.

I enclose the power of attorney of my legal counselor.

Karel [*sic*] Giese.

[rubber stamp Zemský úřad v Brně (Provincial authority in Brno), dated Aug. 1, 1937]

CZECH ORIGINAL:

[p. 1, f. 6]

[rubber stamp:]

Dr. Karel [*sic*] Fein
advokát
BRNO

[end rubber stamp]

Zemskému úřadu v Brně

Karel [*sic*] Giese, archivař [*sic*, archivář] a spisovatel v Brně, Střelecká 8
drem [*sic*] Karlem Feinem, advokátem v Brně, Koliště č. 35

[signature Dr. Fein]

Odvolání
do výměru zemského úřadu v Brně ze dne 8. července 1937 jedn. čís. 22241/I-7
k Ministerstvu vnitra v Praze.

Jednou, plná moc.

[p. 2, f. 6b]

Výměrem zemského úřadu ze dne 8. července 1937 jedn. čís. 22241/I-7 bylo vyhověno mé žádosti o pobyt jen v politických okresech Jihlava, Vel. Meziříčí, Třebíč, Nové Město na Mor. a to platností do 30. října 1937. Do tohoto výměru, pokud jím mi nebyl povolen pobyt v Brně resp. na území celé Československé republiky podávám tímto

odvolání

k Ministerstvu vnitra v Praze z těchto důvodů:

Narodil jsem se v Berlíne dne 18.10.1898. Žil jsem v Berlíne až do 7.5.1933 a pracoval jsem 18 let jako tajemník a archivář v Ústavu sexuální vědu [*sic*, vědy] světoznámého sexuálního badatele profesora Dr. Magnuse Hirschfelda, jenž zemřel v Nice dne 13.

[*sic*, 14.] května 1935. Řečený ústav pro sexuální vědu jest, jak známo, dílo Magnuse Hirschfelda a vzal si za úkol obírati se na vědeckém podkladě otazkami a reformami sexuálními v oborech sexuální biologie, pathologie, sociologie a ethnologie. Nabyl jsem za své dlouholeté činností [*sic*, činnosti] pronikavých vědeckých znalostí tohoto oboru, jež mne uzpůsobily, že jsem byl jedním z nejbližších spolupracovníků Magnuse Hirschfelda. Vědecké názory Hirschfeldovy [*sic*, Hirschfelda] byly v naprostém rozporu s názory o rasismu, jež si osvojil nynější vládnoucí režim v Německu, a tento protiklad názorů vedl k zrušení uvedeného ústavu, jehož vědecký materiál byl v květnu 1933 při pálení knih dílem spálen, dílem zničen. Část mohla býti zachráněna a je v mém držení. Magnus Hirschfeld ustanovil mne [*sic*, mne ustanovil] totiž ve své závěti, jelikož jsem byl svou mnoholetou spoluprací nejlépe obeznámen s jeho dílem a jeho ideami, výslovně svým hmotným a duchovním dědicem. Ustanovil již za svého života, že se mám usídliti v Brně, jelikož pokládal Československou republiku a zejména Brno za nejvhodnější

[p. 3, f. 7]

půdu, kde lze pokračovati ve [*sic*, v] vedecké jeho Xsic, jeho vedeckéX práci. Dr. Hirschfeld byl Československé republice nakloněn, již ze svých dřívějších přednášek, kdy nacházel u úřadů, veřejnosti a tisku vřelé porozumění, spatřuje také v badatelské práci brněnského Gregora Mendla vědeckého předchůdce svých idei. Všechny tyto okolnosti a také osobní vztahy, jež pěstoval se zdejšími osobnostmi, příměli jej, že v roce 1932 navrhl jako předseda Světové ligy pro sexuální reformu, aby byl V. sjezd [*sic*] její – dřívější konány byly v Kodani, Vídni, Berlíně a Londýně – konán v Brně. Skutečně byl také tento V. sjezd [*sic*] v Brně v místnostech Masarykovy university. President Masaryk projevil zájem o tento sjezd a osvědčil jej telegramem tohoto znění:

"Kancelář Presidenta Republiky

číslo: D 5887/32

V Praze, dne 6. září 1932.

Pan [*sic*: Pán]
MUDr. Josef Weisskopf,
generální sekretář V. mezinárodního kongresu světové ligy pro sexuální reformu na vědeckém podkladě [*sic*]
v Brně-Král.[ovo] Pole.

K Vašemu přípisu ze dne 6. července 1932, čís. O 1137/32, sděluje kancelář presidenta republiky, že pan [*sic*, pán] president se nemůže přihlásiti za účastníka V. mezinárodního kongresu světově ligy pro sexuální reformu na vědeckém podkladě v Brně ani osobně se kongresu zučastniti, a žádá, abyste jej laskavě omluvili.
Pan [*sic*, pán] president vzkazu je [*sic*, vzkazuje] všem učastníkům kongresu pozdrav a přeje Vašemu jednání hojně zdaru.

Za kancelář presidenta republiky

podpis nečitelný."

Sjezd vzbudil u nás a v cizině nejživější zájem vynikajících vědeckých pracovníků. Brněnští vědci, profesoři Bělohlávek [*sic*, Bělehrádek], Trýb, Iltis, dále Norman Haire z Londýna, Leunbach z Ko-

[p. 4, f. 7b]

daně, D'Alsace [Dalsace] z Paříže, Lewandovski [*sic*: Lewandowski] z Amsterdámu a mnozí jiní cizozemští vědci zúčastnili se činně sjezdu a rozšířili pověst Brna a čsl. republiky jakožto ohnisko vědeckých a duchovních snah.

Když zemřel v květnu 1935 profesor dr. Magnus Hirschfeld, připadlo mně podle jeho výslovné poslední vůle, abych pokračoval v jeho životní vědecké práci, [*sic*,.] Jeho opatření, která učinil po hmotné stránce, mně umožnila, že jsem mohl zbytky vědeckého materiálu jeho ústavu dopraviti do Brna. Jsem od uplynulého roku zaměstnán prohlížením, pořádáním a sepisováním tohoto materiálu / knih, výstřížků z novin, vědeckých projednání, chorobopisů, rukopisních prací, vědeckých předmětů a obrazů /, abych tak obnovil pro bádání a vědu, co bylo zničeno a vybudoval zase základy pro další vědecký šetření. Stojím uprostřed těchto prací a najal jsem si s velkými hmotnými obětmi dvoupokojový byt, v němž zalozím [sic, založím] tento archiv. Jsem štasten, že jsem našel v Brně domov, kde mohu se věnovati této vědecké práci. Mohu zde používati universitní knihovny a stýkati se s lidmi, kteří mají pro věděcké a světové názory Hirschfeldových děl největší prozumení.

Buď mi dovoleno poukáza ti [sic, poukázati] na to, že zesnulý Magnus Hirschfeld svěřoval veškeré své právní záležitosti, pokud žil v emigraci, mému nynějšímu právnímu zástupci, podepsanému dru. [*sic*] Karlu Feinovi, který je tím nejlépe zasvěcen do všech mých právních záležitostí, jakožto právního nástupce Hirschfeldova. Mám v něm proto a dík jeho praktickým zkušenostem pevnou oporu, což přispívá k mému duševnímu uklidnění, neboť vím, že se tento můj právní zánástupce těšil přízni a důvěře Hirschfeldově. Zůstalo-li by nyní při rozhodnutí zemského úřadu, že mám Brno opustiti a stěhovati.

[p. 5, f. 8]

II.
do některého ze zmíněných míst, pozbyl bych všeho, co je nezbytnou podmínkou mé existence a možnosti pokračovati ve vědecké práci Hirschfeldově. V uvedených malých místech není nijakých předpokladů pro vědeckou práci, nemají vědeckých knihoven ani dostatek časopisů a novin, jsem tam docela cizí, nikoho neznám a nemohu se stýkati s lidmi, týchž vědeckých a duchovních zájmů, aby se mnou pracovali na Hirschfeldově odkazu; a k tomu by ještě prišlo, že bych hmotne utrpěl ohromnou škodu. Přestěhování věcí zabírajících 23 beden ve váze 2000 kg stálo by značné peníze, nehledíc k tomu, že mnohé předměty jsou těžko dopravitelné a že bych všechny věci stěží umístil. Musel bych tyto věci, které sebrány a roztříděny znaleckou rukou představují jako celek značnou hodnotu, zciziti, arci [*sic*] naprosto proti vůli zůstavitelově. Poukazuji ještě k tomu, že jsem podle výslovného nařízení Hirschfeldovy závěti ustanoven dědicem jen s tou podmínkou, že všechnu svou pracovní sílu věnuji vědecké činnosti. V žádném z uvedených míst neměl bych této možnosti a tím byl bych připraven i o hmotné základy své existence.

Není mi známo, jaké úvahy přiměly slavný zemský úřad, aby obmezil můj pobyt na tato místa, takže neuvádím své vývody snad správně, poukazuji-li vysokěmu ministerstvu ješte na tyto další okolnosti.

Ani před svou emigrací ani po její dobu nebyl jsem politicky nikterak činný ani interesován. Nemohu býti též pokládán za politického emigranta, nýbrž stal jsem se, jak jsem již uvedi, jen v souvislosti s mým spolupracovnistvím s Magnusem Hirschfeldem a v zájmu další společné práce jaksi podílníkem na jeho osu-

[p. 6, f. 8b]

du ještě přes jeho skon [*sic*, skonem]. Jsem si vědom, že požívaje [*sic*] pohostinství v cizí zemi musím nejpečlivěji a nejsvědomitěji šetřiti jejích předpisů, zájmů a zásadních názorů. Tato myšlenka tane mi tak před očima, že si vůbec nemohu mysliti, že bych se mohl nějak svým jednáním octnouti v rozporu s čsl. státem. Po celý čas mého pobytu v Brně a jsou tomu nyní s krátkými přestávkami tři roky, žil jsem v nějvětším ústraní, věnuji se své vědecké práci a jedinou zotavenou hledám ve výměně myšlenek s kruhem lidí, kteří, jsouce [*sic*, jsou] se mnou spjati památkou na Hirschfelda, snaží se ve vědeckém jeho životním díle pokračovati.

Z uvedeného jest zřejmé, že opatřením zemského úřadu byla by zničena nejen má skromná existence, ale přímo i životní práce světoznámého vědeckého badatele dra. Magnuse Hirschfelda, takže by byla vydána záhube vědecká činnost, v níž neustati má velký význam též pro badatelskou práci čsl. vědy a to tím více, že právě jméno města Brna bylo účinkem posledního vědeckého kongresu po celém světě spojováno s tímto vědním oborem.

Prosím tudíž, aby mému odvolání bylo vyhověno a napadený výměr změněn v ten smysl, že se mi povoluje pobyt v Československé Republice bez místního omezení s trvalým bydlištěm v Brně.

Kdyby tomuto odvolání nemohlo býti vyhověno, podávám pro ten případ uctivou

žádost,

aby mi byl povolen pobyt Československé Republice bez místního omezení s trvalým bydlištěm v Brně.

Prosím, aby tomuto mému odvolání, pokud se týče žádosti byl ponecán [*sic*, ponechán] odkladný účinek až do právoplatného rozhodnutí, po

[p. 7, f. 11 (!)]

případě vyřízení.

Plnou moc svého právního zástupce přikládám.

Karel [*sic*] Giese.

[rubber stamp Zemský úřad v Brně, dated Aug. 1, 1937]

10. BERLIN, BRNO, PARIS, FRESNES, NICE, VIENNA AND SWITZERLAND ADDRESSES WHERE KARL GIESE LIVED OR STAYED (1898–1938)

- Berlin: 17 Schulstraße, currently Berlin Mitte: October 1898–? (childhood).
- Berlin: December 1914 (?) until *ca.* May 7–8, 1933: 10 In den Zelten / 3 Beethovenstrasse (second-floor room in Magnus Hirschfeld's Institute of Sexual Science).[170]
- Zürich: *ca.* May 7–8, 1933 until *ca.* May 14, 1933 (with Magnus Hirschfeld in a hotel, possibly Hotel Central).
- Ascona-Moscia: *ca.* May 14, 1933 until end of July 1933: Casa Werner (address unknown, villa owned by Hilde Werner).
- Zürich: end of July 1933 until beginning of August 1933: address and host unknown.
- Brno: August 5, 1933 until end of December 1933: 46 Lesnická (Forstgasse) (room rented from Hedi and Emil Tschauner).
- Nice: end of December 1933 until end of February 1934: 25 Promenade des Anglais (Hôtel de la Méditerranée et de la Côte d'Azur).
- Nice: end of February 1934 until end of March 1934: 4 Rue Halévy (Camille Buisson's hotel/pension).
- Paris: end of March 1934 until April 14 or 15, 1934: 24 Avenue Charles Floquet (Magnus Hirschfeld's rental apartment).
- Paris: April 14 or 15, 1934 until June 15, 1934: 42 Rue de la Santé (Prison de la Santé).
- Fresnes: June 15, 1934 until July 15, 1934: 1 Allée des Thuyas (Prison de Fresnes).
- Paris: July 15, 1934 until October 25, 26 or even 27, 1934: 24 Avenue Charles Floquet (Magnus Hirschfeld's rental apartment).
- Brno: November 2, 1934 until January 23, 1935: 5 Hutterteich (Hutterův rybník) (room rented from Ferdinand and Ida Beamt).
- Vienna: January 30, 1935 until *ca.* May 30, 1936: 27 Mariahilferstrasse (in the apartment of Dr. Zalman and Sofie Schneyer).
- Brno: May 30, 1936 until mid-September 1936: 7c U dětské nemocnice (Kinderspitalgasse or also Beim Kinderspital) (in Karl Fein's rental apartment).
- Brno: mid-September 1936 until March 16 or 17, 1938: 8 Střelecká (Schützengasse) (Giese's rental apartment).

170 See the floor plan of the corner building's second floor, 10 In den Zelten / 3 Beethovenstrasse: https://magnus-hirschfeld.de/gedenken/historisches/institut/innenansichten/ (accessed May 21, 2021).

11. BRNO, PRAGUE AND ŁÓDŹ ADDRESSES WHERE KARL FEIN LIVED OR STAYED (1894–1942)

BRNO

- 3 Schreibwaldstrasse (later Lehmstätte or V hlinkách): 1894–96 (childhood).
- 37 Schreibwaldstrasse (later Lehmstätte or V hlinkách): 1896 (childhood).
- 5 Giskra-Strasse (later Kaunitzgasse or Kounicova): 1896 until *ca.* 1900 (childhood).
- 19 Rennergasse (Běhounská): *ca.* 1900 until ? (childhood).
- 6 Jodokstrasse (Joštova): November 27, 1923 until April 25, 1927.
- 41 Legionärenstrasse (třída Legionářů): April 25, 1927 until June 1, 1927.
- 29 Glacis (Koliště): July 19, 1927 until July 18, 1930.
- 1 Rathaussteig (U radnice): July 18, 1930 until October 2, 1930.
- 1 Schlossergasse (Zámečnická): November 29, 1930 until ? / December 9, 1931 until November 1, 1932.
- 7c U dětské nemocnice (Kinderspitalgasse or also Beim Kinderspital): November 26, 1932 until October 3 or 8, 1936.
- 35 Koliště (Glacis): October 3 or 8, 1936 until October 15, 1938.
- 2a Falkensteinerova (Falkensteinergasse): October 15, 1938 until October 31, 1938.
- 2a Akademická (Akademiegasse): October 31, 1938 until July 1, 1939.
- 9 Jesuitská (Jesuitengasse): July 1, 1939 until *ca.* September 8-9, 1939 or October 6, 1939.

PRAGUE

- 969/3 U Půjčovny (Leihamtsgasse) in Praha-Nove Město (Neustadt), Prague II (currently Prague I): October 1939 until July 16, 1940.
- 448/11 Erbenstrasse (Erbenova) in Praha-Karlin (Karolinenthal), Prague X (currently Prague VIII): July 16, 1940 until September 16, 1941.[171]

[171] The street's current name (and address) is 448/2 Urxova, Prague VIII. Riegrova, the original street name, was changed by the Germans during the war.

- 370/4 Gödinger Gasse (Hodonínská) in Praha-Karlin (Karolinenthal), Prague X (currently Prague VIII): June 19, 1941 until October 18, 1941, when Fein was summoned to be deported from Prague.

ŁÓDŹ

- 37 Łagiewnicka (Hanseatengasse) (former children's hospital): October 22, 1941 until *ca.* end of December 1941.
- 15 Franciszkańska (Franzstrasse) (former school building): *ca.* end of December 1941 until?
- 34 Franciszkańska (Franzstrasse): ? until May 2, 1942, the day Fein died.

12. OVERVIEW OF ELISE BRECHER'S LAST ADDRESSES IN BRNO (BRÜNN) BEFORE HER DEPORTATION

Around 1934, Elise Brecher lived at 34 Dr- Bedřich- Macků- Gasse (Dra Bedřicha Macků).[172] From approximately 1938 until at least late summer in 1939, she lived at 8 Mášagasse (Jana Máši).[173] Her last address in Brno before moving to the Jewish hospital was 4 Van der Strass-Gasse (Van der Strassova).[174] We know the names of three other people living at this last address, who were all deported at some point: the divorced lawyer Moritz Hirsch (1871–1942), Amalie Fischer (née Neumann, 1862–1942) and Otto Katz (1864–1942). Otto Katz was accompanied by his wife Helena Katz (née Singer, 1879–1942) on transport "Ah", deporting them from Brno to Terezín on April 4, 1942. On June 13, 1942, Helena Katz was further transferred to an unknown destination.[175] Moritz Hirsch does not seem to have been related to the lawyer Rudolf Hirsch (1895–1944), a collaborator of the JKG in Brno who figured in the main text.[176]

The house on Van der Strass-Gasse (Van der Strassova) where these people lived was owned by Berthold Fink (1880- 1940) and Helena Fink (née Schuschny, 1884-1942?).[177] Helena Fink was deported from Brno to Terezín on transport "Ad" on March 23, 1942. One month after she arrived in Terezín, on April 28, 1942, she was further transferred to Zamošč on transport "Ar". Berthold Fink emigrated to England in July 1939.[178] His name shows up on a list of Czechoslovak refugees who managed to escape to England. He died in England in November 1940.[179] Fink's wife Helena was still living in their house in March 1941 when it was sold by force.[180] The Fink couple had one daughter, Greta (1908–1985), whose married name was Seidl. Greta lived with her father Berthold in Cardiff in Wales, most likely in the company of her daughter Anita (1932–1993).[181] Greta married Emil Kotek (1885–1955) in 1945. In 1961, Anita Kotek married Joe Lewis (1924–2007). The couple had two daughters whom I was not able to identify.

Elise Brecher's very last address in Brno was the one belonging to the Jewish hospital on the first floor of the building at the corner of 27 Mühlgasse (Mlýnská) and 5 Stefansgasse (Štěpánská). She stayed there from January 6, 1942 until May 10, 1943.

[172] *Adreßbuch von Groß-Brünn* 1934, 145.

[173] *Seznam telefonních ústředen* 1938, 30; NA, Praha, fonds n° 375, Arizační spisy, kart. n° 191, sign. 1119, file L. & A. Brecher.

[174] AMB, Brno, fonds Z 1, resident registration card (dated Jan. 6, 1942) Elise Brecher.

[175] See http://encyklopedie.brna.cz/home-mmb/?acc=vyhledavani&q=Van+der+Strassova&search=vyhledat (accessed Nov. 12, 2015).

[176] See http://encyklopedie.brna.cz/home-mmb/?acc=profil_osobnosti&load=16535 (accessed Jul. 25, 2015); email (dated Jul. 29, 2015) from Jana Dosoudilová (AMB, Brno) to the author. I did not follow up on the life story of Moritz Hirsch's former wife, Frida Hirsch, or that of his two children, born in 1903 (Uli) and 1906 (Franz?).

[177] *Adreßbuch von Groß-Brünn* 1934, 190, 753.

[178] AMB, Brno, fonds Z 1, resident registration card Berthold Fink.

[179] See http://www.ushmm.org/online/hsv/person_view.php?PersonId=3730823 (accessed Dec. 7, 2015); England & Wales Death Index, 1916–2007, on Ancestry.com. Original data: General Register Office, indices of civil registrations in England and Wales reported quarterly to the General Register Office in London, deaths registered in October, November, December 1940, volume 1a, 955 (287), FIG-FIN, Marylebone (London).

[180] MZA, Brno, fonds B 392, Vystěhovalecký fond, úřadovna Brno, kart. n° 16, sign. n° 336, Berthold and Helena Fink, f. 33, 34b, 35b, 36.

[181] The National Archives, Kew, London, 1939 Register, reference RG 101/ 7261E, available online in the "1939 England and Wales Register" database on Ancestry.com.

13. OVERVIEW OF THE JEWISH TRANSPORTS FROM BRNO (1941–43)

- Transport "F": November 16, 1941 to Minsk, 1,000 people
- Transport "G": December 2, 1941 to Terezín, 1,000 people
- Transport "K": December 5, 1941 to Terezín, 1,000 people
- Transport "U": January 28, 1942 to Terezín, 1,000 people
- Transport "Ac": March 19, 1942 to Terezín, 1,000 people
- Transport "Ad": March 23, 1942 to Terezín, 1,000 people
- Transport "Ae": March 27 (or 29?), 1942 to Terezín, 1,000 people[182]
- Transport "Af": March 31, 1942 to Terezín, 1,000 people
- Transport "Ah": April 4, 1942 to Terezín, 1,000 people
- Transport "Ai": April 8, 1942 to Terezín, 923 people
- Transport "AAa": May 27, 1942 to Terezín, eighty-one people (or eighty-eight people: on May 10, 1943, seven more names were added post factum to this transport list)[183]
- Transport "Dg": July 1, 1943 to Terezín, sixty people (in fact, only fifty-three people)[184]
- Transport "Ez": September 13, 1943 to Terezín, one person[185]

[182] Kárný et al. 1995, 419; www.holocaust.cz (accessed May 19, 2021). Both give March 29, 1942, as the date of this transport, a date also given by Klementová 2014, 71. However, March 27, 1942, is the transport date given in Klenovský 2002, 18. I looked up the names of Julius Zwicker (1865–1947) and Marianne Waelsch (1865–1942?), both deported on transport "Ae", in the "Ghetto Theresienstadt card file" database at https://collections.arolsen-archives.org/ (accessed May 19, 2021). I noticed that, in both their cases, the date stamp was March 27, 1942, for transport "Ae". This leads me to think that the latter date, March 27, is therefore the correct date of the transport.

[183] See also n. 184 hereafter and chapter 17, p. 672 and n. 9 and n. 10.

[184] See chapter 17, pp. 671-72, for the reason that transport "Dg" only carried fifty-three people. This number is also given in Klenovský 2002, 18.

[185] This person could not be identified. Transport "Ez" is not mentioned on www.holocaust.cz (accessed May 19, 2021). This generic transport number "Ez" was used quite often when transporting only a single person or a small number people between mass transports. See the list of transports in Kárný et al. 1995, 63–74.

[186] MZA, Brno, fonds C 12, Krajský soud trestní Brno, III. manipulace, kart. n° 539, sign. TK XI 1687/32, letter (dated Apr. 29, 1932) to Policejní ředitelství v Brně (tisk ref.[erat], printed matter department), f. 17b.

[187] MZA, Brno, fonds C 12, Krajský soud trestní Brno, III. manipulace, kart. n° 539, sign. TK XI 1687/32, f. 24: "Josef Uher, továrník v Židenicích [Brno-Židenice], Dobrovského 21, dílna Masarykova 23, záznamů nemá". Dobrovského's current name is Gajdošova. Masarykova is today Stará osada. There might be a possible point of confusion here. Until 1927, Dobrovského was known as Masarykova. See https://encyklopedie.brna.cz/home-mmb/?acc=profil_ulice&load=1356 (accessed Mar. 6, 2023).

[188] MZA, Brno, fonds C 12, Krajský soud trestní Brno, III. manipulace, kart. n° 539, sign. TK XI 1687/32, f. 23b, back of resident registration card for Bohdan Hájek(!).

[189] After the war, the couple moved to a house in the same street (then renamed Gajdošova), 14 Gajdošova. They were already living at this address in 1934. See *Adreßbuch von Groß-Brünn* 1934, 489; AMB, Brno, fonds Z 1 and fonds B 1/39, Meldezettel and home certificate Josef Uher.

[190] Smutný 2012, 468.

[191] See, for example, *Adressbuch der Landeshauptstadt Brünn* 1942, 95: "Uher Josef & Comp., Spezial-Metallschraubenfabrik und Fassondreherei, Schimitz /Uher Josef a spol., specielní továrna na šrouby a fass. části, Židenice" (Uher Josef & Associates, Spe-

14. JAKUB OR JOSEF UHER?

There remains some uncertainty regarding the exact identity of one of the founders of the 1932 gay magazine *Kamarád*. The archival sources contain two different first names in connection with the last name Uher: Josef and Jakub. Even the Brno police were confused about exactly whom they were looking for. The matter must remain unresolved, but below are the known factors.

The April 1932 letter to the Brno police, announcing the founding of *Kamarád*, clearly mentions the name Jakub Uher, with the added address of 23 Masarykova in Brno-Židenice. Above the name, there is a question mark, most likely added in pencil by an investigating police officer.[186] This indicates that there were uncertainties about identifying the right man. A later handwritten police report (dated May 15, 1932) listing the people involved in the *Kamarád* case includes reference to "Josef Uher, factory manager in [Brno-]Židenice, 21 Dobrovského, workshop 23 Masarykova, he has no [criminal] records".[187] The same *Kamarád* police file also contains a resident registration card (for someone else) on the back of which is written: "Uher Jakub (Josef) 1883" along with the two aforementioned addresses, 21 Dobrovského and 23 Masarykova.[188]

There indeed existed a Josef Uher (1883–1963), born on March 15, 1883. He was married to Josefa Seifert (1885–1971) and had a daughter named Jaromíra (1910–?). The family lived at 21 Dobrovskýgasse (Dobrovského) in Brno-Židenice.[189] Possibly relevant to us is that Josefa Seifert's father, Adolf Seifert, was a typographer.[190] Josef Uher was a self-made man. He started as a factory worker; however, in 1918, he set up his own company producing special screws and molded parts.[191] In 1929, he joined forces with other business partners and founded the company "Josef Uher and Associates".[192] At the end of the 1930s, the factory employed approximately 120 people. In November 1944, the factory was bombed, killing several people. In 1948, the company was nationalized.[193] Its address, 23 Masarykova in Brno-Židenice, was the one mentioned in the *Kamarád* group's April 29, 1932 letter to the Brno police. Josefa and Josef Uher are buried in the Brno-Židenice cemetery in plot 1, graves 42–43, one of the cemetery's prestigious aisles near one of the entrances. I also found Josef Uher's birth certificate, which makes no mention of the first name Jakub.[194]

In their May 1932 report on the *Kamarád* case, the Brno police claimed that they were dealing with Josef Uher. The peculiar (and confusing) thing is that there was also a Jakub Uher (1878–1937), who, like Josef Uher, was born in Brno-Židenice, where he also lived. Most importantly, Jakub Uher was a business partner of Josef Uher and Associates.[195] The two were likely related since Josef Uher was a witness at the January 1905 wedding of Jakub Uher and Justina Talácek (1883–? >1945).[196]

cialized metal screw factory and molded parts shop, Brünn-Schimitz/Brno-Židenice)

192 Smutný 2012, 468; *Adresář zemského hlavního města Brna 1948* 1948, C: 115; *Adreßbuch von Groß-Brünn* 1934, 724.

193 Smutný 2012, 468.

194 Matriky uložené v Moravském zemském archivu v Brně, Brno-Zábrdovice, Nanebevzetí Panny Marie, birth registers, year 1883, číslo knihy 17268, entry n° 115 (dated Mar. 15, 1883), f. 110-111; available online at http://actapublica.eu/ (accessed November 5, 2021).

195 Leopold Andrýsik (?–?) and Theodor Kodar (?–?) were the third and fourth associated business partners, respectively. See *Adreßbuch von Groß-Brünn* 1932, 710; *Adresář zemského hlavního města Brna 1948* 1948, C: 115.

196 Matriky uložené v Moravském zemském archivu v Brně, Brno-Zábrdovice, Nanebevzetí Panny Marie, číslo knihy n° 17313, Julianov III, year 1905, entry n° 1 (dated Jan. 17, 1905), f. 179; available online at http://actapublica.eu/ (accessed Nov. 5, 2021). Josef and Jakub Uher were not brothers but they may have been cousins. When Josef Uher was married, on May 22, 1909, Jakub Uher was not a witness. Josef Uher's business partner Leopold Andrýsik was one of the two witnesses. See Matriky uložené v Moravském zemském archivu v Brně, Brno-Zábrdovice, Nanebevzetí Panny Marie, číslo knihy n° 17308, Židenice, tomus IX, year 1909, entry n° 40 (dated May 22, 1909), f. 13; available online at http://actapublica.eu/ (accessed Mar. 6, 2023).

It is possible, and even probable, that the Jakub Uher, mentioned in the initial April 1932 *Kamarád* letter to the Brno police, indeed referred to the man who joined the 1932 *Kamarád* project. So, it is interesting to observe that Jakub Uher, when asked where he could be reached, gave his business address, 23 Masarykova, and not his home address.[197] We may wonder if he was trying in this way to conceal these private affairs from his family. Before becoming a business partner of Josef Uher and Associates, Jakub Uher worked for the railroads.[198] Jakub Uher, his wife Justina, and two of their three daughters, Květoslava Provazníková (1907–?) and Jiřina Uhrová (1906–1931), are buried in the Brno-Židenice cemetery, in plot 4, graves 63–64. Their third daughter was Bohuvěra Uherová (1905–?). Finally, as I had done in the case of Josef Uher, I also looked at Jakub Uher's birth certificate, which also gives just one first name, Jacob [*sic*] Uher. A handwritten note was also added to Jacob Uher's entry in the birth register: "non-denominational since February 11, 1926".[199]

So, it is possible that the Brno police confused Jakub Uher with his business partner Josef Uher, whose work address was also 23 Masarykova. Jakub Uher's providing the latter as his supposed home address in the letter to the Brno police was likely the main cause of the confusion. In their registers, the police found the "Josef Uher and Associates" company at this address and likely concluded that Jakub Uher must be Josef Uher. However plausible an explanation this may be for the confusion, there is no definitive proof that Jakub Uher was indeed the right *Kamarád* man.

[197] Jakub Uher lived at 61/1487 Jungmannova in Brno-Židenice. See AMB, Brno, resident registration card and home certificate of Jakub Uher in fonds Z 1 and fonds B 1/39. Since 1933, the name of this street has been Rokycanova.

[198] AMB, Brno, fonds Z 1 and fonds B 1/39, registration card and home certificate of Jakub Uher; also, for example, *Adressbuch von Brünn* 1914, 20.

[199] Matriky uložené v Moravském zemském archivu v Brně, Brno-Zábrdovice, Nanebevzetí Panny Marie, birth registers, číslo knihy n° 17268, year 1878, entry n° 119 (dated Jul. 23, 1878), f. 267; available online at http://actapublica.eu/ (accessed Nov. 5, 2021): "seit 11/2/1926 Konfessionslos".

[200] On the search for Heinrich Brecher, see pp. 674-679.

[201] Email (dated Nov. 26, 2013) from Simon Kramer to the author.

[202] Renate Gautschi, of the Evangelical Reformed parish in Locarno, suggested that the priest may have passed away. Neither of the parish's current *Pfarrers* (pastors) could have known Herta Fein, since they had only held their posts for the previous ten years. See Renate Gautschi's email (dated Nov. 28, 2013) to the author.

[203] Renate Gautschi, of the Evangelical Reformed parish in Locarno, wrote to tell me that this was Andreas Henke, and that he had passed away. See her email (dated Nov. 28, 2013) to the author. Later, it became apparent that the first name she suggested was a mistake. See below.

[204] I thank Renate Gautschi (evangelisch-reformierte Kirchgemeinde, Locarno) for her assistance in this regard.

[205] Henke published in an issue of *Ingegneri e architetti svizzeri = Schweizer Ingenieur und Architekt = Ingénieurs et architectes suisses*, n° 36, 1980, 854.

[206] Email (dated Feb. 21, 2021) from Andreas Henke to the author.

[207] Rüegg et al. 1981, n.p.: "A la soirée de clôture, il y eut un souper chez Alberto, le grand ami de toujours de Jocelyn Fein, qui fut pour elle un vrai frère".

[208] Email (dated Feb. 21, 2021) from Andreas Henke to the author.

[209] Online message (dated Feb. 23, 2021) left at https://www.francacoray.com/le-village-des-racas (accessed Feb. 23, 2021).

[210] See A. O., Jan. 4, 1984, 7; "Postuma di Jocelyn Fein da sabato à Ca[sa] Ruggero", *Giornale del Popolo*, Dec. 15, 1983, 15. The local exhibition ran from December 17, 1983 until January 8, 1984. I thank Stefano Anelli (Archivio di Stato del Cantone Ticino, Bellinzona) for sending me, on March 29, 2021, digital copies of three local newspaper articles about this exhibition. I also sent an email (dated Feb. 23, 2021) to the Museo Casa Rusca (Locarno), asking whether they were in possession of Herta Fein's

15. HERTA FEIN (1902–1981)

Herta Fein (1902–1981), the wife of Karl Fein's brother Gustav, struck me as one of the primary witnesses I needed to locate. Besides Heinrich Brecher (Elise Brecher's youngest son), she was Karl Fein's only direct relative to survive the war.[200]

In 2013, I contacted Dora Bachmann (née Thalmann), who knew Herta Fein. Her son-in-law, Simon Kramer, kindly replied that his ninety-six-year-old mother-in-law could not remember anything more than Herta Fein's name.[201] Neither could anyone help me as regards the exact whereabouts or life story of the priest (*Pfarrer*) Gustav Hess, of the Evangelical Reformed parish (evangelisch-reformierte Kirchgemeinde, Comunità Evangelica riformata) in Locarno, who was Herta Fein's friend.[202]

The Forschungsinstitut Brenner-Archiv also contains a letter, which mentions a certain "Herr Henke", who may have been a good friend or even partner of Herta Fein. He, too, has likely passed away.[203] In January 2014, a message (in German) requesting more information about Herta Fein and Andreas Henke was posted in the three churches of the Evangelical Reformed parish in Locarno. No one responded.[204] In 2021, I contacted the only Andreas Henke living in Locarno, a tunnel engineer.[205] Since Mr. Henke was an honorary member of the Swiss Tunnelling Society, I managed to obtain his contact details by sending an email (dated Feb. 19, 2021) to Davide Fabbri, (then still) the society's vice president. Andreas Henke informed me that, most likely, the name was actually meant to be Alberto Henke, also an engineer.[206] This name also appeared in a text by Graziella Amstutz, an acquaintance of Herta Fein: "On closing night, there was a supper at Alberto's place, Jocelyn Fein's longtime friend, who was like a real brother to her".[207] This man likely died around 2005.[208] In February 2021, an online message was also left on the website of the Swiss writer Franca-Henriette Coray, who seems to have known Alberto Henke well, but there was no reaction.[209]

In 2021, I learned that, between December 1983 and January 1984, an exhibition was set up by Herta Fein's friends in Casa Ruggero-Keller in Locarno showing Herta Fein's drawings. Some of her art was sold, with the proceeds used to support young local artists.[210] The memorial brochure for Herta Fein, published in 1981, also contains four brief testimonies from four Locarno locals who knew her. It was in vain that I tried to contact these people and their current relatives.[211]

estate of approximately 600 drawings – mentioned in Rüegg et al. 1981, n.p. – but there was no answer.

[211] There was, first, Graziella Amstutz-Pedrazzini (1922–?), a Swiss artist. See Rüegg et al. 1981, n.p.; https://www.sikart.ch/kuenstlerinnen.aspx?id=4002669 (accessed Mar. 12, 2021). I sent an email (dated Mar. 12, 2021) to Associazione Famiglie Pedrazzini di Campo Vallemaggia, see http://pedrazzini.org/contatti/, (accessed Mar. 12, 2021), but there was no response. Anita Bianchi (née Pedrazzini, 1936–1992), leader of the Gruppo Tempo Libero in Muralto, was another name I found in the same memorial text for Herta Fein. I tried to make contact with her current relatives, sending a letter (dated Mar. 12, 2021) to Franco Bianchi, the husband or son of Anita Bianchi, but there was no response. Another name in the same memorial text was that of Dr. Nageswara Rao Vege (1932–?), who, besides being a doctor, was an artist and a writer. I was not able to definitively determine the identity of Walter Rüegg, mentioned as an author in Rüegg et al. 1981. Presumably, he was the Swiss-born sociology professor (1918–2015), who was the rector of Frankfurt University between 1965 and 1970. He ended his university career at the University of Bern, where he worked from 1973 until 1986. On November 18, 2021, I also contacted the Archiv für Zeitgeschichte in Zürich and the Bibliothek der Helmut-Schmidt-Universität in Hamburg, which both store parts of his personal and professional archive, but neither of these archival fonds contained anything relating to contact between Rüegg and Herta Fein. See email (dated Nov. 18, 2021) from Gaby Pfyffer (ETH Zürich, Archiv für Zeitgeschichte, Zürich) to the author; and emails (dated Nov. 18, 2021) from Lia Rasim (Universitätsbibliothek Helmut-Schmidt-Universität/Universität der Bundeswehr, Hamburg) to the author. For the archival fonds on Rüegg in the Universitätsbibliothek Helmut-Schmidt-Universität/Universität der Bundeswehr, see https://www.hsu-hh.de/paehis/abgeschlossene-projekte/ (accessed Nov. 18, 2021). Rüegg's more personal archives, deposited in the Deutsches Literaturarchiv, Marbach, do not contain anything related to Herta Fein either. See email (dated Nov. 29, 2021) from Ruth Doersing (Deutsches Literaturarchiv Marbach, Marbach am Neckar) to the author.

16. THE (KNOWN) LECTURES GIVEN BY MAGNUS HIRSCHFELD IN PARIS (1933–34)

Title or topic	Date	Place	Organized by	Source
Présentation	Tuesday, Jul. 4, 1933	Salle Wagram, 39-41 Avenue de Wagram, Paris XVII	Club du Faubourg	*Bec et ongles,* July 2, 1933, 8.
"Das Rassenproblem: von Gobineau bis heute" (The race problem: from Gobineau to today)	Saturday, Sep. 9, 1933	Deutscher Klub, Université du Parthénon, 64 Rue du Rocher, Paris VIII		*Das neue Tagebuch,* Jg. 1, n° 11, Sep. 9, 1933, 266.
On the new German (forced) sterilization law	Saturday, Apr. 14, 1934	Deutschen Klub, Université du Parthénon, 64 Rue du Rocher, Paris VIII		*Pariser Tageblatt,* Apr. 13, 1934, n° 122, 3; *Pariser Tageblatt,* Apr. 14, 1934, n° 123, 3?; *Pariser Tageblatt,* Apr. 16, 1934, n° 125, 4
"Die Sexualwissenschaft" or "La science sexologique" (The science of sexology), given in French, with slides (Lichtbilder), see card in MHG, Berlin, fonds Max Reiss	Wednesday, Jun. 6, 1934	Salle de l'Akadémia Raymond Duncan, 31 Rue de Seine		*Pariser Tageblatt,* Jun. 6, 1934, n° 176, 3
"Was eint und trennt das Menschengeschlecht?" (What unites and divides the human race?)	Wednesday, Oct. 31, 1934	Festsaal, 15 Avenue Hoche	Association des émigrés Israélites d'Allemagne en France	*Pariser Tageblatt,* Oct. 27, 1934, n° 319, 3; *Pariser Tageblatt,* Oct. 28, 1934, n° 320, 5
"La situation actuelle de la pathologie sexuelle" (The current situation of sexual pathology)	Thursday, Nov. 22, 1934	Sorbonne university Paris, amphithéâtre Michelet, 45 Rue Saint-Jacques, Paris V.	Groupe d'études philosophiques et scientifiques pour l'examen des tendances nouvelles	*Pariser Tageblatt,* Nov. 21, 1934, n° 344, 3; see also Bergemann, Dose, Keilson-Lauritz & Dubout 2019, f. 96/137

17. LAST WILL (TESTAMENT) OF MAGNUS HIRSCHFELD (GERMAN ORIGINAL AND ENGLISH TRANSLATION)

Magnus Hirschfeld wrote down the final version of his last will on January 10, 1935, in Nice, France. In 1984, a transcribed copy of the will was discovered by Manfred Baumgardt (1947–) in a 500-page German restitution file. Baumgardt published it in the fourth issue of the *Mitteilungen der Magnus-Hirschfeld-Gesellschaft* shortly afterwards.[212] The text can also be found on the website of the MHG, Berlin.[213] The website of the MHG, Berlin, also includes English translations of excerpts of Hirschfeld's will.[214] This is the very first complete English translation of Hirschfeld's last will, based on the original (and exclusively authentic) handwritten German version found in the ADAM, Nice.[215] A transcript based on the original handwritten German version is presented here. Pictures of this final five-page handwritten will have been added as well.

[212] Baumgardt 1984 and http://www.hirschfeld.in-berlin.de/publikationen/MittMHG_04.pdf (accessed Aug. 9, 2024).

[213] See https://www.magnus-hirschfeld.de/gedenken/historisches/institut/hirschfelds-testament-de/ (accessed Aug. 9, 2024).

[214] See https://www.magnus-hirschfeld.de/gedenken/historisches/institut/hirschfelds-testament-en/ (accessed Aug. 9, 2024).

[215] ADAM, Nice, Archives notariales, minutes notariales étude Pierre Demnard, May 22, 1935, n° 563, cote 03E 148/011.

[f. 1, p. 1]

1. EC 34390 [rubber stamped]

Testament

Ich, der unterzeichnete Dr. Magnus Hirschfeld, zur Zeit wohnhaft in Nice, Hôtel de la Méditerranée, Promenade des Anglais, erkläre hiermit folgendes als meinen letzten Willen:

Artikel 1.

Ich widerrufe hiermit meine sämtlichen früheren Testamente und letztwilligen Verfügungen jeder [underligned in original] Art einschliesslich derjenigen die in notarieller Form oder auf brieflichem Wege errichtet wurden.

Artikel 2.

Der Hauptzweck meines gegenwärtigen Testamentes ist es, da ich keine Leibeserben habe, das in meiner wissenschaftlichen, insbesondere sexualwissenschaftlichen Lebensarbeit enthaltene geistige [underligned in original] Erbe über mein persönliches Ende hinaus zu sichern beziehungsweise zu fördern.

Die persönlichen [underligned in original] Träger und Verwalter dieser Erbschaft sind meine Schüler.

Artikel 3.

Ich wünsche, dass mein Testamentsvollstrecker, soweit gesetzlich zulässig, über den Inhalt dieses Testaments vollständige Diskretion wahrt und den einzelnen Erben und Vermächtnisnehmern nur [underligned in original] diejenigen Teile des Testaments bekannt gibt, die sich auf jeden einzelnen beziehen.

[initial signature „Dr. M. H."]

[f. 1, p. 1]

1. EC 34390 [rubber stamped]

Testament [Last Will]

I, the undersigned Dr. Magnus Hirschfeld, currently residing in Nice, Hôtel de la Méditerranée, Promenade des Anglais, hereby declare the following to be my last will and testament:

Article 1.

I hereby revoke all my previous wills and testamentary dispositions of *any* [underlined in original] kind, including those made in notarial form or by letter.

Article 2.

The main purpose of my present will is, since I have no blood-related heirs, to secure and promote the *intellectual* [underlined in original] legacy contained in my scientific, in particular sexological, life's work after my own death.

The *personal* [underlined in original] bearers and administrators of this inheritance are my students.

Article 3.

I desire that my executor, to the extent permitted by law, shall exercise complete discretion as to the contents of this will and shall disclose to the individual heirs and legatees *only* [underlined in original] those parts of the will which relate to them.

[initial signature «Dr. M. H.»]

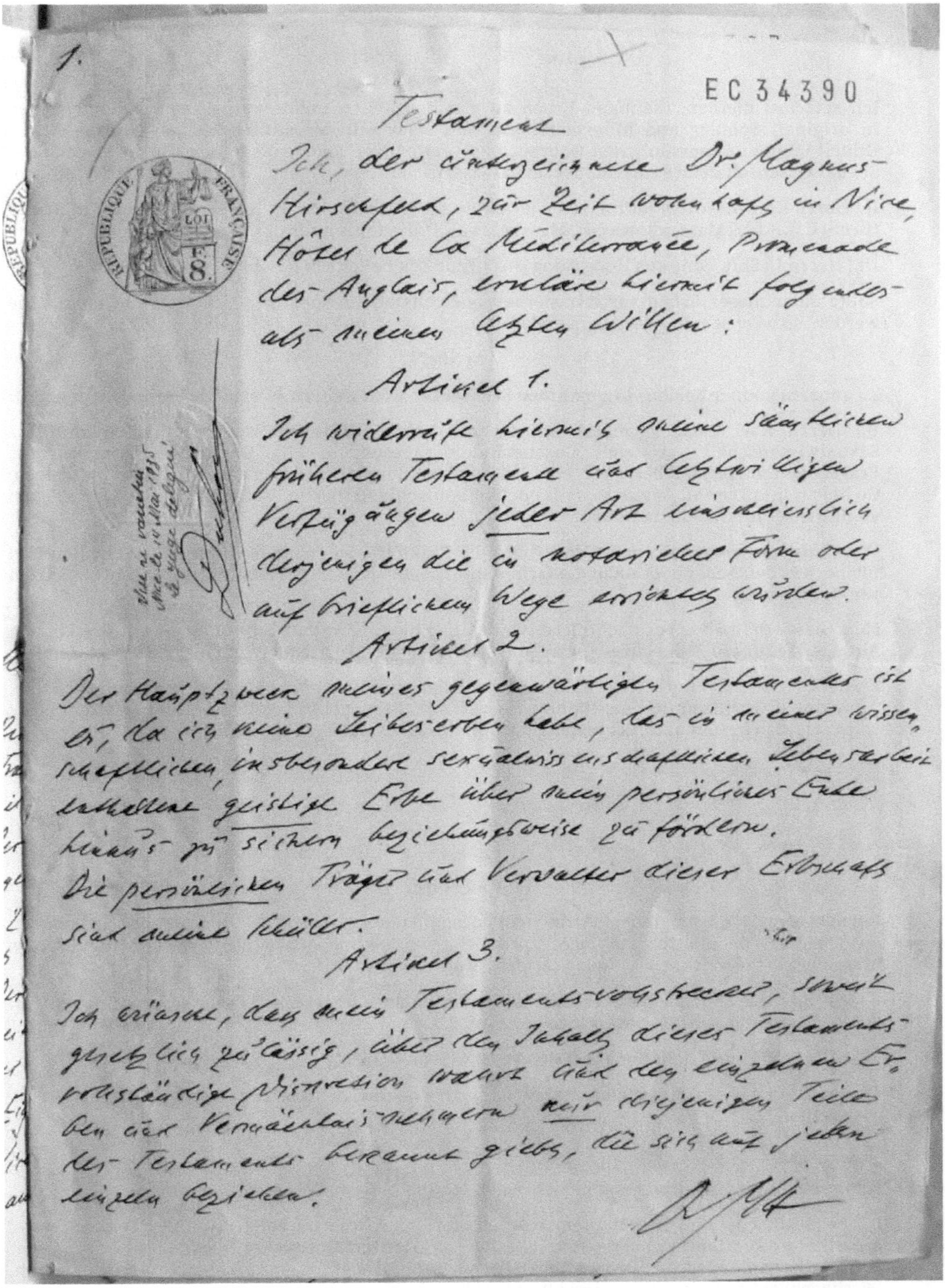

1.

EC 34390

RÉPUBLIQUE FRANÇAISE LOI F. 8.

Testament

Ich, der Unterzeichnete Dr. Magnus Hirschfeld, zur Zeit wohnhaft in Nice, Hôtel de la Méditerranée, Promenade des Anglais, erkläre hiermit folgendes als meinen letzten Willen:

Artikel 1.

Ich widerrufe hiermit meine sämtlichen früheren Testamente und letztwilligen Verfügungen jeder Art einschliesslich derjenigen die in notarieller Form oder auf brieflichem Wege errichtet wurden.

Artikel 2.

Der Hauptzweck meines gegenwärtigen Testamentes ist es, da ich keine Leibeserben habe, das in meiner wissenschaftlichen, insbesondere sexualwissenschaftlichen Lebensarbeit enthaltene geistige Erbe über mein persönliches Erbe hinaus zu sichern beziehungsweise zu fördern.

Die persönlichen Träger und Verwalter dieser Erbschaft sind meine Schüler.

Artikel 3.

Ich wünsche, dass mein Testamentsvollstrecker, soweit gesetzlich zulässig, über den Inhalt dieses Testamentes vollständige Diskretion wahrt und den einzelnen Erben und Vermächtnisnehmern nur diejenigen Teile des Testamentes bekannt gibt, die sich auf jeden einzeln beziehen.

[f. 1, p. 2]

2.

Artikel 4.

Ich setze zu meinen alleinigen Erben zu gleichen Teilen meine *nachgenannten* [underligned in original] Schüler und Mitarbeiter ein und zwar mit der ausdrücklichen Auflage, ihren Erbteil nicht zum persönlichen Gebrauch zu verwenden, sondern lediglich für die Zwecke der Sexualwissenschaft im Sinne meiner sexualwissenschaftlichen Ideen, Arbeiten und Bestrebungen:

I[.] Herrn Karl Giese aus Berlin; seine jeweilige Adresse wird bei Dr. Karl Fein, Advokat in Brünn (Brno) Č.S.R.[,] 6 Masarykowa [*sic*, Masarykova][,] zu erfahren sein.

II[.] Herrn Li Shiu Tong aus Hong Kong [*sic*] [,] zur Zeit bei mir in Nice[.]

Sollte einer dieser Erben vor mir sterben oder aus einem sonstigen Grunde nicht mein Erbe werden, so wächst sein Anteil dem anderen zu.

Artikel 5.

Zu gunsten meiner beiden vorgenannten Schüler setze ich weiterhin folgende Vermächtnisse fest:

I[.] Herrn Karl Giese vermache ich die mit seiner Hülfe aus dem Berliner Institut für Sexualwissenschaft geretteten Gegenstände, insbesondere alle Dokumente, Manuskripte, Fragebogen, Bilder, Bücher[,] etc. etc.[,] die sich zur Zeit teils auf dem garde-meuble von Bedel u. Co in Paris[,] 18 rue St. Augustin, teils noch in Deutschland (Berlin, Wiesbaden) oder Saarbrücken an ihm bekannter Stelle befinden.

Weiterhin vermache ich Herrn Karl Giese die Einkünfte aus meinen sämtlichen Schriften und Büchern in deutscher oder nicht deutscher Sprache incl.[usiv] Übersetzungen sowie aus Lizenzen für Medikamente.

Herr Giese erhält diese Vermächtnisse, wie das in Artikel 4 erwähnte Erbe unter der ausdrücklichen Auflage, sie für ein Archiv bzw. [beziehungsweise] Institut für Sexualwissenschaft zu verwenden.

Fernerhin ist an Frau Ellen Bakgaard [*sic*, Bækgaard], Kopenhagen 4, Aa boulevard [*sic*, Åboulevard] 82.I[,] der für das Studium des Herrn K. Giese mit ihr brieflich vereinbarte Teilbetrag zu zahlen, am besten nach Correspondenz mit ihr in einmaliger Summe.

[f. 1, p. 2]

2.

Article 4.

I appoint as my sole heirs, in equal shares, the following [underlined in original] students and collaborators, on the express condition that their inheritance not be employed for personal use, but only for the purposes of sexology in the sense of my sexological ideas, work and endeavors:

I[.] Mr. Karl Giese of Berlin; his latest address can be obtained from Dr. Karl Fein, lawyer in Brünn (Brno) Č.S.R.[,] 6 Masarykowa [sic, Masarykova].

II[.] Mr. Li Shiu Tong of Hong Kong [sic], at present with me in Nice[.]

Should one of these heirs die before me or for any other reason not become my heir, his share shall accrue to the other.

Article 5.

For the benefit of my two aforementioned pupils, I furthermore make the following bequests:

I[.] I bequeath to Mr. Karl Giese the items rescued with his help from the Berlin Institute of Sexual Science, in particular all documents, manuscripts, questionnaires, pictures, books, etc., etc.[,] which are at present partly in the garde-meuble of Bedel & Co[.] in Paris[,] 18 rue St. Augustin, and partly still in Germany (Berlin, Wiesbaden) or Saarbrücken[,] in places known to him.

Furthermore, I bequeath to Mr. Karl Giese the income from all my writings and books in German and other languages, including translations and licenses for medicines.

Mr. Giese receives these bequests, like the legacy mentioned in Article 4, on the express condition that they be used for an archive or, alternatively, an institute of sexual science.

Furthermore, the partial amount agreed by letter with Mrs. Ellen Bakgaard Bakgaard [sic, Bækgaard], Copenhagen 4, 82.I Aaboulevard [sic, Åboulevard][,] for Mr. K. Giese's studies is to be paid to her, preferably in a lump sum after correspondence with her.

2. Artikel 4.

Ich setze zu meinen alleinigen Erben zu gleichen Teilen meine nachgenannten Schüler und Mitarbeiter ein und zwar mit der ausdrücklichen Auflage, ihren Erbteil nicht zum persönlichen Gebrauch zu verwenden, sondern lediglich für die Zwecke der Sexualwissenschaft im Sinne meiner sexualwissenschaftlichen Ideen, Arbeiten und Bestrebungen:

I Herrn Karl Giese aus Berlin. Seine jeweilige Adresse wird bei Dr. Karl Fein, Advokat in Brünn (Brno) Č.S.R. 6 Masarykova zu erfahren sein.

II Herrn Li Shiu Tong aus Hongkong zur Zeit bei mir in Nice

Sollte einer dieser Erben vor mir sterben oder aus einem sonstigen Grunde nicht mein Erbe werden, so wächst sein Anteil dem anderen zu.

Artikel 5.

Zu Gunsten meiner beiden vorgenannten Schüler setze ich weiterhin folgende Vermächtnisse fest:

I Herrn Karl Giese vermache ich die mit seiner Hilfe aus dem Berliner Institut für Sexualwissenschaft geretteten Gegenstände, insbesondere alle Dokumente, Manuskripte, Fragebogen, Bilder, Bücher etc. etc. die sich zur Zeit teils auf dem gardemeuble von Bedel u. Co in Paris 18 rue St. Augustin, teils noch in Deutschland (Berlin, Wiesbaden) oder Saarbrücken an ihm bekannten Stellen befinden.

Weiterhin vermache ich Herrn Karl Giese die Einkünfte aus meinen sämtlichen Schriften und Büchern in deutscher oder nicht deutscher Sprache incl. Übersetzungen sowie aus Lizenzen.

Herr Giese erhält diese Vermächtnisse, für Medikamente, wie das im Artikel 4 erwähnte Erbe unter der ausdrücklichen Auflage, sie für ein Archiv bzw. Institut für Sexualwissenschaft zu verwenden.

Fernerhin ist an Frau Ellen Bækgaard, Kopenhagen 4, Aaboulevard 82.I der für das Studium des Herrn Li. Giese mit ihr brieflich vereinbarte Teilbetrag zu zahlen, am besten nach Correspondenz mit ihr in einmaliger Summe.

[f. 2, p. 3]

3.

II. Meinem vorgenannten Schüler Li Shiu Tong vermache ich alle Aktien und Shares, welche in einem Bank-Safe auf *seinem* [underligned in original] und meinem Namen zur Zeit in Paris liegen. Mit diesem Vermächtnis soll gleichzeitig die Schuld getilgt sein, die ich infolge meiner Verfolgung in Deutschland nach und nach bei ihm aufzunehmen gezwungen war.

Ferner vermache ich ihm alle Bücher, Papiere, Bilder und sonstigen Gegenstände, die sich zur Zeit meines Ablebens bei mir, ihm oder in gemeinsamer Aufbewahrung z.B. [zum Beispiel] in Paris im Hôtel Quai d'Orsay befinden mit Ausnahme von Geldbeständen (Papiergeld, Devisen, Cheks[,] etc.), aus denen in erster Linie die in den weiteren Artikeln dieses Testaments aufgeführten Familien- u.[nd] sonstigen Legate durch den Testamentsvollstrecker auszubezahlen sind.

Diese Vermächtnisse wende ich meinem Schüler Li Shiu Tong unter der ausdrücklichen Auflage zu, sie nicht für sein persönlichen Gebrauch zu verwenden, sondern lediglich für die Zwecke der Sexualwissenschaft im Sinne meiner Bestrebungen.

Artikel 6.

Ich bestimme weiterhin ausdrücklich, dass meine Schüler Karl Giese und Li Shiu Tong dafür zu sorgen haben, dass die ihnen zur Verwendung für die Zwecke der Sexualwissenschaft zugewandten Gegenstände und Vermögenswerte nach ihrem eigenen Tode diesem Zwecke möglichst erhalten bleiben, eventuell durch die Begründung einer juristischen Person[,] z.B. [zum Beispiel] eines Vereins, zu ihren Lebzeiten.

Artikel 7.

Weiterhin sind an folgende Personen Vermächtnisse zu zahlen, die mit dem Wegfall des betreffenden Vermächtnisnehmers erlöschen:

[initial signature „Dr. M. H."]

[f. 2, p. 3]

3.

II. I bequeath to my aforementioned pupil Li Shiu Tong all shares and stocks [*sic*] which are currently held in a bank safe in *his* [underlined in original] and my name in Paris. With this bequest, the debt that I was gradually compelled to incur to him as a result of my persecution in Germany is to be simultaneously repaid.

Furthermore, I bequeath to him all books, papers, pictures and other items which at the time of my death are either with me, him or in our joint safekeeping, e.g. in Paris at the Hôtel Quai d'Orsay, with the exception of monetary assets (cash, foreign currency, checks[,] etc.), from which, first and foremost, the bequests to family and others listed in the other articles of this will are to be paid out by the executor.

These legacies are to be given to my disciple Li Shiu Tong on the express condition that they not to be employed for his personal use, but only for the purposes of sexology in accordance with my aspirations.

Article 6.

Furthermore, I expressly decree that my students Karl Giese and Li Shiu Tong must ensure that the items and assets given to them to be used for the purposes of sexual science are preserved for this purpose after their own deaths, possibly by establishing a legal entity[,] e.g. an association, during their lifetimes.

Article 7.

Furthermore, bequests shall be made to the following persons, which shall expire upon the death of the respective legatee:

[initial signature "Dr. M. H."]

II. Meinem vorgenannten Schüler Li Shiu Tong vermache ich alle Aktien und Shares, welche in einem Bank-Safe auf seinem und meinem Namen zur Zeit in Paris liegen. Mit diesem Vermächtnis soll gleichzeitig die Schuld getilgt sein, die ich infolge meiner Verfolgung in Deutschland nach und nach bei ihm aufzunehmen gezwungen war.

Ferner vermache ich ihm alle Bücher, Papiere, Bilder und sonstigen Gegenstände, die sich zur Zeit meines Ablebens bei mir, ihm oder in gemeinsamer Aufbewahrung z. B. in Paris im Hôtel Quai d'Orsay befinden mit Ausnahme von Geldbeständen (Papiergeld, Devisen, Checks etc.) aus denen in erster Linie die in den weiteren Artikeln dieses Testaments aufgeführten Familien- u. sonstigen Legate durch den Testamentsvollstrecker auszubezahlen sind.

Diese Vermächtnisse wende ich meinem Schüler Li Shiu Tong unter der ausdrücklichen Auflage zu, sie nicht für seinen persönlichen Gebrauch zu verwenden, sondern lediglich für die Zwecke der Sexualwissenschaft im Sinne meiner Bestrebungen.

Artikel 6.

Ich bestimme weiterhin ausdrücklich, dass meine Schüler Karl Giese und Li Shiu Tong dafür zu sorgen haben, dass die ihnen zur Verwendung für die Zwecke der Sexualwissenschaft zugewandten Gegenstände und Vermögenswerte nach ihrem eigenen Tode diesem Zwecke möglichst erhalten bleiben, eventuell durch die Begründung einer juristischen Person z. B. eines Vereins zu ihren Lebzeiten.

Artikel 7.

Weiterhin sind an folgende Personen Vermächtnisse zu zahlen, die mit dem Wegfall des betreffenden Vermächtnisnehmers erlöschen:

[f. 2, p. 4]

4.

a. 30.000 (dreißigtausend) französische Franken in entsprechender Währung an meine jüngste Schwester Fr.[au] Jenny Hauck[,] zur Zeit Berlin, Halensee[,] Hectorstr.[asse] 3[,] bei Posner, falls verzogen Adresse durch meine ältere Schwester Fr. R.[echa] Tobias, Berlin-Halensee, Joachim[-] Friedrichstr.[asse] 7.

b. 20.000 (zwanzigtausend) französ.[ische] Franken an meine Freundin Margarete Dost, Berlin NW 87, Unionstrasse 2.

c. Je 15.000 (fünfzehntausend) Francs (français) [sic] an die folgenden Nachkommen meiner verstorbenen Geschwister:

c: [*sic*] Nichte Röschen Hirschfeld, Hamburg, Wandsbecker [*sic,* Wandsbeker] Chaussée 87[.]

d: Neffe Walter Mann[,] Berlin, Mommsenstrasse 53/54[.]

e: Großneffe Franz Richard Mann, z. Z. [zur Zeit] in London, Sohn des vorigen Walter Mann, der seine genaue Adresse wissen wird.

f. 5000 [*sic*] (fünftausend) französische Francs an meinen Grossvetter Ernst Maass[,] zur Zeit Mailand, Viale Romagna 65.III.

Ferner soll erhalten:

g. 3000 [*sic*] (dreitausend) franz.[ösische] Francs[,] mein früherer Angestellter Franz Wimmer, Berlin W. 62, Burggrafenstr.[asse] 14[.]

sowie:

h. 10.000 (zehntausend) franz. Franken[,] mein ärztlicher Berater und Freund Dr. Leopold Hönig, Karlsbad, Č.S.R., alte Wiese[.]

Sollten die Mittel meines Nachlasses nicht zur Bezahlung sämtlicher vorstehender Vermächtnisse ausreichen, so sollen diese verhältnismässig gekürzt werden.

Artikel 8.

Für die Errichtung meines Grabmals soll ein Betrag

[f. 2, p. 4]

4.

a. 30,000 (thirty thousand) French francs in corresponding currency to my youngest sister Mrs. Jenny Hauck[,] currently [in] Berlin, Halensee[,] 3 Hectorstr.[aße][,] living with Posner, if the address is no longer valid, [obtain her latest address] through my older sister Mrs. R.[echa] Tobias, Berlin-Halensee, 7 Joachim[-]Friedrichstr.[asse].b. 20,000 (twenty thousand) French francs to my friend Margarete Dost, Berlin NW 87, 2 Unionstrasse.

c. 15,000 (fifteen thousand) francs (French) [*sic*] each to the following descendants of my deceased siblings:

c: [*sic*] Niece Röschen Hirschfeld, Hamburg, 87 Wandsbecker [*sic,* Wandsbeker] Chaussée[.]

d: Nephew Walter Mann[,] Berlin, 53/54 Mommsenstrasse[.]

e: Great-nephew Franz Richard Mann, cur. [currently] in London, son of the previously mentioned Walter Mann, who will know his exact address.

f. 5000 [*sic*] (five thousand) French francs to my great cousin Ernst Maass[,] currently in Milan, 65.III Viale Romagna.

Furthermore, the following must receive:

g. 3000 [*sic*] (three thousand) French francs[,] my former employee Franz Wimmer, Berlin W. 62, 14 Burggrafenstr.[asse][.]

and also:

h. 10,000 (ten thousand) French francs[,] my medical advisor and friend Dr. Leopold Hönig, Karlsbad, Č.S.R., alte Wiese[.]

Should the funds of my estate not be sufficient to pay all of the above bequests, they shall be reduced proportionately.

Article 8.

For the erection of my tombstone an amount

a. 30.000 (dreissig tausend) französische Francs in entsprechender Währung an meine jüngste Schwester Fr. Jenny Hauer zur Zeit Berlin, Halensee Hectorstr. 3 bei Posner, falls verzogen Adresse durch meine ältere Schwester Fr. R. Tobias, Berlin-Halensee, Joachim Friedrichstr. 7.

b. 20.000 (zwanzig tausend) französ. Francs an meine Freundin Margarete Dost, Berlin NW 87, Unionstrasse 2.

c. Je 15.000 (fünfzehn tausend) Francs (français) an die folgenden Nachkommen meiner verstorbenen Geschwister:

c. Nichte Röschen Hindfeld, Hamburg, Wandsbecker Chaussee 87

d. Neffe Walter Mann Berlin. Mommsenstrasse 53/54

e. Grossneffe Franz Richard Mann z. Z. in London, Sohn des vorigen Walter Mann, der seine genauere Adresse wissen wird.

f. 5000 (fünftausend) französische Francs an meinen Grossvetter Ernst Haase zur Zeit Mailand, Viale Romagna 65. IV.

Ferner soll erhalten:

g. 3000 (dreitausend) franz. Francs mein früherer Angestellter Franz Wimmer, Berlin W. 62, Burggrafenstr. 14

sowie:

h. 10.000 (zehntausend) franz. Francs mein ärztlicher Berater und Freund Dr. Leopold König, Karlsbad, C.S.R. Alte Wiese

Sollten die Mittel meines Nachlasses nicht zur Bezahlung sämtlicher vorstehender Vermächtnisse ausreichen, so sollen diese verhältnismässig gekürzt werden.

Artikel 8.

Für die Errichtung meines Grabmals soll ein Betrag

remis à Me Herzfelder le 13. 2. 36.

[f. 3, p. 5]

5. AT 86387 [rubber stamped]

von 15.000 (fünfzehntausend) französischen Franken aufgewendet werden. Mit der Anfertigung des Grabmals ist mein Landsmann[,] der Bildhauer Arnold Zadikow, Paris-Malakoff[,] 27 rue Leplanquais[,] zu beauftragen. Vorraussetzung dabei ist, dass ich in Europa (am liebsten wäre mir Nice oder Paris) bestattet werde.

Die Pflege meines Grabes lege ich in die Hände meines Schülers Li Shiu Tong.

Artikel 9.

Meine Leiche soll verbrannt werden.

Artikel 10.

Zu meinem Testamentsvollstrecker ernenne ich Herrn Dr. Franz Herzfelder, früher Rechtsanwalt in München, jetzt conseil juridique in Nice, Boulevard Carlone no. 6.

Der Testamentsvollstrecker hat alle nach dem Gesetz ihm obliegenden Pflichten und ihm zustehenden Rechte. Er hat insbesondere zwecks Ausführung der Bestimmungen meines Testaments das Recht, den Nachlass in vorläufigen Besitz zu nehmen.

Der Testamentsvollstrecker erhält ein Honorar von 2500 [*sic*] (zweitausendfünfhundert) französischen Francs ausser dem Ersatz seiner notwendigen Auslagen.

Eigenhändig geschrieben und unterschrieben

Nice, im Hôtel de la Méditerranée

am 10[.] Januar 1935[.]

[signed „Dr. Magnus Hirschfeld."]

[f. 3, p. 5]

5. AT 86387 [rubber stamped]

of 15,000 (fifteen thousand) French francs shall be spent. My countryman[,] the sculptor Arnold Zadikow, Paris-Malakoff[,] 27 rue Leplanquais[,] is to be commissioned with the production of the tomb. The condition is that I be buried in Europe (I would prefer Nice or Paris). I leave the care of my grave in the hands of my disciple Li Shiu Tong.

Article 9.

My body shall be cremated.

Article 10.

I appoint Dr. Franz Herzfelder, formerly a lawyer in Munich, now conseil juridique in Nice, n° 6 Boulevard Carlone, as my executor.

The executor has all the duties and rights incumbent upon him under the law. In particular, he has the right to take provisional possession of the estate for the purpose of executing the provisions of my will.

The executor shall receive a fee of 2500 [*sic*] (two thousand five hundred) French francs in addition to the reimbursement of his necessary expenses.

Handwritten by myself and signed

Nice, at the Hôtel de la Méditerranée

on January 10, 1935[.]

[signed "Dr. Magnus Hirschfeld."]

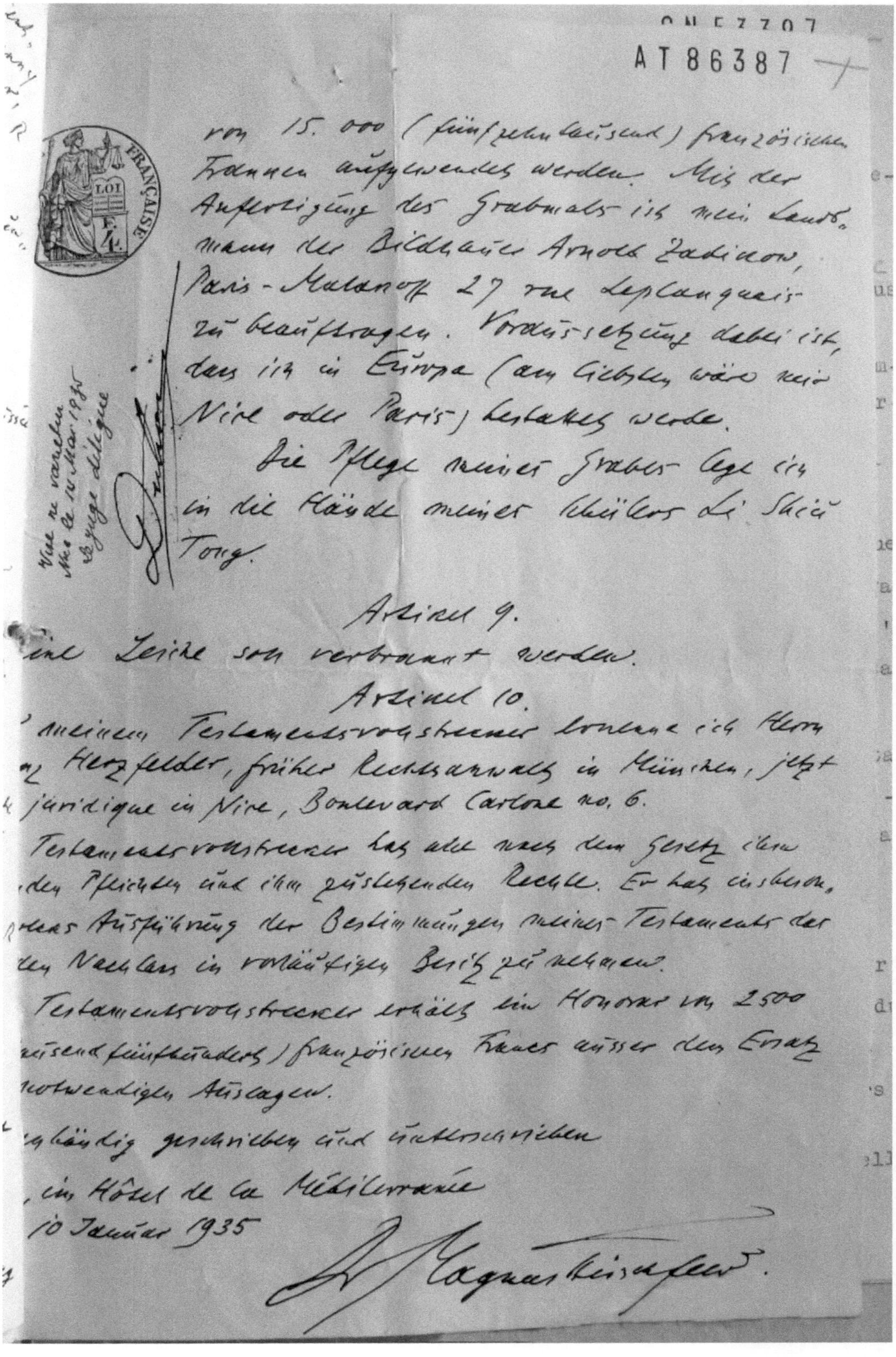

AT 86387

FRANÇAISE LOI

von 15.000 (fünfzehntausend) französischen Francs aufgewendet werden. Mit der Anfertigung des Grabmals ist mein Landsmann der Bildhauer Arnold Zadikow, Paris-Malakoff 27 rue Leplanquais zu beauftragen. Voraussetzung dabei ist, dass ich in Europa (am liebsten wäre mir Nice oder Paris) bestattet werde.

Die Pflege meines Grabes lege ich in die Hände meines Schülers Li Shiu Tong.

Vu ne varietur … le 14 Mai 1935 … juge délégué

Artikel 9.

…ine Leiche soll verbrannt werden.

Artikel 10.

… meinem Testamentsvollstrecker ernenne ich Herrn …nz Herzfelder, früher Rechtsanwalt in München, jetzt … juridique in Nice, Boulevard Carlone no. 6.

… Testamentsvollstrecker hat alle nach dem Gesetz ihm …den Pflichten und ihm zustehenden Rechte. Er hat insbesondere …ecks Ausführung der Bestimmungen meines Testaments den …en Nachlass in vorläufigen Besitz zu nehmen.

… Testamentsvollstrecker erhält ein Honorar von 2500 …tausend fünfhundert) französischen Francs ausser dem Ersatz … notwendigen Auslagen.

…nhändig geschrieben und unterschrieben

…, im Hôtel de la Méditerranée

10 Januar 1935

Magnus Hirschfeld.

Archives and Libraries Consulted

ARCHIVES

AUSTRALIA

University of Sydney Library, Sydney

AUSTRIA

Universität von Innsbruck, Forschungsinstitut Brenner-Archiv, Innsbrück

WStLA, Wien
Wiener Stadt- und Landesarchiv, Wien

DöW, Wien
Dokumentationsarchiv des österreichischen Widerstandes, Wien

BELGIUM

Felix archief, Antwerpen

Rijksarchief Brussel/Archives de l'État à Bruxelles, Brussel/Bruxelles

CANADA

LAC/BAC, Ottawa

Library and Archives Canada/Bibliothèque et archives Canada, Ottawa

CZECH REPUBLIC

ABS, Praha
Archiv bezpečnostních složek, Praha

AHMP, Praha
Archiv hlavního města Prahy, Praha

AMB, Brno
Archiv města Brna, Brno

Archiv Masarykovy univerzity, Brno

Archiv města Ostravy, Ostrava

Archiv Památníku Terezín, Terezín

Katastrální úřad pro Jihomoravský kraj, Brno

Moravské zemské muzeum, Mendelianum, Brno

MZA, Brno
Moravský zemský archiv v Brně, Brno

Muzeum města Brna, Brno

Muzeum Policie ČR, Praha

NA, Praha
Národní archiv Ceské republiky, Praha

NFA, Praha
Národní filmový archiv, Praha

PNP, Praha
Památník národního písemnictví, Praha

Státní okresní archiv Blansko, Blansko

Státní okresní archiv Brno-venkov, Rajhrad

Státní okresní archiv Jihlava, Jihlava

Státní okresní archiv Kroměříž, Kroměříž

Státní okresní archiv Opava, Opava

Státní okresní archiv Příbram, Příbram

Státní okresní archiv Vyškov se sídlem ve Slavkově u Brna, Slavkov u Brna

Ústav dějin Univerzity Karlovy a Archiv Univerzity Karlovy, Praha

Vojenský historický archív, Praha

ŽMP, Praha
Židovské muzeum v Praze, Praha

FRANCE

Archives départementales de la Drôme, Valence

ADAM, Nice
Archives départementales des Alpes-Maritimes, Nice

ADBR, Aix-en-Provence
Archives départementales des Bouches-du-Rhône, Centre d'Aix, Aix-en-Provence

Archives départementales du Haut-Rhin, Colmar

Archives départementales du Val-de-Marne, Créteil

Archives de la Préfecture de Police de Paris, Paris

Archives Municipales, Nice

Archives Nationales, site de Pierrefitte-sur-Seine, Paris

Bibliothèque histoire de la médecine, Paris

Fondation Catherine Gide, Paris

IMEC, Abbaye d'Ardenne, Saint-Germain-la-Blanche-Herbe
Institut mémoires de l'édition contemporaine, Abbaye d'Ardenne, Saint-Germain-la-Blanche-Herbe

Ministère des armées, Service historique de la Défense, Vincennes

GERMANY

Archiv Kurt Hiller Gesellschaft, Neuss

Archiv MHG, Berlin
Archiv Magnus-Hirschfeld-Gesellschaft, Berlin

BA, Berlin-Lichterfelde
Bundesarchiv, Berlin-Lichterfelde

Deutsches Literaturarchiv Marbach, Marbach am Neckar

ELAB, Berlin
Evangelisches Landeskirchliches Archiv in Berlin, Berlin

Hessisches Hauptstaatsarchiv, Wiesbaden

Institut für Zeitungsforschung, Dortmund

Jüdisches Museum, Frankfurt

LAB, Berlin
Landesarchiv, Berlin

Landesarchiv Nordrhein-Westfalen, Abteilung Rheinland, Düsseldorf

Landesarchiv Saarland, Saarbrücken-Scheidt

LKAN, Nürnberg
Landeskirchliches Archiv, Nürnberg

Politisches Archiv des Auswärtigen Amts, Berlin

Sächsisches Staatsarchiv, Leipzig

Stadtarchiv Saarbrücken, Saarbrücken

StadtA WM, Weilheim in Oberbayern
Stadtarchiv, Weilheim in Oberbayern

HUNGARY

Főváros Levéltára, Budapest

ISRAEL

GFHA, Beit Lohamei Haghetaot
The Ghetto Fighters' House Archives, Beit Lohamei Haghetaot

Israel State Archives, Jerusalem

Yad Vashem, The World Holocaust Remembrance Center, Jeruzalem

ITALY

Archivio di Stato del Cantone Ticino, Bellinzona

POLAND

APŁ, Łódź
Archiwum Państwowe w Łodzi, Łódź

Państwowe Muzeum Auschwitz-Birkenau w Oświęcimiu, Oświęcim

SLOVAKIA

Slovenský národný archív, Bratislava

SWEDEN

Arbetarrörelsens arkiv och bibliotek, Stockholm

Landsarkivet i Göteborg, Göteborg

Region- och stadsarkivet i Göteborg, Göteborg

Riksarkivet, Stockholm

SWITZERLAND

BAR/AFS/AFS, Bern
Schweizerisches Bundesarchiv, Archives fédérales suisses, Archivio federale svizzero, Bern

THE NETHERLANDS

IHLIA LGBT Heritage, Amsterdam
Internationaal Homo/Lesbisch Informatiecentrum en Archief, Amsterdam

IISH, Amsterdam
International Institute of Social History, Amsterdam

UNITED KINGDOM

Wellcome collection (formerly Wellcome Institute), London

World Jewish Relief Archives (London)

USA

AJJDC, New York
Archives of the American Jewish Joint Distribution Committee, New York

Kinsey Institute, Bloomington (Indiana)

Leo Baeck Institute, New York

The National Archives at New York City, New York

USHMM, Washington D.C.
United States Holocaust Memorial Museum, Washington D.C.

University of Southern California, USC Shoah Foundation, Los Angeles

U.S. Department of Homeland Security, US Citizenship and Immigration Services, Lee's Summit (Missouri)

Visual History Archive (USC Shoah Foundation), Los Angeles

Washington State Archives, Southwest Regional Branch, Olympia, Washington

YIVO, New York
Institute for Jewish Research, New York

LIBRARIES

Albertina, Brussel/Bruxelles (KBR)

Biblioteca Nacional de Uruguay, Montevideo

Bibliotheek Instituut voor Oorlogs-, Holocaust- en Genocidestudies, Amsterdam (NIOD)

Bibliotheek Studiecentrum Oorlog en Maatschappij/Centre d'Etude Guerre et Société, Brussel/Bruxelles (CEGESOMA)

Bibliotheek Universiteit Gent, Gent

Bibliothèque Nationale, Paris (BN)

Deutsche Nationalbibliothek, Leipzig (DNB)

East Asian Library (Cheng Yu Tung), University of Toronto, Toronto

Klementinum, Praha

Knihovna Židovského muzea v Praze, Praha

Koninklijke Bibliotheek, Den Haag (KB)

Moravská zemská knihovna, Brno (MZK)

National Library, London

Universitäts- und Landesbibliothek Tirol, Innsbruck

Universiteitsbibliotheek, Leuven

Universiteitsbibliotheek, Utrecht

Vědecká knihovna Olomouc, Olomouc

Wellcome Collection (formerly Wellcome Institute) Library, London

Bibliography

[Official program brochure WLSR 1930 Vienna conference.] *IV. Kongress der Weltliga für Sexualreform auf wissenschaftlicher Grundlage.* September 16–23, 1930. Wien [etc.]: Elbemühl Verlag, 1930.

[Announcement leaflet WLSR 1932 Brno conference.] *V. Mezinárodní kongres Světové ligy pro sexuální reformu na vědeckém podkladě - Brno, 20.-26. září 1932 = V. Kongress der Weltliga für Sexualreform auf wissenschaftlicher Grundlage - Brünn (Tschechoslowakei), 20.-26. September 1932 = Vth Congress of the World league for Sexual Reform on* [*sic*] *Scientific Basis - Brno (Czechoslovakia), September 20th to 26th 1932 = 5ième Congrès de la Ligue Mondiale pour la réforme sexuelle sur base scientifique - Brno (Tchécoslovaquie) 20 à 26 Septembre 1932 = V. Kongreso de Tutmonda Ligo por Seksa reformo sur scienca bazo - Brno (Ĉeĥoslovakio), 20.-26. Septembro 1932.*

[Preliminary program brochure WLSR 1932 Brno conference.] *V. Mezinárodní kongres Světové Ligy pro sexuální reformu na vědeckém podkladě = V. Internationaler* [*sic*] *Kongress der Weltliga für Sexualreform auf wissenschaftlicher Grundlage = Vth International Congress of the World League for Sexual Reform on a Scientific Basis = Ve Congrès International de la Ligue Mondiale pour la réforme sexuelle sur une base scientifique = Va Internacia kongreso de la Tutmonda Ligo por seksa reformo sur scienca bazo. September 20–26, 1932. Brno-Brünn, ČSR.*

[Official program brochure WLSR 1932 Brno conference.] *V. Mezinárodní kongres Světové ligy pro sexuální reformu na vědeckém podkladě = V. Internationalen Kongress der Weltliga für Sexualreform auf wissenschaftlicher Grundlage = Vth International Congress of the World league for Sexual Reform on a Scientific Basis = Ve Congrès International de la Ligue Mondiale pour la réforme sexuelle sur une base scientifique = Va Internacia kongreso de la Tutmonda Ligo por seksa reformo sur scienca bazo. September 20–26, 1932 Brno Brünn, ČSR. 20.-26.IX.1932.*

125 Jahre R. Lechner (Walter Krieg), Universitätsbuchhandlung und photographische Manufaktur. 1941.Wien: R. Lechner.

Adresář Protektorátu Čechy a Morava pro průmysl, živnosti, obchod a zemědělství = Adressbuch des Protektorates Böhmen und Mähren für Industrie, Gewerbe, Handel und Landwirtschaft. 1939. Praha: Rudolf Mosse.

Adresář zemského hlavního města Brna 1948. 1948. Brno: Polygrafie.

Adressbuch der Ärzte im Protektorat Böhmen und Mähren = Adresář lékařů protektorátu Čechy a Morava. 1942. Prag: Ärztlicher Revue.

Adressbuch der Landeshauptstadt Brünn 1942 = Adresář zem. hlavního města Brna 1942. 1943. Prag: Verlag Oskar Kuhn & Co.

Adressbuch des Deutschen Buchhandels und der verwandten Geschäftszweige. 1892. Leipzig: Geschäftsstelle des Börsenvereins der Deutschen Buchhändler.

Adreßbuch von groß-Brünn = Adresář Velkého Brna. 1920–1934. Brno/Brünn: Friedr. Irrgang.

Album bývalých příslušníků a zakladatelů 6. střeleckého hanáckého pluku. [1938. Olomouc: M. Lužný].

Allgemeiner Wohnungs-Anzeiger nebst Handels- und Gewerbe-Adressbuch für die Landeshaupstadt Brünn 1881. 1881. Brünn: Rohrer.

Amtliches Fernsprechbuch für Mähren 1941 = Uředni telefonní seznam pro Moravu 1941. N.d. Brünn: Postdirektion.

Annuaire des Alpes-Maritimes: Indicateur de la Principauté de Monaco: Guide de Nice, Cannes, Grasse, Menton, Antibes, Beaulieu, Hyères, Saint-Raphaël, années 52 and 53. 1935 and 1936. Nice: Direction-Administration.

Annuaire du commerce et de l'industrie de Belgique, Tome I, Bruxelles et son banlieue. 1969. Bruxelles: Mertens et Rozez.

Braunbuch über Reichstagsbrand und Hitler-Terror. 1933. Basel: Universum-Bücherei.

Bücherverzeichnis der "Alois Brecher-Bibliothek-Stiftung". 1932. Brünn: Druck Markus Krall.

Čechoslovakische Kurorte. 1931. Karlsbad: L. Eberhart.

Die Bücher des Verlages Julius Püttmann [book catalogue]. 1930. Stuttgart: Julius Püttmann.

Dreiundzwanzigster Jahresbericht der k. k. deutschen Kaiser Franz-Joseph Handelsakademie in Brünn. 1917–18. Brno, Česko:

K.k. deutsche Kaiser Franz Joseph-Handelsakademie.

Gemeinde-Verwaltung und Gemeindestatistik der Landeshauptstadt Brünn. 1896–1917. Brünn: Verlag des Gemeinderathes der Landeshauptstadt Brünn.

Guía telefónica oficial de la República Oriental del Uruguay. 1942. Montevideo, s. n..

Internationales Adressbuch der Antiquar-Buchhändler = International Directory of Second-hand Booksellers = Annuaire international des Librairies d'occasion. 1906. Berlin: W. Junk.

Jüdisches Nachrichtenblatt = Židovské listy [Prague edition]. 1939–1944. Prague: Židovská náboženská obec.

Kurorte, Heilanstalten, Sommerfrischen in der Č.S.R. 1934. Aussig: Selbstverlag.

Liste der angekommenen Kur- und Badegäste in der königl. Stadt Kaiser-Karlsbad im Jahre. 1795–1944. Karlsbad: F.J. Franieck.

Neues Orientirungs-Schema für die Landeshauptstadt Brünn, verfasst auf Grund der neuen Strassenbezeichnung und Häusernummerirung. [1877]. Brno: W. Burkart.

Seznam advokátů. 1904, 1908, 1910, 1926, 1928–37. Brno: Moravská advokátní komora v Brně.

Seznam advokátů v Protektorátu Čechy *a Morava = Verzeichnis der Advokaten im Protektorate Böhmen und Mähren, 1940.* 1940. Praha: Advokátní komora pro Čechy; Moravská advokátní komora.

Seznam telefonních ústředen, hovoren a účastníků pro zemi Moravskoslezskou 1938. 1938. Brno: Polygrafie.

Strassenverzeichnis der Hauptstadt Prag = Seznam ulic hlavního města Prahy. 1941. Prag: Postdirektion.

Terezín-Ghetto [contains the list of persons rescued (*seznam zachráněných osob*)]. 1945. Praha: Repatriační odbor ministerstva ochrany práce a sociální péče Republiky československé.

Věstník Moravské advokátní komory v Brně. 1938–39. Brno: Moravská advokátní komora.

Wohnungs-Adressbuch von Brünn und der Vororte Königsfeld, Hussowitz und Kumrowitz für 1896. 1896. Brünn: Verlag von C. Winkler's Buchhhandlung.

***

A. O. 1984. "L'arte plastica di Jocelyn Fein". *Gazzetta Ticinese*, January 4, 1984, 7.

Abraham, Félix, and Magnus Hirschfeld. 1931. *Perversions sexuelles.* Paris: Aldor.

Adam, Alfons. 2013. *Unsichtbare Mauern: die Deutschen in der Prager Gesellschaft zwischen Abkapselung und Interaktion* (1918–1938/39). Veröffentlichungen zur Kultur und Geschichte im östlichen Europa, vol. 41. Essen: Klartext.

Adámek, Jiří, Milan Kroutil, and Jitka Kučerová. 1981. *Brněnští občané v boji proti fašismu.* Vol. 3 of *Knižnice sborníku Brno v minulosti a dnes.* Brno: Blok.

Adelson, Alan, and Robert Lapides, eds. 1989. *Łódź Ghetto: Inside a Community under Siege.* New York: Viking.

Adler, Hans Günther. 1974. *Der verwaltete Mensch: Studien zur Deportation der Juden aus Deutschland.* Tübingen: Mohr.

Aktives Museum Faschismus und Widerstand in Berlin, ed. 2018. *Berliner Bibliotheken im Nationalsozialismus: eine Sonderausstellung anlässlich der Bücherverbrennungen vor 85 Jahren.* Berlin: Aktives Museum Faschismus und Widerstand in Berlin; Gedenk- und Bildungsstaette Haus der Wannsee-Konferenz.

Albrecht, Berty. 1932. "Ve Congrès de la Ligue Mondiale pour la Réforme Sexuelle". *La grande réforme*, November 1932, 1.

Allendy, René. 1937. "Les conceptions modernes de la sexualité". *Crapouillot*, September 1937, 3–62.

—. 1938. "Le crime et les perversions instinctives". *Crapouillot*, May 1938, 2–65.

Alicke, Klaus-Dieter. 2008. *Lexikon der jüdischen Gemeinden im deutschen Sprachraum.* Gütersloh: Gütersloher Verlagshaus.

Altman, Avraham, and Irene Eber. 2000. "Flight to Shanghai, 1938–1940: The Larger Setting". *Yad Vashem Studies* 28: 51–86. http://www1.yadvashem.org/odot_pdf/Microsoft%20Word%20-%203234.pdf.

Altman, Karel. 2008. *Zmizelý svet brnenských kaváren = Verschwundene Welt der Brünner Cafés.* Brno: Josef Filip.

Anderl, Gabriele, Dirk Rupnow, and Alexandra-Eileen Wenck. 2004. *Die Zentralstelle für jüdische Auswanderung als Beraubungsinstitution.* Wien [etc.]: Oldenbourg.

Anderl, Gabriele. 2004. *"Arisierung" von Mobilien*. Vol 15 of *Veröffentlichungen der Österreichischen Historikerkommission. Vermögensentzug während der NS-Zeit sowie Rückstellungen und Entschädigungen seit 1945 in Österreich.*

Angrick, Andrei, Klaus Hesse, and Stiftung Topographie des Terrors, eds. 2010. *Topographie des Terrors: Gestapo, SS und Reichssicherheitshauptamt in der Wilhelm- und Prinz-Albrecht-Straße; eine Dokumentation.* Berlin: Stiftung Topographie des Terror.

Anonymous. 1992. "175 [Hundertfünfundsiebzig] Jahre Verlagsauslieferung Rudolf Lechner & Sohn". *Buch* 127, n° 3: 6–7.

Anonymous. 2009. "Biografisches Archiv, Juden in Leipzig, Teil 1". *Journal Juden in Sachsen*, March, 3–68.

Antiquariat Bernard Richter. 1995. *Sexualwissenschaft V: perversions* [book catalogue]. Berlin/Baden-Baden.

Apitzsch, Georges. 2006. *Lettres d'un inverti allemand au docteur Alexandre Lacassagne, 1903–1908*, edited by Philippe Artières. Paris: EPEL.

Areco, Victor. 1914. *Das Liebesleben der Zigeuner.* Vol. 3 of *Das Liebesleben aller Zeiten und Völker.* Leipzig: Leipziger Verlag.

Arnal, Elisabeth. 1998. "Le Centre Universitaire Méditerranéen de 1933 à 1947". Master's thesis, Université de Nice-Sophia-Antipolis.

Arnbom, Marie-Theres [*sic*], and Christoph Wagner-Trenkwitz, eds. 2005. *"Grüss mich Gott!": Fritz Grünbaum 1880–1941: ein Biographie.* Wien: C. Brandstätter.

Asprey, Robert B. 1959. *The Panther's Feast.* New York: Putnam.

B. C. 1935. "Magnus Hirschfeld et la lutte contre l'Article 175". *La Grande Réforme* 5, n° 52, August 1935, 3.

Babich, Elena. 2019. "The Fascination with a Person Affected by Hirsutism: Portrait of Helena Antonia from the Velké Losiny Castle Collections". *European Journal of Arts*, n° 3, 74–77.

Bach, Susanne. 1991. *Karussell: von München nach München.* Nürnberg: Frauen in der Einen Welt.

Bach, Ulrich. 2016. "Leo Schidrowitz' *Bilder-Lexikon der erotik* (Wien: 1928–1931)". In *Pornographie in der deutschen Literatur: Texte, Themen, Institutionen*, edited by Hans-Edwin Friedrich, Sven Hanuschek, and Christoph Rauen, 267–74. München: Belleville.

Baculus [Blum, Paul]. 1912. *Brünner Anlagen.* Brünn: L. & A. Brecher.

Bækgaard, Ellen. 1984 (1985). *Das sexualwissenschaftliche Institut in Berlin.* In *Paradiset er ikke til salg, trangen til at være begge køn. København*: Hertoft & Ritzau. Reprinted in *Mitteilungen der Magnus-Hirschfeld-Gesellschaft* 5: 32–35. Citations refer to the reprint edition from 1985.

Bakacsy, Judith. 2003. "Paul Engelmann: (1891–1965); ein biographischer Versuch". PhD diss., Universität Innsbruck. http://www.uibk.ac.at/brenner-archiv/bibliothek/pdf/bakacsy-engelmann-fertig.pdf.

Baránek, Daniel. 2017. *Židé na Ostravsku: dynamika a pluralita židovské společnosti 1832–1942.* Ostrava: Židovská obec v Ostravě.

Barbedette, Gilles, and Michel Carassou. 1981. *Paris Gay 1925.* Paris: Presses de la Renaissance.

Barnes, James J., and Patience P. Barnes. 2005. *Nazis in Pre-War London, 1930–1939: The Fate and Role of Germany Party Members and British Sympathizers.* Brighton: Sussex Academic Press.

Bato, Yomtov Ludwig. 1965. "Vorfahren und Familienangehörige von Rabbiner Dr. Leo Baeck". *Zeitschrift für die Geschichte der Juden* 2, n°s 1–4: 65–68.

Bauer, Heike. 2021. "The Institute of Sexual Science and Sexual Subcultures in 1920s Berlin = Das Institut für Sexualwissenschaft und sexuelle Subkulturen im Berlin der 1920er Jahre". In *Happy in Berlin? English Writers in the City, the 1920s and Beyond = Englische Autor*innen der 1920er und 30er Jahre*, edited by Gesa Stedmann Stefano Evangelista, 75–93. Göttingen: Wallstein. Baumgardt, Manfred. 1984. "Hirschfelds Testament". *Mitteilungen der Magnus-Hirschfeld-Gesellschaft*, n° 4 (October): 7–12.

—, Ralf Dose, Manfred Herzer, Hans-Günter Klein, Ilse Kokula, and Geza Lindemann. 1985. *Magnus Hirschfeld: Leben und Werk: Eine Ausstellung aus Anlass seines 50. Todestags: Katalog.* Vol. 3 of *Schriftenreihe der Magnus-Hirschfeld-Gesellschaft.* Berlin: Verlag rosa Winkel.

—. 2000. "Die Abwicklung des Instituts für Sexualwissenschaft (I.f.S.): Die Prozesse und ihre Folgen (1950–1965)". *Schwule Geschichte*, n° 4 (July): 18–40.

—. 2003. “Kaffeerunde mit Adelheid Schulz”. *Schwule Geschichte*, n° 7, 4–16.

Beachy, Robert. 2014. *Gay Berlin: Birthplace of a Modern Identity*. New York: Knopf.

Bečvová, Romana. 2007. “Beteiligt euch, - es geht um eure Erde: Die Tourneen des politisch-satirischen Kabaretts ‘Die Pfeffermühle’ in der Tschechoslowakei und Analyse ausgewählter Texte”. Master’s thesis, Masaryk University, Faculty of Arts, Department of German, Nordic and Dutch Studies.

Beer, Fritz. 1992. *Hast du auf Deutsche geschossen, grandpa?: Fragmente einer Lebensgeschichte*. Berlin: Aufbau Verlag.

Beier, Klaus M. 2013. “Hirschfelds Erbe und die moderne Sexualmedizin”. *Sexuologie* 20, n°s 1–2: 89–97.

Bellanger, Emmanuel. 2008. *La mort, une affaire publique: histoire du syndicat intercommunal funéraire de la région parisienne, fin XXe-début XXIe siècle*. Ivry-sur-Seine: Éditions de l’Atelier.

Belloc, Hilaire. 1927. *Die Juden*. München: J. Kösel & F. Pustet.

Bendová, Lenka. 2019. “Zámecká knihovna Defurovy Lažany - fond Otokara Kruliše-Randy”. *Acta Musei Nationalis Pragae - Historia litterarum* 64, n°s 1–2: 22–34.

Beneš, František, and Patricia Tošnerová. 1996. *Pošta v ghettu Terezín = Die Post im Ghetto Theresienstadt = Mail Service in the Ghetto Terezín 1941–1945*. Praha: Dům filatelie Profil.

Benjamin, Harry. 1966. *The Transsexual Phenomenon*. New York: Julian Press.

Bergemann, Hans, Ralf Dose, Marita Keilson-Lauritz, and Kevin Dubout, eds. 2019. *Magnus Hirschfelds Exil-Gästebuch*. Leipzig: Hentrich & Hentrich.

—. 2019. “Magnus Hirschfelds Gästebuch im Exil 1933–1935”. In *Magnus Hirschfelds Exil-Gästebuch*, edited by Hans Bergemann, Ralf Dose, Marita Keilson-Lauritz, and Kevin Dubout, 27–35. Leipzig: Hentrich & Hentrich.

—, and Marita Keilson-Lauritz. 2020. “Auszüge über Magnus Hirschfeld aus Max Reiss’ Briefen an seine Eltern, Juni bis August 1934 (Dokumentation)”. *Mitteilungen der Magnus-Hirschfeld-Gesellschaft*, n°s 65–66, 42–46. For the Dutch original, see Broers 2016b.

—, Ralf Dose, and Marita Keilson-Lauritz. 2021. *Magnus Hirschfelds Exil-Gästebuch: Nachträge und Korrekturen*. [Berlin: Magnus-Hirschfeld-Gesellschaft].

Berner, Dieter. 1989a. “Zur Fundgeschichte von Tao Li’s Namenszug”. *Mitteilungen der Magnus-Hirschfeld-Gesellschaft*, n° 13: 5–7.

—. 1989b. “Eine Lektion in Chinesisch”. *Mitteilungen der Magnus-Hirschfeld-Gesellschaft*, n° 14: 5–8.—. 1993. “Nachtrag zur Artikelserie: ‘Hirschfeld im Exil’”. *Gay News*, n° 1: 10–11.

Bernhardt, Heike. 2016. “Die Drei Abhandlungen zur Sexualtheorie von Sigmund Freud kehren in die Bibliothek der Magnus-Hirschfeld-Gesellschaft ‘zurück’”. *Mitteilungen der Magnus-Hirschfeld-Gesellschaft*, n° 54 (June): 24–26.

Beucler, André. 1932. “Berlin secret: Institut für Sexualwissenschaft”. *Voilà* (n° 55), April 9, 1932, 6–7.

—. 1980. *De Saint-Petersbourg à Saint-Germain-des-Prés: souvenirs*. Paris: Gallimard.

Birchall, Frederick T. 1933. “Nazi Book-Burning Fails to Stir Berlin”. *New York Times*, May 11, 1933, 1, 12.

Bircken, Margrid, and Helmut Peitsche, eds. 2003. *Brennende Bücher: Erinnerungen an den 10. Mai 1933*. Potsdam: Brandenburgische Landeszentrale für Politische Bildung.

Bispinck, Henri, and Katharina Hochmuth, eds. 2014. *Flüchtlingslager im Nachkriegsdeutschland: Migration, Politik, Erinnerung*. Berlin: Links.

Bloch, Anny, and Grete Tugendhat. [1937?]. *Bericht über die Tätigkeit der Brünner Arbeitsgemeinschaft der Liga für Menschenrechte in der Tschechoslowakei 1933–1937*. Brünn: Selbstverlag.

Blum, Heinrich. 1905. *Salomon Breier’s Werdegang: humoristisches Lebensbild*. Brünn: L. & A. Brecher.

Boberach, Heinz. 1991. *Teil 1 Reichszentralbehörden, regionale Behörden und wissenschaftliche Hochschulen für die zehn westdeutschen Länder sowie Berlin*. Vol. 3 of *Inventar archivalischer Quellen des NS-Staates: die Überlieferung von Behörden und Einrichtungen des Reiches, der Länder und der NSDAP*, compiled by Werner Röder and Christoph Weisz. Berlin and Boston: Saur.

Bock, Sigrid. 2003. “‘Geglüht und gehärtet’? Zu Funktionen und Folgen der Bücherverbrennung 1933". In *Brennende Bücher: Erinnerungen an den 10. Mai 1933*, edited by Margrid Bircken, and Helmut Peitsch, 58–83. Potsdam: Brandenburgische Landeszentrale für Politische Bildung.

Bohrmann, Hans, and Gabriele Toepser-Ziegert, eds. 1998. *Band 5/January-April 1937. Register*. Vol. 5 of *NS-Presseanweisungen der Vorkriegszeit: Edition und Dokumentation*. Berlin and Boston: Saur.

Bondi, Gustav. 1907. *Fünfundzwanzig Jahre Eigenregie: Geschichte des Brünner Stadttheaters 1882–1907*. Brünn: G. Bondi.

—. 1924. *Geschichte des Brünner deutschen Theaters 1600–1925*. Brünn: Verlag des Deutschen Theatervereines.

Bondy, Hugo. 1921. "Trestnost homosexuality. (K reformě § 129 I. b. tr. z.)". *Revue v neuropsychopathologii, therapii, veřejné hygieně a lékařství* 18, n°s 1–2: 20–24.

—. 1921. "K operativní léčbě homosexuality". *Časopis lékařů českých* (n° 31), July 30, 1921, 468.

—. 1921. "Ustav pro sexuální vědy v Berlíně". *Časopis lékařů českých* (n° 42), October 15, 1921, 677.

—. 1922. "Kolem nového trestního zákona. Homosexualita a §§ 129–130 trest. zák. rak. a čsl". *Československá republika* 243, n° 281, October 13, 1922, 4.

—. 1924. "František Jelínek: Homosexualita ve světle védy". *Časopis lékařů českých* (n° 26), June 28, 1924, 999.

—. 1925. *K trestnosti homosexuality: Příspěvek k reformě § 129 tr. z.* Brno: Sjezdový výbor.

—. 1928. "II. mezinárodní kongres pro pohlavní reformu na podkladě pohlavní vědy". *Časopis lékařů českých* (n° 32), September 21, 1928, 1350–51.

—. 1929. "Die Reformbestrebungen im neueren Entwurf des tsechoslowakischen Gesetzbuches". In *Sexual Reform Congress / Copenhagen 1.-5.: VII: 1928 / W.L.S.R. / World League for Sexual Reform = Weltliga für Sexualreform* = Ligue mondiale pour la réforme sexuelle = Tutmonda ligo por seksoj reformoj / Proceedings of the second congress = *Bericht des zweiten Kongresses = Compte rendu du deuxième congrès = Dokumentaro de la dua kongreso*, edited by Hertha Riese and J. H. Leunbach, 240–253. Copenhagen and Leipzig: Levin & Munksgaard/Georg Thieme Verlag.

—. 1934. "Sexuologie". *Sociálne zdravotní revue* 2, n° 3, March 25, 1934, 59–60.

Bondy, Ruth. 1989. *"Elder of the Jews": Jakob Edelstein of Theresienstadt*. New York: Grove Press.

—. 2003. *Mezi námi řečeno: jak mluvili Židé v Čechách a na Moravě*. Prague: Nakladatelství Franze Kafky.

Bopp, Dominika, ed. & trans.; and Sascha Feuchert, Andrea Löw, Jörg Riecke, Markus Roth, and Elisabeth Turvold, eds. 2020. *Die Enzyklopädie des Gettos Lodz / Litzmannstadt*. Göttingen: Wallstein.

Borchers, Wolf. 2001. *Mannliche Homosexualitat in der Dramatik der Weimarer Republik*. Cologne: Universitat zu Koln. http://webdoc.gwdg.de/ebook/d/2003/uni-koeln/11w1293.pdf

Botsch, Gideon. 2010. "Der Weg studentischer Aktivisten in die Einsatzgruppen der SS". In *Verfemt und Verboten: Vorgeschichte und Folgen der Bücherverbrennungen 1933*, edited by Julius H.Schoeps and Werner Treß, 191–207. Vol. 2 of *Wissenschaftliche Begleitbände im Rahmen der Bibliothek Verbrannter Bücher*. Hildesheim, Zürich, and New York: Georg Olms.

Bourdieu, Pierre. 1979. *La distinction: critique sociale du jugement*. Paris: Minuit.

Brand, Margarethe; Herzer, Manfred and Dieter Berner. 2000. "Besuche in Wilhelmshagen". In *Emanzipation hinter der Weltstadt: Adolf Brand und die Gemeinschaft der Eigenen; Katalog zur Ausstellung vom 7. Oktober bis 17. November 2000 in Berlin-Friedrichshagen*, edited by Marita Keilson-Lauritz and Rolf F. Lang, 87–100. Vol. 4 of *Edition Friedrichshagen*. Berlin-Friedrichshagen: Müggel-Verlag Rolf F. Lang.

Bránský, Jaroslav. 1995. *Osud Židů z Boskovic a bývalého okresu boskovického 1939–1945*. Boskovice: Albert/Muzeum Boskovicka.

—. 1999. *Židé v Boskovicích*. Boskovice: Klub přátel Boskovic/Albert.

Brechelmacher, Angelika. 2015. *Postkarten aus dem Getto Litzmannstadt = Postcards from Litzmannstadt Ghetto*. In *Post 41: Berichte aus dem Getto Litzmannstadt: ein Gedenkbuch = Post 41: Reports from Litzmannstadt Ghetto: A Memorial Book*, edited by Angelika Brechelmacher, Bertrand Perz, and Regina Wonisch. Vienna: Mandelbaum.

Brecher, Elise. 1904. "Über Weininger". *Neues Frauenleben* 16, n° 9, n.p. [book review of

Weiberhass und Weiberverachtung by Grete Meisel-Hess].

—. 1911. "Stimmrechtsbrief aus Mähren". *Neues Frauenleben* 25, n° 8: 213–214.

Břečka, Jan, and Jiří Mitáček, eds. 2014. *In Suffering and Fighting: The Jews of Brno in Fateful Moments of the 20th Century*. Brno: Moravian Museum.

Brenner, Arthur David. 2001. *Emil J. Gumbel: Weimar German Pacifist and Professor*. Boston and Leiden: Brill.

Brenner-Wonschick, Hannelore. 2009. *The Girls of Room 28: Friendship, Hope, and Survival in Theresienstadt*. New York: Schocken Books.

Bringuier, Paul. 1934. "Septembre 33-septembre 34: la patience". *Détective* 7, n° 307, September 13, 1934, 7.

Brocke, Michael, and Julius Carlebach, eds.; and Carsten Wilke. 2004. *Die Rabbiner der Emanzipationszeit in den deutschen, böhmischen und grosspolnischen Ländern 1781–1871*. Vol. 1 of *Biographisches Handbuch der Rabbiner*. Munich: Saur.

Broers, Jean-Bart. 2016a. "Max Reiss – ein Lebensbild". *Mitteilungen der Magnus-Hirschfeld-Gesellschaft*, n°s 55–56 (December): 31–33.

Broers, Jean-Bart. 2016b. Woordelijk gelijkluidende uittreksels uit de brieven van Max Reiss aan zijn ouders. Typescript. For a German translation of this text, see Bergemann & Keilson-Lauritz 2020.

Brummer, Alexandr, and Michal Konečný. 2013 *Brno nacistické: průvodce městem*. Brno: Host.

Brunner, Andreas. 2016. *Das schwule Wien: Der Guide zu Kunst, Kultur & Szene*. [Vienna]: Metroverlag.

Brunner, Andreas, and Hannes Sulzenbacher. 2016. "Die verborgene schwule Topografie der Stadt". In *Sex in Wien: Lust. Kontrolle. Ungehorsam.*, edited by Andreas Brunner, Frauke Kreutler, Michaela Lindinger, Gerhard Milchram, Martina Nußbaumer, Hannes Sulzenbacher, and Wien Museum Karlsplatz, 260–266. Vienna: Metroverlag.

Bryant, Chad. 2007. *Prague in Black: Nazi Rule and Czech Nationalism*. Cambridge, London: Harvard University Press.

Buchhas, Sigrid. 1994. *Der österreichische Buchhandel im Nationalsozialismus: Ein Beitrag zur Geschichte des Buchhandels unter besonderer Berücksichtigung Wiens*. Thesis, University of Vienna.

Bullough, Vern L., W. Dorr Legg, Barrett W. Elcano, and James Kepner. 1976. *An Annotated Bibliography of Homosexuality*, 2 vols. New York: Garland Publishing.

Buot, François. 2013. *Gay Paris: une histoire du Paris interlope entre 1900 et 1940*. Paris: Fayard.

Burian, Michal, Aleš Knížek, Jiří Raylich, and Eduard Stehlík. 2002. *Assassination: Operation Anthropoid 1941–1942*. Prague: Avis. http://www.army.cz/images/id_7001_8000/7419/assassination-en.pdf

Bušek, Michal, and Galerie Roberta Guttmanna, eds. 2007. *"Hope is on the next page": 100 years of the library of the Jewish Museum in Prague*. Prague: Jewish Museum.C.

Čapek, Karel. 1933. "Memento". *Lidové noviny*, May 21, 1933, 1.

Čapková, Kateřina, and Michal Frankl. 2012. *Unsichere Zuflucht: die Tschechoslowakei und ihre Flüchtlinge aus NS-Deutschland und Österreich 1933–1938*. Vienna: Böhlau.

Car, Emmanuel. 1933. "La Sainte Vehme à Paris". *Voilà* 3, n° 136, October 28, 1933, 8–9.

Caron, Vicki. 2008. *L'asile incertain: la crise des refugiés juifs en France, 1933–1942*. Paris: Tallandier.

Caruso, Alexandra. 2015. "… fast wie ein Krieg. Alexandra Caruso im Interview mit Uri Arthur Peled-Feldmann". In *Spurensuche: Die Sammlung Arthur Feldmann und die Albertina*, edited by Achim Gnann and Heinz Schödl, 33–41. Special volume, *Schriftenreihe der Kommission für Provenienzforschung* Cologne.

Celovsky [Čelovský], Boris. 2005. *Germanisierung und Genozid: Hitlers Endlösung der tschechischen Frage; deutsche Dokumente 1933–1945*. Dresden: Neisse; Brno: Stilus.

Černá, Iveta, Kateřina Konečná, Veronika Lukešová, Jakub Pernes, Petr Svoboda, Petra Svobodová, Lucie Valdhansová, and Věra Vystavělová. 2017. Exploring the History of the Textile Industrialists in Brno: Löw-Beer, Stiassni, Tugendhat. [Brno]: Muzeum Brněnska.

Černil, František. 1945. "Anno domini 1939". *Rovnost*, June 29, 1945, 3. (Also published in *Čin*, June 29, 1945, 3).

Černil, Standa [Stanislav]. 1932. "Kamarád". *Kamarád* 1, n° 1, May 28, 1932, 11.

Černý, Bohumil. 1997. "Die Emigration der Juden aus den Böhmischen Ländern 1938–1941". *Theresienstädter Studien und Dokumente*, n° 4, 63–85.

Černý, Vladimír. 2006. "Protipartyzánské operace na Moravě v letech 1944–1945". PhD diss., Masaryk University. https://is.muni.cz/th/16005/ff_d/—. 2018. *Brněnské Gestapo 1939–1945 a poválečné soudní procesy s jeho příslušníky*. Brno: Archiv města Brna; Moravské zemské muzeum.

Čeřovský, František. 1922. "Kolem nového trestního zákona. Homosexualita a §§ 129–130 trest. zák. rak. a čsl". *Československá republika* 243, n° 292, October 24, 1922, 5–6.

—. 1934. "Nutnost reformy trestního zákona stran trestání osob pohlavně odlišně založených (homosexuálních)". *Sociálne zdravotní revue* 2, n° 3, March 25, 1934, 55–59.

—. 1938. "Boj o reformu trest. zákona *(§ 129* l.b tr. z.)". *Hlas přírody* 1, n° 1, September 1938, 3–4.

Chaponnière, Corinne. 2015. *Les quatre coups de la Nuit de cristal: Paris, 7 novembre 1938: L'affaire Grynszpan-vom Rath*. Paris: Albin Michel.

Chickering, Roger. 1998. *Imperial Germany and the Great War, 1914–1918*. Cambridge: Cambridge University Press.

Chlapcová-Gforgjovičová, Julka. 1932. "Pátý mezinárodní sexuologický kongres". *Ženská rada*, 193–94.

Císař, V., and V. D. [Vilém Drexler] Hlubocký. N.d. [1933?]. *Zapomenutý život ...: drama o třech jednáních*. V Brtnici: Josef Birnbaum.

Cohen, Marc. 2002. "Quelques repères biographiques = Einige biographische Eckdaten". In *Henri Nouveau: au-delà de l'abstraction = Henrik Neugeboren: jenseits der Abstraktion: 1901–1959*, edited by Christophe Duvivier, Marius Joachim Tataru, Pavel Liška189–195. Paris: Somogy.

Comité international d'aide aux victimes du fascisme hitlérien. 1933. *Livre brun sur l'incendie du Reichstag et la terreur hitlérienne*. Vol. 1 of *Réquisitoires*. Paris: Éditions du Carrefour.

[Condell, Jennie, ed.]. 2005. *The Day War Ended: Voice and Memories from 1945*. London: Weidenfeld and Nicolson.

Court, Jürgen. 2019. *Institute für Leibesübungen 1920–1925*. Vol. 3 of *Deutsche Sportwissenschaft in der Weimarer Republik und im Nationalsozialismus*. Münster: LIT Verlag.

Crowhurst, Patrick. 2013. *Hitler and Czechoslovakia in World War II: Domination and Retaliation*. London: Tauris.

Cullen, Tom. 2014. *The Man Who Was Norris: The Life of Gerald Hamilton*. Sawtry: Dedalus.

Czech, Danuta. 1990. Auschwitz Chronicle: 1939–1945. New York: Holt.

Dannecker, Martin. 2009. "Hans Giese (1920–1970)". In *Personenlexikon der Sexualforschung*, edited by Volkmar Sigusch and Günter Grau, 226–235. Frankfurt: Campus.

de Buton, Alice. 2007. "Wie arbeitet der Neueingesiedelte im Getto". In *Die Chronik des Gettos Lodz / Litzmannstadt*, edited by Sascha Feuchert, Erwin Leibfried, and Jörg Riecke, 20–23 (including Appendix and Supplements). Göttingen: Wallstein-Verlag.

Demetz, Peter. 2008. *Prague in Danger: The Years of German Occupation, 1939–45: Memories and History, Terror and Resistance, Theater and Jazz, Film and Poetry, Politics and War*. New York: Farrar, Straus and Giroux.

Delpêche, René. 1955. *Les dessous de Paris: souvenirs vécus par l'ex-inspecteur principal de la brigade mondaine Louis Métra*. Paris: Les éditions du Scorpio.

d'Elvert, Christian. 1866. *Zur Cultur-Geschichte Mährens und Oest.-Schlesiens*. Brünn: Rudolf M. Rohrer.

Dereymez, Jean-William, ed. 2008. *Le refuge et le piège: les Juifs dans les Alpes, 1938–1945: actes du colloque, Grenoble, décembre 2004*. Paris: l'Harmattan.

Detering, Heinrich. 1994. *Das offene Geheimnis: zur literarischen Produktivität eines Tabus von Winckelmann bis zu Thomas Mann*. Göttingen: Wallstein.

Diebow, Hans. 1938. *Der ewige Jude: 165 Bilddokumente*. Munich and Berlin: Eher.

[Dobler, Jens], and Norbert Baxmann. 1999. "Die verschwundene Schorer-Bibliothek – Ein Zwischenbericht". *Mitteilungen der Magnus-Hirschfeld-Gesellschaft*, n°s. 29–30 (July): 87–95.

Dobler, Jens. 2003. *Von anderen Ufern: Geschichte der Berliner Lesben und Schwulen in Kreuzberg und Friedrichshain*. Berlin: Bruno Gmünder.

—. 2004. *Prolegomena zu Magnus Hirschfelds Jahrbuch für sexuelle Zwischenstufen (1899 bis 1923): Register – Editionsgeschichte – Inhaltsbeschreibungen*. Vol. 11 of *Schriftenreihe der Magnus-Hirschfeld-Gesellschaft*. Hamburg: von Bockel.

—. 2008. *Zwischen Duldungspolitik und Verbrechensbekämpfung: Homosexuellenverfolgung durch die Berliner Polizei von 1848 bis 1933*. Frankfurt: Verlag für Polizeiwissenschaft.

—. 2016. *Dr. Fritz Flato (1895–1949): Anwalt der ersten Homosexuellenbewegung: eine Expertise im Auftrag der Landesstelle für Gleichbehandlung – gegen Diskriminierung (Landesantidiskriminierungsstelle – LADS), Fachbereich für die Belange von Lesben, Schwulen, Bisexuellen, trans- und intergeschlechtlichen Menschen (LSBTI)*. Berlin: Senatsverwaltung für Justiz, Verbraucherschutz und Antidiskriminierung. Landesstelle für Gleichbehandlung – gegen Diskriminierung.

—. 2020. *Polizei und Homosexuelle in der Weimarer Republik: Zur Konstruktion des Sündenbabels*. Berlin: Metropol.

—. 2022. *You have never seen a dancer like Voo Doo: das unglaubliche Leben des Willi Pape*. Berlin: Berlin Brandenburg.

Dobroszycki, Lucjan, ed. 1984. *The Chronicle of the Łódź Ghetto 1941–1944*, translated by Richard Lourie, Joachim Neugroschel and others. New Haven and London: Yale University Press.

Dokumentationsarchiv des österreichischen Widerstandes, Mary Steinhauser, ed. 1987. *Totenbuch Theresienstadt: damit sie nicht vergessen werden*. Vienna: Junius.

Dose, Ralf. 1993. "Thesen zur Weltliga für Sexualreform – Notizen aus der Werkstatt". *Mitteilungen der Magnus-Hirschfeld-Gesellschaft*, n° 19 (November): 23–39.

—. 1999. "The World League for Sexual Reform: Some Possible Approaches". In *Sexual Cultures in Europe: National Histories*, edited by Franz X. Eder, Lesley Hall, and Gert Hekma, 242–259. Manchester: Manchester University Press.

—. 2003a. "In memoriam Li Shiu Tong (1907–1993). Zu seinem 10. Todestag am 5.10.2003". *Mitteilungen der Magnus-Hirschfeld-Gesellschaft*, n°s 35–36 (December): 9–23.

—, and Pamela Eve Selwyn. 2003b. "The World League for Sexual Reform: Some Possible Approaches". *Journal of the History of Sexuality* 12, n° 1: 1–15.

—. 2005a. Magnus Hirschfeld: Deutscher, Jude, Weltbürger. Teetz: Hentrich & Hentrich.

—, and Rainer Herrn. 2005b. "Um das Erbe Magnus Hirschfelds". *AKMB-news (Informationen zu Kunst, Museum und Bibliothek)* 11, n° 2, 19–23.

—, and Rainer Herrn. 2006. "Verloren 1933: Bibliothek und Archiv des Instituts für Sexualwissenschaft in Berlin". In *Jüdischer Buchbesitz als Raubgut: Zweites Hannoversches Symposium*, edited by Regine Dehnel, 37–51. Special edition, *Zeitschrift für Bibliothekswesen und Bibliographie*, 88. Frankfurt: Vittorio Klostermann.

—, and Marita Keilson-Lauritz. 2010. "'Vielen Dank, Erich Kästner !': Die Berliner Bücherverbrennung – am Morgen nach der Tat". In *Verfemt und Verboten: Vorgeschichte und Folgen der Bücherverbrennungen 1933*, edited by Julius H. Schoeps and Werner Treß, 169–176. Vol. 2 of *Wissenschaftliche Begleitbände im Rahmen der Bibliothek Verbrannter Bücher*, vol. 2. Hildesheim: Georg Olms.

—. 2011 "Es gibt noch einen Koffer in New York – eine vorläufige Bestanssaufnahme". *Mitteilungen der Magnus-Hirschfeld-Gesellschaft*, n°s 46–47 (May): 12–20.

—. 2012. Thirty Years of Collecting Our History – Or: How to Find Treasure Troves. Presentation given at the ALMS conference Amsterdam, August 1–3, 2012, dated June 18, 2012. https://magnus-hirschfeld.de/site/assets/files/1087/dose_alms.pdf.

—. 2014. *Magnus Hirschfeld: The Origins of the Gay Liberation Movement*. New York: Monthly Review Press.

—. 2015. *Das verschmähte Erbe: Magnus Hirschfelds Vermächtnis an die Berliner Universität*. Berlin: Hentrich & Hentrich.

—. 2016. "'Es gab doch für ihn ein sogenanntes bürgerliches Leben schon sehr lange nicht mehr'. Dr. med. Felix Abraham – Fragmente eines Lebens". *Mitteilungen der Magnus-Hirschfeld-Gesellschaft*, n° 54 (June): 9–23.

—. 2019 "Magnus Hirschfeld in Frankreich". In *Magnus Hirschfelds Exil-Gästebuch*, edited by Hans Bergemann, Ralf Dose, Marita Keilson-Lauritz, and Kevin Dubout, 11–25. Leipzig: Hentrich & Hentrich.

—. 2020a. "Jahrestage". In *Liebe und Gerechtigkeit: zum 150. Geburtstag von Magnus Hirschfeld*, edited by Bundestiftung Magnus Hirschfeld, 23–25. Göttingen: Wallstein.

—. 2020b. "Magnus Hirschfeld als Vortragsredner". In *Der Anschlag auf Magnus Hirschfeld: Ein Blick auf das reaktionäre München 1920*, edited by Albert Knoll, 23–39. Munich: Forum Queeres Archiv München.

—. 2021. "Haus-, medizinisches und Verwaltungspersonal des Instituts für Sexualwissenschaft". *Mitteilungen der Magnus-Hirschfeld-Gesellschaft*, n° 67 (July): 9–32.

Douxchamps, Charles. 1907. *De la profession d'avocat et d'avoué*. Brussels: Vve Ferd. Lacier; Paris: A. Pedone.

Dubois, Gaston [Karl Meier]. 1934. "Das falsche Bild". *Schweizerisches Freundschafts-Banner* 2, n° 11, June 1, 1934, 1–2.

Dubout, Kevin and Raimund Wolfert. 2013. "Eigentümliche Städte, sympathische Völker und Sehenswürdigkeiten von großer Schönheit. Zur Skandinavien-Rundreise des WhK-Aktivisten Eugen Wilhelm 1901". *Invertito* 15, 9–44.

Dudek, Peter. 2012. *"Er war halt genialer als die anderen": biografische Annäherungen an Siegfried Bernfeld*. Gießen: Psychosozial-Verlag.

Dušek, Otto. 2020. *Brno # 4*. Brno: Mapcards.net.

du Teil, Roger. 1935. *Spécialisation et évolution: essai pragmatique sur la transcendance nécessaire de la loi morale*. Paris: F. Alcan.

—. 1946. *Vie communautaire, liberté vraie*. Valence: Rassemblement communautaire français.

Duvivier, Christophe, Marius Joachim Tataru, and Pavell Liška, eds. 2002. *Henri Nouveau: au-delà de l'abstraction = Henrik Neugeboren: jenseits der Abstraktion: 1901–1959*. Paris: Somogy.

E. H. 1921. "Das Institut für Sexuologie: ein Tribunal für sexuelle Minderheiten". *Prager Presse*, September 25, 1921, 4.

Eberle, Annette. 1994. *Die Arbeiterkolonie Herzogsägmühle: Beiträge zur Geschichte der bayerischen Obdachlosenhilfe*. Peiting: Selbstverlag.

Ehrlich, Jacques, Monique Ehrlich, and Nicole Ehrlich. 2015. "D'après Mayou. Une femme courageuse à travers le XXème siècle de Königshofen à Nice: des fleurs sous les barbelés". Unpublished typescript. The interview was conducted in 1990–91.

Eichhorn, Maria, Anh-Linh Ngo, and Arno Löbbecke. 2015. Wohnungsfrage. In den Zelten 4 / 5 / 5A / 6 / 7 / 8 / 9 / 9A / 10, Kronprinzenufer 29/30, Beethovenstrasse 1 / 2 / 3 (1832 bis / to 1959) > John-Foster-Dulles-Allee 10 (seit / since 1959), Berlin. Publication in conjunction with the exhibition titled Wohnungsfrage held in the Haus der Kuluren der Welt (Berlin) from October 23, 2015, to December 14, 2015. Berlin: Haus der Kulturen der Welt.

Eisenberg-Bach, Susi. 1986. *Im Schatten von Notre Dame*. London: World of Books; Worms: Verlag Heintz.

Eisermann, Falk. 2001. *"Stimulus amoris": Inhalt, lateinische Ueberliefering, deutsche Uebersetzungen, Rezeption. Münchener Texte und Untersuchungen zur deutschen Literatur des Mittelalters*, vol. 118. Tübingen: Max Niemeyer Verlag.

Elledge, Jim. 2023. *An Angel in Sodom: Henry Gerber and the Birth of the Gay Rights Movement*. Chicago: Chicago Review Press.

Elias, Ruth. 1998. *Triumph of Hope: From Theresienstadt and Auschwitz to Israel*. Translated by Margot Bettauer Dembo. New York: John Wiley.

Eliav, Mordechai, Esriel Hildesheimer, Chana C. Schütz, Hermann Simon, and Jana Caroline Reimer. 2008. *Das Berliner Rabbinerseminar 1873–1938: seine Gründungsgeschichte – seine Studenten*. Vol. 5 of *Schriftenreihe des Centrum Judaicum*. Teetz and Berlin: Hentrich & Hentrich.

Elis, Hugh [Josef Weisskopf?]. 1930. *Liebesparadies: Leitfaden der Liebe und Ehe: Geheimnis der Liebe ohne Folgen*. Brünn: Privatverlag.

Emeis, Harald. 2007. "Les séjours de Roger Martin du Gard à Berlin". In *La littérature des voyages Roger Martin du Gard*, presented by Àngels Santa; edited by Irene Aguilà, 233–43. Vols. 11–12 of *L'ull crític*. Lleida: Edicions de la Universitat de Lleida.

Endlich, Stefanie. 2010. "'Brandspuren': Die Bücherverbrennung in der Erinnerungskultur". In *Verfemt und Verboten. Vorgeschichte und Folgen der Bücherverbrennungen 1933*, edited by Julius H. Schoeps and Werner Treß, 363–377. Vol. 2 of *Wissenschaftliche Begleitbände im Rahmen der Bibliothek Verbrannter Bücher*. Hildesheim: Georg Olms.

Engels, Eve-Marie, and Thomas F. Glick. 2008. *The Reception of Charles Darwin in Europe*. Vols. 1–2 of *The Reception of British and Irish Authors in Europe*. London: Continuum.

Engliš, Karel, and Karl Fein [the elder]. 1920. *Die Steuer von Güterübertragungen und Arbeitsleistungen und die Luxussteuer: Gesetz und Verordnung*. Brünn: Polygrafia.

Epstein, Julius. 1935. "Das neue Homosexuellen-Gesetz Sowjet-Russlands". *Zeitschrift für politische Psychologie und Sexualökonomie* 1, n° 2, 50–51.

Eßl, Julia. 2015. "Die Sammlung Feldmann: Spuren – Fragmente – Dokumente: Weg einer Rekonstruktion". In *Spurensuche: Die Sammlung Arthur Feldmann und die Albertina*, edited by Achim Gnann and Heinz Schödl, 9–23. Special volume, *Schriftenreihe der Kommission für Provenienzforschung* Cologne.

Evreinov, Nikolaj Nikolaevič. 1931. *Die Körperstrafen in der russischen Rechtspflege und Verwaltung*. Leipzig: Verlag für Sexualwissenschaft Schneider & Co.

Fahlman, Betsy. 2004. *Guy Pène du Bois: Painter of Modern Life*. New York: Quantuck Lane Press.

Fanel, Jiří. 2000. *Gay historie*. Prague: Dauphin.

Farcy, Jean-Claude. 1992. *Guide des archives judiciaires et pénitentiaires en France: 1800–1958*. Nanterre: Centre d'histoire de la France contemporaine.

Fein, Karl. 1930. "Gespräch mit Magnus Hirschfeld". *Tagesbote*, November 4, 1930, 3–4; repr. in *Neues Pressburger Tagblatt*, November 5, 1930, 11.

—. 1934a. "Die Homosexuellen und das Gesetz". *Nový hlas*, second German supplement D.Z.N.H. 2, n° 5 (May), 5–7.

—. 1934b. "Die Homosexuellen und das Gesetz (Ende)". *Nový hlas*, third German supplement D.Z.N.H. 2, n° 6 (June), 9–10.

—. 1934. "Die Homosexuellen und das Gesetz". *Freundschafts-Banner* 2, n° 19, October 1, 1934, 1–2.

Fein, Karel [Karl]. 1938. "§ 10. osnovy ministerstva spravedlnosti". *Hlas přírody: orgán "Ligy pro sexální reformu"* 1, n° 1 (September): 6–7.

Feldman, Michèle. 2012. *Le carnet noir: un notable israélite à Paris sous l'Occupation, 1er novembre 1942–12 octobre 1943*. Paris: L'Harmattan.

Feuchert, Sascha, Joanna Ratusinska, Elisabeth Turvold, Ewa Wiatr, Erwin Leibfried, Jörg Riecke, Julian Baranowski, Joanna Podolska, Krystyna Radziszewska, Jacek Walicki, Imke Janssen-Mignon, and Andrea Löw, eds. 2007. *Die Chronik des Gettos Lodz / Litzmannstadt*. 5 vols. Göttingen: Wallstein-Verlag.

—. 2007. "Die Getto-Chronik Entstehung und Überlieferung; Eine Projektskizze". In *Die Chronik des Gettos Lodz / Litzmannstadt*, edited by Sascha Feuchert, Joanna Ratusinska, Elisabeth Turvold, Ewa Wiatr, Erwin Leibfried, Jörg Riecke, Julian Baranowski, Joanna Podolska, Krystyna Radziszewska, Jacek Walicki, Imke Janssen-Mignon, and Andrea Löw, Appendix and Supplement, 167–90. Göttingen: Wallstein-Verlag.

Filip, Vladimír. N.d. *Brno staré pohlednice = Brno alte postkarten = Brno old postcards XI; Staré Brno I = Altbrünn I = Old Brno I*. Brno: Nakladatelství Josef Filip.

—, Vlastimil Schildberger, Jan Břečka, and Lubor Nedbal. 2011. *Brno 1939–1945: roky nesvobody = Brünn 1939–1945: Jahre in Unfreiheit*, vol. 1. Vol. 25 of *Bruna Aeterna*. Brno: Verlag Josef Filip.—, Jan Břečka,, Vlastimil Schildberger, and Lenka Kudělková. 2012. *Brno 1939–1945: roky nesvobody = Brünn 1939–1945: Jahre in Unfreiheit*, vol. 2. Vol. 29 of *Bruna Aeterna*. Brno: Verlag Josef Filip.

—, and Vlastimil Schildberger. 2013. *Brno 1939–1945: roky nesvobody = Brünn 1939–1945: Jahre in Unfreiheit*, vol. 3. Vol. 31 of *Bruna Aeterna*. Brno: Verlag Josef Filip.

Fischer, Ernst. 2013. "'… mit nationalsozialistischer Gründlichkeit': Der 'Anschluss' 1938 und seine Folgen für Verlag und Buchhandel in Österreich". In *Verlage im "Dritten Reich,"* edited by Klaus G. Saur, 189–210. Vol. 60, n° 6 of *Zeitschrift für Bibliothekswesen und Bibliographie*. Frankfurt: Vittorio Klostermann.

Fischer-Defoy, Christine, and Kaspar Nürnberg. 2011. "Zu treuen Händen: Eine Skizze über die Beteiligung von Berliner Speditionen am Kunstraub der Nationalsozialisten". *Aktives Museum Faschismus und Widerstand in Berlin e.V., Mitgliederrundbrief*, n° 65 (Jul): 7–12. http://www.aktives-museum.de/file admin/user_upload/Extern/Dokumente/ rundbrief_65.pdf

Foucart, Claude. 1986. "Le procès Krantz, ou un fait divers qui aurait pu devenir un roman gidien". *Bulletin des Amis d'André Gide*, n° 65 (January): 39–57.

Foucault, Michel. 1976. *La volonté de savoir. Histoire de la sexualité*, vol. 1. Paris: Gallimard.

—; J. P. Joecker, M. Ouerd, and A. Sanzio. 1982. "Histoire et homosexualité: entretien avec Michel Foucault". *Masques*, n° 13 (Spring): 15–24.

Friedjung, Josef R. 1932. "Das Kongreß für Sexualreform darf nicht in Frankreich tagen". *Arbeiter Zeitung*, September 29, 1932, 5.

Friedmann, Franz. 1997. "Rechtsstellung der Juden im Protektorat Böhmen und Mähren – Stand am 31.7.1942 für internen Gebrauch der Jüdischen Kultusgemeinde in Prag". In *Židé v Protektorátu: Hlášení Židovské náboženské obce v roce 1942: dokumenty*, compiled by Helena Krejčová, Jana Svobodová, and Anna Hyndráková, 232–63. Vol. 11 of *Historia nova*. Prague: Ústav pro soudobé dějiny AVČR / Maxdorf. [The original typescript can be found in the Yad Vashem archive, Jerusalem, sign. 07-CZ/4. For the publication of an earlier version, describing the situation in August 1940, see Utermöhle, Walther, H. G. Adler, and Herbert Schmerling. 1940. *Die Rechtsstellung der Juden im Protektorat Böhmen und Mähren: eine systematische Darstellung der gesamten Judengesetzgebung*. Prague: Böhmisch-Mährische Verlags- und Druckerei-Gesellschaft.]

Frischknecht, Beat. 2009. "'Der Racismus – ein Phantom als Weltgefahr': Der Fund eines verschollenen Typoskripts als Auslöser umfangreicher Recherchen". *Mitteilungen der Magnus-Hirschfeld-Gesellschaft*, n°s 43–44 (November): 21–34.

Frommer, Benjamin. 2005. *National Cleansing: Retribution against Nazi Collaborators in Postwar Czechoslovakia*. Cambridge: Cambridge University Press.

Fry, Michael. 1934. *Hitler's Wonderland*. London: John Murray.

Fuhrer, Armin. 2013. *Herschel: das Attentat des Herschel Grynszpan am 7. November 1938 und der Beginn des Holocaust*. Berlin: Berlin-Story.

Führing, Linda. 1996. "Das schnelle Ende von Lechner". *Wirtschaftsblatt*, December 21, 1996. http://wirtschaftsblatt.at/archiv/wirtschaft/992196/print.do

G. D. 1935. "Magnus Hirschfeld als Mensch und Persönlichkeit". *Pariser Tageblatt*, n° 524, May 20, 1935, 1.

G. V. V. 2020. "'Het huwelijk, dat is man en vrouw,' schreef hij". *De Morgen* [Belgium], December 3, 2020, 4.

Galerie Welz. 2006. *Victor Bauer (Wien 1902–1959 Nizza); Ölbilder, Aquarelle, Zeichnungen*; 22. März bis 30. April 2006, Galerie Welz, Salzburg. Salzburg: Galerie Welz.

Gao, Bei. 2013. *Shanghai Sanctuary: Chinese and Japanese Policy toward European Jewish Refugees during World War II*. Oxford: Oxford University Press.

Garcia, Daniel. 1999. *Les années Palace*. Paris: Flammarion.

Gaudet, Michel. 2001. *La Vie du Haut de Cagnes (1930–1980): La Bohème Ensoleillée*. Nice: Demaistre.

Gayraud, Didier. 2005. *Belles demeures en Riviera, 1835–1930*. Nice: Editions Gilletta.

Genger, Angela, and Hildegard Jakobs, eds. 2010. *Düsseldorf/Getto Litzmannstadt. 1941*. Essen: Klartext.

Gerwarth, Robert. 2011. *Hitler's Hangman: The Life of Heydrich*. New Haven: Yale University Press.

Giannini, Adriana. Nov. 30, 1999 (2008). "Les péripéties d'un monument: le xxe siècle accorde à Mendel reconnaissance et célébrations, mais lui réserve aussi quelques déplaisirs". *Les génies*, n° 35, May 1, 2008. https://www.pourlascience.fr/sd/histoire-sciences/les-peripeties-dun-monument-3735.php

Giardini, Cesare. 1935. *Lo strano caso del cavaliere d'Éon: 1728–1810*. Milan: Arnoldo Mondadori.

Giese, Hans. 1959. *L'Homosexualité de l'homme: psychogenèse, psychopathologie, psychanalyse, thérapeutique, étude scientifique à l'usage des éducateurs, des psychologues, des médecins et des juristes*. Paris: Payot.

Giese, Karl. 1921a. "Siber, Jules: Paganini. Ein Roman von alten Göttern und Hexentänzen". *Jahrbuch für sexuelle Zwischenstufen mit besonderer Berücksichtigung der Homosexualität* 21, n°s 3–4, 146–47.

Androgynos [Karl Giese]. 1921b. "Jourgeschichten. Skizzen. V. Die Zwei und die Dame". *Die Freundschaft* 3, n° 5, 3.

Giese, Karl. 1921–22. "Andersens Wesen und Werke". *Der Eigene: Ein Blatt für männliche Kultur* 9, n° 3: 78–83; n° 5: 150–54.

—. 1927. "Vom Institut für Sexualwissenschaft als Forschungs-, Lehr-, Heil- und Zufluchtsstätte". Special issue [titled „Überwindung der Geschlechtsnot"], *Junge Menschen: Monatshefte für Politik, Kunst, Literatur und Leben* 8, vol. 6 (June): 132–33.

—, and Richard Linsert. 1929a. "Hauptmann Barker, ihre Vorgänger und Kollegen". *Arbeiter-Illustrierte-Zeitung* 8, n° 14, 4–5. [On the cover of the magazine the article is announced as "Frauen als Männer" (women as men).]

—. 1929b. "Was unsere Väter pikant fanden". *Die Aufklärung* 1, n° 4, 105–8.

—. 1929c. "Eros im Museum: Ein Gang durch das Archiv des Instituts für Sexualwissenschaft". *Die Aufklärung* 1, n° 5, 139–42.

—. 1930a. "Transvestitismus und Eheberatung". *Die Aufklärung* 2, n° 3, 66–68.

—. 1930b. "Zeichnungen als sexuelles Ausdrucksmittel". *Die Aufklärung* 2, n°s 4–5, 92–94.

—. 1931a. "Liebes-Ersatz: über erotische Ersatzhandlungen". *Die Ehe* 6, n° [?], 292–93.

—. 1931b. "Selbsttötung auf sexueller Grundlage". *Die Ehe* 6, n° [?], 210–11.

—. 1931c. "Erotischer Verkleidungstrieb". *Detektiv* 1, n° [?], 10–12.

—. 1932a. "Sittliches und Modisches: sexualethnologische Betrachtungen". *Die Ehe* 7, n° 5, 134–36.

—. 1932b. "Cleopatra ... Herr William Shakespeare". *Die Ehe* 7, n° [12?], 365–67.

—. 1933. "André Gide: 'Corydon'. Vier Sokratische Dialoge". In *Sexus, Vierteljahreszeitschrift für die gesamte Sexualwissenschaft und Sexualreform*, 64.

—. 1934. "Vraždění homosexuelních (psáno pro Nový hlas)". *Nový hlas* 3, n° 1 (January): 9–10.

— [German version of previous] 2015. "Die Homosexuellenmorde". *Capri*, n° 49 (September): 33–35.

—. N.d. "The sexual causes underlying self-inflicted death". Unpublished manuscript, 3 pages.

Girardet, René. 1933. "La secrète I: la danse des sexes". *Détective* 6, n° 252, August 24, 1933, 12–13.

—. 1933. "La secrète II: [subtitle on consulted microfilm illegible]". *Détective* 6, n° 253, August 31, 1933, 12–13.

Gnann, Achim, and Heinz Schödl, eds. 2015. *Spurensuche: Die Sammlung Arthur Feldmann und die Albertina*. Special volume, *Schriftenreihe der Kommission für Provenienzforschung*. Cologne: Böhlau Verlag.

Godefroy, Christian. 1933. "Chassé de sa patrie, le professeur Hirschfeld nous dit qu'il s'établira probablement à Paris: 'J'avais passé ma vie à l'établissement d'une oeuvre dont il ne reste plus rien qu'un souvenir'". *Paris-Soir*, June 5, 1933, 3.

Gordon, Mel. 2000. *Voluptuous Panic: The Erotic World of Weimar Berlin*. Venice, CA: Feral.

Gorer, Geoffrey. 1934a. *The Revolutionary Ideas of the Marquis de Sade*. London: Wishart.

—. 1934b. *The Marquis de Sade: A Short Account of His Life and Work*. New York: Liveright.

Gosewinkel, Dieter. 2003. *Einbürgern und Ausschließen: die Nationalisierung der Staatsangehörigkeit vom Deutschen Bund bis zur Bundesrepublik Deutschland*. Vol. 150 of *Kritische Studien zur Geschichtswissenschaft*. Göttingen: Vandenhoeck und Ruprecht.

Grau, Günter. 2009. "Serge Voronoff (1866–1951)". In *Personenlexikon der Sexualforschung*, edited by Volkmar Sigusch and Günter Grau, 732–35. Frankfurt [etc.]: Campus.

Greenwell, Garth. 2016. *What Belongs to You: A Novel*. New York: Farrar, Straus and Giroux.

Grenier, Roger, and Georges Lemoine. 2011. *5, rue Sébastien-Bottin*. [Paris]: Gallimard.

Grundmann, E. 1979. "Nekrologe: Hans Herbert Waelsch". *Deutsche Medizinische Wochenschrift* 104, n° 38, September 21, 1979, 1357.

Gruner, Wolf. 2005. "Das Protektorat Böhmen und Mähren und die antijüdische Politik 1939–1941. Lokale Initiativen, regionale Maßnahmen, zentrale Entscheidungen im 'Großdeutschen Reich'". *Theresienstädter Studien und Dokumente*, n° 12, 27–62.

—. 2010. "Protektorat Böhmen und Mähren". In *Das Grossdeutsche Reich und die Juden Nationalsozialistische Verfolgung in den angegliederten Gebieten*, edited by Wolf Gruner and Jörg Osterloh, 139–74. Frankfurt: Campus-Verlag.

—. 2016. *Die Judenverfolgung im Protektorat Böhmen und Mähren: Lokale Initiativen, zentrale Entscheidungen, jüdische Antworten 1939–1945*. Göttingen: Wallstein Verlag.

Gruner, Wolfgang. 2006 *"Ein Schicksal, das ich mit sehr vielen anderen geteilt habe": Alfred Kantorowicz – sein Leben und seine Zeit von 1899 bis 1935*. Kassel: Kassel University Press.

Haarmann, Hermann, Walter Huder, and Klaus Siebenhaar. 1983. *"Das war ein Vorspiel nur ...": Bücherverbrennung Deutschland 1933: Voraussetzungen und Folgen*. Catalogue, and exhibition of the Ausstellung der Akademie der Künste from May 8 to July 3, 1983. Berlin: Medusa.iesner

Haire, Norman, and L. Sp.[Lothar Spielmann]. 1932. "Die Entwicklung der Sexuologie in England: Eine Unterredung mit Norman Haire". *Prager Presse*, September 30, 1932, 5.

Hájková, Alena. 2000. "Ursprung und Zusammensetzung einer Personenkartei der Juden aus der Zeit des Protektorats". *Theresienstädter Studien und Dokumente*, n° 7, 343–52.

Hájková, Anna. 2014. "Israeli Historian Otto Dov Kulka Tells Auschwitz Story of a Czech Family That Never Existed". *Tablet*, October 29, 2014. https://www.tabletmag.com/sections/arts-letters/articles/otto-dov-kulka

—. 2019. "Fredy Hirsch's Lover: Could a Homosexual Love Survive Theresienstadt?" *Tablet*, May 2, 2019. https://www.tabletmag.com/sections/arts-letters/articles/fredy-hirschs-lover

—. 2020. *The Last Ghetto: An Everyday History of Theresienstadt*. New York: Oxford University Press.

Hall, Murray G. "Epitaph auf den Verlag Moritz Perles in Wien, 1869–1938". https://personal.murrayhall.com/epitaph-moritz-perles/

Heilig, Bernard. 2007. "Die ersten sieben Monate in Litzmannstadt-Getto". In *Die Chronik des Gettos Lodz / Litzmannstadt*, edited by Sascha Feuchert, Joanna Ratusinska, Elisabeth Turvold, Ewa Wiatr, Erwin Leibfried, Jörg Riecke, Julian Baranowski, Joanna Podolska, Krystyna Radziszewska, Jacek Walicki, Imke Janssen-Mignon, and Andrea Löw, appendix and supplement, 9–19. Göttingen: Wallstein-Verlag.

Heim, Susanne. 2009. *Deutsches Reich 1938–August 1939*. Vol. 2 of Die *Verfolgung und Ermordung der europäischen Juden durch das nationalsozialistische Deutschland 1933–1945*. Berlin: De Gruyter Oldenbourg.

Hejnová, Miroslava. 2007. *Historické fondy Národní knihovny ČR Pruvodce*. Prague: Národní knihovna České republiky.

Heller, Hermann. 1892. *Mährens Männer der Gegenwart: biographisches Lexicon. Fünfter Theil, Dichter, Schriftsteller, Journalisten, Musiker, Maler, Bildhauer, Schauspieler etc.* Brünn: H. Heller.

Hepp, Michal, ed. 1985. *Listen in chronologischer Reihenfolge*. Vol. 1 of *Die Ausbürgerung deutscher Staatsangehöriger 1933–45 nach den im Reichsanzeiger veröffentlichten Listen*. Munich: Saur.

Herdt, Gilbert, ed. 1993. *Ritualized Homosexuality in Melanesia*. Vol. 2 of *Studies in Melanesian Anthropology*. Berkeley and London: University of California Press.

Hergemöller, Bernd-Ulrich. 1998. *Mann für Mann: biographisches Lexikon zur Geschichte von Freundesliebe und mannmännlicher Sexualität im deutschen Sprachraum*. Hamburg: MännerschwarmSkript-Verlag.

—. 2010. "Friedmann, Hans". In *Mann für Mann: Biographisches Lexikon zur Geschichte von Freundesliebe und mannmännlicher Sexualität im deutschen Sprachraum*, edited by Bernd-Ulrich Hergemöller, vol. 1. Berlin: Lit.h

—. 2010. "Giese, Hans". In *Mann für Mann: Biographisches Lexikon zur Geschichte von Freundesliebe und mannmännlicher Sexualität im deutschen Sprachraum*, edited by Bernd-Ulrich Hergemöller, vol. 1, 402–4. Berlin: Lit.

Herrmann, Robert. 1962. "Zum Wiedergutmachungs-Schlussgesetz: Wuensche der 'Vertriebenen'". *AJR information* 17, n° 2 (February): 1–2.

Herrn, Rainer. 2003. "'Phantom Rasse. Ein Hirngespinst als Weltgefahr'. Anmerkungen zu einem Aufsatz Magnus Hirschfelds". In *Durch Wissenschaft zur Gerechtigkeit? Textsammlung zur kritischen Rezeption des Schaffens von Magnus Hirschfeld*, edited by Andreas Seeck, 111–24. Münster: Lit.

—. 2004. "Vom Traum zum Trauma: Das Institut für Sexualwissenschaft". In *Der Sexualreformer Magnus Hirschfeld: ein Leben im Spannungsfeld von Wissenschaft, Politik und Gesellschaft*, edited by Kotowski Elke-Vera and Julius H. Schoeps, 173–99. Berlin: Be.bra Wissenschaft Verlag.

—. 2008a. "Sex Brennt. Magnus Hirschfelds Institut für Sexualwissenschaft und die Bücherverbrennung - Kunst und Dokumente im Berliner Medizinhistorischen Museum der Charité vom 7. Mai bis 14. September 2008". *Mitteilungen der Magnus-Hirschfeld-Gesellschaft*, n°s 39–40 (May): 9–17.

—. 2008b. "Magnus Hirschfeld, sein Institut für Sexualwissenschaft und die Bücherverbrennung". *Mitteilungen der Magnus-Hirschfeld-Gesellschaft*, n°s 39–40 (May): 18–22.

—. 2008c. [Collection of circa 110 card board cards]. Presented with the exhibition *Sex brennt: Magnus Hirschfelds Institut für Sexualwissenschaft und die Bücherverbrennung*, Museum der Charité Berlin, May 7–September 14, 2008.

—. 2010. "Magnus Hirschfelds Institut für Sexualwissenschaft und die Bücherverbrennung". In *Verfemt und Verboten. Vorgeschichte und Folgen der Büchererbrennungen 1933*, edited by Julius H. Schoeps and Werner Treß, 113–68. Vol. 2 of *Wissenschaftliche Begleitbände im Rahmen der Bibliothek Verbrannter Bücher*. Hildesheim: Georg Olms.

—, Michael Thomas Taylor, and Annette F. Timm. 2017. "Magnus Hirschfeld's Institute for Sexual Science: A Visual Sourcebook". In *Not Straight from Germany: Sexual Publics and Sexual Citizenship since Magnus Hirschfeld*, edited by Michael Thomas Taylor, Annette F. Timm, and Rainer Herrn, 37–79. Ann Arbor: University of Michigan Press.

—. 2022. *Der Liebe und dem Leid: Das Institut für Sexualwissenschaft 1919–1933*. Berlin: Suhrkamp.

Hertl, Hanns, Erich Pillwein, Helmut Schneider, and Karl Walter Siegler. 2000. *Der "Brünner Todesmarsch" 1945: die Vertreibung und Mißhandlung der Deutschen aus Brünn; eine Dokumentation*. S.l.: "BRUNA," Heimatverband der Brünner in der Bundesrepublik Deutschland.

Herzer, Manfred. 1982. *Bibliographie zur Homosexualität: Verzeichnis des deutschsprachigen nichtbelletristischen Schrifttums zur weiblichen und männlichen Homosexualität aus den Jahren 1466 bis 1975 in chronologischen Reihenfolge*. Berlin: Verlag rosa Winkel.

—. 1989. "Die Polizei überwacht Hirschfelds Vorträge". *Mitteilungen der Magnus-Hirschfeld-Gesellschaft*, n° 14 (December): 38–44.

—. 1997a. "In memoriam Günter Maeder (*13.2.1905 in Berlin + 3.1.1993 in Berlin) mit einer Beilage: Vier Briefe von Christopher Isherwood an Günter Maeder". *Capri*, n° 23 (May): 16–18.

—. 1997b. "Schweizerisches Freundschafts-Banner". In *Goodbye to Berlin?: 100 Jahre Schwulenbewegung: eine Ausstellung des Schwulen Museums und der Akademie der Künste*, edited by Andreas Sternweiler and Hans Gerhard Hannesen, 130–34. Berlin: Rosa Winkel.

—, comp. and ed. 1998. "Harald Jepsen Stimmen aus". In *100 Jahre Schwulenbewegung: Dokumentation einer Vortragsreihe in der Akademie der Künste*, 111–128. Berlin: Verlag rosa Winkel.

—. 2001. *Magnus Hirschfeld: Leben und Werk eines jüdischen, schwulen und sozialistischen Sexologen*, 2nd rev. ed. Vol. 28 of *Bibliothek rosa Winkel*; vol. 10 of *Schriften* [*sic*] *der Magnus-Hirschfeld-Gesellschaft*. Hamburg: MännerschwarmSkript Verlag.

—. 2009a. "Plünderung und Raub des Instituts für Sexualwissenschaft". *Zeitschrift für Sexualforschung* 22, n° 2, 151–62.

—. 2009b. "'Pg. Gutjahr' – Der Exterminator in der Beethovenstraße". *Capri*, n° 42 (October): 21–23.

—. 2015. "Bekenntnisse des Hochstaplers Marcel Herckmans: 'Zitate aus den letzten Aussprachen mit Magnus Hirschfeld'". In *Die andere Fakultät: Theorie. Geschichte. Gesellschaft*, edited by Florian Mildenberger, 131–47. Hamburg: Männerschwarm Verlag.

—. 2017. *Magnus Hirschfeld und seine Zeit*. Berlin: de Gruyter Oldenbourg.

Herzfelder, François. 2015. "Une longue marche. Souvenirs et réflexions (Ma longue Marche, Paris, 1976)". In *Die Erfahrung des Exils: Vertreibung, Emigration und Neuanfang; ein Münchner Lesebuch*, edited by Andreas Heusler and Andrea Sinn, 220–29. Berlin: De Gruyter Oldenbourg

—. 1978. *Problèmes relatifs au régime matrimonial en droit international privé français et allemand*. Paris: Litec.

Herzog, Dagmar. 2020. "Liebe und Gerechtigkeit. Magnus Hirschfeld in Vergangenheit, Gegenwart, und Zukunft". In *Liebe und Gerechtigkeit: zum 150. Geburtstag von Magnus Hirschfeld*, edited by Bundestiftung Magnus Hirschfeld, 75–97. Göttingen: Wallstein.

Heusler, Andreas, and Andrea Sinn, eds. 2015. *Die Erfahrung des Exils: Vertreibung, Emigration und Neuanfang; ein Münchner Lesebuch*. Berlin: De Gruyter Oldenbourg.

Hichens, Robert. 1939. *That Which Is Hidden*. London: Cassell.

Hiller, Kurt. 1932–33. "Exekutionskrieg des Völkerbundes". *Aufruf* 3, n° 2 (December–January): 6–7.

—. "Der Sinn eines Lebens: in memoriam Magnus Hirschfeld (zugleich dem Andenken meines Freundes Richard Linsert, 1899-1933)". *Der Kreis / Le Cercle* 16, n° 6 (June): 2–5. Rpt. of *Die Wahrheit* 14 (1935), n° 17, 8. Also rpt. in 1950. *Köpfe und Tröpfe: Profile aus einem Vierteljahrhundert*, 253–58. Hamburg: Rowohlt. [The version in *Der Kreis / Le Cercle* was reprinted on the occasion of the tenth anniversary of Hirschfeld's death.]

—. 1938. "Případ tenisty Cramma". *Hlas přírody: orgán "Ligy pro sexální reformu"* 1, n° 1 (September): 5–6.

—. 1938 [German version of previous]. "Strafrecht: Cramm". *Sozialistische Warte* 13, n° 22, June 3, 1938, 520–21. Rpt.: "Der Fall des Tennisspielers Cramm". *Capri*, n° 49 (September): 41–43.

—. 1948. "Persönliches über Magnus Hirschfeld". *Der Kreis/Le Cercle* 16, n° 5 (May): 3–6. Rpt. 1993. *Zeitschrift für Sexualforschung* 6, n° 4 (December): 350–53.

—. 1969. *Leben gegen die Zeit: Logos*. Reinbek: Rowohlt.

Hindls, Arnold. [1965]. *Einer kehrte zurück: Bericht eines Deportierten*. Stuttgart: Deutsche Verlags-Anstalt.

—. 1966. "Aus meinem Leben". Typescript. Leo Baeck Institute New York, Center for Jewish History, sign. ME 296 / MM 35. https://digipres.cjh.org/delivery/DeliveryManagerServlet?dps_pid=IE8906893

Hirschbiegel, Thomas. 2023. "Die verschollenen Akten des Sex-Forschers: weltweit gesuchte Fragebögen lagen auf dem Flohmarkt". *Morgenpost*, May 6–7, 2023, 46–47.

Hirschfeld, Magnus. 1901. "Die Homosexualität in Wien". *Wiener klinische Rundschau*, n° 42, 788–90.

—. 2001. *Les homosexuels de Berlin (Berlins Drittes Geschlecht) 1908*, edited by Patrick Cardon. Lille: Les Cahiers Question de Genre/GKC.

—. 1910. "Drei deutsche Gräber in fernem Land". *Vierteljahresberichte des wissenschaftlich-humanitären Komitees* 10, 31–35. Rpt. 2006. Michael A. Lombardi-Nash, ed. *Sodomites and Urnings: Homosexual Representations in Classic German Journals*, 41–45. New York: Harrington Park Press.

—. 1915. *Psychobiologischer Fragebogen*, vol. 4. Berlin: Selbstverlag.

—. 1924. *Sexualität und Kriminalität: Ueberblick über Verbrechen geschlechtlichen Ursprungs*. Vienna, Berlin, Leipzig and New York: Renaissance.

—. 1926. "Film und Forschung". *Internationale Filmschau* 8, n° 12, July 20, 1926, 9.

—. 1926–30. *Geschlechtskunde auf Grund dreissigjähriger Forschung und Erfahrung*. Stuttgart: Julius Püttmann.

—, and H. [Hermann] Beck. 1927. *Gesetze der Liebe: Aus der Mappe eines Sexualforschers; nach dem gleichnamigen Kultur- und Spielfilm der Humboldt-Film-Gesellschaft*. Berlin-Hessenwinkel: Verlag der Neuen Gesellschaft.

—. 1929. "10 Jahre Institut für Sexualwissenschaft". *Die Aufklärung* 1, n° 5, 129–31.

—, and Andreas Gaspar, eds. 1930a. *Sittengeschichte des Weltkrieges*. Vienna: Verlag für Sexualgeschichte Schneider & Co.

—, and Ewald Bohm. 1930b. *Sexualerziehung: Der Weg durch Natürlichkeit zur neuen Moral*. Berlin: Universitas.

—, and Richard Linsert. 1930c. *Liebesmittel: Eine Darstellung der geschlechtlichen Reizmittel (Aphrodisiaca)*. Berlin: Man.

—. 2003. "Kein Wiedersehen auf Capri". *Capri*, n° 34 (November): 37. Fragment from *Testament: Heft II* (dated November 26, 1931). [See also Hirschfeld & Dose 2013, f. 60/132.]

—. 1932. "Sexualforschung erobert die Welt: Aus einer Unterredung mit Prof. Magnus Hirschfeld". *Prager Presse*, September 29, 1932, 4.

—. 1933a. "Přece se jde kupředu". *Nový hlas* 2, n° 1, January, 1–2.

—. 1933b. *Die Weltreise eines Sexualforschers*. Brugg: Bözberg.

—. 1933. "L'amour et la science". *Voilà*, n° 119, July 1, 1933, 5–6.

—. 1933. "L'amour et la science, II, Au Japon". *Voilà*, n° 120, July 8, 1933, 10–11.

—. 1933. "L'amour et la science, III, En Chine". *Voilà*, n° 121, July 15, 1933, 12–13.

—. 1933. "L'amour et la science, IV, Les Indes". *Voilà*, n° 122, July 22, 1933, 5–6.

—. 1933. "L'amour et la science, V". *Voilà*, n° 123, July 29, 1933, 10–11.

—. 1933. "En marge de l'affaire Nozières: le démon de la sexualité". *Vu* 6, n° 286, September 6, 1933, 1387. Rpt. in Spanish in *Orto* 2, n° 16, 18–20.

—. 1933. "Les matriarcats". Special issue ("Femmes"). *Vu* 6, December 9, 1933, 66.

—, and Ewald Bohm. 1934a. *Education sexuelle. Collection d'études sexologiques*. Paris: Montaigne.

—. 1934b. "Stand der Bewegung im geistigen Befreiungskampf der Homosexuellen". *Nový Hlas*, first German supplement D.Z.N.H. *1*, n° 4, April, 1–3. Rpt. 2015. *Capri*, n° 49 (September): 37–40.

—. 1934c. "Das Erbgericht: Betrachtungen zum deutschen Sterilisationsgesetz". *Die Sammlung* 1, n° 6, February, 309–19.

—. 1934d. "L'Impuissance Sexuelle". *Archives de neurologie* 53, series 26, n° 5 (May–June): 227–33.

—. 1934e. "Fétichisme et Antifétichisme pathologique". *Archives de neurologie* 53, series 26, n° 8 (October): 403–14.

—. 1934 "Das Erbgericht". *Pariser Tageblatt*, n° 319, February 6, 1934, 4.

—. 1934 "Stérilisés". *Détective* 7, n° 279, March 1, 1934, 12–13.

—. 1934. "Le tourbillon de la danse". *Voilà*, n° 163, May 5, 1934, 12–13.

—. 1934. "Hans-Adalbert von Maltzahn, ein Mittler deutsch-französischer Kultur. + 4. Juni 1934". *Deutsche Freiheit* 2, n° 131, June 10–11, 1934, 7.

H., M. [Magnus Hirschfeld?]. 1934. "Die Probe aufs Exempel: Roehm und die Rassentheorie". *Pariser Tageblatt* 2, n° 205, July 5, 1934, 2.

Hirschfeld, Magnus. 1934. "Die gemordeten und ihre mörder: eine sexualkritische Studie". *Der Aufruf* 4, July 15, 1934, 512–15. [The title of Hirschfeld's article is printed on a colored ribbon wrapped around the cover page of the periodical: "Röhm und Genossen: eine sexualkritische Studie". A version was published under this title in 1934 in the Swiss newspaper *Das Volk*, July 17, 1934. [See Steakley 2021, 147.]

—. 1934. "Männerbünde: Sexualpsychologischer Beitrag zur Roehm-Katastrophe". *Pariser Tageblatt* 2, n° 220, July 20, 1934, 1.

—. 1935a. *L'âme et l'amour: psychologie sexologique*. La science et l'amour. Paris: Gallimard.

—. 1935b. *Sex in Human Relationships*. The International Library of Sexology and Psychology. London: The Bodley Head. [This is the English translation of Hirschfeld 1935a, *L'âme et l'amour*.]

—. 1935c. *Women East and West: Impressions of a Sex Expert*. London: William Heinemann.

— [Magnus Hirshfeld, *sic*]. 1935d. *Curious Sex Customs in the Far East* [originally published as *Men and Women]*. New York: Grosset & Dunlap.

—. 1935e. *Le sexe inconnu*. Collection d'études sexologiques. Paris: Editions Montaigne.

—. 1935f. "Associations masculines: commentaires d'ordre psycho-sexuel sur le drame Roehm". *L'en dehors* 16, n° 281, mid-April, 267. [French translation of Hirschfeld Jul. 20, 1934: "Männerbünde: Sexualpsychologischer Beitrag zur Roehm-Katastrophe"]

Expertus [Magnus Hirschfeld]. 1935. "Die ‚Ausrottung' der Homosexuellen im Dritten Reich". *Pariser Tageblatt* 3, n° 385, January 1, 1935, 1–2. [Excerpts in Zinn 1997, 166–67.]

Hirschfeld, Magnus. 1935. "Riviera-Brief: 'Circus Mensch' – Verklungener Glanz – Geistesaristokratie verdrängt Geburtsaristokratie – Eine Nietzsche-Reminiscenz". *Pariser Tageblatt* 3, n° 446, March 3, 1935, 4.

—. 1935. "Rivierabrief: Das neue 'Centre Universitaire Méditerranéen'". *Pariser Tageblatt* 3, n° 488, April 14, 1935, 4.

H., M. [Magnus Hirschfeld?]. 1935. "Bodo Uhse: 'Sölder und Soldat'". *Pariser Tageblatt* 3, n° 502, April 28, 1935, 4.

Hirschfeld, Magnus. 1936. "Entry name". Autobiographical sketch". In *Encyclopaedia Sexualis: A Comprehensive Encyclopaedia-Dictionary of the Sexual Sciences*, edited by Victor Robinson, 317–21. New York: Dingwall-Rock. Rpt. 1975. Jonathan Ned, ed. *A Homosexual Emancipation Miscellany, c. 1835–1952*. New York: Arno Press.

—. 1937. *Le corps et l'amour*. La science et l'amour. Paris: Gallimard.

—. 1938a. *Racism*, edited and translated by Eden Paul and Cedar Paul. London: Victor Gollancz.

—. 1938b. *Le tour du monde d'un sexologue*. Translated by L. [László] Gara. Paris: Gallimard.

—. 1986. *Von einst bis jetzt: Geschichte einer homosexuellen Bewegung 1897–1922*. Berlin: Verlag rosa Winkel.

—. 2013. *Testament: Heft II*, edited and annotated by Ralf Dose. Berlin: Hentrich & Hentrich.

Hlubocký, V. D. [Vilém Drexler]. 1936. *Bolesti mé duše: básně*. Brno: s. n.

—. 1937. *Listy z deníku*. Brno: s. n.

—. 1938. *Balada o ženách*. Brno: edice Nová tvorba.

—. 1939. *Matka básníkova*. [Brno]: s. n.

—, and Kresba E. Bartoš. 1940. *Věčné milování*. Brno: s. n.

—. 1940. *Žalm o smrti*. Brno: s. n.

Hlubocký, Karel [Vilém Drexler]. 1932. "Oskaru Wildeovo". *Kamarád* 1, n° 1, May 28, 1932, 6.

—. 1932. "Pohádka máje". *Kamarád* 1, n° 1, May 28, 1932, 12–13.

—. 1932. "Dr. Magnus Hirschfeld mezi námi". *Kamarád* 1, n° 1, May 28, 1932, 15–16.

—. 1932. "Kulturní hlídka, Divadla". *Kamarád* 1, n° 1, May 28, 1932, 17–19.

Hlubocký, Luděk [Vilém Drexler], and Vítězslav Šafránek. 1945. *Smrt Abelova: Biblický epos*. Brno: s.n

—, and Václav Palma. 1947. *Hovory s matkou*. Brno: s.n.

Hlusicka, Jirí, Karel Holesovský, Lada Hubatová-Vacková, Alena Krkošková, Marcela Macharáčková, and Lubomír Slavíček. 2002. *Antonín Procházka 1882–1945*. Brno: Brno City Museum and the Moravian Gallery Brno.

Hodann, Max. 1933. *Amour et sexualité dans la biologie et la société*. Collection d'études sexologiques. Paris: Montaigne.

Hohmann, Joachim S., ed. 1981. *Der Eigene: Ein Blatt für männliche Kultur: Ein Querschnitt durch die erste Homosexuellenzeitschrift der Welt*. Frankfurt: Foerster.

Holitscher, Arnold. 1933. "Pozdrav! Begrüssung". *Sociálne zdravotní revue* 1, n° 1, March 10, 1933, 5–6.

Holm, Hans. 1934. "Der deutschen Beilage zum Geleite!" *Nový Hlas*, third German supplement D.Z.N.H., 2, n° 6, June, 10–11.

Holzbauer, Robert. 2000. "'Einziehung volks- und staatsfeindlichen Vermögens im Lande Österreich'. Die 'VUGESTA' – die 'Verwertungsstelle für jüdisches Umzugsgut der Gestapo'". *Spurensuche*, n°s 1–2, 38–50.

Hrubá, Alice. 2008. "Genocida brněnských židů – transport Dg". BA thesis, University of Pardubice. http://dspace.upce.cz/bitstream/10195/28736/1/HrubaA_Genocida%20brnenskych_KR_2008.pdf

Huebner, Karla Tonine. 2008. "Eroticism, Identity, and Cultural Context: Toyen and the Prague avant-garde." PhD diss., University of Pittsburgh. https://d-scholarship.pitt.edu/10323/

Huebner, Karla. 2010. "The Whole World Revolves around It: Sex Education and Sex Reform in First Republic Czech Print Media". *Aspasia* 4, 25–49.

Humbert, Eugène. 1932. "Ve Congrès de la Ligue mondiale pour la réforme sexuelle sur une base scientifique". *La Grande Réforme* 2, n° 16 (August): 1.

Humbert, Jeanne. 1934. *Sous la cagoule: à Fresnes, prison modèle*. Paris: de Lutèce.

—. 1947. *Eugène Humbert. La vie et l'oeuvre d'un néo-malthusien*. Paris: La Grande Réforme.

Hupfer, Georg. 2003. "Zur Geschichte des antiquarischen Buchhandels in Wien". MA thesis, University of Vienna. https://www.wienbibliothek.at/sites/default/files/files/buchforschung/hupfer-georg-antiquariat-wien.pdf

Hyndráková, Anna, Helena Krejčová, and Jana Svobodová. 1996 *Prominenti v ghettu Terezín: (1942–1945)*. Prague: Ústav pro soudobé dějiny AV ČR.

Hynie, Josef. 1933. "Sexualní stesky mladých lidí". *Sociálne zdravotní revue* 1, n° 4, June 10, 1933, 76–80.

Iltis, Hugo. 1921. *Über die Verbreitung der Malariamücken in Mähren und über die Gefahr einer Malariaendemie*. [Brünn]: [L. & A. Brecher, self-published].

—. 1924. *Gregor Johann Mendel: Leben, Werk und Wirkung*. Berlin and Heidelberg: Springer.

—. 1929. *Hranice a možnosti socialistické výchovné a vzdělávací práce*. Prague: Pražská odbočka Dělnické akademie.

—. 1930. *Volkstümliche Rassenkunde*. Jena: Urania.

—. 1932. *Life of Mendel*. Translated by Eden Paul and Cedar Paul. [American edition: New York: W. W. Norton & Co.; British edition: [s.l.]: G. Allen & Unwin.]

—. 1935. "Fünfundachtzig Jahre". *Licht ins Volk!* 7, n° 3, 1.

—. [1936]. *Der Mythus von Blut und Rasse*. Vienna: R. Harand.

—. 2017. *Race, Genetics, and Science: Resisting Racism in the 1930s*. Brno: Masaryk University.

In het Panhuis, Erwin. 2020. "Moralist und Aktivist: Der Ex-Nazi, der für die Rechte monogamer Schwuler kämpfte". www.*queer.*

de, June 26, 2020. https://www.queer.de/detail.php?article_id=36430

—. 2020. "Mordversuch an Magnus Hirschfeld: Die Vorgeschichte". www.queer.de, October 2, 2020. https://www.queer.de/detail.php?article_id=37216

—. 2020. "Mordversuch an Magnus Hirschfeld: Die Tat". www.queer.de, October 3, 2020. https://www.queer.de/detail.php?article_id=37220

—. 2020. "Mordversuch an Magnus Hirschfeld: Die Reaktionen". www.queer.de, October 4, 2020. https://www.queer.de/detail.php?article_id=37223

—. 2020. "Die Reaktionen nach dem Attentat". In *Der Anschlag auf Magnus Hirschfeld: Ein Blick auf das reaktionäre München 1920*, edited by Albert Knoll, 51–73. Munich: Forum Queeres Archiv München.

Isherwood, Christopher. 1977. *Christopher and His Kind*. London: Eyre Methuen.

—. 1988. *De kant van Christopher 1929–1939*. Amsterdam: Querido. [Dutch translation of previous.]

Isnard, Marguerite, and Roger Isnard. 1989. *Sus lu Barri: les pierres racontent Nice*. Breil-sur-Roya: Les Editions du Cabri.

Jackson, Julian. 2009. *Arcadie: la vie homosexuelle en France, de l'après-guerre à la dépénalisation*. Paris: Autrement.

Janás, Robert, and Jana Svobodová. 2004. *"z lásky k umění a sobě pro radost": umělecká sbírka Heinricha Gomperze (1843–1894) = "aus Liebe zur Kunst, welche meine Freude war": die Kunstsammlung Heinrich Gomperz*. Brno: Moravská galerie.

Jančík, Drahomir, and Jiří Daníček, eds. 2001. *Jewish Gold and other Precious Metals, Precious Stones, and Objects made of such Materials - Situation in the Czech Lands in the Years 1939 to 1945: Unlawful Infringement of Property Rights and its Scope; Subsequent Fate of the Jewish Assets affected by this Infringement*. Prague: Sefer/Institute of the Terezin Initiative.

—, and Eduard Kubů. 2006. "Bankéř a finančník: Příklad Karla Engliše". In Lukáš Fasora, Jiří Hanuš, Libor Vykoupil, and Jiří Malíř, *Člověk na Moravě v první polovině 20. Století*, 129–145. Brno: Centrum pro studium demokracie a kultury.

Janota, Otakar, and Jaroslav Šindelář. 1943. *Hyperkinetická a hypokineticko-hypertonická forma hepatolentikulární degenerace u dvou rodných bratří*. Prague: s.n. [self-published].

Jaouen, Romain. 2018. *L'inspecteur et l'"inverti": la police face aux sexualités masculines à Paris, 1919–1940*. Rennes: Presses universitaires de Rennes.

Jelínek, František. 1924. *Homosexualita ve svetle vedy*. Prague: Obelisk.

Jepsen, Harald Hartvig. 1998. "Stimmen aus dem schwulen Prag 1918–1938: Der Kampf der tschechoslowakischen Sexualreformbewegung gegen das Homosexuellenstrafrecht". In *100 Jahre Schwulenbewegung: Dokumentation einer Vortragsreihe in der Akademie der Künste*, selected and published by Manfred Herzer, 111–28. Berlin: Verlag rosa Winkel.

Kämper, Dirk. 2015. *Fredy Hirsch und die Kinder des Holocaust: die Geschichte eines vergessenen Helden aus Deutschland*. Zürich: Orell Füssli.

Kantorowicz, Alfred. 1947. *Der Tag des freien Buches: zum Gedenken an die Bücherverbrennungen vom 10. Mai 1933*. [Berlin]: Deutschen Verwaltung für Volksbildung in der sowjetischen Besatzungszone.

Karkanová, Hana. 2004. "Die Sammlung Gomperz – ein zweites Leben". In Robert Janás, and Jana Svobodová. *"z lásky k umění a sobě pro radost": umělecká sbírka Heinricha Gomperze (1843–1894) = "aus Liebe zur Kunst, welche meine Freude war": die Kunstsammlung Heinrich Gomper*, 47–72. Brno: Moravská galerie.

Kárný, Miroslav. 1994–95 "Vorgeschichte der Regierungsverordnung über die Rechtsstellung der Juden im öffentlichen Leben". *Judaica Bohemiae*, vols. 30–31, 107–17.

—, ed.; and [unknown] others. 1995. *Terezínská pamětní kniha: židovské oběti nacistických deportací z Čech a Moravy 1941–1945*. 2 vols. Prague: Melantrich. [Theresienstädter Gedenkbuch: Jüdische Opfer der nazistischen Deportationen aus Böhmen und Mähren 1941–1945].

—, ed.; and [unknown] others. 1996. *Terezín Memorial Book: Jewish Victims of Nazi Deportations from Bohemia and Moravia 1941–1945: A Guide to the Czech Original with a Glossary of Czech Terms Used in the Lists*. Prague: Melantrich.

—. 1997. "Das Theresienstädter Familienlager (BIIb) in Birkenau (September 1943–Juli 1944)". *Hefte von Auschwitz*, n° 20, 133–237.

—. 1998. "Die Ausschaltung der Juden aus dem öffentlichen Leben des Protektorats und die Geschichte des 'Ehrenariertums'". *Theresienstädter Studien und Dokumente*, n° 5, 7–39.

—. 1999. "'Heydrichiaden': Widerstand und Terror im 'Protektorat Böhmen und Mähren'". In *Von Lidice bis Kalavryta: Widerstand und Besatzungsterror; Studien zur Repressalienpraxis im Zweiten Weltkrieg*, edited by Loukia Droulia and Hagen Fleischer, 51–64. Vol. 8 of *Nationalsozialistische Besatzungspolitik in Europa 1939–1945*. Berlin: Metropol.

Kater, Michael H. 1989. *Doctors under Hitler*. Chapel Hill, NC: University of North Carolina Press.

Keiderling, Thomas. 2008. *Unternehmer im Nationalsozialismus: Machtkampf um den Konzern Koehler & Volckmar AG & Co*, 2nd improved edition. Beucha: Sax-Verlag.

Keilson-Lauritz, Marita. 1997. *Die Geschichte der eigenen Geschichte: Literatur und Literaturkritik in den Anfängen der Schwulenbewegung am Beispiel des Jahrbuchs für sexuelle Zwischenstufen und der Zeitschrift Der Eigene*. Vol. 11 of *Homosexualität und Literatur*. Berlin: Verlag rosa Winkel.

—, and Friedemann Pfäfflin. 1999. "Unzüchtig im Sinne des § 184 des Strafgesetzbuchs. Drei Urteilstexte und ein Einstellungsbeschluß". *Forum Homosexualität und Literatur*, n° 34, 33–98.

—, and Friedemann Pfäfflin. 2000. "Die Sitzungsberichte des wissenschaftlich-humanitären Komitees München 1902–1908". *Capri*, n° 28, 2–33.

—, and Friedemann Pfäfflin. 2003. *100 Jahre Schwulenbewegung an der Isar I: Die Sitzungsberichte des Wissenschaftlich-humanitären Komitees München 1902–1908*. Vol. 10 of *Splitter: Materialien zur Geschichte der Homosexuellen in München und Bayern*. Munich: Forum Homosexualität und Geschichte.

—. 2004a. "Magnus Hirschfeld und seine Gäste. Das Exil-Gästebuch 1933–1935". In *Der Sexualreformer Magnus Hirschfeld: ein Leben im Spannungsfeld von Wissenschaft, Politik und Gesellschaft*, edited by Elke-Vera Kotowski and Julius H. Schoeps, 71–88. Berlin: be.bra Wissenschaft Verlag.

—. 2004b. "Zur 'inneren' Geschichte des Jahrbuchs für sexuelle Zwischenstufen". In Jens Dobler, *Prolegomena zu Magnus Hirschfelds Jahrbuch für sexuelle Zwischenstufen (1899 bis 1923). Register – Editionsgeschichte – Inhaltsbeschreibungen*, 9–32. Hamburg: von Bockel.

—. 2008. "'Ein Rest wird übrig bleiben …': Hirschfelds Gästebuch als biographische Quelle". *Mitteilungen der Magnus-Hirschfeld-Gesellschaft*, n°s 39–40 (May): 36–49.

—, and Ralf Dose. 2009. "Für die Echtheit der Handschrift verbürge ich mich. Ein Tagebuch-Fragment Magnus Hirschfelds im Nachlass von Erich Kästner". *Mitteilungen der Magnus-Hirschfeld-Gesellschaft*, n°s 43–44 (November): 9–20.

Kennedy, Hubert. 1999. *Der Kreis: Eine Zeitschrift und ihr Programm*. Vol. 19 of *Bibliothek rosa Winkel*. Berlin: Verlag rosa Winkel.

Kerchner, Brigitte. 2005. "Körperpolitik. Die Konstruktion des 'Kinderschänders' in der Zwischenkriegszeit". In *Politische Kulturgeschichte der Zwischenkriegszeit 1918–1939*, edited by Wolfgang Hardtwig, 241–78. Göttingen: Vandenhoeck und Ruprecht.

Kirchhoff, Wolfgang. 2017. "Aspekte der Berufswahl und -ausübung deutscher/österreichischer jüdischer Psychoanalytikerinnen im ersten Drittel des 20. Jahrhunderts". In *Jüdinnen und Psyche*, edited by Caris-Petra Heidel, 39–76. Vol. 13 of *Medizin und Judentum*. Frankfurt: Mabuse.

Kirsch, Jonathan. 2013. *The Short, Strange Life of Herschel Grynszpan: A Boy Avenger, a Nazi Diplomat, and a Murder in Paris*. New York: Liveright.

Klarsfeld, Serge. 1978. *Le Mémorial de la déportation des Juifs de France: listes alphabétiques par convois des Juifs déportés de France, historique des convois de déportation, statistiques de la déportation des Juifs de France*. Paris: B. et S. Klarsfeld.

Klatt, Norbert. 2005. "Zur strafrechtlichen Stellung von homoexuellen Männern und Frauen im 'Großdeutschen Reich'". *Invertito* 7, 88–104.

Klein, Peter. 2009. *Die "Gettoverwaltung Litzmannstadt" 1940 bis 1944: eine Dienststelle im Spannungsfeld von Kommunalbürokratie und staatlicher Verfolgungspolitik*. Hamburg: Hamburger Edition.

Klementová, Táňa. 2010. „Poslední nástupiště: Brněnské transporty židů v letech 1941–1945". MA thesis, Masaryk University.

—. 2014. "The final platform: Jewish transports from Brno in 1941–1945". In *Suffering and Fighting: The Jews of Brno in Fateful*

Moments of the 20th Century, edited by Jiří Mitáček, 67–74 Brno: Moravian Museum.

Klenovský, Jaroslav. 1995. *Jewish Monuments in Brno: A Brief History of the Brno Jewish Community*. Brno: Moravian Museum / Jewish Community Litera Foundation.

—. 2002. *Brno židovské: historie a památky osídlení města Brna*. Brno: Vydavatelství ERA.

—. 2016. *Brno židovské: historie a památky židovského osídlení města Brna = Jewish Brno: History and Monuments of the Jewish Settlement in Brno*. Prague: Grada.

Knittel, John. 1934. *Via mala*. Zürich: Orell Füssli.

Knoll, Albert, ed. 2020. *Der Anschlag auf Magnus Hirschfeld: Ein Blick auf das reaktionäre München 1920*. Vol. 16 of *Splitter: Materialien zur Geschichte der Homosexuellen in München und Bayern*. Munich: Forum Queeres Archiv München.

Kohlmann-Viand, Doris. 1991. *NS-Pressepolitik im Zweiten Weltkrieg: die "vertraulichen Informationen" als Mittel der Presselenkung*. Munich: Saur.

Kokošková, Zdeňka, Jaroslav Pažout, and Monika Sedláková. 2019. *Úřady oberlandrátů v systému okupační správy Protektorátu Čechy a Morava a jejich představitelé*. Prague: Scriptorium.

Kopečný, Petr. 2006. *Obrana národa na Brněnsku 15.3.1938–29.2.1940*. Brno: Archiv města Brna.

Kosch, Wilhelm, Carl Ludwig Lang, Konrad Feilchenfeldt, and Lutz Hagestedt, eds. 2000. *Deutsches Literatur-Lexikon – das 20. Jahrhundert: biographisch-bibliographisches Handbuch*, vol. 1 (Aab–Bauer). Zürich; München: Saur/De Gruyter.

Kostelničáková, Anna. 2008. *Čaro ornamentu: Štefan Leonard Kostelničák*. Martin: Matica slovenská.

Král, Václav. 1964. *Die Deutschen in der Tschechoslowakei 1933–1947, Dokumentensammlung*. Acta occupationis Bohemiae et Moraviae. Prague: Academia.

Krantz, Hubert W. 1976. "Die sozial- und gesellschaftspolitischen Vorstellungen Walther Rathenaus". PhD diss., Universität Abteilung für Sozialwissenschaften.

Krčál, Martin. 2011. „Brněnský advokát JUDr. Jaromír Appel a jeho odbojová činnost." *Vlastivědný věstník moravský* 63, n°s 1–4, 214–34.

Kreisler, Karl. 1912. *Junge Jahre: Lyrik*. Brünn: L. & A. Brecher.

—. 1922. *Hieronymus Lorms: Schicksal und Werk*. Brünn: L. & A. Brecher.

Krejčová, Helena, Jana Svobodová, and Anna Hyndráková, comps. 1997. *Židé v Protektorátu: Hlašení Židovské nábozenské obce v roce 1942: dokumenty*. Vol. 11 of *Historia nova*. Prague: Ústav pro soudobé dějiny AV ˇCR: Maxdorf.

—. 1999. "Spezifische Voraussetzungen des Antisemitismus und antijüdische Aktivitäten im Protektorat Böhmen und Mähren". In *Judenemanzipation – Antisemitismus – Verfolgung in Deutschland, Österreich-Ungarn, den Böhmischen Ländern und in der Slowakei*, edited by Jörg K. Hoensch, Stanislav Biman, and Ľubomír Lipták, 175–94. S.l.: Essen.

—, and Mario Vlček. 2008. *Memories Returned: Jewish Property at the Museum of Decorative Arts, Prague*. Translated by Christopher Hopkinson. [Prague]: Institute for Contemporary History/Academy of Sciences of the Czech Republic.

Kroha, Jiří. 1932. "Sexuální reformou osvoboďte člověka od tyranie sexu, třídně zneužívaného". *Dělnická rovnost*, November 2, 1932, 8.

Krupička, Miroslav. 2017. "Die deutsche Sprache auf den Wellen des Tschechoslowakischen Rundfunks 1923–1945 und die Entstehung der Sendungen ins Ausland". In *Hörfunk und Hörfunkpolitik in der Tschechoslowakei und im Protektorat Böhmen und Mähren*, edited by Peter Becher, and Anna Knechtel, 11–18. Berlin: Frank & Timme.

Kubista, Jar. 1922. "Kolem nového trestního zákona. Homosexualita a §§ 129–130 trest. zák. rak. a čsl". *Československá republika* 243, n° 275, October 7, 1922, 1–2.

Kudělková, Lenka. 1998. "Životopis / Curriculum vitae [Otto Eisler]". In *Otto Eisler: 1893–1968*, edited by Petr Pelčák, Jindřich Škrabal, and Ivan Wahla, 23–24. Brno: Spolek Obecní dům.

—. 2007. "Ing. Artur Eisler, podnikatelství staveb, Brno: Příspěvek k dějinám brněnské meziválečné architektury". *Forum Brunense: sborník prací Muzea města Brna*, 177–84. Brno: Společnost přátel Muzea Města Brna.

Kuller, Christiane. 2004. "Finanzverwaltung und Judenverfolgung. Antisemitische Fiskalpolitik und Verwaltungspraxis im nationalsozialistischen Deutschland". *zeiten-*

blicke 3, n° 2. (September 13). http://www.zeitenblicke.historicum.net/2004/02/kuller/index.html

Ladwig-Winters, Simone, and Rechtsanwaltskammer Berlin, eds. 2007. Schicksale jüdische Rechtsanwälte in Deutschland nach 1933. Volume of *Anwalt ohne Recht*. Berlin: be.bra.

Landré, Berta. 1982. "Jüdische Zwangsarbeit in Prag". *Zeitgeschichte* 9, n°s 11–12 (August–September): 365–77.

Lane, A. Thomas. 1995. *Biographical Dictionary of European Labor Leaders*. Westport, CT and London: Greenwood Press.

Lambert, Raymond-Raoul. 1937. "Magnus Hirschfeld: la pensée en exil". *L'Univers israélite*, n° 41, June 18, 1937, 629–30.

—, and Richard I. Cohen. 1984. *Carnet d'un témoin: 1940–1943*. Paris: Fayard.

Lamm, Josef. 1934. *Tschechische Konjugationstabelle*. Brünn: L. & A. Brecher.

Lamprecht, Herbert. 1935. "Magnus Hirschfeld, der Gelehrte und Philantrop: [Teil 1]". *Der Freidenker* 18, n° 22, November 15, 1935, 171–73.

—. 1935. "Magnus Hirschfeld, der Gelehrte und Philantrop: (Schluss)". *Der Freidenker* 18, n° 23, December 1, 1935, 180–81.

Lawson, David, Libuše Salomonovičová, and Hana Šústková. 2018. *Ostrava and its Jews: "Now No-one Sings You Lullabies"*. London and Chicago: Vallentine Mitchell.

LeCaine Agnew, Hugh. 2004. *The Czechs and the Lands of the Bohemian Crown*. Stanford: Hoover Institution/Stanford University Press.

Lechner, Harald. 1951. *Studien zum Wiener Verlagswesen im 18. und 19. Jahrhundert*. Vienna: s.n.

—. [1967]. *Firmengeschichte der Verlags- und Kommissionsbuchhandlung Rudolf Lechner & Sohn*. [Vienna]: [Lechner].

Lehmstedt, Mark. 2002. *Bücher für das "dritte Geschlecht": Der Max Spohr Verlag in Leipzig: Verlagsgeschichte und Bibliographie (1881–1941)*. Wiesbaden: Harrassowitz Verlag.

Lehnerdt, Gotthold. 1928. "Die erste Voronoff-Operation in Berlin". *Die Ehe: Monatsschrift für Ehe-Wissenschaft,-Recht u.-Kultur* 3, n° 2, February 1, 40–41.

Leidinger, Christiane. 2008. *Keine Tochter aus gutem Hause: Johanna Elberskirchen (1864–1943)*. Konstanz: UVK.

Leisching, Julius. 1913. *Das erzherzog Rainer-Museum für Kunst und Gewerbe in Brünn*. Vienna: Anton Schroll. http://bvpb.mcu.es/es/consulta/registro.cmd?id=483317

Leiter, Ferdinand, and Hans H. Thal, eds. 1929. *Liebe im Orient: Das Kamasutram des Vatsyayana: mit einem Anhang das Erotische in der indischen Kunst; Anangaranga: die Bühne des Liebesgottes; Der duftende Garten des Scheik Nefzaui*. With a foreword by Magnus Hirschfeld and Hanns Heinz Ewers. Vienna: Verlag für Sexualwissenschaft Schneider & Co.

Levy-Lenz, Ludwig, ed. 1926. *Sexual-Katastrophen: Bilder aus dem modernen Geschlechts- und Eheleben*. Leipzig: A. H. Payne.

—. 1954. *Erinnerungen eines Sexual-Arztes (aus den Memoiren eines Sexologen)*. Baden-Baden: Wadi.

Lewandowski, Herbert. 1932. "Mijn reis naar het congres voor sexueele hervorming te Brünn (C.S.R.)". *Het Vaderland* ['s-Gravenhage, Den Hague], October 11, 1932, evening edition, 13.

—, and P. J. van Dranen. 1933. *Beschavings- en zedengeschiedenis van Nederland*. Amsterdam: Enum.

Linge, Ina. 2018. "Sexology, Popular Science and Queer History in *Anders als die Andern* (*Different from the Others*)". In "Gender and Historical Film and Television". Special issue, *Gender & history* 30, n° 3 (October): 595–610.

Linhartová, Věra. 2003. *Jan Bělehrádek a jeho cesta ke svobodě ducha*. Prague: Galén.

Lishaugen, Roar. 2007. "Nejistá sezóna jiné literatury: osudy časopisu Hlas sexuální menšiny". *Dějiny a současnost* 29, n° 12, 33–35.

Lišková, Kateřina. 2018. *Sexual Liberation, Socialist Style: Communist Czechoslovakia and the Science of Desire*. Cambridge: Cambridge University Press.

Loewy, Hanno. 1990. *"Unser einziger Weg ist Arbeit": das Getto in Łódź, 1940–1944; eine Ausstellung des Jüdischen Museums Frankfurt am Main*, edited by Gerhard Schoenberner. Vienna: Löcker, 1990.

London, Louise. 2000. *Whitehall and the Jews, 1933–1948: British Immigration Policy, Jew-*

ish Refugees and the Holocaust. Cambridge: Cambridge University Press.

Lourie de la Belleissue, Ariane. 2008. "Mass-produced Aura: Thonet and the Market for Modern Design, 1930–1953". PhD diss., New York University.

Löw, Andrea, and Sascha Feuchert. 2007 (1941). "Vorwort". In *Die Chronik des Gettos Lodz / Litzmannstadt*, edited by Sascha Feuchert, Erwin Liebfried, and Jörg Riecke, 11–16. Göttingen: Wallstein-Verlag.

—, ed. 2012. *Deutsches Reich und Protektorat Böhmen und Mähren September 1939–September 1941*. Vol. 3 of *Die Verfolgung und Ermordung der europäischen Juden durch das nationalsozialistische Deutschland 1933–1945*, edited by Bundesarchiv, Institut für Zeitgeschichte and Lehrstuhl für Neuere und Neueste Geschichte der Universität Freiburg. Munich: De Gruyter Oldenbourg.

Ludwig, Bernard. 2003. "La propagande anti-communiste en Allemagne fédérale: Le 'VFF,' pendant allemand de 'Paix et Liberté'?" *Vingtième Siècle*, n° 80, 33–42. https://www.cairn.info/revue-vingtieme-siecle-revue-d-histoire-2003-4-page-33.htm

Lützenkirchen, Harald. 1992. "Vorläufige Gesamt-Bibliographie der Schriften Kurt Hilers". In *Kurt Hiller: Erinnerungen und Materialien*, edited by Rolf von Bockel and Harald Lützenkirchen, 125–201. Hamburg: von Bockel Verlag.

M. 1933. "Dans Berlin, à la lueur du brasier qui consume les bibliothèques proscrites". *L'Intransigeant*, May 12, 1933, 5.

M. H. D. 1921. "Das Theater des Eros". *Die Freundschaft*, n° 3, 6.

M. J. S. 1935. "Lettre niçoise: la mort du Docteur Magnus Hirschfeld". *La Tribune juive*, n° 22, May 31, 1935, 410.

M. P. 1933. "Proč sexuologický sešit?" *Sociálne zdravotní revue* 1, n° 4, June 10, 1933, 75–76.

Macek, Pavel, and Lubomír Uhlíř. 2001. *Dějiny policie a četnictva. III., Protektorát Čechy a Morava a Slovenský stát (1939–1945)*. Prague: Police History.

Machtan, Lothar. 2001. *Hitlers Geheimnis: das Doppelleben eines Diktators*. Berlin: Fest.

—. 2006. *Der Kaisersohn bei Hitler*. Hamburg: Hoffmann und Campe.

Maeder, Günter. [1993]. "Bruchstücke!" Typescript, 12 pages. Archiv Magnus-Hirschfeld-Gesellschaft, Berlin.

Maier, Hans. 1934. "Expérience pratique de la stérilisation en Suisse". In *Le problème sexuel*, n° 4 (November): 1–6.

Makarova, Elena G., Sergei Makarov, and Victor Kuperman. 2004. *University over the abyss: The Story behind 520 Lecturers and 2,430 Lecturers in KZ Theresienstadt 1942–1944*, 2nd corr. edn., corrected and expanded with feedback from survivors.

Mako, Michal. 2020. "Štefan Leonard Kostelníček: Príbeh známy neznámy". *QYS magazín*, May 29, 2020, 47–50.

Malečková, Jitka. 2016. "The Importance of Being Nationalist". In *Czech Feminisms: Perspectives on Gender in East Central Europe*, edited by Iveta Jusová and Jiřina Šiklová, 46–59. Bloomington: Indiana University Press.

Malt, Ulrik Fredrik, and Miluše Juříčková. 2016. *Leo Eitinger – život a dílo: studie k česko-norským kulturním vztahům*. Boskovice: Albert/Masarykova univerzita.

Mändl Roubíčková, Eva, and Veronika Springmann, eds.; Wolfgang Schellenbacher. 2007. *"Langsam gewöhnen wir uns an das Ghettoleben": ein Tagebuch aus Theresienstadt*. Hamburg: Konkret Literatur Verlag.

Mandon, Maurice. 1999. *Une plume contre Vichy: Jean Rochon (1903–1944) et le journal La Montagne sous l'occupation (1940–1944)*. Clermont-Ferrand: Presses universitaires Blaise Pascal.

Mann, Klaus. 1934. "Die Linke und 'das Laster'". *Europäische Hefte* 1, n°s 36–37, 675–78.

Margolius Kovaly, Heda. 1988. *Prague Farewell*. Translated by Franci Epstein and Helen Epstein. London: Gollancz.

Margolius, Ivan. 2006. *Reflections of Prague: Journeys Through the 20th Century*. Chichester: Wiley.

Margolius Kovály, Heda, Helena Třeštíková, and Ivan Margolius. 2018. *Hitler, Stalin and I: An Oral History*. Los Angeles: DoppelHouse Press.

Marhoefer, Laurie. 2015. Sex and the Weimar Republic: German homosexual emancipation and the rise of the Nazis. Toronto: University of Toronto Press.

Maršálek, Zdenko. 2014. "'Česká,' nebo 'československá' armáda? Národnostní složení československých vojenských jednotek v zahraničí v letech 1939–1945 = "'Czech,' or 'Czechoslovak' Army? The ethnic and Nationality Composition of the Czechoslovak

Military Units-in-Exile in 1939–1945". PhD diss., Univerzita Karlova v Praze/Ústav českých dějin.

Marschik, Matthias. 2016. "Chronist der Sexualität: Leo Schidrowitz (1894–1956). Im Niemandsland zwischen Erotik, Pornografie und Kulturanalyse". In *Sex in Wien: Lust. Kontrolle. Ungehorsam*, edited by Andreas Brunner, Frauke Kreutler, Michaela Lindinger, Gerhard Milchram, Martina Nußbaumer, Hannes Sulzenbacher, and Wien Museum Karlsplatz, 106–11. Vienna: Metroverlag.

Martel, Frédéric. 2019. *Sodoma: enquête au coeur du Vatican*. Paris: de Noyelles.

Matyáš, Imrich. 1931. "Zdravotný radca Dr. Magnus Hirschfeld". *Hlas* 1, n° 2, May 15, 1931, 4–5.

—. 1932 "Jeden homosexuelný mučedník". *Kamarád* 1, n° 1, May 2, 1932, 7–10.

—. 1932. "Osvobozovacia akcia dr. Magnusa Hirschfelda". *Nový hlas* 1, n° 3, July 1, 1932, 3–6.

—. 1933. "65 let Dr. M. Hirschfelda". *Nový hlas* 2, n° 5, May 1933, 72.

McKenna, Neil. 2005. *The Secret Life of Oscar Wilde: An Intimate Biography*. New York: Basic Books.

McLeod, Donald W., and Soetaert, Hans P. 2010. "'Il regarde la mer et pense à son idéal': Die letzten Tage von Magnus Hirschfeld in Nizza, 1934–1935". *Mitteilungen der Magnus-Hirschfeld-Gesellschaft*, n° 45 (July): 14–33.

McLeod, Don. 2012. "Serendipity and the Papers of Magnus Hirschfeld: The Case of Ernst Maass". Presentation given at the ALMS conference Amsterdam August 1–3, 2012. https://tspace.library.utoronto.ca/bitstream/1807/32968/1/Maass.pdf.

Melichar, Leopold. 1905. *Arzneizubereitungen und pharmaceutische Specialitäten*. Leipzig: Deudicke.

Meschede, Friedrich, ed.; Ullmann, Micha. 1999. *Micha Ullmann, Bibliothek*. Amsterdam and Dresden: Verlag der Kunst.

Messaoudi, Alain. 2012. "Deux éditeurs de la Francophonie". *La lettre de l'IMEC*, n° 16 (Autumn): 24.

Mildenberger, Florian. 2009. "Eugen Steinach (1861–1944)". In *Personenlexikon der Sexualforschung*, edited by Volkmar Sigusch and Günter Grau, 663–665. Frankfurt: Campus.

Miller, M. S. [Josef Weisskopf?]. 1932a. *Liebesparadies: Geheimnis der Liebe ohne Folgen. Bücher für Sexual- und Lebenskunde*. Brünn: Kulturverlag.

—. [Josef Weisskopf?]. 1932b. *Ewige Flitterwochen: Geheimnis der Liebe ohne Folgen. Bücher für Sexual- und Lebenskunde*. Vienna: Kulturverlag.

Miller, Michael Laurence. 2011. *Rabbis and Revolution: The Jews of Moravia in the Age of Emancipation*. Stanford: Stanford University Press.

Milotová, Jaroslava. 1997. "Die Zentralstelle für jüdische Auswanderung in Prag. Genesis und Tätigkeit bis zum Anfang des Jahres 1940". *Theresienstädter Studien und Dokumente*, n° 4, 7–30.

—. 1998. "Der Okkupationsaparat und die Vorbereitung der Transporte nach Lodz". *Theresienstädter Studien und Dokumente*, n° 5, 40–69.

Missika, Dominique. 2005. *Berty Albrecht*. N.p.: Perrin.

Morawek. Horst. 2021. *Brünn, meine Jugend, mein Leben, meine Sehnsucht: Horst Morawek erinnert sich an Brünn und an sein Erleben*. Schorndorf: self-published.

Moser, Jonny, Joseph W. Moser, and Kames R. Moser, eds. 2012. *Nisko: die ersten Judendeportationen*. Vienna: Steinbauer.

Müller, Dora. 1997. *Drehscheibe Brünn: deutsche und österreichische Emigranten 1933–1939 = Přestupní stanice Brno: Němečtí* a *rakouští emigranti*. Brno: [Deutscher Kulturverband Region Brünn/Německé kulturní sdružení region Brno].

Munthe, Axel. 1931. *The Story of San Michele*. London: John Murray.

Musial, Petr. 1999. "Postavení homosexuálů v ČSR v letech 1918–38". BA thesis, Charles University.

N. [Karl Fein?]. 1923. "Liebe unter Männern". *Tagesbote*, June 9, 1923, 4.

Nachum, Iris. 2013. "Reconstructing Life after the Holocaust: The Lastenausgleichsgesetz and the Jewish Struggle for Compensation". *Leo Baeck Institute Year Book* 58, 53–67.

Nardi, Peter M. 1999. *Gay Men's Friendships: Invincible Communities*. Chicago: University of Chicago Press.

Navratil, Michael, and Florian Remele, eds. 2021. *Unerlaubte Gleichheit: Homosexualität und mann-männliches Begehren in Kulturgeschichte und Kulturvergleich*. Bielefeld: transcript Verlag.

Nebe, [Arthur], and [?] Werner. 1941. *Organisation und Meldedienst der Reichskriminalpolizei*, edited by Reichskriminalpolizeiamt. With a foreword by Reinhard Heydrich. Vol. 1 of *Schriftenreihe des Reichskriminalpolizeiamtes, Berlin*. Berlin: Praxis Verlag.

Neubauer, Fritz. N.d. "Introduction. Last Letters from the Łódź (Lodsch) Ghetto". JewishGen website, last updated November 9, 2011. http://www.jewishgen.org/databases/Holocaust/0194_Lodz_letters.html

—. N.d. "RG-15.083M_Last Letters from Łódź". Spreadsheet (Index of people). United States Holocaust Memorial Museum (USHMM), Washington. http://collections.ushmm.org/findingaids/RG-15.083M_02_nam_en.pdf

Neumann, Lothar F., ed. 2011. *Victor Bauer 1902–1959: Surrealist, Maler, Antifaschist*. Saint-Paul-de-Vence: Neumann.

Neumann, S. 1937. *Ewige Flitterwochen*. Paris: La Culture.

Niederacher, Sonja. 2010. "Dossier Fritz Grünbaum: Provenienzforschung bm:ukk – LMP". [Vienna]: [Ministerium für Kunst, Kultur, öffentlichen Dienst und Sport]. https://www.bmkoes.gv.at/dam/jcr:e929e27f-0c2a-4ab2-9af7-a8ee72675e94/dossier_gruenbaum.pdf

Nosková, Jana, and Jana Čermáková. 2013. *"Měla jsem moc krásné dětství": vzpomínky německých obyvatel Brna na dětství a mládí ve 20. až 40. letech 20. století = "Ich hatte eine sehr schöne Kindheit": Erinnerungen von Brünner Deutschen an ihre Kindheit und Jugend in den 1920er-1940er Jahren*. Brno: Etnologický ústav AV ČR, Praha – pracoviště Brno; Statutární město Brno: Archiv města Brna.

—. 2016. *"Proč to vyprávím?": první polovina 20. století v písemných vzpomínkách německých obyvatel Brna = "Warum erzähle ich das?": die erste Hälfte des 20. Jahrhunderts in schriftlichen Erinnerungen deutscher Bewohner Brünns*. Brno: Etnologický ústav AV ČR, Praha – pracoviště Brno; Statutární město Brno: Archiv města Brna.

Nováková, Lucie. 2014. *Skupina výtvarných umělců v Brně*. MA thesis, Masaryk University.

Novotný, Bohumil, and Karl Fein [the elder]. 1921. Prováděcí nařízení k zákonu o dani z obratu a dani přepychové a daňové paušály. Prague: Šimek.

Nowak, Kai. 2015. *Projektionen der Moral: Filmskandale in der Weimarer Republik*. Göttingen: Wallstein Verlag.

Ondrichová, Lucie; and Astrid Prackatzsch, trans. 2000. *Fredy Hirsch: von Aachen über Düsseldorf und Frankfurt am Main durch Theresienstadt nach Auschwitz-Birkenau; eine jüdische Biographie 1916–1944*. Konstanz: Hartung-Gorre.

Oprach, Marc. 2006. *Nationalsozialistische Judenpolitik im Protektorat Böhmen und Mähren: Entscheidungsabläufe und Radikalisierung*. Hamburg: Kovač.

Orlow, Dietrich. 2009. *The Lure of Fascism in Western Europe: German Nazis, Dutch and French Fascists, 1933–1939*. New York: Palgrave Macmillan.

Padevět, Jiří. 2013. *Průvodce protektorátní Prahou: místa – události – lidé*. Prague: Academia/Archiv hlavního města Prahy.

—. 2016. *Krvavé léto 1945: poválečné násilí v českých zemích*. Prague: Academia.

—. 2018. *Za dráty: tábory v období 1938–1945 na území dnešní České republiky*. Prague: Academia.

—. 2021. *Kronika protektorátu: represe, rezistence, holokaust, státní a okupační správa, kolaborace, bojové operace, kultura, všední život*. Prague: Academia.

Panýrek, D.[uchoslav]. 1932. "V. mezinárodní sjezd Světové ligy pro sexuální reformu na vědeckém základě v Brně 20. – 26. září 1932". *Praktický lékař* 12, n° 20 (October 20): 597–99; n° 21 (November 5): 628–30.

Pascal, Claire. 1979. *Portraits d'écrivains*. Paris: Arcam.

Patzaková, A. J., and [unknown] others. [1935]. *Prvních deset let československého rozhlasu*. [Prague]: [Radiojournal].

Paulhan, Jean, Dominique Aury, and Jean-Claude Zylberstein. 1986. *Choix de lettres. 1, La Littérature est une fête: 1917–1936*, revised and annotated by Bernard Leuilliot. Paris: Gallimard.

Pawlitschko, Iris. 1996 "Jüdische Buchhandlungen in Wien: 'Arisierung' und Liquidierung in den Jahren 1938–1945". MA thesis, University of Vienna.

Pečírka, Ferdinand. 1922. "Begrüßunfsansprachen". In *Sexualreform und Sexualwissenschaft: Vorträge gehalten auf der I. Internationalen Tagung für Sexualreform auf sexualwissenschaftlicher Grundlage in Ber-*

lin, edited by Arthur Weil, 7–8. Stuttgart: Julius Püttmann.

Peiffer, Lorenz. 2010. "Studierende der 'Deutschen Hochschule für Leibesübungen' als Akteure der 'Aktion wider den undeutschen Geist" im Frühjahr 1933'". In *Verfemt und Verboten: Vorgeschichte und Folgen der Bücherverbrennungen 1933*, edited by Julius H. Schoeps and Werner Treß, 99–111. Vol. 2 of *Wissenschaftliche Begleitbände im Rahmen der Bibliothek Verbrannter Bücher*. Hildesheim: Georg Olms.

Pelčák, Petr, Jindřich Škrabal, and Ivan Wahla, eds. 1998. *Otto Eisler: 1893–1968*. Brno: Spolek Obecní dům.

—, Jan Sapák, and Ivan Wahla. 2000a. *Brněnští židovští architekti, 1919–1939 = Brno's Jewish Architects, 1919–1939 = Ha-adrichalim ha-yehudi'im bi-Brno, 1919–1939*. Brno: Obecní dům Brno.

—. 2000b. "Memories of Otto Eisler". In *Brněnští židovští architekti, 1919–1939 = Brno's Jewish Architects, 1919–1939 = Ha-adrichalim ha-yehudi'im bi-Brno, 1919–1939*, edited by Petr Pelčák, Jan Sapák, and Ivan Wahla, 28. Brno: Obecní dům Brno.

—, and Vladimír Šlapeta. 2015. *Brno architektura 1918–1939 = Brno Architecture 1918–1939*. [Brno]: Centrum architektury.

Pełka, Bolesław, Julian Baranowski, and Piotr Strembski. 2009. *Inwentarz akt Przełożonego Starszeństwa Żydów w Getcie Łódzkim 1939–1944*. Łódz: Archiwum Państwowe w Łodzi.

Pénet, Martin. 2006. "L'expression homosexuelle dans les chansons françaises de l'entre-deux-guerres: entre dérision et ambiguïté". *Revue d'histoire moderne & contemporaine*, n°s 53–54 (April): 106–27.

Peniston, William A. 2004. *Pederasts and Others: Urban Culture and Sexual Identity in Nineteenth-Century Paris*. New York: Harrington Park Press.

Pernauhm, Fritz Geron (Guido Hermann Eckardt), and Wolfram Setz. 2010. *Die Infamen*. Hamburg: Männerschwarm.

Petrův, Helena. 2000. *Právní postavení židů v Protektorátu Čechy a Morava (1939–1941) = Die Rechtsstellung der Juden im Protektorat Böhmen und Mähren (1939–1941)*. Praha: Sefer.

Pettinger, Jürgen. 2021. *Franz: Schwul unterm Hakenkreuz*. Vienna: Kremayr & Scheriau.

Pfäfflin, Friedemann, and Walter v. Murat, eds. 1985. *Mitteilungen des Wissenschaftlich-Humanitären Komitees 1926–1933: Faksimile-Nachdruck*. With an introduction by Friedemann Pfäfflin. Vol. 4. of *Arcana bibliographica: Bibliographien zu Erotik und Sexualwissenschaft*. Hamburg: C. Bell.

—, and Manfred Herzer. 1998. "Die Monatsberichte des Wissenschaftlich-humanitären Komitees aus den Jahren 1902 und 1903". *Capri*, n° 26 (June): 2–21.

Ploto, Achim. 1921. "Sanitätsrat Dr. Magnus Hirschfeld in der Tschecho-Slowakei". *Die Freundschaft*, n° 3, 6.

Polak, E. [1934]. *Liebelei ohne Folgen*. [Brünn]: [E. Foltyn].

Popper, Max. 1934. "Náležejí sexuální úchylky lidí před soud či k lékaři?" *Sociálne zdravotní revue* 2, n° 3, March 25, 1934, 60.

Potthast, Jan Björn. 2000. "Antijüdische Maßnahmen im Protektorat Böhmen und Mähren und das 'Jüdische Zentralmuseum' in Prag". In *"Arisierung" im Nationalsozialismus: Volksgemeinschaft, Raub und Gedächtnis*, edited by Irmtrud Wojak and Peter Hayes, 157–99. Frankfurt: Campus.

—. 2002. *Das jüdische Zentralmuseum der SS in Prag: Gegnerforschung und Völkermord im Nationalsozialismus*. Frankfurt: Campus.

Poznański, Jakub, and Ingo Loose, ed. and trans. 2011. *Tagebuch aus dem Ghetto Litzmannstadt*. Berlin: Metropol.

Pretzel, Andreas. 2013. "Wie Berlin zum Zentrum der Sexualwissenschaft wurde – Überlegungen zum Erbe der Berliner Sexualforschung". *Sexuologie* 20, n°s 1–2, 23–29.

Punkl, Daniela. 2002. *Verlag Moritz Perles: k. u. k. Hofbuchhandlung in Wien*. Vienna: Geistes- und Kulturwissenschaftlichen Fakultät der Universität Wien.

Püttmann, Eduard Oskar. 1921. "Das 'Theater des Eros'". *Die Freundschaft* 3, n° 29, July 23–29, 1921, 1–2.

—. 1922. "Theater des Eros". *Die Freundschaft* 4, n° 26, 1922, 3.

R. O. 1933. "Oeffentliches Autodafe der 'Asphaltliteratur' am 10. Mai". *Wiener Allgemeine Zeitung*, May 7, 1933, 3.

Raith, Andreas. 2011. "Nationalsozialistischer Deutscher Studentenbund (NSDStB), 1926–1945". Last updated May 5, 2020. Historisches Lexikon Bayerns. http://www.historisches-lexikon-bayerns.de/Lexikon/Nationalsozialistischer_Deutscher_Stu dentenbund_(NSDStB),_1926–1945, dated May 6, 2020.

Raková, Zuzana. 2011. *Francophonie de la population Tchèque 1848–2008*. Vol. 38 of *Spisy Masarykovy univerzity v Brně Filosofická fakulta*. Brno: Masarykova univerzita Brno.

Reay, Barry. 2010. *New York Hustlers: Masculinity and Sex in Modern America*. Manchester: Manchester University Press.

Rees, Laurence. 2005. *Auschwitz: The Nazis and "The Final Solution"*. London: BBC.

Reich, Wilhelm. 1936. *Die Sexualität im Kulturkampf: zur sozialistischen Umstrukturierung des Menschen*. 2nd exp. edn. Copenhagen: Sexpol-Verlag.

—, Mary Higgins, and Chester M. Raphael. 1979. *The Bion Experiments on the Origin of Life*. Translated by Derek Jordan and Inge Jordan. New York: Octagon Books.

—. 1938. [German edition of previous]. *Die Bione zur Entstehung des vegetativen Lebens*. Vol. 6 of *Institut für Sexualökonomische Lebensforschung, klinische und experimentelle Berichte*. Oslo: Sexpol-Verlag.

—. 1994. *Beyond Psychology: Letters and Journals, 1934–1939*, edited and with an introduction by Mary Boyd Higgins. Translated by Derek Jordan, Inge Jordan, and Philip Schmitz. New York: Farrar, Straus, and Giroux.

—. 1997. [German version]. *Jenseits der Psychologie: Briefe und Tagebücher 1934–1939*, edited and with an introduction by Mary Boyd Higgins. Cologne: Kiepenheuer und Witsch.

Reifler, David M. [2015]. *Days of Ticho: Empire, Mandate, Medicine, and Art in the Holy Land*. Jerusalem and New York: Gefen.

Rey, Michel. 1989. "Police and Sodomy in Eighteenth-Century Paris: From Sin to Disorder". In *The Pursuit of Sodomy: Male Homosexuality in Renaissance and Enlightenment Europe*, edited by Gerard Kent and Gert Hekma, 129–46. New York: Harrington Park Press.

Rheiner, Rudolf [Karl Meier]. 1934. "Appell an Alle!" *Schweizerisches Freundschafts-Banner* 2, n° 10, May 15, 1934, 1–2.

—. 1934. "Das falsche Bild". *Nový Hlas*, German supplement D.Z.N.H., 2, n° 10, October, 17–19.

Richter, Horst. 1977. *Victor Bauer: Ölbilder und Aquarelle 1934–1959*. Cologne: Galerie Dreiseitel.

Riese, Hertha, and J. H. Leunbach. 1929. *Sexual Reform Congress / Copenhagen 1.-5.: VII: 1928 / W.L.S.R. / World League for Sexual Reform = Weltliga für Sexualreform = Ligue mondiale pour la réforme sexuelle = Tutmonda ligo por seksoj reformoj / Proceedings of the Second Congress* = Bericht des zweiten Kongresses = *Compte rendu du deuxième congrès = Dokumentaro de la dua kongreso*. Copenhagen and Leipzig: Levin & Munksgaard/Georg Thieme Verlag.

Rilke, Rainer Maria, and Inga Junghanns. 1959. *Briefwechsel*. Wiesbaden: Insel.

Rille, Albert. 1907. "Die städtische Heinrich Gomperz-Gemäldesammlung in Brünn". *Zeitschrift des deutschen Vereines für die Geschichte Mährens und Schlesiens* 11, n°s 1–2, 1–58.

Ripa, Alexandra. 2004. "Hirschfeld privat. Seine Haushälterin erinnert sich". In *Magnus Hirschfeld: Ein Leben im Spannungsfeld von Wissenschaft, Politik und Gesellschaft*, edited by Elke-Vera Kotowski and Julius H. Schoeps, 65–70. Vol. 8 of *Sifria. Wissenschaftliche Bibliothek*. Berlin: be.bra wissenschaft.

Roček, Josef. 1923. *Bakteriologie a serologie tuberkulosy, gonorrhoei a syfilis*. Brno: Kurs pro výcvik lékařů v sociální péči zdravotnictví.

Rohrer, Christian. 2006. *Nationalsozialistische Macht in Ostpreußen*. Vol. 7/8 of *Colloquia Baltica*. Munich: Martin Meidenbauer.

Roitner, Ingrid. 2008. "Helena Antonia aus Lüttich: eine Virgo barbata am Hof der Erzherzogin Maria in Graz (+1608)". *Mitteilungen des Instituts für Wissenschaft und Kunst* 63, n°s 1–2, 41–49.

Rose, Andrew. 2009. "Lethal Witness". Talk given on Sir Bernard Spilsbury to the Medico-Legal Society in London on April 2, 2009, 16 unnumbered pages. http://netk.net.au/Forensic/Spilsbury1.pdf

Rosenberg, Clifford. 2006. *Policing Paris: The Origins of Modern Immigration Control between the Wars*. Ithaca: Cornell University Press.

Rosenfeld, Oskar. 1994. *Wozu noch Welt: Aufzeichnungen aus dem Getto Lodz*. Vol. 7 of *Schriftenreihe der Arbeitsstelle Fritz Bauer Institut*. Frankfurt: Verlag Neue Kritik.

Roth, Thomas. 2011. "Die Kriminalpolizei". In *Ordnung und Vernichtung: die Polizei im NS-Staat*, edited by Florian Dierl, Mariana

Hausleitner, Martin Hölzl, and Andreas Mix, 42–53. Dresden: Sandstein.

Rothenberg, Ruth. 2001. "Richard Fry". *AJR Journal* 1, n° 3 (March): 11.

Rothkirchen, Livia. 2005. *The Jews of Bohemia and Moravia: Facing the Holocaust*. Lincoln: University of Nebraska Press.

Rotily, Jocelyne. 2006. *Au sud d'Eden: des Américains dans le Sud de la France, années 1910–1940*. Marseille: Association culturelle France-Amérique.

Roubíčková, R. 1932. "Několik dojmů ze sexuologického sjezdu". *Pokrokový obzor*, October 1, 1932, 5.

Royer, Louis-Charles. 1930. *L'Amour en Allemagne*. Paris: Les éditions de France.

Rückl, Steffen, and Karl-Heinz Noack. 2005. "Studentischer Alltag an der Berliner Universität 1933 bis 1945". In *Die Berliner Universität in der NS-Zeit*, vol. 1, edited by Christoph Jahr, 115–42. Stuttgart: Franz Steiner.

[Rüegg, Walter, Vege Nagaswara Rao, Anita Bianchi-Pedrazzini, and Graziella Amstutz.] [*ca.* 1981]. *H. Jocelyn Fein, 1902–1981: pro Memoria*. [Locarno]: [Bassi].

Rürup, Reinhard. 1999. "Deutsche Studenten 'wider den undeutschen Geist': Die Bücherverbrennungen vom 10. Mai 1933". In *Micha Ullman Bibliothek*, edited by Friedrich Meschede, 26–36. Amsterdam and Dresden: Verlag der Kunst.

Rys, Jan [pseudonym]. 1938. *Židozednářství – metla světa*. Prague: Zednářská korespondence. http://www.vzdelavaci-institut.info/?q=system/files/Zidozednarstvi_metla_sveta-Jan_Rys.pdf

Ryšková, Michaela, and Petra Mertová. 2014. *Kulturní dědictví brněnského vlnařského průmyslu*. Ostrava: Národní památkový ústav/územní odborné pracoviště v Ostravě.

Růžička, Karel. 1922. *Odluka státu od církve*. Brno: nákladem Vydavatelského družstva "Práce".

Salardenne, Roger. 1930. *Les capitales de la débauche*. Paris: Prima.

—. 1931. *Hauptstädte des Lasters: Eine Reportage aus den Vergnügungsvierteln der Weltstädte*. Berlin: Auffenberg.

—. 1933. "Berlin, Babylone moderne". Series of ten articles in *Police Magazine*, n°s 136–145, July 2–September 3, 1933.

Salathé, André. 1997. *"Rolf": Karl Meier (1897–1974); Schauspieler, Regisseur, Herausgeber des "Kreis"*. Frauenfeld: Verlag des Historischen Vereins des Kantons Thurgau.

Sapák, Jan. 2000. "Brno's Jewish Architects". In *Brněnští židovští architekti, 1919–1939 = Brno's Jewish Architects, 1919–1939 = Ha-adrichalim ha-yehudi'im bi-Brno, 1919–1939*, edited by Petr Pelčák, Jan Sapák, and Ivan Wahla, 8–19. Brno: Obecní dům Brno.

Sauder, Gerhard. 2010. "Vorgeschichte und Folgen der Bücherverbrennung im Mai 1933". In *Verfemt und Verboten: Vorgeschichte und Folgen der Bücherverbrennungen 1933*, edited by Julius H. Schoeps and Werner Treß, 31–45. Vol. 2 of *Wissenschaftliche Begleitbände im Rahmen der Bibliothek Verbrannter Bücher*. Hildesheim: Georg Olms.

[Sauer, Barbara]. 2017. "125 Jahre Ärztekammer für Wien". *Doktor in Wien*, n° 1, 16–31.

Schiller, Dieter. 2003. "Tag des verbrannten Buches: Der 10. Mai im Terminkalender des Exils". In *Brennende Bücher: Erinnerungen an den 10. Mai 1933*, edited by Margrid Bircken and Helmut Peitsch, 39–57. Potsdam: Brandenburgische Landeszentrale für Politische Bildung.

Schindler, Franz. 1999. "Prager Besuch am Institut für Sexualwissenschaft im Jahre 1929". *Mitteilungen der Magnus-Hirschfeld-Gesellschaft*, n°s 29–30 (July): 81–86.

—. 2000. "Prager Besuch in Berlin und Wien im Jahre 1931". *Mitteilungen der Magnus-Hirschfeld-Gesellschaft*, n°s 31–32 (March): 51–53.

—. 2001. "Jak se stala Masarykova univerzita centrem světového hnutí pro sexuální reformu". *Univerzitní noviny*, n° 3, 29–32.

Schmidt, Peter. 1928. *Das überwundene Alter: Wege zu Verjüngung und Leistungssteigerung*. Leipzig: Paul List.

Schmidt-Bachem, Heinz. 2011 *Aus Papier: eine Kultur- und Wirtschaftsgeschichte der Papier verarbeitenden Industrie in Deutschland*. Berlin: De Gruyter.

Schock, Axel. 2007. *Schwule Orte: 150 berühmt-berüchtigte Schauplätze in Oesterreich, Deutschland und der Schweiz*. Berlin: Querverlag.

Schoeps, Julius H. 2008. *Orte der Bücherverbrennungen in Deutschland 1933*, edited by Werner Treß. Vol. 1 of *Wissenschaftliche Begleitbände im Rahmen der Bibliothek verbrannter Bücher*. Hildesheim: Olms.

[Schorer, J. A.]. [1922]. *Catalogus van de bibliotheek van het Nederlandsch Wetenschappelijk Humanitair Komitee gevestigd te 's Gravenhage Laan van Meerdervoort 491 ten huize van Jhr. Mr. J. A. Schorer.* ['s Gravenhage]: [self-published].

Schröder, Stefan. 2018. *Freigeistige Organisationen in Deutschland: Weltanschauliche Entwicklungen und strategische Spannungen nach der humanistischen Wende.* Vol. 8 of *Religion and Its Others.* Berlin: De Gruyter.

Schulz, Adelheid, Ralf Dose, Rainer Herrn, and Alexandra Ripa. 2001. "Interview Frau Schulz". Typed transcript of interviews conducted March 13–14, 2001, 124 pages. Berlin: Archiv Magnus-Hirschfeld-Gesellschaft.

Schulze, Franz. 1994. *Philip Johnson: Life and Work.* New York: Knopf, 1994.

Schur, Herbert. 1997. "Terezin Memorial Book: Data on 81,397 Jewish Prisoners". [Review of Miroslav Karny, ed., *Terezinska pametni kniha.* Prague: Melantrich, 1995]. Prague: Melantrich. H-Net Reviews in the Humanities and Social Sciences, January 1997. http://www.h-net.org/reviews/showrev.php?id=759

Schütz, Otto. 1928. "Von den Unentschlossenen". *Tagesbote*, January 15, 1928, 17.

—. 1932. "Worte um Dr. Karl Fein". *Tagesbote*, October 14, 1932, 3–4.

—. 1932a. "Aus polnischen Folterkammern". *Aufruf* 2, n° 6, April, 16–18.

—. 1932b. "Soldatenselbstmorde". *Aufruf* 2, n°s 8–9, June–July, 19–20.

—. 1932. "Nach dem Kongreß". *Tagesbote*, October 2, 1932, 3–4.

—. 1932–33. "Folter in Rumänien". *Aufruf* 3, n° 2, December-January, 4–5.

—. 1933. "Schutz der Demokratie durch Menschlichkeit". *Tagesbote*, December 5, 1933, 3.

—. 1934. "Polizeiliche Emigrantenfürsorge". *Aufruf* 4, n° 24, September 15, 1934, 609–10.

—. 1947. "Farblibene yidishe pleytim fun shvedn zukhn oystsuvandern. Shvere lage fun di etlekhe hundert kranke, vos lign in di shpitoln". *Jedioth*, October 28, 1947, 6–8.

Schwarz, J. [Karl Fein the younger ?]. 1932. "Pravda a právo". *Kamarád* 1, n° 1, May 28, 1932, 3–5.

Schwarz, Ursula. 2003. "Das Wiener Verlagswesen der Nachkriegszeit: Eine Untersuchung der Rolle der öffentlichen Verwalter bei der Entnazifizierung und bei der Rückstellung arisierter Verlage und Buchhandlungen". MA thesis, University of Vienna. https://www.nonstopsystems.com/radio/pdf-hell/article-hell-swrz03.pdf

Scize, Pierre. 1932. "Aux assises des temps nouveaux". *Voilà* 2, n° 80, October 1, 1932, 5–6.

—. 1932. "Aux assises des temps nouveaux". *Voilà* 2, n° 82, October 15, 1932, 5–6.

—. 1932. "Aux assises des temps nouveaux. III. Vers la normalisation des anormaux". *Voilà* 2, n° 83, October 22, 1932, 10–11.

—. 1933. "Le Congrès de la Ligue Mondiale pour la Réforme Sexuelle de Brno". In *Sexus, Vierteljahreszeitschrift für die gesamte Sexualwissenschaft und Sexualreform*, 38–47.

Sedláková, Monika. 2003. "Die Rolle der so genannten Einsatzstäbe bei der Enteignung jüdischen Vermögens". *Theresienstädter Studien und Dokumente* 10, 275–305.

Sedlářová, Jitka. 2001. "Architekt, sochař, medailér a výtvarný pedagog: Viktor Oppenheimer". In Jan Kratochvíl, Karolína Krátká, Martina Horáková, and Hana Sedalová, eds. *Židovská Morava - Židovské Brno = Jewish Moravia - Jewish Brno*, 58–65. Brno: Společnost pro kulturu a dialog K2001.

Seeck, Andreas. 2003. "Aufklärung oder Rückfall? Das Projekt der Etablierung einer 'Sexualwissenschaft' und deren Konzeption als Teil der Biologie". In *Durch Wissenschaft zur Gerechtigkeit? Textsammlung zur kritischen Rezeption des Schaffens von Magnus Hirschfeld*, edited by Andreas Seeck, 173–206. Münster: Lit.

Seidl, Jan. 2007a. "Úsilí o odtrestnění homosexuality za první republiky". PhD diss., Masaryk University. http://is.muni.cz/th/64594/ff_r/stesura_rigo.pdf.

—. 2007b. "'Kde budeme velkou rodinou': Homosexuální spolky v občanské společnosti první republiky". *Dějiny a současnost* 29, n° 12, 36–39. http://dejinyasoucasnost.cz/archiv/2007/12/-kde-budeme-velkou-rodinou-/

—, Lukáš Nozar, and Jan Wintr. 2012. *Od žaláře k oltáři: emancipace homosexuality v českých zemích od roku 1867 do současnosti.* Brno: Host.

—. 2013. "Křižácké tažení, či ostrov relativního bezpečí? Perzekuce homosexuality v protektorátu Čechy a Morava". In *Homosexualita v dějinách a společnosti českých zemí*, edited by Pavel Himl, Jan Seidl, and Franz Schindler, 217–69 Prague: Argo. [The German version of the article ("Kreuzzug oder eine Insel der relativen Sicherheit? Verfolgung der Homosexualität im Protektorat Böhmen und Mähren"), foreseen for the year 2009, was never published in *Theresienstädter Studien und Dokumente* because the periodical stopped being published in 2008. For a French version, see Seidl 2017.]

[—, Ruth Jochanan Weiniger, Ladislav Zikmund Lender, and Lukáš Nozar, eds.]. 2014a. *Queer Prague: A Guide to the LGBT History of the Czech Capital 1380–2000*. [Translated by Katarína Mináriková and Tereza Janáčková]. Brno: Černé pole.

[—, Ruth Jochanan Weiniger, Ladislav Zikmund Lender, and Lukáš Nozar, eds.]. 2014b. *Teplá Praha: průvodce po queer historii hlavního města 1380–2000*. Brno: Černé pole.

—. 2017. "Imbroglio juridique dans le Protectorat de Bohême-Moravie". In *Homosexuel.le.s en Europe pendant la seconde guerre mondiale*, edited by Régis Schlagdenhauffen, in collaboration with Julie Le Gac and Fabrice Virgili, 73–84. [Paris]: Nouveau Monde.

Selerowicz, Anna. 2011. "Portret Brodatej dziewicy". *Aspiracje: pismo Warszawskich uczeni artystycznych* (Spring): 32–37.

Sem-Sandberg, Steve. 2011. *The Emperor of Lies*. Translated by Sarah Death. New York: Farrar, Straus and Giroux.

Senelick, Laurence. 2008. "The Homosexual Theatre Movement in the Weimar Republic". *Theatre Survey* 49, n° 1 (May): 5–35.

Serke, Jürgen. 2006 "Peter oder Petr Kien? Wem gehört der Maler und Dichter aus Warnsdorf?" In *Juden zwischen Deutschen und Tschechen: sprachliche und kulturelle Identitäten in Böhmen 1800–1945*, edited by Marek Nekula and Walter Koschmal, 273–88. München: Oldenbourg.

Seuss, Andrej. 2022. *Der Vice-Malik: Hans-Adalbert von Maltzahn - Berliner Bohème und Pariser Exil*. Berlin: Vergangenheitsverlag.

Shapiro, Robert Moses, ed. 1999. *Holocaust Chronicles: Individualizing the Holocaust Through Diaries and Other Contemporaneous Personal Accounts*. Hoboken, NJ: Ktav.

Sigusch Volkmar. 2008. *Geschichte der Sexualwissenschaft*. Frankfurt and New York: Campus Verlag.

Šišma, Pavel, and Joszef Smolka, eds. 2009. *Zur Geschichte der Deutschen Technischen Hochschule Brünn: Professoren, Dozenten und Assistenten 1849–1945*. Vol. 13 of *Schriftenreihe Geschichte der Naturwissenschaften und der Technik*. Linz: Trauner.

Sládek, Oldřich. 2000. "Standrecht und Standgericht: Die Gestapo in Böhmen und Mähren". In *Die Gestapo im Zweiten Weltkrieg: "Heimatfront" und besetztes Europa*, edited by Paul Gerhard and Klaus-Michael Mallmann, 317–39. [Darmstadt]: Primus-Verlag.

Slavíček, Lubomír. 2002. "Zdroj radosti a přemýšlení: Antonín Procházka & jeho sběratelé v Brně a jinde". In Vojtěch Lahoda, Karel Holešovský, Jiří Hlušička, Marcela Macharáčková, Lubomír Slavíček, Hana Rousová, and Lada Hubatová-Vacková, *Antonín Procházka 1882–1945*, 182–99. Brno: The Brno City Museum/The Moravian Gallery Brno.

Sleutjes, Martien. 1983. *Catalogus Van Leeuwen Bibliotheek: Historische Bibliotheek van de N.V.I.H. COC*. Amsterdam: Van Leeuwen Bibliotheek.

Šmejkal, Pavel, and Jiří Padevět. 2016. *Anthropoid*. Prague: Academia.

Smutný, Bohumír. 2004. "Heinrich Gomperz – Herkunft, Familie und Umgebung". In Robert Janás, and Jana Svobodová. *"z lásky k umění a sobě pro radost": umělecká sbírka Heinricha Gomperze (1843–1894) = "aus Liebe zur Kunst, welche meine Freude war": die Kunstsammlung Heinrich Gomperz*, 9–18. Brno: Moravská galerie.

—. 2012. *Brněnští podnikatelé a jejich podniky 1764–1948: encyklopedie podnikatelů a jejich rodin*. Brno: Statutární město Brno/Archiv města Brna.

Snijders, Paul, and Norbert Baxmann. 1998. *Schorers memorie met bijlagen: documenten over de confiscatie van de bibliotheek van het voormalig Nederlandsch Wetenschappelijk Humanitair Komitee (NWHK) door de Duitse bezetter in 1940 gepubliceerd ter gelegenheid van het 20 jarig bestaan van de Stichting Homo/Lesbisch Dokumentatiecentrum HOMODOK: met bijlagen*. Amsterdam: Paul Snijders, Norbert Baxmann.

Soetaert, Hans P., and Donald W. McLeod. 2010. “Un lion en hiver: les derniers jours de Magnus Hirschfeld à Nice (1934–1935)”. In *Magnus Hirschfeld (1868–1935): Un pionnier du mouvement homosexuel confronté au nazisme*, edited by Hussein Bourgi and Gérard Koskovich, 16–18. Paris: Mémorial de la Déportation Homosexuelle. https://tspace.library.utoronto.ca/bitstream/1807/25932/1/Hirschfeld%20French.pdf

—. 2013. “Karl Giese, Magnus Hirschfeld’s Archivist and Life Partner, and His Attempts at Safeguarding the Hirschfeld Legacy”. *Sexuologie* 20, n°s 1–2, 83–88.

—. 2014. “Succession Hirschfeld: The Handling and Settlement of Magnus Hirschfeld’s Estate in Nice (France), 1935–1936”. *Mitteilungen der Magnus-Hirschfeld-Gesellschaft*, n°s 50–51 (September): 13–77.

—. 2015. “Hirschfelds Fackelträger in der Tschechoslowakei (und in der Schweiz?)”. *Capri*, n° 49 (September): 7–43.

—. 2016. “Karl Giese in Memoriam. Gedenkrede aus Anlass der Stolpersteinverlegung für Karl Giese am 09/02/2016”. Unpublished typescript.

—. 2018. “Robert Gotthelf Kirchberger (1904–1981), the Last Secretary of Magnus Hirschfeld”. *Mitteilungen der Magnus-Hirschfeld-Gesellschaft*, n° 60 (June): 12–20.

—. 2019. “Karl Gieses Pariser ‘Badeanstalts-Affäre’ und ihre Folgen”. *Invertito* 20, 60–95.

—, and Raimund Wolfert. 2016. “Kurzbiographie Karl Giese”. Stolpersteine in Berlin, February 9, 2016. http://www.stolpersteine-berlin.de/de/biografie/7552

—. 2020. “Hans Bergemann, Ralf Dose, Marita Keilson-Lauritz (Hg.): Magnus Hirschfelds Exil-Gästebuch, 2019”. Book review. *Invertito* 22, 152–156. http://www.invertito.de/det4/d_inv2254.html

—. 2024 [2023]. “Jean Genet in Brno”. *Invertito* 25, 69–99.

—. Forthcoming. *Fritz Brecher, Otokar Kruliš-Randa and the Admont Manuscripts.*

Soffé, Emil. 1922. *Charles Sealsfield (Karl Postl).* Brünn: L. & A. Brecher.

Solařik, Bedřich. 1930–31. “Otázce homosexuelní”. *Lidská práva (orgán Ligy pro lidská práva v Československu)*, 77–79.

Spenlé, Jean-Edouard. 1935. “Nietzsche à Nice”. *Mercure de France*, n° 896, October 15, 1935, 227–59.

Spielmann, Lothar. 1932. “Zur Tagung der Sexualforscher in Brünn: Unterredung mit Dr. Magnus Hirschfeld”. *Tagesbote*, July 28, 1932, 4–5.

Staiger, S. 1934. “Die Weltreise eines Sexualforschers”. *Der Freidenker* 17, n° 12, June 15, 1934, 97–99.

Staněk, Tomáš. 2002. *Verfolgung 1945: die Stellung der Deutschen in Böhmen, Mähren und Schlesien (außerhalb der Lager und Gefängnisse).* Vol. 8 of *Buchreihe des Institutes für den Donauraum und Mitteleuropa*. Vienna: Böhlau.

—. 2005. *Poválečné “excesy” v českých zemích v roce 1945 a jejich vyšetřování.* Prague: Ústav pro soudobé dějiny Akademie věd České republiky.

—. 2007. *Internierung und Zwangsarbeit: das Lagersystem in den böhmischen Ländern 1945–1948.* Vol. 92 of *Veröffentlichungen des Collegium Carolinum*. Munich: Oldenbourg.

Staudacher, Anna L. 2009. *“ … meldet den Austritt aus dem mosaischen Glauben”: 18000 Austritte aus dem Judentum in Wien, 1868–1914: Namen, Quellen, Daten.* Frankfurt: Lang.

Steakley, James D. 1985. *The Writings of Dr. Magnus Hirschfeld: A Bibliography.* Vol. 11 of *Canadian Gay Archives Publication Series*; vol. 2 of *Schriftenreihe der Magnus-Hirschfeld-Gesellschaft.* Toronto: Canadian Gay Archives; Berlin: Magnus-Hirschfeld-Gesellschaft.

Steakley, James. 2007. *“Anders als die Andern”: Ein Film und seine Geschichte.* Hamburg: Männerschwarm Verlag.

Steakley, James, comp. 2021. *Magnus Hirschfeld: Ein Schriftenverzeichnis.* Vol. 9 of *Bibliothek rosa Winkel – Sonderreihe Wissenschaft.* Berlin: Männerschwarm; Salzgeber Buchverlage.

Steiner, Herbert ed. 1931. *Sexualnot und Sexualreform: Verhandlungen der Weltliga für Sexualreform: IV. Kongress, abgehalten zu Wien vom 16. bis 23. September 1930.* Vienna: Elbemühl.

Steinert, Hannelore. 2015. “‘Ich bin noch immer ohne Nachricht von Dir …’: beschlagnahmte Post im Getto Litzmannstadt 1940–1944 = ‘I am still without news from you …’: Confiscated Mail in Litzmannstadt Ghetto 1940–1944”. In *Post 41: Berichte aus dem Getto Litzmannstadt: ein Gedenkbuch = Post 41: Reports from Litzmannstadt Ghetto: A Memorial Book*, edited by Angelika

Brechelmacher, Bertrand Perz, and Regina Wonisch, 161–83. Vienna: Mandelbaum.

—, and Angela Genger. 2010. "' ... wir bilden eine unzertrennbare Familie'. Die Deportation von 'Düsseldorfern' aus dem Getto Litzmannstadt im Mai 1942". In *Düsseldorf - Getto Litzmannstadt. 1941*, edited by Angela Genger and Hildegard Jakobs, 153–74 Essen: Klartext.

Steinle, Karl-Heinz. 1999. *Der Kreis: Mitglieder, Künstler, Autoren*. Vol. 2 of *Hefte des Schwulen Museums*. Berlin: Verlag rosa Winkel.

Stelter, René. 1921. "Theater des Eros". *Uranos* 1, n° 9 (September). Rpt. 2002. *Uranos: Unabhängige uranische Monatsschrift. 1. Jahrgang (1921/1922)*, edited by,211–13. Vol. 32 of *Bibliothek rosa Winkel*. Hamburg: MännerschwarmSkript.

Štemberk, Jan. 2007. "Ústrední svaz dopravy 1940–1948". *Acta Oeconomica Pragensia* 5, n° 7, 405–16.

Štěpánek, Zdeněk. 2004. *Nacifikace a moravští lěkaři (1939–1945)*. Brno: Matice moravská.

Sternweiler, Andreas, and Hans Gerhard Hannesen, eds. 1997. *Goodbye to Berlin?: 100 Jahre Schwulenbewegung: eine Ausstellung des Schwulen Museums und der Akademie der Künste*. Berlin: Rosa Winkel.

Steve, Michel. 1989. "A propos de l'architecte Charles Dalmas". *Nice Historique* (July–September): 103–9.

Stiassny, Heda. 1939. "Ankunft jüdischer Kinder in Norwegen". *Hadoar*, November 15, 1939, 2.

Strätz, Hans-Wolfgang. 1968. "Die studentische 'Aktion wider den undeutschen Geist' im Frühjahr 1933". *Vierteljahrshefte für Zeitgeschichte* 16, n° 4 (October): 347–72.

—. 1983. "Die geistige SA rückt ein: Die studentische 'Aktion wider den undeutschen Geist' im Frühjahr 1933". In *10. Mai 1933: Bücherverbrennung in Deutschland und die Folgen*, edited by Ulrich Walberer, 84–114. Frankfurt: Fischer-Taschenbuch-Verlag.

Strick, James E. 2015. *Wilhelm Reich, Biologist*. Cambridge, MA: Harvard University Press.

Strongworth, Baldwin [Josef Weisskopf?]. 1932. *Hochschule der Liebeskunst, vol. I: Liebeserfahrungen der grössten Lebenskünstler: Lexikon der gesamten Liebeswissenschaft*. Brünn: Kulturverlag.

—. 1932. *Hochschule der Liebeskunst, vol. II: Ergänzungsband*. Brünn: Kulturverlag.

Sullivan, Rosemary. 2022. *Het verraad van Anne Frank: Het baanbrekende onderzoek van een internationaal coldcaseteam in Nederland*. Translated by Hans E. van Riemsdijk and Marijke Gheeraert. Amsterdam: Ambo/Anthos.

Sulzenbacher, Hannes. 1999. "'Homosexual' men in Vienna, 1938". In *Opposing Fascism: Community, Authority, and Resistance in Europe*, edited by Tim Kirk and Anthony McElligott, 150–62, 227–29. Cambridge: Cambridge University Press.

Sunnus, Michael. 1990. *Der NS-Rechtswahrerbund (1928–1945): zur Geschichte der nationalsozialistischen Juristenorganisation*. Vol. 78 of *Rechtshistorische Reihe*. Frankfurt: Lang.

Svacina, J. 1976. "Jaroslav Sindelár - sedmdesát let". *Ceskoslovenská neurologie a neurochirurgie* 39, n° 1 (January): 46.

Svoboda, Filip. 2014. "Trestněprávní aspekty pornografie". PhD diss., Charles University. https://doi.org/20.500.11956/68100

Sýkora, Karel. 2013. "Velel i Obraně národa v Nové Bělé". *Novobělský zpravoda* 10, n° 6, December, 7–8.

Szegedi, Gábor. 2014. "Good Health Is the Best Dowry: Marriage Counseling, Premarital Examinations, Sex Education in Hungary, 1920–1952". PhD diss., Central European University.

Taithe, Marcel, and Christian Taithe. 1986. *La pratique des successions*, 12th edn. Paris: Delmas.

Tamagne, Florence. 2006. "Le 'crime du Palace': Homosexualité, médias et politique dans la France des années 1930". *Revue d'histoire moderne et contemporaine*, n°s 53–54 (October–December): 128–49.

—. 2017. *Le crime du Palace: Enquête sur l'une des plus grandes affaires criminelles des années 1930*. Paris: Payot.

Tauchen, Jaromír. 2015. "Legislation on the Disposal of Jewish Property in the Protectorate of Bohemia and Moravia". In *Anti-Semitic Legislation in Slovakia and in Europe: Collection of Papers from the International Scientific Conference Bratislava, September 8–9, 2011*, edited by Martina Fiamová, 110–24. Bratislava: Ústav pamäti národa.

Taylor, Michael Thomas, Annette F. Timm, and Rainer Herrn, eds. 2017. *Not Straight from Germany: Sexual Publics and Sexual Citizenship since Magnus Hirschfeld*. Ann Arbor: University of Michigan Press.

Thalmann, Rolf, ed. 2014. *"Keine Liebe ist an sich Tugend oder Laster": Heinrich Hössli (1784–1864) und sein Kampf für die Männerliebe*. Zürich: Chronos.

Thérenty, Marie-Ève. 2019. "L'esprit Gallimard: Stratégies médiatiques et dispositifs éditoriaux de Détective, Voilà et Marianne (1928–40)". *Journal of European Periodical Studies* (Winter 2019): 122–38. https://ojs.ugent.be/jeps/article/view/10772/13403.

Tichauer, Eva. 1988. *J'étais le numéro 20832 à Auschwitz*. Paris: L'Harmattan.

—. 2017. *Grâce à mes yeux bleus, j'ai survécu*. Paris: Les impliqués.

Tichauer, Theodor. 1926. "Die Ehe als Einrichtung". *Die Ehe: Monatsschrift für Ehe-Wissenschaft, -Recht und -Kultur* 1, n° 2 (July 1): 36–39.

—. 1926. "Soll man einen Ehevertrag schließen?" *Die Ehe: Monatsschrift für Ehe-Wissenschaft,-Recht u.-Kultur* 1, n° 5 (October 1): 126.

—. 1927. "Rechtsfolgen der Scheidung". *Die Ehe: Monatsschrift für Ehe-Wissenschaft, -Recht u.-Kultur* 2, n° 2 (February 1): 45–46.

Ticho, Charles J. 2001. *M'dor l'dor, from Generation to Generation: A Family's Story of Survival*. Woodcliff Lake, NJ: Charles Ticho. https://collections.ushmm.org/search/catalog/bib265430

Ticho, Robert. 1907. *Aus Stunden der Sehnsucht: Gedicht*. Brünn: Brecher.

Tmb. 1944. "Mimořádný sběr starého papíru v Brně". *Lidové noviny*, n° 81, March 22, 1944, 4.

Tomková, Monika. 2010. "Die Kultur der deutschjüdischen Bevölkerung im Raum Brünn". BA thesis, Tomas Bata University in Zlín.

Treß, Werner. 2003. *"Wider den undeutschen Geist": Bücherverbrennung 1933*. Berlin: Parthas.

—. 2008a. "Berlin". In *Orte der Bücherverbrennungen in Deutschland 1933*, edited by Julius H. Schoeps and Werner Treß, 47–142. Vol. 1 of *Wissenschaftliche Begleitbände im Rahmen der Bibliothek verbrannter Bücher*. Hildesheim: Olms.

—. 2008b. "Phasen und Akteure der Bücherverbrennungen in Deutschland". In *Orte der Bücherverbrennungen in Deutschland 1933*, edited by Julius H. Schoeps and Werner Treß, 9–28. Vol. 1 of *Wissenschaftliche Begleitbände im Rahmen der Bibliothek verbrannter Bücher*. Hildesheim: Olms.

Trkan, Tomáš. 2014. "Oskar Judex a Vilém Czerny, brněnští starostové před Mimořádným lidovým soudem Brno". BA thesis, Masaryk University.

Trýb, Antonín. 1933. "Badání sexualní náleží lékařské vědě". *Sociálne zdravotní revue* 1, n° 4 (June 10): 76.

—. 1946a. *Loňské listí*. Blansko: Karel Jelínek.

—. 1946b. *Císař chudých*. Brno: Družstvo Moravského kola spisovatelů.

Tuma von Waldkampf, Marianne. 1911. "I. Internationaler Kongreß für Mutterschutz und Sexualreform". *Neues Frauenleben* 23, n° 11, 296–99.

Turner, Christopher. 2012. *Adventures in the Orgasmatron: The Invention of Sex. London: Fourth Estate.*

Tvrdý, Josef, and Karel Růžička. *1925. T. G. Masaryk: K 75. narozeninám*. Brno: Dělnická akademie "Osvěta" v Brně.

V. 1935. "+ Dr. Magnus Hirschfeld". *Schweizerisches Freundschafts-Banner* 3, n° 11, June 1, 1935, 1.

V., V. [Vladimír Vávra]. 1934a. "Zum Erscheinen einer deutschen Beilage". *Nový hlas*, first German supplement D.Z.N.H. 1, n° 4, April, 4.

—. 1934b. "Die Zeitschrift Simplicus". *Nový hlas*, second *German supplement D.Z.N.H.* 2, n° 5, May 1934, 7.

Valtus, Ondřej. 2015. "Perzekuce homosexuality v obvodu Krajského soudu trestního v Brně ve 30. letech 20. století". MA thesis, Masaryk University.

van Cleeff, G. [Gaston]. 1935. "Un Grand Savant Allemand, le Docteur Magnus Hirschfeld, exilé de sa patrie, vient de mourir à Nice". *L'Eclaireur de Nice et du Sud-Est*, May 16, 1935, 2.

van der Meer, Theo. 2007. *Jonkheer mr. Jacob Anton Schorer (1866–1957): Een biografie van homoseksualiteit*. Amsterdam: Schorer.

van de Velde, Theodoor Hendrik. 1930. *Dokonalé manželství: studie o jeho fysiologii a technice*. Prague: Literární a vědecké nakladatelství.

van Dongen, Luc, S. Roulin, and G. Scott-Smith, eds. 2014. *Transnational Anti-Communism and the Cold War: Agents, Activities, and Networks*. London: Palgrave Macmillan.

Vaňková, Lenka. 2009. "Nová instalace na SZ Velké Losiny". *Sborník Národního památkového ústavu: územního odborného pracoviště v Olomouci*, 120–26.

van Pelt, Robert Jan. 2015. *Lodz and Getto Litzmannstadt: Promised Land and Croaking Hole of Europe*. Toronto: Art Gallery of Ontario.

van Santhorst, [Arent] [Jaap van Leeuwen]. 1953. "Dr H. C. Rogge overleden". *Vriendschap* 8 (December 1953): 4.

Vašek, František and Zdeněk Štěpánek. 2002. *První a druhé stanné právo na Moravě (1941–1942)*. Brno: Šimon Ryšavý.

—, Vladimír Černý and Jan Břečka. 2015. *Místa zkropená krví: Kounicovy studentské koleje v Brně v letech nacistické okupace 1940–1945*. Brno: Archiv města Brna/Moravské zemské Museum.

Veigl, Hans, and Iris Fink, eds. 2012. *Verbannt, verbrannt, vergessen und verkannt: Kurzbiographien zum Thema Verfolgung und Vertreibung österreichischer Kabarett und Kleinbühnenkünstler 1933–1945*. Graz: Österreichisches Kabarettarchiv.

Verdan, Nicolas. 2011. *Le patient du docteur Hirschfeld*. Orbe: Bernard Campiche.

Vermassen, Jef. 2017. Moordenaars en hun motieven. Ghent: Borgerhoff & Lamberigts.

Veselská, Magda. 2012a. "Engel, Alfred". In *(Dvořák–Enz)*, edited by Pavla Vošahlíková, 593. Vol. 15 of *Biografický slovník českých zemí*. Prague: Libri.

—. 2012b. *Archa paměti: cesta pražského židovského muzea pohnutým 20. stoletím*. Prague: Academia/Židovské muzeum v Praze.

—. 2013. "'Sie müssen sich als Jude dessen bewusst sein, welche Opfer zu tragen sind…': Handlungsspielräume der jüdischen Kultusgemeinden im Protektorat bis zum Ende der großen Deportationen". In *Alltag im Holocaust: Jüdisches Leben im Großdeutschen Reich 1941–1945*, edited by Andrea Löw, Doris L. Bergen, and Anna Hájková, 151–66. Vol. 106 of *Schriftenreihe der Vierteljahrshefte für Zeitgeschichte*. Munich: Oldenbourg.

Vespera, Carl [Večeřa, Karel?]. 1930. *Regenera: die Wiedergeburt der Ehe: das grosse Geheimnis der Liebe ohne Folgen*. Brünn: Regenera Verlag.

Vespera [Večeřa], Karel and Jan Svoboda. 1929. *Osvobozené manželství: regenera: (tajemství lásky bez následků)*. Brno: Regenera, Karel Večeřa.

Viereck, George Sylvester. 1930. *Glimpses of the Great*. London: Duckworth.

Voigt, Wolfgang and Uwe Bresan eds. 2002. *Schwule Architekten: Verschwiegene Biografien vom 18. bis zum 20. Jahrhundert = Gay Architects: Silent Biographies from [the] 18th to the 20th Century*. Berlin: Wasmuth & Zohlen.

Vojkůvka, Alois. 1942. *České martyrium (1938–1942)*. Brno: vytiskl J. A. Kajš.

von Benda-Beckmann, Bas. 2020. *Na het Achterhuis: Anne Frank en de andere onderduikers in de kampen*. Amsterdam: Querido.

von Glasenapp, Gabriele and Hans Otto Horch. 2005. *Ghettoliteratur: eine Dokumentation zur deutsch-jüdischen Literaturgeschichte des 19. und frühen 20*. Vols. 53–55 of *Jahrhunderts. Conditio Judaica*. Tübingen: Niemeyer Verlag.

von Praunheim, Rosa, and Hanns G.[rafe]. 1992. "Ein schwuler Teenager als Patient in Magnus Hirschfelds Institut für Sexualwissenschaft: Rosa von Praunheim interviewt Dr. Hanns G. am 13.10.1991 in Berlin". *Capri* 4, n° 3 (February 1992): 11–16.

von Soden, Kristine. 1988. *Die Sexualberatungsstellen der Weimarer Republik 1919–1933*. Berlin: Hentrich.

von Vegesack, Alexander. 1987. *Das Thonet Buch*. Munich: Bangert.

von zur Mühlen, Patrik. 1998. "Ostasien". In *Handbuch der deutschsprachigen Emigration 1933–1945*, edited by Klaus-Dieter Krohn, Patrick von zur Mühlen, Gerhard Paul, and Lutz Winckler, 336–49. Darmstadt: Primus-Verlag.

Vordtriede, Werner. 2002. *Das verlassene Haus: Tagebuch aus dem amerikanischen Exil 1938–1947. Lengwil: Libelle.*

Vrabelová, Renata, Petra Svobodová, and Vladimír Šlapeta. 2016. *Brno moderní: Velký průvodce po architektuře*. Prague: Paseka.

Waddington, Lorna. 2007. *Hitler's Crusade: Bolshevism and the Myth of the International Jewish Conspiracy*. London and New York: Tauris Academic Studies.

Wagner, Patrick. 1996. *Volksgemeinschaft ohne Verbrecher: Konzeptionen und Praxis der Kriminalpolizei in der Zeit der Weimarer Republik und des Nationalsozialismus*. Vol. 34 of *Hamburger Beiträge zur Sozial- und Zeitgeschichte*. Hamburg: Christians.

—. 2002. *Hitlers Kriminalisten: die deutsche Kriminalpolizei und der Nationalsozialismus zwischen 1920 und 1960*. Munich: Beck.

—, and Jürgen *Zarusky*. 2011. *Der Volksgerichtshof im nationalsozialistischen Staat*. Vol. 16 of *Quellen und Darstellungen zur Zeitgeschichte*, expanded new edition. Munich: Oldenbourg.

Walberer, Ulrich, ed. 1983. *10. Mai 1933: Bücherverbrennung in Deutschland und die Folgen*. Frankfurt: Fischer-Taschenbuch-Verlag.

Warmerdam, Hans and Henny Brandhorst. 1995. "Een vergeten voorhoede: De Nederlandse Vereniging voor Sexuele Hervorming 1932–1939". In *Het oog op de lust: 100 jaar seksuologie in Amsterdam*, edited by Gert Hekma and Hugo Röling, 33–40. Amsterdam: Het Spinhuis.

Weigl, Hanuš Z. 2008–2009 ([Jewish year] 5769). "Jiches." *Židovská ročenka*, 100–34. Prague: Federace židovských obcí v České republice.

Weil, Arthur, ed. 1922. *Sexualreform und Sexualwissenschaft: Vorträge gehalten auf der I. Internationalen Tagung für Sexualreform auf sexualwissenschaftlicher Grundlage in Berlin*. Stuttgart: Julius Püttmann.

Weil, Jiří. 1990. *Life with a Star*. Rpt. New York: Farrar, Straus and Giroux.

Weisskopf, Josef. 1931. *Láska a manželství*. Brno: Barvič a Novotný.

—. 1931. "O sexuální reformu". *Praktický lékař* 11, n° 5 (March 5): 139–40.

—. 1932a. *Pohlavní otázky ve výchově dorostu*. Brno: Barvič a Novotný.

—. 1932b. *Škola dílnou pravdy: slovo lékaře o školské reformě k rodičům, vychovatelům a mládeži*. Brno: Josef Weisskopf.

—. 1932. "O sexuální reformu. (K. V. Mezinárodnímu kongresu Světové Ligy pro sexuální reformu v Brně)". *Pokrokový obzor*, September 10, 1932, 2–3.

—. 1932. "Přeji sovětským dělníkům k 15 letému výročí SSSR, aby socialismus zvítězil co nejdříve na celém světě". *Dělnická rovnost*, October 28, 1932, 1.

—. 1933. "Der Brünner Sexualkongreß". In *Sexus, Vierteljahreszeitschrift für die gesamte Sexualwissenschaft und Sexualreform*, 26–33.

Weisskopf, Jos. [Josef]. 1933. "Memento mementu". *Pokrokový obzor*, May 27, 1933, 2.

Weisskopf, Josef. 1934. "Magnus Hirschfeld: Die Weltreise eines Sexualforschers". *Praktický lékař* 14, n° 4, 113–14.

—. 1938. *Krvácející rány:bojovné verše*. Brno: Edice Dnes.

Wendt, Bernhard. 1955. "Walter Krieg zum Gedächtnis". *Börsenblatt für den deutschen Buchhandel*, 6–7. Vol. 55 of *Antiquariatsbeilage des Börsenblattes*.

Wessely, Katharina. 2011. *Theater der Identität: das Brünner deutsche Theater der Zwischen-kriegszeit*. Bielefeld: Transcript.

White, Edmund. 1993. *Genet*. London: Picador.

Wiener, Jan and Erhard Roy Wiehn, eds. 1992. *Immer gegen den Strom: ein jüdisches Überlebensschicksal aus Prag 1939–1950*. Konstanz: Hartung-Gorre Verlag.

Wienerová, Gertruda. N. d. "Racine et les héroïnes de ses [*sic*] tragédies". MA diss., Masaryk University.

Wiesner, Herbert. 2003. "Der Sturm auf Magnus Hirschfelds Institut für Sexualwissenschaft". *Zeitschrift für Geschichtswissenschaft* 51, n° 5, 422–29.

Wildt, Michael. 2003. *Generation des Unbedingten: das Führungskorps des Reichssicherheitshauptamtes*. Hamburg: Hamburger Edition.

Willemin, Véronique. 2009. *La Mondaine: histoire et archives de la police des mœurs*. Paris: Hoëbeke.

Witte, Peter. 1995. "Zwei Entscheidungen in der 'Endlösung der Judenfrage': Deportation nach Lodz und Vernichtung in Chelmno". *Theresienstädter Studien und Dokumente*, n° 2, 38–68.

Wladika, Michael; and Leopold Museum-Privatstiftung. 2009. *Dossier Ing. Moriz Eisler: Provenienzforschung bm:ukk - LMP*. [Vienna]: Leopold Museum-Privatstiftung. https://www.bmkoes.gv.at/dam/jcr:ff30c1a5-d2b4-418d-9465-9234150c393f/dossier_eisler.pdf

Wolfert, Raimund. 2015a. "'Sage, Toni, denkt man so bei euch drüben?': Auf den Spuren von Curt Scharlach alias Charlotte Charlaque (1892–?) und Toni Ebel (1881–1961)". Online-Projekt Lesbengeschichte. Ingeborg Boxhammer, and Christiane Leidinger, March 2015. http://www.lesbengeschichte.org/bio_charlaque_d.html

—. 2015b. *Homosexuellenpolitik in der jungen Bundesrepublik: Kurt Hiller, Hans Giese und das Frankfurter*. Göttingen: Wallstein.

—. 2020. "Walter Mann". Stolpersteine in Berlin, October 28, 2020. https://www.stolpersteine-berlin.de/de/biografie/9305.

—. 2021. *Charlotte Charlaque: Transfrau, Laienschauspielerin, "Königin der Brooklyn Heights Promenade".* Berlin: Hentrich und Hentrich.

Wolff, Charlotte. 1986. *Magnus Hirschfeld: A Portrait of a Pioneer in Sexology.* London: Quartet Books.

Wosyka, Alfred. 1935. "Magnus Hirschfeld". *Morgenpost*, n° 188, May 21, 1935, 2.

Wulf, Joseph. 1963. *Literatur und Dichtung im Dritten Reich: eine Dokumentation.* Gütersloh: Sigbert Mohn.

Wullfen, Erich, and Felix Abraham. 1931. *Fritz Ulbrichs lebender Marmor: Eine Sexualpsychologische Untersuchung des den Mordprozess Lieschen Neumann charakterisierenden Milieus und seiner psychopathologischen Typen.* Vienna: Verlag für Kulturforschung.

Würffel, Reinhard. 2000. *Lexikon deutscher Verlage von A bis Z: 1071 Verlage und 2800 Verlagssignete vom Anfang der Buchdruckerkunst bis 1945.* Berlin: Grotesk.

Würmann, Isaac. 2021. "Lost During Nazi Rule in Germany, One of the World's First Pro-Gay Films Has Finally Been Restored for Modern Viewers". *Xtra Magazine*, September 24, 2021. https://xtramagazine.com/culture/tv-film/laws-of-love-film-restoration-208929

Yagil, Limore. 2015. *Au nom de l'art, 1933–1945: exils, solidarités et engagements.* Paris: Fayard.

Zatloukal, Jaroslav. 1946. *Svědectví Kounicových kolejí.* Brno: Klub Kounicových kolejí.

Zatloukal, Pavel. 2006. *A Guide to the Architecture of Brno 1815–1915.* Brno: Obecní dům/Národní památkový ústav, územní odborné pracoviště v Brně.

Zinn, Alexander. 1997. *Die soziale Konstruktion des homosexuellen Nationalsozialisten: zu Genese und Etablierung eines Stereotyps.* Frankfurt: Lang.

—. 2011. *"Das Glück kam immer zu mir": Rudolf Brazda – das Überleben eines Homosexuellen im Dritten Reich.* Frankfurt: Campus.

Acronyms and Abbreviations

ABS: Archiv bezpečnostních složek, Praha

ACJR: Association of Children of Jewish Refugees, London

ADAM: Archives départementales des Alpes-Maritimes, Nice

ADBR: Archives départementales des Bouches-du-Rhône, Aix-en-Provence

AG: Aktiengesellschaft (joint- stock company)

AHMP: Archiv hlavního města Prahy, Praha

AJJDC: (Archives of the) American Jewish Joint Distribution Committee, New York

AJR: British Association of Jewish Refugees, London

ALMS: LGBTQ Archives, Libraries, Museums and Special Collections

AMB: Archiv města Brna, Brno

APŁ: Archiwum Państwowe w Łodzi, Łódź

ARJ: Ältestenrat der Juden (Jewish Council of Elders)

ASSO: Association des Emigrés Israélites d'Allemagne en France

BA: Bundesarchiv, Berlin-Lichterfelde

BA: Bundesarchiv, Abteilung Militärarchiv, Freiburg im Breisgau

BAR/AFS/AFS: Schweizerisches Bundesarchiv, Archives fédérales suisses, Archivio federale svizzero, Bern

BCRC: British Committee for Refugees from Czechoslovakia

BDC: Berlin Document Center

BN: Bibliothèque Nationale, Paris

CASLIN: Union Catalogue of the Czech Republic

CEGESOMA: Studiecentrum Oorlog en Maatschappij/Centre d'Etude Guerre et Société, Brussel/Bruxelles

COJASOR: Comité Juif d'Action Sociale et de Reconstruction, Paris

CRTF: Czech Refugee Trust Fund

CUM: Centre Universitaire Méditerranéen, Nice

DNB: Deutsche Nationalbibliothek, Leipzig

DOPZ: Družstvo obchodních a průmyslových zaměstnanců, Brno (Haus des Einheitsverbands der Privatangestellten, Cooperative Association of Trade and Industry Employees), Brno

DöW: Dokumentationsarchiv des österreichischen Widerstandes, Wien

ELAB: Evangelisches Landeskirchliches Archiv in Berlin, Berlin

e.V.: eingetragener Verein (registered association)

Gestapo: Geheime Staatspolizei (Secret State Police)

GFHA: The Ghetto Fighters' House Archives, Beit Lohamei Haghetaot (Israel)

IHLIA: Internationaal Homo/Lesbisch Informatiecentrum en Archief, Amsterdam

IISH: International Institute of Social History, Amsterdam

IMEC: Institut mémoires de l'édition contemporaine, Abbaye d'Ardenne, Saint-Germain-la-Blanche-Herbe (France)

ITS: International Tracing Service (Arolsen Archives), Bad Arolsen (Germany)

JDC: (American Jewish) Joint Distribution Committee

JKG: Jüdische Kultusgemeinde (Jewish Religious Community)

KBR: Albertina, Brussel/Bruxelles

Kripo: Kriminalpolizei (Criminal Police)

LAB: Landesarchiv, Berlin

LAC/BAC: Library and Archives Canada/Bibliothèque et archives Canada, Ottawa

LKAN: Landeskirchliches Archiv, Nürnberg

m.b.H.: mit beschränkter Haftung (limited liability)

MHG: Magnus-Hirschfeld-Gesellschaft, Berlin

MZA: Moravský zemský archiv v Brně, Brno

MZK: Moravská zemská knihovna, Brno

NA: Národní archiv Ceské republiky, Praha

NARA: National Archives and Records Administration, Washington D.C.

NFA: Národní filmový archiv, Praha

NIOD: Instituut voor Oorlogs-, Holocaust- en Genocidestudies, Amsterdam

NLM: National Library of Medicine, Bethesda (Maryland)

NOF: Národní obec fašistická (National Fascist Movement)

NPÚ: Národní památkový ústav

NSDAP: Nationalsozialistische Deutsche Arbeiterpartei

NSRB: Nationalsozialistische Rechtswahrerbund

OCLC: Online Computer Library Center, Dublin (Ohio)

OUSŘ: Odbor územního a stavebního řízení, Brno

PNP: Památník národního písemnictví, Praha

QRAB: Queerrörelsens Arkiv och Bibliotek, Göteborg (Sweden)

RAF: Royal Air Force

RGBl.: Reichsgesetzblatt (Reich Legislation Publication)

RKK: Reichskulturkammer (Reich Chamber of Culture)

RSHA: Reichssicherheitshauptamt (Reich Security Main Office)

SA: Sturmabteilung (Storm Division)

SD: Sicherheitsdienst (Security Service)

SNB: Sbor národní bezpečnosti (National security corps)

Sipo: Sicherheitspolizei (Security Police)

SPB: Svaz protifašistických bojovníků (Union of Anti-Fascist Fighters)

StadtA WM: Stadtarchiv, Weilheim in Oberbayern (Germany)

StB: Státní bezpečnost (State Security)

SVU: Skupina výtvarných umělců v Brně (Group of Visual Artists in Brno)

TASIS: American School in Switzerland

TD: tracing document

UNRRA: United Nations Relief and Rehabilitation Administration, Washington D.C.

URO: United Restitution Organization

USHMM: United States Holocaust Memorial Museum, Washington D.C.

USNA: United Service for New Americans

WhK: Wissenschaftlich-humanitären Komitee

WStLA: Wiener Stadt- und Landesarchiv, Wien

YIVO: Institute for Jewish Research, New York

YWCA: Young Women's Christian Association

ŽMP: Židovské muzeum v Praze, Praha

aka = also known as

BA = Bachelor of Arts

Bd. = Band (volume)

ca. = circa, approximately

cf. = compare

ch. = chapter

comp. = compiled

č.o. (**ČO**) = číslo orientační (regular house number)

č.p. (**ČP**) = číslo popisné (conscription number)

d. = deceased

diss. = dissertation

ed. = edited by, editor, edition

eds. = edited by more than one person, editors

f. = folio

ff. = and the following pages or lines

ggl. = gottgläubig (believing in a god without adhering to an organized religion)

ibid. = ibidem (the same source)

ill. = illustration

Jg. = Jahrgang (year volume)

kart. = karton, box

lit. = literally

MA = Master of Arts

n. = (foot)note

n° = number

n.d. = no date

n.p. = no page (number) / no publisher / without place (of publication)

o.c. = opus citatum (in the work cited)

p. = page

PhD = Doctor of Philosophy

qtd. = quoted

rev. = revised

rpt. = reprint(ed)

s.l. = sine loco, without place (of publication)

s.n. = sine nomine, without name (of publisher)

trans. = translated, translator

vol. = volume

Brno Street Names (German-Czech)

Adlergasse: Orlí, currently Orlí
Altbrünnergasse: Starobrněnská, currently Starobrněnská
Am Bergl: Na kopečku, currently Antonína Slavíka
Am Gelben Berg: Na Žlutém kopci, currently Žlutý kopec
Am Rasen: Trávníky, currently Geislerova
Antonína Nováka, currently Leitnerova (Czech name only)
Akademiegasse: Akademická, currently Čápkova
Alleegasse: V aleji (1939–1945), currently třída Kpt. Jaroše
Ausstellungsstrasse: Výstavní, currently Výstavní
Babičkagasse: Babičkova, currently Babičkova
Bäckergasse: Pekařská, currently Pekařská
Basteigasse: Na hradbách, currently Rooseveltova
Beethovenstrasse: Beethovenova, currently Beethovenova
Comeniusplatz: Komenského náměstí, currently Komenského náměstí (before 1918 known as Elisabethplatz)
Cyrillsgasse: Cyrilská, currently Cyrilská
d'Elvertstrasse: d'Elvertova (also known as Lange Gasse or Dlouhá before World War II), currently Staňkova
Dobrovskýgasse: Dobrovského, currently Gajdošova
Dominikanerplatz: Dominikánské náměstí, currently Dominikánské náměstí
Dornich: Dornych, currently Dornych
Dörnrössel: Trnitá, currently Trnitá
Dr-Bedřich-Macků-Gasse: Dra Bedřicha Macků (also known as Talgasse before World War II), currently Údolní
Eichhorner Strasse: Veveří, currently Veveří
Fabriksgasse: Tovární, currently Úzká
Falkensteinergasse: Falkensteinerova, currently Gorkého
Fleischmarktgasse: Masná, currently Masná
Fliedergasse: Šeříková (also known as Grillparzergasse – Grillparzerova during World War II), currently Heinrichiva Freiheitsplatz: náměstí Svobody, currently náměstí Svobody
Gerichtsgasse: Soudní, currently Soudní
Glacis: Koliště, currently Koliště
Hans-Kudlich-Gasse: ulice Hanse Kudlicha, currently Botanická
Hinterm Gärtchen: Za zahrádkou, currently Sochorava
Husgasse: Husova, currently Králova
Hutterova: Huttergasse, currently Traubova
Hutterteich: Hutterův rybník, currently Vrchlického sad
Innere gasse: Vnitřní, currently Vnitřní
Jakobsplatz: Jakubské náměstí, currently Jakubské náměstí
Jeronymgasse: Jeronýmova, currently Jeronýmova
Jesuitengasse: Jesuitská, currently Jesuitská
Jodokstrasse: Joštova, currently Joštova
Johannesgasse: Jánská, currently Jánská
Josef-Pekař-strasse: třída Josefa Pekaře, currently Palackého třída
Josef-Švec-Gasse: Josefa Švece, currently Ševcova
Jungmanngasse: Jungmannova (starting in 1942: Zur Reiteralee - U jízdárenské aleje), currently Jungmannova
Kampelíkgasse: Kampelíkova (from February 1942: Dr Schindler-Gasse - ulice Dra Schindlera), currently Kampelíkova
Karl-Wawra-Gasse: Karla Wawry, currently Havlíčkova
Kinderspitalgasse (also Beim Kinderspital): U dětské nemocnice, currently Helfertova
Kořískogasse: Kořískova, currently Kořískova
Kounicgasse (also Kaunitzgasse): Kounicova (also known as Giskra-Strasse before 1918), currently Kounicova
Krapfengasse: Kobližná, currently Malinovského náměstí
Krautmarkt: Zelný trh, currently Zelný trh
Kreuzgasse: Křížová, currently Křížová
Kroatische Gasse: Chorvatská, currently Charvatská
Kröna: Křenová, currently Křenová

Kuneš-Kunz-Gasse: Kuneše Kunze, currently Kunzova

Lazanskyplatz: Lažanského náměstí, currently Moravské náměstí

Legionärenstrasse: třída Legionářů, currently třída Kapitána Jaroše

Lehmstätte: V hlinkách, currently Hlinky

Leopoldshof: Skořepka, currently Skořepka

Lösselgasse (also Töpfergasse): Lösselova, currently Hrnčířská

Mášagasse: Jana Máši, currently Mášova (Veveří)

Máchagasse: Máchova, currently Máchova (Královo Pole)

Marxgasse: Marxova, currently Spolková

Masarykstrasse: Masarykova (before 1918 known as Ferdinandsgasse), currently Masarykova

Mendelplatz: Mendlovo náměstí, currently Mendlovo náměstí

Merhautgasse: Merhautova (also Senefeldergasse during World War II), currently Merhautova

Mühlgasse: Mlýnská, currently Mlýnská

Neugasse: Nová, currently Lidická

Neumanngasse: Neumannova, currently Neumannova

Neustift: Nové sady, currently Nové sady

Neutorgasse: U Nové brány, currently Novobranská

Obrowitz: Zábrdovice, currently Zábrdovická

Olomoucká: Olmützerstrasse, currently Olomoucká

Palackýstrasse: Palackého třída, currently Palackého třída

Pestalozziplatz: náměstí Pestalozziho, currently Šujanovo náměstí

Pilgramgasse: Pilgramova, currently Divadelní

Plankengasse: Plotní, currently Plotní

Ponawkagasse: Na Ponávce, currently Vlhká

Postgasse: Poštovská, currently Poštovská

Prager Strasse: Pražská, currently Štefánikova

Preßburgerstrasse: Bratislavská, currently Bratislavská

Quergasse: Příční, currently Příční

Rathaussteig: U radnice, currently Průchodní

Rennergasse: Běhounská, currently Běhounská

Rokycanagasse: Rokycanova, currently Rokycanova

Sandstätte: Na pískách, currently Bayerova

Schillergasse: Schillerova, currently Jiříkovského

Schlossergasse: Zámečnická, currently Zámečnická

Schützengasse: Střelecká, currently Domažlická

Schwarze Gasse: Černá, currently Hilleho

Schwarzfeldgasse: V černých polích, currently Černopolní

Smetanagasse: Bedřicha Smetany, currently Smetanova (Královo Pole)

Svatopluk-Čech-Gasse: Svatopluka Čecha, currently Svatopluka Čecha

Obeschitzer Gasse: Soběšická, currently Soběšická

Stephansgasse: Štěpánská, currently Štěpánská

Stiftergasse: Stifterova, currently Klácelova

Stiftgasse: Nadační, currently Přízova

Stojangasse: Stojanova, currently Stojanova

Talgasse, see Dr-Bedřich-Macků-Gasse

Theatergasse: Divadelní, currently Divadelní

Traubengasse: Hroznová, currently Hroznová

Trávníčekgasse: Trávníčkova, currently Trávníčkova

Tschechische Gasse: Česká, currently Česká

Tschechnergasse: Čechyňská, currently Čechyňská

Untere Gasse: Dolní ulice, currently Vranovská

Van der Strass-Gasse: Van der Strassova (before World War II it was known as Gymnasiumgasse - Gymnasijní), currently Kudelova

Waisenhausgasse: Sirotčí, currently Grohova

Wannieckgasse: Wannieckova, currently Podnásepní

Winterhollerplatz: Winterhollerovo náměstí, currently Náměstí 28. října

Winzergasse: Vinařská, currently Vinařská

Zazowitzer Gasse: Cacovická, currently Cacovická

Zeile: Cejl, currently Cejl

Zierotinplatz: Žerotínovo náměstí, currently Žerotínovo náměstí

Photo and Illustration Credits

Every effort has been made to trace the copyright holders and obtain permissions to reproduce these materials. Please get in touch with the publisher for any enquiries or any information relating to these images and their rights holders.

FRONT COVER PICTURE
Bundesarchiv, Berlin, picture n° 183-R70391, unknown photographer.

1. INTRODUCTION
Bundesarchiv, Berlin, picture n° 183-R70391, unknown photographer.

2. KARL GIESE AND MAGNUS HIRSCHFELD

1. Collection author, photo author.
2. The right holders of this image could not be found, courtesy of Filmmuseum Potsdam.
3. Archiv MHG, Berlin, fonds Adelheid Schulz, unknown photographer.
4. Bayerisches Hauptstaatsarchiv (BayHStA), München, Bildersammlung 1876, unknown photographer.
5. University of Sydney Library, Sydney, Norman Haire collection, 3.21, Karl Geise [*sic*, Giese], Typescripts, 1928–1934.
6. Collection author, *Voilà* (Apr. 9, 1932, 7), unknown photographer. The photo was also published in Magnus Hirschfeld's *Geschlechtskunde* (1926–1930, 1930: vol. IV, Bilderteil, picture n° 1393, 892).
7. Archiv MHG, Berlin, fonds Adelheid Schulz, unknown photographer.
8. Collection author, Magnus Hirschfeld's *Geschlechtskunde* (1926–1930, 1930: vol. IV, Bilderteil, picture n° 422, 327), unknown photographer (original), photo author.
9. Archiv MHG, Berlin, picture formerly owned by Dr. Hanns Grafe and donated by Manfred Herzer to the Archiv MHG, Berlin, unknown photographer.
10. Archiv MHG, Berlin, fonds Ernst Maass, unknown photographer (original), photo author.

3. THE SEPTEMBER 1932 WORLD LEAGUE FOR SEXUAL REFORM CONFERENCE IN BRNO

1. MZK, Brno/Digitální knihovna Kramerius, *Časopis lékařů českých* (1911, n° 50, 5), unknown photographer.
2. Collection author, Jelínek 1924, book cover, photo author.
3. Collection author, Miller 1932a, 281, unknown photographer (original), mention foto Lehký Brünn, photo author.
4. http://www.matyas.sk/, unknown photographer.
5. Deutsches Literaturarchiv, Marbach am Neckar, Magnus Hirschfeld Gästebuch (1933–1935), Zugangsnummer 85.451, f. 69, unknown photographer. The photo is also reproduced in Bergemann, Dose, Keilson-Lauritz & Dubout 2019, f. 69/113.
6. Postcard collection author, unknown photographer.
7. https://www.wikipedia.org/, creative commons, posted by user Sprockethead1.
8. Postcard collection author, unknown photographer, mention Metropol company.
9. Postcard collection author, unknown photographer.
10. © Universitätsbibliothek der Humboldt-Universität zu Berlin, Abteilung Historische Sammlungen, Fotosammlung Haeberle-Hirschfeld-Archiv für Sexualwissenschaft (HHA), photographer likely Eugen Faden.
11. Collection author, photo author.
12. Collection author, Lewandowski 1933, image n° 24, unknown photographer (original) but possibly Eugen Faden or Herbert Lewandowski, photo author.
13. Collection author, Patzaková et al. 1935, 534, unknown photographer (original), photo author.
14. Postcard collection author, unknown photographer, mention Bromografia.
15. Collection author, *Voilà* (Oct. 10, 1932, 5), photographer Eugen Faden.
16. Postcard collection author, mention Č.[eněk?] Pozdník (photographer ?) Brno, EPO.
17. Postcard collection author, unknown photographer.
18. Postcard collection author, mention Metropol, unknown photographer.
19. Postcard collection author, mention Fototypia, unknown photographer.

4. THE MAY 1933 LOOTING OF THE INSTITUTE AND THE BERLIN BOOK BURNING

1. Bundesarchiv, Berlin, image n° 183-R70390, Allgemeiner Deutscher Nachrichtendienst – Zentralbild, unknown photographer.
2. Collection author, *Police magazine* (May 21, 1933, 16), unknown photographer.
3. Getty images/Ullstein, image n° 542879957, unknown photographer.
4. USHMM, Washington, photo n° 71188, unknown photographer.

5. Bpk-Bildagentur, Berlin, Deutsches Historisches Museum, Berlin, unknown photographer.
6. Collection author, photo issued in 1984 by Archiv MHG, Berlin, unknown photographer.
7. Collection author, photo author.
8. Collection author, photo author.

5. MAGNUS HIRSCHFELD LANDS IN PARIS AND KARL GIESE TESTS THE WATERS IN BRNO

1. Collection author, *Vu* (May 24, 1933, 1), photo collage.
2. Collection author, *Police Magazine* (Aug. 27, 1933, 6–7), photo collage, unknown photographers (original), photo author.
3. Collection author, *Voilà* (July 1, 1933, 1), unknown photographer, mention Voilà-Heim.
4. Collection author, *Voilà* (July 1, 1933, 5), unknown photographer (original), mention Voilà-Heim, photo author.
5. Collection author, photo author.
6. Verlag Hentrich & Hentrich, Leipzig, Bergemann, Dose, Keilson-Lauritz & Dubout 2019, book cover.
7. Collection author, Miller 1932, book cover.
8. MZA, Brno, fonds C 12, Krajský soud trestní Brno, III. manipulace, kart. n° 968, sign. Hp I 81/38, photo author.

6. KARL FEIN AND THE OPERATION TO BUY BACK INSTITUTE MATERIALS

1. Collection author, Müller 1907, photo author.
2. IHLIA, Amsterdam.
3. ANNO/Österreichische Nationalbibliothek.
4. Collection author, Titus-Perlen brochure, unknown artist.
5. Collection author, photo author.
6. Collection author, photo author.
7. Postcard collection author, mention H. S. B. 1679, [year] 1908, unknown photographer.
8. Muzeum města Brna (Museum of the city of Brno), Brno, item n° 235.790, photographer Herbert Orth. By Courtesy of Museum of the City of Brno.
9. Collection author, photo author.
10. Collection author, *Licht ins Volk!* [1931].
11. Photo archive Nakladatelství Josef Filip, Brno, unknown photographer.

7. ATTEMPTS AT A NEW BEGINNING IN FRANCE AND CZECHOSLOVAKIA

1. Postcard collection author, unknown photographer, mention Edition "La Cigogne", 15, Rue St.-François-de-Paule, Nice.
2. University of Sydney Library, Sydney, Norman Haire collection, 3.20, Magnus Hirschfeld, Typescripts, 1923–1935, letter (dated 11 or 12 Apr., 1934) Magnus Hirschfeld to Norman Haire, p. 2 (II).
3. Collection author, Hirschfeld 1935e, book cover, photo author.
4. Collection author, *Le problème sexuel* (Nov. 1933, cover page).
5. Collection author, undated clipping from unknown magazine acquired online.
6. Collection author, *Voilà* (Dec. 30, 1933, 10), unknown photographer, mention "Hirschfeld" so likely photo from (now lost) private collection Magnus Hirschfeld.
7. Collection author, *Détective* (Mar. 1, 1934, 12–13) photo collage, photographers unknown (original), photo author.
8. Collection author, *Nový hlas* (Sept. 1933, cover page).
9. Collection author, *Détective* (Sept. 13, 1934, 7), Bringuier (Sept. 13, 1934), photo collage, photographers unknown (original), photo author.
10. Staatsarchiv Kanton Thurgau, Frauenfeld (Switzerland), Nachlass Karl Meier, Schauspieler, n° 8'658, 7, photographer René Leier, © Staatsarchiv des Kantons Thurgau.
11. Collection author, *Der Kreis/Le Cercle* (Oct. 1952, cover page).

8. KARL GIESE'S PARIS BATHHOUSE AFFAIR

1. http://nalouisintheair.blogspot.com/2015/03/, photographer Natie/Nalou.
2. AN, site de Pierrefitte-sur-Seine, Ministère de l'intérieur, Direction générale de la sûreté nationale (fonds de Moscou), file on Karl Giese, dossier n° 15843, cote 19940448/186, Prisons de Fresnes, étrangers détenus passibles d'expulsion, notice individuelle Karl Giésé [*sic*, Giese], f. 14b, photo author.
3. Bibliothèque nationale de France, Paris, Agence de presse Meurisse.
4. AN, site de Pierrefitte-sur-Seine, Ministère de l'intérieur, Direction générale de la sûreté nationale (fonds de Moscou), file on Karl Giese, dossier n° 15843, cote 19940448/186, letter (dated Oct. 23, 1934) Magnus Hirschfeld to the French Justice Minister, f. 2, photo author.
5. Archiv MHG, Berlin, fonds Max Reiss/Jean Bart Broers, photographer Max Reiss. The photo is also reproduced in Bergemann, Dose, Keilson-Lauritz & Dubout, 2019, f. 79/123.
6. Archiv MHG, Berlin, fonds Max Reiss/Jean Bart Broers, photographer Max Reiss.
7. Archiv MHG, Berlin, fonds Max Reiss/Jean Bart Broers, unknown photographer.
8. Collection author, photo author.
9. Bibliothèque nationale de France, Paris, Gallica (Bibliothèque numérique de la BnF et de ses partenaires), *Paris-Midi* (Apr. 28, 1935, 2). Unknown artist.
10. Collection author, Abraham & Hirschfeld 1931, front dustcover.
11. Postcard collection author, unknown photographer, mention Photo du Jardin Albert I, Kiosque (Angle Ave[nue] des Phocéens – Nice).
12. Postcard collection author, photographer Pierre Petit, mention AN Paris.

9. THE HANDLING AND SETTLEMENT OF MAGNUS HIRSCHFELD'S ESTATE IN NICE

1. Collection author, photo author.
2. Collection author, photo author.
3. Postcard collection author, photographer Ray(mond) Delvert, Villeneuve sur Lot.

4. Deutsches Literaturarchiv, Marbach am Neckar, Magnus Hirschfeld Gästebuch (1933–1935), Zugangsnummer 85.451, f. 149. The photo is also reproduced in Bergemann, Dose, Keilson-Lauritz & Dubout, 2019, f. 149/193, top photo.
5. Archiv MHG, Berlin, fonds Gaby Cohen. The photo is also reproduced in Bergemann, Dose, Keilson-Lauritz & Dubout, 2019, f. 151/195.
6. Private archive Don McLeod, unknown photographer (original photo), photographer Don McLeod.
7. ADAM, Nice, Archives notariales, minutes notariales, étude Pierre Demnard, Nice, Dépôt du Testament Olographe de Mr. le Dr. Magnus Hirschfeld (dated May 22, 1935), May 16, 1935-May 31, 1935, n° 563, cote 03E 148/011, photo author.
8. AN, site de Pierrefitte-sur-Seine, Ministère de la Justice, Sous-direction des naturalisations (1976–1980), file Franz Herzfelder, dossier n° 52713X38, cote 19770898/197, unknown photographer (original photo), photo author.
9. Collection author, photo author.
10. ADAM, Nice, Archives administratives de 1940 à nos jours, Direction départementale de la sécurité publique des Alpes-Maritimes, Sûreté départementale: unité technique d'aide à l'enquête (caserne Auvare), cote 1060W 0478, file Pierre Demnard, unknown photographer (original), photo author.
11. ADAM, Nice, Archives administratives de 1940 à nos jours, Direction départementale de la sécurité publique des Alpes-Maritimes, Sûreté départementale: unité technique d'aide à l'enquête (caserne Auvare), cote 1292W 0018, file Léopold Hönig, unknown photographer (original), photo author.
12. Collection author, photographer Itale Joseph Maniezzi (or his father Jean Maniezzi), Nice, modern print from glass negative.
13. Collection author, photo author.
14. NA, Praha, Policejní ředitelství Praha II, všeobecná spisovna 1941–1950, kart. n° 12.893, sign. Z 71/7, Arnold Zadikow 1884, unknown photographer (original), photo author.
15. Collection author, photo author.
16. Collection author, photo author.

10. WHAT HAPPENED TO THE INSTITUTE AND HIRSCHFELD MATERIALS AFTER HIRSCHFELD'S DEATH IN NICE?

1. Národní památkový ústav, Olomouc, evidenční list NPÚ, item VL01179a, photographer Chrisula Heckelová.
2. Josephinum, Ethics, Collections and History of Medecine, Medizinische Universität Wien, MUW-FO-IR-000670-0526 [Aufnahme: Kongressausstellung des Forschung im Konzerthaus/Wien], photographer Atelier S. Wagner, Wien.
3. AN, site de Pierrefitte-sur-Seine, Ministère de l'intérieur, Direction générale de la sûreté nationale (fonds de Moscou), fichier central de la Sûreté nationale, fiche (index card) Victor Bauer, cote 19940508/176, unknown photographer (original), photo author.
4. Collection author, Duvivier, Tataru, Liška, [et al.], 2002, 68, unknown photographer.
5. Archiv MHG, Berlin, fonds Ernst Maass, photo author.
6. NA, Praha, Policejní ředitelství Praha II, všeobecná spisovna, 1931–1940, kart. n° 11221, sign. S 6897/20, Ewa Stross 1866, unknown photographer (original), photo author.
7. Private archive Philippe Fabre, photographer Philippe Fabre.
8. Collection author, Giese 1959, book cover.
9. Private archive Don McLeod, photographer Don McLeod.
10. https://makinggayhistory.com/podcast/magnus-hirschfeld/, photographer Ralf Dose.
11. Deutsches Literaturarchiv, Marbach am Neckar, Magnus Hirschfeld Gästebuch (1933–1935), Zugangsnummer 85.451, f. 155. The photo is also reproduced in Bergemann, Dose, Keilson-Lauritz & Dubout, 2019, f. 155/199, unknown photographer (but likely Li Shiu Tong).
12. Archiv MHG, Berlin, fonds Ernst Maass, photo author.

11. KARL GIESE SETTLES DOWN IN BRNO FOR THE THIRD AND LAST TIME

1. Collection author, photo author.
2. Collection author, photo author.
3. Photo archive Nakladatelství Josef Filip, Brno, unknown photographer.
4. Postcard collection author, unknown photographer, mention EPO Brno.
5. Private archive Peter Barber, unknown photographer (original), photo author.
6. Private archive Peter Barber, unknown photographer (original), photographer Peter Barber.
7. Collection author, photo author.
8. AMB, Brno, fonds Z 1, photo author.
9. AN, site de Pierrefitte-sur-Seine, Ministère de l'intérieur, Direction générale de la sûreté nationale (fonds de Moscou), fichier central de la Sûreté nationale, fiche (index card) Milada Luklová (née Tabatznik), cote 19940508/1534, unknown photographer (original), photo author.
10. Private archive Mabel Tuinman-Hesling, unknown photographer.
11. MZK, Brno, periodicals department, *Morgenpost* (Mar. 20, 1938, 1), photo author.
12. Collection author, Hirschfeld 1938a, front dustcover, photo author.
13. MZA, Brno, fonds C 152, Okresní soud civilní Brno, rubber stamped 23/03/1938, ad DV 206/38/2, sign. s.l. 69/38, photo author.
14. Stadtarchiv Kaufbeuren, Kaufbeuren, Antrag auf Ausstellung einer deutschen Kennkarte Walter Lukl, unknown photographer.
15. Postcard collection author, unknown photographer, mention Verlag Foto-Kohlbauer, Pfronten-Allgäu, AKO.

12. THE GIESE-FEIN INHERITANCE CASE

1. Bundesarchiv, Berlin-Lichterfelde, Reichsjustizministerium, Personalakten, N (1877–1945), Franz Nawratil, geb. 4.8.1889, sign. BArch, R 3001/69402, unknown photographer.
2. MZK, Brno, periodicals department, *Brünner Tagblatt* (May 13, 1942, 6), photo author.
3. Postcard collection author, photographer Karel Čuda (or his studio), mention Grafo Čuda Holice.
4. MZA, Brno, fonds C 107, Německý úřední soud Brno (Deutsches Amtsgericht Brünn), kart. n° 256, sign. 5aV 3/41, Zpáteční lístek okresního soudu civilního pro Brno-město, photo author.
5. Postcard collection author, unknown photographer.
6. Rijksarchief/Archives de l'Etat, Brussel/Bruxelles, Ministerie van Justitie, Bestuur der Openbare Veiligheid, Dienst Vreemdelingenpolitie, file Lazare Tcherniak (born 1895), individueel dossier nr. 1.194.274, unknown photographer (original), photo author.
7. MZK, Brno/Digitální knihovna Kramerius, *Salon* (Aug. 15, 1930, 1d).
8. Vědecká knihovna Olomouc, Olomouc, periodicals department, *Hlas přírody* (Sept. 1938), front cover, photo author.
9. NA, Praha, Policejní ředitelství Praha II, všeobecná spisovna 1931–1940, kart. n° 6491, sign. H2086/21, Kurt Hiller 1895, f. 9, unknown photographer (original), photo author.

13. THE HOLOCAUST FATES OF KARL FEIN AND HIS IMMEDIATE FAMILY

1. Postcard collection author, photographer Karel Čuda (or his studio), mention Grafo Čuda Holice.
2. Forschungsinstitut Brenner-Archiv, Universität von Innsbruck, Innsbruck, Nachlass Herta Fein-Erich Messing, Kassette 152, unknown photographer, mention photo Biesk (Prague).
3. Collection author, picture from the photo album of an unidentified Wehrmacht soldier, acquired online, unknown photographer.
4. NA, Praha, fonds n° 375, Arizačni spisy, company Rudolf Schneider, kart. 43, invent. n° 443, unknown photographer (original), photo author.
5. NA, Praha, fonds Policejní ředitelství Praha II, všeobecná spisovna, 1941–1950, kart. n° 9761, sign. S38/1, Salomon Sabovič 1914, unknown photographer (original), photo author.
6. Postcard collection author, unknown photographer.
7. Collection author, photo author.
8. APŁ, Łódź, fonds Przełożony Starszeństwa Żydów, sign. 2316, microfilm L-20930, [Karty pocztowe przeznaczone dla krewnych i znajomych w Generalnej Guberni, Rzeszy i w innych krajach, które nie zostały wysłane z getta przez pocztę], postcard (dated Dec. 8, 1942) Karl Fein to Greta Polatschek, numbered 1669–1670.
9. Collection author, photo author.
10. NA, Praha, Policejní ředitelství Praha II, všeobecná spisovna, 1941–1950, kart. n° 4481, sign. J 1141/7, Jelínek Karel 1894, unknown photographer (original), photo author.
11. Forschungsinstitut Brenner-Archiv, Universität von Innsbruck, Innsbruck, Nachlass Herta Fein-Erich Messing, Kassette 152, unknown photographer.
12. NA, Praha, Policejní ředitelství Praha II, všeobecná spisovna, 1931–1940, kart. n° 5661, sign. F 271/14, Herta Feinová 1902, unknown photographer (original), photo author.
13. Collection author, photo author.

14. WHAT DID KARL FEIN DO (AND NOT DO) WITH THE HIRSCHFELD AND INSTITUTE MATERIALS IN BRNO? ONE LEAD, AND A FIRST APPROACH.

1. Deutsches Literaturarchiv, Marbach am Neckar, Magnus Hirschfeld Gästebuch (1933–1935), Zugangsnummer 85.451, f. 163. The photo is also reproduced in Bergemann, Dose, Keilson-Lauritz & Dubout, 2019, f. 163/201.
2. Collection author, photo author.
3. Collection author, photo author.
4. Collection author, Evreinov 1931, book cover.
5. Private archive Brno, unknown photographer.
6. Collection author, photo author.
7. NA, Praha, fonds Národní obnovy Praha (National restoration fonds, Prague), file confiscation of house 194/68 in Křenová Street, Brno-Zábrdovice, sign. VZ 11073/III/1.
8. Collection author, photo author.
9. Collection author, photo author.
10. Private archive Peter Barber, unknown photographer.
11. NA, Praha, fonds n° 375, Arizačni spisy, kart. n° 205, sign. 1268, file firm Leopold Fleischer, not foliated, photo author.
12. Collection author, photo author.
13. Muzeum města Brna (Museum of the city of Brno), Brno, U 5, photo fonds, inventory number A 10.193/11.323, unknown photographer. By Courtesy of Museum of the City of Brno.
14. Postcard collection author, unknown photographer, mention UKA.
15. Private archive Peter Barber, unknown photographer.

15. KAMARÁD AND THE DISCARDING OF THE INSTITUTE MATERIALS

1. Postcard collection author, unknown photographer.
2. Vědecká knihovna Olomouc, Olomouc, periodicals department, *Kamarád* (May 28, 1932, front cover), photo author.
3. Postcard collection author, unknown photographer.
4. Vědecká knihovna Olomouc, Olomouc, periodicals department, *Nový hlas* (Sept. 1932, 8), photo author.
5. Collection author, Drexler-Hlubocký 1937, front cover.
6. Postcard collection author, unknown photographer, mention Fototypia.

7. Private archive Brno, unknown photographer.
8. Collection author, from the photo album of an unidentified Wehrmacht soldier, photo acquired online, unknown photographer.
9. Vědecká knihovna Olomouc, *Kamarád* (May 28, 1932, 17), unknown photographer, photo author.
10. AMB, Brno, fonds U 5 (photo fonds), photo n° XIII B 144, unknown photographer.
11. AMB, Brno, fonds U 5 (photo fonds), photo Čoupek Kr/7/2/1, photographer Čoupek (?).
12. Collection author, photo author.
13. AMB, Brno, fonds Z 1, photo author.

14a. and 14b. AMB, Brno, fonds Z 1, photos author.

15. Private archive Dagmar Černilová [married name known to author], unknown photographer, mention Agfa.
16. MZK, Brno/Digitální knihovna Kramerius, *Volksdeutsche Zeitung* (Apr. 21, 1943, 6).
17. Private Kratochvila family archive, unknown photographer.
18. Private Kratochvila family archive, unknown photographer.

16. DR. STANISLAV KADĚRKA, ELISE BRECHER AND THE JEWISH HOSPITAL IN BRNO

1. Collection author, photo author.
2. Collection author, photographer (who preferred to remain anonymous) known to author.

3a and 3b. ŽMP, Praha, Shoah-related collections, personal and family related materials and papers, osobní pozůstalosti (personal estates), Albert Ascher (22/07/1899), postcard (dated Mar. 26, 1942) Pikesler to Albert Ascher, collection identifier COLLECTION.JMP.SHOAH/PERS/OP/036.

4. MZA, Brno, fonds B 392, Vystěhovalecký fonds, úřadovna Brno (1939–1945), kart. n° 9, inv. n° 186, f. 78, unknown photographer (original), photo author.
5. MZA, Brno, fonds B 392, Vystěhovalecký fonds, úřadovna Brno (1939–1945), kart. n° 9, inv. n° 186, f. 78, unknown photographer (original), photo author.
6. Private archive Rudy Klein, unknown photographer.
7. Private archive Brno, unknown photographer, mention Foto Tingl, Brno - Sirotčí 23 / Brünn – Waisenhausgasse 23.
8. NA, Praha, fonds n° 1077, Okupační vězeňské spisy (OVS), kart. n° 241, sign. 101–615/5, unknown photographer, photo author.
9. http://www.vilemwalter.cz/mapy/, map Katastrální plán Brna z roku 1906.
10. Postcard collection author, unknown photographer, mention Svět ORBIS.
11. MZK, Brno/Digitální knihovna Kramerius, collection Osobnosti Moravy a Slezska, call number Gr1–1253.294, unknown photographer.
12. GFHA, Beit Lohamei Haghetaot (Israel), Collection of the Schoen-Sima family from Czechoslovakia: documents, albums, and books, catalogue n° 32911, University [*sic*] Karlovy v Praze (Universitatis Carolinae Pragensis), Seznam přednášek (index lectionum) Albert Schön, 1934–1938, unknown photographer.
13. GFHA, Beit Lohamei Haghetaot (Israel), Collection of the Schoen-Sima family from Czechoslovakia: Letters, newspapers and official documents, catalogue n° 32911, ID card (všeobecná občanská legitimace) issued by the Ústřední národní výbor v Ostravě, unknown photographer.
14. GFHA, Beit Lohamei Haghetaot (Israel), Collection of the Schoen-Sima family from Czechoslovakia: Letters, newspapers and official documents, catalogue n° 30069, ID card (všeobecná občanská legitimace, allgemeine bürgerliche Legitimation) issued by the Brno police (Policejní ředitelství v Brně, Polizeidirektion in Brünn), unknown photographer.

17. CONCLUDING ITINERARIES

1. Collection author, photo author.

2–3. NA, Praha, Policejní ředitelství Praha II, všeobecná spisovna 1931–1940, kart. n° 4923, sign. 2781/18, Heinrich Brecher 1904, photos author.

4. Collection author, photo author.
5. Collection author, photo author.
6. Postcard collection author, mention Grafo Čuda Holice, unknown photographer.
7. ABS, Praha, fonds Správa vyšetřování StB (State Security Investigation Headquarters), vyšetřovací spis, spis arch. č. V-650 BN, envelope (obalka) n° 8, Anděla Poláková [*sic*] (born 1898).
8. Collection author, photo author.
9. Collection author, photo author.

18. FEAR

1. Archiv MHG, Berlin, unknown photographer.
2. Archiv MHG, Berlin, fonds Ernst Maass, photo author.
3. Collection author, photo author.

BACK COVER PICTURE

Collection author, photographer Harry Devolder. In the background, the art work "Singularidade" by the Spanish artist Alicia Martín (1964-) (seen in Cidade da Cultura da Galiza, Santiago de Compostela, 2017).

Index

The index applies to the main text, the footnotes and the addenda. Focus is on historical figures treated in the book. With reference to traces of mainly Jewish survival, I have also indexed the names of members of later generations. In the majority of cases, I have omitted the names of staff in the libraries and archives consulted, as well as those of people who helped me. Authors referred to in quoted sources have been left out, unless explicitly named in the main text or the footnotes. The decision to add (or omit) the suffix "ová" in the names of Czech women was arbitrary. When alphabetizing Czech names, I used the English, not the Czech, alphabet.

A

B

C

D

G

R

S

T

Y

Z

Acknowledgments

In October 2009, my good friend Don McLeod from Toronto and I went to Nice (France) to see if we could find traces of Magnus Hirschfeld's stay there in the years 1934–35. We both loved our research trip. It resulted in a co-authored text the following year (McLeod & Soetaert 2010). But it also sparked my interest to pursue research further. The somewhat disregarded figure of Karl Giese, Hirschfeld's secretary and life partner, especially intrigued me. In the years that followed, I conducted research in several archives and libraries in Belgium, France, the Czech Republic, Austria, Germany, Poland, the Netherlands and the UK. I am grateful to the many people who have helped me in the past decade and a half. Here, I wish to thank a few in particular.

Don McLeod maintained an interest in my endeavor and did not hesitate to actively help me where he could. Marita Keilson-Lauritz was one of my main mental coaches, as well as my very first reader, and gave me sound advice. On many occasions, Marita also helped me in deciphering difficult and challenging samples of German handwriting. Knowing this *grande dame* of European gay literature studies is an honor. I also wish to thank Ralf Dose, who was always prompt with helpful replies to every little question I had. He was and remains one of the principal authorities on the life of Magnus Hirschfeld. I doff my hat to the great work undertaken by him, and his friends, volunteers and colleagues in the Magnus-Hirschfeld-Gesellschaft (MHG) in Berlin, to restore Hirschfeld's legacy. Manfred Herzer, another towering figure in German gay studies, also kindly helped me a few times. At intervals, Kevin Dubout would spontaneously send me valuable information, for which I am grateful. Harald Lützenkirchen kindly and helpfully sent me copies from the Kurt Hiller archive.

Since I have no mastery of Czech, and made around ten research trips to Czechia, I had to rely on others for help in reading Czech-language sources. I want to thank in particular my very first and very last translators: Gabriela Patriková and Tomáš Adamec. They proved to be the most loyal, and I thank them for their belief in my project and for supporting it by putting up with my endless inquiries. A warm thank you also to the other students who helped me through the years: Jakub S., Katka Linhardtová, Eva Beránková, Pavla Čonková, Jaroslava Peťková, Irena Janíková and Vojtěch Hrdlička. Marcin Piotr Wojciechowski helped me to read Polish; Veronika Ceuppens aided me to write some letters in German; Benny Gezels and his partner, Andrés Sorin and Rubén Hernández assisted me with Spanish. The late Avi Haimovsky, who took a genuine interest in my work, assisted me with Hebrew. I regret that he did not live to see the end result. Horst Morawek, who, when still very young, had seen Brno often from the front seat of a car helped me to find my way in the pre-war city. At crucial moments, Rainer-Joachim Siegel helped me with several (to me) illegible examples of German handwriting, and I thank Els Snick for her mediation in locating him. In May 2023, Graham Willett, Colin Deinhardt and Alain V. Miller provided valuable tips for polishing the book title in Brussels. My partner Harry helped me with the laborious task of indexing as we faced the final deadline.

I thank Jan Seidl for showing me the ropes at the Klementinum library in Prague in 2011. In the course of this project, I ran into some less friendly – even nasty – academics but, fortunately, there were some very pleasant exceptions: Karla Huebner, Jana Nosková, Petr Pelčák, Magda Veselská and Ewa Wiatr. Thank you for your kindness and assistance.

I was also helped, of course, by many staff members of archives and libraries and thank them for their assistance. A few stood out: Jana Dosoudilová, Markéta Jančíková and especially Petr Houzar, all three of the AMB in Brno. In addition, the help provided by Jana Fasorová (MZA, Brno) was exemplary. Enthusiastic assistance was also provided by Filip Strubbe (Rijksarchief Brussel/Archives de l'Etat Bruxelles), Richard Ratajczak (Rare Books and Special Collections, University of Sydney) and Shawn Wilson (Kinsey Institute, Bloomington, Indiana). Danny Halim and Jack van der Wel (IHLIA, Amsterdam) were always ready to help.

I wish to thank Chris Schön (and Jakob Horstmann) of Ibidem Verlag who, after briefly consulting with Anne Braem and Michiel Van den Bosch of the company Typeface in Leuven, agreed to publish my book. Jens Dobler, and Ralf Dose, kindly assisted me in my attempt to find funding sources, and I am very grateful for that. A generous subvention from the MHG, Berlin was a welcome "band aid" in financing my endeavor.

Lucie Tuzová and her husband Ondřej Tuza, two Czech people who assisted me whenever they could, merit special mention. In crucial places, their help made this book what it is and I want to express my heartfelt gratitude for that. Their children now have yet another reason to be proud of their parents.

Many thanks to Stefano Anelli, Romana Balcarová, Daniel Baránek, Peter Barber, L. Baum, Marianna Becková and her immediate family, Jitka Bílková, Bruno Boigontier, Michal Bušek, Krishna C., Dagmar Černilová (married name known to author), Daniël Christiaens, Marc Cornelis, Charles des Fours-Walderode, Madeleine Duarte, Pavel Dufek, the Ehrlich family in France, Philippe Fabre, Andreas Franck, Šárka Glombíčková, Anna Hájková, Murray G. Hall, Rainer Herrn, David Hubený, Jana Jablonická-Zezulová, Eyal Kahn, Peter Keller, Judy M. King, Rudy Klein, Andreas Kraß, Milan Kratochvila, Miroslava Kučerová, Annette Lechner, Michael Lenarz, Hanno Loewy, Randy Medenwald, Vlasta Měšťánková, Elizabeth Miller, Michael L. Miller, Gilles Mordant, Mary Munk, Anne Newman, Yvonne Oliver, Ludmila Ondráčková, Mark Osenga, John Panofsky, Pascale Paugam, Uri Arthur Peled-Feldmann, Tom Perles, Jaroslava Plosová, Andreas Pretzel, Andres Rodenstein, the current relatives of Jaroslav and Jindra Růžička (who preferred to remain anonymous), Lieven Saerens, Mario Schertz, Ursula A. Schneider, Judith Schuyf, Tal Shohamy, my parents Albrecht Soetaert and Cécile Bleuzé, Carola Staniek, Renée Stern Steinig, Annette Steinsiek, Hannes Sulzenbacher, Helga Sykora, Robert A. Tabatznik, Hermann Teifer, Terezie Tenorová, Eva Tichauer, Charles Ticho, Pol Timmerman, Siegfried Tornow, Mabel Tuinman-Hesling, Lenka Vaňková, Maurice van Lieshout, Miroslav Veselka, Vilém Walter, Claudia Weiss, Gerrit Weßel, Bernhard Wittstock, Raimund Wolfert and Alexander Zinn. Others who helped me are mentioned in the footnotes of the text.

Thank you also to the Jewish community in Miami, without whom I would not be alive today. I am in your eternal debt. I will never forget the lady I met in the hospital, also seated in a semi-recliner next to me. When I asked her about the number tattooed on her forearm, she told me that, when her daughter was still a child, she had told her that it was her phone number, and it was there so that she could remember it. Her daughter is now conducting Holocaust research.

Last, but not least, I want to thank my partner Harry. For more than a decade he put up with my nearly continuous work on this research project in my spare time. I am as glad as he that it has finally come to an end.

Ghent, September 4, 2024.